Fodor's 25th Edition

New England

D1405858

The Guide
for All Budgets

Completely
Updated

Where to Stay,
Eat, and Explore

On and Off
the Beaten Path

When to Go,
What to Pack

Maps, Travel Tips,
and Web Sites

Fodor's Travel Publications • New York, Toronto, London, Sydney, Auckland
www.fodors.com

Fodor's New England

EDITOR: William Travis

Editorial Contributors: Michelle Bodak Acri, Paula Bodah, Andrew Collins, Elizabeth Gehrman, Alexandra Hall, Carolyn Heller, Satu Hummasti, Rene Hertzog, Laura Kidder, Hilary M. Nangle, Bill Scheller, and Kay Scheller

Maps: David Lindroth, *cartographer*; Rebecca Baer and Bob Blake, *map editors*

Design: Fabrizio La Rocca, *creative director*; Guido Caroti, *art director*; Jolie Novak, *senior picture editor*; Melanie Marin, *photo editor*

Cover Design: Pentagram

Production/Manufacturing: Angela L. McLean

Cover Photo (Manchester, Vermont): Craig Aurness/Corbis

Copyright

Important Tip

Although all prices, opening times, and other details in this book are based on information supplied to us at press time, changes occur all the time in the travel world, and Fodor's cannot accept responsibility for facts that become outdated or for inadvertent errors or omissions. So **always confirm information when it matters,** especially if you're making a detour to visit a specific place.

Special Sales

Fodor's Travel Publications are available at special discounts for bulk purchases for sales promotions or premiums. Special editions, including personalized covers, excerpts of existing guides, and corporate imprints, can be created in large quantities for special needs. For more information, contact your local bookseller or write to Special Markets, Fodor's Travel Publications, 280 Park Avenue, New York, NY 10017. Inquiries from Canada should be directed to your local Canadian bookseller or sent to Random House of Canada, Ltd., Marketing Department, 2775 Matheson Boulevard East, Mississauga, Ontario L4W 4P7. Inquiries from the United Kingdom should be sent to Fodor's Travel Publications, 20 Vauxhall Bridge Road, London SW1V 2SA, England.

CONTENTS

Maps

ON THE ROAD WITH FODOR'S

A TRIP TAKES YOU OUT OF YOURSELF. Concerns of life at home completely disappear, driven away by more immediate thoughts—about, say, what marvels will beguile the next day, or where you'll have dinner. That's where Fodor's comes in. We make sure that you know all your options, so that you don't miss something that's around the next bend just because you didn't know it was there. Mindful that the best memories of your trip might have nothing to do with what you came to New England to see, we guide you to sights large and small all over the region. You might set out to discover the Berkshires or Maine's southeastern coast, but back at home you find yourself unable to forget walking amid the opulence of the Breakers in Newport or driving in fall under canopies of trees, ablaze in shades of oranges and reds, in Vermont. With Fodor's at your side, serendipitous discoveries are never far away.

About Our Writers

Our success in showing you every corner of New England is a credit to our extraordinary writers. Although there's no substitute for travel advice from a good friend who knows your style, our contributors are the next best thing—the kind of people you would poll for travel advice if you knew them.

Hilary M. Nangle, formerly travel editor for a daily newspaper in Maine, is now a freelancer based in the state's scenic midcoast. Her Fodor's beat is Maine, and she writes regularly about travel, food, and skiing for publications in the United States and Canada.

Former Fodor's editor and New England native **Andrew Collins,** who updated and expanded the New Hampshire chapter as well as the Martha's Vineyard, Berkshires, and Pioneer Valley sections of Massachusetts, is the author of several books on travel in New England, including handbooks on Connecticut and Rhode Island.

Kay and Bill Scheller, who updated the Vermont chapter have a total of more than 30 years' experience as contributors to Fodor's guides. They are the authors of several books on travel in New England and the Northeast. The Schellers live in northern Vermont.

A number of talented writers worked on the Massachusetts chapter. Food and travel writer **Alexandra Hall,** the features and lifestyle editor of *Boston Magazine,* updated the Boston dining scene. **Elizabeth Gehrman,** a freelance writer based in Boston, served as the Boston shopping maven and explorer extraordinaire. **Carolyn Heller,** a Cambridge-based travel writer, provided the latest updates on Cambridge, Boston side trips, the North Shore, and Cape Cod. She has contributed to several Fodor's New England guidebooks and other publications. Boston lodging updater **Rene Hertzog,** a writer and editor, explored the city's best digs. Nantucket resident Sandy MacDonald updated the Nantucket section.

Rhode Island updater **Paula Bodah** is the editor of *Rhode Island Monthly* and a native of Rhode Island. She's written for *Yankee, Yankee's Travel Guide to New England, Walking* magazine, and Rodale Press cookbooks.

Michelle Bodak Acri, who updated the Connecticut chapter, has lived in the Nutmeg State for 32 years, the last 10 of them working as an editor for *Connecticut* magazine. She enthusiastically shares her state's glories with the uninitiated.

You can rest assured that you're in good hands—and that no property mentioned in the book has paid to be included. Each has been selected strictly on its merits, as the best of its type in its price range.

How to Use This Book

Up front is Smart Travel Tips A to Z, arranged alphabetically by topic and loaded with tips, Web sites, and contact information. Destination: New England helps get you in the mood for your trip. Subsequent chapters in *Fodor's New England* are arranged regionally. All chapters are

New England

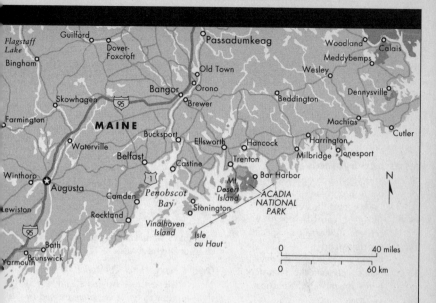

ATLANTIC OCEAN

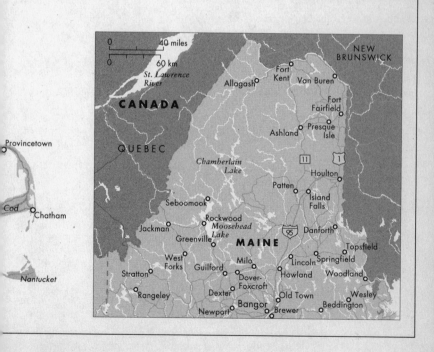

divided geographically; within each area, towns are covered in logical geographical order, and attractive stretches of road between them are indicated by the designation En Route. To help you decide what you'll have time to visit, all chapters begin with our writers' favorite itineraries. (Mix itineraries from several chapters, and you can put together a really exceptional trip.) The A to Z section that ends every chapter lists additional resources.

Icons and Symbols

★   Our special recommendations
✕   Restaurant
   Lodging establishment
✕   Lodging establishment whose restaurant warrants a special trip
   Campgrounds
   Good for kids (rubber duck)
☞   Sends you to another section of the guide for more information
✉   Address
☎   Telephone number
☉   Opening and closing times
   Admission prices (those we give apply to adults; substantially reduced fees are almost always available for children, students, and senior citizens)

Numbers in white and black circles ③ ❸ that appear on the maps, in the margins, and within the tours correspond to one another.

For hotels, you can assume that all rooms have private baths, phones, TVs, and air-conditioning unless otherwise noted and that all hotels operate on the European Plan (with no meals) if we don't specify another meal plan. We always list a property's facilities but not whether you'll be charged extra to use them, so when pricing accommodations, do ask what's included. For restaurants, it's always a good idea to book ahead; we mention reservations only when they're essential or are not accepted. All restaurants we list are open daily for lunch and dinner unless stated otherwise; dress is mentioned only when men are required to wear a jacket or a jacket and tie. Look for an overview of local dining-out habits in Smart Travel Tips A to Z and in the Pleasures and Pastimes section that follows each chapter introduction.

Don't Forget to Write

Your experiences—positive and negative—matter to us. If we have missed or misstated something, we want to hear about it. We follow up on all suggestions. Contact the New England editor at editors@fodors.com or c/o Fodor's at 280 Park Avenue, New York, NY 10017. And have a fabulous trip!

Karen Cure

Karen Cure
Editorial Director

ESSENTIAL INFORMATION

AIR TRAVEL

Most travelers visiting New England will head for a major gateway and then rent a car to enjoy the sights. The New England states form a fairly compact region, with few important destinations more than six hours apart by car. Intraregional air transportation facilities are mainly patronized by business travelers (exceptions include flights to island resort destinations such as Martha's Vineyard and Nantucket from Boston's Logan International Airport). Should you wish to fly, be advised that intraregional fares can be high and flights limited.

BOOKING

When you book **look for nonstop flights** and **remember that "direct" flights stop at least once.** Try to avoid connecting flights, which require a change of plane. Two airlines may operate a connecting flight jointly, so ask if your airline operates every segment of the trip; you may find that the carrier you prefer flies you only part of the way. To find more booking tips and to check prices and make on-line flight reservations, log on to www.fodors.com.

CARRIERS

➤ MAJOR AIRLINES: **American** (☎ 800/433–7300). **Continental** (☎ 800/525–0280). **Delta** (☎ 800/221–1212). **Northwest** (☎ 800/225–2525). **Southwest** (☎ 800/435–9792). **Sun Country** (☎ 800/359–5786). **TWA** (☎ 800/221–2000). **United** (☎ 800/241–6522). **US Airways** (☎ 800/428–4322).

➤ REGIONAL AIRLINES: **Cape Air/Nantucket Airlines** (☎ 508/790–3122 or 800/352–0714). **Midway** (☎ 800/446–4392).

➤ FROM THE U.K.: **American** (☎ 0345/789–789). **British Airways** (☎ 0345/222–111). **Virgin Atlantic** (☎ 01293/747–747).

➤ FROM AUSTRALIA AND NEW ZEALAND: **Qantas** (from Australia, ☎ 13–1313, 0800/808–767, or 09/357–8900; from New Zealand, outside Auckland, ☎ 0800/808–767; from Auckland area, ☎ 09/357–8900).

CHECK-IN AND BOARDING

Always **ask your carrier about its check-in policy.** Plan to arrive at the airport about 2 hours before your scheduled departure time for domestic flights and 2½ to 3 hours before international flights. Assuming that not everyone with a ticket will show up, airlines routinely overbook planes. When everyone does, airlines ask for volunteers to give up their seats. In return, these volunteers usually get a certificate for a free flight and are rebooked on the next flight out. If there are not enough volunteers, the airline must choose who will be denied boarding. The first to get bumped are passengers who checked in late and those flying on discounted tickets, so **get to the gate and check in as early as possible,** especially during peak periods.

Always **bring a government-issued photo ID to the airport;** even when it's not required, a passport is best.

CUTTING COSTS

The least expensive airfares to New England are priced for round-trip travel and must usually be purchased in advance. Airlines generally allow you to change your return date for a fee; most low-fare tickets, however, are nonrefundable. It's smart to **call a number of airlines,** and when you are quoted a good price, **book it on the spot**—the same fare may not be available the next day. Always **check different routings** and look into using alternate airports. Also, price off-peak flights, which may be significantly less expensive than others. Travel agents, especially low-fare specialists (☞ Discounts and Deals), are helpful.

Airlines often post discounted "cyber-fares" on their Web sites. The best bargains are on unsold seats on upcoming flights. If your plans are flexible, you can often save 60% to 70% by booking on-line. Discount travel Web sites such as Travelocity and Priceline.com also offer reduced fares (☞ Discounts and Deals).

Consolidators are another good source. They buy tickets for scheduled international flights at reduced rates from the airlines, then sell them at prices that beat the best fare available directly from the airlines. Sometimes you can even get your money back if you need to return the ticket. Carefully read the fine print detailing penalties for changes and cancellations, purchase the ticket with a credit card, and **confirm your consolidator reservation with the airline.**

➤ CONSOLIDATORS: **Cheap Tickets** (☎ 800/377–1000 or 888/922–8849, WEB www.cheaptickets.com). **Discount Airline Ticket Service** (☎ 800/576–1600). **Unitravel** (☎ 800/325–2222, WEB www.unitravel.com). **Up & Away Travel** (☎ 212/889–2345, WEB www.upandaway.com). **World Travel Network** (☎ 800/409–6753).

ENJOYING THE FLIGHT

State your seat preference when purchasing your ticket, and then repeat it when you confirm and when you check in. For more legroom, you can request one of the few emergency-aisle seats at check-in, if you are capable of lifting at least 50 pounds—a Federal Aviation Administration requirement of passengers in these seats. Seats behind a bulkhead also offer more legroom, but they don't have under-seat storage. Don't sit in the row in front of the emergency aisle or in front of a bulkhead, where seats may not recline.

Ask the airline whether a snack or meal is served on the flight. If you have dietary concerns, **request special meals when booking.** These can be vegetarian, low-cholesterol, or kosher, for example. It's a good idea to pack some healthy snacks and a small (plastic) bottle of water in your carry-on bag. On long flights, try to maintain a normal routine, to help fight jet lag. At night, **get some sleep.** By day, **eat light meals, drink water** (not alcohol), and **move around the cabin** to stretch your legs. For additional jet-lag tips consult *Fodor's FYI: Travel Fit & Healthy* (available at bookstores everywhere).

All flights within the United States are strictly nonsmoking, as are international flights on American-based carriers. Smoking regulations vary among non-U.S.–based carriers, so call if this is important to you. It is uncommon for U.S. airports to allow smoking, although a few permit it in specially designated areas. Airlines have cut back on in-flight meal service. Call ahead to see if you will be served food en route: if not, you might want to bring along a snack or eat beforehand.

FLYING TIMES

Flying time to Boston is 1 hour from New York, 2 hours and 15 minutes from Chicago, 6 hours from Los Angeles, 4 hours from Dallas, and 8 hours from London. Flying time from Sydney, Australia, to Boston (via Los Angeles) is 20 hours; flying time from Auckland, New Zealand, to Boston (via Los Angeles) is 17 hours.

HOW TO COMPLAIN

If your baggage goes astray or your flight goes awry, complain right away. Most carriers require that you **file a claim immediately.** The Aviation Consumer Protection Division of the Department of Transportation publishes *Fly-Rights*, which discusses airlines and consumer issues and is available on-line. At PassengerRights.com, a Web site, you can compose a letter of complaint and distribute it electronically.

➤ AIRLINE COMPLAINTS: **Aviation Consumer Protection Division** (✉ U.S. Department of Transportation, Room 4107, C-75, Washington, DC 20590, ☎ 202/366–2220, WEB www.dot.gov/airconsumer). **Federal Aviation Administration Consumer Hotline** (☎ 800/322–7873).

RECONFIRMING

Check the status of your flight before you leave for the airport. You can do this on your carrier's Web site, by linking to a flight-status checker (many Web booking services offer these), or by calling your carrier or travel agent.

AIRPORTS

The main gateway to New England is Boston's Logan International Airport (BOS), the region's largest. Bradley International Airport (BDL), in Windsor Locks, Connecticut, 12 mi north of Hartford, is convenient to western Massachusetts and all of Connecticut. T. F. Green State Airport (PVD), just outside Providence, Rhode Island, is another major airport. Additional New England airports served by major carriers include Manchester Airport (MHT) in New Hampshire (a rapidly growing, lower-cost alternative to Boston); Portland International Jetport (PWM) in Maine; and Burlington International Airport (BTV) in Vermont. Other airports are in Bangor, Maine, and Hyannis, Massachusetts.

➤ AIRPORT INFORMATION: **Bangor International Airport** (✉ Godfrey Blvd., ☎ 207/947–0384, WEB www.flybangor.com). **Barnstable Municipal Airport** (✉ 480 Barnstable Rd., Hyannis, ☎ 508/775–2020). **Bradley International Airport** (☎ 888/624–1533). **Burlington International Airport** (☎ 802/863–1889). **Logan International Airport** (☎ 800/235–6426). **Manchester Airport** (☎ 603/624–6539). **Portland International Jetport** (☎ 207/774–7301). **T. F. Green State Airport** (☎ 888/268–7222).

BIKE TRAVEL

Cyclists favor New England because overnight destinations are seldom far apart. Inns and B&Bs are plentiful, and some operators provide guided inn-to-inn tours. In general, northern (except for far northern Maine) and western New England have the best cycling opportunities, with plenty of lightly traveled secondary roads and pleasant small towns to explore en route. Make sure you're in shape if you plan to tackle the hills of Vermont and New Hampshire, and **consider a mountain bike** if you're going to be on dirt roads. Both mountain and touring bikes are available for rent in resort areas and in most larger towns and cities for as little as $20 a day.

BIKES IN FLIGHT

Most airlines accommodate bikes as luggage, provided they are dismantled and boxed; check with individual airlines about packing requirements. Airlines sell bike boxes, which are often free at bike shops, for about $15 (bike bags start at $100). International travelers often can substitute a bike for a piece of checked luggage at no charge; otherwise, the cost is about $100. Domestic and Canadian airlines charge $40–$80 each way.

BOAT AND FERRY TRAVEL

Principal ferry routes in New England connect Cape Cod with Martha's Vineyard and Nantucket, and Connecticut with New York's Long Island; other routes provide access to many islands off the Maine coast. In addition, ferries cross Lake Champlain between Vermont and upstate New York. International service between Portland and Bar Harbor, Maine, and Yarmouth, Nova Scotia, is also available. With the exception of the Lake Champlain ferries, which are first-come, first-served, car reservations are always advisable.

FARES AND SCHEDULES

For reservations made by phone, MasterCard and Visa are universally accepted; many ferry services also accept American Express and Discover. When picking up tickets at the station, travelers' checks, credit cards, and cash are approved forms of payment.

BUS TRAVEL

All New England states have bus service; fares are generally moderate and buses normally run on schedule, although service can be infrequent and travel time can be long due to traffic and frequent stops. Be sure to arrive at the terminal at least one hour before the bus is scheduled to depart. Smoking is not permitted on buses.

CUTTING COSTS

Greyhound offers Ameripass, which allows riders to travel throughout New England at discounted fares for varying lengths of time from 7 to 60 days. Tickets purchased at least 7 days in advance are discounted. A

Companion Fare, purchased at least 3 days in advance, allows a companion to ride for free (not available in some destinations and at certain times of the year).

PAYING

Tickets can be purchased at the terminal or by phone; Greyhound offers on-line ticket sales. All major credit cards are accepted.

RESERVATIONS

Greyhound does not accept advance reservations. The only way to reserve a seat on the bus is to purchase a ticket in advance.

➤ BUS INFORMATION: **Bonanza Bus Lines** (☎ 800/556–3815). **Concord Trailways** (☎ 800/639–3317). **Greyhound** (☎ 800/231–2222; 888/454–7277 Ameripass; WEB www.greyhound.com). **Peter Pan Bus Lines** (☎ 800/343–9999). **Vermont Transit** (☎ 800/642–3133 in Vermont; 800/552–8737 elsewhere).

BUSINESS HOURS

Banks in New England are generally open weekdays 9 AM–3 PM, with longer hours on Thursday and Friday. Post offices are open weekdays 8 AM–5 PM; many branches operate Saturday morning hours. Business hours tend to be weekdays 9–5. Banks and post offices close on all national holidays; retail businesses generally close only on Thanksgiving, Christmas, New Year's Day, and Easter. Convenience stores, especially in urban areas, are often open year-round.

GAS STATIONS

Except along major highways, gas stations frequently close at around 10 or 11 PM and reopen at 5 or 6 AM.

MUSEUMS AND SIGHTS

While some major museums and attractions are open daily—at least during peak tourist season, Memorial Day to Columbus Day—Monday closings are common. In resort areas, museums and attractions are frequently closed or on significantly reduced schedules from mid-October to late May. Hours of sights and attractions are denoted throughout this book by the clock icon, ☉ .

PHARMACIES

In larger cities, pharmacies near hospitals and/or medical centers generally stay open 24 hours.

SHOPS

Many stores may not open until 10 or 11 AM, but they remain open until 6 or 7 PM; most carry on brisk business on Saturday and Sunday as well. Suburban shopping malls are generally open seven days a week, with evening hours every day except Sunday. All across New England, convenience stores sell food and sundries until about 11 PM. Along the highways and in major cities you can usually find all-night diners, supermarkets, pharmacies, and convenience stores.

CAMERAS AND PHOTOGRAPHY

Seascapes and fall foliage are the most commonly photographed subjects in New England. Both can make for memorable images, provided you remember that saltwater and autumn leaves photograph better when something else is included in the picture. Look for a lighthouse or fog-shrouded sailboat in your ocean shots and a covered bridge or church steeple tucked among the birches and maples. The *Kodak Guide to Shooting Great Travel Pictures* (available at bookstores everywhere) is loaded with tips.

➤ PHOTO HELP: **Kodak Information Center** (☎ 800/242–2424, WEB www.kodak.com).

EQUIPMENT PRECAUTIONS

Saltwater and sand can damage your equipment. **Keep your camera in its case when not in use,** and wipe the lens and case with a soft cloth if it's sprayed with saltwater. **Don't pack film and equipment in checked luggage,** where it is much more susceptible to damage. X-ray machines used to view checked luggage are becoming much more powerful and therefore are much more likely to ruin your film. Try to **ask for hand inspection of film,** which becomes clouded after repeated exposure to airport X-ray machines, and **keep videotapes and computer disks away from metal**

detectors. Always **keep film, tape, and computer disks out of the sun.** Carry an extra supply of batteries, and **be prepared to turn on your camera, camcorder, or laptop** to prove to airport security personnel that the device is real.

Be careful on sailboat cruises—salt-water can corrode metal camera parts. Remember to **stock up on film at home or in big cities.** Prices are a lot higher in airports, resort areas, and small towns, and the film options are often limited.

CAR RENTAL

Rates in Boston begin at $25 a day and $160 a week for an economy car with air-conditioning, an automatic transmission, and unlimited mileage. This rate does not include taxes and surcharges, which can add as much as 25% if you rent a car at the airport.

➤ MAJOR AGENCIES: **Alamo** (☎ 800/327–9633; WEB www.alamo.com). **Avis** (☎ 800/331–1212; 800/879–2847 in Canada; 02/9353–9000 in Australia; 09/526–2847 in New Zealand; 0870/606–0100 in the U.K.; WEB www.avis.com). **Budget** (☎ 800/527–0700; 0870/156–5656 in the U.K.; WEB www.budget.com). **Dollar** (☎ 800/800–4000; 0124/622–0111 in the U.K.; where it's affiliated with Sixt; 02/9223–1444 in Australia; WEB www.dollar.com). **Hertz** (☎ 800/654–3131; 800/263–0600 in Canada; 020/8897–2072 in the U.K.; 02/9669–2444 in Australia; 09/256–8690 in New Zealand; WEB www.hertz.com). **National Car Rental** (☎ 800/227–7368; 020/8680–4800 in the U.K.; WEB www.nationalcar.com).

CUTTING COSTS

For a good deal, **book through a travel agent who will shop around.** Also, **price local car-rental companies**—whose prices may be lower still, although their service and maintenance may not be as good as those of major rental agencies—and **research rates on-line.** Remember to ask about required deposits, cancellation penalties, and drop-off charges if you're planning to pick up the car in one city and leave it in another. If you're traveling during a holiday period, also make sure that a confirmed reservation guarantees you a car.

INSURANCE

When driving a rented car you are generally responsible for any damage to or loss of the vehicle. You may also be liable for any property damage or personal injury that you may cause while driving. Before you rent, see what coverage you already have under the terms of your personal auto-insurance policy and credit cards.

For about $15 to $20 a day, rental companies sell protection, known as a collision- or loss-damage waiver (CDW or LDW), that eliminates your liability for damage to the car; it's always optional and should never be automatically added to your bill.

In Massachusetts the car-rental agency's insurance is primary; therefore, the company must pay for damage to third parties up to a preset legal limit, beyond which your own liability insurance kicks in. However, **make sure you have enough coverage to pay for the car.** If you do not have auto insurance or an umbrella policy that covers damage to third parties, purchasing liability insurance and a CDW or LDW is highly recommended.

REQUIREMENTS AND RESTRICTIONS

When picking up a rental car, non-U.S. residents need a reservation voucher for any prepaid reservations that were made in the traveler's home country, a passport, a driver's license, and a travel policy that covers each driver. In New England, most agencies won't rent to you if you're under the age of 21.

SURCHARGES

Before you pick up a car in one city and leave it in another, **ask about drop-off charges or one-way service fees,** which can be substantial. Note, too, that some rental agencies charge extra if you return the car before the time specified in your contract. To avoid a hefty refueling fee, **fill the tank just before you turn in the car,** but be aware that gas stations near the rental outlet may overcharge. It's almost never a deal to buy the tank of gas in the car when you rent it; the understanding is that you'll return it empty, but some fuel usually remains. Surcharges may apply if you're under 25. You'll pay extra for child seats (about $6 a day), which are compulsory for children under five, and for additional drivers (about $5 per day).

CAR TRAVEL

Because public transportation is spotty or completely lacking in the outer reaches of New England, a car is the most convenient means of transportation. The region is well served by the interstate highway system, on which you can expect to average 65 mph, except near major metropolitan areas (in rush hour around Hartford and Boston, you will cut that average in half). On other federal and state highways, your average will more likely be 40–50 mph. In northern New England, east–west travel is notoriously slow, due to several mountain ranges and no limited-access highways.

GASOLINE

Self-service gas stations are the norm in New England, though in some of the less-populated regions you'll find stations with one or two pumps and a friendly attendant who provides full service (pumping your gas, checking your tires and oil, washing your windows). Stations are plentiful. Most stay open late (24 hours along large highways and in big cities), except in rural areas, where Sunday hours are limited and where you may drive long stretches without a refueling opportunity. At press time, rates for unleaded regular gas at self-service stations in New England were about $1.40 per gallon (somewhat higher in Boston and Connecticut); rates at full-service stations are often slightly more.

ROAD CONDITIONS

Federal and state highways throughout New England are maintained in excellent condition and are promptly plowed and salted in winter. Secondary roads maintained by local municipalities are sometimes in poor repair, especially in spring, when frost heaves—bumps and dips in the pavement—are caused by melting ground frost. Northern New England has many miles of unpaved roads, but these are usually well graded and

pleasant to travel, except in mud season during late March and early April. Far northern Maine is crisscrossed by privately owned logging roads, for which a pass is frequently required (pay at gates at entrances to logging company lands).

City traffic can be particularly trying in New England, as many streets were laid out centuries ago. Boston's traffic snarls are legendary; avoid driving here if at all possible. Rush hours in the city run roughly from 6 to 9 AM and from 4 to 7 PM.

ROAD MAPS

Each state in New England makes available a free map that has directories, mileage, and other useful information—contact the state offices of tourism (☞ Visitor Information). Jimapco produces detailed maps of Massachusetts. Hagstrom sells maps of Connecticut. Rand McNally prints a detailed map of Rhode Island. Delorme publishes topographical atlases of Connecticut/Rhode Island, Maine, New Hampshire, and Vermont that include most back roads and many outdoor recreation sites. The maps are widely available in the state.

RULES OF THE ROAD

The speed limit in much of New England is 65 mph on interstate and some limited-access highways (55 mph in densely populated areas) and 50 mph on most other roads (25–30 mph in towns and cities). Speed limits are stringently enforced throughout the region, particularly in populated areas. Fines can easily exceed $100 for driving 15–20 mi above the speed limit. In New England, drivers can turn right at a red light (unless signs indicate otherwise) providing they come to a full stop and check to see that the intersection is clear first.

There is zero tolerance for drunk driving. The blood alcohol content that defines legal intoxication for adults varies between .08 and .10 percent, depending on the state, and penalties are severe.

Always **strap children under age 4 or under 40 lbs., regardless of age, into approved child-safety seats.** Children must wear seat belts regardless of where they're seated.

CHILDREN IN NEW ENGLAND

In New England, there's no shortage of things to do with children. Major museums have children's sections, and you'll find children's museums in cities large and small. Many tourist areas have roadside attractions, and miniature golf courses are easy to come by. Attractions such as beaches and boat rides, parks and planetariums, lighthouses and llama treks can be fun for youngsters, as can special events such as crafts fairs and food festivals. *Fodor's Around Boston with Kids* (available in bookstores everywhere) can help you plan your days together.

Be sure to plan ahead and **involve your youngsters** as you outline your trip. When packing, include things to keep them busy en route. On sightseeing days try to schedule activities of special interest to your children. If you are renting a car, don't forget to **arrange for a car seat** when you reserve. For general advice about traveling with children, consult *Fodor's FYI: Travel with Your Baby* (available in bookstores everywhere).

FLYING

If your children are two or older, **ask about children's airfares.** As a general rule, infants under two not occupying a seat fly at greatly reduced fares or even for free.

Experts agree that it's a good idea to use safety seats aloft for children weighing less than 40 pounds. Airlines set their own policies: U.S. carriers usually require that the child be ticketed, even if he or she is young enough to ride free, since the seats must be strapped into regular seats. Do **check your airline's policy about using safety seats during takeoff and landing.** Safety seats are not allowed everywhere in the plane, so get your seat assignments as early as possible.

When reserving, **request children's meals or a freestanding bassinet** (not available at all airlines) if you need them. But note that bulkhead seats, where you must sit to use the bassinet, may lack an overhead bin or storage space on the floor.

LODGING

Chain hotels and motels welcome children, and New England has many family-oriented resorts with lively children's programs. You'll also find farms that accept guests and can be lots of fun for children. Rental houses and apartments abound, particularly around ski areas; off-season, these can be economical as well as comfortable touring bases. Some country inns, especially those with a quiet, romantic atmosphere and those furnished with antiques, are less enthusiastic about little ones, so **be up front about your traveling companions** when you reserve. Many larger resorts and hotels will provide a baby-sitter at an additional cost. Others will provide a list of sitters in the area.

Most hotels in New England allow children under a certain age to stay in their parents' room at no extra charge, but others charge them as extra adults; be sure to **find out the cutoff age for children's discounts.**

Most lodgings that welcome infants and small children will provide a crib or cot, but **be sure to give advance notice** so that one will be available for you. Most resort and hotels with extended amenities will also arrange to have a baby-sitter come to your room. Many family resorts make special accommodations for small children during meals. Be sure to ask in advance.

SIGHTS AND ATTRACTIONS

Places that are especially appealing to children are indicated by a rubber-duckie icon (☺) in the margin.

TRANSPORTATION

Each New England state has specific requirements regarding age and weight requirements for children in car seats. If you're renting a car, **be sure to ask about the state(s) you're planning to drive in.** If you will need a car seat, make sure the agency you select provides them and **reserve well in advance.**

CONSUMER PROTECTION

Whether you're shopping for gifts or purchasing travel services, **pay with a major credit card** whenever possible, so you can cancel payment or get reimbursed if there's a problem (and you can provide documentation). If you're doing business with a particular company for the first time, **contact your local Better Business Bureau and the attorney general's offices** in your state and (for U.S. businesses) the company's home state as well. Have any complaints been filed? Finally, if you're buying a package or tour, always **consider travel insurance** that includes default coverage (☞ Insurance).

➤ BBBs: **Council of Better Business Bureaus** (✉ 4200 Wilson Blvd., Suite 800, Arlington, VA 22203, ☎ 703/276–0100, ℻ 703/525–8277, ☒ www.bbb.org).

CRUISE TRAVEL

Several cruise companies have ships that set sail from Boston to cruise the coast of New England. Many head north to Canada, stopping in Montréal or Halifax. Others head south out of Boston to Newport, Rhode Island. To learn how to plan, choose, and book a cruise-ship voyage, consult *Fodor's FYI: Plan & Enjoy Your Cruise* (available in bookstores everywhere).

➤ CRUISE LINES: **American Canadian Caribbean Line** (☎ 800/556–7450). **Clipper Cruise Line** (☎ 800/325–0010). **Royal Caribbean International** (☎ 800/327–6700).

CUSTOMS AND DUTIES

IN AUSTRALIA

Australian residents who are 18 or older may bring home A$400 worth of souvenirs and gifts (including jewelry), 250 cigarettes or 250 grams of tobacco, and 1,125 ml of alcohol (including wine, beer, and spirits). Residents under 18 may bring back A$200 worth of goods. Prohibited items include meat products. Seeds, plants, and fruits need to be declared upon arrival.

➤ INFORMATION: **Australian Customs Service** (Regional Director, ✉ Box 8, Sydney, NSW 2001; ☎ 02/9213–2000 or 1300/363263; 1800/020504 quarantine-inquiry line; ℻ 02/9213–4043; ☒ www.customs.gov.au).

IN CANADA

Canadian residents who have been out of Canada for at least seven days may bring in C$750 worth of goods duty-free. If you've been away fewer than seven days but more than 48 hours, the duty-free allowance drops to C$200; if your trip lasts 24 to 48 hours, the allowance is C$50. You may not pool allowances with family members. Goods claimed under the C$750 exemption may follow you by mail; those claimed under the lesser exemptions must accompany you. Alcohol and tobacco products may be included in the seven-day and 48-hour exemptions but not in the 24-hour exemption. If you meet the age requirements of the province or territory through which you reenter Canada, you may bring in, duty-free, 1.5 liters of wine *or* 1.14 liters (40 imperial ounces) of liquor *or* 24 12-ounce cans or bottles of beer or ale. If you are 19 or older you may bring in, duty-free, 200 cigarettes and 50 cigars. Check ahead of time with the Canada Customs and Revenue Agency or the Department of Agriculture for policies regarding meat products, seeds, plants, and fruits.

You may send an unlimited number of gifts (only one gift per recipient, however) worth up to C$60 each duty-free to Canada. Label the package UNSOLICITED GIFT—VALUE UNDER $60. Alcohol and tobacco are excluded.

➤ INFORMATION: **Canada Customs and Revenue Agency** (✉ 2265 St. Laurent Blvd. S, Ottawa, Ontario K1G 4K3, ☎ 204/983–3500, 506/636–5064, 800/461–9999, ☒ www.ccra-adrc.gc.ca/).

IN NEW ZEALAND

All homeward-bound residents may bring back NZ$700 worth of souvenirs and gifts; passengers may not pool their allowances, and children can claim only the concession on goods intended for their own use. For those 17 or older, the duty-free allowance also includes 4.5 liters of wine or beer; one 1,125-ml bottle of spirits; and either 200 cigarettes, 250 grams of tobacco, 50 cigars, *or* a combination of the three up to 250 grams. Meat products, seeds, plants, and fruits must be declared upon arrival to the Agricultural Services Department.

➤ INFORMATION: **New Zealand Customs** (Head office: ✉ The Customhouse, 17–21 Whitmore St., Box 2218, Wellington, ☎ 09/300–5399 or 0800/428–786, 🖵 www.customs.govt.nz.

IN THE U.K.

From countries outside the European Union, including the United States, you may bring home, duty-free, 200 cigarettes or 50 cigars; 1 liter of spirits or 2 liters of fortified or sparkling wine or liqueurs; 2 liters of still table wine; 60 ml of perfume; 250 ml of toilet water; plus £145 worth of other goods, including gifts and souvenirs. Prohibited items include meat products, seeds, plants, and fruits.

➤ INFORMATION: **HM Customs and Excise** (✉ Portcullis House, 21 Cowbridge Rd. E, Cardiff CF11 9SS, ☎ 029/2038–6423 or 0845/010–9000, 🖵 www.hmce.gov.uk).

DINING

Thoughts of dining in New England center on seafood, and the coast and many inland locations have restaurants specializing in lobster, clams, scallops, and fresh fish. Restaurants in New England's cities have an impressive variety of menus and price ranges. The best dining in rural areas is often to be found in country inns, the larger of which are often quite proud of their chefs and their commitment to using local meats and produce.

Restaurant prices in New England are generally on a par with those elsewhere in the country, but travelers may experience sticker shock at even more modest seafood restaurants. Catch limits on many favorite ocean species, as well as the premium charged for lobster and other shellfish, have sent prices soaring. Lobsters are sold by the pound ("market price" is the phrase that appears on many menus), and a $20 lobster dinner or a $10 lobster roll is not uncommon.

The restaurants we list are the cream of the crop in each price category. Properties indicated by an ✕🔲 are lodging establishments whose restaurant warrants a special trip. Following is the price chart used in this book; note that prices do not include tax, which is 6% in Connecticut, 5% in Maine (7% on alcohol), 5% in Massachusetts, 8% in New Hampshire, 7% in Rhode Island, and 9% in Vermont (10% on alcohol).

CATEGORY	COST*
$$$$	over $25
$$$	$17–$25
$$	$9–$16
$	under $9

*per person, for a main-course dinner

MEALTIMES

In general, the widest variety of mealtime options in New England is in larger cities and at resort areas.

For an early breakfast, pick places that cater to a working clientele. City, town, and roadside establishments specializing in breakfast for the busy often open their doors at 5 or 6 AM. At country inns and B&Bs, breakfast is seldom served before 8; if you need to get an earlier start, ask ahead of time if your host or hostess can accommodate you.

Unless otherwise noted, the restaurants listed in this guide are open daily for lunch and dinner. Lunch in New England generally runs from around 11 to 2:30; dinner is usually served from 6 to 9 (many restaurants have early-bird specials beginning at 5). Only in the larger cities will you find full dinners being offered much later than 9, although you can usually find a bar or bistro serving a limited menu late into the evening in all but the smallest towns.

Many restaurants in New England are closed on Mondays, although this is never true in resort areas in high season. However, resort-town eateries often shut down completely in the off-season.

Credit cards are accepted for meals throughout New England in all but the most modest establishments.

RESERVATIONS AND DRESS

Reservations are always a good idea; we mention them only when they're essential or not accepted. Book as far ahead as you can, and reconfirm as soon as you arrive. (Large parties should always call ahead to check the reservations policy.) We mention dress only when men are required to wear a jacket or a jacket and tie.

WINE, BEER, AND SPIRITS

New England is no stranger to microbrews. The granddaddy of New England's independent beer makers is Boston's Samuel Adams, producing brews available throughout the region since 1985. Following the Sam Adams lead in offering hearty English-style ales and special seasonal brews are breweries such as Vermont's Long Trail, Maine's Shipyard, and New Hampshire's Old Man Ale.

New England is beginning to earn some respect as a wine-producing region. Varieties capable of withstanding the region's harsh winters have been the basis of promising enterprises such as Rhode Island's Sakonnet Vineyards, Chicama Vineyards on Martha's Vineyard, and Connecticut's Hopkins Vineyard. Even Vermont is getting into the act with the new Snow Farm Vineyard in the Lake Champlain Islands and Boyden Valley Winery in Cambridge.

Although a patchwork of state and local regulations affect the hours and locations of places that sell alcoholic beverages, New England licensing laws are fairly liberal. State-owned or -franchised stores sell hard liquor in New Hampshire, Maine, and Vermont; many travelers have found that New Hampshire offers the region's lowest prices. Look for state-run liquor "supermarkets" on interstate highways in the southern part of the state; these also have good wine selections.

DISABILITIES AND ACCESSIBILITY

➤ LOCAL RESOURCES: **Cape Cod Chamber of Commerce** (✉ U.S. 6 and Rte. 132, Hyannis 02601, ☎ 508/862–0700 or 888/332–2732) produces two publications with accessibility ratings: "Visitor's Guide" and "Accommodations Directory." The **Cape Cod National Seashore** (✉ South Wellfleet 02663, ☎ 508/349–3785) publishes "Cape Cod National Seashore Accessibility." **Connecticut Office of Tourism** (☞ Visitor Information) prints accessibility codes in the *Connecticut Vacation Guide*. **MBTA** (✉ MBTA, Office for Transportation Access, 10 Boylston Pl., Boston 02116, ☎ 617/722–3200; 617/222–5415 TTY) distributes a brochure, "MBTA: Access." The **New Hampshire Office of Travel and Tourism Development's** (☞ Visitor Information) *New Hampshire Guide Book* includes accessibility ratings for lodgings and restaurants. **Vermont Chamber of Commerce** (☞ Visitor Information) includes accessibility codes for attractions in the *Vermont Traveler's Guidebook*. **VSA** (✉ 2 Boylston St., Room 211, Boston 02116, ☎ 617/350–7713, WEB www.accessexpressed.net) sells "Access Expressed! New England."

LODGING

Despite the Americans with Disabilities Act, the definition of accessibility seems to differ from hotel to hotel. Some properties may be accessible by ADA standards for people with mobility problems but not for people with hearing or vision impairments, for example.

If you have mobility problems, ask for the lowest floor on which accessible services are offered. If you have a hearing impairment, check whether the hotel has devices to alert you visually to the ring of the telephone, knock at the door, and a fire/emergency alarm. Some hotels provide these devices without charge. Discuss your needs with hotel personnel if this equipment isn't available, so that a staff member can personally alert you in the event of an emergency.

If you're bringing a guide dog, get authorization ahead of time and write down the name of the person you spoke with.

RESERVATIONS

When discussing accessibility with an operator or reservations agent, **ask hard questions.** Are there any stairs, inside *or* out? Are there grab bars next to the toilet *and* in the shower/tub? How wide is the doorway to the room? To the bathroom? For the most extensive facilities meeting the latest legal specifications, **opt for newer accommodations.** If you reserve through a toll-free number, consider also calling the hotel's local number to confirm the information from the central reservations office. Get confirmation in writing when you can.

SIGHTS AND ATTRACTIONS

In Boston, many sidewalks are brick or cobblestone and may be uneven or sloping; many have curbs cut at one end and not the other. To make matters worse, Boston drivers are notorious for running yellow lights and ignoring pedestrians. Back Bay has flat, well-paved streets; older Beacon Hill is steep and difficult; Quincy Market's cobblestone and brick malls are crisscrossed with smooth, tarred paths. The downtown financial district and Chinatown are accessible, while areas such as the South End and the Italian North End may prove more problematic for people who use wheelchairs.

In Cape Cod, a number of towns such as Wellfleet, Hyannis, and Chatham have wide streets with curb cuts, and the Cape Cod National Seashore has several accessible trails. The narrow streets of Provincetown, the Cape's most-popular destination, are difficult for anyone to navigate. Travelers using wheelchairs would be well advised to visit "P-town" in the off-season, when pedestrian and vehicular traffic is less chaotic.

In Kennebunkport, as in many of Maine's coastal towns south of Portland, travelers with mobility impairments will have to cope with crowds as well as with narrow, uneven steps and sporadic curb cuts. L. L. Bean's outlet in Freeport is fully accessible, and Acadia National Park has some 50 accessible mi of carriage roads that are closed to motor vehicles. In New Hampshire, many of Franconia Notch's natural attractions are accessible.

TRANSPORTATION

Many major rental agencies provide special cars for people with disabilities on request. Most ask that you provide your own handicapped sticker or plate, which will be honored throughout the region. Be sure to reserve well in advance.

➤ COMPLAINTS: **Aviation Consumer Protection Division** (☞ Air Travel) for airline-related problems. **Departmental Office of Civil Rights** (for general inquiries, ✉ U.S. Department of Transportation, S-30, 400 7th St. SW, Room 10215, Washington, DC 20590, ☎ 202/366–4648, FAX 202/366–3571, WEB www.dot.gov/ost/docr/index.htm). **Disability Rights Section** (✉ NYAV, U.S. Department of Justice, Civil Rights Division, 950 Pennsylvania Ave. NW, Washington, DC 20530; ☎ ADA information line 202/514–0301, 800/514–0301, 202/514–0383 TTY, 800/514–0383 TTY, WEB www.usdoj.gov/crt/ada/adahom1.htm).

TRAVEL AGENCIES

In the United States, the Americans with Disabilities Act requires that travel firms serve the needs of all travelers. Some agencies specialize in working with people with disabilities.

➤ TRAVELERS WITH MOBILITY PROBLEMS: **Access Adventures** (✉ 206 Chestnut Ridge Rd., Scottsville, NY 14624, ☎ 716/889–9096), run by a former physical-rehabilitation counselor. **Accessible Vans of America** (✉ 9 Spielman Rd., Fairfield, NJ 07004, ☎ 877/282–8267; 888/282–8267 reservations; FAX 973/808–9713; WEB www.accessiblevans.com). **CareVacations** (✉ No. 5, 5110–50 Ave., Leduc, Alberta T9E 6V4, Canada, ☎ 780/986–6404 or 877/478–7827, FAX 780/986–8332, WEB www.carevacations.com), for group tours and cruise vacations. **Flying Wheels Travel** (✉ 143 W. Bridge St. [Box 382, Owatonna, MN 55060], ☎ 507/451–5005, FAX 507/451–1685, WEB www.flyingwheelstravel.com).

➤ TRAVELERS WITH DEVELOPMENTAL DISABILITIES: **Sprout** (✉ 893 Amsterdam Ave., New York, NY 10025, ☎ 212/222–9575 or 888/222–9575, FAX 212/222–9768, WEB www.gosprout.org).

DISCOUNTS AND DEALS

Be a smart shopper and **compare all your options** before making decisions. A plane ticket bought with a promotional coupon from travel clubs, coupon books, and direct-mail offers or purchased on the Internet may not be cheaper than the least expensive fare from a discount ticket agency. And always keep in mind that what you get is just as important as what you save.

DISCOUNT RESERVATIONS

To save money, **look into discount reservations services** with Web sites and toll-free numbers, which use their buying power to get a better price on hotels, airline tickets, even car rentals. When booking a room, always **call the hotel's local toll-free number** (if one is available) rather than the central reservations number—you'll often get a better price. Always ask about special packages or corporate rates.

➤ AIRLINE TICKETS: ☎ 800/AIR–4LESS. Travelocity (www.travelocity.com). Priceline.com (www.priceline.com).

➤ HOTEL ROOMS: **Accommodations Express** (☎ 800/444–7666, WEB www.accommodationsexpress.com). **Central Reservation Service** (CRS; ☎ 800/548–3311, WEB www.room-connection.net). **Hotel Reservations Network** (☎ 800/964–6835, WEB www.hoteldiscount.com).**Quikbook** (☎ 800/789–9887, WEB www.quik-book.com). **RMC Travel** (☎ 800/245–5738, WEB www.rmcwebtravel.com). **Steigenberger Reservation Service** (☎ 800/223–5652, WEB www.srs-worldhotels.com). **Turbotrip.com** (☎ 800/473–7829, WEB www.turbotrip.com).

PACKAGE DEALS

Don't confuse packages and guided tours. When you buy a package, you travel on your own, just as though you had planned the trip yourself. Fly-drive packages, which combine airfare and car rental, are often a good deal.

ECOTOURISM

Many state parks in New England request that you dispose of your trash after you leave the grounds. Connecticut, Massachusetts, Maine, and Vermont recycle cans and bottles and charge 5¢–15¢ per unit at time of purchase, refundable when the can or bottle is returned to a store or recycling center.

Throughout the region, particularly on beaches and in areas with high cliffs, markers forbid trespassing. These are generally nesting areas for endangered species, such as peregrine falcons in Smugglers' Notch, Vermont, and terns on beaches in Connecticut and Massachusetts.

GAY AND LESBIAN TRAVEL

As one of the country's most socially and politically progressive regions, New England is almost invariably accepting of gay and lesbian travelers. Some exceptions might be found in some areas less frequented by visitors, but in general, people in the tourism business here are hospitable to travelers regardless of sexual orientation.

The capitals of gay New England are Boston and Cambridge and, on Cape Cod, Provincetown. Most sizable college and university towns in New England have gay communities. Alternative publications in all of these areas carry listings of gay bars, nightclubs, and special events. For details about the gay and lesbian scene in Boston and Provincetown, Massachusetts, and in Ogunquit, Maine, consult *Fodor's Gay Guide to the USA* (available in bookstores everywhere).

➤ GAY- AND LESBIAN-FRIENDLY TRAVEL AGENCIES: **Different Roads Travel** (✉ 8383 Wilshire Blvd., Suite 902, Beverly Hills, CA 90211, ☎ 323/651–5557 or 800/429–8747, FAX 323/651–3678). **Kennedy Travel** (✉ 314 Jericho Turnpike, Floral Park, NY 11001, ☎ 516/352–4888 or 800/237–7433, FAX 516/354–8849, WEB www.kennedytravel.com). **Now, Voyager** (✉ 4406 18th St., San Francisco, CA 94114, ☎ 415/626–1169 or 800/255–6951, FAX 415/626–8626, WEB www.nowvoyager.com). **Skylink Travel and Tour** (✉ 1006 Mendocino Ave., Santa Rosa, CA 95401, ☎ 707/546–9888 or 800/225–5759, FAX 707/546–9891, WEB www.skylinktravel.com), serving lesbian travelers.

GUIDEBOOKS

Plan well and you won't be sorry. Guidebooks are excellent tools—and you can take them with you. You may want to check out color-photo-illustrated guides such as *Fodor's Exploring Boston and New England* and the Maine, Vermont, Southern New England, and Boston guides in the Compass American series—all thorough on culture and history. *Fodor's Road Guide USA: Maine, Vermont, and New Hampshire* and *Fodor's Road Guide USA: Connecticut,*

Massachusetts, and Rhode Island are packed with hotel, restaurant, and attractions listings. Also see *Fodor's Cape Cod, Pocket Martha's Vineyard,* and *Pocket Nantucket.* Visiting Boston? Study *Fodor's Boston;* pocket-size *Citypack Boston,* with a supersize city map; *Flashmaps Boston,* for theme maps; or *Fodor's CITYGUIDE Boston,* for residents, packed with listings. All are available at on-line retailers and bookstores everywhere.

HEALTH

LYME DISEASE

Lyme disease, so named for its having been first reported in the town of Lyme, Connecticut, is a potentially debilitating disease carried by deer ticks, which thrive in dry, brush-covered areas, particularly on the coast. Always **use insect repellent;** outbreaks of Lyme disease all over the East Coast make it imperative that you protect yourself from ticks from early spring through summer. To prevent bites, **wear light-colored clothing and tuck pant legs into socks.** Look for black ticks about the size of a pinhead around hairlines and the warmest parts of the body. If you have been bitten, **consult a physician, especially if you see the telltale bull's-eye bite pattern.** Influenza-like symptoms often accompany a Lyme infection. Early treatment is imperative.

PESTS AND OTHER HAZARDS

New England's two greatest insect pests are black flies and mosquitoes. The former are a phenomenon of late spring and early summer and are generally a problem only in the densely wooded areas of the far north. Mosquitoes, however, can be a nuisance just about everywhere in summer—they're at their worst following snowy winters and wet springs. The best protection against both pests is repellent containing DEET; if you're camping in the woods during black fly season, you'll also want to **use fine mesh screening in eating and sleeping areas, and even wear mesh headgear.** A particular pest of coastal areas, especially salt marshes, is the greenhead fly. Their bite is nasty, and they are best repelled by a liberal application of Avon Skin So Soft.

SHELLFISHING

Coastal waters attract seafood lovers who enjoy harvesting their own clams, mussels, and even lobsters; permits are required, and casual harvesting of lobsters is strictly forbidden. Amateur clammers should be aware that New England shellfish beds are periodically visited by red tides, during which microorganisms can render shellfish poisonous. To keep abreast of the situation, inquire when you apply for a license (usually at town halls or police stations) and pay attention to red tide postings as you travel.

HOLIDAYS

Expect banks and post offices to be closed on all national holidays. Exceptions are restaurants and hotels, which, depending on location, may be even busier at holiday times. Christmas in Boston or in ski country, for instance, will require early advance dining and lodging reservations. Public transportation schedules will also be affected on major holidays; in general, schedules will be similar for those of normal Sundays.

Major national holidays include New Year's Day (Jan. 1); Martin Luther King Jr. Day (3rd Mon. in Jan.); Presidents' Day (3rd Mon. in Feb.); Memorial Day (last Mon. in May); Independence Day (July 4); Labor Day (1st Mon. in Sept.); Thanksgiving Day (4th Thurs. in Nov.); Christmas Day (Dec. 25); and New Year's Eve (Dec. 31). Patriots' Day (the Monday closest to Apr. 19) is a state holiday in Massachusetts.

INSURANCE

The most useful travel-insurance plan is a comprehensive policy that includes coverage for trip cancellation and interruption, default, trip delay, and medical expenses (with a waiver for preexisting conditions).

Without insurance you will lose all or most of your money if you cancel your trip, regardless of the reason. Default insurance covers you if your tour operator, airline, or cruise line goes out of business. Trip-delay covers expenses that arise because of bad weather or mechanical delays. Study the fine print when comparing policies.

Always **buy travel policies directly from the insurance company**; if you buy them from a cruise line, airline, or tour operator that goes out of business you probably will not be covered for the agency or operator's default, a major risk. Before making any purchase, **review your existing health and homeowner's policies** to find what they cover away from home.

➤ TRAVEL INSURERS: In the United States: **Access America** (⊠ 6600 W. Broad St., Richmond, VA 23230, ☎ 800/284–8300, FAX 804/673–1491 or 800/346–9265, WEB www.accessamerica.com). **Travel Guard International** (⊠ 1145 Clark St., Stevens Point, WI 54481, ☎ 715/345–0505 or 800/826–1300, FAX 800/955–8785, WEB www.travelguard.com).

FOR INTERNATIONAL TRAVELERS

For information on customs restrictions, *see* Customs and Duties

CAR TRAVEL

Interstate highways—limited-access, multilane highways whose numbers are prefixed by "I–"—are the fastest routes. Interstates with three-digit numbers encircle urban areas, which may have other limited-access expressways, freeways, and parkways as well. Tolls may be levied on limited-access highways. So-called U.S. highways and state highways are not necessarily limited-access but may have several lanes.

Along larger highways, roadside stops with rest rooms, fast-food restaurants, and sundries stores are well spaced. State police and tow trucks patrol major highways and lend assistance. If your car breaks down on an interstate, pull onto the shoulder and wait for help, or have your passengers wait while you walk to an emergency phone. If you carry a cell phone, dial *55, noting your location on the small green roadside mileage markers.

Driving in the United States is on the right. Do **obey speed limits** posted along roads and highways. Watch for lower limits in small towns and on back roads. On weekdays between 6 and 9 AM and again between 4 and 7 PM **expect heavy traffic.** To encourage carpooling, some freeways have special lanes for so-called high-occupancy vehicles (HOV)—cars carrying more than one passenger.

Bookstores, gas stations, convenience stores, and rest stops sell maps (about $3) and multiregion road atlases (about $10).

For more information, *see* Car Travel.

CONSULATES AND EMBASSIES

➤ AUSTRALIA: **Consulate** (⊠ 150 E. 42nd St., 34th floor, New York, NY 10017, ☎ 212/351–6500).

➤ CANADA: **Consulate** (⊠ 3 Copley Pl., Suite 400, Boston, MA 02216, ☎ 617/262–3760).

➤ NEW ZEALAND: **Consulate** (⊠ 780 3rd Ave. NW, Suite 1904, New York, NY 10017-2024, ☎ 212/832–7420)

➤ UNITED KINGDOM: **Consulate** (⊠ 600 Atlantic Ave., Boston, MA 02210, ☎ 617/248–9555).

CURRENCY

The dollar is the basic unit of U.S. currency. It has 100 cents. Coins include the copper penny (1¢); the silvery nickel (5¢), dime (10¢), quarter (25¢), and half-dollar (50¢); and the golden $1 coin, replacing a now-rare silver dollar. Bills are denominated $1, $5, $10, $20, $50, and $100, all green and identical in size; designs vary. The exchange rate at press time was US$1.44 per British pound, $.62 per Canadian dollar, $.52 per Australian dollar, and $.42 per New Zealand dollar. The European Union euro was at $.95 euro to the dollar.

ELECTRICITY

The U.S. standard is AC, 110 volts/60 cycles. Plugs have two flat pins set parallel to each other.

EMERGENCIES

For police, fire, or ambulance, **dial 911.**

INSURANCE

Britons and Australians need extra medical coverage when traveling overseas.

➤ INSURANCE INFORMATION: In Australia: **Insurance Council of Australia** (✉ Level 3, 56 Pitt St., Sydney, NSW 2000, ☎ 02/9253–5100, FAX 02/9253–5111, WEB www.ica.com.au). In Canada: **RBC Insurance** (✉ 6880 Financial Dr., Mississauga, Ontario L5N 7Y5, ☎ 905/816–2400 or 800/668–4342, FAX 905/813–4704, WEB www.rbcinsurance.com). In New Zealand: **Insurance Council of New Zealand** (✉ Level 7, 111–115 Customhouse Quay, Box 474, Wellington, ☎ 04/472–5230, FAX 04/473–3011, WEB www.icnz.org.nz). In the United Kingdom: **Association of British Insurers** (✉ 51 Gresham St., London EC2V 7HQ, ☎ 020/7600–3333, FAX 020/7696–8999, WEB www.abi.org.uk).

MAIL AND SHIPPING

You can buy stamps and aerograms and send letters and parcels in post offices. Stamp-dispensing machines can occasionally be found in airports, bus and train stations, office buildings, drugstores, and the like. You can also deposit mail in the stout, dark blue steel bins at strategic locations everywhere and in the mail chutes of large buildings; pickup schedules are posted.

For mail sent within the United States, you need a 37¢ stamp for first-class letters weighing up to 1 ounce (23¢ for each additional ounce) and 23¢ for postcards. You pay 80¢ for 1-ounce airmail letters and 70¢ for airmail postcards to most other countries; to Canada and Mexico, you need a 60¢ stamp for a 1-ounce letter and 50¢ for a postcard. An aerogram—a single sheet of lightweight blue paper that folds into its own envelope, stamped for overseas airmail—costs 70¢.

To receive mail on the road, have it sent c/o General Delivery at your destination's main post office (use the correct five-digit ZIP code). You must pick up mail in person within 30 days and show a driver's license or passport.

PASSPORTS AND VISAS

When traveling internationally, **carry your passport** even if you don't need one (it's always the best form of ID)

and **make two photocopies of the data page** (one for someone at home and another for you, carried separately from your passport). If you lose your passport, promptly call the nearest embassy or consulate and the local police.

Visitor visas are not necessary for Canadian citizens, or for citizens of Australia and the United Kingdom who are staying fewer than 90 days.

➤ AUSTRALIAN CITIZENS: **Australian State Passport Office** (☎ 131–232, WEB www.passports.gov.au). **United States Consulate General** (✉ MLC Centre, 19–29 Martin Pl., 59th floor, Sydney, NSW 2000, ☎ 02/9373–9200, 1902/941–641 fee-based visa-inquiry line, WEB www.usis-australia.gov/index.html).

➤ CANADIAN CITIZENS: **Passport Office** (to mail in applications: ✉ Department of Foreign Affairs and International Trade, Ottawa, Ontario K1A 0G3, ☎ 819/994–3500 or 800/567–6868, WEB www.dfait-maeci.gc.ca/passport).

➤ NEW ZEALAND CITIZENS: **New Zealand Passport Office** (☎ 04/474–8100 or 0800/22–5050, WEB www.passports.govt.nz). **Embassy of the United States** (✉ 29 Fitzherbert Terr., Thorndon, Wellington, ☎ 04/462–6000 WEB usembassy.org.nz). **U.S. Consulate General** (✉ Citibank Bldg., 3rd floor, 23 Customs St. E, Auckland, ☎ 09/303–2724, WEB usembassy.org.nz).

➤ U.K. CITIZENS: **London Passport Office** (☎ 0870/521–0410, WEB www.passport.gov.uk). **U.S. Consulate General** (✉ Queen's House, 14 Queen St., Belfast, Northern Ireland BT1 6EQ, ☎ 028/9032–8239, WEB www.usembassy.org.uk). **U.S. Embassy** (enclose a SASE to ✉ Consular Information Unit, 24 Grosvenor Sq., London W1 1AE, for general information; ✉ Visa Branch, 5 Upper Grosvenor St., London W1A 2JB, to submit an application via mail; ☎ 09068/200–290 recorded visa information or 09055/444–546 operator service, both with per-minute charges; WEB www.usembassy.org.uk).

TELEPHONES

All U.S. telephone numbers consist of a three-digit area code and a seven-digit local number. Within most local calling areas, you dial only the seven-digit number. Within the same area code, dial "1" first. To call between area-code regions, dial "1" then all 10 digits; the same goes for calls to numbers prefixed by "800," "888," and "877"—all toll-free. For calls to numbers preceded by "900" you must pay—usually dearly.

For international calls, dial "011" followed by the country code and the local number. For help, dial "0" and ask for an overseas operator. The country code is 61 for Australia, 64 for New Zealand, 44 for the United Kingdom. Calling Canada is the same as calling within the United States. Most local phone books list country codes and U.S. area codes. The country code for the United States is 1.

For operator assistance, dial "0." To obtain someone's phone number, call directory assistance, 555–1212 or occasionally 411 (free at public phones). To have the person you're calling foot the bill, phone collect; dial "0" instead of "1" before the 10-digit number.

At pay phones, instructions are usually posted. Usually you insert coins in a slot (10¢–50¢ for local calls) and wait for a steady tone before dialing. When you call long-distance, the operator tells you how much to insert; prepaid phone cards, widely available in various denominations, are easier. Call the number on the back, punch in the card's personal identification number when prompted, then dial your number.

LODGING

Hotel and motel chains provide standard rooms and amenities in major cities and at or near traditional vacation destinations. At small inns, where each room is different and amenities vary in number and quality, price isn't always a reliable indicator; fortunately, when you call to make reservations, most hosts will be happy to give all manner of details about their properties, down to the color scheme of the handmade quilts—so **ask all your questions before you book.** Also **ask if the property has a Web site**; sites may have helpful information and pictures, although

it's always wise to confirm how up-to-date the information is. The rooms in the lodgings reviewed here have private baths unless otherwise indicated.

The lodgings we list are the cream of the crop in each price category. We always list the facilities that are available—but we don't specify whether they cost extra. When pricing accommodations, always ask what's included and what costs extra. Lodgings are indicated in the text by a little house icon, ⌂ ; lodging establishments whose restaurants warrant a special trip, by ✕⌂ . Following is the price chart used in this book; note that prices do not include tax, which is 12% in Connecticut, 5% in Maine, 5% state tax plus up to 7% local tax in some cities in Massachusetts, 8% in New Hampshire, 5% in Rhode Island, and 9% in Vermont.

CATEGORY	BOSTON, THE CAPE, AND THE ISLANDS*	OTHER AREAS*
$$$$	over $220	over $180
$$$	$160–$220	$130–$180
$$	$110–$160	$80–$130
$	under $110	under $80

All prices are for a standard double room during peak season and not including tax or gratuities. Some inns add a 15% service charge.

Assume that hotels operate on the **European Plan** (EP, with no meals) unless we specify that they use the **Continental Plan** (CP, with a Continental breakfast), **Breakfast Plan** (BP, with a full breakfast), **Modified American Plan** (MAP, with breakfast and dinner), or the **Full American Plan** (FAP, with all meals).

APARTMENT RENTALS

If you want a home base that's roomy enough for a family and comes with cooking facilities, **consider a furnished rental.** These can save you money, especially if you're traveling with a group. Home-exchange directories sometimes list rentals as well as exchanges. In New England, you are most likely to find a house, apartment, or condo rental in areas in which ownership of second homes is common, such as beach resorts and ski country. A good strategy is to **inquire about rentals in what would be the off-season** for those resort areas—for instance, it's fairly easy to rent ski chalets during the summer. Home-exchange directories sometimes list rentals as well as exchanges. Another good bet is to **contact real estate agents in the area in which you are interested.**

➤ INTERNATIONAL AGENTS: **Hideaways International** (✉ 767 Islington St., Portsmouth, NH 03801, ☎ 603/430–4433 or 800/843–4433, FAX 603/430–4444, WEB www.hideaways.com; membership $129).

➤ LOCAL AGENTS: **Cyberrentals.com** (✉ 110 Main St., Ludlow, VT 05149, ☎ 802/228–7158, FAX 815/461–5569, WEB www.CyberRentals.com). **Go New England** (✉ Box 322, Harwich Port, MA 02646-0322, WEB www.gonewengland.com).

BED-AND-BREAKFASTS

The bed-and-breakfasts and small inns of New England offer some of the region's most distinctive lodging experiences. Some are homey and casual, others provide a stay in a historic property in a city or out in the country, and still others are modern and luxurious. At even the poshest country inns, rooms frequently lack telephones or televisions; many proprietors feel that their guests are actively escaping from the modern world. These properties are also not likely to feature air-conditioning, which is often superfluous in New England's mountains or seashore. Most inns offer bed-and-breakfast—hence the name bed-and-breakfast—yet this formula varies; at one B&B you may be served muffins and coffee, at another a multicourse feast with fresh flowers on the table. In keeping with the preferences of their guests, most inns and B&Bs prohibit smoking, and some of the inns with antiques or other expensive furnishings do not allow children. Almost all say no to pets. Always be sure to **ask about any restrictions** when you're making a reservation. It's also necessary to **inquire about minimum stays**; many inns require a two-night stay on weekends, for example.

CAMPING

The state offices of tourism (☞ Visitor Information) supply information about privately operated campgrounds and ones in parks run by state agencies and the federal government.

HOME EXCHANGES

If you would like to exchange your home for someone else's, **join a home-exchange organization,** which will send you its updated listings of available exchanges for a year and will include your own listing in at least one of them. It's up to you to make specific arrangements.

➤ EXCHANGE CLUBS: **HomeLink International** (✉ Box 47747, Tampa, FL 33647, ☎ 813/975–9825 or 800/638–3841, FAX 813/910–8144, WEB www.homelink.org; $106 per year). **Intervac Home Exchange** (✉ 30 Corte San Fernando, Tiburon, CA 94920, ☎ 800/756–4663, FAX 415/435–7440, WEB www.intervacus.com; $93 yearly fee includes one catalog and on-line access).

HOSTELS

No matter what your age, you can **save on lodging costs by staying at hostels.** In some 4,500 locations in more than 70 countries around the world, Hostelling International (HI), the umbrella group for a number of national youth-hostel associations, offers single-sex, dorm-style beds and, at many hostels, rooms for couples and family accommodations. Membership in any HI national hostel association, open to travelers of all ages, allows you to stay in HI-affiliated hostels at member rates; one-year membership is about $25 for adults (C$35 for a two-year minimum membership in Canada, £13 in the U.K., A$52 in Australia, and NZ$40 in New Zealand); hostels run about $10–$30 per night. Members have priority if the hostel is full; they're also eligible for discounts around the world, even on rail and bus travel in some countries.

➤ ORGANIZATIONS: **Hostelling International—American Youth Hostels** (✉ 733 15th St. NW, Suite 840, Washington, DC 20005, ☎ 202/783–6161, FAX 202/783–6171,

WEB www.hiayh.org). **Hostelling International—Canada** (✉ 400–205 Catherine St., Ottawa, Ontario K2P 1C3, ☎ 613/237–7884 or 800/663–5777, FAX 613/237–7868, WEB www.hihostels.ca). **Youth Hostel Association of England and Wales** (✉ Trevelyan House, Dimple Rd., Matlock, Derbyshire DE4 3YH, U.K., ☎ 0870/870–8808, FAX 0169/592–702, WEB www.yha.org.uk). **Youth Hostel Association Australia** (✉ 10 Mallett St., Camperdown, NSW 2050, ☎ 02/9565–1699, FAX 02/9565–1325, WEB www.yha.com.au). **Youth Hostels Association of New Zealand** (✉ Level 3, 193 Cashel St., Box 436, Christchurch, ☎ 03/379–9970, FAX 03/365–4476, WEB www.yha.org.nz).

HOTELS

Hotel and motel chains are amply represented in New England. Some of the large chains, such as Holiday Inn, Hilton, Hyatt, Marriott, and Ramada, operate all-suites, budget, business-oriented, or luxury resorts, often variations on the parent corporation's name (Courtyard by Marriott, for example). Though some chain hotels and motels may have a standardized look to them, this "cookie-cutter" approach also means that you can rely on the same level of comfort and efficiency at all properties in a well-managed chain, and at a chain's premier properties—its so-called flagship hotels—the decor and services may be outstanding.

New England is liberally supplied with small, independent motels, which run the gamut from the tired to the tidy. Don't overlook these mom-and-pop operations; they frequently offer cheerful, convenient accommodations at lower rates than the chains.

While reservations are always a good idea, they are particularly recommended in summer and winter resort areas; in college towns during September and at graduation time in the spring; and at areas renowned for autumn foliage.

Most hotels and motels will hold your reservation until 6 PM; **call ahead if you plan to arrive late.** All will hold a late reservation for you if you guarantee your reservation with a credit-card number.

When you call to make a reservation, **ask all the necessary questions up front.** If you are arriving with a car, ask if there is a parking lot or covered garage and whether there is an extra fee for parking. If you like to eat your meals in, ask if the hotel has a restaurant or whether it has room service (most do, but not necessarily 24 hours a day—and be forewarned that it can be expensive). Most hotels and motels have in-room TVs, often with cable movies, but verify this if you like to watch TV. If you want an in-room crib for your child, there will probably be an additional charge.

➤ TOLL-FREE NUMBERS: **Best Western** (☎ 800/528–1234, WEB www.bestwestern.com). **Choice** (☎ 800/221–2222, WEB www.choicehotels.com). **Clarion** (☎ 800/424–6423, WEB www.choicehotels.com). **Colony Resorts** (☎ 800/777–1700). **Comfort Inn** (☎ 800/424–6423, WEB www.choicehotels.com). **Days Inn** (☎ 800/325–2525, WEB www.daysinn.com). **Doubletree and Red Lion Hotels** (☎ 800/222–8733, (WEB www.hilton.com). **Embassy Suites** (☎ 800/362–2779, WEB www.embassysuites.com). **Fairfield Inn** (☎ 800/228–2800, WEB www.marriott.com).**Four Seasons** (☎ 800/332–3442, WEB www.fourseasons.com). **Hilton** (☎ 800/445–8667, WEB www.hilton.com). **Holiday Inn** (☎ 800/465–4329, WEB www.sixcontinentshotels.com). **Howard Johnson** (☎ 800/654–4656, WEB www.hojo.com). **Hyatt Hotels & Resorts** (☎ 800/233–1234, WEB www.hyatt.com). **La Quinta** (☎ 800/531–5900, WEB www.laquinta.com). **Marriott** (☎ 800/228–9290, WEB www.marriott.com). **Quality Inn** (☎ 800/228–5151, WEB www.choicehotels.com). **Radisson** (☎ 800/333–3333, WEB www.radisson.com). **Ramada** (☎ 800/228–2828; 800/854–7854 international reservations; WEB www.ramada.com or www.ramadahotels.com). **Sheraton** (☎ 800/325–3535, WEB www.sheraton.com). **Sleep Inn** (☎ 800/424–6423, WEB www.choicehotels.com). **Westin Hotels & Resorts** (☎ 800/228–3000, WEB www.starwood.com/westin).

MAIL AND SHIPPING

➤ OVERNIGHT SERVICES: **FedEx** (☎ 800/463–3339). **UPS** (☎ 800/742–5877).

MEDIA

NEWSPAPERS AND MAGAZINES

The *New York Times* and the national *USA Today* are available in all but the most remote regions of New England; of the two, the *Times* is by far the more thorough and is considered the United States newspaper of record. The *Boston Globe,* a respected morning daily, is also available throughout the region. Most cities with 10,000 or more inhabitants generally have their own daily newspapers, many of which carry comprehensive listings of local events at least once a week. Larger cities and college towns often have at least one alternative publication that provides extensive coverage on the local cultural and social scene. Among regional magazines, the most noteworthy are *Yankee, Vermont Life, Down East* (Maine), and *Boston.*

RADIO AND TELEVISION

As in the rest of the United States, talk shows are usually found on AM radio stations, while FM stations are devoted primarily to music. National Public Radio (NPR), which has FM affiliates in each New England state, provides a combination of both, including *Morning Edition* and *All Things Considered,* the most comprehensive radio news programs in the U.S.

Although New England's half dozen or so major metropolitan areas each have their own local television stations and public television affiliates, cable and satellite TV bring dozens of channels to most hotels and motels. Cable News Network (CNN) offers the most comprehensive national and international news coverage. Boston's public television affiliate, WGBH, is a flagship station of the U.S. Public Television Network.

MONEY MATTERS

It costs about the same to travel in New England as it does throughout the rest of the northeastern United States. As a rule, this is slightly more expensive than touring just about anywhere else in the country, with the exception of metropolitan California and major resort areas. The regional capital, Boston, is among the more expensive U.S. cities; it's cheaper than New York City and perhaps comparable to San Francisco. Out in the countryside, or in lesser metropolitan centers, you'll find consistent good value, with the exception of places such as Cape Cod and the Massachusetts islands (in summer) and times such as fall foliage season (along the well-traveled routes of western and northern New England).

British, Australian, and New Zealand travelers will find hotel and restaurant tariffs comparable to those they're familiar with at home; Canadians, however, may be in for a bit of sticker shock due to the prevailing exchange rate between the two currencies. However, a number of hotel and resort operators, and places frequented by Canadian travelers, often offer exchange rates at or close to par as a promotional come-on.

Unless you're out slumming or deliberately going posh, figure on paying about $1 for a cup of coffee in New England, $2–$3 for a draft beer, and $4 for a ham sandwich with a few pickles and chips. A 1-mi ride in a Boston taxi will set you back $5, including tip; admission to a major museum such as Boston's Museum of Fine Arts will average about $10.

Prices throughout this guide are given for adults. Substantially reduced fees are almost always available for children, students, and senior citizens. For information on taxes, *see* Taxes.

ATMS

Automatic teller machines (ATMs) are a useful way to obtain cash. A debit card, also known as a check card, deducts funds directly from your checking account and helps you stay within your budget. When you want to rent a car, though, you may still need an old-fashioned credit card. Although you can always *pay* for your car with a debit card, some agencies will not allow you to *reserve* a car with a debit card.

ATMs are located just about everywhere in New England, from big-city banks to Vermont general stores.

CREDIT CARDS

Using a credit card on the road allows you to delay payment and gives you certain rights as a consumer (☞ Consumer Protection).

Throughout this guide, the following abbreviations are used: **AE**, American Express; **D**, Discover; **DC**, Diners Club; **MC**, MasterCard; and **V**, Visa.

➤ REPORTING LOST CARDS: **American Express** (☎ 800/441–0519). **Discover** (☎ 800/347–2683). **Diners Club** (☎ 800/234–6377). **MasterCard** (☎ 800/622–7747). **Visa** (☎ 800/ 847–2911).

NATIONAL PARKS

Look into discount passes to save money on park entrance fees. For $50, the National Parks Pass admits you (and any passengers in your private vehicle) to all national parks, monuments, and recreation areas, as well as other sites run by the National Park Service, for a year. (In parks that charge per person, the pass admits you, your spouse and children, and your parents, when you arrive together.) Camping and parking are extra. The $15 Golden Eagle Pass, a hologram you affix to your National Parks Pass, functions as an upgrade, granting entry to all sites run by the NPS, the U.S. Fish and Wildlife Service, the U.S. Forest Service, and the Bureau of Land Management (BLM). The upgrade, which expires with the parks pass, is sold by most national-park, Fish-and-Wildlife, and BLM fee stations. A percentage of the proceeds from pass sales funds National Parks projects.

Both the Golden Age Passport ($10), for U.S. citizens or permanent residents who are 62 and older, and the Golden Access Passport (free), for those with disabilities, entitle holders (and any passengers in their private vehicles) to lifetime free entry to all national parks, plus 50% off fees for the use of many park facilities and services. (The discount doesn't always apply to companions.) To obtain them, you must show proof of age and of U.S. citizenship or permanent residency—such as a U.S. passport, driver's license, or birth certificate—and, if requesting Golden Access, proof of disability. The Golden Age and Golden Access passes, as well as the National Parks Pass, are available at any NPS-run site that charges an entrance fee. The National Parks Pass is also available by mail and via the Internet.

➤ PASSES BY MAIL AND ON-LINE: **National Park Foundation** (WEB www.nationalparks.org). **National Parks Pass** (✉ 27540 Ave. Mentry, Valencia, CA 91355, ☎ 888/GO–PARKS or 888/467–2757, WEB www.nationalparks.org); include a check or money order payable to the National Park Service for the pass, plus $3.95 for shipping and handling.

OUTDOORS AND SPORTS

See Destination: New England (Chapter 1) for a summary of all New England's sporting opportunities. For further information, call state information offices (☞ Visitor Information).

BIKING

➤ BIKING: **Cambridge Bicycle** (✉ 259 Massachusetts Ave., Cambridge, MA 02139, ☎ 617/876–6555) rents bicycles. **Vermont Bicycle Touring** (✉ Box 711, Bristol, VT 05443, ☎ 802/453–4811 or 800/245–3868) operates tours throughout the region and overseas.

HIKING

➤ HIKING: **Appalachian Mountain Club** (✉ Box 298, Gorham, NH 03581, ☎ 603/466–2725). **Audubon Society of New Hampshire** (✉ 3 Silk Farm Rd., Concord, NH 03301, ☎ 603/224–9909). **Green Mountain Club** (✉ Rte. 100 [Box 650, Waterbury, VT 05677], ☎ 802/244–7037). **White Mountain National Forest** (✉ 719 N. Main St., Laconia, NH 03246, ☎ 603/528–8721).

SKIING

See Destination New England for a skiing information and destination map.

PACKING

The principal rule on weather in New England is that there are no rules. A cold, foggy morning in spring can and often does become a bright, 60° afternoon. A summer breeze can suddenly turn chilly, and rain often appears with little warning. Thus, the best advice on how to dress is to **layer your clothing** so that you can peel off or add garments as needed for comfort. Showers are frequent, so **pack a raincoat and umbrella.** Even in summer you should bring long pants, a sweater or two, and a waterproof windbreaker, for evenings are often chilly and sea spray can make things cool.

Casual sportswear—walking shoes and jeans or khakis—will take you almost everywhere, but swimsuits and bare feet will not: shirts and shoes are required attire at even the most casual venues. Dress in restaurants is generally casual, except at some of the distinguished restaurants of Boston, Newport, and Maine coast towns such as Kennebunkport; a number of inns in the Berkshires; and in Litchfield and Fairfield counties in Connecticut. Upscale resorts will, at the very least, require men to wear collared shirts at dinner, and jeans are often frowned upon.

In summer, **bring a hat and sunscreen.** Remember also to **pack insect repellent;** to prevent Lyme disease you'll need to guard against ticks from early spring through the summer (☞ Health).

In your carry-on luggage, **pack an extra pair of eyeglasses or contact lenses and enough of any medication** you take to last a few days longer than the entire trip. You may also ask your doctor to write a spare prescription using the drug's generic name, since brand names may vary from country to country. In luggage to be checked, **never pack prescription drugs or valuables.** And don't forget to carry with you the addresses of offices that handle refunds of lost traveler's checks. Check *Fodor's How to Pack* (available in bookstores everywhere) for more tips.

To avoid customs and security delays, carry medications in their original packaging. Don't pack any sharp objects in your carry-on luggage, including knives of any size or material, scissors, manicure tools, and corkscrews, or anything else that might arouse suspicion.

CHECKING LUGGAGE

You are allowed one carry-on bag and one personal article, such as a purse or a laptop computer. Make sure that everything you carry aboard will fit under your seat or in the overhead bin. Get to the gate early, so you can board as soon as possible, before the overhead bins fill up.

If you are flying internationally, note that baggage allowances may be determined not by piece but by weight—generally 88 pounds (40 kilograms) in first class, 66 pounds (30 kilograms) in business class, and 44 pounds (20 kilograms) in economy.

Airline liability for baggage is limited to $2,500 per person on flights within the United States. On international flights it amounts to $9.07 per pound or $20 per kilogram for checked baggage (roughly $640 per 70-pound bag) and $400 per passenger for unchecked baggage. You can buy additional coverage at check-in for about $10 per $1,000 of coverage, but it excludes a rather extensive list of items, shown on your airline ticket.

Before departure, **itemize your bags' contents** and their worth, and label the bags with your name, address, and phone number. (If you use your home address, cover it so potential thieves can't see it readily.) Inside each bag, **pack a copy of your itinerary.** At check-in, **make sure that each bag is correctly tagged** with the destination airport's three-letter code. If your bags arrive damaged or fail to arrive at all, file a written report with the airline before leaving the airport.

PASSPORTS AND VISAS

For information on passports for non-U.S. citizens, *see* For International Travelers.

➤ U.S. CITIZENS: **National Passport Information Center** (☎ 900/225–5674 or 888/362–8668, WEB www.travel.state.gov/passport services; calls to the 900 number are 35¢ per minute for automated service, $1.05 per minute for operator service); calls to the 888 number, for Visa, MasterCard, or American Express card holders, are billed at a flat rate of $4.95.

SAFETY

Rural New England is one of the country's safest regions, so much so that residents often leave their doors unlocked. In the cities, particularly in Boston, observe the usual precautions; it's worth noting, however, that crime rates have been dropping in metropolitan areas. You should avoid out-of-the-way or poorly lit areas at night; clutch handbags close to your body and don't let them out of your sight; and be on your guard in subways, not only during the deserted wee hours but in crowded rush hours, when pickpockets are at work. Keep your valuables in hotel safes. Try to use ATMs in busy, well-lighted places such as bank lobbies.

If your vehicle breaks down in a rural area, **pull as far off the road as possible,** tie a handkerchief to your radio antenna (or use flares at night—check if your rental agency can provide them), and stay in your car with the doors locked until help arrives. Don't pick up hitchhikers. If you're planning to leave a car overnight to make use of off-road trails or camping facilities, **make arrangements for a supervised parking area** if at all possible. Cars left at trailhead parking lots are subject to theft and vandalism.

The universal telephone number for crime and other emergencies throughout New England is 911.

SENIOR-CITIZEN TRAVEL

To qualify for age-related discounts, **mention your senior-citizen status up front** when booking hotel reservations (not when checking out) and before you're seated in restaurants (not when paying the bill). Be sure to have identification on hand. When renting a car, ask about promotional car-rental discounts, which can be cheaper than senior-citizen rates.

Members of AARP, an organization for people 50 years of age and older, are often eligible for discounts at attractions, lodgings, and restaurants.

➤ EDUCATIONAL PROGRAMS: **AARP** (✉ 3200 E. Carson St., Lakewood CA 90712, ☎ 800/424–3410). **Elderhostel** (✉ 11 Ave. de Lafayette, Boston, MA 02111-1746, ☎ 877/426–8056, FAX 877/426–2166, WEB www.elderhostel.org). **Interhostel** (✉ University of New Hampshire, 6 Garrison Ave., Durham, NH 03824, ☎ 603/862–1147 or 800/733–9753, FAX 603/862–1113, WEB www.learn.unh.edu).

SHOPPING

SMART SOUVENIRS

Distinctive New England souvenirs include Nantucket lightship baskets; authentic handbag versions are available at several Nantucket shops and will cost several hundred dollars (watch out for imported knockoffs). Less expensive options are Blue Hill pottery, sturdy, brightly colored tableware made in Blue Hill, Maine, and available at several shops in the area; Bennington Pottery, attractive, utilitarian items made in the Vermont town (Bennington Potters North in Burlington sells inexpensive seconds); moccasins of moose and deer hide made by Maine Native Americans and sold throughout the state; and whimsical animal prints by Woody Jackson (cows) and Stephen Huneck (dogs), available at several Vermont galleries.

WATCH OUT

When you're looking for pure maple syrup, a sugarhouse can be the most or the least expensive place to shop, depending on how tourist-oriented it is. Small grocery stores are often a good source of less-expensive syrup. **Look for the word "pure" and the state designation;** much artificially flavored sugarcane syrup is sold as "maple."

With any crafts item, always **be aware that some vendors substitute mass-produced imports** for the real thing; if the price seems too good to be true, it probably is.

As the United States is signatory to treaties involving trade and products made from endangered animal species, you won't need to worry about purchasing souvenirs that you won't be able to bring into your home country. Visitors to New Hampshire should be aware that one item for sale in this state—fireworks, found at many roadside stands—is strictly forbidden as airline baggage and cannot be imported into most countries.

STUDENTS IN NEW ENGLAND

Most major attractions throughout New England offer discount admissions to students. This is particularly true in and around Boston, which has America's highest concentration of colleges and universities.

➤ IDs AND SERVICES: **Council Travel** (✉ 205 E. 42nd St., 15th floor, New York, NY 10017, ☎ 212/822–2700 or 888/226–8624, FAX 212/822–2719, WEB www.counciltravel.com). **Travel Cuts** (✉ 187 College St., Toronto, Ontario M5T 1P7, Canada, ☎ 416/979–2406 or 888/838–2887, FAX 416/979–8167, WEB www.travelcuts.com).

TAXES

See Dining *and* Lodging for information about taxes on restaurant meals and accommodations.

SALES TAX

Sales taxes in New England are as follows: Connecticut 6% (with an exemption on clothing purchases up to $50); Maine 5%; Massachusetts 5%; Rhode Island 7%; Vermont 5% (with an exemption on purchase of individual clothing items costing under $110. No sales tax is charged in New Hampshire. Some states and municipalities levy an additional tax (from 1% to 10%) on lodging or restaurant meals. Alcoholic beverages are sometimes taxed at a higher rate than that applied to meals.

TIME

New England is in the Eastern time zone.

TIPPING

At restaurants, a 15% tip is standard for waiters; up to 20% is expected at more expensive establishments. The same goes for taxi drivers, bartenders, and hairdressers. Coat-check operators usually expect $1; bellhops and porters should get $1 per bag; hotel maids should get about $1.50 per day of your stay. Hotel concierges should be tipped if you utilize their services; the amount varies widely depending on the nature of service. On package tours, conductors and drivers usually get $10 per day from the group as a whole; check whether this has already been figured into your cost. For local sightseeing tours, you may individually tip the driver-guide $1–$5, depending on the length of the tour and the number of people in your party, if he or she has been helpful or informative.

TOURS AND PACKAGES

Because everything is prearranged on a prepackaged tour or independent vacation, you spend less time planning—and often get it all at a good price.

BOOKING WITH AN AGENT

Travel agents are excellent resources. But it's a good idea to collect brochures from several agencies, as some agents' suggestions may be influenced by relationships with tour and package firms that reward them for volume sales. If you have a special interest, **find an agent with expertise in that area**; the American Society of Travel Agents (ASTA; ☞ Travel Agencies) has a database of specialists worldwide.

Make sure your travel agent knows the accommodations and other services of the place being recommended. Ask about the hotel's location, room size, beds, and whether it has a pool, room service, or programs for children, if you care about these. Has your agent been there in person or sent others whom you can contact?

Do some homework on your own, too: local tourism boards can provide information about lesser-known and small-niche operators, some of which may sell only direct.

BUYER BEWARE

Each year consumers are stranded or lose their money when tour operators—even large ones with excellent reputations—go out of business. So **check out the operator.** Ask several travel agents about its reputation, and try to **book with a company that has a consumer-protection program.** (Look for information in the company's brochure.) In the United States, members of the National Tour Association and the United States Tour Operators Association are required to set aside funds to cover your payments and travel arrangements in the event that the company defaults. It's also a good idea to choose a company that participates in the American Society of Travel Agents' Tour Operator Program (TOP); ASTA will act as mediator in any disputes between you and your tour operator.

Remember that the more your package or tour includes the better you can predict the ultimate cost of your vacation. Make sure you know exactly what is covered, and **beware of hidden costs.** Are taxes, tips, and transfers included? Entertainment and excursions? These can add up.

➤ TOUR-OPERATOR RECOMMENDATIONS: **American Society of Travel Agents** (☞ Travel Agencies, *below*). **National Tour Association** (NTA; ✉ 546 E. Main St., Lexington, KY 40508, ☎ 859/226–4444 or 800/682–8886, WEB www.ntaonline.com). **United States Tour Operators Association** (USTOA; ✉ 275 Madison Ave., Suite 2014, New York, NY 10016, ☎ 212/599–6599 or 800/468–7862, FAX 212/599–6744, WEB www.ustoa.com).

TRAIN TRAVEL

State-run and national train service are options in New England: The Massachusetts Bay Transportation Authority (MBTA) connects Boston with outlying areas on the north and south shores of the state; Amtrak offers frequent daily service along its Northeast Corridor route from Washington and New York to Boston. Amtrak's new high-speed *Acela* trains now link Boston and Washington, with a stop at Penn Station in New York. The *Down Easter* connects Boston with Portland, Maine.

Other Amtrak services include the *Vermonter* between Washington, D.C., and St. Albans, Vermont; the *Ethan Allen* between New York and Rutland, Vermont; and the *Lake Shore Limited* between Boston and Chicago, with stops at Worcester and Springfield, Massachusetts. These trains run on a daily basis. Amtrak sells passes good for travel within specific regions for a set period of time and also has a schedule of reduced children's fares. Overnight accommodations exist on only one New England train, the *Lake Shore Limited*. Reservations are required for certain trains and for all overnight accommodations. As a general policy, Amtrack does not permit smoking on its trains. To avoid last-minute confusion, allow 15 to 30 minutes to make train connections.

Private rail lines have scenic train trips throughout New England, particularly during fall foliage season. Several use vintage steam equipment; the most notable is the Cog Railway to Mt. Washington in New Hampshire.

➤ TRAIN INFORMATION: **Amtrak** (☎ 800/872–7245, WEB www.amtrak.com). **Massachusetts Bay Transportation Authority (MBTA;** ☎ 617/722–3200).

TRANSPORTATION AROUND NEW ENGLAND

If you plan to travel around a sizable portion of New England, a car or car rental is a *must*. Frequent rail connections between major cities exist only within Amtrak's Northeast Corridor (most notably New Haven, Providence, and Boston), and regional travel by air is expensive. Buses connect major cities and towns, but schedules are often inconvenient and routes are generally not the most scenic. Since one of New England's primary attractions is its picturesque countryside and innumerable small villages, only the automobile traveler (or bicyclist) can really appreciate all the region has to offer. If, however, you plan to concentrate your trip in and around Boston, where streets and roads are tangled and hectic, you're better off relying on public transportation.

TRAVEL AGENCIES

A good travel agent puts your needs first. Look for an agency that has been in business at least five years, emphasizes customer service, and has someone on staff who specializes in your destination. In addition, **make sure the agency belongs to a professional trade organization.** The American Society of Travel Agents (ASTA)—the largest and most influential in the field, with more than 24,000 members in some 140 countries—maintains and enforces a strict code of ethics and will step in to help mediate any agent-client disputes involving ASTA members if necessary.

ASTA (whose motto is "Without a travel agent, you're on your own") also maintains a Web site that includes a directory of agents. (If a travel agency is also acting as your tour operator, *see* Buyer Beware *in* Tours and Packages).

➤ LOCAL AGENT REFERRALS: **American Society of Travel Agents** (ASTA; ⌧ 1101 King St., Suite 200, Alexandria, VA 22314, ☏ 800/965–2782 24-hr hot line, FAX 703/739–7642, WEB www.astanet.com). **Association of British Travel Agents** (⌧ 68–71 Newman St., London W1T 3AH, ☏ 020/7637–2444, FAX 020/7637–0713, WEB www.abtanet.com). **Association of Canadian Travel Agents** (⌧ 130 Albert St., Suite 1705, Ottawa, Ontario K1P 5G4, ☏ 613/237–3657, FAX 613/237–7052, WEB www.acta.net). **Australian Federation of Travel Agents** (⌧ Level 3, 309 Pitt St., Sydney, NSW 2000, ☏ 02/9264–3299, FAX 02/9264–1085, WEB www.afta.com.au). **Travel Agents' Association of New Zealand** (⌧ Level 5, Tourism and Travel House, 79 Boulcott St., Box 1888, Wellington 10033, ☏ 04/499–0104, FAX 04/499–0827, WEB www.taanz.org.nz).

VISITOR INFORMATION

Each New England state provides a helpful free information kit, including a guidebook, map, and listings of attractions and events. All include listings and/or advertisements for lodging and dining establishments. Each state also has an official Web site with material on sights and lodgings; most of these sites have a calendar of events and other special features.

➤ TOURIST INFORMATION: **Connecticut Office of Tourism** (⌧ 505 Hudson St., Hartford, CT 06106, ☏ 860/270–8081 or 800/282–6863, WEB www.ctbound.org). **Maine Tourism Association** (⌧ 325-B Water St. [Box 2300, Hallowell, ME 04347], ☏ 207/623–0363 or 888/624–6345, WEB www.visitmaine.com). **Massachusetts Office of Travel and Tourism** (⌧ 10 Park Plaza, Suite 4510, Boston, MA 02116, ☏ 617/727–3201; 800/227–6277; 800/447–6277 brochures; WEB www.mass-vacation.com). **New Hampshire Office of Travel and Tourism Development** (⌧ Box 1856, Concord, NH 03302, ☏ 603/271–2343; 800/258–3608 seasonal events; 800/386–4664 brochures; WEB www.visitnh.gov). **Rhode Island Department of Economic Development, Tourism Division** (⌧ 1 W. Exchange St., Providence, RI 02903, ☏ 401/222–2601; 800/556–2484 brochures; WEB www.visitrhodeisland.com). **Vermont Chamber of Commerce, Department of Travel and Tourism** (⌧ Box 37, Montpelier, VT 05601, ☏ 802/223–3443, WEB www.VTchamber.com). **Vermont Department of Tourism and Marketing** (⌧ 134 State St., Montpelier, VT 05602, ☏ 802/828–3237; 800/837–6668 brochures; WEB www.1800VT.com).

➤ IN THE U.K.: **Discover New England** (⌧ Admail 4 International, Greatness La., Sevenoaks, England TN14 5BQ, ☏ 01732/742777, WEB www.discovernewengland.org).

WEB SITES

Do check out the World Wide Web when planning your trip. You'll find everything from weather forecasts to virtual tours of famous cities. Be sure to **visit Fodors.com** (www.fodors.com), a complete travel-planning site. You can research prices and book plane tickets, hotel rooms, rental cars, vacation packages, and more. In addition, you can post your pressing questions in the Travel Talk section. Other planning tools include a currency converter and weather reports, and there are loads of links to travel resources.

CONNECTICUT

The **Connecticut Impressionist Art Trail** has a site at WEB www.arttrail.org; the **Connecticut Wine Trail** is at WEB ctwine.com.

MAINE

MaineToday.com provides travel information at WEB travel.mainetoday.com. Maine's **Nordic Ski Council** provides cross-country info at WEB www.mnsc.com. The site of **Ski Maine** (WEB www.skimaine.com) has information about alpine snow sports.

MASSACHUSETTS

Boston.com, home of the *Boston Globe* on-line, has news and feature articles, ample travel information, and links to towns throughout Massachusetts. The site for Boston's arts and entertainment weekly, the *Boston Phoenix* (WEB www.bostonphoenix.com), has nightlife, movie, restaurant, and fine and performing arts listings. The site of the **Cape Cod Information Center** (WEB www.allcapecod.com) carries events information and has town directories with weather, sightseeing, lodging, and dining entries.

NEW HAMPSHIRE

For information on downhill and cross-country skiing, WEB www.skinh.com is the site of **Ski New Hampshire.**

RHODE ISLAND

The official site of Providence (WEB www.goprovidence.com) tells you what's happening in town.

VERMONT

The **Vermont Ski Areas Association** covers the downhill scene at WEB www.skivermont.com. Up-to-date foliage reports are given at WEB www.1800vermont.com.

GENERAL INTEREST

The Great Outdoor Recreation Page (WEB www.gorp.com) is arranged into three easily navigated categories: attractions, activities, and locations; within most of the "locations" are links to the New England state parks office. The **National Park Service** site (WEB www.nps.gov) lists all the New England's national parks and has extensive historical, cultural, and environmental information. **Visit New England** (WEB www.visitnewengland.com) covers the entire region.

WHEN TO GO

All six New England states are largely year-round destinations. But you might want to **stay away from rural areas during mud season in April and black-fly season from mid-May to mid-June.** Many smaller museums and attractions are open only from Memorial Day to mid-October, at other times by appointment only.

Memorial Day is the start of the migration to the beaches and the mountains, and summer begins in earnest on July 4. Those who are driving to Cape Cod in July or August should know that Friday and Sunday are the days weekenders clog the overburdened Route 6; a better time to visit the beach areas and the islands may be after Labor Day. The same applies to the Maine coast and its feeder roads, I–95 and U.S. 1.

Fall is the most colorful season in New England, a time when many inns and hotels are booked months in advance by foliage-viewing visitors. New England's dense hardwood forests explode in color as the diminishing hours of autumn daylight signal trees to stop producing chlorophyll. As green is stripped away from the leaves of maples, oaks, birches, beeches, and other deciduous species, a rainbow of reds, oranges, yellows, purples, and other vivid hues is revealed. The first scarlet and gold colors emerge in mid-September in northern areas; "peak" color occurs at different times from year to year. Generally, it's best to **visit the northern reaches in late September and early October** and move southward as October progresses.

All leaves are off the trees by Halloween, and hotel rates fall as the leaves do, dropping significantly until ski season begins. November and early December are hunting season in much of New England; those who venture into the woods should wear bright orange clothing.

Winter is the time for downhill and cross-country skiing. New England's major ski resorts are well equipped with snowmaking equipment if nature falls short. Along the coast, bed-and-breakfasts that remain open will often rent rooms at far lower prices than in summer.

In spring, despite mud season, maple sugaring goes on in Maine, New Hampshire, and Vermont, and the fragrant scent of lilacs is never far away.

CLIMATE

In winter, coastal New England is cold and damp; inland temperatures may be lower, but generally drier conditions make them easier to bear. Snowfall is heaviest in the interior mountains and can range up to several hundred inches per year in northern Maine, New Hampshire, and Vermont. Spring is often windy and rainy; in many years it appears as if winter segues almost immediately into summer. Coastal areas can be quite humid in summer, making even moderate temperatures uncomfortable. One of the delights of inland northern New England, particularly at higher elevations, is the prevalence of cool summer nights. Autumn temperatures can be quite mild in more southerly areas well into October, although northern portions of the region can be quite cold by Columbus Day. In some years, a period of unseasonably mild weather occurs in late October and early November.

➤ FORECASTS: **Weather Channel Connection** (☎ 900/932–8437), 95¢ per minute from a Touch-Tone phone.

HARTFORD, CT

Jan.	36F	2C	May	70F	21C	Sept.	74F	23C
	20	– 7		47	8		52	11
Feb.	38F	3C	June	81F	27C	Oct.	65F	18C
	20	– 7		56	13		43	6
Mar.	45F	7C	July	85F	29C	Nov.	52F	11C
	27	– 3		63	17		32	0
Apr.	59F	15C	Aug.	83F	28C	Dec.	38F	3C
	38	3		61	16		22	– 6

BOSTON, MA

Jan.	36F	2C	May	67F	19C	Sept.	72F	22C
	20	– 7		49	9		56	13
Feb.	38F	3C	June	76F	24C	Oct.	63F	17C
	22	– 6		58	14		47	8
Mar.	43F	6C	July	81F	27C	Nov.	49F	9C
	29	– 2		63	17		36	2
Apr.	54F	12C	Aug.	79F	26C	Dec.	40F	4C
	38	3		63	17		25	– 4

BURLINGTON, VT

Jan.	29F	– 2C	May	67F	19C	Sept.	74F	23C
	11	–12		45	7		50	10
Feb.	31F	– 1C	June	77F	25C	Oct.	59F	15C
	11	–12		56	13		40	4
Mar.	40F	4C	July	83F	28C	Nov.	45F	7C
	22	6		59	15		31	– 1
Apr.	54F	12C	Aug.	79F	26C	Dec.	31F	– 1C
	34	1		58	14		16	– 9

PORTLAND, ME

Jan.	31F	– 1C	May	61F	16C	Sept.	68F	20C
	16	– 9		47	8		52	11
Feb.	32F	0C	June	72F	22C	Oct.	58F	14C
	16	– 9		54	15		43	6
Mar.	40F	4C	July	76F	24C	Nov.	45F	7C
	27	– 3		61	16		32	0
Apr.	50F	10C	Aug.	74F	23C	Dec.	34F	1C
	36	2		59	15		22	– 6

FESTIVALS AND SEASONAL EVENTS

➤ JANUARY: The Bethel (ME) **Winter Festival** has snowshoe and cross-country races, sleigh rides, and a snowman contest. Stowe's (VT) festive **Winter Carnival** heats up late in the month. Brookfield (VT) holds its **Ice Harvest Festival,** one of New England's largest. The weeklong **Winter Carnival** in Jackson (NH) includes ski races and ice sculptures.

➤ FEBRUARY: The Camden Snow Bowl in Camden (ME) is the site of the **U.S. National Toboggan Championships.** On tap at the **Brattleboro Winter Carnival** (VT), held during the last week of the month, are jazz concerts and an ice fishing derby. The **Mad River Valley Winter Carnival** (VT) is a week of winter festivities, including dogsled races and ski races and fireworks; Burlington's **Vermont Mozart Festival** showcases the Winter Chamber Music Series. Flower lovers flock to Hartford's (CT) Expo Center for the annual **Flower and Garden Show.**

➤ MARCH: This is the season for **maple-sugaring festivals and events:** throughout the month and into April, New England sugarhouses demonstrate procedures from maple-tree tapping to sap boiling. During **Maine Maple Sunday** Maine sugarhouses open for tours and tastings. Maine's Moosehead Lake has a renowned **Ice-Fishing Derby.** Rangeley's (ME) **New England Sled Dog Races** attract more than 100 teams. Stratton Mountain (VT) hosts the **U.S. Open Snowboarding Championships.** Boston's (MA) **St. Patrick's Day Parade** is one of the nation's largest. Five acres of landscaped gardens bloom at Boston's (MA) **New England Spring Flower Show.** At Lyman Plant House on the Smith College Campus in Northampton (MA), more than 2,500 flowering bulbs and spring flowers are on display at the **Spring Bulb Show.**

➤ APRIL: During **Reggae Weekend** at Sugarloaf/USA (ME), Caribbean reggae bands play outdoors and inside. At Sunday River's (ME) annual **Bust 'n' Burn Mogul Competition,** professional and amateur bump skiers test their mettle. Early blooms are the draw of Nantucket's (MA) **Daffodil Festival,** which celebrates spring with a flower show and a procession of antique cars along roadsides bursting with daffodils. You can gorge on sea grub at Boothbay Harbor's (ME) **Fishermen's Festival,** held on the third weekend in April. Dedicated runners draw huge crowds to the **Boston Marathon** (MA), run each year on Patriot's Day (the Monday nearest April 19). Colonial Minute Men battle the British at the annual **Battle of Lexington and Concord Reenactment** (MA). At the **Maple Festival,** held early each April in St. Albans (VT), you can try Sugar on Snow, a taffylike treat.

➤ MAY: The Shelburne Museum in Shelburne (VT) is awash in purple glory in mid-May, when the **Lilac Festival** blossoms. **Lilac Sunday,** at Boston's Arnold Arboretum (MA), celebrates the blooming of more than 250 varieties. If you want to see a moose, visit Greenville (ME) during **Moosemania,** which runs from mid-May to mid-June. Events include moose safaris and mountain bike and canoe races. **Lobsterfest** kicks off Mystic Seaport's (CT) summer of festivities with live entertainment and good food. Holyoke's (MA) **Shad Fishing Derby** is said to be the largest freshwater fishing derby in North America.

➤ JUNE: In Vermont, you can listen to jazz at Burlington's **Discover Jazz Festival. Lake Champlain International Fishing Derby** (VT) entices anglers to try their fishing skills. **Jacob's Pillow Dance Festival** at Becket (MA) in the Berkshires hosts performers of various dance traditions from June to September. The **Boothbay Harbor Windjammer Days** starts the high season for Maine's boating set. The **Blessing of the Fleet** in Provincetown (MA) culminates a weekend of festivities. Mystic Seaport in Mystic (CT) hosts its annual **Small Craft Weekend.** The **Sea Music Festival,** in Mystic (CT), is a celebration of New England's quintessential folk music. **A Taste of Hartford** lets you eat your way through Connecticut's capital city while enjoying outdoor music, dance, comedy, and magic. Burlington, Vermont's **Green Mountain Chew Chew** offers a variety of entertainment including outdoor music and comedy. New Haven (CT) hosts the two-week **International Festival of Arts and Ideas,** showcasing music, dance, theater, film, visual arts, and literature. During the **Strawberry Festival** in Wiscasset (ME), you can get your fill of strawberry goodies. You can visit Providence's (RI) stately homes, some by candlelight, on one of the **Providence Preservation Society's** tours. At the **Great Chowder Cookoff** in Newport (RI), restaurants compete for the distinction of having the best chowder in New England.

➤ JULY: During Bath's (ME) **Heritage Days,** Independence day is celebrated with concerts, family entertainment, an art show, a parade, and fireworks.Exeter (NH) holds a **Revolutionary War Festival** at the American Independence Museum with battle reenactments and period crafts and antiques. The **Mashpee Powwow** (MA) brings together Native Americans from North and South America for three days of dance contests, drumming, a fireball game, and a clambake. The **Marlboro Music Festival** presents classical music at Marlboro College (VT). Newport's (RI) **Music Festival** brings together celebrated musicians for two weeks of concerts in Newport mansions. Newport's (RI) **Rhythm & Blues Festival** hosts an array of top performers. The **Bar Harbor Festival** (ME) hosts classical, jazz, and popular music concerts into August. The **Tanglewood Music Festival** at Lenox (MA) shifts into high gear with performances by the Boston Symphony Orchestra and major entertainers. Glorious outdoor concert sites and sumptuous picnics are sidelines to fine music at the **Vermont Mozart Festival,** held throughout central and northern Vermont in July and August. The two-day **Stoweflake Hot Air Balloon Festival** in Stowe (VT) is one of the state's most popular events. Admire the furnishings of homes during **Open House Tours** in Litchfield (CT) and Camden (ME). Folks flock to the **Mashantucket Pequot Thames River Fireworks** in New London (CT) to view one of the country's largest fireworks events. In Mystic (CT), vintage powerboats and sailboats are on view at the **Antique and Classic Boat Rendezvous.** The

Yarmouth Clam Festival (ME) is more than a seafood celebration—expect continuous entertainment and a crafts show throughout the three-day event.

➤ AUGUST: **Ben & Jerry's Newport Folk Festival** (RI) is one of the region's most popular musical events. Newport (RI) hosts the **JVC's Jazz Festival.** The historic streets of Essex (CT) rock with sounds of the **Great Connecticut Traditional Jazz Festival.** Stowe (VT) hosts a popular **Antique and Classic Car Rally.** The **Southern Vermont Crafts Fair** in Manchester (VT) features popular arts, crafts, and antiques. The **Outdoor Arts Festival** in Mystic (CT) presents the works of fine local artists. Sellers and collectors throng to the **Maine Antiques Festival** in Union. Waterfront activities, arts and crafts, entertainment, and succulent Maine lobster feature prominently at Rockland's (ME) **Lobster Festival.** Everything's coming up blueberries at the **Wild Maine Blueberry Festival** in Machias (ME). In Rangeley Lake (ME), the blueberry is king at the annual **Blueberry Festival.** Rhode Islanders honor their favorite shellfish at the **International Quahog Festival** in Wickford. A **Bluefish Festival** takes place in Clinton (CT). Brunswick's **Maine Festival** is a four-day celebration of Maine arts. Maine's **Annual Maine Highland Games** features traditional Scottish athletic events and music entertainment. The **Martha's Vineyard Agricultural Fair** (MA) includes animal shows, a carnival, and evening entertainment. In New Bedford (MA), the **Feast of Blessed Sacrament** is the country's largest Portuguese feast.

➤ SEPTEMBER: New England's Labor Day fairs include the **Vermont State Fair** in Rutland, with agricultural exhibits and entertainment. The **Providence Waterfront Festival** (RI) is a weekend of arts, crafts, ethnic foods, music, and boat races. The **International Seaplane Fly-In Weekend** sets Moosehead Lake (ME) buzzing. The **Champlain Valley Fair,** in Burlington (VT), has all the features of a large county fair. The **Rhythm and Roots** festival of Cajun food, music, and dancing is held in Charlestown (RI). Many of the country's finest fiddlers compete at the

National Traditional Old-Time Fiddler's Contest in Barre (VT). Folk music is the highlight at the Rockport Folk Festival in Rockport (ME). In Stratton (VT), artists and performers gather for the Stratton Arts Festival. Providence (RI) shows off its diversity during its Heritage Day Festival. The Common Ground Country Fair in Unity (ME) is an organic farmer's delight. The Deerfield Fair (NH) is one of New England's oldest agricultural fairs. The Eastern States Exposition) is New England's largest agricultural fair–carnival. The six small Vermont towns of Walden, Cabot, Plainfield, Peacham, Barnet, and Groton host the weeklong Northeast Kingdom Fall Foliage Festival. Crafts, entertainment, and fried scallops are served up at the Bourne Scallopfest in Buzzards Bay (MA). For the Martha's Vineyard Striped Bass and Bluefish Derby (MA), from mid-September to mid-October, locals cast their lines in search of a prizewinning whopper. The Eastport Salmon Festival (ME), the first Sunday after Labor Day, hosts entertainers and crafts artists. At the Annual Seafood Festival in Hampton Beach (NH), you can sample seafood specialties, dance to live bands, and watch fireworks.

➤ OCTOBER: The Fryeburg Fair (ME) presents agricultural exhibits, harness racing, and a pig scramble. The Nantucket Cranberry Harvest in Massachusetts is a three-day celebration including bog and inn tours and a crafts fair. Connecticut's Quiet Corner holds a Walking Weekend, with 50 guided scenic walks through the towns, along rivers, and in the woods of this rural area. Hildene Farm, Food and Crafts Fair in Manchester (VT) has farm activities, entertainment, and lots of events for kids.

➤ NOVEMBER: The International Film Festival presents films dealing with environmental, human rights, and political issues for a week in Burlington (VT). The Bradford Wild Game Supper (VT) draws thousands to taste large and small game animals and birds. New Haven's (CT) Annual Celebration of American Crafts exhibits and sells works of more than 400 juried craftspeople.

➤ DECEMBER: The reenactment of the Boston Tea Party takes place on the *Beaver II* in Boston Harbor (MA). In Nantucket (MA), the first weekend of the month sees an early Christmas celebration with elaborate decorations, costumed carolers, theatrical performances, art exhibits, and a tour of historic homes. In Newport (RI), several Bellevue Avenue mansions open for the holidays, and there are candlelight tours of Colonial homes. At Mystic Seaport (CT), costumed guides escort visitors on lantern-light tours. Old Saybrook (CT) has a Christmas Torchlight Parade and Muster of Ancient Fife and Drum Corps, which ends with a carol sing. The little town of Bethlehem (CT) is the site of a large Christmas festival each December. More than 200 spectacularly decorated trees and wreaths grace the Wadsworth Atheneum in Hartford (CT) during its annual Festival of Trees. Historic Strawbery Banke (NH) has a Christmas Stroll, with carolers, through nine historic homes. Christmas Prelude in Kennebunkport (ME) celebrates winter with concerts, caroling, and special events. The final day of the year is observed with festivals, entertainment, and food in many locations during First Night Celebrations. Some of the major cities hosting First Nights are Portland (ME); Burlington, Montpelier, and St. Johnsbury (all in VT); Providence (RI); Boston; and Danbury, Hartford, and Mystic (in CT).

1   DESTINATION: NEW ENGLAND

A NEW ENGLAND PAUL REVERE WOULD RECOGNIZE

Just 20 years after the Declaration of Independence, the Reverend Timothy Dwight, president of Yale College and grandson of the fiery Puritan preacher Jonathan Edwards, set out on the first of a series of annual rambles through his native New England. In his journal, Dwight declared, "A succession of New England villages, composed of neat houses, surrounding neat schoolhouses and churches, adorned with gardens, meadows, and orchards, and exhibiting the universally easy circumstances of the inhabitants, is . . . one of the most delightful prospects this world can afford." More than two hundred years after Dwight's first tour, the graceful small towns he described remain intact: clapboard farmhouses, weather-beaten barns, lovely old churches, and some of the nation's best schools still line the rural routes in all six New England states.

The difference from Dwight's day to our own is that a whole world of cities and suburbs has grown up around these rural villages. New England's first cities—Portland, Boston, Providence, Newport, New London, New Haven—began as harbor towns. In the 17th century, English Puritans, fleeing religious persecution and civil war, were the first Europeans to make their fortunes in these harbors. Merchants, fishermen, and shipbuilders from all over the world thrived here in the years before the American Revolution.

Even as their cities expanded, New Englanders protected their natural resources. The most famous pioneer of conservation and outdoor recreation is poet and naturalist Henry David Thoreau, who led the way in the 1840s with his famous pilgrimages to Walden Pond in Massachusetts and Mount Katahdin in Maine. In the years after the Civil War, New Englanders flocked to the mountains and the seashore seeking relief from the pressures of city life. Nature lovers and amateur mountaineers cut hiking trails and built rustic shelters in the White Mountains of New Hampshire; Massachusetts families camped and tramped in the rolling Berkshire Hills; in Maine, Harvard president

Charles W. Eliot and his fellow "rusticators" conserved craggy cliffs, rocky beaches, and pine forests for future generations by donating land to establish Acadia National Park. By 1910, Vermont hikers had begun work on the 255-mi Long Trail, which connects the Green Mountain summits from Canada to the Massachusetts border. During the Great Depression, conservationists rescued the trail from highway planners who would have paved this favorite mountain footpath.

New England's tangle of turnpikes and highways originated with the area's first inhabitants. The Pocumtucks, Nehantics, Nipmucks, Wampanoags, Pequots, Mohegans, Kennebecs, Penobscots, and Narragansetts created footpaths with skills that modern engineers might envy. This vast trail network extended over rolling hills, through dense woodlands, along riverbanks and the Atlantic coast. The Mohawk Trail—Route 2 on your Massachusetts road map—ran east to west through the Deerfield and Connecticut River valleys to the Hudson River. Seasonal feasts and athletic competitions were held along this route for hundreds of years.

Like well-worn Indian byways, the familiar ingredients of the New England diet have been around since before the *Mayflower*: clams, cranberries, pumpkins, corn, squash, beans, blueberries, cod, and lobster. Clambakes and baked beans were also Native American specialties.

Another New England specialty is education: dedication to the life of the mind is fostered at Harvard, Yale, and hundreds of excellent secondary schools, colleges, and other universities throughout the region.

When it comes to weather, variety is New England's great virtue: all four seasons get full play here. September and October are dazzling as the dying leaves turn color. Foliage enthusiasts take to the rural roads and country inns to observe the way in which warm sunny days and cool autumn nights work together to paint the treetops crimson and gold. Winter usually brings plenty of snow, but if Mother Nature fails to satisfy skiers, resort owners rely on high-tech Yankee know-how (in the form of snowmaking devices) to make up the difference. Spring brings crocuses, muddy boots, and maple syrup—sugaring begins when the days are warm and the nights are still below freezing. Summer is the season to enjoy New England's lakes, beaches, and ocean resorts, from Cape Cod to Bar Harbor.

The streets of Boston, New England's largest city, provide a crash course in the early political history of the United States. The red line of the Freedom Trail begins at Boston Common, America's oldest public park, and winds past a dozen Revolutionary-era memorials, including the Granary Burial Ground, where the victims of the Boston Massacre were laid to rest; Faneuil Hall, the meetinghouse and marketplace that earned the name the "Cradle of Liberty"; Old North Church, immortalized in Longfellow's poem "Paul Revere's Ride"; and the obelisk commemorating the Battle of Bunker Hill. Monuments to 18th-century glory stand alongside glass office towers in the busy financial district; and in the North End, the house where midnight rider Paul Revere lived is just around the corner from some of the best Italian restaurants in town.

The story of the preservation of Boston's most elegant neighborhood gives us clues about the New England character that we know incompletely from novels, films, and history books. The Boston Brahmin, the ingenious Yankee, the doom-laden Puritan, and the straitlaced reformer have contributed as much to our sense of the place as have New England's snug harbors, salty sea air, stone walls, and pine forests. In 1947, Beacon Hill matrons, dressed in felt hats and furs, conducted a sit-in to save the brick sidewalks of this historic neighborhood, whose noteworthy architectural elements include its gaslights, cast-iron fences, and sturdy brownstones. With true New England spirit, these earnest women let their opinions be known. Such a polished group of protesters was impossible to resist. Tradition was properly preserved.

Despite two hundred years of growth and change—and several large cities notwithstanding—the Reverend Dwight would still recognize his beloved New England. And he'd be delighted you've decided to visit.

WHAT'S WHERE

If New England didn't exist, Currier & Ives might have had to invent it. Its immaculate village greens, brilliant white clapboard churches, covered bridges, and lighthouses are national emblems, along with the seasons themselves: the Green Mountains in autumn oranges, the White Mountains mounded with snow, Cape Cod polka-dotted with beach-plum blossoms. But New England is much more than a colossal picture postcard: the historic sites witnessed events still chronicled in classrooms across the country, the antiques shops and discount malls are legendary, and urban pleasures flourish, from lively restaurants to the performing arts. New England is a pleasure trove—if you know where to look.

Maine

Maine is by far the largest state in New England. At its extremes it measures 300 mi by 200 mi; all other New England states could fit within its perimeters. Due to overdevelopment, Maine's southernmost coastal towns won't give you the rugged, "Down East" experience, but the Kennebunks will: classic townscapes, rocky shorelines punctuated by sandy beaches, quaint downtown districts. Purists hold that the Maine coast begins at Penobscot Bay, where the vistas over the water are wider and bluer, the shore a jumble of granite boulders. Acadia National Park is Maine's principal tourist attraction; Bar Harbor is one of the park's gateway towns. Bangor is north of Penobscot Bay on the Penobscot River. The vast North Woods region is a destination for outdoors enthusiasts.

New Hampshire

Portsmouth, the star of New Hampshire's 18-mi coastline, has great shopping, restaurants, music, and theater as well as one of the best historic districts in the nation. Exeter is New Hampshire's enclave of Revolutionary War history. The Lakes Region, rich with historic landmarks, also has good restaurants, several golf courses, hiking trails, and antiquing. People come to the White Mountains to hike and climb, to photograph the dramatic vistas and the vibrant sea of foliage, and to ski. Western and central New Hampshire have managed to keep the water slides and the outlet malls at bay. The lures here include Lake Sunapee and Mt. Monadnock, the second-most-climbed mountain in the world.

Vermont
Southern Vermont has farms, freshly starched New England towns, quiet back roads, bustling ski resorts, and strip-mall sprawl. Central Vermont's trademarks include famed marble quarries, just north of Rutland, and large dairy herds and pastures that create the quilted patchwork of the Champlain Valley. The heart of the area is the Green Mountains, and the surrounding wilderness of the Green Mountain National Forest. Both the state's largest city (Burlington) and the nation's smallest state capital (Montpelier) are in northern Vermont, as are some of the most rural and remote areas of New England. Much of the state's logging, dairy farming, and skiing takes place here. With Montréal only an hour from the border, the Canadian influence is strong, and Canadian accents and currency common.

Massachusetts
Much of what makes Massachusetts famous is in the eastern part of the state: academically endowed Boston, the historic South Shore town of Plymouth, chic Martha's Vineyard, scenic Cape Cod, and cozy Nantucket; witch-obsessed Salem and the port town of Gloucester are on the North Shore, which extends past grimy docklands to the picturesque Cape Ann region. But the western reaches of the state hold attractions as well: the Pioneer Valley is a string of historic settlements, and the Berkshires, in the western end of the state, live up to the storybook image of rural New England.

Rhode Island
Wedged between Connecticut and Massachusetts and occupying a mere 48 mi by 37 mi, Rhode Island is the smallest of the 50 states. Providence, the state capital, is in the northeast portion of the state. To the southeast is Newport, the state's other well-known city and one of the great sailing capitals of the world. The area known as South County contains coastal towns along Route 1, rolling farmland, sparsely populated beaches, and wilderness; it's just a short ferry ride from the South County town of Galilee to scenic Block Island. The Blackstone Valley, in the northern portion of the state, was the cradle of the Industrial Revolution in the United States. The region, which includes the towns of Pawtucket, Woonsocket, and Slatersville, is beginning to blossom as a tourist destination.

Connecticut
Southwestern Connecticut, the richest part of the richest state, is home to commuters, celebrities, and others who seek privacy and rusticity and proximity to New York City. Far less touristy than other parts of the state, the Connecticut River valley is a stretch of small river villages and uncrowded state parks punctuated by a few small cities and one large one: Hartford. The Litchfield Hills have grand old inns, rolling farmlands, and plenty of forests and rivers, making it a popular retreat for New Yorkers. The Quiet Corner, a string of sparsely populated towns in the northeast known chiefly for their antiquing potential, is also becoming a weekend escape from New York City. New Haven is home to Yale and several fine museums. Along the southeastern coast lie quiet shoreline villages, and, a bit inland, Foxwoods Casino draws droves of gamblers to the Mashantucket Pequots' reservation in Ledyard.

PLEASURES AND PASTIMES

Beaches
Long, wide beaches edge the New England coast from southern Maine to southern Connecticut; the most popular are on Cape Cod, Martha's Vineyard, Nantucket, and the shore areas north and south of Boston; on Maine's York County coast; Block Island Sound in Rhode Island; and the coastal region of New Hampshire. Many are maintained by state and local governments and have

lifeguards on duty; they may have picnic facilities, rest rooms, changing facilities, and concession stands. Depending on the locale, you may need a parking sticker to use the lot. The waters are at their warmest in August, though they're cold even at the height of summer along much of the Maine coast. Inland, small lake beaches abound, most notably in New Hampshire and Vermont.

Bicycling

Cape Cod, in Massachusetts, has miles of bike trails, some paralleling the national seashore, most on level terrain. On either side of the Cape Cod Canal is an easy 7-mi straight trail with views of the canal traffic. Other favorite areas for bicycling are the Massachusetts Berkshires, the New Hampshire Lakes Region, and Vermont's Green Mountains and Champlain Valley. Nantucket, Martha's Vineyard, and Block Island can be thoroughly explored by bicycle. Biking in Maine is especially scenic in and around Kennebunkport, Camden, Deer Isle, and the Schoodic Peninsula. The carriage paths in Acadia National Park are ideal. Many ski resorts allow mountain bikes during the summer months.

Boating

Along many of New England's larger lakes, sailboats, rowboats, canoes, and outboards can be rented at local marinas. Sailboats are available for rent at a number of seacoast locations; you may, however, be required to demonstrate competence. Lessons are also frequently available. In Rhode Island, Block Island Sound, Narragansett Bay, and Newport are revered by sailors worldwide. Maine's Penobscot Bay draws boaters, including windjammers. Lakes in New Hampshire and Vermont are splendid for all kinds of boating. In Massachusetts, the Connecticut River in the Pioneer Valley and the Housatonic River in the Berkshires are popular for canoeing. Maine's Allagash Wilderness Waterway is one of the region's premier places to canoe.

Dining

Seafood is king throughout New England. Clam favorites include chowder, made with big, meaty quahogs (with milk or cream, unlike the tomato-based Manhattan version); fried clams; and steamers. Some lobster classics include plain boiled lobster—a staple at "in the rough" picnic-bench-and-paper-plate spots along the Maine coast—and lobster rolls, a lobster meat and mayo (or just melted butter) preparation served in a hot dog bun. The leading fin fish is scrod—young cod or haddock—best sampled baked or broiled.

Inland specialties run to the plain and familiar dishes of old-fashioned Sunday-dinner America—pot roast, roast turkey, baked ham, hefty stacks of pancakes (with local maple syrup, of course), and apple pie. One regional favorite is Indian pudding, a long-boiled cornmeal and molasses concoction that's delicious with vanilla ice cream. As for ethnic menus, New England has welcomed Chinese, Thai, Middle Eastern, and all the other international cuisines popular in America. The region's deeper ethnic traditions, though, take in the hearty Portuguese pork and fish dishes and spicy sausages of southern Massachusetts and Rhode Island; the festival of Italian flavors that is Boston's North End; and the pork pie (*tortière*) and pea soup of northern New England's French-Canadians.

Fishing

Anglers will find sport aplenty throughout the region—surf-casting along the shore; deep-sea fishing in the Atlantic on party and charter boats; fishing for trout in streams; and angling for bass, landlocked salmon, and other fish in freshwater lakes. Maine's Moosehead and Rangeley lakes regions are draws for serious anglers, as are Vermont's Lakes Champlain and Memphremagog and the Connecticut Lakes of far northern New Hampshire. Coastal towns in southeastern Connecticut and Rhode Island (notably Narragansett) are home to scores of deep-sea charter boats. Sporting-goods stores and bait-and-tackle shops are reliable sources for licenses—necessary in fresh waters—and for leads to the nearest hot spots.

Golf

Golf caught on early in New England. The region has an ample supply of public and semiprivate courses, many of which are attached to distinctive resorts or even ski areas. One dilemma facing golfers is keeping their eyes on the ball instead of the scenery: in Manchester, Vermont, the

Gleneagles Course at the Equinox Hotel is ringed by mountain splendor, as are the links at the Balsams Grand Resort in Dixville Notch, New Hampshire, and the nearby course at the splendid old Mount Washington Hotel in Bretton Woods. During prime season, make sure you reserve ahead for tee times, particularly near urban areas and at resorts.

Hiking

Probably the most famous trails are the 255-mi Long Trail, which runs north–south through the center of Vermont, and the Maine-to-Georgia Appalachian Trail, which runs through New England on both private and public land. The Appalachian Mountain Club (AMC) maintains a system of staffed huts in New Hampshire's Presidential Range, with bunk space and meals available by reservation. You'll find good hiking in many state parks throughout the region.

National and State Parks and Forests

National parks and forests provide myriad facilities, including campgrounds, picnic grounds, hiking trails, nature walks, boating, and ranger programs. Contact the state tourism offices or specific national park or forest headquarters for more information on any of these.

Connecticut. Although Connecticut has no national parks or forests, its coastline comprises two components of the National Wildlife Refuge system, Stewart B. McKinney and Salt Meadow National Wildlife refuges. The refuges, whose facilities extend only to limited parking areas, are popular with birders. A 53-mi swath of the Appalachian Trail, which is part of the national park system, also cuts through Litchfield County. The Litchfield Hills have a strong concentration of protected green spaces, of which the best include Kent Falls State Park, Mt. Tom, Dennis Hill, Haystack Mountain, Campbell Falls, Housatonic Meadows, and Burr Pond. Elsewhere in the state, Rocky Neck State Park in Niantic has one of the finest beaches on Long Island Sound; Wadsworth Falls, near Wesleyan University, has a beautiful waterfall and 285 acres of forest; and Dinosaur State Park, north of Middletown in Rocky Hill, has dinosaur tracks dating from the Jurassic period. Gillette Castle State Park, an outrageous

hilltop castle on 117 acres, has excellent hiking and picnicking.

Maine. Acadia National Park, which preserves fine stretches of shoreline and high mountains, covers much of Mount Desert Island and more than half of Isle au Haut and Schoodic Point on the mainland. The 6,700-acre Moosehorn National Wildlife Refuge, in the eastern quarter of Maine near the New Brunswick border, is bounded by Cobscook Bay and the mouth of the Dennys and Whiting rivers. Baxter State Park comprises more than 200,000 acres of wilderness surrounding Katahdin, Maine's highest mountain. Hiking and moose-watching are major activities. The Allagash Wilderness Waterway is a 92-mi corridor of lakes and rivers surrounded by vast commercial forest property. A number of state parks line Maine's fabled rock-bound coast; at Camden Hills State Park, an auto road winds to the top of Mt. Battie for spectacular views of Penobscot Bay.

Massachusetts. Terrain of all kinds unfolds in Massachusetts state parks and forests, ranging from the dwarf pine forests of Myles Standish State Forest near Plymouth to the heights of Mt. Tom State Reservation overlooking the Pioneer Valley near Holyoke to the many public lands in the Berkshire Hills, most spectacular of which is the Mt. Greylock State Reservation surrounding the state's highest peak. Parks in Lowell, Gardner, North Adams, Holyoke, Lawrence, Lynn, Roxbury, and Fall River, which commemorate the Industrial Revolution, have been created as part of the Urban Heritage State Park Program for Economic Revitalization. Cape Cod National Seashore, a 40-mi stretch of the Cape between Chatham and Provincetown, has excellent swimming, biking, bird-watching, and nature walks. Parker River National Wildlife Refuge, near Newburyport, is a jewel of the nation's refuge system, comprising a barrier island rich in bird life and dune vegetation; limited parking and ocean bathing are available.

New Hampshire. New Hampshire state parklands vary widely, even within a region. Major recreation parks are at Franconia Notch, Crawford Notch, and Mt. Sunapee. Rhododendron State Park near Fitzwilliam in the Monadnock region has a singular collection of wild rhododendrons; Mt. Washington Park (White Mountains) is on top of the highest mountain in the

Northeast. Along New Hampshire's short coastline, Hampton Beach and Odiorne Point state parks provide fine ocean swimming. The White Mountain National Forest covers 770,000 acres of northern New Hampshire, including 6,288-ft Mt. Washington, highest point in the Northeast, and the other peaks of the Presidential Range. Several federally designated Wilderness areas lie within its boundaries. Near the city of Portsmouth, Great Bay National Wildlife Refuge has fine birding and canoeing opportunities on a shallow backwater of the Piscataqua River.

Rhode Island. Rhode Island makes up for its small size with 19 preserves, state parks, beaches, and forest areas, including a string of beautifully maintained public beaches along Block Island Sound and Narragansett Bay. Fifteen state parks in Rhode Island permit camping. Its federally protected areas consist entirely of an impressive string of national wildlife refuges along the shores of Rhode Island Sound. These include Ninigret, Pettaquanscutt, and Sachuest National Wildlife refuges.

Vermont. Vermont has one of the Northeast's best developed systems of state parks, many of which are along the shores of lakes ideal for swimming, fishing, and boating. Most have campsites and boat rentals. Several of the most attractive are among the islands of northern Lake Champlain. At the Green River Reservoir in north-central Vermont, you'll find primitive camping along the shores of the motorboat-free reservoir. The 350,000-acre Green Mountain National Forest consists of separate northern and southern portions in the center of the state. Hikers treasure the more than 500 mi of trails; canoeists work its white waters; and campers and anglers find plenty to keep them happy. Among the most popular spots are the Falls of Lana and Silver Lake near Middlebury; Hapgood Pond between Manchester and Peru; and Chittenden Brook near Rochester. The Marsh-Billings-Rockefeller National Historical Park, in Woodstock, is dedicated to the legacy of conservation and land stewardship associated with the trio of local luminaries for which it is named. On the shores of Lake Champlain in the state's northwestern corner, the Missisquoi National Wildlife Refuge provides superb wildfowl habitat; in the Connecticut River Watershed of the state's Northeast Kingdom, the Sylvio Conte National Wildlife Refuge protects thousands of acres of undeveloped lands.

Shopping

Antiques, crafts, maple syrup and sugar, and fresh produce lure shoppers to New England's flea markets, bazaars, yard sales, country stores, and farmers' markets.

Antiques. Best bets for antiquing in Connecticut include U.S. 7 (in Wilton and Ridgefield, and also in western Litchfield County), New Preston, Putnam and Woodstock, Woodbury and Litchfield, and the area of West Cornwall just east of the covered bridge. Antiques stores are plentiful in Newport but are a specialty of Rhode Island's South County: the best places to browse are Wickford, Charlestown, and Watch Hill. In Massachusetts, the North Shore around Essex has a large concentration of antiques stores, but plenty of shops thrive in Salem and Cape Ann and along Boston's Charles Street at the base of Beacon Hill. Also try the Berkshires around Great Barrington, South Egremont, and Sheffield. One of America's biggest open-air antiques markets is held at Brimfield, Massachusetts, on several dates in summer and fall. Particularly in the Monadnock region of New Hampshire, dealers abound in barns and home stores strung along back roads—along Route 119, from Fitzwilliam to Hinsdale; Route 101, from Marlborough to Wilton; and in the towns of Hopkinton, Hollis, and Amherst. In southern New Hampshire, shops flourish along the stretch of U.S. 4 between Durham and Concord. In Vermont, antiques shops and barns are scattered just about everywhere but are especially concentrated along the southern portions of U.S. 7 and along Route 30, particularly in and around Newfane. In Maine, antiques shops are clustered in Wiscasset and Searsport and along U.S. 1 between Kittery and Scarborough.

Crafts. Try Washington Street in South Norwalk, Connecticut; in Massachusetts, Provincetown on Cape Cod and the Berkshires have some good shops. In Vermont, galleries in Burlington, Middlebury, and Windsor sell work by some of the best of the state's craftspeople, although artisans have set up shop throughout the state. The League of New Hampshire Craftsmen operates seven fine shops, including locations in Concord, Exeter, and North Conway. On Maine's Deer Isle, Haystack Mountain School of Crafts attracts internationally renowned craftspeople to its summer institute. The Schoodic Peninsula is home to many skilled artisans. Passamaquoddy baskets can be found in Eastport.

Produce. Opportunities abound for obtaining fresh farm produce from the source; some farms allow you to pick your own strawberries, raspberries, blueberries, and apples. October in Maine is prime time for pumpkins and potatoes. Maple-syrup producers demonstrate the process to visitors, most notably in Vermont. Maple syrup is available in different grades; while Grade AA, "fancy," is the lightest in color and the most refined, many Vermonters prefer grade B, which has a deeper flavor and is often used in cooking. Grade A, medium amber in color, has a light caramel flavor and is often used with pancakes and hot cereals.

Skiing

New England resorts reflect New England values: independence, resourcefulness, thriftiness. No two are alike. Although skiing may have changed the face of some resorts, it hasn't affected the charm of a New England village: the church on the town green, the barns and homesteads brimming with antiques for sale, the country inns.

Blending Old and New. New England areas have attitude and history on their side. Some of the first lifts in North America were located here: a shovel handle tow at Black Mountain, New Hampshire; single chairlifts at Stowe and Mad River Glen, Vermont. Many of these have given way to high-speed chairlifts, trams, and gondolas.

Sugar Hill, in Franconia, New Hampshire, was the site of America's first ski school. Today most areas have instructional programs for adults and children, including clinics for women, tree skiers, bump bashers, and extreme skiers. First-timers should ask about Learn-to-Ski-or-Ride programs that package lessons with equipment and a lift ticket. Discovery Centers at Mt. Snow and Killington, Vermont; Sunday River, Maine; and Attitash Bear Peak, New Hampshire, are excellent programs for families and beginners.

Perhaps nowhere is the blend of old and new more apparent than on the hill. Old-fashioned trails ebb and flow with the mountain's contours, weaving through woods, over knolls, and providing glimpses of the surrounding countryside. Newer trails were built to accommodate snowmaking and grooming equipment; they're usually wide and often follow the fall line. Often at the same mountain, you can cruise down a steep, wide, perfectly groomed slope; experience the thrills of linking tight turns on a narrow, bump-choked trail; or ramble along a trail that takes the least direct route from summit to base.

Advanced skiers have even more options: tree skiers can snake their way through glades at most resorts, with Stowe Mountain and Jay Peak, Vermont, and Sugarloaf/USA and Sunday River, Maine, providing some of the best tree skiing in the country. For the true expert, Tuckerman Ravine in New Hampshire is the Holy Grail. This hike to–only terrain on Mt. Washington, New England's tallest peak, is a rite of passage.

New England's weather can be unpredictable: rain on the coast is often snow in the mountains, and sleet at lower elevations may be feathery powder at higher ones. For the most part modern snowmaking and grooming produce reliable conditions from early December into April. Nevertheless, New England snow is not western-style snow. What New Englanders consider hard-packed powder, Westerners often consider ice. While powder days are a rare treat here, grooming means top-to-bottom cruising runs are the rule. It can get cold, but if you dress in layers and wear a neck warmer and face mask, you'll be prepared. As a general rule, the farther north the ski area, the longer the season and the more natural snow you can expect.

Riding, Gliding, Shoeing. Snowboarding has changed American resorts as riders have come to share the lifts, slopes, and trails with skiers. Most resorts have embraced snowboarding. Halfpipes and terrain parks are popular not only with riders but also with skiers. New snow toys, such as the giant Zorb ball, ski bikes, and Snow Blades, as well as tubing parks, provide alternative activities.

Off-the-hill activities abound. Cross-country centers such as Jackson, Bretton

Woods, and the Balsams Wilderness, New Hampshire; Bethel, Maine; and Stowe, Vermont, have gained international recognition for their climate, terrain, and size. Bretton Woods and the Balsams are self-contained downhill and cross-country resorts anchored by historic grand resort hotels. In Jackson, you can ski from inn to inn, and Stowe has the Trapp Family Lodge. At many cross-country centers you can also snowshoe, a wonderful, easy-to-do sport.

Saving Big by Thinking Small. While day tickets at the bigger resorts approach $50, those at smaller areas can be as low as $20. Some independently owned areas are bona fide bargains for skiers who don't require the glitz of the high-profile resorts. Family pricing, multiday tickets, frequent-skier programs, junior and senior rates, Web-site deals, and lift-and-lodging packages can all lower the price significantly. Midweek prices are often less expensive, and many areas offer incentives then, such as two-for-one days.

Most ski areas have a variety of accommodations—lodges, condominiums, hotels, motels, inns, bed-and-breakfasts—close to the action. For stays of three days or more, a package rate may be the deal. Packages vary in composition, price, and availability; their components may include a room, meals, lift tickets, ski lessons, rental equipment, transfers to the mountain, parties, races, use of a sports center, tips, and taxes. In general, if you're willing to commute a few extra miles, off-site lodging offers good value.

Getting Practical. Rental equipment is available at all ski areas, at ski shops around resorts, and even in cities far from ski areas. Shop personnel will advise you on equipment and how to use it.

Ski areas have devised standards for rating and marking trails and slopes that offer fairly accurate guides. Trails are rated Easier (green circle), More Difficult (blue square), Most Difficult (black diamond), and Expert (double diamond). Keep in mind that trail difficulty is measured relative to that of other trails at the same ski area. A black-diamond trail at one area may rate only a blue square at a neighboring area. Unless you're able to handle any type of terrain, your best bet is to start on green-circle trails and work

your way up in difficulty until you find the terrain where you're most comfortable.

If you're traveling with children, ask about programs geared to their age. Areas renowned for their family emphasis include Smugglers' Notch, Vermont, and Waterville Valley, New Hampshire. Both have plenty of activities, both on the snow and off, for all ages. Child-care centers can be found at virtually all ski areas and often accept children from ages six weeks to six years. Parents must usually supply formula and diapers for infants; reservations are advised at most, essential at some. Most programs also have instructional opportunities for children at least three years of age and older.

FODOR'S CHOICE

Dining

Golden Lamb Buttery, Brooklyn, CT. This is Connecticut's most unusual—and magical—dining experience. *$$$$*

Go Fish, Mystic, CT. This big, bright, colorful restaurant serves up the bounty of the sea. *$$–$$$*

White Barn Inn, Kennebunkport, ME. One of Maine's best restaurants, it combines fine dining with unblemished service in a rustic setting. *$$$$*

Lobstermen's Co-op, Round Pond, ME. For lobster-in-the-rough, you can't beat this dockside takeout. *$–$$*

Biba, Boston, MA. The city's favorite place to see and be seen serves gutsy fare from five continents. *$$$$*

Blantyre, Lenox, MA. If you choose to dine on the imaginative contemporary cuisine here, set aside several hours and dress up. *$$$$*

Chillingsworth, Brewster, MA. The chefs at this formal spot prepare luscious French fare. *$$$$*

The Balsams Wilderness, Dixville Notch, NH. The summer buffet lunch is heaped upon a 100-ft-long table; dinners might include salmon with caviar. *$$$$*

Al Forno, Providence, RI. The Italian dishes here make the most of the region's fresh produce. *$$$*

New England Ski Areas

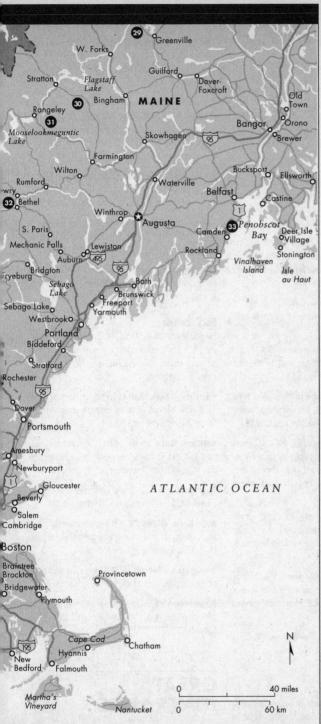

Hemingway's, Killington, VT. The chic seasonal menu celebrates native game and fresh seafood in such dishes as Vermont venison with pumpkin pudding. *$$$$*

Lodging
Boulders Inn, New Preston, CT. This idyllic inn on Lake Waramaug has panoramic views. *$$$$*

Manor House, Norfolk, CT. Twenty stained-glass windows by Louis Comfort Tiffany are a unique feature. *$$–$$$$*

Blair Hill Inn, Greenville, ME. Beautiful gardens and a hilltop location with marvelous views over Moosehead lake distinguish this 1891 estate. *$$$$*

Ullikana, Bar Harbor, ME. Within this Tudor mansion is a riot of color and art. Water views and delicious breakfasts make it a real treat. *$$$–$$$$*

Charlotte Inn, Edgartown, MA. Rooms in one of the region's finest inns are smartly furnished. *$$$$*

Historic Merrell Inn, South Lee, MA. Built as a stagecoach stopover around 1794, this inn has an unfussy style. *$$$*

Manor on Golden Pond, Holderness, NH. The rooms in this English-style manor are filled with luxurious touches. *$$$$*

Snowvillage Inn, Snowville, NH. Rooms in this book-filled inn near North Conway are named after authors; the nicest, with 12 windows, is a tribute to Robert Frost. *$$$–$$$$*

Vanderbilt Hall, Newport, RI. The city's most sophisticated small hotel, a former Vanderbilt family home, exudes elegance. *$$$$*

West Mountain Inn, Arlington, VT. A former 1840s farmhouse anchors a llama ranch with 150 acres of glorious views. *$$$$*

Inn at Shelburne Farms, Shelburne, VT. This Tudor-style inn sits on the edge of Lake Champlain. *$$–$$$$*

Memorable Sights
Long Island Sound from Stonington, CT. Wander past the historic buildings and climb up into the Old Lighthouse Museum for a spectacular view.

Sunrise from Cadillac Mountain, Mount Desert Island, ME. From the summit you have a 360-degree view of the ocean, islands, woods, and lakes.

Cobblestone streets and antique houses, Nantucket, MA. Settled in the mid-17th century, Nantucket has a pristine town center.

Cranberry harvesttime, Cape Cod and Nantucket, MA. Cape Cod's Rail Trail passes salt marshes, cranberry bogs, and ponds. On Nantucket, visit lovely Milestone Bog.

Early October views, Kancamagus Highway, NH. The White Mountain vistas on this 34-mi drive burst into color each fall.

Bellevue Avenue, Newport, RI. Mansions with pillars and marble preside over gardens and lawns that roll to the ocean.

The Appalachian Gap, Route 17, VT. Views from this mountain pass near Bristol are a just reward for the challenging drive.

Ski Resorts
Sugarloaf/USA, ME. At 2,820 ft, Sugarloaf/USA's vertical drop is greater than that of any other New England ski peak except Killington.

Sunday River, ME. Good snowmaking and reliable grooming ensure great snow from November to May.

Attitash Bear Peak, NH. Something innovative is always happening here—from demo days to race camps.

Jay Peak, VT. It gets the most natural snow of any Vermont ski area.

Mad River Glen, VT. The apt motto at this area owned by a skiers cooperative is "Ski It If You Can."

Smugglers' Notch, VT. Morse Mountain at Smugglers' is tops for beginners.

Sugarbush, VT. Sugarbush is an overall great place to ski; nearly everyone will feel comfortable.

GREAT ITINERARIES

Highlights of New England
14 to 19 days. In a nation where distances can often be daunting, New England

13

packs its highlights into a remarkably compact area. Understanding Yankee-dom might take a lifetime—but it's possible to get a good appreciation for the six-state region in a 2- to 2½-week drive.

Hartford *(1 day).* The Mark Twain House resembles a Mississippi steamboat beached in a Victorian neighborhood. Downtown, visit Connecticut's ornate State Capitol and the Wadsworth Atheneum, which houses fine Impressionist and Hudson River School paintings. ☞ *Hartford and the Connecticut River Valley in Chapter 7.*

Lower Connecticut River Valley, Block Island Sound *(1 or 2 days).* Here centuries-old towns such as Essex and Chester coexist with a well-preserved natural environment. In Rhode Island, sandy beaches dot the coast in Watch Hill, Charlestown, and Narragansett. ☞ *Hartford and the Connecticut River Valley in Chapter 7, South County in Chapter 6.*

Newport *(1 day).* Despite its Colonial downtown and seaside parks, to most people Newport means mansions—the most opulent, cost-be-damned enclave of private homes ever built in the United States. Turn-of-the-20th-century "cottages" such as the Breakers and Marble House are beyond duplication today. ☞ *Newport County in Chapter 6.*

Providence *(1 day).* Rhode Island's capital holds treasures in places such as Benefit Street, with its Federal-era homes, and the Museum of Art at the Rhode Island School of Design. Savor a knockout Italian meal on Federal Hill and visit Waterplace Park. ☞ *Providence in Chapter 6.*

Cape Cod *(2 or 3 days).* Meander along Massachusetts' arm-shape peninsula and explore Cape Cod National Seashore. Provincetown, at the Cape's tip, is Bohemian, gay, and touristy, a Portuguese fishing village on a Colonial foundation. In season, you can whale-watch here. ☞ *Cape Cod in Chapter 5.*

Plymouth *(1 day).* "America's hometown" is where 102 weary settlers landed in 1620. You can climb aboard the replica *Mayflower II,* then spend time at Plimoth Plantation, staffed by costumed "Pilgrims." ☞ *Boston in Chapter 5.*

Boston *(2 or 3 days).* In Boston, famous buildings such as Faneuil Hall are not merely civic landmarks but national icons. From the Boston Common, the Freedom Trail extends to encompass foundation stones of American liberty such as Old North Church. Walk the gaslit streets of Beacon Hill, too. On your second day, explore the Museum of Fine Arts and the grand boulevards and shops of Back Bay. Another day, visit the Cambridge campus of Harvard University and its museums. ☞ *Boston in Chapter 5*

Salem and Newburyport *(1 or 2 days).* In Salem, many sites, including the Peabody and Essex Museum, recall the dark days of the 1690s witch hysteria and the fortunes amassed in the China trade. Newburyport's Colonial and Federal-style homes testify to Yankee enterprise on the seas. ☞ *The North Shore in Chapter 5.*

Manchester and Concord *(1 day).* Manchester, New Hampshire's largest city, holds the Amoskeag Textile Mills, a reminder of New England's industrial past. Smaller Concord is the state capital. Near the State House is the fine Museum of New Hampshire History, housing one of the locally built stagecoaches that carried Concord's name throughout the West. ☞ *Western and Central New Hampshire in Chapter 3.*

Green Mountains and Montpelier *(1 or 2 days).* Route 100 travels through the heart of the Green Mountains, whose rounded peaks assert a modest grandeur. Vermont's vest-pocket capital, Montpelier, has the gold-dome Vermont State House and the quirky Vermont Museum. ☞ *Central Vermont and Northern Vermont in Chapter 4.*

White Mountains *(1 day).* U.S. 302 threads through New Hampshire's White Mountains, passing beneath brooding Mt. Washington and through Crawford Notch. In Bretton Woods the Mt. Washington Cog Railway still chugs to the summit, and the Mount Washington Hotel recalls the glory days of White Mountain resorts. ☞ *The White Mountains in Chapter 3.*

Portland *(1 day).* Maine's maritime capital shows off its restored waterfront at the Old Port. Nearby, two lighthouses on Cape Elizabeth, Two Lights and Portland Head, stand vigil. ☞ *Portland to Waldoboro in Chapter 2.*

Fall Foliage Tour

7 to 12 days. In fall, New England's dense forests explode into reds, oranges, yellows, and purples. Like autumn itself, this itinerary works its way south from northern Vermont into Connecticut. Nature's schedule varies from year to year; as a rule, this trip is best begun around the third week of September. Book accommodations well in advance.

Northwestern Vermont *(1 or 2 days).* In Burlington the elms will be turning color on the University of Vermont campus. A ferry ride across Lake Champlain affords great views of Vermont's Green Mountains and New York's Adirondacks. After visiting the resort town of Stowe, continue beneath the cliffs of Smugglers' Notch. The north country's palette unfolds in Newport, where the blue waters of Lake Memphremagog reflect the foliage. ☞ *Northern Vermont in Chapter 4.*

Northeast Kingdom *(1 day).* After a side trip along Lake Willoughby, explore St. Johnsbury, where the St. Johnsbury Athenaeum and Fairbanks Museum reveal Victorian tastes in art and natural-history collecting. In Peacham, stock up for a picnic at the Peacham Store. ☞ *Northern Vermont in Chapter 4.*

White Mountains and Lakes Region *(1 or 2 days).* In New Hampshire, I–93 narrows as it winds through craggy Franconia Notch. Watch for the Old Man of the Mountain, a natural rock profile. The sinuous Kancamagus Highway passes through the mountains to Conway. In Center Harbor in the Lakes Region, you can ride the M/S *Mount Washington* for views of the Lake Winnipesaukee shoreline, or ascend to Moultonborough's Castle in the Clouds for a falcon's-eye look at the colors. ☞ *The White Mountains and Lakes Region in Chapter 3.*

Mt. Monadnock Region *(1 or 2 days).* In Concord stop at the Museum of New Hampshire History and the State House. Several trails climb Mt. Monadnock, near Jaffrey Center, and colorful vistas extend as far as Boston. ☞ *Western and Central New Hampshire in Chapter 3.*

The Mohawk Trail *(1 day).* In Shelburne Falls, Massachusetts, the Bridge of Flowers displays the last of autumn's blossoms. Follow the Mohawk Trail as it ascends into the Berkshire Hills—and stop to take in the view at the hairpin turn just east of North Adams. In Williamstown the Sterling and Francine Clark Art Institute houses a collection of Impressionist works. ☞ *The Pioneer Valley and the Berkshires in Chapter 5.*

The Berkshires *(1 or 2 days).* The scenery around Lenox, Stockbridge, and Great Barrington has long attracted the talented and the wealthy. You can visit the homes of novelist Edith Wharton (the Mount, in Lenox), sculptor Daniel Chester French (Chesterwood, in Stockbridge), and diplomat Joseph Choate (Naumkeag, in Stockbridge). ☞ *The Berkshires in Chapter 5.*

The Litchfield Hills *(1 or 2 days).* This area of Connecticut combines the feel of up-country New England with exclusive exurban polish. The wooded shores of Lake Waramaug harbor country inns and wineries in New Preston and other pretty towns. Litchfield has a village green that could be the template for anyone's idealized New England town center. ☞ *The Litchfield Hills in Chapter 7.*

The Seacoast

8 to 14 days. Every New England state except Vermont borders on salt water. For history buffs, vivid links to the days when the sea was the region's lifeblood abound; for water-sports enthusiasts, it's a guarantee of fun on beaches from the sandy shores of Long Island Sound to the bracing waters of Down East Maine. A journey along the coast also brings the promise of fresh seafood, incomparable sunrises, and a quality of light that has entranced artists from Winslow Homer to Edward Hopper.

Southeastern Connecticut, Newport *(1 to 3 days).* Begin in New London, home of the U.S. Coast Guard Academy, and stop at Groton to tour the *Nautilus* at the Submarine Force Museum. In Mystic the days of wooden ships and whaling adventures live on at Mystic Seaport museum. In Rhode Island, savor the Victorian resort of Watch Hill and the Block Island Sound beaches. See the extravagant summer mansions in Newport. ☞ *New Haven and the Southeastern Coast in Chapter 7, South County and Newport County in Chapter 6.*

Massachusetts' South Shore and Cape Cod *(2 to 4 days).* New Bedford was once a major whaling center; exhibits at the New Bedford Whaling Museum capture this vanished world. Cape Cod can be nearly all things to all visitors, with quiet Colonial villages and lively resorts, gentle bay-side wavelets and crashing surf. In Plymouth visit the *Mayflower II* and Plimoth Plantation, the re-created Pilgrim village. ☞ *Boston and Cape Cod in Chapter 5.*

Boston, The North Shore *(2 days).* To savor Boston's centuries-old ties to the sea, take a half-day stroll by Faneuil Hall and Quincy Market or a boat tour of the harbor. In Salem, America's early shipping fortunes are chronicled in the Peabody and Essex Museum and the Salem Maritime National Historic Site. Spend a day exploring more of the North Shore, including the old fishing port of Gloucester and Rockport, one possible place to buy that seascape painted in oils. Newburyport, with its Federal-style shipowners' homes, is home to the Parker River National Wildlife Refuge, beloved by birders and beach walkers. ☞ *Boston and the North Shore in Chapter 5.*

New Hampshire and Southern Maine *(1 or 2 days).* New Hampshire fronts the Atlantic for a scant 18 mi, but its coastal landmarks range from honky-tonk Hampton Beach to quiet Odiorne Point State Park in Rye and pretty Portsmouth, whose Georgian- and Federal-style mansions once sheltered the cream of pre-Revolutionary society. Visit a few at Strawbery Banke Museum and elsewhere. Between here and Portland, Maine's largest city and the site of a waterfront revival, you will find ocean-side resorts such as Kennebunkport. Near Portland is Cape Elizabeth, with its Portland Head and Two Lights lighthouses. ☞ *The Coast in Chapter 3, and York County Coast and Portland to Waldoboro in Chapter 2.*

Down East *(2 or 3 days).* Beyond Portland ranges the ragged, island-strewn coast that Mainers call Down East. On your first day, travel to Camden or Castine. Some highlights are the retail outlets of Freeport, home of L. L. Bean; Brunswick, with the museums of Bowdoin College; and Bath, with the Maine Maritime Museum and Shipyard. Perhaps you'll think about cruising on one of the schooners that sail out of Rockland. In Camden and Castine, exquisite inns occupy homes built from inland Maine's gold, timber. On your second day, visit the spectacular rocky coast of Acadia National Park, near the resort town of Bar Harbor. If you have another day, drive the desolately beautiful stretch of Maine's granite coast to the New Brunswick border, where President Franklin Roosevelt's "beloved island," Campobello, and Roosevelt Campobello International Park lie across an international bridge. ☞ *Portland to Waldoboro, Penobscot Bay, Mount Desert Island, and Way Down East in Chapter 2.*

2 MAINE

At its extremes Maine measures 300 mi by 200 mi; all the other states in New England could fit within its ample perimeters. The Kennebunks hold classic townscapes, rocky shorelines, sandy beaches, and quaint downtown districts. Portland has the state's best selection of restaurants, shops, and cultural offerings, and Freeport draws outlet shoppers. North of Portland, sandy beaches give way to rocky coast and treasures such as Acadia National Park. Outdoors enthusiasts head to inland Maine's lakes, mountains, and the vast North Woods.

By Hilary
M. Nangle

ON THE MAINE–NEW HAMPSHIRE BORDER is a sign that plainly announces the philosophy of the region: WELCOME TO MAINE: THE WAY LIFE SHOULD BE. Local folk say too many cars are on the road when you can't make it through the traffic signal on the first try. Romantics luxuriate in the feeling of a down comforter on an old, yellowed pine bed or in the sensation of the wind and salt spray on their faces while cruising in a historic windjammer. Families love the unspoiled beaches and safe inlets dotting the shoreline and the clear inland lakes. Hikers and campers are revived by the exalting and exhausting climb to the top of Katahdin. Adventure seekers raft the Kennebec and Penobscot rivers or sea-kayak along the coast, and skiers head for the snow-covered slopes of western and northern Maine.

There is an expansiveness to Maine, a sense of distance between places that hardly exists elsewhere in New England and, along with the sheer size and spread of the place, a variety of terrain. People speak of "coastal" Maine and "inland" Maine as though the state could be summed up under the twin emblems of lobsters and pine trees. Yet the topography and character in this state are a good deal more complicated.

Even the coast is several places in one. Portland may be Maine's largest city, but its attitude is decidedly more big town than small city. South of this rapidly gentrifying city, Ogunquit, Kennebunkport, Old Orchard Beach, and other resort towns predominate along a reasonably smooth shoreline. North of Portland and Casco Bay, secondary roads turn south off U.S. 1 onto so many oddly chiseled peninsulas that it's possible to drive for days without retracing your route. Slow down to explore the museums, galleries, and shops in the larger towns and the antiques and curio shops and harborside lobster shacks in the smaller fishing villages on the peninsulas. Freeport is an entity unto itself, a place where numerous name-brand outlets and specialty stores have sprung up around the retail outpost of famous outfitter L. L. Bean. And no description of the coast would be complete without mention of popular Acadia National Park, with its majestic mountains, and the rugged scenery of the less-visited towns that lie way Down East.

Inland Maine likewise defies easy characterization. For one thing, a lot of it is virtually uninhabited. This is the land Henry David Thoreau wrote about in his evocative mid-19th century portrait, *The Maine Woods*; aside from having been logged over several times, much of it hasn't changed since Thoreau and his Native American guides passed through. Ownership of vast portions of northern Maine by forest-products corporations has kept out subdivision and development, but this, too, is changing; many of the roads here are private, open to travel only by permit.

Wealthy summer visitors, or "sports," came to Maine beginning in the late 1800s to hunt, fish, and play in the clean air and clean water. The state's more than 6,000 lakes and more than 3,000 mi of rivers and streams still attract such people, and more and more families, for the same reasons. Sporting camps still thrive around Greenville, Rangeley, and in the Great North Woods.

Logging in the north created the culture of the mill towns, the Rumfords, Skowhegans, Millinockets, and Bangors that lie at the end of the old river drives. The logs arrive by truck today, but Maine's harvested wilderness still feeds the mills and the nation's hunger for paper.

Maine

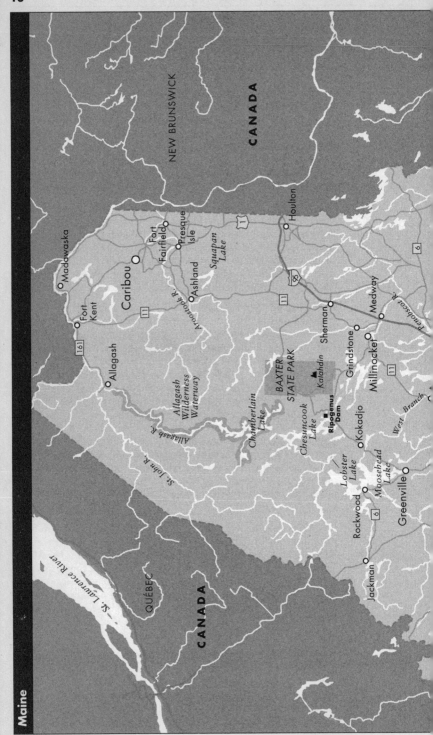

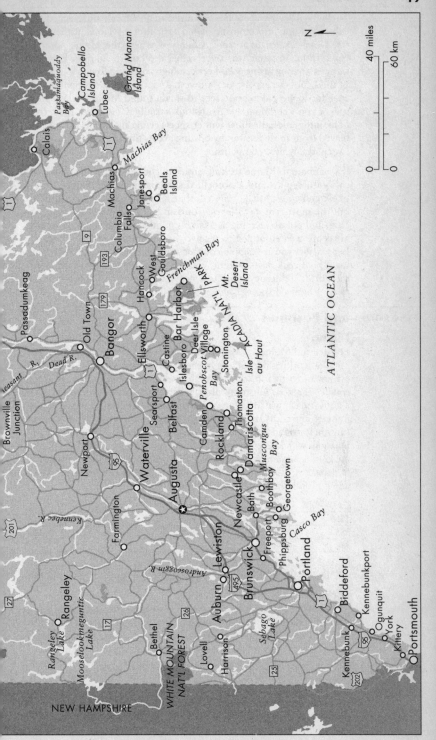

N

40 miles

60 km

Passamaquoddy Bay

Campobello Island

Grand Manan Island

Lubec

Calais

11

Machias Bay

Machias

Jonesport

Beals Island

1

Columbia Falls

9

Gouldsboro

West

193

Hancock

Frenchman Bay

Passadumkeag

179

Old Town

Ellsworth

Bar Harbor

ACADIA NAT'L PARK

Mt. Desert Island

R.

Dead R.

Bangor

Castine

Deer Isle

Brownville Junction

11

Islesboro

Penobscot Bay

Stonington

Isle au Haut

Searsport

Belfast

Camden

Rockland

Thomaston

ATLANTIC OCEAN

Newport

95

Waterville

Damariscotta

Muscongus Bay

201

Augusta

Newcastle

Bath

Boothbay

Georgetown

Farmington

Kennebec R.

Freeport

Phippsburg

Casco Bay

Androscoggin R.

495

Brunswick

Portland

Lewiston

Auburn

Rangeley

27

Rangeley Lake

17

Mooselookmeguntic Lake

26

Bethel

Sebago Lake

Biddeford

Kennebunkport

Lovell

Harrison

WHITE MOUNTAIN NAT'L FOREST

25

Kennebunk

Ogunquit

York

95

Kittery

Portsmouth

201

NEW HAMPSHIRE

The hunger for potatoes has given rise to an entirely different Maine culture, in one of the most isolated agricultural regions of the country. Northeastern Aroostook County is where the Maine potatoes come from. In what was once called the Potato Empire, however, farmers are now as pressed between high costs and low prices as any of their counterparts in the Midwest, and a growing national preference for Idaho baking potatoes to small, round Maine boiling potatoes has only compounded Aroostook's troubles. However, the arrival of an international-caliber winter sports center in 1999 is giving a renewed focus to this region by hosting events that are attracting World Cup and Olympic competitors.

If you come to Maine seeking an untouched fishing village with locals gathered around a potbellied stove in the general store, you'll likely come away disappointed; that innocent age has passed in all but the most remote villages. Tourism has supplanted fishing, logging, and potato farming as Maine's number one industry, and most areas are well equipped to receive the annual onslaught of visitors. But whether you are stepping outside a motel room for a walk or watching a boat rock at its anchor, you can sense the infinity of the natural world. Wilderness is always nearby, growing to the edges of the most urbanized spots.

Pleasures and Pastimes

Dining

Lobster and Maine are synonymous. As a general rule, the closer you are to a working harbor, the fresher your lobster will be. Aficionados eschew ordering lobster in restaurants, preferring to eat them "in the rough" at classic lobster pounds, where you select your dinner out of a pool and enjoy it at a waterside picnic table. Shrimp, scallops, clams, mussels, and crabs are also caught in the cold waters off Maine. Restaurants in Portland and in resort towns prepare shellfish in creative combinations with lobster, haddock, salmon, and swordfish. Wild blueberries are grown commercially in Maine, and local cooks use them generously in pancakes, muffins, jams, pies, and cobblers. In 1999, Maine passed a law prohibiting smoking in restaurants.

CATEGORY	COST*
$$$$	over $25
$$$	$17–$25
$$	$9–$16
$	under $9

*per person, for a main-course dinner

Lodging

The beach communities in the south beckon with their weathered look. Stately digs can be found in the classic inns along the York County Coast. Bed-and-breakfasts and Victorian inns furnished with lace, chintz, and mahogany have joined the family-oriented motels of Ogunquit, Boothbay Harbor, Bar Harbor, and the Camden–Rockport region. Although accommodations tend to be less luxurious away from the coast, Bethel, Carrabassett Valley, and Rangeley have sophisticated hotels and inns. Greenville has the largest selection of restaurants and accommodations in the North Woods region. Lakeside sporting camps, which range from the primitive to the upscale, are popular around Rangeley and the North Woods. Many have cozy cabins heated with woodstoves and serve three hearty meals a day. At some of Maine's larger hotels and inns with restaurants, rates may include breakfast and dinner during the peak seasons.

CATEGORY	COST
$$$$	over $180
$$$	$130–$180
$$	$80–$130
$	under $80

All prices are for a standard double room during peak season and not including tax or gratuities. Some inns add a 15% service charge.

Outdoor Activities and Sports

BOATING

Maine's long coastline is justifiably famous: be sure to get on the water, whether on an excursion headed for Monhegan Island for the day or on a windjammer for a relaxing vacation. Windjammer trips last from just a few hours to a full week. Longer trips include hearty, home-style meals and a traditional lobster bake often held on a remote island. Windjammers may sail past long, craggy fingers of land that jut into a sea dotted with more than 2,000 islands. Sail among these islands and you'll see hidden coves, lighthouses, boat-filled harbors, and quiet fishing villages. Some windjammers, traditional two- or three-masted tall ships, are historic vessels that have been modified to carry human cargo while others have more modern amenities. Most windjammers depart from Rockland, Rockport, or Camden, all ports on Penobscot Bay. Boating trips, including whale-watching, run in season, from mid- to late May through September or mid-October.

HIKING

From seaside rambles to backwoods hikes, Maine has a walk for everyone. This state's beaches are mostly hard-packed and good for walking. Many coastal communities, such as York, Ogunquit, and Bar Harbor, have shoreside paths for people who want to keep sand out of their shoes yet enjoy the sound of the crashing surf and the cliff-top views of inlets and coves. Those who like to walk in the woods will not be disappointed: 90% of the state is forested land. Acadia National Park has more than 150 mi of hiking trails, and within Baxter State Park are the northern end of the Appalachian Trail and Katahdin. At nearly 1 mi high, Katahdin is the tallest mountain in the state.

SKIING

Weather patterns that create snow cover for Maine ski areas may come from the Atlantic or from Canada, and Maine may have snow when other New England states do not—and vice versa. Sunday River and Sugarloaf, both operated by the American Skiing Co., are the state's largest ski areas. Both are full-service destination resorts with a choice of lodging, dining, and shopping as well as more than enough terrain to keep skiers and riders content for days. It's worth the effort to get to Sugarloaf, which provides the only above-tree-line skiing in New England and also has a lively base village.

Saddleback, in Rangeley, has big-mountain skiing at little-mountain prices. Its lift system is sorely out of date, but many would have it no other way, preferring its down-home wilderness ambience. Squaw Mountain in Greenville is similar in character. Its remote location ensures few crowds, and its low prices make it an attractive alternative to other big mountains.

WHITE-WATER RAFTING

From early May through September, Maine has consistent white-water rafting on three dam-controlled, Class III–V rivers: the Kennebec, the Penobscot, and the Dead. About a dozen outfitters are based in and around the Forks, Maine's white-water capital, where the Kennebec and the Dead rivers meet. Both are good day trips, with the Kennebec being the most popular—like a white-water roller coaster; big thrills but few chills. The Penobscot, which flows near Baxter State Park in the shadow of Mt. Katahdin, provides a remote trip with challenging white water and beautiful views of the mountain. It's not uncommon to see moose or deer while on the river. Most outfitters have facilities in this area, and most offer both day and overnight trips.

Exploring Maine

Maine is a large state that offers many different experiences. The York County Coast, in the southern portion of the state, is easily accessible and has long sand beaches, historic homes, and good restaurants. The coastal geography changes in Portland, the economic and cultural center of southern Maine. North of the city, long fingers of land jut into the sea, sheltering fishing villages. Penobscot Bay is famed for its rockbound coast, sailing, and numerous islands. Mount Desert Island lures crowds of people to Acadia National Park, which is filled with stunning natural beauty. Way Down East, beyond Acadia, the tempo changes; fast-food joints and trinket shops all but disappear, replaced by family-style restaurants and artisans' shops. Inland, the western lakes and mountains provide an entirely different experience. Summer camps, ski areas, and small villages populate this region. People head to Maine's North Woods to escape the crowds and to enjoy the great outdoors by hiking, rafting, camping, or canoeing.

Numbers in the text and in the margin correspond to numbers on the maps: Southern Maine Coast, Portland, Penobscot Bay, Mount Desert Island, Way Down East, Western Maine, and the North Woods.

Great Itineraries

You can spend days exploring just the coast of Maine, as these itineraries indicate, so plan ahead and decide whether you want to ski and dogsled in the western mountains, raft or canoe in the North Woods, or simply meander up the coast, stopping at museums and historic sites, shopping for local arts and crafts, and exploring coastal villages and lobster shacks. Trying to see everything in one visit is complicated by the lack of east–west roads in the state and heavy traffic on popular routes, such as U.S. 1 and U.S. 302. Build extra time into your schedule and relax. You'll get there eventually, and in the meantime, enjoy the view.

IF YOU HAVE 2 DAYS

A two-day exploration of the southern coast provides a good introduction to different aspects of the Maine coast. Begin in **Ogunquit** ③ with a morning walk along the Marginal Way. Then head north to **Kennebunks** ⑤, allowing at least two hours to wander through the shops and historic homes around Dock Square. Relax on the beach for an hour or so before heading to ⛪ **Portland** ⑦–⑫. If you thrive on arts and entertainment, spend the night here. Otherwise, continue north to ⛪ **Freeport** ⑮, where you can shop all night at L. L. Bean. On day two, head north, stopping in **Bath** ⑰ to tour the Maine Maritime Museum, and finish up with a lobster dinner on **Pemaquid Peninsula** ⑳.

IF YOU HAVE 4 DAYS

A four-day tour of midcoast Maine up to Acadia National Park is one of New England's classic trips. From New Harbor on **Pemaquid Peninsula** ⑳, take the boat to ⛪ **Monhegan Island** ㉔ for a day of walking the trails and exploring the artists' studios and galleries. The next day, continue northeast to **Rockland** ㉕ and ⛪ **Camden** ㉖. On day four, visit the Farnsworth Museum in Rockland, hike or drive to the top of Mt. Battie in Camden, and meander around Camden's boat-filled harbor. Or bypass midcoast Maine in favor of ⛪ **Mount Desert Island** ㊱–㊹ and Acadia National Park. To avoid sluggish traffic on U.S. 1, from Freeport, stay on I–95 to Augusta and the Maine Turnpike; then take Route 3 to Belfast and pick up U.S. 1 north there.

IF YOU HAVE 8 DAYS

An eight-day trip allows time to see a good portion of the coast. Spend two days wandering through gentrified towns and weather-beaten fishing villages from ⊡ **Kittery** ① to ⊡ **Portland** ⑦–⑫. On your third day explore Portland and environs, including a boat ride to **Eagle Island** ⑭ or one of the other Casco Bay islands and a visit to Portland Head Light and Two Lights in Cape Elizabeth. Continue working your way up the coast, letting your interests dictate your stops: outlet stores in **Freeport** ⑮, Maine Maritime Museum in ⊡ **Bath** ⑰, antiques shops in **Wiscasset** ⑱, fishing villages and a much-photographed lighthouse on **Pemaquid Peninsula** ㉑. Allow at least one day in the **Rockland** ㉕ and ⊡ **Camden** ㉖ region before taking the leisurely route to **Bar Harbor** ㊱via the **Blue Hill** ㉚ peninsula and ⊡ **Deer Isle Village** ㉛. Finish up with two days on ⊡ **Mount Desert Island** ㊱–㊹.

When to Tour Maine

From July to September is the choice time for a vacation in Maine. The weather is warmest in July and August, though September is less crowded. In warm weather, the arteries along the coast and lakeside communities inland are clogged with out-of-state license plates, campgrounds are filled to capacity, and hotel rates are high. Midweek is less busy, and lodging rates are often lower then than on weekends.

Fall foliage can be brilliant in Maine and is made even more so by its reflection in inland lakes or streams or off the ocean. Late September is peak season in the north country, while in southern Maine the prime viewing dates are usually around October 5 to 10. In September and October the days are sunny and the nights crisp.

In winter, the coastal towns almost completely close down. If the sidewalks could be rolled up, they probably would be. Maine's largest ski areas usually open in mid-November and, thanks to excellent snowmaking facilities, provide good skiing often into April.

Springtime is mud season here, as in most other rural areas of New England. Mud season is followed by spring flowers and the start of wildflowers in meadows along the roadsides. Mid-May to mid-June is the main season for black flies, especially inland. It's best to schedule a trip after mid-June if possible, though this is prime canoeing time.

YORK COUNTY COAST

Maine's southernmost coastal towns, most of them in York County, won't give you the rugged, wind-bitten "Down East" experience, but they are easily reached from the south, and most have the sand beaches that all but vanish beyond Portland. These towns are highly popular in summer, an all-too-brief period. Crowds converge and gobble up rooms and dinner reservations at prime restaurants. You'll have to work a little harder to find solitude and vestiges of the "real" Maine here. Still, even day-trippers who come for a few fleeting hours will appreciate the magical warmth of the sand along this coast.

North of Kittery, the Maine coast has long stretches of hard-packed white-sand beach, closely crowded by nearly unbroken ranks of beach cottages, motels, and oceanfront restaurants. The summer colonies of York Beach and Wells Beach have the crowds and ticky-tacky shorefront overdevelopment, but quiet wildlife refuges and land reserves promise an easy escape. York's historic district is on the National Register of Historic Places. Ogunquit is more upscale and offers much to do, from shopping to taking a cliff-side walk.

More than any other region south of Portland, the Kennebunks—and especially Kennebunkport—provide the complete Maine-coast experience: classic townscapes where white clapboard houses rise from manicured lawns and gardens; rocky shorelines punctuated by sandy beaches; quaint downtown districts packed with gift shops, ice cream stands, and visitors; harbors where lobster boats bob alongside yachts; lobster pounds and well-appointed dining rooms. As you continue north, the scents of french fries, pizza, and cotton candy hover in the air above Coney Island–like Old Orchard Beach, known for its amusement pier and 7-mi-long shoreline. These towns are best explored on a leisurely holiday of two days—more if you require a fix of solid beach time. U.S. 1 travels along the coast. Inland, the Maine Turnpike (I–95) is the fastest route if you want to skip some towns.

Kittery

❶ *55 mi north of Boston; 5 mi north of Portsmouth, New Hampshire.*

Kittery, which lacks a large sand beach of its own, hosts a complex of factory outlets that make it a popular destination. As an alternative to shopping, drive north past the outlets and go east on Route 103 for a peek at the hidden Kittery most people miss: hiking and biking trails and, best of all, great views of the water. Also along this winding stretch are two forts, both open in summer.

Built in 1872, **Ft. Foster** (✉ Pocahontas Rd., Kittery Point, ☎ 207/439–3800) was an active military installation until 1949. **Ft. McClary** (✉ Rte. 103, Kittery Point, ☎ 207/384–5160), which dates from 1715, was staffed during five wars.

Dining and Lodging

$–$$ ✕ **Warren's Lobster House.** A local institution, this waterfront restaurant specializes in seafood and has a huge salad bar. The pine-sided dining room leaves the impression that little has changed since the restaurant opened in 1940. In season, you can dine outdoors overlooking the water. ✉ *U.S. 1 and Water St.,* ☎ *207/439–1630. AE, MC, V.*

$$$ ▥ **The Inn at Portsmouth Harbor.** This brick Victorian built in 1889 on the old Kittery town green overlooks the Piscataqua River and Portsmouth Harbor. An easy walk over the bridge takes you to nearby Portsmouth, New Hampshire. English antiques and Victorian watercolors decorate the inn. ✉ *6 Water St., 03904,* ☎ *207/439–4040,* FAX *207/438–9286,* WEB *www.innatportsmouth.com. 5 rooms. In-room data ports, cable TV; no kids under 16, no smoking. AE, MC, V. BP.*

$ ▥ **Academy Street Inn.** Antiques, family photos, and a collection of sleds and snowshoes adorn this grand 1903 home within walking distance of two historic houses, Hamilton House and Sarah Orne Jewett's home. Its location on the New Hampshire border is convenient for exploring both southern Maine and New Hampshire. Rates include big breakfasts served in the formal dining room. ✉ *15 Academy St., South Berwick, 20 mi northwest of Kittery, 03908,* ☎ *207/384–5633. 5 rooms. No air-conditioning, no room phones, no room TVs, no kids under 10, no smoking. AE, D, MC, V. BP.*

Nightlife and the Arts

Hamilton House (✉ 40 Vaughan's La., South Berwick, 20 mi northwest of Kittery, ☎ 603/436–3205; ⊠ $5), the Georgian home featured in Sarah Orne Jewett's historical novel *The Tory Lover,* presents "Sundays in the Garden" in July, a series of concerts ranging from classical to folk music. Concerts ($6) begin at 4. You can also visit **Jewett's**

Southern Maine Coast

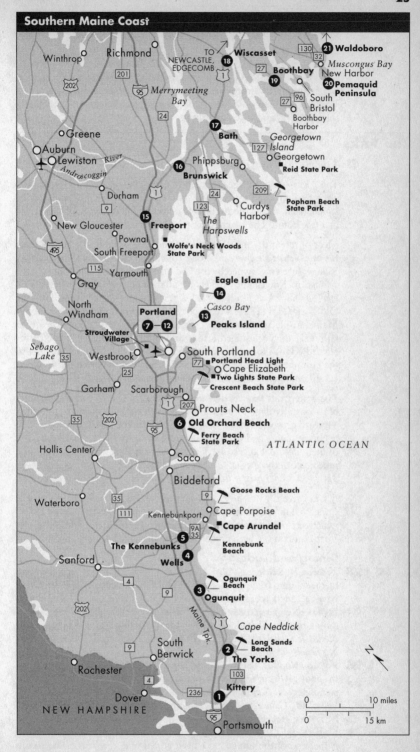

home (⊠ 5 Portland St., South Berwick, ☎ 207/436–3205, ⊠ $5, ☉ Wed.–Sun. 11–5, with tours on the hour until 4) during summer.

Shopping

Kittery has more than 120 outlet stores. Along a several-mile stretch of U.S. 1 you can find just about anything, from hardware to underwear. Among the stores are Crate & Barrel, Eddie Bauer, Jones New York, Esprit, Waterford/Wedgwood, Lenox, Ralph Lauren, Tommy Hilfiger, DKNY, and J. Crew.

The Yorks

② *4 mi north of Kittery.*

The Yorks—York Village, York Harbor, York Beach, and Cape Neddick—are typical of small-town coastal communities in New England and are smaller than most. Many of their nooks and crannies can be explored in a few hours. The beaches are the big attraction here.

Most of the 18th- and 19th-century buildings within the **York Village Historic District** are clustered along York Street and Lindsay Road in York Village; seven are owned by the Old York Historical Society and charge admission. You can buy tickets for all the buildings at the **Jefferds Tavern** (⊠ U.S. 1A at Lindsay Rd.), a restored late-18th-century inn. The **Old York Gaol** (1720) was once the King's Prison for the Province of Maine; inside are dungeons, cells, and the jailer's quarters. Theatrical jailbreak tours are staged Friday and Saturday nights. The 1731 **Elizabeth Perkins House** reflects the Victorian style of its last occupants, the prominent Perkins family. ☎ *207/363–4974,* WEB *www.oldyork.org.* ⊠ *All buildings $7.* ☉ *Mid-June–mid-Oct., Mon.–Sat. 10–5.*

The waterfront **Sayward-Wheeler House** (1718) mirrors the fortunes of a coastal village in the transition from trade to tourism. Jonathan Sayward prospered in the West Indies trade in the 18th century; by 1860 his descendants had opened the house to the public to share the story of their Colonial ancestors. The house, accessible only by guided tour, reflects both these eras. ⊠ *79 Barrell La., York Harbor,* ☎ *603/436–3205.* ⊠ *$5.* ☉ *June–mid-Oct., weekends 11–5; tours on the hr 11–4.*

If you drive down Nubble Road from U.S. 1A and go to the end of Cape Neddick, you can park and gaze out at the **Nubble Light** (1879), which sits on a tiny island just offshore. The keeper's house is a tidy Victorian cottage with gingerbread woodwork and a red roof.

Dining and Lodging

$$$–$$$$ ✕ **Cape Neddick Inn.** Chef Jonathan Pratt's French-based American menu changes frequently at this restaurant and art gallery. Past entrées have included poached lobster in vermouth cream and sautéed sweetbreads in caper parsley butter. Tables are well spaced in the bi-level dining room, which is accented by local artwork. ⊠ *1233 U.S. 1, Cape Neddick,* ☎ *207/363–2899. AE, MC, V. Closed Mon., Mar., and Nov. No lunch.*

$–$$$ ✕ **Cape Neddick Lobster Pound.** At this casual harborside restaurant, the nautical decor reflects the menu. All kinds of seafood, including lobster, is served. A children's menu and outdoor dining are available. ⊠ *Shore Rd., Cape Neddick,* ☎ *207/363–5471. MC, V. Closed Jan.–Mar.*

$$ ✕▥ **York Harbor Inn.** A mid-17th-century fishing cabin with dark
★   timbers and a fieldstone fireplace forms the heart of this inn, to which wings and outbuildings have been added over the years. The rooms are furnished with antiques and country pieces; many have decks overlooking the water, and some have whirlpool tubs or fireplaces. The nicest rooms are in two adjacent buildings, Harbor Cliffs and Harbor Hill.

The dining room ($$$–$$$$; no lunch off-season) has great ocean views. For dinner, start with Maine crab cakes and then try the lobster-stuffed chicken breast or the scallops Dijon. ⊠ *U.S. 1A (Box 573, York Harbor 03911),* ☎ *207/363–5119 or 800/343–3869,* ℻ *207/363–7151,* WEB *www.yorkharborinn.com. 47 rooms, 2 suites. Restaurant, pub, cable TV, meeting rooms; no smoking. AE, DC, MC, V. CP.*

$$–$$$$ ⊞ **Edward's Harborside.** This turn-of-the-20th-century B&B sits on the harbor's edge and is just a two-minute walk from the beach. Rooms share baths, are spacious, and have big windows to take in the water views. One room has a whirlpool tub. ⊠ *Stage Neck Rd. (Box 866, York Harbor 03911),* ☎ *207/363–3037,* ℻ *207/363–1544,* WEB *www. edwardsharborsideinn.com. 4 rooms without bath, 3 suites. Cable TV, dock; no kids under 8, no smoking. MC, V. CP.*

$$ ⊞ **The Riverbed.** An oasis of calm, this clapboard home dating from before the American Revolution provides a nice counterpoint to busy York Beach, a short walk away. Each room is carefully furnished with antiques and family pieces and has a private deck; a private sitting room has TV and phone. The shared back deck, with hot tub, slopes gently down to the Cape Neddick River. ⊠ *154 Cape Neddick Rd. (Rte. 1A), 03910,* ☎ *207/363–3630. 3 rooms. Outdoor hot tub, boating; no air-conditioning, no room phones, no room TVs, no smoking. MC, V. Closed Columbus Day–Memorial Day weekend. BP.*

Nightlife and the Arts

Inn on the Blues (⊠ 7 Ocean Ave., York Beach, ☎ 207/351–3221) is a hopping blues club that attracts national bands.

Outdoor Activities and Sports

U.S. 1A runs right behind **Long Sands Beach,** a 1½-mi stretch of sand in York Beach that has roadside parking and a bathhouse. **Short Sands Beach** in York Beach has a bathhouse and is convenient to restaurants and shops. **Capt. Tom Farnon** (⊠ Rte. 103, Town Dock No. 2, York Harbor, ☎ 207/363–3234) takes passengers on lobstering trips, weekdays 10–2.

Ogunquit

❸ *10 mi north of the Yorks, 39 mi southwest of Portland.*

Probably more than any other south-coast community, Ogunquit blends coastal ambience with style and good eating. The village became a resort in the 1880s and gained fame as an artists' colony. A mini Provincetown, Ogunquit has a gay population that swells in summer; many inns and small clubs cater to a primarily gay and lesbian clientele. Families love the protected beach area and friendly environment. Shore Road, which takes you into downtown, passes the 100-ft Bald Head Cliff, with views up and down the coast. On a stormy day the surf can be quite wild here.

Perkins Cove, a neck of land connected to the mainland by Oarweed Road and a pedestrian drawbridge, has a jumble of sea-beaten fish houses. These have largely been transformed by the tide of tourism to shops and restaurants. When you've had your fill of browsing and jostling ★ the crowds, stroll out along the **Marginal Way,** a mile-long footpath that hugs the shore of a rocky promontory known as Israel's Head. Benches along the route give walkers an opportunity to stop and appreciate the open sea vistas, flowering bushes, and million-dollar homes.

The small but worthwhile **Ogunquit Museum of American Art,** dedicated to 20th-century American art, overlooks the ocean and is set amid a 3-acre sculpture garden. Inside are works by Henry Strater, Marsden Hartley, Winslow Homer, Edward Hopper, Gaston Lachaise, Marguerite Zorach, and Louise Nevelson. The huge windows of the sculpture court command a superb view of cliffs and ocean. ⊠ *543 Shore Rd.,* ☎ *207/646–4909.* ☞ *$4.* ☉ *July–mid-Oct., Mon.–Sat. 10:30–5, Sun. 2–5.*

Dining and Lodging

$$$$ ✕ **Arrows.** Elegant simplicity is the hallmark of this restaurant in an 18th-century farmhouse, 2 mi up a back road. Grilled salmon and radicchio with marinated fennel and baked polenta, and Chinese-style duck glazed with molasses are typical entrées on the daily-changing menu. The Maine crabmeat mousse and lobster risotto appetizers and desserts such as strawberry shortcake with Chantilly cream are also beautifully executed. ⊠ *Berwick Rd.,* ☎ *207/361–1100. Reservations essential. MC, V. Closed Mon. and mid-Dec.–mid-Apr. No lunch.*

$$$–$$$$ ✕ **98 Provence.** Country French ambience provides a fitting backdrop
★ for chef Pierre Gignac's French fare. Begin with the duck foie gras or country-style rabbit pâté, and follow it up with a cassoulet or medallion of veal tenderloin with a wild mushroom cream sauce. ⊠ *104 Shore Rd.,* ☎ *207/646–9898. Reservations essential. MC, V.*

$$–$$$ ✕ **Gypsy Sweethearts.** The multiethnic fare at this popular bistro ranges from shrimp margarita to chili-crusted rack of lamb to Jamaican jerk-rubbed chicken. In the dining area, cobalt-blue glassware accents the white-draped tables. ⊠ *10 Shore Rd.,* ☎ *207/646–7021. MC, V. Closed Mon. and Jan.–Apr. No lunch.*

$$–$$$ ✕ **Hurricane.** Don't let the weather-beaten exterior or the frenzied atmosphere inside deter you—this small seafood bar and grill with spectacular views of the crashing surf turns out first-rate dishes. Start with lobster chowder or a chilled fresh-shrimp spring roll. Entrées may include lobster cioppino, rack of lamb, and fire-roasted red snapper. A second Hurricane is on Dock Square, in Kennebunkport. ⊠ *Oarweed La., Perkins Cove,* ☎ *207/646–6348 or 800/649–6348. AE, D, DC, MC, V. Closed early Jan.*

$$$$ ⚏ **Cliff House.** Elsie Jane Weare opened the Cliff House in 1872, and her granddaughter Kathryn now presides over this sprawling oceanfront resort atop Bald Head Cliff. All rooms have ocean views. Those who favor country decor, intimate areas, and artsy touches may find the rooms lack warmth, but the resort's facilities are the best in the region. A new resort center with full health spa, new pools, and 32 oversize rooms with gas fireplaces opened in 2002. This place has a loyal following, so reserve well in advance. ⊠ *2 E. Shore Rd. (Box 2274, 03907),* ☎ *207/361–1000,* ⨳ *207/361–2122,* 🆆🅴🅱 *www.cliffhousemaine.com. 194 rooms, 2 suites. Restaurant, in-room data ports, cable TV, 2 pools (1 indoor), hot tub, sauna, spa, 2 tennis courts, health club; no smoking AE, D, MC, V. Closed mid-Dec.–late Mar.*

$$–$$$$ ⚏ **The Rockmere.** Midway along Ogunquit's Marginal Way, this shingle-style Victorian cottage is an ideal retreat from the hustle and bustle of Perkins Cove. All the rooms have corner locations and are large and airy, and all but one have ocean views. You'll find it easy to laze the day away on the wraparound porch or in the gardens. ⊠ *150 Stearns Rd. (Box 278, 03907),* ☎ *207/646–2985,* ⨳ *207/646–6947,* 🆆🅴🅱 *www. rockmere.com. 8 rooms. Cable TV; no air-conditioning, no phones, no kids under 16. AE, D, V. CP.*

Nightlife and the Arts

Much of the nightlife in Ogunquit revolves around the precincts of Ogunquit Square and Perkins Cove, where people stroll, often enjoying an after-dinner ice cream cone or espresso. Ogunquit is popular with gay and lesbian visitors, and its club scene reflects this.

Jonathan's Restaurant (✉ 2 Bourne La., ☎ 207/646–4777) hosts live entertainment, usually blues, during peak season, from June to mid-October. The **Ogunquit Playhouse** (✉ U.S. 1, ☎ 207/646–5511), one of America's oldest summer theaters, mounts plays and musicals with name entertainment from late June to Labor Day.

Outdoor Activities and Sports

Ogunquit Beach, a 3-mi-wide stretch of sand at the mouth of the Ogunquit River, has snack bars, a boardwalk, rest rooms, and, at the Beach Street entrance, changing areas. Families gravitate to the ends; gay visitors camp at the beach's middle. The less-crowded section to the north is accessible by footbridge and has portable rest rooms, all-day paid parking, and trolley service. **Finestkind** (✉ Perkins Cove, ☎ 207/646–5227) operates cocktail cruises, lobstering trips, and cruises to Nubble Light.

Wells

❹ *5 mi north of Ogunquit, 34 mi southwest of Portland.*

This family-oriented beach community has 7 mi of densely populated shoreline, along with nature preserves where you can explore salt marshes and tidal pools and see birds and waterfowl.

Extensive trails in the **Wells Reserve** lace the 1,600 acres of meadows, orchards, fields, and salt marshes, as well as two estuaries and 9 mi of seashore. Laudholm Farm, an 18th-century saltwater farm, houses the visitor center, where an introductory slide show is screened. Five rooms have exhibits. In winter, cross-country skiing is permitted. ✉ *342 Laudholm Farm Rd.,* ☎ *207/646–1555.* 🎫 *$2 July–Aug. and weekends Sept.–mid-Oct.* ☉ *Grounds daily 8–5. Visitor center May–Dec., Mon.–Sat. 10–4, Sun. noon–4; Jan.–Apr., Sat. 10–4, Sun. noon–4.*

Rachel Carson National Wildlife Refuge (✉ Rte. 9, ☎ 207/646–9226) has a mile-long-loop nature trail through a salt marsh. The trail borders the Little River and a white-pine forest where migrating birds and waterfowl of many varieties are regularly spotted.

☏ A must for motor fanatics and youngsters, the **Wells Auto Museum** has 70 vintage cars, antique coin games, and a restored Model T you can ride in. ✉ *U.S. 1,* ☎ *207/646–9064.* 🎫 *$5.* ☉ *Memorial Day–Columbus Day, daily 10–5.*

Dining and Lodging

$$–$$$$ ✕ **Billy's Chowder House.** Locals head to this simple restaurant in a salt marsh for the generous lobster rolls, haddock sandwiches, and chowders. Big windows in the bright dining rooms overlook the marsh. ✉ *216 Mile Rd.,* ☎ *207/646–7558. AE, D, MC, V. Closed mid-Dec.–mid-Jan.*

$$–$$$ ✕🖪 **Grey Gull Inn.** This Victorian inn, built in 1893, has views of the open sea and rocks on which seals like to sun themselves. Most of the unpretentious rooms have ocean views. The restaurant ($$–$$$$) serves excellent seafood dishes such as soft-shell crabs almandine and regional fare like Yankee pot roast and chicken breast rolled in walnuts. ✉ *475 Webhannet Dr., at Moody Point,* ☎ *207/646–7501,* 🅵🅰🆇 *207/646–0938,* 🆆🅴🅱 *www.thegreygullinn.com. 5 rooms, 4 with bath. Restaurant, cable TV; no smoking. AE, D, MC, V. CP.*

$$–$$$$ 🖪 **Haven by the Sea.** Spacious rooms, some with marsh views, provide comfort at this renovated 1920s church. One block from the beach, it has four common areas, including one with a fireplace. ✉ *59 Church St., 04090,* ☎ *207/646–4194,* 🅵🅰🆇 *207/646–6883,* 🆆🅴🅱 *www.havenbythesea.com. 6 rooms, 2 suites, 1 apartment. Cable TV, Internet, meeting rooms; no kids under 12, no smoking. AE, MC, V. BP.*

Outdoor Activities and Sports

Kayaking is popular along the coast, and **World Within Sea Kayaking** (☎ 207/646–0455) conducts guided tours with lessons.

Shopping

Douglas N. Harding Rare Books (✉ 2152 Post Rd. [U.S. 1], ☎ 207/ 646–8785) has more than 100,000 old books, maps, and prints. The **Lighthouse Depot** (✉ U.S. 1, ☎ 207/646–0608) calls itself the world's largest lighthouse gift store, with lighthouse-themed gifts and memorabilia. **R. Jorgensen** (✉ 502 Post Rd. [U.S. 1], ☎ 207/646–9444) stocks 18th- and 19th-century formal and country antiques from the British Isles, Europe, and the United States.

The Kennebunks

⑤ *5 mi north of Wells, 29 mi southwest of Portland.*

The Kennebunks encompass Kennebunk, Kennebunk Beach, Goose Rocks Beach, Kennebunkport, Cape Porpoise, and Arundel. This cluster of seaside and inland villages provides a little bit of everything, from salt marshes to sand beaches, jumbled fishing shacks to architectural gems.

Handsome white clapboard homes with shutters give Kennebunk, a shipbuilding center in the first half of the 19th century, a quintessential New England look. If you enjoy shopping, plan to spend the better part of a day exploring the boutiques and galleries in Dock Square. People flock to Kennebunkport mostly in summer; some come in early December when the **Christmas Prelude** is celebrated on two weekends. Santa arrives by fishing boat, and the Christmas trees are lighted as carolers stroll the sidewalks.

Route 35 south leads to Kennebunk's Lower Village. Continue south on Beach Avenue for Kennebunk Beach. To reach Kennebunkport, head east on Route 9/Western Avenue and cross the drawbridge into Dock Square. Continue east on Route 9, or take scenic Ocean Avenue and Wildes District Road to quiet Cape Porpoise. To access Goose Rocks Beach continue east on Route 9, which is now called the Mills Road. Arundel is nestled between Kennebunk and Kennebunkport.

The cornerstone of the **Brick Store Museum,** a block-long preservation of early 19th-century commercial buildings, is **William Lord's Brick Store.** Built as a dry-goods store in 1825 in the Federal style, the building has an open-work balustrade across the roof line, granite lintels over the windows, and paired chimneys. Exhibits chronicle Kennebunk's relationship with the sea. The museum leads architectural walking tours of Kennebunk's historic Summer Street. ✉ *117 Main St., Kennebunk,* ☎ *207/985–4802,* WEB *www.brickstoremuseum.org.* ☑ *$5.* ☉ *Apr.–Dec., Tues.–Sat. 10–4:30.*

The drive from Kennebunk to Kennebunkport will take you by the **Wedding Cake House** (✉ 104 Summer St./Rte. 35, Kennebunk). The legend behind this confection in fancy wood fretwork is that its builder, a sea captain, was forced to set sail in the middle of his wedding; the house was his bride's consolation for the lack of a wedding cake. The home, built in 1826, is not open to the public.

Route 35 merges with Route 9 in Kennebunk and takes you right into Kennebunkport's **Dock Square,** the busy town center. Boutiques, T-shirt shops, art galleries, crafts stores, and restaurants encircle the square and spread out alongside streets and alleys. Although many businesses close in winter, the best bargains often are had in December. Walk onto the drawbridge to admire the tidal Kennebunk River.

The **Nott House,** also known as White Columns, is an imposing Greek Revival mansion with Doric columns that rise the height of the house. The 1853 house is furnished with the belongings of four generations of the Perkins-Nott family. It is a gathering place for village walking tours; call for the schedule. ⊠ *8 Maine St., Kennebunkport,* ☎ *207/ 967–2751,* WEB *www.kporthistory.org.* ⌲ *$5.* ◷ *Mid-June–mid-Oct., Tues.–Fri. 1–4, Sat. 10–1.*

Ocean Avenue follows the Kennebunk River from Dock Square to the sea and winds around the peninsula of **Cape Arundel.** Parson's Way, a small and tranquil stretch of rocky shoreline, is open to all. As you round Cape Arundel, look to the right for the entrance to former president George Bush's summer home at Walker's Point.

★ ☾ The **Seashore Trolley Museum** displays streetcars built from 1872 to 1972 and includes trolleys from major metropolitan areas and world capitals—Boston to Budapest, New York to Nagasaki, and San Francisco to Sydney—all beautifully restored. Best of all, you can take a trolley ride for nearly 4 mi over the tracks of the former Atlantic Shoreline trolley line, with a stop along the way at the museum restoration shop, where trolleys are transformed from junk into gems. Both guided and self-guided tours are available. ⊠ *195 Log Cabin Rd., Kennebunkport,* ☎ *207/967–2800,* WEB *www.trolleymuseum.org.* ⌲ *$7.50.* ◷ *Early May–mid-Oct., daily 10–4:30; reduced hrs in spring and fall.*

Dining and Lodging

$$$$ ✕ **White Barn Inn.** Formally attired waiters, meticulous service, and
★ exquisite food have earned this restaurant accolades as one of the best in New England. Regional New England fare is served in a rustic but elegant dining room. The three-course, prix-fixe menu, which changes weekly, might list steamed Maine lobster nestled on fresh fettuccine with carrots, ginger, and snow peas. ⊠ *37 Beach Ave., Kennebunkport,* ☎ *207/967–2321. Reservations essential. Jacket required. AE, MC, V.*

$$$–$$$$ ✕ **Seascapes.** The emphasis is on seafood at this pretty harbor-front restaurant where the view takes center stage. You can begin with Seascapes smoked chowder, then move on to grilled diver-harvested scallops or try the ginger-garlic rack of lamb. Accompany it all with a selection from the excellent wine list. ⊠ *77 Pier Rd., Cape Porpoise,* ☎ *207/967–8500. AE, D, DC, MC, V. Closed late Oct.–Apr.*

$$$–$$$$ ✕ **Windows on the Water.** Big windows frame Dock Square and the working harbor of Kennebunkport, and almost every window in the airy dining room shares the view. Lobster ravioli and classic Spanish paella are two noteworthy entrées. ⊠ *12 Chase Hill Rd., Kennebunkport,* ☎ *207/967–3313. Reservations essential. AE, D, DC, MC, V.*

$$ ✕ **Grissini.** This popular trattoria draws high praise for its northern Italian cuisine. Dine by the stone hearth on inclement days or on the patio when the weather's fine. You can mix and match appetizers, pizzas, salads, pastas, and entrées from the menu to suit your hunger and budget. ⊠ *27 Western Ave., Kennebunk,* ☎ *207/967–2211. AE, MC, V.*

$–$$ ✕ **Cape Pier Chowder House.** You can watch the surf crash over distant ledges near the Goat Island lighthouse and see lobster boats returning with their day's catch at this oceanfront lobster shack. Seating is on the deck or inside. The fare includes lobster, clams, and fried foods. ⊠ *15 Pier Rd., Cape Porpoise,* ☎ *207/967–4268 or 800/967–4268. MC, V. Closed early Nov.–mid-Apr.*

$$$–$$$$ ✕▥ **Cape Arundel Inn.** This shingle-style inn commands a magnificent ocean view that takes in the Bush estate at Walker's Point. The spacious rooms are furnished with country-style furniture and antiques, and most have sitting areas with ocean views. You can relax on the front porch or in front of the living-room fireplace. In the candlelit dining

room ($$$–$$$$), open to the public for dinner, every table has a view of the surf. The menu changes seasonally. ✉ *208 Ocean Ave., Kennebunkport 04046,* ☎ *207/967–2125,* 𝔽𝔸𝕏 *207/967–1199,* 𝕎𝔼𝔹 *www.capearundelinn.com. 13 rooms, 1 suite. Restaurant; no air-conditioning, no room phones, no TV in some rooms, no smoking. AE, D, MC, V. Closed Jan.–Feb. CP.*

$$$$ 🏠 **The Beach House.** Gooch's Beach is out the front door of this elegant late-19th-century inn. Rooms are individually decorated, with most colored in shades of beige and accented with country antiques that are comfortable rather than fussy. Feather beds and down comforters and pillows add a luxurious touch. Watch the sunrise from the wraparound porch, or sleep in, snuggled beneath a down comforter. You can hunker down by the big stone fireplace on rainy days. ✉ *211 Beach Ave., Kennebunk 04046,* ☎ *207/967–3850,* 𝔽𝔸𝕏 *207/967–4719,* 𝕎𝔼𝔹 *www.beachhseinn.com. 35 rooms. Cable TV, in-room VCRs, some in-room hot tubs, beach, boating, bicycles; no smoking. AE, MC, V. CP.*

$$$$ 🏠 **Captain Lord Mansion.** Of all the mansions in Kennebunkport's historic district that have been converted to inns, the 1812 Captain Lord Mansion is the most stately and sumptuously appointed. Distinctive architecture, including a suspended elliptical staircase, gas fireplaces in all rooms, and near–museum quality accoutrements, make for a formal but not stuffy setting. Six rooms have whirlpool tubs. The extravagant suite has two fireplaces, a double whirlpool, a hydro-massage body spa, a TV/VCR and stereo system, and a king-size canopy bed. ✉ *Pleasant and Green Sts. (Box 800, 04046),* ☎ *207/967–3141,* 𝔽𝔸𝕏 *207/967–3172,* 𝕎𝔼𝔹 *www.captainlord.com. 15 rooms, 1 suite. In-room data ports, Internet, meeting rooms; no room TVs, no kids under 12, no smoking. D, MC, V. BP.*

$$$$ 🏠 **The Seaside.** This handsome seaside property has been in the hands of the Severance family since 1667. The modern motel units, all with sliding-glass doors that open onto private decks or patios (half with ocean views), are appropriate for families; so are the cottages with one to four bedrooms. ✉ *80 Beach Ave., Kennebunk 04046,* ☎ *207/967–4461 or 866/300–6750,* 𝔽𝔸𝕏 *207/967–1135,* 𝕎𝔼𝔹 *www.kennebunkbeach.com. 22 rooms, 11 cottages. Refrigerators, cable TV, beach, playground, laundry service; no pets, no smoking. AE, MC, V. Cottages closed Nov.–May. CP.*

$$$$ 🏠 **White Barn Inn.** For a romantic overnight stay, you need look no
★   further than the exclusive White Barn Inn, known for its attentive, pampering service. No detail has been overlooked in the meticulously appointed rooms, from plush bedding and reading lamps to robes and slippers. Rooms are in the main inn and adjacent buildings. Some have fireplaces, hot tubs, and luxurious baths with steam showers. The ample breakfast includes quiche and freshly baked pastries. The inn is within walking distance of Dock Square and the beach. ✉ *37 Beach Ave. (Box 560C, Kennebunkport 04046),* ☎ *207/967–2321,* 𝔽𝔸𝕏 *207/ 967–1100,* 𝕎𝔼𝔹 *www.whitebarninn.com. 16 rooms, 9 suites. Restaurant, in-room data ports, cable TV, in-room VCRs, pool, bicycles, piano bar, dry cleaning, laundry, concierge, Internet, meeting room; no smoking, no kids under 12. AE, MC, V. BP.*

$$$$ 🏠 **The Yachtsman.** Relaxing in one of the handsome rooms—in muted shades of beige, brown, and black—in this riverfront hotel feels like you're aboard an elegant yacht. Down comforters cover the king-size beds, and nautical artwork adorns the walls. French doors open onto private patios overlooking the marina. A hearty Continental breakfast and afternoon tea are served on the riverfront patio. The shops and restaurants of Dock Square are just a short walk away. ✉ *Ocean Ave. (Box 2609, Kennebunkport 04046),* ☎ *207/967–2511,* 𝔽𝔸𝕏 *207/967–5056,* 𝕎𝔼𝔹 *www.yachtsmanlodge.com. 30 rooms. Refrigerators, boating, bicycles; no smoking. AE, MC, V. Closed early Dec.–Mar. CP*

$$$–$$$$ 🔲 **Bufflehead Cove.** On the Kennebunk River at the end of a winding dirt road, this gray-shingle B&B amid quiet country fields and apple trees is only five minutes from Dock Square. Rooms in the main house have white wicker and flowers hand-painted on the walls. The Hideaway Suite, with a two-sided gas fireplace, king-size bed, and large whirlpool tub, overlooks the river. The Garden Studio has a fireplace and offers the most privacy. ✉ *18 Bufflehead Cove Rd. (Box 499, Kennebunk 04046),* ☎ FAX *207/967–3879,* WEB *www.buffleheadcove.com. 2 rooms, 3 suites, 1 cottage. Internet, dock, boating; no room phones, no TVs in some rooms, no kids, no smoking. D, MC, V. Closed Dec.–May. BP.*

$$–$$$ 🔲 **Rhumb Line.** Although the rooms are standard motel fare, the facilities set this family-friendly motor lodge apart. It's on the trolley line, making getting around Kennebunk-area sites easy. Lobster bakes (extra charge) are held nightly weekends late May–June and daily July–August. ✉ *41 Turbats Creek Rd. (Box 3067, Kennebunkport 04046),* ☎ *207/967–5457 or 800/337–4862,* FAX *207/967–4418,* WEB *www.rhumblinemaine.com. 56 rooms, 3 suites. Snack bar, refrigerators, cable TV, 3 pools (1 indoor), health club, hot tub, sauna, meeting rooms; no-smoking rooms. AE, D, MC, V. CP*

$ 🔲 **St. Anthony's Franciscan Monastery Guest House.** Those in search of a quiet, contemplative retreat may want to choose one of the unadorned, motel-style rooms in a former dormitory on the grounds of a riverside monastery. The guest house is private yet within walking distance of Dock Square and the beach. The landscaped grounds, open to the public, have trails and shrines. The monks live in a Tudor mansion on the property, where Mass is said daily. This place is not recommended for those uncomfortable with Christian symbolism, although no religious participation is required. ✉ *28 Beach Ave., Kennebunkport 04043,* ☎ *207/967–2011. 60 rooms. Cable TV, saltwater pool; no room phones. No credit cards. Closed Sept. 10–June 10.*

Outdoor Activities and Sports

BEACHES

Kennebunk Beach has three parts: Gooch's Beach, Mother's Beach, and Kennebunk Beach. Beach Road, with its cottages and old Victorian boardinghouses, runs right behind them. Gooch's and Kennebunk attract teenagers; Mother's Beach, which has a small playground and tidal puddles for splashing, is popular with families. For parking permits (a fee is charged in summer), go to the **Kennebunk Town Office** (✉ 1 Summer St., ☎ 207/985–2102).

Three-mi-long **Goose Rocks,** a few minutes' drive north of town off Route 9, is a favorite of families with small children. You can pick up a parking permit ($5 a day, $15 a week) at the **Chamber of Commerce** (✉ 17 Western Ave., Lower Village, ☎ 207/967–0857).

BIKING

Cape-Able Bike Shop (✉ 83 Arundel Rd., Kennebunkport, ☎ 207/967–4382) rents bicycles.

BOATING AND FISHING

Cape Arundel Cruises (✉ Kennebunkport Marina, ☎ 207/967–5595) conducts scenic and theater cruises, deep-sea fishing, and whale-watching trips. **First Chance** (✉ 4-A Western Ave., Kennebunk, ☎ 207/967–5507 or 800/967–2628) leads whale-watching cruises and guarantees sightings in season.

Shopping

The **Gallery on Chase Hill** (✉ 10 Chase Hill Rd., Kennebunk, ☎ 207/967–0049) presents original artwork by Maine and New England artists. **Mainely Quilts** (✉ 1 Temple St., Kennebunkport, ☎ 207/967–

3571) sells a nice selection of quilts and Teddy bears. **Marlow's Artisans Gallery** (⊠ 39 Main St., Kennebunk, ☎ 207/985–2931) carries a large and eclectic collection of crafts. **Mast Cove Galleries** (⊠ Mast Cove La., Kennebunkport, ☎ 207/967–3453) sells graphics, paintings, and sculpture by 105 artists. **Tom's of Maine Natural Living Store** (⊠ 64 Main St., Kennebunk, ☎ 207/985–3874) sells all-natural personal-care products.

Old Orchard Beach

❻ *15 mi north of Kennebunkport, 18 mi south of Portland.*

Old Orchard Beach, a few miles north of Biddeford on Route 9, is a 7-mi strip of sand beach with an amusement park that resembles a small Coney Island. Despite the summertime crowds and fried-food odors, the atmosphere can be captivating. During the 1940s and '50s, in the heyday of the Big Band era, the pier had a dance hall where stars of the time performed. Fire claimed the end of the pier, but booths with games and candy concessions still line both sides. Plans are under way to extend the pier and offer dinner-gaming cruises. In summer the town sponsors fireworks (usually on Thursday night). The many places to stay run the gamut from cheap motels to cottage colonies to full-service seasonal hotels. You won't find free parking anywhere in town, but there are ample lots. Amtrak has a seasonal stop here.

A world away from the beach scene is **Ocean Park** (☎ 207/934–9068), on the southwestern edge of town. This vacation community was founded in 1881 as a summer assembly, following the example of Chautauqua, New York. Today the community still hosts a variety of cultural happenings, including movies, concerts, workshops, and religious services. Most are presented in the Temple, which is on the National Register of Historic Places.

🕲 **Palace Playland** (⊠ 1 Old Orchard St., ☎ 207/934–2001), open from Memorial Day to Labor Day, has rides, booths, and a roller coaster
🕲 that drops almost 50 ft. **Funtown/Splashtown** (⊠ U.S. 1, Saco, ☎ 207/284–5139 or 800/878–2900) has more than 30 rides and amusements, including miniature golf, water slides, a wave pool, and Excalibur, a wooden roller coaster.

Dining and Lodging

$$–$$$$ ✕ **Joseph's by the Sea.** Big windows frame the ocean beyond the dunes at this fine restaurant, which offers outdoor dining in season. Appetizers may include goat cheese terrine and lobster potato pancake; try the grilled Tuscan swordfish or seared sea scallops for your main course. ⊠ *55 W. Grand Ave.,* ☎ *207/934–5044. MC, V.*

$$–$$$ 🏨 **Old Orchard Beach Inn.** Dating from 1730, this is Old Orchard Beach's oldest inn. It was saved from demolition in 1997 and was completely renovated. The spacious guest rooms are furnished with antiques, area rugs cover the pine floors, quilts brighten the beds, and lace curtains frame the windows. Many have views over the town of the shimmering Atlantic. ⊠ *6 Portland Ave., 04064,* ☎ *207/934–5834 or 877/700–6624,* FAX *207/934–0782,* WEB *www.oldorchardbeachinn.com. 17 rooms, 1 suite. In-room data ports, cable TV; no air-conditioning, no smoking. AE, D, MC, V. CP.*

Nightlife and the Arts

In season, weekly concerts are held in Town Square every Monday and Tuesday night at 7. Fireworks light the sky Thursdays at 9:30 from late June through Labor Day. Concerts are held most Sunday evenings in Ocean Park.

Outdoor Activities and Sports

Ferry Beach State Park (⊠ Rte. 9, Saco, ☎ 207/283–0067) comprises 117 acres of beach, bike paths, and nature trails. The **Maine Audubon Society** (⊠ Rte. 9, Scarborough, ☎ 207/781–2330; 207/883–5100 from mid-June to Labor Day) operates guided canoe trips and rents canoes in Scarborough Marsh, the largest salt marsh in Maine. Programs at Maine Audubon's Falmouth headquarters (north of Portland) include nature walks and a discovery room for children.

York County Coast A to Z

To research prices, get advice from other travelers, and book travel arrangements, visit www.fodors.com.

AIR TRAVEL

Portland International Jetport is 35 mi northeast of Kennebunk.

BIKE TRAVEL

A bicycle can make it easy to get around the Kennebunks, but the lack of shoulders on some roads can be intimidating. Two good resources are the Bicycle Coalition of Maine and the Maine Department of Transportation.

➤ BIKE INFORMATION: **Bicycle Coalition of Maine** (⊠ Box 5275, Augusta 04332, ☎ 207/623–4511, WEB www.bikemaine.org). **Maine Dept. of Transportation Bike and Pedestrian Section** (WEB www.state.me.us/mdot/biketours.htm).

CAR TRAVEL

U.S. 1 from Kittery is the shopper's route north; other roads hug the coastline. Interstate 95 is usually faster for travelers headed to towns north of Ogunquit, but be forewarned that the Maine Turnpike/I–95 is in the midst of a widening project from Wells to Portland that will result in slowdowns and stops until completion in 2004. The renumbering of exits to coincide with mileage from the border, however, is expected to be completed by 2003.

Route 9 goes from Kennebunkport to Cape Porpoise and Goose Rocks. Parking is tight in Kennebunkport in peak season. Possibilities include the municipal lot next to the Congregational Church ($2 an hour from May to October) and 30 North Street (free year-round).

EMERGENCIES

➤ HOSPITALS AND EMERGENCY SERVICES: **Maine State Police** (⊠ Gray, ☎ 207/793–4500 or 800/482–0730). **Southern Maine Medical Center** (⊠ Rte. 111, Biddeford, ☎ 207/283–7000; 207/283–7100 emergency room). **York Hospital** (⊠ 15 Hospital Dr. York, ☎ 207/351–2157 or 800/283–7234).

LODGING

For home rentals in the Kennebunks, try Port Properties or Sand Dollar Real Estate Sales & Rentals. For rentals on the southern Maine coast, try Seaside Vacation Rentals. Garnsey Bros. rents condominiums and housekeeping cottages in Wells, Moody Beach, and Drakes Island. The Wight Agency specializes in waterfront rentals in Old Orchard.

➤ LODGING: **Garnsey Bros.** (⊠ 510 Webhannet Dr., Wells 04090, ☎ 207/646–8301, WEB www.garnsey.com). **Port Properties** (⊠ Box 799, Kennebunkport 04046, ☎ 207/967–4400 or 800/443–7678, WEB www.portproperties.com). **Sand Dollar Real Estate Sales & Rentals** (⊠ 5 Dyke Rd., Goose Rocks Beach, Kennebunkport, 04046, ☎ 207/967–3421). **Seaside Vacation Rentals** (⊠ Box 2000, York 03909, ☎ 207/

646–7671 or 207/363–1825, WEB www.seasiderentals.com). **The Wight Agency** (✉ 125 W. Grand Ave., Old Orchard Beach 04064, ☎ 207/934–4576).

MEDIA

The *Biddeford Tribune* and the *Portland Press Herald,* the state's largest paper, are published daily. The *Maine Sunday Telegram* is the state's only Sunday paper. The *York County Coast Star* is published weekly.

WMEA 90.1 is the local National Public Radio affiliate. WCSH, channel 6, is the NBC affiliate. WMTW, channel 8, is the ABC affiliate. WGME, channel 13, is the CBS affiliate. WCBB, channel 10, or WMEA, channel 26, is the Maine Public Broadcasting affiliate.

TOURS

Gone with the Wind schedules guided kayak and windsurfing trips. Van tours of southern Maine are operated by Seacoast Tours. Routes include Portland, Ogunquit, Kittery and York, and Kennebunkport; tours are 1¼–4 hours. Intown Trolley conducts 45-minute sightseeing tours of the Kennebunks.

➤ TOUR OPERATORS: **Gone With the Wind** (✉ Biddeford, ☎ 207/283–8446). **Intown Trolley** (✉ Kennebunkport, ☎ 207/967–3686). **Seacoast Tours** (✉ Perkins Cove, Ogunquit, ☎ 207/646–6326 or 800/328–8687).

TRAIN TRAVEL

Amtrak offers rail service from Boston to Portland, with stops in Wells and Saco and a seasonal stop in Old Orchard Beach.
➤ TRAIN INFORMATION: **Amtrak** (☎ 800/872–7245, WEB www. thedowneaster.com).

TRANSPORTATION AROUND YORK COUNTY COAST

Trolleys ($1–$3) serve several areas. A trolley circulates among the Yorks from late June to Labor Day. A trolley fleet serves the major tourist areas and beaches of Ogunquit in July and August. Trolleys circulate in Wells on weekends from Memorial Day to Columbus Day and daily from late June to Labor Day. Trolleys circulate through Kennebunkport to Kennebunk Beach from Memorial Day to Columbus Day; an all-day ticket is $8. Biddeford–Saco–Old Orchard Beach Transit operates a trolley that circulates through Old Orchard Beach and a bus service from Old Orchard to Portland with stops in Scarborough and at the Maine Mall.

VISITOR INFORMATION

➤ TOURIST INFORMATION: **Gateway to Maine Chamber of Commerce** (✉ 191 State Rd., Kittery 03904, ☎ 207/439–7574 or 800/639–9645, WEB www.gatewaytomaine.org). **Kennebunk-Kennebunkport Chamber of Commerce** (✉ Box 740, Kennebunk 04043, ☎ 207/967–0857, WEB www.visitthekennebunks.com). **Maine Tourism Association & Visitor Information Center** (✉ U.S. 1 and I–95, Kittery 03904, ☎ 207/439–1319). **Ogunquit Chamber of Commerce** (✉ U.S. 1 [Box 2289, Ogunquit 03907], ☎ 207/646–2939, WEB www.ogunquit.org). **Old Orchard Beach Chamber of Commerce** (✉ 1st St. [Box 600, Old Orchard Beach 04064], ☎ 207/934–2500 or 800/365–9386, WEB www.oldorchardbeachmaine.com). **Wells Chamber of Commerce** (✉ Box 356, Wells 04090, ☎ 207/646–2451, WEB www.wellschamber.org). The **Yorks Chamber of Commerce** (✉ 571 U.S. 1, York 03903, ☎ 207/363–4422 or 800/639–2442, WEB www.yorkme.org).

PORTLAND TO WALDOBORO

This south–mid-coast area provides an overview of Maine: a little bit of urban life, a little more coastline, and a nice dollop of history and architecture. Maine's largest city, Portland, holds some pleasant surprises, including the Old Port, among the finest urban renovation projects on the East Coast. Freeport, north of Portland, was made famous by its L. L. Bean store, whose success led to the opening of scores of other clothing stores and outlets. Brunswick is best known for Bowdoin College. Bath has been a shipbuilding center since 1607; the Maine Maritime Museum preserves its history. Wiscasset contains many antiques shops and galleries.

The Boothbays—the coastal areas of Boothbay Harbor, East Boothbay, Linekin Neck, Southport Island, and the inland town of Boothbay—attract hordes of vacationing families and flotillas of pleasure craft. The Pemaquid peninsula juts into the Atlantic south of Damariscotta and just east of the Boothbays. Near Pemaquid Beach you can view the objects unearthed at the Colonial Pemaquid Restoration, including the remains of an old customs house, a tavern, a jail, a forge, and homes.

Portland

105 mi northeast of Boston; 320 mi northeast of New York City; 215 mi southwest of St. Stephen, New Brunswick.

Portland's role as a cultural and economic center for the region has given the gentrifying city of 65,000 plenty of attractions that make it well worth a day or two of exploration. Its restored Old Port balances modern commercial enterprise and salty waterfront character in an area bustling with restaurants, shops, and galleries. Water tours of the harbor and excursions to islands of Casco Bay depart from the piers of Commercial Street. Downtown Portland, in a funk for years, is now a burgeoning arts district connected to the Old Port by a revitalized Congress Street, where L. L. Bean operates a factory store.

Portland's first home was built on the peninsula now known as Munjoy Hill in 1632. The British burned the city in 1775, when residents refused to surrender arms, but it was rebuilt and became a major trading center. Much of Portland was destroyed on July 4 in the Great Fire of 1866, when a boy threw a celebration firecracker into a pile of wood shavings; 1,500 buildings burned to the ground. Poet Henry Wadsworth Longfellow said at the time that his city reminded him of the ruins of Pompeii. The Great Fire started not far from where people now wander the streets of the Old Port.

Congress Street runs the length of the peninsular city from alongside the Western Promenade in the southwest to the Eastern Promenade on Munjoy Hill in the northeast, passing through the small downtown area. A few blocks southeast of downtown, the bustling Old Port sprawls along the waterfront. Below Munjoy Hill is India Street, where the Great Fire of 1866 started.

❼ The **Portland Observatory** on Munjoy Hill was built in 1807 by Capt. Lemuel Moody, a retired sea captain. It is the last remaining signal tower in the country and is held in place by 122 tons of ballast. After visiting the small museum at the base, you can climb to the Orb deck and take in views of Portland, the islands, and inland to the White Mountains. ✉ *138 Congress St.,* ☎ *207/774–5561.* ✉ *$3.* ☉ *Memorial Day– Columbus Day, daily 10–5.*

38

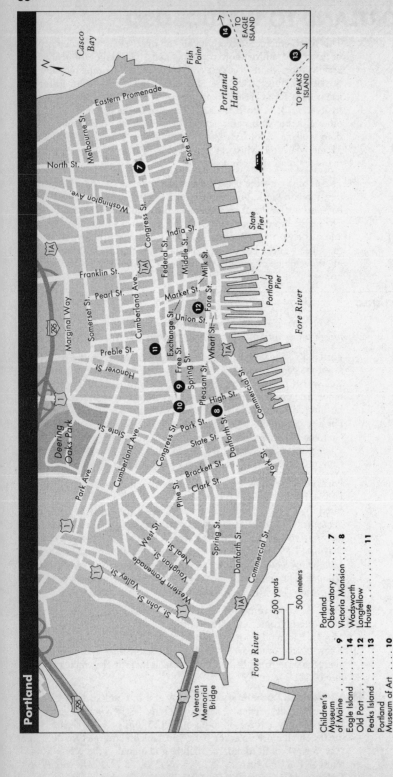

Portland

Casco Bay

Fish Point

Eastern Promenade

Portland Harbor

TO EAGLE ISLAND

TO PEAKS ISLAND

State Pier

Portland Pier

Fore River

North St.

Melbourne St.

Washington Ave.

Congress St.

India St.

Federal St.

Middle St.

Milk St.

Fore St.

Franklin St.

Pearl St.

Cumberland Ave.

Market St.

Union St.

Wharf St.

Commercial St.

Marginal Way

Somerset St.

Preble St.

Exchange St.

Free St.

Spring St.

Pleasant St.

Park St.

High St.

Hanover St.

Congress St.

Cumberland Ave.

State St.

Danforth St.

York St.

State St.

Brackett St.

Clark St.

Pine St.

Spring St.

Danforth St.

Commercial St.

Deering Oaks Park

Park Ave.

West St.

Neal St.

Vaughan St.

Western Promenade

St. John St.

Valley St.

Veterans Memorial Bridge

Fore River

Fore River

500 yards

500 meters

Children's Museum of Maine **9**
Eagle Island **14**
Old Port **12**
Peaks Island **13**
Portland Museum of Art **10**
Portland Observatory **7**
Victoria Mansion **8**
Wadsworth Longfellow House **11**

★ ❽ The Italianate-style Morse-Libby Mansion, known as **Victoria Mansion,** was built between 1858 and 1860 and is widely regarded as the most sumptuously ornamented dwelling of its period remaining in the country. Architect Henry Austin designed the house for hotelier Ruggles Morse and his wife, Olive; the interior design—everything from the plasterwork to the furniture (much of it original)—is the only surviving commission of New York designer Gustave Herter. Inside the elegant brownstone exterior of this National Historic Landmark are colorful frescoed walls and ceilings, ornate marble mantelpieces, gilded gas chandeliers, a magnificent 6- by 25-ft stained-glass ceiling window, and a freestanding mahogany staircase; guided tours cover all the details. ⊠ *109 Danforth St.,* ☎ *207/772–4841,* WEB *www.victoriamansion.org.* 🎟 *$8.* ☉ *May–Oct., Tues.–Sat. 10–4, Sun. 1–5.*

👆 ❾ Touching is okay at the relatively small but fun **Children's Museum of Maine,** where kids can pretend they are fishing for lobster or are shopkeepers or computer experts. The majority of the museum's exhibits, many of which have a Maine theme, are best for children 10 and younger. Camera Obscura, an exhibit about optics, provides fascinating panoramic views of the city. ⊠ *142 Free St.,* ☎ *207/828–1234,* WEB *www.kitetails.com.* 🎟 *Museum $5; Camera Obscura only, $3.* ☉ *Memorial Day–Labor Day, Mon.–Sat. 10–5, Sun. noon–5; early Sept.– Memorial Day, Tues.–Sat. 10–5, Sun. noon–5.*

★ ❿ The **Portland Museum of Art,** Maine's largest public art institution, has a number of strong collections, including fine seascapes and landscapes by Winslow Homer, John Marin, Andrew Wyeth, Edward Hopper, Marsden Hartley, and other painters. Homer's *Pulling the Dory* and *Weatherbeaten,* two quintessential Maine-coast images, are here; the museum owns 17 paintings by Homer. The Joan Whitney Payson Collection of Impressionist and Postimpressionist art includes works by Monet, Picasso, and Renoir. Harry N. Cobb, an associate of I. M. Pei, designed the strikingly modern Charles Shipman Payson building. The renovated McLellan-Sweat House is expected to open in fall 2002 with additional galleries housing the museum's 19th-century collection and decorative art as well as interactive educational stations. ⊠ *7 Congress Sq.,* ☎ *207/775–6148; 800/639–4067 recorded information;* WEB *www.portlandmuseum.org.* 🎟 *$6, free Fri. 5–9.* ☉ *Memorial Day– Columbus Day, Mon.–Wed. and weekends 10–5; Thurs.–Fri. 10–9; Columbus Day–Memorial Day, closed Mon.*

⓫ The **Wadsworth Longfellow House,** the boyhood home of the poet and the first brick house in Portland, is particularly interesting because most of the furnishings are original to the house. The late-Colonial-style structure, built in 1785, sits back from the street and has a small portico over its entrance and four chimneys surmounting the hip roof. The house is part of the Center for Maine History, which includes the adjacent Maine History Gallery and a research library; the gift shop has a good selection of books about Maine. ⊠ *489 Congress St.,* ☎ *207/774–1822,* WEB *www.mainehistory.org.* 🎟 *$6, Center $4.* ☉ *House and Maine History Gallery June–Oct., daily 10–5; library Tues.–Sat., 10–3; last tour at 4.*

★ ⓬ The **Old Port** bridges the gap between the city's 19th-century commercial activities and those of today. Like the Customs House, the brick buildings and warehouses of the Old Port were built following the Great Fire of 1866 and were intended to last for ages. When the city's economy slumped in the mid-20th century, however, the Old Port declined and seemed slated for demolition. Then artists and craftspeople began opening shops in the late 1960s, and restaurants, boutiques, and bookstores followed. Allow a couple of hours to wander at leisure on Market, Exchange, Middle, and Fore streets. You can park your car at the city garage on Fore Street (between Exchange and Union streets) or opposite the U.S. Customs House at the corner of Fore and Pearl streets.

OFF THE
BEATEN PATH

CAPE ELIZABETH – This upscale Portland suburb juts out into the Atlantic. Take Route 77 south and east from Portland and follow signs to Two Lights State Park, home to Two Lights, one of the cape's three lighthouses. You can wander through World War II bunkers and picnic on the rocky coast. Stay on Two Lights Road to the end, where you'll find another lighthouse, privately owned, and the Lobster Shack, a seafood-in-the-rough restaurant. Return to the center of Cape Elizabeth and turn right on Shore Road, which winds along the coast to Portland.

Historic **Portland Head Light,** familiar to many from photographs and Edward Hopper's painting, was commissioned by George Washington in 1791. Besides a harbor view, its park has walking paths and picnic facilities. The keeper's house is now the Museum at Portland Head Light. The lighthouse is about 2 mi from the town center in Fort Williams Park. *Museum:* ⊠ *1000 Shore Rd., Cape Elizabeth,* ☎ *207/799-2661.* ⊑ *$2.* ⊘ *June–Oct., daily 10–4; Apr.–May and Nov.–Dec., weekends 10–4.*

Dining and Lodging

$$–$$$$ ✕ **Street and Co.** Fish and seafood are the specialties here, and you won't
★   find any better or fresher. You enter through the kitchen, with all its wonderful aromas, and dine, amid dried herbs and shelves of staples, at one of a dozen copper-topped tables (so your waiter can place a skillet of steaming seafood directly in front of you). Some good choices are lobster diavolo for two, scallops in Pernod and cream, and sole Française. A vegetarian dish is the only alternative to seafood. ⊠ *33 Wharf St.,* ☎ *207/775–0887. AE, MC, V. No lunch.*

$$$ ✕ **Aubergine.** This casual bistro and wine bar has staked out a prime downtown location, near both L. L. Bean and the Portland Museum of Art. The French-inspired menu changes daily but might list appetizers such as creamy onion soup with fresh tarragon or duck liver pâté and entrées such as roasted Atlantic scallops with tomato Choron or duck breast with mixed peppercorns. Wines by the glass are chosen to complement the dishes. ⊠ *555 Congress St.,* ☎ *207/874–0680. MC, V. Closed Sun.–Mon. No lunch.*

$$$ ✕ **Hugos.** Chef-owner Rob Evans has turned Hugos, always a popular eatery, into one of the city's best restaurants. The subdued yet elegant dining room is a perfect background for Evans' masterful, creative cuisine. The menu, which may include pistachio-crusted lobster or pan-fried Deer Isle scallops, changes weekly. For a splurge, ask for the Chef's Menu, in which Evans will send out multiple courses of his choosing. ⊠ *88 Middle St.,* ☎ *207/774–8538. AE, MC, V. Closed Sun.–Mon. No lunch.*

$$–$$$ ✕ **Fore Street.** Two of Maine's best chefs, Sam Hayward and Dana Street,
★   opened this restaurant in a renovated, cavernous warehouse on the edge of the Old Port. Every table in the two-level main dining room has a view of the enormous brick oven and hearth and the open kitchen, where creative entrées such as roasted Maine lobster, apple-wood-grilled Atlantic swordfish loin, and wood oven–braised cassoulet are prepared. ⊠ *288 Fore St.,* ☎ *207/775–2717. AE, MC, V. No lunch.*

$$–$$$ ✕ **Walter's Cafe.** Brick walls and wood floors in this popular two-story restaurant capture the 19th-century spirit of Old Port. Begin with lobster bisque or deep-fried lemongrass shrimp sticks; then move on to a shrimp and andouille bake. ⊠ *15 Exchange St.,* ☎ *207/871–9258. AE, MC, V. Closed Sun.–Mon. No lunch.*

$–$$$ ✕ **Ri-Ra.** Whether you're in the mood for a pint of beer and corned beef and cabbage or a crock of mussels and whole roasted rainbow trout, Ri-Ra's delivers. Settle into a comfy couch in the downstairs pub or take a table in the upstairs dining room, where walls of windows overlook the busy ferry terminal. ⊠ *72 Commercial St.,* ☎ *207/761–4446. AE, MC, V.*

$–$$ ✕ **Portland Public Market.** Nibble your way through this handsome, airy market where 20 locally owned businesses sell fresh foods, organic produce, and imported specialty items, including fresh baked goods, soups, smoked seafood, rotisserie chicken, aged cheeses, and free-range meats. The market is open Monday–Saturday 9–7, Sunday 10–5; some vendors open at 7. ⊠ *25 Preble St.,* ☎ *207/228–2000.*

$$$$ ✕⚏ **Inn by the Sea.** This all-suites inn welcomes families and dogs. All the spacious suites include kitchens and overlook the Atlantic, and it's just a short walk down a private boardwalk to sandy Crescent Beach, a popular family spot. The Audubon dining room ($$$–$$$$), open to nonguests, serves fine seafood and regional dishes. Dogs are welcomed with a room-service pet menu, evening turndown treats, and oversize beach towels. Its shingle-style design, typical of turn-of-the-20th-century New England shorefront cottages and hotels, includes a varied roofline punctuated by turretlike features and gables, balconies, a covered porch supported by columns, an open deck, and big windows. ⊠ *40 Bowery Beach Rd., Cape Elizabeth 04107 (7 mi south of Portland),* ☎ *207/799–3134 or 800/888–4287,* ℻ *207/799–4779,* ⟨WEB⟩ *www.innbythesea.com. 25 suites, 18 cottages. Restaurant, in-room data ports, kitchens, microwaves, refrigerators, cable TV, in-room VCRs, pool, tennis court, croquet, lobby lounge, baby-sitting, dry cleaning, Internet, meeting rooms; no smoking. AE, D, MC, V.*

$$$$ ⚏ **Black Point Inn.** Toward the tip of the peninsula that juts into the ocean at Prouts Neck stands this stylish, tastefully updated old-fashioned resort with spectacular views up and down the Maine coast. The extensive grounds contain beaches, trails, and sports facilities, including use of tennis courts and golf course of the nearby country club. The Cliff Walk runs along the Atlantic headlands that Winslow Homer (his studio is nearby) often painted. The inn is 12 mi south of Portland and about 10 mi north of Old Orchard Beach by road. ⊠ *510 Black Point Rd., Scarborough 04074,* ☎ *207/883–2500 or 800/258–0003,* ℻ *207/883–9976,* ⟨WEB⟩ *www.blackpointinn.com. 73 rooms, 12 suites. Restaurant, bar, 2 pools (1 indoor), hot tub, golf privileges, croquet, volleyball, boating, bicycles. AE, D, MC, V. MAP.*

$$$$ ⚏ **Inn on Carleton.** After a day of exploring Portland's museums and shops, you'll find a quiet retreat at this elegant brick town house on the city's Western Promenade. Built in 1869, it is furnished throughout with period antiques as well as artwork by contemporary Maine artists. A restored trompe l'oeil painting by Charles Schumacher greets you at the entryway, and more of his work is displayed in the back dining room. ⊠ *46 Carleton St., 04102,* ☎ *207/775–1910 or 800/639–1779,* ℻ *207/761–0956,* ⟨WEB⟩ *www.innoncarleton.com. 6 rooms. Internet; no room phones, no room TVs, no kids under 16, no smoking. D, MC, V. BP.*

$$$$ ⚏ **Portland Regency Hotel.** The only major hotel in the center of the Old Port, the brick Regency building was Portland's armory in the late 19th century. Most rooms have four-poster beds, tall standing mirrors, floral curtains, and love seats. You can walk to shops, restaurants, and museums from the hotel. ⊠ *20 Milk St., 04101,* ☎ *207/774–4200 or 800/727–3436,* ℻ *207/775–2150,* ⟨WEB⟩ *www.theregency.com. 87 rooms, 8 suites. Restaurant, in-room data ports, minibars, cable TV, hot tub, massage, sauna, steam room, health club, dry cleaning, Internet, business services, meeting rooms; no-smoking rooms. AE, D, DC, MC, V.*

$$$–$$$$ ☒ **Pomegranate Inn.** The classic architecture of this handsome inn in the architecturally rich Western Promenade area gives no hint of the surprises within. Vivid hand-painted walls, floors, and woodwork combine with contemporary artwork, and the result is both stimulating and comforting. Rooms are individually decorated, and five have fireplaces. Room 8, in the carriage house, has a private garden terrace. ⊠ *49 Neal St., 04102,* ☎ *207/772–1006 or 800/356–0408,* ℻ *207/773–4426,* 𝗪𝗘𝗕 *www.pomegranateinn.com. 7 rooms, 1 suite. In-room data ports; no kids under 16, no smoking. AE, D, DC, MC, V BP.*

$$$ ☒ **Inn at St. John.** This gem of a small hotel was built by railroad tycoon John Deering in 1897. Victorian accents flavor the rooms, which have a mix of traditional and antique furnishings—no two are alike. It's an uphill walk to downtown attractions from here. ⊠ *939 Congress St., 04102,* ☎ *207/773–6481 or 800/636–9127,* ℻ *207/756–7629,* 𝗪𝗘𝗕 *www.innatstjohn.com. 37 rooms, 22 with bath. Some refrigerators, some microwaves, cable TV with movies, in-room data ports; no-smoking rooms. D, DC, MC, V. CP.*

Nightlife and the Arts

NIGHTLIFE

Asylum (⊠ 121 Center St., ☎ 207/772–8274) oozes with live entertainment and dancing on two levels and a sports bar; it books local and regional rock, pop, and hip-hop groups. **Brian Boru** (⊠ 57 Center St., ☎ 207/780–1506) is an Irish pub with occasional entertainment, ranging from Celtic to reggae, and an outside deck. For laughs, head to **Comedy Connection** (⊠ 6 Custom Wharf, ☎ 207/774–5554). **Gritty's** (⊠ 396 Fore St., ☎ 207/772–2739) brews fine ales and serves British pub fare and seafood dishes. The **Pavilion** (⊠ 199 Middle St., ☎ 207/773–6422) houses one of Portland's most popular dance clubs. **Stone Coast Brewery** (⊠ 14 York St., ☎ 207/773–2337) is a brewpub with billiards and occasional live entertainment. For live blues every night of the week, head to the **Big Easy Blues Club** (⊠ 55 Market St., ☎ 207/871–8817).

THE ARTS

Cumberland County Civic Center (⊠ 1 Civic Center Sq., ☎ 207/775–3458) hosts concerts, sporting events, and family shows. **Portland City Hall's Merrill Auditorium** (⊠ 20 Myrtle St., ☎ 207/874–8200) hosts events by the Portland Symphony Orchestra, Portland Concert Association, Portland Opera Repertory Theater, and the site of numerous theatrical and musical events. On most Tuesdays from mid-June to September, organ recitals ($5 donation) are given on the auditorium's huge 1912 Kotzschmar Memorial Organ. **Portland Performing Arts Center** (⊠ 25A Forest Ave., ☎ 207/761–0591) presents music, dance, and theater performances. **Portland Stage Company** (⊠ 25-A Forest Ave., ☎ 207/774–0465) mounts productions year-round at the Portland Performing Arts Center. Rock concerts and other events are frequently staged at the **State Theatre** (⊠ 609 Congress St., Arts District, ☎ 207/773–2337).

Outdoor Activities and Sports

BALLOON RIDES

Balloon Rides (⊠ 17 Freeman St., ☎ 207/772–4730) operates scenic flights over southern Maine.

BASEBALL

The Class AA **Portland Sea Dogs** (☎ 207/879–9500), a farm team of the Florida Marlins, play at Hadlock Field (⊠ 271 Park Ave.). Tickets cost $4–$6.

BEACHES

Crescent Beach State Park (⊠ Rte. 77, Cape Elizabeth, ☎ 207/767–3625), about 8 mi south of Portland, has a sand beach, picnic tables, a seasonal snack bar, and a bathhouse. Popular with families with young children, it charges a nominal fee for admittance.

BOAT TRIPS

For tours of the harbor, Casco Bay, and the scenic nearby islands, try **Bay View Cruises** (⊠ Fisherman's Wharf, ☎ 207/761–0496). **Casco Bay Lines,** (⊠ Maine State Pier, Waterfront, ☎ 207/774–7871) provides narrated cruises and transportation to Casco Bay Islands. **Eagle Island Tours** (⊠ Long Wharf, ☎ 207/774–6498) conducts daily cruises to Eagle Island and seal-watching cruises. **Old Port Mariner Fleet** (⊠ Long Wharf, ☎ 207/775–0727 or 800/437–3270) leads scenic cruises and whale-watching and fishing trips.

HOCKEY

The **Portland Pirates,** the farm team of the Washington Capitals, play home games at the Cumberland County Civic Center (⊠ 85 Free St., ☎ 207/828–4665). Tickets cost $10–$14.

Shopping

For a city this size, you'll find a plethora of locally owned stores and art and crafts galleries, particularly those in or near the Old Port; trendy Exchange Street is great for browsing.

ART AND ANTIQUES

Abacus (⊠ 44 Exchange St., old port, ☎ 207/772–4880), an appealing crafts gallery, has unusual gift items in glass, wood, and textiles, plus fine modern jewelry. **Greenhut Galleries** (⊠ 146 Middle St., ☎ 207/772–2693) shows contemporary art and sculpture by Maine artists. **F. O. Bailey Antiquarians** (⊠ 141 Middle St., ☎ 207/774–1479), Portland's largest retail showroom, carries antique and reproduction furniture and jewelry, paintings, rugs, and china. **Institute for Contemporary Art** (⊠ 522 Congress St., ☎ 207/879–5742), at the Maine College of Art, showcases contemporary artwork from around the world. The **Pine Tree Shop & Bayview Gallery** (⊠ 75 Market St., ☎ 207/773–3007 or 800/244–3007) has original art and prints by prominent Maine painters. Representing 100 American artists, the spacious **Stein Gallery** (⊠ 195 Middle St., ☎ 207/772–9072) showcases decorative and sculptural contemporary glass.

BOOKS

Carlson and Turner (⊠ 241 Congress St., ☎ 207/773–4200) is an antiquarian-book dealer with an estimated 70,000 titles.

CLOTHING

Family-owned **Casco Bay Wool Works** (⊠ 10 Moulton St., ☎ 207/879–9665) sells beautiful handcrafted wool capes, shawls, blankets, and scarves.

FURNITURE

Made locally, the handsome cherrywood pieces at **Green Design Furniture** (⊠ 267 Commercial St., ☎ 207/775–4234; 800/853–4234 orders) have a classic feel—somewhat Asian, somewhat Mission; a unique system of joinery enables easy assembly after shipping.

MALL

Maine Mall (⊠ 364 Maine Mall Rd., South Portland, ☎ 207/774–0303), 5 mi south of Portland, has 145 stores, including Sears, Filene's, JCPenney, and Macy's.

Casco Bay Islands

The islands of Casco Bay are also known as the Calendar Islands because an early explorer mistakenly thought there was one for each day of the year (in reality there are only 140). These islands range from ledges visible only at low tide to populous Peaks Island, which is a suburb of Portland. Some islands are uninhabited, others support year-round communities as well as stores and restaurants. Fort Gorges commands Hog Island Ledge, and Eagle Island is the site of Arctic explorer Admiral Perry's home. The brightly painted ferries of Casco Bay Lines are the islands' lifeline. There is frequent service to the most-populated ones, including Peaks, Long, Little Diamond, and Great Diamond. A ride on the bay is a great way to experience the Maine coast.

⑬ **Peaks Island,** nearest to Portland, is the most developed of the Calendar Islands, but you can still commune with the wind and the sea, explore an old fort, and ramble along the alternately rocky and sandy shore. The trip to the island by boat is particularly enjoyable at or near sunset. Order a lobster sandwich or cold beer on the outdoor deck of **Jones' Landing** restaurant, steps from the dock. A circle trip without stops takes about 90 minutes. On the far side of the island you can stop on the rugged shoreline and have lunch. A small museum with Civil War artifacts, open in summer, is maintained in the **Fifth Maine Regiment** building. When the Civil War broke out in 1861, Maine was asked to raise only a single regiment to fight, but the state raised 10 and sent the 5th Maine Regiment into the war's first battle, at Bull Run.

⑭ **Eagle Island,** owned by the state and open to the public for day trips in summer, was the home of Admiral Robert E. Peary, the American explorer of the North Pole. Peary built a stone-and-wood house on the 17-acre island as a summer retreat in 1904 but made it his permanent residence. Filled with Peary's stuffed Arctic birds, the quartz he brought home and set into the fieldstone fireplace, and other objects, the house remains as it was when Peary lived in it. A boat ride here offers a classic Maine experience as you pass by forested islands, and the island has a rocky beach and some trails to explore. The *Kristy K.* and *Fish Hawk* depart from Long Wharf in Portland (you can also visit the island from Freeport) and make four-hour narrated tours; tours of Portland Head Light and seal-watching cruises are also conducted. ✉ *Long Wharf,* ☎ *207/774–6498.* 🎫 *$8–$15, depending on tour.* 🕐 *Departures late May–Labor Day, daily beginning 10 AM.*

Freeport

⑮ *17 mi northeast of Portland, 10 mi southwest of Brunswick.*

Freeport, on U.S. 1, has charming backstreets lined with historic buildings and old clapboard houses, and the pretty little harbor on the Harraseeket River in South Freeport, 3 mi from downtown, is a relaxing place to linger. Most people, however, come here simply to shop—L. L. Bean is the store that put Freeport on the map, and plenty of outlets and some specialty stores have settled here. Still, if you choose, you can stay awhile and sample both parts of the Freeport experience: shopping along the town streets and easy access to nearby historic sites and outdoor activities. The **Freeport Historical Society** mounts exhibits pertaining to the town's history. You can also pick up a walking map of the village here. ✉ *45 Main St.,* ☎ *207/865–0477.*

♨ At the **Desert of Maine,** a 40-acre desert, a safari coach tours the sand dunes and you can walk nature trails, hunt for gemstones, and watch sand artists at work. Poor agricultural practices in the late 18th century combined with massive land clearing and overgrazing uncovered this desert, which was actually formed by a glacier during the last Ice Age. ☒ *I–95, Exit 19,* ☎ *207/865–6962,* WEB *www.desertofmaine.com.* ☒ *$7.50.* ☉ *Early May–mid-Oct., daily.*

Dining and Lodging

$–$$$ ✕ **Harraseeket Lunch & Lobster Co.** Seafood baskets and lobster dinners are what this bare-bones place beside the town landing in South Freeport is all about. You can eat outside on picnic tables in good weather. ☒ *On the pier, end of Main St.,* ☎ *207/865–4888. Reservations not accepted. No credit cards. Closed mid-Oct.–Apr.*

$$$–$$$$ ✕☲ **Harraseeket Inn.** Despite modern appointments such as elevators and whirlpool baths in some rooms, this 1850 Greek Revival home provides a pleasantly old-fashioned country-inn experience just a few minutes' walk from L. L. Bean. Guest rooms have print fabrics and reproductions of Federal quarter-canopy beds. The formal Maine Dining Room ($$$–$$$$) specializes in contemporary American regional cuisine such as lamb ragout ravioli and pan-roasted halibut with potato chowder. The casual Broad Arrow Tavern ($–$$$) serves heartier fare. ☒ *162 Main St., 04032,* ☎ *207/865–9377 or 800/342–6423,* FAX *207/ 865–1684,* WEB *www.stayfreeport.com. 82 rooms, 2 suites. 2 restaurants, in-room data ports, some microwaves, some refrigerators, cable TV, indoor pool, croquet, meeting room, some pets allowed (fee); no-smoking rooms. AE, D, DC, MC, V. BP.*

$$$ ☲ **Atlantic Seal Bed & Breakfast.** The nautical theme of this 1850 waterfront Cape Cod home complements the pleasant water views from all three of its rooms. Owner Capt. Thomas Ring provides homemade quilts, antiques, and down comforters for each room; he also leads boat trips. ☒ *25 Main St. (Box 146, South Freeport 04078),* ☎ *207/865– 6112; 877/285–7325 seasonal. 2 rooms, 1 suite. Cable TV, in-room VCRs, boating, mountain biking; no smoking. AE, MC, V. BP.*

$$ ☲ **Isaac Randall House.** On a 5-acre lot within walking distance of downtown shops, this circa-1829 inn is a quiet retreat. Victorian antiques and country pieces fill the rooms. A red caboose in the backyard has been turned into a room that's ideal for families. Two rooms are in the town's former police station, now moved to the property. ☒ *10 Independence Dr., 04032,* ☎ *207/865–9295 or 800/865–9295,* FAX *207/865– 9003,* WEB *www.isaacrandall.com. 11 rooms, 1 suite. Some in-room data ports, some microwaves, some refrigerators, cable TV in some rooms, ice-skating, playground, baby-sitting, some pets allowed; no smoking. AE, D, MC, V. BP.*

$ ☲ **Maine Idyll Motor Court.** The third and fourth generations of the Marsteller family operate this simple 1932 cottage colony. The tidy white cabins are shaded by towering pines and popular with families. Wood floors and paneling enrich the rustic interior of each cabin. ☒ *325 Rte. 1, 04032,* ☎ *207/865–4201. 20 1- to 3-bedroom cottages. Refrigerators, some microwaves, cable TV in some rooms, 2 playgrounds, some pets allowed; no air-conditioning in some rooms, no-smoking rooms. No credit cards. Closed mid-Nov.–mid-Apr. CP.*

Outdoor Activities and Sports

Atlantic Seal Cruises (☒ South Freeport, ☎ 207/865–6112 or 877/285–7325 seasonal) operates day trips to Eagle Island and Seguin Island lighthouse and evening seal and osprey watches.

L. L. Bean's year-round **Outdoor Discovery Schools** (☒ Freeport, ☎ 888/552–3261) include half- and one-day classes, as well as longer trips that teach canoeing, kayaking, fly-fishing, cross-country skiing, and other sports. Classes are for all skill levels; it's best to sign up several months in advance if possible.

STATE PARKS

Wolfe's Neck Woods State Park has 5 mi of good hiking trails along Casco Bay, the Harraseeket River, and a fringe salt marsh. Naturalists lead walks. The park has picnic tables and grills but no camping. ⊠ *Wolfe's Neck Rd. (follow Bow St. opposite L. L. Bean off U.S. 1),* ☎ *207/865–4465.* ⊡ *$2 Memorial Day–Labor Day, $1 off-season.*

Bradbury Mountain State Park has moderate trails to the top of Bradbury Mountain, which has views of the sea. A picnic area and shelter, a ball field, a playground, and 41 campsites are among the facilities. ⊠ *Rte. 9, Pownal (I–95, 5 mi from Freeport-Durham exit),* ☎ *207/ 688–4712.* ⊡ *$2 Memorial Day–Labor Day, $1 off-season.*

Shopping

The *Freeport Visitors Guide* (☎ 207/865–1212; 800/865–1994 for a copy) lists the more than 100 shops and factory outlet stores that can be found on Main Street, Bow Street, and elsewhere, including such big-name designers as Coach, Brooks Brothers, Polo Ralph Lauren, and Cole-Haan. Don't overlook the specialty stores, such as crafts galleries and shops selling unique items.

Cuddledown of Maine (⊠ 237 U.S. 1, ☎ 207/865–1713) has a selection of down comforters, pillows, and luxurious bedding. Head upstairs for discounted merchandise. Kids get their chance to shop at the educational toy store **Play and Learn** (⊠ 140 Main St., ☎ 207/865–6434). **Thos. Moser Cabinetmakers** (⊠ 149 Main St., ☎ 207/865–4519) sells high-quality handmade furniture with clean, classic lines.

Founded in 1912 as a mail-order merchandiser of products for hunters, guides, and anglers, **L. L. Bean** (⊠ 95 Main St. [U.S. 1], ☎ 800/341–4341) attracts 3½ million shoppers a year to its giant store (open 24 hours a day) in the heart of Freeport's shopping district. You can still find the original hunting boots, along with cotton, wool, and silk sweaters; camping and ski equipment; comforters; and hundreds of other items for the home, car, boat, or campsite. The **L. L. Bean Factory Store** (⊠ Depot St., ☎ 800/341–4341) has seconds and discontinued merchandise at discount prices. **L. L. Bean Kids** (⊠ 8 Nathan Nye St., ☎ 800/341–4341) specializes in children's merchandise and has a climbing wall and other activities that appeal to kids.

Brunswick

⑯ *10 mi north of Freeport.*

Lovely brick and clapboard homes and structures are the highlights of the town's Federal Street Historic District, which includes Federal Street and Park Row and the stately campus of Bowdoin College. Pleasant Street, in the center of town, is the business district. Harriet Beecher Stowe wrote *Uncle Tom's Cabin* while living in Brunswick.

The 110-acre campus of **Bowdoin College** (⊠ Maine, Bath, and College Sts., off east end of Pleasant St.) holds an enclave of distinguished architecture, gardens, and grassy quadrangles, along with several museums. Nathaniel Hawthorne, Civil War hero Joshua L. Chamberlain, and the poet Henry Wadsworth Longfellow attended Bowdoin.

Bowdoin's imposing neo-Gothic Hubbard Hall holds the **Peary–MacMillan Arctic Museum,** with photographs, navigational instruments, and artifacts from the first successful expedition to the North Pole, in 1909, by two of Bowdoin's most famous alumni, Admiral Robert E. Peary and Donald B. MacMillan. Changing exhibits document conditions in the Arctic. ☎ *207/725–3416.* ⊡ *Free.* ⊙ *Tues.–Sat. 10–5, Sun. 2–5.*

The **Bowdoin College Museum of Art,** in a splendid Renaissance Revival–style building designed by Charles F. McKim in 1894, displays small but good collections that encompass Assyrian and classical art and works by Dutch, Italian, French, and Flemish old masters; a superb gathering of Colonial and Federal paintings, notably Gilbert Stuart portraits of Madison and Jefferson; and a Winslow Homer Gallery of engravings, etchings, and memorabilia (open in summer only). The museum's collection also includes 19th- and 20th-century American painting and sculpture, with works by Mary Cassatt, Andrew Wyeth, and Robert Rauschenberg. ⊠ *Walker Art Bldg.,* ☎ *207/725–3275.* ⊡ *Free.* ⊙ *Tues.–Sat. 10–5, Sun. 2–5.*

The **General Joshua L. Chamberlain Museum** displays memorabilia and documents the life of Maine's most celebrated Civil War hero. The general, who played an instrumental role in the Union army's victory at Gettysburg, was elected governor in 1867. From 1871 to 1883 he served as president of Bowdoin College. ⊠ *226 Main St.,* ☎ *207/729–6606.* ⊡ *$4.* ⊙ *Late May–mid-Oct., Tues.–Sat. 10–4.*

OFF THE
BEATEN PATH

THE HARPSWELLS – A side trip from Bath or Brunswick on Route 123 or Route 24 takes you to the peninsulas and islands known collectively as the Harpswells. Small coves along Harpswell Neck shelter the boats of lobstermen, and summer cottages are tucked away amid the birch and spruce trees. Along Route 123, signs with blue herons mark the studios and galleries of the Harpswell Craft Guild. For lunch, follow the signs off Route 123 to **Dolphin Marina** restaurant (⊠ end of Basin Point Rd., off Ash Point Rd.) and try the delicious fish stew and a blueberry muffin.

Dining and Lodging

$$ ✕ **The Great Impasta.** You can match your favorite pasta and sauce to create your own dish at this storefront restaurant, a good choice for lunch, tea, or dinner. The seafood lasagna is tasty, too. ⊠ *42 Maine St.,* ☎ *207/729–5858. Reservations not accepted. D, DC, MC, V.*

$ ✕ **Fat Boy Drive-In.** Put your lights on for service at this old-fashioned drive-in restaurant renowned for its BLTs made with Canadian bacon, frappés (try the blueberry), and onion rings. ⊠ *Bath Rd.,* ☎ *207/729–9431. No credit cards. Closed mid-Oct.–mid-Mar.*

$$$ ⊞ **Captain Daniel Stone Inn.** This Federal-style inn overlooks the Androscoggin River and Route 1. No two rooms are furnished identically, but all contain executive-style comforts and many have whirlpool baths, queen-size beds, and pullout sofas. A guest parlor, a breakfast room, and excellent service in the Narcissa Stone Restaurant (no lunch on Saturday) make this an upscale escape from college-town funkiness. ⊠ *10 Water St., 04011,* ☎ *877/573–5151 or* ☎ FAX *207/725–9898,* WEB *www.someplacesdifferent.com. 30 rooms, 4 suites. Restaurant, cable TV; no-smoking rooms. AE, D, DC, MC, V. CP.*

$$–$$$ ⊞ **Captain's Watch Bed and Breakfast and Sail Charter.** Built in 1862 and originally known as the Union Hotel, the Captain's Watch is the oldest surviving hotel on the Maine coast. Although much smaller than originally built, this National Historic Register property retains its distinctive octagonal cupola and a homey, old-fashioned feel. Two guest rooms share access to the cupola. Others have less-inspired but still-pleasant water views. You can arrange to go on a day sail aboard the inn's 37-ft sloop, *Symbion.* ⊠ *926 Cundy's Harbor Rd., Harpswell 04079,* ☎ *207/725–0979. 4 rooms. Internet; no TV in some rooms, no air-conditioning, no room phones, no kids under 10, no smoking. MC, V for deposit only. BP.*

Nightlife and the Arts

Bowdoin Summer Music Festival (☎ 207/725–3322 information; 207/
725–3895 tickets) is a six-week concert series featuring performances
by students, faculty, and prestigious guest artists. **Maine State Music
Theater** (⊠ Pickard Theater, Bowdoin College, ☎ 207/725–8769)
stages musicals from mid-June to September. **Theater Project of Brunswick**
(⊠ 14 School St., ☎ 207/729–8584) performs semiprofessional, children's, and community theater.

Outdoor Activities and Sports

H2Outfitters (⊠ Rte. 24, Orr's Island, ☎ 207/833–5257 or 800/205–
2925) provides sea-kayaking instruction and rentals and conducts day
and overnight trips.

Shopping

ICON Contemporary Art (⊠ 19 Mason St., ☎ 207/725–8157) specializes
in modern art. **Wyler Craft Gallery** (⊠ 150 Maine St., ☎ 207/729–
1321) carries crafts, jewelry, and clothing.

Tontine Fine Candies (⊠ Tontine Mall, 149 Maine St., ☎ 207/729–4462)
sells chocolates and other goodies. A **farmers' market** takes place on
Tuesday and Friday from May to October, on the town mall between
Maine Street and Park Row.

Bath

🔞 *11 mi northeast of Brunswick, 38 mi northeast of Portland.*

Bath has been a shipbuilding center since 1607, so it's appropriate that
a museum here explores the state's rich maritime heritage. These days
the Bath Iron Works turns out guided-missile frigates for the U.S.
Navy and merchant container ships. On Front and Centre streets in
the heart of Bath's historic district, amid 19th-century Victorian homes,
antiques shops and intriguing specialty shops invite browsing. It's a
good idea to avoid Bath and U.S. 1 on weekdays 3:15–4:30 PM, when
BIW's major shift change occurs. The massive exodus can tie up traffic for miles.

★ At the **Maine Maritime Museum**, displays in the Maritime History
Building and in the buildings of the former Percy & Small shipyard
examine the world of shipbuilding and the relationship between Mainers and the sea. The history building contains themed exhibits with maritime paintings, ship models, journals, photographs, artifacts, and
videos. From May to November, one-hour tours (call for times) of the
shipyard explain how wooden ships were built; at other times you can
visit the buildings on your own. You can also watch boatbuilders
wield their tools on classic Maine boats in the boat shop and learn about
lobstering in a special exhibit building. In summer, boat tours sail the
scenic Kennebec River (extra charge); a number of boats, including the
142-ft Grand Banks fishing schooner *Sherman Zwicker,* are on display
when in port. The museum has a gift shop and bookstore, and you can
picnic on the grounds. ⊠ 243 *Washington St.,* WEB *www.bathmaine.com.*
🎫 *$9.50; tickets valid for 2 consecutive days.* ☉ *Daily 9:30–5.*

Sagadahoc Preservation (☎ 207/443–2174) conducts guided walking
tours of private homes and historic buildings from mid-June to early-
September. Call for schedule and fees.

Reid State Park (☎ 207/371–2303), on Georgetown Island, off Route
127, has 1½ mi of sand on three beaches. Facilities include bathhouses,
picnic tables, fireplaces, and a snack bar. Parking lots fill by 11 AM on
summer Sundays and holidays.

OFF THE
BEATEN PATH

POPHAM – Follow Route 209 south from Bath to Popham, the site of the short-lived 1607 Popham Colony, where the *Virginia*, the first English ship built in the Northeast, was launched. Benedict Arnold set off from Popham in 1775 on his ill-fated march against the British in Québec. Granite-walled **Ft. Popham** (⊠ Phippsburg, ☎ 207/389–1335) was built in 1861. **Popham State Park,** at the end of Route 209, has a sand beach, a marsh area, bathhouses, and picnic tables.

Dining and Lodging

$$$
★

✕ **Robinhood Free Meetinghouse.** Chef Michael Gagne, one of Maine's best, prepares his classic and creative multiethnic cuisine in this 1855 Greek Revival–style meetinghouse with cream-color walls, pine floorboards, cherry Shaker-style chairs, and white table linens. You might begin with the artichoke strudel; veal saltimbocca and confit of duck are two entrées. Finish up with Gagne's signature Obsession in Three Chocolates. ⊠ *210 Robinhood Rd., Georgetown,* ☎ *207/371–2188. AE, D, MC, V. Closed some weeknights mid-Oct.–mid-May. No lunch.*

$$–$$$

✕ **Kristina's Restaurant & Bakery.** This restaurant in a frame house with a front deck prepares some of the finest pies, pastries, and cakes on the coast. The satisfying new American cuisine served for dinner usually includes fresh seafood and grilled meats. All meals can be packed to go. ⊠ *160 Centre St.,* ☎ *207/442–8577. D, MC, V. Closed Jan. No dinner Sun. Call ahead in winter.*

$$$$

🏨 **Sebasco Harbor Resort.** This family resort sprawls over 575 oceanfront acres at the foot of the Phippsburg peninsula. The owners have retained the resort's old-fashioned feel while updating and renovating the facilities. Rooms in the Main Inn were renovated in 2002. The antique furnishings remain, but the rooms have been spruced up with new drapes, carpeting, and bedspreads. Lighthouse rooms have the best views and location and were renovated in 1998. A new all-suites building is slated to open in spring 2003. The suites will have kitchenettes, living areas, and decks with ocean views over the gardens. ⊠ *Rte. 217 (Box 75, Sebasco Estates 04565),* ☎ *207/389–1161 or 800/225–3819,* FAX *207/389–2004,* WEB *www.sebasco.com. 115 rooms, 23 cottages. 3 restaurants, cable TV, in-room data ports, saltwater pool, hair salon, sauna, 9-hole golf course, 3-hole golf course, 2 tennis courts, bowling, health club, Ping-Pong, dock, boating, bicycles, video game room, shop, recreation room, lounge, children's programs, playground, Internet, meeting rooms, airport shuttle; no air-conditioning, no-smoking rooms. AE, D, MC, V. Closed Nov.–mid-May. MAP available.*

$$$–$$$$

🏨 **The Inn at Bath.** Filled with antiques, this handsome 1810 Greek Revival inn in the town's historic district makes a convenient and comfortable base for exploring Bath on foot. Five rooms have wood-burning fireplaces, and two have two-person whirlpool tubs. ⊠ *969 Washington St., 04530,* ☎ *207/443–4294 or 800/423–0964,* FAX *207/443–4295,* WEB *www.innatbath.com. 8 rooms, 1 suite. Cable TV, in-room VCRs, in-room data ports, Internet, meeting rooms, some pets allowed; no smoking. AE, D, MC, V. BP.*

$$$–$$$$

🏨 **1774 Inn.** On the National Register of Historic Places, the 1774 Inn is a pre-Revolutionary mansion with handsome interior detailing and magnificent antiques. The inn, on a bend in the Kennebec River, has large corner guest rooms in the main house, two with fireplaces. In the attached ell is a room with a deck overlooking the river. A four-bedroom cottage on the river is available for longer stays. ⊠ *44 Parker Head Rd., Phippsburg Center 04562,* ☎ *207/389–1774,* FAX *207/389–9076. 7 rooms, 1 cottage. No kids under 12, no smoking. MC, V. BP.*

$$–$$$$

🏨 **Popham Beach Bed & Breakfast.** Housed in a former Coast Guard station, this casual bed-and-breakfast sits right on Popham Beach.

Rooms are comfortably but not fancifully furnished. The nicest are the Library, with two walls lined with books, and the Bunkroom; both have queen-size beds and overlook the beach. ⊠ *4 Riverview Ave., Phippsburg 04562,* ☎ *207/389–2409,* FAX *207/389–2379,* WEB *www. pophambeachbandb.com. 4 rooms, 3 with bath; 1 suite. No air-conditioning, no in-room phones, no room TVs, no kids under 15, no smoking. MC, V. BP.*

Nightlife and the Arts

Chocolate Church Arts Center (⊠ 804 Washington St., ☎ 207/442–8455) hosts folk, jazz, and classical concerts, theater productions, and performances for children. The gallery exhibits works in various media by Maine artists.

Shopping

The **Montsweag Flea Market** (⊠ U.S. 1 between Bath and Wiscasset, ☎ 207/443–2809) is a roadside attraction with trash and treasures. It's open on weekends from May to October and also on Wednesday (for antiques) and Friday during the summer. **West Island Gallery** (⊠ 37 Bay Point Rd., Georgetown, ☎ 207/443–9625) carries contemporary Maine art and quality crafts.

Wiscasset

⑱ *10 mi north of Bath, 46 mi northeast of Portland.*

Settled in 1663 on the banks of the Sheepscot River, Wiscasset fittingly bills itself as Maine's Prettiest Village. Stroll through town and you'll pass by elegant sea captains' homes (many now antiques shops or galleries), old cemeteries, churches, and public buildings. Unfortunately, Route 1 doubles as Main Street, and traffic often slows to a crawl and backs up for miles.

The **Nickels-Sortwell House,** maintained by the Society for the Preservation of New England Antiquities, is an outstanding example of Federal architecture. ⊠ *12 Main St.,* ☎ *207/882–6218.* ☒ *$5.* ۞ *June–mid-Oct., Wed.–Sun. 11–5; tours on the hr 11–4.*

The 1807 **Castle Tucker** is known for its extravagant architecture, Victorian appointments, and freestanding elliptical staircase. It's run by the Society for the Preservation of New England Antiquities. ⊠ *Lee and High Sts.,* ☎ *207/882–7364.* ☒ *$5.* ۞ *June–mid-Oct., Wed.–Sun. 11–5; tours on the hr 11–4.*

★   The 1852 **Musical Wonder House,** formerly a sea captain's home, houses a private collection of thousands of antique music boxes from around the world. ⊠ *18 High St.,* ☎ *207/882–7163 or 800/336–3725,* WEB *www. musicalwonderhouse.com.* ☒ *$2; ½-hr presentation on main floor $10; 1-hr full downstairs presentation $18; 3-hr tour of entire house $30 by reservation only, minimum 2 people.* ۞ *Memorial Day–mid-Oct., daily 10–5; last tour usually at 4; call ahead for 3-hr tours.*

Dining and Lodging

$–$$$ ✕ **Le Garage.** The best tables at this automotive garage turned casual restaurant are on the glassed-in porch overlooking the Sheepscot River and Wiscasset's harbor. Entrées include homemade chicken pie, sea scallops au gratin, charbroiled lamb and vegetable kebabs, and pastas and salads. ⊠ *Water St.,* ☎ *207/882–5409. MC, V. Closed Jan.*

$$ ▥ **Marston House.** Two carriage-house rooms provide a quiet retreat from the bustle of Main Street but are just a stone's throw from the action. Both have private entrances and fireplaces and are simply furnished with Shaker- and Colonial-style pieces. The rooms can be joined by opening a door between them. A hearty Continental breakfast is delivered to your room. ⊠ *101 Main St. (Box 517, 04578),* ☎ *207/882–6010 or 800/852–4137,* ꊤ *207/882–6965. 2 rooms. Fans. AE, MC, V. Closed Nov.–Apr. CP.*

Shopping

The Wiscasset area rivals Searsport as a destination for antiquing. Shops line Wiscasset's main and side streets and extend over the bridge into Edgecomb. The **Butterstamp Workshop** (⊠ 55 Middle St., ☎ 207/882–7825) carries handcrafted folk-art designs from antique molds. The **Maine Art Gallery** (⊠ Warren St., ☎ 207/882–7511) presents the works of local artists. **Marston House American Antiques** (⊠ 101 Main St., ☎ 207/882–6010) specializes in 18th- and 19th-century painted furniture and "smalls" (small objects), homespun textiles, and antique garden accessories and tools. The **Wiscasset Bay Gallery** (⊠ Main St., ☎ 207/882–7682) displays a fine collection of the works from 19th- and 20th-century American and European artists. **Treats** (⊠ Main St., ☎ 207/882–6192) dishes up sandwiches, cheeses, bread, and other goodies for a picnic at Waterfront Park.

Boothbay

⑲ *10 mi southeast of Wiscasset, 60 mi northeast of Portland, 50 mi southwest of Camden.*

When Portlanders want a break from city life, many come north to the Boothbay region, which comprises Boothbay proper, East Boothbay, and Boothbay Harbor. This part of the shoreline is a craggy stretch of inlets where pleasure craft anchor alongside trawlers and lobster boats. Commercial Street, Wharf Street, the By-Way, and Townsend Avenue are filled with shops, galleries, and ice cream parlors. You can browse for hours in the trinket and T-shirt shops, crafts galleries, clothing stores, and boutiques that line the streets around the harbor. Excursion boats leave from the piers off Commercial Street. From the harbor, you can catch a boat to Monhegan Island.

Ↄ At the **Boothbay Railway Village,** about 1 mi north of Boothbay, you can ride 1½ mi on a narrow-gauge steam train through a re-creation of a century-old New England village. Among the 24 buildings is a museum with more than 50 antique automobiles and trucks. ⊠ *Rte. 27,* ☎ *207/633–4727,* ꊚ *www.railwayvillage.org.* 🎟 *$7.* ☉ *Memorial Day weekend and early June–Columbus Day, daily 9:30–5; special Halloween and Christmas schedules.*

Ↄ The **Department of Marine Resources Aquarium** has a shark you can pet, touch tanks, and rare blue and multiclawed lobsters. ⊠ *194 McKown Point Rd., West Boothbay Harbor,* ☎ *207/633–9559.* 🎟 *$3.* ☉ *Memorial Day–late Sept., daily 10–5.*

Dining and Lodging

$$–$$$$ ✕ **Christopher's Boathouse.** You can't beat the harbor view or the stylish food at this restaurant in a renovated boathouse where you can watch the chefs at work. The lobster and mango bisque with spicy lobster wontons is noteworthy. Some main-course options are lobster succotash and Asian-spiced tuna steak with Caribbean salsa; finish off with the raspberry almond flan. ⊠ *25 Union St., Boothbay Harbor,* ☎ *207/633–6565. DC, MC, V. Closed Mar., and Mon.–Wed. Jan.–Feb.*

$–$$ ✕ **Lobstermen's Co-op.** Crustacean lovers and landlubbers alike will find something to satisfy their cravings at this dockside working lobster pound. Lobster, steamers, hamburgers, and sandwiches are on the menu. Eat indoors or outside to watch the lobstermen at work. ⊠ *Atlantic Ave., Boothbay Harbor,* ☎ *207/633–4900. D, MC, V. Closed mid-Oct.–mid-May.*

$$$ 🏨 **Admiral's Quarters Inn.** This renovated 1830 sea captain's house is ideally situated for exploring Boothbay Harbor by foot. All rooms have fireplaces, and some have private decks overlooking the harbor. On rainy days you can relax by the woodstove in the solarium. ✉ *71 Commercial St., Boothbay Harbor 04538*, ☎ *207/633–2474 or 800/ 644–1878*, FAX *207/633–5904*, WEB *www.admiralsquartersinn.com. 2 rooms, 5 suites. Cable TV, Internet; no kids under 12, no smoking. D, MC, V. Closed Dec.–mid-Feb. BP.*

$$$ 🏨 **Spruce Point Inn.** Escape the hubbub of Boothbay Harbor at this sprawling resort, which is a short shuttle ride from town, yet a world away. Guest rooms in the main inn are comfortable but not fancy, and most have ocean views, fireplaces, and whirlpool baths. The nearby fog horn blows in inclement weather. ✉ *Atlantic Ave. (Box 237, Boothbay Harbor 04538)*, ☎ *207/633–4152 or 800/553–0289*, FAX *207/ 633–7138*, WEB *www.sprucepointinn.com. 21 rooms, 41 suites, 7 cottages. Restaurant, cable TV, some microwaves, pool, saltwater pool, massage, spa, 2 tennis courts, gym, dock, lounge, meeting rooms, children's programs. AE, D, DC, MC, V. Closed mid-Oct.–late May.*

$$–$$$ 🏨 **Hodgdon Island Inn.** Every room in this 1810 inn, which is within walking distance of a lobster pound and a botanical garden, has a view of the water; two rooms open onto a shared deck. Inside, artwork from New England and the Caribbean graces the walls. ✉ *374 Barters Island Rd., 04571*, ☎ *207/633–7474*, FAX *207/733–0571*, WEB *www.hodgdonislandinn.com. 6 rooms. Fans; no air-conditioning, no room phones, no room TVs, pool, no smoking. D, MC, V. BP.*

$$–$$$ 🏨 **Welch House.** This 1873 sea captain's house sits high on a hill, a few minutes' walk from the center of town. Antiques, artwork, and bric-a-brac from the owner's worldwide travels adorn the rooms. From the shared third-floor deck, you can take in the 180-degree views of the harbor. ✉ *36 McKown St., 04538*, ☎ *207/633–3431 or 800/279– 7313*, WEB *www.welchhouse.com. 16 rooms. Cable TV; no air-conditioning in some rooms, no in-room phones, no kids under 8, no smoking indoors. MC, V. Closed Dec.–Mar. BP.*

Outdoor Activities and Sports

BOAT TRIPS

Balmy Day Cruises (✉ Pier 8, 62 Commercial St., Boothbay Harbor, ☎ 207/633–2284 or 800/298–2284) operates day boat trips to Monhegan Island and tours of the harbor. **Boothbay Whale Watch** (✉ Pier 6, ☎ 207/633–3500 or 800/942–5363) conducts whale-watching tours and evening sunset-nature cruises. **Cap'n Fish's Boat Trips** (✉ Pier 1, Boothbay Harbor, ☎ 207/633–3244 or 800/636–3244) runs regional sightseeing cruises, including puffin-watching excursions, lobster-hauling and whale-watching rides, and trips to Damariscove Harbor, Pemaquid Point, and up the Kennebec River to Bath.

KAYAKING

Tidal Transit Ocean Kayak Co. (☎ 207/633–7140) offers guided tours and rentals.

Shopping

BOOTHBAY HARBOR

Gleason Fine Art (✉ 7 Oak St., ☎ 207/633–6849) showcases fine art—regional and national, early 19th century and contemporary. **House of Logan** (✉ 20 Townsend Ave., ☎ 207/633–2293) stocks upscale casual and fancy attire for men and women. **McKown Square Quilts** (✉ 14-B Boothbay House Hill Rd., ☎ 207/633–2007) displays quilts and fiber art in seven rooms. Beautiful housewares and attractive children's clothes can be found at the **Village Store & Children's Shop** (✉ 34 Townsend Ave., ☎ 207/633–2293).

EDGECOMB

Highly reputable **Edgecomb Potters** (⊠ 727 Boothbay Rd., ☎ 207/882–6802) sells stylish glazed porcelain pottery and other crafts at rather high prices; some discontinued items or seconds are discounted. There's a store in Freeport if you miss this one. **Sheepscot River Pottery** (⊠ U.S. 1, ☎ 207/882–9410) displays hand-painted pottery and a large collection of American-made crafts, including jewelry, kitchenware, furniture, and home accessories.

Pemaquid Peninsula

⑳ *8 mi southeast of Wiscasset.*

A detour off U.S. 1 via Routes 130 and 32 leads to the Pemaquid Peninsula and a satisfying microcosm of coastal Maine. Art galleries, country stores, antiques and crafts shops, and lobster shacks dot the country roads that meander to the tip of the point, where you'll find a much-photographed lighthouse perched on an unforgiving rock ledge, as well as a pleasant beach. Exploring here reaps many rewards, including views of salt ponds, the ocean, and boat-clogged harbors. The twin towns of Damariscotta and Newcastle anchor the region, but small fishing villages such as Pemaquid, New Harbor, and Round Pond give the peninsula its purely Maine flavor.

At what is now the **Colonial Pemaquid Restoration,** on a small peninsula jutting into the Pemaquid River, English mariners established a fishing and trading settlement in the early 17th century. The excavations at Ft. William Henry, begun in the mid-1960s, have turned up thousands of artifacts from the Colonial settlement, including the remains of an old customs house, a tavern, a jail, a forge, and homes. Some items are from even earlier Native American settlements. The state operates a museum displaying many of the artifacts. ⊠ *Off Rte. 130, New Harbor,* ☎ *207/677–2423.* ⊡ *$2.* ⊙ *Memorial Day–Labor Day, daily 9:30–5.*

★ Route 130 terminates at the **Pemaquid Point Light,** which looks as though it sprouted from the ragged, tilted chunk of granite that it commands. The former lighthouse keeper's cottage is now the Fishermen's Museum, with photographs, models, and artifacts that explore commercial fishing in Maine. Here, too, is the Pemaquid Art Gallery, which mounts exhibitions from July to Labor Day. ⊠ *Museum: Rte. 130,* ☎ *207/677–2494.* ⊡ *$1.* ⊙ *Memorial Day–Columbus Day, Mon.–Sat. 10–5, Sun. 11–5.*

Dining and Lodging

$$ ✕ **Round Pond Lobstermen's Co-op.** Lobster doesn't get much rougher,
★ any fresher, or any cheaper than what's served at this no-frills dockside takeout. The best deal is the dinner special: a 1-pound lobster, steamers, and corn-on-the-cob, with a bag of chips. Regulars often bring beer, wine, bread, and salads. Settle in at a picnic table and breathe in the fresh salt air while you drink in the view over dreamy Round Pond Harbor. ⊠ *Round Pond Harbor, off Rte. 32, Round Pond,* ☎ *207/ 529–5725. MC, V.*

$$$–$$$$ ✕🏨 **The Bradley Inn.** Within walking distance of Pemaquid Point Lighthouse, this former rooming house for summer rusticators alternated between abandonment and operation as a B&B until complete renovation in the 1990s. It now houses one of the best dining rooms in the state. The menu ($$$–$$$$; closed Mon.–Wed. Nov.–Mar.) changes nightly and emphasizes fresh and local foods. Guest rooms are comfortable and uncluttered; some have fireplaces and rooms on the third floor have ocean views. ⊠ *3063 Bristol Rd., New Harbor 04554,* ☎ *207/677–2105 or*

800/942–5560, FAX *207/677–3367*, WEB *www.bradleyinn.com. 12 rooms, 4 suites. Restaurant, fans, bicycles, boccie, croquet, lounge, baby-sitting, Internet, meeting rooms; no air-conditioning, no TVs in some rooms, no smoking. AE, MC, V. BP.*

$$$–$$$$ ✕🖿 **Newcastle Inn.** A riverside location and an excellent dining room highlight this classic country inn. All the rooms are filled with country pieces and antiques; some rooms have fireplaces and whirlpool baths. Breakfast is served on the back deck in fine weather. The four-course dinners ($$$$) at the inn, open to the public by reservation, emphasize local seafood. ⊠ *60 River Rd., Newcastle 04553,* ☎ *207/563–5685 or 800/832–8669,* FAX *207/563–6877,* WEB *www.newcastleinn.com. 11 rooms, 4 suites. Restaurant, pub; no air-conditioning in some rooms, no room phones, no room TVs, no kids under 12, no smoking. AE, MC, V. BP.*

$$ 🖿 **Mill Pond Inn.** A quiet residential street holds this circa-1780 inn, which is on a mill pond across the street from Damariscotta Lake. Loons, otters, and bald eagles reside on the lake, and you can arrange a trip with the owner, a Registered Maine Guide, on the inn's 17-ft antique lapstrake boat. The rooms are warm and inviting, though you may find it hard to tear yourself away from the hammocks-for-two overlooking the pond. ⊠ *50 Main St., off Rte. 215 N, Nobleboro 04555,* ☎ *207/563–8014,* WEB *www.millpondinn.com. 6 rooms, 1 suite. Horseshoes, boating, bicycles, pub; no air-conditioning, no room phones, no room TVs, no kids under 12, no smoking. No credit cards. BP.*

$–$$ 🖿 **Hotel Pemaquid.** This 1888 inn is less than 500 ft from the lighthouse at Pemaquid Point. The main building is Victorian in style; cottages and bungalow units have a more contemporary feel; and the carriage-house suite is ideal for honeymooners or others seeking a romantic retreat. ⊠ *3098 Bristol Rd. (Rte. 130), New Harbor 04554,* ☎ *207/677–2312,* WEB *www.hotelpemaquid.com. 21 rooms, 17 with bath; 4 suites; 3 cottages; 1 apartment. No air-conditioning, no room phones, no room TVs, no-smoking rooms. No credit cards. Closed mid-Oct.–mid-May.*

Nightlife and the Arts

Round Top Center for the Arts (⊠ Business Rte. 1, Damariscotta, ☎ 207/563–1507) has a gallery with rotating exhibits and a performance hall where classical, folk, operatic, and jazz concerts are held.

Outdoor Activities and Sports

Pemaquid Beach Park (⊠ off Rte. 130, New Harbor, ☎ 207/677–2754) has a sand beach, a snack bar, changing facilities, and picnic tables overlooking John's Bay.

Shopping

Of the villages on and near the Pemaquid Peninsula, downtown Damariscotta has boutiques, a book shop, clothing stores, and galleries. New Harbor and Round Pond have crafts and antiques shops as well as artisans' studios. Antiques shops dot the main thoroughfares in the region.

If gardening is your passion, **Bramble's** (⊠ Main St., Damariscotta, ☎ 207/563–2800) is the place for tools, sculpture, pots, artwork, and topiary. **Granite Hill Store** (⊠ Backshore Rd., Round Pond, ☎ 207/ 529–5864) has penny candy, kitchen goodies, baskets, and cards on the first floor, antiques and books on the second, and an ice cream window on the side. The work of more than 50 Maine artisans is displayed in the 15 rooms of the **Pemaquid Craft Co-op** (⊠ 2545 Bristol Rd., New Harbor, ☎ 207/677–2077). You never know what you'll find at **Reny's** (⊠ Main St., Damariscotta, ☎ 207/563–5757)—perhaps merchandise from L. L. Bean or a designer coat. This bargain chain has outlets in many Maine towns, but this is its hometown, and there are two outlets: one for clothes, the other for everything else. The **Stable Gallery** (✉ Water St., Damariscotta, ☎ 207/563–1991) is a barn with fine Maine crafts, paintings, and prints by more than 100 artisans.

Waldoboro

㉑ *10 mi northeast of Damariscotta.*

Veer off U.S. 1 onto Main Street or down Route 220 or 32, and you'll discover a seafaring town with a proud shipbuilding past. The town's Main Street is lined with houses and businesses representing numerous architectural styles, including Cape Cod, Queen Anne, Stick, Greek Revival, and Italianate.

The **Waldoborough Historical Society Museum** comprises the one-room Boggs Schoolhouse, built in 1857; the Town Pound, built in 1819; and a barn and museum filled with artifacts and antiques, including hooked rugs, old toys, tools, clothing, and housewares. ✉ *Rte. 220,* ☎ *no phone.* ✍ *Free.* ☉ *July–Labor Day, daily 1–4:30.*

One of the three oldest churches in Maine, the **Old German Church** was built in 1772 on the eastern side of the Medomak River, then moved across the ice to its present site in 1794. Inside you'll find box pews and a 9-ft-tall chalice pulpit. ✉ *Rte. 32,* ☎ *207/832–5639.* ☉ *July–Aug., daily 1–3.*

The **Fawcett's Toy Museum** delights adults and children with collectible toys, from Betty Boop and Charlie Brown to Mickey Mouse and Popeye, and original comic art. ✉ *3506 Rte. 1,* ☎ *207/832–7398.* ✍ *$3.* ☉ *Memorial Day–Columbus Day, Thurs.–Mon. 10–4; Columbus Day–Dec. 24, weekends noon–3:30.*

Dining and Lodging

$–$$$ ✕ **Pine Cone Cafe.** Paintings by local artist Eric Hopkins hang on the
★ walls of this cozy restaurant, which serves up hearty soups, salads, and a mix of home-style and creative entrées. Try the corn-fried soft-shell crab tower or turkey potpie; the crème brûlée is a good choice for dessert. In favorable weather ask for a table on the back deck overlooking the river. ✉ *13 Friendship St.,* ☎ *207/832–6337. MC, V.*

$–$$ ✕ **Moody's Diner.** Settle into one of the well-worn wooden booths or snag a counter stool at this old-style diner for home-cooking fare. Breakfast is served all day; don't miss the legendary walnut pie. ✉ *Rte. 1,* ☎ *207/832–5362. D, MC, V.*

$ 🏠 **Roaring Lion.** Tin walls and ceilings and other Victorian-era architectural details highlight this friendly B&B. Special diets are accommodated. During summer, a used-book sale is held in the barn on Saturday mornings. ✉ *995 Main St., 04572,* ☎ *207/832–4038,* ℻ *207/832–7892,* 🕸 *www.roaringlion.com. 4 rooms, 1 with bath. No air-conditioning, no room phones, no room TVs, no smoking. No credit cards. BP.*

Nightlife and the Arts

The **Waldo Theatre** (✉ 916 Main St., ☎ 207/832–6060), a Greek Revival–style cinema with an Art Deco interior, stages concerts, plays, lectures, and other performances.

Shopping

Glockenspiel Imports (✉ U.S. 1, ☎ 207/832–8000) sells traditional German lace. For a taste of authentic German sauerkraut, visit **Morse's Sauerkraut** (✉ 3856 Washington Rd./Rte. 220 N, ☎ 207/832–5569). The **Waldoboro 5 & 10/Fernald's General Store** (✉ 17 Friendship St., ☎ 207/832–4624) is the oldest continually operated five-and-ten in the country. It has an old-fashioned soda fountain, which serves sandwiches, soups, and ice cream; there's even a penny candy counter.

Portland to Waldoboro A to Z

To research prices, get advice from other travelers, and book travel arrangements, visit www.fodors.com.

BIKE TRAVEL

The craggy fingers of land that dominate this part of the coast are fun for experienced cyclists to explore. The lack of shoulders on most roads combined with heavy tourist traffic can be intimidating. Two good resources are the Bicycle Coalition of Maine and the Maine Department of Transportation, which include information on trails and bike shops around the state.

➤ BIKE INFORMATION: **Bicycle Coalition of Maine** (⊠ Box 5275, Augusta, ☎ 207/623–4511, WEB www.bikemaine.org). **Maine Dept. of Transportation Bike and Pedestrian Section** (WEB www.state.me.us/mdot/biketours.htm).

BOAT AND FERRY TRAVEL

Casco Bay Lines provides ferry service from Portland to the islands of Casco Bay.

➤ BOAT AND FERRY INFORMATION: **Casco Bay Lines** (☎ 207/774–7871, WEB www.cascobaylines.com).

BUS TRAVEL TO AND FROM PORTLAND

Greater Portland's Metro runs seven bus routes in Portland, South Portland, and Westbrook. The fare is $1; exact change ($1 bills accepted) is required. Buses run from 5:30 AM to 11:45 PM.

➤ BUS INFORMATION: **Greater Portland's Metro** (☎ 207/774–0351).

CAR TRAVEL

Congress Street leads from I–295 into the heart of Portland; the Gateway Garage on High Street, off Congress, is a convenient place to leave your car downtown. North of Portland, U.S. 1 brings you to Freeport's Main Street, which continues on to Brunswick and Bath. East of Wiscasset you can take Route 27 south to the Boothbays, where Route 96 is a good choice for further exploration. To visit the Pemaquid region, take Route 129 off Business Route 1 in Damariscotta; then pick up Route 130 and follow it down to Pemaquid Point. Return to Waldoboro and U.S. 1 on Route 32 from New Harbor.

In Portland, metered on-street parking is available at 25¢ per half hour, with a two-hour maximum. Parking lots and garages can be found near the Portland Public Market, downtown, in the Old Port, and on the waterfront; most charge $1 per hour or $8–$12 per day. If you're shopping or dining, remember to ask local vendors if they participate in the Park & Shop program, which provides an hour of free shopping for each participating vendor visited.

EMERGENCIES

➤ HOSPITALS: **Maine Medical Center** (⊠ 22 Bramhall St., Portland, ☎ 207/871–0111). **Mid Coast Hospital** (⊠ 123 Medical Center Dr., Brunswick, ☎ 207/729–0181). **Miles Memorial Hospital** (⊠ Bristol Rd., Damariscotta, ☎ 207/563–1234). **St. Andrews Hospital** (⊠ 3 St. Andrews La., Boothbay Harbor, ☎ 207/633–2121).

LODGING

Your Island Connection manages vacation home rentals in Great, Orr's, and Bailey islands, near Brunswick. A Summer Place and Cottage Connection of Maine rent cottages and condos in the Boothbay region. For rentals in the Pemaquid area, contact Newcastle Square Rentals.

➤ LODGING: **A Summer Place** (✉ Box 165, West Boothbay Harbor 04575, ☎ 207/633–4889, WEB www.asummahplace.com). **Cottage Connection of Maine** (✉ Box 662, Boothbay Harbor 04538, ☎ 207/633–6545 or 800/823–9501, WEB www.cottageconnection.com). **Newcastle Square Rentals** (✉ 18 Main St., Damariscotta 04543, ☎ 207/563–6500, WEB www.cheneycompanies.com). **Your Island Connection** (✉ Box 300, Bailey Island 04003, ☎ 207/833–7705, WEB www.mainerentals.com).

MAIL AND SHIPPING

➤ MAIL AND SHIPPING: **U.S. Post Office** (✉ 125 Forest Ave., Portland, ☎ 207/871–8461), open weekdays 7:30–7, Saturday 7:30–5. **U.S. Post Office Station A** (✉ 622 Congress St., Portland, ☎ 207/871–8449), open weekdays 8:30–5, Saturday 9–noon. **U.S. Post Office and postal store** (✉ 400 Congress St., Portland, ☎ 207/871–8464), open weekdays 8–7, Saturday 9–1.

MEDIA

The *Portland Press Herald* is published Monday–Saturday; the *Maine Sunday Telegram* is published on Sunday. The *Times Record,* which covers the Bath-Brunswick region, publishes Monday–Friday, with an entertainment section on Thursday. A number of weekly newspapers provide local coverage and entertainment listings. These include the *Coastal Journal* (Brunswick through Waldoboro), *Wiscasset Newspaper, Boothbay Register, Lincoln County News* (Wiscasset through Waldoboro), and *Lincoln County Weekly* (Wiscasset through Waldoboro). Two magazines, *Portland Monthly* and the bimonthly *Port City Life,* cover Portland.

WMEA 90.1 is the local National Public Radio affiliate. WCSH, channel 6, is the NBC affiliate; WMTW, channel 8, is the ABC affiliate; and WGME, channel 13, is the CBS affiliate. Channel 10 is the Maine Public Broadcasting affiliate.

OUTDOOR ACTIVITIES AND SPORTS
BOATING

For boat rentals, *see* town listings. The Maine Professional Guides Association represents kayaking guides.

➤ CONTACT: **Maine Professional Guides Association** (✉ Box 847, Augusta 04332, ☎ 207/549–5631, WEB www.maineguides.org).

TOURS
BUS TOURS

In Portland, the informative trolley tours of Mainely Tours cover the city's historical and architectural highlights from Memorial Day through October. Other tours combine a city tour with a bay cruise or a trip to four lighthouses.

➤ TOUR OPERATOR: **Mainely Tours** (✉ 5½ Moulton St., ☎ 207/774–0808).

WALKING TOURS

Greater Portland Landmarks conducts 1½-hour walking tours of the city from July through September; tours begin at the Convention and Visitors Bureau and cost $8. Sagadahoc Preservation leads walking tours of historic homes and buildings in Bath on Tuesday and Thursday afternoons from mid-June to September. Tours begin at the Winter Street Church and cost $10; reservations are recommended.

➤ TOUR OPERATORS: **Convention and Visitors Bureau** (☎ 207/772–5800). **Greater Portland Landmarks** (✉ 165 State St., ☎ 207/774–5561).

Sagadahoc Preservation (✉ 165 State St., ☎ 207/443–2174). **Winter Street Church Center** (✉ 880 Washington St.).

VISITOR INFORMATION

➤ CONTACTS: **Boothbay Harbor Region Chamber of Commerce** (✉ Box 356, Boothbay Harbor 04538, ☎ 207/633–2353, WEB www. boothbayharbor.com). **Chamber of Commerce of the Bath/Brunswick Region** (✉ 45 Front St., Bath 04530, ☎ 207/443–9751; ✉ 59 Pleasant St., Brunswick 04011, ☎ 207/725–8797, WEB www.midcoastmaine.com). **Convention and Visitors Bureau of Greater Portland** (✉ 305 Commercial St., Portland 04101, ☎ 207/772–5800 or 877/833–1374, WEB www.visitportland.com). **Damariscotta Region Chamber of Commerce** (✉ Box 13, Damariscotta 04543, ☎ 207/563–8340, WEB www. damariscottaregion.com). **Freeport Merchants Association** (✉ 23 Depot St., Freeport 04032, ☎ 207/865–1212 or 877/865–1212, WEB www.freeportusa.com). **Greater Portland Chamber of Commerce** (✉ 145 Middle St., Portland 04101, ☎ 207/772–2811, WEB www. portlandregion.com). **Maine Tourism Association** (✉ U.S. 1 [I–95, Exit 17], Yarmouth 04347, ☎ 207/846–0833, WEB www.mainetourism.com).

PENOBSCOT BAY

Purists hold that the Maine coast begins at Penobscot Bay, where the vistas over the water are wider and bluer; the shore a jumble of broken granite boulders, cobblestones, and gravel punctuated by small sand beaches; and the water numbingly cold. Port Clyde, in the southwest, and Stonington, in the southeast, are the outer limits of Maine's largest bay, 35 mi apart across the bay waters but separated by a drive of almost 100 mi on scenic but slow two-lane highways. From Pemaquid Point at the western extremity of Muscongus Bay to Port Clyde at its eastern extent, it's less than 15 mi across the water, but it's 50 mi for the motorist, who must return north to U.S. 1 to reach the far shore. A relaxing sail on a windjammer is a great way to explore the area.

Thomaston, on the western edge of the region, has a fine collection of sea captains' homes. Rockland, the largest town on the bay, is a growing arts center, home of the Maine Lobster Festival, and the port of departure for trips to Vinalhaven, North Haven, and Matinicus islands. The Camden Hills, looming green over Camden's fashionable waterfront, turn bluer and fainter as you head toward Castine, the small town across the bay. In between Camden and Castine are Belfast and the antiques and flea market of Searsport. Deer Isle is connected to the mainland by a slender, high-arching bridge, but Isle au Haut, accessible from Deer Isle's fishing town of Stonington, can be reached by passenger ferry only: More than half of this steep, wooded island is wilderness, the most remote section of Acadia National Park.

The most promising shopping areas are Main Street in Rockland, Main and Bay View streets in Camden, and the Main Streets in Belfast, Blue Hill, and Stonington. Antiques shops are clustered in Searsport and scattered around the outskirts of villages, in farmhouses and barns. Yard sales abound in summer.

Thomaston

㉒ *10 mi northeast of Waldoboro, 72 mi northeast of Portland.*

The Maine State Prison that has loomed over Thomaston for decades has been replaced by a new facility in Warren. Plans call for the dreary monstrosity to be razed and replaced with a park. Prison aside, this is a delightful town, full of beautiful sea captains' homes and dotted with antiques and specialty shops. A National Historic District encompasses parts of High, Main, and Knox streets.

The **Montpelier: General Henry Knox Museum** was built in 1930 as a replica of the late-18th-century mansion of Major General Henry Knox, a general in the Revolutionary War and secretary of war in Washington's Cabinet. Antiques and Knox family possessions fill the interior. Architectural appointments include an oval room and a double staircase. ⊠ *U.S. 1 and Rte. 131,* ☎ *207/354–8062,* WEB *www. generalknoxmuseum.org.* 🖃 *$5.* ☉ *Memorial Day–late Sept., Tues.– Sat. 10–4, Sun. 1–4; tours on the hr and ½ hr 10–3.*

Dining

$$–$$$ ✕ **Thomaston Cafe & Bakery.** A changing selection of works by local artists adorns the walls of this small café. Entrées, prepared with locally grown and produced ingredients, may include seared fresh tuna on soba noodles, lobster ravioli with lobster sauce, or filet mignon with béarnaise sauce. ⊠ *154 Main St.,* ☎ *207/354–8589. MC, V. No dinner Sun.–Thurs.*

Shopping

The **Maine State Prison Showroom Outlet** (⊠ Main St., ☎ 207/354–2535) carries crafts, furniture, and woodwork made by prisoners. Browse the well-chosen selections at **Personal Bookstore** (⊠ 144 Main St., ☎ 207/ 354–8058 or 800/391–8058), which also houses a gallery upstairs.

Tenants Harbor

㉓ *13 mi south of Thomaston.*

Tenants Harbor is a quintessential Maine fishing town, its harbor dominated by lobster boats, its shores rocky and slippery, its center full of clapboard houses, a church, and a general store. The fictional Dunnet Landing of Sarah Orne Jewett's classic *The Country of the Pointed Firs* (1896) is based on this region. It's a favorite with artists, too, and galleries and studios invite browsing.

The keeper's house at the **Marshall Point Lighthouse** has been turned into a museum containing memorabilia from the town of St. George (a few miles north of Tenants Harbor). The setting has inspired Jamie Wyeth and other artists. You can stroll the grounds and watch the boats go in and out of Port Clyde. ⊠ *Marshall Point Rd., Port Clyde,* ☎ *207/372–6450.* 🖃 *Free.* ☉ *June–Sept., weekdays 1–5, Sat. 10–5; May and Oct., weekends 1–5.*

Dining and Lodging

$$–$$$$ ✕🖫 **East Wind Inn & Meeting House.** Built as a sail loft in 1830, this comfortably old-fashioned inn has a dreamy view overlooking an island-studded harbor. Rooms in the main inn are plain and unadorned; those in the Meeting House (a converted sea captain's house) and the Wheeler Cottage have more comforts, including some with fireplaces. The inn's restaurant ($$–$$$) emphasizes local seafood. A take-out restaurant on the wharf serves lobster, clams, and lighter fare. ⊠ *Mechanic St., 04860,* ☎ *207/372–6366 or 800/241–8439,* FAX *207/372– 6320,* WEB *www.eastwindinn.com. 18 rooms, 12 with bath; 3 suites; 4 apartments. 2 restaurants, cable TV in some rooms, some microwaves, meeting rooms, some pets allowed; no air-conditioning. AE, D, MC, V. Closed Dec.–Apr. BP.*

Shopping

Gallery-by-the-Sea (⊠ Port Clyde Village, Port Clyde, ☎ 207/372–8631) carries works by a dozen local artists, including Leo Brooks, Lawrence Goldsmith, and Emily Muir. **Port Clyde Arts & Crafts Society Gallery**

(✉ Rte. 131, Tenants Harbor, ☎ 207/372–0673) showcases members' works in a garden.

Monhegan Island

★ ㉔   *East of Pemaquid Peninsula, 10 mi south of Port Clyde.*

Remote Monhegan Island, with its high cliffs fronting the open sea, was known to Basque, Portuguese, and Breton fishermen well before Columbus "discovered" America. About a century ago Monhegan was discovered again by some of America's finest painters, including Rockwell Kent, Robert Henri, A. J. Hammond, and Edward Hopper, who sailed out to paint its meadows, savage cliffs, wild ocean views, and fishermen's shacks. Tourists followed, and today three excursion boats dock here. The village bustles with activity in summer, when many artists open their studios. You can escape the crowds on the island's 17 mi of hiking trails, which lead to the lighthouse and to the cliffs. Those who overnight here have a quieter experience, since lodging is limited. Bring a lunch if you're visiting during the day, as restaurants can have long waits at lunchtime.

The **Monhegan Museum,** in an 1824 lighthouse, and an adjacent, newly built assistant keeper's house have wonderful views of Manana Island and the Camden Hills in the distance. Inside, artworks and displays depict island life and local flora and birds. ✉ *White Head Rd.,* ☎ *no phone.* 🎫 *Donations accepted.* ☉ *July–mid-Sept., daily 11:30–3:30.*

Lodging

$$$–$$$$ 🛏 **Island Inn.** This three-story inn, which dates from 1807, has a commanding presence on Monhegan's harbor. The waterside rooms are the nicest, with sunset views over the harbor and stark Manana Island. Some of the meadow-view rooms have the distinct disadvantage of being over kitchen vents. The property includes the main inn, the adjacent Pierce Cottage, a small bakery-café, and a dining room that serves breakfast, lunch, and dinner. ✉ *1 Ocean Ave (Box 128, 04852),* ☎ *207/596–0371,* FAX *207/594–5517 (seasonal),* WEB *www.islandinnmonhegan.com. 30 rooms, 15 with bath; 4 suites in 2 buildings. Restaurant, café; no air-conditioning, no room phones, no room TVs. MC, V. Closed Columbus Day–Memorial Day. BP.*

Outdoor Activities and Sports

Port Clyde, a fishing village at the end of Route 131, is the point of departure for the **Laura B.** (☎ 207/372–8848 schedules), the mail boat that serves Monhegan Island. The **Balmy Days** (☎ 207/633–2284 or 800/298–2284) sails from Boothbay Harbor to Monhegan on daily trips in summer. **Hardy Boat Cruises** (☎ 207/677–2026 or 800/278–3346) leave daily from Shaw's Wharf in New Harbor.

Rockland

㉕   *4 mi northeast of Thomaston, 14 mi northeast of Tenants Harbor.*

Once a place to pass through on the way to tonier ports like Camden, Rockland now attracts attention on its own, thanks to the expansion of the Farnsworth Museum. Specialty shops and galleries line Main Street and the side streets, and restaurants and inns continue to open. A large fishing port and the commercial hub of this coastal area, with working boats moored alongside yachts and windjammers, Rockland still holds on to its working-class flavor, but it's fading.

Day trips to Vinalhaven and North Haven islands and distant Matinicus depart from the harbor, the outer portion of which is bisected by a nearly mile-long granite breakwater. At the end of the breakwater is a late-19th-century lighthouse, one of the best places in the area to watch

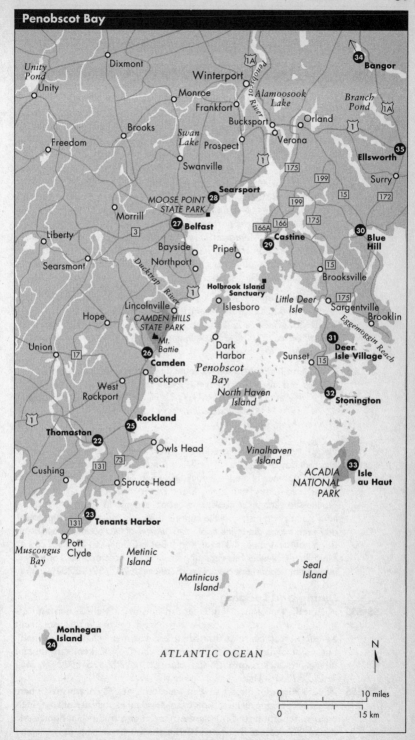

the many windjammers sail in and out of Rockland Harbor. Owl's Head Lighthouse, off Route 73, is also a good vantage point.

★ The **Farnsworth Art Museum,** an excellent small museum of American art, contains works by Andrew, N. C., and Jamie Wyeth; Fitz Hugh Lane; George Bellows; Frank W. Benson; Edward Hopper; Louise Nevelson; and Fairfield Porter. The **Wyeth Center** is devoted to Maine-related works of the Wyeth family. Some works from the personal collection of Andrew and Betsy Wyeth include *The Patriot, Adrift, Maiden Hair, Dr. Syn, The Clearing,* and *Watch Cap.* Works by living Maine artists are shown in the **Jamien Morehouse Wing.** The **Farnsworth Homestead,** a handsome circa-1852 Greek Revival dwelling that is part of the museum, retains its original lavish Victorian furnishings. The museum also operates the **Olson House** (⊠ Hathorn Point Rd., Cushing), which is depicted in Andrew Wyeth's famous painting *Christina's World.* ⊠ *352 Main St.,* ☎ *207/596–6457,* ⓦⒺⒷ *www.farnsworthmuseum.org.* ⚏ *$9; Olson House only, $4.* ☉ *Museum Memorial Day–Columbus Day, daily 9–5; Columbus Day–Memorial Day, Tues.–Sat. 10–5, Sun. 1–5. Homestead Memorial Day–Columbus Day, daily 10–5. Olson House Memorial Day–Columbus Day, daily 11–4.*

☾ The **Shore Village Museum** displays many lighthouse and Coast Guard artifacts and has exhibits of maritime memorabilia. ⊠ *104 Limerock St.,* ☎ *207/594–0311,* ⓦⒺⒷ *www.lighthouse.cc/shorevillage.* ⚏ *Donation suggested.* ☉ *June–mid-Oct., daily 10–4; mid-Oct.–June by chance or appointment.*

☾ **Owls Head Transportation Museum** displays antique aircraft, cars, and engines and stages special events every other weekend May–October. ⊠ *117 Museum La., off Rte. 73, Owls Head (3 mi south of Rockland),* ☎ *207/594–4418,* ⓦⒺⒷ *www.ohtm.org.* ⚏ *$6.* ☉ *Apr.–Oct., daily 10–5; Nov.–Mar., daily 10–4.*

OFF THE **VINALHAVEN –** You can take the ferry from Rockland to this island for a
BEATEN PATH pleasant day of bicycling or walking. A number of parks are within walking distance of the ferry dock, including Armbrust Hill, the site of an abandoned quarry, and Lane's Island Preserve, a 40-acre site of moors, granite shoreline, tidal pools, and beach. You can learn about the island's quarrying history at the Historical Society Museum on High Street and even take a dip in the cool, clear waters of two quarries. Lawson's is 1 mi out on the North Haven Road; Booth Quarry is 1½ mi out East Main Street. Neither has changing facilities, so go prepared. For ferry information, call Maine State Ferry Service (☎ 207/596–2202).

Dining and Lodging

$$–$$$ ✕ **Amalfi.** Delicious Mediterranean cuisine, a well-chosen and af-
★ fordable wine list, and excellent service have made this storefront Mediterranean bistro an immediate hit. The menu changes seasonally but may include the house paella with chorizo, chicken, shrimp, and mussels or duck risotto. ⊠ *421 Main St.,* ☎ *207/596–0012. D, MC, V. Closed Sun.–Mon.*

$$–$$$ ✕ **Café Miranda.** Expect to wait for a table at this cozy bistro, where the daily-changing menu reflects fresh, seasonal ingredients and the chef's creative renditions of both new American and traditional home-style foods. You can make a meal from the 20 or so appetizers, many roasted in the brick oven. The two dozen entrées may include crispy panfried soft-shell crabs with red bean ragout and yellow jasmine rice. The patio is a good choice on nice days. ⊠ *15 Oak St.,* ☎ *207/594–2034. MC, V. Closed Sun.–Mon. No lunch.*

$$-$$$ × **Primo.** At this restaurant, James Beard Award–winning chef Melissa
★   Kelly and baker and pastry chef Price Kushner serve cuisine that combines fresh Maine ingredients with Mediterranean influences. The
weekly changing menu may include wood-roasted black sea bass, local
crab-stuffed turbot, or diver harvested–scallop and basil ravioli. ⊠ *2
S. Main St.,* ☎ *207/594–0770. Reservations essential. AE, D, DC, MC,
V. Closed Tues.–Wed. No lunch.*

$$$$ ⊡ **Samoset Resort.** On the Rockland-Rockport town line next to the
breakwater, this sprawling ocean-side resort has excellent golf and fitness facilities. Most of the spacious rooms, decorated in deep green and
burgundy tones, have views of Penobscot Bay over the fairways; all
have patios or decks. ⊠ *220 Warrenton St., Rockport 04856,* ☎ *207/
594–2511 or 800/341–1650,* FAX *207/594–0722,* WEB *www.samoset.com.
154 rooms, 24 suites. 3 restaurants, in-room data ports, some minibars, cable TV with movies and video games, 18-hole golf course, putting
green, 4 tennis courts, pro shop, 2 pools (1 indoor), health club, hot
tub, massage, sauna, dock, racquetball, lounge, baby-sitting, children's
programs (ages 3–12), playground, dry cleaning, laundry service, concierge, Internet, business services, meeting rooms, airport shuttle; no-
smoking rooms. AE, D, DC, MC, V.*

$$$-$$$$ ⊡ **Berry Manor Inn.** Built in 1898 as the residence of Charles E. Berry,
★   a prominent Rockland merchant, this Victorian shingle-style inn has
been carefully restored. The large guest rooms come elegantly furnished
with antiques and reproduction pieces. All have fireplaces; TVs are avail-
able upon request. A guest pantry is stocked with sweets. ⊠ *81 Tal-
bot Ave., 04841,* ☎ *207/596–7696 or 800/774–5692,* FAX *207/596–9958,*
WEB *www.berrymanorinn.com. 8 rooms. In-room data ports, some in-
room hot tubs, library, meeting room; no kids under 12, no smoking.
AE, MC, V. BP.*

$$-$$$ ⊡ **Limerock Inn.** You can walk to the Farnsworth and the Shore Vil-
★   lage museums from this magnificent Queen Anne–style Victorian on
a quiet residential street. The meticulously decorated rooms include
Island Cottage, with a whirlpool tub and doors that open onto a pri-
vate deck overlooking a garden, and Grand Manan, which has a fire-
place, a whirlpool tub, and a four-poster king-size bed. ⊠ *96 Limerock
St., 04841,* ☎ *207/594–2257 or 800/546–3762,* FAX *207/594–1846,* WEB
*www.limerockinn.com. 8 rooms. In-room data ports, bicycles, croquet;
no air-conditioning, no room phones, no room TVs, no kids under 12,
no smoking. D, MC, V. BP.*

Outdoor Activities and Sports

BOAT TRIPS

Bay Island Yacht Charters (⊠ 120 Tillison Ave., ☎ 207/596–5770 or
800/421–2492) operates bareboats and charters. The **Maine Windjammer
Association** (⊠ Box 1144, Blue Hill 04614, ☎ 800/807–9463) repre-
sents the Rockland-based windjammers *American Eagle, Heritage,
Isaac H. Evans, J&E Riggin, Nathaniel Bowditch, Stephen Taber,* and
Victory Chimes, which sail on three- to eight-day cruises.

TOURS

Downeast Air Inc. (☎ 207/594–2171 or 800/594–2171) operates scenic
flights and lighthouse tours.

Shopping

Archipelago (⊠ 386 Main St., ☎ 207/596–0701) carries work created
by residents of Maine's islands. **Caldbeck Gallery** (⊠ 12 Elm St., ☎
207/596–5935) displays contemporary Maine works by artists such
as William Thon. **Harbor Square Gallery** (⊠ 374 Main St., ☎ 207/
596–8700) has roomfuls of Maine-related arts and crafts.

Camden

26 *8 mi north of Rockland, 19 mi south of Belfast.*

"Where the mountains meet the sea," Camden's longtime publicity slogan, is an apt description, as you will discover when you look up from the harbor. The town is famous not only for geography but for its large fleet of windjammers—relics and replicas from the age of sailing. At just about any hour during the warm months you're likely to see at least one windjammer tied up in the harbor. The excursions, whether for an afternoon or a week, are best from June through September. Eggemoggin Reach is a famous cruising ground for yachts, as are the coves and inlets around Deer Isle and the Penobscot Bay waters between Camden and Castine. Busy downtown Camden has some of the best shopping in the region. The district's compact size makes it perfect for exploring on foot: shops, restaurants, and galleries line Main Street (U.S. 1) and Bayview, as well as side streets and alleys around the harbor.

Although their height may not be much more than 1,000 ft, the hills in **Camden Hills State Park** are lovely landmarks for miles along the low, rolling reaches of the Maine coast. The 5,500-acre park contains 20 mi of trails, including the easy Nature Trail up Mt. Battie. Hike or drive to the top for a magnificent view over Camden and island-studded Penobscot Bay. The 112-site camping area, open from mid-May to mid-October, has flush toilets and hot showers. The entrance is 2 mi north of Camden. ⊠ *U.S. 1,* ☎ *207/236–3109.* 🎫 *Trails and auto road up Mt. Battie $2.* ☉ *Daily dawn–dusk.*

Merryspring Horticultural Nature Park is a 66-acre retreat with herb, rose, rhododendron, hosta, and children's gardens as well as 4 mi of walking trails. ⊠ *Conway Rd., off U.S. 1,* ☎ *207/236–2239.* 🎫 *Free.* ☉ *Daily dawn–dusk.*

☾ **Kelmscott Farm** is a rare-breed animal farm (sheep, pigs, horses, poultry, goats, and cows) with displays, a nature trail, children's activities, a picnic area, heirloom gardens, and special events. ⊠ *Rte. 52, Lincolnville,* ☎ *207/763–4088 or 800/545–9363,* WEB *www.kelmscott.org.* 🎫 *$5.* ☉ *May–Oct., Tues.–Sun. 10–5; Nov.–Apr., Tues.–Sun. 10–3.*

Dining and Lodging

$–$$$ ✕ **Waterfront Restaurant.** A ringside seat on Camden Harbor can be had here; the best view is from the deck, open in warm weather. The fare is primarily seafood, but they also serve plenty of beef, chicken, and salads. Some lunchtime highlights are lobster and crabmeat rolls. ⊠ *Bayview St.,* ☎ *207/236–3747. Reservations not accepted. AE, MC, V.*

$$–$$$ ✕🏠 **The Belmont.** Fresh flowers, gleaming woodwork, comfortable antiques, and Oriental rugs highlight this 19th-century Edwardian-style inn. Most rooms are spacious, and some have fireplaces. Adding to the experience is an elegant dining room, Marquis at the Belmont ($$–$$$$; closed Sun.), open to the public, where the menu might include grilled beef tenderloin with roasted pistachio blue-cheese butter. ⊠ *6 Belmont Ave., 04843,* ☎ *207/230–1226 or 800/237–8053,* FAX *207/236–9872,* WEB *www.thebelmontinn.com. 6 rooms. Restaurant, bar; no air-conditioning in some rooms, no room TVs, no kids, no smoking. AE, MC, V. BP.*

$$–$$$ ✕🏠 **Hartstone Inn.** Michael and Mary Jo Salmon have turned this
★ downtown 1835 Mansard-style Victorian into an elegant and sophisticated retreat and culinary destination. No detail has been overlooked, from soft robes, down comforters, and chocolate truffles in the guest rooms to china, crystal, and silver in the dining room. The five-course, prix-fixe menu ($$$$; reservations essential; closed late

Oct.–May, Mon.–Wed.; June–late Oct., Mon.–Tues.) changes daily. The inn hosts seasonal food festivals and off-season cooking classes. ✉ *42 Elm St., 04843,* ☎ *207/236–4259 or 800/788–4823,* FAX *207/ 235–9575,* WEB *www.hartstoneinn.com. 6 rooms, 4 suites. Restaurant, cable TV in some rooms, in-room data ports; no kids under 12, no smoking.*

$$–$$$ ✕▥ **Whitehall Inn.** One of Camden's best-known inns, just north of town, is an 1843 white clapboard sea captain's home with a wide porch. The Millay Room, off the lobby, preserves memorabilia of the poet Edna St. Vincent Millay, who grew up in the area. The sparsely furnished rooms have dark-wood bedsteads, white bedspreads, and claw-foot tubs. The dining room ($$$), which serves traditional and creative American cuisine, is open to the public for dinner. ✉ *52 High St. (Box 558, 04843),* ☎ *207/236–3391 or 800/789–6565,* FAX *207/236–4427 (seasonal),* WEB *www.whitehall-inn.com. 50 rooms, 45 with bath. Restaurant, tennis court, shuffleboard; no phones in some rooms, no room TVs, no smoking. AE, MC, V. Closed mid-Oct.–mid-May. BP.*

$$–$$$ ✕▥ **Youngtown Inn.** Inside this white Federal-style farmhouse are a French-inspired country retreat and a well-respected French restaurant ($$$). The country location guarantees quiet, and the inn is a short walk from the Fernald Neck Preserve on Lake Megunticook. Simple, airy rooms open to decks with views of the rolling countryside. Four have fireplaces. The restaurant, open to the public for dinner, serves entrées such as rack of lamb and breast of pheasant with foie gras mousse. ✉ *Rte. 52 at Youngtown Rd., Lincolnville 04849,* ☎ *207/763–4290 or 800/291–8438,* FAX *207/763–4078,* WEB *www.youngtowninn.com. 6 rooms, 1 suite. Restaurant, cable TV in some rooms; no room phones, no smoking. AE, MC, V. BP.*

$$$$ ▥ **Inn at Ocean's Edge.** Perched on the ocean's edge, this shingle-style
★ inn looks as if it has been here for decades. In actuality, the original building dates from 1999 and the upper building from 2001. Both were built with modern-day comforts in mind. Every room has a king-size bed, an ocean view, a fireplace, and a whirlpool for two. ✉ *U.S. 1, Lincolnville (Box 704, Camden 04843),* ☎ *207/236–0945,* FAX *207/ 236–0609,* WEB *www.innatoceansedge.com. 26 rooms, 1 suite. In-room data ports, cable TV, in-room VCRs, gym, pub, meeting room; no kids under 14, no smoking. MC, V. BP.*

$$$ ▥ **Victorian by the Sea.** It's less than 10 minutes from downtown Camden, but with a quiet waterside location well off U.S. 1, the Victorian Inn feels a world away. Most rooms and the wraparound porch have magnificent views over island-studded Penobscot Bay. Romantic touches include canopy and brass beds, braided rugs, white wicker furniture, and floral wallpapers. Six guest rooms have fireplaces; four more fireplaces are in common rooms, including the glass-enclosed breakfast room. ✉ *31 Sea View Dr., Lincolnville (Box 1385, Camden 04843),* ☎ *207/236–3785 or 800/382–9817,* FAX *207/236–0017,* WEB *www.victorianbythesea.com. 5 rooms, 2 suites. Fans; no air-conditioning in some rooms, no room phones, no room TVs, no kids under 12, no smoking. AE, MC, V. BP.*

$$–$$$ ▥ **Camden Maine Stay.** This 1802 clapboard inn on the National Reg-
★ ister of Historic Places is within walking distance of shops and restaurants. The grounds are classic and inviting, from the flowers lining the granite walk in summer to the snow-laden bushes in winter. Fresh and colorful, the rooms contain many pieces of Eastlake furniture; six have fireplaces. ✉ *22 High St., 04842,* ☎ *207/236–9636,* FAX *207/236– 0621,* WEB *www.camdenmainestay.com. 5 rooms, 3 suites. No room phones, no cable TV in some rooms, no kids under 10, no smoking. AE, MC, V. BP.*

Nightlife and the Arts

Bay Chamber Concerts (⊠ Rockport Opera House, 6 Central St., Rockport, ☎ 207/236–2823 or 888/707–2770) presents chamber music on Thursday and Friday night during July and August; concerts are given once a month from September to June. **Gilbert's Public House** (⊠ 12 Bay View St., ☎ 207/236–4320) has dancing and live entertainment. **Sea Dog Tavern & Brewery** (⊠ 43 Mechanic St., ☎ 207/236–6863), a popular brewpub in a converted woolen mill, hosts live bands playing blues, rock and jazz. The **Whale's Tooth Pub** (⊠ U.S. 1, Lincolnville Beach, ☎ 207/236–3747) hosts live folk music on weekends.

Outdoor Activities and Sports

The **Betselma** (⊠ Camden Public Landing, ☎ 207/236–4446) operates one- and two-hour powerboat trips. **Brown Dog Bikes** (⊠ 46 Elm St., ☎ 207/236–6664) delivers rental bikes to area lodging. **Maine Sport** (⊠ U.S. 1, Rockport, ☎ 207/236–8797 or 800/722–0826), the best sports outfitter north of Freeport, rents bikes, camping and fishing gear, canoes, kayaks, cross-country skis, ice skates, and snowshoes. It also conducts skiing and kayaking clinics and trips. The **Maine Windjammer Association** (⊠ Box 1144, Blue Hill 04614, ☎ 800/807–9463) represents the Camden-based windjammers *Angelique, Grace Bailey, Lewis R. French, Mary Day,* and *Mercantile* and the Rockport-based *Timberwind.* Cruises last three to eight days.

Shopping

Center for Maine Contemporary Art (⊠ 162 Russell Ave., Rockport, ☎ 207/236–2875) specializes in contemporary Maine art. **Maine Gathering** (⊠ 21 Main St., ☎ 207/236–9004) sells a well-chosen selection of crafts, including Passamaquoddy and Penobscot baskets. **Maine's Massachusetts House Galleries** (⊠ U.S. 1, Lincolnville, ☎ 207/789–5705) display regional art, including bronzes, carvings, sculptures, and landscapes and seascapes in pencil, oil, and watercolor.

ABCD Books (⊠ 23 Bay View St., ☎ 207/236–3903 or 888/236–3903) has a discriminating selection of quality antiquarian and rare books. The **Owl and Turtle Bookshop** (⊠ 8 Bay View St., ☎ 207/236–4769) sells books, CDs, cassettes, and cards. The two-story shop has rooms devoted to marine and children's books. The **Pine Tree Shop & Bayview Gallery** (⊠ 33 Bay View St., ☎ 207/236–4534) specializes in original art, prints, and posters, almost all with Maine themes. **Stone Soup Books** (⊠ 35 Main St., second floor, ☎ no phone) stocks used contemporary fiction and is a great place to pick up a cache of books to read on inclement days. The **Windsor Chairmakers** (⊠ U.S. 1, Lincolnville, ☎ 207/789–5188 or 800/789–5188) sells custom-made handcrafted beds, chests, china cabinets, dining tables, highboys, and chairs.

Ski Areas

CAMDEN SNOW BOWL

The Maine coast isn't known for skiing, but this small, lively park has skiing, snowboarding, tubing, and tobogganing—plus magnificent views over Penobscot Bay. ⊠ *Hosmer Pond Rd. (Box 1207, 04843),* ☎ *207/236–3438.*

Downhill. The park has a 950-ft-vertical mountain, a small lodge with a cafeteria, a ski school, and ski and toboggan rentals. Camden Snow Bowl has 11 trails accessed by one double chair and two T-bars. It also has night skiing.

Other Activities. Camden Snow Bowl has a small lake that is cleared for ice-skating, a snow-tubing park, and a 400-ft toboggan run that shoots sledders out onto the lake. The North American Tobogganing

Championships, a tongue-in-cheek event open to anyone, is held annually in early February

CROSS-COUNTRY SKIING
There are 16 km (10 mi) of cross-country skiing trails at **Camden Hills State Park** (✉ U.S. 1, ☎ 207/236–9849). **Tanglewood 4-H Camp** (✉ U.S. 1, ☎ 207/789–5868), about 5 mi away in Lincolnville, has 20 km (12½ mi) of trails.

Belfast

㉗ *19 mi north of Camden, 46 mi east of Augusta.*

Like many other Maine towns, Belfast has ridden the tides of affluence and depression since its glory days in the 1800s, when it was a shipbuilding center and home to many sea captains. Today it's high-tech, namely credit-card giant MBNA, that has helped rescue the city's economy. The upswing has brought the revival of the old-fashioned redbrick Victorian downtown and a lively waterfront, as well as affordable lodging and dining. The houses on Church Street are a veritable glossary of 19th-century architectural styles; pick up a map with a walking tour at the visitor center at the foot of Main Street.

The **Belfast & Moosehead Lake Railroad** (✉ 44 Front St., ☎ 207/948–5500 or 800/392–5500, WEB www.belfastrailroad.com) operates a 90-minute trip from July to mid-October ($15) between Belfast and Waldo, providing views of Belfast Harbor, Lake Winnecook and area towns. Narrators discuss the region's history and folklore.

Dining and Lodging

$$–$$$ ✕ **Spring Street Cafe.** Don't let the unassuming small Cape Cod–style house tucked on a side street fool you; this restaurant prepares such eclectic fare as Mediterranean halibut cake, Spring Street pad Thai, and Cuban-style roasted pork. Both small plates, ideal for those not too hungry, and large plates are served. ✉ *38 Spring St.,* ☎ *207/338–4603. MC, V.*

$–$$ ✕ **Darby's.** Tin ceilings and an old-fashioned bar create a comfortable ambience for the creative casual fare served here. The eclectic menu lists hearty soups and sandwiches as well as dishes with an international flavor, such as Moroccan lamb and pad Thai. ✉ *155 High St.,* ☎ *207/338–2339. AE, D, DC, MC, V.*

$$–$$$ 🏨 **Jeweled Turret Inn.** Turrets, columns, gables, and magnificent woodwork embellish this inn, originally built in 1898 as the home of a local attorney. The inn is named for the jewel-like stained-glass windows in the stairway turret; the gem theme continues in the den, where the ornate rock fireplace is said to include rocks from every state in the Union. Elegant Victorian pieces furnish the rooms: The Opal room has a marble bath with whirlpool tub in addition to a French armoire and a four-poster. ✉ *40 Pearl St., 04915,* ☎ *207/338–2304 or 800/696–2304,* WEB *www.jeweledturret.com. 7 rooms. No air-conditioning in some rooms, no room phones, no room TVs, no kids under 12, no smoking indoors. AE, MC, V. BP.*

$$–$$$ 🏨 **The White House.** This 1840–1842 landmark by Maine architect Calvin Ryder is considered one of the most sophisticated examples of Greek Revival architecture in New England. An eight-side cupola tops the house; inside are ornate plaster ceiling medallions, Italian marble fireplaces, an elliptical flying staircase, and intricate moldings. Crystal chandeliers, Oriental rugs, and antiques and reproduction pieces elegantly decorate the spacious rooms. You can relax in the English garden, in the gazebo, or under the enormous copper beech tree. ✉ *1 Church St., 04915,* ☎ *207/338–1901 or 888/290–1901,* FAX *207/338–*

5161, WEB www.mainebb.com. 4 rooms, 2 suites. Some in-room hot tubs, some cable TV, some in-room VCRs, meeting room, some pets allowed; no kids under 12, no smoking. D, MC, V. BP.

Outdoor Activities and Sports

KAYAKING

Belfast Kayak Tours (⊠ Belfast City Pier, ☎ 207/382–6204) provides fully outfitted trips and instruction.

PARKS

Belfast City Park (⊠ High St., 1 mi east of downtown) has a playground, tennis courts (lighted at night), a baseball diamond, and an outdoor swimming pool with lockers and showers. Use of the park is free.

Moose Point State Park (⊠ U.S. 1 between Belfast and Searsport, ☎ 207/548–2882) is ideal for easy hikes and picnics overlooking Penobscot Bay.

Shopping

Belfast's main and side streets house an eclectic selection of shops that mirror the city's economic base. Shoppers who prefer upscale boutiques rub elbows with those who bargain-hunt in thrift stores.

Visit the **Belfast Co-op** (⊠ 123 High St., ☎ 207/338–2352), the region's premier natural foods store, for healthful snacks and goodies. The Co-op also has a café with soups, sandwiches, and other fare. You can dine inside, outdoors on picnic tables, or have your order prepared to go. The **Green Store** (⊠ 71 Main St., ☎ 207/338–4045) sells environmentally friendly products, from lightbulbs to clothing. The **Gothic Cafe** (⊠ 108 Main St., ☎ 207/338–9901) sells melt-in-your-mouth pastries and to-die-for ice cream as well as architectural antiques.

Searsport

❷❽ *11 mi northeast of Belfast, 57 mi east of Augusta.*

Searsport, Maine's second-largest deepwater port (after Portland), has a rich shipbuilding and seafaring history. In the 1880s, 10% of all captains under deepwater sail hailed from here. Many of the former sea captains' homes are now bed-and-breakfasts. They make an ideal base for exploring the multitude of antiques shops and flea markets lining U.S. 1 that have earned Searsport the title Maine's Antiques Capital.

★ The fine holdings within the nine historic and five modern buildings of the **Penobscot Marine Museum** provide fascinating documentation of the region's seafaring way of life. These buildings, including a still-active church and a sea captain's house, remain in their original spots in town. The museum's outstanding collection of marine art includes the largest collection of works by Thomas and James Buttersworth in the country. Also of note are photos of 284 local sea captains, a collection of China-trade articles, artifacts of the whaling industry (including lots of scrimshaw), navigational instruments, treasures collected by seafarers around the globe, and models of famous ships. The museum's newest building, a boat barn, opened in 2001 with exhibits of small craft. ⊠ 5 U.S. 1, at Church St., ☎ 207/548–2529, WEB www.penobscotmarinemuseum.org. ☞ $8. ☉ Memorial Day–late Oct., Mon.–Sat. 10–5, Sun. noon–5; late Oct.–Memorial Day by appointment.

Dining and Lodging

$$$ ✕ **The Rhumb Line.** The upscale restaurant in this 18th-century sea captain's home delivers fine dining, with formally attired waitstaff and excellent food. Pepper-glazed pork tenderloin, orange-glazed duck with

potato pancakes, and horseradish-crusted salmon are typical entrées. ⊠ *200 E. Main St. (U.S. 1),* ☎ *207/548–2600. MC, V. No lunch.*

$$ 🏠 **Brass Lantern.** This antiques-filled Victorian bed-and-breakfast is an elegant retreat after a day of shopping at nearby flea markets and antiques shops. Two rooms have water views. The multicourse breakfasts are served on china and crystal by candlelight in the tin-ceiling dining room. ⊠ *81 W. Main St. (U.S. 1), 04874,* ☎ *207/548–0150 or 800/691–0150,* FAX *207/548–0304,* WEB *www.brasslanternmaine.com. 5 rooms. No air-conditioning, no room phones, no room TVs, no kids under 12, no smoking. D, MC, V. BP.*

$–$$ 🏠 **Homeport Inn.** This 1861 inn, a former sea captain's home, provides an opulent Victorian environment that might put you in the mood to rummage through the nearby antiques and treasure shops. The back rooms downstairs have private decks and views of the bay. Families often stay in the housekeeping cottages. ⊠ *121 E. Main St. (U.S. 1),* ☎ *207/548–2259 or 800/742–5814,* WEB *www.bnbcity.com/inns/20015. 10 rooms, 7 with bath; 2 cottages. Some pets allowed; no air-conditioning, no room phones, no room TVs, no kids under 3, no smoking. AE, D, MC, V. BP.*

Shopping

Museum-quality model-ship kits can be found at **Bluejacket Shipcrafters** (⊠ 160 E. Main St. [U.S. 1], ☎ 207/548–9970). Hundreds of teddy bears can be found at **Cranberry Hollow** (⊠ 157 W. Main St. [U.S. 1], ☎ 207/548–2647); the owner also makes custom bears from old fur coats. **Pumpkin Patch Antiques** (⊠ 15 W. Main St. [U.S. 1], ☎ 207/ 548–6047) displays such items as quilts, nautical memorabilia, and painted and wood furniture from about 20 dealers. It's open April through Thanksgiving or by appointment. More than 70 dealers show their wares in the two-story **Searsport Antique Mall** (⊠ 149 E. Main St. [U.S. 1], ☎ 207/548–2640); look for everything from linens and silver to turn-of-the-20th-century oak.

Castine

㉙ *30 mi southeast of Searsport.*

Set on the tip of a peninsula, Castine is a quiet, peaceful place to escape most of the coastal crowds. The French, the British, the Dutch, and the Americans fought over the town from the 17th century to the War of 1812. Signs explaining this history are posted throughout town, making it ideal for a walking tour. Present-day Castine's many appealing attributes include its lively harbor front, Federal and Greek Revival houses, and town common; the two small museums and the ruins of a British fort are also worth exploring. For a nice stroll, park your car at the landing and walk up Main Street toward the white Trinitarian Federated Church, which has a tapering spire. Among the white clapboard buildings that ring the town common are the Ives House (once the summer home of the poet Robert Lowell), the Abbott School, and the Unitarian Church, capped by a whimsical belfry. The Maine Maritime Academy is also here, and its training ship often can be seen in port. You can pick up a map detailing the town's businesses, history, and historic sites at most local businesses.

The **Castine Historical Society Museum**'s changing exhibits relating to Castine's tumultuous history include the town's Bicentennial Quilt, created in 1996 to celebrate the town's 200th birthday. ⊠ *Town Common (Box 238, 04421),* ☎ *207/326–4118.* 🎫 *Free.* ⊙ *Tues.–Sat. 10– 4, Sun. 1–4.*

Castine's **Soldiers and Sailors Monument** (⊠ Castine Town Common) honors the state's participation in the Civil War. The memorial was dedicated in May 1887 to the veterans of that conflict.

The **Wilson Museum** comprises four buildings. The main building houses anthropologist-geologist John Howard Wilson's collection of prehistoric artifacts from around the world, including rocks, minerals, and other intriguing objects. The **John Perkins House** is a restored Colonial house built in 1763 and enlarged in 1774 and 1783. The **Blacksmith Shop** holds demonstrations showing all the tricks of this old-time trade. Inside the **Hearse House** you can see the summer and winter hearses that serviced Castine more than a century ago. ⊠ *Perkins St.,* ☎ *207/677–2423.* ▣ *Museum, Blacksmith Shop, and Hearse House free; John Perkins House $4.* ☉ *Museum late May–late Sept., Tues.– Sun. 2–5. Guided tours of John Perkins House and demonstrations at Blacksmith Shop July–Aug., Sun. and Wed. 2–5. Hearse House, July– Aug., Sun. and Wed. 2–5*

Dining and Lodging

$–$$$ ✕ **Dennett's Wharf.** When you need a break from exploring Castine, this casual waterfront restaurant with indoor and outdoor tables serves a diverse menu, from burgers to lobster. ⊠ *15 Sea St.,* ☎ *207/326– 9045. MC, V. Closed Columbus Day–May.*

$$–$$$ ✕▣ **Manor Inn.** Bordering a 95-acre conservation forest with trails leading to the bay, this 1895 English manor–style inn provides a quiet retreat. Yoga classes are held in a fully equipped studio. Rooms are individually decorated, and four have fireplaces. The dining room ($$–$$$), which specializes in regional cuisine, is on the front porch and overlooks the expansive lawn and side gardens. The pub serves lighter fare. ⊠ *15 Manor Dr., off Battle Ave., 04421,* ☎ *207/326–4861 or 877/626–6746,* ℻ *207/326–0891,* 🕸 *www.manor-inn.com. 10 rooms, 2 suites. Restaurant, pub, some pets allowed (fee); no air-conditioning in some rooms, no room TVs, no-smoking rooms. AE, DC, MC, V. BP.*

$$ ✕▣ **Castine Inn.** Upholstered easy chairs and fine prints and paintings
★ adorn this inn's airy and simply decorated rooms. The well-respected dining room ($$$–$$$$; closed Tues.), decorated with a wraparound mural of Castine, is open to the public for breakfast and dinner; the creative menu includes entrées such as oil-poached salmon. After dinner, unwind in the snug, English-style pub just off the lobby. ⊠ *33 Main St. (Box 41, 04421),* ☎ *207/326–4365,* ℻ *207/326–4570,* 🕸 *www. castineinn.com. 15 rooms, 4 suites. Restaurant, sauna, pub; no air- conditioning, no room phones, no room TVs, no kids under 8, no smoking. MC, V. Closed Nov.–late Apr. BP.*

Outdoor Activities and Sports

Castine Kayak Adventures (⊠ Dennett's Wharf, ☎ 207/326–9045) operates tours with a registered Maine guide. The **Steam Launch *Laurie Ellen*** (⊠ Dennett's Wharf, ☎ 207/326–9045 or 207/266–2841), the only wood-fired, steam-powered, USCG-inspected passenger steam launch in the country, conducts cruises around Castine Harbor and up the Bagaduce River.

Shopping

H.O.M.E. (⊠ U.S. 1, Orland, ☎ 207/469–7961) is a cooperative crafts village with a crafts and pottery shop, weaving shop, flea market, market stand, and woodworking shop. **Leila Day Antiques** (⊠ 53 Main St., ☎ 207/326–8786) specializes in antiques, quilts, folk art, and nautical accessories. **McGrath-Dunham Gallery** (⊠ 9 Main St., ☎ 207/ 326–9175) carries paintings, sculpture, original prints, and pottery.

Blue Hill

30 *19 mi east of Castine.*

Snugged between 943-ft Blue Hill Mountain and Blue Hill Bay, Blue Hill has a dramatic perch over the harbor that's popular with sailors and sea-kayakers. Originally know, for its granite quarries, copper mining, and shipbuilding, today the town flourishes with pottery and artisans. You'll find a plethora of galleries, small shops and studios, as well as bookstores and antiques shops. The Blue Hill Fair, held Labor Day weekend, is a traditional country fair with agricultural exhibits, food, and entertainment. It is renowned for its pottery and is a good spot for shopping and gallery hopping.

Jonathan Fisher was the first settled minister of Blue Hill. The **Parson Fisher House,** which he built from 1814 to 1820, provides a fascinating look at his many accomplishments and talents, which included writing and illustrating books and poetry, farming, painting, building furniture, and making a camera obscura. Also on view is a wooden clock he crafted while a student at Harvard; the face holds messages about time written in English, Greek, Latin, Hebrew, and French. ⊠ *Rtes. 15/176,* ☎ *no phone.* ⌸ *$3.* ☉ *July–mid-Sept., Mon.–Sat. 2–5.*

Dining and Lodging

$$$ ✕ **Arborvine.** Antiques, fireplaces, hardwood floors covered with Asian Oriental rugs, and candlelight set an inviting tone in each of the four dining rooms in this renovated, Cape Cod–style house. The menu emphasizes fresh native fish in season as well as entrées such as noisettes of lamb chasseur. A take-out lunch is available at the adjacent Moveable Feasts deli. ⊠ *Main St.,* ☎ *207/374–2119. MC, V. Closed Mon.– Tues. No lunch.*

$$$–$$$$ ⊞ **Blue Hill Inn.** Rambling and antiques-filled, this 1830 inn is a com-
★ forting place to relax after exploring nearby shops and galleries. Original pumpkin pine and painted floors set the tone for the mix of Empire and early Victorian pieces that fill the two parlors and guest rooms; five rooms have fireplaces. The Cape House Suite, with full kitchen and cable TV, is open all year. ⊠ *40 Union St. (Box 403, 04614),* ☎ *207/374–2844 or 800/826–7415,* ᶠᴬˣ *207/374–2829,* ᵂᴱᴮ *www. bluehillinn.com. 11 rooms, 1 suite. Internet; no air-conditioning in some rooms, no room phones, no room TVs, no kids, no smoking. AE, MC, V. Closed Nov.–mid-May. BP.*

$$$–$$$$ ⊞ **Oakland House.** An inn, dining hall, and cottages are tucked among the towering pines at this sprawling oceanfront property. Owner Jim Littlefield is a fourth-generation innkeeper. The Shore Oaks seaside inn, built in 1907 in the Arts and Crafts style, retains an elegant turn-of-the-20th-century ambience. Cottages, most with kitchenettes and fireplaces, are rustic but fully equipped. The inn has ½ mi of ocean shorefront on Eggemoggin Reach as well as a lake beach. ⊠ *435 Herrick Rd., Brooksville 04617,* ☎ *207/359–8521 or 800/359–7352,* ᶠᴬˣ *207/359–9865,* ᵂᴱᴮ *www.oaklandhouse.com. 10 rooms, 7 with bath; 15 cottages. Dining room, some microwaves, lake, hiking, beaches, boating, recreation room, playground; no air-conditioning, no phones in some rooms, no TVs in some rooms, no-smoking rooms. MC, V. MAP.*

Nightlife and the Arts

Kneisel Hall Chamber Music Festival (⊠ Kneisel Hall, Rte. 15, ☎ 207/ 374–2811) has concerts on Sunday and Friday in summer.

Outdoor Activities and Sports

Holbrook Island Sanctuary (⊠ off Cape Rosier Rd., Brooksville, ☎ 207/326–4012) has a gravel beach with splendid views, a picnic area, and hiking trails.

Shopping

Big Chicken Barn (⊠ U.S. 1, Ellsworth, ☎ 207/374–2715) has three floors filled with books, antiques, and collectibles. **Handworks Gallery** (⊠ Main St., ☎ 207/374–5613) carries unusual crafts, jewelry, and clothing. **Leighton Gallery** (⊠ Parker Point Rd., ☎ 207/374–5001) shows oil paintings, lithographs, watercolors, and other contemporary art in the gallery, and sculpture in its garden. **Mark Bell Pottery** (⊠ Rte. 15, ☎ 207/374–5881) has received national acclaim for his porcelain bowls, bottles, and vases.

North Country Textiles (⊠ Main St., ☎ 207/374–2715) specializes in fine woven shawls, place mats, throws, baby blankets, and pillows in subtle patterns and color schemes. **Rackliffe Pottery** (⊠ Rte. 172, ☎ 207/374–2297) is famous for its vivid blue pottery, including plates, tea and coffee sets, pitchers, casseroles, and canisters. **Rowantrees Pottery** (⊠ Union St., ☎ 207/374–5535) has an extensive selection of styles and patterns in dinnerware, tea sets, vases, and decorative items.

En Route   Scenic Route 15 south from Blue Hill passes through Brooksville and takes you over the graceful suspension bridge that crosses Eggemoggin Reach to Deer Isle. The turnout and picnic area at **Caterpillar Hill,** 1 mi south of the junction of Routes 15 and 175, commands a fabulous view of Penobscot Bay, hundreds of dark-green islands, and the Camden Hills across the bay.

Deer Isle Village

③ *16 mi south of Blue Hill.*

In Deer Isle Village, thick woods give way to tidal coves. Stacks of lobster traps populate the backyards of shingled houses, and dirt roads lead to summer cottages. The region is prized by craftsman and artists, and studios and galleries are plentiful.

Haystack Mountain School of Crafts attracts internationally renowned glassblowers, potters, sculptors, jewelers, blacksmiths, printmakers, and weavers to its summer institute. You can attend evening lectures or visit artists' studios (by appointment only). ⊠ *Rte. 15, south of Deer Isle Village (turn left at Gulf gas station and follow signs for 6 mi),* ☎ 207/ 348–2306. 🎟 *Free.* ☉ *June–Sept.*

Dining and Lodging

$$$$ ✕🏠 **Pilgrim's Inn.** A deep-red, four-story gambrel-roof house, this inn
 ★   dates from about 1793 and overlooks a mill pond and harbor in Deer Isle Village. Wing chairs and Oriental rugs fill the library; a downstairs taproom has a huge brick fireplace and pine furniture. Guest rooms are individually decorated. The dining room ($$$$; reservations essential; no lunch) is rustic yet elegant, with farm implements, French oil lamps, and tiny windows. The four-course menu changes nightly but might list rack of lamb or fresh seafood. ⊠ *20 Main. St. (Rte. 15A), 04627,* ☎ *207/348–6615 or 888/778–7505,* 🅵🅰🆇 *207/346–6615,* 🆆🅴🅱 *www. pilgrimsinn.com. 12 rooms, 3 seaside cottages. Restaurant, bicycles, some pets allowed; no air-conditioning, no in-room phones, no in-room TVs, no kids under 10 in inn, no smoking. AE, MC, V. Closed mid-Oct.–mid-May. BP, MAP.*

$$$–$$$$ ✕🏠 **Goose Cove Lodge.** A country lane leads to this spectacular oceanfront property, where cottages and suites are scattered in the woodlands and on the shore along a sandy beach. At low tide, you can cross a sandbar to a nature preserve. Units vary in size; all but three have fireplaces. Dinner at the restaurant ($$–$$$; reservations essential) is superb, and the contemporary American fare includes at least one vegetarian entrée. On Monday night in July and August, there's a lobster feast on the beach.

✉ *300 Goose Cove Rd. (Box 40, Sunset 04683),* ☎ *207/348–2508 or 800/728–1963,* FAX *207/348–2624,* WEB *www.goosecovelodge.com. 2 rooms, 7 suites, 13 cottages. 2 restaurants, hiking, beach, boating; no air-conditioning, no room phones, no room TVs, no smoking. D, MC, V. All but 3 units closed mid-Oct.–mid-May. BP.*

Shopping

Blue Heron Gallery & Studio (✉ Rte. 15, ☎ 207/348–6051) sells the work of the Haystack Mountain School of Crafts faculty. **Harbor Farm** (✉ 29 Little Deer Isle Rd., Little Deer Isle, ☎ 207/348–7737) carries wonderful products for the home, such as pottery, furniture, dinnerware, linens, and folk art. **Nervous Nellie's Jams and Jellies** (✉ 598 Sunshine Rd., ☎ 800/777–6825) sells jams and jellies and operates a café. The outdoor sculpture garden is a hit with kids. **Old Deer Isle Parish House Antiques** (✉ 7 Church St., ☎ 207/348–9964) is a place for poking around in jumbles of old kitchenware, glassware, books, and linens. **Turtle Gallery** (✉ 61 N. Deer Isle Rd., ☎ 207/348–9977) shows contemporary painting and sculpture.

Stonington

③② *7 mi south of Deer Isle.*

Stonington's isolation at the tip of the Deer Isle peninsula has helped it retain its fishing-village flavor. This is changing now, as boutiques and galleries open in summer now line its main thoroughfare. Still, Stonington remains a working port town—the principal activity is at the waterfront, where fishing boats arrive with the day's catch. At night, the town can be rowdy. The high, sloped island that rises beyond the archipelago known as Merchants Row is Isle au Haut, which contains a remote section of Acadia National Park; it's accessible by mail boat from Stonington.

The tiny **Deer Isle Granite Museum** documents Stonington's quarrying tradition. The museum's centerpiece is an 8- by 15-ft working model of quarrying operations on Crotch Island and the town of Stonington in 1900. ✉ *Main St.,* ☎ *207/367–6331.* 🎫 *Free.* ☉ *Memorial Day–Labor Day, Mon.–Sat. 10–5, Sun. 1–5.*

Dining and Lodging

$$–$$$ ✕ **Cafe Atlantic.** Whether you want ice cream, tasty boiled lobster, or a fancier meal, you'll find it at this harbor-front eatery. Country linens and antiques decorate the restaurant, which serves fresh seafood as well as chicken and steak. For lobster in the rough, head to the deck overhanging the water. ✉ *Main St.,* ☎ *207/367–6373. AE, D, MC, V. Closed Nov.–Apr.*

$$–$$$ ✕ **Lily's.** Local artwork embellishes the three dining rooms in this old Victorian house. The bistro-style menu emphasizes fresh, seasonal foods and may include entrées such as fresh salmon with a sesame butter sauce or curried chicken. The desserts are legendary. ✉ *Rte. 15,* ☎ *207/367–5936. MC, V. Closed weekends.*

$$ 🏨 **Inn on the Harbor.** From the front, this inn composed of four 100-year-old Victorian buildings is as plain and unadorned as Stonington itself. But out back it opens up, with an expansive deck over the harbor—a pleasant spot for a morning breakfast. Rooms on the harbor side have views, and some have fireplaces and private decks. Those on the street side lack the views and can be noisy at night. ✉ *Main St. (Box 69, 04681),* ☎ *207/367–2420 or 800/942–2420,* FAX *207/367–5165,* WEB *www.innontheharbor.com. 14 rooms, 2 suites. Coffee shop, cable TV, in-room data ports; no air-conditioning, no kids under 12, no smoking inside. AE, D, MC, V. CP.*

The Arts
Stonington Opera House (⊠ School St., ☎ 207/367–2788) hosts live theater, music, and dance events.

Outdoor Activities and Sports
The registered Maine guides of **Granite Island Guide Service** (☎ 207/367–2788) lead kayaking and canoe trips. **Old Quarry** (☎ 207/367–8977, WEB www.oldquarry.com) operates a charter and boat-taxi service; rents canoes, kayaks, and bicycles; and conducts guided kayak trips. Call for directions.

Shopping
The **Clown** (⊠ Main St., ☎ 207/367–6348) has fine art, antiques, a good wine selection, and specialty foods. **Dockside Books & Gifts** (⊠ W. Main St., ☎ 207/367–2652), on the harbor front, stocks an eclectic selection of books, crafts, and gifts. **Eastern Bay Gallery** (⊠ Main St., ☎ 207/367–6368) carries contemporary Maine crafts; summer exhibits highlight the works of specific artists. **Firebird Gallery** (⊠ W. Main St., ☎ 207/367–0955) sells fine contemporary crafts.

Isle au Haut

㉝ *14 mi south of Stonington.*

Isle au Haut thrusts its steeply ridged back out of the sea south of Stonington. Accessible only by passenger mail boat (☎ 207/367–5193), the island is worth visiting for the ferry ride itself, a half-hour cruise amid the tiny islands of Merchants Row, where you might see terns, guillemots, and harbor seals.

More than half the island is part of **Acadia National Park**: 17½ mi of trails extend through quiet spruce and birch woods, along beaches and seaside cliffs, and over the spine of the central mountain ridge. (For more information on the park, *see* Bar Harbor *and* Acadia National Park.) From mid-June to mid-September, the mail boat docks at **Duck Harbor** within the park. The small campground here, with five lean-tos, is open from mid-May to mid-October and fills up quickly. Reservations, which are essential, can be made after April 1 by writing to Acadia National Park (⊠ Box 177, Bar Harbor 04609).

Lodging
$$$$ 🏨 **The Keeper's House.** Thick spruce forest surrounds this converted lighthouse keeper's house on a rock ledge. There is no electricity, but everyone receives a flashlight upon registering; you dine by candlelight and oil chandelier on seafood or chicken and read in the evening by kerosene lantern. Trails link the inn with Acadia National Park's Isle au Haut trail network, and you can walk to the village. The spacious rooms contain simple, painted-wood furniture and local crafts. A separate cottage, the Oil House, has no indoor plumbing. ⊠ *Lighthouse Rd. (Box 26, 04645),* ☎ *207/367–2261,* WEB *www.keepershouse.com. 4 rooms without bath, 1 cottage. Dock, bicycles; no air-conditioning, no room phones, no room TVs. No credit cards. Closed Nov.–Apr. FAP.*

Penobscot Bay A to Z

To research prices, get advice from other travelers, and book travel arrangements, visit www.fodors.com.

BIKE TRAVEL
Like many parts of Maine, the roads in this region are narrow, winding and often without shoulders. As in most places on the Maine Coast, it's smart to stay off heavily traveled Route 1. Experienced cyclers should try the back roads around Camden to Belfast or explore

the Blue Hill Peninsula region. Islesboro, Vinalhaven, and North Haven islands are popular day trips for cyclists, and traffic is light on both. You can take bicycles on the ferries at an extra fee. Be forewarned that island residents expect cyclists to obey the rules of the road.

➤ BIKE INFORMATION: **Brown Dog Bikes** (✉ 46 Elm. St., Camden, ☎ 207/236–6664, WEB www.browndogbike.com). **Maine Sport Outfitters** (✉ Rte. 1, Rockport, ☎ 207/236–7120 or 888/236–8797, WEB www.mainesport.com). **Old Quarry** (✉ R.R. 1, Box 700, Stonington, ☎ 207/367–8977, WEB www.oldquarry.com).

CAR TRAVEL

U.S. 1 follows the west coast of Penobscot Bay, linking Rockland, Rockport, Camden, Belfast, and Searsport. On the east side of the bay, Route 175 (south from U.S. 1) takes you to Route 166A (for Castine) and Route 15 (for Blue Hill, Deer Isle, and Stonington). A car is essential for exploring the bay area.

EMERGENCIES

➤ HOSPITALS: **Blue Hill Memorial Hospital** (✉ Water St., Blue Hill, ☎ 207/374–2836). **Island Medical Center** (✉ Airport Rd., Stonington, ☎ 207/367–2311). **Penobscot Bay Medical Center** (✉ U.S. 1, Rockport, ☎ 207/596–8000). **Waldo County General Hospital** (✉ 56 Northport Ave., Belfast, ☎ 207/338–2500).

LODGING

Camden Accommodations lists rental cottages and camps from Friendship to Searsport. For rentals on Monhegan Island, call Shining Sails. Coastal Cottage Rental Co. and Peninsula Property Rentals list properties on the Blue Hill Peninsula. For rentals in Stonington, try Island Vacation Rentals.

➤ LODGING: **Camden Accommodations** (✉ 43 Elm St., Camden 04614, ☎ 207/236–6090 or 800/344–4830, WEB www.camdenac.com). **Coastal Cottage Rental Company** (✉ Box 835, Blue Hill 04575, ☎ 207/374–3500, WEB www.vacationcottages.com). **Island Vacation Rentals** (✉ Box 446, Stonington 04681, ☎ 207/367–5095). **Peninsula Property Rentals** (✉ Box 611, Blue Hill 04614, ☎ 207/374–2428). **Shining Sails** (✉ Box 346, Monhegan 044852, ☎ 207/596–0041, WEB www.shiningsails.com).

MEDIA

Daily newspapers serving the region include the *Bangor Daily News,* published Monday–Friday; the *Portland Press Herald,* published Monday–Saturday; and the *Maine Sunday Telegram,* published on Sunday. The *Courier Gazette* (Rockland) is published thrice weekly.

WMEH 90.0 is the local National Public Radio affiliate. WCSH, channel 6, or WLBZ, channel 2, is the NBC affiliate. WMTW, channel 8, or WVII, channel 7, is the ABC affiliate. WGME, channel 13, or WABI, channel 5, is the CBS affiliate. WCBB, channel 10, or WMEB, channel 12, is the Maine Public Broadcasting affiliate.

OUTDOOR ACTIVITIES AND SPORTS
BOATING

For boat rentals, *see* individual listings by town. The Maine Windjammer Association represents 13 windjammers offering multiday sails along the Maine Coast. The Maine Professional Guides Association represents kayaking guides.

➤ CONTACTS: **Maine Windjammer Association** (✉ Box 1144, Blue Hill 04614, ☎ 800/807–9463, WEB www.sailmainecoast.com). **Maine Professional Guides Association** (✉ Box 847, Augusta 04332, ☎ 207/549–5631, WEB www.maineguides.org).

VISITOR INFORMATION
➤ CONTACTS: **Belfast Area Chamber of Commerce** (✉ 1 Main St. [Box 58, Belfast 04915], ☎ 207/338–5900, WEB www.belfastmaine.org). **Blue Hill Peninsula Chamber of Commerce** (✉ Box 520, Blue Hill 04614, ☎ 207/374–3242, WEB www.bluehillmaine.com). **Castine Town Office** (✉ Emerson Hall, Court St., Castine 04421, ☎ 207/326–4502). **Deer Isle–Stonington Chamber of Commerce** (✉ Box 459, Stonington 04681, ☎ 207/348–6124, WEB www.deerislemaine.com). **Rockland–Thomaston Area Chamber of Commerce** (✉ Box 508, Harbor Park, Rockland 04841, ☎ 207/596–0376 or 800/562–2529, WEB www.midcoast.com/~rtacc). **Rockport-Camden-Lincolnville Chamber of Commerce** (✉ Public Landing, Box 919, Camden 04843, ☎ 207/236–4404 or 800/223–5459, WEB www.camdenme.org). **Waldo County Regional Chamber of Commerce** (✉ School St., Unity 04988, ☎ 207/948–5050 or 800/870–9934, WEB palermo.org/wccc).

BANGOR TO MOUNT DESERT ISLAND

Just over an hour from the coast, along the Penobscot River, Bangor anchors northern and eastern Maine. Its plethora of cultural and shopping spots and its convenient access, via Bangor National Airport, make it an ideal starting point for visits to Maine's Great North Woods and Acadia National Park. Acadia is the informal name for the area east of Penobscot Bay that includes Mount Desert Island (pronounced "dessert") as well as Blue Hill Bay and Frenchman Bay. Mount Desert, 13 mi across, is Maine's largest island, and it encompasses most of Acadia National Park, an astonishingly beautiful preserve with rocky cliffs, crashing surf, and serene mountains and ponds. Maine's number one tourist attraction, it draws more than 4 million visitors a year. The 40,000 acres of woods and mountains, lake and shore, footpaths, carriage roads, and hiking trails that make up the park extend to other islands and some of the mainland. Outside the park, on Mount Desert's eastern shore, Bar Harbor has become a busy tourist town. Less commercial and congested are the smaller island towns, such as Southwest Harbor and Northeast Harbor, and the outlying islands.

Bangor

❸❹ *133 mi northeast of Portland, 46 mi north of Bar Harbor.*

Bangor is Maine's second largest city and the unofficial capital of northern Maine. The city rose to prominence in the 19th century, when its location on the Penobscot River and proximity to the North Woods helped it become the largest lumber port in the world. A 31-ft-tall statue honoring legendary lumberman Paul Bunyan stands in front of the Bangor Auditorium. Today the river is the focus of Bangor's economic redevelopment. Through 2004, the **National Folk Festival,** a free celebration of traditional arts, will take place in the revitalized riverfront and downtown. ✉ ☎ *800/916–6673,* WEB *www.nationalfolkfestival.com.* ✆ *Free.*

☪ The **Maine Discovery Museum,** opened in 2001, is the largest children's museum in the state. It has three floors of interactive and hands-on exhibits. Kids can explore Maine's ecosystem in Nature Trails, travel to foreign countries in Passport to the World, and walk through Maine's literary classics in Booktown, among other displays. ✉ *74 Main St.,* ☎ *207/262–7200,* WEB *www.mainediscoverymuseum.org.* ✆ *$5.50.* ☺ *Tues.–Thurs. and Sat. 9:30–5, Fri. 9:30–8, Sun. 11–5.*

Trained docents lead tours through the beautifully restored **Thomas A. Hill House,** an 1836 Greek Revival home listed on the National Reg-

ister of Historic Places. ✉ *159 Union St.,* ☎ *207/942–5766.* ✍ *$5.*
🕐 *June–Sept., Tues.–Sat. noon–4; Oct.–Dec., weekdays noon–4.*

The **Cole Land Transportation Museum** chronicles the history of transportation in Maine through historical photographs and more than 200 vehicles. ✉ *405 Perry Rd.,* ☎ *207/990–3600,* WEB *www.colemuseum.org.* ✍ *$5.* 🕐 *May–mid-Nov., daily 9–5.*

Dining and Lodging

$–$$$$ ✗ **Ichiban.** A calming minimalistic interior, sushi bar, and traditional fare have earned this restaurant a dedicated local following. ✉ *226 3rd St., at Union St.,* ☎ *207/262–9308. MC, V. No lunch Sun.*

$$–$$$ ✗ **J. B. Parker's.** The extensive menu here serves everything from grilled polenta with a trio of sauces for vegetarians to veal oscar with lobster, for those who can't decide between meat or fish. White-draped tables and deep red chairs fill the dining areas, local artwork covers the walls, and jazz or classical music is performed live on weekends. ✉ *167 Center St.,* ☎ *207/947–0167. MC, V. Closed Sun. No lunch Sat.*

$$–$$$ ✗ **Thistle's.** Paintings by local artists adorn the walls in this bright storefront restaurant. The diverse menu includes entrées such as Argentinian steak with chimichurri sauce, pickled ginger salmon picatta, and roast duckling. Musicians often perform during dinner. ✉ *175 Exchange St.,* ☎ *207/945–5480. MC, V. Closed Sun.*

$$–$$$$ 🏨 **The Lucerne Inn.** Conveniently located midway between Bangor and Ellsworth, a good dining room, and views over Phillips Lake make this country inn a pleasant stop. Every room has a gas fireplace and whirlpool, and most have lake views. ✉ *Rte. 1A (R.R. 3, Box 540, Dedham 04429),* ☎ *207/843–5123 or 900/325–5123,* FAX *207/843–6138,* WEB *www.lucernneinn.com. 21 rooms, 4 suites. Restaurant, cable TV, pool, golf privileges, lounge, meeting rooms; no-smoking rooms. MC, V. CP.*

$$–$$$ 🏨 **The Phenix Inn.** Inside a renovated 1873 National Historic Register property in downtown Bangor, this inn has comfortable but plain guest rooms, some of which overlook the Kenduskeag River. ✉ *20 Broad St., 04401,* ☎ *207/947–0411,* FAX *207/947–0255,* WEB *www.phenixinn.com. 29 rooms, 2 suites, 1 apartment. In-room data ports, cable TV, gym, some pets allowed; no-smoking rooms. AE, D, DC, MC, V. CP.*

The Arts

The **Bangor Symphony Orchestra** (✉ 44 Central St., ☎ 207/942–5555 or 800/639–3221) performs at the Bangor Opera House, from September to April. The **Penobscot Theatre Company** (✉ 183 Main St., ☎ 207/942–3333) stages live classic and contemporary plays from October to May. From mid-July to mid-August, it hosts the **Maine Shakespeare Festival** on the riverfront.

Ellsworth

㉟ *140 mi northeast of Portland, 28 mi south of Bangor.*

Ellsworth, the shire town of Hancock county, clogs with traffic during the summer months. Route 1 passes through an inviting downtown lined with shops and a strip of shopping plazas and factory outlets, including L. L. Bean, between downtown and where Route 3 splits to Mount Desert.

At the 130-acre **Stanwood Homestead Museum and Bird Sanctuary** you can hike its trails and visit the 1850 Stanwood House Museum, a Cape Cod–style house. Cordelia Stanwood, born in 1856, was one of Maine's earliest ornithologists. ✉ *Rte. 3,* ☎ *207/667–8460.* ✍ *Free; donations accepted.* 🕐 *Trails daily sunrise–sunset; museum mid-May–mid-Oct., daily 10–4.*

Between 1824 and 1828, Col. John Black built **Woodlawn,** an elegant Georgian mansion. Inside are an especially fine elliptical flying staircase and period artifacts from the three generations of the Black family who lived here. ⊠ *Rte. 172,* ☎ *207/667–8671.* ⊡ *$5.* ⊙ *June–mid-Oct., Mon.–Sat. 10–4:30.*

ⓒ The **Acadia Zoo** shelters about 45 species of wild and domestic animals, including reindeer, wolves, monkeys, and a moose in its pastures, streams, and woods. A converted barn serves as a rain-forest habitat for monkeys, birds, reptiles, and other Amazon creatures. ⊠ *446 Bar Harbor Rd. (Rte. 3), Trenton,* ☎ *207/667–3244.* ⊡ *$7.50.* ⊙ *May–Dec., daily 9:30–dusk.*

Outdoor Activities and Sports
BICYCLING

Bar Harbor Bicycle Shop (⊠ 193 Main St., Ellsworth, ☎ 207/667–6886, WEB www.barharborbike.com) rents both recreational and high-performance bikes by the half or full day.

Bar Harbor

③⑥ *160 mi northeast of Portland, 22 mi southeast of Ellsworth on Rte. 3.*

An upper-class resort town in the 19th century, Bar Harbor now serves visitors to Acadia National Park with inns, motels, and restaurants. Most of its grand mansions were destroyed in a fire that devastated the island in 1947, but many surviving estates have been converted into inns and restaurants. Motels abound, yet the town retains the beauty of a commanding location on Frenchman Bay. Shops, restaurants, and hotels are clustered along Main, Mount Desert, and Cottage streets. Take a stroll down West Street, a National Historic District, where you can see some of the grand cottages that survived the fire.

The **Bar Harbor Historical Society Museum** displays photographs of Bar Harbor from the days when it catered to the very rich. Other exhibits document the fire of 1947. ⊠ *33 Ledgelawn Ave.,* ☎ *207/288–3807 or 207/288–0000.* ⊡ *Free.* ⊙ *June–Oct., Mon.–Sat. 1–4 or by appointment.*

★ The **Abbe Museum,** with its collection of Native American artifacts, opened a new downtown museum in 2001. The museum's collections contain 50,000 objects spanning 10,000 years of Native American history, archaeology, and culture in Maine; many are on display in both permanent and changing exhibitions. A glass-walled archaeological laboratory allows you to observe staff and volunteers working with artifacts found during the museum's scientific excavations. The 1893 building, the former home of the YMCA, is eligible for the National Register of Historic Places. Its facade is an example of the eclectic Shingle Style often used for coastal summer homes at the turn of the 20th century. ⊠ *26 Mount Desert St.,* ☎ *207/288–3519,* WEB *www.abbemuseum.org.* ⊡ *$4.50.* ⊙ *Memorial Day–mid-Oct., Sun.–Wed. 10–5, Thurs.–Sat. 10–9; mid-Oct.–Memorial Day, Thurs.–Sun. 10–5.*

ⓒ The small **Natural History Museum** at the College of the Atlantic has wildlife exhibits, a hands-on discovery room, interpretive programs, and a self-guided nature trail. ⊠ *Rte. 3,* ☎ *207/288–5015.* ⊡ *$3.50.* ⊙ *Mid-June–Labor Day, Mon.–Sat. 10–5; Labor Day–mid-June, Thurs.–Fri. and Sun. 1–4, Sat. 10–4.*

Dining and Lodging
$$$$ ✕ **George's.** Candles, flowers, and linens grace the tables, and art fills
★   the walls of the four small dining rooms in this old house. Try the char-grilled swordfish with Mediterranean salsa over couscous or lobster

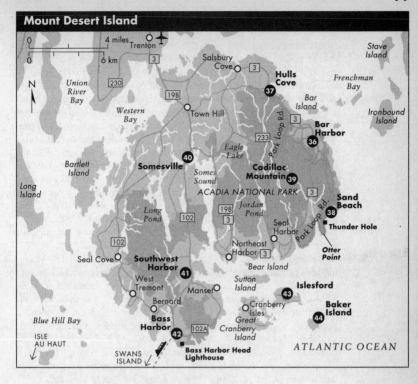

Mount Desert Island

strudel with chanterelle ragout from the prix-fixe menu. Jazz musicians perform nightly in peak season. ✉ *7 Stephen's La.,* ☎ *207/288–4505. AE, D, DC, MC, V. Closed Nov.–mid-June. No lunch.*

$$–$$$$ ✕ **Havana.** Pumpkin-color walls, soft jazz, wood floors, and cloth-cov-
★ ered tables set the tone at this storefront restaurant on the fringe of downtown Bar Harbor. The Latin-influenced menu emphasizes local natural and organic ingredients and changes weekly. The menu may include crab-and-roasted-corn cakes or grilled swordfish, marinated in ginger and lime and finished with a scallion vinaigrette. ✉ *318 Main St.,* ☎ *207/288–2822. Reservations essential. MC, V. Closed Sun.–Tues. late Oct.–mid-May.*

$$$ ✕ **The Burning Tree.** Fresh is the key word at this casual restaurant just
★ outside town. The ever-changing menu emphasizes seafood and organic produce and chicken; entrées include pan-sautéed monkfish, Cajun lob-ster, crab au gratin, chicken pot roast, and two or three vegetarian choices. Local contemporary art adorns the walls in the two dining rooms and on the porch. ✉ *Rte. 3, Otter Creek,* ☎ *207/288–9331. D, MC, V. Closed Tues. and mid-Oct.–late May.*

$$$ ✕ **Mache.** It's the food that's bright at this small, dark bistro. The menu changes twice weekly but might include stew of braised fish and shell-fish with organic veggies or crisp rendered duck breast with spiced plum–enriched juice. ✉ *135 Cottage St.,* ☎ *207/388–0447. MC, V.*

$$–$$$ ✕ **Café This Way.** Jazz, unmatched tables and chairs, and a few couches provide a relaxing background for the creative, internationally in-spired menu at this restaurant tucked in a backstreet. You might begin with crab cakes with tequila-lime sauce and then move on to cashew-crusted chicken over sautéed greens with sesame-ginger aioli or per-haps Thai seafood pot. Save room for the homemade desserts. ✉ *14½ Mount Desert St.,* ☎ *207/288–4483. MC, V.*

$$ ✕ **Thrumcap.** Dark wood and gleaming hardwood floors exude elegance at this casual café and wine bar. You can mix and match plates from three price groupings. Menu choices include shrimp and boursin ravioli, grilled marinated quail with plum sauce, and coconut-fried lobster with black bean and tropical-fruit salsa. ✉ *123 Cottage St.,* ☎ *207/288–3884. MC, V. Closed Sun. and Nov.–May.*

$$$–$$$$ ✕▥ **Bar Harbor Inn.** This genteel inn dates from the 1880s. Rooms are spread out over three buildings on nicely landscaped waterfront property, just a short walk from town. Most rooms have balconies, hot tubs, fireplaces, and great views. Rooms in the Oceanfront Lodge have private decks or patios overlooking the ocean, while those in the Newport Lodge, behind it, are more simply furnished and smaller. The formal waterfront Reading Room ($$$–$$$$) serves mostly Continental fare but has such Maine specialties as lobster pie and a scrumptious Indian pudding. ✉ *Newport Dr., 04609,* ☎ *207/288–3351 or 800/248–3351,* FAX *207/288–5296,* WEB *www.barharborinn.com. 138 rooms, 15 suites. 2 restaurants, cable TV, pool, gym, business services, meeting room; no-smoking rooms. AE, D, DC, MC, V. CP.*

$$$$ ▥ **Balance Rock Inn.** This grand summer cottage built in 1903 commands a prime, secluded waterfront location but is only two blocks from downtown. Rooms are spacious and meticulously furnished with reproduction pieces—four-poster and canopy beds in guest rooms, crystal chandeliers and a grand piano in common rooms. Some rooms have fireplaces, saunas, steam rooms, or porches; service is thoughtful. ✉ *21 Albert Meadow, 04609,* ☎ *207/288–2610 or 800/753–0494,* FAX *207/288–5534,* WEB *www.barharborvacations.com. 13 rooms, 1 suite, 3 apartments. In-room data ports, cable TV, in-room VCRs, pool, gym, bar, concierge. AE, D, MC, V. Closed late Oct.–early May. BP.*

$$$–$$$$ ▥ **Nannau.** For a taste of 19th-century Bar Harbor, stay at this seaside 1904 estate, a National Register property secluded among towering evergreens just 1 mi from downtown Bar Harbor. The shingle-style house is comfortably furnished with period pieces and fabrics and wallpapers. All rooms have ocean views; two have fireplaces. The 4-acre property borders Compass Harbor and a section of Acadia National Park. ✉ *396 Lower Main St. (Box 710, 04609),* ☎ *207/288–5575,* WEB *www. nannau.com. 3 rooms, 1 suite. No air-conditioning, no in-room TVs, no in-room phones, no smoking. MC, V. Closed Nov.–June. BP.*

$$$–$$$$ ▥ **Sunset on West.** Contemporary artwork fills this 1960 cottage over-
★   looking Bar Island and Frenchman's Bay. Some of the carefully appointed rooms have porches, fireplaces, and whirlpool tubs; most have water views. ✉ *115 West St., 04609,* ☎ *207/288–4242 or 877/406–4242,* FAX *207/288–4545,* WEB *www.sunsetonwest.com. 2 rooms, 2 suites. Cable TV, in-room VCRs; no kids under 16. MC, V. BP.*

$$$–$$$$ ▥ **Ullikana.** Inside the stucco-and-timber walls of this traditional
★   Tudor cottage, the interior juxtaposes antiques with contemporary country pieces, vibrant color with French country wallpapers, and abstract art with folk creations. The combination not only works—it shines. Rooms are large, many have fireplaces, and some have decks. Breakfast is an elaborate multicourse affair. The refurbished Yellow House across the drive has six additional rooms decorated in traditional Old Bar Harbor style. ✉ *16 The Field, 04609,* ☎ *207/288–9552,* FAX *207/288–3682,* WEB *www.ullikana.com. 16 rooms. No air-conditioning in some rooms, no kids, no smoking. MC, V. Closed Nov.–May. BP.*

$$ ▥ **Cromwell Harbor Motel.** Less than 1 mi from downtown Bar Harbor is this clean and pleasant motel set amidst pretty gardens. You can walk to a quiet section of Acadia National Park. ✉ *359 Main St., 04069,* ☎ *207/288–3201 or 800/544–3201,* WEB *www.cromwellharbor.com. 24 rooms. Cable TV, some refrigerators, some microwaves, pool; no-smoking rooms. MC, V.*

$$ ⊡ **Seacroft Inn.** It's an easy walk to town or the Shore Path from this rambling multigabled inn, which is a good choice for families. One room has a fireplace, another a kitchen, yet another a private deck. A breakfast basket is delivered to your room each morning. ⊠ *18 Albert Meadow, 04609,* ☎ *207/288–4669 or 800/824–9694. 3 rooms, 1 with bath; 1 suite; 1 studio; 1 efficiency. Cable TV, microwaves, refrigerators. MC, V. CP.*

Nightlife and the Arts

For dancing, try **Carmen Verandah** (⊠ 119 Main St., upstairs, ☎ 207/288–2766); the venue also hosts live blues, jazz, reggae, rock, and pop bands. The art deco–style **Criterion Theater** (⊠ 35 Cottage St., ☎ 207/288–3441) stages concerts, movies, and theatrical performances. **Geddy's Pub** (⊠ 19 Main St., ☎ 207/288–5077) has live entertainment early in the evening followed by a DJ spinning discs. At the **Lompoc Cafe & Brewpub** (⊠ 30 Rodick St., ☎ 207/288–9513) you can relax in a garden setting and play a game of boccie. Comfortable chairs, pizza, and beer make the viewing easy at **Reel Pizza Cinerama** (⊠ 33-B Kennebec Pl., ☎ 207/288–3811).

Arcady Music Festival (☎ 207/288–3151) schedules concerts (primarily classical) at locations around Mount Desert Island and at some off-island sites, year-round. **Bar Harbor Music Festival** (⊠ 59 Cottage St., ☎ 207/288–5744) arranges jazz, chamber music, string-orchestra, and pop concerts by young professionals from July to early August.

Outdoor Activities and Sports

BIKING

Acadia Bike & Canoe (⊠ 48 Cottage St., ☎ 207/288–9605 or 800/526–8615) rents and sells mountain bikes. **Bar Harbor Bicycle Shop** (⊠ 141 Cottage St., ☎ 207/288–3886 or 800/824–2453) rents both recreational and high-performance bikes by the half or full day.

BOATING

Acadia Bike & Canoe rents canoes and sea kayaks. **National Park Sea Kayak Tours** (⊠ 39 Cottage St., ☎ 207/288–0342 or 800/347–0940) leads guided kayak tours. **Coastal Kayaking Tours** (⊠ 48 Cottage St., ☎ 207/288–9605 or 800/526–8615) conducts tours led by registered Maine guides. The four-mast schooner **Margaret Todd** (⊠ Bar Harbor Inn Pier, ☎ 207/288–4585) operates 1½- to 2-hour tours daily between mid-May and October.

STATE PARK

On Frenchman Bay but off Mount Desert Island, the 55-acre **Lamoine State Park** (⊠ Rte. 184, Lamoine, ☎ 207/667–4778) has a boat-launching ramp, a fishing pier, a children's playground, and a 61-site campground that's open mid-May–mid-October.

WHALE-WATCHING

Acadian Whale Watcher (⊠ Golden Anchor Pier, 52 West St., ☎ 207/288–9794 or 800/421–3307) runs 3½-hour whale-watching cruises from June to mid-October. **Bar Harbor Whale Watch Co.** (⊠ 1 West St., ☎ 207/288–3322 or 800/508–1499) operates the catamaran *Friendship V,* for whale-watching, and the *Katherine,* for lobster fishing and seal watching.

Shopping

Bar Harbor in summer is prime territory for browsing for gifts, T-shirts, and novelty items. For bargains, head for the outlets that line Route 3 in Ellsworth, which have good discounts on shoes, sportswear, cookware, and more.

The **Alone Moose–Fine Crafts** (⊠ 78 West St., ☎ 207/288–4229) has art glass and works in clay, pottery, wood, and fiberglass. Pick up a treat for your pet at **Bark Harbor** (⊠ 200 Main St., ☎ 207/288–0404), a specialty shop for pet owners. **Ben and Bill's Chocolate Emporium** (⊠ 66 Main St., ☎ 207/288–3281) is a chocolate lover's nirvana; the adventurous should try the lobster ice cream. **Birdsnest Gallery** (⊠ 12 Mount Desert St., ☎ 207/288–4054) sells fine art, paintings, and sculpture. The **Eclipse Gallery** (⊠ 12 Mount Desert St., ☎ 207/288–9048) carries handblown glass, ceramics, art photography, and wood furniture. **Island Artisans** (⊠ 99 Main St., ☎ 207/288–4214) sells basketry, pottery, fiber work, and jewelry created by Maine-based artisans. **Songs of the Sea** (⊠ 47 West St., ☎ 207/288–5653) specializes in folk music and sells handcrafted Irish, Scottish, and world instruments.

Acadia National Park

4 mi northwest of Bar Harbor (to Hulls Cove).

There is no one Acadia. The park holds some of the most spectacular and varied scenery on the eastern seaboard: a rugged coastline of surf-pounded granite and an interior graced by sculpted mountains, quiet ponds, and lush deciduous forests. Cadillac Mountain, the highest point of land on the eastern coast, dominates the park. Although it's rugged, Acadia National Park also has graceful stone bridges, horse-drawn carriages, and the elegant Jordan Point Tea House. The 27-mi Park Loop Road provides an excellent introduction, yet to truly appreciate the park you must get off the main road and experience it by walking, biking, or taking a carriage ride on the carriage trails, by hiking or perhaps sea kayaking. If you get off the beaten path, you'll find places in the park that you can have practically to yourself, despite the millions of visitors who descend in summer.

★ ③⑦ The popular **Hulls Cove** approach to Acadia National Park, northwest of Bar Harbor on Route 3, brings you to the start of the **Park Loop Road.** Even though it is often clogged with traffic in summer, the road provides the best introduction to the park. You can drive it in an hour, but allow at least half a day or more to explore the many sites along the route. At the start of the loop, the visitor center shows a free 15-minute orientation film. Acadia Rangers lead nature walks, children's programs, mountain hikes, photography programs, and evening talks. A schedule of programs is available here. You can also pick up the *Acadia Beaver Log* (the park's free newspaper detailing guided hikes and other ranger-led programs), books, maps of hiking trails and carriage roads, the schedule for naturalist-led tours, and cassettes for drive-it-yourself tours. Traveling south on the Park Loop Road, you'll reach a small ticket booth where you pay the $10-per-vehicle entrance fee, good for seven consecutive days. ⊠ *Visitor center, Park Loop Rd. off Rte. 3,* ☎ *207/288–3338,* WEB *www.nps.gov/acad.* ☉ *Park daily. Visitor center mid-June–Aug., daily 8–6; mid-Apr.–mid-June and Sept.–Oct., daily 8–4:30.*

③⑧ **Sand Beach** is a small stretch of pink sand backed by the mountains of Acadia and the odd lump of rock known as the Beehive. The **Ocean Trail,** which runs alongside the Park Loop Road from Sand Beach to the Otter Point parking area, is an easily accessible walk with some of the most awesome scenery in Maine: huge slabs of pink granite heaped at the ocean's edge, ocean views unobstructed to the horizon, and Thunder Hole, a natural seaside cave into which the ocean rushes and roars.

★ ③⑨ **Cadillac Mountain,** at 1,532 ft, is the highest point on the eastern seaboard. From the smooth, bald summit you have an awesome 360-

degree view of the ocean, islands, jagged coastline, and woods and lakes of Acadia and its surroundings. You can drive or hike to the summit.

The original **Abbé Museum** (a larger museum opened in downtown Bar Harbor in 2001) displays its collection of Maine's Native American history, including arrowheads, moccasins, tools, jewelry, and a well-documented collection of baskets. ☒ *Sieur de Monts Spring exit from Rte. 3 or Acadia National Park Loop Rd.,* ☎ *207/288–3519.* 🎫 *$2.* ☉ *July–Aug., daily 9–5; late May–June and Sept.–late Oct., daily 10–4.*

The **Wild Gardens of Acadia** present a miniature view of the plants that grow on Mount Desert Island. ☒ *Rte. 3 at the Sieur de Monts Spring exit,* ☎ *207/288–3400.* 🎫 *Free.*

Dining and Lodging

$$–$$$ ✕ **Jordan Pond House.** Come for tea and the oversize popovers with homemade strawberry jam and ice cream, a century-old tradition at this restaurant overlooking Jordan Pond. If you choose to sit on the terrace or lawn, be forewarned that bees are more than a nuisance. The menu has both lunch and dinner items, including lobster stew, but these get mixed reviews. ☒ *Park Loop Rd.,* ☎ *207/276–3316. AE, D, MC, V. Closed late Oct.–mid-May.*

$ ⚠ **Blackwoods and Seawall.** These two campgrounds with a total of 530 campsites, fill up quickly during the summer. Space at Seawall is a first-come, first-served basis, starting at 8 AM. Reservations for a May 1–October visit to Blackwoods can be made four months in advance. *Blackwoods:* ☒ *Rte. 3, Otter Creek,* ☎ *800/365–2267.* ☉ *Year-round. Seawall:* ☒ *Rte. 102A, Southwest Harbor,* ☎ *207/244–3600. Closed late Sept.–late May.*

Outdoor Activities and Sports

BIKING

The carriage roads that wind through the woods and fields of Acadia National Park are ideal for biking and jogging when the ground is dry and for cross-country skiing in winter. You can pick up trail maps at the Hulls Cove Visitor Center.

HIKING

Acadia National Park maintains nearly 200 mi of foot and carriage paths, from easy strolls along flatlands to rigorous climbs that involve ladders and hand holds on rock faces. Among the more rewarding hikes are the Precipice Trail to Champlain Mountain, the Great Head Loop, the Gorham Mountain Trail, and the path around Eagle Lake. The Hulls Cove Visitor Center has trail guides and maps and will help you match a trail with your interests and abilities.

Around Acadia

There's plenty to explore on Mount Desert Island beyond the 27-mi Park Loop Road. You can continue an auto tour of the island by heading west on Route 233 for the villages on Somes Sound, a true fjord—the only one on the East Coast—that almost bisects the island.

40 **Somesville,** the oldest settlement on the island (1621), is a carefully preserved New England village of white clapboard houses and churches, neat green lawns, and bits of blue water visible behind them.

41 **Southwest Harbor,** south from Somesville on Route 102, combines the salty character of a working port with the refinements of a summer resort community. From the town's Main Street (Route 102), turn left onto Clark Point Road to reach the harbor.

☾ **Mount Desert Oceanarium** has exhibits in two locations on the fishing and sea life of the Gulf of Maine, a live-seal program, a lobster hatchery, and hands-on exhibits such as a touch tank. ⊠ *Clark Point Rd., Southwest Harbor,* ☎ *207/244–7330;* ⊠ *Rte. 3, Thomas Bay, Bar Harbor,* ☎ *207/288–5005.* ☞ *Call for admission fees (combination tickets available).* ☉ *Mid-May–late Oct., Mon.–Sat. 9–5.*

Wendell Gilley Museum of Bird Carving showcases bird carvings by Gilley, has carving demonstrations and workshops and natural-history programs, and exhibits wildlife art. ⊠ *4 Herrick Rd., Southwest Harbor,* ☎ *207/244–7555,* WEB *www.acadia.net/gilley.* ☞ *$3.50.* ☉ *July–Aug., Tues.–Sun. 10–5; June and Sept.–Oct., Tues.–Sun. 10–4; May and Nov.–Dec., Fri.–Sun. 10–4.*

㊷ **Bass Harbor,** 4 mi south of Southwest Harbor (follow Route 102A when Route 102 forks), is a tiny lobstering village with cottages for rent, inns, a restaurant, and a gift shop. You can visit the **Bass Harbor Head lighthouse,** which clings to a cliff at the eastern entrance to Blue Hill Bay. It was built in 1858. Also here is the **Maine State Ferry Service**'s car-and-passenger ferry (☎ 207/244–3254), which travels to Swans Island and Frenchboro.

Dining and Lodging

$–$$$ ✕ **Beal's Lobster Pier.** You can watch lobstermen bring in their catch at this working lobster pound. Order lobster at one take-out window and fried foods, burgers, and dessert at another. ⊠ *End of Clark Point Rd., Southwest Harbor,* ☎ *207/244–3202, 207/244–7178, or 800/244–7178. AE, MC, V. Closed mid-Oct.–mid-May.*

$–$$ ✕ **Seaweed Café.** This unpretentious restaurant serves natural and organic seafood with an Asian touch. Entrées include sushi, sashimi, and noodle dishes. ⊠ *Rte. 102, Southwest Harbor,* ☎ *207/244–0572. Reservations essential. No credit cards. Closed Sun.–Tues. No lunch.*

$$$ ⌂ **Claremont Hotel.** Built in 1884 and operated continuously as an inn, the Claremont calls up memories of the long, leisurely vacations of days gone by. The inn commands a view of Somes Sound. Croquet is played on the lawn, and cocktails and lunch are served at the Boat House in summer. Rooms are simply—some would say sparsely—decorated; cottages are more rustic. The menu in the water-view dining room, open to the public for breakfast and dinner, changes weekly; reservations are essential, and a jacket is required for dinner. ⊠ *Off Clark Point Rd. (Box 137, Southwest Harbor 04679),* ☎ *207/244–5036 or 800/ 244–5036,* FAX *207/244–3512,* WEB *www.theclaremont.com. 30 rooms, 2 suites, 14 cottages. Restaurant, tennis court, dock, boating, bicycles, croquet; no air-conditioning, no phones in some rooms, no room TVs, no smoking. No credit cards. Hotel and restaurant closed mid-Oct.– mid-June; cottages closed Nov.–mid-May. BP, MAP.*

$$ ⌂ **Island House.** This sweet B&B on the quiet side of the island has four simple and bright rooms in the main house. The carriage-house suite comes complete with a sleeping loft and a kitchenette. ⊠ *121 Clark Point Rd. (Box 1006, Southwest Harbor 04679),* ☎ *207/244– 5180,* WEB *www.acadia.net/islandhouse. 4 rooms, 1 suite. No air-conditioning, no room phones, no room TVs, no kids under 5, no smoking. MC, V. BP.*

$–$$ ⌂ **Moorings Inn & Cottages.** Nothing is fancy here except the jaw-dropping view of Somes Sound. The main house dates to the late 18th century, its rooms decorated with antiques and country touches. The rooms in the attached motel wing lack the appointments of the main house but have sliding glass doors onto decks. The homey cottages have the most privacy and offer cooking facilities. Lookout Front has a fireplace, screened porch, and king-size bed. ⊠ *135 Shore Rd., Manset (Box 744, Southwest Harbor 04679),* ☎ *207/244–5523, 207/244–3210, or 800/596–5523,* WEB *www.mooringsinn.com. 13 rooms, 5 cottages,*

1 apartment. Some refrigerators, some microwaves, dock, bicycling, boating; no air-conditioning, no room phones, no room TVs. No credit cards. Closed mid-Oct.–mid-May. CP.

Outdoor Activities and Sports

BIKING

Southwest Cycle (⊠ Main St., Southwest Harbor, ☎ 207/244–5856) rents bicycles.

BOATING

Manset Yacht Service (⊠ Shore Rd., Manset, ☎ 207/244–4040) charters powerboats and sailboats. **Mansell Boat and Marine** (⊠ Rte. 102A, Manset, ☎ 207/244–5625) rents small powerboats and sailboats. **National Park Canoe and Kayak Rentals** (⊠ Pretty Marsh Rd., Somesville, at the head of Long Pond, ☎ 207/244–5854) rents canoes and kayaks. **Island Cruises** (⊠ Shore Rd., Bass Harbor, ☎ 207/244–5785) takes passengers on a 40-ft lobster boat through the islands of Blue Hill Bay.

Shopping

E. L. Higgins (⊠ Bernard Rd., off Rte. 102, Bernard, ☎ 207/244–3983) carries antique wicker, furniture, and glassware. **Marianne Clark Fine Antiques** (⊠ Main St., Southwest Harbor, ☎ 207/244–9247) sells formal and country furniture, American paintings, and accessories from the 18th and 19th centuries. **Port in a Storm Bookstore** (⊠ Main St., Somesville, ☎ 207/244–4114) stocks well-chosen inventory and is conducive to browsing, with soaring ceilings and comfy chairs.

Excursions to the Cranberry Isles

Off the southeast shore of Mount Desert Island at the entrance to Somes Sound, the five Cranberry Isles—Great Cranberry, Islesford (or Little Cranberry), Baker Island, Sutton Island, and Bear Island—escape the hubbub that engulfs Acadia National Park in summer. Sutton and Bear islands are privately owned. The **Beal & Bunker passenger ferry** (☎ 207/244–3575) serves Great Cranberry from Northeast Harbor. **Cranberry Cove Boating Company** (☎ 207/244–5882) serves Great Cranberry, Sutton, and Islesford from Southwest Harbor. Baker Island is reached by the summer cruise boats of the **Islesford Ferry Company** (☎ 207/276–3717) from Northeast Harbor.

㊸ Islesford comes closest to having a village: a collection of houses, a church, a fishermen's co-op, a market, and a post office near the ferry dock.

The **Islesford Historical Museum,** run by Acadia National Park, has displays of tools and documents relating to the island's history. ⊠ *Islesford,* ☎ *207/244–9224.* 🆓 *Free.* 🕙 *Mid-June–late Sept., daily 10–noon and 12:30–4:30.*

㊹ The 123-acre **Baker Island,** the most remote of the Cranberry Isles, looks almost black from a distance because of its thick spruce forest. The Islesford Ferry cruise boat from Northeast Harbor conducts a 4½-hour narrated tour, during which you are likely to see ospreys, harbor seals, and cormorants. Because Baker Island has no natural harbor, you take a fishing dory to get to shore.

Bangor to Mount Desert Island A to Z

To research prices, get advice from other travelers, and book travel arrangements, visit www.fodors.com.

BUS TRAVEL

The free Island Explorer shuttle services the entire island from mid-June through Labor Day. Concord Trailways operates shuttle service from Bangor airport to Bar Harbor with stops in Bangor and Ellsworth. Greyhound Bus Lines services Bangor. Vermont Transit services Bangor and Bar Harbor. Downeast Transportation operates buses from Ellsworth to various locations on Mount Desert, Bangor, the Schoodic Peninsula, and the Blue Hill Peninsula.

➤ Bus Information: **Concord Trailways** (☎ 207/942–8686 or 888/741–8686, WEB www.concordtrailways.com). **Downeast Transportation** (☎ 207/667–5796). **Greyhound Bus Lines** (☎ 800/231–2222, WEB www.greyhound.com). **Island Explorer** (☎ 207/667–5796). **Vermont Transit** (☎ 207/772–6587 or 800/451–3292, WEB www.vermonttransit.com).

CAR TRAVEL

Route 1A east connects Bangor to Route 1 in Ellsworth. Route 3 leads to Mount Desert Island. North of Bar Harbor, the scenic 27-mi Park Loop Road leaves Route 3 to circle the eastern quarter of Mount Desert Island, with one-way traffic from Sieur de Monts Spring to Seal Harbor and two-way traffic between Seal Harbor and Hulls Cove. Route 102, which serves the western half of Mount Desert, is reached from Route 3 just after it enters the island or from Route 233 west from Bar Harbor. All these island roads pass through the precincts of Acadia National Park.

EMERGENCIES

➤ Hospitals: **Eastern Maine Medical Center** (✉ 489 State St., Bangor, ☎ 207/973–8000). **Maine Coast Memorial Hospital** (✉ 50 Union St., Ellsworth, ☎ 207/667–5311). **Mount Desert Island Hospital** (✉ 10 Wayman La., Bar Harbor, ☎ 207/288–5081). **Southwest Harbor Medical Center** (✉ Herrick Rd., Southwest Harbor, ☎ 207/244–5513).

LODGING

Maine Island Properties lists private home rentals throughout the Acadia region. Mount Desert Properties specializes in private home rentals in the Mount Desert region. The Davis Agency has properties on the island as well as from Blue Hill to Hancock.

➤ Lodging: **The Davis Agency** (✉ 363 Main St., Southwest Harbor 04679, ☎ 207/244–3891), WEB www.daagy.com. **Maine Island Properties** (✉ Box 1025, Mount Desert 04660, ☎ 207/244–4348, WEB www.maineislandproperties.com). **Mount Desert Properties** (✉ Box 536, Bar Harbor 04609, ☎ 207/288–4523, WEB www.barharborvacationhome.com).

MEDIA

Daily newspapers serving the region include the *Bangor Daily News,* published Monday–Friday. Weekly papers include the *Bar Harbor Times, Ellsworth American,* and *Ellsworth Weekly.*

Community radio station WERU 89.9 FM in Blue Hill has eclectic programming. WMEH 90.0 is the local National Public Radio affiliate. WLBZ, channel 2, is the NBC affiliate. WVII, channel 7, is the ABC affiliate. WABI, channel 5, is the CBS affiliate. WMEB, channel 12, is the Maine Public Broadcasting affiliate.

OUTDOOR ACTIVITIES AND SPORTS
BOATING

For boat rentals, *see* listings by town. The Maine Professional Guides Association represents kayaking guides.
➤ Contact: **Maine Professional Guides Association** (✉ Box 847, Augusta 04332, ☎ 207/549–5631, WEB www.maineguides.org).

TOURS

Acadia National Park Tours operates a 2½-hour bus tour of Acadia National Park, narrated by a naturalist, from May to October, and 2½-hour narrated trolley tours. Bar Harbor Taxi and Tours conducts half-day historic and scenic tours of the area. Downeast Nature Tours leads personalized and small-group tours highlighting the island's flora and fauna.

Acadia Air, on Route 3 in Trenton, between Ellsworth and Bar Harbor at Hancock County Airport, rents aircraft and flies seven aerial sightseeing routes, from spring to fall. A Step Back in Time uses Victorian-costumed guides to lead walking tours that highlight the 1890s in Bar Harbor. Tours leave from 48 Cottage Street.

➤ CONTACTS: **A Step Back in Time** (☎ 207/288–9605). **Acadia Air** (☎ 207/667–5534). **Acadia National Park Tours** (☎ 207/288–3327). **Bar Harbor Taxi and Tours** (☎ 207/288–4020). **Downeast Nature Tours** (☎ 207/288–8128).

VISITOR INFORMATION

➤ CONTACTS: **Acadia National Park** (✉ Box 177, Bar Harbor 04609, ☎ 207/288–3338, WEB www.nps.gov/acad). **Bangor Convention and Visitors Bureau** (✉ 115 Main St., Bangor 04401, ☎ 207/947–5205 or 800/926–6673, WEB www.bangorcvb.org). **Bangor Region Chamber of Commerce** (✉ 519 Main St., Bangor 04401, ☎ 207/947–0307, WEB www.bangorregion.com). **Bar Harbor Chamber of Commerce** (✉ 93 Cottage St. [Box 158, Bar Harbor 04609], ☎ 207/288–3393, 207/288–5103, or 800/288–5103, WEB www.barharborinfo.com). **Southwest Harbor/Tremont Chamber of Commerce** (✉ Main St. [Box 1143, Southwest Harbor 04679], ☎ 207/244–9264 or 800/423–9264, WEB www.acadiachamber.com).

WAY DOWN EAST

East of Ellsworth on U.S. 1 is a different Maine, a place pretty much off the beaten path that seduces with a rugged, simple beauty. Red-hued blueberry barrens dot the landscape, and scraggly jack pines hug the highly accessible shoreline. The quiet pleasures include hiking, birding, and going on whale-watching and puffin cruises. Many artists live in the region; you can often purchase works directly from them.

Hancock

45 *9 mi east of Ellsworth.*

As you approach the small town of Hancock and the summer colony of cottages at Hancock Point, stunning views await, especially at sunset, over Frenchman Bay toward Mount Desert.

Dining and Lodging

$$$$ ✕🏠 **Le Domaine.** Owner-chef Nicole L. Purslow whips up classic French haute cuisine ($$$–$$$$; closed Sun.–Mon.), the perfect accompaniments to which can be found amid the more than 5,000 bottles of French wine in the restaurant's cellar. Le Domaine is known primarily for its food, but its Provence-inspired guest rooms are also inviting; the two suites have fireplaces. Although the building fronts on U.S. 1, the rooms open to private decks overlooking the perennial gardens, private pond, and trails that meander the property's 100 acres, and the building is well insulated to block out road noise. ✉ U.S. 1 (HC 77, Box 496, 04640), ☎ 207/422–3395 or 800/554–8498, FAX 207/422–2316, WEB *www.ledomaine.com. 5 rooms, 2 suites. Restaurant, in-room data ports, hiking, some pets allowed (fee); no room TVs. AE, D, MC, V. Closed late Oct.–mid-June. BP.*

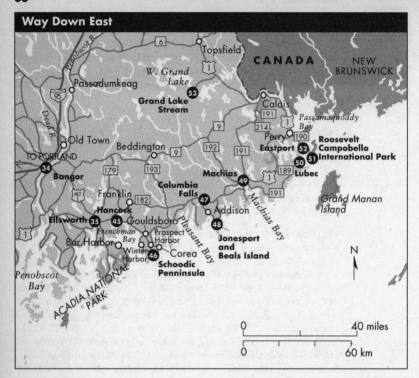

Way Down East

$$$ ✕🔲 **Crocker House Inn.** Set amid tall fir trees, this century-old shingle-style cottage is a mere 200 yards from the water and holds comfortable rooms decorated with antiques and country furnishings. The accommodations in the Carriage House, which also has a TV room and a hot tub, are best for families. The inn's dining room ($$$), which serves New American cuisine, draws Maine residents from as far away as Bar Harbor. ✉ *Hancock Point Rd. (HC 77, Box 171, 04640),* ☎ *207/422–6806 or 877/715–6017,* 🆁🅰🆇 *207/422–3105,* 🆆🅴🅱 *www.crockerhouse.com. 11 rooms. Restaurant, hot tub, bicycles, some pets allowed; no smoking. AE, D, MC, V. BP.*

Nightlife and the Arts

Pierre Monteux School for Conductors (✉ off U.S. 1, ☎ 207/422–3931) presents orchestral and chamber concerts from mid-June through mid-August.

Shopping

Hog Bay Pottery (✉ 245 Hog Bay Rd., Franklin, ☎ 207/565–2282) sells pottery by Charles Grosjean and handwoven rugs by Susanne Grosjean. **Spring Woods Gallery** (✉ 40-A Willowbrook La., Sullivan, ☎ 207/422–3006) carries contemporary art by Paul and Ann Breeden and other artists, as well as Native American pottery, jewelry, and instruments. **Sullivan Harbor Farm** (✉ U.S. 1, Sullivan, ☎ 207/422–3735 or 800/422–4014) cold-smokes salmon in the traditional Scottish manner. **Sullivan Harbor Gallery** (✉ Town Office Building, U.S. 1, Sullivan, ☎ no phone) displays the work of local artisans.

Schoodic Peninsula

46 *23 mi southeast of Hancock, 32 mi east of Ellsworth.*

The landscape of the Schoodic Peninsula makes it easy to understand why the overflow from Bar Harbor's wealthy summer population settled in Winter Harbor: the views over Frenchman's Bay to Mount Desert, the craggy coastline, and the towering evergreens. A drive through the community of Grindstone Neck shows what Bar Harbor might have been like before the Great Fire of 1947. Artists and craftspeople have opened galleries in and around Winter Harbor. No visit to Winter Harbor is complete without a stop at **Gerrish's Store** (⊠ Main St., ☎ 207/ 963–5575), which has an old-fashioned ice cream counter.

★ The Schoodic section of **Acadia National Park** (⊠ off Rte. 186, ☎ 207/ 288–3338), 2 mi east of Winter Harbor, has a scenic 6½-mi one-way loop that edges around the tip of the peninsula and yields views of Winter Harbor, Grindstone Neck, and Winter Harbor Lighthouse. At the tip of the point, huge slabs of pink granite lie jumbled along the shore, thrashed unmercifully by the crashing surf, and jack pines cling to life amid the rocks. The Fraser Point Day-Use Area at the beginning of the loop is an ideal place for a picnic. Work off your lunch with a hike up Schoodic Head for the panoramic views up and down the coast. Admission is free.

Prospect Harbor, on Route 186 northeast of Winter Harbor, is a small fishing village nearly untouched by tourism. There's little to do in **Corea,** at the tip of Route 195, other than watch the fishermen at work, pick your way over stone beaches, or gaze out to sea—and that's what makes it so special. **Petit Manan National Wildlife Refuge** (⊠ Pigeon Hill Rd. off Rte. 1, ☎ 207/546–2124) is a 2,166-acre refuge of fields, forest, and rocky shorefront on the peninsula east of Schoodic. You can explore the property on two walking trails; the wildlife viewing and bird-watching is renowned. Admission is free, parking is limited.

Dining and Lodging

$$$$ ✕ **Kitchen Garden.** This restaurant just off U.S. 1 in an old Cape Cod–style house is a wonderful surprise. The five-course, fixed-price menu emphasizes organic foods, home-grown produce, and Jamaican specialties. Bring your own wine or beer. ⊠ *335 Village Rd., Steuben,* ☎ *207/546–2708. Reservations essential. No credit cards. Closed July–Aug. Mon.–Tues. and Sept.–June. No lunch.*

$$–$$$ ✕ **Fisherman's Inn.** The menu at this popular establishment emphasizes local foods and wines. The house specialty is lobster pie, but beef, chicken, seafood, and Italian dishes also appear on the menu. ⊠ *7 Newman St., Winter Harbor,* ☎ *207/963–5585. AE, D, MC, V. Closed mid-Oct.–Memorial Day.*

$–$$ ✕ **West Bay Lobsters in the Rough.** Lobsters, steamers, corn-on-the-cob, coleslaw, baked beans, and homemade blueberry pie are among the dishes served. Eat at the outdoor tables or set up a picnic on nearby Schoodic Point. ⊠ *Rte. 186, Prospect Harbor,* ☎ *207/963–7021. AE, D, DC, MC, V. Closed Nov.–May.*

$$–$$$ ▦ **Oceanside Meadows.** Inspired by the ocean out the front door; fields,
★   woods, and a salt marsh out back; and moose, eagles, and other wildlife, the owners created the Institute for the Arts and Sciences, an environmental center with lectures, musical performances, art shows, and other events held weekly in the barn. Rooms, furnished with antiques, country pieces, and family treasures, are spread out among two white clapboard buildings; many have ocean views. Breakfast is an extravagant multicourse affair. ⊠ *Corea Rd. (Rte. 195), Prospect Harbor 04669,* ☎ *207/963–5557,* ℻ *207/963–5928,* ⬛ *www.oceaninn.com. 12 rooms, 3 suites. Boating, croquet, hiking, horseshoes, beach, concert hall, Internet, meeting rooms, some pets allowed (fee); no air-conditioning, no room TVs, no-smoking rooms. AE, D, MC, V. Closed Nov.–Apr. BP.*

$$ ▦ **Black Duck.** This small bed-and-breakfast has comfortable public areas and guest rooms, tastefully decorated with antiques and art. Two tiny cottages perch on the harbor. ⊠ *Crowley Island Rd., Corea*

04624, ☎ 207/963–2689 or 877/963–2689, FAX 207/963–7495, WEB
*www.blackduck.com. 2 rooms, 1 suite, 2 cottages. No air-condition-
ing, no room phones, no room TVs, no kids ages 1–8, no smoking.
MC, V. Closed Nov.–Mar. BP.*

$ 🏨 **The Pines.** This motel's location, right at the beginning of the Sc-
hoodic Point Loop, makes it a good value. The property includes a motel,
cottages, and log cabins, all with hand-stitched quilts. ⊠ *17 Rte. 186,
Winter Harbor 04693,* ☎ *207/963–2296,* WEB *www.ayuh.net. 3 rooms,
4 cottages, 2 cabins. Snack bar, cable TV, some kitchenettes, playground;
no air-conditioning. MC, V.*

Outdoor Activities and Sports
Moose Look Guide Service (⊠ Rte. 186, Gouldsboro, ☎ 207/963–7720)
provides kayak tours and rentals, rowboat and canoe rentals, and bike
rentals; it also conducts guided fishing trips and all-terrain-vehicle tours.

Shopping
The wines sold at the **Bartlett Maine Estate Winery** (⊠ off Rte. 1, Gouldsboro, ☎ 207/546–2408) are produced from locally grown apples,
pears, blueberries, and other fruit. **Lee Art Glass Studio** (⊠ Main St.,
Winter Harbor, ☎ 207/963–7004) carries fused-glass tableware and
other items. **U.S. Bells** (⊠ Rte. 186, Prospect Harbor, ☎ 207/963–7184)
produces hand-cast bronze wind and door bells. **Works of Hand** (⊠
430 Main St., Winter Harbor, ☎ 207/963–2547) is a basket-making
shop that also carries the works of local artisans.

Columbia Falls

47 *41 mi east of Ellsworth, 78 mi west of Calais.*

Columbia Falls, founded in the late 18th century, is a small, pretty village on the Pleasant River. Once a prosperous shipbuilding center, it
still has a number of stately homes dating from that era.

★ Judge Thomas Ruggles, a wealthy lumber dealer, store owner, postmaster,
and Justice of the Court of Sessions, built **Ruggles House** in 1818. The
house's distinctive Federal architecture, flying staircase, Palladian window, and woodwork were crafted over a period of three years by
Massachusetts wood-carver Alvah Peterson with a penknife. ⊠ *Main
St.,* ☎ *207/483–4637.* 🎟 *$3 donation requested.* ⊙ *June–mid-Oct.,
weekdays 9:30–4:30, Sun. 11–4:30.*

Lodging
$ 🏨 **Pleasant Bay Inn and Llama Keep.** This Cape Cod–style inn takes
advantage of its riverfront location. You can stroll the nature paths on
the property, which winds around a peninsula and out to Pleasant Bay;
you can even take a llama with you for company. The rooms, all with
water views, are decorated with antiques and have country touches.
⊠ *386 West Side Rd. (Box 222, Addison 04606),* ☎ *207/483–4490,*
FAX *207/483–4653. 3 rooms, 1 with bath; 1 suite. Some refrigerators;
no air-conditioning, no phones in some rooms, no smoking, no TV in
some rooms. MC, V. BP.*

Shopping
Columbia Falls Pottery (⊠ Main St., ☎ 207/483–4075) stocks stoneware
and a sampling of Maine foods.

Jonesport and Beals Island

48 *12 mi south of Columbia Falls, 20 mi southwest of Machias.*

Jonesport and Beals Island, two fishing communities joined by a bridge
over the harbor, are less polished than the towns on the Schoodic

Peninsula. The birding here is superb. **Norton of Jonesport** (☎ 207/ 497–5933) takes passengers on day trips to Machias Seal Island, where there's a large puffin colony.

Great Wass Island Preserve (☎ 207/729–5181) a 1,540-acre nature conservancy at the tip of Beals Island, protects rare plants, stunted pines, and raised peat bogs. Trails lead through the woods and emerge onto the undeveloped, raw coast, where you can make your way along the rocks and boulders before retreating into the forest. To get to the preserve from Jonesport, cross the bridge over Moosabec Reach to Beals Island. Go through Beals to Great Wass Island. Follow the road, which eventually becomes unpaved, to Black Duck Cove, about 3 mi from Beals, where there is a parking area on the left. Admission is free.

Dining and Lodging

$$–$$$$ ✕ **Seafarer's Wife and Old Salt Room.** These two restaurants share a central kitchen. Allow at least a couple of hours to dine at the Seafarer's Wife, where a five-course meal with main dishes such as a seafood platter and baked stuffed chicken is presented at a leisurely pace in a candlelit dining room. The casual Old Salt Room specializes in fresh fish and seafood. Bring your own wine—neither restaurant has a liquor license. ⊠ *Rte. 187, Jonesport,* ☎ *207/497–2365. MC, V. Closed Jan.– Mar. No lunch.*

$$ ★ ⊞ **Harbor House.** The two spacious rooms on the third floor of this harbor-front building have big windows to take in the water view. Both are tastefully furnished with Victorian touches such as cabbage rose wallpaper and Oriental-style rugs, and both have separate sleeping and sitting areas. An alcove is stocked with books, coffee, tea, and snacks. Breakfast is served on the porch, and the owners will prepare a lobster dinner if asked in advance. ⊠ *Sawyer Square (Box 468, Jonesport 04649),* ☎ *207/497–5417,* ℻ *207/497–3211,* ⓦⓔⓑ *www.harborhs.com. 2 rooms. Cable TV, Internet; no air-conditioning, no room phones, no kids under 12. MC, V. BP.*

$ ⊞ **Raspberry Shores.** This comfortably furnished Victorian sits on Main Street, but its backyard slopes down to a small beach on Jonesport Harbor. Rooms in the back of the house share the view, but the nicest room is in the turret and right on the road, which can be noisy. Owner Nan Ellis will prepare a Continental breakfast if you're taking an early morning boat trip. ⊠ *Rte. 187 (Box 409, Jonesport 04649),* ☎ *207/497–2463 or 877/710–3268,* ⓦⓔⓑ *www.jonesportmaine.com. 3 rooms without bath. Beach, boating, bicycles, some pets allowed; no air-conditioning, no room phones, no room TVs, no kids under 15, no smoking. MC, V. Closed Nov.–Apr. BP.*

Machias

49 *20 mi northeast of Jonesport.*

Machias claims to be the site of the first naval battle of the Revolutionary War. On June 12, 1775, despite being outnumbered and outarmed, a small group of Machias men under the leadership of Jeremiah O'Brien captured the armed British schooner *Margaretta* in a battle now known as the Lexington of the Sea. The town's other claim to fame is wild blueberries. The Machias Wild Blueberry Festival, held annually during the third weekend in August, is a true community celebration complete with parade, crafts fair, concerts, and plenty of blueberry dishes. Machias is the county seat of Washington County and is home to a campus of the University of Maine.

★ The **Burnham Tavern Museum,** in a 1770 building, details the colorful history of Job Burnham, Mary O'Brien (his wife), and other early residents of the area. It was here that the men of Machias laid the plans that culminated in the capture of the *Margaretta*. ⊠ *Rte. 192,* ☎ *207/ 255–4432.* 🎫 *$2.50.* ⊙ *Mid-June–late Sept., weekdays 9–5; late Sept.– mid-June, by appointment.*

Although small, the **Art Galleries at the University of Maine at Machias** have a strong selection of paintings by John Marin and other Maine artists. Two galleries showcase rotating exhibitions of works from the permanent collection, the Marin Foundation collection, and visiting shows. Don't miss the William Zorach sculpture just outside the front door. ⊠ *Powers Hall, University of Maine at Machias, 9 O'Brien Ave.,* ☎ *207/255–1200.* 🎫 *Free.* ⊙ *Weekday afternoons or by appointment.*

Built by Nathan Gates in 1810, the **Gates House** houses the Machiasport Historical Society. It contains an extensive collection of photographs, tools, period furniture, housewares, memorabilia, and a genealogical library. ⊠ *Rte. 92, Machiasport,* ☎ *207/255–8461.* 🎫 *$1.* ⊙ *Mid-June–early-Sept., Tues.–Fri. 12:30–4:30.*

The **O'Brien Cemetery** dates from the late 18th century; many of Machias's earliest settlers and heroes are buried here. ⊠ *Bad Little Falls Park off Rte. 92, Machias (walk through the park toward the water and look for a stairway on your right, which leads to a path; follow it along the river until you see a white fence on a hill to your right; a small side path leads to the cemetery.)*

OFF THE BEATEN PATH   **JASPER BEACH–** No sand exists here, just smooth, heather-color jasper and rhyolite stones polished by the sea. ⊠ *Rte. 92, Buck's Harbor (9½ mi south of Machias).*

Dining and Lodging

$$–$$$ ✕ **Artist's Cafe.** The white-walled dining rooms in this old house provide a simple backdrop for artwork and creative food. The menu usually has a choice of four entrées such as a catch of the day, a rib-eye steak, and "The Mex," the house vegetarian dish. You might start with Horses Standing Still, handmade Thai dumplings filled with chicken and shrimp and served with a dipping sauce. ⊠ *3 Hill St.,* ☎ *207/255– 8900. MC, V. Closed Sun.*

$$ ✕🏠 **Riverside Inn & Restaurant.** The Victorian era is captured in the furnishings and linens of this restored sea captain's home overlooking the East Machias River. Suites in the guest house have balconies, and one has a full kitchen. The restaurant ($$), open to the public for dinner Thursday–Saturday, is the best in the area, serving four-course feasts of contemporary American fare by candlelight. ⊠ *U.S. 1 (Box 373, 04630),* ☎ *207/255–4134,* 🆑 *207/255–3580,* 🌐 *www.riversideinn-maine.com. 2 rooms, 2 suites. Restaurant, cable TV; no air-conditioning, no room phones, no smoking. AE, MC, V. BP.*

Outdoor Activities and Sports

Machias Bay Boat Tours and Sea Kayaking (⊠ Buck's Harbor, Machiasport, ☎ 207/259–3338) operates day trips aboard the *Martha Ann* to see seals, islands and lighthouses, salmon aquaculture, and historical sites. Guided fishing and sea-kayaking trips are also conducted.

Lubec

⑤⓪   *28 mi east of Machias.*

Lubec is the first town in the United States to see the sunrise. Its rural beauty outshines this once thriving shipbuilding and sardine-packing site. Lubec is best appreciated by those who enjoy outdoor pleasures;

there are few shops and little entertainment. It also makes a good base for day trips to Campobello Island.

★ **Quoddy Head State Park,** the easternmost point of land in the United States, is marked by candy-striped West Quoddy Head Light. The mystical 2-mi path along the cliffs here yields magnificent views of Canada's Grand Manan island. Whales can often be sighted offshore. The 483-acre park has a picnic area. ⊠ *S. Lubec Rd. off Rte. 189,* ☎ *no phone.* 🎟 *$1.* ☉ *Memorial Day–mid-Oct., daily 8–sunset; Apr.– Memorial Day and mid-Oct.–Dec., weekends 9–sunset.*

At **Cottage Garden** paths lead through perennial, rose, rock, water, herb, and vegetable gardens and through sections with woods, rhododendrons, dwarf conifers, and shrubs. ⊠ *S. Lubec Rd. off Rte. 189,* ☎ *207/733–2902.* 🎟 *Free.* ☉ *June–Aug., daily dawn–dusk.*

⑤ **Roosevelt Campobello International Park,** a joint project of the American and Canadian governments, has hiking trails and historical displays. Neatly manicured Campobello Island has always had a special appeal for the wealthy and famous. It was here that the Roosevelt family spent its summers. The 34-room **Roosevelt Cottage** was presented to Eleanor and Franklin as a wedding gift. The island can be reached by land only by crossing the International Bridge from Lubec. Stop at the information booth for an update on tides—specifically, when you will be able to walk out to East Quoddy Head Lighthouse—and details on walking and hiking trails. Once you've crossed the bridge, you're in the Atlantic time zone. ⊠ *Rte. 774, Welshpool, Campobello Island, New Brunswick, Canada,* ☎ *506/752–2922.* 🎟 *Free.* ☉ *House mid-May–mid-Oct., daily 10–6; grounds daily.*

Dining and Lodging

$–$$ ✕🏠 **Home Port Inn.** Lubec's grandest accommodations are in this 1880 Colonial-style house atop a hill. The spacious rooms, some with water views, are furnished with antiques and family pieces. There are two sitting areas, and the living room has a fireplace and a television. The dining room ($$–$$$), the best in town, is open to the public for dinner. The menu emphasizes seafood. ⊠ *45 Main St., 04652,* ☎ *207/733–2077 or 800/457–2077,* ᴡᴇʙ *www.homeportinn.com. 7 rooms. Restaurant; no air-conditioning, no room phones, no room TVs, no smoking. AE, D, MC, V. Closed mid-Oct.–mid-June. CP.*

$ 🏠 **Peacock House.** Four generations of the Peacock family lived in this 1860 Victorian before it was converted into an inn. A few of the simply furnished rooms have water views through lace-curtained windows. ⊠ *27 Summer St., 04652,* ☎ ꜰᴀx *207/733–2403 or 888/305–0036,* ᴡᴇʙ *www.peacockhouse.com. 2 rooms, 3 suites. No air-conditioning in some rooms, no TV in some rooms, no room phones, no kids under 7. MC, V. Closed mid-Oct.–mid-May. BP.*

En Route The road to Eastport leads through the Pleasant Point Indian Reservation, where the **Waponahki Museum and Resource Center** explains the culture of the Passamaquoddy, or "People of the Dawn." Tools, baskets, beaded artifacts, historic photos, and arts and crafts are displayed. ⊠ *Rte. 190, Perry,* ☎ *207/853–4001.* 🎟 *Free.* ☉ *Weekdays 8:30–11 and noon–4.*

Eastport

⑤² *39 mi north of Lubec, 102 mi east of Ellsworth.*

Eastport is a small island connected to the mainland by a granite causeway. In the late 19th century, 14 sardine canneries operated in Eastport. The decline of that industry in the 20th century has left the city economically depressed, though a commercial port facility, growing aquaculture, and an increase in tourism bode well for the future. From the waterfront, you can take a ferry to Deer Island and Campobello.

The **National Historic Waterfront District** extends from the Customs House, down Water Street to Bank Square and the Peavey Library. Pick up a walking map at the **Chamber of Commerce** (⊠ 78 Water St., ☎ 207/853–4644) and wander through streets lined with historic homes and buildings. You can also take the waterfront walkway to watch the fishing boats and freighters. The tides fluctuate as much as 28 ft, which explains the ladders and steep gangways necessary to access boats.

Raye's Mustard Mill is the only remaining mill in the U.S. producing stone-ground mustard. Historically, this mill served the sardine-packing industry. You can purchase mustards made on the premises at the mill's Pantry Store; Maine-made crafts and other foods are also for sale. ⊠ 85 Washington St., ☎ 207/853–4451 or 800/853–1903. ☑ Free. ☉ Jan.–May, weekdays 8–5; June–Dec., daily 9–4:30. Tours on the hr Memorial Day–Labor Day; rest of yr subject to guide availability.

The short hike to **Shakford Head** (⊠ behind Washington County Technical College on Deep Cove Rd.) affords views over Passamaquoddy Bay to Campobello. From here you can see the pens for Eastport's salmon-farming industry as well as the port facility.

Lodging

$–$$ 🏠 **Weston House.** A Federal-style home built in 1810, this antiques-
★   filled inn overlooks Eastport and Passamaquoddy Bay from a prime in-town location. The family room, with a fireplace and a TV, is a casual place to plan the day's activities. An elegant multicourse breakfast is served in the formal dining room, and dinner is available by advance reservation. ⊠ 26 Boynton St., 04631, ☎ 207/853–2907 or 800/853–2907, FAX 207/853–0981. 4 rooms without bath. No air-conditioning, no room phones, no room TVs, no smoking. No credit cards. BP.

Outdoor Activities and Sports

Harris Whale Watching (⊠ Harris Point Rd., ☎ 207/853–2940 or 207/853–4303) operates three-hour tours. **Tidal Trails** (⊠ Water St., ☎ 207/726–4799) conducts boat charters, natural-history tours, and guided bird-watching, canoeing, sea-kayaking, and saltwater-fishing trips.

Shopping

Dog Island Pottery (⊠ 224 Water St., ☎ 207/853–4775) stocks stoneware pottery and local crafts. The **Eastport Gallery** (⊠ 69 Water St., ☎ 207/853–4166) displays works by area artists. **45th Parallel** (⊠ U.S. 1, Perry, ☎ 207/853–9600) stocks a mix of antiques, crafts, and home furnishing. **Joe's Basket Shop** (⊠ Rte. 190, Pleasant Point, ☎ 207/853–2840) has fancy and coarse (work) baskets and jewelry made by the Passamaquoddy. **Quoddy Wigwam** (⊠ Rte. 1, Perry, ☎ 207/853–2488) sells handcrafted Maine moccasins.

Grand Lake Stream

② 50 mi northwest of Eastport, 108 mi east of Bangor.

This tiny community, on Grand Lake Stream between West Grand Lake and Big Lake, was once one of the largest tannery centers in the world. Today it's renowned for fishing, especially for land-locked salmon and smallmouth bass, and for the Grand Laker, a stable, square-ended wooden canoe built specifically for use on the big and often windy lakes in this region. Outdoors lovers will find lakes and rivers for swimming, boating, and fishing; trails for hiking; and plenty of places to spot wildlife.

On the last full weekend of July, the town holds a juried folk arts festival, which attracts thousands of visitors.

The tiny **Grand Lake Stream Historical Society & Museum** is jampacked with artifacts from the town's early days. Here you can learn more about the Grand Lake canoes, the town's tannery years, and its fishing heritage. ☎ 207/796–5562. ✉ *Donation accepted.* ☉ *By chance or appointment.*

Lodging

$$$$ ⊡ **Leen's Lodge.** Ten rustic cabins varying in size from one to four bedrooms are nestled on 23 wooded acres on West Grand Lake. All have woodstoves or fireplaces and big windows to take in the views. A country-style breakfast and a hearty, home-style dinner are served in a central lodge, where you'll also find a TV/VCR, card tables, books, and games. The lodge can arrange guided fishing trips, wildlife or photographic safaris, and other excursions. Boat rentals are available. ⊠ *Box 40, 04637,* ☎ *207/796–5575 or 800/995–3367,* WEB *www. leenslodge.com. 10 cabins. Some kitchenettes, hiking, beach, boating, recreation room, some pets allowed; no air-conditioning, no room phones, no room TVs. MC, V. Closed Nov.–Apr. MAP.*

$$$$ ⊡ **Weatherby's.** Nicknamed "the fishermen's resort," Weatherby's is ideal for those who want to be in the center of the action in Grand Lake Stream. Fifteen cottages, each with an open brick or Franklin fireplace, surround the main lodge, where you can take breakfast and dinner daily. Lunch is available upon request. The main lodge also has a library, television, and piano. ⊠ *Grand Lake Stream 04637,* ☎ *207/796–5558,* WEB *www.weatherbys.com. 15 cottages. No air-conditioning, no room phones, no room TVs. MC, V. Closed mid-Oct.–Apr. MAP.*

Outdoor Activities and Sports

The **Grand Lake Stream Guides Association** (⊠ Grand Lake Stream 04637) maintains more than 25 launch sites on area lakes. Guides lead fishing, family, boating, hiking, photographic, and wildlife trips.

Shopping

Shamel Boat & Canoe Works (⊠ Tough End Rd., ☎ 207/796–8199) specializes in building canoes.

Way Down East A to Z

To research prices, get advice from other travelers, and book travel arrangements, visit www.fodors.com.

BIKE TRAVEL

Narrow roads, most without shoulders, are the rule here, but you'll find some beautiful routes on the long fingers of land that stretch toward the ocean as well as on the inland side of Route 1, where you'll see plenty of lakes. Be aware that most land owned by logging companies is not open for bicycling.

BOAT AND FERRY TRAVEL

East Coast Ferries, Ltd. provides ferry service between Eastport and Deer Island and Deer Island and Campobello from late June to mid-September. Ferries run on Atlantic time, which is one hour earlier than Eastern time.

➤ BOAT AND FERRY INFORMATION: **East Coast Ferries, Ltd.** (☎ 506/747–2159, WEB www.eastcoastferries.nb.ca).

CAR TRAVEL

U.S. 1 is the primary coastal route, with smaller roads leading to the towns on the long fingers of land in this region. Route 182 is a pleasant inland route; Route 186 loops through the Schoodic Peninsula. The most direct route to Lubec is Route 189, but Route 191, between East Machias and West Lubec, is a scenic coastal drive.

LODGING

Black Duck Properties specializes in properties on the Schoodic Peninsula. Hearts of Maine has waterfront listings in the Machias region.
➤ LODGING: **Black Duck Properties** (✉ Box 39, Corea 04624, ☎ 207/963–2689, WEB www.acadia.net/blackduck). **Hearts of Maine** (✉ 10 High St., Machias 04564, ☎ 207/255–4210, WEB www.boldcoast.com/mainecottages).

MEDIA

The *Bangor Daily News* is published Monday–Friday. Weekly newspapers include *Calais Advertiser, Downeast Times* (Calais), *Downeast Coastal Press* (Cutler), *Machias Valley News Observer,* and the twice-monthly *Quoddy Tides* (Eastport).

WMEH 90.0 or WMED 89.7 is the local National Public Radio affiliate. WLBZ, channel 2, is the NBC affiliate. WVII, channel 7, is the ABC affiliate. WABI, channel 5, is the CBS affiliate. WMEB, channel 12, or WMED, channel 13, is the Maine Public Broadcasting affiliate.

OUTDOOR ACTIVITIES AND SPORTS

BOATING

For boat rentals, *see* listings by town. The Maine Professional Guides Association represents kayaking guides.
➤ CONTACT: **Maine Professional Guides Association** (✉ Box 847, Augusta 04332, ☎ 207/549–5631, WEB www.maineguides.org).

FISHING

For information about fishing and licenses, contact the Maine Department of Inland Fisheries and Wildlife.
➤ CONTACT: **Maine Department of Inland Fisheries and Wildlife** (✉ 41 State House Station, Augusta 04333, ☎ 207/287–8000, WEB www.state.me.us/ifw).

TOURS

Quoddy Air has scenic flights. Scenic Island Tours leads tours of Eastport in a 1947 Dodge Woody bus.
➤ TOUR OPERATORS: **Quoddy Air** (✉ Eastport Municipal Airport, County Rd., Eastport, ☎ 207/853–0997). **Scenic Island Tours** (✉ 37 Washington St., Eastport, ☎ 207/853–2840).

VISITOR INFORMATION

➤ CONTACTS: **Downeast Coastal Chamber of Commerce** (✉ Box 331, Harrington 04643, ☎ 207/483–2131, WEB www.downeastcoastalchamber.org). **Eastport Area Chamber of Commerce** (✉ 72 Water St. [Box 254, Eastport 04631], ☎ 207/853–4644, WEB www.nemaine.com/eastportcc). **Grand Lake Stream Chamber of Commerce** (✉ Box 124, Grand Lake Stream 046337, ☎ 207/448–3000, WEB www.grandlakestream.com). **Lubec Area Chamber of Commerce** (✉ Box 123, Lubec 04652, ☎ 207/733–4522). **Machias Bay Area Chamber of Commerce** (✉ 378 Main St. [Box 606, Machias 04654], ☎ 207/255–4402, WEB www.nemaine.com/mbacc). **Quoddy Coastal Tourism Association of New Brunswick and Maine** (✉ Box 1171, St. Andrews, New Brunswick, Canada E0G 2X0, ☎ 800/377–9748). **Schoodic Peninsula Chamber of Commerce** (✉ Box 381, Winter Harbor 04693, ☎ 207/963–7658 or 800/231–3008, WEB www.acadia-schoodic.org).

WESTERN LAKES AND MOUNTAINS

Less than 20 mi northwest of Portland and the coast, the sparsely populated lake and mountain areas of western Maine stretch north along the New Hampshire border to Québec. In winter this is ski country; in summer the woods and waters draw vacationers.

The Sebago–Long Lake region bustles with activity in the summer. Harrison and the Waterfords are quieter. Bridgton attracts lake visitors in summer and skiers in winter, while Lovell is a dreamy escape. Kezar Lake, tucked away in a fold of the White Mountains, has long been a hideaway of the wealthy. Children's summer camps dot the region. Bethel, in the Androscoggin River valley, is a classic New England town, its town common lined with historic homes. The more rural Rangeley Lake area brings long stretches of pine, beech, spruce, and sky—and stylish inns and bed-and-breakfasts with access to golf, boating, fishing, and hiking. Snow sports, especially snowmobiling, are popular winter pastimes. Carrabassett Valley, just north of Kingfield, is home to Sugarloaf/USA, a major ski resort with a challenging golf course.

Sebago Lake

54 *17 mi northwest of Portland.*

Sebago Lake, which provides all the drinking water for Greater Portland, is Maine's best-known lake after Moosehead (☞ The North Woods). Many camps and year-round homes surround Sebago, which is popular with water-sports enthusiasts. At the north end of the lake, the **Songo Lock** (☎ 207/693–6231), which permits the passage of watercraft from Sebago Lake to Long Lake, is the lone surviving lock of the Cumberland and Oxford Canal. Built of wood and masonry, the original lock dates from 1830 and was expanded in 1911; today it sees heavy traffic in summer.

The 1,300-acre **Sebago Lake State Park** on the north shore of the lake provides swimming, picnicking, camping (250 sites), boating, and fishing (salmon and togue). ⊠ *11 Park Access Rd., Casco,* ☎ *207/693– 6613 May–mid-Oct.; 207/693–6231 mid-Oct.–Apr.* ⊡ *$2.50.* ⊙ *Daily 9–8.*

The **Jones Museum of Glass & Ceramics** houses more than 8,000 glass, pottery, stoneware, and porcelain objects from around the world. Also on the premises are a research library and gift shop. ⊠ *35 Douglas Mountain Rd., off Rte. 107, Sebago,* ☎ *207/787–3370.* ⊡ *$5.* ⊙ *Mid-May–mid-Nov., Mon.–Sat. 10–5, Sun. 1–5; tours by appointment.*

OFF THE
BEATEN PATH

SABBATHDAY LAKE SHAKER MUSEUM – Established in the late 18th century, this is the last active Shaker community in the United States. Members continue to farm crops and herbs, and you can see the meetinghouse of 1794—a paradigm of Shaker design—and the ministry shop with 14 rooms of Shaker furniture, folk art, tools, farm implements, and crafts from the 18th to the early 20th century. There is also a small gift shop, but don't expect to find furniture or other large Shaker items. On the busy road out front, a farmer usually has summer and fall vegetables for sale. In autumn, he sells cider, apples, and pumpkins. ⊠ *707 Shaker Rd. (Rte. 26), New Gloucester (20 mi north of Portland, 12 mi east of Naples),* ☎ *207/926–4597.* ⊡ *Tour $6.* ⊙ *Memorial Day– Columbus Day, Mon.–Sat. 10–4:30.*

Naples

55 *32 mi northwest of Portland.*

Naples occupies an enviable location between Long and Sebago lakes. On clear days, the view down Long Lake takes in the Presidential Range of the White Mountains, highlighted by often-snowcapped Mt. Washington. The Causeway, which divides Long Lake from Brandy Pond pulses with activity: Cruise and rental boats sail and motor on the lakes, moving between the two through a swing bridge; open-air cafés overflow and throngs of families parade along the sidewalk edging Long Lake. The town swells with seasonal residents and visitors in summer and all but shuts tight for winter.

Songo River Queen II, a 92-ft stern-wheeler, takes passengers on hourlong cruises on Long Lake and longer voyages down the Songo River and through Songo Lock. ⊠ *U.S. 302, Naples Causeway,* ☎ *207/693–6861.* ⊠ *Long Lake cruise $8, Songo River ride $11.* ⊙ *July–Labor Day, 5 cruises daily; call for spring and fall hrs.*

Lodging

$$$$ 🏠 **Migis Lodge.** The lodge's pine-panel cottages, scattered among 100 shorefront acres, have fieldstone fireplaces and are handsomely furnished with braided rugs and handmade quilts. A warm, woodsy feeling pervades the main inn. The deck has views (marvelous at sunset) of Sebago Lake. All kinds of outdoor and indoor activities are included in the room rate, and canoes, kayaks, and sailboats are available. Three fancy meals are served daily in the main dining room. ⊠ *Migis Lodge Rd., off U.S. 302 (Box 40, South Casco 04077),* ☎ *207/655–4524,* FAX *207/655–2054,* WEB *www.migis.com. 29 cottages, 6 rooms. Dining room, cable TV, refrigerators, 2 tennis courts, gym, massage, spa, beach, boating, waterskiing, fishing, playground, recreation room, meeting rooms; no air-conditioning in some rooms. No credit cards. FAP.*

$$–$$$ 🏠 **Augustus Bove House.** Built as the Hotel Naples in the 1820s, this rambling brick B&B sits across from the Naples Causeway and has views down Long Lake. Rooms are furnished with antiques. ⊠ *Rte. 302 (R.R. 1, Box 501, 04055),* ☎ *207/693–6365 or 888/806–6249,* WEB *www.naplesmaine.com. 10 rooms, 8 with bath; 2 suites. Cable TV, in-room VCRs, some refrigerators, some microwaves, Internet; no smoking. AE, D, DC MC, V. BP.*

Outdoor Activities and Sports

U.S. 302 cuts through Naples, and in the center at the Naples Causeway are rental craft for fishing or cruising. Sebago, Long, and Rangeley lakes are popular areas for sailing and motorboating. For motorboat rentals, try **Mardon Marine** (⊠ U.S. 302, ☎ 207/693–6264). **Naples Marina** (⊠ U.S. 302 and Rte. 114, ☎ 207/693–6254) also rents motorboats. **Long Lake Marina** (⊠ U.S. 302, ☎ 207/693–3159) rents fishing boats and canoes.

Shopping

The **Cry of the Loon** (⊠ U.S. 302, South Casco, ☎ 207/655–5060) complex includes a gift shop: the Nest, a country home-furnishings shop, and the Barn, which carries specialty foods, nautical gifts, and other items.

Harrison

56 *10 mi north of Naples, 25 mi south of Bethel.*

Harrison anchors the northern end of Long Lake but is less commercial than Naples. The combination of woods, lakes, and views makes it a good choice for leaf-peepers. The nearby towns of North Water-

Western Maine

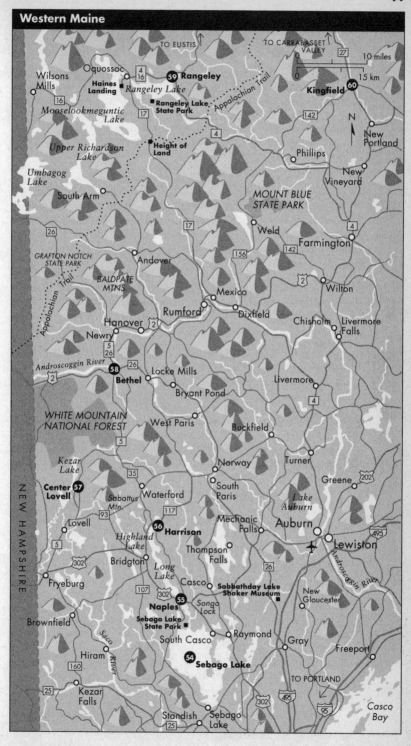

TO EUSTIS

TO CARRABASSET VALLEY

0   10 miles
0   15 km

Wilsons Mills

Oquossoc

4 / 16

59 Rangeley

Kingfield **60**

Haines Landing

Rangeley Lake

Rangeley Lake State Park

Appalachian Trail

142

N

Mooselookmeguntic Lake

16

17

New Portland

Upper Richardson Lake

Height of Land

4

Phillips

New Vineyard

Umbagog Lake

South Arm

MOUNT BLUE STATE PARK

26

17

Weld

Farmington

GRAFTON NOTCH STATE PARK

Andover

156

142

Wilton

BALDPATE MTNS

Mexico

Dixfield

Chisholm

Livermore Falls

Appalachian Trail

Rumford

Hanover

2

Newry

5 / 26

Androscoggin River

Livermore

58 Bethel

26

Locke Mills

4

2

Bryant Pond

WHITE MOUNTAIN NATIONAL FOREST

West Paris

5

Buckfield

Kezar Lake

35

Norway

Turner

Greene

202

57 Center Lovell

Sabattus Mtn.

Waterford

South Paris

Lake Auburn

NEW HAMPSHIRE

Lovell

93

117

Mechanic Falls

Auburn

495

5

56 Harrison

Highland Lake

Thompson Falls

Lewiston

302

Bridgton

Long Lake

Casco

26

Androscoggin River

Fryeburg

107

302

Sabbathday Lake Shaker Museum

New Gloucester

Brownfield

Saco River

55 Naples

Songo Lock

Sebago Lake State Park

South Casco

Raymond

Gray

Freeport

Hiram

160

54 Sebago Lake

TO PORTLAND

Kezar Falls

25

495

95

Casco Bay

Standish

25

Sebago Lake

302

ford, South Waterford, and tiny Waterford, a National Historic District, are ideal for outdoors lovers who prefer to get away from the crowds.

Lodging

$$ 🏨 **Bear Mountain Inn.** After swimming at the private beach on Bear
★ Lake or hiking up Bear Mountain (across the street), it's nice to return to this rambling farmhouse inn, which the owner has meticulously decorated in a woodsy theme. The luxurious Great Grizzly Suite has a fireplace, whirlpool bath for two, and mesmerizing views, while the cozy Sugar Bear Cottage is a romantic retreat. Breakfast is served in the dining room, which has a fieldstone fireplace and lake views. ⊠ *Rte. 35, South Waterford 04084,* ☎ *207/583–4404,* FAX *207/ 583–2437,* WEB *www.bearmtninn.com. 8 rooms, 6 with bath; 1 suite; 1 cottage. Cable TV in some rooms, some in-room VCRs, Internet, badminton, croquet, horseshoes, volleyball, beach, boating, fishing, ice-skating, cross-country skiing, snowmobiling; no kids under 8, no smoking. MC, V. BP.*

$$ 🏨 **Harrison House.** When it was built in 1867, this house at the head of Long Lake was one of the most costly and elegant residences in town. Today it charms with feather beds, quilts, and a porch swing. The living room, dining room, and three guest rooms have lake views. All rooms have private baths, but four of the baths are adjacent to or across the hall from the rooms. ⊠ *16 Waterford Rd., 04040,* ☎ *207/583–6564. 5 rooms. No air-conditioning, no room phones, no room TVs, no smoking. AE, MC, V. BP.*

$$ 🏨 **Waterford Inne.** This gold-painted house on a hilltop provides a good home base for trips to lakes, ski trails, and antiques shops. The bedrooms have lots of nooks and crannies. The Nantucket, with a whale motif, and the Chesapeake, with a private porch and a fireplace, are the nicest. A converted woodshed holds five additional rooms, and though they have less character than the rooms in the inn, four have sunny decks. ⊠ *258 Chadbourne Rd. (Box 149, Waterford 04088),* ☎ FAX *207/583–4037. 7 rooms, 5 with bath; 1 suite. Ice-skating, cross-country skiing, some pets allowed (fee); no air-conditioning, no room phones, no room TVs, no smoking. AE. Closed Apr. BP.*

Nightlife and the Arts

From late June through Labor Day, **Deertrees Theater and Cultural Center** (⊠ Deertrees Rd. off Rte. 117, ☎ 207/583–6747) stages musicals, dramas, dance performances, shows for children, concerts, and other events in a theater listed on the National Register of Historic Places.

Outdoor Activities and Sports

For guided fishing trips, call **Carl Bois** (☎ 207/925–6262) in Lovell. **Mutiny Brook Stables** (⊠ Sweden Rd., South Waterford, ☎ 207/583–6650) outfits horseback tours in the Maine woods.

Center Lovell

🔟 *17 mi northwest of Harrison, 28 mi south of Bethel.*

At Center Lovell you can barely glimpse the secluded Kezar Lake to the west, the retreat of wealthy and very private people. Sabattus Mountain, which rises behind Center Lovell, has a public hiking trail and stupendous views of the Presidential Range from the summit.

Dining and Lodging

$$$$ ✕🏨 **Quisisana.** This delightful cottage resort on Kezar Lake may inspire music lovers. After dinner, the staff—students and graduates of some of the country's finest music schools—perform everything from Broadway tunes to concert piano pieces at the music hall. One night

dinner ($$$$) might be lobster and blueberry pie; the next it might be saddle of lamb with a black-olive tapenade or salmon-and-leek roulade. Most of the white-clapboard cottages have screened porches, pine-paneled living areas and fireplaces, and are simply furnished with wicker and country pieces. For most of the resort's season, a one-week stay beginning Saturday is required. ⊠ *Pleasant Point Rd., 04016,* ☎ *207/925–3500,* FAX *207/925–1004 in season,* WEB *www.quisisanaresort.com. 11 rooms in 2 lodges, 32 cottages. Restaurant, 3 tennis courts, windsurfing, boating, waterskiing, Ping-Pong, recreation room; no air-conditioning, no room phones, no room TVs, no smoking. No credit cards. Closed Sept.–mid-June. FAP.*

$–$$ ✕☲ **Center Lovell Inn.** The current owners won this rambling old-fashioned country inn in an essay contest in 1993. The eclectic furnishings blend mid-19th and mid-20th centuries in a pleasing, homey style. The best tables for dining ($$$–$$$$) are on the wraparound porch, which has sunset views over Kezar Lake and the White Mountains. Entrées may include pan-seared muscovy duck, fillet of bison, or fresh swordfish. Rooms are upstairs and in the adjacent Harmon House. ⊠ *Rte. 5 (Box 261, 04016),* ☎ *207/925–1575 or 800/777–2698,* WEB *www.centerlovellinn.com. 6 rooms, 4 with bath; 1 suite. Restaurant; no air-conditioning, no room phones, no room TVs, no smoking. D, MC, V. Closed Nov.–late Dec. and Apr.–mid-May.*

Outdoor Activities and Sports

BOATING AND FISHING

For guided fishing trips, call **Carl Bois** (☎ 207/925–6262) in Lovell. **Kezar Lake Marina** (⊠ West Lovell Rd. at The Narrows, Lovell, ☎ 207/925–3000) rents boats.

CANOEING

Two scenic canoeing routes on the Saco River (near Fryeburg) are the gentle stretch from Swan's Falls to East Brownfield (19 mi) and from East Brownfield to Hiram (14 mi). For rentals, try **Saco River Canoe and Kayak** (⊠ Rte. 5, Fryeburg, ☎ 207/935–2369).

DOGSLEDDING

Winter Journeys (☎ 207/928–2026) in Lovell operates day and multiday dogsledding trips.

Bethel

58 *28 mi north of Lovell, 66 mi north of Portland.*

Bethel is pure New England, a town with white clapboard houses and white-steeple churches and a mountain vista at the end of every street. In winter, this is ski country: Sunday River ski area in Newry is only a few miles north.

A stroll in Bethel should begin at the Bethel Historical Society's **Regional History Center.** The center's campus comprises two buildings, the 1821 O'Neil Robinson House and the 1813 Dr. Moses Mason House; both are listed on the National Register of Historic Places. The Robinson House has exhibits pertaining to the region's history and a small gift shop. The Moses Mason House has nine period rooms and a front hall and stairway wall decorated with murals by Rufus Porter. Pick up materials here for a walking tour of Bethel Hill Village, most of which is on the National Register of Historic Places. ⊠ *14 Broad St.,* ☎ *207/824–2908 or 800/824–2910,* WEB *www.bethelhistorical.org.* ⊠ *$3.* ☉ *O'Neil Robinson House July–Aug. and Dec., Tues.–Sun. 1–4; Sept.–Oct. and Jan.–June, Tues.–Fri. 1–4. Moses Mason House July–Aug., Tues.–Sun. 1–4; Sept.–June by appointment.*

The **Major Gideon's House** on Broad Street has a columned-front portico typical of the Greek Revival style. The severe white **West Parish Congregational Church** (1847), with an unadorned triangular pediment and a steeple supported on open columns, is on Church Street, around the common from the Major Gideon Hastings House. The campus of **Gould Academy** (✉ Church St., ☎ 207/824–7777), a preparatory school, opened its doors in 1835; the dominant style of the school buildings is Georgian.

Dining and Lodging

$$$ ✕🏨 **Gideon Hastings House.** Lace curtains, gleaming hardwood floors, and tin ceilings welcome you to this historic inn and restaurant. The two spacious guest rooms can be connected as a family suite. The restaurant's menu ($$–$$$; closed Tues.) ranges from pizzas to entrées such as filet mignon and chicken stuffed with goat cheese, artichoke hearts, and sun-dried tomatoes. ✉ 22 Broad St., 04217, ☎ 207/824–3496, WEB www.gideonhastingshouse.com. 2 rooms with shared bath, 2 suites. Restaurant, in-room data ports, in-room VCRs, boccie, bar; no air-conditioning. MC, V. BP.

$$ ✕🏨 **L'Auberge.** Built as a barn in the late 1850s, L'Auberge has evolved into a casual inn with a French country accent and one of the area's best restaurants. The inn is on 5 acres just off the Bethel Common. The menu ($$$; closed Tues.–Wed.) changes seasonally but might include hors d'oeuvres such as pâté de campagne or escargots and entrées such as sea bass Provençal or caramelized duck breast. ✉ 24 Mill Hill Rd., 04217, ☎ 207/824–2774 or 800/760–2774, WEB www.laubergecountryinn.com. 6 rooms, 1 apartment. Restaurant, baby-sitting, Internet, some pets allowed; no air-conditioning, no room TVs, no room phones. AE, D, MC, V. BP.

$$ ✕🏨 **Victoria Inn.** It's hard to miss this turreted inn, with its beige-, mauve-, and teal-painted exterior and attached carriage house topped with a cupola. Inside, Victorian details include ceiling rosettes, stained-glass windows, elaborate fireplace mantels, and gleaming oak trim. Guest rooms vary in size; most are furnished with reproductions of antiques. The restaurant, open to the public for dinner ($$–$$$; closed Mon.), has three rooms, one with a wraparound mural of Italian scenes. Choose from entrées such as lobster ravioli and filet mignon. ✉ 32 Main St. (Box 249, 04217), ☎ 207/824–8060 or 888/774–1235, FAX 207/824–3926, WEB www.victoria-inn.com. 15 rooms. Restaurant, cable TV, in-room data ports; no smoking. AE, MC, V. BP.

$–$$ ✕🏨 **Briar Lea.** At this Georgian-style inn, you can snuggle under a down comforter at night in rooms decorated in a warm and inviting country style. The dining room ($$–$$$; no lunch) is open to the public for breakfast and dinner. Entrées may include pork chops, rainbow trout, and crispy roast duck. A children's menu is available. ✉ 150 Mayville Rd. (Rte. 2), 04217, ☎ 207/824–4717 or 877/311–1299, FAX 207/824–7121, WEB www.briarlearestaurant.com. 6 rooms. Restaurant, cable TV, some pets allowed (fee); no-smoking. AE, D, MC, V. Call ahead Nov.–late Dec., Apr.–May. BP.

$$$ 🏨 **Jordan Grand Resort Hotel.** A hit with Sunday River skiers, this condominium hotel provides ski-in, ski-out access to the Jordan Bowl trails. After a day on the slopes, you can relax in the heated outdoor pool. Room rates include lift tickets. ✉ 1 Grand Cir., off Skiway Rd. and U.S. 2 (Box 450, Newry 04217), ☎ 207/824–5000 or 800/543–2754, FAX 207/824–5399. 195 condominiums. 2 restaurants, some kitchenettes, café, pool, health club, baby-sitting, meeting room. AE, D, MC, V.

$$$ 🏨 **Sunday River Inn.** This homey chalet on the Sunday River ski-area access road has private rooms for families and dorm rooms (bring your sleeping bag) for groups and students, all within easy access of the slopes. A hearty breakfast and dinner are served buffet-style, and a stone hearth dominates the comfortable living room. The inn operates an excellent ski-touring center; rates include touring ticket. ✉ *213 Skiway Rd., Newry 04261,* ☎ *207/824–2410,* ℻ *207/824–3181,* WEB *www.sundayriverinn.com. 19 rooms, 3 with private bath; 5 dorms with shared bath. Hot tub, sauna, cross-country skiing, downhill skiing; no air-conditioning, no room TVs, no room phones, no smoking. AE, D, MC, V. Closed Apr.–late Nov. MAP.*

Nightlife and the Arts

For a quiet evening, head to the piano bar at the **Bethel Inn and Country Club** (✉ Village Common, ☎ 207/824–2175). At Sunday River, the **Bumps Pub** (✉ Whitecap Lodge, ☎ 207/824–5269) has après-ski and evening entertainment. Tuesday night is comedy night, ski movies are shown on Wednesday, and rock/pop bands play on weekends and holidays. **Sunday River Brewing Company** (✉ U.S. 2, ☎ 207/824–4253) has pub fare and live entertainment—usually progressive rock bands—on weekends. The **Sudbury Inn** (✉ 151 Main St., ☎ 207/824–2174) draws the après-ski crowd with mostly live blues.

Outdoor Activities and Sports

CANOEING

Bethel Outdoor Adventures (✉ 121 Mayville Rd., ☎ 207/824–4224) rents canoes, kayaks, bikes, and snowmobiles.

DOGSLEDDING

Mahoosuc Guide Service (✉ Bear River Rd., Newry, ☎ 207/824–2073) leads day and multiday dogsledding expeditions on the Maine–New Hampshire border.

HIKING

Telemark Inn & Llama Treks (✉ King's Hwy., Mason Township, ☎ 207/836–2703) operates one- to six-day llama-supported hiking trips in the White Mountain National Forest.

HORSEBACK RIDING

Sparrowhawk Mountain Ranch (✉ 600 Fleming Rd., ☎ 207/836–2528) leads one-hour to day-long trail rides and also has an indoor arena.

SNOWMOBILING

Sun Valley Sports (✉ 129 Sunday River Rd., ☎ 207/824–7533 or 877/851–7533, WEB www.sunvalleysports.com) rents snowmobiles and gives tours. It also operates fly-fishing trips, canoe and kayak rentals, and moose and wildlife safaris.

NATIONAL FORESTS AND PARKS

At **Grafton Notch State Park** (✉ Rte. 26, 14 mi north of Bethel, ☎ 207/824–2912) you can take an easy nature walk to Mother Walker Falls or Moose Cave and see the spectacular Screw Auger Falls, or you can hike to the summit of Old Speck Mountain, the state's third-highest peak. If you have the stamina and the equipment, you can pick up the Appalachian Trail here, hike over Saddleback Mountain, and continue on to Katahdin. The **Maine Appalachian Trail Club** (✉ Box 283, Augusta 04330) publishes a map and trail guide.

White Mountain National Forest straddles New Hampshire and Maine. Although the highest peaks are on the New Hampshire side, the Maine section has magnificent rugged terrain, camping and picnic areas, and hiking from hour-long nature loops to a 5½-hour scramble up Speckled Mountain. ✉ *Evans Notch Visitor Center, 18 Mayville Rd., 04217,* ☎ *207/824–2134.* ⛺ *Parking pass (good 1–7 days) $5.* ☯ *Center early May–mid-Oct., daily 8–5; mid-Oct.–early May, daily 8:30–4:30.*

Shopping

Bonnema Potters (⌧ 146 Lower Main St., ☎ 207/824–2821) sells plates, lamps, tiles, and vases in colorful modern designs. The **Lyons' Den** (⌧ U.S. 2, Hanover, ☎ 207/364–8634), a great barn of a place near Bethel, stocks antique glass, china, tools, prints, rugs, hand-wrought iron, and some furniture. **Mt. Mann Jewelers** (⌧ 57 Main St., ☎ 207/824–3030) carries contemporary jewelry with unusual gems.

Ski Areas

SUNDAY RIVER

What was once a sleepy little ski area with minimal facilities has evolved into a sprawling resort that attracts skiers from as far away as Europe. Spread throughout the valley are three base areas, two condominium hotels, trailside condominiums, town houses, and a ski dorm. Sunday River is home to the Maine Handicapped Skiing program, which provides lessons and services for skiers with disabilities. ⌧ *Sunday River Rd. off U.S. 2, Newry (Box 450, Bethel 04217), ☎ 207/824–3000; 207/824–5200 snow conditions; 800/543–2754 reservations.*

Downhill. White Heat has gained fame as the steepest, longest, widest lift-served trail in the East; but skiers of all abilities will find plenty of suitable terrain, from a 5-km (3-mi) beginner run to steep glades, in-your-face bumps, and terrain parks. The area has 127 trails, the majority of them in the intermediate range. Expert and advanced runs are grouped from the peaks, and most beginner slopes are near the base. Trails spreading down from eight peaks have a total vertical descent of 2,340 ft and are served by nine quads, four triples, and two double chairlifts and three surface lifts.

Other activities. The Entertainment Center at White Cap has a lighted halfpipe, a lighted ice-skating rink, a tubing area, a teen center, and a nightclub with live music.

Child care. Three licensed day-care centers accommodate children ages 6 weeks–6 years. Coaching for children ages 3–18 is available in the Children's Center at the South Ridge base area.

Summer and year-round activities. Within the housing complexes are indoor pools, outdoor heated pools, saunas, hot tubs, and four tennis courts. In summer, a mountain park attracts families with hiking and mountain biking.

CROSS-COUNTRY SKIING

Bethel Inn Touring Center (⌧ Village Common, ☎ 207/824–6276) has 40 km (25 mi) of trails and provides ski and snowshoe rentals and lessons. **Carter's Cross-Country Ski Center** (⌧ 786 Intervale Rd., ☎ 207/539–4848) has 50 km (31 mi) for all levels of skiers; a center in Oxford has 35 km (22 mi) of trails for novice and intermediate skiing. Both centers provide lessons and snowshoe, ski, and sled rentals. **Sunday River Cross-Country Ski Center** (⌧ 23 Skiway Rd., Newry, ☎ 207/824–2410), based at the Sunday River Inn, has 40 km (25 mi) of trails; all are tracked and most have skating lanes. A special trail is designated for skiing with dogs. Lessons and rentals are available.

En Route   The routes north from Bethel to the Rangeley district are all scenic, particularly in the autumn when the maples are aflame with color. In the town of Newry, make a short detour to the **Artist's Bridge** (turn off Route 26 onto Sunday River Road and drive about 3 mi), the most painted and photographed of Maine's eight covered bridges. Route 26 continues north to the gorges and waterfalls of **Grafton Notch State Park.** Past the park, Route 26 continues to Errol, New Hampshire, where

Route 16 will return you east around the north shore of Mooselook-meguntic Lake, through Oquossoc, and into Rangeley.

A more direct route (if marginally less scenic) from Bethel to Range-ley still allows a stop in Newry. Follow U.S. 2 north and east from Bethel to the twin towns of Rumford and Mexico, where Route 17 continues north to Oquossoc, about an hour's drive. The high point of this route is **Height of Land,** with its unforgettable views of mountains ranges and the island-studded blue mass of Mooselookmeguntic Lake. At **Haines Landing** on Mooselookmeguntic Lake, you can stand at 1,400 ft above sea level and face the same magnificent scenery you admired at 2,400 ft from Height of Land on Route 17.

Rangeley

59 *67 mi north of Bethel.*

Rangeley, north of Rangeley Lake on Route 4/16, has long lured an-glers and winter-sports enthusiasts to its more than 40 lakes and ponds and 450 square mi of woodlands. Equally popular in summer or win-ter, Rangeley has a rough, wilderness feel to it. Lodgings are in the woods, around the lake, and along the golf course.

The **Wilhelm Reich Museum** interprets the life and work of controver-sial physician-scientist Wilhelm Reich (1897–1957), who believed that a force called orgone energy was the source of neurosis. The Orgone Energy Observatory, designed for Reich in 1948, exhibits biographi-cal materials, inventions, and the equipment used in his experiments. Also on view are Reich's library, personal memorabilia, and artwork. Trails lace the 175-acre grounds, and the observatory deck has mag-nificent views of the countryside. ⊠ *Dodge Pond Rd.,* ☎ *207/864–3443,* WEB *www.rangeleymaine.com/wilhelmreich.* ⊡ *$4.* ☉ *July–Aug., Wed.–Sun. 1–5; Sept., Sun. 1–5.*

OFF THE
BEATEN PATH

SANDY RIVER & RANGELEY LAKES RAILROAD – You can ride a mile through the woods along a narrow-gauge railroad on a century-old train drawn by a replica of the *Sandy River No. 4* locomotive. ⊠ *Bridge Hill Rd., Phillips (20 mi southeast of Rangeley),* ☎ *207/778–3621,* WEB *www.srrl-rr.org.* ⊡ *$3.* ☉ *June–Oct., 1st and 3rd Sun. each month; rides hourly 11–3.*

Dining and Lodging

$$–$$$ ✕ **Gingerbread House.** A big fieldstone fireplace, well-spaced tables, and an antique marble soda fountain, all with views of the woods be-yond, make for comfortable surroundings at this gingerbread-trim house, which is open for breakfast, lunch, and dinner. Soups, salads, and sandwiches at lunch give way to entrées such as shrimp scampi, roasted cranberry-maple chicken, and Maine crab cakes. ⊠ *Rtes. 17 and 4, Oquossoc,* ☎ *207/864–3602. AE, D, MC, V. Closed Mon. No dinner Sun.*

$$–$$$ ✕ **Porter House Restaurant.** This popular restaurant, seemingly in the middle of nowhere, draws diners from Rangeley, Kingfield, and Canada with its good service, excellent food, and casual surroundings. Of the 1908 farmhouse's four dining rooms, the front one downstairs, which has a fireplace, is the most intimate and elegant. The broad Continental-style menu includes entrées for diners with light appetites. On the heavier side are porterhouse steak and roast duckling. ⊠ *Rte. 27, Eu-stis (20 mi north of Rangeley),* ☎ *207/246–7932. Reservations essential. AE, D, MC, V. Closed Mon.–Tues.*

$$ ✕🏨 **Country Club Inn.** Built in the 1920s on the Mingo Springs Golf Course, this retreat has a secluded hilltop location and sweeping lake

and mountain views. Fieldstone fireplaces anchor both ends of the inn's living room. Rooms downstairs in the main building and in the 1950s motel-style wing are cheerfully if minimally decorated. The glassed-in dining room ($$–$$$)—open to nonguests by reservation only—has linen-draped tables set well apart. The menu lists entrées such a veal Gruyère and roast duck Montmorency. ⊠ *1 Country Club Rd., 04970,* ☎ *207/864–3831,* WEB *www.countryclubinnrangeley.com. 19 rooms. Restaurant, cable TV, 18-hole golf course, pool, bar; no air-conditioning, no-smoking rooms. AE, MC, V. Closed Apr.–mid-May and mid-Oct.– late Dec. BP, MAP.*

$$ ✕🏨 **Rangeley Inn and Motor Lodge.** From Main Street you see only the three-story blue inn building (circa 1907), but behind it is a motel wing with views of Haley Pond, a lawn, and a garden. Some of the inn's sizable rooms have iron-and-brass beds and subdued wallpaper, some have claw-foot tubs, and others have whirlpool tubs. The dining room ($$$–$$$$) has Continental-style choices, including chicken in creamy champagne sauce and filet mignon; the tavern serves casual fare such as soups, sandwiches, steaks, and ribs. You can choose to include breakfast and dinner in the rate. ⊠ *51 Main St. (Box 160, 04970),* ☎ *207/864–3341 or 800/666–3687,* FAX *207/864–3634,* WEB *www.rangeleyinn.com. 36 inn rooms, 15 motel rooms, 2 cabins. Restaurant, cable TV, some microwaves, some refrigerators, bar, Internet, meeting rooms, some pets allowed (fee); no air-conditioning. AE, D, MC, V.*

$$$$ 🏨 **Grant's Kennebago Camps.** People have been roughing it in comfort at this traditional sporting camp on Kennebago Lake for more than 85 years, lured by the mountain views, excellent fly-fishing, and hearty home-cooked meals. The wilderness setting is nothing less than spectacular. The cabins, whose screened porches overlook the lake, have woodstoves and are finished in knotty pine. Meals are served in the cheerful waterfront dining room. ⊠ *Off Rte. 16 (Box 786, 04970),* ☎ *207/864–3608 or 800/633–4815,* WEB *www.grantscamps.com. 18 cabins. Dining room, lake, windsurfing, boating, fishing, mountain bikes, hiking, playground, some pets allowed (fee); no air-conditioning, no room phones, no room TVs. D, MC, V. Closed Oct.–mid-May. FAP.*

$$–$$$ 🏨 **Hunter Cove on Rangeley Lake.** These rustic lakeside cabins, which sleep from two to six people, provide all the comforts of home. The interiors are unfinished knotty pine and include kitchens, full baths, and comfortable if plain living rooms. Cabin No. 1 has a fieldstone fireplace, and others have wood-burning stoves. Cabin Nos. 5 and 8 have hot tubs. If you visit in summer, you can take advantage of a sand swimming beach, boat rentals, and a nearby golf course. In winter, snowmobile right to your door or ski nearby (cross-country and downhill). ⊠ *334 Mingo Loop Rd.,* ☎ *207/864–3383,* WEB *www.huntercove.com. 8 cabins. Cable TV, in-room VCRs, microwaves, beach, boating, some pets allowed (fee). AE.*

Nightlife and the Arts

Rangeley Friends of the Arts (⊠ Box 333, 04970, ☎ no phone) sponsors musical theater, fiddlers' contests, rock and jazz, classical, and other summer fare, mostly at Lakeside Park.

Outdoor Activities and Sports

BOATING

Rangeley and Mooselookmeguntic lakes are good for canoeing, sailing, and motorboating. For fishing and paddleboat rentals, call **Oquossoc Cove Marina** (⊠ Oquossoc, ☎ 207/864–3463). **Dockside Sports Center** (⊠ Town Cove, ☎ 207/864–2424) rents boats, canoes, and other crafts. **River's Edge Sports** (⊠ Rte. 4/16, Oquossoc, ☎ 207/864–5582) rents canoes.

FISHING

Fishing for brook trout and salmon is at its best in May, June, and September; the Rangeley area is especially popular with fly-fishers. **West-wind Charters and Guide Service** (☎ 207/864–5437) provides fishing guides and services.

SNOWMOBILING

More than 100 mi of maintained trails link lakes and towns to wilderness camps in the Rangeley area. The **Maine Snowmobile Association** has information about Maine's nearly 8,000-mi trail system.

STATE PARK

On the south shore of Rangeley Lake, **Rangeley Lake State Park** (⊠ off Rte. 17, ☎ 207/864–3858) has superb lakeside scenery, swimming, picnic tables, a boat ramp, showers, and 50 campsites.

Ski Areas

SADDLEBACK SKI AND SUMMER LAKE PRESERVE

A down-home atmosphere prevails at Saddleback, where the quiet and the absence of crowds, even on holiday weekends, draw return visitors—many of them families. The Appalachian Trail crosses Saddleback's summit ridge. ⊠ *Saddleback Rd. off Rte. 4 (Box 490, 04970),* ☎ *207/864–5671; 207/864–3380 snow conditions; 207/864–5364 reservations;* WEB *www.saddlebackskiarea.com.*

Downhill. The terrain is short and concentrated at the top of the mountain, accessible only by a T-bar. The middle of the mountain is mainly intermediate, with a few meandering easy trails; the beginner or novice slopes are toward the bottom. Two double chairlifts and three T-bars carry skiers to the 41 trails on the 1,830-ft mount.

Cross-country. Forty kilometers (25 miles) of groomed cross-country trails spread out from the base area and circle Saddleback Lake and several ponds and rivers.

Child care. The nursery takes children ages 6 weeks–8 years. Ski classes and programs for kids of different levels and ages are offered.

Summer activities. Hiking is the big sport in warm weather.

Kingfield

⑥⓪ *33 mi east of Rangeley, 15 mi west of Phillips.*

In the shadows of Mt. Abraham and Sugarloaf Mountain, Kingfield has everything a "real" New England town should have: a general store, historic inns, and a white clapboard church. Sugarloaf/USA has golf and tennis in summer.

The **Stanley Museum** houses a collection of original Stanley Steamer cars built by the Stanley twins, Kingfield's most famous natives. ⊠ *40 School St.,* ☎ *207/265–2729.* ☜ *$2.* ☉ *May–Oct., Tues.–Sun. 10–4; Nov.–Apr., weekdays 1–4.*

Nowetah's American Indian Museum displays an extensive collection of baskets as well as artifacts from native peoples of North and South America. This small museum is part of a store. ⊠ *Rte. 27, New Portland,* ☎ *207/628–4981.* ☜ *Free.* ☉ *Daily 10–5.*

Dining and Lodging

$–$$$ ✕ **Gepetto's.** Gepetto's combines efficient service with a diverse menu including homemade soups, hearty salads, burgers, pizza, vegetarian pasta, and fresh seafood. Hanging plants brighten the pine-paneled dining rooms, and big windows let you watch skiers as they schuss the slopes or walk through the village. ⊠ *Sugarloaf Base Village, Carrabassett Valley,* ☎ *207/237–2953. MC, V.*

$–$$ ✕🏠 **Sugarloaf Inn.** Guest rooms at this country inn could use a face lift, but you can't beat the ski-on access to Sugarloaf/USA. Rooms range from king-size on the fourth floor to dorm-style (bunk beds) on the ground floor. A greenhouse section of the Seasons Restaurant ($$–$$$) affords views of the slopes. At breakfast the sunlight pours into the dining room, and at dinner you can watch the snow-grooming machines prepare your favorite run. The in-house brewpub is a comfortable après-ski spot. ⊠ *Sugarloaf Access Rd. (R.R. 1, Box 5000, Carrabassett Valley 04947),* ☎ *207/237–6814 or 800/843–5623,* 𝔽𝔸𝕏 *207/237–3773,* 𝕎𝔼𝔹 *www.sugarloaf.com. 38 rooms, 4 dorm-style rooms. Restaurant, cable TV, golf privileges, pool, health club, cross-country skiing, downhill skiing, pub, video game room, meeting room; no smoking. AE, D, MC, V.*

$ ✕🏠 **One and Three Stanley Avenue.** These sister properties, a fine-dining restaurant and a simple B&B, are in adjacent Victorian houses. The quiet neighborhood is a few minutes' walk from downtown Kingfield and about a 20-minute drive from Sugarloaf/USA. Both are decorated with period furnishings. The restaurant ($$$–$$$$; closed May–mid-Nov.) specializes in creative Continental fare and emphasizes fresh Maine ingredients. ⊠ *3 Stanley Ave. (Box 169, 04947),* ☎ *207/265–5541,* 𝕎𝔼𝔹 *www.stanleyavenue.com. 6 rooms, 3 with bath. Restaurant; no air-conditioning, no room phones, no smoking. MC, V. BP.*

$–$$$ 🏠 **Grand Summit.** New England ambience and European-style service are combined at this six-story brick hotel at the base of the lifts at Sugarloaf/USA. Oak and redwood paneling in the main rooms is enhanced by contemporary furnishings. Valet parking, ski tuning, and lockers are available. ⊠ *R.R. 1, Box 2299, Carrabassett Valley 04947,* ☎ *207/237–4205 or 800/527–9879,* 𝔽𝔸𝕏 *207/237–2874,* 𝕎𝔼𝔹 *www.sugarloaf.com. 100 rooms, 19 suites. Restaurant, cable TV with video games, some microwaves, some refrigerators, hot tub, massage, sauna, spa, video game room, meeting room; no-smoking rooms. AE, D, DC, MC, V.*

Nightlife and the Arts

Monday is blues night at the **Bag & Kettle** (☎ 207/237–2451), which is the best choice for pizza and burgers. A microbrewery on the access road, the **Sugarloaf Brewing Company** (☎ 207/237–2211) pulls in revelers who come for après-ski brewskies. **Widowmaker Lounge** (☎ 207/237–6845) frequently presents live entertainment in the base lodge.

Outdoor Activities and Sports

T.A.D. Dog Sled Services (⊠ Rte. 27, Carrabassett Valley, ☎ 207/246–4461) conducts short 1½-mi rides near Sugarloaf/USA; sleds accommodate up to two adults and two children.

Ski Areas

SUGARLOAF/USA

Abundant natural snow, a huge mountain, and the only above-treeline skiing in the East have made Sugarloaf one of Maine's best-known ski areas. Two slope-side hotels and hundreds of slope-side condominiums provide ski-in, ski-out access, and the base village has restaurants and shops. Once you are here, a car is unnecessary—a shuttle connects all mountain operations. Summer is much quieter than winter, but you can bike, hike, golf, and fish. ⊠ *Sugarloaf Access Rd. (R.R. 1, Box 5000, Carrabassett Valley 04947),* ☎ *207/237–2000; 207/237–6808 snow conditions; 800/843–5623 reservations.*

Downhill. With a vertical of 2,820 ft, Sugarloaf is taller than any other New England ski peak except Killington in Vermont. The advanced terrain begins with the steep snowfields on top, wide open and treeless. Coming down the face of the mountain, black-diamond runs are everywhere, often blending into easier terrain. Many intermediate trails can be found down the front face, and a couple more come off the summit. Easier runs are predominantly toward the bottom, with a few long, winding runs that twist and turn from higher elevations. The mountain has three terrain parks and a halfpipe. Serving the resort's 129 trails are two high-speed quad, two quad, one triple, and eight double chairlifts and one T-bar.

Cross-country. The Sugarloaf Ski Outdoor Center has 105 km (62 mi) of cross-country trails that loop and wind through the valley. Trails connect to the resort.

Other activities. Snowshoeing and ice skating are available at the Outdoor Center. On Wednesday and Saturday nights, you can take a Sno-Cat to **Bullwinkles,** a mid-mountain restaurant, for a multicourse dining adventure (☎ 207/237–2000;$85 per person, reservations essential).

Child care. A nursery takes children ages 10 weeks–5 years. Children's ski programs begin at age 3. A night nursery is open on Thursday and Saturday 6–10 PM by reservation. Instruction is provided on a half-day or full-day basis for children ages 4–14.

Summer and year-round activities. The resort has a superb 18-hole, Robert Trent Jones Jr.–designed golf course and six tennis courts for public use in warmer months. The Original Golf School operates from late June to late October. You can get advice on planning mountain biking and hiking trips, and the resort has canoe and bike rentals and can arrange fly-fishing instruction. The **Sugarloaf Sports and Fitness Club** (☎ 207/237–6946) has an indoor pool, six indoor and outdoor hot tubs, racquetball courts, full fitness and spa facilities, and a beauty salon. Use of club facilities is included in all lodging packages. The **Anti-Gravity Center** (☎ 207/237–5566) has a climbing wall, weight room, basketball court, trampolines, and indoor skate park.

Western Lakes and Mountains A to Z

To research prices, get advice from other travelers, and book travel arrangements, visit www.fodors.com.

AIR TRAVEL
Mountain Air Service provides air access to remote areas, scenic flights, and charter-fishing trips. Naples Seaplane Service operates charter and scenic flights over the lakes region.
➤ AIRLINES AND CONTACTS: **Mountain Air Service** (⊠ Rangeley, ☎ 207/ 864–5307). **Naples Seaplane Service** (⊠ Rte. 302, Naples Causeway, Naples, ☎ 207/693–5138).

BIKE TRAVEL
Numerous back roads provide plenty of mountain biking. As in other parts of the state, few roads have shoulders.
➤ BIKE INFORMATION: **Bethel Outdoor Adventures** (⊠ 121 Mayville Rd., Bethel, ☎ 207/824–4224 or 800/533–3607, WEB www. BethelOutdoorAdventure.com). **Rangeley Mountain Bike Touring** (⊠ 53 Main St. Rangeley, ☎ 207/864–5799). **Ride On!** (⊠ Village Center, Sugarloaf Resort, Carrabassett Valley, ☎ 207/237–6986).

BUS TRAVEL
The Mountain Express is a free shuttle bus that operates between Bethel village and Sunday River. The Sunday River Trolley links hotels and con-

dos at the ski resort with lifts and lodges. Sunday River's Jordan Shuttle vans operate between the Jordan Grand and South Ridge Base Lodge during the day and the White Cap Base Lodge in the evening.

CAR TRAVEL

A car is essential to tour the western lakes and mountains. To travel from town to town in the order described in this section, drive U.S. 302 to Naples, then Route 35 to Harrison and the Waterfords. Take the Sweden Road, an ideal pick for autumn due to its vistas of the White Mountains, across to Lovell and pick up Route 5 to Bethel. From there, take Route 26 to U.S. 2 to Route 17 to Oquossoc, then head east on Route 16 through Rangeley to Kingfield.

EMERGENCIES

➤ HOSPITALS: **Bethel Family Health Center** (⊠ 42 Railroad St., Bethel, ☎ 207/824–2193 or 800/287–2292). **Mt. Abram Regional Health Center** (⊠ Depot St., Kingfield, ☎ 207/265–4555). **Northern Cumberland Memorial Hospital** (⊠ S. High St., Bridgton, ☎ 207/647–8841). **Rangeley Regional Health Center** (⊠ Main St., Rangeley, ☎ 207/ 864–3303).

LODGING

Krainin Real Estate specializes in lakefront rentals in the Sebago area. In the Bethel area, try Maine Street Realty. Morton & Furbish has extensive rental listings in the Rangeley Lakes region.
➤ LODGING: **Krainin Real Estate** (⊠ Rte. 302, South Casco, ☎ 207/655– 3811 or 800/639–2321, WEB www.krainin.com). **Maine Street Realty** (⊠ 57 Main St., Bethel, ☎ 800/824–2141, WEB www.mainestreetrealty.com). **Morton & Furbish** (⊠ Rangeley, ☎ 207/864–5777 or 888/218–4882, WEB www.rangeleyrentals.com). **Sugarloaf Area Reservations Service** (☎ 207/235–2100 or 800/843–2732).

MEDIA

The *Portland Press Herald* is published Monday–Saturday; the *Maine Sunday Telegram* is published on Sunday. The *Lewiston Sun Journal* is published daily. Weekly newspapers include the *Bethel Citizen, Bridgton News, Irregular* (Kingfield), and *Suburban News* (Windham).

WMEA 90.1 is the public broadcasting affiliate for the Sebago Lakes region. WCSH, channel 6, is the NBC affiliate. WMTW, channel 8, is the ABC affiliate. WGME, channel 13, is the CBS affiliate. WCBB, channel 10, is the Maine Public Broadcasting affiliate.

OUTDOOR ACTIVITIES AND SPORTS
FISHING

For information about fishing and licenses, contact the Maine Department of Inland Fisheries and Wildlife.
➤ CONTACT: **Maine Department of Inland Fisheries and Wildlife** (⊠ 41 State House Station, Augusta 04333, ☎ 207/287–8000, WEB www .state.me.us/ifw).

SKIING

Sunday River is one of the state's largest alpine areas. Family-friendly Mt. Abram also has night skiing. Saddleback delivers a back-to-basics ski experience. You can cross-country ski at Nordic centers with groomed trails or go on a backcountry excursion. For information on cross-country ski centers, shops, and lodging packages, contact the Maine Nordic Ski Council. For information on alpine skiing, contact Ski Maine.
➤ CONTACTS: **Maine Nordic Ski Council** (⊠ Box 645, Bethel 04217, ☎ 207/824–3694 or 800/754–9263, WEB www.mnsc.com). **Ski Maine**

(✉ Box 7566, Portland 04112, ☎ 207/622–6983; 207/761–3774; 888/624–6345 snow conditions; WEB www.skimaine.com).

VISITOR INFORMATION

Bethel's Chamber of Commerce has a reservations service. For reservations at Sugarloaf/USA, contact Sugarloaf Area Reservations Service. ➤ CONTACTS: **Bethel Area Chamber of Commerce** (✉ 30 Cross St. [Box 439, Bethel 04217], ☎ 207/824–2282, WEB www.bethelmaine.com). **Bethel's Chamber of Commerce Reservation Service** (☎ 207/824–3585 or 800/442–5826). **Greater Bridgton–Lakes Region Chamber of Commerce** (✉ U.S. 302 [Box 236, Bridgton 04009], ☎ 207/647–3472, WEB www.mainelakeschamber.com). **Greater Windham Chamber of Commerce** (✉ U.S. 302 [Box 1015, Windham 04062], ☎ 207/892–8265, WEB windhamchamber.sebagolake.org). **Maine Tourism Association Welcome Center** (✉ U.S. 2 [Box 1084, Bethel 04217], ☎ 207/824–4582). **Naples Business Association** (✉ Box 412, Naples 04055, ☎ 207/693–3285 summer). **Rangeley Lakes Region Chamber of Commerce** (✉ Main St. [Box 317, Rangeley 04970], ☎ 207/864–5571 or 800/685–2537, WEB www.rangeleymaine.com). **Sugarloaf Area Chamber of Commerce** (✉ R.R. 1, Box 2151, Kingfield 04947, ☎ 207/235–2100).

THE NORTH WOODS

Maine's North Woods, the vast area in the north-central section of the state, is best experienced by canoe or raft, hiking trail, or on a fishing trip. Some great theaters for these activities are Moosehead Lake, Baxter State Park, and the Allagash Wilderness Waterway—as well as the summer resort town of Greenville. Maine's largest lake, Moosehead supplies more in the way of rustic camps, restaurants, guides, and outfitters than any other northern locale. Its 420 mi of shorefront, three-quarters of which is owned by paper manufacturers, is virtually uninhabited.

Greenville

61 *160 mi northeast of Portland, 71 mi northwest of Bangor.*

Greenville, the largest town on Moosehead Lake, is an outdoors-lover's paradise. Boating, fishing, and hiking are popular in summer; snowmobiling and skiing in winter. The town has the greatest selection of shops, restaurants, and inns in the region, though many of these are closed mid-October–mid-June.

The **Greenville Historical Society** leads guided tours of the Eveleth-Crafts-Sheridan House, a late-19th-century Victorian mansion filled with period antiques. Special exhibits and displays change annually. A small lumberman's museum and a fine exhibit of Native American artifacts dating from 9,000 BC are in the Carriage House. ✉ *Pritham Ave.,* ☎ *207/695–2909,* WEB *www.mooseheadhistory.org.* 🎟 *$2.* ⊙ *Mid-June–Sept., Wed.–Fri. 1–4.*

Moosehead Marine Museum has exhibits on the local logging industry and the steamship era on Moosehead Lake, plus photographs of the Mount Kineo Hotel. ✉ *Main St.,* ☎ *207/695–2716.* 🎟 *$3.* ⊙ *Late May–early Oct., daily 10–4.*

★ The Moosehead Marine Museum runs three- and five-hour trips on Moosehead Lake aboard the *Katahdin,* a 1914 steamship (now diesel). The 115-ft ship, also called *The Kate,* carried passengers to Kineo until 1942 and then was used in the logging industry until 1975. ✉ *Main St. (boarding on shoreline by museum),* ☎ *207/695–2716,* WEB *www.katahdincruises.com.* 🎟 *$20–$26.* ⊙ *July–Columbus Day.*

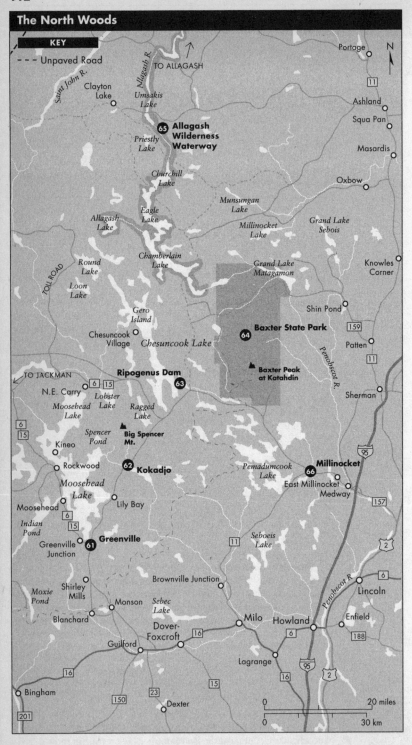

The North Woods

KEY

- - - Unpaved Road

N

TO ALLAGASH

Portage

11

Saint John R.

Allagash R.

Clayton Lake

Umsakis Lake

Ashland

Squa Pan

65 **Allagash Wilderness Waterway**

Priestly Lake

Masardis

Churchill Lake

Oxbow

Munsungan Lake

Eagle Lake

Millinocket Lake

Grand Lake Sebois

Allagash Lake

Knowles Corner

Chamberlain Lake

Grand Lake Matagamon

Round Lake

Shin Pond

TOLL ROAD

Loon Lake

159

Gero Island

Baxter State Park

Patten

64

11

Chesuncook Village

Chesuncook Lake

Penobscot R.

TO JACKMAN

Ripogenus Dam

Baxter Peak at Katahdin

Sherman

N.E. Carry

6 15

63

Lobster Lake

Moosehead Lake

Ragged Lake

95

6 15

Spencer Pond

Big Spencer Mt.

Kineo

Pemadumcook Lake

66 **Millinocket**

Rockwood

62 **Kokadjo**

East Millinocket

Moosehead Lake

Medway

157

Lily Bay

Moosehead

6

Indian Pond

15

Seboeis Lake

2

61 **Greenville**

Greenville Junction

11

Shirley Mills

Brownville Junction

6

Moxie Pond

Monson

Sebec Lake

Lincoln

Blanchard

Dover-Foxcroft

Milo

Howland

Enfield

Guilford

16

6

188

16

Lagrange

16

95

Bingham

150

23

15

2

201

Dexter

0 _____ 20 miles

0 _____ 30 km

OFF THE
BEATEN PATH

KINEO – Once a thriving summer resort, the original Mount Kineo Hotel (built in 1830 and torn down in the 1940s) was accessed primarily by steamship. Today Kineo makes a pleasant day trip. You can take the Kineo Shuttle, which departs from the State Dock in Rockwood (☎ 207/534–8812), or rent a motorboat in Rockwood and make the journey across the lake in about 15 minutes. You can hike the Kineo's summit for awesome views down the lake. A map is available at the Moosehead Area Chamber of Commerce.

Dining and Lodging

$$$$
★

✕🏨 **Blair Hill Inn.** Beautiful gardens and a hilltop location with marvelous views over the lake distinguish this 1891 estate. Guest rooms are spacious, and four have fireplaces. A restaurant, open to the public by reservation, serves a five-course dinner ($$$$) from late May to mid-October on Friday and Saturday nights. Arrive early to enjoy cocktails on the wraparound porch. The inn hosts a music series from June through September and cooking school weekends in the off-season. ⊠ *Lily Bay Rd. (Box 1288, 04441),* ☎ *207/695–0224,* FAX *207/695–4324,* WEB *www.blairhill.com, 8 rooms, 2 suites. Restaurant, cable TV in some rooms, outdoor hot tub, gym, Internet; no air-conditioning, no room phones, no kids under 10, no smoking. D, MC, V. BP.*

$$$

✕🏨 **Greenville Inn.** The ornate cherry and mahogany paneling, Oriental rugs, and lead glass create an aura of masculine ease in this 1985 former lumber baron's mansion. Some rooms and cottages have lake views as does the restaurant ($$$; reservations essential; closed Nov.–Apr.; no lunch). Revised daily, the menu reflects the owners' Austrian background with choices such as spicy maple-glazed salmon fillets with potato pancakes and pork tenderloin with paprika sauce and spaetzle. ⊠ *Norris St. (Box 1194, 04441),* ☎ *207/695–2206 or 888/695–6000,* FAX *207/695–0335,* WEB *www.greenvilleinn.com. 4 rooms, 1 suite in main inn; 1 suite in carriage house; 6 cottages. Restaurant, cable TV in some rooms; no air-conditioning, no room phones, no kids under 8. D, MC, V. CP.*

$$$$

🏨 **Attean Lake Lodge.** The Holden family has owned and operated this island lodge about an hour and a half northwest of Greenville since 1900. Log cabins, which sleep from two to six people, provide a secluded environment. Look for lobster, beef, and veal at the substantial meals; cookouts and picnic lunches add variety. ⊠ *Off Rte. 201, Birch Island (Box 457, Jackman 04945),* ☎ *207/668–3792,* FAX *207/668–4016,* WEB *www.atteanlodge.com. 18 cabins. Beach, boating, recreation room, library. AE, MC, V. Closed Oct.–May. FAP.*

$$$$

🏨 **Little Lyford Pond Camps.** When you want to get away from everything—electricity, plumbing, phones—this remote and rustic wilderness retreat with llamas and sheep, dogs, and chickens casts a magical spell. Gulf Hagas is a half-day hike, moose are abundant, and the fly-fishing is excellent. Cabins have woodstoves, gas lanterns, and small libraries. The home-cooked fare is vegetarian oriented with some fish and poultry. Winter access is by cross-country ski. ⊠ *(Box 340, 04441),* ☎ *207/695–3288,* WEB *www.littlelyford.com. 9 cottages. Ponds, sauna (winter), boating, fishing, hiking, cross-country skiing, some pets allowed (fee); no air-conditioning, no room TVs, no phones, no smoking. No credit cards. Closed Apr. and Nov.–early Dec. FAP.*

$$$–$$$$

🏨 **Lodge at Moosehead Lake.** All rooms in this grand manor overlooking Moosehead Lake have fireplaces and hand-carved four-poster beds; some have lake views. The carriage-house suites open on to private patios. The dining room, where breakfast is served, has a spectacular view of the water. Four-course, prix-fixe dinners are occasionally available; entrées may include pan-seared salmon with citrus. ⊠ *Lily*

Bay Rd. (Box 1167, 04441), ☎ *207/695–4400,* FAX *207/695–2281,*
WEB *www.lodgeatmooseheadlake.com. 5 rooms, 3 suites. Dining room,
cable TV, in-room VCRs, hot tubs, snowmobiling, lobby lounge; no
kids under 14, no smoking. D, MC, V. Closed late Oct.–late Dec. and
mid-Mar.–mid-May.*

$$ 🏠 **Lakeview House.** You get nearly the same sweeping views over
Moosehead Lake at this small, minimally decorated B&B as you do
from the more exclusive and expensive Lodge at Moosehead Lake. ⊠
358 Lily Bay Rd. (Box 1102, 04441), ☎ *207/695–2229,* FAX *207/695–
8951,* WEB *www.lakeviewhouse.com. 2 rooms, 1 suite. Cable TV, some
pets allowed; no room phones, no smoking. Call ahead in winter. BP.*

$ 🏠 **Chalet Moosehead.** Fifty yards off Route 6/15 and right on Moose-
head Lake, this property has efficiencies (with two double beds, a liv-
ing room, and a kitchenette), motel rooms, and cabins, all with picture
windows to capture the view. The attractive grounds include a pri-
vate beach and dock. Some rooms have private balconies overlook-
ing the lake. ⊠ *Rte. 6/15 (Box 327, Greenville Junction 04442),* ☎
207/695–2950 or 800/290–3645, WEB *www.mooseheadlodging.com.
19 rooms, 8 efficiencies. Cable TV, some in-room hot tubs, some kitch-
enettes, some refrigerators, dock, beach, boating, horseshoes, snow-
mobiling, some pets allowed (fee); no air-conditioning, no-smoking
rooms. AE, D, MC, V.*

Outdoor Activities and Sports

Beaver Cove Marina (☎ 207/695–3526) rents boats and snowmobiles.
Big Lake Marina (☎ 207/695–4487) is a full-service marina with boat
rentals. **Moose Country Safaris and Dogsled Trips** (☎ 207/876–4907)
leads moose safaris, dogsled trips, and canoe and kayak trips. **North-
woods Outfitters** (☎ 207/695–3288) outfits a variety of sports and of-
fers tours, moose safaris, dogsledding, and trail advice.

FISHING

Togue, landlocked salmon, and brook and lake trout lure thousands
of anglers to the region from ice-out in mid-May until September; the
hardiest return in winter to ice-fish. Call for current **information** (☎
207/695–3756 or 800/322–9844) on water levels.

RAFTING

The Kennebec and Dead rivers and the west branch of the Penobscot
River provide thrilling white-water rafting (guides are strongly rec-
ommended). These rivers are dam-controlled, so trips run rain or shine
daily from May to October (day and multiday trips are conducted).
Most guided raft trips on the Kennebec and Dead rivers leave from
the Forks, southwest of Moosehead Lake, on Route 201; Penobscot
River trips leave from either Greenville or Millinocket. Many rafting
outfitters operate resort facilities in their base towns. **Raft Maine** (☎
800/723–8633) has lodging and rafting packages and information
about outfitters.

STATE PARK

Lily Bay State Park (⊠ Lily Bay Rd., ☎ 207/695–2700; 🎫 $2), 8 mi
northeast of Greenville, has a good swimming beach, two boat-launch-
ing ramps, and two campgrounds with 91 sites.

Shopping

Indian Hill Trading Post (⊠ Rte. 6/15, ☎ 207/695–2104) stocks just
about anything you might need for a North Woods vacation, includ-
ing sporting and camping equipment, canoes, and fishing licenses;
there's even an adjacent grocery store. You enter **Moosehead Traders**
(⊠ Moosehead Center Mall, Rte. 6/15, ☎ 207/695–3806) through an
antler archway; inside are books, clothing, and antiques and artifacts.

Ski Areas

BIG SQUAW MOUNTAIN RESORT

At this remote but pretty resort overlooking Moosehead Lake, the emphasis is on affordable family skiing—prices are downright cheap compared with those at other in-state areas. ⊠ *Rte. 6/15 (Box D, 04441),* ☎ *207/695–1000.*

Downhill. Trails are laid out according to difficulty, with the easy slopes toward the bottom, intermediate trails weaving from midpoint, and steeper runs high up off the 1,750-vertical-ft peak. The 22 trails are served by one triple and one double chairlift and two surface lifts.

Child care. The nursery takes children from infants through age six. The ski school has daily lessons and racing classes for children of all ages.

Kokadjo

62 *22 mi northeast of Greenville.*

Kokadjo, population "not many," has a sign that reads "Keep Maine green. This is God's country. Why set it on fire and make it look like hell?" This is the last outpost before you enter the North Woods. As you leave Kokadjo, bear left at the fork and follow signs to Baxter State Park. A drive of 5 mi along this road (now dirt) brings you to the Sias Hill checkpoint, where from June to November a fee may be charged to travel the next 40 mi. Access is through a forest where you're likely to encounter logging trucks (which have the right of way), logging equipment, and work in progress. Drive carefully; sightings of moose, deer, and even bear are common.

Ripogenus Dam

63 *20 mi northeast of Kokadjo, 25 mins southeast of Chesuncook Village by floatplane.*

Ripogenus Dam and the granite-walled Ripogenus Gorge are on Ripogenus Lake, east of Chesuncook Lake. The gorge is the jumping-off point for the famous 12-mi West Branch of the Penobscot River whitewater rafting trip and the most popular put-in point for Allagash canoe trips. The Penobscot River drops more than 70 ft per mi through the gorge, giving rafters a hold-on-for-your-life ride. The best spot to watch the Penobscot rafters is from Pray's Big Eddy Wilderness Campground, overlooking the rock-choked Crib Works Rapid (a Class V rapid). To get here, follow the main road northeast and turn left on Telos Road; the campground is about 10 yards after the bridge.

En Route   From Pray's Big Eddy Wilderness Campground, take the main road (here called the Golden Road for the amount of money it took the Great Northern Paper Company to build it) southeast toward Millinocket. The road soon becomes paved. After you drive over the one-lane Abol Bridge and pass through the Debsconeag checkpoint, bear left to reach Togue Pond Gatehouse, the southern entrance to Baxter State Park.

Baxter State Park

★ **64** *24 mi northwest of Millinocket.*

Few places in Maine are as remote or as beautiful as Baxter State Park and the ☞ Allagash Wilderness Waterway. Baxter, a gift from Governor Percival Baxter, is the jewel in the crown of northern Maine, a 204,733-acre wilderness area that surrounds Katahdin, Maine's highest mountain (5,267 ft at Baxter Peak) and the terminus of the Appalachian Trail. There are 46 mountain peaks and ridges, 18 of which exceed an elevation of 3,000 ft. Day-use parking areas fill quickly in season; it's best to arrive early, before 8 AM. The park is intersected by more than 180 mi of trails. No pets, domestic animals, oversize vehicles, cell phones, radios, all-terrain vehicles, motorboats, or motorcycles are allowed in the park, and there are no pay phones, gas stations, stores, or running water or electricity. The one visitor center is at Togue Pond, for which Millinocket is the nearest gateway. ⊠ *Mailing address: 64 Balsam Dr., Millinocket 04462,* ☎ *207/723–5140.* ☜ *$8 per vehicle; free to Maine residents.*

OFF THE
BEATEN PATH

LUMBERMAN'S MUSEUM – This museum comprises 10 buildings filled with exhibits depicting the history of logging, including models, dioramas, and equipment. ⊠ *Shin Pond Rd. (Rte. 159), Patten (22 mi east of Baxter State Park),* ☎ *207/528–2650,* WEB *www.lumbermensmuseum. org.* ☜ *$5.* ⊙ *July–Aug., Fri.–Sun. 10–4; Memorial Day–June and Sept.–Columbus Day, Tues.–Sun. 10–4.*

Lodging

$ ⚠ **Baxter State Park Authority.** Camping spaces at the 10 campgrounds here can be reserved only by mail or in person. Reservations can be made beginning the first working day in January—some sites are fully booked for midsummer weekends soon after that. The state also maintains primitive backcountry sites. ⊠ *64 Balsam Dr., Millinocket 04462,* ☎ *207/723–5140.*

Outdoor Activities and Sports

Katahdin, in Baxter State Park, draws thousands of hikers every year for the daylong climb to the summit and the stunning views of woods, mountains, and lakes from the hair-raising Knife Edge Trail along its ridge. The crowds can be formidable on clear summer days, so if you crave solitude, tackle one of the 45 other mountains in the park, all of which are accessible from a 150-mi network of trails. South Turner can be climbed in a morning (if you're fit)—it has a great view of Katahdin across the valley. On the way you'll pass Sandy Stream Pond, where moose are often seen at dusk. The Owl, the Brothers, and Doubletop Mountain are good day hikes.

Allagash Wilderness Waterway

⑥⑤ *22 mi north of Ripogenus Dam.*

The Allagash is a spectacular 92-mi corridor of lakes and rivers that cuts across 170,000 acres of wilderness, beginning at the northwest corner of Baxter State Park and running north to the town of Allagash, 10 mi from the Canadian border. For information, contact the **Allagash Wilderness Waterway** (⊠ 106 Hogan Rd., Bangor 04401, ☎ 207/ 941–4014).

Outdoor Activities and Sports

The Allagash rapids are ranked Class I and Class II (very easy and easy), but that doesn't mean the river is a piece of cake; river conditions vary greatly with the depth and volume of water, and even a Class I rapid can hang your canoe up on a rock, capsize you, or spin you around. On the lakes, strong winds can halt your progress for days. The Allagash should not be undertaken lightly or without planning; the complete 92-mi course requires 7 to 10 days. The canoeing season along the Allagash is from mid-May to October, although it's wise to remember that the black-fly season ends about July 1. The best bet for a novice is to go with a guide; a good outfitter will help plan your route and provide your craft and transportation.

Millinocket

⑥⑥ *19 mi southeast of Baxter State Park, 70 mi north of Bangor, 90 mi northwest of Greenville.*

Millinocket, a paper-mill town with a population of 7,000, is a gateway to Baxter State Park and Maine's North Woods. Most visitors to this region come to hike, camp, canoe or raft, not to explore Millinocket itself. Although it has a smattering of motels and restaurants, Millinocket is the place to stock up on supplies, fill your gas tank, or grab a hot meal or shower before heading into the wilderness. Numerous rafting and canoeing outfitters and guides are based here.

OFF THE
BEATEN PATH

KATAHDIN IRON WORKS – For a worthwhile day trip from Millinocket, take Route 11 and head southwest to a trailhead 5 mi north of Brownville Junction. Drive the gravel road 6 mi to Katahdin Iron Works, the site of a mining operation that employed nearly 200 workers in the mid-1800s; a deteriorated kiln, a stone furnace, and a charcoal-storage building are all that remain. From here, a hiking trail leads over fairly rugged terrain to **Gulf Hagas,** with natural chasms, cliffs, a 3½-mi gorge, waterfalls, pools, exotic flora, and rock formations.

Lodging

$$$$ ▥ **Bradford Camps.** It's tempting to laze the day away on the front porch of these rustic lakefront log cabins (no electricity) or by the massive fieldstone fireplace in the main lodge. But alas, you have miles of trails, woods, and roads to explore, rivers and lakes to fish and canoe, and even the Allagash is close enough for a day trip. Rates include three hearty, home-style meals. Floatplane transportation is available from Millinocket and other locations. ⊠ *Box 729, Ashland 04732,* ☏ *207/746–7777 May–Nov.; 207/439–6364 Dec.–Apr.;* ⓦⓔⓑ *www.bradfordcamps.com. 8 cabins. Dining room, lake, hiking, boating; no air-conditioning, no room phones, no room TVs. Closed late Nov.–May.*

$$$$ ▥ **Libby Camps.** Matt Libby, along with his wife, Ellen, represent the fifth generation of Libbys to run this sporting camp on Millinocket Lake, the headwaters of the Allagash and Aroostook rivers. Skylights brighten the well-kept cabins, where handmade quilts cover the beds and woodstoves keep the chill at bay (there's no electricity). The main lodge is open and airy with a magnificent central stone fireplace. Rates include all meals as well as use of sea kayaks, canoes, and sail and motor boats. ⊠ *Box 810, Ashland 04732,* ☏ *207/435–8274,* ⒻⒶⓍ *207/435–3230,* ⓦⓔⓑ *www.libbycamps.com. 8 cabins, 10 rustic outpost cabins. Hiking, beach, boating, fishing; no air-conditioning, no room phones, no room TVs. MC, V. Closed late Nov.–Apr. FAP.*

$ ▥ **Big Moose Inn.** There's nothing fancy about this old-fashioned inn and the cabins and campsites nestled between Ambejesus and Millinocket lakes, just 8 mi from the entrance to Baxter State Park. The inn has a big stone-and-brick fireplace decorated with a moose trophy and snowshoes; inn rooms are comfortably furnished with country pieces. The popular dining room, open for dinner Wednesday–Saturday, emphasizes seafood. Canoes and a store are other amenities. ⊠ *Baxter State Park Rd. (Box 98, 04462),* ☏ *207/723–8391,* ⒻⒶⓍ *207/ 723–8199,* ⓦⓔⓑ *www.bigmoosecabins.com. 11 rooms without bath, 11 cabins, 44 campsites. Restaurant, boating, fishing, hiking, snowmobiling; no air-conditioning, no room phones, no room TVs. MC, V. Closed late Nov.–May. CP.*

$ ▥ **Gateway Inn.** After roughing it in the woods, this motel just off I-95 provides clean facilities. Book a room with a deck facing Katahdin for the best views. ⊠ *Rte. 157 (Box 637, Medway 04460),* ☏ *207/ 746–3193,* ⒻⒶⓍ *207/746–3430,* ⓦⓔⓑ *www.medwaygateway.com. 30* *rooms, 8 efficiencies. Cable TV, some kitchenettes, gym, indoor pool, hot tub, sauna, snowmobiling, meeting room, some pets allowed; no-smoking rooms. AE, D, MC, V. CP.*

Outdoor Activities and Sports

Katahdin Outfitters (✉ Baxter State Park Rd., ☎ 800/862–2663 or 207/723–5700) outfits canoeing expeditions. **New England Outdoor Center** (☎ 207/723–5438 or 800/766–7238) rents snowmobiles and offers guided trips.

The North Woods A to Z

To research prices, get advice from other travelers, and book travel arrangements, visit www.fodors.com.

AIR TRAVEL

Charter flights, usually by seaplane, from Bangor, Greenville, or Millinocket to smaller towns and remote lake and forest areas can be arranged with a number of flying services, which will transport you and your gear and help you find a guide.

➤ AIRLINES AND CONTACTS: **Currier's Flying Service** (✉ Greenville Junction, ☎ 207/695–2778). **Folsom's Air Service** (✉ Greenville, ☎ 207/695–2821). **Katahdin Air Service** (✉ Millinocket, ☎ 207/723–8378). **Scotty's Flying Service** (✉ Shin Pond, ☎ 207/528–2626).

AIRPORTS

Bangor International Airport is the closest airport (☞ Maine A to Z).

BIKE TRAVEL

Mountain biking is popular in the Greenville area, but no bikes are allowed on logging roads. Expect to pay $20–$25 for a rental bicycle.

➤ BIKE INFORMATION: **Northwoods Outfitters** (✉ Main St., Greenville, ☎ 207/695–3288, WEB www.maineoutfitter.com).

CAR TRAVEL

A car is essential to negotiate this vast region but may not be useful to someone spending a vacation entirely at a wilderness camp. Public roads are scarce in the north country, but lumber companies maintain private roads that are often open to the public (sometimes by permit only). When driving on a logging road, always give lumber-company trucks the right of way. Be aware that loggers often take the middle of the road and will neither move over nor slow down for you.

I–95 provides the quickest access to the North Woods. U.S. 201 is the major route to Jackman and to Québec. Route 15 connects Jackman to Greenville and Bangor. The Golden Road is a private, paper company–operated road that links Greenville to Millinocket. Be sure to have a full tank of gas before heading on the many private roads in the region.

EMERGENCIES

➤ HOSPITALS: **Charles A. Dean Memorial Hospital** (✉ Pritham Ave., Greenville, ☎ 207/695–2223 or 800/260–4000). **Mayo Regional Hospital** (✉ 75 W. Main St., Dover-Foxcroft, ☎ 207/564–8401). **Millinocket Regional Hospital** (✉ 200 Somerset St., Millinocket, ☎ 207/723–5161).

LODGING

CAMPING

Reservations for state park campsites (excluding Baxter State Park) can be made through the Bureau of Parks and Lands, which can also tell you if you need a camping permit and where to obtain one. Maine Sporting Camp Association publishes a list of its members, with details on the facilities available at each camp.

The Maine Campground Owners Association publishes a helpful annual directory of its members. The Maine Forest Service, Department of Conservation will direct you to the nearest place to get a fire permit. Maine Tourism Association publishes a listing of private campsites and cottage rentals. North Maine Woods maintains 500 primitive campsites on commercial forest land.

➤ CONTACTS: **Bureau of Parks and Lands** (✉ State House Station 22, Augusta 04333, ☎ 207/287–3821; 800/332–1501 in Maine). **Maine Campground Owners Association** (✉ 655 Main St., Lewiston 04240, ☎ 207/782–5874, WEB www.campmaine.com). **Maine Forest Service, Department of Conservation** (✉ State House Station 22, Augusta 04333, ☎ 207/287–2791). **Maine Sporting Camp Association** (✉ Box 119, Millinocket 04462, WEB www.mainesportingcamps.com). **Maine Tourism Association** (✉ 325-B Water St., Hallowell 04347, ☎ 207/623–0363; 800/533–9595 outside Maine). **North Maine Woods** (✉ 41 Main St. [Box 425, Ashland 04732], ☎ 207/435–6213, WEB www.northmainewoods.org).

MEDIA

The *Bangor Daily News* is published Monday–Friday. Weekly newspapers include *Katahdin Times* (Millinocket) and *Moosehead Messenger* (Greenville).

WMEH 90.0, a public broadcasting affiliate, reaches southern portions of the North Woods region. WLBZ, channel 2, is the NBC affiliate. WVII, channel 7, is the ABC affiliate. WABI, channel 5, is the CBS affiliate. WMEB, channel 12, is the Maine Public Broadcasting affiliate.

OUTDOOR ACTIVITIES AND SPORTS
CANOEING

Most canoe rental operations will arrange transportation, help plan your route, and provide a guide. Transport to wilderness lakes can be arranged through the flying services listed under Air Travel.

The Bureau of Parks and Lands (☞ Lodging) provides information on independent Allagash canoeing and camping. Allagash Canoe Trips operates guided trips on the Allagash Waterway, plus the Moose, Penobscot, and St. John rivers. Canoe Maine with Gil Gilpatrick conducts fully outfitted canoeing trips on Maine rivers. Mahoosuc Guide Service runs guided trips on the Penobscot, Allagash, and Moose rivers.

Northwoods Outfitters rents equipment and leads trips on regional lakes and rivers, including the Allagash and the West Branch of the Penobscot. North Woods Ways is a Maine Master guide service on the state's rivers and lakes. Sunrise International outfits trips on eastern and northern Maine waterways and other locations. Willard Jalbert Camps has been leading guided Allagash trips since the late 1800s. North Maine Woods has maps, a canoeing guide for the St. John River, and lists of outfitters, camps, and campsites.

➤ CONTACTS: **Allagash Canoe Trips** (✉ Box 713, Greenville 04441, ☎ 207/695–3668). **Canoe Maine with Gil Gilpatrick** (✉ Box 461, Skowhegan 04976, ☎ 207/453–6959). **Mahoosuc Guide Service** (✉ Bear River Rd., Newry 04261, ☎ 207/824–2073). **North Maine Woods** (✉ Box 425, Ashland 04732, ☎ 207/435–6213). **Northwoods Outfitters** (✉ Maine St. [Box 160, Greenville 04441], ☎ 207/695–3288). **North Woods Ways** (✉ R.R. 2, Box 159A, Guilford 04443, ☎ 207/997–3723). **Sunrise International** (✉ 4 Union Pl., Suite 21, Bangor

04401, ☎ 207/942–9300 or 800/980–2300). **Willard Jalbert Camps** (✉ 6 Winchester St., Presque Isle 04769, ☎ 207/764–0494).

FISHING

For information about fishing and licenses, contact the Maine Department of Inland Fisheries and Wildlife. Guides are available through most wilderness camps, sporting goods stores, and canoe outfitters. For assistance in finding a guide, contact Maine Professional Guides Association or North Maine Woods (☞ Canoeing).

➤ CONTACTS: **Maine Department of Inland Fisheries and Wildlife** (✉ 41 State House Station, Augusta 04333, ☎ 207/287–8000, WEB www.state.me.us/ifw). **Maine Professional Guides Association** (✉ Box 336, Augusta 04332, ☎ 207/622–6241, WEB www.maineguides.org).

HORSEBACK RIDING

North Woods Riding Adventures, owned by registered Maine guides Judy Cross-Strehlke and Bob Strehlke, conducts one-day, two-day, and week-long pack trips (10 people maximum) through parts of Piscataquis County. A popular two-day trip explores the Whitecap–Barren Mountain Range, near Katahdin Iron Works.

➤ CONTACT: **North Woods Riding Adventures** (✉ 64 Garland Line Rd., Dover-Foxcroft 04426, ☎ 207/564–3451).

RAFTING

Raft Maine is an association of white-water outfitters licensed to lead trips down the Kennebec and Dead rivers and the West Branch of the Penobscot River. Rafting season begins May 1 and continues through mid-October.

➤ CONTACT: **Raft Maine** (☎ 800/723–8633, WEB www.raftmaine.com).
➤ CONTACT: **Maine Snowmobile Association** (✉ Box 77, Augusta 04332, ☎ 207/622–6983; 207/626–5717 trail conditions; WEB www.mesnow.com).

VISITOR INFORMATION

➤ CONTACTS: **Baxter State Park Authority** (✉ 64 Balsam Dr., Millinocket 04462, ☎ 207/723–5140). **Katahdin Area Chamber of Commerce** (✉ 1029 Central St., Millinocket 04462, ☎ 207/723–4443, WEB www.katahdinmaine.com). **Moosehead Lake Region Chamber of Commerce** (✉ Rte. 6/15 [Box 581, Greenville 04441], ☎ 207/695–2702, WEB www.mooseheadlake.org).

MAINE A TO Z

To research prices, get advice from other travelers, and book travel arrangements, visit www.fodors.com.

AIR TRAVEL

Regional flying services, operating from regional and municipal airports, provide access to remote lakes and wilderness areas as well as to Penobscot Bay islands.

AIRPORTS

Portland International Jetport is served by Air Nova, American, Business Express, Continental, Delta, Northwest, TWA, United, and US Airways. Bangor International Airport is served by Business Express, Continental, Delta/Comair, and US Airways. Hancock County Airport, 8 mi northwest of Bar Harbor, is served by US Airways Express. Knox County Regional Airport, in Owls Head, 3 mi south of Rockland, has flights to Boston and Bar Harbor on US Airways Express.

➤ AIRPORT INFORMATION: **Portland International Jetport** (✉ Westbrook St. off Rte. 9, ☎ 207/774–7301, WEB www.portlandjetport.org).

Bangor International Airport (✉ Godfrey Blvd., ☎ 207/947–0384, WEB www.flybangor.com.org). Hancock County Airport (✉ Rte. 3, Trenton, ☎ 207/667–7329, WEB www.bhairport.co). Knox County Regional Airport (✉ off Rte. 73, ☎ 207/594–4131, WEB knoxcounty. midcoast.com).

BIKE TRAVEL

For information on bicycling in Maine and a list of companies operating tours, contact the Bicycle Coalition of Maine. The Maine Department of Transportation Web site has information on bike tours.
➤ CONTACTS: Bicycle Coalition of Maine (✉ Box 5275, Augusta, ☎ 207/623–4511, WEB www.bikemaine.org). Maine Department of Transportation Bike and Pedestrian Section (WEB www.state.me.us/mdot/ biketours.htm).

BOAT AND FERRY TRAVEL

Northumberland/Bay Ferries operates the Cat, a high-speed car-ferry service on a catamaran, between Yarmouth, Nova Scotia, and Bar Harbor from mid-May to mid-October. The crossing takes three hours, and the Cat has everything from a casino to sightseeing decks. Prince of Fundy Cruises operates a car ferry from May to October between Portland and Yarmouth, Nova Scotia. Maine State Ferry Service provides service from Rockland, Lincolnville, and Bass Harbor to islands in Penobscot and Blue Hill bays. East Coast Ferries operates between Deer Island, New Brunswick, and Eastport.
➤ BOAT AND FERRY INFORMATION: East Coast Ferries (☎ 506/747–2159). Maine State Ferry Service (☎ 207/596–2202 or 800/491–4883, WEB www.state.me.us/mdot/opt/ferry/ferry.htm). Northumberland/Bay Ferries (☎ 888/249–7245, WEB www.nfl-bay.com). Prince of Fundy Cruises (☎ 800/341–7540; 800/482–0955 in Maine; WEB www. scotiaprince.com).

BUS TRAVEL

Concord Trailways provides service to Bangor, Bath, Belfast, Brunswick, Camden/Rockport, Damariscotta, Lincolnville, Orono, Portland, Rockland, Searsport, Waldoboro, and Wiscasset. Greyhound Bus Lines serves Augusta, Bangor, Bath, Belfast, Brunswick, Camden, Damariscotta, Lewiston, Lincolnville, Orono, Portland, Rockland, Searsport, Waldoboro, Waterville, and Wiscasset. Vermont Transit provides service to Augusta, Bangor, Bar Harbor, Brunswick, Caribou, Ellsworth, Houlton, Lewiston, Old Orchard Beach, Portland, and Waterville.
➤ BUS INFORMATION: Concord Trailways (☎ 800/639–3317, WEB www.concordtrailways.com). Greyhound Bus Lines (☎ 800/231–2222, WEB www.greyhound.com). Vermont Transit (☎ 207/772–6587 or 800/451–3292, WEB www.vermonttransit.com).

CAR RENTAL

➤ MAJOR AGENCIES: Alamo (✉ 1000 Westbrook St., Portland, ☎ 207/ 775–0855; 800/327–9633 in Portland). Avis (✉ Portland International Jetport, Portland, ☎ 207/874–7500; ✉ Bangor International Airport, Bangor, ☎ 207/947–8383 or 800/831–2847, WEB www.avis.com). Budget (✉ 1128 Westbrook St., Portland, ☎ 800/527–7000; ✉ Bangor International Airport, Bangor, ☎ 207/945–9429 or 800/527–0700, WEB www.budgetmaine.com). Hertz (✉ 1049 Westbrook St., Portland International Jetport, Portland, ☎ 207/774–4544; ✉ Bangor International Airport, Bangor, ☎ 207/942–5519 or 800/654–3131, WEB www.hertz.com). National (✉ Portland International Jetport, Portland, ☎ 207/773–0036; ✉ Bangor International Airport, Bangor, ☎ 207/ 947–0158 or 800/227–7368, WEB www.nationalcar.com).

CAR TRAVEL

Interstate 95 is the fastest route to and through the state from coastal New Hampshire and points south, turning inland at Brunswick and going on to Bangor and the Canadian border. U.S. 1, more leisurely and scenic, is the principal coastal highway from New Hampshire to Canada. U.S. 302 is the primary access to the Sebago Lake region, while Route 26 leads to the western mountains and Route 27 leads to the Rangeley and Sugarloaf regions. U.S. 201 is the fastest route to Québec, and Route 9 is the inland route from Bangor to Calais.

The maximum speed limit is 65 mph, unless otherwise posted, on I–95 and the Maine Turnpike. For condition and updates on construction on the Maine Turnpike, contact the Maine Turnpike Authority. Local municipalities post speed limits on roads within their jurisdictions. State law requires drivers to stop for pedestrians. Drivers can make right turns on red if no sign prohibits such turns. Note that Maine law requires drivers to turn on their lights when windshield wipers are operating.

In many areas a car is the only practical means of travel. The *Maine Map and Travel Guide,* available for a small fee from the Maine Tourism Association, is useful for driving throughout the state; it has directories, mileage charts, and enlarged maps of city areas. DeLorme's *Maine Atlas & Gazetteer,* sold at local bookstores, includes enlarged, detailed maps of every part of the state.

➤ CONTACT: **Maine Turnpike Authority** (☎ 800/698–7747), WEB www. maineturnpike.com.

LODGING

CAMPING

Reservations for state park campsites (excluding Baxter State Park) can be made from January until August 23 through the Bureau of Parks and Lands. Make reservations as far ahead as possible (at least seven days in advance), because sites go quickly. The Maine Campground Owners Association has a statewide listing of private campgrounds.

➤ CONTACTS: **Bureau of Parks and Lands** (☎ 207/287–3824; 800/332–1501 in Maine). **Maine Campground Owners Association** (✉ 655 Main St., Lewiston 04240, ☎ 207/782–5874, FAX 207/782–4497, WEB www.campmaine.com).

OUTDOOR ACTIVITIES AND SPORTS

BIRDING

The Maine Audubon Society provides information on birding in Maine and hosts field trips for novice to expert birders.

➤ CONTACT: **Maine Audubon Society** (✉ 20 Gilsland Farm Rd., Falmouth 04105, ☎ 207/781–6180, WEB www.maineaudubon.org).

FISHING

For information about fishing and licenses, contact the Maine Department of Inland Fisheries and Wildlife. The Maine Professional Guides Association maintains and mails out listings of its members and their specialties.

➤ CONTACTS: **Maine Department of Inland Fisheries and Wildlife** (✉ 41 State House Station, Augusta 04333, ☎ 207/287–8000, WEB www.state.me.us/ifw). **Maine Professional Guides Association** (✉ Box 847, Augusta 04332, ☎ 207/549–5631, WEB www.maineguides.org).

KAYAKING

A number of outfitters provide sea-kayaking instruction as well as tours along the Maine coast.

➤ CONTACTS: **Maine Island Kayak Co.** (✉ 70 Luther St., Peaks Island, 04018, ☎ 207/766–2373 or 800/796–2376). **Maine Sport Outfitters**

(✉ U.S. 1, Rockport 04856, ☎ 207/236–8797 or 800/722–0826). **Sunrise County Canoe & Kayak** (✉ Cathance Lake, Grove Post 04657, ☎ 207/454–7708 or 800/980–2300).

PARKS AND PUBLIC LANDS

The Bureau of Parks and Public Lands publishes the brochure "Outdoors in Maine," a listing of state parks, public reserved lands, state historic trails, boat access sites, snowmobile trails, and all-terrain-vehicle trails.

➤ CONTACT: **Bureau of Parks and Public Lands** (✉ 22 State House Station, Augusta 04333, ☎ 207/287–3821, WEB www.state.me.us/doc/parks).

RAFTING

Raft Maine provides information on white-water rafting on the Kennebec, Penobscot, and Dead rivers.

➤ CONTACT: **Raft Maine** (✉ Box 3, Bethel 04217, ☎ 800/723–8633, WEB www.raftmaine.com).

SKIING

For information on alpine skiing, contact Ski Maine. For information on cross-country ski centers, shops, and lodging packages, contact the Maine Nordic Ski Council.

➤ CONTACTS: **Maine Nordic Ski Council** (✉ Box 645, Bethel 04217, ☎ 207/824–3694 or 800/754–9263, WEB www.mnsc.com). **Ski Maine** (✉ Box 7566, Portland 04112, ☎ 207/622–6983; 207/761–3774; 888/624–6345 snow conditions; WEB www.skimaine.com).

SNOWMOBILING

The Maine Snowmobile Association distributes an excellent statewide trail map of about 8,000 mi of trails.

➤ CONTACT: **Maine Snowmobile Association** (✉ Box 77, Augusta 04332, ☎ 207/622–6983; 207/626–5717 trail conditions; WEB www.mesnow.com).

SPORTING CAMPS

Maine Sporting Camp Association publishes a directory of sporting camps throughout the state.

➤ CONTACT: **Maine Sporting Camp Association** (✉ Box 89, Jay 04249, WEB www.mainesportingcamps.com).

WINDJAMMING

The Maine Windjammer Association represents 13 schooners offering multiday cruises along the Maine coast.

➤ CONTACT: **Maine Windjammer Association** (✉ Box 1144, Blue Hill 04614, ☎ 800/807–9463, WEB www.sailmainecoast.com).

TRAIN TRAVEL

Amtrak's Downeaster operates between Boston and Portland with stops in Saco and Wells year-round and in Old Orchard Beach in the summer. At press time, Acadian Railway is scheduled to begin operating luxury excursion trains in Maine's North Woods in spring 2002. Trains will depart from New York, Boston, Portland, and Montreal, and many excursions will travel from Maine to the Canadian Maritimes with stops in Greenville.

➤ TRAIN INFORMATION: **Acadian Railway** (☎ 800/659–7602, WEB www.AcadianRailway.com). **Amtrak** (☎ 800/872–7245, WEB www.amtrak.com or www.thedowneaster.com).

VISITOR INFORMATION

The Maine Tourism Association operates a welcome center on U.S. 2 in Bethel. State of Maine Visitor Information Centers are on Union Street in Calais, Route 203 in Fryeburg, I–95 and U.S. 1 in Kittery, and on U.S. 1 in Yarmouth, I–95, Exit 17. For a brochure describing eight art museums along the Maine coast, write the Maine Art Museum Trail. The Maine Crafts Association publishes a "Guide to Crafts and Culture." "The Maine Archives and Museums Directory" lists museums, historical societies, archives, and historic sites statewide. Call the Maine Garden and Landscape Trail for a map and guide. The Web site, www.mainemusic.org, lists music-related events around the state.

➤ CONTACTS: **The Maine Archives and Museums Directory** (✉ 60 Community Dr., Augusta 04330, ☎ 800/452–8786, WEB www. mainemuseums.org). **Maine Art Museum Trail** (✉ 75 Russell St., Lewiston 04240 ☎ 800/782–6497, WEB www.maineartmuseums.org). **Maine Crafts Association** (✉ 15 Walton St., Portland 04103, WEB www.mainecrafts.maine.com). **Maine Garden and Landscape Trail** (✉ ☎ 800/782–6497). **Maine Innkeepers Association** (✉ 305 Commercial St., Portland 04101, ☎ 207/773–7670, WEB www. maineinns.com). **Maine Office of Tourism** (✉ 33 Stone St., Augusta 04333, ☎ 888/624–6345, WEB www.visitmaine.com). **Maine Tourism Association** (✉ 325-B Water St. [Box 2300, Hallowell 04347], ☎ 207/623–0363 or 888/624–6345, WEB www.mainetourism.com).

3 NEW HAMPSHIRE

Ocean, mountains, lakes—New Hampshire has them all. The engaging coastal city of Portsmouth is a gateway to smaller towns with sandy beaches. The Lakes Region is a summer and fall haven for fishing, swimming, and boating. The White Mountains attract people who come to gaze on Mt. Washington, the East's tallest peak, to ski and snowboard, to hike, and to shop at North Conway's outlet stores. Western and central New Hampshire have a string of cities along I–93 as well as unspoiled historical villages.

By Paula
J. Flanders

Updated and
revised by
Andrew Collins

CRUSTY, AUTONOMOUS NEW HAMPSHIRE is often defined more by what it is not than by what it is. It lacks Vermont's folksy charm, and its coast isn't nearly as grand as that of Maine. Its politics tend toward conservative (with a distinctly libertarian slant), unlike the decidedly more liberal Massachusetts. It was the first colony to declare independence from Great Britain, the first to adopt a state constitution, and the first to require that constitution to be referred to the people for approval.

From the start, New Hampshire residents took their hard-won freedoms seriously. Twenty years after the Revolutionary War's Battle of Bennington, New Hampshire native Gen. John Stark, who led the troops to that crucial victory, wrote a letter to be read at the reunion he was too ill to attend. In it, he reminded his men, "Live free or die; death is not the worst of evils." The first half of that sentiment is now the Granite State's motto. Nothing symbolizes those freedoms more than voting, not only for government officials but also on issues during an annual town meeting. And residents truly relish their role as host of the nation's earliest presidential primary.

New Hampshire's independent spirit, mountain peaks, clear air, and sparkling lakes have attracted trailblazers and artists for centuries. The first hiker to reach the top of Mt. Washington was Darby Field, in 1642. The first summer home appeared on one of the state's many lakes in 1763. Ralph Waldo Emerson, Henry David Thoreau, Nathaniel Hawthorne, and Louisa May Alcott all visited and wrote about the state, sparking a strong literary tradition that continues today. Filmmaker Ken Burns, writer J. D. Salinger, and poet Donald Hall all make their homes here.

Portsmouth has several theater groups, both cutting-edge and mainstream. New Hampshire's oldest professional troupe, Tamworth's Barnstormers, claims the son of a president as its founder. Shops throughout the state often display the work of local artisans. On back roads and in small towns, you can find makers of fine furniture, glassblowers, potters, weavers, and woodworkers. The League of New Hampshire Craftsmen operates eight stores and runs the nation's oldest crafts fair each year in early August.

The state's diverse terrain makes it popular with everyone from avid adventurers to young families looking for easy access to nature. You can ski, snowboard, hike, and fish as well as explore on snowmobiles, sailboats, and mountain bikes. Rock climbing and snowshoeing are popular, too. Natives have no objection to others' enjoying the state's beauty as long as they leave some money behind. New Hampshire has long resisted both sales and income taxes, so tourism adds much-needed revenue to the government coffers.

With a few of its cities consistently rated among the most livable in the nation, New Hampshire has seen considerable growth over the past decade or two. Longtime residents worry that the state will soon take on two personalities: one of rapidly growing cities to the southeast and the other of quiet villages to the west and north. Although the influx of newcomers has brought change, the independent nature of the people and the state's natural beauty remain constant.

Pleasures and Pastimes

Dining

New Hampshire prides itself on seafood—not just lobster but also salmon pie, steamed mussels, fried clams, and seared tuna. Across the state you'll

New Hampshire

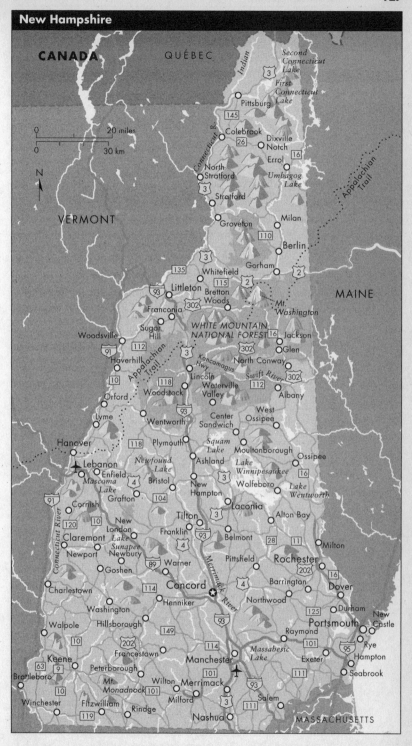

find country taverns with upscale Continental and American menus, many of them embracing regional ingredients and cutting-edge preparations. Alongside a growing number of contemporary eateries are such state traditions as greasy-spoon diners, pizzerias, and pubs that serve hearty comfort fare.

CATEGORY	COST*
$$$$	over $25
$$$	$17–$25
$$	$9–$16
$	under $9

per person, for a main-course dinner

Lodging

In the mid-19th century, wealthy Bostonians took imposing country homes during the summer months. Many of these houses have been converted into handsome inns. The smallest have only a couple of rooms and are typically done in period style. The largest contain 30 or more rooms and have in-room fireplaces and even hot tubs. Pampering amenities increase each year at some of these inns, which, along with bed-and-breakfasts, dominate New Hampshire's lodging scene. You'll also find a great many well-kept, often family-owned motor lodges—particularly in the White Mountains and Lakes regions. A few of the grand old resorts still stand, with their world-class cooking staffs and tradition of top-notch service. In the Merrimack River valley, as well as along major highways, chain hotels and motels prevail.

CATEGORY	COST
$$$$	over $180
$$$	$130–$180
$$	$80–$130
$	under $80

All prices are for a standard double room during peak season and not including tax or gratuities. Some inns add a 15% service charge.

National and State Parks and Forests

The awesome White Mountain National Forest covers 770,000 acres in northern New Hampshire, and Mt. Washington Park crowns the Northeast's highest peak. You can camp, picnic, hike, fish, swim, bike, and ski at numerous other park and recreation areas, including Franconia Notch, Crawford Notch, and Mt. Sunapee. Rhododendron State Park, in Fitzwilliam in the Monadnock region, has a singular collection of wild rhododendrons.

Outdoor Activities and Sports

BEACHES AND LAKES

New Hampshire makes the most of its 18-mi coastline with several good beaches, among them Hampton Beach and Wallis Sands in Rye. For warmer, fresh waters, head to pristine Lake Winnipesaukee, Lake Sunapee, Squam Lake, and Newfound Lake.

BIKING

A safe, scenic route along New Hampshire's seacoast is the bike path along Route 1A, for which you can park at Odiorne Point and follow the road 14 mi south to Seabrook. (Some bikers begin at Prescott Park in Portsmouth and take Route 1B into New Castle, but beware of the traffic.) Another pretty route is from Newington Town Hall to the Great Bay Estuary. White Mountains routes are detailed in "The White Mountain Ride Guide," sold at area sports and bookshops. There's also a bike path in Franconia Notch State Park at the Lafayette Campground and a mountain-biking center, Great Glen Trails, at the base of Mt. Washington. Many ski areas have lift-serviced mountain biking in summer.

Brook and rainbow trout, salmon, smallmouth bass, pickerel, and horned pout are just some of the species that swim in the fresh waters of the Lakes, Sunapee, and Monadnock regions. In winter, ice fishing from huts known as "ice bobs" is common throughout the state. Alton Bay has an "Ice Out" salmon derby in spring. Between April and October, deep-sea anglers take to the ocean for cod, mackerel, and bluefish.

Scandinavian settlers who came to New Hampshire's high, handsome, rugged peaks in the late 1800s brought their skis with them. Skiing got its modern start here in the 1920s with the cutting of trails on Cannon Mountain. You can now ski or snowboard at nearly 20 areas, from the old, established slopes (Cannon, Cranmore, Wildcat) to more contemporary ones (Attitash, Loon, Waterville Valley). Packages assembled by the ski areas allow you to sample different resorts.

Shopping

The absence of sales tax makes New Hampshire a hugely popular shopping destination. Outside the outlet meccas of North Conway and Tilton, this pastime revolves around antiques and local crafts, though in the southern Lakes Region and Hampton Beach, tacky souvenirs are the norm.

Summertime fairs, such as the one operated by the League of New Hampshire Craftsmen at Mt. Sunapee State Park, are a good way to see the best arts and crafts. Look for pottery, jewelry, and wooden boxes. Antiques shops appear in clusters along U.S. 4, between Route 125 and Concord; along Route 119, from Fitzwilliam to Hinsdale; along Route 101, from Marlborough to Wilton; and in the towns of North Conway, North Hampton, Hopkinton, Hollis, and Amherst. In the Lakes Region, most shops are along the eastern side of Winnipesaukee, near Wolfeboro. Many stores are in barns and homes along back roads; quite a few are open by chance or by appointment. Depression glass, silverware, and china abound, with high-quality furniture becoming scarcer and more expensive.

Exploring New Hampshire

The main attraction of southern New Hampshire's coast are historical Portsmouth and bustling Hampton Beach; several somewhat quieter communities such as Durham and Exeter are a bit farther inland. The east-central Lakes Region has good hiking trails, antiques shops, and, of course, water sports. To hike, ski, and photograph vibrant foliage, head to the north's White Mountains. The southwest is hemmed in to the east by the central Merrimack Valley, which has a string of fast-growing communities along I–93 and U.S. 3.

Numbers in the text and in the margin correspond to numbers on the maps: New Hampshire Coast, New Hampshire Lakes, The White Mountains, Dartmouth–Lake Sunapee, and Monadnock Region and Central New Hampshire.

Great Itineraries

Some people come to New Hampshire to hike or ski the mountains, fish and sail the lakes, or cycle along the back roads. Others prefer to drive through scenic towns, visiting museums and shops. Although New Hampshire is a small state, roads curve around lakes and mountains, making distances longer than they appear. You can get a taste of the coast, lake, and mountain areas in three to five days; eight days gives you time to make a comprehensive loop.

IF YOU HAVE 3 DAYS

Drive along Route 1A to see the coast or take a boat tour of the Isles of Shoals before exploring **Portsmouth** ①. The next day visit **Wolfeboro** ㉒, on the eastern edge of Lake Winnipesaukee, good for an overnight stop. The following morning drive across the scenic **Kancamagus Highway** ㊲ (Route 112) from Conway to **Lincoln** ㉕ to see the granite ledges and sparkling streams of the White Mountains.

IF YOU HAVE 5 DAYS

After visiting **Portsmouth** ① and **Wolfeboro** ㉒, explore Squam and Ossipee lakes and the charming towns near them: **Moultonborough** ⑱, **Center Harbor** ⑮, and **Tamworth** ⑲. Spend your third night in the White Mountains town of **Jackson** ㉝. After crossing the **Kancamagus Highway** ㊲ (Route 112) to **Lincoln** ㉕, tour the western part of the White Mountain National Forest via Route 112 to Route 118. Take Route 25A and then Route 10 south through the upper Connecticut River valley to **Hanover** ㊺, home of Dartmouth College, for an overnight. Follow I–89 back by way of **Newbury** ㊸ and the Lake Sunapee region.

IF YOU HAVE 8 DAYS

Spend your first two nights in **Portsmouth** ①, allowing a chance to visit Strawbery Banke Museum and soak up the city's history as well as explore the short, scenic shoreline. Then follow the five-day itinerary above as far as **Hanover** ㊺. From here, visit the Shaker Community at **Enfield** ㊹; then take either Route 12A along the Connecticut River or Route 10 south to **Keene** ㊾. Route 119 leads east to Rhododendron State Park in **Fitzwilliam** ㊿.

When to Tour New Hampshire

In summer, people flock to seaside beaches, mountain trails, and lake boat ramps. In the cities, festivals showcase music, theater, and crafts. Fall brings leaf-peepers, especially to the White Mountains and along the Kancamagus Highway (Route 112). Skiers take to the slopes in winter, when Christmas lights and carnivals brighten the long, dark nights. Spring's unpredictable weather—along with April's mud and late May's black flies—tends to deter visitors. Still, the season has its joys, not the least of which is the appearance of the state flower, the purple lilac, from mid-May to early June.

THE COAST

New Hampshire's 18-mi stretch of coastline packs in a wealth of scenery and diversions. The honky-tonk of Hampton Beach gets plenty of attention, good and bad, but first-timers are often surprised by the significant chunk of shoreline that remains pristine—especially through the town of Rye. This tour begins in the regional hub, Portsmouth; cuts down the coast to the beaches; branches inland to the quintessential prep school town of Exeter; and then runs back up north through Dover, Durham (home to the University of New Hampshire), and Rochester. From here it's a short drive to the Lakes Region.

Portsmouth

★ ❶ *47 mi southeast of Concord; 50 mi southwest of Portland, Maine; 56 mi north of Boston.*

Settled in 1623 as Strawbery Banke, Portsmouth became a prosperous port before the Revolutionary War, and like similarly wealthy Newport, Rhode Island, it harbored many Tory sympathizers throughout the campaign. Filled with grand residential architecture spanning the 18th through early 20th centuries, this city of 23,000 has numerous house-museums, including the collection of buildings that make up the Strawbery Banke Museum. With hip eateries, quirky shops, swank cocktail bars, respected theaters, and jumping live-music venues, this sheltered harbor city is a hot destination. Downtown, especially around elegant Market Square, buzzes with conviviality.

The **Portsmouth Harbour Trail** passes more than 70 18th- and 19th-century structures downtown, through the South End, and along State and Congress streets. You can purchase a tour map ($2.50) at the information kiosk in Market Square, at the chamber of commerce, and at several house-museums. Guided walks are conducted late spring to early fall ☎ *603/436–3988 for guided tour,* WEB *www.seacoastnh.com/ harbourtrail.* ☒ *$7 for guided tour.* ☉ *May–mid-Oct., Thurs.–Mon.*

The **Portsmouth Black Heritage Trail** (☎ 603/431–2768, WEB www. seacoastnh.com/blackhistory) is a self-guided walk that visits sites important to African-American history in Portsmouth. Included are the **New Hampshire Gazette Printing Office**, where skilled slave Primus Fowle operated the paper's printing press for some 50 years beginning in 1756, and the city's 1866 **Election Hall,** outside of which the city's black citizens held annual celebrations of the Emancipation Proclamation.

The yellow, hip-roof **John Paul Jones House** was a boardinghouse when the Revolutionary War hero lived here while supervising shipbuilding for the Continental Navy. The 1758 structure, now the headquarters of the Portsmouth Historical Society, contains furniture, costumes, glass, guns, portraits, and documents from the late 18th century. ☒ *43 Middle St.,* ☎ *603/436–8420,* WEB *www.seacoastnh.com/ touring/jpjhouse.html.* ☒ *$4.* ☉ *June–mid-Oct., Mon.–Sat. 10–4, Sun. noon–4.*

The period interior of the **Moffatt-Ladd House,** built in 1763, tells the story of Portsmouth's merchant class through portraits, letters, and fine furnishings. The Colonial Revival garden includes a horse chestnut tree planted by Gen. William Whipple when he returned home after signing the Declaration of Independence in 1776. ☒ *154 Market St.,* ☎ *603/436–8221.* ☒ *$5, garden tour $1.* ☉ *Mid-June–mid-Oct., Mon.– Sat. 11–5, Sun. 1–5.*

NEED A BREAK?	Drop by **Annabelle's Natural Ice Cream** (☒ 49 Ceres St., ☎ 603/436–3400) for a dish of Ghirardelli chocolate chip or Almond Joy ice cream. **Cafe Brioche** (☒ 14 Market Sq., ☎ 603/430–9225) serves coffee, thick deli sandwiches, and fresh-baked pastries.

The first English settlers named the area around today's Portsmouth for the wild strawberries abundant along the shores of the Piscataqua River. ★ **Strawbery Banke Museum,** the city's largest and most-impressive museum, now uses the name. The 10-acre compound has 46 buildings that date from 1695 to 1820 as well as period gardens, exhibits, and craftspeople. Ten furnished homes represent 300 years of history in one continuously occupied neighborhood. Half the interior of the Drisco House, built in 1795, depicts its history as a Colonial dry-goods store, while the living room and kitchen are decorated as they were in the 1950s, showing how buildings are adapted. The Shapiro House has been restored to reflect the life of the Russian Jewish immigrant family who lived in the home in the early 1900s. Perhaps the most opulent house, done in decadent Victorian style, is the 1860 Goodwin Mansion, former home of Gov. Ichabod Goodwin. ☒ *Marcy St.,* ☎ *603/433–1100,* WEB *www.straw-*

berybanke.org. ⊠ *$12.* ⊙ *May–Oct., daily 10–5; Nov.–Dec. and Feb.–Apr., Wed.–Sat. 10–2.*

Picnicking is popular in **Prescott Park,** on the waterfront between Strawbery Banke Museum and the Piscataqua River. A large formal garden with fountains is perfect for whiling away an afternoon. The park also contains Point of Graves, Portsmouth's oldest burial ground, and two 17th-century warehouses.

☺ Nineteen hands-on exhibits, geared toward kids under 11, at the **Children's Museum of Portsmouth** explore lobstering, sound and music, computers, space travel, and other subjects. Some programs require reservations. ⊠ *280 Marcy St.,* ☎ *603/436–3853,* WEB *www.childrens-museum.org.* ⊠ *$5.* ⊙ *Tues.–Sat. 10–5, Sun. 1–5; also Mon. 10–5 in summer and during school vacations.*

The **Wentworth-Coolidge State Historic Mansion,** a National Historic Landmark that's now part of Little Harbor State Park, was originally the residence of Benning Wentworth, New Hampshire's first royal governor (1753–70). Notable among its period furnishings is the carved pine mantelpiece in the council chamber. Wentworth's imported lilac trees bloom each May. The visitor center stages lectures and exhibits. ⊠ *Little Harbor Rd., near South Street Cemetery,* ☎ *603/436–6607.* ⊠ *$2.50.* ⊙ *Grounds daily; mansion June–Sept., Tues. and Thurs.–Sat. 10–3, Sun. 1–6.*

Docked at the **Port of Portsmouth Maritime Museum** in Albacore Park is the USS *Albacore*, built here in 1953. You can board this prototype submarine, which was a floating laboratory assigned to test an innovative hull design, dive brakes, and sonar systems for the navy. The nearby Memorial Garden and its reflecting pool are dedicated to those who have lost their lives in submarine service. ⊠ *600 Market St.,* ☎ *603/436–3680.* ⊠ *$5.* ⊙ *Daily 9:30–5:30.*

The **Redhook Ale Brewery,** visible from the Spaulding Turnpike, conducts tours that end with a beer tasting. If you don't have time to tour, you can stop in the Cataqua Public House to sample the fresh ales and have a bite to eat (open daily, lunch and dinner). ⊠ *Pease International Tradeport, 35 Corporate Dr.,* ☎ *603/430–8600,* WEB *www.redhook.com.* ⊠ *$1.* ⊙ *Tours weekdays at 2, weekends at 2 and 4.*

Dining and Lodging

$$$–$$$$ ✕ **Dunfey's Aboard the *John Wanamaker*.** Portsmouth's floating restaurant, on a restored 1920s tugboat, prepares such creative delicacies as tandoori game hen, marinated in buttermilk, chilies, ginger, garlic, and cilantro, and then slow-roasted and served with a turmeric-pomodoro sauce, sautéed spinach, and polenta. You can enjoy the bistrolike main dining room or unwind in the Wheelhouse Bar. The upper-level deck is a favorite on starry summer nights for light meals, a glass of wine, or dessert and cappuccino. Reservations are a good idea on weekends. ⊠ *1 Harbour Pl.,* ☎ *603/433–3111. AE, MC, V. Closed Mon. No lunch winter.*

$$$–$$$$ ✕ **The Library.** Most of this 1785 mansion, a former luxury hotel, has been converted to condominiums, but the restaurant retains hand-carved mahogany paneling, a marble-top bar, and bookcases on every wall. Although the kitchen churns out such light dishes as sesame-encrusted tuna with a soy reduction, the mainstays are traditional dishes like char-grilled rib chop and pan-seared rack of lamb with a blackberry sauce. The check arrives between the pages of a vintage best-seller. Order an ale in the English-style pub. Sunday brunch is a big to-do. ⊠ *401 State St.,* ☎ *603/431–5202. Reservations essential. AE, D, DC, MC, V.*

$$–$$$$ ✕ **Lou's Upstairs Grill.** Movers and shakers favor this snazzy spot for power lunches and after-work cocktails. The space is dramatic—with tall windows and a bold red, white, and gray color scheme—and the kitchen reinterprets conventional American recipes. The surf-and-turf here pairs tournedos of beef tenderloin with seared sea scallops over basmati rice with horseradish cream. The fried chicken comes lightly crisped with sour-cream mashed potatoes. ⊠ *100 Market St.,* ☎ *603/ 766–4745. AE, D, MC, V.*

$$–$$$ ✕ **Blue Mermaid World Grill.** The chefs at Blue Mermaid prepare globally influenced fare on a wood-burning grill. Specialties include lobster-and-shrimp pad thai; pan-seared cod with a coconut cream sauce and plantain chips; and polenta lasagna layered with cilantro, adobo, goat cheese, and roasted tomatoes. In summer you can eat on a deck that overlooks the historical Hill neighborhood. Entertainers perform (outdoors in summer) on Friday and Saturday. ⊠ *409 Hanover St.,* ☎ *603/ 427–2583. AE, D, DC, MC, V.*

$$–$$$ ✕ **Jumping Jay's.** A wildly popular spot downtown, this offbeat, dimly lit eatery presents a changing menu of world-beat cooking, and nary a red-meat platter is served. Try the steamed Prince Edward Island mussels with a spicy lemongrass and saffron sauce, the lobster risotto, or the Chilean sea bass with a ginger-orange marinade. Singles often gather at the central bar for dinner and schmoozing. ⊠ *150 Congress St.,* ☎ *603/766–3474. D, MC, V. No lunch.*

$$–$$$ ✕ **Porto Bello Ristorante Italiano.** In the second-story dining room of
★ this family-run Neapolitan restaurant overlooking the harbor, you can savor daily antipasto specials ranging from grilled calamari to fresh mozzarella. Pastas include spinach gnocchi and lobster tails over fettuccine. Veal *carciofi*—a 6-ounce cutlet served with artichokes—is a specialty. ⊠ *67 Bow St.,* ☎ *603/431–2989. AE, D, MC, V. Closed Mon.– Tues. No lunch.*

$–$$ ✕ **Muddy River Smokehouse.** Red-check tablecloths and murals of trees and meadows evoke an outdoor summer barbecue joint—even when the weather turns cold. Roll up your sleeves and dig into corn bread and molasses baked beans as well as blackened catfish or a burger. Devotees swear by the Pig City platter of grilled ribs, smoked sweet sausage, and pulled pork. ⊠ *21 Congress St.,* ☎ *603/430–9582. AE, MC, V.*

$–$$ ✕ **Poco's.** Sure, Poco's boisterous downstairs bar and spacious out-
★ side deck have earned it a reputation as a collegiate hangout, but the upstairs dining room turns out exceptional Southwestern and pan-Latin cuisine—and at great prices. Avocado-wrapped fried oysters with chipotle tartar sauce and lobster quesadilla with Brie, caramelized onions, and roasted corn–tomato salsa are among the better choices. Most tables have great views of the Piscataqua River. ⊠ *37 Bow St.,* ☎ *603/431–5967. AE, D, MC, V.*

$$$–$$$$ ⊞ **Sheraton Harborside Portsmouth Hotel.** Portsmouth's only luxury hotel, this five-story redbrick building is within easy walking distance of shops and attractions. Many rooms have large windows overlooking Portsmouth Harbor and the Piscataqua River. Suites have full kitchens and living rooms. The Harbor's Edge Restaurant serves a popular Sunday brunch. ⊠ *250 Market St., 03801,* ☎ *603/431–2300 or 800/325–3535,* ℻ *603/431–7805,* WEB *www.sheratonportsmouth.com. 179 rooms, 24 suites. 2 restaurants, room service, in-room data ports, some kitchens, indoor pool, health club, sauna, bar, nightclub, business services, meeting rooms. AE, D, DC, MC, V.*

$$$ ⊞ **Sise Inn.** Each room at this 1880s Queen Anne–style town house is decorated in Victorian style, with designer fabrics, antiques, and reproductions. Some rooms have fireplaces, and about half are in a 1980s addition that blends well with the older section. It's close to Market Square. ⊠ *40 Court St., 03801,* ☎ *877/747–3466,* ☎ ℻ *603/433–*

1200, WEB *www.someplacesdifferent.com/sise.htm. 26 rooms, 8 suites. Some in-room hot tubs, in-room VCRs, laundry service, meeting rooms. AE, DC, MC, V. CP.*

$$-$$$ ⊞ **Wren's Nest Village Inn.** With standard rooms, suites, efficiencies, and cottages, the Wren's Nest draws lots of families and groups of friends; many regulars rent for weeks at a time. Guest quarters are clean, well maintained, and decorated with nautical artwork, and the 4 acres of lawns and gardens are attractive. It's a 10-minute drive south of downtown Portsmouth and convenient to Rye and the beaches. ⊠ *3548 Lafayette Rd. (U.S. 1), 03801,* ☎ *603/436–2481,* WEB *www.portsmouthnh. com/wrensnest. 35 units. Some in-room hot tubs, some kitchens, refrigerators, some in-room VCRs, volleyball. AE, D, MC, V.*

$$ ⊞ **Inn at Christian Shore.** Perennial gardens surround this handsome, yellow-clapboard Federal house, which is equidistant to downtown and the Maritime Museum. Original beam ceilings and rough-hewn hardwood floors reveal the building's rich history, and an eclectic mix of pre-Columbian, African, and European art makes a distinctive statement. The breakfast is memorable—the frittata-like Spanish tortillas are a specialty. ⊠ *335 Maplewood Ave., 03801,* ☎ *603/431–6770,* WEB *www.portsmouthnh.com/christianshore. 5 rooms. No room phones, no room TVs, no kids, no-smoking rooms. MC, V. BP.*

$$ ⊞ **Martin Hill Inn.** Within walking distance of the historic district and the waterfront, this inn consists of extensive gardens around a building from 1815 and another from 1850. The quiet rooms are furnished with antiques and decorated in formal Colonial or country-Victorian styles. The Greenhouse Suite has a solarium. ⊠ *404 Islington St., 03801,* ☎ *603/436–2287,* WEB *www.portsmouthnh.com/martinhillinn. 4 rooms, 3 suites. No room phones, no room TVs, no-smoking rooms. MC, V. BP.*

Nightlife and the Arts

NIGHTLIFE

The late-night coffeehouse **Breaking New Grounds** (⊠ 16 Market St., ☎ 603/436–9555) buzzes with a festive vibe and a mixed-age clientele. **King Tiki** (⊠ 2 Bow St., ☎ 603/430–5228), a bar-restaurant that oozes Polynesian kitsch, delights scenesters, poseurs, and other revelers with karaoke nights, retro music, and goofy drinks.

The **Portsmouth Gas Light Co.** (⊠ 64 Market St., ☎ 603/430–9122), a brick-oven pizzeria and restaurant, hosts local rock bands in its lounge or courtyard. People come from as far away as Boston and Portland to hang out at the **Press Room** (⊠ 77 Daniel St., ☎ 603/431–5186), which showcases folk, jazz, blues, and bluegrass performers.

THE ARTS

Beloved for its acoustics, the 1878 **Music Hall** (⊠ 28 Chestnut St., ☎ 603/436–2400 or 603/436–9900 film line) brings the best touring events to the seacoast—from classical and pop concerts to dance and theater. The hall also hosts art-house film series. From September through June the **Players' Ring** (⊠ 105 Marcy St., ☎ 603/436–8123) stages more than 15 original and well-known plays and performances by local theater groups.

The **Pontine Movement Theatre** (⊠ 135 McDonough St., ☎ 603/436–6660) presents dance performances in a renovated warehouse. The company also tours throughout northern New England. The **Prescott Park Arts Festival** (⊠ 105 Marcy St., ☎ 603/436–2848) presents theater, dance, and musical events outdoors June–August. The **Seacoast Repertory Theatre** (⊠ 125 Bow St., ☎ 603/433–4472 or 800/639–7650) has a year-round schedule of musicals, classic dramas, and works by up-and-coming playwrights, as well as a youth theater.

Outdoor Activities and Sports

Just inland from Portsmouth, the **Great Bay Estuarine Research Reserve** is one of southeastern New Hampshire's most precious assets. Amid its 4,471 acres of tidal waters, mudflats, and about 48 mi of inland shoreline, you can spot blue herons, ospreys, and snowy egrets, particularly during spring and fall migrations. Winter eagles also live here. The best public access is via the **Sandy Point Discovery Center** (⊠ 89 Depot Rd., off Rte. 101, Stratham, ☎ 603/778–0015, WEB www.greatbay.org). The facility has year-round interpretive programs, indoor and outdoor exhibits, a library and bookshop, and a 1,700-ft boardwalk as well as other trails through mudflats and upland forest. The center, about 15 mi southeast of Durham and 6 mi west of Exit 3 from I–95 in Portsmouth, also distributes maps and information. ⊠ *Information: New Hampshire Fish & Game Dept., 37 Concord Rd., Durham 03824,* ☎ *603/868–1095.* ⊠ *Free.* ☉ *Daily dawn–dusk.*

Portsmouth doesn't have sandy stretches, but the **Seacoast Trolley** (☎ 603/431–6975 or 800/828–3762, WEB www.locallink.com/seacoast-trolley), which operates from mid-June through Labor Day, departs from Market Square on the hour (daily 10–5) for Portsmouth sights and area beaches. The **Urban Forestry Center** (⊠ 45 Elwyn Rd., ☎ 603/431–6774) has gardens and marked trails appropriate for short hikes on its 180 acres.

Shopping

Market Square, in the center of town, has gift and clothing boutiques, book and card shops, and exquisite crafts stores. **Byrne & Carlson** (⊠ 121 State St., ☎ 888/559–9778) produces handmade chocolates in the finest European tradition. **Kumminz Gallery** (⊠ 65 Daniel St., ☎ 603/433–6488) carries pottery, jewelry, and fiber art by New Hampshire artisans. **N. W. Barrett** (⊠ 53 Market St., ☎ 603/431–4262) specializes in leather, jewelry, pottery, and fiber and other arts and crafts. It also sells furniture, including affordable steam-bent oak pieces and one-of-a-kind lamps and rocking chairs.

Pierce Gallery (⊠ 105 Market St., ☎ 603/436–1988) has prints and paintings of the Maine and New Hampshire coasts. The **Portsmouth Bookshop** (⊠ 1–7 Islington St., ☎ 603/433–4406) carries old and rare books and maps. At **Salamandra Glass Studios** (⊠ 67 Bow St., ☎ 603/436–1038), you'll find hand-blown glass vases, bowls, and other items.

Isles of Shoals

❷ *10 mi southeast of Portsmouth, by ferry.*

Many of these nine small, rocky islands (eight at high tide) retain the earthy names—Hog and Smuttynose, to cite but two—given them by transient 17th-century fishermen. A history of piracy, murder, and ghosts surrounds the archipelago, long populated by an independent lot who, according to one writer, hadn't the sense to winter on the mainland. Not all the islands lie within the state's border: after an ownership dispute, five went to Maine and four to New Hampshire.

Celia Thaxter, a native islander, romanticized these islands with her poetry in *Among the Isles of Shoals* (1873) and celebrated her garden in *An Island Garden* (1894; now reissued with the original color illustrations by Childe Hassam). In the late 19th century, **Appledore Island** became an offshore retreat for Thaxter's coterie of writers, musicians, and artists. The island is now used by the Marine Laboratory of Cornell University. **Star Island** contains a nondenominational conference center and is open to those on guided tours.

New Castle

❸ *3 mi southeast of Portsmouth.*

Though it consists of a single square mile of land, the small island of New Castle was once known as Great Island. The narrow roads lined with pre-Revolutionary houses and upscale condos and homes make the island, which is accessible from the mainland by car, perfect for a stroll.

Wentworth by the Sea, the last of the state's great seaside resorts, is impossible to miss as you approach New Castle on Route 1B. Empty these days, it was the site of the signing of the Russo-Japanese Treaty in 1905, a fact that attracts many Japanese tourists. The current owners and the town have reached an agreement to bring this grand hotel back to life; renovations were under way at press time.

Ft. Constitution was built in 1631 and then rebuilt in 1666 as Ft. William and Mary, a British stronghold overlooking Portsmouth Harbor. The fort earned notoriety in 1774, when patriots raided it in one of Revolutionary America's first overtly defiant acts against King George III. The rebels later used the captured munitions against the British at the Battle of Bunker Hill. Panels throughout the fort explain its history. ⊠ *Rte. 1B at the Coast Guard Station,* ☎ *603/436–1552.* ⬚ *Free.* ◷ *Mid-June–Labor Day, daily 9–5; Labor Day–mid-June, weekends 9–5.*

Rye

❹ *8 mi south of Portsmouth.*

In 1623 the first Europeans established a settlement at Odiorne Point in what is now the largely undeveloped and picturesque town of Rye, making it the birthplace of New Hampshire. Today the area's main draws are a lovely state park, oceanfront beaches, and the views from Route 1A.

★ ⓒ **Odiorne Point State Park** encompasses more than 330 acres of protected land, on the site where David Thompson established the first permanent European site in what is now New Hampshire. Stroll several nature trails with interpretive panels describing the park's military history or simply enjoy the vistas of the nearby Isles of Shoals. The rocky shore's tidal pools shelter crabs, periwinkles, and sea anemones. Throughout the year, the Seacoast Science Center conducts guided walks and interpretive programs and has exhibits on the area's natural history. Displays trace the social history of Odiorne Point back to the Ice Age, and the tidal-pool touch tank and 1,000-gallon Gulf of Maine deepwater aquarium are popular with kids. Day camp is offered for grades K–8 throughout the summer and during school vacations. ⊠ *570 Ocean Blvd. (Rte. 1A), north of Wallis Sands, Rye State Beach,* ☎ *603/436–8043 science center; 603/436–1552 park;* ⓦⒺⒷ *www.seacentr.org.* ⬚ *Science center $1 (guided walks and some interpretive programs $4); park Memorial Day–Columbus Day and weekends $3.* ◷ *Science center daily 10–5, park daily 8 AM–dusk.*

Dining and Lodging

$$–$$$ ✕ **Saunders at Rye Harbor.** Folks have been lazing about on the waterfront deck at sunset or over lunch since this place opened in the 1920s. Fresh-caught lobster, broiled scallops with a butter-and-crumb topping, and baked-stuffed shrimp are among the specialties. ⊠ *175 Harbor Rd.,* ☎ *603/964–6466. AE, MC, V. Closed Tues.*

$$–$$$ ✕ **Wildflowers Cafe.** You might think that this weathered bungalow near Jenness Beach is just another vacation hideaway rather than a sun-

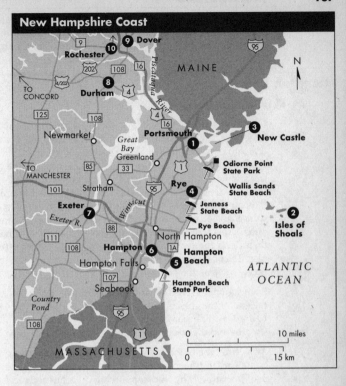

New Hampshire Coast

filled eatery serving memorable home-cooking. For breakfast, try the scallops, bacon, spinach, and poached eggs topped with hollandaise sauce. The savory smoked-cheddar cheesecake with tomato, thyme, and roasted–red pepper coulis makes a wonderful dinner entrée. Owner Roberta Daly bakes all her own breads and desserts. ⊠ *2197 Ocean Blvd.,* ☎ *603/964–5132. MC, V. No dinner Mon.–Tues.*

$$–$$$$ 🏨 **Rock Ledge Manor.** Built out on a point, this mid-19th-century gambrel-roof house with a wraparound porch once anchored a resort colony. Rooms have water views, brass-and-iron beds, and marble-top dressers; the family suite has a balcony. Owners Stan and Stella Smith serve breakfast in the sunny dining room overlooking the Atlantic. ⊠ *1413 Ocean Blvd., 03870,* ☎ *603/431–1413,* WEB *www.rockledge-manor.com. 2 rooms, 1 suite. Dining room; no room phones, no room TVs, no kids under 11, no smoking. No credit cards. BP.*

Outdoor Activities and Sports

BEACHES

Good for swimming and sunning, **Jenness State Beach,** on Route 1A, is a favorite with locals. The facilities include a bathhouse, lifeguards, and metered parking. **Wallis Sands State Beach,** on Route 1A, is a swimmers' beach with bright white sands and a bathhouse. There's plenty of parking; rates are $8 on weekends, $5 weekdays in summer.

FISHING

For a full- or half-day deep-sea angling charter, try **Atlantic Fishing Fleet** (⊠ Rye Harbor, ☎ 603/964–5220 or 800/942–5364).

Shopping

Although Rye isn't known for its shopping, **Antiques at Rye Center** (⊠ 655 Wallis Rd., ☎ 603/964–8999) is worth searching out for well-presented antiques from hand-painted porcelain to early toys.

En Route   On Route 1A as it winds south through Rye to North Hampton, you'll pass a group of late-19th- and early 20th-century mansions known as **Millionaires' Row.** Because of the way the road curves, the drive south along this route is especially breathtaking.

Hampton Beach

❺ *8 mi south of Rye.*

Hampton Beach, from Route 27 to where Route 1A crosses the causeway, is an authentic seaside amusement center—the domain of fried-dough stands, loud music, arcade games, palm readers, parasailing, and bronzed bodies. An estimated 150,000 people visit the town and its free public beach on the Fourth of July, and it draws plenty of people until late September, when things close up. The 3-mi boardwalk, where kids can play games and see how saltwater taffy is made, looks as if it were snatched out of the 1940s; in fact, the whole community remains remarkably free of modern franchises. Free outdoor concerts are held on many a summer evening, and once a week there's a fireworks display. Talent shows and karaoke performances take place in the Seashell Stage, right on the beach.

Each summer locals hold a children's festival in August and celebrate the end of the season with a huge seafood feast on the weekend after Labor Day. For a quieter time, stop by for a sunrise stroll, when only seagulls and the occasional jogger interrupt the serenity.

Away from the beach crowds, you'll find **Fuller Gardens,** a late-1920s estate garden (the mansion was razed in 1961) designed in the Colonial Revival style by landscape architect Arthur Shurtleff, with a 1938 addition by the Olmsted brothers. With 2,000 rosebushes, a hosta garden, an annual display garden, a tropical conservatory, and a Japanese garden, it blooms all summer long. The Fuller Foundation is currently restoring the grounds according to original blueprints. ⊠ *10 Willow Ave., North Hampton,* ☎ *603/964–5414,* WEB *www.fullergardens.org.* ☞ *$6.* ☉ *Mid-May–mid-Oct., daily 10–6.*

Dining and Lodging

$$$–$$$$ ✕ **Ron's Landing at Rocky Bend.** Amid the motels lining Ocean Boulevard is this casually elegant restaurant. Pan-seared ahi over mixed greens with a Thai peanut dressing makes a tempting starter. For an entrée, try the oven-roasted salmon with a hoisin (soybeans, garlic, and chili peppers) glaze, a Fra Angelico cream sauce, slivered almonds, and sliced apple or the baked haddock stuffed with scallops and lobster and served with lemon-dill butter. From many tables you can enjoy a sweeping Atlantic view. ⊠ *379 Ocean Blvd.,* ☎ *603/929–2122. AE, D, DC, MC, V. No lunch Mon.–Sat.*

$$–$$$$ ✕🏨 **Ashworth by the Sea.** This family-owned hotel was built across the street from Hampton Beach in 1912, though furnishings vary from period to contemporary. Most rooms have decks, though you should request a beachside room for an ocean view; otherwise you'll look out onto the pool or street. The Ashworth Dining Room ($$–$$$) serves steaks, poultry, and seafood. Of the seven lobster variations, the lobster meat wrapped in haddock with a crawfish-sherry sauce stands out. ⊠ *295 Ocean Blvd., 03842,* ☎ *603/926–6762 or 800/345–6736,* FAX *603/926–2002,* WEB *www.ashworthhotel.com. 105 rooms. 3 restaurants, pool. AE, D, DC, MC, V.*

$$$ 🏨 **D. W.'s Oceanside Inn.** The square front and simple awnings of this inn look much the same as those on all the other buildings lining Ocean Boulevard. Individually decorated rooms have carefully selected antiques and collectibles. You can curl up with a book by the

fireplace in the living room or watch the waves from the second-floor veranda. Should Hampton Beach's crush of people and noise begin to overwhelm, you'll appreciate the soundproofing. A separate three-bedroom cottage sleeps up to six guests and has a kitchen. ⊠ *365 Ocean Blvd., 03842,* ☎ FAX *603/926–3542,* WEB *www.oceansideinn.com. 9 rooms, 1 cottage. In-room safes, some kitchens; no kids, no-smoking rooms. AE, D, MC, V. Closed mid-Oct.–mid-May. BP.*

Nightlife

Despite its name, the **Hampton Beach Casino Ballroom** (⊠ 169 Ocean Blvd., ☎ 603/929–4100) isn't a gambling establishment but rather a late-19th-century, 2,000-seat performance venue that has hosted everyone from Janis Joplin to Jerry Seinfeld to Barenaked Ladies. Performances are scheduled weekly from April through October.

Outdoor Activities and Sports

BEACHES

Hampton Beach State Park (⊠ Rte. 1A, ☎ 603/926–3784) is a quiet stretch of sand that shares its name with the town. The park, on the southwestern edge of town at the mouth of the Hampton River, has picnic tables, a store (seasonal), parking ($8 on summer weekends, $5 weekdays in summer), and a bathhouse.

FISHING AND WHALE-WATCHING

Several companies conduct whale-watching excursions as well as half-day, full-day, and nighttime cruises. Most leave from the Hampton State Pier on Route 1A. **Al Gauron Deep Sea Fishing** (☎ 603/926–2469) maintains a fleet of four boats for whale-watching cruises and fishing charters. **Eastman Fishing Fleet** (⊠ Seabrook, ☎ 603/474–3461) offers whale-watching and fishing cruises, with evening and morning charters. **Smith & Gilmore** (☎ 603/926–3503) conducts deep-sea fishing expeditions and whale-watching trips.

Hampton

❻ *3 mi northwest of Hampton Beach, 11 mi southwest of Portsmouth, 45 mi north of Boston.*

One of New Hampshire's first towns, Hampton was settled in 1638. Its name in the 17th century was Winnacunnet, which means "beautiful place of pines." Today busy U.S. 1 defines its center and makes it a crossroads for anyone traveling along the seacoast. Hampton's early hub was **Meeting House Green,** where 42 stones represent the founding families. It's still a tranquil place surrounded by pine trees.

Tuck Museum, across from Meeting House Green, contains displays on the town's early history. The grounds also include a 19th-century schoolhouse, a farm museum, and a fire-fighting museum. ⊠ *40 Park Ave.,* ☎ *603/929–0781; 603/926–2543 appointments.* 🎟 *Free.* ☉ *June–Sept., Tues.–Fri. and Sun. 1–4* PM *and by appointment.*

At 400-acre **Applecrest Farm Orchards** you can pick your own apples and berries or buy fresh fruit pies and cookies. Fall brings cider pressing, hay rides, pumpkins, and music on weekends. In winter a cross-country ski trail traverses the orchard. ⊠ *133 Rte. 88, Hampton Falls,* ☎ *603/926–3721,* WEB *www.applecrest.com.* ☉ *Daily 9–5.*

Lodging

$$–$$$ 🏨 **Hampton Falls Inn.** Intricate Burmese wall hangings and leather furniture fill the lobby of this modern motel only 3½ mi from Hampton Beach. The bright, airy rooms and minisuites are large, and many have a view of the neighboring farm. An enclosed porch looks out over the woods and fields. ⊠ *11 Lafayette Rd., 03844,* ☎ *603/926–9545*

or 800/356–1729, FAX *603/926–4155,* WEB *www.hamptonfallsinn.com.*
33 rooms, 15 suites. Restaurant, minibars, some microwaves, some re-
frigerators, indoor pool, hot tub, meeting room. AE, D, DC, MC, V.

$$ 🏨 **Victoria Inn.** Easygoing innkeepers Ron and Marina Mansfield run
this romantic B&B half a mile from Hampton Beach. The 1875 struc-
ture, built as a carriage house, is decorated with plush Victorian an-
tiques and fabrics. The wraparound porch and the gazebo are great
spots to relax with a book on a warm summer afternoon. The dining
room overlooks the former summer home of President Franklin Pierce.
✉ *430 High St., 03842,* ☎ *603/929–1437 or 800/291–2672,* FAX *603/
929–0747,* WEB *www.thevictoriainn.com. 3 rooms, 2 suites. Dining
room, bicycles. AE, MC, V. BP.*

$ ⛺ **Tidewater Campground.** This camping area has 200 sites, a large
playground, a pool, a game room, and a basketball court. ✉ *160
Lafayette Rd., 03842,* ☎ *603/926–5474. MC, V. Closed mid-Oct.–mid-
May.*

Shopping

Antiques shops line U.S. 1 (Lafayette Rd.) in Hampton and neighbor-
ing Hampton Falls. The more than 50 dealers at **Antiques at Hamp-
ton Falls** (✉ Lafayette Rd., ☎ 603/926–1971) have all types of antiques
and collectibles. **Antiques New Hampshire** (✉ Lafayette Rd., ☎ 603/
926–9603) is a group shop with 35 dealers and a range of items. **An-
tiques One** (✉ 80 Lafayette Rd., ☎ 603/926–5332) carries everything
but furniture, including books and maps. The prodigious **Barn Antiques
at Hampton Falls** (✉ 44 Lafayette Rd., ☎ 603/926–9003) is known
for American and European furniture.

Exeter

❼ *9 mi northwest of Hampton, 52 mi north of Boston, 47 mi southeast
of Concord.*

In Exeter's center, contemporary shops mix well with the buildings of
the esteemed Phillips Exeter Academy, which opened in 1783, and other
equally historical structures. During the Revolutionary War, Exeter was
the state capital, and it was here amid intense patriotic fervor that the
first state constitution and the first Declaration of Independence from
Great Britain were put to paper. These days Exeter shares more in ap-
pearance and personality with Boston's blue-blooded satellite com-
munities than the rest of New Hampshire—indeed, plenty of locals
commute to Beantown.

The **American Independence Museum,** adjacent to Phillips Exeter
Academy in the Ladd-Gilman House, celebrates the birth of our na-
tion. The story of the Revolution unfolds during each guided tour, on
which you'll see drafts of the U.S. Constitution and the first Purple Heart.
Other items include letters and documents written by George Wash-
ington and the household furnishings of John Taylor Gilman, one of
New Hampshire's early governors. The museum also hosts a Revolu-
tionary War Festival in June. ✉ *1 Governor's La.,* ☎ *603/772–2622,*
WEB *www.independencemuseum.org.* 🎫 *$5.* ☉ *May–Oct., Wed.–Sun.
noon–5 (last tour at 4).*

Dining and Lodging

$$–$$$ ✕ **Tavern at River's Edge.** A convivial downtown gathering spot on
the Exeter River, this tavern pulls in parents of prep school kids, UNH
students, and suburban yuppies. It may be informal, but the kitchen
turns out surprisingly sophisticated chow. You might start with sautéed
ragout of Portobello and shiitake mushrooms, sun-dried tomatoes,
roasted shallots, garlic, Madeira, and Asiago cheese. Move on to gin-

gered Atlantic salmon with lemon-and-jicama slaw, a crispy fried won-ton, and a *ponzu* glaze. ✉ *163 Water St.,* ☎ *603/772–7393. AE, D, DC, MC, V. No lunch.*

$–$$ ✗ **Loaf and Ladle.** Chowders, soups, and stews as well as huge sand-wiches on homemade bread are served cafeteria-style at this under-stated eatery overlooking the river. Check the blackboard for the ever-changing rotation of specials, breads, and desserts, and don't miss the fresh salad bar. ✉ *9 Water St.,* ☎ *603/778–8955. Reservations not accepted. AE, D, DC, MC, V.*

$$–$$$ ✗⊞ **Inn and Conference Center of Exeter.** This brick Georgian-style inn on the Phillips Exeter Academy campus has been the choice of vis-iting parents since it opened in the 1930s. It's furnished with antique and reproduction pieces and possesses plenty of modern amenities. Among the Terrace Restaurant's ($$–$$$$) specialties are mustard-glazed American bison and pecan-encrusted Atlantic salmon with a pineap-ple salsa. On Sunday, the line forms early for brunch. ✉ *90 Front St., 03833,* ☎ *603/772–5901 or 800/782–8444,* ⅎₐₓ *603/778–8757,* ⱳₑᵦ *www.someplacesdifferent.com/exeter.htm. 43 rooms, 3 suites. Restau-rant, meeting rooms. AE, D, DC, MC, V.*

$$–$$$ ⊞ **Governor Jeremiah Smith House Inn.** Named for the Colonial gov-ernor who eulogized George Washington, this dignified 1730s house sits squarely in Exeter's impressive historic district, just a couple of blocks from the river. Rooms capture the inn's spirit—period draperies, hand-made quilts, wrought-iron sewing stands, gas stoves, canopy beds, and oak antiques are typical. One efficiency is outfitted for longer stays. Tea is served in the parlor each afternoon. ✉ *41 Front St., 03833,* ☎ *603/ 778–7770,* ⱳₑᵦ *www.portsmouthnh.com/jeremiahsmithinn. 8 rooms. No room phones, no TV in some rooms, no smoking. MC, V. BP.*

$$–$$$ ⊞ **Inn by the Bandstand.** Common rooms in this 1809 Federal man-sion are decorated in period style. Seven guest rooms have working fire-places; some have marble baths and curtained four-poster beds. After a day of sightseeing, you can relax with a glass of complimentary sherry. ✉ *4 Front St., 03833,* ☎ *603/772–6352 or 877/239–3837,* ⅎₐₓ *603/778–0212,* ⱳₑᵦ *www.innbythebandstand.com. 5 rooms, 4 suites. In-room data ports, some in-room hot tubs, business services; no smoking. AE, D, MC, V. CP.*

$ ⚠ **Exeter Elms Family Campground.** This 50-acre campground has 200 sites (some riverfront), a swimming pool, a playground, canoe rentals, a video arcade, and a recreation program. ✉ *188 Court St., 03833,* ☎ ⅎₐₓ *603/778–7631,* ⱳₑᵦ *www.ucampnh.com/exeterelms. MC, V. Closed mid-Sept.–mid-May.*

Shopping

A Picture's Worth a Thousand Words (✉ 65 Water St., ☎ 603/778–1991) stocks antique and contemporary prints, old maps, town his-tories, and rare books. The **Travel and Nature Bookshop** (✉ 59 Water St., ☎ 603/772–5573) has a wide selection of travel books including guides to New Hampshire hiking spots and other specialized titles. **Water Street Books** (✉ 125 Water St., ☎ 603/778–9731) carries new fiction and nonfiction with an emphasis on New Hampshire authors.

Durham

❽ *12 mi north of Exeter, 11 mi northwest of Portsmouth.*

Settled in 1635 and home of Gen. John Sullivan, a Revolutionary War hero and three-time New Hampshire governor, Durham was where Sul-livan and his band of rebel patriots stored the gunpowder they cap-tured from Ft. William and Mary in New Castle. Easy access to Great Bay via the Oyster River made Durham a maritime hub in the 19th century. Among the lures today are the water, farms that welcome visitors, and the University of New Hampshire (UNH), which occupies much of the town's center.

The **Art Gallery** at UNH occasionally exhibits items from a permanent collection of about 1,100 pieces but generally uses its space to host traveling exhibits. Noted items in the collection include 19th-century Japanese wood-block prints and American landscape paintings. ✉ *Paul Creative Arts Center, 30 College Rd.,* ☎ *603/862–3712,* WEB *www.arts.unh.edu/gallery.html.* ✆ *Free.* ☾ *Sept.–May, Mon.–Wed. 10–4, Thurs. 10–8, weekends 1–5.*

Emery Farm, which has been in the same family for 11 generations, sells fruits and vegetables in summer (including pick-your-own raspberries, strawberries, and blueberries), pumpkins in fall, and Christmas trees in December. The farm shop carries breads, pies, and local crafts. Children can pet the resident goats and sheep and attend the storytelling events that are often held on Tuesday mornings in July and August. ✉ *U.S. 4, 1½ mi east of Rte. 108,* ☎ *603/742–8495.* ☾ *Late Apr.–Dec., daily 9–6.*

Several dozen American bison roam the **Little Bay Buffalo Farm.** The on-site Drowned Valley Trading Post sells bison-related gifts and top-quality bison meat. ✉ *50 Langley Rd.,* ☎ *603/868–3300.* ☾ *Trading Post daily 10–5, observation area daily 10 AM–dusk.*

Dining and Lodging

$$$–$$$$ ✕⊡ **Three Chimneys Inn.** This stately yellow structure has graced a hill overlooking the Oyster River since 1649. Rooms in the house and the 1795 barn are named after plants from the gardens and filled with Georgian- and Federal-style antiques and reproductions, canopy or four-poster beds with Edwardian drapes, and Oriental rugs; half have fireplaces. Specialties in the Maples dining room ($$$–$$$$) include mussel salad and braised bison short ribs with blackberries, blue cheese, watercress, and caramelized-onion mash. The comfy Frost Sawyer Tavern ($–$$) serves simpler fare as does the outdoor conservatory, which is open spring through fall. ✉ *17 Newmarket Rd., 03824,* ☎ *603/868–7800 or 888/399–9777,* FAX *603/868–2964,* WEB *www.threechimneysinn.com. 23 rooms. 3 restaurants, in-room data ports, some in-room hot tubs, business services, meeting room; no smoking. AE, D, MC, V. BP.*

$$–$$$ ✕⊡ **New England Conference Center and Hotel.** In a wooded area on the UNH campus, this contemporary hotel is large enough to be a full-service conference center but quiet enough to seem like a retreat. The Acorns Restaurant ($$–$$$) specializes in American regional cuisine and is a favorite place for Sunday brunch. A signature dish is blackened red snapper with pineapple chutney. ✉ *15 Strafford Ave., 03824,* ☎ *603/ 862–2801 or 800/909–6931,* FAX *603/862–4897,* WEB *www.necc.unh.edu. 115 rooms. 2 restaurants, in-room data ports, health club, bar, Internet, business services, meeting rooms. AE, DC, MC, V.*

Nightlife and the Arts

Students and local yupsters head to the **Stone Church** (✉ 5 Granite St., Newmarket, ☎ 603/659–6321)—in an authentic 1835 former Methodist church—to listen to live rock, jazz, blues, and folk.

The **Celebrity Series** (☎ 603/862–2290) at UNH brings music, theater, and dance to several venues. The **UNH Department of Theater and Dance** (✉ Paul Creative Arts Center, 30 College Rd., ☎ 603/862–2919) produces a variety of shows. UNH's **Whittemore Center Arena** (✉ 128 Main St., ☎ 603/862–4000) hosts everything from Boston Pops concerts to home shows, plus college sports.

Outdoor Activities and Sports

You can take a picnic to or hike several trails at 130-acre **Wagon Hill Farm** (⌧ U.S. 4 across from Emery Farm, ☏ no phone), overlooking the Oyster River. The old farm wagon on the top of a hill is one of the most-photographed spots in New England. Park next to the farmhouse and follow walking trails to the wagon and through the woods to the picnic area by the water. Sledding and cross-country skiing are winter activities.

Dover

❾ *6 mi northeast of Durham.*

Dover Point was settled in 1623 by fishermen who worked Great Bay. By the end of the century, the town center had moved inland to its present location. The falls on the Cocheco River made Dover a prolific textile-mill town. Many of the brick mill buildings have been converted to restaurants and shops.

The **Woodman Institute** consists of three buildings: the 1675 William Damm Garrison House, the 1813 J. P. Hale House (home to abolitionist Senator John P. Hale from 1840 to 1873), and the 1818 Woodman House. Exhibits focus on early American cooking utensils, clothing, furniture, New Hampshire's involvement in the Civil War, and natural history. ⌧ *182–190 Central Ave.,* ☏ *603/742–1038,* ⓦⒺⒷ *www. seacoastnh.com/woodman.* ⌧ *$3.* ☉ *Apr.–Nov., Wed.–Sun. 12:30–4:30; Dec.–Jan., weekends 12:30–4:30.*

Dining

$$–$$$ ✕ **Firehouse One.** A fire station was transformed to create this dramatic bi-level eatery complete with exposed brick, pressed-tin walls, and a vaulted ceiling. Through tall, arched windows you can admire the vintage mills of downtown Dover. The main restaurant serves jazzed-up comfort fare, from chicken satay with Thai sesame-peanut sauce to grilled Delmonico rib-eye rubbed with cracked black pepper and served with roasted-corn salsa. On the upper level, Garrison City Tavern has dancing and one of the state's longest granite bars. ⌧ *1 Orchard St.,* ☏ *603/749–2220. AE, D, MC, V.*

$–$$$ ✕ **Newick's Seafood Restaurant.** Newick's, which also has locations in Hampton and Merrimack, might serve the best lobster roll on the New England coast, but regulars cherish the scallop pies and onion rings, too. This oversize shack serves seafood in heaping portions. Picture windows allow terrific views over Great Bay. ⌧ *431 Dover Point Rd.,* ☏ *603/742–3205. AE, D, MC, V.*

Shopping

Downtown Dover Crafts (⌧ 464 Central Ave., ☏ 603/749–4952) showcases country-style crafts by local artisans who are part of a collective. **Just the Thing!** (⌧ 451 Central Ave., ☏ 603/742–9040) carries an engaging mix of vintage collectibles and contemporary handicrafts. You can watch artisans work at **Salmon Falls Stoneware** (⌧ Oak Street Engine House, ☏ 603/749–1467 or 800/621–2030), which is known for its salt-glaze stoneware made using a method favored by early American potters. **Tuttle's Red Barn** (⌧ 151 Dover Point Rd., ☏ 603/742–4313) carries jams, pickles, and other farm products.

Rochester

❿ *10 mi north of Dover, 22 mi northwest of Portsmouth, 21 mi south of Wakefield.*

This old mill factory city on the Cocheco River may not be as quaint as the state's coastal communities and lake hamlets, but it's an excellent base for exploring either region and has plenty of fine Victorian architecture. Stroll around the central intersection at Main, Wakefield, and Congress streets to get a feel for the town's heritage, or drive up along the mighty Salmon Falls River, which once powered the town's many manufacturers—everything from shoes to carbonated beverages to bricks has been produced here.

Dining and Lodging

$$–$$$　✕▦ **Governor's Inn.** Just north of downtown, this pair of neighboring, early 20th-century Georgian-style mansions are the former homes of state governors (and brothers) Huntley and Roland Spaulding. Guests now make their way about the homes' stately marble fireplaces, elliptical staircases, garden patios, and lavishly furnished bedrooms. The restaurant ($$–$$$; closed Mon.) presents an often-changing menu of regional American dishes such as Cajun rabbit roasted with an andouille–and–corn bread stuffing. ⊠ *78 Wakefield St., 03867,* ☎ *603/332–0107,* ᴘᴀx *603/335–1985,* ᴡᴇʙ *www.governorsinn.com. 16 rooms, 4 suites. Restaurant, inroom data ports, some kitchenettes, bar; no-smoking rooms. D, MC, V.*

The Coast A to Z

To research prices, get advice from other travelers, and book travel arrangements, visit www.fodors.com.

AIRPORTS

Manchester Airport is a one-hour drive from the coastal region (☞ New Hampshire A to Z).

AIRPORT TRANSFERS

Hampton Shuttle links the region's towns to both Manchester Airport and Boston's Logan Airport.

➤ INFORMATION: **Hampton Shuttle** (☎ 603/659–9893 or 800/225–6426).

BUS TRAVEL

C&J Trailways, Concord Trailways, and Vermont Transit provide bus service to and from the coast. UNH Wildcat Transit provides limited service to coastal-area towns.

➤ BUS INFORMATION: **C&J Trailways** (☎ 603/430–1100 or 800/258–7111). **Concord Trailways** (☎ 603/228–3300 or 800/639–3317). **UNH Wildcat Transit** (☎ 603/862–2328). **Vermont Transit** (☎ 800/552–8737).

CAR TRAVEL

The main (and fastest) route to New Hampshire's coast from other states is I–95, which runs from the Massachusetts border to that of Maine. Coastal Route 1A has views of water, beaches, and summer estates. The more convenient U.S. 1 travels inland. The Spaulding Turnpike (Route 16) and U.S. 4 connect Portsmouth with Dover, Durham, and Rochester. Route 108 links Durham and Exeter.

EMERGENCIES

➤ EMERGENCY SERVICES: **Exeter Hospital** (⊠ 10 Buzell Ave., Exeter, ☎ 603/778–7311). **New Hampshire State Police** (☎ 603/271–3636 or 800/852–3411). **Portsmouth Regional Hospital** (⊠ 333 Borthwick Ave., Portsmouth, ☎ 603/436–5110).

➤ PHARMACY: **Rite Aid** (⊠ 800 Islington St., Portsmouth, ☎ 603/436–2454).

OUTDOORS AND SPORTS

FISHING

Many companies offer rentals and charters for deep-sea fishing and cruises. For information about fishing and licenses, call the New Hampshire Fish and Game Department.

➤ CONTACT: **New Hampshire Fish and Game Department** (☎ 603/271–3211).

HIKING

An excellent 1-mi trail reaches the summit of Blue Job Mountain, where a fire tower has a good view. The trailhead is on Crown Point Road, off Route 202A, 13 mi northwest of Dover. The New Hampshire Division of Parks and Recreation maintains the Rockingham Recreation Trail, which wends 27 mi from Newfields, just north of Exeter, to Manchester and is open to hikers, bikers, snowmobilers, and cross-country skiers.

➤ CONTACT: **New Hampshire Division of Parks and Recreation** (☎ 603/271–3556).

TOURS

Portsmouth Livery Company gives narrated horse-and-carriage tours through Colonial Portsmouth and Strawbery Banke. The Isles of Shoals Steamship Company runs island cruises, river trips, foliage excursions, and whale-watching expeditions from April to January out of Portsmouth. Capt. Jeremy Bell hosts these voyages aboard the M/V *Thomas Laighton,* a replica of a Victorian steamship, and the smaller and more modern M/V *Oceanic.* Lunch and light snacks are available on board, or you can bring your own. Some trips include a stop at Star Island and include a walking tour.

New Hampshire Seacoast Cruises conducts naturalist-led whale-watching tours and narrated Isles of Shoals cruises aboard the 150-passenger M/V *Granite State* from May to October out of Rye Harbor State Marina. From May to October, Portsmouth Harbor Cruises operates tours of Portsmouth Harbor, trips to the Isles of Shoals, foliage trips on the Cocheco River, and sunset cruises aboard the M/V *Heritage.*

➤ TOUR-OPERATOR RECOMMENDATIONS: **Isles of Shoals Steamship Company** (✉ Barker Wharf, 315 Market St., Portsmouth, ☎ 603/431–5500 or 800/441–4620). **New Hampshire Seacoast Cruises** (✉ Rye Harbor State Marina, Rte. 1A, Rye, ☎ 603/964–5545 or 800/964–5545). **Portsmouth Harbor Cruises** (✉ Ceres Street Dock, Portsmouth, ☎ 603/436–8084 or 800/776–0915). **Portsmouth Livery Company** (✉ Market Sq., ☎ 603/427–0044).

VISITOR INFORMATION

➤ TOURIST INFORMATION: **Exeter Area Chamber of Commerce** (✉ 120 Water St., Exeter 03833, ☎ 603/772–2411, WEB www.exeterarea.org). **Greater Dover Chamber of Commerce** (✉ 299 Central Ave., Dover 03820, ☎ 603/742–2218, WEB www.dovernh.org). **Greater Portsmouth Chamber of Commerce** (✉ 500 Market St., Portsmouth 03802, ☎ 603/436–1118, WEB www.portcity.org). **Hampton Beach Area Chamber of Commerce** (✉ 409 Lafayette Rd., Hampton 03842, ☎ 603/926–8718, WEB www.hamptonbeaches.com).

➤ WEB SITE: WEB www.seacoastnh.com.

LAKES REGION

Lake Winnipesaukee, a Native American name for "smile of the great spirit," is the largest of the dozens of lakes scattered across the eastern half of central New Hampshire. With about 240 mi of shoreline full of inlets and coves, it's the largest in the state. Some claim Winnipesaukee has an island for each day of the year, but the total actually falls well short: 274.

In contrast to Winnipesaukee's summer-long bustle, the more secluded Squam Lake has a dearth of public-access points. Its tranquillity no doubt attracted the producers of *On Golden Pond*; several scenes of the Oscar-winning film were shot here. Nearby Lake Wentworth is named for the state's first royal governor, who, in building his country manor here, established North America's first summer resort.

Well-preserved Colonial and 19th-century villages are among the region's many landmarks, and you'll find hiking trails, good antiques shops, and myriad water-oriented activities. This tour begins at Laconia, just off I–93, and more or less circles Lake Winnipesaukee clockwise, with several side trips.

Laconia

⑪ *27 mi north of Concord, 94 mi north of Boston.*

The arrival in Laconia—then called Meredith Bridge—of the railroad in 1848 turned the once-sleepy hamlet into the Lakes Region's chief manufacturing hub. It acts today as the area's supply depot, a perfect role given its accessibility to both Winnisquam and Winnipesaukee lakes as well as I–93. Come here when you need to find a chain superstore or fast-food restaurant.

Belknap Mill (⊠ Mill Plaza, 25 Beacon St., ☎ 603/524–8813), the oldest unaltered, brick-built textile mill in the United States (1823), contains a knitting museum devoted to the textile industry and a year-round cultural center that sponsors concerts, workshops, exhibits, and a lecture series.

Dining and Lodging

$$–$$$ ✕ **Hickory Stick Farm.** The scent of duckling roasting (before being served with an herb stuffing and an orange-sherry sauce) frequently fills this restaurant inside a 200-year-old Cape. In fact, the duck dinners have become so renowned that the restaurant has developed a mail-order business for them. Other favorites from the mostly Continental and American menu include prime rib and vegetarian lasagna. ⊠ *66 Bean Hill Rd., Belmont (4 mi south of Laconia),* ☎ *603/524–3333. AE, D, MC, V. Closed Mon. No lunch Tues.–Sat.*

$$–$$$ ✕ **Le Chalet Rouge.** This yellow house with two small dining rooms recalls a country-French bistro. To start, try the house pâté, escargots, or steamed mussels. The steak au poivre is tender and well spiced, and the duckling is prepared with seasonal sauces: rhubarb in spring, raspberry in summer, orange in fall, creamy mustard in winter. ⊠ *385 W. Main St., Tilton (10 mi west of Laconia),* ☎ *603/286–4035. Reservations essential. MC, V. Closed Mon.–Tues. No lunch.*

$$ ⌂ **Ferry Point House.** Built in the 1800s as a summer retreat for the Pillsbury family of baking fame, this red Victorian farmhouse has superb views of Lake Winnisquam. White wicker furniture and hanging baskets of flowers grace the 60-ft veranda, and the gazebo by the water's edge is a pleasant place to lounge and listen for loons. A pedal boat and a rowboat await those eager to get in the water. The pretty rooms have Oriental rugs and Victorian furniture. ⊠ *100 Lower Bay Rd., Sanbornton 03269,* ☎ *603/524–0087,* WEB *www.new-hampshire-inn.com. 6 rooms. Beach, boating, fishing; no room phones, no room TVs, no-smoking rooms. No credit cards. Closed Nov.–Mar. BP.*

Outdoor Activities and Sports

Bartlett Beach (⊠ Winnisquam Ave.) has a playground and picnic area. **Opechee Park** (⊠ N. Main St.) has dressing rooms, a baseball field, tennis courts, and picnic areas.

Shopping

The **Belknap Mall** (⊠ U.S. 3, ☎ 603/524–5651) has boutiques, crafts shops, and a New Hampshire State Liquor Store. The 53 stores at the

Lakes Region Factory Stores (⊠ 120 Laconia Rd., I–93 Exit 20, Tilton, ☎ 888/746–7333) include Brooks Brothers, Eddie Bauer, Coach, Geoffrey Beene, and Black & Decker.

OFF THE BEATEN PATH	**CANTERBURY SHAKER VILLAGE –** Shaker furniture and inventions are well regarded, and this National Historic Landmark helps illuminate the world of the people who created them. Established as a religious community in 1792, the village flourished in the 1800s and practiced equality of the sexes and races, common ownership, celibacy, and pacifism. The last member of the community passed away in 1992. Shakers invented such household items as the clothespin and the flat broom and were known for the simplicity and integrity of their designs. Engaging 90-minute tours pass through some of the 694-acre property's 24 restored buildings, many of them still with original Shaker furnishings, and crafts demonstrations take place daily. The Creamery Restaurant serves lunch daily and candlelight dinners Friday–Saturday (reservations essential). A large shop sells fine Shaker reproductions. ⊠ *288 Shaker Rd., 15 mi south of Laconia via Rte. 106, Canterbury,* ☎ *603/783–9511 or 866/783–9511,* WEB *www.shakers.org.* ⊠ *$10, good for 2 consecutive days.* ☉ *May–Oct., daily 10–5; Apr. and Nov.–Dec., weekends 10–4.*

Gilford

⑫ *4 mi northeast of Laconia.*

One of the larger public beaches on Lake Winnipesaukee is in Gilford. When the town was incorporated in 1812, the inhabitants asked the oldest resident to name it. A veteran of the Battle of the Guilford Courthouse, in North Carolina, he borrowed that town's name—though apparently he didn't know how to spell it. Quiet and peaceful, Gilford remains decidedly uncommercial.

Lodging

$$–$$$ 🛏 **B. Mae's Resort Inn.** All the rooms in this contemporary resort and conference center are large, if nondescript, and have a deck or patio; some are suites with kitchens. Close to the Gunstock ski area and within walking distance of Lake Winnipesaukee, B. Mae's is popular with skiers in winter and boaters in summer. ⊠ *Rtes. 11 and 11B, 03246,* ☎ *603/293–7526 or 800/458–3877,* FAX *603/293–4340,* WEB *www. bmaesresort.com. 60 rooms, 24 suites. 2 restaurants, in-room data ports, in-room safes, some kitchens, some in-room VCRs, 2 pools (1 indoor), hot tub, gym, bar, recreation room. AE, D, DC, MC, V.*

$–$$ 🛏 **Gunstock Inn & Fitness Center.** The original building of this Colonial-style inn, just up the road from the Gunstock ski area, was constructed in the 1930s by Civilian Conservation Corps workers who cut the area's first ski trails. The inn has individually decorated rooms, some of which are large enough to accommodate families. Many rooms have views of the mountains and Lake Winnipesaukee. The snug tavern serves everything from seafood to burgers. In the fitness center, you can take water aerobics and body-toning classes free of charge. ⊠ *580 Cherry Valley Rd., 03246,* ☎ *603/293–2021 or 800/ 654–0180,* FAX *603/293–2050,* WEB *www.gunstockinn.com. 23 rooms, 2 suites. Restaurant, some refrigerators, indoor pool, health club, sauna, steam room. AE, MC, V. BP.*

$ 🏕 **Gunstock Campground.** The campground at the Gunstock ski and recreation area has a pool and 300 tent and trailer sites as well as several cabins. ⊠ *Rte. 11A (Box 1307, Laconia 03247),* ☎ *603/293–4341 or 800/486–7862. AE, D, MC, V.*

Nightlife and the Arts

The outdoor stage (with 2,500 covered seats) at **Meadowbrook Farm**

New Hampshire Lakes

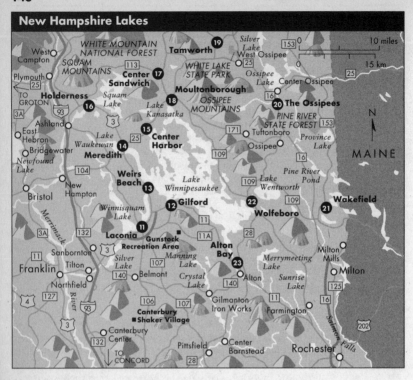

(⊠ 72 Meadowbrook La., off Rte. 11B, ☎ 603/293–4700 or 888/563–2369) hosts top music acts, from Nanci Griffith to 98°. The **New Hampshire Music Festival** (⊠ 88 Belknap Mountain Rd., ☎ 603/524–1000) presents award-winning orchestras from early July to mid-August.

Outdoor Activities and Sports

Ellacoya State Beach (⊠ Rte. 11, ☎ 603/293–7821) covers just 600 ft along the southwestern shore of Lake Winnipesaukee. In season, there's a bathhouse, picnic tables, and a fee ($3 from mid-May to Labor Day) for parking.

Shopping

Pepi Herrmann Crystal (⊠ 3 Waterford Pl., ☎ 603/528–1020) sells hand-cut crystal chandeliers and stemware. You can take a tour and watch the artists at work.

Ski Area

GUNSTOCK USA

High above Lake Winnipesaukee, this all-purpose area dates from the 1930s. It once had the country's longest rope tow lift—an advantage that helped local downhill skier and Olympic silver medalist Penny Pitou perfect her craft. Gunstock allows patrons to return lift tickets for a cash refund for absolutely any reason within 75 minutes of purchase. Thrill Hill, a snowtubing park, has 10 runs, multipassenger tubes, and lift service. ⊠ *Rte. 11A (Box 1307, Laconia 03247),* ☎ *603/293–4341 or 800/486–7862,* WEB *www.gunstock.com.*

Downhill. Clever trail cutting along with grooming and surface sculpting three times daily have made this otherwise pedestrian mountain good for intermediates. That's how most of the 44 trails are rated, with a few more challenging runs as well as designated sections for slow skiers and learners. Lower Ramrod trail is set up for snowboarding. Chairlifts include one quad, two triples, two doubles as well as two surface tows. At night, you'll find 15 lighted trails and five lifts in operation, making this the state's largest night-skiing facility.

Cross-country. Gunstock has 50 km (30 mi) of trails for skiing and snowshoeing. Some 15 km (9 mi) are for advanced skiers, and there are backcountry trails as well.

Child care. The nursery takes children ages 6 months and up; the ski school teaches children ages 3–14.

Summer activities. In summer, Gunstock has a swimming pool, a playground, hiking trails, mountain-bike rentals and trails, a skateboarding-blading park, guided horseback rides, pedal boats, and a campground.

Weirs Beach

⑬ *10 mi northwest of Gilford, 8 mi north of Laconia.*

Weirs Beach is Lake Winnipesaukee's center for arcade activity. Anyone who loves souvenir shops, fireworks, water slides, and hordes of children will feel right at home. Several cruise boats depart from the town dock.

The period cars of the **Winnipesaukee Scenic Railroad** carry you along the lakeshore on one- or two-hour rides; boarding is at Weirs Beach or Meredith. Special trips that include certain meals are also available. ⊠ *U.S. 3, Weirs Beach,* ☎ *603/279–5253 or 603/745–2135,* WEB *www.hoborr.com.* ⊠ *$9.95–$24.50.* ☉ *July–mid-Sept., daily; Memorial Day–late June and mid-Sept.–mid-Oct. weekends only. Call for hrs and for special Santa trains in Dec.*

♺ Day or night you can work your way through the miniature golf course, 20 lanes of bowling, and more than 500 games at **Funspot** (⊠ Rte. 11B, at U.S. 3, ☎ 603/366–4377). For a full aquatic experience,
♺ visit **Surf Coaster** (⊠ U.S. 3, ☎ 603/366–4991), which has seven slides,
♺ a wave pool, and a large area for young children. A giant **Water Slide** (⊠ U.S. 3, ☎ 603/366–5161) overlooks the lake.

Outdoor Activities and Sports
Thurston's Marina (⊠ U.S. 3 at the bridge, ☎ 603/366–4811 or 800/834–4812) rents pontoon boats, powerboats, and personal watercraft.

Meredith

⑭ *5 mi northwest of Weirs Beach, 41 mi north of Concord.*

Meredith, a one-time workaday mill town on U.S. 3 at Lake Winnipesaukee's western end, has watched its fortunes change for the better over the past decade or so. The opening and constant expansion of Inns at Mills Falls have attracted hundreds of visitors, and crafts shops and art galleries have sprung up. You can pick up area information at a kiosk across from the town docks.

At **Annalee's Doll Museum,** you can view a collection of the famous felt dolls and learn about the woman who created them. Annalee Davis Thorndike began making these poppets after her graduation from high school in 1933. They caught on with collectors, and the company has grown into an empire. ⊠ *Hemlock Dr. off Rte. 104,* ☎ *603/279–3333 or 800/433–6557,* WEB *www.annalee.com.* ⊠ *Free.* ☉ *Memorial Day–mid-Oct.; call for hrs.*

Dining and Lodging

$$–$$$ ✕ **Mame's.** This 1820s tavern, once the home of the village doctor, now contains a warren of convivial dining rooms with exposed-brick walls, wooden beams, and wide-plank floors. Expect mostly American standbys of the seafood, steak, veal, and chicken variety; the mud pie is highly recommended. ⊠ *8 Plymouth St.,* ☎ *603/279–4631. AE, D, MC, V.*

$$–$$$$ ✕🖭 **Inns at Mill Falls.** Overlooking Lake Winnipesaukee and incor-
★ porating sections of the 19th-century Meredith Linen Mills, this complex has all the amenities of a full resort as well as warmth and personality. The central-most Inn at Mills Falls, which adjoins an 18-shop market, has a pool and 54 spacious rooms. The lakefront Inn at Bay Point has 24 rooms—most with balconies, some with fireplaces. The 23 rooms at the lake-view Chase House at Mill Falls all have fireplaces; some have balconies. The upscale Boathouse Grill ($$–$$$) serves such contemporary dishes as pan-seared almond-and-cornmeal-crusted trout with apple butter. The rustic-cabin motifs and the cedar-plank salmon will delight you at Camp ($$–$$$). For breakfast or lunch, try the Waterfall Cafe ($), which overlooks 40-ft cascades. Giuseppe's ($–$$), an Italian eatery, has live cabaret many nights. ⊠ *U.S. 3 at Rte. 25, 03253,* ☎ *603/279–7006 or 800/622–6455,* 𝔽𝔸𝕏 *603/279–6797,* 𝕎𝔼𝔹 *www.millsfalls.com. 101 rooms. 4 restaurants, some in-room hot tubs, indoor pool, sauna, beach, dock, boating, ice-skating, bar, shops, meeting rooms. AE, D, DC, MC, V.*

$ ⚠ **Clearwater Campground.** This wooded tent and RV campground on Lake Pemigewasset has 153 shady sites, several cabins, a large sandy beach, a recreation building, a playground, basketball and volleyball courts, and boat rentals and slips. ⊠ *26 Campground Rd., off Rte. 104, 03253,* ☎ *603/279–7761,* 𝕎𝔼𝔹 *www.clearwatercampground.com. Closed mid-Oct.–mid-May.*

The Arts

The **Lakes Region Summer Theatre** (⊠ Interlakes Auditorium, Rte. 25, ☎ 603/279–9933) presents Broadway musicals.

Outdoor Activities and Sports

BEACHES

Wellington State Beach (⊠ off Rte. 3A, Bristol, 12 mi west of Meredith, ☎ 603/744–2197), on Newfound Lake's western shore, is beautiful. You can swim, picnic, hike along the ½-mi shoreline, or use the boat launch.

BOATING

Meredith Marina and Boating Center (⊠ Bayshore Dr., ☎ 603/279–7921) rents powerboats. **Wild Meadow Canoes & Kayaks** (⊠ Rte. 25 between Center Harbor and Meredith, ☎ 603/253–7536 or 800/427–7536) has canoes and kayaks for rent.

GOLF

Waukewan Golf Club (⊠ off U.S. 3 and Rte. 25, ☎ 603/279–6661) is an 18-hole, par-71 course. Greens fees are $22–$28.

Shopping

About 170 dealers operate out of the three-floor **Burlwood Antique Center** (⊠ U.S. 3, ☎ 603/279–6387), open May–October. The **Meredith League of New Hampshire Craftsmen** (⊠ 279 U.S. 3, ½ mi north of Rte. 104, ☎ 603/279–7920) sells works by area artisans. **Mill Falls Marketplace** (⊠ U.S. 3 at Rte. 25, ☎ 603/279–7006), part of the Inns at Mills Falls, contains shops with clothing, gifts, and books. The **Old Print Barn** (⊠ 1008 Winona Rd., ☎ 603/279–6479) carries rare prints—Currier & Ives, antique botanicals, and more—from around the world.

Center Harbor

⓯ *5 mi northeast of Meredith.*

In the middle of three bays at the northern end of Lake Winnipesaukee, the town of Center Harbor also borders Squam, Waukewan, and Winona lakes. This prime location, which takes in views of the White Mountains to the north, has long made it popular in summer, especially with boaters.

Outdoor Activities and Sports

Red Hill, a hiking trail on Bean Road off Route 25, northeast of Center Harbor, really does turn red in autumn. The reward at the end of the route is a view of Squam Lake and the mountains.

Shopping

Keepsake Quilting & Country Pleasures (✉ Senter's Marketplace, Rte. 25B, ☎ 603/253–4026), reputedly America's largest quilt shop, contains 5,000 bolts of fabric, hundreds of quilting books, and countless supplies as well as handmade quilts.

Holderness

⓰ *8 mi northwest of Center Harbor, 8 mi northwest of Meredith.*

Routes 25B and 25 lead to the small, prim town of Holderness, between Squam and Little Squam lakes. *On Golden Pond,* starring Katharine Hepburn and Henry Fonda, was filmed on Squam, whose quiet beauty attracts nature lovers.

★ ℭ Trails at the 200-acre **Squam Lakes Natural Science Center** include a ¾-mi path that passes black bears, bobcats, otters, and other native wildlife in trailside enclosures. Educational events include the "Up Close to Animals" series in July and August, at which you can study a species in an intimate setting. The Gordon Children's Activity Center has interactive exhibits. A ride on a 28-ft pontoon boat is the best way to tour the lake and observe the loons. ✉ *Rtes. 113 and 25,* ☎ *603/968–7194,* WEB *www.nhnature.org.* ☞ *$9, $7 May–June and Sept.–Oct.* ☉ *May–Oct., daily 9:30–4:30 (last entry at 3:30).*

Dining and Lodging

$$$$ ✕▥ **Manor on Golden Pond.** Built in 1903, this dignified inn has 14
★ acres of well-groomed grounds and a dock with canoes and pedal boats. You can stay in the main inn, the cottages, or, in summer and fall, the carriage house. Sixteen rooms have wood-burning fireplaces; eight have two-person whirlpool baths. Three-, four-, or five-course prix-fixe dinners ($$$$; reservations essential) may include roasted breast and confit of Maine duck on a bed of creamy polenta served with glazed root vegetables and a port wine sauce. ✉ *U.S. 3 and Shepard Hill Rd., 03245,* ☎ *603/968–3348 or 800/545–2141,* FAX *603/968–2116,* WEB *www.manorongoldenpond.com. 20 rooms, 3 cottages, 1 carriage house. Restaurant, in-room data ports, some in-room hot tubs, 2 tennis courts, pool, beach, boating, fishing, badminton, croquet, pub; no kids under 12. AE, MC, V. BP.*

$$–$$$ ▥ **Glynn House Inn.** Jim and Gay Dunlop run this swanky, three-story, 1890s Queen Anne–style home with a turret and wraparound porch. Many rooms have fireplaces; the bi-level Honeymoon Suite has a whirlpool tub and fireplace downstairs and a four-poster bed and skylights above. Breakfast usually includes fresh-baked strudel. Squam Lake is minutes away. ✉ *43 Highland St., Ashland 03217,* ☎ *603/968–3775 or 800/637–9599,* FAX *603/968–3129,* WEB *www.glynnhouse.com. 3 rooms, 6 suites. Some in-room hot tubs, in-room VCRs; no smoking. MC, V. BP.*

$$ ⊞ **Inn on Golden Pond.** This informal country home, built in 1879 and set on 50 wooded acres, is just up the road from Squam Lake. Rooms have hardwood floors, braided rugs, easy chairs, and calico-print bedspreads and curtains. The homemade jam at breakfast is made from rhubarb grown on the property. ⊠ *U.S. 3 (Box 680, 03245),* ☎ *603/968-7269,* FAX *603/968-9226,* WEB *www.innongoldenpond.com. 7 rooms, 1 suite. Hiking; no room phones, no room TVs, no kids under 12, no smoking. AE, MC, V. BP.*

$-$$ ⚠ **Yogi Bear's Jellystone Park.** This family-oriented camping resort has wooded, open, or riverfront sites; basic and deluxe cabins; and trailers. There's also a pool, a water playground, a hot tub, a miniature golf course, a basketball court, canoe and kayak rentals, and daily supervised activities. ⊠ *Rte. 132 (R.R. 1, Box 396, Ashland 03217),* ☎ *603/968-9000,* WEB *www.jellystonenh.com. 275 sites, 43 cabins, 7 trailers.*

Outdoor Activities and Sports

White Mountain Country Club (⊠ N. Ashland Rd., Ashland, ☎ 603/536-2227) has an 18-hole, par-71 golf course. Greens fees are $28-$34.

Center Sandwich

★ ⑰ *12 mi northeast of Holderness.*

With Squam Lake to the west and the Sandwich Mountains to the north, Center Sandwich claims one of the prettiest settings of any Lakes Region community. So appealing are the town and its views that John Greenleaf Whittier used the Bearcamp River as the inspiration for his poem "Sunset on the Bearcamp." The town attracts artisans—crafts shops abound among its clutch of charming 18th- and 19th-century buildings.

The **Historical Society Museum** traces Center Sandwich's history through the faces of its inhabitants. Works by mid-19th-century portraitist and town son Albert Gallatin Hoit hang alongside a local photographer's exhibit portraying the town's mothers and daughters. The museum houses a replica country store and local furniture and other items. ⊠ *4 Maple St.,* ☎ *603/284-6269,* WEB *www.sandwichnh.com/history.* ▨ *Free.* ☉ *Late June-mid-Oct., Tues.-Sat. 11-5.*

Dining

$$-$$$ ✕ **Corner House Inn.** The restaurant, in a converted barn adorned with local arts and crafts, serves classic American fare. Before you get to the white-chocolate cheesecake with key-lime filling, try the chef's lobster-and-mushroom bisque or tasty garlic-and-horseradish-crusted rack of lamb. There's storytelling Thursday evening. ⊠ *Rtes. 109 and 113,* ☎ *603/284-6219 or 800/832-7829. AE, MC, V. Closed Mon. Nov.-May. No lunch.*

Moultonborough

⑱ *5 mi south of Center Sandwich.*

Moultonborough claims 6½ mi of shore on Lake Kanasatka, a large chunk of Lake Winnipesaukee, and even a small piece of Squam.

The **Old Country Store and Museum** (⊠ Moultonborough Corner, ☎ 603/476-5750) has been selling maple products, cheeses aged on site, penny candy, and other items since 1781. Much of the equipment still used in the store is antique, and the museum (free) displays old farming and forging tools.

Castle in the Clouds is an odd, elaborate stone mansion built without nails; it has 16 rooms, 8 bathrooms, and doors made of lead. Construction began in 1911 and continued for three years. Owner Thomas Gustave Plant spent $7 million, the bulk of his fortune, on this project and died penniless in 1946. A tour includes the mansion and the Castle Springs Microbrewery and spring-water facility on this 5,200-acre property; there's also hiking and pony and horseback rides. ⊠ *Rte. 171,* ☎ *603/ 476–2352 or 800/729–2468,* WEB *www.castlesprings.com.* ⊡ *With tour $12, without tour $6.* ☉ *Mid-May–late May, weekends 9–5; early June–early Sept., daily 9–5; early Sept.–late Oct., daily 9–4.*

The **Loon Center** at the **Frederick and Paula Anna Markus Wildlife Sanctuary** is the headquarters of the Loon Preservation Committee, an Audubon Society project. This bird, recognizable for its eerie calls and striking black-and-white coloring, resides on many New Hampshire lakes but is threatened by boat traffic, poor water quality, and habitat loss. The center presents changing exhibits about the birds. Two trails wind through the 200-acre property; vantage points on the Loon Nest Trail overlook the spot resident loons sometimes occupy in late spring and summer. ⊠ *Lees Mills Rd.,* ☎ *603/476–5666,* WEB *www.loon.org.* ⊡ *Free.* ☉ *July–Columbus Day, daily 9–5; Columbus Day–June, Mon.–Sat. 9–5.*

Dining

$$–$$$ ✕ **The Woodshed.** Farm implements and antiques hang on the walls of this enchanting, romantic 1860 barn. The fare is mostly traditional New England—sea scallops baked in butter and lamb chops with mint sauce— but the exceptionally fresh ingredients are sure to please. ⊠ *128 Lee Rd.,* ☎ *603/476–2311. AE, D, DC, MC, V. Closed Mon. No lunch.*

Tamworth

⓳ *12 mi northeast of Moultonborough, 20 mi southwest of North Conway.*

President Grover Cleveland summered in what remains a village of almost unreal quaintness—it's equally photogenic in verdant summer, during fall foliage, or under a blanket of winter snow. Cleveland's son, Francis, returned to stay and founded the acclaimed Barnstormers Theatre in 1931. Tamworth has a clutch of villages within its borders. At one of them—Chocorua—the view through the birches of Chocorua Lake has been so often photographed that you may experience déjà vu.

For 99 years, Dr. Edwin Remick and his father provided medical services to the Tamworth area and operated a family farm. At the **Remick Country Doctor Museum and Farm,** exhibits focus on the life of a country doctor and on the activities of the still-working farm. There are always hands-on activities, but try to visit when ice harvesting, stone-wall building, or the like is scheduled. ⊠ *58 Cleveland Hill Rd.,* ☎ *603/ 323–7591 or 800/686–6117,* WEB *www.remickmuseum.org.* ⊡ *Free.* ☉ *Nov.–June, weekdays 10–4; July–Oct., Mon.–Sat. 10–4.*

Dining and Lodging

$$$–$$$$ ✕▦ **Tamworth Inn.** This 1833 Victorian inn is a great base both for ★ exploring the lakes and skiing in the White Mountains. Common rooms range from a beamed-ceiling pub to a dining room where tables are laid with white linen and crystal. Guest rooms have brass or antique beds, down comforters, and Caswell-Massey toiletries. The dining room ($$–$$$; closed Sun.–Mon. in summer and Sun.–Wed. in winter) serves seasonal cuisine with specialties such as grilled salmon brushed with olive oil and cracked black pepper and served with Yukon potato hash. ⊠ *Main St., 03886,* ☎ *603/323–7721 or 800/642–*

7352, FAX 603/323–2026, WEB *www.tamworth.com. 16 rooms. Restaurant, some in-room hot tubs, pool, pub, some pets allowed (fee); no room phones, no room TVs, no smoking. AE, MC, V. Closed Apr. and 2 wks in Nov. BP, MAP.*

$–$$ ⊞ **Mt. Chocorua View House.** What began as a stagecoach stop has been operating as an inn almost continuously since 1845. Ideally located between the Lakes Region and the White Mountains, it draws many hikers and skiers. Guest rooms are welcoming with floral wallpapers, quilts, ceiling fans, and other personal touches. Common areas include a guest kitchen and a screened porch that might make hiking nearby Mt. Chocorua seem like too much work. ⊠ *Rte. 16 (Box 348, Chocorua 03817),* ☎ *603/323–8350 or 888/323–8350,* FAX *603/323–3319,* WEB *www.mtchocorua.com. 6 rooms, 3 with bath; 1 suite. Gym; no room phones, no room TVs. AE, D, MC, V. BP.*

Nightlife and the Arts

The **Arts Council of Tamworth** (☎ 603/323–8104) produces concerts—soloists, string quartets, revues, children's programs—from September through June and an arts show in late July. **Barnstormers Summer Theatre** (⊠ Main St., ☎ 603/323–8500) has performances in July and August. The box office opens in June.

Outdoor Activities and Sports

The 72-acre stand of native pitch pine at **White Lake State Park** (⊠ Rte. 16, ☎ 603/323–7350) is a National Natural Landmark. The park has hiking trails, a sandy beach, trout fishing, canoe rentals, two camping areas, a picnic area, and swimming.

Shopping

The many theme rooms—a Christmas room, a bride's room, a children's room, among them—at the **Country Handcrafters & Chocorua Dam Ice Cream Shop** (⊠ Rte. 16, Chocorua, ☎ 603/323–8745) contain handcrafted items. When you're done shopping, try the ice cream, coffee, or tea and scones.

The Ossipees

⑳ *6 mi southeast of Tamworth, 21 mi south of North Conway.*

Route 16 between West Ossipee and Center Ossipee passes Ossipee Lake, known for fine fishing and swimming. Around these hamlets you'll find several antiques shops and galleries.

Dining

$$ ✕ **Jake's Seafood.** Oars and nautical trappings adorn the wood-paneled walls at this stop between West and Center Ossipee. The kitchen serves some of eastern New Hampshire's freshest and tastiest seafood, notably lobster pie, fried clams, and seafood casserole; other choices include steak, ribs, and chicken dishes. ⊠ *2055 Rte. 16,* ☎ *603/539–2805. MC, V. Closed Mon.–Wed.*

$–$$ ✕ **Yankee Smokehouse.** This down-home barbecue joint's logo depict-
★   ing two happy pigs foreshadows the gleeful enthusiasm with which patrons dive into the hefty sandwiches of sliced pork and smoked chicken and immense platters of baby back ribs and smoked sliced beef. Ample sides of slaw, beans, fries, and garlic toast complement the hearty fare. Born-and-bred Southerners have been known to come away impressed. ⊠ *Rtes. 16 and 25,* ☎ *603/539–7427. No credit cards. Closed Tues.–Wed.*

Shopping

Local craftspeople create much of the jewelry, turned wooden bowls, pewter goblets, and glassware sold at **Tramway Artisans** (⊠ Rte. 16, West Ossipee, ☎ 603/539–5700).

Wakefield

㉑ *21 mi south of West Ossipee, 43 mi north of Portsmouth, 64 mi northeast of Concord.*

East of Lake Winnipesaukee, seven laid-back villages combine to form Wakefield, a town with 10 lakes. Wakefield's 26-building historic district, just off Route 16 near the Maine border, consists of a church, houses, and an 18th-century inn. A few miles down Route 153 in Sanbornville you'll find Wakefield's present-day commercial district.

The **Museum of Childhood** displays a one-room schoolhouse, a child's room and a kitchen from 1890, model trains, antique sleds, teddy bears, 3,500 dolls, and 44 furnished dollhouses. Special events are scheduled most Fridays. ⊠ *2784 Wakefield Rd.,* ☎ *603/522-8073.* ☜ *$3.* ☉ *Memorial Day–Labor Day, Mon. and Wed.–Sat. 11–4, Sun. 1–4.*

OFF THE BEATEN PATH

NEW HAMPSHIRE FARM MUSEUM – Roughly 10 mi south of Wakefield in northern Milton, a sleepy Colonial village that stretches along the Salmon Falls River, this facility houses more than 60,000 artifacts, retelling New Hampshire farm life from 1700 to the early 1900s. Take a guided tour through the Jones Farmhouse and then explore the Grand Barn—filled with vehicles and implements—the gardens, and the nature trails at your leisure. Special events demonstrating farm-related crafts take place throughout the season. ⊠ *Rte. 125/White Mountain Hwy.,* ☎ *603/652-7840,* WEB *www.farmmuseum.org.* ☜ *$5.* ☉ *June–Oct., Wed.–Sun. 10–4.*

Lodging

$$ **Wakefield Inn.** The restoration of this 1804 stagecoach inn, a high-
★ light of Wakefield's historic district, has been handled with care. The dining-room windows retain the original panes and shutters, but the centerpiece is the freestanding spiral staircase, which rises three stories. The large rooms, named for famous guests or past owners, have wide-board pine floors, big sofas, and handmade quilts. In late fall and early spring, you can learn how to quilt as part of the weekend Quilting Package. ⊠ *2723 Wakefield Rd., 03872,* ☎ *603/522-8272 or 800/245-0841,* WEB *www.wakefieldinn.com. 7 rooms. Dining room; no room phones, no room TVs, no kids under 10, no-smoking rooms. MC, V. BP.*

Wolfeboro

㉒ *21 mi south of West Ossipee, 28 mi northwest of Rochester, 49 mi northwest of Portsmouth.*

Quietly upscale and decidedly preppy Wolfeboro has been a resort since Royal Governor John Wentworth built his summer home on the shores of Lake Wentworth in 1768. The town center, bursting with tony boutiques, fringes Lake Winnipesaukee and sees about a tenfold population increase each summer. The century-old, white-clapboard buildings of the Brewster Academy prep school bracket the town's southern end. Expect none of the exuberant commercialism of Weirs Beach—Wolfeboro marches to a steady, relaxed beat, comfortable for all ages.

Uniforms, vehicles, and other artifacts at the **Wright Museum** illustrate the contributions of those on the home front to America's World War II effort. ⊠ *77 Center St.,* ☎ *603/569-1212,* WEB *www.wrightmuseum.org.* ☜ *$6.* ☉ *May–Oct., Mon.–Sat. 10–4, Sun. noon–5; Nov.–Apr., Sat. 10–4, Sun. noon–4.*

NEED A
BREAK?

Brewster Academy students and summer folk converge upon groovy little **Lydia's** (✉ 30 N. Main St., ☎ 603/569–3991) for espressos, hearty sandwiches, homemade soups, bagels, and desserts.

The artisans at the **Hampshire Pewter Company** (✉ 43 Mill St., ☎ 603/569–4944 or 800/639–7704) use 16th-century techniques to make pewter tableware and accessories. Free tours are conducted at 9:30, 11, 1:30, and 3 most days, Memorial Day–Columbus Day, and by appointment at other times. The gift shop is open year-round.

Dining and Lodging

$$–$$$ ✕ **The Bittersweet.** This converted barn 2 mi north of downtown delights with its display of old quilts, pottery, sheet music, and china. Locals also love the nightly specials—the lobster pie is particularly popular. The upper level has antique tables and chairs and dining by candlelight. The lower-level lounge, with Victorian wicker furniture, serves lighter fare. ✉ Rte. 28, ☎ 603/569–3636. AE, D, MC, V. No dinner Sun. No lunch Mon.–Sat.

$–$$$ ✕ **Wolfetrap Grill and Raw Bar.** The seafood at this festive shanty on Lake Winnipesaukee comes right from the adjacent fish market. You'll find all your favorites here, including a renowned clam boil for one that includes steamers, corn on the cob, onions, baked potatoes, sweet potatoes, sausage, and a hot dog. The raw bar has oysters and clams on the half shell. ✉ 19 Bay St., ☎ 603/569–1503. MC, V. Closed mid-Oct.–mid-May.

$$$–$$$$ ✕🏨 **Wolfeboro Inn.** Built in the early 1800s, this white clapboard house has later additions with lake views. Rooms have polished cherry and pine furnishings, armoires, stenciled borders, and country quilts but could stand a little updating, especially the bathrooms and toiletries. Pub fare and more than 70 brands of beer are available at Wolfe's Tavern ($–$$), where fireplaces take the chill off cool evenings. The 1812 Steakhouse ($$–$$$) serves a popular slow-roasted prime rib. ✉ 90 N. Main St. (Box 1270, 03894), ☎ 603/569–3016 or 800/451–2389, FAX 603/569–5375, WEB www.wolfeboroinn.com. 41 rooms, 3 suites, 1 apartment. 2 restaurants, some refrigerators, beach, boating, bar, meeting room. AE, D, MC, V. CP.

Outdoor Activities and Sports

BEACHES

Wentworth State Beach (✉ Rte. 109, ☎ 603/569–3699) has good swimming, picnicking areas, ball fields, and a bathhouse.

BOATING

Winnipesaukee Kayak Company (✉ 17 Bay St., ☎ 603/569–9926) gives kayak lessons and leads group excursions on the lake. **Wetwolfe Boat Rentals** (✉ 17 Bay St., ☎ 603/569–1503) rents motorboats and personal watercraft.

GOLF

The Donald Ross–designed **Kingswood Golf Club** (✉ Rte. 28, ☎ 603/569–3569) has an 18-hole, par-72 course; greens fees are $35.

HIKING

A short (¼-mi) hike to the 100-ft post-and-beam **Abenaki Tower,** followed by a more rigorous climb to the top, rewards you with a vast view of Lake Winnipesaukee and the Ossipee mountain range. The trailhead is a few miles north of town on Route 109.

WATER SPORTS

Scuba divers can explore a 130-ft-long cruise ship that sank in 30 ft of water off Glendale in 1895. **Dive Winnipesaukee Corp.** (✉ 4 N. Main

St., ☎ 603/569–8080) runs charters out to wrecks and offers rentals, repairs, scuba sales, and lessons in waterskiing and windsurfing.

Shopping

Architectural Attic (✉ 49 Center St., Wolfeboro Falls, ☎ 603/569–8989) mixes an amazing array of antiques and housewares in with its architectural elements. You'll find an excellent regional-history section and plenty of children's titles at Wolfeboro's fine general-interest bookstore, the **Country Bookseller** (✉ 9 Railroad Ave., ☎ 603/569–6030). **Made on Earth** (✉ Main St., ☎ 603/569–9100) carries New Age gifts, clothing, books, and crafts.

Alton Bay

❷❸ *10 mi southwest of Wolfeboro, 20 mi southeast of Laconia*

Lake Winnipesaukee's southern shore is alive with visitors from the moment the first flower blooms until the last maple sheds its leaves. Two mountain ridges hold 7 mi of the lake in Alton Bay, which is the name of both the inlet and the town at its tip. Cruise boats dock here, and small planes land here year-round, on both the water and the ice. There's a dance pavilion, along with miniature golf, a public beach, and a Victorian-style bandstand.

Mt. Major, 5 mi north of Alton Bay on Route 11, has a 2½-mi trail with views of Lake Winnipesaukee. At the top is a four-sided stone shelter built in 1925.

Dining

$$$$ ✕ **Crystal Quail.** This 12-seat restaurant, inside an 18th-century farmhouse, is worth the drive. The prix-fixe contemporary menu changes daily but might include saffron-garlic soup, a house pâté, quenelle-stuffed sole, or goose confit with apples and onions. ✉ *202 Pitman Rd., Center Barnstead (12 mi south of Alton Bay),* ☎ *603/269–4151. Reservations essential. No credit cards. BYOB. Closed Mon.–Tues. No lunch.*

Lakes Region A to Z

To research prices, get advice from other travelers, and book travel arrangements, visit www.fodors.com

AIRPORTS AND TRANSFERS
Manchester Airport is about an hour to 90 minutes away by car (☞ New Hampshire A to Z).

AIRPORT TRANSFERS
Greater Laconia Transit Agency has door-to-door minibus service from Manchester Airport to anywhere within a 10-mi radius of Laconia. The cost is $110 one-way (for up to eight people).
➤ Shuttle: **Greater Laconia Transit Agency** (☎ 603/528–2496 or 800/294–2496).

BUS TRAVEL
Concord Trailways connects Boston's South Station and Logan Airport, via Concord and Manchester, with Center Harbor, Chocorua, Laconia, Meredith, Moultonborough, Plymouth, Tilton, and West Ossipee. Greater Laconia Transit Agency has regional bus service to Laconia, Ashland, Holderness, Tilton, Meredith, Plymouth, Belmont, and Franklin. In summer it also runs a trolley between Meredith and Weirs Beach.
➤ Bus Information: **Concord Trailways** (☎ 603/228–3300 or 800/639–3317). **Greater Laconia Transit Agency** (☎ 603/528–2496 or 800/294–2496).

CAR TRAVEL

On the western side of the Lakes Region, I–93 is the principal north–south artery. Exit 20 leads to U.S. 3 and Route 11 and the southwestern side of Lake Winnipesaukee. Take Exit 23 to Route 104 to Route 25 and the region's northwestern corner. From the coast, the Spaulding Turnpike (Route 16) heads to the White Mountains, with roads leading to the lakeside towns.

EMERGENCIES

➤ HOSPITAL: **Lakes Region General Hospital** (✉ 80 Highland St., Laconia, ☎ 603/524–3211).

LODGING

For longer stays in the Lakes Region consider renting a lakeside house or condominium. Among the agencies are Preferred Vacation Rental, Inc. and Strictly Rentals, Inc.

APARTMENT AND VILLA RENTALS

➤ LOCAL AGENTS: **Preferred Vacation Rentals, Inc.** (✉ Rte. 25 [Box 161, Center Harbor 03226], ☎ 603/253–7811, WEB www.preferredrentals.com). **Strictly Rentals, Inc.** (✉ 285 Rte. 25 [Box 695, Center Harbor 03226], ☎ 603/253–9800, WEB www.strictlyrentals.biz).

OUTDOORS AND SPORTS

The Lakes Region Association provides boating advice. The New Hampshire Fish and Game Department has information about fishing and licenses. The Alexandria headquarters of the Appalachian Mountain Club has trail information, as does the Laconia Office of the U.S. Forest Service.

➤ CONTACTS: **Appalachian Mountain Club** (☎ 617/523–0636). **Laconia Office of the U.S. Forest Service** (☎ 603/528–8721). The **Lakes Region Association** (☎ 603/744–8664 or 800/605–2537). **New Hampshire Fish and Game Department** (☎ 603/271–3211).

TOURS

The 230-ft M/S *Mount Washington* makes 2½-hour scenic cruises of Lake Winnipesaukee from Weirs Beach, mid-May–late October, with stops in Wolfeboro, Alton Bay, Center Harbor, and Meredith. Evening cruises include live music and a buffet dinner. The same company operates the M/V *Sophie C.*, which has been the area's floating post office for more than a century. The boat departs from Weirs Beach with mail and passengers Monday–Saturday, mid-June–Labor Day; call for stops. Additionally, the M/V *Doris E.* runs between Meredith and Weirs Beach throughout the summer.

From May to late October, Squam Lake Tours takes up to 24 passengers on a two-hour pontoon-boat tour of "Golden Pond." The company also operates guided fishing trips and private charters. Sky Bright operates airplane and helicopter tours and provides instruction on aerial photography.

➤ TOUR OPERATORS: **M/S *Mount Washington*** (☎ 603/366–5531 or 888/843–6686, WEB www.msmountwashington.com). **Sky Bright** (✉ Laconia Airport, Rte. 11, ☎ 800/639–6012, WEB www.skybright.com). **Squam Lake Tours** (☎ 603/968–7577, WEB www.squamlaketours.com).

VISITOR INFORMATION

➤ TOURIST INFORMATION: **Lakes Region Association** (✉ Rte. 104, just off I–93 Exit 23 [Box 430, New Hampton 03256], ☎ 603/744–8664 or 800/605–2537, WEB www.lakesregion.org). **Squam Lakes Area Chamber of Commerce** (✉ Box 665, Ashland 03217, ☎ 603/968–4494, WEB www.squamlakeschamber.com). **Wolfeboro Chamber of Commerce**

(✉ 32 Central Ave. [Box 547, Wolfeboro 03894], ☎ 603/569–2200 or 800/516–5324, WEB www.wolfeboroonline.com/chamber).

THE WHITE MOUNTAINS

Sailors approaching East Coast harbors frequently mistake the pale peaks of the White Mountains—the highest range in the northeastern United States—for clouds. It was 1642 when explorer Darby Field could no longer contain his curiosity about one mountain in particular. He set off from his Exeter homestead and became the first man to climb what would eventually be called Mt. Washington. The 6,288-ft peak must have presented Field with formidable obstacles—its peak claims the highest wind velocity ever recorded and it can see snow every month of the year.

More than 350 years after Field's climb, curiosity about the mountains has not abated. Today, an auto road and a railway lead to the top of Mt. Washington, and people come here by the tens of thousands to hike and climb, to photograph the vistas, and to ski. The White Mountain National Forest consists of roughly 770,000 acres and includes the Presidential Range, whose peaks—like Mt. Washington—are all named after early presidents. Among the forest's scenic notches (deep mountain passes) are Pinkham, Franconia, and Crawford.

This tour begins in Waterville Valley, off I–93, and continues to North Woodstock. It then follows portions of the White Mountains Trail, a 100-mi loop designated as a National Scenic & Cultural Byway.

Waterville Valley

㉔ *60 mi north of Concord.*

In 1835, visitors began arriving in Waterville Valley, a 10-mi-long cul-de-sac cut by one of New England's several Mad rivers and circled by mountains. It was first a summer resort and then more of a ski area. Although it's now a year-round getaway, Waterville Valley still has a small-town charm. There are inns, condos, restaurants, shops, conference facilities, a grocery store, and a post office.

Dining and Lodging

$–$$ ✕ **Chile Peppers.** Southwest-inspired Chile Peppers caters to skiers with fajitas, tacos, enchiladas, and other Tex-Mex staples. The food here may not be authentic Mexican, but it's well priced and filling. If you're solely into Tex, the lineup includes ribs, steak, seafood, and chicken. ✉ *Town Square,* ☎ 603/236–4646. *AE, DC, MC, V.*

$$$–$$$$ ▣ **Golden Eagle Lodge.** Waterville's premier condominium property—with its steep roof punctuated by dozens of gabled dormers—recalls the grand hotels of an earlier era. Rooms, however, are contemporary with upscale light-wood furniture and well-equipped kitchens; many have views of the surrounding peaks. The full-service complex has a two-story lobby and a capable front-desk staff. Guests have access to the White Mountain Athletic Club. ✉ *6 Snow's Brook Rd. (Box 495, 03215),* ☎ *603/236–4600 or 888/703–2453,* FAX *603/236–4947,* WEB *www.goldeneaglelodge.com. 139 condominiums. Kitchenettes, indoor pool, sauna, recreation room. AE, D, DC, MC, V.*

$$–$$$ ▣ **Black Bear Lodge.** This family-oriented property has one-bedroom suites that sleep up to six and have full kitchens. Each unit is individually owned and decorated. Children's movies are shown at night in season, and there's bus service to the slopes. Guests can use the White Mountain Athletic Club. ✉ *Village Rd. (Box 357, 03215),* ☎ *603/236–4501 or 800/349–2327,* FAX *603/236–4114,* WEB *www.black-bear-*

lodge.com. 107 suites. Kitchens, indoor-outdoor pool, hot tub, sauna, steam room, gym, recreation room. AE, D, DC, MC, V.

$$–$$$ 🖼 **Snowy Owl Inn.** You're treated to afternoon wine and cheese in the atrium lobby, which has a three-story fieldstone fireplace and many prints and watercolors of snowy owls. The fourth-floor bunk-bed lofts are ideal for families; first-floor rooms are suitable for couples seeking a quiet getaway. Four restaurants are within walking distance. Guests have access to the White Mountain Athletic Club. ⊠ *Village Rd. (Box 407, 03215),* ☎ *603/236–8383 or 800/766–9969,* 🆑 *603/236–4890,* 🕸 *www.snowyowlinn.com. 85 rooms. In-room data ports, some in-room hot tubs, some kitchens, some in-room VCRs, 2 pools (1 indoor), gym, meeting rooms. AE, D, DC, MC, V. BP.*

Outdoor Activities and Sports

The **White Mountain Athletic Club** (⊠ Rte. 49, ☎ 603/236–8303) has tennis, racquetball, and squash as well as a 25-meter indoor pool, a jogging track, exercise equipment, whirlpools, saunas, steam rooms, and a games room. The club is free to guests of many area lodgings.

Ski Area

WATERVILLE VALLEY

Former U.S. ski-team star Tom Corcoran designed this family-oriented resort. The lodgings and various amenities are about 1 mi from the slopes, but a shuttle renders a car unnecessary. ⊠ *1 Ski Area Rd. (Rte. 49) (Box 540, 03215),* ☎ *603/236–8311; 603/236–4144 snow conditions; 800/468–2553 lodging;* 🕸 *www.waterville.com.*

Downhill. Mt. Tecumseh has been laid out with great care. This ski area has hosted more World Cup races than any other in the East, so most advanced skiers will be challenged. Most of the 52 trails are intermediate: straight down the fall line, wide, and agreeably long. A 7-acre tree-skiing area adds variety. Snowmaking coverage of 100% ensures good skiing even when nature doesn't cooperate. There's lift-service snow tubing and a snowboard terrain park that includes a timed boardercross course. The lifts serving the 2,020 ft of vertical rise include two high-speed detachable quads, two triple, three double, and four surface lifts.

Cross-country. The Waterville Valley cross-country network, with the ski center in the town square, has 105 km (65 mi) of trails. About two-thirds of them are groomed; the rest are backcountry.

Child care. The nursery takes children 6 months–4 years. SKIwee instruction accepts children ages 3–12. The Kinderpark, a children's slope, has a slow-running lift.

Summer activities. Hiking, mountain biking, tennis, and golf are popular activities. Mountain bikes are available for rent in the town square.

Lincoln/North Woodstock

㉕ *14 mi northwest of Waterville Valley, 63 mi north of Concord.*

Lincoln and North Woodstock, at the western end of the Kancamagus Highway (Route 112) or at Exit 32 off I–93, combine to make one of the state's liveliest resort areas. They appeal more to the social set and families than to couples seeking romantic retreats. Festivals, such as the New Hampshire Scottish Highland Games in mid-September, keep Lincoln swarming with people year-round; North Woodstock maintains more of a village feel.

ℭ   A ride on the **Hobo Railroad** yields scenic views of the Pemigewasset River and the White Mountain National Forest. The narrated excur-

The White Mountains

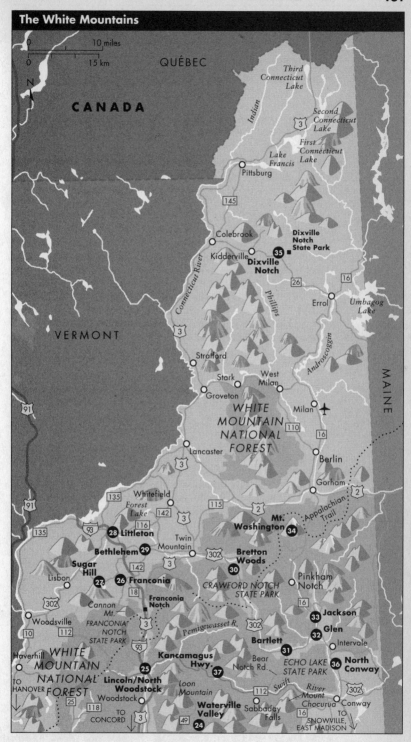

QUÉBEC

CANADA

VERMONT

MAINE

Third Connecticut Lake

Second Connecticut Lake

First Connecticut Lake

Lake Francis

Indian

3

145

Pittsburg

Colebrook

Kidderville **Dixville Notch** **35** ■ **Dixville Notch State Park**

26

16

Errol

Umbagog Lake

Connecticut River

Phillips

Androscoggin

Stratford

Stark

West Milan

Groveton

WHITE MOUNTAIN NATIONAL FOREST

Milan ✈

91

110

16

Lancaster

3

Berlin

91

135

Whitefield

Forest Lake

142

3

115

2

Gorham

2

Mt. Washington **34**

Appalachian Trail

116

93 **28** **Littleton**

Twin Mountain

302

Bethlehem **29**

Sugar Hill

Lisbon

142

3

115

Bretton Woods **30**

CRAWFORD NOTCH STATE PARK

Pinkham Notch

27 **26** **Franconia**

18

Franconia Notch

16

Jackson **33**

Cannon Mt.

FRANCONIA NOTCH STATE PARK

3

Pemigewasset R.

302

Glen **32**

Woodsville

10

112

93

Bartlett **31**

Intervale

ECHO LAKE STATE PARK

36 **North Conway**

Haverhill

WHITE MOUNTAIN NATIONAL FOREST

TO HANOVER ↓

25

Kancamagus Hwy. **37**

Loon Mountain

Bear Notch Rd.

Swift

River

302

25 **Lincoln/North Woodstock**

Woodstock

118

3

112

Mount Chocorua

Conway

Sabbaday Falls

16

TO SNOWVILLE, EAST MADISON ↓

TO CONCORD ↓

49

Waterville Valley **24**

0 —— 10 miles

0 —— 15 km

N

sions take 80 minutes. ✉ *Kancamagus Hwy. (Rte. 112), Lincoln,* ☎ *603/745–2135,* WEB *www.hoborr.com.* 🎟 *$8.50.* ☼ *June–Labor Day, daily; May and Sept.–Oct., weekends; call for schedule.*

☾ At the **Whale's Tale Water Park,** you can float on an inner tube along a gentle river, careen down one of five water slides, take a trip in a multipassenger tube, or body-surf in the large wave pool. Whale Harbor and Orca Park Play Island contain water activities for small children and toddlers. ✉ *U.S. 3, I–93 Exit 3, North Lincoln,* ☎ *603/745–8810,* WEB *www.whalestalewaterpark.com.* 🎟 *$20.* ☼ *Mid-June–Labor Day, daily 10–6.*

Dining and Lodging

$$–$$$ ✕🏠 **Woodstock Inn.** Run by the Rice family since 1982, this social but laid-back inn has rooms in four buildings. Rooms range from simple to romantic (with canopy beds and free champagne), and many accommodate groups. The restaurants include the elegant Clement Room Grill ($$–$$$), where the Mediterranean seafood sauté is a favorite, and the Woodstock Station ($), where the menu lists everything from meat loaf to fajitas. The Woodstock Inn Brewery ($) serves the same dishes as the Woodstock Station as well as six year-round brews and four seasonal ones. ✉ *U.S. 3 (Box 118, North Woodstock 03262),* ☎ *603/745–3951 or 800/321–3985,* FAX *603/745–3701,* WEB *www.woodstock-innnh.com. 23 rooms, 19 with bath; 1 suite. 2 restaurants, some in-room hot tubs, refrigerators, outdoor hot tub, bar. AE, D, MC, V. BP.*

$$$–$$$$ 🏠 **Mountain Club on Loon.** This first-rate resort has an assortment of accommodations: suites that sleep as many as eight, studios with Murphy beds, and 117 units with kitchens. Many can be combined to form larger units. All rooms are within walking distance of the lifts, and condominiums are on or near the slopes. Entertainers perform in the lounge on most winter weekends. ✉ *Kancamagus Hwy. (Rte. 112), Lincoln 03251,* ☎ *603/745–2244 or 800/229–7829,* FAX *603/745–2317,* WEB *www.mtnclubonloon.com. 234 units. Restaurant, some kitchens, 2 tennis courts, 2 pools (1 indoor), health club, massage, sauna, aerobics, racquetball, squash, bar, lounge, video game room. AE, D, MC, V.*

$$–$$$ 🏠 **Indian Head Resort.** Views across the 180 acres of this motel near the Loon and Cannon Mountain ski areas are of Indian Head Rock Profile and the Franconia Mountains. Cross-country ski trails and a mountain-bike trail from the resort connect to the Franconia Notch trail system. The Profile Room restaurant serves standard American fare. ✉ *U.S. 3 (R.R. 1, Box 99, North Lincoln 03251),* ☎ *603/745–8000 or 800/343–8000,* FAX *603/745–8414,* WEB *www.indianheadresort.com. 100 rooms, 40 cottages. Restaurant, refrigerators, tennis court, 2 pools (1 indoor), lake, outdoor hot tub, sauna, fishing, bicycles, cross-country skiing, ice-skating, bar, recreation room. AE, D, DC, MC, V.*

Nightlife and the Arts

Skiers head to the **Granite Bar** (✉ Kancamagus Hwy./Rte. 112, ☎ 603/745–5267) in the Mountain Club at the Loon Mountain resort. The **Olde Timbermill Pub** (✉ Mill at Loon Mountain, Kancamagus Hwy./Rte. 112, ☎ 603/745–3603) has live dance music on weekends. The draws at the **Thunderbird Lounge** (✉ Indian Head Resort, U.S. 3, North Lincoln, ☎ 603/745–8000) are nightly entertainment year-round and a large dance floor.

The **North Country Center for the Arts** (✉ Papermill Theatre, Kancamagus Hwy./Rte. 112, Lincoln, ☎ 603/745–6032; 603/745–2141 box office) presents theater for children and adults and art exhibitions from July to September.

Outdoor Activities and Sports

 At **Lost River in Kinsman Notch** (⊠ Kancamagus Hwy./Rte. 112, 6 mi west of North Woodstock, ☎ 603/745–8720 or 800/346–3687, WEB www.findlostriver.com) you can hike along the sheer granite river gorge and view such geological wonders as the Guillotine Rock and the Lemon Squeezer or pan for gemstones. A cafeteria, garden, and gift shop round out the amenities. It's open daily from mid-May to mid-October; admission is $8.50. **Pemi Valley Excursions** (⊠ Main St., I–93 Exit 32, Lincoln, ☎ 603/745–2744, WEB www.i93.com/pvsr) offers moose and wildlife bus tours June–October and guided snowmobile tours through the White Mountains in winter.

Shopping

The **Curious Cow** (⊠ Main St., North Woodstock, ☎ 603/745–9230) is a multidealer shop selling country crafts. **Millfront Marketplace, Mill at Loon Mountain** (⊠ Kancamagus Hwy./Rte. 112, Lincoln, ☎ 603/745–6261), a former paper factory, contains restaurants, boutiques, a bookstore, and a post office. **Sunburst Fashions** (⊠ 108 Main St., North Woodstock, ☎ 603/745–8745) stocks handcrafted gemstone jewelry and imported gifts.

Ski Area

LOON MOUNTAIN

A modern resort on the Kancamagus Highway (Route 112) and the Pemigewasset River, Loon Mountain opened in the 1960s and was greatly developed in the 1980s. In the base lodge and around the mountain are many food-service and lounge facilities. There's day and nighttime lift-service snow tubing on the lower slopes. Loon's Equestrian Center runs riverside horseback-riding trips. ⊠ *Kancamagus Hwy. (Rte. 112),* ☎ *603/745–8111; 603/745–8100 snow conditions; 800/227–4191 lodging;* WEB *www.loonmtn.com.*

Downhill. Wide, straight, and consistent intermediate trails prevail at Loon. Beginner trails and slopes are set apart. Most advanced runs are grouped on the North Peak section farther from the main mountain. Snowboarders have a halfpipe and their own park; an alpine garden with bumps and jumps provides thrills for skiers. The vertical is 2,100 ft; a four-passenger gondola, one high-speed detachable quad, two triple and three double chairlifts, and one surface lift serve the 44 trails and slopes.

Cross-country. The touring center at Loon Mountain has 35 km (22 mi) of cross-country trails.

Child care. The day-care center takes children from 6 weeks–8 years. The ski school runs several programs for children of different age groups. Children 5 and under ski free.

Summer activities. In summer and fall you can ride New Hampshire's longest gondola to the summit for panoramic mountain views. Among the daily activities at the summit are lumberjack shows, storytelling by a mountain man, and nature tours. You can also take self-guided walks to glacial caves or go horseback riding, mountain biking, and in-line skating and skateboarding in a state park.

Franconia

26 *16 mi northwest of Lincoln/North Woodstock.*

Travelers have long passed through the White Mountains via Franconia Notch, and in the late 18th century a town evolved just to the north. It and the region's jagged rock formations and heavy coat of evergreens have stirred the imaginations of Washington Irving, Henry Wadsworth

Longfellow, and Nathaniel Hawthorne, who penned a short story about the Old Man of the Mountain. The town remains enchanting, if sleepy, touched though it is by I–93 (a.k.a. the Franconia Notch Parkway) and modern ski resorts.

At **Frost Place,** Robert Frost's home from 1915 to 1920, the poet wrote one of his most-remembered works, "Stopping by Woods on a Snowy Evening." Two rooms host occasional readings and contain memorabilia and signed editions of his books. Outside, you can follow short trails marked with lines from Frost's poetry. ⊠ *Ridge Rd., off Rte. 116,* ☏ *603/823–5510.* ⌨ *$3.* ☉ *Memorial Day–June, weekends 1–5; July–Columbus Day, Wed.–Mon. 1–5.*

The **Old Man of the Mountain,** a rock-formation profile high above the notch, defines New Hampshire; you can't easily—and shouldn't—miss glimpsing this granite icon. Nathaniel Hawthorne wrote about it, New Hampshire resident Daniel Webster bragged about it, and P. T. Barnum tried to buy it. Stop at the posted turnouts from I–93 north- or southbound or along the shore of Profile Lake for the best views. There's also a small, free Old Man of the Mountain Museum administered by Franconia Notch State Park at the southbound viewing area (by the Cannon Mountain tram parking area); it's open daily 9–5.

The **Flume** is an 800-ft-long chasm with narrow walls that give the gorge's running water an eerie echo. The route through it has been built up with a series of boardwalks and stairways. The visitor center has exhibits on the region's history. ⊠ *Franconia Notch Pkwy., Exit 2,* ☏ *603/745–8391,* WEB *www.nhparks.state.nh.us/parkops/parks/franconia.html.* ⌨ *$8.* ☉ *Early May–late Oct., daily 9–5.*

Dining and Lodging

$$$ ✕⊡ **Franconia Inn.** At this 107-acre, family-friendly resort, you can play tennis, swim in the pool, hike, and even try soaring. The cross-country ski barn doubles as a horseback-riding center in the warmer months. Rooms have designer chintzes, canopy beds, and country furnishings; some have fireplaces. The restaurant ($$–$$$$) prepares standard American fare with upscale twists. Try the grilled black Angus beef with sweet onion confit, Yukon gold mashed potatoes, and bourbon-peppercorn demiglace. Meal plans are available. ⊠ *1300 Easton Rd., 03580,* ☏ *603/823–5542 or 800/473–5299,* WEB *www.franconiainn.com. 29 rooms, 3 suites. Restaurant, some in-room hot tubs, some kitchenettes, 4 tennis courts, pool, hot tub, bicycles, badminton, croquet, hiking, horseback riding, cross-country skiing, ice-skating, sleigh rides, bar. AE, MC, V. Closed Apr.–mid-May.*

$$ ⊡ **Horse and Hound Inn.** Off the beaten path yet convenient to the Cannon Mountain tram, this inn is on 8 acres surrounded by the White Mountain National Forest. Antiques and assorted collectibles add cheer, and the grounds are laced with 65 km (39 mi) of cross-country ski trails. ⊠ *205 Wells Rd., 03580,* ☏ *603/823–5501 or 800/450–5501,* FAX *603/823–5501. 10 rooms, 8 with bath. Restaurant, cross-country skiing, bar, some pets allowed (fee); no room phones, no room TVs. AE, D, DC, MC, V. Closed Apr.–mid-May and mid-Oct.–Thanksgiving. BP, MAP.*

$ △ **Lafayette Campground.** This campground has hiking and biking trails, 97 tent sites, showers, a camp store, a bike trail, and easy access to the Appalachian Trail. ⊠ *U.S. 3 and I–93, Franconia Notch State Park, 03580,* ☏ *603/271–3628, 603/823–9513, or 877/647–2757 for reservations. MC, V.*

Nightlife

Hillwinds (⊠ Main St., ☏ 603/823–5551), a restaurant and bar, has live entertainment on weekends.

Shopping

Stores in the **Franconia Marketplace** (⊠ Main St., ☎ 603/823–5368) include the Grateful Bread Quality Bakery and Magoons Natural Foods.

Ski Areas

CANNON MOUNTAIN

The staff at this state-run facility in Franconia Notch State Park is attentive to skier services, family programs, snowmaking, and grooming. All this makes Cannon—one of the nation's first ski areas—a very sound value. **The New England Ski Museum** (☎ 603/823–7177, WEB www.skimuseum.org) sits at the base of the tramway and traces the history of the sport with displays of early gear as well as photos, books, and videos. Admission is free, and the museum is open daily noon–5 from late December through March and late May through mid-October. ⊠ *Franconia Notch State Park, I–93 Exit 3, 03580,* ☎ *603/ 823–8800; 603/823–7771 snow conditions; 800/237–9007 lodging;* WEB *www.cannonmt.com.*

Downhill. Cannon's 42 trails present challenges—among them narrow, steep pitches off the peak of a 2,146 ft of vertical rise—rarely found in New Hampshire, particularly after a fresh fall of snow. The nicely contoured cruising trails are great for intermediates; beginners can head to the Brookside learning slope. There are also two glade-skiing trails—Turnpike and Banshee—and a lift-service tubing park. A 70-passenger tramway, two quads, three triples, and one surface lift all move you upward.

Cross-country. Nordic skiing is on a 13-km (8-mi) multiuse recreational path.

Child care. Cannon's Peabody Base Lodge takes children 1 and up. All-day and half-day SKIwee programs cater to kids 4–12, and season-long instruction can be arranged.

Summer activities. A multiuse recreational path runs parallel to the Franconia Notch Parkway (I–93). For $10 round-trip, the Cannon Mountain Aerial Tramway can transport you up 2,022 ft. It's an eight-minute ride to the top, where marked trails lead to an observation platform. The tram runs daily from mid-May through late October.

FRANCONIA VILLAGE CROSS-COUNTRY SKI CENTER

The ski center at the Franconia Inn has 65 km (39 mi) of groomed trails and 40 km (24 mi) of backcountry trails. One popular route leads to Bridal Veil Falls, a great spot for a picnic lunch. There are horse-drawn sleigh rides as well as ice-skating on a lighted rink. ⊠ *1300 Easton Rd., 03580,* ☎ *603/823–5542 or 800/473–5299,* FAX *603/823–8078.*

Sugar Hill

㉗ *6 mi west of Franconia.*

Sugar Hill, a village of 500 people, is deservedly famous for its spectacular sunsets and views of the Franconia Mountains, best seen from Sunset Hill, where a row of grand hotels and summer "cottages" once stood. Quiet country charm and good-quality B&Bs make Sugar Hill a romantic place.

Sugar Hill may be small, but the well-done **Sugar Hill Historical Museum** proves the town has a big history. Permanent and changing exhibits cover everything from settlement to the resort era to the present day. ⊠ Rte. 117, ☎ 603/823–5336. ☜ *$2.* ☉ *July–mid-Oct., Thurs. and weekends 1–4.*

Dining and Lodging

$ ✕ **Polly's Pancake Parlor.** Originally a carriage shed built in 1830, this local institution was converted to a tearoom during the Depression, when the Dexters began serving all-you-can-eat pancakes, waffles, and French toast for 50¢. The prices have gone up some, but the descendants of the Dexters continue to serve pancakes and waffles made from grains ground on the property, their own country sausage, and pure maple syrup. ⊠ *Rte. 117,* ☎ *603/823–5575. D, MC, V. No dinner.*

$$–$$$$ ✕🏨 **Sunset Hill House.** Since opening in 1882, this inn has been fa-
★   mous as one of the best places in New England to watch the sun go down. It's along a 1,700-ft ridge with views not just west toward the sun but also east out toward the Presidential Range. Many of the meticulously kept rooms have antiques dating from the inn's early years; gas fireplaces and decks grace the upper units. The restaurant ($$–$$$$) is highly acclaimed; try the pan-seared ostrich with a raspberry beurre blanc and then move on to roasted game hen with a lemon-spinach cream. A tavern ($–$$) serves lighter fare. ⊠ *Sunset Hill Rd., 03585,* ☎ *603/823–5522 or 800/786–4455,* WEB *www.sunsethillhouse.com. 28 rooms. 2 restaurants, some in-room hot tubs, pool, mountain bikes, hiking, cross-country skiing, ice-skating, bar; no room TVs. AE, D, MC, V. BP, MAP.*

$$–$$$$ ✕🏨 **Sugar Hill Inn.** The lawn's old carriage and the wraparound porch's wicker chairs put you in a nostalgic mood before you even enter this converted 1789 farmhouse. Antiques-filled guest quarters are in the main house or one of three cottages. Many rooms and suites have hand-stenciled walls and views of the Franconia Mountains; some have fireplaces. Bette Davis visited friends in this house—the room with the best vistas is named after her. The restaurant ($$$; reservations essential) serves such haute American fare as roasted duckling with a cranberry-orange glaze; the homemade desserts are always delicious. ⊠ *Rte. 117 (Box 954, 03585),* ☎ *603/823–5621 or 800/548–4748,* WEB *www.sugarhillinn.com. 13 rooms, 5 suites. Restaurant, some in-room hot tubs, cross-country skiing, sleigh rides, pub; no room phones, no room TVs, no smoking. AE, MC, V. BP, MAP required during fall foliage season.*

$$–$$$ 🏨 **Foxglove.** Extensive gardens with hammocks are among the sybaritic delights at this rambling turn-of-the-20th-century home next to Lovers Lane. Common areas have a country French style and are furnished with antiques. Each guest room has a different motif. The Serengeti Room, for example, has animal-print linens, a chandelier with carnival glass shades, and black and brass bath fixtures. ⊠ *Rte. 117, 03585,* ☎ *603/823–8840 or 888/343–2220,* FAX *603/823–5755,* WEB *www. foxgloveinn.com. 6 rooms. No room phones, no room TVs, no kids under 10, no smoking. BP.*

$$–$$$ 🏨 **Hilltop.** Staying here is just like dropping by Grandma's. Rooms in the 1895 farmhouse have a quirky mix of antiques as well as handmade quilts and piles of pillows. Watch one of the hundreds of videos in the TV room or take in the sunset from one of the rockers on the porch. Roughly 20 acres of backcountry terrain is perfect for cross-country skiing. The large country breakfast includes homemade jams, pancakes made with homegrown berries, soufflés, and smoked meats. ⊠ *Rte. 117, 03585,* ☎ *603/823–5695 or 800/770–5695,* FAX *603/ 823–5518,* WEB *www.hilltopinn.com. 3 rooms, 3 suites. Cross-country skiing, bar, library, some pets allowed; no room phones, no room TVs, no kids under 4, no-smoking rooms. D, MC, V. BP.*

Littleton

❷⑧   *9 mi northeast of Sugar Hill, 7 mi north of Franconia, 86 mi north of Concord.*

One of northern New Hampshire's largest towns is on a granite shelf along the Ammonoosuc River, whose swift current and drop of 235 ft enabled the community to flourish as a mill center in its early days. Later, the railroad came through, and Littleton grew into the region's commerce hub. In the minds of many, it's more a place to stock up on supplies than a bona fide destination, but few communities have worked harder at revitalization. Today, intriguing shops and eateries line the main street, whose tidy 19th- and early 20th-century buildings suggest a set in a Jimmy Stewart movie.

Just off Main Street, stop by the **Littleton Grist Mill** (⊠ 22 Mill St., ☎ 603/444–7478), a restored 1798 mill that contains a shop selling New England–made pottery, kitchenware, home accessories, and stone-ground flour products. You'll also find original mill equipment on display.

NEED A
BREAK?

Beside the Littleton Grist Mill, the **Miller's Fare** (⊠ 16 Mill St., ☎ 603/444–2146) serves coffees, microbrews and wines, baked goods, sandwiches, and salads. In warm weather dine on a deck overlooking the Ammonoosuc River.

OFF THE
BEATEN PATH

WHITEFIELD – Like Dixville Notch and Bretton Woods, Whitefield became a prominent summer resort in the late 19th century, when wealthy industrialists flocked here to golf, ski, play polo, and hobnob. This rolling valley village tucked between two precipitous promontories may yet reclaim its vaunted past. The rambling, yellow-clapboard Mountain View Hotel has been fully refurbished. At this writing, the owners planned to open it as a hotel (with a 9-hole golf course, tennis courts, pools, and restaurants) in a year or two. Regardless, it's worth driving through the courtly Colonial Whitefield, 11 mi northeast of Littleton, and up Route 116 just beyond town to see this magnificent structure atop a bluff overlooking the Presidentials.

LANCASTER – About 8 mi north of Whitefield via U.S. 3, the affable seat of Coos County sits at the confluence of the Connecticut and Israel rivers, surrounded by low serrated peaks. Before becoming prosperous through commerce, Lancaster was an agricultural stronghold; at one time the only acceptable currency was the bushel of wheat. It's still an intimate mountain town. Like Littleton, though, it has restored much of its main street, which now has a dapper mix of Victorian homes, funky artisan and antiques shops, and prim churches and civic buildings. If you're peckish, pop inside the **Common Ground Cafe** (⊠ 55 Main St., ☎ 603/788–4379), a tiny bakery–espresso bar that serves sandwiches and snacks; it's inside a fine country clothier and shoe store called Simon the Tanner.

Dining and Lodging

$$–$$$

✕🏠 **Beal House Inn.** Pencil-post beds, marble nightstands, and fluffy upholstered chairs set a low-key, refined tone at this white 1833 Federal-style house. You can rent the two-bedroom suite—with a claw-foot tub, TV/VCR, kitchenette, and fireplace—by the night or the week. The cozy Flying Moose restaurant ($$–$$$) has an eclectic menu. From a classic escargots appetizer, you might move on to wood-grilled chicken in a spinach curry. Chef-owners José Luis and Catherine Pawelek prepare everything from scratch, including breakfast's specialty banana buttermilk pancakes. ⊠ 2 W. Main St., 03561, ☎ 603/444–2661 or 888/616–2325, FAX 603/444–6224, WEB www.bealhouseinn.com. 3 rooms, 5 suites. Restaurant, some kitchenettes, some in-room VCRs. MC, V. BP.

$ 🏨 **Thayer's Inn.** Although stately, this 1843 Greek Revival hotel, isn't
★ luxurious. The clean, well-kept rooms (some share a bath) are quaintly
old-fashioned, with creaky floorboards, exposed pipes, vintage steam
radiators, high ceilings, and comfy wing chairs. The friendly staff welcomes passersby for a look at a small third-floor room set up as it would
have appeared in the 1840s or for a visit to the sixth-floor cupola, with
its 360-degree views. There's no elevator—good to know if you planned
to book an upper-floor room. ⊠ *111 Main St., 03561,* ☎ *603/444–
6469 or 800/634–8179,* WEB *www.thayersinn.com. 31 rooms, 7 suites.
Some refrigerators, some in-room VCRs. MC, V.*

Shopping

Potato Barn Antiques Center (⊠ U.S. 3, Northumberland, 6 mi north
of Lancaster, ☎ 603/636–2611) has several dealers under one roof—
specialties include vintage farm tools, clothing, and costume jewelry.
In a restored mill on the Ammonoosuc River, the **Tannery Marketplace**
(⊠ 111 Saranac St., ☎ 603/444–1200) contains an amazing array of
architectural relics, antiques, collectibles, and estate leftovers. The **Village Book Store** (⊠ 81 Main St., ☎ 603/444–5263) has comprehensive selections of both nonfiction and fiction titles.

Bethlehem

㉙ *5 mi southeast of Littleton.*

In the days before antihistamines, hay-fever sufferers came by the bus
load to Bethlehem, elevation 1,462 ft, whose crisp air has a blissfully
low pollen count. Today this hamlet is notable for its distinctive arts
and crafts, Victorian and Colonial homes, art deco movie theater, and
shops and eateries on its main street.

Dining and Lodging

$$–$$$ ✕ **Tim-bir Alley.** For eight months of the year, this restaurant serves din-
ner in the Adair B&B's elegant dining rooms. The menu, which changes
weekly, utilizes regional American ingredients in creative ways. Main
dishes have included pork tenderloin with maple-balsamic glaze and
apple-almond relish as well as sunflower-encrusted salmon with a
smoked-tomato puree. Save room for such desserts as chocolate-glazed
espresso cheesecake. The hours here change seasonally (and they're sometimes sporadic within a given season); it's best to call ahead. ⊠ *80 Guider
La.,* ☎ *603/444–6142. No credit cards. No lunch.*

$$$–$$$$ 🏨 **Adair.** In 1927 attorney Frank Hogan built this three-story Geor-
★ gian Revival home as a wedding present for his daughter, Dorothy Adair.
Today it's a luxurious country inn, with walking paths that wind
through gardens on 200 acres. Rooms, which have garden or moun-
tain views, are furnished with period antiques and reproductions;
many have fireplaces. One suite has a large two-person hot tub, a fire-
place, a balcony, and a king-size sleigh bed. ⊠ *80 Guider La., 03574,*
☎ *603/444–2600 or 888/444–2600,* WEB *www.adairinn.com. 7 rooms,
2 suites, 1 cottage. Restaurant, some in-room hot tubs, tennis court,
billiards; no room phones, no room TVs, no kids under 12, no smok-
ing. AE, D, MC, V. BP.*

Outdoor Activities and Sports

The Society for the Protection of New Hampshire Forests owns two
properties in Bethlehem open to visitors. **Bretzfelder Park** (⊠ Prospect
St., ☎ 603/444–6228), a 77-acre nature and wildlife park, has a pic-
nic shelter, hiking, and cross-country ski trails. The **Rocks Christmas
Tree Farm** (⊠ 113 Glessner Rd., ☎ 603/444–6228) is a working
Christmas-tree farm with walking trails, historical buildings, and ed-
ucational programs.

Bretton Woods

③ *14 mi southeast of Bethlehem, 28 mi northeast of Lincoln/Woodstock.*

In the early 1900s private rail cars brought the elite from New York and Philadelphia to the Mount Washington Hotel, the jewel of Bretton Woods. The hotel was the site of a famous World Monetary Fund conference in 1944, which greatly affected the post–World War II economy. The area is also known for its cog railway and eponymous ski resort.

★ ☙ In 1858 Sylvester Marsh petitioned the state legislature for permission to build a steam railway up Mt. Washington. A politico retorted that he'd have better luck building a railroad to the moon. Just 11 years later, the **Mt. Washington Cog Railway** chugged up to the summit, and so it remains one of the state's most beloved attractions—a thrill in either direction. Allow three hours round-trip; call for schedule information. ⊠ *U.S. 302, 6 mi northeast of Bretton Woods,* ☎ *603/278–5404; 800/922–8825 outside New Hampshire;* WEB *www.thecog.com.* 🎫 *$49.* ☉ *Late Apr.–late May, weekends; late May–early Nov., daily.*

En Route Scenic U.S. 302 winds through the steep, wooded mountains on either side of spectacular Crawford Notch, southeast of Bretton Woods, and passes through **Crawford Notch State Park** (⊠ U.S. 302, Harts Location, ☎ 603/374–2272), where you can picnic and take a short hike to Arethusa Falls or the Silver and Flume cascades. The visitor center has a gift shop and a cafeteria; there's also a campground.

Dining and Lodging

$$–$$$$ ✕🏨 **Bretton Woods Mountain Resort.** Of Bretton Woods's three ho-
★ tels, the most famous is the leviathan 1902 Mount Washington, a grand resort with a 900-ft-long veranda and full views of the Presidentials. With stately public rooms and large, Victorian-style guest quarters, the hotel retains an early 20th-century formality. A jacket and tie are required in the dining room ($$$$), which serves such seasonal dishes as lemon lobster ravioli with shrimp and scallops or roast pork with onions and mushrooms. The mid-priced rooms at the 1896 Bretton Arms Country Inn are less formal. On arrival, make reservations for its contemporary dining room ($$–$$$). Rooms at the more modern Bretton Woods Motor Inn have balconies or patios. The Continental cuisine at its Darby's Restaurant ($$) is served around a fireplace; the bar is a skier hangout. For long stays, look into the 55 town homes. ⊠ *U.S. 302, 03575,* ☎ *603/278–1000 or 800/258–0330,* FAX *603/278–8838,* WEB *www.mtwashington.com. 339 units. 8 restaurants, some in-room hot tubs, some kitchens, driving range, 27-hole golf course, 12 tennis courts, 2 pools (1 indoor), health club, hot tub, massage, sauna, fishing, bicycles, hiking, horseback riding, cross-country skiing, downhill skiing, sleigh rides, 5 bars, recreation room, baby-sitting, children's programs (ages 5–12), meeting rooms. AE, D, MC, V. MAP*

$ ⛺ **Dry River Campground.** This rustic campground in Crawford Notch State Park has 30 tent sites and is a popular base for hiking the White Mountain National Forest. ⊠ *U.S. 302, Harts Location (Box 177, Twin Mountain 03595),* ☎ *603/271–3628,* WEB *www.nhparks.state.nh.us/parkops/parks/crawford.html. Closed mid-Dec.–mid-May.*

Ski Area

BRETTON WOODS

This expansive, well-run ski area has a tri-level base lodge, convenient parking and drop-off areas, and an uncrowded setting. The views of Mt. Washington alone are worth the visit; the scenery is especially beautiful from the Top o' Quad restaurant and from the former Cog Railway car atop West Mountain. ⊠ *U.S. 302, 03575,* ☎ *603/278–3320;*

603/278–3333 weather conditions; 800/232–2972 information; 800/ 258–0330 lodging; WEB *www.brettonwoods.com.*

Downhill. Although its 76 trails will appeal mostly to novice and intermediate skiers, steeper pitches near the top of the 1,500-ft vertical and glade skiing will satisfy experts. Skiers and snowboarders can try a terrain park with jumps and a halfpipe. The Accelerator halfpipe is for snowboarders only. One high-speed detachable quad, one fixed-grip quad, one triple, and three double chairlifts service the trails. The area has night skiing and snowboarding on Friday, Saturday, and holidays. A limited lift-ticket policy helps keep lines short.

Cross-country. The large, full-service cross-country ski center has 100 km (62 mi) of groomed and double-track trails, many of them lift-serviced. You can also rent snowshoes.

Child care. The nursery takes children ages 2 months–5 years. The ski school has an all-day program for children ages 4 to 12. There's also a snowboarding program for children 8–12. Rates include lifts, lessons, equipment, lunch, and supervised play.

Bartlett

③   *18 mi southeast of Bretton Woods.*

With Bear Mountain to its south, Mt. Parker to its north, Mt. Cardigan to its west, and the Saco River to its east, Bartlett, incorporated in 1790, has an unforgettable setting. Lovely Bear Notch Road (closed in winter) has the only midpoint access to the Kancamagus Highway (Route 112).

Lodging

$$–$$$$ 🏨 **Grand Summit Hotel & Conference Center.** The gables and curves of this resort mimic the slopes of nearby Attitash Bear Peak. Luxurious contemporary-style rooms have kitchenettes, VCRs, and stereos. The main dining room serves passable American fare; dishes at Crawford's Pub and Grill are lighter. ⊠ *U.S. 302 (Box 429, 03812),* ☎ *603/ 374–1900 or 888/554–1900,* FAX *603/374–3040,* WEB *www.attitash.com. 143 rooms. 2 restaurants, room service, in-room data ports, some kitchens, in-room VCRs, pool, health club, hot tub, massage, steam room, downhill skiing, bar, recreation room, laundry facilities. AE, D, MC, V.*

$$–$$$ 🏨 **Attitash Mountain Village.** The style at this condo-motel complex is alpine contemporary, and the staff is young and enthusiastic. Units, some with fireplaces, accommodate from 2 to 14 people. The restaurant, with a varied and family-friendly menu, has unobstructed mountain views. ⊠ *U.S. 302, 03812,* ☎ *603/374–6501 or 800/862–1600,* FAX *603/374–6509,* WEB *www.attitashmtvillage.com. 300 units. Restaurant, some in-room hot tubs, some kitchens, 2 tennis courts, 2 pools (1 indoor), sauna, fishing, mountain bikes, hiking, gym, cross-country skiing, downhill skiing, ice-skating, pub, recreation room, playground, laundry service, meeting rooms. AE, D, MC, V.*

Ski Area

ATTITASH BEAR PEAK

This high-profile resort, which hosts many special events, continues to expand and improve its infrastructure. Lodging at the base of the mountain is in condos and motel-style units. Attitash has a computerized lift-ticket system that allows skiers to pay as they run. Skiers can share the ticket, which is good for two years. ⊠ *U.S. 302 (Box 302, 03812),* ☎ *603/374–2368; 800/223–7669 snow conditions; 800/223– 7669 lodging;* WEB *www.attitash.com.*

Downhill. Enhanced with massive snowmaking (98%), the trails number 70 on two peaks, both with full-service base lodges. The bulk of the skiing and boarding is geared to intermediates and experts, with some steep pitches and glades. Beginners enjoy good terrain on the lower mountain and some runs from the top. At 500 ft, the Ground Zero halfpipe is New England's longest. The Attitash Adventure Center has a rental shop, lessons desk, and children's programs. Serving the 36 km (22 mi) of trails and the 1,750-ft vertical drop are two high-speed quads, one fixed-grip quad, three triple and three double chairlifts, and three surface tows.

Cross-country. The **Bear Notch Ski Touring Center** (☎ 603/374–2277) has more than 70 km (43 mi) of cross-country trails, more than 60 km (37 mi) of which are skate groomed and tracked. Backcountry skiing is unlimited, and there are 35 acres of tree skiing. Guests staying at the Grand Summit Hotel can rent equipment, get trail passes, and connect to the trails from the hotel door.

Child care. The Attitash Adventure Center nursery takes children ages 6 months to 5 years. Other programs accommodate children up to 16.

Summer activities. Attitash Bear Park has two dry alpine slides, four water slides, Buddy Bear's Playpool for children, horseback riding, lift-serviced mountain biking, and a driving range. A chairlift whisks passengers to the White Mountain Observation Tower, which delivers 270-degree views of the Whites.

Glen

③② *6 mi northeast of Bartlett; 89 mi northeast of Concord; 71 mi northwest of Portland, Maine.*

Glen is hardly more than a crossroads between North Conway and Jackson, but its central location has made it the home of a few noteworthy attractions and dining and lodging options.

That cluster of fluorescent buildings on Route 16 is **Story Land,** a theme park with life-size storybook and nursery-rhyme characters. The 16 rides and four shows include a flume ride, a Victorian-theme river-raft ride, and a farm-family variety show. In early spring and late fall, when only parts of the park are open, admission is reduced to $14. ⊠ *Rte. 16,* ☎ *603/383–4186,* ⓦⒺⒷ *www.storylandnh.com.* 🎫 *$19.* ⊙ *Mid-June–Labor Day, daily 9–6; Memorial Day–mid-June and Labor Day–Columbus Day, weekends 10–5.*

Heritage New Hampshire uses theatrical sets, sound effects, and animation to render the state's history. You can "sail" on the *Reliance* from a village in 1634 England to the New World and then saunter along Portsmouth's streets in the late 1700s. Exhibits continue through the present day. ⊠ *Rte. 16,* ☎ *603/383–4186,* ⓦⒺⒷ *www.heritagenh.com.* 🎫 *$10.* ⊙ *Memorial Day–mid-June, weekends 9–5; mid-June–mid-Oct., daily 9–5.*

Dining and Lodging

$–$$$ ✕ **Red Parka Pub.** Practically an institution, the Red Parka Pub has been in downtown Glen for more than two decades. The menu has everything a family could want, from an all-you-can-eat salad bar to scallop pie. The barbecued ribs are favorites, and you'll find hand-carved steaks of every type, from aged New York sirloin to prime rib. ⊠ *U.S. 302,* ☎ *603/383–4344. Reservations not accepted. AE, D, MC, V.*

$–$$ ✕ **Margarita Grill.** Après-ski and hiking types congregate here—in the dining room in cold weather and on the covered patio when it's warm—for homemade salsas, wood-fired steaks, ribs, burgers, and a smattering of Tex-Mex and Cajun specialties. Unwind at the tequila bar after a day on the mountains. ⊠ *U.S. 302,* ☎ *603/383–6556. AE, D, MC, V.*

$$–$$$ ✕▥ **Bernerhof Inn.** With its hardwood floors, hooked rugs, and mix of antique and reproduction furniture, this hotel seems right at home in an alpine setting. The fanciest six rooms have brass beds and spa-size tubs; one suite has a Finnish sauna. The menu at the Rare Bear Bistro ($–$$$) includes Swiss specialties such as fondue and Wiener schnitzel as well as new American dishes—seared scallops with sage butter and butternut-squash sauce is a favorite. The Black Bear pub ($–$$) pours microbrews and serves sandwiches, pastas, bratwurst, and fish-and-chips. ⊠ *U.S. 302 (Box 240, 03838),* ☎ *603/383–9132 or 800/548–8007,* FAX *603/383–0809,* WEB *www.bernerhofinn.com. 7 rooms, 2 suites. Restaurant, some in-room hot tubs, pub; no smoking. AE, D, MC, V. BP.*

$$–$$$ ▥ **Storybook Resort Inn.** On a hillside near Attitash Bear Peak, this motor inn with large rooms is well suited to families. Copperfield's Restaurant serves gingerbread, sticky buns, omelets, and a children's menu. ⊠ *Intersection of U.S 302 and Rte. 16 (Box 129, Glen Junction 03838),* ☎ *603/383–6800,* FAX *603/383–4678,* WEB *www.storybookresort.com. 78 rooms. Restaurant, picnic area, refrigerators, tennis court, 2 pools (1 indoor), wading pool, gym, sauna, Ping-Pong, bar, recreation room, playground, laundry facilities. AE, DC, MC, V.*

Jackson

★ ㉝ *5 mi north of Glen.*

Just off Route 16 via a red covered bridge, Jackson has retained its storybook New England character. Art and antiques shopping, tennis, golf, fishing, and hiking to waterfalls are among the draws. When the snow falls, Jackson becomes the state's cross-country skiing capital. Four downhill ski areas are nearby.

Dining and Lodging

$–$$$ ✕ **Red Fox Pub & Restaurant.** Some say this restaurant overlooking the Wentworth Golf Club gets its name from a wily fox with a penchant for stealing golf balls off the fairway. The wide-ranging menu has barbecue ribs and blue-cheese-and-bacon burgers as well as more substantial dishes such as seared sea scallops with an Asiago cream sauce. The Sunday jazz breakfast buffet draws raves. ⊠ *Rte. 16A,* ☎ *603/ 383–6659. AE, D, MC, V.*

$$$$ ✕▥ **Inn at Thorn Hill.** Architect Stanford White designed this 1895 Vic-
★ torian house, which is just steps from cross-country trails and Jackson village. The main inn's romantic touches include rose-motif wallpaper and such antiques as a blue-velvet fainting couch; many rooms have gas fireplaces. Carriage-house quarters are woodsy, and the cottages are secluded. The restaurant ($$$–$$$$; reservations essential) serves fine contemporary fare: the cider-and-chipotle-glazed shrimp with toasted barley and herbed-sausage risotto is a good bet. ⊠ *Thorn Hill Rd. (Box A, 03846),* ☎ *603/383–4242 or 800/289–8990,* FAX *603/383– 8062,* WEB *www.innatthornhill.com. 12 rooms, 4 suites, 3 cottages. Restaurant, some in-room hot tubs, some in-room VCRs, pool, hot tub, croquet, cross-country skiing, pub; no TV in some rooms, no smoking. AE, MC, V. BP, MAP.*

$$$–$$$$ ✕▥ **Christmas Farm Inn.** Despite its wintery name, this 1778 inn is an all-season retreat. Rooms in the main building and the saltbox next door have Laura Ashley and Ralph Lauren prints. Suites have beamed ceilings and fireplaces. Standbys in the restaurant ($$$–$$$$) are grilled maple-glaze pork loin and tomato-fennel-saffron bouillabaisse. ⊠ *Rte. 16B (Box CC, 03846),* ☎ *603/383–4313 or 800/443–5837,*

FAX 603/383–6495, WEB *www.christmasfarminn.com. 41 units. Restaurant, some in-room hot tubs, pool, health club, hot tub, massage, sauna, volleyball, cross-country skiing, pub, recreation room; no-smoking rooms. AE, MC, V. MAP.*

$$$–$$$$ ✕🖻 **Wentworth.** This pale-yellow 1869 Victorian charms with individually decorated rooms—many with fireplaces—accented with antiques. The dining room ($$–$$$) serves a five-course candlelight dinner with a menu that changes seasonally. Good choices are oven-poached lemon sole in a lobster-vanilla broth, and cider-glazed chicken skewers with thyme-whipped potatoes. ⊠ *Rte. 16A, 03846,* ☎ *603/383–9700 or 800/637–0013,* FAX *603/383–4265,* WEB *www.thewentworth.com. 60 rooms in summer, 52 in winter. Restaurant, some in-room hot tubs, tennis court, pool, billiards, cross-country skiing, ice-skating, sleigh rides, bar. AE, D, DC, MC, V. MAP.*

$$$–$$$$ 🖻 **Ellis River House.** Most of the Victorian-style rooms in this un-
★ abashedly romantic inn on the Ellis River have fireplaces; some have balconies. In winter, a snow bridge across the river connects you with the Ellis River Trail and Jackson's cross-country trail system. ⊠ *Rte. 16 (Box 656, 03846),* ☎ *603/383–9339 or 800/233–8309,* FAX *603/383–4142,* WEB *www.erhinn.com. 15 rooms, 3 suites, 1 cottage. Restaurant, some in-room hot tubs, pool, hot tub, sauna, billiards, cross-country skiing, pub; no kids under 12, no-smoking rooms. AE, D, DC, MC, V. BP.*

$$–$$$$ 🖻 **Inn at Jackson.** The builders of this 1902 Victorian, which overlooks the village, followed a design by Stanford White. Although the foyer's staircase is grand, everything else—from the braided rugs on the hardwood floors to the smattering of antiques—is unpretentious. The airy guest rooms have oversize windows; six have fireplaces. ⊠ *Thorn Hill Rd. (Box 807, 03846),* ☎ *603/383–4321 or 800/289–8600,* FAX *603/383–4085,* WEB *www.innatjackson.com. 14 rooms. Hot tub, cross-country skiing. AE, D, DC, MC, V. CP.*

$$–$$$$ 🖻 **Nordic Village Resort.** The light woods and white walls of these condos are as Scandinavian as the snowy views. Larger units have fireplaces and full kitchens. The 165-acre property is part of Luxury Mountain Getaways, which operates several upscale condos and hotels in the area. ⊠ *Rte. 16, 03846,* ☎ *603/383–9101 or 800/472–5207,* FAX *603/383–9823,* WEB *www.luxurymountaingetaways.com. 140 condominiums. Some in-room hot tubs, some kitchens, tennis court, 3 pools (1 indoor), hot tub, steam room, basketball, hiking, volleyball, cross-country skiing, ice-skating, sleigh rides. D, MC, V.*

$$–$$$ 🖻 **Eagle Mountain House.** With downhill slopes nearby and cross-country trails beginning at this 1879 country estate, skiing is the order of the day. Public areas are rustic but elegant, and the large guest rooms are furnished with late-Victorian pieces. On a warm day, you can nurse a drink in a rocking chair on the wraparound deck. ⊠ *Carter Notch Rd., 03846,* ☎ *603/383–9111 or 800/966–5779,* FAX *603/383–0854,* WEB *www.eaglemt.com. 93 rooms. 2 restaurants, 9-hole golf course, 2 tennis courts, pool, health club, hot tub, sauna, cross-country skiing, video game room, playground. AE, D, DC, MC, V.*

$$ 🖻 **Wildcat Inn & Tavern.** After a day of skiing, you can collapse on a comfy sofa by the fire at this 19th-century inn. The fragrance of home baking permeates into the suite-style guest rooms, which are full of knick-knacks and furniture of various periods. The tavern, where bands often perform, attracts skiers. In summer, dining is available in the garden. ⊠ *Rte. 16A, 03846,* ☎ *603/383–4245 or 800/228–4245,* FAX *603/383–6456,* WEB *www.wildcatinnandtavern.com. 6 rooms, 4 with bath; 7 suites; 1 cottage. 2 restaurants, some kitchenettes, in-room VCRs, bar. AE, MC, V. BP, MAP.*

$–$$ 🏨 **Briarcliff Motel.** This bright and clean motel is a short drive from outlet shopping and ½ mi south of North Conway Village along Route 16. Rooms have mini-refrigerators, coffeemakers, and utilitarian but perfectly pleasant furnishings. ⊠ *Rte. 16/U.S. 302 (Box 504, 03860),* ☎ *603/356–5584 or 800/338–4291,* WEB *www.briarcliffmotel.com. 18 rooms. Refrigerators, pool. AE, D, DC, MC. BP.*

Outdoor Activities and Sports

Nestlenook Farm (⊠ Dinsmore Rd., ☎ 603/383–9443) maintains an outdoor ice-skating rink with rentals, music, and a bonfire. Going snow-shoeing or taking a sleigh ride are other winter options; in summer you can fly-fish or ride in a horse-drawn carriage.

Ski Areas

BLACK MOUNTAIN

Friendly, informal Black Mountain has a warming southern exposure. The Family Passport, which allows two adults and two juniors to ski at discounted rates, is a good value. Midweek rates here are usually the lowest in Mt. Washington valley. ⊠ *Rte. 16B, 03846,* ☎ *603/383–4490; 800/475–4669 snow conditions; 800/698–4490 lodging;* WEB *www.blackmt.com.*

Downhill. The 55 trails and six glades on the 1,100-vertical-ft mountain are evenly divided among beginner, intermediate, and expert. There are triple and double chairlifts and two surface tows. In addition to trails, snowboarders can use two terrain parks and the halfpipe.

Child care. The nursery takes children 6 months–5 years. Kids 3–12 can take classes at the ski school.

JACKSON SKI TOURING FOUNDATION

One of the nation's top four cross-country skiing areas has 154 km (97 mi) of trails. About 96 km (60 mi) are track groomed and 85 km (53 mi) are skate groomed. There are roughly 63 km (39 mi) of marked backcountry trails. You can arrange lessons and rentals at the lodge, in the center of Jackson village. ⊠ *Main St., 03846,* ☎ *603/383–9355,* WEB *www.jacksonxc.org.*

Mt. Washington

★ ③④   *20 mi northwest of Jackson.*

In summer, you can drive to the top of Mt. Washington, the highest peak (6,288 ft) in the northeastern United States and home of a weather station that has recorded the world's highest winds. The Mt. Washington Auto Road, opened in 1861 and said to be the nation's first manufactured tourist attraction, begins at the Glen House, a gift shop and rest stop 15 mi north of Glen on Route 16. Allow two hours round-trip and check your brakes first. Cars with automatic transmissions that can't shift down into first gear aren't allowed on the road.

If you prefer not to drive on a curving, narrow road, take a guided tour in one of the "stages" (vans) that leave from Great Glen Trails Outdoors Center. In winter, they're refitted with snowmobile-like treads and can travel to just above the tree line. You have the option of cross-country skiing or snowshoeing down. (In summer, you can also take the Mt. Washington Cog Railway to the summit; ☞ Bretton Woods.)

Up top, visit the **Sherman Adams Summit Building,** which contains a museum of memorabilia from each of the three hotels that have stood on this spot and a display of native plant life and alpine flowers. Stand in the glassed-in viewing area to hear the wind roar. ☎ *603/466–3988,* WEB *www.mt-washington.com.* 🎫 *Auto road $16 per car and* *driver, plus $6 for each adult passenger; van fare $22.* ☉ *Private cars, mid-May–late Oct.; van tours daily.*

Although not a town per se, scenic **Pinkham Notch** covers Mt. Washington's eastern side and includes several ravines, including Tuckerman Ravine, famous for spring skiing. The Appalachian Mountain Club maintains a large visitor center here on Route 16 that provides information to hikers and travelers and has guided hikes, outdoor skills workshops, a cafeteria, lodging, regional topography displays, and an outdoors shop.

Lodging

$–$$ 🏠 **Joe Dodge Lodge at Pinkham Notch.** The Appalachian Mountain Club operates this rustic lodge at the base of Mt. Washington. Accommodations range from single-sex bunk rooms (rented by the bunk) for as many as five people to private rooms—all have gleaming wood, cheerful quilts, and reading lights. The restaurant serves buffet breakfasts and lunches and family-style dinners. Packages include breakfast and dinner, plus skiing at Great Glen Trails and/or Wildcat Ski Area. ✉ *Rte. 16 (Box 298, Gorham 03581),* ☎ *603/466–2727,* FAX *603/466–3871,* WEB *www.outdoors.org. 102 beds without bath. Restaurant, no room phones, no room TVs, no-smoking rooms. MC, V. MAP.*

Ski Areas

GREAT GLEN TRAILS OUTDOOR CENTER

A fire destroyed the center's large, sunny base lodge in spring 2001, but at this writing plans were under way to build an impressive 16,000-square-ft replacement. Cross-country skiers will use the center in winter, and hikers, mountain bikers, and backpackers will be able to take advantage of it in summer. Amenities will include a huge ski-gear and sports shop, food court, climbing wall, observation deck, and fieldstone fireplace. ✉ *Rte. 16 (Box 300, Gorham 03581),* ☎ *603/466–2333,* WEB *www.mt-washington.com/ggt.*

Cross-country. There are 40 km (24 mi) of cross-country trails—some with snowmaking—as well as access to more than 1,100 acres of backcountry. It's even possible to ski or snowshoe the lower half of the Mt. Washington Auto Road. Trees shelter most of the trails, so Mt. Washington's famous weather won't be a concern.

Summer activities. Great Glen Trails will put its extensive trail network to use for hiking, trail running, and mountain biking. The center will also have programs in canoeing, kayaking, and fly-fishing.

WILDCAT

Glade skiers favor Wildcat, with 28 acres of official tree skiing. Runs include some stunning double-black-diamond trails. Skiers who can hold a wedge should check out the 4-km-long (2½-mi-long) Polecat. Experts can zip down the Lynx. Views of Mt. Washington and Tuckerman Ravine are superb. The trails are classic New England—narrow and winding. ✉ *Rte. 16, Pinkham Notch, Jackson 03846,* ☎ *603/466–3326; 888/754–9453 snow conditions; 800/255–6439 lodging;* WEB *www.skiwildcat.com.*

Downhill. Wildcat's expert runs deserve their designations and then some. Intermediates have mid-mountain–to–base trails, and beginners will find gentle terrain and a broad teaching slope. Snowboarders have several terrain parks and the run of the mountain. The 44 runs, with a 2,100-ft vertical drop, are served by one high-speed detachable quad and three triple chairlifts.

Child care. The child-care center takes children ages 2 months and up. Kids ages 5–12 can participate in SKIwee instruction on designated slopes.

Dixville Notch

35 *63 mi north of Mt. Washington, 66 mi northeast of Littleton, 149 mi north of Concord.*

Just 12 mi from the Canadian border, this tiny community is known for two things. It's the home of the Balsams Wilderness, one of New Hampshire's oldest and most celebrated resorts. And Dixville Notch and Harts Location are the first election districts in the nation to vote in the presidential primaries and general elections. At midnight on Election Day, the 30 or so Dixville Notch voters gather in the little meeting room beside a hotel service bar to cast their ballots and make national news.

One of the favorite pastimes in this area is spotting moose, those large, ungainly, yet elusive members of the deer family. Although you may catch sight of one or more yourself, **Northern Forest Moose Tours** (☎ 603/752–6060 or 800/992–7480) conducts bus tours of the region that have a 97% success rate for spotting moose.

OFF THE BEATEN PATH

PITTSBURG – Well north of the White Mountains, in the great north woods, Pittsburg contains the four Connecticut Lakes and the springs that form the Connecticut River. The state's northern tip—a chunk of about 250 square mi—lies within the town's borders, the result of a dispute between the United States and Canada. The two countries couldn't decide on a border, so the region's inhabitants declared themselves independent of both countries in 1832. They named their nation the Indian Stream Republic, after the river that passes through the territory; its capital was Pittsburg. In 1835 the feisty, 40-man Indian Stream militia invaded Canada, with limited success. The Indian Stream War ended more by common consent than surrender; in 1842 the Webster-Ashburton Treaty fixed the international boundary. Indian Stream was incorporated as Pittsburg, New Hampshire's largest township.

Remote though it is, this frontier town teems with hunters, boaters, fishermen, hikers, and photographers from early summer through winter. Especially in the colder months, moose sightings are common. The town has more than a dozen lodges and several informal eateries. It's about a 90-minute drive from Littleton and 40-minute drive from Dixville Notch; add another 30 minutes to reach Fourth Connecticut Lake, nearly at the Canadian border. On your way, as you pass the village of Stewartson, note the sign along U.S. 3 marking the 45th Parallel, the point exactly midway between the Equator and the North Pole.

Dining and Lodging

$$$$ ✕🖬 **The Balsams Wilderness.** Nestled in the pine groves of the north
★ woods, this lavish grande dame has been rolling out the red carpet since 1866. It draws families, golf enthusiasts, skiers, and others for a varied slate of activities—from dancing to cooking demonstrations. The individually decorated rooms vary in size but are generally spacious and comfortably furnished; all have mountain views. In the dining room ($$–$$$$; jacket and tie), you might sample a chilled strawberry soup spiked with Grand Marnier, followed by poached salmon with golden caviar sauce. Rates, though steep, include breakfast and dinner and unlimited use of the facilities. ⊠ *Rte. 26, 03576,* ☎ *603/255–3400; 800/ 255–0600; 800/255–0800 in New Hampshire;* FAX *603/255–4221;* WEB *www.thebalsams.com. 204 rooms. 3 restaurants, some in-room hot tubs, driving range, 18-hole golf course, 6 tennis courts, pool, gym, massage, boating, fishing, mountain bikes, hiking, cross-country skiing, downhill skiing, ice-skating, bar, shops, children's programs (ages 1–12), dry cleaning, laundry service, business services. AE, D, MC, V. Closed late Mar.–mid-May and mid-Oct.–mid-Dec. MAP winter, FAP spring–fall.*

$$$ 🏠 **The Glen.** This rustic lodge with stick furniture, fieldstone, and cedar is on First Connecticut Lake and surrounded by log cabins, seven of which are right on the water. The cabins have efficiency kitchens and mini-refrigerators—not that you'll need either, because rates include meals in the lodge restaurant. ✉ *77 Glen Rd., 1 mi off U.S. 3, Pittsburg 03592,* ☎ *603/538–6500 or 800/445–4536,* WEB *the-glen.org. 8 rooms, 10 cabins. Restaurant, kitchenettes, lake; no room phones, no room TVs. No credit cards. Closed mid-Oct.–mid-May. FAP.*

Outdoor Activities and Sports

Dixville Notch State Park (✉ Rte. 26, ☎ 603/323–2087), in the northernmost notch of the White Mountains, has picnic areas, a waterfall, and hiking trails.

Ski Area

THE BALSAMS WILDERNESS

Skiing was originally provided as an amenity for hotel guests at the Balsams, but the area has become popular with day-trippers as well. ✉ *Rte. 26, 03576,* ☎ *603/255–3400; 603/255–3951 snow conditions; 800/255–0600; 800/255–0800 in New Hampshire;* FAX *603/255–4221.*

Downhill. Slopes with such names as Sanguinary, Umbagog, and Magalloway may sound tough, but they're only moderately difficult, leaning toward intermediate. There are 14 trails and four glades for every skill level from the top of the 1,000-ft vertical. One double chairlift and two T-bars carry you up the mountain. There's a halfpipe for snowboarders.

Cross-country. The Balsams has 95 km (59 mi) of cross-country skiing, tracked and groomed for skating. Natural-history markers annotate some trails; you can also try telemark and backcountry skiing, and there are 29 km (18 mi) of snowshoeing trails.

Child care. The ski -lodge nursery takes children ages 6 months–5 years at no charge to hotel guests. Lessons are for kids 3 and up.

North Conway

㊱ *76 mi south of Dixville Notch, 7 mi south of Glen, 41 mi east of Lincoln/North Woodstock.*

Before the arrival of the outlet stores, the town drew visitors for its inspiring scenery, ski resorts, and access to White Mountain National Forest. Today, however, shopping is as big a sport as skiing, and businesses line Route 16 for several miles.

☕ The **Conway Scenic Railroad** operates trips of varying durations in vintage coaches pulled by steam or diesel engines. The views are fine in the dome observation coach on the 5½-hour trip through Crawford Notch. Lunch is served aboard the dining car on the Valley Train to Conway or Bartlett. The 1874 station displays lanterns, old tickets and timetables, and other railroad artifacts. Reserve early during foliage season for the dining excursions. ✉ *Rte. 16/U.S. 302 (38 Norcross Cir.),* ☎ *603/356–5251 or 800/232–5251,* WEB *www.conwayscenic.com.* ✇ *$9.50–$46.* ☉ *Mid-Apr.–late Dec; call for times.*

At **Echo Lake State Park,** you needn't be a rock climber to catch views from the 700-ft White Horse and Cathedral ledges. From the top you'll see the entire valley, in which Echo Lake shines like a diamond. An unmarked trailhead another 7/10 mi on West Side Road leads to Diana's Baths, a series of waterfalls. ✉ *Off U.S 302,* ☎ *603/356–2672.* ✇ *$3.* ☉ *Late May–mid-June, weekends dawn–dusk; mid-June–early Sept., daily dawn–dusk.*

🕐 The **Hartmann Model Railroad Museum** houses 14 operating layouts (from G to Z scales), about 2,000 engines, and more than 5,000 cars and coaches. A café, a crafts store, a hobby shop, and an outdoor ride-on train are on-site. ⊠ *Rte. 16/U.S. 302 and Town Hall Rd., Intervale,* ☎ *603/356–9922,* 🖳 *www.hartmannrr.com.* 🖾 *$6.* ☉ *Mid-June–mid-Oct., daily 9–5; mid-Oct.–mid-June, daily 10–5.*

The hands-on exhibits at the **Weather Discovery Center** teach how weather is monitored and how it affects us. The facility is a collaboration between the National and Atmospheric Administration Forecast Systems lab and the Mt. Washington Observatory at the summit of Mt. Washington. ⊠ *Rte. 16/U.S. 302, ⅓ mi north of rail tracks,* ☎ *603/356–2137,* 🖳 *www.mountwashington.org/discovery.* 🖾 *$2.* ☉ *Fri.–Tues. 10–5.*

Dining and Lodging

$–$$ ✕ **Delaney's Hole in the Wall.** This casual restaurant has eclectic memorabilia that includes autographed baseballs and an early photo of skiing at Tuckerman Ravine hanging over the fireplace. Entrées range from fish-and-chips to fajitas to mussels and scallops sautéed with spiced sausage and Louisiana seasonings. ⊠ *Rte. 16, ¼ mi north of North Conway,* ☎ *603/356–7776. D, MC, V.*

$–$$ ✕ **Muddy Moose.** Especially popular with younger singles and families, the Muddy Moose is inviting and rustic thanks to its fieldstone walls, exposed wood, and understated lighting. Dig into a Greek salad, grilled chicken Caesar wrap, char-grilled pork chops with a maple-cider glaze, or muddy moose pie. ⊠ *Rte. 16, just south of North Conway,* ☎ *603/356–7696. AE, D, MC, V.*

$$$–$$$$ ✕🏨 **Snowvillage Inn.** Journalist Frank Simonds built the gambrel-
   ★   roof main house in 1916. To complement the inn's tome-jammed bookshelves, guest rooms are named for famous authors. The nicest of the rooms, with 12 windows that look out over the Presidential Range, is a tribute to Robert Frost. Two additional buildings—the carriage house and the chimney house—also have libraries. Menu highlights in the candlelit dining room ($$$; reservations essential) include grilled hanger steak with a roasted onion and Stilton sauce. For a different outdoors experience, reserve a place on an organized llama trek up Foss Mountain. Trips include a picnic with champagne. ⊠ *Stuart Rd., 5 mi southeast of Conway (Box 68, Snowville 03849),* ☎ *603/447–2818 or 800/ 447–4345,* 🖷 *603/447–5268,* 🖳 *www.snowvillageinn.com. 18 rooms. Restaurant, sauna, cross-country skiing; no room phones, no room TVs, no kids under 6, no smoking. AE, D, MC, V. BP, MAP.*

$$$–$$$$ ✕🏨 **White Mountain Hotel and Resort.** Rooms in this hotel at the base of Whitehorse Ledge have mountain views. Proximity to the White Mountain National Forest and Echo Lake State Park makes you feel farther away from the outlet malls than you actually are. Dinner at the Ledges restaurant ($$$) might include chicken saltimbocca or mustard-roasted rack of lamb with a jalapeño relish. ⊠ *West Side Rd. (Box 1828, 03860),* ☎ *800/533–6301,* ☎ 🖷 *603/356–7100,* 🖳 *www. whitemountainhotel.com. 69 rooms, 11 suites. 2 restaurants, 9-hole golf course, tennis court, pool, health club, hot tub, sauna, hiking, cross-country skiing, bar, meeting rooms. AE, D, MC, V. BP, MAP.*

$$–$$$$ ✕🏨 **Darby Field Inn.** After a day of activity in the White Mountains, warm up by this inn's fieldstone fireplace or by the bar's woodstove. Most rooms in this unpretentious 1826 farmhouse have mountain views; three have fireplaces. The restaurant ($$$–$$$$) prepares such haute regional American fare as roast duckling in a Chambord sauce and rack of lamb with a merlot sauce. The dark-chocolate pâté with white-chocolate sauce is a knockout dessert. ⊠ *185 Chase Hill (Box D, Albany 03818),* ☎ *603/447–2181 or 800/426–4147,* 🖷 *603/447–*

5726, WEB *www.darbyfield.com. 12 rooms, 3 suites. Restaurant, some in-room hot tubs, some in-room VCRs, pool, hot tub, massage, mountain bikes, croquet, hiking, cross-country skiing, sleigh rides, bar; no-smoking rooms. AE, MC, V. Closed Apr. BP, MAP.*

$$–$$$$ ⊡ **Buttonwood Inn.** A tranquil 17-acre oasis in this busy resort area, the Buttonwood is on Mt. Surprise, 2 mi northeast of North Conway village. Rooms in the 1820s farmhouse are furnished in Shaker style. Wide pine floors, quilts, and period stenciling add warmth. Two rooms have gas fireplaces. Innkeepers Peter and Claudia Needham supply many thoughtful extras, such as backpacks and picnic baskets. ⊠ *Mt. Surprise Rd. (Box 1817, 03860),* ☎ *603/356–2625 or 800/258–2625,* FAX *603/356–3140,* WEB *www.buttonwoodinn.com. 8 rooms, 2 suites. Some in-room hot tubs, pool, hiking, cross-country skiing; no room TVs, no-smoking rooms. AE, D, MC, V. BP.*

$$ ⊡ **Cranmore Inn.** This gambrel-roof country inn opened in 1863, and many of its furnishings date from the mid-1800s. The stables have been remodeled to contain condo-style rooms with kitchens. A mere ⅓ mi from the base of Mt. Cranmore, the inn is within walking distance of North Conway village. Guests have privileges at a nearby health club. ⊠ *Kearsarge St. (Box 1349, 03860),* ☎ *603/356–5502,* WEB *www. cranmoreinn.com. 18 rooms. Restaurant, some kitchens, pool. AE, MC, V. BP.*

Nightlife and the Arts

Horsefeather's (⊠ Main St., ☎ 603/356–6862), a restaurant and bar, often has music on weekends. **Mt. Washington Valley Theater Company** (⊠ Eastern Slope Playhouse, Main St., ☎ 603/356–5425) stages productions from mid-June to Labor Day. The Resort Players, a local group, gives pre- and postseason performances.

Shopping

ANTIQUES

The **Antiques & Collectibles Barn** (⊠ 3425 Main St., ☎ 603/356–7118), 1½ mi north of North Conway village, is a 35-dealer colony with furniture, jewelry, coins, and other collectibles. Northern New England's largest multidealer shop, **North Conway Antiques & Collectibles** (⊠ Rte. 16/U.S. 302, ☎ 603/356–6661) has more than 80 stalls. **Richard Plusch Antiques** (⊠ Rte. 16/U.S. 302, ☎ 603/356–3333) deals in period furniture and accessories, including glass, sterling silver, Oriental porcelains, rugs, and paintings.

CRAFTS

The **Basket & Handcrafters Outlet** (⊠ Kearsarge St., ☎ 603/356–5332) sells gift baskets, dried-flower arrangements, and country furniture. **Handcrafters Barn** (⊠ Main St., ☎ 603/356–8996) stocks the work of 350 area artists and artisans. The **League of New Hampshire Craftsmen** (⊠ 2526 Main St., ☎ 603/356–2441) carries the creations of the state's best artisans. **Zeb's General Store** (⊠ Main St., ☎ 603/356–9294 or 800/676–9294) looks just like an old-fashioned country store; it sells food items, crafts, and other products—all made in New England.

FACTORY OUTLETS

More than 150 factory outlets—including L. L. Bean, Timberland, Pfaltzgraff, London Fog, Anne Klein, and Reebok—line Route 16.

SPORTSWEAR

A top pick for skiwear is **Joe Jones** (⊠ 2709 Main St., ☎ 603/356–9411).

Ski Areas

CRANMORE MOUNTAIN RESORT

This ski area on the outskirts of North Conway has been a favorite of families since it began operating in 1938. Five glades have opened more skiable terrain. ✉ *Skimobile Rd. (Box 1640, 03860),* ☎ *603/356–5543; 603/356–8516 snow conditions; 800/786–6754 lodging;* WEB *www. cranmore.com.*

Downhill. The 39 trails are well laid out and fun to ski. Most runs are naturally formed intermediates that weave in and out of glades. Beginners have several slopes and routes from the summit; experts must be content with a few short, steep pitches. In addition to the trails, snowboarders have a terrain park and a halfpipe. One high-speed quad, one triple, and three double chairlifts carry skiers to the top. There are also two surface lifts. Night skiing is an option from Thursday to Saturday and during holidays.

Other activities. Other winter activities are outdoor skating, snowshoeing, and tubing.

Child care. The nursery takes children ages 6 months–5 years. There's instruction for children ages 3–12.

Summer and year-round activities. You can take a chairlift to the top for a panoramic view of the White Mountains or mountain bike on selected trails. The fitness center has an indoor climbing wall, tennis courts, exercise equipment, and a pool.

CROSS-COUNTRY

Sixty-four kilometers (40 miles) of groomed cross-country trails weave through North Conway and the countryside along the **Mt. Washington Valley Ski Touring Association Network** (✉ Rte. 16, Intervale, ☎ 603/356–9920 or 800/282–5220).

KING PINE SKI AREA AT PURITY SPRING RESORT

King Pine, some 9 mi south of Conway, has been a family-run ski area for more than 100 years. Some ski-and-stay packages include free skiing for midweek resort guests. Among the facilities and activities are an indoor pool and fitness complex, ice-skating, and tubing. ✉ *Rte. 153, East Madison 03849,* ☎ *603/367–8896 or 800/367–8897; 800/ 373–3754 snow conditions,* WEB *www.purityspring.com.*

Downhill. King Pine's gentle slopes are ideal for beginner and intermediate skiers; experts won't be challenged except for a brief pitch on the Pitch Pine trail. The 16 trails are serviced by two triple chairs, a double chair, and two surface lifts. There's tubing on Saturday and Sunday afternoons and night skiing and tubing on Friday and Saturday.

Cross-country. King Pine has 15 km (9 mi) of cross-country skiing.

Child care. Children from infants up to 6 years are welcome (8:30–4) at the base lodge's nursery. Children ages 4 and up can take lessons.

Kancamagus Highway

★ ❸ *36 mi between Conway and Lincoln/North Woodstock.*

Interstate 93 is the fastest way to the White Mountains, but it's hardly the most appealing. The section of Route 112 known as the Kancamagus Highway passes through mountains with some of the state's most unspoiled scenery. This stretch, punctuated by overlooks and picnic areas, erupts into fiery color each fall, when photo-snapping drivers can really slow things down. Prepare yourself for a leisurely pace. There are also campgrounds off the highway. In bad weather, check with the White Mountains Visitors Bureau for road conditions.

Outdoor Activities and Sports

A couple of short hiking trails off the Kancamagus Highway (Route 112) yield great rewards for relatively little effort. The **Lincoln Woods Trail** starts from the large parking lot of the Lincoln Woods Visitor Center, 4 mi east of Lincoln. You can purchase the recreation pass ($5 per vehicle, good for seven consecutive days) needed to park in any of the White Mountain National Forest lots or overlooks here; stopping briefly to take photos or to use the rest rooms at the visitor center is permitted without a pass. The trail crosses a suspension bridge over the Pemigewasset River and follows an old railroad bed for 3 mi along the river. The parking and picnic area for **Sabbaday Falls,** about 15 mi west of Conway, is the trailhead for an easy ½-mi route a multilevel cascade that plunges through two potholes and a flume.

The White Mountains A to Z

To research prices, get advice from other travelers, and book travel arrangements, visit www.fodors.com

AIRPORTS

Manchester Airport is about a 60- to 90-minute drive from the region. Charters and private planes land at Franconia Airport & Soaring Center and Mt. Washington Regional Airport.

➤ AIRPORT INFORMATION: **Franconia Airport & Soaring Center** (⊠ Easton Rd., Franconia, ☎ 603/823–8881). **Mt. Washington Regional Airport** (⊠ Airport Rd., Whitefield, ☎ 603/837–9532).

BUS TRAVEL

Concord Trailways connects Boston's South Station and Logan Airport with Berlin, Conway, Franconia, Gorham, Jackson, Lincoln/North Woodstock, Littleton, and Pinkham Notch.

➤ BUS INFORMATION: **Concord Trailways** (☎ 603/228–3300 or 800/639–3317).

CAR TRAVEL

I–93 and U.S. 3 bisect the White Mountain National Forest, running north from Massachusetts to Québec. The Kancamagus Highway (Route 112), the east–west thoroughfare through the White Mountain National Forest, is a scenic drive. U.S. 302, a longer, more leisurely east–west path, connects I–93 to North Conway. From the seacoast, Route 16 is the popular choice.

EMERGENCIES

➤ HOSPITAL: **Memorial Hospital** (⊠ 3073 Main St., North Conway, ☎ 603/356–5461).

LODGING

Country Inns in the White Mountains handles reservations for a wide variety of B&Bs and inns throughout the region.

APARTMENT AND VILLA RENTALS

➤ LOCAL AGENT: **Country Inns in the White Mountains** (☎ 603/356–9460, WEB www.countryinnsinthewhitemountains.com).

CAMPING

White Mountain National Forest campground reservations has 20 campgrounds with more than 900 campsites spread across the region; only some take reservations. All sites have a 14-day limit.

➤ CONTACT: **White Mountain National Forest** (✉ U.S. Forest Service, 719 N. Main St., Laconia 03246, ☎ 603/528–8721 or 877/444–6777).

OUTDOOR ACTIVITIES AND SPORTS

CANOEING AND KAYAKING

River outfitter Saco Bound Canoe & Kayak leads gentle canoeing expeditions, guided kayak trips, and white-water rafting on seven rivers and provides lessons, equipment, and transportation.

➤ CONTACT: **Saco Bound Canoe & Kayak** (✉ Rte. 16/U.S. 302, Conway, ☎ 603/447–2177, WEB www.sacobound.com).

FISHING

For trout and salmon fishing, try the Connecticut Lakes, though any clear White Mountain stream (there are 650 mi of them in the national forest alone) will do. Many streams are stocked. Conway Lake—the largest of the area's 45 lakes and ponds—noted for smallmouth bass and, early and late in the season, good salmon fishing. The New Hampshire Fish and Game Department has information on fishing conditions. Hunter's North Country Angler schedules intensive guided fly-fishing weekends.

➤ CONTACTS: **Hunter's North Country Angler** (✉ 3643 White Mountain Hwy., Intervale, ☎ 603/356–6000, WEB www.flyfishamerica.com/nca). **New Hampshire Fish and Game Department** (☎ 603/271–3211).

HIKING

With 86 major mountains in the area, the hiking possibilities are endless. Innkeepers can usually point you toward the better nearby trails; some inns schedule guided day trips for guests. The White Mountain National Forest has information on hiking as well as on the parking passes ($5) that are required in the national forest.

The Appalachian Mountain Club headquarters at Pinkham Notch has lectures, workshops, slide shows, and outdoor skills instruction year-round. Accommodations include a 100-bunk main lodge, a 24-bed hostel in Crawford Notch, and two rustic cabins. The club's eight trailside huts provide meals and dorm-style lodging on several trails from June to October. The rest of the year the huts are self-serve. New England Hiking Holidays conducts hikes with lodging in country inns for two to eight nights. Hikes, each with two guides, allow for different levels of ability and cover between 5 and 10 mi per day.

➤ CONTACTS: **Appalachian Mountain Club** (✉ Rte. 16 [Box 298, Gorham 03581], ☎ 603/466–2721; 603/466–2727 reservations; WEB www.mountwashington.com/amc). **New England Hiking Holidays** (☎ 603/356–9696 or 800/869–0949, WEB www.nehikingholidays.com). **White Mountain National Forest** (✉ U.S. Forest Service, 719 Main St., Laconia 03246, ☎ 603/528–8721; 877/444–6777 campground reservations; WEB www.fs.fed.us/r9/white).

VISITOR INFORMATION

➤ TOURIST INFORMATION: **Mt. Washington Valley Chamber of Commerce** (✉ Box 2300, North Conway 03860, ☎ 603/356–5701, WEB www.4seasonresort.com). **North Country Chamber of Commerce** (✉ Box 1, Colebrook 03576, ☎ 603/237–8939 or 800/698–8939, WEB www.northcountrychamber.org). **White Mountains Trail** (WEB www.whitemountainstrail.com). **White Mountains Visitors Bureau** (✉ Kancamagus Hwy./Rte. 112 at I–93 [Box 10, North Woodstock 03262], ☎ 603/745–8720 or 800/346–3687, WEB www.whitemtn.org).

WESTERN AND CENTRAL NEW HAMPSHIRE

Western and Central New Hampshire mix village charm with city hustle across three distinct regions. The Merrimack River valley has the state's largest and fastest-growing cities of Nashua, Manchester, and Concord. To the northwest of this region are Lake Sunapee—with its year-round sporting activities and its nearby mountains and Colonial villages—and Hanover, home to the famous Dartmouth College. The least developed of the three areas, the Monadnock region occupies the state's sleepy southwestern corner. Here you'll find plenty of hiking trails as well as peaceful hilltop hamlets that appear barely changed in the past two centuries. Mt. Monadnock, southern New Hampshire's largest peak, stands guard over the area.

When you're done climbing and swimming and visiting the past, look for small studios of area artists. The region has long been an informal artists' colony where people come to write, paint, and weave in solitude. The towns in this region, beginning with Nashua, are described in counterclockwise order.

Nashua

38 *98 mi south of Lincoln/North Woodstock, 48 mi northwest of Boston, 36 mi south of Concord, 50 mi southeast of Keene.*

Once a prosperous manufacturing town that drew thousands of immigrant workers in the late 1800s and early 1900s, Nashua declined following World War II, as many factories shut down or moved to where labor was cheaper. Since the 1970s, however, the metro area has jumped in population, developing into a charming, old-fashioned community. Its low-key downtown has classic redbrick buildings along the Nashua River, a tributary of the Merrimack River, which skirts the east side of town. Though not visited by tourists as much as other communities in the region, Nashua has some good restaurants and an engaging museum.

The city's impressive industrial history is retold at the **Florence Hyde Speare Memorial Building,** which houses the Nashua Historical Society. In this two-story museum you'll find artifacts, early furnishings, photos, a vintage printing press, and a research library. Adjacent to the museum, the Federal-style **Abbot-Spalding House** is furnished with 18th and 19th-century antiques, art, and household items. You can only visit it on a guided tour, which is held at 1 on the third Saturday of every month from April through October. ⊠ *5 Abbot St.,* ☎ *603/883-0015.* ⚑ *Free.* ☉ *Tues.–Thurs. and Sat. 10–4.*

Dining

$$–$$$ ✕ **Michael Timothy's Urban Bistro.** Part hip bistro, part jazzy wine bar
★ (with live music many nights), Michael Timothy's is so popular that even foodies from Massachusetts drive here. The regularly changing menu might offer a fricassee of seasonal mushrooms, oven-dried tomatoes, asparagus tips, and pearl onions in an herb-vegetable broth over mushroom risotto. Wood-fired pizzas are also a specialty. ⊠ *212 Main St.,* ☎ *603/595-9334. AE, D, MC, V.*

$$–$$$ ✕ **Villa Banca.** On the ground floor of a dramatic, turreted office building, this airy spot with high ceilings and tall windows specializes in both traditional and contemporary Italian cooking. Try the baked salmon topped with pistachio crumbs, shrimp scampi, tomatoes, and scallions and served over garlic-Parmesan risotto, or sample chicken-and-sausage lasagna. Note the exotic-martinis menu—a big draw at happy hour. ⊠ *194 Main St.,* ☎ *603/598-0500. AE, D, DC, MC, V.*

Monadnock Region and Central New Hampshire

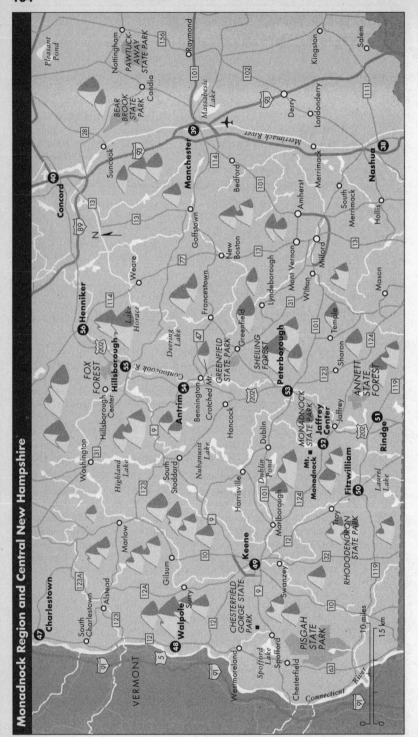

$-$$ ✕ **Martha's Exchange.** A casual spot with copper brewing vats, original marble floors, and booth seating, Martha's appeals both to the after-work set and office workers on lunch breaks. Burgers and sandwiches, maple-stout-barbecued chicken and ribs, Mexican fare, seafood and steak grills, and salads—all in large portions—are your options here. There's also a sweets shop attached, and you can buy half-gallon jugs of house-brewed beers to go. ✉ *185 Main St.,* ☎ *603/883–8781. AE, DC, MC, V.*

The Arts

American Stage Festival (✉ 14 Court St., ☎ 603/886–7000 winter; 603/673–7515 summer), the state's largest professional theater, presents Broadway-style and newer works, music concerts, and a children's-theater series from March through October.

Manchester

㊴ *18 mi north of Nashua, 53 mi north of the Boston.*

Manchester, with just over 100,000 residents, is New Hampshire's largest city. The town grew around the power of the Amoskeag Falls on the Merrimack River, which fueled small textile mills through the 1700s. By 1828, Boston investors had bought the rights to the Merrimack's water power and built on its eastern bank the Amoskeag Textile Mills, which became a testament to New England's manufacturing capabilities. In 1906, the mills employed 17,000 people and churned out more than 4 million yards of cloth per week. This vast enterprise formed Manchester's entire economic base; when it closed in 1936, the town was devastated.

Today Manchester is mainly a banking and business center. As part of an economic recovery plan, the old mill buildings have been converted into warehouses, classrooms, restaurants, museums, and office space. The city is also home to the state's major airport, and the Verizon Wireless Arena, which hosts minor-league hockey matches, concerts, and conventions.

☾ The **Amoskeag Mills** houses both restaurants and museums. The **SEE Science Center** is a hands-on science lab and children's museum. The **Millyard Museum** contains state-of-the-art exhibits depicting the region's history, from when Native Americans lived alongside and fished the Merrimack River to the heyday of Amoskeag Mills. The interactive Discovery Gallery is geared toward kids; there's also a lecture-concert hall and a large museum shop. ✉ *Mill No. 3, 200 Bedford St. (entrance at 255 Commercial St.),* ☎ *603/625–2821; 603/669–0400 Science Center; 603/625–2821 Millyard Museum;* ⬛ *www.mv.com/org/mha.* ✉ *Science Center $4, Millyard Museum $5.* ☺ *Science Center weekdays 10–3, weekends noon–5; Millyard Museum Tues.–Sat. 10–4, Sun. noon–4.*

At the neoclassical redbrick (1931) headquarters of the **Manchester Historic Association,** you'll find a few exhibits on this city's history and information on the Amoskeag Mills. ✉ *129 Amherst St.,* ☎ *603/622–7531,* ⬛ *www.mv.com/org/mha.* ✉ *Free.* ☺ *Tues.–Sat. 10–4.*

The **Currier Gallery of Art,** in a 1929 Italianate building, has a permanent collection of European and American paintings, sculpture, and decorative arts from the 13th to the 20th century, including works by Monet, Picasso, Hopper, and O'Keeffe. Also part of the museum is the Frank Lloyd Wright–designed Zimmerman House, built in 1950. Wright called this sparse, utterly functional living space "Usonian." It's New England's only Wright-designed residence open to the public. ⊠ *201 Myrtle Way,* ☎ *603/669–6144; 603/626–4158 Zimmerman House tours;* W̲E̲B̲ *www.currier.org.* ▨ *Gallery $5, free Sat. 10–1; Zimmerman House $9 (reservations essential).* ☉ *Sun.–Mon. and Wed.–Thurs. 11–5, Fri. 11–8, Sat. 10–5; call for tour times.*

🐟 Salmon, shad, and river herring "climb" the **Amoskeag Fishways** fish ladder near the Amoskeag Dam from May to mid-June. The visitor center has an underwater viewing window, year-round interactive exhibits and programs about the Merrimack River, and a hydroelectric-station viewing area. ⊠ *Fletcher St.,* ☎ *603/626–3474,* W̲E̲B̲ *www.amoskeagfishways.org.* ▨ *$2.* ☉ *Mon.–Sat. 9–5.*

Dining and Lodging

$$$–$$$$ ✕ **Baldwin's on Elm.** Chef Nathan Baldwin has earned raves for his
  ★   creative renderings of regional American fare. The caramelized Nantucket Bay scallops with a celery root-and-truffle puree, squash, and pumpkin seeds is sublime. Consider the spring roll with jasmine rice pudding, mangos, coconut, and rum anglaise for dessert. ⊠ *1105 Elm St.,* ☎ *603/622–5975. AE, D, DC, MC, V. No lunch.*

$$$–$$$$ ✕ **Richard's Bistro.** Whether you want to celebrate a special occasion or you just crave first-rate regional American cuisine, head to this romantic downtown bistro. The kitchen uses traditional New England ingredients in worldly preparations: try the char-broiled filet mignon with Gorgonzola, baked-stuffed potato, and strawberries or the broiled haddock topped with shrimp and scallops on an herb-risotto cake with a honey-peach sauce. ⊠ *36 Lowell St.,* ☎ *603/644–1180. AE, D, MC, V. No lunch Sat.*

$$–$$$ ✕ **Cotton.** Mod lighting and furnishings and an arbored patio set a
  ★   swanky tone at this restaurant inside one of the old Amoskeag Mill buildings. The kitchen churns out updated comfort food. Start with mussels in a red curry of coconut milk, lemongrass, and Kaffir-lime leaves. Stellar entrée picks include a casserole with yellowfin tuna, julienne vegetables, and pappardelle tossed with wild-mushroom cream and toasted lemony crumbs. ⊠ *75 Arms Park,* ☎ *603/622–5488. AE, D, DC, MC, V.*

$–$$ ✕ **Fratello's.** Despite a seemingly endless supply of seating, the wait for a table at this restaurant can be long on the weekends. The huge bi-level space inside a redbrick building at the north end of Amoskeag Mills has high timber ceilings and exposed ducts. The kitchen prepares Italian food from a lengthy menu. Try any of several mix-and-match pastas and sauces, one of the wood-fired pizzas, or one of the many grills. ⊠ *155 Dow St.,* ☎ *603/624–2022. AE, D, MC, V.*

✕ **Red Arrow Diner.** A mix of hipsters and oldsters, including comedian and Manchester native Adam Sandler, favor this neon-streaked, 24-hour greasy spoon, which has been going strong since 1922. Filling fare— platters of kielbasa, French toast, and the diner's famous panfries—keep patrons happy. ⊠ *61 Lowell St.,* ☎ *603/626–1118. MC, V.*

✕🏨 **Bedford Village Inn.** The hayloft and milking rooms of this 1810 Federal farmstead, just a few miles southwest of Manchester, now contain lavish suites with king-size four-poster beds. The restaurant ($$$–$$$$)—a warren of elegant dining rooms with fireplaces and wide-pine floors—presents contemporary fare that might include a starter of Maine Jonah crab cakes with Asian slaw, a chili-soy vinaigrette, and wasabi cream, followed by apricot-and-stout-marinated venison loin with a crisp potato cake, roasted oyster mushrooms, and fennel. There's also a casual tavern ($$–$$$). ⊠ *2 Village Inn La., Bedford 03110,* ☎ *603/472–2001 or 800/852–1166,* F̲A̲X̲ *603/472–2379,* W̲E̲B̲ *www.bedfordvillageinn.com. 12 suites, 2 apartments. Restaurant, some in-room hot tubs, bar, meeting room; no-smoking rooms. AE, DC, MC, V.*

🎬 **Holiday Inn Manchester.** Of Manchester's many chain properties, the 12-story Holiday Inn has the central-most location—just steps from the Amoskeag Mills and the great dining along Elm Street. Rooms are simple and clean, perfect for business travelers. ⊠ *700 Elm St., 03101,* ☎ *603/625–1000,* FAX *603/625–4595,* WEB *www.holiday-inn.com. 244 rooms, 6 suites. 2 restaurants, in-room data ports, indoor pool, hot tub, sauna, gym, bar, business services, meeting rooms, parking (fee). AE, D, DC, MC, V.*

Nightlife and the Arts

Club Merrimack (⊠ 201 Merrimack St., ☎ 603/623–9362) is New Hampshire's most popular lesbian and gay disco. Revelers come from all over to drink and mingle at the **Yard** (⊠ 1211 S. Mammoth Rd., ☎ 603/623–3545), which is also a steak house and seafood restaurant.

The **Palace Theatre** presents musicals and plays throughout the year. It also hosts the state's Philharmonic and symphony orchestras and the Opera League of New Hampshire. ⊠ *80 Hanover St.,* ☎ *603/668– 5588 theater; 603/647–6476 Philharmonic; 603/669–3559 symphony; 603/647–6564 opera.*

Shopping

The enormous **Mall of New Hampshire** (⊠ 1500 S. Willow St., ☎ 603/ 669–0433) has every conceivable store and is anchored by Sears and Filene's.

Spectator Sport

The **Manchester Monarchs** (⊠ Elm St. and Lake Ave., ☎ 603/626–7825 or 603/868–7300), a minor-league affiliate of hockey's Los Angeles Kings, play at the Verizon Wireless Arena. The season runs from October through early April.

Concord

❹⓪ *20 mi northwest of Manchester, 67 mi northwest of Boston, 46 mi northwest of Portsmouth.*

New Hampshire's capital (population 38,000) is a quiet town that tends to the state's business but little else—the sidewalks roll up promptly at 6. The **Concord on Foot** walking trail winds through the historic district. Maps are available from the **Chamber of Commerce** (⊠ 40 Commercial St., ☎ 603/224–2508) or stores along the trail.

The **Pierce Manse** is the Greek Revival home in which Franklin Pierce lived before moving to Washington to become the 14th U.S. president. ⊠ *14 Penacook St.,* ☎ *603/225–2068 or 603/224–5954.* ⊠ *$3.* ⊙ *Mid-June–Labor Day, weekdays 11–3.*

At the neoclassical, gilt-domed **State House,** the legislature still meets in its original chambers. The building, which dates from 1819, is the oldest in the United States in continuous use as a state capitol. ⊠ *107 N. Main St.,* ☎ *603/271–2154,* WEB *www.ci.concord.nh.us/tourdest/ statehs.* ⊙ *Weekdays 8–4:30; guided tours by reservation.*

Among the artifacts at the **Museum of New Hampshire History** is an original Concord Coach. During the 19th century, when more than 3,000 such conveyances were built in Concord, this was about as technologically perfect a vehicle as you could find—many say it's the coach that won the West. Other exhibits provide an overview of state history, from the Abenaki to the settlers of Portsmouth up to current residents. ⊠ *6 Eagle Sq.,* ☎ *603/226–3189,* WEB *www.nhhistory.org/ museum.html.* ⊠ *$5.* ⊙ *Jan.–June and mid-Oct.–Nov., Tues.–Wed. and Fri.–Sat. 9:30–5, Thurs. 9:30–8:30, Sun. noon–5; Dec. and July–*

mid-Oct., Mon.–Wed. and Fri.–Sat. 9:30–5, Thurs. 9:30–8:30, Sun. noon–5.

ⓒ The **Christa McAuliffe Planetarium** presents shows on the solar system, constellations, and space exploration that incorporate computer graphics, sound, and special effects in a 40-ft dome theater. Children love seeing the tornado tubes, magnetic marbles, and other hands-on exhibits. Outside, explore the scale-model planet walk and the human sundial. The planetarium was named for the Concord teacher—and first civilian in space—who was killed in the Space Shuttle *Challenger* explosion in 1986. ⊠ *New Hampshire Technical Institute campus, 2 Institute Dr.,* ☎ *603/271–7831,* WEB *www.starhop.com.* 🎫 *Exhibit area free, shows $8.* ☉ *Tues.–Thurs. 9–5, Fri. 9–7, weekends 10–5. Call for show times and reservations.*

Dining and Lodging

✕ **Siam Orchid.** This dark, attractive Thai restaurant with a colorful rickshaw gracing its dining room serves spicy and reasonably authentic Thai food. Try the fiery broiled swordfish with shrimp curry sauce or the pine-nut chicken in an aromatic ginger sauce. ⊠ *15 N. Main St.,* ☎ *603/228–3633. D, MC, V. No lunch weekends.*

✕ **Foodee's Pizzas.** A local chain with additional parlors in Keene, Dover, Lincoln, Milford, and Wolfeboro, Foodee's serves creative pizzas with especially delicious crusts (sourdough, six-grain, deep-dish). The capital branch is in the heart of downtown and serves such pies as the Polish (with kielbasa, sauerkraut, and three cheeses) and the El Greco (with sweet onions, sliced tomatoes, olive oil, and feta). You can also order pastas, salads, and calzones. ⊠ *2 S. Main St.,* ☎ *603/ 225–3834. MC, V.*

✕🏠 **Centennial Inn.** Built in 1892 for widows of Civil War veterans, this imposing brick-and-stone building is set back from busy Pleasant Street. Much of the original woodwork has been preserved. Each room is decorated with antiques and reproduction pieces, and all have ceiling fans. The kitchen at the somewhat stodgy Franklin Pierce Dining Room ($$–$$$$) turns out surprisingly appealing Continental fare. ⊠ *96 Pleasant St., 03301,* ☎ *603/225–7102 or 800/360–4839,* FAX *603/ 225–5031,* WEB *www.someplacesdifferent.com/centennialinn.htm. 27 rooms, 5 suites. Restaurant, in-room data ports, in-room VCRs, bar, meeting rooms. AE, D, DC, MC, V.*

Nightlife and the Arts

The **Capitol Center for the Arts** (⊠ 44 S. Main St., ☎ 603/225–1111) has been restored to reflect its Roaring '20s origins. It hosts touring Broadway shows, dance companies, and musical acts. The lounge at **Hermanos Cocina Mexicana** (⊠ 11 Hills Ave., ☎ 603/224–5669) has live jazz Sunday through Thursday nights.

Outdoor Activities and Sports

Hannah's Paddles (⊠ 15 Hannah Dustin Dr., ☎ 603/753–6695) rents canoes for use on the Merrimack River, which runs through Concord.

Shopping

CRAFTS

Capitol Craftsman and Romance Jewelers (⊠ 16 N. Main St., ☎ 603/ 224–6166), adjoining shops, sell fine jewelry and handicrafts. The **Den of Antiquity** (⊠ 74 N. Main St., ☎ 603/225–4505) carries handcrafted country gifts and accessories. The **League of New Hampshire Craftsmen** (⊠ 36 N. Main St., ☎ 603/228–8171) exhibits crafts in many media. **Mark Knipe Goldsmiths** (⊠ 2 Capitol Plaza, Main St., ☎ 603/ 224–2920) sets antique stones in rings, earrings, and pendants.

Steeplegate Mall (⊠ 270 Loudon Rd., ☎ 603/228–0025) has more than 75 stores, including chain department stores and some smaller crafts shops.

Warner

41 *22 mi northwest of Concord.*

Three New Hampshire governors were born in this quiet agricultural town just off I–89. Buildings dating from the late 1700s and early 1800s, and a charming library welcomes you to the town's main street.

Mt. Kearsarge Indian Museum, Education and Cultural Center gives guided tours of an extensive collection of Native American artistry, including moose-hair embroidery, quilt work, and basketry. Signs on the Medicine Woods trail identify plants and explain how Native Americans use them as foods, medicines, and dyes. ⊠ *Kearsarge Mountain Rd., 03278,* ☎ *603/456–2600,* WEB *www.indianmuseum.org.* ⊡ *$6.50.* ☉ *May–Oct., Mon.–Sat. 10–5, Sun. noon–5; Nov.–Dec., Sat. 10–5, Sun. noon–5.*

A 3½-mi scenic auto road at **Rollins State Park** (⊠ off Rte. 103) snakes up the southern slope of Mt. Kearsarge, where you can then hike the ½-mi trail to the summit. The road is closed November through mid-May; park admission is $3.

New London

42 *16 mi northwest of Warner, 25 mi west of Tilton.*

New London, the home of Colby-Sawyer College (1837), is a good base for exploring the Lake Sunapee region. A campus of stately Colonial-style buildings fronts the vibrant commercial district, where you'll find several cafés and boutiques. At the 10,000-year-old **Cricenti's Bog,** off Business Route 11, a short trail shows off the shaggy mosses and fragile ecosystem of this ancient pond.

Dining and Lodging

✕ **Peter Christian's Tavern.** Exposed beams, wooden tables, a smattering of antiques, and half shutters on the windows make Peter Christian's a cool summer oasis and a warm winter haven. The fare tends toward the traditional and the hearty, from beef stew to mustard-chicken cordon bleu. ⊠ *186 Main St.,* ☎ *603/526–4042. AE, D, MC, V.*

✕ **Four Corners Grille and Flying Goose Brew Pub.** South of downtown, this little restaurant and pub is known for massive burgers, pit-barbecued meats, calamari in basil pesto, great ales, and exceptional views of Mt. Kearsarge. There's live folk and light rock music many nights. ⊠ *Rtes. 11 and 114,* ☎ *603/526–6899. D, MC, V.*

✕▥ **Inn at Pleasant Lake.** This 1790s inn lies just across Pleasant Lake from majestic Mt. Kearsarge. Its spacious rooms have country antiques and modern bathrooms. The restaurant ($$$$; reservations essential) presents a nightly changing prix-fixe menu that draws raves for such entrées as roast tenderloin of Angus beef with a Calvados demiglace and watercress pesto and such desserts as white-chocolate mousse with a trio of sauces. ⊠ *125 Pleasant St. (Box 1030, 03257),* ☎ *603/526–6271 or 800/626–4907,* FAX *603/526–4111,* WEB *www. innatpleasantlake.com. 12 rooms. Restaurant, some in-room hot tubs, gym, beach, boating, meeting rooms; no room phones, no room TVs, no smoking. MC, V.*

✕▥ **New London Inn.** The two porches of this rambling 1792 inn overlook Main Street. Rooms have Victorian decor; some have views of the Colby-Sawyer campus. The restaurant's ($$–$$$) nouvelle-in-

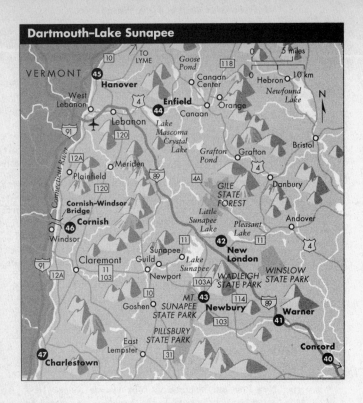

Dartmouth–Lake Sunapee

spired menu has such starters as butternut squash with a sun-dried cranberry pesto and such entrées as grilled cilantro shrimp with a saffron risotto. ⊠ *140 Main St. (Box 8, 03257),* ☎ *603/526–2791 or 800/526–2791,* FAX *603/526–2749. 29 rooms. Restaurant; no smoking. AE, D, MC, V. CP.*

⊞ **Follansbee Inn.** Built in 1840, this quintessential country inn on the shore of Kezar Lake is a perfect fit in the 19th-century village of North Sutton, about 4 mi south of New London. The common rooms and bedrooms are loaded with collectibles—a traveling trunk here, a wooden school desk there. In winter, you can ice-fish on or ski across the lake; in summer you can swim or boat from the inn's pier. A 3-mi walking trail circles the lake. ⊠ *Rte. 114, North Sutton 03260,* ☎ *603/927–4221 or 800/626–4221,* WEB *www.follansbeeinn.com. 23 rooms, 11 with bath; 1 cottage. Some in-room hot tubs, lake, windsurfing, boating, fishing, bicycles, hiking, cross-country skiing, ice-skating; no room phones, no room TVs, no kids under 10, no smoking. MC, V. BP.*

⚠ **Otter Lake Camping Area.** The 28 sites on Otter Lake have plenty of shade, and boating and fishing are available. Facilities include a beach, a playground, and canoe and pedal boat rentals. ⊠ *55 Otterville Rd., 03257,* ☎ *603/763–5600. No credit cards.*

The Arts

The **New London Barn Playhouse** (⊠ 209 Main St., ☎ 603/526–6710 or 800/633–2276) presents Broadway-style and children's plays every summer in New Hampshire's oldest continuously operating theater.

Shopping

Artisan's Workshop (⊠ Peter Christian's Tavern, 186 Main St., ☎ 603/526–4227) carries jewelry, glass, and other local handicrafts.

Ski Area

NORSK CROSS COUNTRY AND SNOWSHOE CENTER

The 70 km (43 mi) of scenic cross-country ski trails here include 45 km (28 mi) that are tracked and 24 km (15 mi) that are skate-groomed. Snowshoers have 19 km (12 mi) of groomed and backcountry trails. ⊠ *Rte. 11,* ☎ *603/526–4685 or 800/426–6775,* WEB *www.skinorsk.com.*

Newbury

 8 mi southwest of New London.

Newbury is on the edge of Mt. Sunapee State Park. The mountain, which rises to an elevation of nearly 3,000 ft, and the sparkling lake are the region's outdoor recreation centers. The popular League of New Hampshire Craftsmen's Fair is held at the base of Mt. Sunapee each August.

John M. Hay, who served as private secretary to Abraham Lincoln and secretary of state for presidents McKinley and Roosevelt, built **The Fells** on Lake Sunapee as a summer home in 1890. House tours focus on his life in Newbury and Washington. Hay's son is responsible for the extensive gardens, a mix of formal and informal styles that include a 75-ft perennial border and a hillside planted with heather. More than 800 acres of the former estate are open for hiking and picnicking. ⊠ *Rte. 103A,* ☎ *603/763–4789,* WEB *www.thefells.org.* ⌹ *$4.* ☉ *House Memorial Day–mid-Oct., weekends 10–5; grounds daily dawn–dusk.*

Lodging

⚠ **Crow's Nest Campground.** This campground has 100 sites, some directly on the Sugar River, as well as cabins with baths. The facilities include a recreation hall, a pool, a children's wading pool, miniature golf, and a warm-up room with a fireplace. River swimming and fishing are summer pastimes; you can skate or sled in the winter, and area snowmobile trails connect to the campground. ⊠ *529 S. Main St., Newport 03773,* ☎ *603/863–6170,* WEB *www.crowsnestcampground.com. D, MC, V. Closed mid-Oct.–Nov. and Apr.–mid-May.*

Outdoor Activities and Sports

BEACHES

Sunapee State Beach has picnic areas, a beach, and a bathhouse. You can rent canoes here, too. ⊠ *Rte. 103,* ☎ *603/763–5561.* ⌹ *$3.* ☉ *Daily dawn–dusk.*

FISHING

Lake Sunapee has brook and lake trout, salmon, smallmouth bass, and pickerel.

Shopping

Overlooking Lake Sunapee's southern tip, **Outspokin' Bicycle and Sport** (⊠ Rtes. 103 and 103A, at the harbor, ☎ 603/763–9500) has a tremendous selection of biking, hiking, skateboarding, snow- and waterskiing, and snowboarding clothing and equipment.

Ski Area

MOUNT SUNAPEE

Although the resort is state-owned, it's managed by Vermont's Okemo Mountain resort, known for being family friendly. The agreement has allowed the influx of capital necessary for operating extensive lifts, snow-making (97% coverage), and trail grooming. ⊠ *Rte. 103 (Box 2021, 03772),* ☎ *603/763–2356; 603/763–4020 snow conditions; 877/687–8627 lodging;* WEB *www.mtsunapee.com.*

Downhill. This mountain is 1,510 vertical ft and has 60 trails, mostly intermediate. Experts can take to a dozen slopes, including three nice double-black diamonds. The beginner's section is well away from other trails and has a quad chairlift. Boarders have a 420-ft-long half-pipe and a terrain park with music. Two base lodges and a summit lodge supply the essentials. One high-speed detachable quad, one fixed-grip quad, two triple and two double chairlifts, and three surface lifts transport skiers.

Child care. The Mother Goose Day Care takes children ages 1–5. Children's programs in skiing or snowboarding are available for kids 4 and up.

Summer activities. The Sunapee Express Quad zooms you to the summit. From here, it's just under a mile hike to Lake Solitude. Mountain bikers can use the lift to many trails, and an in-line skate park has beginner and advanced sections (plus equipment rentals).

Enfield

④ *33 mi northwest of Newbury.*

In 1782, two Shaker brothers from Mount Lebanon, New York, arrived at a community on Mascoma Lake's northeastern side. Eventually, they formed Enfield, the 9th of 18 Shaker communities in this country, and moved it to the lake's southern shore, where they erected more than 200 buildings.

The **Enfield Shaker Museum** preserves the legacy of the Shakers, who numbered 330 members at the village's peak. By 1923, interest in the society had dwindled, and the last 10 members joined the Canterbury community. A self-guided walking tour takes you through 13 of the remaining buildings, among them the Great Stone Dwelling (now the Shaker Inn) and an 1849 stone mill. Demonstrations of Shaker crafts techniques and numerous special events take place year-round. ⊠ *24 Caleb Dyer La.,* ☎ *603/632–4346,* WEB *www.shakermuseum.org.* 🖾 *$7.* ☉ *Memorial Day–late Oct., Mon.–Sat. 10–5, Sun. noon–5; late Oct.–Memorial Day, Sat. 10–4, Sun. noon–4.*

Dining and Lodging

✕🏨 **The Shaker Inn.** Built between 1837 and 1841, the Great Stone Dwelling on Lake Mascoma is the largest main dwelling ever built by a Shaker community. Adjacent to the Enfield Shaker Museum, it's now an inn, and the guest rooms in the original Shaker sleeping chambers have reproduction Shaker furniture and the simplicity of style for which the religious community was known. The dining room ($$) serves Shaker-inspired contemporary cuisine such as panfried buttermilk chicken breast with Vermont cheddar–whipped potatoes. ⊠ *447 Rte. 4A, 03748,* ☎ *603/632–7810 or 888/707–4257,* WEB *www.theshakerinn.com. 24 rooms. Restaurant, lake, baby-sitting; no room phones, no room TVs, no smoking. AE, D, MC, V. BP.*

Outdoor Activities and Sports

Anglers can try for rainbow trout, pickerel, and horned pout in **Lake Mascoma.**

Hanover

㊺ *12 mi northwest of Enfield, 62 mi northwest of Concord.*

Eleazer Wheelock founded Hanover's Dartmouth College in 1769 to educate the Abenaki "and other youth." When he arrived, the town consisted of about 20 families. The college and the town grew symbiotically, with Dartmouth becoming the northernmost Ivy League school. Today Hanover is still synonymous with Dartmouth, but the attractive town is also a respected medical and cultural center for the upper Connecticut River valley.

Robert Frost spent part of a brooding freshman semester at Ivy League **Dartmouth College** before giving up college altogether. The buildings that cluster around the green include the **Baker Memorial Library,** which houses such literary treasures as 17th-century editions of Shakespeare's works. The library is also well known for the 3,000-square-ft murals by Mexican artist José Clemente Orozco that depict the story of civilization on the American continents. If the towering arcade at the entrance to the **Hopkins Center** (☎ 603/646–2422) appears familiar, it's probably because it resembles the project that architect Wallace K. Harrison completed just after designing it: New York City's Metropolitan Opera House at Lincoln Center. The complex includes a 900-seat theater for film showings and concerts, a 400-seat theater for plays, and a black-box theater for new plays. The Dartmouth Symphony Orchestra performs here, as does the Big Apple Circus. In addition to African, Peruvian, Oceanic, Asian, European, and American art, the **Hood Museum of Art** owns the Picasso painting *Guitar on a Table,* silver by Paul Revere, and a set of Assyrian reliefs from the 9th century BC. Rivaling the collection is the museum's architecture: a series of austere, copper-roofed, redbrick buildings arranged around a courtyard. Free guided tours are available on request. ✉ *Museum: Wheelock St.,* ☎ *603/646–2808,* ⓦⒺⒷ *www.dartmouth.edu/~hood.* 🖾 *Free.* ☉ *Tues. and Thurs.–Sat. 10–5, Wed. 10–9, Sun. noon–5.*

NEED A BREAK?	Take a respite from museum-hopping with a cup of espresso, a ham-and-cheese scone, or a fresh-baked brownie at the **Dirt Cowboy** (✉ 7 S. Main St., ☎ 603/643–1323), a café across from the green and beside a used bookstore.

OFF THE BEATEN PATH	**THE UPPER VALLEY –** From Hanover, you can make a 60-mi drive up Route 10 all the way to Littleton for a highly scenic tour of the upper Connecticut River valley. You'll have views of the river and Vermont's Green Mountains from many points. The road passes through groves of evergreens, over leafy ridges, and through delightful hamlets. Grab gourmet picnic provisions at **Pat Tony's General Store** (☎ 603/650–2015) on Lyme's village common, and stop at the bluff-top village green in historical Haverhill (28 mi north of Hanover) for a picnic amid the panorama of classic Georgian- and Federal-style mansions and faraway farmsteads. You can follow this scenic route all the way to the White Mountains region, or loop back south from Haverhill—along Route 25 to Route 118 to U.S. 4 west—to Enfield, a drive of about 45 mi (and 75 minutes).

Dining and Lodging

✕ **Murphy's.** Students, visiting alums, and locals regularly descend upon this pub, whose walls are lined with shelves of old books. The varied menu ranges from sliced, grilled emu with caramelized onions and applewood-smoked bacon vinaigrette to Cajun salmon Caesar salads. Check out the extensive beer list. ✉ *11 S. Main St.,* ☎ *603/643–4075. AE, D, DC, MC, V.*

✕ **Lui Lui.** The creatively topped thin-crust pizzas and huge pasta portions are only part of the draw at this chatter-filled eatery. It also has a dramatic setting inside a former power station on the Mascoma River. Favorite pizza picks include the BLT and the barbecue-chicken pie. Pasta fans should dive into a bowl of linguine with prosciutto, spinach, and mushrooms. The owners also run Molly's Restaurant and Jesse's Tavern, which are both nearby. ⊠ *Adjacent to Powerhouse Mall, off Rte. 12A,* ☎ *603/298–7070. AE, D, DC, MC, V.*

✕ **Panda House/Bamboo Garden.** In a region with few decent Asian restaurants, these two offer a welcome taste of Chinese and Japanese fare. They occupy a sedate basement space of the Hanover Park shopping arcade. Try the sashimi-sushi platters from the Bamboo Garden kitchen; Panda House favorites include the tangerine beef and the crispy fish with a spicy Hunan sauce. ⊠ *3 Lebanon St.,* ☎ *603/643–1290. AE, D, DC, MC, V.*

✕ **Lou's.** A Hanover tradition for decades, this diner-cum-café-cum-bakery serves possibly the best breakfast in the valley—a plate of *migas* (eggs, cheddar, salsa, and guacamole mixed with tortilla chips) can fill you up for the better part of the day; blueberry-cranberry buttermilk pancakes also satisfy. Or grab a seat at the old-fashioned soda fountain and order an ice cream sundae. ⊠ *30 S. Main St.,* ☎ *603/643–3321. No credit cards. No dinner.*

✕🔝 **Hanover Inn.** Owned by Dartmouth College, this sprawling, Georgian-style brick structure rises four white-trimmed stories. The original building was converted to a tavern in 1780, and this expertly run inn, now greatly enlarged, has been operating ever since. Rooms have Colonial reproductions, Audubon prints, and large sitting areas. The formal Daniel Webster Room ($$–$$$$) serves regional American dishes such as grilled monkfish with tempura lobster tail and soba noodles. The swank Zins Wine Bistro ($–$$) prepares lighter but still highly innovative fare. ⊠ *The Green (Box 151, 03755),* ☎ *603/643–4300 or 800/443–7024,* 🅵🅰🆇 *603/646–3744,* 🆆🅴🅱 *www.hanoverinn.com. 92 rooms. 2 restaurants, bar, business services, meeting rooms. AE, D, DC, MC, V.*

🔝 **Trumbull House.** The sunny guest rooms of this white Colonial-style house—on 16 acres in Hanover's outskirts—have king- or queen-size beds, window seats, writing desks, and other comfortable touches. Breakfast, with a choice of entrées, is served in the formal dining room or in front of the living room fireplace. Rates include use of a nearby health club. ⊠ *40 Etna Rd., 03755,* ☎ *603/643–2370 or 800/651–5141,* 🅵🅰🆇 *603/643–2430,* 🆆🅴🅱 *www.trumbullhouse.com. 4 rooms, 1 suite. Dining room, some in-room data ports, some in-room hot tubs, some in-room VCRs, pond, basketball, hiking, business services, meeting room; no smoking. AE, MC, V. BP.*

🔝 **Dowds Country Inn.** This 1780 Georgian-style house on 6 pastoral acres faces the village green and the vintage country store in the frozen-in-time river village of Lyme, about 10 mi north of Hanover. Rooms have a crisp, unfussy look, with Colonial antiques, quilted bedspreads, stenciled walls, and wide-plank floors. It's a relaxed and reasonably priced alternative to the accommodations in bustling Hanover. ⊠ *On the Common (Box 58, 03768),* ☎ *603/795–4712 or 800/482–4712,* 🅵🅰🆇 *603/795–4220,* 🆆🅴🅱 *www.dowdscountryinn.com. 20 rooms, 3 suites. Pond, meeting room; no room phones, no room TVs. D, DC, MC, V. BP.*

Outdoor Activities and Sports

Ledyard Canoe Club of Dartmouth (☎ 603/643–6709) provides canoe and kayak rentals and classes on the swift-flowing Connecticut River, which isn't suitable for beginners and is safest after mid-June.

Shopping

Shops, mostly of the independent variety but with a few upscale chains sprinkled in, line Hanover's main street. The commercial district blends almost imperceptibly with Dartmouth's campus. West Lebanon, south of Hanover on the Vermont border, has many more shops. Goldsmith

Paul Gross of **Designer Gold** (⊠ 3 Lebanon St., ☎ 603/643–3864) designs settings for gemstones—all one-of-a-kind or limited-edition.

The **Mouse Menagerie of Fine Crafts** (⊠ Rte. 12A, West Lebanon, ☎ 603/298–7090) sells its signature collector's series of toy mice, plus furniture, wind chimes, and other gifts. The **Powerhouse Mall** (⊠ Rte. 12A, 1 mi north of I–89 Exit 20, West Lebanon, ☎ 603/298–5236), a former power station, comprises three buildings of specialty stores, boutiques, and restaurants.

En Route From Hanover follow Route 10 south to Route 12A, and exactly 3⅓ mi south of I–89, bear right onto scenic **River Road.** It hugs the shore of the Connecticut River, affording outstanding views of Vermont's countryside (try to ignore the occasional glimpse of busy I–91). The bucolic road also passes several old mansions, including Plainfield's stately Home Hill Inn. The narrow lane is slow-going in places, all the better to take in the views. After about 7 mi, River Road puts you back onto the more prosaic Route 12A in Cornish.

Cornish

46 *22 mi south of Hanover.*

Today Cornish is best known for its four covered bridges and for being the home of reclusive author J. D. Salinger, but at the turn of the 20th century the village was known primarily as the home of the country's then most popular novelist, Winston Churchill (no relation to the British prime minister). His novel *Richard Carvell* sold more than a million copies. Churchill was such a celebrity that he hosted Teddy Roosevelt during the president's 1902 visit. At that time Cornish was an enclave of artistic talent. Painter Maxfield Parrish lived and worked here, and sculptor Augustus Saint-Gaudens set up his studio and created the heroic bronzes for which he is known.

★ Just south of Plainfield, where River Road rejoins Route 12A, a small lane leads to the **Saint-Gaudens National Historic Site.** Here you can tour sculptor Augustus Saint-Gaudens's (1848–1907) house, studio, gallery, and 150 acres of grounds and gardens. Scattered throughout are full-size casts of his works. The property has two hiking trails, the longer of which is the Blow-Me-Down Trail. Concerts are held every Sunday afternoon in July and August. ⊠ *Off Rte. 12A,* ☎ *603/675–2175,* WEB *www.sgnhs.org.* ⌑ *$4.* ⊙ *Buildings mid-May–Oct., daily 9–4:30; grounds daily dawn–dusk.*

1½ mi south of the Saint-Gaudens National Historic Site you'll reach the 460-ft **Cornish-Windsor Bridge,** which connects New Hampshire to Vermont across the Connecticut River. It dates from 1866 and is the longest covered bridge in the United States.

Dining and Lodging

✗⊡ **Home Hill Inn.** Set back from the Connecticut River on 25 acres of meadow and woods, this tranquil 1818 mansion is best suited to adults. The owners have given the inn a French influence with 19th-century antiques and collectibles. Rooms in the main house have canopy or four-poster beds; four have fireplaces. The suite in the carriage house is romantic. The airy dining room ($$$$; closed Mon.–Tues.) serves inspired French and Mediterranean cuisine. Chef-owner Victoria du Roure runs the on-site L'École Culinaire; cooking classes are held one weekend each month in winter and spring and include two nights' accommodation and several meals. ⊠ *River Rd., Plainfield 03781,* ☎ *603/675–6165,* WEB *www.homehillinn.com. 9 rooms, 2 suites, 1 seasonal cottage. Restaurant, putting green, tennis court,* *pool, cross-country skiing, meeting rooms; no room phones, no room TVs, no-smoking rooms. AE, D, MC, V. CP.*

The Arts

The restored 19th-century **Claremont Opera House** (⊠ Tremont Sq., Claremont, ☎ 603/542–4433) hosts plays and musicals from September to May.

Outdoor Activities and Sports

Northstar Canoe Livery (⊠ Rte. 12A, Balloch's Crossing, ☎ 603/542–5802) rents canoes for half- or full-day trips on the Connecticut River.

Charlestown

47 *20 mi south of Cornish, 63 mi northwest of Keene.*

Charlestown has the state's largest historic district. About 60 homes, handsome examples of Federal, Greek Revival, and Gothic Revival architecture, are clustered about the town center; 10 of them were built before 1800. Several merchants on the main street distribute brochures that contain an interesting walking tour of the district.

In 1747, the **Fort at No. 4** was an outpost on the periphery of Colonial civilization. That year fewer than 50 militia men at the fort withstood an attack by 400 French soldiers, ensuring that northern New England remained under British rule. Today, costumed interpreters at this living-history museum cook dinner over an open hearth and demonstrate weaving, gardening, and candle making. Each year the museum holds reenactments of militia musters and battles of the French and Indian War. ⊠ *Rte. 111, ½ mi north of Charlestown, ☎ 603/826–5700 or 888/367–8284, WEB www.fortat4.com. ☜ $8. ☉ Mid-May–Oct., daily 10–4.*

On a bright, breezy day you might want to detour to the **Morningside Flight Park** (⊠ off Rte. 12/11, ☎ 603/542–4416, WEB www.flymorningside.com), not necessarily to take hang-gliding lessons, although you could. You can watch the bright colors of the gliders as they take off from the school's 450-ft peak.

Lodging

MapleHedge. The innkeepers live in the oldest section of this home, which dates from about 1755. Guest rooms, in the 1820 Federal-style part, are furnished with carefully chosen antiques. The Cobalt Room showcases an extensive collection of cobalt glass, stencil-pattern wallpaper, and mahogany furnishings. In Lt. R.A.D.'s Quarters, Marine Corps memorabilia and dark pine wainscoting lend a military academy air. A three-course breakfast is served in the formal dining room. ⊠ *355 Main St. (Box 638, 03603), ☎ 800/962–7539, ☎ FAX 603/826–5237, WEB www.maplehedge.com. 5 rooms. Internet, business services; no room TVs, no kids under 12, no-smoking rooms. MC, V. Closed Jan.–Mar. BP.*

Walpole

48 *13 mi south of Charlestown.*

Walpole possesses one of the state's perfect town greens. This one, bordered by Elm and Washington streets, is surrounded by homes built about 1790, when the townsfolk constructed a canal around the Great Falls of the Connecticut River and brought commerce and wealth to the area. The town now has 3,200 inhabitants, more than a dozen of whom are millionaires.

OFF THE
BEATEN PATH

SUGARHOUSES – Maple-sugar season occurs about the first week in March when days become warmer but nights are still frigid. A drive along maple-lined back roads reveals thousands of taps and buckets catching the labored flow of unrefined sap. Plumes of smoke rise from nearby sugarhouses, where sugaring off, the process of boiling down this precious liquid, takes place. Many sugarhouses are open to the public; after a tour and demonstration, you can sample the syrup—with unsweetened doughnuts and maybe a pickle or over fresh snow. **Bacon's Sugar House** (⊠ 243 Dublin Rd., Jaffrey, ☎ 603/532–8836) ushers in the season with sugar parties that are open to the public. **Bascom Maple Farm** (⊠ Mt. Kingsbury, off Rte. 123A, Alstead, ☎ 603/835–6361) serves maple pecan pie and maple milk shakes. **Stuart & John's Sugar House & Pancake Restaurant** (⊠ Rtes. 12 and 63, Westmoreland, ☎ 603/399–4486) conducts a tour and serves a pancake breakfast.

Shopping

Boggy Meadow Farm (⊠ River Rd. S, ☎ 603/756–3300) sells the farm's Fanny Mason Farmstead Swiss cheese in its store. A window overlooks the cheese-making area. **Burdick Chocolates** (⊠ Main St., ☎ 603/756–3701) is renowned for its chocolate mice, which are shipped to trendy restaurants in New York and other cities. The staff also serves espresso and light lunches in the café; dinner is available some nights.

Keene

49 *17 mi southeast of Walpole; 20 mi northeast of Brattleboro, Vermont; 56 mi southwest of Manchester.*

Keene is the largest city in the state's southwest corner. Its rapidly gentrifying main street, with several engaging boutiques and cafés, is America's widest. Each year, on the Saturday before Halloween, locals use that street to hold a Pumpkin Festival, where they seek to retain their place in the record books for the most carved, lighted jack-o'-lanterns—more than 24,000 some years.

Keene State College, hub of the local arts community, is on the tree-lined main street. The **Thorne-Sagendorph Art Gallery** (☎ 603/358–2720) houses George Ridci's *Landscape* and presents traveling exhibitions. The **Putnam Lecture Hall** (☎ 603/358–2160) shows foreign and art films.

OFF THE
BEATEN PATH

CHESTERFIELD'S ROUTE 63 – If you're in the mood for a country drive or bike ride, head west from Keene along Route 9 to Route 63 (about 11 mi), and turn left toward the hilltop town of Chesterfield. This is an especially rewarding journey at sunset, as from many points along the road you can see west out over the Connecticut River valley and into Vermont. The village center consists of little more than a handful of dignified granite buildings and a small general store. You can loop back to Keene via Route 119 east in Hinsdale and then Route 10 north—the entire journey is about 40 mi.

Dining and Lodging

✕ **176 Main.** This grand old brick house near the campus of Keene State College in the heart of downtown has a menu that runs the gamut from pad Thai noodles to blackened catfish. The bar stocks an extensive selection of draft beers. Weekend brunch is a big event. ⊠ *176 Main St.,* ☎ *603/357–3100. AE, D, MC, V.*

✕▥ **Chesterfield Inn.** Surrounded by gardens, the Chesterfield sits above Route 9, the main road between Keene and Brattleboro, Vermont. Fine antiques and Colonial-style fabrics adorn the spacious guest quarters; eight have fireplaces, and eight have private decks or terraces that face the gardens and verdant Vermont hills. In the restaurant ($$$–$$$$) leg of venison with cranberry-port sauce and baked fusilli with roast squash, ham, spinach, and Asiago are among the highlights. ⊠ *Rte. 9 (Box 155, Chesterfield 03443),* ☎ *603/256–3211 or 800/365–5515,* FAX *603/256–6131,* WEB *www.chesterfieldinn.com. 13 rooms, 2 suites. Restaurant, some in-room hot tubs, some pets allowed. AE, D, MC, V. BP.*

🏨 **E. F. Lane Hotel.** Lending a rare touch of urbanity to the sleepy Monadnocks, this upscale redbrick hotel is inside a retrofitted department store on Keene's gentrified Main Street. It's within earshot of local church bells and is a 10-minute walk from Colony Marketplace. Rooms are furnished with reproduction Victorian antiques. The sky-lighted Salmon Chase Bistro and Lounge serves American and Continental fare. ⊠ *30 Main St., 03431,* ☎ *603/357–7070 or 888/ 300–5056,* FAX *603/357–7075,* WEB *www.someplacesdifferent.com/ eflane.htm. 33 rooms, 7 suites. Restaurant, in-room data ports, some in-room hot tubs, bar, Internet, meeting rooms. AE, D, MC, V. CP.*

🏨 **Carriage Barn.** Antiques and wide pine floors give this inn across from Keene State College charm. An expansive buffet is served each morning in the breakfast room, but many guests savor a second cup of coffee in the summerhouse. ⊠ *358 Main St., 03431,* ☎ *603/357– 3812,* WEB *www.carriagebarn.com. 4 rooms. No room phones, no room TVs, no smoking. AE, D, MC, V. CP.*

⛺ **Swanzey Lake Camping Area.** This 82-site campground for tents and RVs has a sandy beach, a dock, a ball field, a recreation area, and boat rentals. ⊠ *88 E. Shore Rd. (Box 115, W. Swanzey 03469),* ☎ *603/352–9880,* WEB *www.swanzeylake.com.*

Nightlife and the Arts

The **Colonial Theatre** (⊠ 95 Main St., ☎ 603/352–2033) opened in 1924 as a vaudeville stage. It now hosts folk and jazz concerts and has the town's largest movie screen. **Elm City Brew Co.** (⊠ 222 West St., ☎ 603/355–3335), at the Colony Mall, serves light food and draws a mix of college students and young professionals. The **Redfern Arts Center at Brickyard Pond** (⊠ 229 Main St., ☎ 603/358–2168) has year-round music, theater, and dance performances.

Outdoor Activities and Sports

The Monadnock region has more than 200 lakes and ponds. Rainbow trout, smallmouth and largemouth bass, and some northern pike swim in Chesterfield's **Spofford Lake. Goose Pond** in West Canaan, just north of Keene, holds smallmouth bass and white perch.

Shopping

ANTIQUES

The more than 200 dealers at **Antiques at Colony Mill** (⊠ 222 West St., ☎ 603/358–6343) sell everything from furniture to dolls. Just touring the six furniture- and collectibles-filled rooms is part of the fun at **Stone House Antiques** (⊠ Rte. 9, Chesterfield, ☎ 603/363–4866), a stately, restored stagecoach tavern.

BOOKS

The extraordinary collection of used books at the **Homestead Bookshop** (⊠ Rtes. 101 and 124, Marlborough, ☎ 603/876–4213) includes biographies, cookbooks, and town histories.

GIFTS

Country Artisans (⊠ 53 Main St., ☎ 603/352–6980) showcases the stoneware, textiles, prints, and glassware of regional artists. **Hannah Grimes Marketplace** (⊠ 42 Main St., ☎ 603/352–6862) overflows with mostly New Hampshire–made pottery, toys, kitchenwares, soaps, greeting cards, and specialty foods.

SHOPPING CENTERS

Colony Mill Marketplace (⊠ 222 West St., ☎ 603/357–1240), an old mill building, holds 30-plus stores and boutiques such as the Toadstool Bookshop, which carries many children's and regional travel and history books, and Ye Goodie Shoppe, whose specialty is handmade confections. There's also a food court.

Fitzwilliam

50 *14 mi southeast of Keene.*

A well-preserved historic district of Colonial and Federal-style houses has made the town of Fitzwilliam, on Route 119, the subject of thousands of postcards. Many show views of its landscape in winter, when a fine white snow settles on the oval common. Town business is still conducted in the 1817 meetinghouse.

The **Amos J. Blake House,** maintained by the Fitzwilliam Historical Society, contains a museum with period antiques and artifacts and the law office of its namesake. A town walking-tour pamphlet is available here, too. ⊠ *Village green,* ☎ *603/585–7742.* 🎟 *Free.* ☉ *Late May–mid-Oct., Sat. 1–4 or by appointment.*

More than 16 acres of wild rhododendrons bloom in mid-July at **Rhododendron State Park,** which has the largest concentration of *Rhododendron maximum* north of the Allegheny Mountains. Bring a picnic lunch and sit in a nearby pine grove, or follow the marked footpaths through the flowers. ⊠ *Off Rte. 12, 2½ mi northwest of village green,* ☎ *603/239–8153.* 🎟 *$3 weekends and holidays; free at other times.* ☉ *Daily 8–sunset.*

Lodging

🏨 **Inn at East Hill Farm.** If you have kids, you'll be happy at this 1830 farmhouse resort, where children are not only allowed but seem to be expected. They can milk the cows; feed the animals; and try arts and crafts, storytelling, and hiking. The innkeepers arrange weekly sleigh (or hay) and pony rides. Twice weekly in July and August, trips are scheduled to a nearby lake for boating, waterskiing, and fishing. Rates include most activities and three meals in a camplike dining hall. ⊠ *460 Monadnock St., Troy 03465,* ☎ *603/242–6495 or 800/242–6495,* FAX *603/242–7709,* WEB *www.east-hill-farm.com. 65 rooms. Restaurant, tennis court, 3 pools (1 indoor), wading pool, sauna, hiking, horseback riding, sleigh rides, recreation room, Internet, baby-sitting, some pets allowed (fee); no room phones, no TV in some rooms, no smoking. D, MC, V. FAP.*

$–$$ 🏨 **Hannah Davis House.** This 1820 house just off the village green has retained its Federal elegance. The original beehive oven still sits in the kitchen, and one suite has two Count Rumford fireplaces. Pumpkin pine floors, antique quilts, and braided rugs give the rooms cheer. Your host has the scoop on area antiquing. ⊠ *106 Rte. 119, 03447,* ☎ *603/585–3344. 3 rooms, 3 suites. No room phones, no room TVs, no smoking. MC, V. BP.*

Shopping

ANTIQUES

You'll find about 35 dealers at **Bloomin' Antiques** (⊠ Rte. 12, 3 mi south of Rte. 119, ☎ 603/585–6688). The wares of some 40 dealers are for sale at **Fitzwilliam Antiques Centre** (⊠ Rtes. 12 and 119, ☎ 603/585–9092).

Rindge

51 *8 mi southeast of Fitzwilliam.*

Tiny, hilltop Rindge overlooks the Monadnock region. Most diversions center on outdoor activities.

Cathedral of the Pines is an outdoor memorial to American soldiers and civilians who have sacrificed their lives in service to their country. There's an inspiring view of Mt. Monadnock and Mt. Kearsarge from the Altar of the Nation, which is composed of rock from every U.S. state and territory. All faiths are welcome to hold services here; organ meditations take place at midday from Tuesday to Thursday in July and August. The Memorial Bell Tower, with a carillon of bells from around the world, is built of native stone. Norman Rockwell designed the bronze tablets over the four arches. Flower gardens, an indoor chapel, and a museum of military memorabilia share the hilltop. ⊠ *75 Cathedral Entrance Rd., off Rte. 119,* ☎ *603/899–3300.* ☑ *Free; donations suggested.* ☉ *May–Oct., daily 9–5.*

Dining and Lodging

✕ **Lilly's on the Pond.** An appealing choice either for lunch or dinner, this rustic-timber dining room overlooks a small mill pond. The extensive menu of mostly American fare includes chicken sautéed with lime and tequila, shrimp scampi, and burgers. ⊠ *U.S. 202,* ☎ *603/ 899–3322. D, MC, V. Closed Mon.*

🏠 **Woodbound Inn.** A favorite with families and outdoors enthusiasts, this 1819 farmhouse became an inn in 1892. It occupies 200 acres on the shores of Contoocook Lake. Accommodations are functional but clean and cheerful; they range from quirky rooms in the main inn to modern hotel-style rooms in the Edgewood building to cabins by the water. ⊠ *62 Woodbound Rd., 03461,* ☎ FAX *603/532–8341,* ☎ *800/ 688–7770,* WEB *www.woodboundinn.com. 46 rooms, 42 with bath; 11 cottages. Restaurant, some refrigerators, lake, 9-hole golf course, tennis court, fishing, croquet, hiking, horseshoes, shuffleboard, volleyball, cross-country skiing, ice-skating, tobogganing, bar, recreation room. AE, MC, V. BP, MAP.*

🏠 **Cathedral House Bed and Breakfast.** This 1850s farmhouse on the edge of the Cathedral of the Pines was the home of the memorial's founders. Rooms have high ceilings, floral wallpaper, quilts, and well-stocked cookie jars, all of which create the sense that you've just arrived at Grandma's house. Innkeepers Don and Shirley Mahoney are well versed in area history. ⊠ *63 Cathedral Entrance Rd., 03461,* ☎ *603/899–6790 or 866/229–4519,* WEB *www.cathedralpines.com/ cathedralhouse.html. 5 rooms, 1 with bath. No room phones, no room TVs, no smoking. MC, V. BP.*

Jaffrey Center

52 *8 mi northwest of Rindge, 7 mi northeast of Fitzwilliam.*

Novelist Willa Cather came to Jaffrey Center in 1919 and stayed in the Shattuck Inn, which now stands empty on Old Meeting House Road. Not far from here, she pitched the tent in which she wrote several chapters of *My Antonia.* She returned nearly every summer thereafter until her death and was buried in the Old Burying Ground. **Amos Fortune Forum,** near the Old Burying Ground, brings nationally known speakers to the 1773 meetinghouse on summer evenings.

The oft-quoted statistic about Mt. Monadnock in **Monadnock State Park** is that it's America's most-climbed mountain—second in the world to Japan's Mt. Fuji. Whether this is true or not, locals agree that it's never lonely at the top. Some days more than 400 people crowd its bald peak. Monadnock rises to 3,165 ft, and on a clear day the hazy Boston skyline is visible from its summit. The park maintains picnic grounds and a small campground (RVs welcome, but no hookups). Five trailheads branch into more than two dozen trails of varying difficulty that wend their way to the top. Allow between three and four hours for any round-trip hike. A visitor center has free trail maps as well as exhibits documenting the mountain's history. ✉ *Off Rte. 124, 2½ mi north of Jaffrey Center, 03452,* ☎ *603/532–8862.* 🎫 *$3.* ⏲ *Daily dawn–dusk.*

Dining and Lodging

✕🏨 **Inn at Jaffrey Center.** Rooms here are painted in lively lavenders, yellows, or peaches. Although full of period furnishings, they have a hip sensibility as well as high-thread-count bedding, fluffy towels, and fine toiletries. The restaurant ($$–$$$; no lunch Sat.) offers a mix of American, Asian, and Italian dishes; good bets include the veal chops with fennel and honey, the pan-seared orange-ginger scallops, or the sole piccata. Sunday brunch is impressive. ✉ *379 Main St. (Box 484, 03452),* ☎ *603/532–7800 or 877/510–7019,* FAX *603/532–7900,* WEB *www.theinnatjaffreycenter.com. 9 rooms, 2 suites. Restaurant, bar; no TV in some rooms, no-smoking rooms. MC, V. CP.*

🏨 **Benjamin Prescott Inn.** Thanks to the working dairy farm surrounding this 1853 Colonial house—with its stenciling and wide pine floors—you feel as though you're miles out in the country rather than just minutes from Jaffrey Center. A full breakfast of Welsh miner's cakes and baked French toast with fruit and maple syrup prepares you for a day of antiquing or hiking. ✉ *Rte. 124, 03452,* ☎ *603/532–6637 or 888/950–6637,* FAX *603/532–6637,* WEB *www.benjaminprescottinn.com. 10 rooms, 3 suites. No room phones, no room TVs, no kids under 10, no-smoking rooms. AE, MC, V. BP.*

Peterborough

(53) *9 mi northeast of Jaffrey Center, 30 mi northwest of Nashua.*

The nation's first free public library opened in Peterborough in 1833. The town, which was the first in the region to be incorporated (1760), is still a commercial and cultural hub.

The **MacDowell Colony** was founded by the composer Edward MacDowell in 1907 as an artists' retreat. Willa Cather wrote part of *Death Comes for the Archbishop* here. Thornton Wilder was in residence when he wrote *Our Town* (Peterborough's resemblance to the play's Grover's Corners is no coincidence). Only a small portion of the still-active colony is open to visitors. ✉ *100 High St.,* ☎ *603/924–3886.*

In **Miller State Park,** 3 mi east of town, an auto road takes you almost 2,300 ft up Pack Monadnock Mountain. The road is closed mid-November through mid-April. ✉ *Rte. 101,* ☎ *603/924–3672.* 🎫 *$3.*

Dining and Lodging

✕ **Acqua Bistro.** People like to congregate at the long bar of this smart bistro. You might join them before dining on a thin-crust pizza or an entrée of wild Arctic char with roasted vegetable-dill couscous and basil-walnut pesto. Save room for the bittersweet chocolate soufflé. ✉ *9 School St.,* ☎ *603/924–9905. MC, V. No lunch.*

✕🏨 **Hancock Inn.** This Federal-style 1789 inn is the pride of the idyllic town it anchors. Common areas possess the warmth of a tavern, with fireplaces, big wing chairs, couches, dark-wood paneling, and Rufus Porter murals. Rooms, done in Colonial style, have antique four-poster beds. Updated Yankee fare is served by candlelight in the dining room

($$$–$$$$); a specialty is roast duckling with maple-whipped sweet potatoes and a blackberry cognac sauce. ⊠ *33 Main St. (Box 96, Hancock 03449)*, ☎ *603/525–3318*, FAX *603/525–9301*, WEB *www. hancockinn.com. 11 rooms, 4 suites. Restaurant, bar; no smoking. AE, D, DC, MC, V. BP.*

✕📷 **Inn at Crotched Mountain.** Three of the nine fireplaces in this 1822 inn—with stunning views of the Monadnocks—are in Colonial-style guest rooms. In the restaurant ($$–$$$) the menu lists cranberry-port pot roast as well as Indonesian charbroiled swordfish with a sauce of ginger, green pepper, onion, and lemon. Weekend rates include breakfast and dinner. ⊠ *534 Mountain Rd., Francestown 03043 (12 mi northeast of Peterborough)*, ☎ *603/588–6840*, FAX *603/588–6623. 13 rooms. Restaurant, 2 tennis courts, pool, cross-country skiing, bar, some pets allowed. No credit cards. Closed Apr. and Nov. BP, MAP.*

✕📷 **Birchwood Inn.** Thoreau slept here, probably on his way to climb Monadnock or to visit Jaffrey or Peterborough. Country furniture and handmade quilts outfit the bedrooms, just as they did in 1775, when the house was new. Allow time to linger in the dining room ($$$; reservations essential; BYOB; closed Sun.–Mon.; no lunch). Rufus Porter murals cover the walls; she-crab soup, shrimp Parmesan, and pumpkin-applesauce tea bread are among the choices. ⊠ *Rte. 45 (Box 197, Temple 03084)*, ☎ *603/878–3285*, FAX *603/878–2159. 7 rooms, 5 with bath. Restaurant; no room phones, no smoking. No credit cards. BP.*

📷 **Apple Gate Bed and Breakfast.** With 90 acres of orchards across the street, this B&B is appropriately named. The four rooms (and the resident yellow labrador) are named for types of apples. Some guest quarters are small, but Laura Ashley prints and stenciling make them cheery. The house dates from 1832, and the original beams and fireplace still grace the dining room. A music and reading room has a piano and a TV with a VCR tucked in the corner. From June to October, there's a two-night minimum on weekends. ⊠ *199 Upland Farm Rd., 03458,* ☎ FAX *603/924–6543. 4 rooms. No room phones, no room TVs, no kids under 12, no smoking. MC, V. BP.*

📷 **Jack Daniels Motor Inn.** With so many dowdy motels in southwestern New Hampshire, it's a pleasure to find one as bright and clean as the Jack Daniels, just ½ mi north of downtown Peterborough. The rooms are large and furnished with attractive cherrywood reproduction antiques. ⊠ *U.S. 202, 03458,* ☎ *603/924–7548,* FAX *603/924–7700,* WEB *www.jackdanielsmotorinn.com. 17 rooms. AE, D, MC, V.*

The Arts

From early July to mid-September, **Monadnock Music** (☎ 603/924–7610 or 800/868–9613) produces a series of solo recitals, chamber music concerts, and orchestra and opera performances by renowned musicians. Events take place throughout the area in the evening at 8 and on Sunday at 4; many are free. In winter, the **Peterborough Folk Society** (☎ 603/827–2905) presents folk music concerts. The **Peterborough Players** (⊠ Stearns Farm, off Middle Hancock Rd., ☎ 603/924–7585) have performed for more than 60 seasons. Productions are staged in a converted barn.

Outdoor Activities and Sports

You can rent bikes or get yours serviced at **Spokes and Slopes** (⊠ 30 Grove St., ☎ 603/924–9961). At the Donald Ross–designed **Tory Pines Golf Course** (⊠ off Rte. 47 [near Bennington town line], Francestown, ☎ 603/588–2923), you'll find a hilly, rolling 18-hole layout with nice view of the Monadnocks. Greens fee are $28–$38.

Shopping

The corporate headquarters and retail outlet of **Eastern Mountain**

Sports (⊠ 1 Vose Farm Rd., ☎ 603/924–7231) sells everything from tents to skis to hiking boots, gives hiking and camping classes, and conducts kayaking and canoeing demonstrations. **Harrisville Designs** (⊠ Mill Alley, Harrisville, ☎ 603/827–3333) sells hand-spun and hand-dyed yarn as well as looms. The shop also conducts classes in knitting and weaving. **North Gallery at Tewksbury's** (⊠ Rte. 101, ☎ 603/924–3224) stocks sconces, candlestick holders, and woodworkings. **Sharon Arts Downtown** (⊠ Depot Sq., ☎ 603/924–2787) has a gallery that exhibits locally made pottery, fabric, and woodwork and other crafts.

Antrim

54 *13 mi north of Peterborough.*

Little Antrim, an attractive mill town of neatly preened brick and clapboard structures, merits a look. Shovel, tool, and cutlery factories hummed along the Contoocook River's dammed rapids for many decades, and still today—at the south end of town, just off U.S. 202—the massive redbrick Monadnock Paper Company employs hundreds of locals. Its huge, red-neon sign glows purposefully, plumes of smoke rising from its mighty stacks day and night.

Dining and Lodging

✕ **Rynborn Restaurant and Blues Club.** You may be surprised to find a blues club in such a quiet community, but this place serves up some vibrant sounds. The menu consists of mostly regional American fare such as blackened Cajun shrimp and pecan-crusted chicken in a honey mustard sauce. ⊠ *76 Main St., ☎ 603/588–6162. AE, D, MC, V. No lunch.*

🏨 **Maplehurst Inn.** Since 1794 this lodging in the heart of Antrim has welcomed travelers. At first glance it looks like a slightly faded boardinghouse. But wander in and you'll find a well-kept hotel with 14 comfy rooms; one has a fireplace, and several have claw-foot tubs. A fireplace glows all winter long in the homey tavern, which serves a standard lineup of American and Continental dishes. ⊠ *67 Main St. (Box 155, 03440), ☎ FAX 603/588–8000, WEB www.bitwizard.com/maplehurst. 14 rooms. Restaurant; no TV in some rooms, no-smoking rooms. AE, MC, V. CP.*

Hillsborough

55 *8 mi northeast of Antrim, 23 mi southwest of Concord.*

Hillsborough comprises four villages, the most prominent of which lies along the Contoocook River and grew up around a thriving woolen and hosiery industry in the mid-1800s. This section, which is really considered Hillsborough proper, is what you'll see as you roll through town on Route 9/U.S. 202.

Turn north from downtown up School Street, however, and continue 3 mi past Fox State Forest to reach one of the state's best-preserved historic districts, Hillsborough Center, where 18th-century houses surround a green. Continue north 6 mi through the similarly quaint village of East Washington, and another 6 mi to reach the Colonial town center of Washington. One of the highest-elevation villages in New Hampshire, this picturesque arrangement of white clapboard buildings made the cover of *National Geographic* several years back. You can loop back to Hillsborough proper via Route 31 south.

The nation's 14th president, Franklin Pierce, was born in Hillsborough and lived here until he married. The **Pierce Homestead,** operated by the Hillsborough Historical Society, welcomes visitors for guided tours. The house is much as it was during Pierce's life. ⊠ *Rte. 31 just north*

of Rte. 9, ☎ 603/478–3165, WEB *www.conknet.com/~hillsboro/pierce.*
🖼 *$3.* ☉ *June and Sept., Sat. 10–4, Sun. 1–4; July–Aug., Mon.–Sat. 10–4, Sun. 1–4.*

NEED A BREAK?	Families have been coming to **Diamond Acres Dairy Bar** (⊠ Rte. 9, ¼ mi west of Rte. 31, ☎ 603/478–3121), a short-order shanty attached to a gas station, for years to devour superfresh clam platters, lobster rolls, and frozen sweets.

Outdoor Activities and Sports
Fox State Forest (⊠ Center Rd., ☎ 603/464–3453) has 20 mi of hiking trails and an observation tower.

Shopping
At **Gibson Pewter** (⊠ 18 E. Washington Rd., ☎ 603/464–3410), Raymond Gibson and his son Jonathan create and sell museum-quality pewter pieces.

Henniker

56 *7 mi northeast of Hillsborough, 16 mi southwest of Concord.*

Governor Wentworth, New Hampshire's first Royal Governor, named this town in honor of his friend John Henniker, a London merchant and member of the British Parliament (residents delight in their town's status as "the only Henniker in the world"). Once a mill town producing bicycle rims and other light-industrial items, Henniker reinvented itself after the factories were damaged, first by spring floods in 1936 and then by the hurricane and flood of 1938. New England College was established in the following decade. One of the area's covered bridges is on its campus.

Dining and Lodging
✕🏠 **Colby Hill Inn.** There's no shortage of relaxing activities at this farmhouse: you can curl up with a book by the parlor fireplace, stroll through the gardens and meadows, or play badminton out back. Rooms in the main house contain antiques, Colonial reproductions, and lace curtains. In carriage-house rooms, plain country furnishings, stenciled walls, and exposed beams are the norm. The frequently changing menu ($$$–$$$$) is excellent—one fine choice is boneless breast of chicken stuffed with Maine lobster, leeks, and Boursin. ⊠ *3 The Oaks (Box 779, 03242),* ☎ *603/428–3281 or 800/531–0330,* FAX *603/428–9218,* WEB *www.colbyhillinn.com. 16 rooms. Restaurant, in-room data ports, pool, badminton, recreation room; no smoking. AE, D, DC, MC, V. BP.*

✕🏠 **Meeting House Inn & Restaurant.** The owners of this 200-year-old farmhouse tout it as a lovers' getaway and start each day by serving you breakfast in bed. The old barn has become a restaurant ($$$; closed Mon.–Tues.; no dinner Sun.) that specializes in leisurely, romantic dining. Try seared medallions of pork tenderloin with spiced apples, toasted pecans, and a maple cream sauce; the chocolate-raspberry frozen mousse comes in the shape of a heart. ⊠ *Rte. 114/Flanders Rd., 03242,* ☎ *603/428–3228,* FAX *603/428–6334,* WEB *www.conknet.com/ ~meetinghouse. 6 rooms. Restaurant, hot tub, sauna; no smoking. MC, V. BP.*

Nightlife
There's often live folk music at **Daniel's Restaurant and Pub** (⊠ Main St., ☎ 603/428–7621), which occupies a rambling wood-frame building with great views of the Contoocook River.

Shopping

The **Fiber Studio** (⊠ 9 Foster Hill Rd., ☎ 603/428–7830) sells beads, hand-spun natural-fiber yarns, spinning equipment, and looms.

Ski Area

PATS PEAK

A quick trip up I–93 from the Mass border, Pats Peak is geared to families. Base facilities are rustic, and friendly personal attention is the rule. ⊠ *Rte. 114, 03242,* ☎ *603/428–3245; 888/728–7732 snow conditions;* WEB *www.patspeak.com.*

Downhill. Despite Pats Peak's short 710 vertical ft rise, the 21 trails and slopes have something for everyone. New skiers and snowboarders can take advantage of a wide slope and several short trails; intermediates have wider trails from the top; and experts have a couple of real thrillers. Night skiing and snowboarding take place in January and February. One triple and three double chairlifts and three surface lifts serve the runs. Pats Peak also has afternoon snowtubing on weekends and holidays.

Child care. The nursery takes children ages 6 months–5 years. Ski programs operate on weekends and during vacations for kids 4–12; all-day lessons for self-sufficient skiers in this age range are scheduled daily.

Western and Central New Hampshire A to Z

To research prices, get advice from other travelers, and book travel arrangements, visit www.fodors.com

AIRPORTS

Manchester Airport is the main airport in western and central New Hampshire. Lebanon Municipal Airport, near Dartmouth College, is served by Colgan Air (an affiliate of US Airways) from Boston and by US Airways Express from Philadelphia and New York. Private planes and charters fly to Keene Dillant-Hopkins Airport.

➤ AIRPORT INFORMATION: **Keene Dillant-Hopkins Airport** (⊠ 80 Airport Rd., off Rte. 12 south of Keene, North Swanzey, ☎ 603/357–9835). **Lebanon Municipal Airport** (⊠ 5 Airpark Rd., West Lebanon, ☎ 603/298–8878).

BUS TRAVEL

Concord Trailways runs from Concord, Londonderry, and Manchester to Boston. Dartmouth Coach connects Boston's South Station and Logan Airport with Hanover, Lebanon, and New London. Vermont Transit links Nashua, Manchester, Concord, Keene, and White River Junction, Vermont (near Hanover) with major cities in the eastern United States. Advance Transit shuttles between Hanover, West Lebanon, Enfield, Canaan, and Lebanon. Keene City Express buses serves the town from 6 AM to 7:30 PM. Manchester Transit Authority has hourly local bus service around town and to Bedford from 6 AM to 6 PM.

➤ BUS INFORMATION: **Advance Transit** (☎ 802/295–1824). **Concord Trailways** (☎ 603/228–3300 or 800/639–3317). **Dartmouth Coach** (☎ 603/448–2800 or 800/637–0123 out of state). **Keene City Express** (☎ 603/352–8494). **Manchester Transit Authority** (☎ 603/623–8801). **Vermont Transit** (☎ 800/552–8737).

CAR TRAVEL

Most people who travel up from Massachusetts do so on I–93, which passes through Manchester and Concord before cutting a path through the White Mountains. I–89 connects Concord, in the Merrimack Valley, with Vermont. Route 12 runs north–south along the Connecticut River. Farther south, Route 101 connects Keene and Manchester, then continues to the seacoast. On the western border of the state, Routes 12 and 12A are picturesque but slow-moving. U.S. 4 crosses the region, winding between Lebanon and the seacoast. Other pretty drives include Routes 101, 202, and 10.

EMERGENCIES

➤ HOSPITALS: **Cheshire Medical Center** (✉ 580 Court St., Keene, ☎ 603/354–5400). **Concord Hospital** (✉ 250 Pleasant St., Concord, ☎ 603/225–2711). **Dartmouth Hitchcock Medical Center** (✉ 1 Medical Center Dr., Lebanon, ☎ 603/650–5000). **Elliot Hospital** (✉ 1 Elliot Way, Manchester, ☎ 603/669–5300). **Monadnock Community Hospital** (✉ 452 Old Street Rd., Peterborough, ☎ 603/924–7191). **Southern New Hampshire Medical Center** (✉ 8 Prospect St., Nashua, ☎ 603/577–2200).

➤ 24-HOUR PHARMACIES: **CVS Pharmacy** (✉ 271 Mammoth Rd., Manchester, ☎ 603/623–0347; ✉ 240–242 Main St., Nashua, ☎ 603/886–1798).

LODGING

Town & Country Realty has a wide range of Lake Sunapee–area long-term rentals.

APARTMENT AND VILLA RENTALS

➤ LOCAL AGENT: **Town & Country Realty** (☎ 603/763–2334 or 800/639–9960).

OUTDOOR ACTIVITIES AND SPORTS

FISHING

For word on what's biting where, contact the New Hampshire Fish and Game Department.

➤ CONTACT: **New Hampshire Fish and Game Department** (☎ 603/271–3211).

TOURS

Narrated cruises aboard the M/V *Mt. Sunapee II* provide a closer look at Lake Sunapee's history and mountain scenery. Dinner cruises are held on the M/V *Kearsarge*. Both boats leave from the dock at Sunapee Harbor and run from late May through mid-October.

➤ CONTACTS: **M/V *Kearsarge*** (☎ 603/763–4030). **M/V *Mt. Sunapee II*** (✉ Main St., Sunapee, ☎ 603/763–4030).

VISITOR INFORMATION

➤ TOURIST INFORMATION: **Concord Chamber of Commerce** (✉ 40 Commercial St., Concord 03301, ☎ 603/224–2508, WEB www.concordnhchamber.com). **Keene Chamber of Commerce** (✉ 48 Central Sq., Keene 03431, ☎ 603/352–1303). **Lake Sunapee Region Chamber of Commerce** (✉ Box 532, Sunapee 03782, ☎ 603/526–6575 or 877/526–6575, WEB sunapeevacations.com). **Manchester Chamber of Commerce** (✉ 889 Elm St., Manchester 03101, ☎ 603/666–6600, WEB www.manchester-chamber.org). **Monadnock Travel Council** (✉ 58 Central Sq. [Box 358, Keene 03431], ☎ 800/432–7864, WEB www.monadnocktravel.com).

NEW HAMPSHIRE A TO Z

To research prices, get advice from other travelers, and book travel arrangements, visit www.fodors.com

AIRPORTS

Manchester Airport, the state's largest airport, has rapidly become a cost-effective, hassle-free alternative to Boston's Logan International

Airport. It has nonstop service to more than 20 cities thanks to scheduled flights by Air Canada, American Eagle, Continental, Delta, Northwest, Southwest, United, and US Airways. Lebanon Municipal Airport has commuter flights by US Airways.

➤ AIRPORT INFORMATION: **Lebanon Municipal Airport** (✉ 5 Airpark Rd., West Lebanon, ☎ 603/298–8878).

Manchester Airport (✉ 1 Airport Rd., Manchester 03103, ☎ 603/624–6539).

BIKE TRAVEL

Bike the Whites, Monadnock Bicycle Touring, and New England Hiking Holidays organize bike tours.

➤ CONTACTS: **Bike the Whites** (☎ 800/448–3534, WEB www.bikethewhites.com). **Monadnock Bicycle Touring** (☎ 603/827–3925). **New England Hiking Holidays** (☎ 603/356–9696 or 800/869–0949, WEB www.nehikingholidays.com).

BUS TRAVEL

C&J Trailways serves the seacoast area of New Hampshire. Concord Trailways links Boston's South Station and Logan Airport with points all along I–93 and, around Lake Winnipesaukee and the eastern White Mountains, along Route 16. Vermont Transit links the cities of western and southern New Hampshire with major cities in the eastern United States.

➤ BUS INFORMATION: **C&J Trailways** (☎ 603/430–1100 or 800/258–7111). **Concord Trailways** (☎ 603/228–3300 or 800/639–3317). **Vermont Transit** (☎ 800/552–8737).

CAR TRAVEL

Interstate 93 is the principal north–south route through Manchester, Concord, and central New Hampshire. To the west, I–91 traces the Vermont–New Hampshire border. To the east, I–95, which is a toll road, passes through southern New Hampshire's coastal area on its way from Massachusetts to Maine. Interstate 89 travels from Concord to Montpelier and Burlington, Vermont.

Speed limits on interstate and limited-access highways are generally 65 mph, except in heavily settled areas, where 55 mph is the norm. On state and U.S. routes, speed limits vary considerably. On any given stretch, the limit may be anywhere from 25 mph to 55 mph, so watch the signs carefully. Right turns are permitted on red lights unless indicated.

Official state maps are available free from the New Hampshire Office of Travel and Tourism Development. They cite useful telephone numbers and information about bike, snowmobile, and scenic routes.

EMERGENCIES

➤ CONTACTS: **Ambulance, fire, police** (☎ 911).

LODGING
CAMPING

New Hampshire Campground Owners Association publishes a guide to private, state, and national-forest campgrounds.

➤ CONTACT: **New Hampshire Campground Owners Association** (✉ Box 320, Twin Mountain 03595, ☎ 603/846–5511 or 800/822–6764, WEB www.ucampnh.com).

OUTDOOR ACTIVITIES AND SPORTS
BIRD-WATCHING

Audubon Society of New Hampshire schedules monthly field trips throughout the state and a fall bird-watching tour to Star Isle and other parts of the Isles of Shoals.

➤ CONTACT: **Audubon Society of New Hampshire** (✉ 3 Silk Farm Rd., Concord 03301, ☎ 603/224–9909, WEB www.nhaudubon.org).

FISHING

For information about fishing and licenses, call the New Hampshire Fish and Game Department.

➤ CONTACT: **New Hampshire Fish and Game Department** (☎ 603/271–3211).

FOLIAGE AND SNOW HOT LINES

A snow and fall-foliage hot line is regularly updated with information on leaf-peeping and skiing conditions.

➤ CONTACT: **Foliage and Snow hot line** (☎ 800/258–3608).

SKIING

Ski New Hampshire has information on downhill and cross-country snow sports in the state.

➤ CONTACT: **Ski New Hampshire** (✉ Box 10, North Woodstock 03262, ☎ 603/745–9396 or 800/887–5464, WEB www.skinh.com).

VISITOR INFORMATION

➤ TOURIST INFORMATION: **New Hampshire Office of Travel and Tourism Development** (✉ 172 Pembroke Rd. [Box 1856, Concord 03302], ☎ 603/271–2343; 800/386–4664 free vacation packet; WEB www.visitnh. gov). **New Hampshire Parks Department** (☎ 603/271–3556, WEB www. nhparks.state.nh.us). **New Hampshire State Council on the Arts** (✉ 40 N. Main St., Concord 03301, ☎ 603/271–2789, WEB www.state. nh.us/nharts).

4 VERMONT

Southern Vermont has manicured landscapes, immaculate villages, and summer theaters, as well as a surprisingly large chunk of wilderness in the Green Mountain National Forest. Central Vermont is home to the state's largest ski resort, Killington, along with the rolling farmland vistas of the lower Lake Champlain valley. Up north, Vermont attractions include the state's largest city, cosmopolitan and collegiate Burlington; the nation's smallest state capital, Montpelier; the legendary slopes of Stowe; and the leafy back roads of the Northeast Kingdom.

Updated by
Kay and Bill
Scheller

E VERYWHERE YOU LOOK IN VERMONT, the evidence is clear: this is not the state it was 30 years ago. That may be true for the rest of New England as well, but the contrasts between the present and recent past seem all the more sharply drawn in the Green Mountain State, if only because an aura of timelessness has always been at the heart of the Vermont image. Vermont was where all the quirks and virtues outsiders associate with up-country New England were supposed to reside. It was where the Yankees were Yankee-est and where cows outnumbered people.

Not that you should be alarmed if you haven't been here in a while; Vermont hasn't become southern California, or even, for that matter, southern New Hampshire. The state's population, which increased from 335,000 to only 390,000 from 1860 to 1960, began to climb sharply as interstate highways and resort development made their impact. By 1990 the state had 563,000 residents; today, a population of approximately 600,000 indicates some leveling off in the rate of growth. This is still the most rural state in the Union (meaning that it has the smallest percentage of citizens living in statistically defined metropolitan areas), and it still turns out most of New England's milk, even though people finally outnumber cows. Vermont remains a place where cars occasionally have to stop while a dairy farmer walks his herd across a secondary road; and up in Essex County, in what George Aiken dubbed the Northeast Kingdom, there are townships with zero population. And the kind of scrupulous, straightforward, plainspoken politics practiced by Governor (later Senator) Aiken for 50 years has not become outmoded in a state that still turns out on town-meeting day.

How has Vermont changed? In strictly physical terms, the most obvious transformations have taken place in and around the two major cities, Burlington and Rutland, and near the larger ski resorts, such as Stowe, Killington, Stratton, and Mt. Snow. Burlington's Church Street, once a paradigm of all the sleepy redbrick shopping thoroughfares in northern New England, is now a pedestrian mall with chic bistros; outside the city, suburban development has supplanted farms in towns where someone's trip to Burlington might once have been an item in a weekly newspaper. As for the ski areas, it's no longer enough simply to have the latest in chairlift technology. Slope-side hotels and condos have boomed, especially in the southern part of the state, turning ski areas into big-time resort destinations. And once-sleepy Manchester has become one of New England's factory-outlet meccas.

The real metamorphosis in the Green Mountains, however, has to do more with style, with the personality of the place, than with development. The past couple of decades have seen a tremendous influx of outsiders—not only skiers and "leaf peepers" but people who have come to stay year-round—and many of them are determined either to freshen the local scene with their own idiosyncrasies or to make Vermont even more like Vermont than they found it. On the one hand, this translates into the fact that Vermont is the only state represented in Washington by an independent socialist congressman; on the other, it means that sheep farming has been reintroduced to the state, largely to provide a high-quality product for the hand-weaving industry.

This ties in with another local phenomenon, one best described as Made in Vermont. Once upon a time, maple syrup and sharp cheddar cheese were the products that carried Vermont's name to the world. The market niche that they created has since been widened by Vermonters—a great many of them refugees from more hectic arenas of commerce—

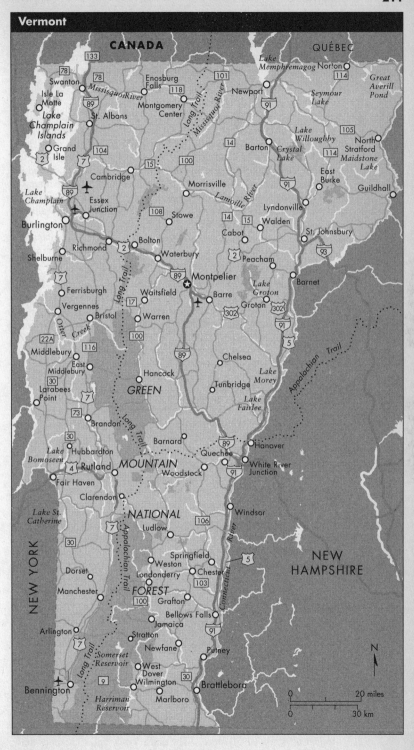

Vermont

who now sell a plethora of goods with the ineffable cachet of Vermont manufacture, from Vermont wood toys and Vermont apple wines to Vermont chocolates and even Vermont vodka. The most successful Made in Vermont product is Ben & Jerry's ice cream, which absorbs a significant portion of Vermont's milk output.

The character and appearance of the landscape are what most readily ignite preservationists' passions in Vermont. Farming may be changing—sheep, goats, llamas, emus, and even elk graze the Green Mountain foothills—but farms are farms, valued for their open-space counterpoint to Vermont forests and villages. The Vermont Land Trust has saved thousands of acres of farmland through the purchase of development rights; meanwhile, vast tracts of northern woodlands have been preserved for wildlife habitat, recreation, and low-impact forestry. The challenge is to bring Vermont into the 21st century while making sure it still looks like Vermont. The model might be an old farmhouse, with fiber-optic cables hidden in its walls.

Pleasures and Pastimes

Dining

Over the past few years, Vermont chefs have been working hard to fulfill two distinct responsibilities. One is the need to honor the traditions of Yankee cooking— the realm of pot roast and Indian pudding, sticky buns, and homemade corn relish. Two is to satisfy the sophisticated palate of travelers and residents, who seek ethnic cuisines, lighter adaptations of classics, and new American treatments of seasonal ingredients that now characterize urban menus.

The more ambitious restaurants and inn kitchens have not only managed to balance these two gastronomic imperatives but also have succeeded in combining them. The trick is to take an innovative approach with Vermont game and local produce, introduce fresh herbs and other seasonings, and change menus to suit the season. Look for imaginative approaches to native New England foods such as fiddlehead ferns (available only for a short time in the spring), maple syrup (Vermont is the largest U.S. producer), dairy products (especially cheese), native fruits and berries, "new Vermont" products such as salsa and salad dressings, and venison, quail, pheasant, and other game.

Your chances of finding a table for dinner vary with the season: many restaurants have lengthy waits during peak seasons (when it's always a good idea to make a reservation) and then shut down during the slow months of April and November. Some of the best dining is found at country inns.

CATEGORY	COST*
$$$$	over $25
$$$	$17–$25
$$	$9–$16
$	under $9

per person, for a main-course dinner

Lodging

Vermont's largest hotels are in Burlington and near the major ski resorts. Burlington has a dearth of inns and bed-and-breakfasts, though chain hotels provide dependable accommodations. Elsewhere you'll find inns, B&Bs, and small motels. The many lovely and sometimes quite luxurious inns and B&Bs provide what many people consider the quintessential Vermont lodging experience. Rates are highest during foliage season, from late September to mid-October, and lowest in late spring and November, when many properties close. Many of the larger hotels offer package rates.

CATEGORY	COST*
$$$$	over $180
$$$	$130–$180
$$	$80–$130
$	under $80

All prices are for a standard double room during peak season and not including tax or gratuities. Some inns add a 15% service charge.

National Forests

The two sections of the 355,000-acre Green Mountain National Forest (GMNF) are central and southern Vermont's primary stronghold of woodland and high mountain terrain. Like all other national forests, it contains sections on which timber leases are sometimes granted, but it's possible to travel through much of this preserve without seeing significant evidence of human intrusion. In addition to the paved public highways that traverse the GMNF, many of the occasional logging roads are maintained for public use, and although unpaved, these are kept in good condition during snow-free times of the year.

The Forest Service maintains a number of picnic areas and primitive campgrounds; complete information is available from the Forest Supervisor. Fishing, subject to state laws and seasonal closings and limits, is allowed throughout the GMNF. Canoeing, cross-country skiing, and hiking are also popular; the Appalachian and Long trails run the length of the forest. Snowmobiles and other forms of motorized transportation, such as all-terrain vehicles, are permitted on marked trails, except within roadless areas designated as wilderness.

Outdoor Activities and Sports

BIKING

Vermont, especially the often deserted roads of the Northeast Kingdom, is great bicycle-touring country. Many companies lead weekend tours and weeklong trips throughout the state. If you'd like to go it on your own, most chambers of commerce have brochures highlighting good cycling routes in their area, including *Vermont Life* magazine's "Bicycle Vermont" map and guide, and many bookstores sell *25 Bicycle Tours in Vermont* by John Freidin.

FISHING

Central Vermont is the heart of the state's warm-water lake and pond fishing. Harriman and Somerset reservoirs have both warm- and cold-water species; Harriman has a greater variety. Lake Dunmore produced the state-record rainbow trout; Lakes Bomoseen and St. Catherine are good for rainbows and largemouth bass. In the east, Lakes Fairlee and Morey hold bass, perch, and chain pickerel, while the lower part of the Connecticut River contains smallmouth bass, walleye, and perch; shad are returning via the fish ladders at Vernon and Bellows Falls.

In northern Vermont, rainbow and brown trout inhabit the Missisquoi, Lamoille, Winooski, and Willoughby rivers. Lakes Seymour, Willoughby, and Memphremagog and Great Averill Pond in the Northeast Kingdom are good for salmon and lake trout. The Dog River near Montpelier has one of the best wild populations of brown trout in the state, and landlocked Atlantic salmon are returning to the Clyde River following removal of a controversial dam.

Lake Champlain, stocked annually with salmon and lake trout, has become the state's ice-fishing capital; walleye, bass, pike, and channel catfish are also taken. Ice fishing is also popular on Lake Memphremagog.

SKIING

The Green Mountains run through the middle of Vermont like a bumpy spine, visible from almost every point in the state; generous accumulations of snow make the mountains an ideal site for skiing. Increased snowmaking capacity and improved, high-tech computerized equipment at many areas virtually assure a good day on the slopes. Vermont has 26 alpine ski resorts with nearly 1,000 trails and some 5,000 acres of skiable terrain. Combined, the resorts operate nearly 200 lifts and have the capacity to carry some 215,000 skiers per hour. Though grooming is sophisticated at all Vermont areas, conditions usually run to a typically Eastern hard pack, with powder a rare luxury and ice a bugbear after January thaw. The best advice for skiing in Vermont is to keep your skis well tuned.

Route 100 is also known as Skier's Highway, passing by 13 of the state's ski areas. Vermont's major resorts are Stowe, Jay Peak, Sugarbush, Killington, Okemo, Mt. Snow, and Stratton. Midsize, less-hectic areas to consider include Ascutney, Bromley, Smugglers' Notch, Pico, Mad River Glen, Burke Mountain, and Bolton Valley Holiday Resort.

Exploring Vermont

Vermont can be divided into three regions. The southern part of the state, flanked by Bennington on the west and Brattleboro on the east, played an important role in Vermont's Revolutionary War–era drive to independence (yes, there was once a Republic of Vermont) and its eventual statehood. The central part is characterized by rugged mountains and the gently rolling dairy lands near Lake Champlain. Northern Vermont is the site of the state's capital, Montpelier, and its largest city, Burlington, yet it is also home to Vermont's most rural area, the Northeast Kingdom.

Numbers in the text correspond to numbers in the margin and on the Southern Vermont, Central Vermont, and Northern Vermont maps.

Great Itineraries

There are many ways to take advantage of Vermont's beauty—skiing or hiking its mountains, biking or driving its back roads, fishing or sailing its waters, shopping for local products, visiting its museums and sights, or simply finding the perfect inn and never leaving the front porch. Distances in Vermont are relatively short, yet the mountains and many back roads will slow a traveler's pace. You can see a representative north–south section of Vermont in a few days; if you have up to a week you can hit the highlights around the state.

IF YOU HAVE 3 DAYS

Spend a few hours in historic **Bennington** ⑤ in the southern part of Vermont; then travel north to see Hildene and stay in 🏨 **Manchester** ⑦. On your second day take Route 100 through Weston and travel north through the Green Mountains to Route 125, where you turn west to explore 🏨 **Middlebury** ㉖. On day three, enter the Champlain Valley, which has views of the Adirondack Mountains to the west. Stop at Shelburne Farms and carry on to **Burlington** ㊲; catch the sunset from the waterfront and take a walk on Church Street.

IF YOU HAVE 5 TO 7 DAYS

You can make several side trips off Route 100 and also visit the Northeast Kingdom on a trip of this length. Visit **Bennington** ⑤ and 🏨 **Manchester** ⑦ on day one. Spend your second day walking around the small towns of **Chester** ⑫ and 🏨 **Grafton** ⑬. On day three head north to explore **Woodstock** ㉑ and 🏨 **Quechee** ⑳, stopping at either the Billings Farm Museum and Marsh-Billings-Rockefeller National Historical Park or the Vermont Institute of Natural Science. Head leisurely on your fourth day toward **Middlebury** ㉖, along one of Vermont's most inspiring mountain drives, Route 125 west of Route 100. Between Hancock and Middlebury, you'll pass nature trails and the picnic spot at Texas Falls Recreation Area, then traverse a moderately steep mountain pass. Spend day five in **Burlington** ㊲. On day six head east to **Waterbury** ㉛ and then north to **Stowe** ㉝ and Mt. Mansfield for a full day. Begin your last day with a few hours in **Montpelier** ㉚ on your way to **Peacham** ㊽, **St. Johnsbury** ㊼, **Lake Willoughby** ㊺, and the serenity and back roads of the Northeast Kingdom. Especially noteworthy are U.S. 5, Route 5A, and Route 14.

When to Tour Vermont

The number of visitors and the rates for lodging reach their peaks along with the color of the leaves during foliage season, from late September to mid-October. But if you have never seen a kaleidoscope of autumn colors, it is worth braving the slow-moving traffic and paying the extra money. In summer the state is lush and green. Winter, of course, is high season at Vermont's ski resorts. Rates are lowest in late spring and November, although many properties close during these times.

SOUTHERN VERMONT

The Vermont tradition of independence and rebellion began in southern Vermont. Many towns founded in the early 18th century as frontier outposts or fortifications were later important as trading centers. In the western region the Green Mountain Boys fought off both the British and the claims of land-hungry New Yorkers—some say their descendants are still fighting. In the 19th century, as many towns turned to manufacturing, the farmers here retreated to hillier regions and, as the modern ski and summer-home booms got under way, retreated even farther.

The first thing you'll notice upon entering the state is the conspicuous lack of billboards along the highways and roads. The foresight back in the 1960s to prohibit them has made for a refreshing absence of aggressive visual clutter that allows unencumbered views of working farmland, fresh-as-paint villages, and quiet back roads—but does not hide the reality of abandoned dairy barns, bustling ski resorts, and strip-mall sprawl. Reaching Vermont via the well-settled districts around Brattleboro and Bennington, you'll discover beautifully desolate woodlands nestled between these gateways. Much of the Green Mountain National Forest's southern section occupies rugged uplands where homesteads and farms once thrived more than 400 years ago.

The towns are listed in counterclockwise order, beginning in the east, south of the junction of I–91 and Route 9 in Brattleboro, and following the southern boundary of the state toward Bennington, then north up to Manchester and Weston and south back to Newfane.

Brattleboro

❶ *60 mi south of White River Junction.*

Its downtown bustling with activity, Brattleboro, with about 13,000 inhabitants, is the center of commerce for southeastern Vermont. This town at the confluence of the West and Connecticut rivers originated as a frontier scouting post and became a thriving industrial center and resort town in the 1800s. Since the late 1960s the area has drawn political activists and a raft of earnest counterculturists.

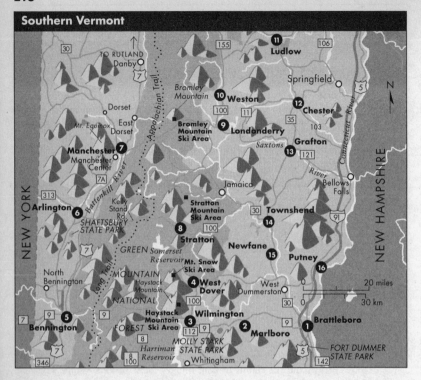

Southern Vermont

The **Brattleboro Museum and Art Center,** housed in historic Union Station, presents changing exhibits created by locally, nationally, and internationally renowned artists. Each year the museum focuses on a unifying theme, which provides a structure for that year's exhibits and programs. The theme for 2002 is "Earth, Air, Fire, Water." ⊠ *Vernon and Main Sts.,* ☎ *802/257-0124,* ⓦⒺⒷ *www.brattleboromuseum.org.* 🖾 *$3.* ☽ *May–Dec., Tues.–Sun. noon–6.*

Dining and Lodging

$$$ ✕ **Peter Havens.** In a town better known for tofu than toniness, this chic little bistro knows just what to do with a filet mignon—serve it with Roquefort walnut butter, of course. Look for the house-cured gravlax made with lemon vodka and fresh seasonal seafood, which even includes a spring fling with soft-shell crabs. The wine list is superb. ⊠ *32 Elliot St.,* ☎ *802/257-3333. MC, V. Closed Sun.–Mon. No lunch.*

$$ ✕ **Sarkis Market.** Gail Sarkis's Lebanese grandmother gave her many of the recipes she uses to create Middle Eastern delicacies such as falafel, stuffed grape leaves, hummus, and *kibbe*—a layered meat loaf stuffed with ground lamb, pine nuts, and onions. Undecided about what to order? Go for the combination plate and finish with a wedge of homemade baklava. ⊠ *50 Elliot St.,* ☎ *802/258-4906. AE, MC, V. Call for hrs.*

$–$$ ✕ **Top of the Hill Grill.** Hickory-smoked ribs and beef brisket, apple smoked turkey, and pulled pork are a few of the "divinely inspired" favorites at this barbecue just out of town. Those looking to cross the border can try the tortilla roll-ups and fajitas. Larger parties can opt for "family-style" dinners. Homemade pecan pie is the dessert of choice. You can sit indoors in the informal dining with big windows, but the best seats are outdoors at picnic tables overlooking the West River. ⊠ *632 Putney Rd.,* ☎ *802/258-9178. No credit cards. Closed Oct.–Apr.*

$ ✕ **Common Ground.** The political posters and concert fliers that line the staircase here attest to Vermont's progressive element. The stairs lead to loftlike, rough-hewn dining rooms. Owned cooperatively by the staff and volunteer-run, this mostly organic vegetarian restaurant serves cashew burgers, veggie stir-fries, curries, hot soup and stew, and a humble bowl of brown rice. All the desserts, including a chocolate cake with peanut butter frosting, are made without white sugar. Sunday brunch is served 11–2. ⊠ *25 Elliot St.,* ☎ *802/257–0855. No credit cards. Closed Mon.–Wed. No lunch Thurs.–Sat.*

$$ ╳⊡ **Latchis Hotel.** Front rooms at this 1938 downtown Art Deco landmark overlook busy—and often noisy—Main Street. All the rooms are furnished comfortably, many with their original restored 1930s furniture; the suites are a bargain. Muffins are delivered to your room late in the evening or early in the morning, and you can catch a movie under the zodiac ceiling of the adjoining Latchis Theater. The hotel's restaurant, ($$) the Lucca Brasserie and Bistro, serves lunch on weekends and dinner nightly. ⊠ *50 Main St., 05301,* ☎ *802/254–6300,* FAX *802/254–6304,* WEB *www.brattleboro.com/latchis. 30 rooms, 3 suites. Restaurant, cable TV, pub. AE, MC, V. CP.*

$$$–$$$$ ⊡ **Forty Putney Road.** Owners Mimi and Rob Hamlin's French-style home provides elegant yet comfortable accommodations. Rooms are furnished with antiques; the suite has a gas fireplace. A separate cottage with a full kitchen sleeps four. In warm weather, breakfast is served on the patio of the formally landscaped grounds, which lead to the shores of the West River. The inn is a popular spot to celebrate Civil Unions. ⊠ *40 Putney Rd., 05301,* ☎ *802/254–6268 or 800/941–2413,* FAX *802/258–2673,* WEB *www.putney.net/40putneyrd. 3 rooms, 1 suite, 1 cottage. In-room VCRs, pub, some pets allowed. AE, D, MC, V. BP.*

Nightlife and the Arts

Common Ground (⊠ 25 Elliot St., ☎ 802/257–0855) hosts live music, mostly from local bands. **Mole's Eye Cafe** (⊠ 4 High St., ☎ 802/257–0771) hosts an open-mike night every Thursday and live bands Friday and Saturday.

Outdoor Activities and Sports

BIKING

Brattleboro Bicycle Shop (⊠ 165 Main St., ☎ 802/254–8644 or 800/272–8245) rents and repairs hybrid bikes. **Burrows Specialized Sports** (⊠ 105 Main St., ☎ 802/254–9430) services bikes, skis, and snowboards and rents skis and snowshoes.

CANOEING

Vermont Canoe Touring Center (⊠ U.S. 5, ☎ 802/257–5008) conducts guided and self-guided tours, rents canoes and kayaks, and provides a shuttle service.

SKATING

Nelson Withington Skating Rink (⊠ Memorial Park, 4 Guilford St., ☎ 802/257–2311) rents skates.

STATE PARK

The hiking trails at **Fort Dummer State Park** (⊠ S. Main St., 2 mi south of Brattleboro, ☎ 802/254–2610) afford views of the Connecticut River valley; campsites are available.

Shopping

The **Book Cellar** (⊠ 120 Main St., ☎ 802/254–6026) stocks two floors with a variety of local titles. You can watch **Tom and Sally's Homemade Chocolates** being made just around the corner from their shop (⊠ 55 Elliott St., ☎ 802/258–3065), which also sells the famous chocolate Vermont Meadow Muffins. **Vermont Artisan Designs** (⊠ 106 Main St., ☎ 802/257–7044) displays ceramics, glass, wood, clothing, jewelry, and furniture.

Marlboro

❷ *10 mi west of Brattleboro.*

Tiny Marlboro draws musicians and audiences from around the world each summer to the Marlboro Music Festival, founded by Rudolf Serkin and joined for many years by Pablo Casals. **Marlboro College,** high on a hill off Route 9, is the center of musical activity. The college's white-frame buildings have outstanding views of the valley below, and the campus is studded with apple trees.

The **Southern Vermont Natural History Museum** houses one of New England's largest collections of mounted birds, specimens of three extinct birds, and a complete collection of mammals native to the Northeast. The museum also has weather displays and live hawk and owl exhibits. ⊠ *Rte. 9,* ☎ *802/464–0048.* ⊡ *$3.* ☉ *Memorial Day–late Oct., daily 10–5; late Oct.–Memorial Day, weekends 10–4, weather permitting.*

Nightlife and the Arts

The **Marlboro Music Festival** (⊠ Marlboro Music Center, Marlboro College, ☎ 802/254–2394; 215/569–4690 Sept.–June) presents chamber music at weekend concerts from mid-July to mid-August. The **New England Bach Festival** (☎ 802/257–4523) is held at Marlboro College in October.

Wilmington

❸ *8 mi west of Marlboro.*

Wilmington is the shopping and dining center for the Mt. Snow ski area (☞ West Dover) to the north. Main Street has a cohesive assemblage of 18th- and 19th-century buildings, many of them listed on the National Register of Historic Places. For a town stroll, pick up a self-guided tour map from the **Mount Snow Valley Chamber of Commerce** (⊠ W. Main St./Rte. 9, ☎ 802/464–8092 or 877/887–6884, WEB www. visitvermont.com).

North River Winery, which occupies a converted farmhouse and barn, produces fruit wines such as Green Mountain Apple and Vermont Pear. ⊠ *Rte. 112, 6 mi south of Wilmington, Jacksonville,* ☎ *802/368–7557.* ⊡ *Free.* ☉ *Daily 10–5; tours late May–Dec.*

OFF THE BEATEN PATH

SCENIC TOUR – To begin a scenic (though well-traveled) 35-mi circular tour with panoramic views of the region's mountains, farmland, and abundant cow population, drive west on Route 9 to the intersection with Route 8. Turn south and continue to the junction with Route 100; follow Route 100 through Whitingham (the birthplace of the Mormon prophet Brigham Young), and stay with the road as it turns north again and takes you back to Route 9.

Dining and Lodging

$$$–$$$$ ✕ **Le Petit Chef.** Chef Betty Hillman prepares a tasty selection of French-inspired dishes in her cozy white-clapboard farmhouse restaurant. Appetizers include her hallmark Bird's Nest, a shoestring-potato basket filled with savory delicacies. The rack of lamb served table-side for two is a stand-out. Desserts are all made in-house and include crunch meringue pie and strawberry-rhubarb shortcake. ⊠ *Rte. 100, 05363,* ☎ *802/464–8437. Reservations essential. AE, D, MC, V. Closed Tues.*

$$$–$$$$ ▥ **White House of Wilmington.** The grand staircase in this Federal-style mansion leads to rooms with antique bathrooms and brass wall sconces;

some rooms have fireplaces and lofts. You'll also find a cross-country ski touring and snowshoeing center, a tubing hill, and 12 km (7 mi) of groomed trails. You can dine at the restaurant for a fixed price of $35. ⊠ *178 Rte. 9 E, 05363,* ☎ *802/464–2135 or 800/541–2135,* FAX *802/464–5222,* WEB *www.whitehouseinn.com. 25 rooms. Restaurant, 2 pools (1 indoor), some in-room hot tubs, sauna, cross-country skiing, pub; no-smoking rooms, no kids under 8. AE, D, MC, V. BP.*

$$$ 🏨 **Trail's End, A Country Inn.** This cozy four-season lodge is set on 10 acres 4 mi from Mt. Snow. The inn's centerpiece is its cathedral-ceiling living room with catwalk loft seating and a 21-ft fieldstone fireplace. Guest rooms are comfortable; some have fireplaces. Dinner is served during the holiday season only. Cross-country ski trails are nearby. ⊠ *5 Trail's End La., 05363,* ☎ *802/464–2727 or 800/859–2585,* FAX *802/464–5532,* WEB *www.trailsendvt.com. 13 rooms, 2 suites. Some refrigerators, some microwaves, tennis court, pool, pond, fishing; no kids under 6. AE, D, MC, V. BP.*

Nightlife and the Arts

A year-round roster of music, theater, film, and fine art is presented at the **Memorial Hall Center for the Arts** (⊠ 14 W. Main St., ☎ 802/464–8411). In addition to steak and Mexican specialties, the standard fare on weekends at **Poncho's Wreck** (⊠ S. Main St., ☎ 802/464–9320) is acoustic jazz or mellow rock. **Sitzmark** (⊠ Rte. 100, ☎ 802/464–3384) hosts rock bands on weekends.

Outdoor Activities and Sports

SLEIGH RIDES

Adams Farm (⊠ 15 Higley Hill Rd., ☎ 802/464–3762) has three double-traverse sleighs drawn by Belgian draft horses. Rides include a narrated tour and hot chocolate. The farm store sells more than 200 handmade quilts and sweaters. An indoor petting farm is open Wednesday–Sunday from November to April, and an outdoor version is open daily the rest of the year.

STATE PARK

Molly Stark State Park (⊠ Rte. 9, east of Wilmington, ☎ 802/464–5460) has campsites and a hiking trail that leads to a vista from a fire tower on Mt. Olga.

WATER SPORTS

Lake Whitingham (Harriman Reservoir), just west of Wilmington, is the largest lake in the state, with good fishing. Boat-launch areas are at Wards Cove, Whitingham, Mountain Mills, and the Ox Bow. **Green Mountain Flagship Company** (⊠ Rte. 9, 2 mi west of Wilmington, ☎ 802/464–2975) runs a cruise boat on Lake Whitingham and rents canoes, kayaks, surf bikes, and sailboats from May to late October.

Shopping

Quaigh Design Centre (⊠ W. Main St./Rte. 9, ☎ 802/464–2780) sells New England crafts, artwork from Britain and New England—including works by Vermont woodcut artists Sabra Field and Mary Azarian—and Scottish woolens and tartans. **Wilmington Flea Market** (⊠ Rtes. 9 and 100 S, ☎ 802/464–3345) sells antiques on weekends from Memorial Day to mid-October.

West Dover

❹ *6 mi north of Wilmington.*

The Congregational church in small West Dover, a classic New England town, dates from the 1700s. The year-round population of about 1,000 swells on winter weekends as skiers flock to Mt. Snow/Haystack

Ski Resort. The many condos, lodges, and inns at the base of the mountain accommodate them.

Dining and Lodging

$$$$ ✕🏨 **Inn at Saw Mill Farm.** One of Vermont's two Relais & Châteaux
★ inns (the other is the Pitcher Inn), this inn has all the upscale amenities expected at these properties. English chintzes, antiques, and dark wood set a comfortable tone in the common room. Each of the guest rooms is individually decorated, and many have sitting areas and fireplaces. The 22 landscaped acres are perfect for hiking. The restaurant's ($$$$) seasonal menu might include potato-crusted black sea bass with wild mushrooms and orzo or a grilled veal chop with wild mushroom risotto and rosemary sauce. The wine selection, with more than 30,000 bottles, is superb. ⊠ *Rte. 100 and Crosstown Rd., 05356,* ☏ *800/493–1133 or 802/464–8131,* FAX *802/464–1130,* WEB *www.vermontdirect.com/sawmill. 21 rooms. Restaurant, tennis court, pool, fishing; no room phones, no room TVs, no kids under 6. AE, DC, MC, V. Closed Easter–late May. MAP.*

$$$ ✕🏨 **Doveberry Inn.** After a day's skiing, this handsome country inn just a few minutes from the slopes provides a welcome haven. You can warm up by the fireplace in the living room with a glass of wine from the bar. Guest rooms are cheerful and bright; one room has a fireplace. The restaurant ($$$; closed Tues.) serves northern Italian specialties such as wood-grilled veal chop with wild mushrooms and pan-seared salmon with herbed risotto in intimate, candlelit dining rooms. ⊠ *Rte. 100, 05356,* ☏ *802/464–5652 or 800/722–3204,* FAX *802/464–6229,* WEB *www.doveberryinn.com. 8 rooms. Restaurant, some in-room VCRs, bar; no kids under 8. AE, MC, V. BP.*

$$ ✕🏨 **Deerhill Inn and Restaurant.** A huge fireplace at this English-style
★ country inn dominates the living room, and English hand-painted yellow wallpaper, a garden-scene mural, and collections of antique plates accent the dining rooms. Several guest rooms have hand-painted murals and fireplaces. The three spacious balcony rooms have great views. The restaurant's ($$$–$$$$; closed Wed. in summer, Tues.–Wed. in winter) upscale comfort food might include a veal medallion with wild mushrooms in a lemon cream sauce or a black-pepper sirloin steak. ⊠ *Valley View Rd. (Box 136, 05356),* ☏ *802/464–3100 or 800/993–3379,* FAX *802/464–5474,* WEB *www.deerhill.com. 15 rooms, 2 suites. Restaurant, some cable TV, pool; no-smoking rooms, no kids under 8. AE, MC, V. BP, MAP.*

Nightlife and the Arts

Deacon's Den Tavern (⊠ Rte. 100, ☏ 802/464–9361) hosts bands on weekends from Thanksgiving through Easter. The **Snow Barn** (⊠ near the base of Mt. Snow, ☏ 802/464–1100 ext. 4693) has live music several nights a week.

Ski Areas

MT. SNOW/HAYSTACK SKI RESORT

One of the state's premier family resorts has a full roster of year-round activities. Since it opened in the 1950s as one of Vermont's first ski areas, the almost 800-acre facility has grown to encompass the Grand Summit Hotel and Crown Club (☏ 800/451–4211), a 201-room slope-side condo, hotel, and conference center; a golf course; a 45-mi mountain-biking park; and an extensive network of hiking trails. One lift ticket lets you ski at Mt. Snow and at nearby Haystack. A free shuttle connects the two ski areas. Haystack is open on weekends and holidays only. ⊠ *400 Mountain Rd., Mt. Snow 05356,* ☏ *802/464–3333; 800/245–7669 lodging; 802/464–2151 snow conditions;* WEB *www.mountsnow.com.*

Downhill. Mt. Snow has five separate mountain faces, each with its own personality. More than half of the 132 trails down its 1,700-ft vertical summit are intermediate, wide, and sunny. Most of the beginner slopes are toward the bottom; most of the expert terrain is on the North Face, where there's excellent fall-line skiing. The trails are served by 23 lifts, including three high-speed quads, one regular quad, 10 triple chairs, four double chairs, and three Magic Carpets (similar to an escalator). Snow-making covers 85% of the terrain. The ski school's Perfect Turn instruction program is designed to help skiers of all ages and abilities.

Child care. The well-organized child-care center (reservations essential) takes children ages 6 weeks–6 years. The center has age-appropriate toys and balances indoor play—including arts and crafts—with trips outdoors. The Pre-ski program is for 3-year-olds, and a Perfect Kids program for ages 4–12 teaches skiing and snowboarding.

Summer activities. Mt. Snow offers two- to seven-day Grand Summer Vacation packages with activities, including golf at the 18-hole Mt. Snow Golf Course, mountain biking on ski trails and forest roads, and use of the health club, with a pool, hot tubs, and spa. The Summit Local triple chairlift transports riders to the 3,600-ft peak. Swimming, boating, and a children's water-play pool are available at the resort's Snow Lake. A hiking center, in-line skating park, climbing wall, and BMX track provide other summer fun.

CROSS-COUNTRY SKIING/SNOWSHOEING

Three cross-country-trail areas within 4 mi of Mt. Snow/Haystack provide more than 150 km (90 mi) of varied terrain. The **Hermitage** (⊠ Coldbrook Rd., Wilmington, ☎ 802/464–3511) has 50 km (30 mi) of groomed trails. **Timber Creek** (⊠ Rte. 100, north of the Mt. Snow entrance, ☎ 802/464–0999) is appealingly small with 16 km (10 mi) of thoughtfully groomed trails. The groomed trails at the **White House of Wilmington** (⊠ Rtes. 9 and 100, ☎ 802/464–2135) cover 50 km (30 mi).

Snowmobile Tours

At **Sitzmark** (⊠ East Dover Rd., Wilmington, ☎ 802/464–3384) guides lead snowmobile tours across a golf course and through 50 acres of woods and fields.

Bennington

 21 mi west of Wilmington.

Bennington, college town and commercial focus of Vermont's southwest corner, lies at the edge of the Green Mountain National Forest. It has retained much of the industrial character it developed in the 19th century, when paper mills, gristmills, and potteries formed the city's economic base. It was in Bennington, at the Catamount Tavern, that Ethan Allen organized the Green Mountain Boys, who helped capture Ft. Ticonderoga in 1775. Here also, in 1777, American general John Stark urged his militia to attack the British-paid Hessian troops across the New York border: "There are the redcoats; they will be ours or tonight Molly Stark sleeps a widow!"

A brochure available at the Chamber of Commerce describes a self-guided walking tour of **Old Bennington,** a National Register Historic District west of downtown. Impressive white-column Greek Revival and sturdy Federal-style brick homes stand around the village green. In the graveyard of the **Old First Church,** at Church Street and Monument Avenue, the tombstone of the poet Robert Frost proclaims, "I had a lover's quarrel with the world."

The **Bennington Battle Monument,** a 306-ft stone obelisk with an elevator to the top, commemorates General Stark's victory over the British, who attempted to capture Bennington's stockpile of supplies. The battle, which took place near Walloomsac Heights in New York State on August 16, 1777, helped bring about the surrender two months later of the British commander "Gentleman Johnny" Burgoyne at Saratoga in New York. ⊠ *15 Monument Ave.,* ☎ *802/447–0550.* 🖾 *$1.50.* ☉ *Mid-Apr.–Oct., daily 9–5.*

The **Bennington Museum**'s rich collections include vestiges of rural life, a percentage of which are packed into towering glass cases. The decorative arts are well represented; one room is devoted to early Bennington pottery. Two rooms cover the history of American glass and contain fine Tiffany specimens. The museum displays the largest public collection of the work of Grandma Moses (1860–1961), the popular self-taught folk artist who lived and painted in the area. Among the 30 paintings and assorted memorabilia are her only self-portrait and the famous painted caboose window. Also here are the only surviving automobile of Bennington's Martin company, a 1925 Wasp, and the Bennington Flag, one of the oldest versions of the Stars and Stripes in existence. ⊠ *W. Main St./Rte. 9,* ☎ *802/447–1571,* WEB *www.benningtonmuseum.com.* 🖾 *$6.* ☉ *Nov.–May, daily 9–5; June–Oct., daily 9–6.*

Built in 1865 and once home to two Vermont governors, the **Park-McCullough House** is a 35-room classic French Empire–style mansion furnished with period pieces. Several restored flower gardens grace the landscaped grounds, and a stable houses a collection of antique carriages. Call for details on the summer concert series, Victorian Christmas, and other special events. ⊠ *Corner of Park and West Sts., North Bennington,* ☎ *802/442–5441,* WEB *www.park/mccullough.org.* 🖾 *$6.* ☉ *Mid-May–mid-Oct., Thurs.–Mon. 10–4; last tour at 3.*

Contemporary stone sculpture and white-frame neo-Colonial dorms surrounded by acres of cornfields punctuate the green meadows of **Bennington College**'s placid campus. The small liberal arts college, one of the most expensive to attend in the country, is noted for its progressive program in the arts. ⊠ *Rte. 67A, off U.S. 7 (look for stone entrance gate),* ☎ *800/833–6845 tour information.*

Dining and Lodging

$ ✕ **Blue Benn Diner.** Breakfast is served all day in this authentic diner, where the eats include turkey hash and breakfast burritos, with scrambled eggs, sausage, and chilies, plus pancakes of all imaginable varieties. The menu lists many vegetarian selections. Lines may be long, especially on weekends. ⊠ *U.S. 7 N,* ☎ *802/442–5140. Reservations not accepted. No credit cards. No dinner Sat.–Tues.*

$$$–$$$$ 🛏 **South Shire Inn.** Canopy beds in lushly carpeted rooms, ornate plaster moldings, and a dark mahogany fireplace in the library re-create the grandeur of the Victorian past; fireplaces in some rooms add warmth. The South Shire is in a quiet residential neighborhood within walking distance of the bus depot and downtown stores. Breakfast is served in the burgundy-and-white dining room. ⊠ *124 Elm St., 05201,* ☎ *802/447–3839,* FAX *802/442–3547,* WEB *www.southshire.com. 9 rooms. Cable TV, some in-room hot tubs; no kids under 12. AE, MC, V. BP.*

$–$$ 🛏 **Molly Stark Inn.** Tidy blue-plaid wallpaper, gleaming hardwood floors, antique furnishings, and a wood-burning stove in a brick alcove of the sitting room add country charm to this 1860 Queen Anne Victorian. Molly's Room, at the back of the building, gets less noise from Route 9; the attic suite is the most spacious. Three cottages have fireplaces and are more secluded. ⊠ *1067 E. Main St./Rte. 9, 05201,* ☎ *802/442–9631 or 800/356–3076,* FAX *802/442–5224,* WEB *www.mollystarkinn.com. 9 rooms. Some cable TV, some in-room hot tubs; no air-conditioning in some rooms, no kids under 10. AE, D, MC, V. BP.*

Nightlife and the Arts

The **Bennington Center for the Arts** (⊠ Rte. 9 at Gypsy La., ☎ 802/442–7158) hosts cultural events, including exhibitions by local and nationally recognized artists, and of wildlife and Native American art. The **Oldcastle Theatre Co.** (☎ 802/447–0564) at the Bennington Center for the Arts, whose season runs from May through October, is one of the Northeast's finest regional theaters.

Outdoor Activities and Sports

Cutting Edge (⊠ 160 Benmont Ave., ☎ 802/442–8664) rents and repairs bicycles and also sells and rents snowboards and cross-country skis. It has one of Vermont's few skateboarding parks, open Monday–Saturday 10–6, and Sunday noon–6.

HIKING

Four miles east of Bennington, the **Long Trail** crosses Route 9 and runs south to the top of Harmon Hill. Allot two or three hours for this hike.

STATE PARKS

Lake Shaftsbury State Park (⊠ Rte. 7A, 10½ mi north of Bennington, ☎ 802/375–9978) is one of a few parks in Vermont with group camping. It has a swimming beach, nature trails, boat and canoe rentals, and a snack bar. **Woodford State Park** (⊠ Rte. 9, 10 mi east of Bennington, ☎ 802/447–7169) has an activities center on Adams Reservoir, campsites, a playground, boat and canoe rentals, and nature trails.

Shopping

The **Apple Barn and Country Bake Shop** (⊠ U.S. 7 S, ☎ 802/447–7780) sells home-baked goodies, fresh cider, Vermont cheeses, and maple syrup. The showroom at the **Bennington Potters Yard** (⊠ 324 County St., ☎ 802/447–7531 or 800/205–8033) stocks first-quality pottery and antiques in addition to seconds from the famed Bennington Potters. On the free tour you can follow the clay through production and hear about the Potters Yard, in business for five decades. Tours begin at 10 and 2 in spring, summer, and fall. **Hawkins House Craftsmarket** (⊠ 262 North St./U.S. 7, ☎ 802/447–0488) showcases jewelry, wooden ware, glass, pottery, rugs, and clothing from more than 450 craftspeople.

Arlington

 15 mi north of Bennington.

Don't be surprised to see familiar-looking (if considerably aged) faces among the roughly 2,200 people of Arlington. The illustrator Norman Rockwell lived here from 1939 to 1953, and many of the models for his portraits of small-town life were his neighbors. First settled in 1763, Arlington was called Tory Hollow for its Loyalist sympathies—even though a number of the Green Mountain Boys lived here, too. Smaller than Bennington and more down-to-earth than upper-crust Manchester to the north, Arlington exudes a certain Rockwellian folksiness. Dorothy Canfield Fisher, a novelist popular in the 1930s and 1940s, also lived here.

Although no original paintings are displayed at the **Norman Rockwell Exhibition,** the rooms are crammed with reproductions of the illustrator's works, arranged in every way conceivable: chronologically, by subject matter, and juxtaposed with photos of the models—several of whom work here. ⊠ *Main St./Rte. 7A,* ☎ *802/375–6423,* WEB *www.*

normanrockwellexhibit.com. ✉ *$2.* ☉ *May–Oct., daily 9–5; Nov.–Dec. and Feb.–Apr., daily 10–4.*

Dining and Lodging

$$$$ ✕🏨 **West Mountain Inn.** Spectacular views, labyrinthine gardens, and
★ pet llamas are hallmarks of this inn, built in the 1840s on 150 acres
as an elegant summer retreat. The children's room, brightly painted
with life-size Disney characters, is stocked with games, stuffed animals,
and a TV with VCR. Six-course prix-fixe dinners ($$$$) highlighting
updated Continental cuisine are served in a low-beam candlelit dining
room. Request a table by the window. ✉ *West Mountain Inn Rd., 05250,*
☎ *802/375–6516,* FAX *802/375–6553,* WEB *www.westmountaininn.com.*
*18 rooms, 6 suites. Restaurant, some microwaves, hiking, cross-coun-
try skiing, bar, meeting room; no phones in some rooms. AE, D, MC,
V. MAP.*

$$–$$$$ ✕🏨 **Arlington Inn.** Greek Revival columns at this 1848 home lend it
★ an imposing presence, but the atmosphere is hardly forbidding. Vic-
torian-style wallpaper and original moldings and wainscoting are high-
lights. King-size rooms have fireplaces and two-person hot tubs. The
five rooms in the carriage house have country-French and Queen Anne
furnishings. The restaurant serves regional American dishes ($$$–
$$$$). The grounds have a garden, gazebo, pond, and waterfall. ✉
Rte. 7A, 05250, ☎ *802/375–6532 or 800/443–9442,* FAX *802/375–6534,*
WEB *www.arlingtoninn.com. 13 rooms, 5 suites. Restaurant, cable TV,
meeting rooms. AE, D, MC, V. BP.*

$$ 🏨 **Hill Farm Inn.** This homey inn on the Battenkill River has the feel
of the country farmhouse it used to be. The fireplace in the informal
living room, the sturdy antiques, and the spinning wheel in the upstairs
hallway all convey a relaxed, friendly environment. The Battenkill
Suite has a beamed cathedral ceiling, and from its porch you can see
Mt. Equinox. The rooms in the 1790 guest house are private; the
charming one- and two-bedroom cabins are open from spring through
fall. ✉ *458 Hill Farm Rd., off Rte. 7A, 05250,* ☎ *802/375–2269 or
800/882–2545,* FAX *802/375–9918,* WEB *www.hillfarminn.com. 5 rooms,
6 suites, 4 cabins. Some kitchenettes, some refrigerators, in-room
VCRs; no air-conditioning in some rooms. D, MC, V. BP.*

Outdoor Activities and Sports

Battenkill Canoe, Ltd./Vermont Canoe Trips (✉ Rte. 7A, ☎ 802/362–
2800 or 800/421–5268) rents canoes and runs inn-to-inn tours and day
trips on the Battenkill.

Shopping

Equinox Valley Nursery (✉ Rte. 7A between Arlington and Man-
chester, ☎ 802/362–2610) is known for its perennials (more than
1,000 varieties). The nursery has 17 greenhouses and a conservatory,
sells 150 varieties of herbs, and carries many Vermont-made products
in the large gift shop.

Manchester

★ **❼** *9 mi northeast of Arlington.*

Manchester, where Ira Allen proposed financing Vermont's participa-
tion in the American Revolution by confiscating Tory estates, has been
a popular summer retreat since the mid-19th century. Manchester Vil-
lage's tree-shaded marble sidewalks and stately old homes reflect the
luxurious resort lifestyle of a century ago. Manchester Center's upscale
factory outlets appeal to the affluent 20th-century ski crowd drawn
by nearby Bromley and Stratton mountains. Warning: shoppers come
in droves at times, giving the place the feel of a crowded mall on the

weekend before Christmas. If you're coming here from Arlington, take pretty Route 7A, which passes directly by a number of sights.

★ **Hildene,** the summer home of Abraham Lincoln's son and onetime Pullman company chairman Robert Todd Lincoln, is a beautifully preserved 412-acre estate. The 24-room mansion, with its Georgian Revival symmetry, welcoming central hallway, and grand curved staircase, is unusual in that its rooms are not roped off. When the 1,000-pipe Aeolian organ is played, the music reverberates as though from the mansion's very bones. Tours include a short film on the owner's life and a walk through the elaborate formal gardens. When snow conditions permit, you can cross-country ski on the property, which has views of nearby mountains. ⊠ *Rte. 7A,* ☎ *802/362–1788,* WEB *www.hildene.org.* ☜ *$8.* ☉ *Mid-May– Oct., daily 9:30–5:30; visitor center daily 9–5:30. Tours on the ½ hr (first tour at 9:30, last tour at 4). Candlelight tours Dec. 27–29 at 5 PM.*

The **American Museum of Fly Fishing,** which houses the largest collection of fly-fishing equipment in the world, displays more than 1,500 rods, 800 reels, 30,000 flies, and the tackle of famous people such as Winslow Homer, Bing Crosby, and Jimmy Carter. Its library of 2,500 books is open by appointment. ⊠ *Rte. 7A at Seminary Ave.,* ☎ *802/362–3300,* WEB *www.amff.com.* ☜ *$3.* ☉ *Mon.–Sat. 10–4.*

The **Southern Vermont Arts Center** showcases rotating exhibits and its permanent collection of more than 700 pieces of 19th- and 20th-century American art in a 12,500-square-ft museum. The Arts Center's original building, a graceful Georgian mansion set on 375 acres, is the frequent site of concerts, performances, and film screenings. In summer and fall, a pleasant restaurant with magnificent views opens for business. ⊠ *West Rd.,* ☎ *802/362–1405,* WEB *www.svac.org.* ☜ *$6.* ☉ *May–Oct., Tues.– Sat. 10–5, Sun. noon–5; Nov.–Apr., Mon.–Sat. 10–5.*

You may want to keep your eye on the temperature gauge of your car as you drive the 5-mi toll road to the top of 3,825-ft **Mt. Equinox.** Along the way you'll see the Battenkill trout stream and the surrounding Vermont countryside. Picnic tables line the drive, and you can look down both sides of the mountain from a notch known as the Saddle. ⊠ *Off Rte. 7A, south of Manchester,* ☎ *802/362–1114.* ☜ *Car and driver $6, each additional adult $2.* ☉ *May–Oct., daily 8 AM–10 PM.*

Green Mountain Railroad operates **Vermont Valley Flyer,** a vintage passenger coach that travels along the Battenkill River to Arlington (with fall excursions extending to North Bennington). It departs from the junction of Routes 11 and 30. ☎ *802/463–3069 or 800/707–3530,* WEB *www.rails-vt.com.* ☜ *$14.* ☉ *July 4–Sept. 1 and mid-Sept.–mid-Oct., Wed.–Mon. Train departs several times daily; call for schedule.*

Dining and Lodging

$$$$ ✕ **Chantecleer.** Intimate dining rooms have been created in a former dairy barn with a large fieldstone fireplace. The menu reflects the chef's Swiss background: appetizers include *Bündnerfleisch* (air-dried Swiss beef) and frogs' legs in garlic butter; rack of lamb, whole Dover sole filleted table-side, and veal chops highlight the entrées. The restaurant is 5 mi north of Manchester. ⊠ *Rte. 7A, East Dorset,* ☎ *802/362– 1616. Reservations essential. AE, DC, MC, V. Closed Tues. in summer; Mon.–Tues. in winter; and late Oct.–Thanksgiving and mid-Apr.– mid-May. No lunch.*

$$–$$$ ✕ **Bistro Henry's.** This airy restaurant on the outskirts of town attracts a devoted clientele for authentic Mediterranean fare. The menu lists fresh fish, seasonal game, and eclectic dishes such as rare tuna with wasabi and soy. The wine list is extensive. ⊠ *Rte. 11/30,* ☎ *802/362– 4982. AE, D, DC, MC, V. Closed Mon. No lunch.*

$$$$ ✕⊞ **The Equinox.** Even before Abe Lincoln's family began summering here, this grand white-column resort was a local fixture. The spacious, sunny rooms are furnished with antique reproductions. The main hotel houses rooms and Presidential Suites; the Orvis Inn has one- and two-bedroom suites; and more rooms are in the Town House. Richly upholstered settees and fireplace in the Marsh Tavern create a plush traditional ambience. Men are requested to wear jackets in the elegant Colonnade restaurant ($$$–$$$$). The Sunday brunch is spectacular. ⊠ *3567 Main St./Rte. 7A, Manchester Village 05254,* ☎ *802/362–4700 or 800/362–4747,* ℻ *802/362–1595,* ⬜ *www.equinoxresort.com. 163 rooms, 14 suites. 3 restaurants, 18-hole golf course, 3 tennis courts, 2 pools (1 indoor), health club, sauna, steam room, fishing, mountain bikes, croquet, horseback riding, cross-country skiing, ice-skating, snowmobiling, bar, meeting rooms; no smoking rooms. AE, D, DC, MC, V. MAP.*

$–$$$ ✕⊞ **Barrows House.** This 200-year-old Federal-style inn and miniresort 8 mi from Bromley has guest rooms in eight buildings spread over 11 acres. Some have gas or wood-burning fireplaces and afford great privacy. Dinner ($$$)—served in the spacious main dining room, the greenhouse room, and the tavern—includes perennial favorites such as rack of lamb as well as nightly specials, which might include native grilled trout. ⊠ *Rte. 30 (Box 98, Dorset 05251),* ☎ *802/867–4455 or 800/ 639–1620,* ℻ *802/867–0132,* ⬜ *www.barrowshouse.com. 18 rooms, 10 suites. Restaurant, cable TV, 2 tennis courts, pool, sauna, bicycles, cross-country skiing, some pets allowed. AE, D, DC, MC, V. BP, MAP.*

$$$$ ⊞ **Inn at Ormsby Hill.** Once a stop on the Underground Railroad, this ★ 1774 Federal-style building has guest rooms furnished with antiques and canopied or four-poster beds and fireplaces. Some have mountain views. Breakfasts are in the conservatory—entrées may include baked, stuffed French toast with an apricot brandy sauce. ⊠ *1842 Main St./Rte. 7A, 05255,* ☎ *802/362–1163 or 800/670–2841,* ℻ *802/362– 5176,* ⬜ *www.ormsbyhill.com. 10 rooms. In-room hot tubs; no kids. D, MC, V. BP.*

$$$–$$$$ ⊞ **Wilburton Inn.** Overlooking the Battenkill Valley, this turn-of-the-20th-century Tudor mansion has 11 lovingly furnished bedrooms and suites, and richly paneled common rooms decorated with part of the owners' vast art collection. Five guest buildings are spread over the grounds, dotted with sculpture. Eight rooms have private decks with mountain views. A buffet breakfast is served in the Terrace Room, and dinner is served in the handsome Billiard Room. One note: weddings take place here most summer weekends. ⊠ *River Rd., 05254,* ☎ *802/362–2500 or 800/648– 4944,* ℻ *802/362–1107,* ⬜ *www.wilburton.com. 30 rooms, 4 suites. Restaurant, some cable TV, some microwaves, 3 tennis courts, pool. AE, MC, V. BP.*

$$–$$$$ ⊞ **1811 House.** At this mansion once owned by President Lincoln's ★ granddaughter, you can experience life in an English country home without crossing the Atlantic. Three acres of lawn are landscaped in the English floral style. Rooms contain period antiques; six have fireplaces and eight have four-poster beds. Bathrooms are old-fashioned but serviceable. Three rooms in the cottage have fireplaces and modern baths. ⊠ *Rte. 7A (Box 39, 05254),* ☎ *802/362–1811 or 800/432–1811,* ℻ *802/362–2443,* ⬜ *www.1811house.com. 13 rooms, 1 suite. Pub, video game room; no kids under 16. AE, D, MC, V. BP.*

$–$$ ⊞ **Aspen Motel.** A rare find in this area, the immaculate, family-owned Aspen is set well back from the highway and moderately priced. The spacious, tastefully decorated rooms have Colonial-style furnishings; a common room has a fireplace. ⊠ *Rte. 7A N, 05255,* ☎ *802/362– 2450,* ℻ *802/362–1348,* ⬜ *www.thisisvermont.com/aspen. 24 rooms, 1 cottage. Pool, some refrigerators, playground. AE, D, MC, V.*

Nightlife and the Arts

The two pre–Revolutionary War barns of the **Dorset Playhouse** (✉ off town green, Dorset, ☎ 802/867–5777) host a community group in winter and a resident professional troupe in summer. The **Marsh Tavern** (☎ 802/362–4700) at the Equinox hosts cabaret music and jazz from Wednesday to Sunday in summer and on weekends in winter. **Mulligan's** (✉ Rte. 7A, ☎ 802/362–3663) is a popular hangout in Manchester Village, especially for the après-ski set.

Outdoor Activities and Sports

BIKING

The 20-mi Dorset–Manchester trail runs from Manchester Village north on West Street to Route 30, turns west at the Dorset village green onto West Road, and heads back south to Manchester. **Battenkill Sports** (✉ 1240 Depot St. [U.S. 7, Exit 4], ☎ 802/362–2734 or 800/340–2734) rents and repairs bikes and provides maps and route suggestions.

FISHING

Battenkill Anglers (✉ 6204 Main St., Manchester Center, ☎ 802/362–3184) teaches the art and science of fly-fishing in both private and group lessons. The **Orvis Co.** (✉ Rte. 7A, Manchester Center, ☎ 800/235–9763) hosts a nationally known fly-fishing school on the Battenkill, the state's most famous trout stream, with 2½-day courses given weekly between April and October.

HIKING

One of the most popular segments of Vermont's **Long Trail** starts at Route 11/30 west of Peru Notch and goes to the top of Bromley Mountain. The round-trip trek takes about four hours.

The **Mountain Goat** (✉ 4676 Main St., ☎ 802/362–5159) sells hiking, backpacking, and climbing equipment and rents snowshoes and cross-country and telemark skis. The shop also conducts rock- and ice-climbing clinics.

STATE PARK

Emerald Lake State Park (✉ U.S. 7, North Dorset, ☎ 802/362–1655), 9 mi north of Manchester, has campsites, a marked nature trail, an on-site naturalist, boat and canoe rentals, and a snack bar.

Shopping

ART AND ANTIQUES

Carriage Trade (✉ Rte. 7A north of Manchester Center, ☎ 802/362–1125) contains room after room of Early American antiques and has a fine collection of ceramics. **Danby Antiques Center** (✉ ⅛ mi off U.S. 7, Danby, ☎ 802/293–5990), 13 mi north of Manchester, has 11 rooms and a barn filled with furniture and accessories, folk art, textiles, and stoneware. Vermont-based artists display their oils, watercolors, and sculptures at **Gallery North Star** (✉ Rte. 7A, ☎ 802/362–4541). The **Peel Gallery of Fine Art** (✉ Peel Gallery Rd., Danby, ☎ 802/293–5230), which has celebrated its third decade in business, represents 40 professional American artists. **Tilting at Windmills Gallery** (✉ Rte. 11/30, ☎ 802/362–3022) exhibits the works of well-known artists such as Douglas Flackman of the Hudson River School.

BOOKS

Northshire Bookstore (✉ Main St., ☎ 802/362–2200 or 800/437–3700), a community bookstore for more than 20 years, carries many travel and children's books and sponsors readings year-round.

CLOTHING AND SPECIALTY ITEMS

Alfred Baier (✉ Butternut La., ☎ 802/362–3371) makes and sells pipes in his studio-workshop. **Orvis Fly Fishing Outlet** (✉ Union St.,

☎ 802/362–6455) sells discounted fishing supplies in what was Orvis's shop in the 1800s.

FISHING GEAR

Orvis Retail Store (✉ Rte. 7A, ☎ 802/362–3750), one of the largest suppliers of fishing gear in the Northeast, also carries clothing, gifts, and hunting supplies.

MALLS AND MARKETPLACES

Manchester Designer Outlets (✉ U.S. 7 and Rte. 11/30, ☎ 802/362–3736 or 800/955–7467) has such big-city names as Joan & David, Baccarat, Coach, Ralph Lauren, and Cole-Haan. At **Manchester Square** (✉ Rte. 11/30 and Richville Rd.) you'll find outlet stores for Giorgio Armani, Yves Delorme/Palais Royal, Vermont Toy Chest, Brooks Brothers, Levi Strauss, Escada, and more.

Ski Areas

BROMLEY MOUNTAIN

The first trails at Bromley were cut in 1936. The area has a comfortable red-clapboard base lodge, built when the ski area first opened; it was later expanded. Many families appreciate the resort's conviviality, with its large ski shop and a condominium village adjacent to the slopes. A reduced-price, two-day lift pass is available, as is a snowboard park-only lift ticket. Kids six and under ski free when accompanied by an adult. Eighty percent of the area is covered by snowmaking. ✉ *Rte. 11 (Box 1130, Manchester Center 05255), ☎ 802/ 824–5522 information and snow conditions; 800/865–4786 lodging;* WEB *www.bromley.com.*

Downhill. Most ski areas are laid out to face the north or east, but Bromley faces south, making it one of the warmer spots to ski in New England. Its 43 trails are equally divided into beginner, intermediate, and advanced terrain; the last is serviced by the Blue Ribbon quad chairlift on the east side. The vertical drop is 1,334 ft. Four double chairlifts, two quad lifts, a J-bar, and two surface lifts for beginners provide transportation. The high-speed quad lift takes skiers from the base to the summit in just six minutes.

Child care. Bromley is one of the region's best places to bring children. Besides a nursery for children ages 6 weeks–4 years, ski instruction is provided for children ages 3–12.

Summer activities. The area becomes a veritable playground in summer. At the DevalKart and the Alpine Slide, passengers ride up on a chairlift and come down on wheeled sleds (or ride back down on the chair). There's also a helium-filled, parachute-harnessed tethered balloon; a climbing wall; kiddie bumper cars; and a huge trampoline.

CROSS-COUNTRY SKIING

The **Meadowbrook Inn** (✉ Rte. 11, Landgrove, ☎ 802/824–6444 or 800/498–6445) maintains 21 km (16 mi) of marked trails for cross-country skiing and snowshoeing. The inn, which has eight guest rooms and a restaurant, has rental gear and provides lessons.

Stratton

8 *18 mi southeast of Manchester.*

Stratton, home to the famous Stratton Mountain Resort, has a self-contained town center with shops, restaurants, and lodgings clustered at the base of the slopes. There's plenty of activity year-round between skiing and summer sports.

Lodging

$$–$$$$ ⊡ **Stratton Mountain Inn and Village Lodge.** This complex not only comprises the largest inn on the mountain but is the only slope-side hotel at Stratton. The inn is within walking distance of the lifts. Ski packages that include lift tickets bring down room rates. ⊠ *Middle Ridge Rd., 05155,* ☎ *802/297–2500; 877/887–3767 lodging;* FAX *802/297–1778;* WEB *www.strattonmountain.com. 120 rooms, 91 lodge units. Restaurant, minibars, microwaves, refrigerators, golf course, 2 tennis courts, outdoor pool (summer only), hot tub, sauna, cross-country skiing, downhill skiing, lounge, video game room, meeting rooms; no air-conditioning in some rooms, no-smoking rooms. AE, DC, MC, V. BP mid-Apr.–mid–Dec.*

$–$$ ⊡ **Red Fox Inn.** Tom and Cindy Logan's "white house," just 4 mi from Stratton and 8 mi from Bromley, provides pleasant and comfortable accommodations. Each room has a private bath, and the suite has a fireplace and hot tub. Dinner is served nightly in the restaurant next door; a full roster of entertainment in the Tavern includes Irish and folk music as well as rock and roll. A special 50%-off room rate is offered Sunday–Thursday. ⊠ *Winhall Hollow Rd., Bondville 05340,* ☎ *802/297–2488,* FAX *802/297–02156,* WEB *www.redfoxxinn.com. 9 rooms. Restaurant, bar, some pets allowed. MC, V.*

Nightlife and the Arts

Popular **Mulligan's** (⊠ Mountain Rd., ☎ 802/297–9293) hosts bands or DJs in the late afternoon and on weekends. The **Red Fox Inn** (⊠ Winhall Hollow Rd., Bondville, ☎ 802/297–2488) hosts Irish music Tuesday night in winter; live folk music on Sunday night; an open mike on Thursday night; and rock and roll at other times.

Ski Areas

STRATTON MOUNTAIN

Since its creation in 1961, Stratton has undergone physical transformations and upgrades, yet the area's sophisticated character has been retained. It is a popular destination for affluent families and young professionals from the New York–southern Connecticut corridor. An entire village, with a covered parking structure for 700 cars, is at the base of the mountain. Adjacent to the base lodge are a condo-hotel, restaurants, and about 25 shops lining a pedestrian mall. Stratton is 4 mi up its own access road off Route 30 in Bondville, about 30 minutes from Manchester's popular shopping zone. ⊠ *R.R. 1, Box 145, Stratton Mountain 05155,* ☎ *802/297–2200; 800/843–6867; 802/297–4211 snow conditions; 800/787–2886 lodging;* WEB *www.stratton.com.*

Downhill. Stratton's skiing is in three sectors. The first is the lower mountain directly in front of the base lodge-village-condo complex; several lifts reach mid-mountain from this entry point, and practically all skiing is beginner or low-intermediate. Above that, the upper mountain, with a vertical drop of 2,000 ft, has a high-speed, 12-passenger gondola, Starship XII. Down the face are the expert trails, and on either side are intermediate cruising runs with a smattering of wide beginner slopes. The third sector, the Sun Bowl, is off to one side with two high-speed, six-passenger lifts and two expert trails, a full base lodge, and plenty of intermediate terrain. Snowmaking covers 85% of the terrain. Stratton hosts the U.S. Open Snowboarding championships; its snowboard park has a 380-ft halfpipe. A Ski Learning Park provides its own Park Packages for novice skiers. In all, Stratton has 11 lifts that service 90 trails and 90 acres of glades.

Cross-country. The resort has more than 30 km (18 mi) of cross-country skiing and two Nordic centers: Sun Bowl and Country Club.

Child care. The day-care center takes children from ages 6 weeks–5 years for indoor activities and outdoor excursions. There is a ski school for children ages 4–12. A junior racing program and special instruction groups are geared toward more experienced young skiers.

Summer and year-round activities. Stratton has 15 outdoor tennis courts, 27 holes of golf, horseback riding, mountain biking and hiking accessed by a gondola to the summit, and instructional programs in tennis and golf. The sports center, open year-round, contains two indoor tennis courts, three racquetball courts, a 25-meter indoor swimming pool, a hot tub, a steam room, a fitness facility with Nautilus equipment, and a restaurant. Stratton also hosts summer entertainment and family activities, including a skating park and climbing wall.

Londonderry

❾ *12 mi north of Stratton.*

Within 20 minutes of Stratton and Bromley and Magic mountains, Londonderry is one of the area's major shopping centers, with lodgings convenient to ski areas yet tucked away from on-site hustle and bustle.

Dining and Lodging

$–$$ ✕🏠 **Swiss Inn & Restaurant.** Guest rooms are large and comfortable at this relaxing and homey onetime dairy farm, which also houses a popular Swiss-German restaurant ($$–$$$). Among the specialties are raclette and Wiener schnitzel. Continental fare includes shrimp à la Marseilles. A lighter tavern menu is also available. ⊠ *249 Rte. 11, 05148,* ☎ *802/824–3442 or 800/847–9477,* 𝖥𝖠𝖷 *802/824–3957,* 𝖶𝖤𝖡 *www. swissinn.com. 19 rooms. Cable TV, tennis court, pool, pond, lounge. MC, V. BP.*

$$$ 🏠 **Londonderry Inn.** This inn is particularly inviting for groups and families with small children. Rooms, with patchwork quilts, hand-hooked rugs, and teddy bears, are spacious and comfortable, and many can be used as suites to accommodate larger parties. The rambling inn, an 1826 farmhouse on 9 acres, is a state-awarded "Green" hotel, which recognizes it as an environmentally sensitive lodging. ⊠ *Rte. 100, South Londonderry 05155,* ☎ *802/824–5226,* 𝖥𝖠𝖷 *802/824–3146,* 𝖶𝖤𝖡 *www.londonderryinn.com. 24 rooms. Pool, cross-country skiing, cinema. AE, D, MC, V. BP.*

Shopping

J. J. Hapgood Store (⊠ off Rte. 11, Peru, ☎ 802/824–5911) is an old-fashioned country store, complete with a potbellied stove.

Weston

❿ *5 mi north of Londonderry.*

Although perhaps best known for the Vermont Country Store, Weston is famed as one of the first Vermont towns to have discovered its own intrinsic loveliness—and marketability. With its summer theater, pretty town green, and Victorian bandstand, as well as an assortment of shops offering variety without modern sprawl, the little village really lives up to its vaunted image.

The **Mill Museum,** down the road from the Vermont Country Store, has numerous hands-on displays depicting the engineering and mechanics of one of the town's mills. The many old tools on view kept towns like Weston running smoothly in their early days. ⊠ *Rte. 100,* ☎ *802/824–3119.* 🎟 *Donations accepted.* ☉ *July–Aug., Wed.–Sun. 1–4; Sept.–mid-Oct., weekends 1–4.*

Dining and Lodging

$$$–$$$$ ✕⊡ **Inn at Weston.** Country elegance best describes this 1848 village inn and adjoining Coleman House. Some rooms and suites have fireplaces. The restaurant ($$$–$$$$; closed Mon.) serves contemporary regional cuisine amid candlelight. Vermont cheddar cheese and Granny Smith apple omelets are popular at breakfast. ⊠ *Rte. 100 (Box 66, 05161),* ☎ *802/824–6789,* ℻ *802/824–3073,* WEB *www.innweston.com. 13 rooms. Restaurant, some in-room hot tubs, pub; no TV in some rooms, no kids under 12. AE, DC, MC, V. BP.*

$–$$ ⊡ **Colonial House Inn & Motel.** You'll find warmth and charm at this family-friendly complex just 2 mi south of the village. Relax on comfortable furniture in the large living room or enjoy the sun in the solarium. Homey, country furnishings adorn both of the two inn rooms and the motel units. The complimentary breakfast includes fresh goodies from the on-site bakery; a family-style dinner is served Friday and Saturday nights. ⊠ *287 Rte. 100, 05161,* ☎ *802/824–6286 or 800/639–5033,* ℻ *802/824–3934,* WEB *www.cohoinn.com. 9 motel units, 2 inn rooms with shared bath. Cable TV. D, MC, V. BP.*

Nightlife and the Arts

The members of the **Weston Playhouse** (⊠ Village Green, off Rte. 100, ☎ 802/824–5288), the oldest professional theater in Vermont, produce Broadway plays, musicals, and other works. Their season runs from late June to early September.

The **Kinhaven Music School** (⊠ Lawrence Hill Rd., ☎ 802/824–3365) stages free student concerts on Friday at 4 PM and Sunday at 2:30 in July and August.

Shopping

The **Vermont Country Store** (⊠ Rte. 100, ☎ 802/824–3184, WEB www. vtcountrystore.com) sets aside one room of its old-fashioned emporium for Vermont Common Crackers and bins of fudge and other candy. For years the retail store and its mail-order catalog have carried nearly forgotten items such as Lilac Vegetal aftershave, Monkey Brand black tooth powder, Flexible Flyer sleds, and tiny wax bottles of colored syrup, but have also sold plenty of practical items such as sturdy outdoor clothing and even a manual typewriter. Nostalgia-evoking implements dangle from the store's walls and ceiling. (There's another store on Route 103 in Rockingham.)

Drury House Antiques (⊠ Village Green, ☎ 802/824–4395) specializes in antique clocks, fly rods, and other fishing-related objects. The **Todd Gallery** (⊠ 614 Main St., ☎ 802/824–5606) exhibits paintings, prints, and sculptures by Vermont artists and craftspeople.

Ludlow

⑪ *9 mi northeast of Weston.*

Ludlow was once a nondescript factory town that just happened to have a major ski area—Okemo—on its outskirts. Today the old General Electric plant is gone, its premises recycled into a rambling, block-long complex of shops and restaurants, and the town seems much more integrated into the ski scene. A beautiful, often-photographed historic church overlooks the town green.

Dining and Lodging

$–$$$ ✕ **Pot Belly Pub.** Après-ski fun seekers pile into this popular restaurant-nightspot for house specialties such as Belly burgers, smoked ribs, steaks, applejack pork, and fresh seafood. Live entertainment—from jazz and rhythm-and-blues to swing—keeps patrons warm on winter weekends. ✉ *130 Main St.,* ☎ *802/228–8989. AE, DC, MC, V.*

$$–$$$$ ✕▥ **Governor's Inn.** This 19th-century Victorian country home on the village green is a welcome retreat for those looking for gracious accommodations and creative, contemporary fare. The second- and third-floor guest rooms are decorated with antique furnishings; the third-floor rooms, including the suite, have gas-lit fire stoves. Chef–co-owner Kathy Kubec prepares prix-fixe, six-course dinners Thursday–Sunday ($$$$; reservations essential). An elegant breakfast is served at individual tables for two. ✉ *86 Main St., 05149,* ☎ *802/228–8830 or 800/ 468–3766,* FAX *802/228–2961,* WEB *www.thegovernorsinn.com. 9 rooms. Some cable TV; no kids under 12. AE, D, MC, V. BP.*

$$$–$$$$ ▥ **Andrie Rose Inn.** Many of the antiques-filled rooms at this 1829 inn and adjacent buildings have whirlpool tubs and mountain views. Two-person luxury suites have whirlpool tubs, fireplaces, and steam showers for two. Full-floor condo suites in the 1883 Victorian Town House sleep up to 12, and two family suites have fireplaces and kitchens. Candlelight breakfast is included in standard rooms; a breakfast basket is delivered to the luxury suites. A four-course dinner with a seasonal menu is served Friday and Saturday. ✉ *13 Pleasant St., 05149,* ☎ *802/223– 4846 or 800/223–4846,* FAX *802/228–7910,* WEB *www.andrieroseinn.com. 9 rooms, 14 suites. Restaurant, some cable TV, some refrigerators, some microwaves, bicycles, bar; no air-conditioning in some rooms, no phones in some rooms. AE, V. BP.*

$$$–$$$$ ▥ **Okemo Mountain Lodge.** The one-bedroom contemporary country condominiums clustered around the base of Okemo's ski lifts come with fireplaces and decks. The restaurant is open for breakfast and lunch only. The Okemo Mountain Lodging Service rents one- to five-bedroom units in the Kettle Brook, Winterplace, and Solitude slope-side condominiums. Ski-and-stay packages are available for three or more non-holiday nights. ✉ *77 Okemo Ridge Rd., off Rte. 103, 05149,* ☎ *802/228–5571, 802/228–4041, or 800/786–5366,* FAX *802/228–2079,* WEB *www.okemo.com. 55 rooms. Restaurant, kitchens, in-room VCRs, cross-country skiing, downhill skiing, bar. AE, MC, V.*

Outdoor Activities and Sports

Cavendish Trail Horse Rides (✉ 20 Mile Stream Rd., Proctorsville, ☎ 802/226–7821) operates horse-drawn sleigh rides in snowy weather, wagon rides at other times, and guided trail rides from mid-May to mid-October.

Ski Areas

OKEMO MOUNTAIN RESORT

An ideal ski area for families with children, family-owned Okemo has evolved into a major year-round resort. The main attraction is a long, broad, gentle slope with two beginner lifts just above the base lodge. All the facilities at the bottom of the mountain are close together, so family members can regroup easily during the ski day. The resort offers numerous ski and snowboarding packages. ✉ *77 Okemo Ridge Rd./Rte. 100,* ☎ *802/228–4041; 800/786–5366 lodging; 802/228–5222 snow conditions;* WEB *www.okemo.com.*

Downhill. Above the broad beginner's slope at the base, the upper part of Okemo has a varied network of trails: long, winding, easy trails for beginners; straight fall-line runs for experts; and curving, cruising slopes for intermediates. Fifty percent of the trails have an intermediate rating; 25% are rated novice, and 25% are rated for experts. The 98 trails are served by an efficient lift system of 14 lifts, including seven quads, three triple chairlifts, and four surface lifts; 95% are covered by snowmaking. From the summit to the base lodge, the vertical drop is 2,150 ft, the highest in southern Vermont. Okemo has a self-contained snowboarding area serviced by a surface lift; the mile-long park has two halfpipes, including the 400-ft-long Super Pipe. There's also a snowboard park for beginners.

Cross-country skiing/snowshoeing. The **Okemo Valley Nordic Center** (⊠ Fox La., ☎ 802/228–1396) has 28 km (16 mi) of groomed cross-country trails and 10 km (6 mi) of dedicated snowshoe trails and rents equipment.

Child care. The area's nursery, for children ages 6 weeks–8 years, has many indoor activities and supervised outings. The MiniStar Ski Program is for children ages 3–4; the SnowStar program is for kids ages 4–7. Nursery reservations are essential. Okemo also runs a Kids' Night Out evening child-care program on Saturdays during the regular season and certain holiday weeks.

Summer activities. The Okemo Valley Golf Club has an 18-hole, par-71, 6,000-yard course. Seven target greens, a putting green, a golf academy, and an indoor putting green, swing stations, and a simulator provide plenty of ways to improve your game.

Chester

⑫ *11 mi east of Weston.*

Gingerbread Victorians frame Chester's town green. The local pharmacy on Main Street has been in continuous operation since the 1860s. The stone village on North Street on the outskirts of town, two rows of buildings constructed from quarried stone, was built by two brothers and is said to have been used during the Civil War as a station on the Underground Railroad.

In Chester's restored 1852 train station you can board the **Green Mountain Flyer** for a 26-mi, two-hour round-trip journey to Bellows Falls, on the Connecticut River at the eastern edge of the state. The cars that date from the golden age of railroading travel past covered bridges and along the Brockway Mills gorge. The fall foliage trips are spectacular. ⊠ *Rte. 103,* ☎ *802/463–3069 or 800/707–3530,* WEB *www.rails-vt.com.* ☑ *$11 in summer, $12 in fall.* ☼ *Late June–mid-Sept., Tues.–Sun.; mid-Sept.–late-Oct., daily. Train departs several times daily; call for schedule.*

Dining and Lodging

$$–$$$ ✕ **Raspberries and Thyme.** Breakfast specials, homemade soups, a large selection of salads, homemade desserts, and a menu listing more than 40 sandwiches make this one of the area's most popular spots for casual dining. ⊠ *On the Green,* ☎ 802/875–4486. AE, D, MC, V. *No dinner Tues.*

$$–$$$ 🏠 **Chester House Inn.** All of the rooms in this handsomely restored 1780 historic inn on the Green have private baths. Five have fireplaces, and three have hot tubs or steam showers. Breakfast and dinner are served in the elegant Keeping Room, which has a fireplace. ⊠ *266 Main St., 05143,* ☎ *802/875–2205 or 888/875–2205,* FAX *802/875–6602,* WEB *www.chesterhouseinn.com. 7 rooms. Restaurant, some in-room hot tubs, bar. D, DC, MC, V.*

$$ 🏠 **Fullerton Inn.** Guest rooms with country quilts and lace curtains vary in size and amenities at this three-story, wooden 19th-century building with a big porch. Some favorites are the bright corner rooms and Nos. 8 and 10, which share a private porch. The restaurant serves breakfast Tuesday–Saturday in winter and Monday–Saturday in summer. Dinner is served every night except Wednesday. A shuttle bus to local attractions and ski areas stops in front of the inn. ⊠ *40 Common, on the Green, 05143,* ☎ *802/875–2444,* [FAX] *802/875–6414,* [WEB] *www.fullertoninn.com. 21 rooms, 3 suites. Restaurant, lounge, shop; no kids under 13. AE, D, MC, V. BP.*

Outdoor Activities and Sports

A 26-mi **driving or biking loop** out of Chester follows the Williams River along Route 103 to Pleasant Valley Road north of Bellows Falls. At Saxtons River, turn west onto Route 121 and follow along the river to connect with Route 35. When the two routes separate, follow Route 35 north back to Chester.

Shopping

The **National Survey Charthouse** (⊠ Main St., ☎ 802/875–2121) is a pleasant place for a rainy-day browse, especially for map lovers. More than 125 dealers sell antiques and country crafts at **Stone House Village Antiques Center** (⊠ Rte. 103 S, ☎ 802/875–4477).

Grafton

★ ⑬ *8 mi south of Chester.*

Like many Vermont villages its size, Grafton enjoyed its heyday as an agricultural community well before the Civil War, when its citizens grazed some 10,000 sheep and spun their wool into sturdy yarn for locally woven fabric. Unlike most other out-of-the-way country towns, though, Grafton was born again, following a long decline, by preservationists determined to revitalize not only its centerpiece, the Old Tavern, but many other commercial and residential structures in the village center. Beginning in 1963, the Windham Foundation—Vermont's second-largest private foundation—commenced the rehabilitation of Grafton. The **Historical Society** documents the town's renewal. ⊠ *Townshend Rd.,* ☎ *802/843–2584 visitor center information.* ☜ *$1.* ◯ *June–late Sept., weekends 1:30–4; late Sept.–Oct., daily 1:30–4.*

Dining and Lodging

$$$$ ✕▥ **Old Tavern at Grafton.** White-column porches on both stories wrap around the main building of this commanding 1801 inn. The main building has 11 rooms; the rest are dispersed among six other buildings in town. Two dining rooms ($$$), one with formal Georgian furniture, the other with rustic paneling and low beams, serve inspired Continental fare. The inn runs the nearby Grafton Ponds Cross-Country Ski Center. ⊠ *Rte. 121, 05146,* ☎ *802/843–2231 or 800/843–1801,* [FAX] *802/843–2245,* [WEB] *www.old-tavern.com. 48 rooms, 7 suites. Restaurant, café, tennis court, pond, mountain bikes, paddle tennis, cross-country skiing, ice-skating, bar, Internet, meeting rooms. AE, MC, V. Closed Apr. BP.*

Shopping

Gallery North Star (⊠ Townshend Rd., ☎ 802/843–2465) exhibits the oils, watercolors, lithographs, and sculptures of Vermont-based artists.

Townshend

⑭ *9 mi south of Grafton.*

One of a string of pretty villages along the banks of the West River, Townshend embodies the Vermont ideal of a lovely town green presided over by a gracefully proportioned church spire. The spire belongs to the 1790 Congregational Meeting House, one of the state's oldest houses of worship. Just north on Route 30 is the Scott Bridge (closed to traffic), the state's longest single-span covered bridge.

At **Townshend State Park,** you'll find a sandy beach and a trailhead for the rigorous, 2.7-mi hike to the top of Bald Mountain. Campsites are available. ⊠ *Rte. 30 N,* ☎ *802/365–7500.*

Dining and Lodging

$ ✕ **Townshend Dam Diner.** Folks come from miles around to enjoy traditional fare such as Mom's meat loaf, chili, and roast beef croquettes, as well as Townshend-raised bison burgers, and creative daily specials. Breakfast, served all day every day, includes such tasty treats as raspberry chocolate-chip walnut pancakes and homemade French toast. ⊠ *Rte. 30,* ☎ *802/874–4107. No credit cards. Closed Tues.*

$$$$ ✕🖫 **Windham Hill Inn.** Period antiques, Oriental carpets, and locally made furniture are hallmarks of this 1825 brick farmhouse and white barn annex house. Most rooms have fireplaces; all have magnificent views of the West River valley. A prix-fixe four-course candlelight dinner ($$$; à la carte menu also available) is served in the Frog Pond Dining Room. ⊠ *311 Lawrence Dr., West Townshend 05359,* ☎ *800/944–4080,* FAX *802/874–4702,* WEB *www.windhamhill.com. 21 rooms. Restaurant, tennis court, pool, hiking, cross-country skiing, ice-skating; no kids under 12. BP.*

$ 🖫 **Boardman House.** This handsome Greek Revival home on the town green combines modern comfort with the relaxed charm of a 19th-century farmhouse. The uncluttered guest rooms are furnished with Shaker-style furniture, colorful duvets, and paintings. Both the breakfast room and front hall have trompe l'oeil floors. ⊠ *On the Green, 05353,* ☎ *802/365–4086,* WEB *www.southvermont.com/townshend/ boardmanhouse. 5 rooms, 1 suite. Some cable TV, sauna. No credit cards. BP.*

Outdoor Activities and Sports

You can rent canoes, kayaks, tubes, cross-country skis, and snowshoes at **Townshend Outdoors** (⊠ Rte. 30, ☎ 802/365–7309).

Shopping

The **Big Black Bear Shop** at Mary Meyer Stuffed Toys Factory, the state's oldest stuffed toy company, offers discounts of up to 70% on bear-related products (⊠ Rte. 30, ☎ 888/758–2327).

Newfane

🅕 *15 mi south of Grafton.*

With a village green surrounded by pristine white buildings, Newfane is sometimes described as the quintessential New England small town. The 1839 First Congregational Church and the Windham County Court House, with 17 green-shuttered windows and a rounded cupola, are often open. The building with the four-pointed spire is Union Hall, built in 1832.

Dining and Lodging

$$–$$$ ✕🖫 **Four Columns.** Rooms in this white-columned, 1834 Greek Revival mansion are decorated with a mix of antiques and turn-of-the-20th-century reproductions. Most of the suites have cathedral ceilings; all have double whirlpool baths and gas fireplaces. Two third-floor suites in the old section afford the most privacy. The elegant restaurant ($$$–$$$$; closed Tues.) serves new American cuisine. ⊠ *West St. (Box 278, 05345),* ☎ *802/365–7713 or 800/787–6633,* FAX *802/ 365–0022,* WEB *www.fourcolumnsinn.com. 9 rooms, 6 suites. Restaurant, pool, hiking, bar, Internet, some pets allowed (fee). AE, D, DC, MC, V. CP.*

Shopping

The **Newfane Country Store** (✉ Rte. 30, ☎ 802/365–7916) carries many quilts (which can also be custom ordered), homemade fudge, and other Vermont foods, gifts, and crafts. Collectibles dealers from across the state sell their wares at the **Newfane Flea Market** (✉ Rte. 30, ☎ 802/365–7771), held every weekend during summer and fall. Corn-cob-smoked ham and bacon and Vermont cheeses are just a few of the delectable goodies at **Lawrence's Smoke House** (✉ Rte. 30, ☎ 802/365–7372).

Putney

16 *7 mi east of Newfane, 9 mi north of Brattleboro.*

Putney, a Connecticut River valley town just upriver from Brattleboro, was a prime destination for many of the converts to alternative rural lifestyles who swarmed into Vermont during the late 1960s and early '70s. Those who remain maintain a tradition of progressive schools, artisanship, and organic farming.

Harlow's Sugar House (✉ U.S. 5, ☎ 802/387–5852), 2 mi north of Putney, has a working cider mill and sugarhouse, as well as berry picking in summer and apple picking in autumn. You can buy cider, maple syrup, and other items in the gift shop.

Tours are given of the **Green Mountain Spinnery,** a factory-shop that sells yarn, knitting accessories, and patterns. ✉ *Depot Rd. at Exit 4 off I–91,* ☎ *802/387–4528 or 800/321–9665.* ☉ *Tours at 1:30 on the 1st and 3rd Tues. of month.*

Dining and Lodging

$$–$$$ ✕▥ **Putney Inn.** The inn's main building dates from the 1790s and was later part of a seminary—the present-day pub was the chapel. Two fireplaces dominate the lobby. The spacious, modern rooms in an adjacent building have Queen Anne mahogany reproductions and are 100 yards from the banks of the Connecticut River. The restaurant ($$$) serves regionally inspired cuisine—seafood, New England potpies, a wild-game mixed grill, and burgers with Vermont cheddar—marked by innovative flourishes. ✉ *Depot Rd., 05346,* ☎ *802/387–5517 or 800/653–5517,* FAX *802/387–5211,* WEB *www.putneyinn.com. 25 rooms. Restaurant, lounge, meeting rooms, some pets allowed (fee). AE, D, MC, V. BP.*

$$$ ▥ **Hickory Ridge House Bed and Breakfast.** On the National Register of Historic Places, this 1808 Federal-style mansion with Palladian windows and a parlor with a Rumford fireplace has large, comfortable guest rooms filled with antiques and country furnishings. Five rooms have wood-burning fireplaces and private baths. A two-bedroom cottage, with a full kitchen and fireplace, can be rented as a unit or the rooms can be rented separately. ✉ *53 Hickory Ridge Rd., 05346,* ☎ *802/387–5709 or 800/380–9218,* FAX *802/387–4328,* WEB *www.hickoryridgehouse.com. 6 rooms, 1 cottage. Hiking, cross-country skiing. AE, MC, V. BP.*

Shopping

Allen Bros. (✉ U.S. 5 north of Putney, ☎ 802/722–3395) bakes apple pies, makes cider doughnuts, and sells Vermont foods and products.

Southern Vermont A to Z

To research prices, get advice from other travelers, and book travel arrangements, visit www.fodors.com.

BUS TRAVEL

Vermont Transit links Bennington, Manchester, and Brattleboro.
➤ BUS INFORMATION: **Vermont Transit** (☎ 800/552–8737).

CAR TRAVEL

In the south the principal east–west highway is Route 9, the Molly Stark Trail, from Brattleboro to Bennington. The most important north–south roads are U.S. 7; the more scenic Route 7A; Route 100, which runs through the state's center; I–91; and U.S. 5, which runs along the state's eastern border. Route 30 from Brattleboro to Manchester is a scenic drive.

EMERGENCIES

➤ HOSPITALS: **Brattleboro Memorial Hospital** (⊠ 9 Belmont Ave., Brattleboro, ☎ 802/257–0341). **Southwestern Vermont Medical Center** (⊠ 100 Hospital Dr., Bennington, ☎ 802/442–6361).

VISITOR INFORMATION

➤ CONTACTS: **Bennington Area Chamber of Commerce** (⊠ Veterans Memorial Dr., Bennington 05201, ☎ 802/447–3311 or 800/229–0252, WEB www.bennington.com). **Brattleboro Area Chamber of Commerce** (⊠ 180 Main St., Brattleboro 05301, ☎ 802/254–4565, WEB www.brattleboro.com). **Chamber of Commerce, Manchester and the Mountains** (⊠ 5046 Main St., Manchester 05255, ☎ 802/362–2100, WEB www.manchestervermont.net). **Mt. Snow Valley Chamber of Commerce** (⊠ W. Main St. [Box 3, Wilmington 05363], ☎ 802/464–8092 or 877/887–6884, WEB www.visitvermont.com).

CENTRAL VERMONT

Central Vermont's economy once centered on the mills and railroad yards of Rutland and the marble quarries that honeycomb nearby towns. Vermont's "second city" is still a busy commercial hub, but today, as in much of the rest of the state, it's tourism that drives the economic engine. The center of the dynamo is the massive ski-and-stay infrastructure around Killington, the East's largest downhill resort.

However, Central Vermont has more to discover than high-speed chairlifts and slope-side condos. The protected (except for occasional logging) lands of the Green Mountain National Forest surround the spine of Vermont's central range; off to the west, the rolling dairy land of the southern Lake Champlain valley is one of the truly undiscovered corners of the state. To the east, in the Connecticut River valley, are towns as diverse as Calvin Coolidge's Plymouth, a Yankee Brigadoon, and busy, polished-to-perfection Woodstock, where upscale shops are just a short walk from America's newest national park.

The coverage of towns begins with Windsor, on U.S. 5 near I–91 at the state's eastern edge; winds westward toward U.S. 7; then continues north before heading over the spine of the Green Mountains.

Windsor

🄻 *50 mi north of Brattleboro, 42 mi east of Rutland.*

Windsor justly bills itself as the birthplace of Vermont. An interpretive exhibit on Vermont's constitution, the first in the United States to prohibit slavery and establish a system of public schools, is housed in the **Old Constitution House.** The site, where in 1777 grant holders declared Vermont an independent republic, contains 18th- and 19th-century furnishings, American paintings and prints, and Vermont-made tools, toys, and kitchenware. ⊠ N. Main St., ☎ 802/828–3211. 🖭 *$1.* ⊘ *Late May–mid-Oct., Wed.–Sun. 11–5.*

The firm of Robbins & Lawrence became famous for applying the "American system" (the use of interchangeable parts) to the manufacture

Central Vermont

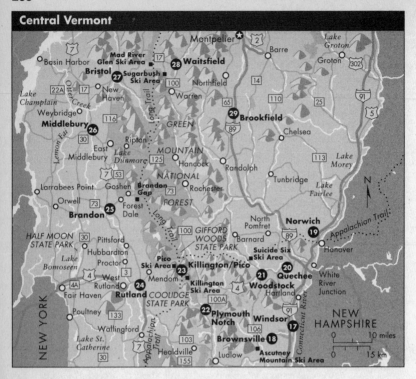

of rifles. Although the company no longer exists, the **American Precision Museum** extols the Yankee ingenuity that created a major machine-tool industry here in the 19th century. The museum contains the largest collection of historically significant machine tools in the country and presents changing exhibits. ⊠ *196 Main St.,* ☎ *802/674–6628.* ⊡ *$5.* ☺ *Memorial Day–Nov. l, daily 10–5.*

The mission of the **Vermont State Craft Gallery,** in the restored 1846 Windsor House, is to, advance the appreciation of Vermont crafts through education and exhibition. The center presents crafts exhibitions and operates a small museum. ⊠ *54 Main St.,* ☎ *802/674–6729.* ☺ *Mon.–Sat. 10–5, Sun. 1–5.*

Glass blowers demonstrate their art at **Simon Pearce** (⊠ U.S. 5, ☎ 802/ 674–6280 or 800/774–5277), where there's also a retail shop.

At 460 ft, the **Cornish–Windsor Covered Bridge** off U.S. 5, which spans the Connecticut River between Windsor and Cornish, New Hampshire, is the longest in the state.

Dining and Lodging

$$–$$$ ✕ **Windsor Station.** This converted main-line railroad station serves such entrées as chicken Kiev, filet mignon, and prime rib. The booths, with their curtained brass railings, were created from the high-back railroad benches of the depot. ⊠ *Depot Ave.,* ☎ *802/674–2052. AE, MC, V. Closed Mon. in fall and winter. No lunch.*

$$–$$$$ ✕☰ **Juniper Hill Inn.** An expanse of green lawn with Adirondack chairs and a garden of perennials sweeps up to the portico of this turn-of-the-20th-century Greek Revival mansion. Eleven of the antiques-furnished bedrooms have fireplaces. Four-course dinners ($$$$; reservations essential) are served in the candlelit dining room at 7 PM. Tuesday–Saturday may include sautéed scallops with glazed garlic and champagne sauce. ⊠ *153 Pembroke Rd., 05089,* ☎ *802/674–5273 or 800/359–*

2541, 🅵🅰🅇 802/674–2041, 🆆🅴🅱 *www.juniperhillinn.com. 16 rooms. Restaurant, pool, hiking, meeting room; no kids under 12. AE, D, MC, V. BP.*

Nightlife and the Arts

Destiny (⊠ U.S. 5, Windsor, ☎ 802/674–6671) hosts rock bands most days and has a DJ on Sunday.

Brownsville

🔞 *5 mi southwest of Windsor.*

Brownsville, a small village at the foot of Ascutney Mountain, has everything a village needs: a country store, post office, town hall, and historic grange building. The Ascutney Mountain ski area is a self-contained four-season resort.

Lodging

$$–$$$$ 🎿 **Ascutney Mountain Resort Hotel.** One of the big attractions of this five-building resort hotel–condo complex is the ski lift outside the main door. The comfortable, well-maintained suites come in different configurations and sizes—some with fireplaces and decks. Slope-side multilevel condos have three bedrooms, three baths, and private entrances. The Ascutney Harvest Inn, within the complex, serves Continental cuisine. ⊠ *Hotel Rd., off Rte. 44 (Box 699, 05037),* ☎ *802/ 484–7711 or 800/243–0011,* 🅵🅰🅇 *802/484–3117. 212 units. 3 restaurants, some kitchens, 2 pools (1 indoor), hot tub, health club, racquetball, ice-skating. AE, MC, V.*

$–$$ 🎿 **Mill Brook.** This Victorian farmhouse, built in 1880, is directly across from the Ascutney ski slopes. Making après-ski idleness easy are the four sitting rooms, decorated with antiques and contemporary furnishings. The honeymoon suite has a separate dressing room with a claw-foot bathtub; the other suites are perfect for families. Rates include afternoon tea. ⊠ *Rte. 44 (Box 410, 05037),* ☎ *802/484–7283,* 🆆🅴🅱 *www.millbrookbb.com. 2 rooms, 3 suites. Hot tub, some pets allowed (fee). AE, MC, V. BP.*

Nightlife and the Arts

Crow's Nest Club (⊠ Ascutney Mountain Resort Hotel, Hotel Rd., off Rte. 44, ☎ 802/484–7711) hosts live blues, country, rock and folk on weekends.

Ski Areas

ASCUTNEY MOUNTAIN RESORT

The Plausteiner family, whose patriarch, John, was instrumental in operations at Mt. Snow and White Face Mountain, in Lake Placid, New York, purchased this resort in the mid-1990s and since then has been continually making improvements. The self-contained resort has a 10-acre Learning Park with its own chairlift and surface lift, 95% snowmaking coverage, and a Sports and Fitness Center. The five buildings of the resort village include ski-in, ski-out hotel suites and condominium units. ⊠ *Rte. 44, off I–91 (Box 699, Brownsville 05037),* ☎ *802/484–7711; 800/243–0011 lodging.*

Downhill. Fifty-six trails with varying terrain are serviced by six lifts, including a mile-long North Peak Express high-speed quad, three triple chairs, one double chair, and a surface lift. Beginner and novice skiers stay toward the base, while intermediates enjoy the band that wraps the midsection. For experts, tougher black-diamond runs top the mountain. One disadvantage to Ascutney is that there is no easy way down from the summit, so novice skiers should not make the trip. Ascutney is popular with families because it provides some of the least-expensive junior lift tickets in the region.

Cross-country skiing. The resort has 32 km (19 mi) of groomed cross-country trails and offers rentals.

Child care. Day care is available for children from ages 6 weeks–6 years, with learn-to-ski options and rental equipment for toddlers and up. There are half- and full-day instruction programs for children ages 3–12; a Mini-Olympians program for ages 4 to 6; and a Young Olympians program for ages 7–12.

Summer and year-round activities. Ascutney Mountain Resort Hotel has a sports-and-fitness center with full-size indoor and outdoor pools, a hot tub, racquetball, aerobics facilities and classes, weight training, and massage. Summer activities include mountain biking, hiking, and tennis.

Norwich

🔟 *6 mi north of White River Junction, 22 mi north of Brownsville.*

Norwich, comprised of beautifully kept 18th- and 19th- century homes surrounding a handsome green, is home to Dartmouth College and an excellent science museum.

★ ☾ Numerous hands-on exhibits at the **Montshire Museum of Science** explore space, nature, and technology; there are also living habitats, aquariums, and many children's programs. A maze of trails wind through 100 acres of pristine woodland. An ideal destination for a rainy day, this is one of the finest museums in New England. ⊠ *1 Montshire Rd.,* ☎ *802/649–2200,* WEB *www.montshire.org.* ⊡ *$6.50.* ☾ *Daily 10–5.*

Shopping
The shelves at **King Arthur Flour Baker's Store** (⊠ 135 Rte. 5 S, ☎ 802/649–3881) are stocked with all the tools and ingredients in the company's Baker's Catalogue, including mixes and flours, and local products. A bakery with a viewing area enables you to watch products being made.

Quechee

🔟 *11 mi south of Norwich, 6 mi west of White River Junction.*

Quechee is perched astride the Ottauquechee River. Quechee Gorge, 165 ft deep, is impressive though sometimes overrun by tourists. You can see the mile-long gorge, carved by a glacier, from U.S. 4, but many people picnic nearby or scramble down one of several descents for a closer look.

More than a decade ago Simon Pearce set up **Simon Pearce,** an eponymous glassblowing factory in an old mill by a waterfall here, using the water power to drive his furnace. Today the glassblowing factory is at the heart of a handsome, upscale shopping complex that also houses a weaver (demonstrations Tuesday–Sunday) and a pottery studio. You can watch the glassblowers at work daily and then purchase their wares in the gift shop or enjoy food served on seconds in the restaurant, which overlooks the waterfall. ⊠ *The Mill, Main St.,* ☎ *802/295–2711,* WEB *www.simonpearceglass.com.* ☾ *Store daily 9–9.*

Dining and Lodging
$$–$$$ ✕ **Simon Pearce.** Candlelight, sparkling glassware from the studio downstairs, contemporary dinnerware, exposed brick, and large windows that overlook the roaring Ottauquechee River create an ideal setting for contemporary American cuisine. Sesame-crusted tuna with noodle cakes and wasabi as well as roast duck with mango chutney sauce are house specialties; the wine cellar holds several hundred vintages. ⊠ *Main St.,* ☎ *802/295–1470. AE, D, DC, MC, V.*

$$$ ✕⛻ **Quechee Inn at Marshland Farm.** Each room in this handsomely restored 1793 country home is decorated with Queen Anne–style furnishings and period antiques. Activities include cross-country skiing on groomed ski trails, bike and canoe rentals, a fly-fishing school, and privileges at the Quechee Country Club. The dining room's ($$$) creative dishes include entrées such as duck confit and seared sesame tuna. ⊠ *Clubhouse Rd., 05059,* ☎ *802/295–3133 or 800/235–3133,* ᴲᴬᵡ *802/ 295–6587,* ᵂᴱᴮ *www.quecheeinn.com. 22 rooms, 2 suites. Restaurant, golf privileges, fishing, bicycles, cross-country skiing, meeting room. AE, D, DC, MC, V. BP.*

$$–$$$ ✕⛻ **Parker House.** The peach-and-blue rooms of this 1857 Victorian mansion are named for former residents: Emily has a marble fireplace and Joseph has a view of the Ottauquechee River. The elegant dining room ($$$) prepares sophisticated American comfort cuisine such as loin of venison with a port and balsamic vinegar sauce. You also have access to the Quechee Country Club's facilities. ⊠ *1792 Quechee Main St. (Box 0780, 05059),* ☎ *802/295–6077,* ᴲᴬᵡ *802/296–6696,* ᵂᴱᴮ *www.theparkerhouseinn.com. 7 rooms. Restaurant, golf privileges; no air-conditioning in some rooms. AE, MC, V. BP.*

Outdoor Activities and Sports

FISHING

The **Vermont Fly Fishing School/Wilderness Trails** (⊠ Quechee Inn, Clubhouse Rd., ☎ 802/295–7620) leads workshops, rents fishing gear and mountain bikes, and arranges canoe and kayak trips. In winter, the company conducts cross-country and snowshoe treks.

POLO

Quechee Polo Club (⊠ Dewey's Mill Rd., ½ mi north of U.S. 4, ☎ 802/ 295–7152) draws hundreds of spectators on summer Saturdays to its matches near the Quechee Gorge. Admission is $3 per person or $6 per carload.

Shopping

The 40 dealers at the **Hartland Antiques Center** (⊠ U.S. 4, ☎ 802/457– 4745) stock furniture, paper items, china, glass, and collectibles. More than 350 dealers sell their wares at the **Quechee Gorge Village** (⊠ U.S. 4, ☎ 802/295–1550 or 800/438–5565), an antiques and crafts mall in an immense reconstructed barn that also houses a country store and a classic diner. A merry-go-round and a small-scale working railroad operate when weather permits.

Ottauquechee Valley Winery (⊠ 5967 Woodstock Rd./U.S. 4, ☎ 802/ 295–9463), in a historic 1870s barn complex, has a tasting room and sells fruit wines, such as apple and blueberry.

Scotland by the Yard (⊠ U.S. 4, ☎ 802/295–5351 or 800/295–5351) is the place to shop for all things Scottish, from kilts to Harris tweed jackets and tartan ties.

Woodstock

★ ㉑ *4 mi west of Quechee.*

Perfectly preserved Federal-style houses surround Woodstock's tree-lined village green, and streams flow around the town center, which is anchored by a covered bridge. The town owes much of its pristine appearance to the Rockefeller family's interest in historic preservation and land conservation. Woodstock's history of conservation dates from the 19th century: town native George Perkins Marsh, a congressman and diplomat, wrote the pioneering book *Man and Nature* in 1864 and was closely involved in the creation of the Smithsonian Institution in Washington, D.C.

The **Billings Farm and Museum,** on the grounds of George Perkins Marsh's boyhood home, was founded by Frederick Billings in 1870 as a model of conservation and is one of the oldest dairy farms in the country. Billings, a lawyer and businessman, put into practice Marsh's ideas about the long-term effects of farming and grazing. Exhibits in the reconstructed Queen Anne farmhouse, school, general store, workshop, and former Marsh homestead demonstrate the lives and skills of early Vermont settlers. ⊠ *Rte. 12, ½ mi north of Woodstock,* ☎ *802/457–2355,* WEB *www.billingsfarm.org.* ▦ *$8.* ☉ *May–late Oct., daily 10–5; call for Thanksgiving and Dec. weekend schedules.*

The 500-acre **Marsh-Billings-Rockefeller National Historical Park,** which opened in 1998, is Vermont's only national park and the nation's first to focus on conservation and stewardship of natural resources. The park encompasses the forest lands planned by Frederick Billings according to the principles of George Perkins Marsh, as well as Billings' mansion, gardens, and carriage roads. The entire property was the gift of Laurance S. Rockefeller, who lived here with his late wife, Mary, Frederick Billings' granddaughter. It is adjacent to the ☞ Billings Farm and Museum. The residential complex is accessible by guided tour only, but you can explore the extensive network of carriage roads and trails on your own. ⊠ *Rte. 12,* ☎ *802/457–3368,* WEB *www.nps.marshbillings.com.* ▦ *Tour $6.* ☉ *Memorial Day–Oct., daily for guided tours only (call for schedules); grounds daily dawn–dusk.*

Period furnishings of the Woodstock Historical Society fill the white clapboard **Dana House,** built circa 1807. Exhibits include the town charter, furniture, maps, and locally minted silver. The converted barn houses the Woodstock Works exhibit, an economic portrait of the town. ⊠ *26 Elm St.,* ☎ *802/457–1822.* ▦ *$2.* ☉ *Mid-May–mid-Oct., Mon.–Sat. 10–4, Sun. noon–4; mid-Oct.–mid-May, by appointment only.*

The Raptor Center of the **Vermont Institute of Natural Science** (VINS) houses 23 species of birds of prey, among them bald eagles, peregrine falcons, and 3-ounce saw-whet owls. There are also ravens, turkey vultures, and snowy owls. All the caged birds have been found injured and unable to survive in the wild. This nonprofit, environmental research and education center is on a 77-acre nature preserve with walking trails. ⊠ *Church Hill Rd.,* ☎ *802/457–2779,* WEB *www.vinsweb.org.* ▦ *$7.* ☉ *Mon.–Sat. 10–4.*

Dining and Lodging

$$$–$$$$ ★ ✕ **Prince & the Pauper.** Modern French and American fare with a Vermont accent is the focus of this candlelit Colonial restaurant. The grilled duck breast might have an Asian five-spice sauce; lamb and pork sausage in puff pastry comes with a honey-mustard sauce. A three-course prix-fixe menu is available for $38; a less-expensive bistro menu is available in the lounge. ⊠ *24 Elm St.,* ☎ *802/457–1818. AE, D, MC, V. No lunch.*

$–$$ ✕ **Pane & Salute.** Regional Italian breads are a specialty, but this restaurant serves a lot more. Try the Tuscan pizzas and pasta entrées such as penne with spinach, pine nuts, raisins, and garlic. Add a glass of Chianti and *mangia bene.* Desserts include meringues with whipped cream and raspberry sauce. Sunday brunch is served from 10 to 2. ⊠ *61 Central St.,* ☎ *802/457–4882. D, MC, V. Closed Tues.–Wed.*

$$$$ ★ ✕▥ **Jackson House Inn.** European antiques, Oriental rugs, and French-cut crystal fill the formal parlor and cozy library at this inn. One wing

houses suites with gas fireplaces, down duvets, and thermal massage tubs; the other wing has the restaurant ($$$$), whose focal point is a granite, open-hearth fireplace. Herb-crusted cod with an artichoke ragout and lamb shanks braised in red wine and port typify the lighter, contemporary cuisine. You can choose from a prix-fixe, three-course menu or the five-course chef's tasting menu ($65). ⊠ *114-3 Senior La., 05091,* ☎ *802/457–2065 or 800/448–1890,* FAX *802/457–9290,* WEB *www.jacksonhouse.com. 9 rooms, 6 suites. Restaurant, gym, sauna, Internet, meeting room; no kids under 14. AE, MC, V. BP.*

$$$$ ✕⊞ **Woodstock Inn and Resort.** Resort entrepreneur Laurance Rockefeller, long a Woodstock resident, made this elegant country inn a flagship property of his Rockresorts chain. Rooms are spacious, serene, and set well back from Woodstock's often noisy main street. Dinner ($$$–$$$$), served by candlelight, highlights classic American and nouvelle New England. Lighter fare is served in the more casual café. You can ski free midweek at the inn-owned Suicide Six. ⊠ *14 The Green, U.S. 4, 05091,* ☎ *802/457–1100 or 800/448–7900,* FAX *802/457–6699,* WEB *www.woodstockinn.com. 144 rooms, 7 suites. 2 restaurants, 2 18-hole golf courses, 12 tennis courts, 2 pools (1 indoor), health club, sauna, croquet, racquetball, squash, cross-country skiing, meeting room. AE, MC, V. MAP.*

$$$–$$$$ ✕⊞ **Kedron Valley Inn.** Two 19th-century buildings, including the 13-
★ room Main House, and a 1968 log structure make up this inn on 15 acres. Many of the rooms have a fireplace or a Franklin stove, two have decks, one has a veranda, and another has a terrace overlooking a stream. The motel units in back are decorated with country antiques and reproductions. In the restaurant ($$$–$$$$), the chef creates French masterpieces such as fillet of Norwegian salmon stuffed with herb seafood mousse in puff pastry. ⊠ *Rte. 106, 05071,* ☎ *802/457–1473 or 800/ 836–1193,* FAX *802/457–4469,* WEB *www.kedronvalleyinn.com. 21 rooms, 7 suites. Restaurant, pond, beach, bar, meeting room, some pets allowed (fee); no air-conditioning in some rooms. AE, D, MC, V. Closed Apr. and 10 days before Thanksgiving. BP, MAP.*

$$$$ ⊞ **Twin Farms.** At the center of this exclusive 300-acre resort— Vermont's most sumptuous and most expensive—stands the 1795 farmhouse where writers Sinclair Lewis and Dorothy Thompson lived. Twin Farms' rooms and cottages are fantasy environments, drawing their inspiration from Moorish, Scandinavian, Japanese, and Adirondack design. There are fireplaces throughout, along with museum-quality artworks. The rich contemporary cuisine emphasizes local ingredients. ⊠ *Stage Rd., off Rte. 12, 8 mi north of Woodstock (Box 115, Barnard 05031),* ☎ *802/234–9999 or 800/894–6327,* FAX *802/234–9990,* WEB *www. twinfarms.com. 6 rooms, 9 cottages. Dining room, Japanese baths, gym, spa, boating, bicycles, ice-skating, cross-country skiing, downhill skiing, recreation room, meeting room; no kids. AE, DC, MC, V. FAP.*

$$–$$$ ⊞ **Shire Motel.** Some rooms in this immaculate motel have decks overlooking the Ottauquechee River and the Billings Farm. All have four-poster beds and wing chairs; the suites have hot tubs and fireplaces. Complimentary coffee is served each morning. ⊠ *46 Pleasant St., 05091,* ☎ *802/457–2211,* FAX *802/457–5836,* WEB *www.shiremotel.com. 33 rooms, 3 suites. Refrigerators. AE, D, MC, V.*

$$–$$$ ⊞ **Winslow House.** Jeff and Kathy Bendis take great pride in their beau-
★ tifully restored 200-year-old farmhouse, which has hardwood and wide pine flooring, fine architectural details, and lovely but simple antique furnishings. The two guest rooms on the first floor include a suite with a private sitting room and a day bed; the three second-floor accommodations include two suites with private sitting rooms and a spacious room with a cathedral ceiling and private balcony. Breakfast is served by candlelight. ⊠ *492 Woodstock Rd./U.S. 4, 05091,* ☎ *802/*

457–1820, WEB *www.thewinslowhousevt.com. 2 rooms, 3 suites. Re-frigerators, some pets allowed; no kids under 8. MC, V. BP.*

$$ ⊡ **Deer Brook Inn B&B.** Each spacious, immaculate guest room at this 1820 Colonial-style farmhouse has comfortable, unpretentious furnishings. The quilts are handmade by the inn's owner, Rosemary McGinty, who will bring her two golden retrievers out to meet you on request. The Deer Brook is 5 mi from downtown Woodstock and 10 mi from Killington. ⊠ *535 U.S. 4, 05091,* ☎ *802/672–3713,* WEB *www.bbhost.com/deerbrookinn. 4 rooms, 1 suite. AE, MC, V. BP.*

Outdoor Activities and Sports

BIKING

Cyclery Plus (⊠ 36 U.S. 4 W, West Woodstock, ☎ 802/457–3377) rents, sells, and services bikes and also distributes a free touring map of local rides.

GOLF

Robert Trent Jones Sr. designed the 18-hole, par-69 course at **Woodstock Country Club** (⊠ South St., ☎ 802/457–2114), which is run by the Woodstock Inn. Greens fees are $32–$75; cart rentals are $38.

HORSEBACK RIDING

Kedron Valley Stables (⊠ Rte. 106, South Woodstock, ☎ 802/457–2734 or 800/225–6301) gives lessons and conducts guided trail rides and excursions in a sleigh and a wagon. The stable also organizes year-round, inn-to-inn four-day riding packages.

STATE PARK

Coolidge State Park (⊠ Rte. 100A, 2 mi north of Rte. 100, ☎ 802/672–3612) abuts Coolidge State Forest and has campsites (log lean-tos from the 1930s).

Shopping

The **Marketplace at Bridgewater Mills** (⊠ U.S. 4, west of Woodstock, ☎ 802/672–3332) houses shops and attractions in a three-story converted woolen mill. There's an antiques and crafts center, a bookstore, Miranda Thomas pottery, and handsome Charles Shackleton furniture. Sample Vermont stocks foods and gifts.

Stephen Huneck Studio (⊠ 49 Central St., ☎ 802/457–3206) invites canines and humans to visit the artist's gallery, filled with whimsical animal carvings, prints, and furniture. **Taftsville Country Store** (⊠ U.S. 4, Taftsville, ☎ 802/457–1135 or 800/854–0013) sells an excellent selection of Vermont cheeses, moderately priced wines, and Vermont specialty foods. The **Village Butcher** (⊠ Elm St., ☎ 802/457–2756) is an emporium of Vermont comestibles. **Who Is Sylvia?** (⊠ 26 Central St., ☎ 802/457–1110), in the old firehouse, sells vintage clothing and antique linens, lace, and jewelry.

Sugarbush Farm Inc. (⊠ 591 Sugarbush Farm Rd., ☎ 802/457–1757 or 800/281–1757) taps 5,000 maple trees to make syrup each spring. You can purchase syrup here and take a self-guided tour at any time of the year. The farm also makes excellent cheeses. The road can be messy, so call for conditions and directions.

Ski Areas

SUICIDE SIX

The site of the first ski tow in the United States (1934), this resort is owned and operated by the Woodstock Inn and Resort. The inn's package plans are remarkably inexpensive, considering the high quality of the accommodations. ⊠ *Pomfret Rd., 05091,* ☎ *802/457–6661; 800/448–7900 lodging; 802/457–6666 snow conditions.*

Downhill. Despite Suicide Six's short vertical of only 650 ft, the skiing is challenging. There are steep runs down the mountain's face, intermediate trails that wind around the hill, and glade skiing. Beginner terrain is mostly toward the bottom. Two double chairlifts and one surface lift service the 23 trails and slopes. The resort also has a snowboard area with a halfpipe. Snowmaking covers 50% of the area's terrain.

Child care. The ski area has no nursery, but baby-sitting can be arranged through the Woodstock Inn if you're a guest. Lessons for children are given by the ski-school staff, and there's a children's ski-and-play park for kids ages three to seven.

Summer and year-round activities. Outdoor tennis courts, lighted paddle courts, croquet, and an 18-hole golf course are open in summer. The **Woodstock Health and Fitness Center** (☎ 802/457–6656), open year-round, has an indoor lap pool; indoor tennis, squash, and racquetball courts; whirlpool, steam, sauna, and massage rooms; and exercise and aerobics rooms.

CROSS-COUNTRY

The **Woodstock Ski Touring Center** (☎ 802/457–6674), headquartered at the Woodstock Country Club (⊠ Rte. 106), has 60 km (37 mi) of trails. Equipment and lessons are available.

Plymouth Notch

㉒ *14 mi southwest of Woodstock.*

U.S. president Calvin Coolidge was born and buried in Plymouth Notch, a town that shares his character: low-key and quiet. The perfectly preserved 19th-century buildings of the **Plymouth Notch Historic District** look more like a large farm than a town; in addition to the homestead there's the general store once run by Coolidge's father, a visitor center, a cheese factory (with tasty cheeses for sale), and a one-room schoolhouse. Coolidge's grave is in the cemetery across Route 100A. The Aldrich House, which mounts changing historical exhibits, is open on some weekdays during the off-season. ⊠ *Rte. 100A, 6 mi south of U.S. 4, east of Rte. 100,* ☎ *802/672–3773.* ☞ *$5.* ☺ *Late May–mid-Oct., daily 9:30–5.*

Killington/Pico

㉓ *11 mi (Pico) and 15 mi (Killington) east of Rutland.*

The intersection of U.S. 4 and Route 100 is the heart of central Vermont's ski country, with the Killington, Pico, and Okemo resorts nearby. Unfortunate strip development characterizes the Killington access road, but the views from the top of the mountain are worth the drive.

Dining and Lodging

$$$$ ✕ **Hemingway's.** With a national reputation, Hemingway's is as good
★ as dining gets in central Vermont. Among the house specialties are the cream of garlic soup and a seasonal kaleidoscope of dishes based on native game, fresh seafood, and prime meats. Weekends, diners can opt for the prix-fixe, three- to six-course menu or the four-course wine-tasting menu. An à la carte menu is available during the week. Request seating in either the formal, vaulted dining room or the intimate wine cellar. ⊠ *U.S. 4,* ☎ *802/422–3886. AE, D, DC, MC, V. Closed most Mon.–Tues., early Nov., and mid-Apr.–mid-May. No lunch.*

$$$$ ✕▥ **Red Clover Inn.** Elegant accommodations and fine dining ($$$–$$$$)
★ are the attractions at this romantic 1840s hideaway on 13 mountain acres 5 mi from Killington. Among the antiques-filled rooms in the inn

and carriage house are three with fireplaces and whirlpool tubs for two. Many rooms have mountain views. A four-course candlelight dinner, with choice of menu, is served Monday–Saturday evenings. *Wine Spectator* magazine cited the inn's wine list as one of the world's most outstanding. ⊠ *7 Woodward Rd., Mendon 05701,* ☎ *802/775–2290 or 800/752–0571,* FAX *802/773–0594,* WEB *www.redcloverinn.com. 14 rooms. Dining room, cable TV in some rooms, pool, hiking, meeting rooms, some pets allowed (fee); no kids under 12. D, MC, V. Closed Apr.–Memorial Day. BP, MAP.*

$$$ ✕🖬 **Birch Ridge Inn.** A slate-covered carriageway leads to one of Killington's newest inns, a former executive retreat that has been converted into an upscale getaway. Rooms range in styles from Colonial and Shaker to Mission, and all have a sitting area. Six rooms have gas fireplaces, and four of these also have whirlpool baths. In the intimate dining room ($$$$), you can choose either a four-course meal or an à la carte menu ($$$–$$$$), which includes dishes such as pan-seared duckling breast. ⊠ *Butler Rd., at Killington Rd., 05751,* ☎ *802/422–4293 or 800/435–8566,* FAX *802/422–3406,* WEB *www.birchridge.com. 10 rooms. Restaurant, lounge; no air-conditioning in some rooms, no kids under 12. AE, MC, V. BP, MAP.*

$$$ ✕🖬 **Summit Lodge.** Three miles from Killington Peak, this rustic two-story country lodge caters to a varied crowd of ski enthusiasts, who are warmly met by the lodge's mascots—a pair of Saint Bernards. Country appointments and antiques blend with modern conveniences to create relaxing surroundings. The restaurant ($$–$$$) serves Continental specialties such as rack of lamb and chicken Birmingham—a boneless breast of chicken with spinach, garlic, feta cheese, and sun-dried tomatoes. ⊠ *Killington Rd., 05751,* ☎ *802/422–3535 or 800/635–6343,* FAX *802/422–3536,* WEB *www.summitlodgevermont.com. 43 rooms, 2 suites. Restaurant, pool, pond, hot tub, massage, sauna, ice-skating, bar, nightclub, video game room, meeting rooms; no-smoking rooms. AE, DC, MC, V. BP; MAP only certain vacation/holiday periods.*

$$–$$$$ 🖬 **Cortina Inn & Resort.** Close to the ski resort, this large lodge provides comfortable accommodations and a host of year-round activities. The contemporary country rooms have private balconies or terraces; deluxe rooms have mountain or garden views. Two-room family suites have bunk beds. Amenities include guided snowmobile, fly-fishing, and mountain-biking tours. ⊠ *U.S. 4, Killington 05751,* ☎ *802/773–3333 or 800/451–6108,* FAX *802/775–6948,* WEB *www.cortinainn.com. 89 rooms, 7 suites. 2 restaurants, some cable TV, 8 tennis courts, indoor pool, health club, hot tub, sauna, horseback riding, ice-skating, sleigh rides, some pets allowed (fee). AE, D, DC, MC, V. BP.*

$$–$$$ 🖬 **Mountain Meadows Lodge.** Simple but comfortable accommodations and a plethora of activities for both kids and adults make this lakefront resort a perfect family getaway. Mountain Meadow Munchkins provides child care. Dinner is served Friday and Saturday nights, and a light menu is available Sunday–Thursday. ⊠ *285 Thundering Brook Rd., 05751,* ☎ *802/775–1010 or 800/370–4567,* FAX *802/773–4459,* WEB *www.mtmeadowslodge.com. 20 rooms, 1 suite. Restaurant, pool, lake, sauna, boating, fishing, hiking, cross-country skiing, tobogganing, recreation room, children's programs. AE, D, MC, V. Closed mid-Oct.–mid-Nov. BP, MAP.*

Nightlife and the Arts

The pub at the **Inn at Long Trail** (⊠ U.S. 4, ☎ 802/775–7181) hosts Irish music on weekends. The **Pickle Barrel** (⊠ Killington Rd., ☎ 802/422–3035), a favorite with the après-ski crowd, presents pop and rock acts and can get pretty rowdy. Dance to blues and rock at the **Wob-**

bly Barn (✉ Killington Rd., ☎ 802/422–3392), open only during ski season.

Outdoor Activities and Sports

FISHING

Gifford Woods State Park's Kent Pond (✉ Rte. 100, ½ mi north of U.S. 4, ☎ 802/775–5354) is a terrific fishing hole; campsites are available.

GOLF

The 18-hole, par-71 **Green Mountain National Golf Course** (✉ Rte. 100 N, Shelburne, ☎ 802/422–4653) has earned accolades as one of the state's best. Greens fees are $52 midweek and $57 weekends in May and June; $57 midweek and $62 weekends from late June through fall. Cart rental is $18 per person. At its namesake resort, **Killington Golf Course** (✉ 4763 Killington Rd., 05751, ☎ 802/422–6700) has a challenging 18-hole course. Greens fees are $51; carts run for $16.

ICE-SKATING

Cortina Inn has an ice-skating rink and runs sleigh rides; you can also skate on Summit Pond.

Ski Areas

KILLINGTON

"Megamountain," "Beast of the East," and plain "huge" are apt descriptions of Killington. The American Skiing Company operates Killington and its neighbor, Pico, and over the past several years has improved lifts, snowmaking capabilities, and lodging options. The resort has the longest ski season in the East as well as the country's most extensive snowmaking system. Killington's après-ski activities are plentiful and have been rated best in the East by the national ski magazines. With a single call to Killington's hot line or a visit to its Web site, skiers can plan an entire vacation: choose accommodations; book air or railroad transportation; and arrange for rental equipment and ski lessons. Killington ticket holders can also ski at Pico: a shuttle connects the two areas. ✉ *4763 Killington Rd., 05751,* ☎ *802/422–6200; 800/621–6867 lodging; 802/422–3261 snow conditions;* WEB *www.killington.com.*

Downhill. It would probably take several weeks to test all 200 trails on the seven mountains of the Killington complex, even though all except Pico interconnect. About 70% of the 1,182 acres of skiing terrain can be covered with machine-made snow. Transporting skiers to the peaks of this complex are 32 lifts, including two gondolas, 12 quads (including six high-speed express quads), six triples, and a Magic Carpet. The K-1 Express Gondola goes to the area's highest elevation, at 4,241 ft off Killington Peak, and a vertical drop of 3,050 ft to the base of the Skyeship, the world's fastest and first heated eight-passenger lift. The Skyeship base station has a rotisserie, food court, and a coffee bar. The skiing includes everything from Outer Limits, one of the steepest and most challenging mogul trails anywhere in the country, to the 6½-mi Great Eastern Trail. In the Fusion Zones, underbrush and low branches have been cleared away to provide tree skiing. Killington's Superpipe is one of the best-rated in the East. Two alpine parks and a 420 ft-long superpipe are set-up for snowboarders.

Child care. Nursery care is available for children ages 6 weeks–6 years old. Instruction programs are available for youngsters from ages 3–8; those from 6 to 12 can join an all-day program.

Summer activities. The Killington-Pico complex has a host of activities including an alpine slide, a golf course, a "Bungee Thing" ride, two water slides, a skateboard park, and a swimming pool. The resort rents mountain bikes and advises hikers. The **K1 Express Gondola** (☎ 802/422–6200) takes you up the mountain on the Killington Skyeship.

PICO SKI RESORT

Although it's only 5 mi down the road from Killington, Pico—one of the state's first ski areas—has long been a favorite among people looking for old New England–style skiing, with lots of glades and winding and narrow trails. A village square lies at the base, with condo-hotel, restaurants, and shops. ⊠ *Rte. 4, Killington 05751,* ☎ *802/422–3333; 800/621–6867 lodging; 802/422–3261 snow conditions.*

Downhill. Many of the 48 trails are advanced to expert, with two intermediate bail-out trails for the timid. The rest of the mountain's 2,000 ft of vertical terrain is mostly intermediate or easier. The mountain has seven lifts including two high-speed quads, two triples, and three double chairs and has 75% snowmaking coverage. Snowboarding is permitted everywhere on Pico, and there is a Terrain Park. For instruction of any kind, head to the Alpine Learning Center.

Child care. Pico's nursery takes children ages 6 months–6 years and provides indoor activities and outdoor play. The ski school has full- and half-day instruction programs for children ages 3–12.

Summer and year-round activities. A sports center (☎ 802/773–1786) at the base of the mountain has fitness facilities, a 75-ft pool, whirlpool tub, saunas, and a massage room. You can also take advantage of activities at Killington.

CROSS-COUNTRY SKIING

Mountain Meadows (⊠ Thundering Brook Rd., ☎ 802/775–7077 or 800/221–0598) has 57 km (34½ mi) of groomed trails and 10 km (6 mi) of marked outlying trails. You can also access 500 acres of back-country skiing. **Mountain Top Inn and Resort** (☎ 802/483–6089 or 800/445–2100) is mammoth, with 120 km (72 mi) of trails, 80 km (49 mi) of which are groomed.

Rutland

㉔ *15 mi southwest of Killington, 32 mi south of Middlebury, 31 mi west of Woodstock, 47 mi west of White River Junction.*

On and around U.S. 7 in Rutland are strips of shopping centers and a seemingly endless row of traffic lights, although the mansions of the marble magnates who made the town famous still command whatever attention can be safely diverted from the traffic. Rutland's compact downtown, one of only a handful of urban centers in Vermont, has experienced a modest revival and is worth an hour's stroll. The area's traditional economic ties to railroading and marble, the latter an industry that became part of such illustrious structures as the central research building of the New York Public Library in New York City, have been rapidly eclipsed by the growth of the Pico and Killington ski areas to the east. If you're planning to visit more than one of the area's attractions, ask about the "One Great Day" admission at the Vermont Marble Exhibit, New England Maple Museum, or Wilson Castle.

The **Chaffee Center for the Visual Arts** (⊠ 16 S. Main St., ☎ 802/775–0356) exhibits and sells the output of more than 250 Vermont artists who work in various media. It's closed Tuesday.

The highlight of the Rutland area, the **Vermont Marble Exhibit** includes a sculptor-in-residence who transforms stone into finished works of art or commerce (you can choose first-hand the marble for a custom-built kitchen counter). The gallery illustrates the many industrial and artistic applications of marble—such as the hall of presidents and a replica of Leonardo da Vinci's *Last Supper* in marble—and depicts the industry's history via exhibits and a video. Factory seconds and foreign and domestic marble items are for sale. ⊠ *62 Main St., Proctor (4 mi north of Rutland, off Rte. 3),* ☎ *802/459–2300 or 800/427–1396.* ☜ *$6.* ⊗ *Mid-May–Oct., daily 9–5:30.*

A 32-room mansion built in 1888 by a doctor, **Wilson Castle** comes complete with turrets, towers, stained glass, and 13 fireplaces. It's magnificently furnished with European and Asian objets d'art. Head west out of Rutland on Route 4A and follow signs. ⊠ *West Proctor Rd., Proctor,* ☎ *802/773–3284,* WEB *www.wilsoncastle.com.* ☜ *$7.* ⊗ *Late May–mid-Oct., daily 9–5:30.*

Dining and Lodging

$-$$$ ✕ **The Palms.** When this Rutland landmark opened its doors on Palm Sunday in 1933 it was the first restaurant in the state to serve pizza. It's still owned by the same family. The menu is primarily southern Italian, with specialties such as fried mozzarella; antipasto Neapolitan (with provolone, pepperoni, mild peppers, anchovies, and house dressing); and the chef's personal creation, veal à la Palms—veal scallops topped with mushrooms, two kinds of cheese, and a special tomato sauce. Dessert choices are fairly pedestrian. ⊠ *36 Strongs St.,* ☎ *802/773–2367. AE, MC, V. Closed Sun. No lunch.*

$$$$ ⌂ **Mountain Top Inn and Resort.** On 500 acres overlooking Chittenden Reservoir and the Green Mountain National Forest, this is a year-round outdoor enthusiast's inn. There's an equestrian center and golf school, and activities include swimming and canoeing. A tip: opt for the more-expensive deluxe rooms, which are larger and have spectacular views. ⊠ *195 Mountaintop Rd., Chittenden 05737,* ☎ *802/483–2311 or 800/445–2100,* FAX *802/483–6373,* WEB *www.mountaintopinn.com. 35 rooms, 6 cottages, 6 chalets. Restaurant, driving range, pool, beach, boating, fishing, horseback riding, cross-country skiing, ice-skating, sleigh rides. AE, MC, V. Closed late Oct.–late Dec. and mid-Mar.–mid-May. BP, MAP.*

$$-$$$ ⌂ **Inn at Rutland.** One alternative to Rutland's chain motel accommodations is this renovated Victorian mansion. The ornate oak staircase lined with heavy embossed gold and leather wainscoting leads to rooms that blend modern bathrooms with late-19th-century touches such as elaborate ceiling moldings and frosted glass. The two large common rooms, one with a fireplace, have views of surrounding mountains and valleys. The meal plan varies. Afternoon tea is served daily. ⊠ *70 N. Main St., 05701,* ☎ *802/773–0575 or 800/808–0575,* FAX *802/775–3506,* WEB *www.innatrutland.com. 11 rooms. Cable TV, library AE, D, MC, V.*

Nightlife and the Arts

Crossroads Arts Council (⊠ 39 E. Center St., ☎ 802/775–5413) presents music, opera, dance, jazz, and theater year-round at venues throughout the region.

Outdoor Activities and Sports

Half Moon State Park's principal attraction is Half Moon Pond (⊠ Town Rd., 3½ mi off Rte. 30, west of Hubbardton, ☎ 802/273–2848). The park has nature trails, campsites, and boat and canoe rentals.

Shopping

Tuttle Antiquarian Books (⊠ 28 S. Main St., ☎ 802/773–8229) stocks rare and out-of-print books, genealogies, local histories, and miniature books; you also find a large collection of books on Asia.

Brandon

㉕ *15 mi northwest of Rutland.*

Straddling busy U.S. 7, Brandon nevertheless has broad side streets lined with gracious Victorian houses, lodging at the landmark Brandon Inn or at smaller B&Bs, and ready access to the mountain scenery and recreation of nearby Brandon Gap.

The **Stephen A. Douglas Birthplace** commemorates the "Little Giant" (he stood only 5 ft, 2 inches tall), best known for his debates with Abraham Lincoln in 1858. Douglas, who became a U.S. representative and senator from Illinois, was born here on April 23, 1813. His boyhood home and a monument to his memory are just north of the village, next to the Baptist church. ⊠ *U.S. 7.* ☎ *802/247–6569 or 802/247–6332.* 🎫 *Donations welcome.* ⊙ *By appointment.*

Maple syrup is Vermont's signature product, and the **New England Maple Museum and Gift Shop** explains the history and process of turning maple sap into syrup with murals, exhibits, and a slide show. ⊠ *U.S. 7, Pittsford (9 mi south of Brandon),* ☎ *802/483–9414.* 🎫 *Museum $2.50.* ⊙ *Late May–Oct., daily 8:30–5:30; Nov.–Dec. and mid-Mar.–late May, daily 10–4.*

Dining and Lodging

$$$$ ✕🏨 **Blueberry Hill Inn.** In the Green Mountain National Forest and 5½ mi off a mountain pass on a dirt road, the inn has lush gardens and a pond with a wood-fired sauna on its bank. Many rooms have views of the mountains; all are furnished with antiques and quilts. The restaurant prepares a four-course ($$$$) dinner nightly, with dishes such as venison fillet with cherry sauce. The ski-touring center has 80 km (50 mi) of trails. ⊠ *1307 Goshen–Ripkin Rd., Goshen 05733,* ☎ *802/247–6735 or 800/448–0707,* ⅢX *802/247–3983,* WEB *www.blueberryhillinn.com. 12 rooms. Restaurant, sauna, mountain bikes, hiking, volleyball, cross-country skiing, some pets allowed. MC, V. MAP.*

$$$ ✕🏨 **Lilac Inn.** The bridal suite at this Greek Revival mansion has a pewter canopy bed, whirlpool bath for two, and fireplace. The other rooms, all furnished and with claw-foot tubs and handheld European shower heads, are also charming. The elegant dining room ($$$), overlooking the gardens, serves dishes such as fig-mango pork short ribs and green tea–encrusted yellowfin tuna. The inn is a popular spot for weddings on summer weekends. ⊠ *53 Park St./Rte. 73, 05733,* ☎ *802/247–5463 or 800/221–0720,* ⅢX *802/247–5499,* WEB *www.lilacinn.com. 9 rooms. Restaurant, meeting rooms, some pets allowed (fee); no kids under 12. AE, MC, V. BP.*

$$–$$$$ 🏨 **The Brandon Inn.** Built in 1786, this National Register of Historic Places inn in the center of town has the state's oldest elevator (circa 1901), comfortable and spacious guest rooms, and Victorian-furnished common rooms that feel like they've been frozen in time. Moderately priced fare, including the house-special barbecued spareribs, are served in the elegant, multipillared dining room. ⊠ *20 Park St., 05733,* ☎ *800/639–8685,* ⅢX *802/247–5768,* WEB *www.brandoninn.com. 35 rooms. Restaurant, pool, recreation room. AE, D, MC, V. BP.*

Outdoor Activities and Sports

Moosalamoo (☎ 800/448–0707) is the name given by a partnership of public and private entities to a 20,000-acre chunk of Green Mountain National Forest land (along with several private holdings) just northeast of Brandon. More than 60 mi of trails take hikers, mountain bikers, and cross-country skiers through some of Vermont's most gorgeous mountain terrain. Attractions include Branbury State Park, on the shores of Lake Dunmore; secluded Silver Lake; and sections of both the Long Trail and Catamount Trail (the latter is a Massachusetts-to-Québec ski trail). Both the Blueberry Hill Inn and **Churchill House Inn** (☎ 802/247–3078) have direct public access to trails.

GOLF

Neshobe Golf Club (✉ Rte. 73, east of Brandon, ☎ 802/247–3611) has 18 holes of par-72 golf on a bent-grass course totaling nearly 6,500 yards. The Green Mountain views are terrific. Several local inns offer golf packages.

HIKING

About 8 mi east of Brandon on Route 73, a trail that takes an hour to hike starts at Brandon Gap and climbs steeply up **Mt. Horrid.** South of Lake Dunmore on Route 53, a large turnout marks a trail (a hike of about two hours) to the **Falls of Lana.** Four trails—two short ones of less than 1 mi each and two longer ones—lead to the old abandoned Revolutionary War fortifications at **Mt. Independence**; to reach them, take the first left turn off Route 73 west of Orwell and go right at the fork. The road will turn to gravel and once again will fork; take a sharp left-hand turn toward a small marina. The parking lot is on the left at the top of the hill.

Shopping
The **Warren Kimble Gallery & Studio** (✉ off Rte. 73 E, ☎ 802/247–3026 or 800/954–6253) is the workplace, gallery, and gift shop of the nationally renowned folk artist.

Middlebury

★ ㉖ *17 mi north of Brandon, 34 mi south of Burlington.*

In the late 1800s Middlebury was the largest Vermont community west of the Green Mountains: an industrial center of river-powered wool, grain, and marble mills. This is Robert Frost country; Vermont's late poet laureate spent 23 summers at a farm east of Middlebury. Otter Creek, the state's longest river, traverses the town center. Still a cultural and economic hub amid the Champlain Valley's serene pastoral patchwork, the town and countryside invite a day of exploration.

Smack in the middle of town, **Middlebury College** (☎ 802/443–5000), founded in 1800, was conceived as a more godly alternative to the worldly University of Vermont. The college has no religious affiliation today, however. The early 19th-century stone buildings contrast provocatively with the postmodern architecture of the Center for the Arts and the sports center. Music, theater, and dance performances take place throughout the year at the **Wright Memorial Theatre** and **Center for the Arts.**

The **Middlebury College Museum of Art** has a permanent collection of paintings, photography, works on paper, and sculpture. ✉ *Center for the Arts, Rte. 30,* ☎ *802/443–5007.* ☑ *Free.* ☉ *Mid-Jan.–mid Dec., Tues.–Fri. 10–5, weekends noon–5.*

The **Vermont Folklife Center** exhibits photography, antiques, folk paintings, manuscripts, and other artifacts and contemporary works that examine facets of Vermont life. The center is in the basement of the restored 1801 home of Gamaliel Painter, the founder of Middlebury College. ✉ *3 Court St.,* ☎ *802/388–4964.* ☑ *Donations accepted.* ☉ *Gallery May–Dec., Tues.–Sat. 11–4. Oral history archive weekdays 10–4.*

The **Henry Sheldon Museum of Vermont History,** an 1829 marble merchant's house, is the oldest community museum in the country. The period rooms contain Vermont-made textiles, furniture, toys, clothes, kitchen tools, and paintings. ⊠ *1 Park St.,* ☎ *802/388–2117.* ▦ *$4.* ⊙ *Mon.–Sat. 10–5.*

More than a crafts store, the **Vermont State Craft Center at Frog Hollow** mounts changing exhibitions and displays exquisite work in wood, glass, metal, clay, and fiber by more than 250 Vermont artisans. The center, which overlooks Otter Creek, sponsors classes taught by some of those artists. Burlington and Manchester also have centers. ⊠ *1 Mill St.,* ☎ *802/388–3177,* 〚WEB〛 *www.froghollow.org.* ⊙ *Call for hrs.*

The Morgan horse—the official state animal—has an even temper, good stamina, and slightly truncated legs in proportion to its body. The University of Vermont's **UVM Morgan Horse Farm,** about 2½ mi west of Middlebury, is a breeding and training center where in summer you can tour the stables and paddocks. ⊠ *74 Battell Dr., off Horse Farm Rd. (follow signs off Rte. 23), Weybridge,* ☎ *802/388–2011.* ▦ *$4.* ⊙ *May–Oct., daily 9–5 (last tour at 4).*

About 10 mi east of town on Route 125 (1 mi west of Middlebury College's Bread Loaf campus), the easy ¾-mi **Robert Frost Interpretive Trail** winds through quiet woodland. Plaques along the way bear quotations from Frost's poems. A picnic area is across the road from the trailhead.

OFF THE
BEATEN PATH
FORT TICONDEROGA FERRY – Established in 1759, the Fort Ti cable ferry crosses Lake Champlain between Shoreham and Fort Ticonderoga, New York, at one of the oldest ferry crossings in North America in just six minutes. ⊠ *4675 Rte. 74 W,18 mi southwest of Middlebury, Shoreham* ☎ *802/897–7999.* ▦ *Cars, pickups, and vans with driver and passenger $7; pedestrians $1.* ⊙ *May–last Sun. of Oct.*

Dining and Lodging

$$–$$$ ✕ **Fire & Ice.** A 55-item salad bar (with peel-and-eat shrimp), prime rib, steak, fish, and a house specialty—homemade mashed potatoes—are all choices at this family-friendly spot. Although large, the space is divided into several rooms (each with a different theme) and has numerous intimate nooks and crannies for diners who seek privacy. Families may want to request a table next to the "children's corner," which is outfitted with cushions and a VCR. Sunday dinner begins at 1. ⊠ *26 Seymour St.,* ☎ *802/388–7166 or 800/367–7166. AE, D, DC, MC, V. No lunch Mon.*

$$–$$$ ✕ **Roland's Place.** Chef Roland Gaujac prepares classic French and
★   American dishes in a 1796 house. Some dishes use locally raised lamb, turkey, and venison; other entrées include shrimp with chipotle and roasted garlic vinaigrette on fried ravioli. A prix-fixe menu is available, and a special menu served daily from 5 to 6 lists numerous à la carte dishes. ⊠ *U.S. 7, New Haven,* ☎ *802/453–6309. AE, D, DC, MC, V. Hrs vary; call ahead*

$ ✕ **Baba's Market & Deli.** Authentic Lebanese dishes are the specialty in this cheerful, informal spot near the college. Among the standouts are kibbe, stuffed grape leaves, moussaka, and pizza prepared in a wood-fired oven. ⊠ *54 College St.,* ☎ *802/388–6408. MC, V.*

$$–$$$$ ▥ **Middlebury Inn.** Since 1827 gracious New England–style hospitality has been the hallmark of this three-story brick Georgian inn. The property also encompasses a contemporary motel with Early American–style furnishings and the Victorian-era Porter House Mansion. Complimentary afternoon tea is served daily between 3 and 4 except holidays. In nice weather, you can have lunch on the wicker-furnished porch. Rooms facing the lovely town green can be noisy if the window is open. ⊠ *14 Courthouse Sq., 05753,* ☎ *802/388–4961 or*

800/842–4666, FAX 802/388–4563, WEB *www.middleburyinn.com. 75 rooms. Restaurant, some pets allowed; no smoking rooms. AE, D, MC, V. CP, MAP.*

$$–$$$ ★ 🏠 **Swift House Inn.** The Georgian home of a 19th-century governor contains white-panel wainscoting, mahogany, and marble fireplaces. The rooms—most with Oriental rugs and nine with fireplaces—have period reproductions such as canopy beds, curtains with swags, and claw-foot tubs. Some bathrooms have double whirlpool tubs. Rooms in the gatehouse suffer from street noise but are charming; a carriage house holds six luxury accommodations. ⊠ *25 Stewart La., 05753,* ☎ *802/388–9925,* FAX *802/388–9927,* WEB *www.swifthouseinn.com. 21 rooms, 1 suite. Sauna, steam room, pub, meeting room; no smoking rooms. AE, D, DC, MC, V. CP.*

$ 🏠 **Lemon Fair.** This unfussy, family-friendly bed-and-breakfast was tiny Bridport's first church before it was moved to its present location overlooking the town green in 1819. Furnishings are Early American and the grounds are spacious. The common room is a cozy spot in which to curl up by the fireplace. The inn is just 8 mi from downtown Middlebury. The owners live next door and will rent out the entire house. ⊠ *Crown Point Rd., Bridport 05734,* ☎ *802/ 758–9238,* FAX *802/758–2135,* WEB *www.lemonfair.com. 3 rooms, 1 suite. Pool. No credit cards. BP.*

Outdoor Activities and Sports

The **Bike Center** (⊠ 74 Main St., ☎ 802/388–6666) has ski and bike sales, rentals, and repairs.

HIKING

On Route 116, about 5½ mi north of East Middlebury, a U.S. Forest Service sign marks a dirt road that forks to the right and leads to the start of the two- to three-hour hike to **Abbey Pond,** which has a beaver lodge and dam as well as a view of Robert Frost Mountain.

Shopping

Historic Marble Works (⊠ Maple St., ☎ 802/388–3701), a renovated marble manufacturing facility, is a collection of unique shops set amid quarrying equipment and factory buildings. **Danforth Pewterers** (☎ 802/388–0098) sells handcrafted pewter vases, lamps, and tableware. **De Pasquale's** (☎ 802/388–3385) prepares subs and fresh fried-fish platters for takeout and sells imported Italian groceries and wines. **Holy Cow** (⊠ 44 Main St., ☎ 802/388–6737) is where Woody Jackson sells his Holstein cattle–inspired T-shirts, memorabilia, and paintings.

Bristol

㉗ *13 mi northeast of Middlebury.*

At the northeastern threshold of the Green Mountain National Forest, where the rolling farmlands of the Champlain Valley meet the foothills of Vermont's main mountain chain, Bristol has a redbrick 19th-century Main Street that reflects the town's prosperous heyday as the center of a number of wood-products industries. Almost overshadowing the still-busy little downtown are the brooding heights of the Bristol Cliffs Wilderness Area, a section of national forest that has been assured permanent status as a primitive, roadless tract.

Dining

$$$–$$$$ ✕ **Mary's at Baldwin Creek.** This restaurant and B&B in a 1790 farmhouse provides a truly inspired culinary experience. The innovative fare includes a superb garlic soup and Vermont rack of lamb with a rosemary-mustard sauce. Farmhouse dinners on Wednesday in summer highlight Vermont products. A café menu is also available. Four rooms above the restaurant have simple, comfortable furnishings. ⊠ *Rte. 116,* ☎ *802/453–2432. AE, DC, MC, V. Closed Mon.–Tues. No lunch.*

Outdoor Activities and Sports

A challenging 32-mi bicycle ride starts in Bristol. Take North Street from the traffic light in town and continue north to Monkton Ridge and on to Hinesburg. To return, follow Route 116 south through Starksboro and back to Bristol.

Shopping

Folkheart (⊠ 18 Main St., ☎ 802/453–4101) carries unusual jewelry, toys, and crafts from around the world.

En Route From Bristol, Route 17 winds eastward up and over the **Appalachian Gap,** one of Vermont's most panoramic mountain passes. The views from the top and on the way down the other side toward the ski town of Waitsfield are a just reward for the challenging drive.

Waitsfield

㉘ *20 mi east of Bristol, 55 mi north of Rutland, 32 mi northeast of Middlebury, 19 mi southwest of Montpelier.*

Although close to Sugarbush and Mad River Glen ski areas, the Mad River valley towns of Waitsfield and Warren are decidedly low-key. The gently carved ridges cradling the valley and the swell of pastures and fields lining the river seem to keep further notions of ski-resort sprawl at bay. With a map from the Sugarbush Chamber of Commerce you can investigate back roads off Route 100 that have exhilarating valley views.

Dining and Lodging

$$$–$$$$ ✕ **Spotted Cow.** Jay and Renate Young attract a steady clientele to their intimate dining room decorated with contemporary furnishings and warm woods. Lunch items include a fresh spinach salad with fried oysters and Bermuda codfish cakes. For dinner, try a ragout of seafood in puff pastry or the house specialty: sautéed medallions of New Zealand venison finished in lingonberry crème fraîche. Sunday brunch is served 10:30–3. ⊠ *Bridge St.,* ☎ *802/496–5151. MC, V. Closed Mon.*

$$–$$$ ✕ **American Flatbread.** For ideologically and gastronomically sound pizza, you won't find a better place in the Green Mountains than this modest haven between Waitsfield and Warren. Organic flour and produce fuel mind and body, and Vermont hardwood fuels the earth-and-stone oven. The "punctuated equilibrium flatbread," made with olive-pepper goat cheese and rosemary, is a dream, as are more traditional pizzas. It's open Monday–Thursday 7:30 AM–8 PM for takeout, Friday and Saturday 5:30–9:30 for dinner. ⊠ *Rte. 100,* ☎ *802/496–8856. Reservations not accepted. MC, V. Closed Sun.*

$$–$$$ ✕ **Common Man.** *Pescespada de merida* (grilled New England swordfish steak) and ravioli *alla calabrese* share the menu with French classics such as braised rabbit, *entrecôte maison* (sirloin steak with an herb and garlic butter sauce), rack of lamb, and roast duck. The restaurant, a local institution since 1972, is housed in a mid-1800s barn with hand-hewn rafters and crystal chandeliers. Dinner is served by candlelight. ⊠ *German Flats Rd., Warren,* ☎ *802/583–2800. AE, D, MC, V. Closed Mon. Easter–Christmas. No lunch.*

$$$$ ✕🏠 **Pitcher Inn.** Each guest room at this Relais & Châteaux property ★ has its own motif. A curved ceiling in the Mallard gives the illusion of a duck blind, and the windows are etched and frosted in the likeness of the banks of a marsh. All rooms have stereos; nine have fireplaces and six have steam showers. The formal dining room ($$$–$$$$) specializes in local produce and wild game; you can also dine in the pri-

vate wine cellar. ✉ *275 Main St. (Box 347, Warren 05674),* ☎ *802/ 496–6350 or 888/867–4824,* ℻ *802/496–6354,* ⓦⓔⓑ *www. pitcherinn.com. 9 rooms, 2 suites. Restaurant, in-room data ports, hot tub, billiards; no kids under 16 (except in suites). AE, MC, V. BP.*

$$ ✕🏨 **Tucker Hill Lodge.** Guest rooms in this country inn, convenient to both Sugarbush and Wild Cat, are adorned in country-casual furnishings. There are fireplaces in three guest rooms and in the living room, dining room, and pub. The menu at the Steak Place ($$–$$$$) includes a 24-ounce steak and barbecue ribs, as well as fish and vegetarian choices. Lighter fare is served in the pub area for late-night patrons. Dinner can be included in the room rate if desired. ✉ *65 Marble Hill Rd./Rte. 17, 05673,* ☎ *802/496–3983 or 800/543–7841,* ℻ *802/496–9837,* ⓦⓔⓑ *www.tuckerhill.com. 18 rooms, 6 suites. Restaurant, in-room data ports, tennis court, pool, hiking, bar, meeting rooms; no air-conditioning in some rooms. AE, MC, V. CP.*

$$–$$$$ 🏨 **Inn at the Round Barn Farm.** A Shaker-style round barn (one of only eight in the state) dominates the farm's 215 acres. The inn's guest rooms, inside an 1806 farmhouse, are sumptuous, with eyelet-trimmed sheets, elaborate four-poster beds, rich-colored wallpapers, and brass wall lamps for easy bedtime reading. Seven have fireplaces, four have whirlpool tubs, and five have steam showers. The inn also arranges snowshoe packages and tours. ✉ *1661 E. Warren Rd., 05673,* ☎ *802/496–2276,* ℻ *802/ 496–8832,* ⓦⓔⓑ *www.innatroundbarn.com. 12 rooms. Indoor pool, cross-country skiing, library, recreation room. AE, D, MC, V. BP.*

Nightlife and the Arts

The Back Room at **Chez Henri** (✉ Sugarbush Village, ☎ 802/583–2600) has a pool table and is popular with the après-ski and late-night dance crowds. Local bands play music at **Gallagher's** (✉ Rtes. 100 and 17, ☎ 802/496–8800).

The **Green Mountain Cultural Center** (✉ Inn at the Round Barn Farm, E. Warren Rd., ☎ 802/496–7722), a nonprofit organization, brings concerts and art exhibits, as well as educational workshops, to the Mad River valley. The **Valley Players** (✉ Rte. 100, ☎ 802/496–9612) present musicals, dramas, follies, and holiday shows.

Outdoor Activities and Sports

BIKING

The popular 14-mi Waitsfield–Warren loop begins when you cross the covered bridge in Waitsfield. Keep right on East Warren Road to the four-way intersection in East Warren; continue straight and then bear right, riding down Brook Road to the village of Warren. Return by turning right (north) on Route 100 back toward Waitsfield.

Clearwater Sports (✉ Rte. 100, ☎ 802/496–2708) rents canoes, kayaks, and camping equipment and leads guided river trips and whitewater instruction in the warm months; in the winter, the store leads snowshoe tours and rents telemark equipment, snowshoes, and one-person Mad River Rocket sleds.

GOLF

Great views and challenging play are the trademarks of the Robert Trent Jones–designed 18-hole, par-72 course at **Sugarbush Resort** (✉ Golf Course Rd., ☎ 802/583–6727). The greens fee runs from $32 to $52; a cart (sometimes mandatory) costs $17.

SLEIGH RIDES

The 100-year-old sleigh of the **Lareau Farm Country Inn** (✉ Rte. 100, ☎ 802/496–4949 or 800/833–0766) cruises along the banks of the Mad River.

Shopping

Cabin Fever Quilts (⊠ Rte. 100, ☎ 802/496–2287), which shares a building with Luminosity Stained Glass Studios, sells fine handmade quilts. **Luminosity Stained Glass Studios** (☎ 802/496–2231), inside the converted Old Church on Route 100, specializes in stained glass, custom lighting, and art glass.

All Things Bright and Beautiful (⊠ Bridge St., ☎ 802/496–3997) is a 12-room Victorian house jammed to the rafters with stuffed animals of all shapes, sizes, and colors as well as folk art, prints, and collectibles. **Warren Village Pottery** (⊠ Main St., Warren, ☎ 802/496–4162) sells handcrafted wares from its retail shop and specializes in functional stoneware pottery.

Ski Areas

The hundreds of shareholders who own Mad River Glen are dedicated, knowledgeable skiers devoted to keeping skiing what it used to be—a pristine alpine experience. Mad River's unkempt aura attracts rugged individualists looking for less-polished terrain: the area was developed in the late 1940s and has changed relatively little since then. It remains one of only a handful of resorts in the country that ban snowboarding. Skiers can use their tickets at nearby Sugarbush; a free shuttle bus runs between the two areas. ⊠ *Rte. 17, 05673,* ☎ *802/496–3551; 800/850–6742 cooperative office; 802/496–2001 snow conditions;* WEB *www.madriverglen.com.*

Downhill. Mad River is steep, with natural slopes that follow the contours of the mountain. The terrain changes constantly on the 45 interconnected trails, of which 30% are beginner, 30% are intermediate, and 40% are expert. Intermediate and novice terrain is regularly groomed. Five lifts, including a single 1940s chairlift that may be the only lift of its vintage still carrying skiers, service the mountain's 2,037-ft vertical drop. Most of Mad River's trails (85%) are covered only by natural snow.

Telemark/snowshoe. The "Mecca of Free-Heel Skiing" sponsors telemark programs through the season and each March hosts the North America Telemark Organization, which attracts up to 1,200 skiers. There is a $5 fee to use the snowshoe trails, and rentals are available.

Child care. The nursery is for infants to 6 years. The ski school runs classes for little ones ages 4 to 12. Junior racing is available weekends and during holidays.

In the Warren-Waitsfield ski world, Sugarbush is Mad River Glen's alter ego. The Slide Brook Express quad connects the two mountains, Sugarbush South and Sugarbush North. A computer-controlled system for snowmaking has increased coverage to nearly 70%. At the base of the mountain is a village with condominiums, restaurants, shops, bars, and a sports center. Skiers can use their tickets at nearby Mad River Glen; a free shuttle bus runs between the two areas. ⊠ *Sugarbush Access Rd., accessible from Rte. 100 or Rte. 17 (Box 350, Warren 05674),* ☎ *802/ 583–6300; 800/537–8427 lodging; 802/583–7669 snow conditions;* WEB *www.sugarbush.com.*

Downhill. Sugarbush is two distinct, connected mountain complexes. The Sugarbush South area is what old-timers recall as Sugarbush Mountain: with a vertical of 2,400 ft, it is known for formidable steeps toward the top and in front of the main base lodge. Sugarbush North offers what South has in short supply—beginner runs. North also has steep fall-line pitches and intermediate cruisers off its 2,650 vertical ft. There are 115 trails in all: 23% beginner, 48% intermediate, 29% expert. The resort has 18 lifts: seven quads (including four high-speed versions), three triples, four doubles, and four surface lifts.

Child care. The Sugarbush Day School accepts children ages 6 weeks–6 years; older children have indoor play areas and can go on outdoor excursions. There's half- and full-day instruction available for children ages 4–11. Kids have their own Magic Carpet lift. Sugarbear Forest, a terrain garden, has fun bumps and jumps.

Summer and year-round activities. The **Sugarbush Mountain Biking & Technical Hiking Center** (☎ 802/583–6572) has bike rentals and miles of terrain; it provides guided tours and instruction. Open year-round, the **Sugarbush Health and Racquet Club** (☎ 802/583–6700), near the ski lifts, has Nautilus and Universal equipment; tennis, squash, and racquetball courts; a whirlpool, a sauna, and steam rooms; one indoor pool; and a 30-ft-high climbing wall.

CROSS-COUNTRY SKIING

Blueberry Lake Cross-Country Ski Area (⊠ Plunkton Rd., Warren, ☎ 802/496–6687) has 30 km (18 mi) of groomed trails through thickly wooded glades. **Ole's** (⊠ Airport Rd., Warren, ☎ 802/496–3430) runs a cross-country center and small restaurant out of the tiny Warren airport; it has 50 km (37 mi) of groomed European-style trails that span out into the surrounding woods from the landing strips.

Brookfield

㉙ *26 mi southeast of Waitsfield, 15 mi south of Montpelier.*

The residents of secluded Brookfield have voted several times to keep the town's roads unpaved and even turned down an offered I–89 exit when the interstate highway was being built in the '60s. Route 14 east of town is a scenic road. Crossing the nation's only **floating bridge** (⊠ Rte. 65 between Rtes. 12 and 14) feels like driving on water. The bridge, supported by nearly 400 barrels, sits at water level. It's the scene of the annual ice-harvest festival in January, though it's closed to traffic in winter.

Dining and Lodging

$$$ ✕ **Ariel's.** Reserve a seat on the porch overlooking the lake (summer and fall), and put yourself in the capable hands of Culinary Institute of America–trained chef Lee Duberman, who prepares eclectic treats such as sautéed breast and confit leg of duck as well as seared fillet of salmon. Husband-sommelier Ricard Fink recommends selections from the wine cellar. The full menu is offered Friday and Saturday; a pub menu is served Wednesday, Thursday, and Sunday. ⊠ *Main St.,* ☎ *802/276–3939. D, MC, V. Closed Mon.–Tues.*

$$–$$$ ✮ ⊞ **Green Trails Inn.** The enormous fieldstone fireplace that dominates the living and dining area of this historic inn overlooking Sunset Lake is symbolic of the stalwart hospitality of new innkeepers Nina Gaby and Craig Smith. Comfortably elegant rooms in two buildings have antiques and Oriental rugs. The suite has a fireplace, and two rooms have whirlpool tubs. Dinner is prepared on request. ⊠ *Main St., 05036,* ☎ *802/276–3412 or 800/243–3412,* WEB *www.greentrailsinn.com. 13 rooms, 9 with bath. Dining room, lake, boating, cross-country skiing, ski shop, sleigh rides. D, MC, V. BP.*

Central Vermont A to Z

To research prices, get advice from other travelers, and book travel arrangements, visit www.fodors.com.

BUS TRAVEL

Vermont Transit links Rutland, White River Junction, Burlington, and many smaller towns.

➤ Bus INFORMATION: **Vermont Transit** (☎ 800/552–8737).

CAR TRAVEL

The major east–west road is U.S. 4, which stretches from White River Junction in the east to Fair Haven in the west. Route 125 connects Middlebury on U.S. 7 with Hancock on Route 100; Route 100 splits the region in half along the eastern edge of the Green Mountains. Route 17 travels east–west from Waitsfield over the Appalachian Gap through Bristol and down to the shores of Lake Champlain. Interstate–91 and the parallel U.S. 5 follow the state's eastern border; U.S. 7 and Route 30 are the north–south highways in the west. Interstate–89 links White River Junction with Montpelier to the north.

EMERGENCIES

➤ HOSPITALS: **Porter Hospital** (⊠ South St., Middlebury, ☎ 802/388–7901). **Rutland Medical Center** (⊠ 160 Allen St., Rutland, ☎ 802/775–7111; 800/649–2187 in Vermont).

LODGING

Sugarbush Reservations and the Woodstock Area Chamber of Commerce provide lodging referral services.

➤ RESERVATION SERVICES: **Sugarbush Reservations** (☎ 800/537–8427). **Woodstock Area Chamber of Commerce** (☎ 802/457–3555 or 888/496–6378).

TOURS

Country Inns Along the Trail arranges self-guided and guided hiking and skiing trips and provides self-guided biking trips from inn to inn in Vermont. The Vermont Icelandic Horse Farm conducts year-round guided riding expeditions on easy-to-ride Icelandic horses. Full-day, half-day, and hourly rides as well as weekend tours and inn-to-inn treks are available.

➤ TOUR OPERATORS: **Country Inns Along the Trail** (⊠ 834 Van Cortland Rd., Brandon 05733, ☎ 802/247–3300 or 800/838–3301). **Vermont Icelandic Horse Farm** (⊠ N. Fayston Rd., Waitsfield 05673, ☎ 802/496–7141).

VISITOR INFORMATION

➤ TOURIST INFORMATION: **Addison County Chamber of Commerce** (⊠ 2 Court St., Middlebury 05753, ☎ 802/388–7951 or 800/733–8376, WEB www.midvermont.com). **Quechee Chamber of Commerce** (⊠ 1789 Quechee St. [Box 106, Quechee 05059], ☎ 802/295–7900 or 800/295–5451, WEB www.quechee.com). **Rutland Region Chamber of Commerce** (⊠ 256 N. Main St., Rutland 05701, ☎ 802/773–2747 or 800/756–8880, WEB www.rutlandvermont.com). **Sugarbush Chamber of Commerce** (⊠ Rte. 100 [Box 173, Waitsfield 05673], ☎ 802/496–3409 or 800/828–4748, WEB www.madrivervalley.com). **Woodstock Area Chamber of Commerce** (⊠ 18 Central St. [Box 486, Woodstock 05091], ☎ 802/457–3555 or 888/496–6378, WEB www.woodstockvt.com).

NORTHERN VERMONT

Vermont's northernmost region reveals the state's greatest contrasts. To the west, along Lake Champlain, Burlington and its Chittenden County suburbs have grown so rapidly that rural wags now say that Burlington's greatest advantage is that it's "close to Vermont." The north country also harbors Vermont's tiny capital, Montpelier, and its highest mountain, Mt. Mansfield, site of the famous Stowe ski slopes. To the northeast of Burlington and Montpelier spreads a sparsely populated and heavily wooded territory, the domain of loggers as much as farmers, where French spills out of the radio and the last snows melt toward the first of June.

You'll find plenty to do in the region's cities (Burlington, Montpelier, St. Johnsbury, and Barre), in the bustling resort area of Stowe, in the Lake Champlain Islands, and—if you like the outdoors—in the wilds of the Northeast Kingdom.

The coverage of towns in this area begins in the state capital, Montpelier; moves west toward Waterbury, Stowe, and Burlington; then goes north through the Lake Champlain Islands, east along the boundary with Canada toward Jay Peak and Newport, and south into the heart of the Northeast Kingdom before completing the circle in Barre.

Montpelier

30 *38 mi southeast of Burlington, 115 mi north of Brattleboro.*

With only about 8,000 residents, Montpelier is the country's least populous state capital. The intersection of State and Main streets is the city hub, bustling with the activity of state and city workers during the day. It's a pleasant place to spend an afternoon shopping and browsing; in true small-town Vermont fashion, though, the streets become deserted at night.

The **Vermont State House**—with a gleaming gold dome and columns of Barre granite 6 ft in diameter—is impressive for a city this size. The goddess of agriculture tops the dome. The Greek Revival building dates from 1836, although it was rebuilt after a fire in 1859; the latter year's Victorian style was adhered to in a lavish 1994 restoration. Interior paintings and exhibits make much of Vermont's sterling Civil War record. ⊠ *115 State St.,* ☎ *802/828–2228.* ☞ *Donation.* ☉ *Weekdays 8–4; tours July–mid-Oct., weekdays every ½ hr 10–3:30 (last tour at 3:30), Sat. 11–3 (last tour at 2:30). Self-guided tours available when building is open.*

Perhaps you're wondering what the last panther shot in Vermont looked like? Why New England bridges are covered? What a niddy-noddy is? Or what Christmas was like for a Bethel boy in 1879? ("I skated on my new skates. In the morning Papa and I set up a stove for Gramper.") The **Vermont Museum,** on the ground floor of the Vermont Historical Society offices in Montpelier, satisfies the curious with intriguing and informative exhibits. At press time it was scheduled to reopen, after extensive renovations, in late 2002. ⊠ *109 State St.,* ☎ *802/828–2291,* WEB *www.state.vt.us/vhs.* ☞ *$3.* ☉ *Call for hrs.*

Dining and Lodging

$$–$$$ ✕ **Chef's Table.** Nearly everyone working here is a student at the New
★ England Culinary Institute. Although this is a training ground, the quality and inventiveness are anything but beginner's luck. The menu changes daily. Dining is more formal than that of the sister operation downstairs, the Main Street Bar and Grill (open daily for lunch and

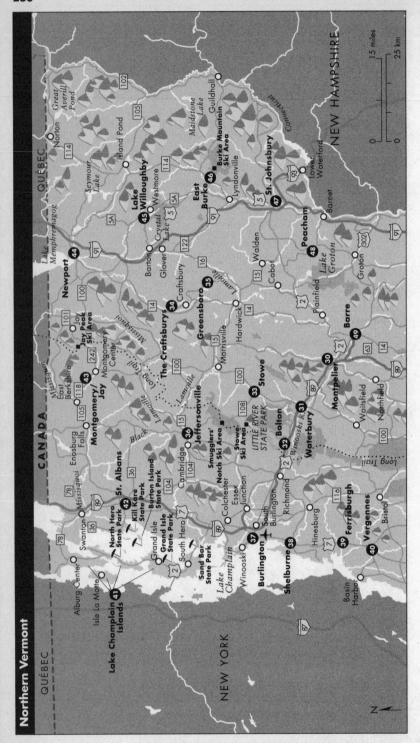

Northern Vermont

dinner). A 15% gratuity is added to the bill. ⊠ *118 Main St.,* ☎ *802/ 229–9202; 802/223–3188 grill. AE, D, DC, MC, V. Closed Sun. No lunch Sat.*

$$ ✕ **River Run Restaurant.** Mississippi-raised chef Jimmy Kennedy has brought outstanding Southern fare to the shores of the Winooski River. Fried catfish, hush puppies, collard greens, and whiskey cake are just a few of the surprises awaiting diners at this tiny restaurant housed in a former speakeasy. Try the buttermilk biscuits at breakfast. ⊠ *Main St., Plainfield,* ☎ *802/454–1246. No credit cards. BYOB. Closed Mon.–Tues.*

$$ ✕ **Sarducci's.** Legislative lunches have been a lot more leisurely ever since Sarducci's came along to fill the trattoria void in Vermont's capital. These bright, cheerful rooms alongside the Winooski River are a great spot for pizza fresh from wood-fired ovens, wonderfully textured homemade Italian breads, and imaginative pasta dishes such as pasta pugliese, which marries penne with basil, black olives, roasted eggplant, Portobello mushrooms, and sun-dried tomatoes. ⊠ *3 Main St.,* ☎ *802/ 223–0229. Reservations not accepted. AE, MC, V. No lunch Sun.*

$$–$$$ ▣ **Inn at Montpelier.** This inn built in the early 1800s was renovated with the business traveler in mind, but the architectural detailing, antique four-poster beds, Windsor chairs, and classical guitar on the stereo attract the leisure trade as well. The formal sitting room has a wide wraparound Colonial Revival porch, perfect for reading a book or watching the townsfolk stroll by. The rooms in the annex, also a 19th-century building, are equally spiffy. ⊠ *147 Main St., 05602,* ☎ *802/223–2727,* FAX *802/223–0722,* WEB *www.innatmontpelier.com. 19 rooms. Meeting room. AE, D, DC, MC, V. CP.*

Waterbury

③ *12 mi northwest of Montpelier.*

The face of Waterbury's compact downtown is changing as coffee shops, restaurants, and galleries begin to move into the brick buildings that once housed tired-looking furniture and hardware stores. But the anchor here remains the huge state office complex that formerly served as a hospital. The little red train station comes to life only when Amtrak's *Vermonter* stops in town, once a day in each direction. The principal draws for visitors, however, are north of I–89, along Route 100.

Ben & Jerry's Ice Cream Factory is the Valhalla for ice cream lovers. Ben and Jerry began selling ice cream from a renovated gas station in Burlington in the 1970s. Famous for their social and environmental consciousness, the boys do good works while living off the butterfat of the land. The tour only skims the surface of the behind-the-scenes goings-on at the plant—a flaw forgiven when the free samples are dished out. ⊠ *Rte. 100, 1 mi north of I–89,* ☎ *802/846–1500; 802/882–1260 recorded information;* WEB *www.benjerry.com.* ▦ *Tour $2.* ☉ *June, daily 9–5; July–late Aug., daily 9–8; late Aug.–Oct., daily 9–6; Nov.–May, daily 10–5. Tours every ½ hr in winter, more frequent in summer. Gift and scoop shops stay open an hr later.*

Dining and Lodging

$$–$$$$ ✕ **Mist Grill Cafe, Bakery, Roastery.** The fare is best described as country bistro at this casual contemporary restaurant in a renovated gristmill overlooking Thatcher Brook Falls. The menu includes handmade breakfast treats and a ploughman's lunch. Grilled rib steak and pork loin are served Thursday–Saturday evenings, and Sunday "supper" dishes up traditional comfort foods. ⊠ *92 Stowe St.,* ☎ *802/244–2233. AE, MC, V. Closed Mon.*

$-$$ ✕⊞ **Thatcher Brook Inn.** Twin gazebos poised on both ends of the front porch of this sprawling 1899 inn define its space on busy Route 100. Three buildings hold comfortable guest rooms of all sizes, with modern bathroom fixtures and Laura Ashley–style floral wallpaper. Some rooms have fireplaces and whirlpool tubs. The pine-paneled tavern is a popular socializing spot, and classic French cuisine ($$–$$$) is served in the dining room. ⊠ *Rte. 100, 05676,* ☎ *802/244–5911 or 800/292–5911,* FAX *802/244–1294,* WEB *www.thatcherbrook.com. 21 rooms, 1 suite. Restaurant, some cable TV, pub; no air-conditioning in some rooms. AE, D, DC, MC, V. BP.*

$-$$ ⊞ **Old Stagecoach Inn.** Unwind in the spacious, comfortable rooms at this former-stagecoach stop, now a beautifully restored inn. Antiques embellish all of the individually decorated rooms. The suites, in a separate section, are perfect if you're traveling with kids or pets. An elegant breakfast buffet is served daily. A two-minute walk takes you to restaurants and shops. ⊠ *18 N. Main St., 05676,* ☎ *800/262–2206,* WEB *www.oldstagecoach.com. 8 rooms, 7 with bath; 3 suites. Bar. AE, D, MC, V.*

Outdoor Activities and Sports

Mt. Mansfield State Forest and Little River State Park (⊠ U.S. 2, 1½ mi west of Waterbury, ☎ 802/244–7103) have extensive trail systems for hiking, including one that reaches the headquarters of the Civilian Conservation Corps unit that was stationed here in the 1930s. At Little River State Park, you'll find campsites and trails leading to Mt. Mansfield and Camel's Hump.

Shopping

The **Cold Hollow Cider Mill** (⊠ Rte. 100, 3 mi north of I–89, ☎ 802/244–8771 or 800/327–7537) sells cider, baked goods, Vermont produce, and specialty foods. Tastes of fresh-pressed cider are served while you watch how it is made. **Green Mountain Chocolate Complex** (⊠ Rte. 100, 2½ mi north of I–89, ☎ 802/244–1139) houses specialty shops including the Cabot Cheese Annex Store (☎ 802/244–6334) and the Shimmering Glass Studio and Gallery (☎ 802/244–8134). The **Red Hen Baking Company** (⊠ Rte. 100 S, ☎ 802/244–0966) bakes wonderful artisan breads. The **Vermont Clay Studio & Gallery** (⊠ Rte. 100, ☎ 802/244–1126) displays works by artists from around the country.

Bolton

③② *8 mi northwest of Waterbury, 20 mi northwest of Montpelier, 20 mi southeast of Burlington.*

There isn't much to the town of Bolton itself, but Bolton Valley Holiday Resort bustles with activity.

Dining and Lodging

$$-$$$ ✕⊞ **Black Bear Inn.** Teddy bears in all shapes and sizes decorate this mountaintop inn near the Bolton resort and overlooking the Green Mountains. Twelve rooms have glass-door fire stoves and balconies, and six have private hot tubs. Owner-chef Ken Richardson, a graduate of the Culinary Institute of America, serves dishes ($$–$$$) such as grilled Atlantic salmon with a maple-Dijon mustard glaze. ⊠ *Bolton Access Rd., 05477,* ☎ *802/434–2126; 800/395–6335 outside Vermont;* FAX *802/434–5161;* WEB *www.blkbearinn.com. 24 rooms. Restaurant, pool, outdoor hot tub, kennel. MC, V. BP, MAP.*

$$$ ⊞ **Bolton Resort Hotel and Condominiums.** This slope-side complex includes functional, contemporary rooms, all with mountain views and most with balconies. Studios and suites with kitchens and fireplaces are available, as are condominiums. You can use the resort's sports cen-

ter, including a pool, sauna, and indoor tennis courts. Ski packages are available. ⊠ *Mountain Rd., 05477,* ☎ *802/434–3444 or 877/926–5866,* FAX *802/434–2131,* WEB *www.boltonvalleyvt.com. 60 rooms, 50 suites, 100 condominiums. AE, MC, V.*

Ski Areas

BOLTON VALLEY HOLIDAY RESORT

Although the area continues to struggle through difficult financial times, a face-lift in 2000 put Bolton well on the way to its goal of becoming a four-season destination. The minivillage at the base of the mountain encompasses a hotel, several restaurants, a wine and cheese shop, and a sports shop. The major attraction, however, is the downhill ski facility. ⊠ *Bolton Access Rd., 05477,* ☎ *802/434–3444 or 877/926–5866,* WEB *www.boltonvalley.com.*

Downhill. Bolton's six lifts include a quad chair, four double chairs, and a surface lift, which service 52 trails covering 157 acres of skiable terrain. The majority of the trails are rated for intermediates; the longest is the 2½-mi Cobrass Run. The vertical drop is 1,625 ft. The resort has 60% snowmaking coverage and provides top-to-bottom night skiing Monday–Saturday until 10 PM. There's a 1,500-ft terrain park for snowboarders.

Cross-country skiing. A Nordic center has cross-country ski, telemark, and snowshoe rentals and lessons. The resort has 35 km (22 mi) of groomed trails and 65 km (40 mi) of natural trails, including some where dogs are permitted. Naturalist-led snowshoe tours are scheduled daily.

Child care. The licensed Honey Bear Child Care Center provides care for children 6 weeks–6 years of age. There are ski programs for ages 3–15.

Summer and year-round activities. The resort has a mountain bike center that rents bikes; indoor and outdoor tennis courts; and hiking trails. A chairlift transports hikers to the top of the mountain but not down. The sports center, open year-round, houses the indoor tennis courts and a pool, sauna, whirlpool, and weight room.

Stowe

★ *16 mi northeast of Bolton, 22 mi northwest of Montpelier, 36 mi east of Burlington.*

Ever since the Civilian Conservation Corps cut the first downhill trails on Mt. Mansfield, ever since Austrian instructors first told weekenders to "bend mit der knees," Stowe has been the spiritual home of Vermont skiing. The village itself is tiny, just a few blocks of shops and restaurants clustered around a snow-white church spire—but it serves as the anchor for the Mountain Road, which leads north past more places to dine, stay, and shop on its way to those fabled slopes.

To many, Stowe rings a bell as the place where the von Trapp family, of *Sound of Music* fame, chose to settle after fleeing Austria. Set amid acres of pastures that fall away and allow for wide-angle panoramas of the mountains beyond, the **Trapp Family Lodge** (⊠ Luce Hill Rd., ☎ 802/253–8511 or 800/826–7000) is the site of a popular outdoor music series in summer and an extensive cross-country ski-trail network in winter. The **Vermont Ski Museum** (☎ 802/253–9911), with exhibits documenting the history of skiing in Vermont, was scheduled at press time to open in the Old Meeting House on Main Street in July 2002.

For more than a century the history of Stowe has been determined by the town's proximity to **Mt. Mansfield,** at 4,393 ft the highest elevation in the state. As early as 1858, the intrepid were trooping to the area to view the mountain, which has a shape that suggests the profile of the face of a man lying on his back. If hiking to the top isn't your idea of a good time, in summer you can take the 4½-mi toll road to the top for a short scenic walk and a magnificent view. ⊠ *Mountain Rd., 7 mi from Rte. 100,* ☎ *802/253–3000.* ☜ *Toll road $14.* ☉ *Mid-May–mid-Oct., daily 10–5.*

Mt. Mansfield's upper reaches are accessible by the eight-seat **gondola** that continuously shuttles up to the area of "the Chin" and the **Cliff House Restaurant** (☎ 802/253–3000 ext. 237), where lunch is served daily 11–2:30. ⊠ *Mountain Rd., 8 mi off Rte. 100,* ☎ *802/253–3000.* ☜ *Gondola $14.* ☉ *Mid-June–mid-Oct., daily 10–5; early Dec.–late Apr., daily 8–4 for skiers.*

Dining and Lodging

$$–$$$ ✕ **Chelsea Grill.** Stowe's newest "in" dinner spot successfully blends the accoutrements of a traditional Vermont country restaurant with the glitz and ambition of a big-city dining room. The chef describes his cuisine as "refined country comfort food," with such appetizers as a deviled fried-oyster salad with smoked bacon and lemon parsley vinaigrette, and entrées such as grilled rack of lamb with roasted peppers and pan-roasted sea bass with citrus couscous. The homemade desserts are every bit as creative. ⊠ *18 Edson Hill Rd.,* ☎ *802/253–3075. MC, V.*

$$–$$$ ✕ **Mes Amis.** At this small bistro, locals queue up for house special-
★ ties such as fresh oysters, lobster bisque, braised lamb shanks, roast duck (secret recipe), and bananas Foster. You can dine in the candlelit dining room or outside on the patio, especially on a warm summer's night. ⊠ *311 Mountain Rd.,* ☎ *802/253–8669. D, MC, V. Closed Mon.*

$–$$ ✕ **Miguel's Stowe Away.** Miguel's serves up all the Tex-Mex standards along with tasty surprises such as coconut-fried shrimp, chicken Santa Fe, and a maple flan. Steaks and burgers round out the gringo menu. The cozy front room has a pool table (no quarters required) and a bar stocked with frosty Corona beer. Miguel's has an outpost on the Sugarbush Access Road in Warren (☎ 802/583–3858). ⊠ *3148 Mountain Rd.,* ☎ *802/53–7574 or 800/245–1240. AE, D, MC, V. No lunch.*

$$$$ ✕⬚ **Topnotch at Stowe Resort and Spa.** One of the state's poshest resorts occupies 120 acres overlooking Mt. Mansfield. Floor-to-ceiling windows, a freestanding circular stone fireplace, and cathedral ceilings distinguish the lobby. Country-decorated rooms have thick carpeting and accents such as painted barn-board walls or Italian prints. The large European spa provides 20 massage-treatment rooms and fitness programs. Maxwell's restaurant serves contemporary Continental cuisine. ⊠ *Mountain Rd., 05672,* ☎ *802/253–8585 or 800/451–8686,* ℻ *802/253–9263,* ⓦⓔⓑ *www.topnotch-resort.com. 77 rooms, 13 suites, 30 town houses. 2 restaurants, 10 tennis courts (4 indoor), 2 pools (1 indoor), massage, sauna, spa, horseback riding, cross-country skiing, sleigh rides, bar, video game room; no-smoking rooms. AE, D, DC, MC, V. MAP.*

$$$–$$$$ ✕⬚ **Edson Hill Manor.** At this French-Canadian–style manor atop 225
★ acres of rolling hills Oriental rugs accent the dark wide-board floors, and a huge stone fireplace in the living room provides a cozy ambience. Guest rooms have fireplaces, canopy beds, and down comforters. The dining room ($$$–$$$$; closed Sun.–Thurs. Apr.–May; no lunch) has walls of windows, wildflower paintings, and vines climbing to the ceiling. The contemporary cuisine might include rack of lamb or pan-seared salmon. ⊠ *1500 Edson Hill Rd., 05672,* ☎ *802/253–7371 or 800/621–0284,* ℻ *802/253–4036,* ⓦⓔⓑ *www.stowevt.com. 25 rooms. Restaurant, some cable TV, pool, hiking, horseback riding, cross-coun-*

try skiing, sleigh rides, meeting room; no air-conditioning in some rooms. D, MC, V. BP, MAP.

$$$$ ⊡ **Stone Hill Inn.** The amenities of a fine hotel and the intimacy of a B&B characterize this adult-oriented inn just off the Mountain Road. Each elegantly decorated (and soundproof) guest room has a king-size bed, sitting area, and two-person whirlpool bath in front of a fireplace. Common areas include a sitting room and a game room, and the 10 acres of grounds are beautifully landscaped with gardens and waterfalls. ⊠ *89 Houston Farm Rd., 05672,* ☎ *802/253–6282,* FAX *802/253–7415,* WEB *www.stonehillinn.com. 9 rooms. Golf privileges, outdoor hot tub, hiking, tobogganing, recreation room. AE, D, DC, MC, V. BP.*

$$$–$$$$ ⊡ **Stoweflake Mountain Resort and Spa.** You'll find scenic mountain views and accommodations here, from comfortable, country-inn rooms to luxurious suites with fireplaces, wet bars, refrigerators, and balconies. This full-service resort also has one- to three-bedroom fully equipped town houses and hosts Stowe's annual Hot Air Balloon Festival. ⊠ *1746 Mountain Rd. (Box 369, 05672),* ☎ *802/253–7355,* FAX *802/253–6858,* WEB *www.stoweflake.com. 94 rooms, 30 town houses. 2 restaurants, some kitchenettes, some microwaves, driving range, putting green, 2 tennis courts, pool, hair salon, sauna, spa, bicycles, sleigh rides, recreation room, business services, meeting rooms. AE, D, DC, MC, V. BP, MAP.*

$$ ⊡ **Inn at Turner Mill.** Families will feel particularly welcome at this simple inn tucked well off the main road. Accommodations range from a one-bedroom unit to a two-bedroom apartment with two private baths, full kitchen, and fireplace. The inn is close to the ski area, a short walk from a swimming hole, and just across the road from miles of hiking trails. You can rent snowshoes here or purchase a pass to a nearby health club. ⊠ *56 Turner Mill La., 05672,* ☎ *802/253–2062 or 800/992–0016,* WEB *www.turnermill.com. 5 units. Some kitchens. AE, MC, V. BP.*

$–$$ ⊡ **Sunset Motor Inn.** Strategically set among northern Vermont's big-three ski areas, this family-owned, family-friendly motel has clean and comfortable accommodations. Rooms numbered 70–87 are larger and have whirlpool baths and refrigerators; the best are the ones facing the back of the motel. There's a restaurant next door. ⊠ *Junction of Rtes. 15 and 100, Morrisville 05661,* ☎ *802/888–4956 or 800/544–2347,* FAX *802/888–3698,* WEB *www.sunsetmotorinn.com. 55 rooms. Pool, some refrigerators; no-smoking rooms. AE, D, MC, V. CP.*

Nightlife and the Arts

NIGHTLIFE

The **Matterhorn Night Club** (⊠ Mountain Rd., ☎ 802/253–8198) hosts live music and dancing Thursday–Saturday nights and a DJ Sunday evenings. Live weekend entertainment takes place at **Stoweflake Mountain Resort and Spa** (☎ 802/253–7355). Entertainers perform at the **Topnotch at Stowe** (☎ 802/253–8585) lounge on weekends.

THE ARTS

Stowe Performing Arts (☎ 802/253–7792) sponsors a series of classical and jazz concerts during July in the Trapp Family Lodge meadow. **Stowe Theater Guild** (⊠ Town Hall Theater, Main St., ☎ 802/253–3961 summer only) performs musicals in July and August.

Outdoor Activities and Sports

A **recreational path** begins behind the Community Church in the center of town and meanders for 5⅓ mi along the river valley, with many entry points along the way. Whether you're on foot, skis, bike, or in-line skates, it's a tranquil spot to enjoy the outdoors.

BIKING

The junction of Routes 100 and 108 is the start of a 21-mi tour with scenic views of Mt. Mansfield; the course takes you along Route 100 to Stagecoach Road, to Morristown, over to Morrisville, and south on Randolph Road. The **Mountain Sports and Bike Shop** (⊠ Mountain Rd., ☎ 802/253–7919; 800/682–4534 outside Stowe area) supplies equipment and rents bicycles.

CANOEING AND KAYAKING

Umiak Outdoor Outfitters (⊠ 849 S. Main St./Rte. 100, just south of Stowe Village, ☎ 802/253–2317) specializes in canoes and kayaks, rents them for day trips, and leads overnight excursions. The store also operates a rental outpost at Lake Elmore State Park in Elmore, on the Winooski River off Route 2 in Waterbury, at North Beach in Burlington, and on the Lamoille River in Jeffersonville.

FISHING

The **Fly Rod Shop** (⊠ Rte. 100, 3 mi south of Stowe, ☎ 802/253–7346 or 800/535–9763) provides a guiding service; gives fly-tying, casting, and rod-building classes in winter; rents fly tackle; and sells equipment, including classic and collectible firearms.

GOLF

Stowe Country Club (⊠ Mountain Rd., ☎ 802/253–4893) has a scenic 18-hole, par-72 course; a driving range; and a putting green. Greens fee is $35–$65; cart rental is $16.

HIKING

An ascent of **Mt. Mansfield** makes for a scenic day hike. Trails lead from Route 108 (the Mountain Road) to the summit ridge, where they meet the north-to-south Long Trail. An option is to take the gondola at Stowe to the top and walk down along a ski trail. Views from the summit take in New Hampshire's White Mountains, New York's Adirondacks across Lake Champlain, and southern Québec. The Green Mountain Club has a trail guide.

For the two-hour climb to **Stowe Pinnacle,** go 1½ mi south of Stowe on Route 100 and turn east on Gold Brook Road opposite the Nichols Farm Lodge; turn left at the first intersection, continue straight at an intersection by a covered bridge, turn right after almost 2 mi, and travel 2⅓ mi to a parking lot on the left. The trail crosses an abandoned pasture and takes a short, steep climb to views of the Green Mountains and Stowe Valley.

ICE-SKATING

Jackson Arena (⊠ Park St., ☎ 802/253–6148 or 802/253–4402) is a public ice-skating rink, with skate rentals available.

SLEIGH RIDES

Charlie Horse Sleigh and Carriage Rides (⊠ Mountain Rd., ☎ 802/ 253–2215) operates rides daily from 11 to 7; reservations are suggested for evening rides.

TENNIS

Topnotch at Stowe Resort and Spa has 10 outdoor and 4 indoor courts. Public courts are at Stowe's elementary school.

Shopping

Mountain Road is lined with shops from town up toward the ski area.

Ski Areas

STOWE MOUNTAIN RESORT

To be precise, the name of the village is Stowe and the name of the mountain is Mt. Mansfield, but to generations of skiers, the area, the complex, and the region are just plain Stowe. The resort is a classic that dates from the 1930s. Even today the area's mystique attracts as many serious skiers as social skiers. Improved snowmaking, new lifts, and free shuttle buses that gather skiers from lodges, inns, and motels along Mountain Road have added convenience to the Stowe experience. Yet the traditions remain: the Winter Carnival in January, the Sugar Slalom in April, ski weeks all winter. Three base lodges provide the essentials, including two on-mountain restaurants. A 10-year expansion plan scheduled to begin in 2003 will include base lodges, a hotel, retail shops, and a golf course. ⊠ *5781 Mountain Rd., 05672,* ☎ *802/ 253–3000; 800/253–4754 lodging; 802/253–3600 snow conditions.*

Downhill. Mt. Mansfield, with an elevation of 4,395 ft and a vertical drop of 2,360 ft, is one of the giants among Eastern ski mountains and the highest in Vermont. The mountain's symmetrical shape allows skiers of all abilities long, satisfying runs from the summit. The famous Front Four (National, Liftline, Starr, and Goat) are the intimidating centerpieces for tough, expert runs, yet there is plenty of mellow intermediate skiing, with 59% of the runs rated at that level. One long beginner trail, the Toll Road Trail, is 3⅔ mi. Mansfield's satellite sector is a network of intermediate trails and one expert trail off a basin served by a gondola. Spruce Peak, separate from the main mountain, is a teaching hill and a pleasant experience for intermediates and beginners. In addition to the high-speed, eight-passenger gondola, Stowe has 11 lifts, including a quad, one triple, and six double chairlifts, plus one handle tow, to service its 48 trails. Night-skiing trails are accessed by the gondola. The resort has 73% snowmaking coverage. Snowboard facilities include a halfpipe and two terrain parks—one for beginners, at Spruce Peak, and one for experts, on the Mt. Mansfield side.

Cross-country. The resort has 35 km (22 mi) of groomed cross-country trails and 40 km (24 mi) of backcountry trails. Four interconnecting cross-country ski areas have more than 150 km (90 mi) of groomed trails within the town of Stowe.

Child care. The child-care center takes children ages 6 weeks–6 years, with kids' ski-school programs for ages 6 to 12. A center on Spruce Peak is headquarters for programs for children ages 3–12, including a program for teenagers 13–17.

Summer activities. The resort provides hiking, in-line skating, an alpine slide, gondola rides, and an 18-hole golf course.

The Craftsburys

❸❹ *27 mi northeast of Stowe.*

The three villages of the Craftsburys—Craftsbury Common, Craftsbury, and East Craftsbury—are among Vermont's finest and oldest towns. Handsome white houses and barns, the requisite common, and terrific views make them well worth the drive. Craftsbury General Store in Craftsbury Village is a great place to stock up on picnic supplies and local information. The rolling farmland hints at the way Vermont used to be: the area's sheer distance from civilization and its rugged weather have kept most of the state's development farther south.

Dining and Lodging

$$$$ ✕▥ **Inn on the Common.** All rooms at this Federal-style complex contain antique reproductions and contemporary furnishings; deluxe rooms have seating areas and fireplaces. Cocktails are served in the cozy library, and five-course dinners ($$$$; reservations essential) are served in the dining room overlooking the gardens. You have access to the facilities at the Craftsbury Sports Center and Albany's Wellness Barn. Cross-country ski trails connect with those at the Craftsbury Nordic Center. ⊠ *On the common, 05827,* ☎ *802/586–9619 or 800/521–2233,*

FAX *802/586–2249,* WEB *www.innonthecommon.com. 15 rooms, 1 suite. Dining room, tennis court, pool, cross-country skiing, lounge, library. AE, MC, V. MAP.*

$$$–$$$$ 🏨 **Craftsbury Outdoor Center.** This outdoors enthusiast's haven has standard accommodations and sporting packages. Cross-country skiing is terrific on 135 km (80 mi) of trails (85 km [50 mi] groomed); the rest of the year, sculling and running camps are held. You can ski, mountain bike, and canoe at day-use rates; equipment rental is available. Meals are served buffet-style. ⊠ *Lost Nation Rd. (Box 31, 05827),* ☎ *802/586–7767 or 800/729–7751,* FAX *802/586–7768,* WEB *www.craftsbury.com. 49 rooms, 10 with bath; 4 cottages; 2 efficiencies. Dining room, boating, mountain bikes, cross-country skiing, meeting room. MC, V.*

$ 🏨 **Craftsbury Bed & Breakfast.** Craftsbury's longest-operating traditional B&B is a lovely place to unwind. Owner Margaret Ramsdell creates an air of peaceful informality at her farmhouse, right down to the absence of a TV. Common rooms include a spacious country kitchen with a woodstove and a living room. In summer, relax on lawn chairs in the big yard; in winter, ski on the property's cross-country ski trails, which are part of a 105-km (65-mi) network. ⊠ *Wylie Hill, 05827,* ☎ *802/586–2206,* WEB *www.scenesofvermont.com/craftsburybb. 6 rooms with shared bath. MC, V. BP.*

Greensboro

㉟ *10 mi southeast of Craftsbury Common.*

Greensboro, tucked along the southern shore of Caspian Lake, has been a summer resort for literati, academics, and old-money types for more than a century. It exudes an unpretentious, genteel character of such places with a small village center where most of the people running about their errands seem to know each other. A town beach is right off the main street.

Lodging

$$$$ 🏨 **Highland Lodge.** Tranquillity reigns at this 1860 house overlooking a pristine lake. The lodge's 120 acres of rambling woods and pastures are laced with hiking and skiing trails (ski rentals available). Comfortable guest rooms have Early American–style furnishings; most have views of the lake. The one- to three-bedroom cottages are more private (four with gas stoves stay open in winter). The traditional dinner menu might include entrées such as roasted leg of lamb. ⊠ *1608 Craftsbury Rd., 05841,* ☎ *802/533–2647,* FAX *802/533–7494,* WEB *www.highlandlodge.com. 11 rooms, 11 cottages. Restaurant, tennis court, lake, boating, hiking, cross-country skiing, recreation room; no air-conditioning. D, MC, V. Closed mid-Mar.–late May and mid-Oct.–mid-Dec. MAP.*

Shopping

The **Miller's Thumb** (⊠ Main St., ☎ 802/533–2960 or 800/680–7886) sells Italian pottery, Vermont furniture, crafts and antiques, and April Cornell clothing and linens. **Willey's Store** (⊠ Main St., ☎ 802/533–2621), with wooden floors and tin ceilings, warrants exploration. Foodstuffs, baskets, candy, kitchen paraphernalia, and more are packed to the rafters.

Jeffersonville

㊱ *36 mi west of Greensboro, 18 mi north of Stowe, 28 mi northeast of Burlington.*

Mt. Mansfield and Madonna Peak tower over Jeffersonville, whose activities are closely linked with those of Smugglers' Notch Ski Resort.

Boyden Valley Winery (⊠ junction of Rtes. 15 and 104, Cambridge, ☎ 802/644–8151) conducts tours of its microwinery and showcases an excellent selection of Vermont specialty products and local handicrafts, including fine furniture. The winery is closed Monday in summer and Monday–Thursday in winter.

Lodging

$$$$ 🏨 **Smugglers' Notch Resort.** Most of the condos at this large year-round resort have fireplaces and decks. The resort is known for its many family programs. Rates include lift tickets and ski lessons in season, and kids six weeks to two years of age get free care if parents stay three or more nights. ⊠ *Rte. 108, 05464,* ☎ *802/644–8851 or 800/451–8752,* FAX *802/644–1230,* WEB *www.smugs.com. 502 condominiums. 3 restaurants, 6 tennis courts, pool, gym, hot tub, sauna, downhill skiing, ice-skating, bar, recreation room, baby-sitting, children's programs (ages 3–17), playground. AE, DC, MC, V.*

$–$$ 🏨 **Mannsview Inn.** Bette and Kelley Mann operate what may be Vermont's only B&B, canoe touring center, and antiques center. Decorated with a Victorian accents, the inn furnishes its charming guest rooms with antiques, high poster beds, whirlpool baths, and fireplaces. An antique pool table fills one side of the living room, and breakfast is served in a glassed-in room overlooking the mountains. ⊠ *Rte. 108, 05464,* ☎ *802/644–8321 or 888/937–6266,* FAX *802/644–2006,* WEB *www.mannsview.com. 6 rooms. Outdoor hot tub. AE, D, MC, V. BP*

$ 🏨 **Deer Run Motor Inn.** This comfortable two-story motel may be the north country's best bargain. Although it's right on busy Route 15, the rooms are set well back (second-floor rooms with queen-size beds face the rear), and each has a coffeemaker, deck, and sliding glass doors. Other amenities include a swing set and grills. ⊠ *80 Deer Run Loop, 05464,* ☎ *802/644–8866 or 800/354–2728,* WEB *www.deerrunmotorinn.com. 25 units. Picnic area, cable TV, pool, some pets allowed (fee); no-smoking rooms. AE, D, MC, V.*

Outdoor Activities and Sports

Applecheek Farm (⊠ 567 McFarlane Rd., Hyde Park, ☎ 802/888–4482) runs daytime and evening (by lantern) hay and sleigh rides, llama treks, and farm tours. **Green River Canoe & Kayak** (☎ 802/644–8336 or 802/644–8714), at the junction of Route 15 and 108 behind Jana's Restaurant, rents canoes and kayaks on the Lamoille River and leads guided canoe trips to Boyden Valley Winery. **Northern Vermont Llamas** (⊠ 766 Lapland Rd., Waterville, ☎ 802/644–2257) conducts half- and full-day treks from May through October along the cross-country ski trails of Smugglers' Notch. The llamas carry everything, including snacks and lunches. Advance reservations are essential.

Smugglers' Notch Canoe Touring (⊠ Rte. 108, ☎ 802/644–8321 or 888/937–6266) provides canoes, kayaks, and shuttle service on the Lamoille River from Mannsview Inn. Tubing is also available. **Smugglers' Notch State Park** (⊠ Rte. 108, 10 mi north of Mt. Mansfield, ☎ 802/253–4014) is good for picnicking and hiking on wild terrain among large boulders. **Vermont Horse Park** (⊠ Rte. 108, ☎ 802/644–5347) leads rides on authentic horse-drawn sleighs as well as trail rides when weather permits.

Shopping

ANTIQUES

The **Buggy Man** (⊠ Rte. 15, 7 mi east of Jeffersonville, ☎ 802/635–2110) sells American furniture and collectibles including horse-drawn vehicles. **Mel Siegel** (⊠ Rte. 15, 7 mi east of Jeffersonville, ☎ 802/635–7838) specializes in 19th-century American furniture and glassware.

Smugglers Notch Antique Center (⊠ Rte. 108, ☎ 802/644–8321) sells antiques and collectibles of 60 dealers in a rambling barn.

CLOTHING

The **Forget-Me-Not Shop.** (⊠ Rte. 15, 6½ mi east of Jeffersonville, ☎ 802/635–2335) sells men's and women's designer clothing, military surplus, and jewelry at incredibly low prices. **Johnson Woolen Mills** (⊠ Main St., Johnson, 9 mi east of Jeffersonville, ☎ 802/635–2271) is an authentic factory store with deals on woolen blankets, yard goods, and the famous Johnson outerwear.

CRAFTS

Vermont Rug Makers (⊠ Rte. 100C, East Johnson, 10 mi east of Jeffersonville, ☎ 802/635–2434) weaves imaginative rugs and tapestries from fabrics, wools, and exotic materials. Its International Gallery displays rugs and tapestries from countries throughout the world. The shop has a branch on Main Street in Stowe.

Ski Areas

SMUGGLERS' NOTCH RESORT

This sprawling resort complex consistently wins accolades for its family programs. Its children's ski school is one of the best in the country—possibly *the* best. But skiers of all levels come here (Smugglers' was the first ski area in the East to designate a triple-black-diamond run—the Black Hole). All the essentials are available in the village at the base of the Morse Mountain lifts, including lodgings, restaurants, and several shops. ⊠ *Rte. 108, 05464,* ☎ *802/644–8851 or 800/451–8752,* WEB *www.smuggs.com.*

Downhill. Smugglers' has three mountains. The highest, Madonna, with a vertical drop of 2,610 ft, is in the center and connects with a trail network to Sterling (1,500-ft vertical). The third mountain, Morse (1,150-ft vertical), is adjacent to Smugglers' "village" of shops, restaurants, and lodgings; it's connected to the other peaks by trails and a shuttle bus. The wild, craggy landscape lends a pristine wilderness feel to the skiing experience on the two higher mountains. The tops of each of the mountains have expert terrain—a couple of double-black diamonds make Madonna memorable. Intermediate trails fill the lower sections. Morse has many beginner and advanced beginner trails. Smugglers' 70 trails are served by eight lifts, including six chairs and two surface lifts. Top-to-bottom snowmaking on all three mountains allows for 62% coverage. Several terrain parks are provided for snowboarders, including Prohibition Park, at 3,500 ft one of the longest in Vermont. Night skiing and snowboarding classes are given at the new Learning and Fun Park.

Cross-country/snowshoeing. The area has 27 km (18 mi) of groomed and tracked cross-country trails and 20 km (12 mi) of snowshoe trails.

Other activities. The self-contained village has ice-skating and sleigh rides. The numerous snowshoeing programs include family walks and backcountry trips. The FunZone at SmuggsCentral has an indoor pool, playground, slides, miniature golf, a hot tub, ice-skating rink, and Nordic Center. A Teen Center is open from 5 PM until midnight.

Child care. The state-of-the-art Alice's Wonderland Child Care Center accepts children ages 6 weeks–6 years. Ski camps for kids ages 3–17 provide excellent instruction, plus movies, games, and other activities.

Summer and year-round activities. Smugglers' has a full roster of summertime programs, including a pool, complete with waterfalls and water slides; the Giant Rapid River Ride (the longest water ride in the state); lawn games; and mountain biking and hiking programs. It also has an indoor sports center, the FunZone. Horseback riding is available in summer and fall.

Burlington

★ ❸ *31 mi southwest of Jeffersonville, 76 mi south of Montréal, 349 mi north of New York City, 223 mi northwest of Boston.*

Cited in survey after survey as one of America's most livable small cities, Burlington has the vibrant character of a college town in which a lot of the graduates have stayed behind to put down roots. The largest population center in Vermont, the city was founded in 1763 and is now the center of a rapidly growing suburban area. It has held its own against highway malls by cleverly positioning itself in the "festival marketplace" retail style, as well as by trading on its incomparable location on Lake Champlain. The Church Street Marketplace—a pedestrian mall of boutiques, restaurants, sidewalk cafés, crafts vendors, and street performers—is an animated downtown focal point. The Burlington area's eclectic population includes many transplants from larger urban areas as well as roughly 20,000 students from the area's four colleges. For years it was the only city in America with a socialist mayor—now the nation's sole socialist congressional representative.

Crouched on the shores of Lake Champlain, which shimmers in the shadows of the Adirondacks to the west, Burlington's revitalized waterfront teems with outdoors enthusiasts who stroll along its recreation path and ply the waters in sailboats and motor craft in summer. A 500-passenger, three-level cruise vessel, **Shoreline Cruise's** *The Spirit of Ethan Allen III,* takes people on narrated cruises and on dinner and sunset sailings that drift by the Adirondacks and the Green Mountains. ⊠ *Burlington Boat House, College St. at Battery St.,* ☎ *802/862–8300.* ☞ *$9.95.* ☺ *Cruises late May–mid-Oct., daily 10–9.*

Part of the waterfront's revitalization and still a work in progress, the ☾ **Center for Lake Champlain** was closed at this writing for renovations and scheduled to reopen in June 2003. Check the Web site for updates. ⊠ *1 College St.,* ☎ *802/864–1848,* WEB *www.lakechamplaincenter.org.*

Crowning the hilltop above Burlington is the campus of the **University of Vermont** (☎ 802/656–3480), known simply as UVM for the abbreviation of its Latin name, Universitas Viridis Montis—the University of the Green Mountains. With more than 10,000 students, UVM is the state's principal institution of higher learning. The most architecturally interesting buildings face the Green, which contains some of the grandest surviving specimens of the elm trees that once shaded virtually every street in Burlington, as well as a statue of UVM founder Ira Allen, Ethan's brother. The **Robert Hull Fleming Art Museum** (⊠ Colchester Ave., ☎ 802/656–0750), just behind the Ira Allen Chapel, houses American portraits and landscapes, including works by Sargent, Homer, and Bierstadt; two Corots and a Fragonard; and an Egyptian mummy. Contemporary Vermont works are also exhibited.

Burlington's **Intervale** encompasses 700 acres of open land along the Winooski River. You can rent canoes, bike the 2-mi trail (which connects with Burlington's 10-mi Cycle the City loop), take a river tour, or hike the trails. Gardener's Supply Company (⊠ 128 Intervale Rd., ☎ 802/660–3505, WEB www.gardeners.com), a major direct-mail gardening company, with greenhouses and outdoor display gardens, oversees the project. The company also provides maps, information, and a schedule of the many seasonal events held there. One of the earliest residents of the Intervale was Ethan Allen, Vermont's Revolutionary-era guerrilla fighter, who remains a captivating figure. Exhibits at the

Ethan Allen Homestead visitor center answer questions about his flamboyant life. The house contains such frontier hallmarks as rough sawcut boards and an open hearth for cooking. A re-created Colonial kitchen garden resembles the one the Allens would have had. After the tour and multimedia presentation, you can stretch your legs on scenic trails along the Winooski River. ⊠ *North Ave. off Rte. 127, north of Burlington,* ☎ *802/865–4556,* 〖WEB〗 *www.sover.net/~eahome.com.* ⊡ *$5.* ⊙ *Call for schedule.*

OFF THE
BEATEN PATH **GREEN MOUNTAIN AUDUBON NATURE CENTER –** This is a wonderful place to discover Vermont's outdoor wonders. The center's 300 acres of diverse habitats are a sanctuary for all things wild, and the 5 mi of trails provide an opportunity to explore the workings of differing natural communities. Events include dusk walks, wildflower and birding rambles, nature workshops, and educational activities for kids and adults. The center is 18 mi southeast of Burlington. ⊠ *Huntington–Richmond Rd., Richmond,* ☎ *802/434–3068.* ⊡ *Donations accepted.* ⊙ *Grounds daily dawn–dusk, center Mon.–Sat. 8–4.*

Dining and Lodging

$$–$$$ ✕ **Leunig's Bistro.** Church Street's café delivers alfresco dining, bistro cuisine, and live jazz Tuesday–Thursday evenings. Favorite entrées include herb-crusted rack of lamb and pine nut chicken breast with a red grape white wine sauce. A prix-fixe dinner for two for $30, served Sunday–Thursday 5–6, is one of the city's best bargains. ⊠ *115 Church St.,* ☎ *802/863–3759. AE, D, DC, MC, V.*

$$–$$$ ✕ **NECI Commons.** The initials stand for New England Culinary Institute, the respected Montpelier academy whose students and teachers run this all-under-one-roof café, bakery, market, restaurant, and bar. The deli counter can get a little pricey, but everything is fresh and tasty. It's open daily for lunch and dinner and on Sunday for brunch. Mornings, homemade pastries and muffins are served in the market area. ⊠ *25 Church St.,* ☎ *802/862–6324. AE, D, MC, V.*

$$–$$$ ✕ **Trattoria Delia.** Didn't manage to rent that villa in Umbria this year?
★   The next best thing, if your travels bring you to Burlington, is this superb Italian country eatery just around the corner from City Hall Park. Local game and produce are the stars, as in roast rabbit marinated in herbs, wine, and olive oil. The chef's passion for the truly homemade extends to wild boar sausage, salami, and fresh mozzarella. Wood-grilled items are a specialty. ⊠ *152 St. Paul St.,* ☎ *802/864–5253. AE, D, DC, MC, V. No lunch.*

$$ ✕ **Junior's.** New York–style pizza and freshly made calzones share the menu with spaghetti and meatballs, shrimp *fra diavola,* and penne àla vodka with prosciutto, onions, and mushrooms at this pizzeria. Weekend reservations are recommended for dinner seating in the second floor, white-tableclothed dining room. ⊠ *6 Roosevelt Hwy., Colchester,* ☎ *802/655–5555. AE, MC, V.*

$$ ✕ **Old Heidelberg German Restaurant.** This chef-owned restaurant, graciously appointed with linens and fresh flowers, serves such tasty Teutonic standards as sauerbraten, pork and veal schnitzels, and homemade bratwurst; hearty homemade goulash and potato soups round out the luncheon and appetizer menus. German cuisine is the original "comfort food"—perfect for a cold northern Vermont winter night. German beers and wines are available. ⊠ *1016 Shelburne Rd./Rte. 7,* ☎ *802/ 865–4423. AE, D, DC, MC, V. Closed Mon.*

$$ ✕ **Parima Thai Restaurant.** Chef's specials such as crispy roasted duck in tamarind sauce and seafood *phuket* (shrimp, mussels, cod, and squid sautéed in basil sauce) join a menu of traditional Thai including curries and pad Thai (stir-fried noodles with shrimp or chicken). This

handsomely appointed restaurant has one of the most elegant bars in town and a seasonal patio. Lunch is served weekdays. ⊠ *185 Pearl St.,* ☎ *802/864–7917. AE, D, DC, MC, V.*

$–$$ ✕ **Ri Ra.** Brought to Burlington from Ireland in pieces and reassembled on-site, this Irish pub serves classic fare such as bangers and mash and fish-and-chips, along with burgers and fish. The luncheon buffet serves traditional Irish carvery. ⊠ *123 Church St.,* ☎ *802/860–9401. MC, V.*

$$$$ ✕▦ **Inn at Essex.** About 10 mi from downtown Burlington—next to Essex Outlet Fair—is a state-of-the-art inn and conference center dressed in country clothing. Rooms have flowered wallpaper and reproduction period desks; 30 have fireplaces. The two restaurants ($$$–$$$$) are run by the New England Culinary Institute. Butlers serve dishes such as sweet dumpling squash with ginger-garlic basmati rice. Five-onion soup and daily flatbread pizza specials are among the highlights at the Tavern. ⊠ *70 Essex Way, off Rte. 15, Essex Junction 05452,* ☎ *802/878–1100 or 800/727–4295,* ℻ *802/878–0063,* 𝖂𝖤𝖡 *www.innatessex.com. 120 rooms. 2 restaurants, pool, billiards, bar, library, business services, meeting rooms. AE, D, DC, MC, V. CP.*

$$–$$$$ ▦ **Willard Street Inn.** High in the historic hill section of Burlington, this
★ grand house with an exterior marble staircase and English gardens incorporates elements of Queen Anne and Colonial–Georgian Revival styles. The stately foyer, paneled in cherry, leads to a more formal sitting room with velvet drapes. The solarium is bright and sunny with marble floors, many plants, and big velvet couches for contemplating views of Lake Champlain. All the rooms have down comforters and phones; some have lake views and canopied beds. Orange French toast is among the breakfast favorites. ⊠ *349 S. Willard St., 05401,* ☎ *802/651–8710 or 800/ 577–8712,* ℻ *802/651–8714,* 𝖂𝖤𝖡 *www.willardstreetinn.com. 14 rooms. AE, D, MC, V. BP.*

Nightlife and the Arts

NIGHTLIFE

The music at the **Club Metronome** (⊠ 188 Main St., ☎ 802/865–4563) ranges from cutting-edge sounds to funk, blues, and reggae. National and local musicians come to **Higher Ground** (⊠ 1 Main St., Winooski, ☎ 802/654–8888). The band Phish got its start at **Nectar's** (⊠ 188 Main St., ☎ 802/658–4771). This place is always jumping to the sounds of local bands and never charges a cover. **Red Square Bar and Grill** (⊠ 136 Church St., ☎ 802/859–8909) hosts a Sunday gospel brunch from late January through early March and live music, including funk, jazz, and other eclectic selections, Monday–Saturday. Food is served on the garden patio in nice weather. **Ri Ra** (⊠ 123 Church St., ☎ 802/ 860–9401) hosts live entertainment with an Irish flair. **Vermont Pub and Brewery** (⊠ 144 College St., ☎ 802/865–0500) makes its own beer and fruit seltzers and is arguably the most popular spot in town. Folk musicians play here regularly.

THE ARTS

City Hall's **Burlington City Arts** (☎ 802/865–7166; 802/865–9163 24-hr Artsline) has up-to-date arts-related information. The **Fire House Art Gallery** (⊠ 135 Church St., ☎ 802/865–7165) exhibits works by local artists. **Flynn Theatre for the Performing Arts** (⊠ 153 Main St., ☎ 802/652–4500 information; 802/863–5966 tickets; 𝖂𝖤𝖡 www.flynncenter.org), a grandiose old structure, is the cultural heart of Burlington; it schedules the Vermont Symphony Orchestra, theater, dance, big-name musicians, and lectures. The **Lyric Theater** (☎ 802/658–1484) stages musical productions in the fall and spring at the Flynn Theatre. **St. Michael's Playhouse** (⊠ St. Michael's College, Rte. 15, Colchester, ☎ 802/654–2281 box office; 802/654–2617 administrative office) performs in the McCarthy Arts Center Theater. The **UVM Lane Series** (☎ 802/656–4455 programs and times; 802/656–3085 box office) sponsors classical as well as folk music concerts in the Flynn Theatre, Ira Allen Chapel, and the UVM Recital Hall. The **Vermont Symphony Orchestra** (☎ 802/874–5741) performs throughout the state year-round and at the Flynn from October through May.

Outdoor Activities and Sports

BEACHES

The **North Beaches** are on the northern edge of Burlington: North Beach Park (✉ off North Ave., ☎ 802/864–0123), Bayside Beach (✉ Rte. 127 near Malletts Bay), and Leddy Beach (✉ Leddy Park Rd., off North Ave.), which is popular for sailboarding.

BIKING

Burlington's 10-mi Cycle the City loop runs along the waterfront, connecting several city parks and beaches. It also passes the Community Boathouse and runs within several blocks of downtown restaurants and shops. **North Star Cyclery** (✉ 100 Main St., ☎ 802/863–3832) rents bicycles and provides maps of bicycle routes. **Ski Rack** (✉ 81 Main St., ☎ 802/658–3313 or 800/882–4530) rents and services bikes and provides maps.

WATER SPORTS

Burlington Community Boathouse (✉ foot of College St., Burlington Harbor, ☎ 802/865–3377) rents Jet Skis, sailboards, sailboats from 13 ft to 40 ft, and motorboats (some captained); the boathouse also gives lessons. **Malletts Bay Marina** (✉ 228 Lakeshore Dr., Colchester, ☎ 802/862–4072) has facilities for mooring, sells gasoline, and repairs boats. **Marble Island Resort** (✉ Colchester, ☎ 802/864–6800) has a marina and a 9-hole golf course. **Point Bay Marina** (✉ 1401 Thompson's Point Rd., Charlotte, ☎ 802/425–2431) provides full service and repairs.

Shopping

ANTIQUES

Architectural Salvage Warehouse (✉ 53 Main St., ☎ 802/658–5011) is a great place to hunt for claw-foot tubs, stained-glass windows, mantels, andirons, and other similar items. The large rhinoceros head bursting out of the **Conant Custom Brass** (✉ 270 Pine St., ☎ 802/658–4482) storefront may tempt you in to see the custom work, including decorative lighting and bathroom fixtures.

CRAFTS

In addition to its popular pottery, **Bennington Potters North** (✉ 127 College St., ☎ 802/863–2221 or 800/205–8033) stocks interesting gifts, glassware, furniture, and other housewares. **Vermont State Craft Center** (✉ 85 Church St., ☎ 802/863–6458) displays contemporary and traditional crafts by more than 200 Vermont artisans. **Yankee Pride** (✉ Champlain Mill, E. Canal St., Winooski, ☎ 802/655–0500) has a large inventory of quilting fabrics and supplies as well as Vermont-made quilts.

MALLS AND MARKETPLACES

The remodeled **Burlington Square Mall** (✉ Church St., ☎ 802/658–2545) has a Starbucks, a large Filene's department store, and a few dozen other shops. The **Champlain Mill** (✉ U.S. 2/7, northeast of Burlington, ☎ 802/655–9477), a former woolen mill on the banks of the Winooski River, holds three floors of stores, including several clothing shops and restaurants. **Church Street Marketplace** (✉ Main St. to Pearl St., ☎ 802/863–1648), a pedestrian thoroughfare, is lined with boutiques, cafés, and street vendors. Look for bargains at the rapidly growing **Essex Outlet Fair** (⊠ junction of Rtes. 15 and 289, Essex, ☎ 802/878–2851), with such outlets as Brooks Brothers, Polo Ralph Lauren, and Levi's, among others. **University Mall** (⊠ Dorset St., ☎ 802/863–1066), housing Sears, Bon Ton, and JCPenney, continues to expand.

Shelburne

③ *5 mi south of Burlington.*

Once a village surrounded by small farms and lakeshore estates, Shelburne is now largely a bedroom community for Burlington. It's distinguished by one of the nation's premier repositories of Americana and by a tycoon's gilded-age fiefdom that has become a model farm and agricultural education center.

★ A few miles south of Burlington, the Champlain Valley gives way to fertile farmland, affording stunning views of the rugged Adirondacks across the lake. You can trace much of New England's history simply by wandering the 45 acres and 37 buildings of the **Shelburne Museum.** The outstanding 80,000-object collection of Americana consists of 18th- and 19th-century period homes and furniture, fine and folk art, farm tools, more than 200 carriages and sleighs, Audubon prints, an old-fashioned jail, and even a private railroad car from the days of steam. The museum also has an assortment of duck decoys, an old stone cottage, a display of early toys, and the *Ticonderoga*, an old side-wheel steamship, grounded amid lawn and trees. ⊠ *U.S. 7,* ☎ *802/985–3346 or 802/985–3344,* WEB *www.shelburnemuseum.org.* ☞ *$17.50 for 2 consecutive days.* ☉ *Mid-May–late Oct., daily 10–5; late Apr.–mid-May, daily 1–4.*

★ ☾ Founded in the 1880s as a private estate, the 1,400-acre **Shelburne Farms** is an educational and cultural resource center with, among other things, a working dairy farm, a Children's Farmyard, and a spot for watching the farm's famous cheddar cheese being made. Frederick Law Olmsted, co-creator of New York's Central Park, designed the magnificent grounds overlooking Lake Champlain. For an additional charge of $5, you can tour the 1891 breeding barn. ⊠ *West of U.S. 7 at Harbor and Bay Rds.,* ☎ *802/985–8686,* WEB *www.shelburnefarms.org.* ☞ *Day pass $6, tour an additional $5.* ☉ *Visitor center and shop daily 10–5; tours mid-May–mid-Oct. (last tour at 3:30); mid-Oct.–mid-May, walking trails open, weather permitting.*

☾ On the 25-minute tour of the **Vermont Teddy Bear Company,** you'll hear more puns than you ever thought possible and learn how a few homemade bears, sold from a cart on Church Street, have turned into a multimillion-dollar business. A children's play tent is set up outdoors in summer, and you can wander the beautiful 57-acre property. ⊠ *2236 Shelburne Rd.,* ☎ *802/985–3001.* ☞ *Tour $2.* ☉ *Tours Mon.–Sat. 9:30–5, Sun. 10:30–4; store Mon.–Sat. 9–6, Sun. 10–5.*

At the 6-acre **Vermont Wildflower Farm,** the display along the flowering pathways changes constantly: violets in the spring, daisies and black-eyed Susans for summer, and, for fall, flowers with colors that rival those of the trees' foliage. You can buy wildflower seeds, crafts, and books here. ⊠ *U.S. 7, Charlotte, 5 mi south of the Shelburne Museum,* ☎ *802/425–3641,* WEB *www.americanmeadows.com.* ☞ *$3.* ☉ *Early May–late Oct., daily 10–5.*

Dining and Lodging

$$$ ✕ **Café Shelburne Français.** This popular restaurant serves creative
★ French bistro cuisine. Some specialties are sweetbreads in a port wine

and mushroom sauce in puff pastry and homemade fettucine with prunes. Desserts such as the sweet chocolate layered terrine and maple-syrup mousse with orange terrine are fabulous. ⊠ *U.S. 7,* ☎ *802/985–3939. AE, MC, V. Closed Sun.–Mon. No lunch.*

$–$$ ✕ **La Villa Mediterranean.** Made-to-order pasta dishes, pizza (in three sizes), grilled items such as salmon and lamb chops, and an assortment of tasty appetizers make this family-friendly restaurant a popular choice for lunch and dinner. The large, open dining room seats 60 at candlelit, linen-covered tables. Diners can watch chefs prepare their meals near the open kitchen.⊠ *Rte. 7, Tenneybrook Square,* ☎ *802/ 985–2596. MC, V. Closed Sun.*

$$–$$$$ ✕▥ **Inn at Shelburne Farms.** This turn-of-the-20th-century Tudor-
★   style inn, once the home of William Seward and Lila Vanderbilt Webb, overlooks Lake Champlain, the distant Adirondacks, and the sea of pastures that make up this 1,400-acre working farm. Each room is different, from the wallpaper to the period antiques. The dining room ($$$–$$$$) defines elegance, and Sunday brunch (not served in May) is one of the area's best. ⊠ *Harbor Rd., 05482,* ☎ *802/985–8498,* 𝔽𝔸𝕏 *802/ 985–8123,* ⓌⒺⒷ *www.shelburnefarms.org. 24 rooms, 17 with bath. Restaurant, tennis court, lake, boating, fishing, billiards, hiking. AE, D, DC, MC, V. Closed mid-Oct.–mid-May.*

$$–$$$$ ▥ **Heart of the Village Inn.** Each of the elegantly furnished rooms at this handsomely restored 1886 B&B across from Town Hall (and within walking distance of the Café Shelburne Français) provides coziness and comfort. Four rooms and a suite in the carriage barn are more spacious and have modern accommodations. ⊠ *5347 Shelburne Rd./Rte. 7, 05482,* ☎ *802/985–2800 or 877/808–7031,* 𝔽𝔸𝕏 *802/985–2870,* ⓌⒺⒷ *www.heartofthevillage.com. 8 rooms, 1 suite. Cable TV. AE, MC, V. BP.*

Outdoor Activities and Sports

A moderately easy 18½-mi bike trail begins at the blinker on U.S. 7 in Shelburne and follows Mt. Philo Road, Hinesburg Road, Route 116, and Irish Hill Road.

Shopping

When you enter **Shelburne Country Store** (⊠ Village Green, off U.S. 7, ☎ 802/985–3657) you'll step back in time. Walk past the potbellied stove and take in the aroma emanating from the fudge neatly piled behind huge antique glass cases. The store specializes in candles, weather vanes, glassware, and local foods.

Ferrisburg

㊴   *9 mi south of Shelburne*

A bedroom community for nearby Burlington, rural Ferrisburg is home to one of Vermont's oldest resorts, a museum, a fine restaurant, and Button Bay and Kingsland Bay state parks.

Rokeby Museum, the onetime home of 19th-century author and illustrator Rowland E. Robinson, was once a stop on the Underground Railroad. Today the National Historic Landmark is preserved as a time capsule, incorporating more than 200 years of family treasures. The property includes eight historic outbuildings and hiking trails. Guided tours are given at 11, 12:30, and 2. ⊠ *Rte. 7,* ☎ *802/877–3406.* ▤ *$4.* ☉ *Mid-May–mid-Oct., Thurs.–Sun.*

Dining

$$–$$$ ✕ **Starry Night Cafe.** Since it opened, this chic restaurant housed in an old cider mill has become one of the hottest spots around, increasing in size to meet growing demand. Appetizers include house specials such as honey-chili glazed shrimp and gazpacho. Among the entrées are lobster-stuffed sole, pan-seared scallops, and grilled New York steak. ✉ *5467 Rte. 7,* ☎ *802/877–0316. MC, V.*

Shopping

Dakin Farm (✉ Rte. 7, ☎ 800/993–2546) sells cob-smoked ham, aged cheddar cheese, and other specialty foods; come in for free samples. The **Ferrisburg Artisans' Guild** (✉ 303 Cherry St./Rte. 7, ☎ 802/877–3668), next to the Starry Night Cafe, provides work space for potters, sculptors, and furniture makers and exhibits the works of local craftspeople.

Vergennes

40 *3 mi south of Ferrisburg*

Vermont's oldest city, founded in 1788, is also the third oldest in New England. The downtown area is a compact district of Victorian homes and public buildings. Main Street slopes down to Otter Creek Falls, where cannonballs were made during the War of 1812. The statue of Thomas MacDonough on the Green immortalizes the victor of the Battle of Plattsburgh in 1814.

OFF THE BEATEN PATH

LAKE CHAMPLAIN MARITIME MUSEUM – A replica of Benedict Arnold's Revolutionary War gunboat is part of this museum, which documents centuries of activity on the historically significant lake. The museum commemorates the days when steamships sailed along the coast of northern Vermont carrying logs, livestock, and merchandise bound for New York City. Among the 13 exhibit areas is a blacksmith's shop. A one-room stone schoolhouse built in the early 19th century houses historic maps, nautical prints, and maritime objects. Also on site are a nautical archaeology center, a conservation laboratory, and a restaurant. ✉ *Basin Harbor Rd., Basin Harbor (14 mi west of Bristol, 7 mi west of Vergennes),* ☎ *802/475–2022.* ✍ *$8.* ☉ *May–mid–Oct., daily 10–5.*

Dining and Lodging

$$$–$$$$ ✕ **Christophe's on the Green.** Amid simple elegance—high ceilings, crisp linens, fresh flowers—inside an old hotel in the center of town, this restaurant serves classic, artfully prepared French cuisine. Among the specialties are braised rabbit and Cornish hen in a phyllo pastry. The three-course fixed-price dinner for $45 is an excellent value. ✉ *5 Green St.,* ☎ *802/877–3414. MC, V. Closed mid-Oct.–mid-May and Sun.–Mon.*

$$$–$$$$ ✕🏨 **Basin Harbor Club.** On 700 acres overlooking Lake Champlain
★ this family resort provides luxurious accommodations, a full roster of amenities including an 18-hole golf course, boating (with a 40-ft tour boat), and daylong children's programs. Some rooms have fireplaces, decks, or porches. The restaurant menu ($$–$$$) is classic American, the wine list excellent. Coats and ties are required in common areas after 6 PM from mid-June through Labor Day. ✉ *Basin Harbor Rd., Vergennes 05491,* ☎ *802/475–2311 or 800/622–4000,* 🅵🅰🆇 *802/475– 6545,* 🆆🅴🅱 *www.basinharbor.com. 36 rooms, 2 suites in 3 guest houses, 77 cottages. 2 restaurants, 18-hole golf course, 5 tennis courts, pool, health club, boating, bicycles, children's programs (ages 3–15). MC, V. Closed mid-Oct.–mid-May. FAP July–Aug.; BP spring and fall.*

$$–$$$ 🏨 **Whitford House.** Antiques and original art adorn the walls of this late-18th-century country farmhouse on 37 acres of meadowlands. All three bedrooms in the main house have spectacular views of rolling dairy lands and the distant Adirondacks. The guest cottage, which sleeps four, has a microwave, refrigerator, and wet bar. Dinner is prepared by request. ✉ *912 Grandey Rd., Addison 05491,* ☎ *802/758–2704*

or 800/746–2704, FAX *802/758–2089,* WEB *www.whitfordhouseinn.com.*
3 rooms, 1 cottage. Library, some pets allowed. MC, V. BP.

Shopping

Kennedy Brothers Marketplace (✉ Rte. 22A, ☎ 802/877–2975), in a
renovated creamery, displays the wares of craftspeople, woodworkers,
and antiques and collectibles dealers.

Lake Champlain Islands

④ *43 mi from Vergennes, 20 mi northwest of Shelburne, 15 mi north-*
west of Burlington.

South Hero, North Hero, Isle La Motte, and the Alburg peninsula compose the elongated archipelago that stretches southward from the
Canadian border. Because of their temperate climate, the islands hold
several apple orchards and numerous state parks and are a center of
water recreation in summer and ice fishing in winter. A scenic drive
through the islands on U.S. 2 begins at I–89 and travels north to Alburg Center; Route 78 takes you back to the mainland.

Snow Farm Vineyard and Winery has self-guided tours, a tasting room,
and free concerts on the lawn for 10 Thursday evenings, beginning in
mid-June. ✉ *190 W. Shore Rd., South Hero,* ☎ *802/372–9463.* ☞ *Free.*
☼ *May–Dec., daily 10–5; tours at 11 and 2.*

Hyde Log Cabin, built in 1783 on South Hero, is often cited as the country's oldest surviving log cabin. ✉ *U.S. 2, Grand Isle,* ☎ *802/828–3051.*
☞ *$3.* ☼ *July 4–Labor Day, Thurs.–Mon. 11–5.*

The **Royal Lipizzaner Stallions,** descendants of the noble white horses
bred in Austria since the 16th century, perform intricate dressage maneuvers at their summer home on the islands. ✉ *U.S. 2, North Hero,*
☎ *802/372–5683.* ☞ *Barn visits free between performances; shows*
$15 adults, $8 children. ☼ *Mid-July–late Aug., Thurs.–Fri. at 6 PM,*
weekends at 2:30 PM.

St. Anne's Shrine marks the site where French soldiers and Jesuits put
ashore in 1665 and built a fort, creating Vermont's first European settlement. The state's first Roman Catholic Mass was celebrated here
on July 26, 1666. ✉ *W. Shore Rd., Isle La Motte,* ☎ *802/928–3362.*
☞ *Free.* ☼ *Mid-May–mid-Oct., daily 9–7.*

On the mainland east of the Alburg Peninsula, the **Missisquoi Na-**
tional Wildlife Refuge (✉ off Rte. 78, Swanton, 36 mi north of Burlington, ☎ 802/868–4781) consists of 6,300 acres of federally protected
wetlands, meadows, and woods. It's a beautiful area for bird-watching, canoeing, or walking nature trails.

Dining and Lodging

$$–$$$ ✕ **Ruthcliffe Lodge & Restaurant.** Good food and splendid scenery
make this off-the-beaten-path motel and restaurant overlooking Lake
Champlain worth the drive. Owner-chef Mark Infante specializes in
Italian pasta, fish, and meat dishes; save room for the homemade
desserts. Fixed-price dinners include soup, salad, bread, and coffee or
tea. Seven of the nine motel rooms overlook the lake. ✉ *Old Quarry*
Rd., Isle La Motte, ☎ *802/928–3200. MC, V. Closed Columbus Day–*
mid-May. No lunch mid-May–June and Sept.–Columbus Day.

$$–$$$$ 🏨 **North Hero House Inn and Restaurant.** A classic country inn, North
Hero House overlooks Lake Champlain and has four buildings, in-
cluding the 1891 Colonial Revival main house with nine guest rooms,
the restaurant, a pub room, library, and sitting room. Many rooms
have water views, and each is decorated with country furnishings and

antiques. Dinner is served in the informal glass greenhouse or Colonial-style dining room, or on the glassed-in veranda. Friday evenings in summer there's a lobster bake on the beach. ☒ *U.S. 2, North Hero 05474,* ☎ *802/372–4732 or 888/525–3644,* FAX *802/372–3218,* WEB *www.northherohouse.com. 26 rooms. Restaurant, hot tub, boating, pub, library, meeting rooms; no air-conditioning in some rooms. AE, MC, V. CP.*

$$–$$$ 🛏 **Shore Acres Inn and Restaurant.** This lakefront motel well off the main road has clean, comfortable rooms overlooking the water and ½ mi of private lakeshore. Breakfast and dinner are served in the restaurant overlooking the lake. You have free access to a 9-hole, par-3 golf course. ☒ *U.S. 2, North Hero 05474,* ☎ *802/372–8722,* WEB *www. shoreacres.com. 23 rooms. Restaurant, 9-hole golf course, 2 tennis courts. AE, MC, V. Closed Nov.–Apr.; 4 rooms in annex open year-round.*

Outdoor Activities and Sports

BIKING

Bike Shed Rentals (☒ W. Shore Rd., Isle La Motte, ☎ 802/928–3440) rents bikes of all sizes and shapes. **Hero's Welcome** (☒ U.S. 2, North Hero, ☎ 802/372–4161 or 800/372–4376) rents bikes for adults and children.

BOATING

Apple Island Resort (☒ U.S. 2, South Hero, ☎ 802/372–3922) rents sailboats, rowboats, canoes, and motorboats. **Henry's Sportsman's Cottages** (☒ 218 Poor Farm Rd., Alburg, ☎ 802/796–3616) rents motorboats. **Hero's Welcome** (☒ U.S. 2, North Hero, ☎ 802/372–4161 or 800/372–4376) has canoes and kayaks for rent. **Sea Trek Charters** (☒ Tudhope Sailing Center, U.S. 2, Grand Isle, ☎ 802/372–5391) on South Hero Island conducts full-day fishing and sightseeing trips aboard a 25-ft cruiser.

STATE PARKS

Alburg Dunes State Park, one of the state's newest parks, has a sandy beach and some fine examples of rare flora and fauna along the hiking trails. ☒ *Off U.S. 2, Alburg,* ☎ *802/796–4170.* 🎟 *$2.50.* ☉ *Late May–Labor Day, daily dawn–dusk.*

Grand Isle State Park has a fitness trail, hiking trails, and boat rentals. ☒ *U.S. 2, Grand Isle,* ☎ *802/372–4300.* 🎟 *$2.* ☉ *Late May–Labor Day, daily dawn–dusk.*

North Hero State Park's 400 acres hold a swimming beach, nature trail, and campsites. You can rent rowboats and canoes. ☒ *North Hero,* ☎ *802/372–8727.* 🎟 *$2.* ☉ *Late May–Labor Day, daily dawn–dusk.*

Sand Bar State Park, with one of Vermont's best swimming beaches, has a snack bar, changing room, and boat rental concession. ☒ *U.S. 2, South Hero,* ☎ *802/893–2825.* 🎟 *$2 weekdays, $3 weekends.* ☉ *Late May–Labor Day, daily dawn–dusk.*

Shopping

Open July–December, **Allenholm Farm** (☒ 111 South St., South Hero, ☎ 802/372–5566) has a farm store that stocks local produce.

St. Albans

42 *18 mi south of Alburg Center.*

Don't let the suburban sprawl on the outskirts of St. Albans fool you. The city's compact Victorian downtown, built during its heyday as a bustling railroad center, is alive with shops, restaurants, and cafés. St.

Albans' centerpiece is Taylor Park, a broad green space graced with an ornate bronze fountain and lined with churches and an array of imposing 19th-century municipal buildings. St. Albans was the scene of the northernmost action of the Civil War, an 1864 robbery of the city's banks by a band of Confederate soldiers disguised as civilians. The **St. Albans Historical Museum** is inside an 1861 three-story brick house (⊠ Church St., ☎ 802/527–7933).

Dining and Lodging

$$–$$$　✕ **Jeff's Maine Seafood.** Long one of the area's best spots for seafood, this deli has an attractive adjoining dining room and serves appetizers such as crispy salmon potato cakes topped with sour cream and caviar and entrées including sautéed sea scallops, plum tomatoes, and scallions in an artichoke Parmesan sauce over linguine. Meat and poultry are also on the menu. A Light Fare menu is available Tuesday, Wednesday, and Thursday evenings. ⊠ *65 N. Main St.,* ☎ *802/524–6135. AE, DC, MC, V. Closed Sun. No dinner Mon.*

$–$$$　✕ **Chow! Bella.** This narrow, handsomely decorated Victorian parlor of the former St. Albans Opera House complements chef-owner Connie Jacobs Warden's culinary creations. Pastas, individual flatbreads such as Bella Greek Shrimp with tomatoes, calamata olives and spinach, and Black Angus New York strip steak with Gorgonzola Berkshire shiitake sauce are all worth sampling. For dessert, try the baklava cheesecake or Italian walnut tort. ⊠ *28 N. Main St.,* ☎ *802/524–1405. AE, D, MC, V. Closed Sun. No dinner Mon.*

$　✕ **Kept Writer Book Shop & Café.** Pairing soft classical music and the aroma of freshly brewed coffee with a fine selection of used tomes, this bookstore and café exudes warmth. The menu includes such light fare as sandwich croissants and *spanakopita* (spinach pie), locally baked goodies, and moderately priced wine and beer. It's a cozy retreat perfect for curling up with a good book or the newspaper. ⊠ *5 Lake St.,* ☎ *802/527–6242. MC, V. Closed Mon.*

$$$$　🖬 **The Tyler Place Family Resort.** Even newborns are kept busy at this family resort on 165 acres overlooking Lake Champlain. The staff provides an ongoing roster of children's programs and daily activities for all ages. Accommodations include two-bedroom family suites in the inn and cottages with two to four bedrooms, decorated with simple country furnishings including colorful quilts, unfussy antiques and handcrafts. Parents can dine *sans enfants* by candlelight. ⊠ *Old Dock Rd./Rte 7, Highgate Springs 05460,* ☎ *802/868–4000,* ｆａｘ *802/868–5621,* ⅦＥＢ *www.tylerplace.com. 29 cabins, 12 suites. Pool, aerobics, boating, biking. One-week minimum stay; $89/child for ages 2½–16. D, MC, V. Closed mid-Sept.–late May. FAP.*

$$　🖬 **Highgate Manor.** Breakfast is served on the grand veranda overlooking the perennial gardens of this imposing 1850s Victorian mansion just a few minutes from St. Albans. Rooms are decorated with Victorian furnishings with touches such as antique iron bedsteads, claw-foot bathtubs, wicker furniture, antique armoires, and plush settees. Three of the five guest rooms have private baths; one has a gas stove. The Lovers' Suite has a fireplace and huge jetted claw-foot tub. The manor is a popular spot for weddings, parties, and civil union celebrations. ⊠ *464 Highgate Rd./Rte. 207, Highgate Falls 05459,* ☎ *802/868–5610,* ｆａｘ *802/868–5610,* ⅦＥＢ *www.highgatemanor.com. 4 rooms, 2 with bath; 1 suite. Library. MC, V. BP.*

Shopping

Rail City Market (⊠ 8 S. Main St.) sells an excellent selection of natural foods, teas, spices and coffees, and body creams and soaps.

Montgomery/Jay

43 *51 mi northeast of Burlington.*

Montgomery is a small village near the Canadian border and Jay Peak ski resort. Amid the surrounding countryside are seven historic covered bridges. **Kilgore's Store** (⊠ Main St., Montgomery Center, ☎ 802/326–3058), an old-time country store with an antique soda fountain, is a great place to stock up on picnic supplies, eat a hearty bowl of soup and an overstuffed sandwich, and check out local crafts.

Lodging

$$$ 🏨 **Hotel Jay & Jay Peak Condominiums.** Cheerful simplicity and convenience make this a popular skiers' retreat. Rooms on the southwest side have a view of Jay Peak, and those on the north overlook the valley; upper floors have balconies. The studio to three-bedroom condominiums (most slope-side) have fireplaces, modern kitchens, and washers and dryers. In winter, a minimum two-night stay is required. The meal plan varies during the year; breakfast and dinner are included in ski season. ⊠ *Rte. 242, 05859,* ☎ *802/988–2611; 800/451–4449 outside Vermont;* ℻ *802/988–4049;* ⊞ *www.jaypeakresort.com. 48 rooms, 94 condominiums. Restaurant, 2 tennis courts, pool, hot tub, sauna, downhill skiing, bar, recreation room, children's programs. AE, D, DC, MC, V. CP, MAP.*

$$ 🏨 **Black Lantern.** Built in 1803 as a stagecoach stop, the inn has been providing bed and board ever since. Though the feeling is country, touches of sophistication abound. All the suites have whirlpools and fireplaces. An outdoor hot tub, sheltered by a gazebo, overlooks the mountains. The restaurant menu includes pan-seared salmon dishes and rack of lamb. ⊠ *Rte. 118, Montgomery Village 05470,* ☎ *802/326–4507 or 800/255–8661,* ℻ *802/326–4077,* ⊞ *www.blacklantern.com. 9 rooms, 6 suites. Restaurant, some cable TV, hot tub, some pets allowed (fee). AE, D, DC, MC, V. BP.*

$$ 🏨 **Inn on Trout River.** Guest rooms at this 100-year-old inn are decorated in either English country cottage style or country Victorian, and all have down quilts and flannel sheets in winter. The back lawn rambles down to the river, and llama treks are available for groups. The restaurant specializes in American and Continental fare with a heart-healthy emphasis. ⊠ *Main St., Montgomery Center 05471,* ☎ *802/326–4391 or 800/338–7049,* ℻ *802/326–3194,* ⊞ *www.troutinn.com. 9 rooms, 1 suite. Restaurant, pub, library. AE, D, MC, V. BP, MAP.*

Ski Areas

JAY PEAK

Sticking up out of the flat farmland, Jay averages 351 inches of snowfall a year—more than any other Vermont ski area. Its proximity to Québec attracts Montréalers and discourages eastern seaboarders; hence, the prices are moderate and the lift lines shorter than at other resorts. The area is renowned for its glade skiing, powder, and long season. ⊠ *Rte. 242, Jay 05859,* ☎ *802/988–2611; 800/451–4449 outside VT;* ⊞ *www.jaypeakresort.com.*

Downhill. Jay Peak is in fact two mountains with 75 trails, the highest reaching nearly 4,000 ft with a vertical drop of 2,153 ft. The area is served by seven lifts, including Vermont's only tramway, which transports skiers to the top of the mountain in just seven minutes, and the longest detachable quad in the East. The area also has a quad, a triple, and a double chairlift and two T-bars. The smaller mountain has more straight-fall-line, expert terrain, and the tram-side peak has many curving and meandering trails perfectly suited for intermediate and beginning skiers. Jay, highly rated for gladed skiing by major skiing publications, has 19 gladed trails. The longest trail, Ullr's Dream, is 3 mi. Every morning at 9 AM the ski school conducts a free tour, from the tram down one trail. Jay has 75% snowmaking coverage. The area has a halfpipe and snowboard terrain for snowboarders.

Cross-country. A touring center at the base of the mountain has 20 km (12 mi) of groomed cross-country trails. There is a $5 trail fee. A network of 200 km (124 mi) of trails is in the vicinity.

Other activities. Snowshoes and snowmobiles can be rented, and guided walks are led by a naturalist. Telemark rentals and instruction are available.

Child care. The child-care center for youngsters ages 3 to 5 is open from 9 AM to 9 PM. If you're staying at Hotel Jay and the Jay Peak Condominiums, you receive this nursery care free, as well as free skiing for children ages 6 and under, evening care, and supervised dining at the hotel. Infant care is available on a fee basis with advanced reservations. Children ages 5–10 can participate in a daylong Mountain Explorers program, which includes lunch; a MINIrider program for snowboarders ages 5–10 is also available.

Summer activities. Jay Peak runs tram rides to the summit from mid-June through September ($10) and rents mountain bikes.

CROSS-COUNTRY SKIING

Hazen's Notch Cross Country Ski Center and B&B (⊠ Rte. 58, ☎ 802/326–4708), delightfully remote at any time of the year, has 50 km (31 mi) of marked and groomed trails and rents equipment and snowshoes.

En Route   The descent from Jay Peak on Route 101 leads to Route 100, which can be the beginning of a scenic loop tour of Routes 14, 5, 58, and back to 100, or it can take you east to the city of Newport on Lake Memphremagog. You will encounter some of the most unspoiled areas in all Vermont on the drive south from Newport on either U.S. 5 or I–91 (I–91 is faster, but U.S. 5 is prettier). This region, the Northeast Kingdom, is named for the remoteness and stalwart independence that have helped preserve its rural nature.

Newport

🔟 *20 mi east of Jay Peak.*

From its rough-and-tumble days as a logging town, Newport passed through a long stretch of doldrums and decline before discovering that revitalization lay in taking advantage of its splendid location on the southern shores of Lake Memphremagog, Vermont's second-largest lake (only the southern 3 mi of the lake lie within the state; the northern 30 mi are in Canada). Only a block from the waterfront, downtown's main street has evolved into a busy shopping district. The waterfront city dock has a handsome public boathouse where tours of the lake begin. One of the best ways to explore the lake on both sides of the border is aboard the 49-passenger *Stardust Princess,* which sails from the city dock from mid-May through Labor Day. ⊠ *Newport City Dock,* ☎ *802/334–6617.*

Dining and Lodging

$–$$$ ✕ **The East Side.** With an outdoor deck that overlooks the lake, this popular spot serves American fare such as beef stew and prime rib and specialties such as Crab Chicken—a boneless breast of chicken stuffed with crabmeat and topped with lobster sauce. Homemade soups and desserts also share the menu, and daily specials include overstuffed sandwiches. ⊠ *Lake St.,* ☎ *802/334–2340. D, MC, V.*

$–$$ 🏨 **Newport City Motel.** Rooms at this reasonably priced, two-story motel, a short distance from the center of town, are clean, modern, and nicely furnished. ✉ *444 E. Main St., 05855,* ☎ *800/338–6558,* FAX *802/334–6557. 64 rooms, 1 suite. Indoor pool, exercise equipment, hot tub, video game room, laundry service. AE, D, DC, MC, V.*

Outdoor Activities and Sports

The **Great Outdoors of Newport** (✉ 177 Main St., ☎ 802/334–2831) rents boats, kayaks, and canoes, as well as cross-country skis and snowshoes. The store sells fishing supplies and bicycles.

Shopping

Bogner Haus Factory Outlet (✉ 150 Main St., ☎ 802/334–0135) sells first-quality men's and women's skiwear and golf apparel as well as snowboarding and active wear.

Lake Willoughby

45 *30 mi southeast of Montgomery (summer route; 50 mi by winter route), 28 mi north of St. Johnsbury.*

Flanking the eastern and western shores of Lake Willoughby, the cliffs of surrounding Mts. Pisgah and Hor drop to water's edge, giving this glacially carved, 500-ft-deep lake a striking resemblance to a Norwegian fjord. The beautiful lake is popular for summer and winter recreation, and the trails to the top of Mt. Pisgah reward hikers with glorious views.

The **Bread and Puppet Museum** is a ramshackle barn that houses a surrealistic collection of props used in past performances by the world-renowned Bread and Puppet Theater. The troupe, whose members live communally on the surrounding farm, have been performing social and political commentary with the towering (they're supported by people on stilts), eerily expressive puppets for about 30 years. ✉ *Rte. 122, Glover, 1 mi east of Rte. 16,* ☎ *802/525–3031.* 🎫 *Donations accepted.* ☉ *June–Oct., daily 9–5; other times by appointment.*

Lodging

$$$ 🏨 **WilloughVale Inn.** At the northern end of Lake Willoughby, this handsome inn, with wraparound veranda, has eight spacious, nicely furnished rooms overlooking the lake. The dining room is open for dinner Thursday–Saturday in winter, Thursday–Monday in summer. The shorefront housekeeping cottages have fireplaces, screened porches, and private docks and sleep up to four persons. Cottages rent by the week in July and August. ✉ *Rte. 5A, Westmore 05860,* ☎ *802/525–4123 or 800/594–9102,* FAX *802/525–4514,* WEB *www.willoughvale.com. 8 rooms, 4 cottages. Dining room, boating. AE, MC, V. CP.*

East Burke

46 *17 mi south of Lake Willoughby.*

A jam-packed general store, a post office, and a couple of great places to eat are in the center of East Burke, near the Burke Mountain ski area. A major attraction are the 100 mi of old logging, fire, and country roads, which are good for self-guided hiking, mountain biking, cross-country skiing, and snowshoeing. The **Kingdom Trails Association** (✉ Box 204, East Burke 05832, ☎ 802/626–0737, WEB www.kingdomtrails.org) manages the trails and provides information.

Dining and Lodging

$$–$$$ ✕ **River Garden Café.** You can eat outdoors on the enclosed porch or the patio and view the perennial gardens that rim the grounds, or dine inside the bright and cheerful café. The fare includes lamb tenderloin, warm artichoke dip, bruschetta, pastas, and fresh fish. A lighter menu is served nightly. ⊠ *Rte. 114, East Burke,* ☎ *802/626–3514. AE, D, MC, V. Closed Mon., Nov., and 1 wk in Apr.*

$$$ ✕⊡ **Inn at Mountain View Farm.** The renovated 1890 creamery on a hilltop amid 440 acres of hills and meadows has second-floor guest rooms handsomely furnished with antiques and handmade quilts. Cross-country ski, snowshoe, hiking, and mountain-biking trails are right at the doorstep. Darling's Country Bistro ($$–$$$; no lunch Thurs.–Sun.) serves hearty fare such as beef carbonnade with caramelized onions as well as fish and vegetarian dishes. ⊠ *Darling Hill Rd. (Box 355, 05832),* ☎ *802/626–9924 or 800/572–4509,* WEB *www.innmtnview.com. 15 rooms. Restaurant, hiking, cross-country skiing, sleigh rides, meeting room; no air-conditioning in some rooms. AE, MC, V. Closed Apr. and Nov. BP.*

$$ ✕⊡ **Wildflower Inn.** The hilltop views are breathtaking at this ram-
★ bling, family-oriented complex of old farm buildings on 500 acres. Guest rooms in the restored Federal-style main house and three other build-ings are furnished with reproductions and contemporary furnishings. Rooms in the carriage house have kitchenettes and bunk beds. The restau-rant ($$–$$$) serves dishes such as a seasonal tricolor peppercorn-cognac breast of duck and blackened prime rib. ⊠ *2059 Darling Hill Rd., west of East Burke, Lyndonville 05851,* ☎ *802/626–8310 or 800/627–8310,* FAX *802/626–3039,* WEB *www.wildflowerinn.com. 10 rooms, 11 suites. Restaurant, tennis court, pool, hot tub, sauna, fishing, soccer, ice-skating, skiing, sleigh rides, snowmobiling, recreation rooms, meet-ing room; no air-conditioning in some rooms. MC, V. Closed Apr. and Nov. BP.*

$ ✕⊡ **Old Cutter Inn.** Inside this small converted farmhouse only ½ mi from the Burke Mountain base lodge are quaint inn rooms in the main building and comfortable, if less charming, accommodations in an annex. The restaurant ($$–$$$) serves fare that reflects the Swiss chef-owner's heritage, as well as superb, good-value Continental cuisine in-cluding osso buco, chateaubriand, and veal piccata. ⊠ *143 Pinkham Rd., 05832,* ☎ *802/626–5152 or 800/295–1943,* WEB *www.pbpub.com/ cutter.htm. 9 rooms, 5 with bath; 1 suite. Restaurant, pool, hiking, bi-cycles, cross-country skiing, bar. D, MC, V. Restaurant closed Wed., Apr., and Nov. MAP.*

Outdoor Activities and Sports

Village Sport Shop (⊠ 4 Broad St., Lyndonville, ☎ 802/626–8448) rents canoes, kayaks, bikes, rollerblades, paddleboats, snowshoes, and cross-country and downhill skis.

Shopping

Bailey's & Burke, Inc. (⊠ Rte. 114, ☎ 802/626–9250) sells baked goods, pizza and sandwiches, wine, clothing, and sundries.

Ski Areas

BURKE MOUNTAIN

This low-key, moderately priced resort has plenty of terrain for beginners, but intermediate skiers, experts, racers, telemarkers, and snowboard-ers will find time-honored narrow New England trails. Many pack-ages at Burke are significantly less expensive than those at other Vermont areas. ⊠ *Mountain Rd., East Burke 05832,* ☎ *802/626–3322; 802/626–1390 snow conditions; 802/748–6137 reservations;* WEB *www.skiburke.com.*

Downhill. With a 2,000-ft vertical drop and 43 trails and glades, Burke is something of a sleeper among the larger Eastern ski areas. It has greatly increased its snowmaking capability (76%), which is enhanced by the mountain's northern location and exposure, assuring plenty of natural snow. A 5-acre snowboard park (with a halfpipe and snowmaking capabilities) invites all levels. Burke has one quad, one double chairlift, and two surface lifts. Lift lines, even on weekends and holidays, are light to nonexistent.

Child care. In the Children's Center, the nursery takes children ages 6 months–6 years on weekends and holidays. SKIwee and MINIriders lessons through the ski school are available to children ages 4–16.

Summer activities. Hiking, biking (rentals are available), and a children's swing are summer options.

CROSS-COUNTRY SKIING

Burke Ski Touring Center (☎ 802/626–8338) has 80 km (50 mi) of trails (65 km [39 mi] groomed); some lead to high points with scenic views. There's a snack bar at the center.

St. Johnsbury

47 *16 mi south of East Burke, 39 mi northeast of Montpelier.*

St. Johnsbury is the southern gateway to the Northeast Kingdom. Though the town was chartered in 1786, its identity was not firmly established until 1830, when Thaddeus Fairbanks invented the platform scale, a device that revolutionized weighing methods that had been in use since the beginning of recorded history. Because of the Fairbanks family's philanthropic efforts, the city, with its distinctly 19th-century industrial feel, has a strong cultural and architectural imprint.

Opened in 1891, the **Fairbanks Museum and Planetarium** attests to the Fairbanks family's inquisitiveness about all things scientific. The red-brick building in the squat Romanesque Revival architectural style of H. H. Richardson houses Vermont plants and animals, as well as ethnographic and natural history collections from around the globe. There's also a 50-seat planetarium and a hands-on exhibit room for kids. On the third Saturday in September, the museum sponsors the Festival of Traditional Crafts, with demonstrations of early American household and farm skills such as candle and soap making. ⊠ *Main and Prospect Sts.,* ☎ *802/748–2372,* WEB *www.fairbanksmuseum.org.* 🖃 *Museum $5, planetarium $3.* ☉ *Mon.–Sat. 9–4, Sun. 1–5. Planetarium shows July–Aug., daily at 11 and 1:30; Sept.–June, weekends at 1:30.*

★ The **St. Johnsbury Athenaeum,** with its dark rich paneling, polished Victorian woodwork, and ornate circular staircases that rise to the gallery around the perimeter, is one of the oldest art galleries in the country. The gallery at the back of the building specializes in Hudson River School paintings and has the overwhelming *Domes of Yosemite* by Albert Bierstadt. ⊠ *1171 Main St.,* ☎ *802/748–8291,* WEB *www.stjathenaeum.org.* 🖃 *Free.* ☉ *Mon. and Wed. 10–8, Tues. and Thurs.–Fri. 10–5:30, Sat. 9:30–4.*

Take a tour of the world's oldest and largest maple candy factory at **Maple Grove Maple Museum and Factory.** Be sure to visit the museum, where a film shows how maple syrup is made. ⊠ *1052 Portland St., Rte 2,* ☎ *802/748–5141,* WEB *www.maplegrove.com.* 🖃 *Tour $1.* ☉ *Daily 8–3.*

Dog Mountain is artist–dog lover Stephen Huneck's art gallery (works are for sale) and sculpture garden, complete with a chapel where humans and their canine companions can meditate. ⊠ *Off Spaulding Rd.,* ☎ *802/748–2700 or 800/449–2580,* WEB *www.huneck.com.* 🖃 *Free.* ☉ *June–Oct., Mon.–Sat. 10–5, Sun. 11–4, and by appointment.*

OFF THE
BEATEN PATH

CABOT CREAMERY – The biggest cheese producer in the state, a dairy cooperative, has a visitor center with an audiovisual presentation about the dairy and cheese industry. You can taste samples, purchase cheese, and tour the plant. The center is midway between Barre and St. Johnsbury. ⊠ *2870 Main St./Rte. 215, 3 mi north of U.S. 2, Cabot,* ☎ *802/563–3393; 800/639–4031 orders only.* ⊠ *$1.* ☻ *June–Oct., daily 9–5; Nov.–Dec. and Feb.–May, Mon.–Sat. 9–4; call ahead to check cheese-making days.*

Dining and Lodging

$$$$ ✕⊡ **Rabbit Hill Inn.** Many of the elegant rooms at this classic, white-
★ columned inn have fireplaces and views of the Connecticut River and New Hampshire's White Mountains. The intimate candlelit dining room serves a five-course fixed-price dinner ($$$$) featuring contemporary new American and regional dishes such as grilled venison loin with cranberry juniper orange glaze. Meat and fish are smoked on the premises. ⊠ *Rte. 18, Lower Waterford, 11 mi south of St. Johnsbury, 05848,* ☎ *802/748–5168 or 800/762–8669,* ℻ *802/748–8342,* Ⓦ *www.rabbithillinn.com. 19 rooms. Restaurant, some in-room hot tubs, hiking, cross-country skiing, pub; no kids under 13. AE, MC, V. Closed 1st 3 wks in Apr., 1st 2 wks in Nov. MAP.*

$$ ⊡ **Emergo Farm.** Bebo and Lori Webster rent out three guest rooms in their 1890, 15-room farmhouse on a 240-acre dairy farm that has been in the Webster family for five generations. Lori collects antiques, which are liberally sprinkled throughout the house and in the second-floor guest rooms. One room has its own bath. The other two, which share a bath, have a kitchen and can be rented out as a suite to sleep up to six. The view from the hilltop picnic grove is spectacular. ⊠ *261 Webster Hill Rd., Danville 05828,* ☎ *802/684–2215. 3 rooms, 1 with bath. BP.*

Shopping

The **Trout River Brewing Co.** (⊠ 58 Broad St., Lyndonville, ☎ 802/626–9396 or 888/296–2739) brews all-natural premium ales and lagers and has six styles on tap daily. The tasting room is open Wednesday–Sunday 11 AM–6 PM.

Peacham

㊽ *10 mi southwest of St. Johnsbury.*

Tiny Peacham's stunning scenery and 18th-century charm have made it a favorite with urban refugees, artists seeking solitude and inspiration, and movie directors looking for the quintessential New England village. *Ethan Frome,* starring Liam Neeson, was filmed here.

Gourmet soups and hearty lamb and barley stew are among the seasonally changing take-out specialties at the **Peacham Store** (⊠ Main St., ☎ 802/592–3310). You can browse through the locally made crafts while waiting for your order. Next door, the **Peacham Corner Guild** sells local handcrafts.

Barre

㊾ *7 mi southeast of Montpelier, 35 mi southwest of St. Johnsbury.*

Barre has been famous as the source of Vermont granite ever since two men began working the quarries in the early 1800s; the number of immigrant laborers attracted to the industry made the city prominent in the early years of the American labor movement. Downtown, at the corner of Maple and North Main, look for the statue of a representative Italian stonecutter of a century ago. On Route 14, just north of Barre, stop at Hope Cemetery to see spectacular examples of carving.

The attractions of the **Rock of Ages granite quarry** range from the awe-inspiring (the quarry resembles the Grand Canyon in miniature) to the mildly ghoulish (you can consult a directory of tombstone dealers throughout the country). You might recognize the sheer walls of the quarry from *Batman and Robin,* the film starring George Clooney and Arnold Schwarzenegger. At the crafts center, skilled artisans sculpt monuments; at the quarries themselves, 25-ton blocks of stone are cut from sheer 475-ft walls by workers who clearly earn their pay. ⊠ *Exit 6 off I–89, follow Rte. 63,* ☎ *802/476–3119.* ☞ *Tour of active quarry $4, craftsman center and self-guided tour free.* ☉ *Visitor center May–Oct., Mon.–Sat. 8:30–5, Sun. noon–5; narrated tours every 45 mins 9:15–3 weekdays June–mid-Oct.*

Dining and Lodging

$–$$　✕ **A Single Pebble.** Chef and co-owner Steve Bogart has been cooking creative, authentic Asian dishes for more than 30 years. He prepares traditional clay-pot dishes as well as wok specialties such as sesame catfish and kung po chicken. The dry fried green beans (sautéed with flecks of pork, black beans, preserved vegetables, and garlic) is a house specialty. All dishes can be made without meat. ⊠ *135 Barre–Montpelier Rd.,* ☎ *802/476–9700. Reservations essential. D, MC, V. Closed Sun.–Mon. No lunch.*

$$　✕🛏 **Autumn Harvest Inn.** You'll be tempted to spend the whole day on the porch that graces the front of this casual inn, built in 1790. It sits atop a knoll overlooking a 46-acre workhorse farm and the surrounding valley. Rooms are functional and uncluttered, with an emphasis on comfort and simplicity. One suite has a fireplace. Prime rib and veal dishes are among the highlights of the seasonal country menu at the restaurant ($$–$$$; no lunch), where dinner is served by candlelight Tuesday–Saturday (Wednesday–Saturday in winter). ⊠ *118 Clark Rd., Williamstown 05679,* ☎ *802/433–1355,* 🅵🅰🆇 *802/433–5501,* 🆆🅴🅱 *www.central-vt.com/web/autumn. 18 rooms. Restaurant, pond, horseback riding, cross-country skiing, sleigh rides, bar, some pets allowed. AE, MC, V. MAP.*

Northern Vermont A to Z

To research prices, get advice from other travelers, and book travel arrangements, visit www.fodors.com.

BOAT AND FERRY TRAVEL

Lake Champlain Ferries, in operation since 1826, operates three ferry crossings during the summer months and one—between Grand Isle and Plattsburgh, New York—in winter through thick lake ice. Ferries leave from the King Street Dock in Burlington, Charlotte, and Grand Isle. This is a convenient means of getting to and from New York State, as well as a pleasant way to spend an afternoon.
➤ BOAT AND FERRY INFORMATION: **Lake Champlain Ferries** (☎ 802/864–9804).

BUS TRAVEL

Vermont Transit links Burlington, Waterbury, Montpelier, St. Johnsbury, and Newport.
➤ BUS INFORMATION: **Vermont Transit** (☎ 800/231–2222 or 802/864–6811).

CAR TRAVEL

In north-central Vermont, I–89 heads west from Montpelier to Burlington and continues north to Canada. Interstate 91 is the principal north–south route in the east, and Route 100 runs north–south through the center of the state. North of I–89, Routes 104 and 15 provide a major east–west transverse. From Barton, near Lake Willoughby, U.S. 5 and Route 122 south are beautiful drives. Strip-mall drudge bogs down the section of U.S. 5 around Lyndonville.

EMERGENCIES

➤ HOSPITALS AND EMERGENCY SERVICES: **Copley Hospital** (✉ Washington Hwy., Morrisville, ☎ 802/999–4231). **Fletcher Allen Health Care** (✉ 111 Colchester Ave., Burlington, ☎ 802/847–2434), 24-hour emergency health care information. **Northeastern Vermont Regional Hospital** (✉ Hospital Dr., St. Johnsbury, ☎ 802/748–8141).

OUTDOOR ACTIVITIES AND SPORTS

HIKING

The Green Mountain Club maintains the Long Trail—the north–south border-to-border footpath that runs the length of the spine of the Green Mountains—as well as other trails nearby. The club headquarters sells maps and guides, and experts dispense advice.
➤ CONTACT: **Green Mountain Club** (✉ Rte. 100, Waterbury, ☎ 802/244–7037).

TOURS

P.O.M.G. Bike Tours of Vermont leads weekend and five-day adult camping-bike tours. True North Kayak Tours operates a guided tour of Lake Champlain and a natural-history tour and will arrange a custom multiday trip. The company also coordinates special trips for kids.
➤ TOUR OPERATORS: **P.O.M.G. Bike Tours of Vermont** (✉ Richmond, ☎ 802/434–2270). **True North Kayak Tours** (✉ 53 Nash Pl., Burlington, ☎ 802/860–1910).

TRAIN TRAVEL

The *Champlain Flyer* transports passengers between Burlington and Charlotte—with a stop in Shelburne—in just 25 minutes. Fare is $1 one-way, and $2 round-trip. The *Champlain Valley Weekender* runs between Middlebury and Burlington, with stops in Vergennes and Shelburne. The views from the coach cars, which date from the 1930s, are of Lake Champlain, the valley farmlands, and surrounding mountains.
➤ TRAIN INFORMATION: *Champlain Flyer* (☎ 802/951–4010). *Champlain Valley Weekender* (☎ 802/463–3069 or 800/707–3530).

VISITOR INFORMATION

➤ TOURIST INFORMATION: **Lake Champlain Islands Chamber of Commerce** (✉ 3537 Rte. 2, Suite 100 [Box 213, North Hero 05474], ☎ 802/372–5683, WEB www.Champlain Islands.com). **Lake Champlain Regional Chamber of Commerce** (✉ 60 Main St., Suite 100, Burlington 05401, ☎ 802/863–3489 or 877/686–5253, WEB www.vermont.org). **Northeast Kingdom Chamber of Commerce** (✉ 357 Western Ave., St. Johnsbury 05819, ☎ 802/748–3678 or 800/639–6379, WEB www.vermontnekchamber.org). **Northeast Kingdom Travel and Tourism Association** (✉ Box 465, Barton 05822, ☎ 802/525–4386 or 888/884–8001, WEB www.travelthekingdom.com). **Smugglers' Notch Area Chamber of Commerce** (✉ Box 364, Jeffersonville 05464, ☎ 802/644–2239, WEB www.smugnotch.com). The **Stowe Area Association** (✉ Main St. [Box 1320, Stowe 05672], ☎ 802/253–7321 or 877/603–8693, WEB www.stoweinfo.com). **Vermont North Country Chamber of Commerce** (✉ The Causeway, Newport 05855, ☎ 802/334–7782 or 800/635–4643, WEB www.vtnorthcountry.com).

VERMONT A TO Z

To research prices, get advice from other travelers, and book travel ar-rangements, visit www.fodors.com.

AIRPORTS AND TRANSFERS

Continental, Delta, United, Jet Blue, and US Airways fly into Burling-ton International Airport (BTV). Rutland State Airport (RUT) has daily service to and from Boston on US Airways Express. West of Ben-nington and convenient to southern Vermont, Albany International Air-port (ALB) in New York State is served by 10 major U.S. carriers.

➤ AIRPORT INFORMATION: **Albany International Airport** (⊠ 737 Albany Shaker Rd., Albany, ☎ 518/869–3021, WEB www.albanyairport.com). **Burlington International Airport** (⊠ Airport Dr., 4 mi east of Burling-ton off U.S. 2, ☎ 802/863–2874). **Rutland State Airport** (⊠ 1002 Air-port Rd., North Clarendon, ☎ 802/747–7101).

AIRPORT TRANSFERS

Aircraft charters are available at Burlington International Airport from Heritage Flight Services. Mansfield Heliflight provides helicopter trans-portation throughout New England. Chittenden Country Transportation Authority buses connect Burlington International Airport with down-town Burlington. Buses leave the airport for the downtown depot at Cherry and Church streets at 10 minutes after and 20 minutes before each hour, 6:15 AM–10:30 PM; they leaven downtown at 15 minutes before and 5 minutes after the hour.

➤ SHUTTLES: **Chittenden Country Transportation Authority** (☎ 802/ 864–0211). **Heritage Flight Services** (☎ 802/863–3626 or 800/782– 0773, WEB www.heritageflgt.com). **Mansfield Heliflight** (⊠ Milton, ☎ 802/893–1003 or 800/872–0884, WEB www.mansfieldheliflight.com).

BIKE TRAVEL

Vermont is a popular destination for cyclists, who find villages and towns—with their inns, B&Bs, and restaurants—spaced closely enough for comfortable traveling. Secondary roads in the western part of the state, in the relatively gentle terrain of the Champlain Valley and is-lands, are best for cyclists who prefer not to be challenged by steep hills. Roads that follow the major east–west river valleys—the Winooski, Lamoille and Missisquoi—are similarly forgiving. For cyclists in top shape, hundreds of miles of twisting blacktop and gravel roads criss-cross the Green Mountains. Especially challenging are Middlebury, Lin-coln and Brandon gaps in north-central Vermont, and punishing Smugglers' Notch north of Stowe.

In general, touring bikes with 10 or more gears are preferable; for gravel roads, hybrid or mountain bikes are recommended. Several of the larger ski areas, such as Killington, Smugglers' Notch, and Jay Peak, as well as the Green Mountain National Forest maintain mountain bike trails.

BUS TRAVEL

Bonanza Bus Lines connects New York City and Providence with Ben-nington. Service is twice daily (morning and afternoon) from each city. Vermont Transit connects Bennington, Brattleboro, Burlington, Rutland, and other Vermont cities and towns with Boston, Springfield, Albany, New York, Montréal, and cities in New Hampshire. Local ser-vice in Burlington and surrounding communities is provided by Chit-tenden County Transportation Authority.

➤ BUS INFORMATION: **Bonanza Bus Lines** (☎ 800/556–3815). **Chittenden Country Transportation Authority** (☎ 802/864–0211). **Vermont Tran-sit** (☎ 800/552–8737).

CAR TRAVEL

Interstate 91, which stretches from Connecticut and Massachusetts in the south to Québec in the north, reaches most points along Vermont's eastern border. Interstate–89, from New Hampshire to the east and Québec to the north, crosses central Vermont from White River Junction to Burlington. Southwestern Vermont can be reached by U.S. 7 from Massachusetts and U.S. 4 from New York.

The official speed limit in Vermont is 50 mph, unless otherwise posted; on the interstates it's 65 mph. Right turns are permitted on a red light unless otherwise indicated. You can get a state map, which has mileage charts and enlarged maps of major downtown areas, free from the Vermont Department of Tourism and Marketing. The *Vermont Atlas and Gazetteer,* sold in many bookstores, shows nearly every road in the state and is great for driving on the back roads.

CHILDREN IN VERMONT

Popular attractions such as the Shelburne Museum, Shelburne Farms, Montshire Museum of Science, Billings Farm and Museum, and Southern Vermont Art Center frequently host events for children; inquire directly or check local newspapers. Larger, family-oriented resorts such as the Basin Harbor Club, Tyler Place, Smugglers' Notch, and Mountain Meadows Lodge have ongoing children's programs with full supervision.

BABY-SITTING

Baby-sitting agencies are uncommon in Vermont. Instead, parents generally rely on services provided or arranged by hotels and resorts. Rates generally run $8–$10 per hour, more if more than one child is involved.

EMERGENCIES

➤ EMERGENCY SERVICES: **Ambulance, fire, police** (☎ 911). **Vermont Poison Control Center** (✉ Burlington, ☎ 802/847–3456). **Vermont State Police** (☎ 800/525–5555).

LODGING

The Vermont Chamber of Commerce (☞ Visitor Information) publishes the *Vermont Travelers' Guidebook,* which is an extensive list of lodgings, and additional guides to country inns and vacation rentals. The Vermont Department of Tourism and Marketing (☞ Visitor Information) has a brochure that lists lodgings at working farms.

CAMPING

Call Vermont's Department of Forests, Parks, and Recreation for a copy of the "Vermont Campground Guide," which lists state parks and other public and private camping facilities. Call the following numbers from the second Tuesday in January through May 1; after that, call the individual parks. Between Labor Day and January, reservations are not accepted.

➤ CONTACTS: **Department of Forests, Parks, and Recreation** (☎ 802/241–3655; ☎ 802/885–8891 or 800/299–3071 in southeastern Vermont; ☎ 802/483–2001 or 800/658–1622 in southwestern Vermont; ☎ 802/879–5674 or 800/252–2363 in northwestern Vermont; ☎ 802/479–4280 or 800/658–6934 in northeastern Vermont).

MEDIA

Vermont's largest newspaper, available throughout the state, is the *Burlington Free Press,* a member of the Gannett chain. For upcoming event and performances, see its Thursday "Weekend" section. The *Rutland Herald,* winner of a 2001 Pulitzer Prize for editorial writing, carries *New York Times* wire service stories and is also available throughout much of the state. *Seven Days* is a Burlington-based, free alternative weekly with wide distribution and extensive arts and entertainment listings.

Vermont's two leading magazines are *Vermont Life,* published quarterly by the state, and the privately owned *Vermont,* a bimonthly that covers political as well as lifestyle issues and has a more upscale slant. *Yankee,* published 10 times yearly in Dublin, New Hampshire, covers all New England and has events listings for each state.

Vermont television stations include affiliates of CBS (WCAX, channel 7); NBC (WPTZ, channel 5); ABC (WVNY, channel 22); and Fox (channel 44). Vermont Public Television is on channel 33 throughout much of the state. Vermont Public Radio (VPR) broadcasts local and National Public Radio (NPR) programs through the state; frequency is 107.9 through much of northern Vermont; check local newspaper listings for frequencies elsewhere. Northern Vermont listeners can also pick up the excellent programming of the Canadian Broadcasting Company (CBC) at frequency 93.5.

OUTDOOR ACTIVITIES AND SPORTS

A hot line has tips on peak viewing locations and times and up-to-date snow conditions.
➤ CONTACT: **Foliage and Snow Hot Line** (☎ 802/828–3239).

CANOEING

Umiak Outdoor Outfitters has shuttles to nearby rivers for day excursions and customized overnight trips. Vermont Canoe Trippers/Battenkill Canoe, Ltd. organizes canoe tours (some are inn-to-inn) and fishing trips.
➤ CONTACTS: **Umiak Outdoor Outfitters** (✉ 849 S. Main St., Stowe, ☎ 802/253–2317). **Vermont Canoe Trippers/Battenkill Canoe, Ltd.** (✉ River Rd., off Rte. 7A, Arlington, ☎ 802/362–2800).

FISHING

For information about fishing, including licenses, call the Vermont Fish and Wildlife Department. Strictly Trout will arrange a fly-fishing trip on any Vermont stream or river, including the Battenkill.
➤ CONTACTS: **Strictly Trout** (☎ 802/869–3116). **Vermont Fish and Wildlife Department** (☎ 802/241–3700, WEB www.anr.state.vt.us/fur/furhome).

HIKING

The Green Mountain Club publishes hiking maps and guides. The club also manages the Long Trail, the north–south trail that traverses the entire state.
➤ CONTACT: **Green Mountain Club** (✉ Rte. 100, Waterbury, ☎ 802/244–7037, WEB www.greenmountainclub.org).

HORSEBACK RIDING

Kedron Valley Stables has one- to six-day riding tours with lodging in country inns.
➤ CONTACT: **Kedron Valley Stables** (✉ South Woodstock, ☎ 802/457–1480 or 800/225–6301).

SKIING

For information, contact Ski Vermont/Vermont Ski Area Association.
➤ CONTACT: **Ski Vermont/Vermont Ski Area Association** (✉ 26 State St. [Box 368, Montpelier 05601], ☎ 802/223–2439, WEB www.skivermont.com).

STATE PARKS

Vermont state parks open during the last week in May and close after the Labor Day or Columbus Day weekend, depending on location. Day-use charges are $2.50 per person for ages 14 and up, $2 for ages 4–13; children under 4 are free. Call individual parks or the Department of Forests, Parks, and Recreation for information.

➤ CONTACT: **Department of Forests, Parks, and Recreation** (☎ 802/241–3655, WEB www.vtstateparks.com).

TOURS

Bicycle Holidays helps you plan your own inn-to-inn tour by providing route directions and booking your accommodations. Vermont Bicycle Touring leads numerous tours in the state and the region. New England Hiking Holidays leads guided walks with lodging in country inns. North Wind Hiking and Walking Tours conducts guided walking tours through Vermont's countryside.

➤ TOUR OPERATORS: **Bicycle Holidays** (✉ Munger St., Middlebury, ☎ 802/388–2453 or 800/292–5388). **New England Hiking Holidays** (✉ North Conway, NH, ☎ 603/356–9696 or 800/869–0949). **North Wind Hiking and Walking Tours** (✉ Waitsfield, ☎ 802/496–5771 or 800/496–5771). **Vermont Bicycle Touring** (✉ Monkton Rd., Bristol, ☎ 802/453–4811 or 800/245–3868).

TRAIN TRAVEL

Amtrak's *Vermonter* is a daytime service linking Washington, D.C., with Brattleboro, Bellows Falls, White River Junction, Montpelier, Waterbury, Essex Junction, and St. Albans. The *Adirondack,* which runs from Washington, D.C., to Montréal, serves Albany, Ft. Edward (near Glens Falls), Ft. Ticonderoga, and Plattsburgh, allowing relatively convenient access to western Vermont. The *Ethan Allen Express* connects New York City with Fair Haven and Rutland.

➤ TRAIN INFORMATION: **Amtrak** (☎ 800/872–7245, WEB www.amtrak.com).

VISITOR INFORMATION

➤ TOURIST INFORMATION: **Forest Supervisor, Green Mountain National Forest** (✉ 231 N. Main St., Rutland 05701, ☎ 802/747–6700). **Vermont Chamber of Commerce** (✉ Box 37, Montpelier 05601, ☎ 802/223–3443). **Vermont Department of Tourism and Marketing** (✉ 134 State St., Montpelier 05602, ☎ 802/828–3237 or 800/837–6668). There are **state information centers** on the Massachusetts border at I–91, the New Hampshire border at I–89, the New York border at Route 4A, and the Canadian border at I–89.

5   MASSACHUSETTS

Only a half dozen states are smaller than
Massachusetts, but few have influenced
American life more profoundly. Generations
of Bay State merchants, industrialists, and
computer executives have charted the course
of the country's economy; Massachusetts
writers, artists, and academics have
enriched American culture; and from the
meetinghouse to the White House, the
state's politicians, philosophers, and pundits
have fueled national debates.

MASSACHUSETTS SEABOARD TOWNS—from Newburyport to Provincetown—were built before the Revolution, during the heyday of American shipping. These coastal villages evoke a bygone world of clipper ships, robust fishermen, and sturdy sailors bound for distant Cathay. Lowell, on the Merrimack River, was the first American city to be planned around manufacturing. This textile town introduced the rest of the nation to the routines of the Industrial Revolution. In our own time, the high-tech firms of the greater Boston area helped launch the information age, and the Massachusetts Institute of Technology (MIT) and Harvard supplied intellectual heft to deliver it to the wider world.

The Massachusetts town meeting set the tone for politics in the 13 original colonies. A century later, Boston was a hotbed of rebellion—Samuel Adams and James Otis, the "Sons of Liberty," started a war with words, inciting action against British Colonial policies with patriotic pamphlets and fiery speeches at Faneuil Hall. Twentieth-century heirs to Adams include Boston's flashy mid-century mayor James Michael Curley; Thomas "Tip" O'Neill, the late Speaker of the House; and, of course, the Kennedys. In 1961, the young senator from the Boston suburb of Brookline, John Fitzgerald Kennedy, became president of the United States. JFK's service to Massachusetts was family tradition: in the years before World War I, Kennedy's grandfather John "Honey Fitz" Fitzgerald served in Congress and as mayor of Boston. But political families are nothing new here—Massachusetts has sent both a father and a son (John Adams and John Quincy Adams) to the White House.

Massachusetts has an extensive system of parks, protected forests, beaches, and nature preserves. Like medieval pilgrims, readers of *Walden* come to Concord to visit the place where Henry David Thoreau wrote his prophetic essay. Thoreau's disciples can be found hiking to the top of the state's highest peak, Mt. Greylock; shopping for organic produce in an unpretentious college burg like Williamstown; or strolling the beaches of Cape Cod. For those who prefer the hills to the ocean, the rolling Berkshire terrain defines the landscape from North Adams to Great Barrington in the western part of the state. A favorite vacation spot since the 19th century, when eastern aristocrats built grand summer residences, the Berkshire Hills have been described as an inland Newport. This area attracts vacationers seeking superb scenery and food and an active cultural scene.

The list of Bay State writers, artists, and musicians who have shaped American culture is long indeed. The state has produced great poets in every generation: Anne Bradstreet, Phillis Wheatley, Emily Dickinson, Henry Wadsworth Longfellow, William Cullen Bryant, e. e. cummings, Robert Lowell, Elizabeth Bishop, Sylvia Plath, and Anne Sexton. Massachusetts writers include Louisa May Alcott, author of the enduring classic *Little Women*; Nathaniel Hawthorne, who re-created the Salem of his Puritan ancestors in *The Scarlet Letter*; Herman Melville, who wrote *Moby-Dick* in a house at the foot of Mt. Greylock; Eugene O'Neill, whose early plays were produced at a makeshift theater in Provincetown on Cape Cod; Lowell native Jack Kerouac, author of *On the Road*; and John Cheever, chronicler of suburban angst. Painters Winslow Homer and James McNeill Whistler both hailed from the Commonwealth. Norman Rockwell, the quintessential American illustrator, lived and worked in Stockbridge. Celebrated composer and Boston native Leonard Bernstein was the first American to conduct the New York Philharmonic. Joan Baez got her start singing in Harvard Square, and contemporary Boston singer-songwriter Tracy Chapman picked up the beat with folk songs for the new age.

Pleasures and Pastimes

Dining

Massachusetts invented the fried clam, which appears on many North Shore and Cape Cod menus. Creamy clam chowder is another specialty. Eating seafood "in the rough"—from paper plates in shacklike buildings—is a revered local custom.

Boston restaurants serve New England standards and cutting-edge cuisine. At country inns in the Berkshires and the Pioneer Valley you'll find creative contemporary fare that makes the most of local ingredients, as well as traditional New England "dinners" strongly reminiscent of old England: double-cut pork chops, rack of lamb, game, Boston baked beans, Indian pudding, and the dubiously glorified "New England boiled dinner." On the Cape, ethnic specialties such as Portuguese kale soup and linguiça sausage appear on menus along with plenty of seafood. The Cape's sophisticated first-rate restaurants (with prices to match) include several in Brewster; on Nantucket and Martha's Vineyard, top-of-the-line establishments prepare traditional and innovative fare.

On the North Shore, Rockport is a "dry" town, though you can almost always take your own alcohol into restaurants; most places charge a nominal corkage fee. This law leads to early closing hours—many Rockport dining establishments close by 9 PM.

CATEGORY	COST*
$$$$	over $25
$$$	$17–$25
$$	$9–$16
$	under $9

*per person, for a main-course dinner

Lodging

Boston has everything from luxury hotels to charming B&Bs. The signature accommodation outside Boston is the country inn; in the Berkshires, where magnificent mansions have been converted into lodgings, the inns reach a very grand scale indeed. Less extravagant and less expensive are bed-and-breakfast establishments, many of them in private homes. On Cape Cod, inns are plentiful, and rental homes and condominiums are available for long-term stays. Be sure to make reservations for inns well in advance during peak periods: summer on the Cape and islands, summer through winter in the Berkshires.

CATEGORY	BOSTON, THE CAPE, AND THE ISLANDS*	OTHER AREAS*
$$$$	over $220	over $180
$$$	$160–$220	$130–$180
$$	$110–$160	$80–$130
$	under $110	under $80

*All prices are for a standard double room during peak season and not including tax or gratuities. Some inns add a 15% service charge.

Outdoor Activities and Sports

BEACHES

Massachusetts has many excellent beaches, especially on Cape Cod, where the waves are gentle and the water cool. Southside beaches, on Nantucket Sound, have rolling surf and are warmer. Open-ocean beaches on the Cape Cod National Seashore are cold and have serious surf. Parking lots can fill up by 10 AM in summer. Beaches not restricted to residents charge parking fees; for weekly or seasonal passes, contact the local town hall.

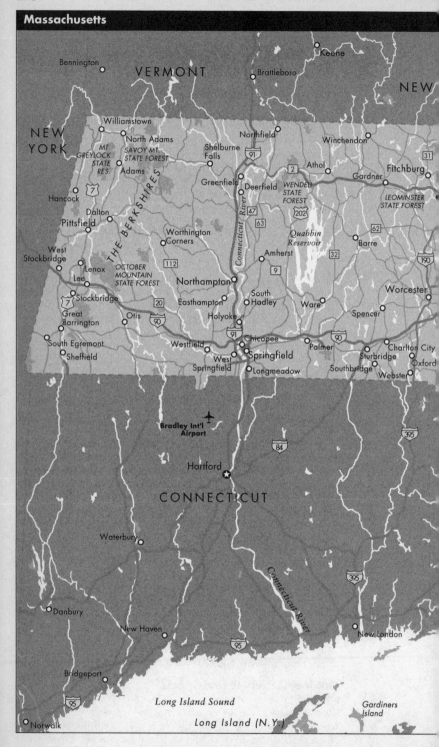

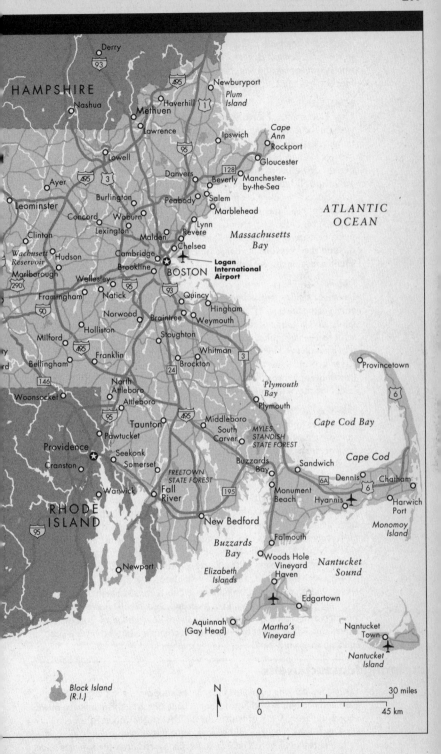

Bostonians head for wide sweeps of sand along the North Shore (beware of biting blackflies in late May and early June), among them Singing Beach in Manchester, Plum Island in Newburyport, and Crane Beach in Ipswich. Boston city beaches are not particularly attractive and definitely not for swimming, though the ongoing rehabilitation of Boston Harbor has made them somewhat cleaner.

BOATING

Cape Cod and the North Shore are centers for oceangoing pleasure craft, with public mooring available in many towns—phone numbers for public marinas are listed in the regional A to Z sections, or you can contact local chambers of commerce. Sea-kayaking is popular along the marshy coastline of the North Shore, where freshwater canoeing is also an option. Inland, the Connecticut River in the Pioneer Valley is navigable by all types of craft between the Turners Falls Dam, just north of Greenfield, and the Holyoke Dam. The large dams control the water level daily, so you will notice a tidal effect; if you have a large boat, beware of sandbanks. Canoes can travel north of Turners Falls beyond the Vermont border; canoeing is also popular in the lakes and small rivers of the Berkshires.

FISHING

Deep-sea fishing trips depart from Boston, Cape Cod, and the South and North shores; surf casting is popular on the North Shore. The rivers, lakes, and streams of the Pioneer Valley and Berkshire County abound with fish—bass, pike, and perch, to name but a few. Stocked trout waters include the Hoosic River (south branch) near Cheshire; the Green River around Great Barrington; Notch Brook and the Hoosic River (north branch) near North Adams; Goose Pond and Hop Brook around Lee; and the Williams River around West Stockbridge.

WHALE-WATCHING

In summer and fall, boats leave Boston, Cape Cod, and Cape Ann two or more times a day to observe the whales feeding a few miles offshore. It's rare not to have the extraordinary experience of seeing several whales, most of them extremely close up.

Shopping

Boston has many high-quality shops, especially in the Newbury Street and Beacon Hill neighborhoods, and most suburban communities have at least a couple of main-street stores selling old furniture and collectibles. Antiques can be found on the South Shore in Plymouth; on the North Shore in Essex, Newburyport, Marblehead, and elsewhere; in the northern towns of the Pioneer Valley (especially in Amherst or along the Mohawk Trail); and just about everywhere in the Berkshires, with particularly rich hunting grounds around Sheffield and Great Barrington. On Cape Cod, Provincetown and Wellfleet are centers for fine arts and crafts. Bookstores, gift shops, jewelers, and clothing boutiques line Main Street in Hyannis. Chatham's Main Street is a pretty, upscale shopping area.

Exploring Massachusetts

Boston has the museums, the history, the shopping, and the traffic; Cape Cod and the North and South shores have beaches, more history, more shopping, and plenty of traffic. In the Berkshires and the Pioneer Valley you'll find centuries-old towns, antiques shops, green hills, and a little less traffic. There's beauty to be discovered after the tourists have gone, wandering through snowy fields or braving the elements on a winter beach, and sipping hot cider at the hearth of a local inn.

Numbers in the text and in the margin correspond to numbers on the maps: Cape Cod, Martha's Vineyard, Nantucket, The North Shore, The Pioneer Valley, and The Berkshires.

Great Itineraries

Massachusetts is a small state but one packed with appealing sights; you could easily spend several weeks exploring it. In a few days you can get a feeling for Boston and some of the historic towns near the city. Those who have a week and like to explore several areas should spend a few days in Boston and then head west for some historic and scenic highlights in the Pioneer Valley and the Berkshires. A leisurely one-week trip to Cape Cod and Martha's Vineyard is a classic summer vacation.

IF YOU HAVE 3 DAYS

Spend two days touring ⚏ **Boston.** You can hit highlights such as the Public Garden, Beacon Hill, and the Freedom Trail on the first day; check out the Museum of Fine Arts or the Isabella Stewart Gardner Museum the morning of the next day; and either explore Harvard and Cambridge or do some shopping on Newbury Street in the afternoon. On the third day either swing west on Route 2 and tour **Lexington** and **Concord** or north on Route 1A and east on Route 129 to **Marblehead** ㉘. Explore Marblehead and have lunch there before heading west on Route 114 and north on Route 1A to **Salem** ㉙.

IF YOU HAVE 7 DAYS

Follow the three-day itinerary above, and spend your third night in **Salem** ㉙. On day four take the Massachusetts Turnpike (I–90) out of Boston and make a half-day stop at Old Sturbridge Village in **Sturbridge** ㊺. Afterward, continue west on I–90 and north on I–91, stopping briefly in **Northampton** ㊶ before heading to ⚏ **Deerfield** ㊴, where you'll spend the night and day five. On day six head to the Berkshires—from Deerfield head north on I–91 to Greenfield, where you'll take Route 2 west to ⚏ **Williamstown** ㊼. On the morning of day seven tour the Sterling and Francine Clark Art Institute in Williamstown. U.S. 7 south takes you through **Pittsfield** ㊾; detour west on U.S. 20 to Hancock Shaker Village before heading on to ⚏ **Lenox** �.

IF YOU HAVE 7 DAYS TO SPEND ON THE CAPE

Head south from Boston (take I–93 to Route 3 to U.S. 6). Stop in **Plymouth** and visit Plimoth Plantation. Have lunch in **Sandwich** ① and tour the town before continuing on U.S. 6 to ⚏ **Chatham** ⑪, where you'll stay the night (have dinner and stroll Main Street in the evening). The next day, drive to **Orleans** ⑫ and spend the day at Nauset Beach. On day three continue on U.S. 6 to ⚏ **Provincetown** ⑯, stopping briefly in **Wellfleet** ⑭ to tour the galleries and detouring east off U.S. 6 to Cahoon Hollow Beach. After dinner take a walk down Commercial Street. On morning four head to Race Point Beach, go on a whale-watching cruise, or take a dune-buggy tour. On day five take U.S. 6 to **Hyannis** ⑤, where you can catch the ferry to ⚏ **Martha's Vineyard** ⑰–㉔.

When to Tour Massachusetts

Fall is the best time to visit western Massachusetts, and it's the perfect season to see Boston as well. Everyone else knows this, so make reservations well ahead. Summer is ideal for visits to the Cape and the beaches. Bostonians often find their city to be too hot and humid in July and August, but if you're visiting from points south, the cool evening coastal breezes might strike you as downright refreshing. Many towns save their best for Christmas—lobster boats parade around Gloucester harbor adorned with lights, inns open their doors for goodies and caroling, shops serve eggnog, and tree-lighting ceremonies are often magical moments. The off-season is the perfect time to try cross-country skiing, take a walk on a stormy beach, or spend a night by the fire, tucked under a quilt catching up on Hawthorne or Thoreau.

BOSTON

Updated by
Elizabeth
Gehrman,
Carolyn Heller,
Rene Hertzog,
and Alexandra
Hall

New England's largest and most important city and the cradle of American independence, Boston is more than 370 years old, far older than the republic its residents helped create. The city's most famous buildings are not merely civic landmarks but national icons, and its local heroes are known to the nation: John and Samuel Adams, Paul Revere, John Hancock, and many more who live at the crossroads of history and myth.

At the same time, Boston is a contemporary center of high finance and high technology, a place of granite and glass towers rising along what once were rutted village lanes. Its many students, artists, academics, and young professionals have made the town a haven for the arts, international cinema, late-night bookstores, ethnic food, alternative music, and unconventional politics.

Best of all, Boston is meant for walking. Most of its historical and architectural attractions are in compact areas. Its varied and distinctive neighborhoods reveal their character to visitors who take the time to stroll through them. Should you need to make short or long hops between neighborhoods, the "T"—the safe, easy-to-ride trains of the Massachusetts Bay Transportation Authority—covers the city.

Beacon Hill and Boston Common

Contender for the "Most Beautiful" award among the city's neighborhoods and the hallowed address of many literary lights, Beacon Hill is Boston at its most Bostonian. The redbrick elegance of its narrow, cobbled streets transports you back to the 19th century. From the gold-topped splendor of the State House to the neoclassical panache of its mansions, Beacon Hill exudes power, prestige, and a calm yet palpable undercurrent of history.

Beacon Hill is bounded by Cambridge Street to the north, Beacon Street to the south, the Charles River Esplanade to the west, and Bowdoin Street to the east. In contrast to "the Hill," nearby Boston Common, the country's oldest public park, has a more egalitarian feel. Beginning with its use as public land for cattle grazing, the Common has always accommodated the needs and desires of Bostonians.

Numbers in the text and in the margin correspond to numbers on the Boston map.

A Good Walk

Stock up on brochures at the **Visitor Information Center** on Tremont Street before heading into the **Boston Common** ① to see Frog Pond and the Central Burying Ground. Head back to **Beacon Street** near the corner of Park Street to reach Augustus Saint-Gaudens's Robert Gould Shaw Memorial, a commemoration of Boston's Civil War unit of free blacks. Facing the memorial, head left toward Park Street, then right on Tremont to pass the **Park Street Church** ② and the **Granary Burying Ground** ③, the final resting place of some of Boston's most illustrious figures. Return to Beacon, turn left, and you'll arrive at the **Boston Athenaeum** ④. Retrace your steps to the neoclassical **State House** ⑤. Continue ahead two blocks to Arlington Street and, to your right, the footbridge that leads to the **Esplanade** ⑥. (The **Museum of Science** ⑦, best reached by car or T, is north of the Esplanade across the Charles

River.) A pedestrian overpass at the Charles/Massachusetts General Hospital T stop connects the Esplanade with **Charles Street.** Head south on Charles, east on **Chestnut Street,** and north on Willow. This will land you at photogenic **Acorn Street** ⑧. Continue on Willow across **Mt. Vernon Street** to **Louisburg Square** ⑨. Turn east (to the right) on Pinckney Street and follow it to Joy Street: Two blocks north on Smith Court is the **Museum of Afro-American History** ⑩, where you can pick up a brochure for the **Black Heritage Trail.**

TIMING

Allow yourself the better part of a day for this walk, particularly if you want to linger in the Common or browse through the antiques shops on Charles Street.

Sights to See

⑧ Acorn Street. Surely the most-photographed street in the city, Acorn is Ye Olde Colonial Boston at its best. Almost toylike row houses once owned by 19th-century artisans line one side; on the other are the doors to Mt. Vernon Street's hidden gardens. The cobblestone street is rough going for some.

Beacon Street. One of the city's most famous thoroughfares, Beacon Street epitomizes Boston. From the magnificent **State House** to the stately patrician mansions, the street is lined with architectural treasures. The **Boston Athenaeum** is on this street, as are the **Appleton Mansions,** at Nos. 39 and 40. Only a few buildings have panes like those of the mansions: sunlight on the imperfections in a shipment of glass sent to Boston around 1820 resulted in an amethystine mauve shade. The mansions are not open to the public.

Black Heritage Trail®. The mention of Beacon Hill conjures up images of wealthy Boston Brahmins; yet until the end of the 19th century, its north side was also home to many free blacks. The 1½-mi Black Heritage Trail celebrates that community, stitching together 14 Beacon Hill sites. Tours guided by National Park Service rangers meet at the Shaw Memorial on the Beacon Street side of the Boston Common.

❹ Boston Athenaeum. Only 1,049 proprietary shares exist for membership in this cathedral of scholarship, and most have been passed down for generations—though the Athenaeum is open for use by qualified scholars who may choose to become members on a yearly basis. Generally the first floor is open to the public and houses an art gallery with rotating exhibits, marble busts, porcelain vases, lush oil paintings, and leather-bound books. Take the guided tour to spy one of the most marvelous sights in the world of Boston academe, the fifth-floor Reading Room, said by poet David McCord to combine "the best elements of the Bodleian, Monticello, the frigate *Constitution,* a greenhouse, and an old New England sitting room." At press time, the Athenaeum was closed for renovation; call ahead for the latest information. ⊠ *10½ Beacon St., Beacon Hill,* ☎ *617/227–0270,* WEB *www.bostonathenaeum.org.* ☞ *Free.* ☉ *Call ahead for hrs and tour availability. T stop: Park St.*

❶ Boston Common. The oldest public park in the United States is the largest and undoubtedly the most famous of the town commons around which New England settlements were traditionally arranged. As old as the city around it (it dates from 1634) and originally set aside as the spot where the freemen of Boston could graze their cattle, the Common contains intriguing sights. On the Beacon Street side of the Common—actually, just outside the park's gates—is the **Robert Gould Shaw Memorial,** executed in deep-relief bronze by Augustus Saint-Gaudens in 1897. It honors the 54th Massachusetts Regiment, the first Civil War unit made up of free blacks, led by the young Robert Gould Shaw; the regiment's

Boston

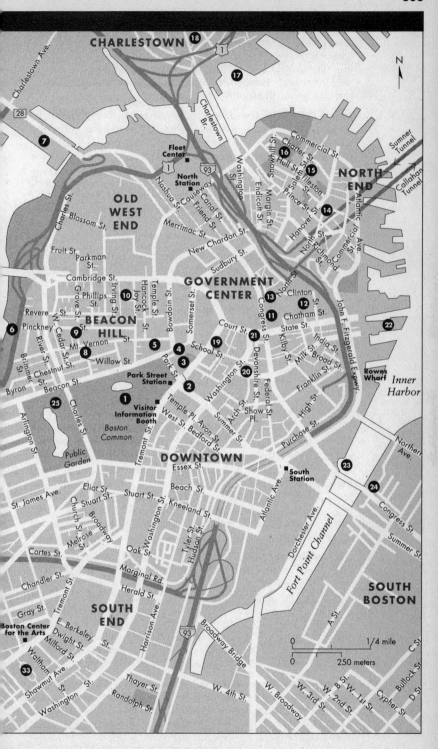

stirring saga inspired the 1989 movie *Glory*. Just below the monument is the **Frog Pond**—a tame and frogless concrete depression, used as a children's wading pool during steamy summer days and for ice skating in winter—which is perhaps the Common's most recognizable feature. The **Central Burying Ground,** along the Boylston Street side, is the final resting place of Tories and Patriots, as well as many British casualties of the Battle of Bunker Hill.

Charles Street. With few exceptions, Beacon Hill lacks commercial development, but the section of Charles Street north of Boston Common more than makes up for it. Antiques shops, bookstores, small restaurants, and flower shops vie for attention, but tastefully: even the 7-Eleven storefront conforms to the Colonial aesthetic. The contemporary activity would present a curious sight to the elder Oliver Wendell Holmes, the publisher James T. Fields (of the famed Boston firm Ticknor & Fields), and many others who lived here when the neighborhood belonged to establishment literati. Charles Street sparkles at dusk from gas-fueled lamps, making it a romantic place for an evening stroll.

Chestnut Street. Delicacy and grace characterize virtually every structure along this street, from the fanlights above the entryways to the wrought-iron boot scrapers on the steps. The **Swan Houses,** at Nos. 13, 15, and 17, have elegant entrances, marble columns, and recessed arches commissioned from Charles Bulfinch by Hepzibah Swan as dowry gifts for her three daughters.

❻ Esplanade. At the northern end of Charles Street is one of several footbridges crossing Storrow Drive to the Esplanade, which stretches along the Charles River. The scenic patch of green is a great place to jog, picnic, and watch the sailboats along the river. For the almost nightly entertainment in the summer, hordes of Bostonians haul chairs and blankets to the lawn in front of the **Hatch Memorial Shell.**

★ Freedom Trail. A 2½-mi tour of the sites of the American Revolution, the Freedom Trail is a crash course in history. There are 16 sites, beginning at the Boston Common and ending at the Bunker Hill Monument in Charlestown; depending on how many are visited in depth, the walk can take an aerobic 90 minutes or a leisurely full day. Trail walks led by National Park Service rangers take place from mid-April to November and begin at the Boston National Historical Park Visitor Center; call for times. Self-guided tour maps are available here and at the Visitor Information Center on Boston Common.

❸ Granary Burying Ground. "It is a fine thing to die in Boston," essayist A. C. Lyons once remarked—alluding to Boston's cemeteries, among the most picturesque and historic in America. If you found a resting place here at the Old Granary (as it's affectionately called), just to the right of Park Street Church, chances are your headstone would have been eloquently ornamented and your neighbors would have been mighty eloquent, too: Samuel Adams, John Hancock, Benjamin Franklin's parents, and Paul Revere. ⊠ *Entrance on Tremont St., Beacon Hill.* ☉ *Dec.–Apr., daily 9–dusk; May–Nov., daily 9–5. T stop: Park St.*

Greater Boston Convention and Visitors' Bureau. You can pick up pamphlets, flyers, maps, and coupons at this kiosk at the center of the Common's Tremont Street side. ⊠ *147 Tremont St., Beacon Hill,* ☏ *617/536–4100 or 888/733–2678,* ⓦⒺⒷ *www.bostonusa.com.* ☉ *Daily 9–5. T stop: Park St.*

★ ❾ Louisburg Square. One of the most appealing corners in a neighborhood that epitomizes charm, Louisburg (pronounce the "s" as the locals do) Square is the very heart of Beacon Hill. Its houses—many built in the 1840s—have seen their share of famous tenants, including the Alcotts at No. 10 (Louisa May died here in 1888, on the day of her father's funeral). In 1852 the popular Swedish singer Jenny Lind was married in the parlor of No. 20, the residence of Samuel Ward, brother of Julia Ward Howe. *T stop: Park St.*

★ ⑩ **The Museum of Afro-American History** is an umbrella historical site that encompasses the Abiel Smith School, the African Meeting House next door, and the African Meeting House on Nantucket Island. Throughout the 19th century, abolition was the cause célèbre for Boston's intellectual elite, and during that time the black community thrived on Beacon Hill. The museum was founded in 1964 to promote this history. The first public school for black children in the United States, the **Abiel Smith School,** was open from 1835 to 1855 and educated about 200 students. The school's exhibits highlight the hardships encountered by the schoolchildren, who endured grossly inadequate learning conditions, and their will to learn. **The African Meeting House,** built in 1806, was the black community's center of social, educational, and political activity and a hotbed of abolitionist fervor. In 1832 the New England Anti-Slavery Society was formed here under the leadership of William Lloyd Garrison. At press time, the Museum of Afro-American History had plans to renovate the African Meeting House, so call ahead for the latest information. The five residences on nearby **Smith Court** are typical of the homes of black Bostonians during the 1800s, including No. 3, the 1799 clapboard house where William C. Nell, America's first published black historian and a crusader for school integration, boarded from 1851 to 1865. ✉ *8 Smith Ct., Beacon Hill,* ☎ *617/ 725–0022,* WEB *www.afroammuseum.org.* ☞ *Free.* ☉ *Abiel Smith School Memorial Day–Labor Day, daily 10–4; Labor Day–May, Mon.– Sat. 10–4. African Meeting House, call ahead for hrs. T stop: Charles/MGH.*

☝ ⑦ **Museum of Science.** With 15-ft lightning bolts in the Theater of Electricity and a 20-ft-high T-rex model, this is just the place to ignite any child's Jurassic spark. In 1999 the Museum of Science joined forces with the Computer Museum, debuting its first permanent Computer Museum exhibit, the **Virtual Fish Tank,** shortly thereafter. The distinction will soon disappear as the Computer Museum is gradually subsumed. The museum, astride the Charles River Dam, has a restaurant, a gift shop, a planetarium, and a theater you can visit separately. The **Charles Hayden Planetarium,** with its sophisticated multi-image system, produces exciting programs on astronomical discoveries. The **Mugar Omni Theater** has a five-story domed screen and 27,000 watts of power driving its 84 loudspeakers. ✉ *Science Park at the Charles River Dam, Old West End,* ☎ *617/723–2500,* WEB *www.mos.org.* ☞ *$11, or with CityPass.* ☉ *Museum July 5–Labor Day, Sat.–Thurs. 9–7, Fri. 9–9; Labor Day– July 4, Sat.–Thurs. 9–5, Fri. 9–9. T stop: Science Park.*

Nichols House. The only Mt. Vernon Street home open to the public, the Nichols House—built in 1804 and attributed to Charles Bulfinch— belonged to Beacon Hill eccentric, philanthropist, peace advocate Rose Standish Nichols, who was also one of the first female landscape designers. Although the Victorian furnishings passed to Miss Nichols by descent, she added a number of Colonial-style pieces, resulting in a delightful mélange of styles. ✉ *55 Mt. Vernon St., Beacon Hill,* ☎ *617/ 227–6993,* WEB *www.nicholshousemuseum.org.* ☞ *$5.* ☉ *May–Oct., Tues.–Sat. 12:15–4:15; Nov.–Dec. and Feb.–Apr., Thurs.–Sat. noon– 4. Tours on the ½ hr. T stop: Park St.*

② **Park Street Church.** If the Congregationalist Park Street Church could talk, what a joyful noise it would make. Samuel Smith's hymn "America" debuted here on July 4, 1831; two years earlier, William Lloyd Garrison began his long public campaign for the abolition of slavery. The 1810 church—designed by Peter Banner and called "the most impressive mass of brick and mortar in America" by Henry James—is easily recognized by its 217-ft steeple, considered by many to be the most beautiful in New England. ⊠ *1 Park St., Beacon Hill,* ☎ *617/523–3383,* WEB *www.parkstreet.org.* ☉ *Tours mid-June–Aug., Tues.–Sat. 9:30–3:30. Sun. services at 8:30, 11, 4:30, and 6:30. T stop: Park St.*

❺ State House. Charles Bulfinch's magnificent State House, one of the greatest works of classical architecture in America, is so striking that it hardly suffers for having been expanded in three directions by bureaucrats and lesser architects. The neoclassical design is poised between Georgian and Federal; its finest features are the delicate Corinthian columns of the portico, the graceful pediment and window arches, and the vast yet visually weightless dome, sheathed in copper from the foundry of Paul Revere. Unfortunately, much of the beauty of the State House is to be hidden for the next couple of years; the facade is being cleaned. The restoration is due to be finished in 2003; until then, it's still worth the trip to tour the interior. ⊠ *Beacon St. between Hancock and Bowdoin Sts., Beacon Hill,* ☎ *617/727–3676,* WEB *state.ma.us/sec/trs.* ☑ *Free.* ☉ *Tours weekdays 10–3:30. T stop: Park St.*

Government Center and the North End

Government Center is the section of town Bostonians love to hate. Not only does it house that which they cannot fight—City Hall—but it also holds some of the bleakest architecture since the advent of poured concrete. The sweeping brick plaza beside City Hall and the twin towers of the John F. Kennedy Federal Office Building begins at the junction where Cambridge Street becomes Tremont Street.

Separating the Government Center area from the North End is the Fitzgerald Expressway, which will eventually be replaced with an underground highway in a massive construction project dubbed "the Big Dig" by locals. In the meantime, calling the area a mess is putting it mildly. Driver alert: the rerouting of traffic and constant reconfiguration of one-way streets have changed what was once a conquerable puzzle into a nearly impenetrable maze. Trust no maps.

Opposite the pedestrian tunnel beneath the Fitzgerald Expressway is the North End, the oldest neighborhood in Boston and one of the oldest in the New World. People walked these narrow byways when Shakespeare was not yet 20 years buried and Louis XIV was new to the throne of France. In the 17th century the North End *was* Boston—much of the rest of the peninsula was still underwater or had yet to be cleared.

Today's North End is almost entirely a creation of the late 19th century, when brick tenements began to fill up with European immigrants—first the Irish, then the Eastern European Jews, then the Portuguese, and finally the Italians. Despite a recent influx of yuppies of all ethnicities, you'll still find dozens of authentic Italian restaurants, along with old world–style groceries, bakeries, churches, social clubs, and cafés.

Numbers in the text and in the margin correspond to numbers on the Boston map.

A Good Walk

The stark expanse of Boston's City Hall Plaza introduces visitors to the urban renewal age, but across Congress Street is **Faneuil Hall** ⑪, a site of political speech making since Revolutionary times. Just beyond that is **Quincy Market** ⑫, where shop-'til-you-droppers can sample a profusion of international taste treats. For more Bostonian fare, walk back toward Congress Street to the **Blackstone Block** ⑬ and the city's oldest restaurant, the Union Oyster House, for some oysters and ale. Around the corner to the north on Blackstone Street are the open-air produce stalls of **Haymarket,** always aflutter with activity on Friday and Saturday. To sample Italian goodies, make your way through a pedestrian tunnel underneath the Fitzgerald Highway and enter the North End at Salem Street. Follow to Parmenter Street, turn right, and continue past Hanover Street, one of the North End's main thoroughfares; here Parmenter becomes Richmond Street. At North Street, turn left, following the Freedom Trail, to the **Paul Revere House** ⑭. Take Prince Street to Hanover Street, and then continue on Hanover to St. Stephen's, the only remaining church designed by Charles Bulfinch. Directly across the street is the Prado, or Paul Revere Mall, dominated by a statue of the patriot and hero. At the end of the mall is the **Old North Church** ⑮, of "One if by land, two if by sea" fame. Continue following the Freedom Trail to Hull Street and **Copp's Hill Burying Ground** ⑯, the resting place of many Revolutionary War heroes.

TIMING

You can explore Faneuil Hall and Quincy Market in about an hour, more if you linger in the food stalls or shop. Give yourself another two to three hours to stroll through the North End. Finish the day with an Italian meal or at least a cappuccino.

Sights to See

⑬ **Blackstone Block.** For decades the butcher trade dominated the city's oldest commercial block. Today, the block is Boston at its time-machine best, with more than three centuries of architecture on view. The centerpiece of the block is the **Union Oyster House,** whose patrons have included Daniel Webster and John F. Kennedy. ⊠ *Blackstone St., between North and Hanover Sts., Government Center T stop: Government Center.*

⑯ **Copp's Hill Burying Ground.** An ancient and melancholy air hovers over this Colonial-era burial ground like a fine mist. Many headstones were chipped by practice shots fired by British soldiers during the occupation of Boston, and a number of musket-ball pockmarks can still be seen. ⊠ *Between Hull and Snowhill Sts., North End,* ᵂᴱᴮ *www. cityofboston.gov/parks/buryinggrounds.* ☉ *Apr.–Nov., daily 9–5; Dec.– Mar., daily 9–dusk. T stop: North Station.*

★ ⑪ **Faneuil Hall.** Faneuil Hall was erected in 1742 to serve as a place for town meetings and a public market. Inside are the great mural *Webster's Reply to Hayne,* Gilbert Stuart's portrait of Washington at Dorchester Heights, several worthwhile shops in the basement, and, on the top floors, the headquarters and museum of the Ancient and Honorable Artillery Company of Massachusetts, the oldest militia in the Western Hemisphere (1638). ⊠ *Faneuil Hall Sq., Government Center,* ᵂᴱᴮ *www.faneuilhallmarketplace.com.* ⊡ *Free.* ☉ *Daily 9–5. T stop: Government Center, State St.*

Holocaust Memorial. At night, its six 50-ft-high glass-and-steel towers glow like ghosts who vow never to forget; during the day, though, the monument seems at odds with the 18th-century streetscape of Blackstone Square behind it. Recollections by Holocaust survivors are set into the glass-and-granite walls; the upper levels of the towers are etched with 6 million numbers in random sequence symbolizing the Jewish victims of the Nazi horror. ⊠ *Union St., Government Center T stop: Government Center.*

★ ⓲ **Old North Church.** Also known as Christ Church, Old North is famous not only for its status as the oldest in Boston (1723) but for the two lanterns that glimmered from its steeple on the night of April 18, 1775, signaling the departure by water of the British regulars to Lexington and Concord. Longfellow's poem aside, the lanterns—hung by a young sexton named Robert Newman—were not a signal *to* Paul Revere but *from* him to the citizens of Charlestown across the harbor. The Episcopal church was designed by William Price from a study of Christopher Wren's London churches. ⊠ *193 Salem St., North End,* ☏ *617/523–6676,* WEB *www.oldnorth.com.* ☼ *June–Oct., daily 9–6; Nov.–May, daily 9–5. Sun. services at 9, 11, and 5. T stop: Haymarket, North Station.*

ⓒ ⓮ **Paul Revere House.** It is an interesting coincidence that the oldest house standing in one of the oldest sections of Boston should also have been the home of Paul Revere, patriot activist and silversmith. And it *is* a coincidence, since many homes of famous Bostonians have burned or been demolished over the years. It was saved from oblivion in 1902 and restored to an approximation of its original 17th-century appearance. The house was built nearly a hundred years before Revere's 1775 midnight ride through Middlesex County, on a site once occupied by the parsonage of the Reverend Increase Mather's Second Church of Boston. A few Revere furnishings are on display. Special events are scheduled throughout the year, many designed with children in mind. The immediate neighborhood surrounding the house also has Revere associations. The little park in North Square is named after Rachel Revere, his second wife, and the adjacent brick **Pierce-Hichborn House** once belonged to relatives of Revere. The garden connecting the Revere House and the Pierce-Hichborn House is planted with flowers and medicinal herbs favored in Revere's day. ⊠ *19 North Sq., North End,* ☏ *617/523–2338,* WEB *www.paulreverehouse.org.* ☞ *$2.50, $4 with Pierce-Hichborn House.* ☼ *Jan.–Mar., Tues.–Sun. 9:30–4:15; Nov.–Dec. and first 2 wks of Apr., daily 9:30–4:15; mid-Apr.–Oct., daily 9:30–5:15. T stop: Haymarket, Aquarium, Government Center.*

⓬ **Quincy Market.** Also known as Faneuil Hall Marketplace, this pioneer effort at urban recycling set the tone for many similar projects throughout America. The market consists of three block-long annexes: Quincy, North, and South markets, each 535 ft long and built to the 1826 design of Alexander Parris. Abundance and variety have been the watchwords of Quincy Market since its reopening in 1976. Some people consider it hopelessly commercial, though in the peak summer season 50,000 or so visitors a day rather enjoy the extravaganza. At the east end of Quincy Market, **Marketplace Center** has tempting boutiques and food shops. ⊠ *Between Clinton and Chatham Sts., Government Center,* ☏ *617/338–2323.* ☼ *Mon.–Sat. 10–9, Sun. noon–6. Restaurants and bars generally daily 11 AM–2 AM; food stalls open earlier. T stop: Haymarket, Government Center, State St.*

Charlestown

Charlestown was a thriving settlement a year before Colonials headed across the Charles River to found Boston proper. The district holds two of the most visible—and vertical—monuments in Boston's history: the Bunker Hill Monument and the USS *Constitution*.

Numbers in the text and in the margin correspond to numbers on the Boston map.

A Good Walk

Charlestown can be reached by foot via the Charlestown Bridge; by Bus 93 from Haymarket Square, Boston; or on the MBTA water shuttle, which runs every 15 or 30 minutes year-round, from Long Wharf in downtown Boston. If you're walking, start at Copp's Hill Burial Ground; follow Hull Street to Commercial Street, and turn left to reach the bridge. The Charlestown Navy Yard will be on your right; ahead is the **USS Constitution** ⑰ museum and visitor center. From here, you can follow the red line of the Freedom Trail to the **Bunker Hill Monument** ⑱.

TIMING

Give yourself two or three hours for a Charlestown walk; the lengthy stroll across the bridge calls for endurance in cold weather. Many save Charlestown's stretch of the Freedom Trail for a second-day outing. You can avoid backtracking by taking the water shuttle back to Long Wharf.

Sights to See

⑱ **Bunker Hill Monument.** British troops sustained heavy losses on June 17, 1775, at the Battle of Bunker Hill—one of the earliest major confrontations of the Revolutionary War. Most of the battle took place on Breed's Hill, which is where the monument, dedicated in 1843, actually stands. The famous war cry "Don't fire until you see the whites of their eyes" may not have been uttered by American colonel William Prescott or General Israel Putnam, but if either did shout it, he was quoting an old Prussian command that was necessary due to the inaccuracy of the musket. No matter. The Americans employed a deadly delayed-action strategy and proved themselves worthy fighters. Though they lost the battle, the engagement made clear that the British could be challenged. The monument's top is reached by a flight of 294 steps. There is no elevator, but the views from the observatory are worth the arduous climb—for those in good condition. In the lodge at the base, dioramas tell the story of the battle, and ranger programs are conducted regularly. ✉ *Main St. to Monument St., then straight uphill, Charlestown,* ☎ *617/242–5641.* ⊡ *Free.* ☽ *Lodge daily 9–5, monument daily 9– 4:30. T stop: Community College.*

☞ ⑰ **USS Constitution.** Better known as "Old Ironsides," the more than two-centuries-old USS *Constitution* is docked at the Charlestown Navy Yard. Launched in 1797, the oldest commissioned ship in the U.S. fleet is from the days of "wooden ships and iron men"—when she and her crew of 200 helped to assert the sovereignty of an improbable new nation. The ship's principal service was in the War of 1812. After her 42 engagements, her record was 42–0. The adjacent **Constitution Museum** (☎ 617/426–1812) has artifacts and hands-on exhibits. It's open May–October, daily 9–6; November–April, daily 10–5. ✉ *Charlestown Navy Yard, off Water St., Charlestown,* ☎ *617/242–5670,* WEB *www. ussconstitution.navy.mil or or www.ussconstitutionmuseum.org.* ⊡ *Free.* ☽ *Daily noon–sunset; continuous tour (last one about 15 mins before sunset). T stop: Haymarket; then MBTA Bus 92 or 93 to Charlestown City Sq. Or MBTA water shuttle from Long Wharf to Pier 4.*

Downtown Boston

The Financial District—what Bostonians usually refer to as "downtown"—may seem off the beaten track for people who are concentrating on following the Freedom Trail, yet there is much to see in a walk of an hour or two. There is little logic to the streets here; they were, after all, village lanes that only now happen to be lined with 40-story office towers.

Downtown is home to some of Boston's most idiosyncratic neighborhoods. The Leather District directly abuts Chinatown, which is also bordered by the Theater District (and the buildings of the New England Medical Center) farther west; to the south, the red light of the once brazen and now decaying Combat Zone flickers weakly.

Numbers in the text and in the margin correspond to numbers on the Boston map.

A Good Walk

After viewing the dramatic interior of **King's Chapel** ⑲ at the corner of Tremont (that's *Treh*-mont, not *Tree*-mont) Street, visit the burying ground next door. Walk southeast on School Street, past the Globe Corner Bookstore, to Washington Street; turn right to see the **Old South Meeting House** ⑳, which seethed with Revolutionary fervor in the 1770s. Retrace your steps on Washington and continue toward Court Street to get to the **Old State House** ㉑. In a traffic island in front is a circle of stones that marks the site of the Boston Massacre, a 1770 riot in which five townspeople were killed by British troops. Follow State Street east to the harbor and the **New England Aquarium** ㉒, on Central Wharf. From here you can walk south to **Rowes Wharf,** Boston's most glamorous waterfront development. Continue on Atlantic Avenue— most likely a wall of traffic due to the construction of an underground central-artery highway nearby—to Congress Street, and then turn left onto the bridge to reach the **Boston Tea Party Ship and Museum** ㉓ aboard the *Beaver II,* a re-creation of the hapless British ship that was carrying tea in 1773. Continue over the Congress Street Bridge to the **Children's Museum** ㉔. If you're starting to crave refreshment, cross back to Atlantic Avenue and continue south past South Station toward the distinctive gate marking **Chinatown.**

TIMING

If you are traveling with small children, you may wish to limit this walk to the area around the New England Aquarium and the Children's Museum. (In fact, you'll probably want to spend two or three hours just in the museums.) Otherwise budget about three hours for the walk, and be prepared for the often cool wind coming off the harbor.

Sights to See

Boston Harbor Islands National Park Area. The focal point of the 31 Boston Harbor Islands, a national park area, is 28-acre George's Island, on which the pre–Civil War Fort Warren stands, partially restored and partially in ruins. From May to October, you can reach George's Island on the Boston Harbor Cruises ferry; from June to September, free water shuttles run from George's to several other islands. Bumpkin and Gallops are small and easily explored within an hour; Lovell's and Grape each cover about 60 acres. You can fish, hike, and picnic— there are plenty of ruins to explore, and beautiful views. Lovell's has a rocky swimming beach with a lifeguard on duty; you can swim unsupervised on Gallops and Grape islands. No dogs are allowed on the islands. ⊠ *Boston Harbor Cruises,* ☎ *617/227–4321 or 617/223–8666,* WEB *www.bostonislands.com.* ⊡ *Trip to George's Island $8.* ☉ *Early June–Oct., daily T stop: State St.*

Boston National Historical Park Visitor Center. National Park Service ranger-led tours of the Freedom Trail leave from the center, which stocks brochures about many attractions and walking tours and has rest rooms. ⊠ *15 State St., near the Old State House, Downtown,* ☎ *617/ 242–5642,* WEB *www.nps.gov/bost.* ⊡ *Free.* ☉ *Daily 9–5. Tours mid-Apr.–Nov.; call for hrs, which change seasonally.*

㉓ **Boston Tea Party Ship and Museum.** Until an August 2001 lightning strike caused a fire that sent it into storage, the *Beaver II,* a replica of one of the ships forcibly boarded and unloaded the night Boston Harbor became a teapot, bobbed in the Fort Point Channel at the Congress Street Bridge. The Tea Party people are taking the opportunity to make improvements to their exhibits. At press time they hope to reopen in early 2003. The site of the actual Boston Tea Party—a revolt over a tax on tea that the British had levied—is marked by a plaque on the corner of Atlantic Avenue and the Northern Avenue bridge. ⊠ *Congress St. Bridge, Downtown,* ☎ *617/269–7150,* ⃞WEB *www. bostonteapartyship.com. T stop: South Station.*

🅒 ㉔ **Children's Museum.** Hands-on exhibits at this popular museum include computers, video cameras, and displays designed to help children understand cultural diversity, their own bodies, the nature of disabilities, and more. Don't miss the Japanese House, Arthur's World, or Boats Afloat, where children can build a wooden boat and float it down a 15-ft replica of the Fort Point Channel. The museum also has a full schedule of special exhibits, festivals, and performances. ⊠ *300 Congress St., Downtown,* ☎ *617/426–6500; 617/426–885 recorded information;* ⃞WEB *www.bostonkids.org.* ▧ *$7.* ☉ *Sat.–Thurs. 10–5, Fri. 10–9. T stop: South Station.*

Chinatown. Boston's Chinatown may be geographically small, but it is home to the third-largest concentration of Chinese-Americans in the United States, after San Francisco's and New York City's Chinatowns. Beginning in the 1870s, Chinese immigrants began to trickle in, many setting up tents in a strip they called Ping On Alley. The trickle increased to a wave when immigration restrictions were lifted in 1968. In recent years, Vietnamese, Korean, Japanese, Thai, and Malaysian eateries have popped up alongside the Chinese restaurants—most along Beach and Tyler streets and Harrison Avenue. A three-story pagoda-style arch at the end of Beach Street welcomes visitors to the district. *T stop: Chinatown.*

⑲ **King's Chapel.** Somber yet dramatic, King's Chapel looms over the corner of Tremont and School streets. The distinctive shape of the 1754 structure was not achieved entirely by design; for lack of funds it was never topped with the steeple that architect Peter Harrison had planned. The interior is a masterpiece of elegant proportion and Georgian calm. The chapel's bell is Paul Revere's largest and, in his judgment, his sweetest-sounding. Take the path to the right from the entrance of the **King's Chapel Burying Ground,** the oldest cemetery in the city. On the left is the gravestone (1704) of Elizabeth Pain, the model for Hester Prynne in Hawthorne's *The Scarlet Letter.* Elsewhere, you'll find the graves of the first Massachusetts governor, John Winthrop, and several generations of his descendants. ⊠ *58 Tremont St., at School St., Downtown,* ☎ *617/227–2155,* ⃞WEB *www.kings-chapel.org.* ☉ *Mid-Apr.–Nov., Mon. and Fri.–Sat. 10–4; Dec.–mid-Apr., Sat. 10–4. Year-round music program Tues. 12:15–1; services Sun. at 11, Wed. at 12:15. T stop: Park St., Government Center.*

★ 🅒 ㉒ **New England Aquarium.** More than just another pretty fish, this aquarium challenges you to really imagine life under (and around) the sea. Seals bark outside the West Wing, its glass-and-steel exterior constructed to mimic fish scales. This facility has a café, a gift shop, and changing exhibits, beginning with "Living Links," about animals that cross more than one habitat. Inside the main building are examples of more than 2,000 species of marine life from sharks to jellyfish, many of which make their homes in a four-story ocean-reef tank. Don't miss the five-times-a-day feeding time, a fascinating procedure that lasts nearly an hour. Educational programs, like the "Science at Sea" cruise, take place year-round. Sea lion shows are held aboard *Discovery,* a floating marine mammal pavilion; and whale-watch cruises ($27) leave from the aquarium's dock from April to early November. ⊠ *Central Wharf* *(between Central and Milk Sts.), Downtown,* ☎ *617/973–5200 or 617/973–5277,* WEB *www.neaq.org.* ✆ *$13, or with CityPass.* ☉ *July–early Sept., Mon.–Tues. and Fri. 9–6, Wed.–Thurs. 9–8, weekends 9–7; early Sept.–June, weekdays 9–5, weekends 9–6. T stop: Aquarium, State St.*

㉒ Old South Meeting House. Some of the most fiery pre-Revolutionary town meetings were held at Old South, culminating in the tumultuous gathering of December 16, 1773, convened by Samuel Adams to address the question of dutiable tea that activists wanted returned to England. This was also the congregation of Phillis Wheatley, the first published African-American poet. A permanent exhibition, "Voices of Protest," celebrates Old South as a forum for free speech from Revolutionary days to the present. ✉ *310 Washington St., Downtown,* ☎ *617/482–6439,* WEB *www.oldsouthmeetinghouse.org.* ✆ *$3.* ☉ *Apr.–Oct., daily 9:30–5; Nov.–Mar., daily 10–4. T stop: State St., Downtown Crossing.*

㉑ Old State House. The brightly gilded lion and unicorn, symbols of British imperial power, that adorn the State Street gable of this landmark structure were pulled down in 1776 but restored in 1880. This was the seat of the Colonial government from 1713 until the Revolution, and after the evacuation of the British from Boston it served the independent Commonwealth until its replacement on Beacon Hill was completed in 1798. The permanent collection traces Boston's Revolutionary War history. ✉ *206 Washington St., at the corner of State St., Downtown,* ☎ *617/720–3290,* WEB *www.bostonhistory.org.* ✆ *$3.* ☉ *Daily 9–5. T stop: State St.*

The Back Bay

In the folklore of American neighborhoods, the Back Bay stands with New York's Park Avenue and San Francisco's Nob Hill as a symbol of propriety and high social standing. The main east–west streets—Beacon, Marlborough, Commonwealth, Newbury, and Boylston—are bisected by eight streets named in alphabetical order from Arlington to Hereford. Note that Huntington Avenue is also known as the Avenue of the Arts, but you'll hear locals use Huntington.

Numbers in the text and in the margin correspond to numbers on the Boston map.

A Good Walk

A walk through the Back Bay properly begins with the **Boston Public Garden** ㉕, the oldest botanical garden in the United States. Wander its paths to the corner of Commonwealth Avenue and Arlington Street. Walk up Arlington to Beacon Street and turn left to visit the **Gibson House** ㉖ museum. Follow Beacon to Berkeley and turn left to return to Commonwealth Avenue. Stroll the avenue to Clarendon, turn left, and head into **Copley Square** ㉗, where you will find **Trinity Church,** the Boston Public Library, and the **John Hancock Tower** ㉘. From Copley Square, you can walk north on Dartmouth to **Newbury Street** and its posh boutiques. For a dose of the avant-garde turn left on Hereford Street and right on Boylston and drop into the **Institute of Contemporary Art** ㉙. From there, proceed one block farther on Boylston Street to Massachusetts Avenue. Turn left to reach the **First Church of Christ, Scientist** ㉚ and **Symphony Hall** ㉛.

The Boston Public Garden is such a delight in the spring and summer that you should give yourself at least an hour to explore it if this is when you're visiting. Distances between sights are a bit longer here than in other parts of the city, so allow one or two hours for a walk down

Newbury Street. The Museum of Contemporary Art and the First Church of Christ, Scientist can each be explored in an hour.

Sights to See

Back Bay mansions. If you like nothing better than to imagine how the other half lives, you'll suffer no shortage of old homes to sigh over in Boston's Back Bay. Most, unfortunately, are off-limits to visitors, but there's no law against gawking from the outside.

Among the grander Back Bay houses is the **Baylies Mansion** (⊠ 5 Commonwealth Ave., Back Bay), of 1904, now the home of the Boston Center for Adult Education; you can enter to view its first-floor common room. The **Burrage Mansion** (⊠ 314 Commonwealth Ave., Back Bay) is a gem, built in 1899 in an extravagant French château style, complete with turrets and gargoyles, that reflects a cost-be-damned attitude uncommon even among the wealthiest Back Bay families. It now houses an assisted-living residence for senior citizens, and walk-in visitors are not encouraged.

The **Cushing-Endicott House** (⊠ 163 Marlborough St., Back Bay) was built in 1871 and later served as the home of William C. Endicott, secretary of war under President Grover Cleveland; this was dubbed "the handsomest house in the whole Back Bay" by the author Bainbridge Bunting. The opulent **Oliver Ames Mansion** (⊠ 55 Commonwealth Ave., corner of Massachusetts Ave., Back Bay) was built in 1882 for a railroad baron and Massachusetts governor; it's now an office building. The **Ames-Webster House** (⊠ 306 Dartmouth St., Back Bay), built in 1872 and remodeled in 1882 and 1969, is one of the city's finest houses; it's still a private home.

★ ☾ ㉕ **Boston Public Garden.** The oldest botanical garden in the United States is beloved by Bostonians and visitors alike. The park's pond has been famous since 1877 for its foot pedal-powered **Swan Boats,** which make leisurely cruises during warm months. Its dominant statuary is Thomas Ball's equestrian **George Washington** (1869); the granite and red-marble **Ether Monument,** which commemorates the advent of anesthesia at nearby Massachusetts General Hospital; and its charming fountains—though the hands-down favorite sculpture of kids (and many adults) is the *Make Way for Ducklings* **bronze statue group,** a tribute to the 1941 classic children's story by Robert McCloskey. The garden gates are always open, but it's not a good idea to visit after dark. ☎ 617/522–1966 or 617/635–4505, WEB *www.swanboats.com.* ⌨ *Swan Boats $2.* ☾ *Swan Boats mid-Apr.–mid-June, daily 10–4; mid-June–Labor Day, daily 10–5; Labor Day–mid-Sept., weekdays noon–4, weekends 10–4. T stop: Arlington.*

★ **Boston Public Library.** When this venerable institution opened in 1895, it confirmed the status of architects McKim, Mead & White as apostles of the Renaissance Revival style while reinforcing Boston's commitment to an enlightened citizenry. You don't need a library card to enjoy the building's magnificent art. The murals at the head of the staircase, depicting the nine muses, are the work of the French artist Puvis de Chavannes; those in the book-request processing room to the right are Edwin Abbey's interpretations of the Holy Grail legend. Upstairs, in the public areas leading to the fine arts, music, and rare-books collections, is John Singer Sargent's mural series on the subject of Judaism and Christianity. Among the library's architectural perks is a Renaissance-style courtyard, where a covered arcade furnished with chairs rings a garden and fountain; the main entrance hall, with its immense stone lions by Louis Saint-Gaudens, vaulted ceiling, and marble staircase; and **Bates Hall,** one of Boston's most sumptuous interior spaces, 218 ft long and with a barrel-arch ceiling 50 ft high. ⊠ *700 Boylston St., at Copley Sq., Back Bay,* ☎ *617/536–5400,* WEB *www.bpl.org.* ☉ *June–Sept., Mon.–Thurs. 9–9, Fri.–Sat. 9–5; Oct.–May, Mon.–Thurs. 9–9, Fri.–Sat. 9–5, Sun. 1–5. Free guided art and architecture tours Mon. at 2:30, Tues. and Thurs. at 6, Fri.–Sat. at 11, Sun. at 2. T stop: Copley.*

㉗ **Copley Square.** For thousands of folks in April, a glimpse of this square is a welcome sight; this is where Boston Marathon runners end their 26-mi race. The Boston Public Library, the Copley Plaza Hotel, and ☞ **Trinity Church** border the square. Copley Place, an upscale glass-and-brass urban mall, comprises two major hotels, shops, and restaurants. The ☞ **John Hancock Tower** looms over all. *T stop: Copley.*

㉚ **First Church of Christ, Scientist.** The world headquarters of the Christian Science faith mixes an old-world basilica with a sleek office complex designed by I. M. Pei. This church was established here by Mary Baker Eddy in 1879. Mrs. Eddy's original granite First Church of Christ, Scientist (1894) has since been enveloped by the domed Renaissance basilica, added to the site in 1906. The 670-ft reflecting pool is a splendid sight on a hot summer day. In the publishing arm's lobby is the fascinating **Mapparium,** a huge stained-glass globe whose 30-ft interior can be traversed on a footbridge. The Mapparium was closed for renovations at press time; it was due to reopen at the end of 2002, with computer projections updating the borders and country names that have changed since the room's completion in 1935. Call ahead for the latest information. ⊠ *175 Huntington Ave., Back Bay,* ☎ *617/ 450–3790,* WEB *www.tfccs.com or www.marybakereddylibrary.org.* ☉ *Free church tours Mon.–Sat. 10–4, Sun. 11:30. Sun. services Sept.–June at 10 and 7; Wed. services at noon and 7:30. T stop: Prudential.*

㉖ **Gibson House.** One of the first Back Bay residences (1859), the Gibson House has been preserved as a museum with all its Victorian fixtures and furniture intact. A Gibson scion lived here until the 1950s and left things as they had always been. ⊠ *137 Beacon St., Back Bay,* ☎ *617/267–6338,* WEB *www.thegibsonhouse.org.* ☜ *$5.* ☉ *Tours Wed.–Sun. at 1, 2, and 3. T stop: Arlington.*

㉙ **Institute of Contemporary Art.** Multimedia art, installations, film and video series, and a variety of other events are showcased in this cutting-edge institution inside a 19th-century police station and firehouse. Over the years the institute has backed many groundbreaking artists, including Edvard Munch, Egon Schiele, Andy Warhol, Robert Rauschenberg, and Roy Lichtenstein. ⊠ *955 Boylston St., Back Bay,* ☎ *617/ 266–5152,* WEB *www.icaboston.org.* ☜ *$6, free Thurs. 5–9.* ☉ *Wed. and Fri. noon–5, Thurs. noon–9, weekends 11–5. Tours on select Sun. at 2:30 and 1st Thurs. of month at 6:30. T stop: Hynes Convention Center.*

㉘ **John Hancock Tower.** The tallest building in New England is a stark and graceful reflective blue rhomboid tower designed by I. M. Pei. Bostonians originally feared the Hancock's stark modernism would overwhelm nearby Trinity Church, but its shimmering sides reflect the older structure's image, actually enlarging its presence. The Tower is closed to the public. ⊠ *200 Clarendon St., Back Bay. T stop: Copley.*

㉛ **Symphony Hall.** The home of the Boston Symphony Orchestra since 1900, the hall was designed by the architectural firm McKim, Mead & White, but it's the acoustics, not the design, that make this a special place for performers and concertgoers. ⊠ *301 Massachusetts Ave., Back Bay,* ☎ *888/266–1200 box office; 617/638–9392 volunteer office;* WEB *www.bso.org.* ☉ *Free walk-up tours every Wed. at 4:30 and 1st Sat. of month at 1:30. T stop: Symphony.*

Trinity Church. In his 1877 masterpiece, architect Henry Hobson Richardson brought his Romanesque Revival style to maturity; all the aesthetic elements for which he was famous—bold masonry, careful arrangement of masses, sumptuously carved interior woodwork— come together magnificently. The Episcopal church remains the centerpiece of Copley Square. ⊠ *206 Clarendon St., Back Bay,* ☎ *617/ 536–0944,* WEB *www.trinitychurchboston.org.* 🔊 *Tours $5, self-guided tours $3.* ☉ *Daily 8–6. Sun. services at 8, 9, 11:15, and 6; services Mon.– Thurs. at 7:30, 12:10, and 5:30, Fri. at 7:30. Tours weekdays at 1, 2, and 3 (call to confirm). T stop: Copley.*

The South End

History has come full circle in the South End. Once a fashionable neighborhood, it was deserted by the well-to-do for the Back Bay toward the end of the 20th century. Solidly back in fashion, it is today a polyglot of upscale eateries and ethnic enclaves, with redbrick row houses in various states of refurbished splendor or genteel decay. The Back Bay is French-inspired, but the South End's architectural roots are English, the houses continuing the pattern established on Beacon Hill (in a uniformly bowfront style), though aspiring to a more florid standard of decoration.

There is a substantial Latino and African-American presence in the South End, particularly along Columbus and Massachusetts avenues, which mark the beginning of the predominantly black neighborhood of Roxbury. Harrison Avenue and Washington Street at the north side of the South End lead to Chinatown, and consequently there is a significant Asian influence. But today the South End is known primarily for its large and well-connected gay community, which started the area's gentrification more than two decades ago and has brought with it a friendly, neighborly feel.

Numbers in the text and in the margin correspond to numbers on the Boston map.

A Good Walk

From the Back Bay, walk down Massachusetts Avenue to Columbus Avenue; turn left and follow it to **Rutland Square** ㉜ on your right. Cross to Tremont, walk northeast on Tremont, and turn right at **Union Park** ㉝. Walk south through the park to Shawmut Street, which holds a mixture of ethnic outlets and retail spaces. Walk northeast along Shawmut to East Berkeley Street, and then turn left and head back to Tremont. On Tremont Street near Clarendon is the **Boston Center for the Arts.** After a break at one of the many trendy restaurants and shops along Tremont, retrace your steps to Arlington and traverse the walkway over the Massachusetts Turnpike to reach **Bay Village,** on your right.

TIMING

You can walk through the South End in two to three hours. It's a good option on a pleasant day; go elsewhere in inclement weather, as most of what you'll see here is outdoors.

Sights to See

Bay Village. This neighborhood is a pocket of early 19th-century brick row houses that appears to be an almost toylike replication of Beacon Hill. It seems improbable that so fine and serene a neighborhood can exist in the shadow of busy Park Square; a developer might easily have leveled these blocks in an afternoon, yet they remain frozen in time, another Boston surprise. To get to Bay Village—where Edgar Allen Poe once lived—follow Columbus Avenue almost into Park Square, turn right on Arlington Street, then left onto one of the narrow streets of this neighborhood.

Boston Center for the Arts. Of Boston's many arts organizations, the city-sponsored arts and culture complex is the one that is closest "to the people." Here you can see the work of budding playwrights, view exhibits on Haitian folk art, or walk through an installation commemorating World AIDS Day. The BCA houses three small theaters, the Mills Art Gallery, and studio space for some 60 artists. ⊠ *539 Tremont St., South End,* ☎ *617/426–5000; 617/426–7700 recorded information; 617/426–8835 Mills Gallery;* WEB *www.bcaonline.org.* ☞ *Free.* ☉ *Weekdays 9–5. Mills Gallery Wed. and Sun. 1–4, Thurs.– Sat. 1–4 and 7–10. T stop: Back Bay.*

③② **Rutland Square.** Reflecting a time in which the South End was Boston's most prestigious address, this slice of park is framed by lovely Italianate bowfront houses. ⊠ *Between Columbus Ave. and Tremont St., South End.*

③③ **Union Park.** Cast-iron fences, Victorian town houses, and a grassy knoll add up to one of Boston's most charming miniscapes, dating to the 1850s. ⊠ *Between Tremont St. and Shawmut Ave., South End.*

The Fens

The marshland known as the Back Bay Fens gave this section of Boston its name, but two quirky institutions give it its character: Fenway Park, where hope for another World Series pennant springs eternal, and the Isabella Stewart Gardner Museum, the legacy of a 19th-century bon vivant Brahmin. Kenmore Square, a favorite haunt of college students, adds a bit of funky flavor to the mix.

The Fens mark the beginning of Boston's Emerald Necklace, a loosely connected chain of parks designed by Frederick Law Olmsted that extends along the Fenway, Riverway, and Jamaicaway to Jamaica Pond, the Arnold Arboretum, and Franklin Park.

Numbers in the text and in the margin correspond to numbers on the Boston map.

A Good Tour

The attractions in the Fens are best visited separately. The **Museum of Fine Arts** ③④, between Huntington Avenue and the Fenway, and the **Isabella Stewart Gardner Museum** ③⑤ are just around the corner from each other. **Kenmore Square** is at the west end of Commonwealth Avenue, a five-minute walk from **Fenway Park** ③⑥.

TIMING
The MBTA Green Line stops near the attractions on this tour. The Gardner is much smaller than the Museum of Fine Arts, but each can take up an afternoon if you take a break at their cafés.

Sights to See

③⑥ **Fenway Park.** Fenway may be one of the smallest parks in the major leagues (capacity 34,000), but it is one of the most loved. Since its construction in 1912, there has been no shortage of heroics: Babe Ruth pitched here when the place was new; Ted Williams and Carl Yastrzemski had epic careers here. ⊠ *4 Yawkey Way, between Van Ness and Lansdowne Sts., The Fens,* ☎ *617/267–1700 box office; 617/267–8661 recorded information; 617/236–6666 tours;* WEB *www.redsox.com/ fenway.* ☞ *Tours $5.* ☉ *Tours May–Sept. weekdays at 10, 11, and noon on day-game days; additional tour at 2 on nongame or night-game days.*

★ ㉟ **Isabella Stewart Gardner Museum.** A spirited young society woman named Isabella Stewart came from New York in 1860 to marry John Lowell Gardner. When it came time to create a permanent home for the old master paintings and Medici treasures she and her husband had acquired in Europe, she decided to build the Venetian palazzo of her dreams along Commonwealth Avenue. The building, whose top floor she occupied until her death in 1924, stands as a monument to one woman's extraordinary taste.

Despite the loss of several masterpieces in a film-worthy 1990 robbery, there is much to see: a trove of spectacular paintings—including masterpieces like Titian's *Rape of Europa,* Giorgione's *Christ Bearing the Cross,* Piero della Francesca's *Hercules,* and John Singer Sargent's *El Jaleo*—as well as rooms bought outright from great European houses, Spanish leather panels, Renaissance hooded fireplaces, and Gothic tapestries. An intimate restaurant overlooks the courtyard, and in the spring and summer tables and chairs spill outside. To fully conjure up the spirit of days past, attend one of the concerts held from September to May in the elegant Tapestry Room. ⌂ *280 The Fenway, Fens,* ☎ *617/566–1401; 617/566–1088 café;* WEB *www.gardnermuseum.org.* 🎟 *$10.* ☉ *Museum Tues.–Sun. 11–5, café Tues.–Sun. 11:30–4. Weekend concerts at 1:30. T stop: Museum.*

Kenmore Square. The Kenmore Square area is home to fast-food joints, rock-and-roll clubs, an abundance of university students, and an enormous sign advertising Citgo gasoline. The red, white, and blue neon sign put up in 1965 is so thoroughly identified with the area that historic preservationists have successfully fought to save it—proof that Bostonians are an open-minded lot who do not insist that all their landmarks be identified with the American Revolution. ⌂ *Intersection of Commonwealth Ave., Brookline Ave., and Beacon St., Fens. T stop: Kenmore Sq.*

★ ㉞ **Museum of Fine Arts.** The MFA's holdings of American art surpass those of all but two or three other U.S. museums. There are more than 50 works by John Singleton Copley, Colonial Boston's most celebrated portraitist, plus major paintings by Winslow Homer, John Singer Sargent, and Edward Hopper. Other artists represented include Mary Cassatt, Georgia O'Keeffe, and Berthe Morisot. The museum also has a sublime collection of French Impressionists—including the largest collection of Monet's work outside France—and renowned collections of Asian, Egyptian, and Nubian art. Three excellent galleries showcase the art of Africa, Oceania, and the Ancient Americas, expanding the MFA's emphasis on civilizations outside the Western tradition. In the West Wing are changing exhibits of contemporary arts, prints, and photographs. The museum has a gift shop, two restaurants, a cafeteria, and a gallery café. ⌂ *465 Huntington Ave., Fens,* ☎ *617/267–9300,* WEB *www.mfa.org.* 🎟 *$14, or with CityPass; by donation Wed. 4–9:45.* ☉ *Museum Mon.–Tues. and weekends 10–5:45, Wed.–Fri. 10–9:45. West Wing only Thurs.–Fri. 5–10. 1-hr tours available weekdays. Garden Apr.–Oct., Tues.–Sun. 10–4. T stop: Museum.*

Cambridge

Pronounced with either prideful satisfaction or a smirk, the nickname "The People's Republic of Cambridge" sums up this independent city of nearly 100,000 west of Boston. Cambridge not only houses two of the country's greatest educational institutions—Harvard University and the Massachusetts Institute of Technology—it has a long history as a haven for freethinkers, writers, and activists of every stamp. Once a center for publishing, Cambridge is now known for its high-tech and biotechnology firms

Cambridge

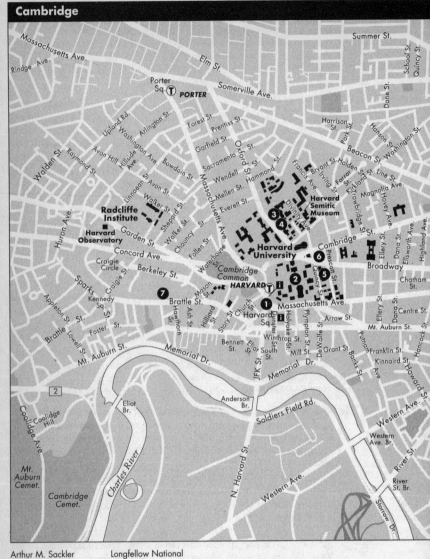

0   550 yards
0   500 meters

Munroe St.
Walnut St.
Stone Ave.
Bow St.
Washington St.
Mansfield St.
Medford St.
Linwood St.
Poplar St.
Joy St.
Somerville Ave.
Rossmore St.
Merriam St.
Linden St.
Allen St.
Marion St.
Newton St.
Concord Ave.
Oak St.
Dickinson St.
Houghton St.
Dimick St.
Webster Ave.
Tremont St.
McGrath Hwy.
LECHMERE
Charlestown Ave.
Winter St.
Gore St.
South St.
Porter St.
Warren St.
Willow St.
Cambridge St.
Otis St.
3rd St.
Sciarappa St.
7th St.
Thorndike St.
8th St.
Spring St.
Fulkerson St.
Hurley St.
Charles St.
6th St.
Bent St.
Roger St.
5th St.
Binney St.
Commercial Ave.
Cambridge St.
Prospect St.
Hampshire St.
Lincoln St.
York St.
Berkshire St.
Portland St.
Windsor St.
Bristol St.
Binney St.
Munroe St.
Athenaeum St.
1st St.
2nd St.
Longfellow Br.
Maple Ave.
Fayette St.
Antrim St.
Amory St.
Inman St.
Norfolk St.
Elm St.
Market St.
Broadway
Kendall Sq.
Harvard St.
MIT List Visual Arts Center
KENDALL
Ames St.
Main St.
West St.
Lee St.
Clinton St.
Bigelow St.
Prospect St.
Essex St.
Washington St.
York St.
Carleton St.
Amherst St.
Hayward St.
City Hall
Bishop Richard Allen Dr.
8
Amest St.
CENTRAL
Massachusetts Ave.
Main St.
MIT Museum
Memorial Dr.
Green St.
Franklin St.
Western Ave.
River St.
Auburn St.
Sidney St.
Cross St.
MIT Chapel
Harvard Bridge
Storrow Drive
Joy St.
Pleasant St.
Magazine St.
Pearl St.
Brookline St.
Pacific St.
Landsdowne St.
Purrington St.
Albany St.
Vassar St.
Allston St.
Putnam St.
Waverly St.
Amherst Alley
Beacon St.
Massachusetts Ave.
Henry St.
Charles River
HYNES CONVENTION CENTER/ ICA (AUDITORIUM)
Boylston St.

Cambridge is easily reached on the Red Line train. The Harvard Square area is notorious for limited parking. If you insist on driving into Cambridge, you may want to avoid the local circling ritual by pulling into a garage.

Numbers in the text and in the margin correspond to numbers on the Cambridge map.

A Good Walk

Begin your tour in **Harvard Square** ① near the T station entrance. Enter Harvard Yard for a look at one of the country's premier educational institutions: **Harvard University** ②. Just past Memorial Hall (ask any student for directions) is Kirkland Street; turn right and then take a quick left onto Divinity Avenue. At 11 Divinity, you'll find an entrance to the complex of the **Peabody Museum of Archaeology and Ethnology** ③ and the **Harvard Museum of Natural History** ④. From Harvard Square, it's about a 10-minute walk to Harvard's **Fogg Art Museum** ⑤, on Quincy Street, and **Arthur M. Sackler Museum** ⑥, on Broadway. The **Longfellow National Historic Site** ⑦, closed for remodeling into 2002, is a 15-minute walk west of Harvard Square on Brattle Street.

In good weather, you can walk along Massachusetts Avenue through the bustle and ethnic diversity of urban Central Square and into the warehouselike openness of the Kendall Square area, where the campus of the **Massachusetts Institute of Technology** ⑧ dominates the neighborhood. If the weather is poor, take the T Red Line heading inbound from Harvard Square two stops to Kendall Square.

TIMING

Budget at least two hours to explore Harvard Square, plus at least three more if you plan to go to Harvard's museums. The walk down Massachusetts Avenue to MIT will take an additional 30 to 45 minutes, and you could easily spend an hour or two on the MIT campus admiring its architecture and visiting its museum or the List Visual Arts Center.

Sights to See

❻ **Arthur M. Sackler Museum.** The richness of the East and artistic treasures of the ancient Greeks, Egyptians, and Romans fill three of the four floors of this modern structure. The changing exhibits are first-rate, but if time is limited, make a beeline for the Ancient and Asian art galleries on the fourth floor, where you can gaze at bronze relics from a Chinese dynasty, Buddhist sculptures, Greek friezes, or Roman marbles. The fee for the Sackler gains you entrance to the ☞ **Fogg Art Museum.** ⊠ *485 Broadway,* ☎ *617/495–9400,* WEB *www.artmuseums.harvard.edu.* ⊠ *$5, free all day Wed. and Sat. 10–noon.* ☉ *Mon.–Sat. 10–5, Sun. 1–5.*

★ ❺ **Fogg Art Museum.** Harvard's most famous art museum owns 80,000 works of art from every major period and from every corner of the world. The Fogg, behind Harvard Yard on Quincy Street, was founded in 1895; its collection focuses primarily on European, American, and East Asian works, with notable 19th-century French Impressionist and medieval Italian paintings. A ticket to the Fogg also gains admission to the Arthur M. Sackler Museum and the **Busch-Reisinger Museum** (☎ 617/495–9400), in the Werner Otto Hall and entered through the Fogg. From the serenity of the Fogg's old masters, you step into the jarring, mesmerizing world of German Expressionists and other 20th-century artists. Also included with Fogg admission is the **Sert Gallery**, in the adjacent Carpenter Center for the Visual Arts. The Sert hosts changing exhibits of contemporary works and also houses a café. ⊠ *32 Quincy St.,* ☎ *617/495–9400,* WEB *www.artmuseums.harvard.edu.* ⊠ *$5, free all day Wed. and Sat. 10–noon.* ☉ *Mon.–Sat. 10–5, Sun. 1–5.*

④ Harvard Museum of Natural History. Many museums promise something for every member of the family; the Harvard museum complex actually delivers. One fee admits you to all three museums. In the **Botanical Museum**, the glass flowers, including 3,000 models of 847 plant species, were meticulously created from 1887 to 1936; everything is, indeed, made of glass. The **Museum of Comparative Zoology** traces the evolution of animals (including dinosaurs) and humans. Oversize garnets and crystals are among the holdings of the **Mineralogical and Geological Museum,** which also has an extensive collection of meteorites. ⊠ *26 Oxford St.,* ☎ *617/495–3045,* WEB *www.hmnh. harvard.edu.* ⌸ *$6.50; free Sun. 9–noon, and Wed. 3–5 (Sept.–May only).* ☉ *Daily 9–5.*

① Harvard Square. Gaggles of students, street musicians, people hawking the paper *Spare Change* (as well as asking for some), end-of-the-world preachers, and political-cause proponents make for a nonstop pedestrian flow at this most celebrated of Cambridge crossroads. Harvard Square is where Massachusetts Avenue (locally, Mass Ave.), coming from Boston, turns and widens into a triangle broad enough to accommodate a brick peninsula (beneath which the MBTA station is located). Sharing the peninsula is the Out-of-Town newsstand, a local institution that occupies the restored 1928 kiosk that used to be the entrance to the MBTA station. Harvard Square is walled on two sides by banks, restaurants, and shops and on the third by Harvard University. The **Cambridge Visitor Information Booth** (☎ 617/497–1630, WEB www.cambridge-usa.org), just outside the T station entrance, is a volunteer-staffed kiosk with maps and brochures. The booth, which is open weekdays 9–5, Saturday 10–3, and Sunday 1–5, has maps for historic and literary walking tours of the city and an excellent guide to the bookstores in the Square and beyond.

② Harvard University. In 1636 the Great and General Court of the Massachusetts Bay Colony established the country's first college here. Named in 1639 for John Harvard, a young Charlestown clergyman who died in 1638, leaving the college his entire library and half his estate, Harvard remained the only college in the New World until 1693, by which time it was firmly established as a respected center of learning. Students run the **Harvard University Events and Information Center,** which has maps of the university area. You can take a free hour-long walking tour of Harvard Yard. ⊠ *Holyoke Center, 1350 Massachusetts Ave.,* ☎ *617/495–1000 general information,* WEB *www.harvard.edu.*

List Visual Arts Center. Founded by Albert and Vera List, pioneer collectors of modern art, this MIT center has three galleries showcasing exhibitions of cutting-edge art and mixed media. Artworks such as Thomas Hart Benton's painting *Fluid Catalytic Crackers* are in keeping with the center's mission to explore the cultural as well as scientific contexts that surround us. ⊠ *Wiesner Bldg., 20 Ames St., off Main St.,* ☎ *617/253–4680,* WEB *web.mit.edu/lvac/www.* ⌸ *Free.* ☉ *Oct.–June, Tues.–Thurs. noon–6, Fri. noon–8, weekends noon–6.*

⑦ Longfellow National Historic Site. Henry Wadsworth Longfellow—the poet whose stirring renditions about the Village Blacksmith, Evangeline, Hiawatha, and Paul Revere's midnight ride thrilled 19th-century America—once lived in this elegant mansion. The house and park reopened in 2002 after a multiyear renovation project; call to confirm hours and admission. ⊠ *105 Brattle St.,,* ☎ *617/876–4491,* WEB *www.nps.gov/long.* ⌸ *$3.* ☉ *May–Oct., Wed.–Sun. 10–4:30.*

⑧ Massachusetts Institute of Technology. MIT, at Kendall Square, occupies 135 acres 1½ mi southeast of Harvard, bordering the Charles River.

The West Campus has some extraordinary buildings: the Kresge Auditorium, designed by Eero Saarinen with a curving roof and unusual thrust, rests on three, instead of four, points; the nondenominational MIT Chapel is a circular Saarinen design. Free campus tours leave from the **MIT Information Center** on weekdays at 10 and 2. ⊠ *77 Massachusetts Ave.,* ☎ *617/253–1000; 617/253–4795 information center;* WEB *web.mit.edu.*

MIT Museum. A place where art and science meet, the museum showcases photos, paintings, and scientific instruments and memorabilia. A popular ongoing exhibit is "The Hall of Hacks," a look at the pranks MIT students have played over the years. Most notable is a rare photo of Oliver Reed Smoot Jr., a 1958 MIT Lambda Chi Alpha pledge. Smoot's future fraternity brothers used the diminutive freshman to measure the distance of the nearby Harvard Bridge, which spans the Charles. Every 5 ft or so became "One Smoot." To this day, the markings remain painted on the bridge. ⊠ *265 Massachusetts Ave.,* ☎ *617/253–4444,* WEB *web.mit.edu/museum.* 🖭 *$5.* ⊙ *Tues.–Fri. 10–5, weekends noon–5.*

➌ **Peabody Museum of Archaeology and Ethnology.** The Peabody holds one of the world's most outstanding anthropological collections; exhibits focus on Native American and Central and South American cultures. The admission fee includes entrance to the ☞ **Harvard Museum of Natural History** as well. ⊠ *11 Divinity Ave.,* ☎ *617/496–1027,* WEB *www.peabody.harvard.edu.* 🖭 *$6.50; free Sun. 9–noon, and Wed. 3–5 (Sept.–May only).* ⊙ *Daily 9–5.*

Radcliffe Institute for Advanced Study. The famed women's college, with its lovely, serene yard, was founded in 1879 and wedded to Harvard University in 1977. It was subsumed under Harvard in 1999 and continues to specialize in gender issues. The **Schlesinger Library** (☎ 617/495–8647), in Radcliffe Yard, houses more than 50,000 volumes on the history of women in America, including the papers of Harriet Beecher Stowe, Julia Child, Betty Friedan, and other notable females. The library is also known for its extensive culinary collections. ⊠ *10 Garden St.,* ☎ *617/495–8601,* WEB *www.radcliffe.edu.*

Dining

Back Bay/Beacon Hill
CONTEMPORARY

$$$$ ✕ **Biba.** Chef and owner Lydia Shire's head-turning cuisine remains
★ the cream of Boston's culinary crop. And for good reason: the adventurous menu encourages inventive combinations, unusual cuts of meat, haute comfort food, and big postmodern desserts. Indulge in "classic lobster pizza" or challenge your palate with vanilla chicken with chestnut puree. Try to finagle a seat near the windows on the second floor for a terrific view of the Public Garden. ⊠ *272 Boylston St., Back Bay,* ☎ *617/426–7878. Reservations essential. AE, D, DC, MC, V.*

$$$$ ✕ **Clio.** Years ago when Ken Oringer opened his snazzy leopard skin–
★ lined hot spot in the tasteful boutique Eliot Hotel, the hordes were fighting over reservations. Things have quieted down since then, but the food hasn't. Luxury ingredients pack the menu, from the now-ubiquitous Hudson Valley foie gras to more-adventurous rarities—for instance, tiny eels called elvers that Oringer has been known to serve when he can get them in season. ⊠ *Eliot Hotel, 370 Commonwealth Ave., Back Bay,* ☎ *617/536–7200. Reservations essential. AE, MC, V.*

$$$$ ✕ **The Federalist.** Now that the initial buzz has calmed, you can actu-
★ ally get a Saturday-night reservation less than a month in advance at this

sophisticated restaurant in the swanky Fifteen Beacon hotel. Chef David Daniels' menu is a melding of modern and traditional that's driven by local ingredients; look for dishes such as native quail breast with foie gras. The wine list, with more than 1,000 entries, is an impressive but expensive proposition. ☒ *Fifteen Beacon hotel, 15 Beacon St., Beacon Hill,* ☎ *617/670–2515. Reservations essential. AE, D, DC, MC, V.*

FRENCH

$$$$ ✕ **L'Espalier.** From sole with black truffles to foie gras with quince,
★ chef-owner Frank McClelland's masterpieces are every bit as impeccable and elegant as the Victorian town house in which they are served. You can skip the opulent menu by choosing a prix-fixe tasting menu, such as the innovative and flat-out fabulous vegetarian dégustation. With two fireplaces and subtle decor in earthy colors, this is one of Boston's most romantic places. ☒ *30 Gloucester St., Back Bay,* ☎ *617/ 262–3023. Reservations essential. AE, D, DC, MC, V. Closed Sun. No lunch.*

$$–$$$$ ✕ **Torch.** A little slice of the Marais hit Charles Street when Evan Deluty and his wife, Candice, opened Torch. Deluty is a keen culinary editor, tweaking dishes with enough ingredients to enhance, but not obscure, the main flavors; witness the sweetly simple seared sea scallops with corn, bacon, and mâche. Delicate roasted potatoes punctuate the decadent Long Island duck breast. Follow it with the thoughtfully chosen cheese plate or a deep-chocolate mousse. ☒ *26 Charles St., Beacon Hill,* ☎ *617/723–5939. Reservations essential. AE, D, DC, MC, V. Closed Mon. No lunch.*

PERSIAN

$$–$$$ ✕ **Lala Rokh.** Persian miniatures and medieval maps cover the walls
★ of this beautifully detailed and delicious fantasy of food and art. The menu focuses on the Azerbaijanian corner that is now northwest Iran, and it includes both exotically flavored specialties and dishes as familiar (but superb here) as eggplant puree, pilaf, kebabs, *fesanjoon* (the classic pomegranate-walnut sauce), and lamb stews. The staff obviously enjoys explaining the menu, and the wine list is well selected for foods that often defy wine matches. ☒ *97 Mt. Vernon St., Beacon Hill,* ☎ *617/720–5511. AE, DC, MC, V.*

SEAFOOD

$–$$$ ✕ **Legal Sea Foods.** What began as a tiny restaurant upstairs over a Cambridge fish market has grown to important regional status, with more than 20 East Coast locations. The hallmark is the freshest possible seafood, whether you have it wood-grilled, in New England chowder, or accompanied by an Asia-inspired sauce. The smoked-bluefish pâté is delectable. A preferred-seating list allows calls ahead. ☒ *26 Park Sq., Theater District,* ☎ *617/426–4444;* ☒ *255 State St., Financial District,* ☎ *617/227–3115;* ☒ *5 Cambridge Center, Kendall Sq., Cambridge,* ☎ *617/864–3400;* ☒ *Logan Airport, Terminal C, East Boston,* ☎ *617/ 569–4622. Reservations not accepted. AE, D, DC, MC, V.*

STEAK

$$$–$$$$ ✕ **Grill 23 & Bar.** Pinstriped suits, dark paneling, comically oversize
★ flatware, and waiters in white jackets give this steak house a posh, men's-club ambience. But the menu is anything other than predictable, offering dishes such as rotisserie tenderloin with Roquefort mashed potatoes. Seafood dishes such as grilled Maine salmon give beef sales a run for their money. Desserts, like the wonderfully tangy lemon cheesecake and the super-rich fallen chocolate soufflé cake, are far above those of the average steak house. ☒ *161 Berkeley St., Back Bay,* ☎ *617/542–2255. Reservations essential. AE, D, DC, MC, V. No lunch.*

Boston Dining and Lodging

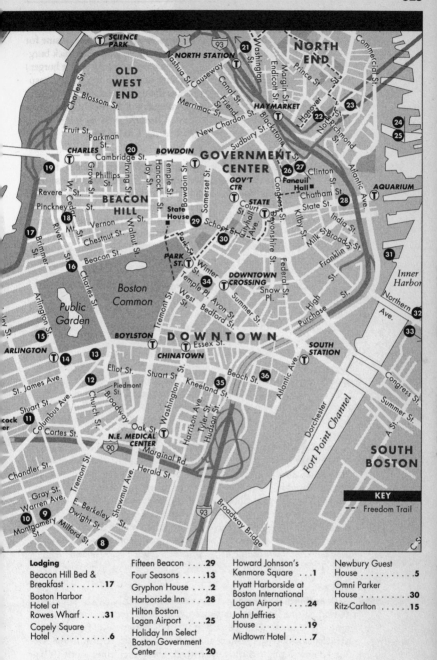

Cambridge

AMERICAN

$–$$ ✕ **Mr. and Mrs. Bartley's Burger Cot[...]** the student metabolism: a huge variety [...] ers, french fries, and onion rings. (The[...] The nonalcoholic Raspberry Lime R[...] berry juice, sweetener, and soda wate[...] tables in a crowded space make it a [...] dropping. ⊠ 1246 Massachusetts A[...] Reservations not accepted. No cre[...]

CONTEMPORARY

$$$–$$$$ ✕ **Harvest Restaurant.** The lavish [...] with a little comfort food—mashe[...] Starters include raw seafood and a [...] clam chowder with finnan haddie [...] lamb are among the recommen[...] tion of Very Important Desserts, a[...] figure Lee Napoli and her up-and-coming protégée, Alice Weib[...] The open kitchen makes some noise, but customers at the ever-popular bar don't seem to mind. ⊠ 44 Brattle St.,at 1 Mifflin Pl., Cambridge, ☎ 617/868–2255. Reservations essential. AE, D, DC, MC, V.

$$$ ✕ **Blue Room.** Totally hip, funky, and Cambridge, the Blue Room, led by Steve Johnson, the convivial owner-chef, blends a host of international cuisines with fresh, local ingredients. Brightly colored furnishings, counters where you can meet others while you eat, and a friendly staff add up to a good-time place that's serious about food. Try the seared scallops with hoisin sauce and sesame, or perhaps the barrel-aged-bourbon crème brûlée with hazelnut biscotti. An extraordinary buffet brunch with grilled meats and vegetables, as well as regular breakfast fare and a gorgeous array of desserts, is served on Sunday. ⊠ 1 Kendall Sq., Cambridge, ☎ 617/494–9034. AE, D, DC, MC, V. No lunch.

$$–$$$ ✕ **East Coast Grill and Raw Bar.** Owner-chef-author Chris Schlesinger
★ built his national reputation on grilled foods and red-hot condiments. The Jamaican jerk, North Carolina pulled pork, and habañero-laced "pasta from Hell" are still here, but this restaurant has made an extraordinary play to establish itself in the front ranks of fish restaurants. Spices and condiments are more restrained, and Schlesinger has compiled a wine list bold and flavorful enough to match the highly spiced food. The dining space is completely informal. Brunch is served on Sunday. ⊠ 1271 Cambridge St., Cambridge, ☎ 617/491–6568. AE, D, MC, V. No lunch.

ECLECTIC

$$$–$$$$ ✕ **Chez Henri.** Although French cuisine with a Cuban twist sound like an odd pairing, the combination works for this sexy, confident restaurant. The dinner menu gets serious with duck tamale and ancho chile, garlicky salsify-oyster bisque, and a creamy, tangy lime tart. At the cozy bar you can sample turnovers, fritters, and grilled three-pork Cuban sandwiches. The place fills quickly with Cantabrigian locals—an interesting mix of students, professors, and sundry intelligentsia. ⊠ 1 Shepard St., Cambridge, ☎ 617/354–8980. AE, DC, MC, V. No lunch.

MEDITERRANEAN

$$$–$$$$ ✕ **Rialto.** The ultraposh dining room continues a pleasant drift from its Mediterranean beginnings toward more French techniques and New England ingredients, such as Maine crab cakes and Macomber turnips (a local, sweet white turnip). But the savory tarts and the Tuscan-style sirloin steak with Portobello and arugula salad are lifetime commitments. ⊠ *Charles Hotel, 1 Bennett St., Harvard Sq., Cambridge,* ☎ *617/661–5050. AE, DC, MC, V. No lunch.*

$$–$$$ ✕ **Casablanca.** Long before *The Rocky Horror Picture Show,* Harvard and Radcliffe types would put on trench coats and head to the Brattle Theatre to see *Casablanca,* rising to recite the Bogart and Bergman lines in unison. Then it was on to this restaurant for more of the same. The path to this local institution is still well worn, thanks to phyllo-wrapped shrimp and grilled quail with almond-honey butter. ⊠ *40 Brattle St., Cambridge,* ☎ *617/876–0999. AE, D, DC, MC, V.*

Charlestown
MEDITERRANEAN

$$$–$$$$ ✕ **Olives.** No longer will you see chef Todd English tending the wood-★ fired brick oven here—these days he's too busy watching over Olives offshoots in New York and elsewhere. But don't worry, English's recipes are in good hands. Witness smart signature offerings such as the appetizer Olives Tart, with goat cheese, marinated olives, caramelized onions, and anchovies. Crowded seating, noise, long lines, and abrupt service only add to the legend. Come early or late or be prepared for an extended wait: dinner reservations are taken only for groups of six or more at 5:30 or 8:30. ⊠ *10 City Sq., Charlestown,* ☎ *617/242–1999. AE, D, DC, MC, V. Closed Sun. No lunch.*

Chinatown
CHINESE

$–$$$$ ✕ **Jumbo Seafood.** Although this Cantonese/Hong Kong–style restaurant has much to be proud of, it's happily unpretentious. Try a whole sea bass with ginger and scallion to see what all the fuss is about. Nonoceanic plates are equally outstanding. The Hong Kong influence results in a lot of fried food; crispy fried calamari with salted pepper is a standout. The waiters are very understanding, though some don't speak English fluently. ⊠ *7 Hudson St., Chinatown,* ☎ *617/542–2823. AE, MC, V.*

Downtown
CONTINENTAL

$$$$ ✕ **Locke-Ober Café.** Biba chef-owner Lydia Shire has taken the reins, giving this Old Boston spot a much-needed update. The ornate woodwork gleams again and the once-stodgy kitchen is turning out classics with flair—and a slightly lighter touch. Traditionalists needn't worry, though; many favorites remain on the menu, including the Indian pudding, which has never been better. There is valet parking after 6 PM. ⊠ *3 Winter Pl., Downtown,* ☎ *617/542–1340. Reservations essential. AE, D, DC, MC, V. No lunch weekends.*

FRENCH

$$$–$$$$ ✕ **Les Zygomates.** *Les zygomates* is the French expression for the ★ muscles on the human face that make you smile—and this combination wine bar–bistro inarguably lives up to its name, with classic French bistro fare that is both simple and simply delicious. The menu beautifully matches the ever-changing wine list, with all wines served by the 2-ounce taste, 6-ounce glass, or bottle. Prix-fixe menus are available at lunch and dinner and could include oysters by the half dozen or pancetta-wrapped venison with roasted pears. ⊠ *129 South St., Downtown,* ☎ *617/542–5108. Reservations essential. AE, D, DC, MC, V. Closed Sun. No lunch Sat.*

Faneuil Hall
AMERICAN

$$–$$$$ ✕ **Union Oyster House.** Established in 1826, this is Boston's oldest continuing restaurant. Consider having what Daniel Webster had—oys-

Cambridge Dining and Lodging

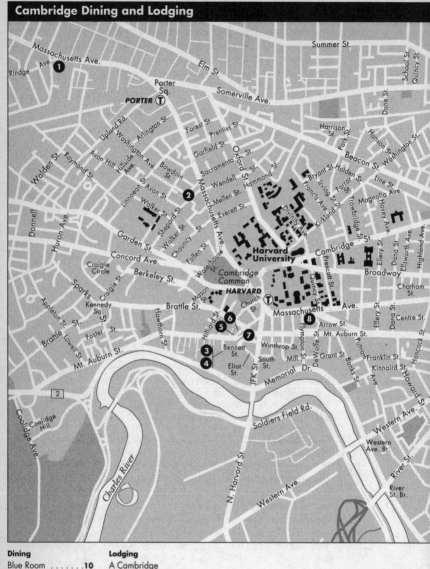

Dining

Blue Room **10**

Casablanca **6**

Chez Henri **2**

Harvest Restaurant . . **5**

East Coast Grill
and Raw Bar **9**

Mr. and Mrs.
Bartley's
Burger Cottage **8**

Rialto **4**

Lodging

A Cambridge
House Bed and
Breakfast **1**

The Charles Hotel . . .**3**

Harvard Square
Hotel **7**

Royal Sonesta
Hotel **11**

ters on the half shell at the ground-floor raw bar, which is the oldest part of the restaurant and still the best. The rooms at the top of the narrow staircase are dark and have low ceilings—very Ye Olde New England—and plenty of nonrestaurant history. Uncomfortably small tables and chairs tend to undermine the simple, decent, but pricey food. There is valet parking after 5:30 PM. ⊠ *41 Union St., Faneuil Hall, ☎ 617/227–2750. AE, D, DC, MC, V.*

$–$$$ ✕ **Durgin Park.** You should be hungry enough to cope with enormous portions, yet not so hungry you can't tolerate a long wait. Durgin Park was serving its same hearty New England fare (Indian pudding, baked beans, corned beef and cabbage, and a prime rib that hangs over the edge of the plate) back when Faneuil Hall was a working market instead of a tourist attraction. The service is famously brusque bordering on rude bordering on good-natured. ⊠ *340 Faneuil Hall Marketplace, North Market Bldg., Faneuil Hall, ☎ 617/227–2038. AE, D, DC, MC, V.*

North End

ITALIAN

$$$–$$$$ ✕ **Bricco.** A sophisticated but unpretentious enclave of nouveau Ital-
★   ian, Bricco has carved out quite a following. And no wonder: the velvety butternut-squash soup alone is argument for a reservation. Simple but well-balanced main courses such as roasted rabbit loin wrapped in pancetta have a sweet smokiness that lingers. You're likely to want to linger in the warm room, too, gazing through the floor-to-ceiling windows while sipping a glass of Sangiovese. ⊠ *241 Hanover St., North End, ☎ 617/248–6800. Reservations essential. AE, D, DC, MC, V.*

$$$–$$$$ ✕ **Mamma Maria.** Don't let the clichéd name fool you: Mamma Maria is one of the most elegant and romantic restaurants in the North End, from the smoked-seafood ravioli appetizer to the innovative sauces and entrées to some of the best desserts in the North End. You can't go wrong with the daily tiramisu or such specials as chocolate-hazelnut cake with a cold champagne sabayon and raspberry compote. ⊠ *3 North Sq., North End, ☎ 617/523–0077. AE, D, DC, MC, V. No lunch.*

South End

CONTEMPORARY

$$$–$$$$ ✕ **Hamersley's Bistro.** Gordon Hamersley has earned a national rep-
★   utation, thanks to such signature dishes as a grilled mushroom-and-garlic sandwich, duck confit, and souffléed lemon custard. He's one of Boston's great chefs and likes to sport a Red Sox cap instead of a toque. His place has a full bar, a café area with 10 tables for walk-ins, and a larger dining room that's a little more formal and decorative than the bar and café, though nowhere near as stuffy as it looks. ⊠ *553 Tremont St., South End, ☎ 617/423–2700. AE, D, DC, MC, V.*

$$ ✕ **Franklin Cafe.** This place has jumped to the head of the class by keeping things simple yet effective. (Its litmus: local chefs gather here to wind down after work.) Try anything with the great chive mashed potatoes. The vibe is generally more bar than restaurant, so be forewarned: it can get loud and smoky. Desserts are not served. ⊠ *278 Shawmut Ave., South End, ☎ 617/350–0010. Reservations not accepted. AE, MC, V. No lunch.*

FRENCH

$–$$ ✕ **Le Gamin.** Equal parts delicious, fast, and inexpensive, Le Gamin
★   makes it hard to understand why crepes haven't permanently caught on in the United States. The small bistro strikes a friendly but French pose with specials such as the buckwheat crepe with smoked salmon, basil cream, and veggies. Sweeter options include a cognac-driven flambé crepe and a sweetly sour fresh-fruit version. Regular sand-

wiches, pastry, and coffee are also good options, but the real draws here are the Parisian pancakes. ⊠ *550 Tremont St., South End,* ☎ *617/654–8969. No credit cards.*

Waterfront

SEAFOOD

$$$–$$$$ ✕ **Anthony's Pier 4.** This massive theme park of a restaurant rolls along, somewhat uncertainly, hosting celebration dinners for Bostonians and visitors alike. The main drawback: the infamous long wait for a table, designed—some complain—to sell drinks. Once seated, you can dine very well on the top-quality seafood if you remember that simple preparations tend to be the best here. The wine list is remarkable, and there are scads of older wines at low prices. Reservations are virtually essential. ⊠ *140 Northern Ave., Waterfront,* ☎ *617/423–6363 or 617/482–6262. Jacket required. AE, D, DC, MC, V.*

$–$$$ ✕ **Barking Crab Restaurant.** It is, believe it or not, a seaside clam shack plunk in the middle of Boston, with a stunning view of the downtown skyscrapers. An outdoor lobster tent in summer, in winter it retreats indoors to a warmhearted version of a waterfront dive, with chestnuts roasting on a cozy woodstove. Look for the classic New England clambake—chowder, lobster, steamed clams, corn on the cob—or the spicier crab boil. The fried food lags. ⊠ *88 Sleeper St. (Northern Ave. Bridge), Waterfront,* ☎ *617/426–2722. AE, DC, MC, V.*

Lodging

If your biggest dilemma is deciding whether to spend $300 per night on old-fashioned elegance or extravagant modernity, you've come to the right city. The bulk of Boston's accommodations are not cheap, yet visitors with limited cash will find choices among the smaller, older establishments; the modern motels; or—perhaps the best option (if you can take early morning small talk)—the bed-and-breakfast inn.

Back Bay

$$$$ 🏨 **Four Seasons.** Overlooking the Public Garden, the Four Seasons is
★ famed for luxurious personal service. Its antiques-filled public spaces are serenely elegant. Guest rooms, even with the king-size beds, swim with space. Suites are enhanced with stereos and private bars. The 51-ft lap pool, inside the health club on the 8th floor, has views of the Public Garden. Aujourd'hui, one of the restaurants here, is among Boston's best. Relax in the Bristol Lounge over afternoon tea or with a cocktail in the evening, when a pianist livens up the bar. Children under 18 stay free in their parents' room. A complimentary car service drops you off downtown. ⊠ *200 Boylston St., Back Bay, 02116,* ☎ *617/338–4400 or 800/332–3442,* FAX *617/423–0154,* WEB *www.fourseasons.com. 202 rooms, 72 suites. 2 restaurants, room service, in-room data ports, in-room safes, minibars, pool, health club, baby-sitting, laundry service, concierge, business services, parking (fee); no-smoking floor. AE, D, DC, MC, V.*

$$$–$$$$ 🏨 **Copley Square Hotel.** This hotel has a quirky turn-of-the-20th-century charm—and its convenient Back Bay location is an all-around plus. The circa 1891 hotel, one of the city's oldest, is busy and comfortable, with winding corridors and repro-antique furniture. The idiosyncratic rooms have a few common denominators (television, coffeemaker) and some have couches. Complimentary afternoon tea is served daily in the lobby. Children under 17 stay free in their parents' room. ⊠ *47 Huntington Ave., Back Bay, 02116,* ☎ *617/536–9000 or 800/225–7062,* FAX *617/267–3547,* WEB *www.copleysquarehotel.com. 143 rooms, 6 suites. 2 restaurants, coffee shop, room service, in-room data ports, in-room safes, 2 bars; no-smoking rooms. AE, D, DC, MC, V.*

$$–$$$$ ⊡ **Midtown Hotel.** Comfortable rooms at reasonable rates and a convenient location near the Prudential Center, Symphony Hall, and the Christian Science Center enable this motel-style hotel to hold its own against its large, expensive neighbors. Rooms have a pale gray and cranberry color scheme; most are doubles, but king-size beds are also available. DSL is also available in each guest room for a small additional fee. Children under 18 stay free in their parents' room. ⊠ *220 Huntington Ave., Back Bay, 02115,* ☎ *617/262–1000 or 800/343–1177,* ℻ *617/262–8739,* ⊞ *www.midtownhotel.com. 159 rooms. Restaurant, in-room data ports, pool, hair salon, baby-sitting, business services, free parking; no-smoking rooms. AE, D, DC, MC, V.*

$$–$$$ ⊡ **Newbury Guest House.** This elegant redbrick and brownstone 1882
★   row house is wildly successful because it's smartly managed, well furnished, and on Boston's most fashionable shopping street—be sure to book a few months in advance. Rooms with queen-size beds, natural pine floors, and elegant reproduction Victorian furnishings open off an oak staircase; prints from the Museum of Fine Arts enliven the walls. Some rooms have bay windows; others have decorative fireplaces. Limited parking is available at $15 for 24 hours, a good deal for the area. ⊠ *261 Newbury St., Back Bay, Boston 02116,* ☎ *617/437–7666 or 800/437–7668,* ℻ *617/262–4243,* ⊞ *www.newburyguesthouse.com. 32 rooms. In-room data ports, parking (fee). AE, D, DC, MC, V. CP.*

Beacon Hill

$$$$ ⊡ **Fifteen Beacon.** At this stylish boutique hotel, inside a 1903 Beaux
★   Arts building, old and new tastes are carefully juxtaposed—for instance, the lobby has cage elevators and a newel post, while an abstract painting dominates the sitting area. Choose from two-room suites or convertible adjoining rooms. The rooms come with many small luxuries, from fresh flowers to 300-thread-count sheets. All are done in soothing taupe, cream, and espresso shades, and each has a four-poster queen-size bed, a gas fireplace, and surround-sound stereo. Bathrooms have whirlpool tubs, huge mirrors, and heated towel bars. ⊠ *15 Beacon St., Beacon Hill, 02108,* ☎ *617/670–1500 or 617/982–3226,* ℻ *617/670–2525,* ⊞ *www.xvbeacon.com. 59 rooms, 2 suites. Restaurant, room service, in-room data ports, in-room safes, minibars, gym, bar, concierge, parking (fee). AE, D, DC, MC, V.*

$$$–$$$$ ⊡ **Beacon Hill Bed and Breakfast.** Staying at this six-story Victorian row house on Beacon Hill gives you a tiny taste of the elegant Brahmin lifestyle. The front overlooks the Gothic Revival Church of the Advent and a narrow cobblestone street with gaslights. From the rear, bay windows look out on the Charles River Esplanade. The three guest rooms are huge—one has a built-in bookcase, and all include sofa beds, Victorian antiques, Oriental rugs, and private bathrooms. Parking is scarce (many guests use the garage under the Common), but shops, restaurants, and the T are all within walking distance. ⊠ *27 Brimmer St., Beacon Hill, Boston 02108,* ☎ *617/523–7376. 3 rooms. No smoking. No credit cards. BP.*

$$–$$$$ ⊡ **Holiday Inn Select Boston Government Center.** This business-class hotel sits near Massachusetts General Hospital, state and city offices, and Beacon Hill. A brisk 10-minute walk takes you to Faneuil Hall, the FleetCenter, the Boston Common, or even across Longfellow Bridge into Cambridge. The meeting space on the 15th floor offers great views of the city through floor-to-ceiling windows. Children under 12 stay free in their parents' room. ⊠ *5 Blossom St., Old West End, 02114,* ☎ *617/742–7630 or 800/465–4329,* ℻ *617/742–4192,* ⊞ *www. holiday-inn.com. 303 rooms, 2 suites. Restaurant, room service, in-room data ports, pool, gym, bar, dry cleaning, laundry facilities, concierge, parking (fee); no-smoking floor. AE, D, DC, MC, V.*

$–$$$
★ **John Jeffries House.** Once a housing facility for nurses, this turn-of-the-20th-century building across from Massachusetts General Hospital is now an elegant four-story inn. The Federal-style double parlor has a cluster of floral-pattern chairs and sofas where you can relax with afternoon tea or coffee (Continental breakfast is also served here.) Guest rooms are furnished with handsome upholstered pieces, and nearly all have pale-green kitchenettes. Triple-glazed windows block virtually all noise from busy Charles Circle; many rooms have views of the Charles River. ⊠ *14 David G. Mugar Way, Beacon Hill, 02114,* ☎ *617/367–1866,* ℻ *617/742–0313. 23 rooms, 23 suites. Parking (fee); no smoking. AE, D, DC, MC, V. CP.*

Cambridge

$$$$
★ **Charles Hotel.** This first-class hotel is right on Harvard Square. The New England Shaker interior is contemporary yet homey; antique quilts done by local artists hang throughout. Guest rooms come with terry robes, quilted down comforters, and Bose radios. If you're looking for a river or skyline view, ask for something above the seventh floor. Rooms facing the courtyard look down on an herb garden. Both of the hotel's restaurants—Rialto and Henrietta's Table—are excellent, and the Regattabar jazz club attracts world-class musicians. Children under 16 stay free in their parents' room. ⊠ *1 Bennett St., Cambridge 02138,* ☎ *617/864–1200 or 800/882–1818,* ℻ *617/864–5715,* 𝚆𝙴𝙱 *www.charleshotel.com. 293 rooms, 44 suites. 2 restaurants, café, room service, in-room data ports, in-room safes, minibars, indoor pool, health club, spa, 3 bars, library, nightclub, baby-sitting, dry cleaning, laundry service, concierge, business services, meeting room, parking (fee); no-smoking floors. AE, DC, MC, V.*

$$$$
★ **Royal Sonesta Hotel.** The Sonesta's East Cambridge location makes it a good base for visiting the Museum of Science or strolling along the Charles. The 10-floor building offers superb views of Beacon Hill and the Boston skyline across the Charles River. An impressive collection of modern art is spread throughout the hotel, and the guest rooms' earth tones keep things mellow. All rooms include CD clock radios, coffeemakers, Sony Playstation, and high-speed Internet access. Children under 18 stay free in their parents' room, and the hotel offers great family excursion packages such as Summerfest, which includes boat rides, ice cream, and free bicycle rental. ⊠ *5 Cambridge Pkwy., Cambridge 02142,* ☎ *617/806–4200 or 800/766–3782,* ℻ *617/806–4232,* 𝚆𝙴𝙱 *www.sonesta.com/boston. 377 rooms, 23 suites. 2 restaurants, room service, in-room data ports, minibars, pool, health club, spa, bicycles, 2 bars, dry cleaning, business services, parking (fee); no-smoking rooms. AE, D, DC, MC, V.*

$$–$$$$
A Cambridge House Bed and Breakfast. A gracious 1892 Greek Revival home listed on the National Register of Historic Places, A Cambridge House is on busy Mass Ave. but set well back from the road. Inside is richly carved cherry paneling, a grand cherry fireplace, elegant Victorian antiques, and polished wood floors overlaid with Oriental rugs. One of the 15 antiques-filled guest rooms has fabric-covered walls, and many have gas fireplaces or four-poster canopy beds. Rooms in the adjacent carriage house are smaller, but all have fireplaces. A full breakfast, hors d'oeuvres, and beverages are all complimentary. Harvard Square is fairly distant, but public transportation is nearby. ⊠ *2218 Massachusetts Ave., Cambridge 02140,* ☎ *617/491–6300 or 800/232–9989,* ℻ *617/868–2848,* 𝚆𝙴𝙱 *www.acambridgehouse.com. 15 rooms. Cable TV, free parking; no smoking, no kids under 6. AE, D, MC, V. BP.*

$$–$$$$
Harvard Square Hotel. Casual and family-friendly, this hotel is an affordable option in the heart of Harvard Square, just steps from the

neighborhood's many restaurants, shops, and lively street corners. Rooms are simple but clean and decorated in a pleasing classic burgundy and cream style. The desk clerks are particularly helpful, assisting with everything from faxing to making restaurant reservations. There's a computer with Internet access in the lobby. Continental breakfast is available for an additional charge. Children under 16 stay free in their parents' room. ⊠ *110 Mt. Auburn St., Cambridge 02138,* ☎ *617/864–5200 or 800/ 458–5886,* ℻ *617/864–2409,* WEB *www.theinnatharvard.com. 73 rooms. Café, in-room data ports, laundry service, car rental, parking (fee); nosmoking rooms. AE, D, DC, MC, V.*

Downtown

$$$$ ⊞ **Boston Harbor Hotel at Rowes Wharf.** Travelers who arrive from
★ Logan Airport via water shuttle come straight to the back door of this deluxe harborside hotel and its dramatic entrance: an 80-ft archway topped by a rotunda. The lobby, equally stunning, has marble archways and antique maps. All guest rooms have marble bathrooms, custom-made desks, 300-thread-count sheets, and down comforters. The Rowes Wharf Restaurant offers a spectacular, if pricey, Sunday brunch. Call ahead for up-to-the-minute driving directions, as the hotel is near the heart of the Big Dig construction and road closings are common. Children under 18 stay free in their parents' room. ⊠ *70 Rowes Wharf, Downtown, 02110,* ☎ *617/439–7000 or 800/752–7077,* ℻ *617/330–9450,* WEB *www.bhh.com. 204 rooms, 26 suites. 2 restaurants, café, room service, minibars, indoor pool, health club, hot tub, massage, sauna, spa, steam room, bar, shop, concierge, business services, meeting room, airport shuttle, parking (fee); no-smoking rooms. AE, D, DC, MC, V.*

$$–$$$$ ⊞ **Omni Parker House.** The oldest continuously operating hotel in the United States, the Parker House's original building opened in 1856 and counted Charles Dickens among its guests (his first reading of *A Christmas Carol* was in the Parker). A Colonial style adorns the lobby and guest rooms, which have custom-built furniture to accommodate the rooms' small size. Parker's Restaurant is known for two things: Parker House rolls and Boston cream pie, both of which were invented here and are still served today. This historic hotel stands opposite old City Hall, on the Freedom Trail. ⊠ *60 School St., Downtown, 02108,* ☎ *617/227–8600 or 800/843–6664,* ℻ *617/742–5729,* WEB *www. omnihotels.com. 551 rooms, 21 suites. Restaurant, room service, inroom data ports, gym, 2 bars, laundry service, concierge, business services, meeting room, parking (fee). AE, D, DC, MC, V.*

$–$$$$ ⊞ **Harborside Inn.** What was once a 19th-century mercantile warehouse
★ is now a plush, sedate inn with exposed brick and granite walls, hardwood floors, Turkish rugs, and Victorian-style furnishings. Many of the snug, variously shaped rooms have windows overlooking the small, open lobby, which extends eight stories up to the roof. (If an outdoor view is important to you, request a room with a city view.) The inn's Margo bistro is a popular lunchtime spot. Children under 12 stay free in their parents' room (though the inn is not especially geared toward families). Harborside is closed for the week around Christmas. ⊠ *185 State St., Downtown, 02109,* ☎ *617/723–7500,* ℻ *617/670–6015,* WEB *www.hagopianhotels.com. 52 rooms, 2 suites. Restaurant, café, room service, in-room data ports, gym, bar, concierge; no-smoking floor. AE, D, DC, MC, V.*

Kenmore Square

$$$–$$$$ ⊞ **Gryphon House.** All the suites in this four-story 19th-century brown-
★ stone are thematically decorated; one evokes a Victorian parlor, another a medieval castle. Among the many amenities—including gas fireplace, wet bar, TV/VCR, CD player, free local calls, and private voice

mail—the enormous bathrooms with oversize Kohler tubs and separate showers are the best. Even the staircase is extraordinary: a 19th-century wallpaper mural, *El Dorado*, wraps along the walls. (There is no elevator.) Trompe l'oeil paintings and murals by local artist Michael Ernest Kirk decorate the common spaces and some rooms. ⊠ *9 Bay State Rd., Kenmore Sq., 02215,* ☎ *617/375–9003,* ⅢＸ *617/425–0716,* Ⅲᴱ *www.innboston.com. 8 suites. In-room data ports, refrigerators, free parking; no-smoking rooms. AE, D, DC, MC, V. CP.*

$$–$$$$ ⊞ **Howard Johnson's Kenmore Square.** Convenient to Boston University's campus, Fenway Park, and the city's vibrant nightlife scene stretched along Lansdowne Street, this Howard Johnson has many rooms with balcony views of the city or the Charles River. Children under 18 stay free in their parents' room. Because of its proximity to BU, the hotel can fill up with students, especially during breaks, and they may not share your desire for a peaceful night's sleep (although the hotel claims to control noise levels by concentrating students in one section of the building). ⊠ *575 Commonwealth Ave., Kenmore Sq., 02215,* ☎ *617/267–3100 or 800/654–2000,* ⅢＸ *617/424–1045,* Ⅲᴱ *www.hojo. com. 178 rooms, 1 suite. Restaurant, in-room data ports, pool, lobby lounge, baby-sitting, free parking; no-smoking rooms. AE, D, DC, MC, V.*

Logan Airport

$$–$$$$ ⊞ **Hilton Boston Logan Airport.** You can practically see duty free from here—the hotel is right on the grounds of Logan Airport. Old maps of Boston hang in the guest rooms and public spaces, and generous amounts of wood are used throughout, from the lobby's paneling to the doors of the guest rooms. All rooms have granite counters in the baths, desks with ergonomic chairs, and high-speed Internet access (for an additional fee). Besides 24-hour shuttle service to the airport, there's a skywalk to some terminals. The Berkshire's restaurant has a New England–style menu, and there's an Irish pub with nightly live music. Children under 17 stay free in their parents' room. ⊠ *85 Terminal Rd., Logan Airport (East Boston), 02128,* ☎ *617/568–6700,* ⅢＸ *617/568–6800,* Ⅲᴱ *www.hilton.com. 555 rooms, 4 suites. Restaurant, coffee shop, room service, in-room data ports, minibars, indoor pool, health club, massage, sauna, spa, steam room, pub, concierge floor, business services, meeting room, parking (fee). AE, D, DC, MC, V.*

$$–$$$$ ⊞ **Hyatt Harborside at Boston International Logan Airport.** A 15-story glass structure punctuates this luxury hotel, on a point of land separating Boston Harbor from the Atlantic Ocean. Half of the rooms have sweeping views of either the Boston skyline or the ocean. It's easy to get anywhere from here; the Hyatt operates its own 24-hour shuttle to all Logan Airport terminals and the airport T stop, and guests get a discount on the water shuttle that runs between the airport and downtown. All rooms are soundproof. The hotel's partnership with Thrifty car rental allows for convenient pick-up and drop-off services. ⊠ *101 Harborside Dr., Logan Airport (East Boston), 02128,* ☎ *617/ 568–1234 or 800/233–1234,* ⅢＸ *617/567–8856,* Ⅲᴱ *www.boston. hyatt.com. 259 rooms, 11 suites. Restaurant, room service, in-room data ports, indoor pool, gym, sauna, bar, lounge, dry cleaning, laundry service, concierge, business services, parking (fee); no-smoking floors. AE, D, DC, MC, V.*

Nightlife and the Arts

Nightlife

Good sources of nighttime happenings are the *Boston Globe* Thursday "Calendar" section, the *Boston Herald* Friday "Scene" section, and the listings in the *Boston Phoenix*, a free weekly that comes out on Thursday. The Friday "Music" and Sunday "Arts" sections in the *Boston Globe* and the Saturday and Sunday "Arts" sections in the *Boston Herald* also contain recommendations for the week's top events. *Boston* magazine's "On the Town" gives a somewhat less detailed but still useful monthly overview. Call clubs to check cover charges, hours, and theme nights.

BARS AND LOUNGES

Black Rose (✉ 160 State St., Faneuil Hall, ☎ 617/742–2286), an authentic Irish pub, draws as many tourists as locals, but music by contemporary and traditional Irish musicians makes it worth the crowds. **Boston Beer Works** (✉ 61 Brookline Ave., Fens; ✉ 112 Canal St., West End, ☎ 617/536–2337) serves up its own brews to students, young professionals, and baseball fans from nearby Fenway Park. **Bull & Finch Pub** (✉ 84 Beacon St., Back Bay, ☎ 617/227–9605), best known for inspiring the TV series *Cheers,* still often attracts long lines of tourists and students. **John Harvard's Brew House** (✉ 33 Dunster St., Harvard Sq., Cambridge, ☎ 617/868–3585), an English-style pub, dispenses a range of ales, lagers, pilsners, and stouts brewed on the premises. **Sonsie** (✉ 327 Newbury St., Back Bay, ☎ 617/351–2500) is a European-style see-and-be-seen bistro. The bar crowd is full of trendy, cosmopolitan types and professionals; in warm weather, the crowd spills out to sidewalk tables. **Top of the Hub** (✉ Prudential Center, 800 Boylston St., Back Bay, ☎ 617/536–1775) has live jazz and fabulous views, making the steep drink prices worthwhile.

BLUES, RHYTHM AND BLUES, FOLK CLUBS

Club Passim (✉ 47 Palmer St., Harvard Sq., Cambridge, ☎ 617/492–5300 or 617/492–7679) is one of the country's most famous venues for live folk music. The spare, light basement room has closely spaced tables and a separate coffee bar–restaurant counter. **House of Blues** (✉ 96 Winthrop St., Harvard Sq., Cambridge, ☎ 617/491–2583) hosts live blues nightly at 10; this ramshackle house has a gospel brunch on Sunday. **Johnny D's Uptown** (✉ 17 Holland St., Davis Sq., Somerville, ☎ 617/776–9667 or 617/776–2004) books an eclectic mix of performers and musical styles: Cajun, country, Latin, blues, jazz, swing, acoustic, and more.

CAFÉS AND COFFEEHOUSES

Caffè Vittoria (✉ 296 Hanover St., North End, ☎ 617/227–7606) is the biggest and the best of the Italian neighborhood's cafés. Stop in after dinner for coffee and tiramisu or cannoli. **Tealuxe** (✉ 0 Brattle St., Harvard Sq., Cambridge, ☎ 617/441–0077) is a "tea bar," with Bombay flare, more than 100 different herbal and traditional blends, an assortment of teatime snacks—and just one type of coffee. **1369 Coffee House** (✉ 757 Massachusetts Ave., Central Sq., ☎ 617/576–4600; ✉ 1369 Cambridge St., Inman Sq., Cambridge, ☎ 617/576–1369) serves coffee and tea in individual pots, as well as soups, salads, sandwiches, and pastries. The coffeehouse even provides outlets for portable computers.

COMEDY

Comedy Connection (✉ Faneuil Hall Marketplace, 245 Quincy Market, Faneuil Hall, ☎ 617/248–9700) books local and nationally known acts nightly. **Dick Doherty's Comedy Vault** (✉ 124 Boylston St., Downtown, ☎ 617/482–0110 or 781/729–2565), tucked away in a former bank vault, presents sketch, stand-up, improv, and open-mike comedy Thursday–Sunday nights, with a cover charge. **ImprovBoston** (✉ Back Alley Theater, 1253 Cambridge St., Cambridge, ☎ 617/576–1253) presents improv competitions and its own TV-style sitcom show—compiled on the spot from suggestions—Thursday through Saturday nights.

Reservations are essential. **Nick's Comedy Stop** (✉ 100 Warrenton St., Theater District, ☎ 617/482–0930) presents local comics Thursday–Saturday nights. Reservations are essential.

DANCE CLUBS

Axis (✉ 13 Lansdowne St., Fens, ☎ 617/262–2437) has high-energy dancing for more than 1,000 people. Friday is "X Night," starring DJs from alternative radio station WFNX. Dress creatively or in black rather than in khakis or jeans. Cover charge varies. **Man Ray** (✉ 21 Brookline St., Central Sq., Cambridge, ☎ 617/864–0400) is home to Boston's alternative and goth scene, with industrial, house, techno, disco, and trance music. Friday night is "Fetish Night." Wear black; dress code is enforced. The club is closed Sunday–Tuesday. The **Roxy** (✉ 279 Tremont St., Theater District, ☎ 617/338–7699), one of Boston's biggest nightclubs, is renowned for theme events such as its reggae, salsa, swing, and Top 40 nights. **Trattoria Il Panino & Club** (✉ 295 Franklin St., Downtown, ☎ 617/338–1000) attracts mostly well-heeled professionals. The multifloor complex offers informal and formal dining, a jazz bar, and dancing. Go dressy.

GAY AND LESBIAN CLUBS

For more on gay and lesbian nightlife, see the *Boston Phoenix* or *Bay Windows* newspaper.

Trendy **Buzz Boston/Europa** (✉ 51–67 Stuart St., Theater District, ☎ 617/482–3939), known as Europa most nights, attracts a well-heeled, largely Euro crowd. On Saturday it becomes Buzz Boston, catering to a gay crowd. It's 21-plus every night. **Club Café & Lounge** (✉ 209 Columbus Ave., South End, ☎ 617/536–0966) is among the smartest spots in town for gay men and lesbians. It has a stylish restaurant, a piano bar, and a video bar.

JAZZ

Regattabar (✉ Charles Hotel, Bennett and Eliot Sts., Harvard Sq., Cambridge, ☎ 617/864–1200; 617/876–7777 tickets) headlines top names in jazz. Reservations are essential. **Ryles Jazz Club** (✉ 212 Hampshire St., Inman Sq., Cambridge, ☎ 617/876–9330) is one of the best places for both new and established performers, with a different group playing on each floor. Sunday jazz brunches are a local institution. **Wally's Café** (✉ 427 Massachusetts Ave., South End, ☎ 617/424–1408) has a loyal clientele hooked on jazz and blues. The performers are mostly locals. Wally's is open every night of the year.

ROCK CLUBS

Avalon (✉ 15 Lansdowne St., Fens, ☎ 617/262–2424) hosts concerts by alternative, rock, and dance acts, then turns into a dance club. Themes include "Euro Night," Top 40, and techno. Ticketmaster (☎ 617/931–2000) sells advance tickets. **Lizard Lounge** (✉ 1667 Massachusetts Ave., between Harvard and Porter Sqs., Cambridge, ☎ 617/547–0759), one of the area's hottest nightspots, presents national and lesser-known folk, rock, acid jazz, and pop bands Wednesday–Saturday and a "poetry jam" on Sunday. **Middle East Café** (✉ 472 Massachusetts Ave., Central Sq., Cambridge, ☎ 617/497–0576 or 617/864–3278, WEB www.mideastclub.com) showcases live local and national acts as well as belly dancing, folk, jazz, and even the occasional country-tinged rock band. There's a restaurant upstairs.

The Arts

BosTix (☎ 617/482–2849, WEB www.bostix.org) is Boston's official entertainment information center and the city's largest ticket agency. It is a full-price Ticketmaster outlet, and beginning at 11 AM, it sells half-price tickets for same-day performances; the "menu board" in front of the booth announces the available events. Only cash and traveler's checks are accepted. ⊠ *Faneuil Hall Marketplace.* ☉ *Tues.–Sat. 10–6, Sun. 11–4;* ⊠ *Copley Sq., near corner of Boylston and Dartmouth Sts.* ☉ *Mon.–Sat. 10–6, Sun. 11–4.*

NEXT Ticketing (☎ 617/423–6398), a Boston-based outlet, handles tickets for many area theaters and nightclubs. The service, which uses a completely automated 24-hour ticket reservation system, also sells tickets on-line. **Ticketmaster** (☎ 617/931–2000 or 617/931–2787, WEB www.ticketmaster.com) allows phone charges to major credit cards, weekdays 9 AM–10 PM, weekends 9–8. There are no refunds or exchanges, and you pay a service charge. It also has outlets in local stores; call for the nearest address.

DANCE

Boston Ballet (⊠ 19 Clarendon St., South End, ☎ 617/695–6950 or 800/447–7400), the city's premier dance company, performs classical and modern works, primarily at the Wang Center. Its annual *Nutcracker* is a Boston holiday tradition. **Dance Complex** (⊠ 536 Massachusetts Ave., Central Sq., Cambridge, ☎ 617/547–9363) presents varied dance styles by local and visiting choreographers in its own studios and other venues.

FILM

The **Brattle Theatre** (⊠ 40 Brattle St., Harvard Sq., Cambridge, ☎ 617/876–6837, WEB www.brattlefilm.org) is a small downstairs cinema catering to classic-movie buffs and fans of new foreign and independent films. **Harvard Film Archive** (⊠ Carpenter Center for the Visual Arts, 24 Quincy St., Cambridge, ☎ 617/495–4700, WEB www.harvardfilmarchive.org) screens the works of directors not usually shown at commercial cinemas.

MUSIC

Berklee Performance Center (⊠ 136 Massachusetts Ave., Back Bay, ☎ 617/266–1400; 617/266–7455 recorded information) is best known for its jazz programs, but it also hosts folk performers such as Arlo Guthrie and pop and rock stars such as Bryan Ferry. **Hatch Memorial Shell** (⊠ off Storrow Dr., at the embankment, Beacon Hill, ☎ 617/727–9547) is a jewel of an acoustic shell where the Boston Pops perform free summer concerts. **Jordan Hall at the New England Conservatory** (⊠ 30 Gainsborough St., Back Bay, ☎ 617/536–2412), ideal for everything from chamber music to a full orchestra, is home to the Boston Philharmonic. **Kresge Auditorium** (⊠ 42 Massachusetts Ave., Cambridge, ☎ 617/253–2826 or 617/253–4003) is MIT's hall for pop and classical concerts. **Orpheum Theatre** (⊠ 1 Hamilton Pl., off Tremont St., Theater District, ☎ 617/679–0810) is a popular forum for national and local rock acts. **Pickman Recital Hall** (⊠ Longy School of Music, 27 Garden St., Cambridge, ☎ 617/876–0956) is Longy School of Music's excellent acoustical setting for smaller ensembles and recitals. **Symphony Hall** (⊠ 301 Massachusetts Ave., Back Bay, ☎ 617/266–1492 or 800/274–8499), one of the world's most perfect acoustical settings, is home to the Boston Symphony Orchestra, conducted by Seiji Ozawa, and the Boston Pops, conducted by Keith Lockhart.

OPERA

Boston Lyric Opera Company (⊠ Shubert Theatre, 265 Tremont St., Theater District, ☎ 617/542–6772 or 800/447–7400) stages four full productions each season, which usually includes one 20th-century work. During the 2001–2002 season, it performed Verdi's *Don Carlos* and Puccini's *La Bohème.*

PERFORMANCE VENUES

The **Colonial Theatre** (✉ 106 Boylston St., Theater District, ☎ 617/426–9366) has welcomed stars from W. C. Fields to Fanny Brice to Katharine Hepburn. More recently, the theater welcomed *The Graduate*, starring Kathleen Turner, Jason Biggs, and Alicia Silverstone. **Shubert Theatre** (✉ 265 Tremont St., Theater District, ☎ 617/482–9393, WEB www.wangcenter.org) has become the home for the Boston Lyric Opera Company. **Wang Center for the Performing Arts** (✉ 270 Tremont St., Theater District, ☎ 617/482–9393, WEB www.wangcenter.org) stages large-scale productions, such as the Boston Ballet season, and concerts by performers like Harry Connick Jr. **Wilbur Theatre** (✉ 246 Tremont St., Theater District, ☎ 617/423–4008, WEB www.broadwayinboston.com), the smallest of the traditional theater houses in the Theater District, has staged such off-Broadway hits as *Stomp*.

THEATER

The **Boston Center for the Arts** (✉ 539 Tremont St., South End, ☎ 617/426–7700) houses more than a dozen quirky low-budget troupes in four spaces. **Charles Playhouse** (✉ 74 Warrenton St., Theater District, ☎ 617/426–6912) presents two long-running shows: the avant-garde *Blue Man Group* (☎ 617/426–6912) and *Shear Madness* (☎ 617/426–5225), an audience-participation whodunit. **Emerson Majestic Theatre** (✉ 219 Tremont St., Theater District, ☎ 617/824–8000) hosts everything from dance to drama to classical concerts. The **Huntington Theatre Company** (✉ 264 Huntington Ave., Back Bay, ☎ 617/266–0800, WEB www.bu.edu/huntington), affiliated with Boston University, performs a mix of established 20th-century plays and classics. The **Loeb Drama Center** (✉ 64 Brattle St., Harvard Sq., Cambridge, ☎ 617/495–2268 or 617/547–8300, WEB www.amrep.org) is home to the acclaimed American Repertory Theater, which produces classic and experimental works.

Outdoor Activities and Sports

Participant Sports

Most public recreational facilities, including skating rinks and tennis courts, are operated by the **Metropolitan District Commission** (MDC; ✉ 20 Somerset St., ☎ 617/727–5114 ext. 555 events hot line, WEB www.state.ma.us/mdc).

BIKING

The **Dr. Paul Dudley White Bikeway,** approximately 18 mi long, follows both banks of the Charles River as it winds from Watertown Square to the Museum of Science. **Community Bicycle Supply** (✉ 496 Tremont St., at E. Berkeley St., South End, ☎ 617/542–8623) rents cycles from April through September, at rates of $20 for 24 hours or $5 per hour (minimum two hours).

BILLIARDS

Flat Top Johnny's (✉ 1 Kendall Sq., Bldg. 200, Cambridge, ☎ 617/494–9565) is the hippest billiards hall around. Members of Boston's better local bands often hang out here on their nights off. At **Jillian's Billiard Club** (✉ 145 Ipswich St., Fens, ☎ 617/437–0300, WEB www.jilliansboston.com) businesspeople bump elbows with students and locals around 56 high-quality pool tables. Professional lessons are available, and the three bars, café, darts, shuffleboard, table tennis, and high-tech games keep everyone entertained.

IN-LINE SKATING

From April through October, **Memorial Drive** on the Cambridge side of the Charles River is closed to auto traffic on Sunday 11 AM–7 PM, when the area between the Western Avenue Bridge and Eliot Bridge is transformed into **Riverbend Park.** Downstream, on the Boston side of the river, the **Esplanade** area swarms with skaters (and joggers) on weekends. **Beacon Hill Skate Shop** (⊠ 135 S. Charles St., off Tremont St., near the Wang Center for the Performing Arts, South End, ☎ 617/482–7400) rents blades and safety equipment for $8 per hour or $20 for 24 hours. You need a credit card for a deposit.

PHYSICAL FITNESS

The extensive facilities of the **Greater Boston YMCA** (⊠ 316 Huntington Ave., Fens, ☎ 617/536–7800) are available for $5 per day to members of other YMCAs in the Boston area. If you have out-of-state YMCA membership, you can use the Boston Y free for up to two weeks. Nonmembers pay $10 a day or $75 for one month. The site has pools, squash and racquetball courts, cardiovascular equipment, free weights, aerobics, track, and sauna.

Spectator Sports

The **Boston Bruins** (⊠ 1 FleetCenter, West End, ☎ 617/624–1000; 617/931–2222 Ticketmaster) of the National Hockey League hit the ice at the FleetCenter from October until April. The **Boston Celtics** (⊠ FleetCenter, West End, ☎ 617/624–1000; 617/931–2222 Ticketmaster) of the National Basketball Association shoot their hoops at the FleetCenter from October to May. The **Boston Red Sox** (⊠ Fenway Park, Fens, ☎ 617/267–1700 tickets) play American League baseball at Fenway Park from April to early October. The **New England Patriots** (⊠ CMGI Field, 60 Washington St. Foxboro, ☎ 508/543–1776 or 800/543–1776) of the National Football League play their games at CMGI Field in Foxborough, 45 minutes south of the city, from August (exhibition games) to January.

Every Patriots' Day (the Monday closest to April 19), fans gather along the Hopkinton-to-Boston route of the **Boston Marathon** to cheer the more than 12,000 runners from all over the world. The race ends near Copley Square in the Back Bay. For information, call the Boston Athletic Association (☎ 617/236–1652).

Shopping

Boston's shops are generally open Monday–Saturday 9 or 10–6 or 7 and Sunday noon–6. Many stay open until 8 PM one night a week, usually Thursday. Malls are open Monday–Saturday 9 or 10–8 or 9 and Sunday noon–6. Most stores accept major credit cards and traveler's checks. There is no state sales tax on clothing. However, there is a 5% luxury tax on clothes priced higher than $175 per item; the tax is levied on the amount in excess of $175. The daily newspapers, the *Globe* and the *Herald,* are the best places to learn about sales.

Shopping Districts

The best shopping is in the area bounded by Quincy Market, the Back Bay, downtown, and Copley Square. Though locals complain that there are too many chain stores, Boston's strength remains its idiosyncratic boutiques, handcrafts shops, and galleries. Although there are few outlet stores in the city, you'll nevertheless find bargains, particularly in the Downtown Crossing area.

BOSTON

Pretty **Charles Street,** one of the oldest streets in the city, is crammed with antiques stores and boutiques, though they're generally a bit pricey, due to their high Beacon Hill rents. **Copley Place** (⊠ 100 Huntington Ave., Back Bay, ☎ 617/369–5000) and the **Prudential Center** are Back Bay malls connected by a glass skywalk over Huntington Avenue. Copley packs more wallet-wallop, while "the Pru" contains moderately priced chain stores. **Downtown Crossing** is a jumble: entrenched independents coexist with prosaic chains, outlets snuggle against downmarket competitors, and pushcarts thrive alongside the city's two largest department stores, Macy's and Filene's (with the famous Filene's Basement beneath it). Historic **Faneuil Hall Marketplace** (☎ 617/338–2323) is an enormous complex that's hugely popular with visitors, perhaps because it successfully combines the familiar with the unique, as such chains as the Disney Store and Banana Republic provide the backdrop for street performers and one of the area's truly great casual dining experiences. In just eight blocks, **Newbury Street** in the Back Bay goes from New York's 5th Avenue stylish to SoHo funky. The gentrified **South End** has become a retailing force, specializing in offbeat home furnishings and gift shops.

CAMBRIDGE

CambridgeSide Galleria (⊠ 100 CambridgeSide Pl., ☎ 617/621–8666), accessible from the Green Line Lechmere T stop and by shuttle from the Kendall T stop, is a basic three-story mall with a food court. Traveling west along Massachusetts Avenue toward Harvard Square, you will pass through eclectic **Central Square,** which holds a mix of furniture stores, used-record shops, ethnic restaurants, and small, hip performance venues. **Harvard Square** comprises just a few blocks but contains more than 150 stores selling clothes, books and records, furnishings, and a range of specialty items. **Porter Square,** on Massachusetts Ave., has several distinctive clothing and home furnishings stores, crafts shops, natural food markets, and restaurants.

Department Stores

Filene's (⊠ 426 Washington St., Downtown, ☎ 617/357–2100; ⊠ CambridgeSide Galleria, 100 CambridgeSide Pl., Cambridge, ☎ 617/621–3800), a full-service department store, carries American name-brand and designer-label men's and women's clothing. Jewelry, shoes, cosmetics, bedding, towels, and luggage are found at the Downtown Crossing store. A standout is **Filene's Basement** (⊠ 426 Washington St., Downtown, ☎ 617/542–2011), a Boston institution where items are automatically reduced in price according to the number of days they've been on the rack. **Lord & Taylor** (⊠ 760 Boylston St., Back Bay, ☎ 617/262–6000) is a reliable, if somewhat overstuffed, stop for classic clothing. **Macy's** (⊠ 450 Washington St., Downtown, ☎ 617/357–3000) carries men's and women's clothing, including top designers, as well as housewares, furniture, and cosmetics. It has direct access to the Downtown Crossing T station. **Neiman Marcus** (⊠ 5 Copley Pl., Back Bay, ☎ 617/536–3660), the flashy Texas retailer, has three levels of high fashion, cosmetics, and housewares. **Saks Fifth Avenue** (⊠ Prudential Center, 1 Ring Rd., Back Bay, ☎ 617/262–8500) stocks top-of-the-line clothing, from more traditional styles to avant-garde apparel, plus accessories and cosmetics.

Specialty Stores

ANTIQUES

Though Newbury Street and the South End have several worthwhile shops, Charles Street has a clutch of stores where you can find everything from 18th-century paintings and early etchings of Boston landmarks to Chinese vases and complete sets of dinnerware. Don't miss the **Boston Antique Co-op** (⊠ 119 Charles St., Beacon Hill, ☎ 617/227–9810 or 617/227–9811), a two-story, flea market–style collection of dealers that carries everything from vintage photos and paintings to porcelain, silver, bronzes, and furniture. **Cambridge Antique Market** (⊠ 201 Monsignor O'Brien Hwy., Cambridge, ☎ 617/868–9655) is a bit off the beaten track but has a selection bordering on overwhelming, with four floors of dealers.

BOOKS

If Boston and Cambridge have bragging rights to anything, it is their independent bookstores, many of which stay open late and sponsor author readings and literary programs. Besides the unique places listed below, there are plenty of major chains. The **Barnes & Noble** in Kenmore Square may stock more Boston University memorabilia than books, though it has a pretty fair selection of those, too (⊠ 395 Washington St., Downtown, ☎ 617/426–5184 or 617/426–5502; ⊠ 660 Beacon St., Kenmore Sq., ☎ 617/267–8484; ⊠ Prudential Center, 800 Boylston St., Back Bay, ☎ 617/536–2606). The **Borders** in Downtown Crossing (⊠ 10–24 School St., Downtown, ☎ 617/557–7188) has 2½ floors of books, as well as a music section and a café that offers a respite from the hubbub; it also hosts periodic readings by such authors as John Irving, Robert Parker, and Amy Tan. **Avenue Victor Hugo** (⊠ 339 Newbury St., Back Bay, ☎ 617/266–7746 or 800/798–7746) can divulge some startling secondhand finds (a first edition of Michelangelo's poems), plus fiction, art books, and magazines dating back to the 1800s. If the book you want is out of print, **Brattle Bookstore** (⊠ 9 West St., Downtown, ☎ 617/542–0210 or 800/447–9595) has it or can probably find it. Hands down, the **Globe Corner Bookstore** (⊠ 28 Church St., Cambridge, ☎ 617/497–6277 or 800/358–6013) is the best source in town for domestic and international travel books and maps; it also has a good selection of books about New England. The literary and academic community is well served at the **Harvard Bookstore** (⊠ 1256 Massachusetts Ave., Cambridge, ☎ 617/661–1515). **Trident Bookseller and Café** (⊠ 338 Newbury St., Back Bay, ☎ 617/267–8688) carries books, tapes, and magazines and stays open until midnight daily. **We Think the World of You** (⊠ 540 Tremont St., South End, ☎ 617/574–5000 or 800/251–9917), in the heart of the South End, stocks gay- and lesbian-oriented publications and is a great source of posted information for the neighborhood's active gay community.

CLOTHING

The terminally chic shop on Newbury Street, the hip hang in Harvard Square, and everyone goes downtown for the real bargains.

The Euro-dominated **Alan Bilzerian** (⊠ 34 Newbury St., Back Bay, ☎ 617/536–1001) sells avant-garde men's and women's fashions. The **April Cornell** outlet (⊠ Faneuil Hall Marketplace, North Market Bldg., Faneuil Hall, ☎ 617/248–0280; ⊠ 43 Brattle St., Cambridge, ☎ 617/661–8910) carries frilly bohemian women's clothing, furniture, linens, and toiletries at 50% off original prices. **Betsy Jenney** (⊠ 114 Newbury St., Back Bay, ☎ 617/536–2610) sells well-made, comfortable women's lines at moderate prices. Young trendsetters will be happiest at **Calypso** (⊠ 115 Newbury St., Back Bay, ☎ 617/421–1887). **Louis Boston** (⊠ 234 Berkeley St., Back Bay, ☎ 617/262–6100) is *the* place for the well-dressed and well-heeled to shop. **Wish** (⊠ 49 Charles St., Beacon Hill, ☎ 617/227–4441) carries everything a hip young woman could wish for, from such designers as Katayone Adeli and Nanette Lepore.

GIFTS AND HOUSEHOLD ITEMS

You can travel back in time or to another country at many Boston gift shops. **Buckaroo's Mercantile** (⊠ 1297 Cambridge St., Cambridge, ☎ 617/492–4792) rocks with retro kitsch, from pink poodle skirts to Barbie lamp shades—along with everything Elvis. **Flat of the Hill** (⊠ 60 Charles St., Beacon Hill, ☎ 617/619–9977) has something for everyone on your list—including Fido—with seasonal items, gourmet foods, hard-to-find toiletries, dolls, toys, pillows, and pet products. **Kybele**

(✉ 583 Tremont St., South End, ☎ 617/262–5522) is like a well-designed Bedouin tent, with handwoven Turkish rugs, extra-deep shag area rugs, hookahs, and delicate cut-glass hanging lamps. **Mayan Weavers** (✉ 268 Newbury St., Back Bay, ☎ 617/262–4342) stocks reasonably priced boldly colored woven textiles, hand-carved furniture, and hand-painted tchotchkes. **Mohr & McPherson** (✉ 281–290 Concord Ave., Cambridge, ☎ 617/354–6662, 617/520–2000, or 617/520–2007; ✉ 75 Moulton St., Cambridge, ☎ 617/520–2000) is a visual exotic feast of cabinets, tables, chairs, and lamps from Japan, India, China, and Indonesia. **Nomad** (✉ 1741 Massachusetts Ave., Cambridge, ☎ 617/497–6677) carries clothing as well as Indian good-luck *torans* (wall hangings), Mexican *milagros* (charms), silver jewelry, and curtains made from sari silk. **Tibet Emporium** (✉ 103 Charles St., Charlestown, ☎ 617/723–8035) goes beyond the usual masks and quilted wall hangings with delicate beaded silk pillowcases, pashmina wraps in every color imaginable, and finely wrought but affordable silver jewelry.

Boston A to Z

To research prices, get advice from other travelers, and book travel arrangements, visit www.fodors.com.

AIRPORTS AND TRANSFERS

Logan International, across the harbor from downtown Boston, receives flights from most major domestic airlines and some carriers from outside the United States. If you're driving from Logan to downtown Boston, the most direct route is by way of the Sumner Tunnel ($2 toll inbound; no toll outbound). On weekends and holidays and after 10 PM weekdays, you can get around Sumner Tunnel backups by using the Ted Williams Tunnel ($2 toll inbound; no toll outbound), which will steer you onto the Southeast Expressway south of downtown Boston. Follow the signs to I–93 northbound to head back into the downtown area.

Cabs can be hired outside each terminal. Fares to and from downtown average about $15–$18 including tip via the most direct route, the Sumner Tunnel, assuming no major traffic jams. The Sumner Tunnel is also the most direct route to Cambridge and the Massachusetts Turnpike (I–90). The Ted Williams Tunnel is the best bet for southbound travelers. It's usually open only to taxis and commercial traffic during the day on weekdays but is open to all traffic after 10 PM daily. Lighted signs on major highways alert drivers to tunnel schedule changes.

The Airport Water Shuttle crosses Boston Harbor in about seven minutes, running between Logan Airport and Rowes Wharf (a free shuttle bus operates between the ferry dock and airline terminals). Adult fare is $10 one-way. The MBTA subway, or T, from Airport Station is one of the fastest ways to reach downtown from the airport. The subway's Blue Line runs from the airport to downtown Boston in about 20 minutes; from there, you can reach the Red, Green, or Orange Line, or commuter rail.

Shuttle bus 22 runs between Terminals A and B and the subway. Shuttle bus 33 goes to the subway from Terminals C, D, and E. US Shuttle provides door-to-door van service 24 hours a day between the airport and Boston, Cambridge, and many suburban destinations. Call and request a pickup when your flight arrives. To go to the airport, call for reservations 24 to 48 hours in advance. Sample one-way fares are $8 to downtown or the Back Bay, $16 to Cambridge.

➤ AIRPORT INFORMATION: **Logan International** (✉ I–93 N, Exit 24, ☎ 617/561–1800; 800/235–6426 24-hr information about parking and the ground transportation options). **Airport Water Shuttle** (☎ 800/235–6426). **MBTA** (☎ 617/222–3200 or 800/392–6100).

BUS TRAVEL TO AND FROM BOSTON

South Station is the depot for most of the major bus companies that serve Boston.

➤ Bus Information: **South Station** (✉ Atlantic Ave. and Summer St., ☎ 617/345–7451).

BUS TRAVEL WITHIN BOSTON

Buses of the Massachusetts Bay Transportation Authority (MBTA) crisscross the metropolitan area and travel farther into suburbia than subway and trolley lines. Buses run roughly from 5:30 AM to 12:30 AM; the new Night Owl service runs limited routes until 2:30 AM Friday and Saturday nights.

➤ Bus Information: **MBTA** (☎ 617/222–3200; 617/722–5146 TTY; WEB www.mbta.com).

CAR TRAVEL

Boston is not an easy city to drive in because of the many one-way streets, the many streets with the same name, the many streets that abruptly *change* name in the middle, and the many illogical twists and turns. If you must bring a car, bring a good map, keep to the main thoroughfares, and park in lots rather than on the street to avoid tickets (signage is confusing at best, and meter patrol is preternaturally quick), accidents, or theft. Some neighborhoods have strictly enforced residents-only rules, with just a handful of two-hour visitor's spaces.

Interstate 95 (also called Route 128 in some parts) skirts the western edge of Boston. Interstate 93 connects Boston to the north and to New Hampshire. The section of I–93 that runs through the city is scheduled to be turned into an underground highway as part of the massive Central Artery Project, or "Big Dig"; expect construction and delays here through at least 2004. Interstate 90 (a toll road technically known as the Massachusetts Turnpike but called "the Mass Pike" or just "the Pike" by locals) enters the city from the west. Route 9, roughly parallel to I–90, passes through Newton and Brookline on its way into Boston from the west. Route 2 enters Cambridge from the northwest.

PARKING

Major public lots are at Government Center and Quincy Market, beneath Boston Common (entrance on Charles Street), beneath Post Office Square, at the Prudential Center, at Copley Place, off Clarendon Street near the John Hancock Tower, and at several hotels. Smaller lots are scattered throughout downtown. Most are expensive (expect to pay $10 and up for an evening out, $20 and up to park all day). The few city-run garages are a bargain at about $10 per day—but try finding a space in them.

DISCOUNTS AND DEALS

The Arts Boston coupon book offers two-for-one admission to 60 museums, attractions, and tour services in and around Boston. The booklets, which cost $9, can be purchased at BosTix booths in Copley Square, the Faneuil Hall Marketplace, and at the Holyoke Center in Harvard Square, Cambridge. Half-price, same-day dance, music, and theater tickets can also be purchased, with cash only, at BosTix beginning at 11 AM daily.

The CityPass is a reduced-fee combination ticket to six major Boston sights: the John F. Kennedy Library and Museum, Prudential Center Skywalk, the Museum of Fine Arts, the Museum of Science, the New

England Aquarium, and the Harvard University Museum of Natural History. The passes cost $30.25 and are available at participating attractions and the Greater Boston Convention and Visitors Bureau information booths (☞ Visitor Information).

MBTA visitor passes are available for unlimited travel on subway, local bus, and inner-harbor ferry for one-, three-, and seven-day periods (fares: $6, $11, and $22 respectively).

EMERGENCIES

➤ DOCTORS AND DENTISTS: **Physician Referral Service** (☎ 617/726–5800). **Dental Emergency** (☎ 508/651–3521). **Dental Referral** (☎ 800/917–6453).

➤ EMERGENCY SERVICES: **Ambulance, fire, police** (☎ 911). **Poison control** (☎ 617/232–2120).

➤ HOSPITAL: **Massachusetts General Hospital** (☎ 617/726–2000).

➤ 24-HOUR PHARMACIES: **CVS** (✉ Porter Square Shopping Plaza, Massachusetts Ave., Cambridge, ☎ 617/876–5519; ✉ 155 Charles St., ☎ 617/227–0437 or 800/746–7287; ☎ 617/227–0437; 800/746–7287 other locations).

LODGING
BED-AND-BREAKFASTS
Bed and Breakfast Reservation Agency of Boston can book a variety of accommodations ranging from historic B&Bs to modern condominiums.

➤ RESERVATION SERVICE: **Bed and Breakfast Reservation Agency of Boston** (✉ 47 Commercial Wharf, 02110, ☎ 617/720–3540; 800/248–9262; 0800/895128 in the U.K.; WEB www.boston-bnbagency.com).

SUBWAY, TRAINS, AND TROLLEY TRAVEL
Boston's public transportation system, the MBTA or "T" for short, is superlative; it's easy and inexpensive and can get you quickly from one end of the city to another or from Boston to Cambridge or other outlying towns. The "T" operates subways, elevated trains, and trolleys along four lines. Trains operate from about 5:30 AM to about 12:30 AM. Current T fares are $1 for adults, 50¢ for children ages 5–11. An extra fare is required heading inbound from distant Green Line stops and in both directions for certain distant Red Line stops. The **Red Line** originates at Braintree and Mattapan to the south; the routes join near South Boston and proceed through downtown Boston (including South Station) to the western edge of Cambridge. The **Green Line,** a combined underground and elevated surface line, uses trolleys that operate underground in the central city. It originates at Cambridge's Lechmere, heads south, and divides into four routes; these end at Boston College (Commonwealth Avenue), Cleveland Circle (Beacon Street), Riverside, and Heath Street (Huntington Avenue). Buses connect Heath Street to the old Arborway terminus. The **Blue Line** runs on weekdays from Bowdoin Square and on weeknights and weekends from Government Center to the Wonderland Racetrack in Revere, north of Boston. Logan Airport is among its stops. The **Orange Line** runs from Oak Grove in north suburban Malden to Forest Hills near the Arnold Arboretum. Park Street Station (on the Common) and State Street are the major downtown transfer points.

➤ CONTACT: **Massachusetts Bay Transportation Authority** (MBTA; ☎ 617/222–3200 or 800/392–6100; 617/222–5854 TTY; WEB www.mbta.com.

TAXIS
Cabs are not easily hailed on the street; if you need to get somewhere in a hurry, use a hotel taxi stand or telephone for a cab. Taxis also gen-

Boston MBTA (the "T")

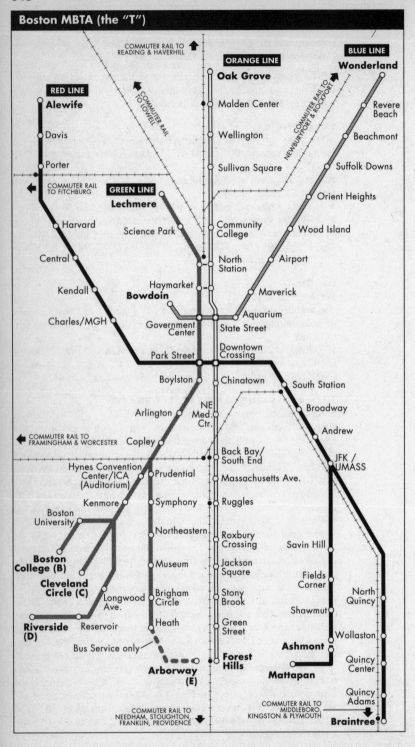

RED LINE
Alewife
Davis
Porter
COMMUTER RAIL TO FITCHBURG
Harvard
Central
Kendall
Charles/MGH

COMMUTER RAIL TO READING & HAVERHILL
COMMUTER RAIL TO LOWELL

GREEN LINE
Lechmere
Science Park
Haymarket
Bowdoin
Government Center
Park Street
Boylston
Arlington
Copley
Hynes Convention Center/ICA (Auditorium)
Kenmore
Boston University
Boston College (B)
Cleveland Circle (C)
Longwood Ave.
Riverside (D)
Reservoir
Bus Service only
Arborway (E)
Heath
Brigham Circle
Museum
Northeastern
Symphony
Prudential

ORANGE LINE
Oak Grove
Malden Center
Wellington
Sullivan Square
Community College
North Station
NE Med. Ctr.
Chinatown
Back Bay/South End
Massachusetts Ave.
Ruggles
Roxbury Crossing
Jackson Square
Stony Brook
Green Street
Forest Hills

BLUE LINE
Wonderland
Revere Beach
Beachmont
Suffolk Downs
Orient Heights
Wood Island
Airport
Maverick
Aquarium
State Street
Downtown Crossing

COMMUTER RAIL TO NEWBURYPORT & ROCKPORT

South Station
Broadway
Andrew
JFK/UMASS
Savin Hill
Fields Corner
Shawmut
Ashmont
Mattapan
North Quincy
Wollaston
Quincy Center
Quincy Adams
Braintree

COMMUTER RAIL TO FRAMINGHAM & WORCESTER

COMMUTER RAIL TO NEEDHAM, STOUGHTON, FRANKLIN, PROVIDENCE

COMMUTER RAIL TO MIDDLEBORO, KINGSTON & PLYMOUTH

erally line up in Harvard Square, around South Station, near Faneuil Hall Marketplace, or in the Theater District. A taxi ride within the city of Boston starts at $1.50, plus 25¢ for the first ¼ mi and 25¢ for each ⅛ mi thereafter. One-way streets often make circuitous routes necessary and increase your cost. Companies offering 24-hour service include Boston Cab Association; Checker; Green Cab Association; Independent Taxi Operators Association; Town Taxi; and Cambridge Checker Cab.

➤ TAXI COMPANIES: **Boston Cab Association** (☎ 617/536–3200). **Cambridge Checker Cab** (✉ Cambridge, ☎ 617/497–1500). **Checker** (☎ 617/536–7000). **Green Cab Association** (☎ 617/628–0600). **Independent Taxi Operators Association** (ITOA; ☎ 617/426–8700). **Town Taxi** (☎ 617/536–5000).

TOURS

BOAT TOURS

Boston Harbor Cruises runs harbor tours and other cruises (including whale-watching, sunset, and evening entertainment cruises; prices vary) from mid-April to October. The Charles Riverboat Co. offers a 55-minute narrated tour of the Charles River Basin. Tours depart from the CambridgeSide Galleria mall at 10:30 AM and then on the hour from noon to 5 daily from June to August and on weekends in April, May, and September; the fare is $9. Massachusetts Bay Lines operates evening cruises with rock, blues, or reggae music and dancing, concessions, and cash bar, as well as daily harbor tours and sunset cruises. Prices vary.

Boston Duck Tours uses World War II amphibious vehicles for 80-minute tours on the city's streets and the Charles River. Tours begin and end at the Huntington Avenue entrance to the Prudential Center, at 101 Huntington Avenue. From April to November, tours leave every half hour from 9 AM till dark; the fare is about $22. Tickets are sold inside the Prudential Center 9–8 Monday–Saturday and 9–6 Sunday; weekend tours often sell out early.

➤ TOUR OPERATORS: **Boston Duck Tours** (✉ 790 Boylston St., Plaza Level, ☎ 617/723–3825). **Boston Harbor Cruises** (✉ 1 Long Wharf, ☎ 617/227–4321). **Charles Riverboat Co.** (☎ 617/621–3001, WEB www.charlesriverboat.com). **Massachusetts Bay Lines** (✉ 60 Rowes Wharf, ☎ 617/542–8000). *Museum of Science*

ORIENTATION TOURS

The red Beantown Trolleys make more than 20 stops; get on and off as many times as you like. Cost is $22. Trolleys run every half hour from 9 AM until 4 PM. Tickets are available from hotel concierges, at many attractions, and sometimes on board. From March to November Brush Hill/Gray Line picks up passengers from hotels for a 2-hour Boston tour or a 3½-hour Cambridge–Lexington–Concord tour. Fees are $21–$45, depending on the destination. The orange-and-green Old Town Trolley runs every 20 minutes from 9 AM to 3 or 4 PM; fare is $23. Specialty tours, such as "JFK's Boston," "Ghost and Gravestones," "The Original Chocolate Tour," and "The Holly Jolly Christmas Trolley" are available.

➤ TOUR OPERATORS: **Beantown Trolleys** (✉ Transportation Bldg., 16 Charles St. S, ☎ 617/720–6342 or 800/343–1328, WEB www.brushhilltours.com). **Brush Hill/Gray Line** (✉ Transportation Bldg., 16 Charles St. S, ☎ 781/986–6100 or 800/343–1328, WEB www.brushhilltours.com). **Old Town Trolley** (✉ 380 Dorchester Ave., South Boston, ☎ 617/269–7010 or 800/868–7482, WEB www.trolleytours.com).

The Black Heritage Trail, a self-guided walk, explores Boston's 19th-century black community, passing 14 sites; free guided tours meet at the Shaw Memorial on Beacon Hill, Memorial Day weekend through Labor Day weekend daily at 10 AM, noon, and 2 PM. The 2½-mi Freedom Trail follows a red line past 16 of Boston's most important historic sites. The nonprofit Historic Neighborhoods Foundation covers the North End, Chinatown, Beacon Hill, the waterfront, and other urban areas on 90-minute guided walks from Wednesday to Saturday between April and November. Tours cost $5 and up. The Society for the Preservation of New England Antiquities conducts a walking tour of Beacon Hill that focuses on the neighborhood as it was in the early 1800s. Tours are given Saturday May through October at 11 PM; tours cost $10. The Old State House and the Boston National Historic Park Service Visitor Center sell maps ($5) and a guidebook ($9.95), which is also available in the bookstores of most historic sites.

➤ TOUR OPERATORS: **Black Heritage Trail** (☎ 617/742–5415 or 617/725–0022, WEB www.afroammuseum.org). **Freedom Trail** (☎ 617/242–5642). **Historic Neighborhoods Foundation** (✉ 99 Bedford St., ☎ 617/426–1885, WEB www.historic-neighborhoods.org). **Society for the Preservation of New England Antiquities** (SPNEA; ✉ 141 Cambridge St., ☎ 617/227–3956).

TRAIN TRAVEL

Boston is served by Amtrak at South Station and Back Bay Station, which accommodates frequent departures for and arrivals from New York, Philadelphia, and Washington, D.C. Amtrak's pricey high-speed *Acela* train has cut the travel time between Boston and New York from 4½ hours to 3½ hours. South Station is also the eastern terminus of Amtrak's *Lake Shore Limited,* which travels daily between Boston and Chicago by way of Albany, Rochester, Buffalo, and Cleveland. An additional Amtrak station with ample parking is just off Route 128 in suburban Canton, southwest of Boston.

➤ TRAIN INFORMATION: **Amtrak** (☎ 617/482–3660 or 800/872–7245, WEB www.amttrak.com).

VISITOR INFORMATION

The Boston Visitor Information Pavilion is open daily 9–5. The Boston Welcome Center is open Sunday–Thursday 9–5 and Friday–Saturday 9–6 for most of the year; it's open until 7 except Sunday during the summer. Greater Boston Convention and Visitors Bureau has brochures and information.

➤ TOURIST INFORMATION: **Boston Common Information Kiosk** (✉ Tremont St. where the Freedom Trail begins, Boston, ☎ 617/426–3115 or 800/733–2678, WEB www.bostonusa.com). **Greater Boston Convention and Visitors Bureau** (✉ 2 Copley Pl., Suite 105, Boston 02116, ☎ 617/536–4100 or 800/888–5515, FAX 617/424–7664, WEB www.bostonusa.com).

AROUND BOSTON

Lexington

16 mi northwest of Boston.

Updated by
Carolyn Heller

The events of the American Revolution are very much a part of present-day Lexington, a modern suburb that sprawls out from the historic sites near the town center. Although the downtown area is generally lively, with ice cream and coffee shops, boutiques, and a great little movie theater, the town becomes especially animated each Patriots' Day (celebrated on the third Monday in April), when costume-clad groups re-create the minutemen's battle maneuvers and "Paul Revere" rides again.

On April 18, 1775, Paul Revere went to the **Hancock-Clarke House** and roused patriots John Hancock and Sam Adams, who were in Concord to attend the Provincial Congress then in session. After Hancock and Adams got the message, they fled to avoid capture. The house, a par-sonage built in 1698, is a 10-minute walk from Lexington Common. Inside are the pistols of the British major John Pitcairn as well as pe-riod furnishings and portraits. ⊠ *36 Hancock St.,* ☎ *781/861–0928,* WEB *www.lexingtonhistory.org.* ✍ *$5; $12 combination ticket includes Buckman Tavern and Munroe Tavern.* ☉ *Mid-Apr.–Oct., Mon.–Sat. 10–5, Sun. 1–5.*

The minutemen gathered at the **Buckman Tavern** (1690) on the morn-ing of April 19, 1775. A half-hour tour takes in the tavern's seven rooms, which have been restored to the way they looked in the 1770s. Among the items on display is an old front door with a hole made by a British musket ball. ⊠ *1 Bedford St.,* ☎ *781/862–5598,* WEB *www.lexingtonhistory. org.* ✍ *$5; $12 combination ticket includes Hancock-Clarke House and Munroe Tavern.* ☉ *Mid-Mar.–Oct., Mon.–Sat: 10–5, Sun. 1–5.*

It was on **Battle Green,** a 2-acre triangle of land, that minuteman cap-tain John Parker assembled his men in advance of the British soldiers, who were marching from Boston. (The minutemen were so called be-cause they were able to prepare themselves at a moment's notice.) Parker's role in the American Revolution is commemorated in Henry Hudson Kitson's renowned 1900 sculpture, the *Minuteman* Statue. Facing downtown Lexington at the tip of Battle Green, the statue's in a traf-fic island and therefore makes for a difficult photo op.

The pleasant **Lexington Visitor Center,** near Battle Green, has a diorama of the 1775 clash on the green, plus a gift shop. ⊠ *Lexington Cham-ber of Commerce, 1875 Massachusetts Ave.,* ☎ *781/862–1450,* WEB *www.lexingtonchamber.org.* ☉ *Mid-Apr.–Nov., daily 9–5; Dec.–mid-Apr., daily 10–4.*

As April 19, 1775, dragged on, British forces met fierce resistance in Concord. Dazed and demoralized after the battle at Concord's Old North Bridge, the British backtracked and regrouped at the **Munroe Tavern** (1695) while the Munroe family hid in nearby woods. The troops then retreated through what is now the town of Arlington. After a bloody battle there, they returned to Boston. The tavern is 1 mi east of Lex-ington Common; tours last about 30 minutes. ⊠ *1332 Massachusetts Ave.,* ☎ *781/674–9238,* WEB *www.lexingtonhistory.org.* ✍ *$5; $12 com-bination ticket includes Hancock-Clarke House and Buckman Tavern.* ☉ *Mid-Apr.–Oct., Mon.–Sat. 10–5, Sun. 1–5.*

★ The **National Heritage Museum,** displays items and artifacts from all facets of American life, putting them in social and political context. An ongoing exhibit, "Lexington Alarm'd," outlines events leading up to April 1775 and illustrates Revolutionary-era life through everyday objects such as blacksmithing and farming tools, scalpels and blood-letting paraphernalia, and dental instruments, including a "tooth key" used to extract teeth. ⊠ *33 Marrett Rd. (Rte. 2A at Massachusetts Ave.),* ☎ *781/861–6559,* WEB *www.monh.org.* ✍ *Free; donation suggested.* ☉ *Mon.–Sat. 10–5, Sun. noon–5.*

West of Lexington's center stretches the 800-acre Minute Man National Historical Park, which also extends into Lincoln and Concord. Begin your park visit at Lexington's **Minute Man National Historical Park Vis-**

itor Center to see its free multimedia presentation, "The Road to Revolution," a captivating introduction to the events of April 1775. Then, continuing along Route 2A toward Concord, you pass the point where Revere's midnight ride ended with his capture by the British; it's marked with a boulder and plaque. You can also visit the 1732 **Hartwell Tavern** (open May–October, daily 10–5), a restored drover's tavern staffed by park employees in period costume; they frequently demonstrate musket firing or open-hearth cooking, and children are likely to enjoy the reproduction Colonial toys. ⊠ *Rte. 2A, ½ mi west of Rte. 128,* ☎ *978/369–6993 or 781/862–7753,* ⓌⒺⒷ *www.nps.gov/mima.* ☉ *May–Oct., daily 9–5; Nov.–Apr., daily 9–4.*

Dining

\$–\$\$\$ ✕ **Bertucci's.** Part of a popular chain, this family-friendly Italian restaurant offers good food, reasonable prices, a large menu. Specialties include ravioli, calzones, and a wide assortment of brick-oven baked pizzas. ⊠ *1777 Massachusetts Ave.,* ☎ *781/860–9000. AE, D, DC, MC, V.*

\$–\$\$\$ ✕ **Dabin.** This relaxing restaurant serves traditional Japanese and Korean fare. Lunch specials include udon or soba noodles, sushi combinations, and *bento* boxes of tempura, Korean-style grilled beef, or broiled salmon. It's one block off Massachusetts Avenue. ⊠ *10 Muzzey St.,* ☎ *781/860–0171. AE, D, DC, MC, V. No lunch Sun.*

Concord

About 10 mi west of Lexington, 21 mi northwest of Boston.

The Concord of today is a modern suburb with a busy center filled with arty shops, places to eat, and (recalling the literary history made here) old bookstores. Autumn lovers, take note: Concord is a great place to start a fall foliage tour. From Boston, head west along Route 2 to Concord, and then continue on to find harvest stands and do-it-yourself apple-picking around Harvard and Stow.

To reach Concord from Lexington, take Routes 4/225 through Bedford and Route 62 west to Concord; or pick up Route 2A west from Massachusetts Avenue (known locally as Mass Ave.) at the National Heritage Museum or Waltham Street south from Lexington Center.

The **Minute Man National Historical Park,** along Route 2A, is a two-parcel park with more than 800 acres straddling Lexington, Concord, and Lincoln. The park contains many of the sites important to Concord's role in the Revolution, including the Old North Bridge, as well as two visitor centers, one each in Concord and Lexington. ⊠ *Between Monument and Liberty Sts., about ½ mi from Concord center,* ⓌⒺⒷ *www.nps.gov/mima.* ☉ *Daily dawn–dusk.*

You can reach the North Bridge section of the Minute Man park by water if you rent a canoe at the **South Bridge Boat House** and paddle along the Sudbury and Concord rivers. ⊠ *496 Main St.,* ☎ *978/369–9438.* ☉ *Apr.–Oct., weekdays 10–dusk, weekends 9–dusk.*

At the **Old North Bridge,** ½ mi from Concord center, the Concord minutemen turned the tables on the British in the morning of April 19, 1775. The Americans didn't fire first, but when two of their own fell dead from a redcoat volley, Major John Buttrick of Concord roared, "Fire, fellow soldiers, for God's sake, fire." The minutemen released volley after volley, and the redcoats fled. Daniel Chester French's famous statue *The Minuteman* (1875) honors the country's first freedom fighters. The lovely wooded surroundings give a sense of what the landscape was like in more rural times.

Of the confrontation, Ralph Waldo Emerson wrote in 1837: "By the rude bridge that arched the flood / Their flag to April's breeze unfurled / Here once the embattled farmers stood / And fired the shot heard round the world." (The lines are inscribed at the foot of *The Minuteman* statue). Concord claims the right to the "shot," believing that native son Emerson was, of course, referring to the North Bridge standoff.

The Reverend William Emerson, grandfather of Ralph Waldo Emerson, watched rebels and redcoats battle from behind his home, the **Old Manse,** which was within sight of the Old North Bridge. The house, built in 1770, was occupied constantly by the Emerson family, except for the 3½-year period during which Nathaniel Hawthorne rented the Manse and wrote. Furnishings date from the late 18th century. Tours run throughout the day and last 45 minutes, with a new tour starting within 15 minutes of when the first person signs up. ⊠ *269 Monument St.,* ☎ *978/369–3909,* WEB *www.thetrustees.org.* ⊠ *$7.* ☉ *Mid-Apr.–Oct., Mon.–Sat. 10–5, Sun. noon–5 (last tour at 4:30).*

Now displaying a series of rotating art exhibits of work by the more than 500 members of the Concord Art Association, the **Jonathan Ball House,** built in 1753, was a station on the Underground Railroad for runaway slaves during the Civil War. Ask to see the secret room. The garden and waterfall are refreshing sights. ⊠ *Art Association, 37 Lexington Rd.,* ☎ *978/369–2578,* WEB *www.concordart.org.* ⊠ *Free.* ☉ *Tues.–Sat. 10–4:30, Sun. noon–4.*

The 19th-century essayist and poet Ralph Waldo Emerson lived briefly in the Old Manse in 1834–35, then moved to what is known as the **Ralph Waldo Emerson House,** where he lived until his death in 1882. Here he wrote the *Essays.* Except for items from Emerson's study, now at the nearby Concord Museum, the Emerson House furnishings have been preserved as the writer left them, down to his hat resting on the newel post. You must join one of the half-hour-long tours to see the interior. ⊠ *28 Cambridge Turnpike, at Lexington Rd.,* ☎ *978/369–2236.* ⊠ *$5.* ☉ *Mid-Apr.–mid Oct., Thurs.–Sat. 10–4:30, Sun. 2–4:30.*

The original contents of Emerson's private study, as well as the world's largest collection of Thoreau artifacts, are in the **Concord Museum.** The museum, set in a 1930 Colonial Revival building just east of the town center, provides a good overview of the town's history, from its original Native American settlement to the present. Start in the "Why Concord?" exhibit, which considers why so many important historical and cultural events happened in Concord. Highlights include Native American artifacts, furnishings from Thoreau's Walden Pond cabin, and one of the two lanterns hung at Boston's Old North Church to signal that the British were coming by sea. The 15-minute "Exploring Concord" film highlights the town's historic places. If you've brought the children, ask for a free family activity pack. ⊠ *200 Lexington Rd. (entrance on Cambridge Turnpike),* ☎ *978/369–9763,* WEB *www.concordmuseum. org.* ⊠ *$7.* ☉ *Apr.–Dec., Mon.–Sat. 9–5, Sun. noon–5; Jan.–Mar., Mon.–Sat. 11–4, Sun. 1–4.*

The dark brown exterior of Louisa May Alcott's family home, **Orchard House,** sharply contrasts with the light, wit, and energy so much in evidence inside. Named for the apple orchard that once surrounded it, Orchard House was the Alcott family home from 1857 to 1877. Here, Louisa wrote *Little Women,* based on her life with her three sisters, and her father, Bronson, founded his school of philosophy; the building remains behind the house. Because Orchard House had just one owner after the Alcotts left and because it became a museum in 1911, many of the original furnishings remain, including the semicircular shelf-desk where Louisa wrote *Little Women*. The gift shop has a generous selection of Alcott books. The 30-minute tours start about every half hour from April through October; call for the off-season tour schedule. ⊠ *399 Lexington Rd.,* ☎ *978/369–4118,* WEB *www.louisamayalcott.org.* 🖾 *$7.* ☉ *Apr.–Oct., Mon.–Sat. 10–4:30, Sun. 1–4:30; Nov.–Dec. and mid-Jan.–Mar., weekdays 11–3, Sat. 10–4:30, Sun. 1–4:30.*

Nathaniel Hawthorne lived at the Old Manse in 1842–45, working on stories and sketches; he then moved to Salem (where he wrote *The Scarlet Letter*) and later to Lenox (*The House of the Seven Gables*). In 1852 he returned to Concord, bought a rambling structure called **The Wayside,** and lived here until his death in 1864. The subsequent owner, Margaret Sidney, wrote the children's book *Five Little Peppers and How They Grew* (1881). Before Hawthorne moved in, the Alcotts lived here, from 1845 to 1848. An exhibit center, in the former barn, provides information about the Wayside authors and links them to major events in American history. Hawthorne's tower-study is substantially as he left it, complete with his stand-up writing desk. ⊠ *455 Lexington Rd.,* ☎ *978/369–6975 or 978/369–6993,* WEB *www.nps.gov/mima/ wayside.* 🖾 *Tours $4, exhibit center free.* ☉ *Early May–Oct., Thurs.– Tues. 10–5.*

Each Memorial Day, Louisa May Alcott's grave in the nearby **Sleepy Hollow Cemetery** is decorated in commemoration of her death. Along with Emerson, Thoreau, and Hawthorne, Alcott is buried in a section of the cemetery known as Author's Ridge. ⊠ *Bedford St./Rte. 62,* ☎ *978/318–3233.* ☉ *Daily dawn–dusk.*

★   A trip to Concord can include a pilgrimage to **Walden Pond,** Henry David Thoreau's most famous residence. Here, in 1845, at age 28, Thoreau moved into a one-room cabin—built for $28.12—on the shore of this 100-ft-deep kettle hole, formed 12,000 years ago by the retreat of the New England glacier. Living alone for the next two years, Thoreau discovered the benefits of solitude and the beauties of nature. The essays in *Walden,* published in 1854, are a mixture of philosophy, nature writing, and proto-ecology. The site of the first cabin is staked out in stone. A full-size, authentically furnished replica of the cabin stands about ½ mi from the original site, near the Walden Pond State Reservation parking lot. Even when it's closed, you can peek through its windows. Now, as in Thoreau's time, the pond is a delightful summertime spot for swimming, fishing, and rowing, and there's hiking in the nearby woods. To get to Walden Pond State Reservation from the center of Concord—a trip of only 1½ mi—take Concord's Main Street a block west from Monument Square, turn left onto Walden Street, and head for the intersection of Routes 2 and 126. Cross over Route 2 onto Route 126, heading south for ½ mi. ⊠ *Rte. 126,* ☎ *978/369– 3254,* WEB *www.magnet.state.ma.us/dem/parks/wldn.htm.* 🖾 *Free; mid-Apr.–Labor Day, $5 per vehicle to park across road from pond.* ☉ *Daily until about ½ hr before sunset. Replica of Thoreau's cabin daily 8–½ hr before sunset.*

Dining

$$$ ✕ **Walden Grille.** In this old brick firehouse turned dining room, satisfy your appetite with tempting contemporary dishes. Lighter options include salads (such as rare lamb over arugula) and sandwiches (try grilled chicken with red pepper rémoulade or the hummus and cucumber wrap). Heartier entrées may range from wild-mushroom ravioli to grilled shrimp with risotto-polenta cakes. ⊠ *24 Walden St.,* ☎ *978/371– 2233. AE, D, DC, MC, V.*

$ ✕ **La Provence.** This little taste of France, a casual café and take-out shop opposite the Concord train station, makes a good stop for a light meal. In the morning, you can start off with a croissant or a brioche, and at midday, you can pick up sandwiches (perhaps pâté and cheese or French ham), quiches, or salads. Leave room for an éclair or a petite fruit tart. Just don't plan a late night here; it closes at 7 PM during the week and at 5:30 on Saturday. ⊠ *105 Thoreau St.,* ☎ *978/371–7428. AE, D, MC, V. Closed Sun.*

Lowell

30 mi northwest of Boston.

Everyone knows that the American Revolution began in Massachusetts. But the Commonwealth, and in particular the Merrimack Valley, also nurtured the Industrial Revolution. Lowell's first mill opened in 1823; by the 1850s, 40 factories employed thousands of workers and produced 2 million yards of cloth every week. By the mid-20th century, much of the textile industry had moved South, but the remnants of redbrick factories and murky canals remain. Lowell's noted son was the late Beat poet and novelist Jack Kerouac, born here in 1922. Kerouac's memory is honored in the **Eastern Canal Park** on Bridge Street (near the Boott Cotton Mills Museum), where plaques bear quotes from his Lowell novels and from *On the Road.* Every October "Lowell Celebrates Kerouac" stages academic symposia, music, and coffeehouse poetry.

The **Lowell National Historical Park** tracks the history of a gritty era when the power loom was the symbol of economic power and progress. It encompasses several blocks in the downtown area, including former mills turned museums, a network of canals, and a helpful visitor center in the 1902 Market Mills. The center makes a good starting point: the city's museums and historic sights spread out in three directions from here. Pick up a map for a self-guided walking tour that highlights aspects of local history. Park rangers lead guided tours on foot year-round and on turn-of-the-20th-century trolleys and canal barges from Memorial Day to Columbus Day. ⊠ *246 Market St.,* ☎ *978/970–5000,* WEB *www.nps.gov/lowe.* ☞ *Free; barge tours generally $6.* ☉ *July–Labor Day, daily 9–6; Labor Day–June, daily 9–5.*

The **Boott Cotton Mills Museum,** about a 10-minute walk northeast from the National Park Visitor Center, is the first major National Park Service museum devoted to the history of industrialization. The textile worker's grueling life is shown with all its grit, noise, and dust. You know you're in for an unusual experience when you're handed earplugs—they're for the re-creation of a 1920s weave room, authentic down to the deafening roar of 88 working power looms. Other exhibits at the complex, which dates from the mid-19th century, include weaving artifacts, cloth samples, video interviews with workers, and a large, meticulous scale model of 19th-century production. ⊠ *400 Foot of John St.,* ☎ *978/970–5000.* ☞ *$4.* ☉ *Apr.–late Nov., daily 9:30–5; late Nov.–Mar., Mon.–Sat. 9:30–4:30, Sun. 11–4:30.*

The **American Textile History Museum,** a short walk southwest along Dutton Street from the National Park Visitor Center, is in a former Civil War–era mill. The museum's collection of working machines ranges from an 18th-century waterwheel to an 1860s power loom to a 1950s "weave room" where fabrics are still made. Special exhibitions, such as a display of the late Princess of Wales's clothing, are held periodically; these have an extra admission fee. ⊠ *491 Dutton St.,* ☎ *978/441–0400,* WEB *www.athm.org.* ☞ *$6.* ☉ *Tues.–Fri. 9–4, weekends 10–5.*

The **Whistler House Museum of Art** displays the museum's permanent collections, including a number of American artist James McNeill

Whistler's etchings, as well as works by late-19th- and early 20th-century American representational artists. ⊠ *243 Worthen St.,* ☎ *978/452-7641,* WEB *www.whistlerhouse.org.* ⊡ *$3.* ☉ *Mar.–Dec., Wed.–Sat. 11–4.*

Dining

$–$$ ✕ **The Olympia.** Lowell has a large Greek-American community. Specialties at this family-run Greek restaurant include lamb, moussaka, and fish dishes. It's about five blocks from the National Park Visitor Center. ⊠ *457 Market St.,* ☎ *978/452–8092. AE, DC, MC, V.*

Plymouth

40 mi south of Boston.

On December 26, 1620, 102 weary men, women, and children disembarked from the *Mayflower* to found the first permanent European settlement north of Virginia. Today, Plymouth is characterized by narrow streets, clapboard mansions, shops, antiques stores, and a scenic waterfront. To mark Thanksgiving, the town holds a parade, historic-house tours, and other activities. Historic statues dot the town, including depictions of William Bradford on Water Street, a Pilgrim maiden in Brewster Gardens, and Massasoit (chief of the local Wampanoag tribe) on Carver Street.

★ ℭ   Over the entrance of the **Plimoth Plantation** is the caution: "You are now entering 1627." Believe it. Against the backdrop of the Atlantic Ocean, a Pilgrim village has been carefully re-created, from the thatch roofs, cramped quarters, and open fireplaces to the long-horned livestock. Throw away your preconception of white collars and funny hats; through ongoing research, the Plimoth staff has developed a portrait of the Pilgrims that's more complex than the dour folk in school textbooks. Listen to the accents of the "residents," who never break out of character. You might see them plucking ducks, cooking rabbit stew, or tending garden. Feel free to engage them in conversation about their life, but expect only curious looks if you ask about anything that happened after 1627.

Elsewhere on the plantation is **Hobbamock's Homestead,** where descendants of the Wampanoag Indians re-create the life of a Native American who chose to live near the newcomers. In the **Carriage House Craft Center** you can see items created using the techniques of 17th-century English craftsmanship—that is, effects that the Pilgrims might have imported. (You can also buy samples.) At the **Nye Barn,** you can see goats, cows, pigs, and chickens. Most of the animals were bred from 17th-century gene pools and are probably similar to those raised in the original plantation. The visitor center has gift shops, a cafeteria, and multimedia presentations. Dress for the weather, since many exhibits are outdoors. Admission tickets are good for two consecutive days; if you have time, you may want to spread out your plantation visit to take in all the sights. ⊠ *Warren Ave. (Rte. 3A),* ☎ *508/746–1622,* WEB *www.plimoth.org.* ⊡ *$20; $22 ticket includes Mayflower II.* ☉ *Apr.–Nov., daily 9–5.*

The **Mayflower II,** a replica of the 1620 *Mayflower,* is manned by staff in period dress. The ship was built in England through research and a bit of guesswork, then sailed across the Atlantic in 1957. ⊠ *State Pier,* ☎ *508/746–1622,* WEB *www.plimoth.org.* ⊡ *$8 or as part of Plimoth Plantation fee.* ☉ *Apr.–Nov., daily 9–5.*

A few dozen yards from the *Mayflower II* is **Plymouth Rock,** popularly believed to have been the Pilgrims' stepping stone when they left the ship. Given the stone's unimpressive appearance—it's little more than a boulder—and dubious authenticity (as explained on a nearby plaque), the grand canopy overhead seems a trifle ostentatious.

Several historic houses are open for visits, including the 1640 **Sparrow House,** Plymouth's oldest structure. You can peek into several rooms furnished in the spartan style of the Pilgrims' era. The contemporary crafts gallery also on the premises seems somewhat out of place, but the works on view are high-quality. ⊠ *42 Summer St.,* ☎ *508/747–1240.* ⌨ *$2, gallery free.* ☉ *Apr.–Dec., Thurs.–Fri. and Sun.–Tues. 10–5, Sat. 10–dusk.*

From the waterfront sights, it's a short walk to one of the country's oldest public museums. The **Pilgrim Hall Museum,** established in 1824, transports you back to the time before the Pilgrims' landing, with items carried by those weary travelers to the New World. Included are a carved chest, a remarkably well preserved wicker cradle, Myles Standish's sword, John Alden's Bible, Native American artifacts, and the remains of the *Sparrow Hawk,* a sailing ship that was wrecked in 1626. ⊠ *75 Court St./Rte. 3A,* ☎ *508/746–1620,* ᗯᗴᗷ *www.pilgrimhall.org.* ⌨ *$5.* ☉ *Feb.–Dec., daily 9:30–4:30.*

Imagine an entire museum devoted to a Thanksgiving side dish. But the Ocean Spray–operated **Cranberry World** is amazingly popular. After viewing details of how this major state crop is grown, harvested, and processed, you can sip juices and sample other cranberry products. ⊠ *158 Water St.,* ☎ *508/747–2350.* ⌨ *$2.* ☉ *May–Nov., daily 9:30–5.*

Dining

$$–$$$ ✕ **Bert's Cove.** This local landmark, just off the entrance to Plymouth Beach, has great ocean views and a straightforward menu that emphasizes fresh seafood and steaks. The traditional fare has some contemporary touches: instead of standard coleslaw, there's a vegetable slaw that uses Asian flavors. ⊠ *140 Warren Ave./Rte. 3A,* ☎ *508/746–3330. AE, D, MC, V. Closed Mon. Nov.–Feb.*

$–$$ ✕ **All-American Diner.** The look is nostalgia—red, white, and blue with movie posters. The specialty is beloved American foods—omelets and pancakes for breakfast; burgers, salads, and soups for lunch. ⊠ *60 Court St.,* ☎ *508/747–4763. AE, DC, MC, V. No dinner.*

New Bedford

45 mi southwest of Plymouth, 50 mi south of Boston.

In 1652, colonists from Plymouth settled in the area that now includes the city of New Bedford. The city has a long maritime tradition, beginning as a shipbuilding center and small whaling port in the late 1700s. By the mid-1800s, the city had developed into a center of North American whaling. Today, New Bedford has the largest fishing fleet on the East Coast. Although much of the town is industrial, the restored historic district near the water is a delight. It was here that Herman Melville set his masterpiece, *Moby-Dick,* a novel about whaling.

The city's whaling tradition is commemorated in the **New Bedford Whaling National Historical Park,** which takes up 13 blocks of the waterfront historic district. The park visitor center, housed in an 1853 Greek Revival building that was once a bank, provides maps and information about whaling-related sites. Free walking tours of the park leave from the visitor center at 10 AM and noon in July and August. You can also view an orientation film about American whaling and the New Bedford historic sites; the film is free and is shown on the hour, daily

10–3, at the nearby New Bedford Whaling Museum. ⊠ *33 William St.*, ☎ *508/996–4095,* WEB *www.nps.gov/nebe.* ☉ *Daily 9–5.*

⊘ The **New Bedford Whaling Museum,** established in 1903, is the world's largest museum of its kind. A highlight is the skeleton of a 66-ft blue whale, one of only three on view anywhere. An interactive exhibit lets you listen to the underwater sounds of whales, dolphins, and other sea life—plus the sounds of a thunderstorm and a whale-watching boat—as a whale might hear them. You can also peruse the collection of scrimshaw, visit exhibits on regional history, and climb aboard an 89-ft, half-scale model of the 1826 whaling ship *Lagoda*—the world's largest ship model. ⊠ *18 Johnny Cake Hill,* ☎ *508/997–0046,* WEB *www. whalingmuseum.org.* ⊡ *$7.* ☉ *Daily 9–5; Memorial Day–Labor Day until 9 on Thurs.*

The **New Bedford Art Museum,** a compact gallery space housed in the 1918 Vault Building, a former bank, showcases the work of area artists. Among the works are paintings by 19th- and early 20th-century New Bedford artists Albert Bierstadt, William Bradford, and Charles Henry Gifford. ⊠ *608 Pleasant St.,* ☎ *508/961–3072,* WEB *www.newbedfordartmuseum.org.* ⊡ *$3.* ☉ *Memorial Day–Labor Day, Mon.–Wed. and Fri.–Sun. 10–5, Thurs. 10–7; Labor Day–Memorial Day, Wed. and Fri.–Sun. noon–5, Thurs. noon–7.*

For a glimpse of upper-class life during New Bedford's whaling heyday, head ½ mi south of downtown to the **Rotch-Jones-Duff House and Garden Museum.** This 1834 Greek Revival mansion, set amid a full city block of gardens, housed three prominent families in the 1800s and is filled with elegant furnishings from the era, including a mahogany piano, a massive marble-top sideboard, and portraits of the house's occupants. A self-guided audio tour is available. ⊠ *396 County St.,* ☎ *508/997–1401,* WEB *www.rjdmuseum.org.* ⊡ *$4.* ☉ *Mon.–Sat. 10–4, Sun. noon–4.*

Dining

$$–$$$ ✕ **Davy's Locker.** A huge seafood menu is the main draw at this spot overlooking Buzzards Bay. Choose from more than a dozen shrimp preparations or a healthy-choice entrée—dishes prepared with olive oil, vegetables, garlic, and herbs. For landlubbers, chicken, steak, ribs, and the like are also served. ⊠ *1480 E. Rodney French Blvd.,* ☎ *508/992–7359. AE, D, DC, MC, V.*

$–$$$ ✕ **Antonio's.** You can sample the traditional fare of New Bedford's large Portuguese population at the friendly, unadorned Antonio's. It serves up hearty portions of pork and shellfish stew, *bacalau* (salt cod), and grilled sardines, often on plates piled high with crispy fried potatoes and rice. ⊠ *267 Coggeshall St., near intersection of I–195 and Rte. 18,* ☎ *508/990–3636. No credit cards.*

AROUND BOSTON A TO Z

To research prices, get advice from other travelers, and book travel arrangements, visit www.fodors.com.

BUS TRAVEL

The Massachusetts Bay Transportation Authority, or MBTA, operates buses to Lexington from Alewife station in Cambridge. Buses 62 and 76 make the trip in 25–30 minutes. American Eagle Motorcoach Inc. offers service from Boston to New Bedford. Plymouth & Brockton Street Railway links Plymouth and the South Shore to Boston's South Station with frequent bus service.

➤ BUS INFORMATION: **American Eagle Motorcoach Inc.** (☎ 800/453–

5040). **MBTA** (☎ 617/222–3200, WEB www.mbta.com). **Plymouth & Brockton Street Railway** (☎ 508/746–0378, WEB www.p-b.com).

CAR TRAVEL

From Boston to Lexington, pick up Memorial Drive in Cambridge, and continue to the Fresh Pond Parkway, then to Route 2 west. Exit Route 2 at Routes 4/225 if your first stop is the National Heritage Museum; from Routes 4/225, turn left on Mass Ave. For Lexington center, take the Waltham Street/Lexington exit from Route 2. Follow Waltham Street just under 2 mi to Mass Ave.; you'll be just east of the Battle Green. The drive takes about 30 minutes. To reach Concord by car, continue west on Route 2. Or take I–90 (the Massachusetts Turnpike) to I–95 north, and then exit at Route 2, heading west. Driving time is 40–45 minutes.

Lowell lies near the intersection of I–495 and Route 3. From Boston, take I–93 north to I–495. Go south on I–495 to Exit 35C, the Lowell Connector. Follow the Lowell Connector to Exit 5B, Thorndike Street. Travel time is 45 minutes to an hour. To get to Plymouth, take the Southeast Expressway I–93 south to Route 3 (toward Cape Cod); Exits 6 and 4 lead to downtown Plymouth. To reach New Bedford from Boston, take I–93 to Route 24 south to Route 140 south, and continue to I–195 east. Allow about one hour from Boston to Plymouth and about one hour from Plymouth to New Bedford.

EMERGENCIES

➤ CONTACTS: **Police** (☎ 911). **Emerson Hospital** (✉ 133 Ornack [off Rte. 2], Concord, ☎ 978/369–1400, WEB www.emersonhospital.org). **Jordan Hospital** (✉ 275 Sandwich St., Plymouth, ☎ 508/746–2000, WEB www.jordan.org). **Newton-Wellesley Hospital** (✉ 2014 Washington St./Rte. 16, Newton, ☎ 617/243–6000, WEB www.nwh.org). **St. Luke's Hospital** (✉ 101 Page St., New Bedford, ☎ 508/997–1515).

TRAIN TRAVEL

The purple line, the MBTA's commuter rail, runs from North Station to Concord in about 40 minutes and to Lowell in about 45 minutes. Concord's station is a short walk away from the town center. The Lowell station is about ½ mi from the historic attractions. Public shuttle buses run between Lowell station and downtown every 15 minutes weekdays 6–6 and every half hour Saturday 10–4. MBTA commuter rail service is available to Plymouth. Travel time is about one hour. From the station, take the Plymouth Area Link buses to the historic attractions.

➤ TRAIN INFORMATION: **Lowell Regional Transit Authority** (✉ 145 Thorndike St., Lowell, ☎ 978/452–6161, WEB www.lrta.com). **MBTA** (☎ 617/222–3200, WEB www.mbta.com).

VISITOR INFORMATION

➤ TOURIST INFORMATION: **Concord Chamber of Commerce** (✉ 105 Everett St., Concord, ☎ 978/369–3120, WEB www.concordmachamber. org). **Concord Visitor Center** (✉ 58 Main St., Concord, ☎ 978/369–3120). **Destination Plymouth** (✉ 170 Water St., Suite 10C, Plymouth 02360, ☎ 800/872–1620, WEB www.visit-plymouth.com). **Lexington Visitor Center** (✉ 1875 Massachusetts Ave., Lexington, ☎ 781/862–1450, WEB www.lexingtonchamber.org). **New Bedford Office of Tourism** (✉ Waterfront Visitors Center, Pier 3, New Bedford 02740, ☎ 508/979–1745 or 800/508–5353, WEB www.ci.new-bedford.ma.us). **Plymouth Waterfront Visitor Information Center** (✉ 130 Water St., at Rte. 44, Plymouth 02360, ☎ 508/747–7525).

CAPE COD

Updated by
Carolyn Heller

A Patti Page song from the 1950s promises that "If you're fond of sand dunes and salty air, quaint little villages here and there, you're sure to fall in love with old Cape Cod." The tourism boom since the '50s has certainly proved her right. Continually shaped by ocean currents, this windswept land of sandy beaches and dunes has compelling natural beauty. Everyone comes for the seaside, yet the crimson cranberry bogs, forests of birch and beech, freshwater ponds, and marshlands that grace the interior are just as splendid. Local history is equally fascinating; whale-watching provides an exhilarating experience of the natural world; cycling trails lace the landscape; shops purvey everything from antiques to pure kitsch; and you can dine on simple fresh seafood, creative contemporary cuisine, or most anything in between.

Separated from the Massachusetts mainland by the 17½-mi Cape Cod Canal—at 480 ft the world's widest sea-level canal—and linked to it by two heavily trafficked bridges, the Cape is always likened in shape to an outstretched arm bent at the elbow, its Provincetown fist turned back toward the mainland. The Cape "winds around to face itself" is how the writer Philip Hamburger has put it.

Each of the Cape's 15 towns is broken up into villages, which is where things can get complicated. The town of Barnstable, for example, consists of Barnstable, West Barnstable, Cotuit, Marstons Mills, Osterville, Centerville, and Hyannis. The terms Upper Cape and Lower Cape can also be confusing. **Upper Cape**—think upper arm, as in the shape of the Cape—refers to the towns of Bourne, Falmouth, Mashpee, and Sandwich. **Mid Cape** includes Barnstable, Yarmouth, and Dennis. Brewster, Harwich, Chatham, Orleans, Eastham, Wellfleet, Truro, and Provincetown make up the **Lower Cape.** The **Outer Cape,** as in outer reaches, is essentially synonymous with Lower Cape, though technically it includes only Wellfleet, Truro, and Provincetown.

Three major roads traverse the Cape. U.S. 6 is the fastest way to get from the mainland to Orleans. Route 6A winds along the north shore through scenic towns; Route 28 dips south through some of the overdeveloped parts of the Cape. If you want to avoid malls, heavy traffic, and tacky motels, avoid Route 28 from Falmouth to Chatham. Past Orleans on the way out to Provincetown, the roadside clutter of much of U.S. 6 masks the beauty of what surrounds it.

Cape Cod is only about 70 mi from end to end—you can make a cursory circuit of it in about two days. But it is really a place for relaxing—for swimming and sunning; for fishing, boating, and playing golf or tennis; for attending the theater, hunting for antiques, and making the rounds of art galleries; for buying lobster and fish fresh from the boat; or for taking leisurely walks, bike rides, or drives along timeless country roads.

Sandwich

★ ❶ *3 mi east of the Sagamore Bridge, 11 mi west of Barnstable.*

The oldest town on Cape Cod, Sandwich was established in 1637 by some of the Plymouth Pilgrims and incorporated in 1638. Today it is a well-preserved, quintessential New England village with a white-columned town hall and streets lined with 18th- and 19th-century homes.

From 1825 until 1888, the main industry in Sandwich was the production of vividly colored glass, made in the Boston and Sandwich Glass Company's factory. The **Sandwich Glass Museum** contains relics of the town's early history, a diorama of the factory in its heyday, and displays of shimmering blown and pressed glass. Glassmaking demonstrations are held in summer, and a gift shop sells attractive glass pieces. ⊠ *129 Main St.,* ☎ *508/888–0251,* WEB *www.sandwichglassmuseum.org.* ⬛ *$3.50.* ☉ *Apr.–Dec., daily 9:30–5; Feb.–Mar., Wed.–Sun. 9:30–4.*

★ **Heritage Plantation,** a fine complex of museum buildings, gardens, and a café, sits on 76 acres overlooking Shawme Pond. The Shaker Round Barn displays historic cars, including a 1930 yellow-and-green Duesenberg built for movie star Gary Cooper. The Military Museum houses antique firearms, military uniforms, and a collection of miniature soldiers. At the Art Museum are an extensive Currier & Ives collection, antique toys, and a working 1912 Coney Island–style carousel. The grounds are planted with flowers, hostas, heather, fruit trees, and rhododendrons. Concerts are held in the gardens on summer afternoons and evenings. ⊠ *Grove and Pine Sts.,* ☎ *508/888–3300,* WEB *www. heritageplantation.org.* ⬛ *$12.* ☉ *Mid-May–Oct., Sat.–Wed. 9–6, Thurs.–Fri. 9–8; Nov.–Apr., Tues.–Sun. 10–4.*

The **Sandwich Boardwalk,** built over a salt marsh, a creek, and low dunes, leads to Town Neck Beach. Cape Cod Bay stretches out around the beach at the end of the walk, where a platform provides fine views, especially at sunset. From town cross Route 6A on Jarves Street, and at its end turn left, then right, and continue to the boardwalk parking lot.

Dining and Lodging

$$–$$$ ✕ **Aqua Grille.** The far-ranging menu and lively atmosphere at this smart-casual bistro by the marina make it a good choice for large groups. Fried or grilled seafood, pastas, and steaks are all available. The superb lobster salad is a hearty serving of greens, avocados, baby green beans, and meaty lobster chunks. ⊠ *14 Gallo Rd.,* ☎ *508/888–8889,* WEB *www.aquagrille.com. AE, MC, V. Closed mid-Oct.–Mar.*

$$$ ✕▦ **Dan'l Webster Inn.** Built in 1971, the Dan'l Webster is a contemporary hotel with old New England friendliness and hospitality. Chef's specials at the restaurant ($$$–$$$$) might include horseradish-crusted salmon served over cucumber and jicama salad. You can choose to include some meals in the room price. Lodgings are in the main inn and wings or in two nearby historic houses with four suites each. All rooms have floral fabrics, reproduction mahogany and cherry furnishings, and some antiques. The eight rooms on the second floor of the Jarves Wing are particularly spacious and have fireplaces. ⊠ *149 Main St., 02563,* ☎ *508/888–3622 or 800/444–3566,* FAX *508/888–5156,* WEB *www. danlwebsterinn.com. 45 rooms, 9 suites. 2 restaurants, room service, some in-room hot tubs, pool; no-smoking rooms. AE, D, DC, MC, V. MAP.*

$–$$$ ✕▦ **Belfry Inn & Bistro.** Housed in a 1902 former church and the adjacent "painted-lady" Victorian rectory, this inn retains many of the church's original features—arches, stained-glass windows—in its six stylish rooms. In the Drew House next door, the eight rooms blend Laura Ashley prints and pastel-painted furnishings. The bistro ($$$), a dramatic space in the former sanctuary, serves contemporary fare such as filet mignon with mascarpone mashed potatoes or duck breast with wild mushroom risotto. ⊠ *8 Jarves St., 02563,* ☎ *508/888–8550 or 800/844–4542,* FAX *508/888–3922,* WEB *www.belfryinn.com. 14 rooms. Restaurant, bar; no air-conditioning in some rooms, no kids under 10. AE, D, DC, MC, V. No dinner Sun.–Mon. No lunch. BP.*

$$ ▦ **Wingscorton Farm.** This enchanting oasis is a working farm. The main house, built in 1756, has two second-floor suites, each with a fireplace, Oriental rugs, and wainscoting. Also on the property are a

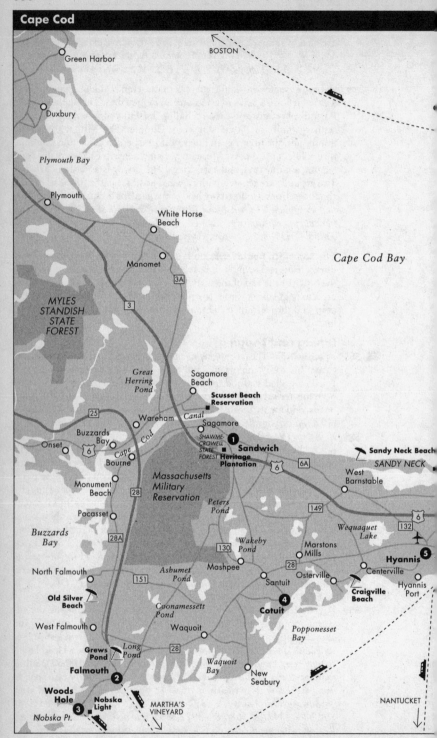

BOSTON

Green Harbor

Duxbury

Plymouth Bay

Plymouth

White Horse
Beach

Manomet

3A

Cape Cod Bay

3

MYLES
STANDISH
STATE
FOREST

*Great
Herring
Pond*

Sagamore
Beach

**Scusset Beach
Reservation**

Canal

25

Wareham

Sagamore

Cod

*SHAWME-
CROWELL
STATE
FOREST*

1

Buzzards
Bay

Cape

**Heritage
Plantation**

Sandwich

6A

West
Barnstable

Sandy Neck Beach

SANDY NECK

Onset

6

Bourne

Monument
Beach

28

*Massachusetts
Military
Reservation*

*Peters
Pond*

149

132

6

Pocasset

*Buzzards
Bay*

28A

*Wakeby
Pond*

130

*Wequaquet
Lake*

Marstons
Mills

Hyannis

5

North Falmouth

151

*Ashumet
Pond*

Mashpee

28

Santuit

Osterville

Centerville

Hyannis
Port

**Old Silver
Beach**

*Coonamessett
Pond*

4

**Craigville
Beach**

West Falmouth

Waquoit

Cotuit

*Popponesset
Bay*

28

*Grews
Pond*

*Long
Pond*

*Waquoit
Bay*

New
Seabury

Falmouth

2

NANTUCKET

**Woods
Hole**

3

**Nobska
Light**

MARTHA'S
VINEYARD

Nobska Pt.

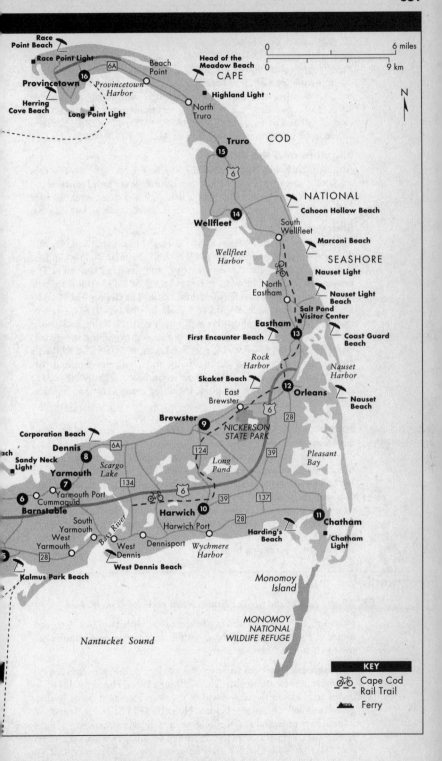

Race
Point Beach

Race Point Light

Provincetown
6A
Provincetown
Harbor
16
Beach
Point

Head of the
Meadow Beach
CAPE

Herring
Cove Beach

Long Point Light

North
Truro

Highland Light

COD

Truro
15
6

NATIONAL

Cahoon Hollow Beach

Wellfleet
14
South
Wellfleet

Marconi Beach

SEASHORE

Wellfleet
Harbor

North
Eastham

Nauset Light

Nauset Light
Beach

Salt Pond
Visitor Center

Eastham
13

Coast Guard
Beach

First Encounter Beach

Rock
Harbor

Nauset
Harbor

Skaket Beach

East
Brewster

12
Orleans

Nauset
Beach

Brewster
9
6
28

NICKERSON
STATE PARK

Corporation Beach

Dennis
8
6A

124

Long
Pond

39

Pleasant
Bay

Sandy Neck
Light

Yarmouth
7

Scargo
Lake

134

6

39

137

Barnstable
6

Yarmouth Port
Cummaquid

Harwich
10

Harwich Port

11
Chatham

South
Yarmouth
West
Yarmouth

West
Dennis

Dennisport

28

Harding's
Beach

Chatham
Light

28

West Dennis Beach

Wychmere
Harbor

Kalmus Park Beach

Monomoy
Island

Nantucket Sound

MONOMOY
NATIONAL
WILDLIFE REFUGE

KEY

Cape Cod
Rail Trail

Ferry

detached two-bedroom cottage and a converted stone carriage house. A private bay beach is a five-minute walk away. ⊠ *11 Wing Blvd., off Rte. 6A, about 4½ mi east of Sandwich Center, East Sandwich 02537,* ☎ *508/888–0534,* FAX *508/888–0545. 2 suites, 1 carriage house, 1 cottage. No air-conditioning. AE, MC, V. BP.*

$ ⚠ **Shawme-Crowell State Forest.** Open-air campfires are allowed at the 285 wooded tent and RV campsites here, and campers have free access to Scusset Beach. The forest is less than a mile from the Cape Cod Canal. ⊠ *Rte. 130, 02563,* ☎ *508/888–0351; 877/422–6762 reservations;* WEB *www.reserveamerica.com. MC, V. Closed Oct.–Mar.*

Nightlife and the Arts

Atmospheric **Bobby Byrne's Pub** (⊠ 65 Rte. 6A, ☎ 508/888–6088) is a relaxing, convivial place to stop for a drink. **Town band concerts** (⊠ Henry T. Wing Elementary School, Rte. 130 and Beale Ave., ☎ 508/ 888–5144) are held on Thursday at 7:30 PM from July to late August.

Shopping

The **Bee-Hive General Store** (⊠ 385 Rte. 6A, East Sandwich, ☎ 508/ 833–4907) sells a hodgepodge of clever and kitsch, including candles, lawn ornaments, jam, 5¢ candy, toys, and assorted souvenirs.The **Brown Jug** (⊠ 155 Main St., at Jarves St., ☎ 508/833–1088) specializes in antique glass and Staffordshire china. The **Giving Tree** (⊠ 550 Rte. 6A, East Sandwich, ☎ 508/888–5446 or 888/246–3551), a gallery and sculpture garden, shows contemporary crafts, jewelry, and prints; it also has walking paths through a bamboo grove along the marsh. **Horsefeathers** (⊠ 454 Rte. 6A, East Sandwich, ☎ 508/888–5298) sells antique linens, lace, and vintage baby and children's clothing. **Titcomb's Bookshop** (⊠ 432 Rte. 6A, East Sandwich, ☎ 508/888–2331) stocks used, rare, and new books, including many Cape and nautical titles.

OFF THE
BEATEN PATH

ROUTE 6A – If you're traveling to Orleans and you're not in a hurry, take this lovely road, which heads east from Sandwich, passing through the oldest settlements on the Cape. Part of the Old King's Highway historic district, this stretch is protected from development. Classic inns and enticing antiques shops alternate with traditional gray-shingled homes on the tree-lined route, and the woods periodically give way to broad vistas across the marshes. In autumn the foliage along the road is bright—maples with their feet wet in ponds and marshes put on a good display. Along 6A east of Sandwich center, you can stop to watch the harvesting of cranberries in flooded bogs.

Falmouth

❷ *15 mi south of the Bourne Bridge, 4 mi north of Woods Hole.*

Falmouth, the Cape's second-largest town, was settled in 1660. Although much of Falmouth is suburban, with a large year-round population, the town still includes sights from earlier times.

The **Falmouth Historical Society** conducts free walking tours in season and maintains two museums. The 1790 **Julia Wood House** retains wonderful architectural details—a widow's walk, wide-board floors, leaded-glass windows. The smaller **Conant House,** a 1794 half Cape next door, has military memorabilia, whaling items, sailors' valentines, and a genealogical and historical research library. ⊠ *Village Green, off Palmer Ave.,* ☎ *508/548–4857,* WEB *www.falmouthhistoricalsociety.org.* ☜ *$4.* ⊙ *June–Aug., Tues.–Sat. 10–4; Sept.–Nov., weekends 1–4.*

Dining and Lodging

$–$$$ ✕ **TraBiCa.** Part trattoria, part bistro, and part café (thus the unusual name), this appealing restaurant in a snug gray-shingle house mixes Italian classics with a changing menu of more sophisticated Mediterranean fare. The selection is fairly innovative for this part of the Cape, and the broad menu should please everyone from tots to great-aunt Tillie. ⊠ *327 Gifford St.,* ☎ *508/548–9861. MC, V. Closed Mon. Nov.–Apr. No lunch.*

$$$–$$$$ ✕☷ **Coonamessett Inn.** With plenty of art, wood, and hanging plants
   ★ all around, this is one of the best and oldest inn-restaurants on the Cape. One- or two-bedroom suites are in five buildings around a broad lawn that spills down to a wooded pond. Rooms are casually decorated, with bleached wood or pine paneling and New England antiques or reproductions. The menu ($$$–$$$$) in the lovely main dining room is traditional; the many seafood choices include swordfish with grilled vegetable slaw and baked, stuffed lobster. ⊠ *311 Gifford St., at Jones Rd., 02540,* ☎ *508/548–2300,* 𝔽𝔸𝕏 *508/540–9831,* 𝕎𝔼𝔹 *www.capecodrestaurants.org. 28 suites, 1 cottage. No-smoking rooms. AE, D, MC, V. CP.*

$$$–$$$$ ☷ **La Maison Cappellari at Mostly Hall.** Looking very much like a pri-
   ★ vate estate, this imposing 1849 house has a wraparound porch and a dramatic widow's walk. Several bedrooms are decorated in an upscale European style, each with a colorful mural; in the Tuscan Room, the walls are painted to suggest an intimate Italian garden. Three rooms are more traditionally decorated, with floral wallpaper, canopy beds, and other antiques. Although the inn is only steps from the town center, you can lounge in the lush gardens and feel a world away. ⊠ *27 Main St., 02540,* ☎ *508/548–3786 or 800/682–0565,* 𝔽𝔸𝕏 *508/548–5778,* 𝕎𝔼𝔹 *www.mostlyhall.com. 6 rooms. Bicycles, library; no smoking, no kids under 16. AE, D, MC, V. Closed mid-Dec.–mid-Apr. BP.*

$$$ ☷ **Wildflower Inn.** The innkeepers here call their decorating style "old
   ★ made new again": tables are constructed from early 1900s pedal sewing-machine bases, and the living room's sideboard was a '20s electric stove. Guest rooms, two of which have whirlpool tubs, are also innovatively decorated, from the romantic Moonflower Room to the bright, cheerful Geranium Room. The five-course breakfast might include sunflower crepes, calendula corn muffins, or other delicious concoctions using the edible wildflowers grown out back. ⊠ *167 Palmer Ave., 02540,* ☎ 𝔽𝔸𝕏 *508/548–9524 or 800/294–5459,* 𝕎𝔼𝔹 *www.wildflower-inn.com. 5 rooms, 1 cottage. No smoking. AE, MC, V. Closed Jan.–Feb. BP.*

Nightlife and the Arts

The **Nimrod Inn** (⊠ 100 Dillingham Ave., ☎ 508/540–4132) presents jazz and contemporary music at least six nights a week. **Town band concerts** (⊠ Marina Park, Scranton Ave., ☎ 508/548–8500 or 800/526–8532) take place on summer Thursdays at 8 PM.

Outdoor Activities and Sports

BEACHES

Grews Pond, in Goodwill Park, is a pretty tree-lined freshwater pond with a sandy beach and lifeguarded swimming area. Popular with local families, it has picnic tables, rest rooms, and free parking. Enter the park from Route 28 just north of Jones Road or from Gifford Street opposite St. Joseph's Cemetery.

Old Silver Beach, a long crescent of white sand, is especially good for small children because a sandbar keeps it shallow at one end and creates tidal pools full of crabs and minnows. There are lifeguards, rest rooms, showers, and a snack bar. ⊠ *Off Quaker Rd., North Falmouth.* ☷ *Parking $10 in summer.*

BIKING

The **Shining Sea Trail** is an easy 3½-mi route between Locust Street in Falmouth and the Woods Hole ferry parking lot.

FISHING

Freshwater ponds are good for perch, pickerel, and trout; the required license is available at **Eastman's Sport & Tackle** (⊠ 150 Main St., ☎ 508/548–6900).

TENNIS

Falmouth Sports Center (⊠ 33 Highfield Dr., ☎ 508/548–7433) has three all-weather and six indoor tennis courts, plus racquetball-hand-ball courts and a health club.

Woods Hole

❸ *4 mi southwest of Falmouth, 19 mi south of the Bourne Bridge.*

Woods Hole is home to several major scientific institutions: the Woods Hole Oceanographic Institution (WHOI), the Marine Biological Laboratory (MBL), the National Marine Fisheries Service, and the U.S. Geological Survey's Branch of Marine Geology. The town is also the departure point for ferries to Martha's Vineyard.

The WHOI is the largest independent private oceanographic laboratory in the world. Its staff led the successful U.S.–French search for the *Titanic* (found about 400 mi off Newfoundland) in 1985. Although the **Oceanographic Institution** is not open to the public, you can learn about it at the small **WHOI Exhibit Center**. ⊠ *15 School St., ☎ 508/289–2663,* WEB *www.whoi.edu.* ☞ *Suggestion donation $2.* ☉ *Memorial Day–Labor Day, Mon.–Sat. 10–4:30, Sun. noon–4:30; Apr. and Nov.–Dec., Fri.–Sat. 10–4:30, Sun. noon–4:30; early May–Memorial Day and Labor Day–Oct., Tues.–Sat. 10–4:30, Sun. noon–4:30.*

☾ The exhibition tanks at the **National Marine Fisheries Service Aquarium** contain regional fish and shellfish. You can see things up close through magnifying glasses. Several hands-on pools hold banded lobsters, crabs, snails, sea stars, and other creatures. The star attractions are two harbor seals, which can be seen in the outdoor pool near the entrance. The exhibits aren't sophisticated and the facility could be better maintained, but this place is definitely kid-friendly. At press time, the aquarium had closed temporarily while staff implemented new security procedures; call to confirm hours before visiting. ⊠ *Albatross and Water Sts., ☎ 508/495–2267; 508/495–2001 recorded information;* WEB *www.nefsc. nmfs.gov/nefsc/aquarium.* ☞ *Free.* ☉ *Call for hrs.*

Dining

$$–$$$ ✕ **Fishmonger's Café.** The ambitious contemporary menu at this restau-
★   rant on the sound includes a fried calamari appetizer with a hot-pepper sauce and grilled seafood dishes with tropical fruit sauces. The mango and cilantro sauce over grilled salmon is particularly delectable. ⊠ *56 Water St., ☎ 508/540–5376. Reservations not accepted. AE, MC, V. Closed Dec.–mid-Feb. and Tues. Labor Day–Mar.*

Cotuit

❹ *16 mi northeast of Woods Hole.*

The center of this picturesque town is not much more than a cross-roads with a coffee shop, pizza parlor, and general store, which all seem unchanged since the 1940s. Nearby Mashpee is one of two Massachusetts towns (the other is Aquinnah, formerly known as Gay Head, on Martha's Vineyard) that have municipally governed, as well as Native

American–governed, areas. Mashpee also encompasses the resort community of New Seabury.

The **Cahoon Museum of American Art** is in a 1775 Georgian Colonial farmhouse that was once a tavern and an overnight way station for travelers on the Hyannis–Sandwich Stagecoach line. Its several rooms display American primitive paintings by Ralph and Martha Cahoon along with other 19th- and early 20th-century art. ⊠ *4676 Falmouth Rd./Rte. 28,* ☎ *508/428–7581,* WEB *www.cahoonmuseum.org.* ⊠ *Suggested donation $3.* ☉ *Feb.–Dec., Tues.–Sat. 10–4.*

Dining and Lodging

$$$–$$$$ ✕ **Regatta of Cotuit.** The classic yet original fare here includes pâtés of rabbit, veal, and venison and a signature seared loin of lamb with cabernet sauce, surrounded by chèvre, spinach, and pine nuts. The restored Colonial stagecoach inn is plushly filled with wood, brass, and Oriental carpets, and the cozy taproom has its own bar menu. ⊠ *4613 Falmouth Rd./Rte. 28,* ☎ *508/428–5715. AE, MC, V. Reservations essential. No lunch.*

$$$$ ✕ ⚇ **New Seabury Resort and Conference Center.** This self-contained
★ resort community on a 2,000-acre point surrounded by Nantucket Sound contains furnished apartments—available for overnight stays or longer—in some of its 13 villages. Among the amenities are fine waterfront dining ($$–$$$), a restaurant overlooking the fairways ($$–$$$), and a private beach. The resort's golf courses are open to the public from September to May. ⊠ *Rock Landing Rd. (Box 549, New Seabury 02649),* ☎ *508/477–9400 or 800/999–9033,* FAX *508/477–9790,* WEB *www.newseabury.com. 140 1- and 2-bedroom units. 2 restaurants, 2 18-hole golf courses, 16 tennis courts, 2 pools, health club, beach, boating, bicycles, shops. AE, DC, MC, V.*

Hyannis

❺ *11 mi northeast of Cotuit, 23 mi east of the Bourne Bridge.*

Perhaps best known for its association with the Kennedy clan, Hyannis is the Cape's year-round commercial and transportation hub. Nearby strip malls have taken their toll on Main Street, but there are plenty of fun and fancy eateries here.

The enlarged and annotated photographs at the **John F. Kennedy Hyannis Museum** document JFK's Cape years (1934–63). ⊠ *Old Town Hall, 397 Main St.,* ☎ *508/790–3077.* ⊠ *$5.* ☉ *Mid-Apr.–Oct., Mon.–Sat. 10–4, Sun. 1–4 (last admission at 3:30); Nov.–mid-Dec. and mid-Feb.–mid-Apr., Wed.–Sat. 10–4.*

Hyannis Port, 1½ mi south of Hyannis, was a mecca for Americans during the Kennedy presidency, when the **Kennedy Compound** became the summer White House. More recently, Kennedy family members waited here for news of John Kennedy Jr.'s missing plane; while he was en route to a cousin's wedding in Hyannis in 1999, his plane crashed off Martha's Vineyard, killing the young Kennedy, his wife, and her sister. The Kennedy mystique is such that tourists still seek out the compound; the best way to get a glimpse of it is from the water on one of the many harbor tours or cruises.

Dining and Lodging

$$$–$$$$ ✕ **The Paddock.** The Paddock is synonymous with excellent formal din-
★ ing—in the authentically Victorian main dining room or the breezy old-style-wicker summer porch. Steak au poivre with five varieties of crushed peppercorns is but one of the many traditional yet innovative preparations. The superb Pacific Rim chicken is a grilled breast topped

with oranges and mangoes, served on mixed greens and Asian noodles. Manhattans are the drink of choice in the lounge, where musicians perform in the evening. ⊠ *W. Main St. rotary, next to Melody Tent,* ☏ *508/775–7677,* WEB *www.capecodtravel.com/paddock. AE, DC, MC, V. Closed mid-Nov.–Mar.*

$$–$$$ ✕ **RooBar.** A bit of Manhattan on Main Street, RooBar has a dark, sophisticated feel, with good music and a hip bar scene at night. From the wood-fired oven come pizzas like scallop and prosciutto with asparagus and goat cheese. Also try the Big-Ass Grilled Shrimp in a red curry-coconut sauce and the fire-roasted chicken rubbed with toasted fennel and cumin seeds. There's a second location in Falmouth (⊠ 285 Main St., ☏ 508/548–8600). ⊠ *586 Main St.,* ☏ *508/778–6515. Reservations essential. AE, MC, V.*

$–$$ ✕ **Baxter's Fish N' Chips.** The delicious fried clams here are served with homemade tartar sauce. Picnic tables make it possible for you to lose no time in the sun while you dine on lobster, burgers, or delicacies from the excellent raw bar. ⊠ *Pleasant St.,* ☏ *508/775–4490. Reservations not accepted. AE, MC, V. Closed Columbus Day–Apr. and weekdays Labor Day–Columbus Day.*

$$–$$$$ ▥ **Breakwaters.** If you were any closer to the water, you'd be in it—
★ that's how close these charming weathered gray-shingle cottages are to Nantucket Sound. The one-, two-, and three-bedroom condos provide all the comforts of home. The units have one or two bathrooms; kitchens with microwaves, coffeemakers, refrigerators, toasters, and stoves; and a deck or patio with a grill. Most have water views. An added plus is daily (except Sunday) maid service. ⊠ *432 Sea St. (Box 118, 02601),* ☏ FAX *508/775–6831,* WEB *www.capecod.com/breakwaters. 19 cottages (weekly rentals only June–Aug.). Pool, beach, baby-sitting; no smoking. No credit cards. Closed mid-Oct.–Apr.*

$–$$ ▥ **Sea Breeze Inn.** The rooms at this cedar-shingle seaside B&B have antique or canopied beds and are decorated with well-chosen antiques. The nicest of the three detached cottages is the three-bedroom Rose Garden, which has two baths, a TV room, a fireplace, and a washer and dryer. Innkeeper Patricia Gibney's breakfasts, served in the dining room or the gazebo, are worth rising early for. ⊠ *270 Ocean Ave., at Sea St., 02601,* ☏ *508/771–7213,* FAX *508/862–0663,* WEB *www.seabreezeinn.com. 14 rooms, 3 cottages. No smoking. AE, D, MC, V. CP.*

Nightlife and the Arts

The **Cape Cod Melody Tent** (⊠ 21 W. Main St., ☏ 508/775–9100, WEB www.melodytent.com) presents pop concerts and comedy shows. The **Prodigal Son** (⊠ 10 Ocean St., ☏ 508/771–1337) hosts live music most nights; the lineup includes acoustic, blues, jazz, rock, and even spoken word performers. **Town band concerts** (⊠ Village Green, Main St., ☏ 508/362–5230 or 800/449–6647) take place at 7:30 PM on Wednesday in July and August.

Outdoor Activities and Sports

Kalmus Park Beach is a wide beach with a section for windsurfers and a sheltered area for children. It has a snack bar, rest rooms, showers, and lifeguards. ⊠ *South end, Ocean St.* ◻ *Parking $10.* ☉ *Memorial Day–Labor Day.*

Barnstable

❻ *4 mi north of Hyannis, 11 mi east of Sandwich.*

Barnstable is the second-oldest town on the Cape (it was founded in 1639), and you'll get a feeling for its age in Barnstable Village, a lovely area of large old homes dominated by the Barnstable County Superior Courthouse. Barnstable is also known for beautiful Sandy Neck Beach.

Dining and Lodging

$–$$ ✕ **Mill Way Fish and Lobster.** This seafood market–lunch place on Barnstable Harbor has only a few outside picnic tables, but the fried clams and fish sandwiches are worth the inevitable wait. Try the fat onion rings or the almost-too-big-for-lunch clambake, which comes with chowder, lobster, steamers, and an ear of corn. Mill Way closes at 7 PM. ✉ *275 Mill Way,* ☎ *508/362–2760. AE, D, MC, V. Closed Oct.– Mar.*

$$–$$$ ⬛ **Beechwood Inn.** This yellow and pale-green 1853 Queen Anne is
★ trimmed with gingerbread, wrapped by a wide porch with a glider swing, and shaded by beech trees. The parlor is pure mahogany-and-red-velvet Victorian; the guest rooms are decorated with antiques in lighter, earlier Victorian styles. ✉ *2839 Main St./Rte. 6A, 02630,* ☎ *508/362–6618 or 800/609–6618,* FAX *508/362–0298,* WEB *www.beechwoodinn.com. 6 rooms. Refrigerators, bicycles; no smoking, no kids under 12. AE, D, MC, V. BP.*

$$ ⬛ **Honeysuckle Hill.** The airy, country-style guest rooms in this gray-shingle 1810 Queen Anne–style cottage have lots of white wicker, feather beds, checked curtains, and pastel-painted floors. But it's the little touches that count here: a fridge stocked with sodas and water bottles, beach chairs with umbrellas (perfect for nearby Sandy Neck Beach), and an always-full cookie jar in the sunny dining room. ✉ *591 Rte. 6A, West Barnstable 02668,* ☎ *508/362–8418 or 866/444–5522,* FAX *508/362–8386,* WEB *www.honeysucklehill.com. 4 rooms, 1 suite. No kids under 12, no smoking. AE, D, MC, V. BP.*

Outdoor Activities and Sports

Hovering above Barnstable Harbor and the 4,000-acre Great Salt Marsh, **Sandy Neck Beach** stretches 6 mi across a peninsula that ends at Sandy Neck Light. The beach is one of the Cape's most beautiful—dunes, sand, and sea spread east, west, and north. The lighthouse, a few feet from the eroding shoreline at the tip of the neck, has been out of commission since 1952. The main beach at Sandy Neck has lifeguards, a snack bar, rest rooms, and showers. ✉ *Sandy Neck Rd. off Rte. 6A, West Barnstable,* ☎ *508/362–8300.* ☜ *Parking $10 Memorial Day– Labor Day.* ☼ *Daily 9–9, but staffed only until 5.*

Yarmouth and Yarmouth Port

❼ *4 mi east of Barnstable, 21 mi east of the Sagamore Bridge.*

Yarmouth was settled in 1639 by farmers from the Plymouth Bay Colony. By 1829, when Yarmouth Port was incorporated as a separate village, the Cape had begun a thriving maritime industry. Many impressive sea captains' houses—some now B&Bs and museums—still line the streets, and Yarmouth Port has some real old-time stores.

For a peek into the past, stop at **Hallet's,** a country drugstore preserved as it was in 1889, when the current owner's grandfather Thatcher Hallet opened it. ✉ *139 Main St./Rte. 6A, Yarmouth Port,* ☎ *508/362– 3362.* ☜ *Free.* ☼ *Call for hrs.*

One of Yarmouth Port's most beautiful spots is Bass Hole, which
★ ☾ stretches from Homer's Dock Road to the salt marsh. **Bass Hole Board-walk** extends over a marshy creek. The 2½-mi **Callery-Darling nature trails** meander through salt marshes, vegetated wetlands, and upland woods. Gray's Beach is a little crescent of sand with calm waters. ✉ *Trail entrance on Center St. near the Gray's Beach parking lot.*

Dining and Lodging

$$–$$$ ✕ **Inaho.** Yuji Watanabe's sushi and sashimi are artistically presented,
★ and his tempura is fluffy and light. The authentic Japanese ambience

(there's a traditional garden out back), the attention to detail, and the remarkably high quality of the ingredients may make you forget you're still on old Cape Cod. ✉ *157 Main St./Rte. 6A, Yarmouth Port,* ☎ *508/362–5522. MC, V. Closed Mon. No lunch.*

$–$$ ✕ **Jack's Outback.** Tough to find, tough to forget, this eccentric little serve-yourself-pretty-much-anything-you-want joint goes by the motto "Good food, lousy service." Solid breakfasts give way to thick burgers and traditional favorites like Yankee pot roast. Jack's has no liquor license, and you can't BYOB. ✉ *161 Main St./Rte. 6A, Yarmouth Port,* ☎ *508/362–6690. Reservations not accepted. No credit cards. No dinner.*

$$–$$$ ⊞ **Wedgewood Inn.** This handsome white-painted 1812 Greek Revival
★ building is on the National Register of Historic Places. Inside, the sophisticated country decor is a mix of fine Colonial antiques, handcrafted cherry pencil-post beds, antique quilts, and maritime paintings. ✉ *83 Main St./Rte. 6A, Yarmouth Port 02675,* ☎ *508/362–5157 or 508/ 362–9178,* ℻ *508/362–5851,* 𝖶𝖤𝖡 *www.wedgewood-inn.com. 4 rooms, 5 suites. No smoking. AE, MC, V. BP.*

$–$$$ ⊞ **Blueberry Manor.** This quiet, early 19th-century Greek Revival house now serves as a wonderfully sophisticated yet homey B&B. The living room pairs Victorian furnishings and a marble fireplace with modern amenities, including a TV/VCR, a stereo, and a stash of games and books. Upstairs, the guest rooms feel crisp and clean; while the furnishings are traditional, there are no fussy lace treatments or curio shelves. The Lavender Room has a queen-size four-poster bed with a handmade quilt and an antique armoire. ✉ *438 Main St./Rte. 6A, Yarmouth Port 02675,* ☎ *508/362–7620,* ℻ *508/362–0053,* 𝖶𝖤𝖡 *www.blueberrymanor.com. 3 rooms, 1 suite. No smoking. AE, MC, V. BP.*

Shopping

Cummaquid Fine Arts (✉ 4275 Rte. 6A, Cummaquid, ☎ 508/362–2593) displays works by Cape Cod and New England artists. **Parnassus Book Service** (✉ 220 Main St./Rte. 6A, Yarmouth Port, ☎ 508/362– 6420), in an 1840 former general store, specializes in Cape Cod, maritime, and antiquarian books. **Peach Tree Designs** (✉ 173 Main St./Rte. 6A, Yarmouth Port, ☎ 508/362–8317) carries home furnishings and accessories made by local craftspeople.

Dennis

❽ *4 mi northeast of Yarmouth, 7 mi west of Brewster.*

Hundreds of sea captains lived in Dennis when fishing, salt making, and shipbuilding were the main industries. The elegant houses they constructed still line the streets. The town has conservation areas, nature trails, and numerous ponds for swimming.

The holdings of the **Cape Museum of Fine Arts** include more than 850 works by Cape-associated artists. The museum hosts film festivals, lectures, and art classes. ✉ *60 Hope La. (on the grounds of the Cape Playhouse), off Rte. 6A,* ☎ *508/385–4477,* 𝖶𝖤𝖡 *www.cmfa.org.* ☞ *$7.* ☺ *Late May–mid-Oct., Mon.–Sat. 10–5, Sun. 1–5; late Oct.–mid-May, Tues.–Sat. 10–5, Sun. 1–5.*

Dining and Lodging

$$$ ✕ **Gina's by the Sea.** In a funky old building tucked into a sand dune, the aroma of fine northern Italian cooking blends with a fresh breeze off the bay. Look for lots of fresh pasta and seafood, and if you don't want a long wait, come early or late. ✉ *134 Taunton Ave.,* ☎ *508/ 385–3213. Reservations not accepted. AE, MC, V. Closed Dec.–Mar. and Mon.–Wed. Oct.–Nov. No lunch Apr.–June and Sept.–Nov.*

$$ ⊡ **Isaiah Hall B&B Inn.** Lilacs and pink roses trail the white fence out-
★ side this 1857 Greek Revival farmhouse on a residential road on the
bay side. Guest rooms are decorated with country antiques, floral-print
wallpapers, and homey quilts. In the carriage house, rooms have sten-
ciled white walls and knotty pine, and some have small balconies over-
looking gardens. ⊠ *152 Whig St., 02638,* ☎ *508/385–9928 or 800/
736–0160,* FAX *508/385–5879,* WEB *www.isaiahhallinn.com. 9 rooms,
1 suite. Picnic area, badminton, croquet; no kids under 7, no smok-
ing. AE, MC, V. Closed mid-Oct.–early May. CP.*

$–$$ ⊡ **Four Chimneys Inn.** This three-story, four-chimney 1881 Queen Anne
gem is a relaxing getaway. The rooms, with hand-stenciled trim, are taste-
fully furnished with cherry four-poster, wicker, antique pine, or oak beds;
all have views of either Scargo Lake or of the surrounding woods and
gardens. ⊠ *946 Main St./Rte. 6A, 02638,* ☎ *508/385–6317 or 800/
874–5502,* FAX *508/385–6285,* WEB *www.fourchimneysinn.com. 7 rooms.
No air-conditioning in some rooms, no kids under 8, no smoking. AE,
MC, V. CP.*

Nightlife and the Arts

The oldest professional summer theater in the country is the **Cape Playhouse** (⊠ 820 Main St./Rte. 6A, ☎ 508/385–3911 or 877/385–3911,
WEB www.capeplayhouse.com), which produces Broadway-style plays
as well as children's shows. The **Reel Art Cinema** (☎ 508/385–4477)
at the Cape Museum of Fine Arts shows avant garde, classic, art, and
independent films on weekends; call for a schedule.

Outdoor Activities and Sports

BEACHES

Parking at these beaches is $10 per day for nonresidents from Memo-
rial Day to Labor Day. Dennis's **Corporation Beach** (⊠ Corporation
Rd.) on Cape Cod Bay is a beautiful crescent of white sand backed by
low dunes; there are lifeguards, showers, rest rooms, and a food stand.
On the south shore, one of the best beaches is the long, wide **West Dennis Beach** (⊠ Davis Beach Rd., West Dennis), which has bathhouses,
lifeguards, a playground, and food concessions.

Brewster

⑨ *7 mi northeast of Dennis, 5 mi west of Orleans.*

Brewster is the perfect place to learn about the natural history of the
Cape: the area contains conservation lands, state parks, forests, freshwater ponds, and marshes. When the tide is low in Cape Cod Bay, you
can stroll the beaches and explore tidal pools up to 2 mi from the shore
on the Brewster flats.

☙ For nature enthusiasts, a visit to the **Cape Cod Museum of Natural History** is a must. In the museum and on the grounds are a library, nature
and marine exhibits, and trails through 80 acres of forest and marshland rich in birds and wildlife. The exhibit hall upstairs has a display
of aerial photographs documenting the process by which the Chatham
sandbar split in two. The museum also offers guided canoe and kayak
trips from May through September and several cruises that explore different Cape waterways: Nantucket Sound, Pleasant Bay, and Nauset
Marsh. ⊠ *869 Main St./Rte. 6A,* ☎ *508/896–3867; 800/479–3867 in
Massachusetts;* WEB *www.ccmnh.org.* ⊡ *$5.* ☉ *Mon.–Sat. 9:30–4:30,
Sun. 11–4:30.*

The **Brewster Store** (⊠ 1935 Main St./Rte. 6A, at Rte. 124, ☎ 508/896–
3744, WEB www.brewsterstore.com) is a local landmark. Built in 1852,
this typical New England general store provides such essentials as the
daily papers, penny candy, and benches out front for conversation.

Dining and Lodging

$$$$ ✕ **Chillingsworth.** This crown jewel of Cape restaurants is extremely
★ formal, terribly pricey, and completely upscale. The classic French
menu and wine cellar continue to win award after award. The seven-
course table d'hôte menu includes an assortment of appetizers, entrées—
like super-rich risotto, roast lobster, or grilled venison—and
"amusements." At dinner, a modest bistro menu is served in the Garden Room, a patiolike area in the front of the restaurant. ⊠ *2449 Main
St./Rte. 6A,* ☎ *508/896–3640,* WEB *www.chillingsworth.com. Reservations essential. AE, DC, MC, V. Closed Mon. mid-June–Thanksgiving;
some weekdays Memorial Day–mid-June and mid-Oct.–Thanksgiving;
and entirely Thanksgiving–Memorial Day.*

$$–$$$ ✕ **Spark Fish.** "Spark" refers to a wood-fire grill, which the kitchen
uses often. The menu emphasizes simple ingredients—fresh herbs, garlic, and fruit salsas—and lets the flavors of local seafood, quality
meats, and good vegetables shine through. The understated interior is
as unfussy as the menu. In the off-season, there's comfortable fireside
dining. ⊠ *2671 Rte. 6A,* ☎ *508/896–1067. MC, V.*

$$–$$$$ ☷ **Captain Freeman Inn.** The opulent details at this splendid 1866 Vic-
★ torian include a marble fireplace, herringbone-inlay flooring, ornate Ital-
ian ceiling medallions, and 12-ft ceilings. Guest rooms have hardwood
floors, antiques, and eyelet spreads. The eight "luxury rooms" truly de-
serve the name. ⊠ *15 Breakwater Rd., 02631,* ☎ *508/896–7481 or 800/
843–4664,* FAX *508/896–5618,* WEB *www.captainfreemaninn.com. 12
rooms. Pool, bicycles, badminton, croquet; no kids under 10, no smok-
ing. MC, V. BP.*

$–$$ ☷ **Old Sea Pines Inn.** Fronted by a white-column portico, the Old Sea
Pines evokes the summer estates of an earlier time. A sweeping stair-
case leads to rooms decorated with framed old photographs and antique furnishings. Rooms in a newer building are sparsely but well
decorated. The rooms with shared baths are *very* small but a steal in
summer. ⊠ *2553 Main St./Rte. 6A (Box 1070, 02631),* ☎ *508/896–
6114,* FAX *508/896–7387,* WEB *www.oldseapinesinn.com. 24 rooms, 19
with bath; 3 suites; 2 family-size rooms. Restaurant; no smoking. AE,
D, DC, MC, V. Closed Jan.–Mar. BP.*

$ ⚠ **Nickerson State Park.** Some of the popular sites at this 2,000-acre
park are right on the edges of ponds. The facilities include showers,
bathrooms, barbecue areas, and a store. ⊠ *3488 Main St./Rte. 6A,
02631,* ☎ *508/896–3491; 877/422–6762 reservations;* FAX *508/896–
3103;* WEB *www.state.ma.us/dem/parks/nick.htm. 418 sites. No credit
cards.*

Outdoor Activities and Sports

BIKING

The **Cape Cod Rail Trail** cuts through Brewster at Long Pond Road, Underpass Road, Millstone Road, and other points.

BOATING

Jack's Boat Rentals (⊠ Nickerson State Park, Flax Pond, Rte. 6A, ☎
508/896–8556) rents canoes, kayaks, Seacycles, Sunfish, pedal boats,
and sailboards.

GOLF

Captain's Golf Course (⊠ 1000 Freeman's Way, ☎ 508/896–5100, WEB
www.captainsgolfcourse.com) is a great 18-hole, par-72 public course
with a greens fee ranging from $20 to $60; cart fees range from $4 to
$28. **Ocean Edge Golf Course** (⊠ Villagers Dr./Rte. 6A, ☎ 508/896–
5911, WEB www.oceanedge.com), an 18-hole, par-72 course winding
around five ponds, has a greens fee that ranges from $25 to $64; carts,
mandatory at certain times, cost $15.

STATE PARK

The 1,961 acres of **Nickerson State Park** (⊠ 3488 Rte. 6A, ☎ 508/896–3491) consist of oak, pitch pine, hemlock, and spruce forest dotted with freshwater kettle ponds formed by glacial action. Recreational opportunities include fishing, boating, biking along 8 mi of trails, cross-country skiing, and bird-watching. **Flax Pond** has picnic areas, a bathhouse, and water-sports rentals.

Shopping

Kemp Pottery (⊠ 258 Main St./Rte. 6A, ☎ 508/385–5782) has functional and decorative stoneware and porcelain. **Kingsland Manor** (⊠ 440 Main St./Rte. 6A, ☎ 508/385–9741) sells everything "from tin to Tiffany." The **Spectrum** (⊠ 369 Main St./Rte. 6A, ☎ 508/385–3322) purveys American arts and crafts, including art glass and pottery. **Sydenstricker Galleries** (⊠ 490 Main St./Rte. 6A, ☎ 508/385–3272) is a working glass studio.

Harwich

⑩ *3 mi south of Brewster.*

Originally known as Setucket, Harwich separated from Brewster in 1694 and was renamed after the famous seaport in England. Like other townships on the Cape, Harwich is actually a cluster of seven small villages, including bustling Harwich Port. Three naturally sheltered harbors on Nantucket Sound make the town, like its English namesake, a popular spot for boaters. Each September Harwich holds a Cranberry Festival to celebrate the importance of this indigenous berry.

Once a private school, the pillared 1844 Greek Revival building of **Brooks Academy** now houses the museum of the **Harwich Historical Society.** In addition to a large photo-history collection and exhibits on artist Charles Cahoon (grandson of Alvin Cahoon, the principal cranberry grower in 1840s Harwich), the socio-technological history of the cranberry culture, and shoe making, the museum displays antique clothing and textiles, china and glass, fans, toys, and much more. There is also an extensive genealogical collection for researchers. On the grounds is a powder house that was used to store gunpowder during the Revolutionary War, as well as a restored 1872 outhouse. ⊠ *80 Parallel St.,* ☎ *508/432–8089.* 🎫 *Donations accepted.* ☉ *June–mid-Oct., Wed.–Sun. 1–4.*

Dining and Lodging

$–$$$ ✗ **Brax Landing.** In this local stalwart, perched alongside busy Saquatucket Harbor, you'll pass by tanks full of steamers and lobsters in the corridor leading to the dining room. The restaurant sprawls around a big bar that serves drinks like the "Moxie" (pink lemonade and vodka, "calm seas guaranteed"). The swordfish and the Chatham scrod are favorites, both served simply and well. There's a notable children's menu, and Sunday brunch, served from 10 to 2, is an institution. ⊠ *Rte. 28 at Saquatucket Harbor, Harwich Port,* ☎ *508/432–5515. Reservations not accepted. AE, DC, MC, V.*

$$$–$$$$ 🏨 **Augustus Snow House.** This grand Victorian epitomizes elegance. ★   The stately dining room is the setting for the three-course breakfast, with dishes like baked pears in a raspberry-cream sauce. Guest rooms, which all have fireplaces, are decorated with Victorian-print wallpapers, luxurious carpets, and fine antiques and reproduction furnishings. ⊠ *528 Main St., Harwich Port 02646,* ☎ *508/430–0528 or 800/320–0528,* FAX *508/432–6638 ext. 15,* WEB *www.augustussnow.com. 5 rooms, 1 suite. No kids under 12. AE, D, MC, V. BP.*

Outdoor Activities and Sports

Cape Water Sports (⊠ 337 Main St., Harwich Port, ☎ 508/432–7079) rents Sunfish, Hobie Cats, Lasers, powerboats, day sailers, and canoes. Fishing trips are operated from spring to fall on the **Golden Eagle** (⊠ Wychmere Harbor, Harwich Port, ☎ 508/432–5611). **Cranberry Valley Golf Course** (⊠ 183 Oak St., ☎ 508/430–7560, WEB www.cranberrygolfcourse.com) has a championship 18-hole, par-72 layout. The greens fee is $55; an optional cart costs $26.

Chatham

⓫ *5 mi east of Harwich.*

At the bent elbow of the Cape, Chatham has all the charm of a quiet seaside resort, with relatively little commercialism. And it *is* charming: gray-shingle houses with tidy awnings and cheerful flower gardens, an attractive Main Street with crafts and antiques stores alongside homey coffee shops, and a five-and-ten. It's well-to-do without being ostentatious, casual and fun but refined, and never tacky.

The view from **Chatham Light** (⊠ Main St., near Bridge St., ☎ 508/945–0719)—of the harbor, the sandbars, and the ocean beyond—justifies the crowds that gather to share it. The lighthouse is especially dramatic on a foggy night, as the beacon's light pierces the mist. Coin-operated telescopes allow a close look at the famous Chatham Break, the result of a fierce 1987 nor'easter that blasted a channel through a barrier beach just off the coast.

Monomoy National Wildlife Refuge is a 2,500-acre preserve including the Monomoy Islands, a fragile, 9-mi-long barrier-beach area south of Chatham. A paradise for bird-watchers, the islands are an important stop along the North Atlantic flyway for migratory waterfowl and shore birds. The Cape Cod Museum of Natural History and the Massachusetts Audubon Society in South Wellfleet conduct island tours. The **Monomoy National Wildlife Refuge headquarters,** on Morris Island, has a visitor center (⊠ off Morris Island Rd., ☎ 508/945–0594), open daily 8–4, where you can pick up pamphlets.

Dining and Lodging

$$–$$$ ✕ **Christian's.** The influences at this landmark town establishment stem from two continents. Downstairs, an Old Cape–country-French motif prevails in the decor and on the menu: boneless roast duck with raspberry sauce and flaky sautéed sole with lobster and lemon-butter sauce are typical entrées. Upstairs is casual and great for families, with a seafood-based menu (with some Mexican influences), and a mahogany-paneled piano bar. ⊠ *443 Main St.,* ☎ *508/945–3362,* WEB *www.christiansrestaurant.com. AE, D, DC, MC, V. Closed weekdays Jan.–Mar.*

$$–$$$ ✕ **Vining's Bistro.** Chatham's restaurants tend to serve conservative fare,
★   but the cuisine at this bistro is among the most inventive in the area. The wood grill, where the chef employs zesty spices from all over the globe, is the center of attention. The exotic Bangkok fishermen's stew, the spit-roasted Jamaican chicken, and the Portobello mushroom sandwich are among the best dishes. ⊠ *595 Main St.,* ☎ *508/945–5033,* WEB *www.viningsbistro.com. Reservations not accepted. AE, D, MC, V. Closed mid-Jan.–Apr.*

$$$$ 🏨 **Wequassett Inn Resort & Golf Club.** This exquisite traditional resort
★   offers accommodations in 20 Cape-style cottages and an attractive hotel complex along a bay and on 22 acres of woods. Luxurious dining, attentive service, evening entertainment, and plenty of sunning and sporting opportunities are among the draws. Spacious rooms have country

pine furniture and such homey touches as handmade quilts and duck decoys. ⊠ *173 Orleans Rd./Rte. 28, Pleasant Bay 02633,* ☎ *508/432–5400 or 800/225–7125,* FAX *508/432–5032,* WEB *www.wequassett.com. 102 rooms, 2 suites. Restaurant, grill, piano bar, room service, 4 tennis courts, pool, gym, windsurfing, boating. AE, D, DC, MC, V. Closed Nov.–Apr. FAP.*

$$$–$$$$ ▥ **Queen Anne Inn.** Built in 1840 as a wedding present for the daughter of a famous clipper-ship captain, this grand structure has large rooms furnished in a casual yet elegant style. Some have working fireplaces, private balconies, and hot tubs. Lingering and lounging are encouraged—around the large pool, on the veranda, in front of the fireplace in the sitting room, and in the plush parlor. ⊠ *70 Queen Anne Rd., 02633,* ☎ *508/945–0394 or 800/545–4667,* FAX *508/945–4884,* WEB *www.queenanneinn.com. 31 rooms. Restaurant, 3 tennis courts, pool, bar. AE, D, MC, V.*

$$–$$$ ▥ **Moses Nickerson House.** Each room in this 1839 B&B has its own
★ look: one has dark woods, leather, Ralph Lauren fabrics, and English hunting antiques; another has a high canopy bed and a hand-hooked rug. All rooms have queen-size beds and complete modem and computer hookups. ⊠ *364 Old Harbor Rd., 02633,* ☎ *508/945–5859 or 800/628–6972,* FAX *508/945–7087,* WEB *www.capecodtravel.com/ mosesnickersonhouse. 7 rooms. In-room data ports; no kids under 12, no smoking. AE, D, MC, V. BP.*

Nightlife and the Arts

Monomoy Theatre (⊠ 776 Main St., ☎ 508/945–1589) presents summer productions by the Ohio University Players. Chatham's summer **town band concerts** (⊠ Kate Gould Park, Main St., ☎ 508/945–5199) begin at 8 PM on Friday and draw up to 6,000 people.

Outdoor Activities and Sports

Harding's Beach (⊠ Harding's Beach Rd., off Barn Hill Rd.), west of Chatham center, is open to the public and charges daily parking fees to nonresidents in season.

Shopping

Cape Cod Cooperage (⊠ 1150 Queen Anne Rd., at Rte. 137, ☎ 508/ 432–0788) sells traditional wooden ware made by an on-site cooper. At **Chatham Glass Co.** (⊠ 758 Main St., ☎ 508/945–5547) you can watch glass being blown and buy it, too. **Marion's Pie Shop** (⊠ 2022 Main St./Rte. 28, West Chatham, ☎ 508/432–9439) sells fruit breads, pastries, prepared foods, and, of course, pies, both savory and sweet. **Yellow Umbrella Books** (⊠ 501 Main St./Rte. 28, ☎ 508/945–0144) has an excellent selection of new and used books.

Orleans

⑫ *8 mi north of Chatham, 35 mi east of the Sagamore Bridge.*

Incorporated in 1797, Orleans is part quiet seaside village and part bustling commercial center. A walk along Rock Harbor Road, a winding street lined with gray-shingled houses, white picket fences, and neat gardens, leads to the bay-side **Rock Harbor,** the base of a small commercial fishing fleet whose catch hits the counters at the fish market here. Sunsets over the harbor are memorable.

Dining and Lodging

$$$–$$$$ ✕ **Nauset Beach Club.** Locals say this intimate restaurant has never been
★ better, serving regional Italian cuisine that emphasizes locally harvested seafood and produce. Choose from a fixed-price option (offered at two early seatings) or the regular menu for such favorites as pistachio-crusted roast rack of lamb or tagliatelle with lobster. The pastas

and desserts are all homemade. ⊠ *222 Main St., East Orleans,* ☎ *508/ 255–8547. AE, D, DC, MC, V. Reservations essential. No lunch.*

$$–$$$ ✕ **Kadee's Lobster & Clam Bar.** A summer landmark, Kadee's serves good clams and fish-and-chips that you can grab on the way to the beach from the take-out window. Or you can sit down in the dining room for steamers and mussels, pasta and seafood stews, or the Portuguese kale soup. There's a miniature golf course out back. The only drawback here is the prices. ⊠ *212 Main St.,* ☎ *508/255–6184. Reservations not accepted. MC, V. Closed day after Labor Day–wk before Memorial Day and weekdays in early June.*

$$ ▣ **Kadee's Gray Elephant.** A mile from Nauset Beach, this centuries-old house contains small vacation studio and one-bedroom apartments. They are a cheerful riot of color, from wicker painted lavender or green to beds layered in quilts and comforters mixing plaids and florals. The kitchens are equipped with microwaves, attractive glassware, irons and boards—and even lobster crackers. ⊠ *216 Main St. (Box 86, East Orleans 02643),* ☎ *508/255–7608,* FAX *508/240–2976. 6–8 apartments. Restaurant, miniature golf. MC, V.*

Nightlife and the Arts

The **Academy Playhouse** (⊠ 120 Main St., ☎ 508/255–1963, WEB www.apa1.org) hosts a dozen or so productions year-round, including original works. The **Cape & Islands Chamber Music Festival** (☎ 508/ 255–1386, WEB www.capecodchambermusic.org) presents three weeks of top-caliber performances in August.

Outdoor Activities and Sports

BEACHES

Nauset Beach (⊠ Beach Rd.)—not to be confused with Nauset Light Beach at Cape Cod National Seashore—is a 10-mi-long sweep of sandy ocean beach with low dunes and large waves good for bodysurfing or boardsurfing. There are lifeguards, rest rooms, showers, and a food concession. Daily parking fees are $8. **Skaket Beach** (⊠ Skaket Beach Rd., ☎ 508/240–3775) on Cape Cod Bay is a sandy stretch with calm, warm water good for children. There are rest rooms, lifeguards, and a snack bar. Daily parking fees are $8.

BOATING AND FISHING

Arey's Pond Boat Yard (⊠ 43 Arey's La., off Rte. 28, South Orleans, ☎ 508/255–0994, WEB www.by-the-sea.com/areyspondboatyard) has a sailing school where individual and group lessons are taught. **Goose Hummock Shop** (⊠ 15 Rte. 6A, off the U.S. 6 rotary, ☎ 508/255–0455) sells licenses, which are required for fishing in Orleans's freshwater ponds. **Rock Harbor Charter Boat Fleet** (⊠ Rock Harbor, ☎ 508/255–9757; 800/287–1771 in Massachusetts) goes for bass and blues in the bay from spring to fall. Walk-ons are welcome.

Shopping

Addison Holmes Fine Art Gallery (⊠ 43 Rte. 28, ☎ 508/255–6200), housed in four rooms of a brick-red Cape, represents area artists. **Hannah** (⊠ 47 Main St., ☎ 508/255–8234) has unique women's fashions. **Tree's Place** (⊠ Rte. 6A at Rte. 28, ☎ 508/255–1330), one of the Cape's most original shops, displays works of New England artists.

Eastham

⓭ *3 mi north of Orleans.*

Like many other Cape towns, Eastham (incorporated in 1651) started as a farming community, later turning to the sea and to salt making for its livelihood. A more atypical industry here was asparagus growing; from the late 1800s through the 1920s, Eastham was known as the Asparagus Capital.

The park on busy U.S. 6 at Samoset Road has as its centerpiece the **Eastham Windmill,** the oldest windmill on Cape Cod. ⊠ *U.S. 6.* 🏷 *Free.* ☉ *Late June–Labor Day, Mon.–Sat. 10–5, Sun. 1–5.*

★ Along 30 mi of shoreline from Chatham to Provincetown, the 27,000-acre **Cape Cod National Seashore** encompasses superb ocean beaches, rolling dunes, wetlands, pitch pine and scrub oak forest, wildlife, and several historic structures. Self-guided nature, hiking, biking, and horse trails lace these landscapes. **Salt Pond Visitor Center** has a museum and offers guided tours, boat trips, and lectures, as well as evening beach walks and campfire talks in summer. ⊠ *Visitor center, Doane Rd., off U.S. 6,* ☎ *508/255–3421,* WEB *www.nps.gov/caco.* 🏷 *Free; beach parking $7 per day mid-June–Labor Day or $20 for yearly pass good at all national seashore beaches.* ☉ *Mar.–June and Sept.–Dec., daily 9–4:30; July–Aug., daily 9–5; Jan.–Feb., weekends 9–4:30.*

Roads and bicycle trails lead to Coast Guard and Nauset Light beaches, which begin an unbroken 30-mi stretch of barrier beach extending to Provincetown—the "Cape Cod Beach" of Thoreau's 1865 classic, *Cape Cod.* You can still walk its length, as Thoreau did. Tours of the much-photographed red and white **Nauset Light** (⊠ Ocean View Dr. and Cable Rd., ☎ 508/240–2612, WEB www.nausetlight.org) are given on weekends in season; call for schedule.

Lodging

$$$-$$$$ 🏨 **Penny House Inn.** Antiques and collectibles decorate the rooms in this rambling inn sheltered by a wave of privet hedge. Common areas include the Great Room, with a fireplace and lots of windows, a combination sunroom-library, and a garden patio set with umbrella tables. ⊠ *4885 County Rd./U.S. 6, 02642,* ☎ *508/255–6632 or 800/554–1751,* FAX *508/255–4893,* WEB *www.pennyhouseinn.com. 12 rooms. No smoking. AE, D, MC, V. BP.*

$$$-$$$$ 🏨 **Whalewalk Inn.** With windows galore, this 1830 whaling master's home on 3 acres of rolling lawns and gardens has an airy feeling. Wide-board pine floors, fireplaces, and 19th-century country antiques provide historical appeal. The spacious rooms have floral fabrics and antique or reproduction furniture. ⊠ *220 Bridge Rd., 02642,* ☎ *508/ 255–0617 or 800/440–1281,* FAX *508/240–0017,* WEB *www. whalewalkinn.com. 11 rooms, 5 suites. Bicycles; no kids under 12, no smoking. MC, V. BP.*

$ ⛺ **Atlantic Oaks Campground.** Primarily an RV camp, this campground forest is less than 1 mi north of the Salt Pond Visitor Center. RV hookups, including cable TV, cost $45 for two people; tent sites are $32 for two people. Showers are free. ⊠ *3700 U.S. 6, 02642,* ☎ *508/255–1437 or 800/332–2267,* WEB *www.atlanticoaks.com. 100 RV sites, 30 tent sites. Bicycles, playground, laundry facilities. D, MC, V. Closed Nov.–Apr.*

Outdoor Activities and Sports

Low grass and heathland back the long **Coast Guard Beach** (⊠ off Ocean View Dr.). It has no parking lot, so park at the Salt Pond Visitor Center or the lot up Doane Road from the center and take the free shuttle or walk the 1¾-mi Nauset Trail to the beach. A great spot for watching sunsets over the bay, **First Encounter Beach** (⊠ Samoset Rd., off U.S. 6) is laden with history. Near the parking lot (daily parking fees are $5 in season), a bronze marker commemorates the first encounter between local Indians and passengers from the *Mayflower,* who explored the area for five weeks in late 1620.

Wellfleet

⑭ *10 mi northwest of Eastham, 13 mi southeast of Provincetown.*

Tastefully developed Wellfleet attracts many artists and writers because of its fine restaurants, historic houses, and many art galleries.

★ The **Massachusetts Audubon Wellfleet Bay Sanctuary,** a 1,000-acre haven for more than 250 species of birds, is a superb place for walking, birding, and looking west over the salt marsh and bay at wondrous sunsets. The Audubon Society hosts naturalist-led wildlife tours year-round; reservations are essential. ☒ *Off U.S. 6 (Box 236, South Wellfleet),* ☎ *508/349–2615,* WEB *www.wellfleetbay.org.* ☒ *$3.* ☉ *Daily 8 AM–dusk.*

A good stroll around town would take in Commercial and Main streets and end at **Uncle Tim's Bridge** (☒ off E. Commercial St.). The short walk across this arcing landmark—with its much-photographed view over marshland and a tidal creek—leads to a small wooded island.

For a **scenic loop** through a classic Cape landscape near Wellfleet's Atlantic beaches—with scrub and pines on the left, heathland meeting cliffs and the ocean below on the right—take LeCount Hollow Road north of the Marconi Station turnoff. Access to the first and last of four beaches on this stretch, **LeCount Hollow** and **Newcomb Hollow,** is restricted to residents in season. Between the two hollows are the lovely public Atlantic beaches **White Crest** and **Cahoon Hollow.** Backtrack to Cahoon Hollow Road and turn west for the southernmost entrance to the town of Wellfleet proper, across U.S. 6.

Dining and Lodging

$$$–$$$$ ✕ **Aesop's Tables.** Inside this 1805 captain's house—a worthy choice
★   for a special dinner—are five dining rooms; aim for a table on the porch overlooking the town center. This is a great place to sample various preparations of local seafood; the signature dish is an exotic bouillabaisse with mounds of fresh-off-the-boat seafood. Death by Chocolate is a popular dessert. On some nights in summer, the tavern hosts jazz musicians. ☒ *316 Main St.,* ☎ *508/349–6450. AE, DC, MC, V. Closed Columbus Day–Mother's Day. No lunch.*

$$–$$$ ✕ **Finely JP's.** The dining room is noisy, but the wonderful Italian-in-
★   fluenced fish and pasta dishes are worth it. The appetizers, among them the warm spinach and scallop salad and the blackened beef with charred-pepper relish, are especially good, and the Wellfleet paella draws raves. ☒ *U.S. 6, South Wellfleet,* ☎ *508/349–7500. Reservations not accepted. D, MC, V. Closed Mon.–Wed. Thanksgiving–Memorial Day; Mon.–Tues. Memorial Day–mid-June and Oct.–Thanksgiving; Tues. Labor Day–Oct.*

$$–$$$ ⌂ **Surf Side Colony Cottages.** These one- to three-bedroom cottages
★   on the Atlantic shore of the Outer Cape have fireplaces, kitchens, and screened porches. The exteriors are retro-Florida, but the knotty-pine interiors are classic Cape Cod. ☒ *Ocean View Dr. (Box 937, South Wellfleet 02663),* ☎ *508/349–3959,* FAX *508/349–3959,* WEB *www.surfsidevacation.com. 18 cottages. Picnic area, laundry facilities. MC, V. 1- to 2-wk minimum in summer. Closed Nov.–Mar.*

$–$$ ⌂ **Holden Inn.** If you're watching your budget and can deal with modest basics, try this old-time place just out of the town center. The lodge has shared baths, an outdoor shower, and a screened-in porch with a view of the bay. Rooms with private baths that have old porcelain sinks are available in adjacent 1840 and 1890 buildings. All rooms are clean and simple. ☒ *140 Commercial St., 02667,* ☎ *508/349–3450. 25 rooms, 10 with bath. No credit cards. Closed mid-Oct.–mid-Apr.*

Nightlife and the Arts

The **Beachcomber** (⊠ Ocean View Dr., Cahoon Hollow Beach, off U.S. 6, ☎ 508/349–6055) has live music and dancing in summer. The drive-in movie is alive and well at the **Wellfleet Drive-In Theater** (⊠ 51 U.S. 6, Eastham-Wellfleet line, ☎ 508/349–7176 or 508/255–9619). Art galleries host cocktail receptions during the **Wellfleet Gallery Crawl,** on Saturday evenings in July and August. The **Wellfleet Harbor Actors Theater** (⊠ Kendrick St., past E. Commercial St., ☎ 508/349–6835, WEB www.what.org) stages American plays, satires, and farces mid-May–mid-October.

Outdoor Activities and Sports

BEACHES

The spectacular dune-bordered Atlantic **public beaches** White Crest and Cahoon Hollow charge daily parking fees of $10 to nonresidents in season only. Cahoon Hollow has lifeguards, rest rooms, and a restaurant and music club on the sand. **Marconi Beach,** part of Cape Cod National Seashore, charges $7 for daily parking or $20 for a yearly pass that provides access to all seven national seashore beaches. **Mayo Beach,** just west of Wellfleet Harbor, is free.

BOATING

Jack's Boat Rentals (⊠ Gull Pond, ☎ 508/349–7553) rents canoes, kayaks, sailboats, and sailboards.

Shopping

Blue Heron Gallery (⊠ 20 Bank St., ☎ 508/349–6724), one of the Cape's best galleries, carries contemporary works. **Karol Richardson** (⊠ 11 W. Main St., ☎ 508/349–6378) designs women's wear in luxurious fabrics. **Kendall Art Gallery** (⊠ 40 E. Main St., ☎ 508/349–2482) carries contemporary art and has a serene sculpture garden.

Truro

⑮ *2 mi north of Wellfleet, 7 mi southeast of Provincetown.*

Truro, a town of high dunes and rivers fringed by grasses, is a popular retreat for artists, writers, and politicos. Edward Hopper, who summered here from 1930 to 1967, found the Cape light ideal for his austere realism. At **Pamet Harbor,** off Depot Road, you can walk out on the flats at low tide and discover the creatures of the salt marsh.

Lodging

$$ 🖿 **Moorlands Inn.** The artful touches at this proud Victorian beauty include the creative works—both visual and musical—of innkeepers Bill and Skipper Evaul. Antiques adorn the bright, uncluttered rooms in the main house, and the spacious penthouse provides a full kitchen, two bedrooms, and plenty of living space. Guests can gather in the communal hot tub out back. ⊠ *11 Hughes Rd., North Truro 02652,* ☎ *508/487–0663. 5 rooms, 1 apartment, 3 cottages. Outdoor hot tub, croquet. MC, V. BP.*

Outdoor Activities and Sports

BEACH

Head of the Meadow Beach (⊠ off U.S. 6, North Truro), a relatively uncrowded part of the national seashore, has only temporary rest-room facilities available in summer and no showers. The daily parking fee is $7 mid-June–Labor Day or $20 for an annual pass.

BIKING

The **Head of the Meadow Trail** is 2 mi of easy cycling between dunes and salt marshes from the Head of the Meadow Beach parking lot to

High Head Road, off Route 6A in North Truro. Bird-watchers love this area.

GOLF

Highland Golf Links (⊠ Lighthouse Rd., North Truro, ☎ 508/487–9201), a 9-hole, par-36 course on a cliff overlooking the Atlantic, has a greens fee of $16; an optional cart costs $13.

Provincetown

★ ⑯ *7 mi northwest of Truro, 27 mi north of Orleans, 62 mi from the Sagamore Bridge.*

Provincetown's shores form a curled fist at the very tip of the Cape. The town was for decades a bustling seaport, with fishing and whaling as its major industries. Fishing is still an important source of income for many Provincetown natives, although the town is a major whale-watching, rather than hunting, mecca.

One of the first of many historically important visitors to anchor in this hospitable natural harbor was Bartholomew Gosnold, who arrived in 1602 and named the area Cape Cod after the abundant codfish he found in the local waters. The Pilgrims arrived on Monday, November 21, 1620, when the *Mayflower* dropped anchor in Provincetown Harbor after a difficult 63-day voyage; while in the harbor they signed the Mayflower Compact, the first document to declare a democratic form of government in America. They stayed in the area for five weeks before moving on to Plymouth. During the American Revolution, Provincetown Harbor was controlled by the British, who used it as a port from which to sail to Boston and launch attacks on Colonial and French vessels.

Provincetown is the nation's oldest continuous arts colony: painters began coming here in 1899 for the unique Cape Cod light. Eugene O'Neill's first plays were written and produced here, and the Fine Arts Work Center continues to have in its ranks some of the most important writers of our time. In the busy downtown, Portuguese-American fishermen mix with painters, poets, writers, whale-watching families, cruise-ship passengers on brief stopovers, and many lesbian and gay residents and visitors, for whom P-town, as it's almost universally known, is one of the most popular East Coast seashore spots.

In summer, Commercial Street, the main thoroughfare, is packed with sightseers and shoppers browsing through the galleries and crafts shops. At night, raucous music and people spill out of bars, drag shows, and sing-along lounges. It's a fun, crazy place, with the extra dimension of the fishing fleet unloading the day's catch at MacMillan Wharf, in the center of the action. On the wharf are a municipal parking facility and the Chamber of Commerce, so it's a sensible place to start a tour of town.

Driving from one end of 3-mi-long Commercial Street to the other could take forever in season—walking is definitely the way to go. Many architectural styles—Victorian, Second Empire, Gothic, and Greek Revival, to name a few—were used to build houses for sea captains and merchants. The Provincetown Historical Society publishes walking-tour pamphlets, available for about $1 at many shops in town. Free Provincetown gallery guides are also available.

The quiet East End of town is mostly residential, with some top galleries. The similarly quiet West End has a number of small inns with neat lawns and elaborate gardens.

The **Pilgrim Monument,** which stretches incongruously into the sky over the low-rise town, commemorates the first landing of the Pilgrims in the New World and their signing of the Mayflower Compact, America's first rules of self-governance. Climb the 252-ft-high tower (116 steps and 60 ramps) for a panoramic view—dunes on one side, harbor on the other, and the entire bay side of Cape Cod beyond. At the base is a museum of Lower Cape and Provincetown history. ⊠ *High Pole Hill,* ☎ *508/487–1310,* WEB *www.pilgrim-monument.org.* ☑ *$6.* ☉ *Apr.–June and Sept.–Nov., daily 9–5; July–Aug., daily 9–7 (last admission 45 mins before closing).*

Founded in 1914 to collect and show the works of Provincetown-associated artists, the **Provincetown Art Association and Museum** (PAAM) houses a 1,650-piece permanent collection. Exhibits here combine the works of up-and-comers with established artists of the 20th century. ⊠ *460 Commercial St.,* ☎ *508/487–1750,* WEB *www.paam.org.* ☑ *$3.* ☉ *Nov.–Apr., weekends noon–4 and by appointment; Memorial Day– Labor Day, daily noon–5 and 8–10; May (until Memorial Day) and Labor Day–Oct., Fri.–Sun. noon–5..*

Near the Provincetown border, **massive dunes** meet the road in places, turning U.S. 6 into a sand-swept highway. Scattered among the dunes are primitive cottages, called dune shacks, built from flotsam and other found materials, that have provided atmospheric as well as cheap lodgings to artists and writers over the years—among them Eugene O'Neill, e. e. cummings, Jack Kerouac, and Norman Mailer.

The **Province Lands,** scattered with ponds, cranberry bogs, and scrub, begin at High Head in Truro and stretch to the tip of Provincetown. Bike and walking trails wind through forests of stunted pines, beech, and oak and across desertlike expanses of rolling dunes—these are the "wilds" of the Cape. A national seashore visitor center is in this area. ⊠ *Visitor center, Race Point Rd.,* ☎ *508/487–1256.* ☉ *Apr.–Nov., daily 9–5.*

Dining and Lodging

$$$–$$$$ ✕ **Chester.** Elegant and understated, this golden-hued dining room in a Greek Revival sea captain's house has earned notice for its memorable, beautifully presented contemporary fare. The small menu changes regularly and emphasizes local ingredients. Try seasonal choices such as asparagus-and-fiddlehead risotto and lamb with cranberry jus, potatoes, and vegetables. ⊠ *404 Commercial St.,* ☎ *508/487–8200,* WEB *www.chesterrestaurant.com. Reservations essential. AE, MC, V. Closed part of Dec.–Mar; call for Dec. dates.*

$$–$$$ ✕ **Café Edwige.** Delicious contemporary cuisine, friendly service, a homey setting—Café Edwige delivers night after night. Two good starters are the Maine crab cake and the warm goat cheese on crostini; for an entrée try lobster and Wellfleet scallops over pasta with a wild mushroom and tomato broth. Don't pass on the wonderful desserts. ⊠ *333 Commercial St.,* ☎ *508/487–2008. AE, MC, V. Closed Nov.–May.*

$$–$$$ ✕ **Front Street.** Many consider this the best restaurant in town. Well
★ versed in classic Italian cooking, chef-owners Donna Aliperti and Kathleen Cotter also venture into other Mediterranean regions. Duck smoked in Chinese black tea is served with a different lusty sauce every day—one of the best is fresh tropical fruit with mixed peppercorns. The wine list is a winner. Call well ahead for a reservation. ⊠ *230 Commercial St.,* ☎ *508/487–9715. Reservations essential. AE, D, MC, V. Closed Jan.–mid-May.*

$$–$$$ ✕ **Lobster Pot.** Provincetown's Lobster Pot is fit to do battle with all the Lobster Pots anywhere on the Cape. As you enter you'll pass through one of the hardest-working kitchens on the Cape, which consistently turns out fresh New England classics and some of the best chowder around. ⊠ *321 Commercial St.,* ☎ *508/487–0842,* WEB *www. ptownlobsterpot.com. Reservations not accepted. AE, D, DC, MC, V. Closed Jan.*

$$–$$$ ✕ **Napi's.** The zesty meals on Napi's internationally inspired menu include many vegetarian choices and Greco-Roman items like delicious
★   shrimp feta (shrimp flambé in ouzo and Metaxa, served with a tomato, garlic, and onion sauce). Both the food and the whimsically tasteful interior share a penchant for unusual, striking juxtapositions. ⊠ *7 Freeman St.,* ☎ *508/487–1145,* WEB *www.provincetown.com/napis. Reservations essential. AE, D, DC, MC, V. No lunch June–mid-Sept.*

$$ ✕ **Bubala's by the Bay.** Personality abounds at this funky restaurant inside a building painted bright yellow and adorned with campy carved birds. The kitchen serves three meals, with lots of local seafood, and the wine list is priced practically at retail. The bar scene picks up in the evening. ⊠ *183 Commercial St.,* ☎ *508/487–0773,* WEB *www. capecodaccess.com/bubala's. AE, D, MC, V. Closed Oct. 31–Mar.*

$–$$ ✕ **Mojo's.** At Provincetown's fast-food institution, the tiniest of kitchens turns out everything from fresh-cut french fries to fried clams, tacos,
★   and tofu burgers. How they crank it out so fast and so good is anybody's guess. ⊠ *5 Ryder St. Ext.,* ☎ *508/487–3140. Reservations not accepted. No credit cards. Closed mid-Oct.–early May, depending on weather and crowds; call ahead.*

$$$$ 🏨 **Brass Key.** Convenient to Commercial Street's restaurants, shops,
★   and nightlife, this gay-popular complex is fast becoming Provincetown's most luxurious resort. Rooms have antique furniture and decidedly modern amenities; all have Bose stereos, mini-refrigerators, and TV/VCRs. Deluxe rooms have gas fireplaces and whirlpool baths. In season, complimentary cocktails are served in the courtyard. ⊠ *67 Bradford St., 02657,* ☎ *508/487–9005 or 800/842–9858,* FAX *508/487–9020,* WEB *www.brasskey.com. 36 rooms. In-room safes, pool; no kids under 16, no smoking. AE, D, MC, V. Closed early Nov.–mid-Apr. CP.*

$$–$$$$ 🏨 **Bayshore and Chandler House.** A great option for longer stays, this
★   apartment complex is on the water, ½ mi from the town center. Many of the units have fireplaces, decks, and large water-view windows. Rentals are mostly by the week in season. Pets are welcome. ⊠ *493 Commercial St., 02657-2413,* ☎ *508/487–9133,* FAX *508/487–0520,* WEB *www.provincetown.com/bayshore. 25 apartments. Kitchens, beach. AE, MC, V.*

$$–$$$$ 🏨 **Fairbanks Inn.** This comfortable inn a block from Commercial Street includes a 1776 main house and auxiliary buildings. Many rooms have four-poster or canopy beds, fireplaces, Oriental rugs on wide-board floors, and antique furnishings. The wicker-filled sunporch and the garden are good places to take your afternoon cocktail. ⊠ *90 Bradford St., 02657,* ☎ *508/487–0386 or 800/324–7265,* FAX *508/487–3540,* WEB *www.fairbanksinn.com. 13 rooms, 1 efficiency. Free parking. AE, MC, V. CP.*

$–$$$$ 🏨 **The Masthead.** Hidden away in the quiet west end of Commercial Street, this charming cluster of shingled houses overlooks a lush lawn, a 450-ft-long boardwalk, and a private beach. Spacious rooms, efficiencies, apartments, and cottages are among the lodging options. The cottages, which sleep four to seven, are ideal for families or larger groups and for longer stays. ⊠ *31–41 Commercial St. (Box 577, 02657),* ☎ *508/487–0523 or 800/395–5095,* FAX *508/487–9251,* WEB *www. capecodtravel.com/masthead. 9 rooms, 7 apartments, 3 cottages, 2 efficiencies. Beach, dock. AE, D, DC, MC, V.*

Nightlife and the Arts

NIGHTLIFE

During the summer the **Boatslip Beach Club** (✉ 161 Commercial St., ☎ 508/487–1669, WEB www.boatslipbeachclub.com) holds a mixed gay and lesbian tea dance daily from 4 to 7 on the outdoor deck. A pianist plays easy-listening tunes on weekends (nightly in season) at **Napi's** (✉ 7 Freeman St., ☎ 508/487–1145). The **Pied Piper** (✉ 193-A Commercial St., ☎ 508/487–1527) draws hordes of gay men to its post–tea dance gathering. Later in the evening, the crowd is mostly, though not exclusively, women.

THE ARTS

The **Provincetown Playhouse Mews Series** (✉ Town Hall, 260 Commercial St., ☎ 508/487–0955) presents varied summer concerts. The **Provincetown Repertory Theatre** (☎ 508/487–0600) mounts productions of classic and modern drama in the summer. The **Provincetown Theatre Company** (☎ 508/487–8673) stages classics, modern drama, and new works by local authors year-round.

Outdoor Activities and Sports

BEACHES

Herring Cove Beach, a national seashore beach, is calmer (and a little warmer) than Race Point Beach, though it's not as pretty since the parking lot isn't hidden behind dunes. But the lot to the right of the bathhouse is a great place to watch the sunset, and there's a hot-dog stand. From mid-June through Labor Day, parking costs $7 per day, or $20 for a yearly pass good at all national seashore beaches. **Race Point Beach** (✉ Race Point Rd.), at the end of U.S. 6, has a remote feeling, with a wide swath of sand stretching around the point. Because it faces north, the beach gets sun all day long.

BIKING

The **Province Lands Trail** is a fairly strenuous 5¼-mi loop off the Beech Forest parking lot on Race Point Road in Provincetown, with spurs to Herring Cove and Race Point beaches and to Bennett Pond.

FISHING

You can go for fluke, bluefish, and striped bass on a walk-on basis from spring to fall with **Cap'n Bill & Cee Jay** (✉ MacMillan Wharf, ☎ 508/487–4330 or 800/675–6723).

GUIDED TOUR

Art's Dune Tours are hour-long narrated van tours through the national seashore and the dunes around Provincetown. ✉ *Standish and Commercial Sts.,* ☎ *508/487–1950; 800/894–1951 in Massachusetts;* WEB *www·artsdunetours.com.* ☐ *$12 daytime, $15 sunset.* ☉ *Tours mid-Apr.–late Oct.; call for schedule.*

WHALE-WATCHING

One of the joys of Cape Cod is spotting whales while they're swimming in and around the feeding grounds at Stellwagen Bank, about 6 mi off the tip of Provincetown. Many people also come aboard for birding, especially during spring and fall migration. Several tour operators take whale-watchers out to sea for three- to four-hour morning, afternoon, or sunset trips.

The naturalist-narrated **Cape Cod Whale Watch** trips leave three times daily from MacMillan Wharf. *SeaVentures* sets sail on select Sundays for a full day of wildlife watching. ✉ *Tickets: MacMillan Wharf or 293 Commercial St.,* ☎ *508/487–4079 or 877/487–4079,* WEB *www.capecodwhalewatch.com.* ☐ *$20 (seasonal variations); SeaVentures $50.* ☉ *Tours Apr.–Oct. Call for hrs.*

Dolphin Fleet tours are accompanied by scientists from the Center for Coastal Studies in Provincetown who know many of the whales by name and tell you about their habits and histories. Reservations essential. ⊠ *Tickets: MacMillan Wharf, Chamber of Commerce building,* ☎ *508/ 349–1900 or 800/826–9300,* WEB *www.whalewatch.com.* ⊞ *$20 (varies with season).* ⊘ *Tours Apr.–Oct.*

Shopping

Berta Walker Gallery (⊠ 208 Bradford St., ☎ 508/487–6411) represents Provincetown-affiliated artists working in various media. **Giardelli Antonelli** (⊠ 417 Commercial St., ☎ 508/487–3016) specializes in handmade clothing by local designers. **Remembrances of Things Past** (⊠ 376 Commercial St., ☎ 508/487–9443) deals in articles from the 1920s to the 1960s. **West End Antiques** (⊠ 146 Commercial St., ☎ 508/487–6723) specializes in variety: $4 postcards, a $3,000 model ship, handmade dolls, and glassware.

Cape Cod A to Z

To research prices, get advice from other travelers, and book travel arrangements, visit www.fodors.com.

AIRPORTS

Barnstable Municipal Airport, the Cape's main air gateway, is served by Cape Air/Nantucket Airlines, and US Airways Express. Provincetown Municipal Airport has Boston service through Cape Air.
➤ AIRPORT INFORMATION: **Barnstable Municipal Airport** (⊠ 480 Barnstable Rd., Hyannis, ☎ 508/775–2020). **Provincetown Municipal Airport** (⊠ Race Point Rd., ☎ 508/487–0241).

BIKE TRAVEL

The Cape's premier bike path, the Cape Cod Rail Trail, follows the paved right-of-way of the old Penn Central Railroad. About 25 mi long, the easy-to-moderate trail passes salt marshes, cranberry bogs, ponds, and Nickerson State Park. The trail starts at the parking lot off Route 134 south of U.S. 6, near Theophilus Smith Road in South Dennis, and it ends at the post office in South Wellfleet. If you want to cover only a segment, there are parking lots in Harwich (across from Pleasant Lake Store on Pleasant Lake Avenue) and in Brewster (at Nickerson State Park). For bike and trailer rentals, try Bert & Carol's Lawnmower & Bicycle Shop; the Little Capistrano Bike Shop; or the Rail Trail Bike Shop.
➤ BIKE RENTALS: **Bert & Carol's Lawnmower & Bicycle Shop** (⊠ 347 Orleans Rd., North Chatham, ☎ 508/945–0137). **Little Capistrano Bike Shop** (⊠ Salt Pond Rd. across from the Salt Pond Visitor Center, Eastham, ☎ 508/255–6515). **Rail Trail Bike Shop** (⊠ 302 Underpass Rd., Brewster, ☎ 508/896–8200).

BOAT AND FERRY TRAVEL

Bay State Cruise Company makes the three-hour trip between Commonwealth Pier in Boston and MacMillan Wharf in Provincetown Friday, Saturday, and Sunday from Memorial Day to Labor Day. The company also runs a two-hour express boat from Boston to Provincetown's Fisherman's Wharf daily from Memorial Day to Columbus Day. *3-hr boat $18 one-way, $5 bicycles; same-day round-trip $30, $10 bicycles. 2-hr express boat $28 one-way, $5 bicycles; same-day round-trip $49, $10 bicycles.*
➤ BOAT AND FERRY INFORMATION: **Bay State Cruise Company** (☎ 617/ 748–1428 in Boston; 508/487–9284 in Provincetown; WEB www. baystatecruisecompany.com).

BUS TRAVEL

Bonanza Bus Lines operates direct service to Bourne, Falmouth, and Woods Hole from Boston and Providence. Plymouth & Brockton Street Railway provides bus service to Provincetown from Boston and Logan Airport, with stops in several Cape towns en route.

The Cape Cod Regional Transit Authority operates its SeaLine service along Route 28 daily except Sunday between Hyannis and Woods Hole and connects in Hyannis with the Plymouth & Brockton line. The driver will stop when signaled along the route. The "b-bus" is a fleet of mini-vans that transport passengers daily door-to-door anywhere on the Cape. Make reservations, which are essential, no later than 11 AM on the day before you want to depart. The H2O Line operates scheduled service several times daily, year-round, between Hyannis and Orleans along Route 28.

➤ BUS INFORMATION: **Bonanza Bus Lines** (☎ 508/548–7588 or 800/556–3815, WEB www.bonanzabus.com). **Plymouth & Brockton Street Railway** (☎ 508/746–0378, WEB www.p-b.com). The **Cape Cod Regional Transit Authority** (☎ 508/385–8326; 800/352–7155 in Massachusetts; WEB www.capecodtransit.org).

CAR RENTAL

Budget rents cars at the Barnstable and Provincetown airports.
➤ MAJOR AGENCY: **Budget** (☎ 508/790–1614 or 800/527–0700, WEB www.budgetrentacar.com).

CAR TRAVEL

From Boston (60 mi), take Route I–93 south to Route 3 south, across the Sagamore Bridge, which becomes U.S. 6, the Cape's main artery. From western Massachusetts, northern Connecticut, and northeastern New York State, take I–84 east to the Massachusetts Turnpike (I–90 east) and take I–495 south and east to the Bourne Bridge. From New York City, and all other points south and west, take I–95 north toward Providence, where you'll pick up I–195 east (toward Fall River/New Bedford) to Route 25 east to the Bourne Bridge.

From the Bourne Bridge, you can take Route 28 south to Falmouth and Woods Hole (about 15 mi), or go around the rotary, following the signs to U.S. 6; this will take you to the Lower Cape and central towns more quickly. On summer weekends, avoid arriving in the late afternoon. U.S. 6, Route 6A, and Route 28 are heavily congested eastbound on Friday evening, westbound on Sunday afternoon, and in both directions on summer Saturdays. When approaching one of the Cape's numerous rotaries (traffic circles), keep in mind that vehicles already in the rotary have the right of way.

EMERGENCIES

➤ HOSPITALS: **Cape Cod Hospital** (✉ 27 Park St., Hyannis, ☎ 508/771–1800). **Falmouth Hospital** (✉ 100 Ter Heun Dr., Falmouth, ☎ 508/548–5300).
➤ LATE-NIGHT PHARMACIES: **CVS** (✉ 105 Davis Straits, Falmouth, ☎ 508/540–4307; ✉ 176–182 North St., Hyannis, ☎ 508/775–8346; WEB www.cvs.com).

LODGING

APARTMENT AND VILLA RENTALS

Commonwealth Associates can assist in finding rentals in the Harwiches. Donahue Real Estate lists apartments and houses in the Falmouth area. Vacation Cape Cod lists apartments and houses on the Outer Cape
➤ LOCAL AGENTS: **Commonwealth Associates** (✉ 551 Main St., Harwich Port 02646, ☎ 508/432–2618, WEB www.commonwealthrealestate.com).

Donahue Real Estate (✉ 850 Main St., Falmouth 02540, ☎ 508/548–5412, WEB www.falmouthhomes.com). **Vacation Cape Cod** (✉ Main St./U.S. 6 Mercantile Unit 19, Eastham 02642, ☎ 508/240–7600 or 800/724–1307, WEB www.vacationcapecod.com).

BED-AND-BREAKFASTS

➤ RESERVATION SERVICES: **Bed and Breakfast Cape Cod** (✉ Box 1312, Orleans 02653, ☎ 508/255–3824 or 800/541–6226, FAX 508/240–0599, WEB www.bedandbreakfastcapecod.com).

CAMPING

The Cape Cod Chamber of Commerce (☞ Visitor Information) maintains a list of private campgrounds.

OUTDOOR ACTIVITIES AND SPORTS

BASEBALL

The Cape Cod Baseball League, considered the country's best summer collegiate league, is scouted by all the major-league teams. Ten teams play a 44-game season from mid-June to mid-August; games held at all 10 fields are free.

➤ CONTACT: The **Cape Cod Baseball League** (☎ 508/432–6909, WEB www.capecodbaseball.org).

FISHING

The Cape Cod Chamber of Commerce's *Sportsman's Guide* describes fishing regulations and surf-fishing access locations and contains a map of boat-launching facilities. The Division of Fisheries and Wildlife has a book of maps of Cape ponds. Freshwater fishing licenses are available for a nominal fee at bait and tackle shops. The Cape Cod Canal is a good place to fish; the Army Corps of Engineers operates a canal fishing hot line.

➤ CONTACTS: **Army Corps of Engineers canal fishing hot line** (☎ 508/759–5991).

TAXIS

➤ CONTACTS: **All Village Taxi** (Falmouth, ☎ 508/540–7200). **Cape Cab** (Provincetown, ☎ 508/487–2222). **Checker Taxi** (☎ 508/771–8294). **Eldredge Taxi** (Chatham, ☎ 508/945–0068).

TOURS

The Cape Cod Central Railroad offers two-hour, 42-mi scenic rail tours from Hyannis to the Cape Cod Canal and back. It's open late May–October, Tuesday–Sunday; off-season, call for schedule.

➤ TOUR-OPERATOR RECOMMENDATIONS: **Cape Cod Central Railroad** (✉ Hyannis Train Depot, 252 Main St., Hyannis, ☎ 508/771–3800 or 888/797–7245, WEB www.capetrain.com).

VISITOR INFORMATION

➤ TOURIST INFORMATION: **Army Corps of Engineers 24-hour recreation hot line** (☎ 508/759–5991). **Cape Cod Chamber of Commerce** (✉ U.S. 6 and Rte. 132, Hyannis, ☎ 508/862–0700 or 888/332–2732, WEB www.capecodchamber.org). **Tide, marine, and weather forecast hot line** (☎ 508/771–5522).

MARTHA'S VINEYARD

Updated by
Andrew Collins

Far less developed than Cape Cod yet more cosmopolitan than Nantucket, Martha's Vineyard is an island with a double life. From Memorial Day through Labor Day the quieter, some might say real, Vineyard quickens into a vibrant, star-studded frenzy. The busy main port, Vineyard Haven, welcomes day-trippers fresh off a ferry or private yacht.

Oak Bluffs, where pizza and ice cream emporiums reign supreme, has the air of a Victorian boardwalk. Edgartown is flooded with seekers of chic who wander tiny streets that hold boutiques, stately whaling captains' homes, and charming inns. Summer regulars include a host of celebrities, among them William Styron, Walter Cronkite, and Sharon Stone. If you're planning to stay overnight on a summer weekend, be sure to make reservations well in advance; spring is not too early. Things stay busy on September and October weekends, a favorite time for weddings, but begin to slow down soon after. In many ways the Vineyard's off-season persona is even more appealing than its summer self. There's more time to linger over pastoral and ocean vistas, free from the throngs of cars, bicycles, and mopeds.

The island is roughly triangular and about 100 square mi—when planning a visit, keep in mind that distances can be substantial. The Down-Island end comprises Vineyard Haven, Oak Bluffs, and Edgartown, the most popular and most populated towns; ferry docks, shops, and centuries-old houses and churches line the main streets. Up-Island, the west end of the Vineyard, remains remarkably rural and free of commercialism. In Chilmark, West Tisbury, and Aquinnah (formerly called Gay Head), country roads meander through woods and tranquil farmland.

The Vineyard, except for Oak Bluffs and Edgartown, is "dry": there are no liquor stores, and restaurants don't serve liquor. Most restaurants in dry towns allow you to bring your own beer or wine.

Vineyard Haven (Tisbury)

⑰ *7 mi southeast of Woods Hole, 3½ mi west of Oak Bluffs, 8 mi northwest of Edgartown.*

The past and the present blend with a touch of the bohemian in Vineyard Haven (officially named Tisbury), the island's busiest year-round community. **William Street,** one block west of commercial Main, is a quiet stretch of white picket fences and Greek Revival houses. Part of a National Historic District, the street recalls the town's 19th-century past.

Beautiful and green, exclusive **West Chop,** about 2 mi north of Vineyard Haven along Main Street, claims some of the island's most distinguished residents. The 52-ft white-and-black brick **West Chop Lighthouse** (⊠ W. Chop Rd.) was built in 1838. On the point beyond the lighthouse is a landscaped scenic overlook with benches.

Dining and Lodging

$$$-$$$$ ✕ **Le Grenier.** Calling a restaurant French in a dry town is a stretch, but the cuisine here is authentic and expert. You might sample such delicacies as quail flambéed with cognac and grapes, or rack of lamb with a rosemary-currant sauce. The intimate dining room is airy and informal. ⊠ *Upper Main St.,* ☎ *508/693–4906,* ᵂᴱᴮ *www.tiac.net/users/lgrenier. AE, MC, V. BYOB. No lunch.*

$$-$$$$ ✕ **Cafe Moxie.** A favorite with those-in-the-know, this casually chic restaurant maintains a relatively low profile despite serving some of the most interesting regional American fare on the island. Occupying a simple, dapper space with small varnished tables, hardwood floors, and a pressed-tin ceiling, Moxie serves such kicky creations as seared confit of duck leg with herbed crepes and pan-seared sea scallops with a butternut squash. ⊠ *Main St.,* ☎ *508/693–1484. MC, V. BYOB. Closed Mon.–Tues. No lunch weekdays.*

$$-$$$ ✕ **Black Dog Tavern.** This island landmark (widely known for its T-shirts and other merchandise) serves all the usual suspects, often with inventive spins. Grilled New York strip steak with caramelized Vidalia

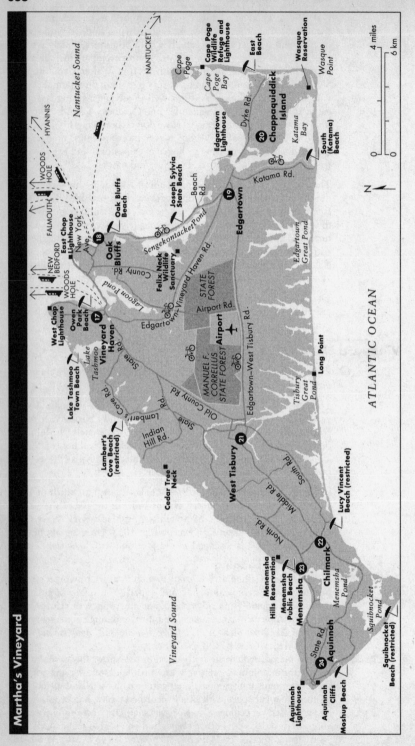

Martha's Vineyard

onions and smoked bayou bacon makes a delicious entrée. Breakfast and lunch are dependable, too. Waiting for a table is something of a tradition, although locals have generally adopted Yogi Berra's line: it's so crowded, no one goes there anymore. ⊠ *Beach St. Ext.,* ☎ *508/693–9223,* WEB *www.theblackdog.com. Reservations not accepted. AE, D, MC, V. BYOB.*

$$$$ 🔲 **Martha's Place.** This handsomely appointed, beautifully restored
★ Greek Revival mansion on Main Street sits just across the street from Owen Park Beach. Light-filled, airy rooms are furnished with fine antiques, Waverly drapes, fluffy beds with Egyptian cotton sheets and down comforters, CD stereos, and elegant bathrooms. Breakfast is served on fine china with silver. The inn also leads sightseeing tours on its own boat. ⊠ *114 Main St. (Box 1182, 02568),* ☎ *508/693–0253,* WEB *www.marthasplace.com. 5 rooms, 1 suite. Some in-room hot tubs; no room phones, no room TVs, no smoking. MC, V. BP.*

$$$$ 🔲 **Thorncroft Inn.** Fine Colonial and Renaissance Revival antiques and
★ tasteful reproductions adorn the somewhat formal main inn, a 1918 Craftsman bungalow set on 3½ acres of woods. Ten rooms have working fireplaces; some rooms have whirlpool baths or canopy beds. It's about a mile from the ferry. Continental breakfast is served in bed on request; rooms in the carriage house are secluded and romantic. ⊠ *460 Main St. (Box 1022, 02568),* ☎ *508/693–3333 or 800/332–1236,* FAX *508/693–5419,* WEB *www.thorncroft.com. 14 rooms, 1 cottage. Some in-room hot tubs, in-room VCRs; no kids under 13, no smoking. AE, D, DC, MC, V. BP.*

$$$–$$$$ 🔲 **Hanover House.** This charming inn within walking distance of the ferry has comfortable rooms decorated in casual country style with antiques and reproduction furniture. The three suites in the carriage house are roomy, with private decks or patios. Homemade breads and muffins and a special house cereal are served each morning on the sunporch. ⊠ *28 Edgartown Rd. (Box 2107, 02568),* ☎ *508/693–1066 or 800/339–1066,* FAX *508/696–6099,* WEB *www.hanoverhouseinn.com. 13 rooms, 3 suites. Some kitchenettes; no smoking. AE, D, MC, V. Closed Dec.–Mar. CP.*

$ 🔺 **Martha's Vineyard Family Campground.** Wooded sites, recreational facilities, a camp store, bicycle rentals, and electrical and water hookups are among the amenities at this campground, which also holds 12 rustic cabins (with electricity, refrigerators, and gas grills). No dogs or motorcycles are allowed. ⊠ *569 Edgartown Rd. (Box 1557, 02568),* ☎ *508/693–3772,* FAX *508/693–5767,* WEB *www.campmvfc.com. 180 sites, 12 cabins. Picnic area, laundry facilities. D, MC, V. Closed mid-Oct.–mid-May.*

Nightlife and the Arts

Town band concerts (☎ 508/693–0085) take place every other Sunday in summer at 8 PM at Owen Park off Main Street. The **Vineyard Playhouse** (⊠ 24 Church St., ☎ 508/693–6450 winter; 508/696–6300 summer; WEB www.vineyardplayhouse.org) presents community theater and Equity productions, including summer programs at a natural amphitheater.

Outdoor Activities and Sports

Lake Tashmoo Town Beach, at the end of Herring Creek Road, has swimming in a warm, relatively shallow lake or in the cooler Vineyard Sound. There is parking, and lifeguards are on duty. **Owen Park Beach,** a small harbor beach off Main Street, has a children's play area and lifeguards. **Public tennis courts** are on Church Street; they're open in season only, and a fee is charged (reserve with the attendant the previous day). **Wind's Up!** (⊠ 199 Beach Rd., ☎ 508/693–4252) rents catamarans, surfboards, sea kayaks, canoes, Sunfish, and Windsurfers.

Shopping

Bramhall & Dunn (⊠ 19 Main St., ☎ 508/693–6437) carries crafts, linens, hand-knit sweaters, and fine antique country-pine furniture. **Bunch of Grapes Bookstore** (⊠ 44 Main St., ☎ 508/693–2291) sells new books and sponsors book signings. **C. B. Stark Jewelers** (⊠ 126 Main St., ☎ 508/693–2284) creates one-of-a-kind pieces, including island charms. **Inspirations** (⊠ 56 Main St., ☎ 508/696–6886) sells custom-made bookshelves, armoires, benches, signs, and other folk and country American furnishings at quite reasonable prices. Carly Simon co-owns **Midnight Farm** (⊠ 18 Water-Cromwell La., ☎ 508/693–1997), a shop filled with outrageously expensive but eye-catching gifts, furnishings, and both women's and men's clothing.

Oak Bluffs

⓲ *3½ mi east of Vineyard Haven.*

Circuit Avenue is the bustling center of the Oak Bluffs action, with most of the town's shops, bars, and restaurants. Colorful gingerbread-trimmed guest houses and food and souvenir joints enliven Oak Bluffs Harbor, once the setting for several grand hotels (the 1879 Wesley Hotel on Lake Avenue is the last remaining one). This small town is more high-spirited than haute, more fun than refined.

On the way from Vineyard Haven to Oak Bluffs, **East Chop Lighthouse** stands atop a bluff with views of Nantucket Sound. The 40-ft tower was built of cast iron in 1876. ⊠ *E. Chop Dr., off Highland Dr.,* ☎ *508/627–4441.* ✆ *$2.* ☼ *Late June–mid-Sept., hr before sunset–hr after sunset.*

☺ The **Flying Horses Carousel,** a National Historic Landmark, is the nation's oldest continuously operating carousel. The carousel was hand-crafted in 1876—the horses have real horse hair and glass eyes. ⊠ *Oak Bluffs Ave.,* ☎ *508/693–9481,* WEB *www.vineyard.net/org/mvpt/carousel.html.* ✆ *Rides $1; book of 10 $8.* ☼ *Easter–Columbus Day; call for hrs.*

★ The **Oak Bluffs Camp Ground,** a 34-acre warren of streets off Circuit Avenue, contains more than 300 Carpenter Gothic Victorian cottages gaily painted in pastels and with wedding-cake trim. Methodist summer camp meetings have been held here since 1835. Each year on Illumination Night, the end of the season is celebrated with lights, song, and open houses. Because of the overwhelming crowds of onlookers, the date is not announced until the week before the event.

Dining and Lodging

$$$$ ✕ **Sweet Life Café.** An island favorite—even with Bill and Hillary
★   Clinton—this 1870s Victorian cottage has an interior so subdued you may feel like you've entered someone's home, but the cooking is highly polished. Cod may be served Basque style, with chorizo, peppers, onion, and local clams, while the black bass may be prepared with an artichoke ragout and potato soufflé. Desserts are superb. ⊠ *63 Upper Circuit Ave.,* ☎ *508/696–0200. Reservations essential. AE, D, MC, V. Closed Jan.–Mar.*

$$$–$$$$ ✕ **Lola's.** This boisterous spot draws a party crowd, with live music several nights a week. Ribs and Louisiana standards such as jambalaya with swordfish, tuna, salmon, sausage, and crawfish fill the long menu; Sunday mornings are reserved for an all-you-can-eat buffet brunch, often with live gospel or jazz. A pub serves surprisingly well-executed pub-style fare (you can order from the main menu, too). ⊠ *Beach Rd., a 1 mi from Oak Bluffs,* ☎ *508/693–5007,* WEB *www.lolassouthernseafood.com. D, MC, V.*

$$–$$$ ✕ **Smoke 'n Bones.** This is the island's only rib joint, with a smoker out back and hickory, apple, oak, and mesquite wood stacked around the lot. The place has a cookie-cutter, prefab feeling, but it's fun, with details kids can really enjoy, like a hole in each tabletop for a bucket to hold discarded ribs. As the menu says, "Bone appetit." ⊠ *Siloam Rd., about 7 blocks from Oak Bluffs,* ☎ *508/696–7427. Reservations not accepted. No credit cards. Closed Nov.–Apr.*

$$$ 🏠 **Oak House.** The wraparound veranda of this pastel-painted 1872
★ Victorian looks across a busy street to the beach. The well-preserved wood of the inn's name provides a solid backdrop (in ceilings and wainscoting) for the choice antique furniture and nautical-theme accessories. An elegant afternoon tea with cakes and cookies is served in a glassed-in sunporch. ⊠ *75 Sea View Ave. (Box 299, 02557),* ☎ *508/693–4187 or 800/245–5979,* ℻ *508/696–7385,* 🕸 *www.vineyard.net/biz/inns/oakhouse. 8 rooms, 2 suites. No kids under 10, no smoking. AE, D, MC, V. Closed mid-Oct.–mid-May. CP.*

$$–$$$ 🏠 **Dockside Inn.** This ornate gingerbread Victorian inn decked with broad porches sits right by the dock, steps from the ferry landing and downtown shops, restaurants, and bars. Many rooms overlook the harbor, and furnishings are attractive but unfancy. The Sail Loft apartment has its own private roof deck. It's one of the better values on the island, especially the suites, which have kitchens and sleep up to four. Continental breakfast is served in the garden each morning. ⊠ *Circuit Ave. Exit (Box 1206, 02557),* ☎ *508/693–2966 or 800/245–5979,* ℻ *508/696–7293,* 🕸 *www.vineyardinns.com. 17 rooms, 5 suites, 2 apartments. Some kitchens. AE, D, MC, V. Closed late Oct.–mid-May. CP.*

Nightlife and the Arts

Atlantic Connection (⊠ 124 Circuit Ave., ☎ 508/693–7129) hosts reggae, R&B, funk, and blues performers and has a strobe-lit dance floor. **Offshore Ale** (⊠ Kennebec Ave., ☎ 508/693–2626), the island's only brewpub, has live entertainment (usually jazz) and good food. **Town band concerts** take place every other Sunday in summer at 8 PM at the gazebo in Ocean Park on Beach Road.

Outdoor Activities and Sports

BEACH

Joseph A. Sylvia State Beach (⊠ off Beach Rd.), between Oak Bluffs and Edgartown, is a 2-mi-long beach with calm water and a view of Cape Cod. Vendors sell tasty short-order seafood and other snacks, and you can park along the roadside.

BOATING AND FISHING

Dick's Bait and Tackle (⊠ 108 New York Ave., ☎ 508/693–7669) rents gear, sells bait, and has a current list of fishing regulations. The party boat *Skipper* (☎ 508/693–1238) leaves for deep-sea fishing trips out of Oak Bluffs Harbor in summer. **Martha's Vineyard Water Sports** (⊠ Dockside Marketplace, Oak Bluffs Harbor, ☎ 508/693–8476) rents Boston Whalers, wave runners, and kayaks.

GOLF

Farm Neck Golf Club (⊠ County Rd., ☎ 508/693–3057), a semiprivate club, has 18 holes in a par-72 championship layout. Reservations are required at least 48 hours in advance.

TENNIS

Niantic Park (☎ 508/693–6535) has courts that cost a small fee to use.

Shopping

Book Den East (⊠ New York Ave., ☎ 508/693–3946) stocks 20,000 out-of-print, antiquarian, and paperback books. **Laughing Bear** (⊠ 138

Circuit Ave., ☎ 508/693–9342) carries women's wear made of Balinese or Indian batiks plus jewelry and accessories from around the world.

Edgartown and Chappaquiddick Island

6 mi southeast of Oak Bluffs.

⑲ Once a well-to-do whaling town, **Edgartown** remains the Vineyard's toniest town and has preserved some of its elegant past. Sea captains' houses from the 18th and 19th centuries, ensconced in well-manicured gardens and lawns, line the streets, including the architecturally pristine upper section of North Water Street. The many shops here attract see-and-be-seen crowds. The **Old Whaling Church** (⊠ 89 Main St., ☎ 508/627–8619 for tour), built in 1843 as a Methodist church and now a performing-arts center, has a six-column portico, unusual triple-sash windows, and a 92-ft clock tower. The stylish 1840 **Dr. Daniel Fisher House** (⊠ 99 Main St.) has a wraparound roof walk, a small front portico with fluted Corinthian columns, and a side portico with thin fluted columns.

The Martha's Vineyard Historical Society administers a complex of buildings and lawn exhibits that constitute the **Vineyard Museum and Oral History Center.** The Francis Foster Museum houses the Gale Huntington Reference Library and 19th-century miniature photographs of 110 Edgartown whaling masters. The **Capt. Francis Pease House,** an 1850s Greek Revival structure, exhibits Native American, prehistoric, pre-Columbian, and more recent artifacts. ⊠ *School St.,* ☎ *508/627–4441,* WEB *www.marthasvineyardhistory.org.* ⊠ *$7.* ☉ *Mid-June–mid-Oct., Tues.–Sat. 10–5; mid-Oct.–late Dec. and late Mar.–mid-June, Wed.–Fri. 1–4, Sat. 10–4; late Dec.–late Mar., Sat. 10–4.*

★ ☾ The 350-acre **Felix Neck Wildlife Sanctuary,** a Massachusetts Audubon Society preserve 3 mi out of Edgartown toward Oak Bluffs and Vineyard Haven, has 2 mi of hiking trails traversing marshland, fields, woods, seashore, and waterfowl and reptile ponds. Naturalist-led events include sunset hikes, stargazing, snake or bird walks, and canoeing. ⊠ *Edgartown–Vineyard Haven Rd.,* ☎ *508/627–4850,* WEB *www. massaudubon.org.* ⊠ *$4.* ☉ *Center June–Sept., daily 8–4; Oct.–May, Tues.–Sun. 8–4. Trails daily sunrise–7 PM.*

⑳ **Chappaquiddick Island,** a sparsely populated area with many nature preserves, makes for a pleasant day trip or bike ride on a sunny day. The island is actually connected to the Vineyard by a long sand spit that begins in South Beach in Katama. It's a spectacular 2¾-mi walk, or you can take the On Time ferry, which departs about every five minutes from 7 AM to midnight in season.

★ The 200-acre **Wasque Reservation** (pronounced *wayce*-kwee) connects Chappaquiddick Island with the Vineyard and forms Katama Bay. **Wasque Beach** is accessed by a flat boardwalk with benches overlooking the west end of Swan Pond. Beyond that are beach, sky, and boat-dotted sea. From the picnic grove, a long boardwalk leads down amid the grasses to **Wasque Point.** There's plenty of wide beach here to sun on, but swimming is dangerous because of strong currents. ⊠ *East end of Wasque Rd., 5 mi from Chappaquiddick ferry landing,* ☎ *508/627–7260.* ⊠ *$3 per vehicle, plus $3 per adult, Memorial Day–mid-Sept.; free rest of yr.* ☉ *Property daily; gatehouse Memorial Day–Columbus Day, daily 9–5.*

At the end of Dyke Road is the **Dyke's Bridge,** infamous as the scene of the 1969 accident in which a young woman died in a car allegedly driven by Senator Edward M. Kennedy. The **Cape Poge Wildlife Refuge,** across Dyke's Bridge, is more than 6 mi of wilderness—dunes, woods, cedar thickets, moors, salt marshes, ponds, tidal flats, and barrier beach. The best way to get to the refuge is as part of a naturalist-led jeep drive (☎ 508/627–3599). Permits for four-wheel-drive vehicles (the cost ranges from $90 to $110) are available on-site or through Coop's Bait and Tackle. ⊠ *East end of Dyke Rd., 3 mi from Chappaquiddick ferry landing.*

Dining and Lodging

$$$$ ✕ **Atria.** Set inside an attractive white house on the main road into town,
★ Atria took the island's culinary scene by storm with its delicious contemporary menu. Try the rare ahi-tuna tempura with miso vinaigrette, sea greens, tobiko, and pickled ginger before moving on to seared filet mignon with over-roasted foie gras, quail eggs, asparagus, whipped potatoes, and a red-wine reduction. A cozy cellar pub with exposed-brick walls has live music and a less pricey pub menu. In summer, you can dine in the rose garden on a brick terrace. ⊠ *137 Main St.,* ☎ *508/ 627–5850. Reservations essential. AE, D, MC, V. No lunch.*

$$–$$$ ✕ **Lattanzi's Restaurant and Pizzeria.** This is no ordinary pasta and pizza joint—Lattanzi's serves first-rate Tuscan fare in a courtly dining room with Italian country–inspired furnishings and lighter but still highly creative food in the adjacent pizzeria, where the light and flavorful pies are wood-fired in a stone oven. A specialty in the restaurant is the antipasti of grilled Portobello mushrooms, freshly made mozzarella, and vine-ripened tomatoes. ⊠ *Old Post Office Sq.,* ☎ *508/627–8854; 508/627–9084 pizzeria. AE, D, MC, V. Restaurant closed Tues. Oct.– May; no lunch. Pizzeria closed Oct.–June.*

$$$$ ✕🖬 **Charlotte Inn.** As you approach the Scottish barrister's desk at check-
★ in, you enter a tasteful and elegant bygone era. Beautiful antique furnishings and paintings fill the property. At L'Étoile ($$$$; reservations essential; no lunch), one of the island's finest restaurants, dine on classic yet creative French food. Not to be missed are a terrine of grilled vegetable appetizer, roasted ivory king salmon with a horseradish and scallion crust, and Black Angus sirloin with zinfandel and oyster sauce. ⊠ *27 S. Summer St., 02539,* ☎ *508/627–4751; 508/627–5187 L'étoile;* FAX *508/627–4652;* WEB *www.relaischateaux.com. 21 rooms, 2 suites. Restaurant. AE, MC, V. CP.*

$$$$ 🖬 **Harbor View Hotel.** This historic hotel, centered in an 1891 grayshingle main building with wraparound veranda and a gazebo, is part of a complex in a residential neighborhood a few minutes from town and overlooking Edgartown Harbor and Chappaquiddick. Town houses have cathedral ceilings, decks, kitchens, and large living areas with sofa beds. Rooms in other buildings, however, resemble upscale motel rooms. A good beach for walking stretches ¾ mi from the hotel's dock. ⊠ *131 N. Water St., 02539,* ☎ *508/627–7000 or 800/225–6005,* FAX *508/742–1042,* WEB *www.harbor-view.com. 102 rooms, 22 suites. 2 restaurants, room service, refrigerators, 2 tennis courts, pool, laundry service, concierge, business services. AE, DC, MC, V.*

$$$$ 🖬 **Hob Knob Inn.** This 19th-century Greek Revival Inn a short walk
★ from the harbor blends the amenities and service of a luxury hotel with the ambience and charm of a small B&B. Rooms are gracious and large by island standards; the upper floors have dormer windows and a cozy configuration. Furnishings are carefully chosen and include down comforters, fresh flowers, and art and antiques that capture the island's rural, seaside charm—many overlook the spectacular gardens. It's on the main road into town but far enough out to avoid crowds. The inn also arranges fishing charters on its 27-ft Boston Whaler. ⊠ *128 Main St., 02539,* ☎ *508/627–9510 or 800/696–2723,* FAX *508/627–9510,* WEB *www.hobknob.com. 20 rooms. Massage, gym, sauna, bicycles, meeting rooms; no kids under 10, no smoking. AE, MC, V. BP.*

$$$$ 🏨 **Winnetu Inn and Resort.** A departure from most properties on the island, Winnetu both welcomes families and provides a contemporary seaside resort experience. This all-suites property has units that sleep from 2 to 11 people, all of them with decks or patios and views either of the ocean, the pool, or the pristine dunes. Room decor is stylish and modern with preppy fabrics and color schemes and a casual enough aesthetic that kids will feel right at home. The resort arranges bicycling and kayaking trips, lighthouse tours, and other island activities. ✉ *Katama Rd. (RFD 270, 02539),* ☎ *508/627–4747 or 978/443–1733,* WEB *www.winnetu.com. 22 suites. 2 restaurants, some kitchenettes, in-room VCRs, tennis, pool, gym, beach, library, children's programs, laundry facilities, concierge, meeting rooms. MC, V. Closed Dec.–mid-Apr.*

Outdoor Activities and Sports

East Beach on Chappaquiddick Island, one of the area's best beaches, is accessible only by boat or jeep from the Wasque Reservation. The relatively isolated strand, a good place to bird-watch, has heavy surf. **South Beach** (✉ Katama Rd.), also called Katama Beach, is the island's largest, a 3-mi ribbon of sand on the Atlantic with strong surf and occasional riptides. Check with the lifeguards before swimming here. Parking is limited.

Big Eye Charters (☎ 508/627–3649) operates fishing charters that leave from Edgartown Harbor. **Coop's Bait and Tackle** (✉ 147 W. Tisbury Rd., ☎ 508/627–3909) sells accessories and bait, rents fishing gear, and has a list of fishing regulations.

Shopping

Bickerton & Ripley Books (✉ Main and S. Summer Sts., ☎ 508/627–8463, WEB www.bickertonandripley.com) carries current and island-related titles. **Edgartown Scrimshaw Gallery** (✉ 43 Main St., ☎ 508/627–9439) stocks some antique pieces, as well as Nantucket lightship baskets and nautical paintings. The **Old Sculpin Gallery** (✉ 58 Dock St., next to the Chappaquiddick Ferry, ☎ 508/627–4881) displays original works by island artists.

West Tisbury

㉑ *8 mi west of Edgartown, 6½ mi south of Vineyard Haven.*

Very much the small New England village, complete with a white steepled church, West Tisbury has a vibrant agricultural life, with several active horse and produce farms. The **West Tisbury Farmers' Market**—Massachusetts' largest—is held mid-June to mid-October on Saturday from 9 to noon and Wednesday from 2:30 to 5:30 at the 1859 **Old Agricultural Hall** (✉ South Rd., ☎ 508/693–9549) near the town hall.

Chicama Vineyards was started in 1971 by George and Cathy Mathiesen and their six children. From 3 acres of trees and rocks, they created a winery that today produces nearly 100,000 bottles a year from chardonnay, cabernet, and other European grapes. ✉ *Stoney Hill Rd.,* ☎ *508/693–0309 or 888/244–2262,* WEB *www.chicamavineyards.com.* 🎫 *Free tours and tastings.* ☉ *Memorial Day–Columbus Day, Mon.–Sat. 11–5, Sun. 1–5; call for off-season hrs and tastings.*

Long Point Wildlife Refuge, a 632-acre preserve, is an open area of grassland and heath bounded on the east by the freshwater Homer's Pond, on the west by the saltwater West Tisbury Great Pond, and on the south by a mile of fantastic South Beach on the Atlantic Ocean. Arrive early on summer days if you're coming by car—the lot fills quickly. ✉ *Mid-June–mid-Sept., turn left onto unmarked dirt road (Waldron's Bottom Rd.; look for mailboxes) ³⁄₁₀ mi west of airport on Edgartown–West*

Tisbury Rd.; at end, follow signs to Long Point parking lot. Mid-Sept.–mid-June, follow unpaved Deep Bottom Rd. (1 mi west of airport) 2 mi to lot; ☎ *508/693–3678,* WEB *www.thetrustees.org.* 🎟 *Mid-June–mid-Sept., $7 per vehicle, $3 per adult; free rest of yr.* ☉ *Daily 9–6 (dawn–dusk in winter).*

★ At the center of the island, the **Manuel F. Correllus State Forest** is a 5,000-acre pine and scrub-oak forest crisscrossed with 15 mi of hiking and paved biking trails (mopeds are prohibited). There's a 2-mi nature trail, a 2-mi course for exercisers, and horse trails. ✉ *Headquarters on Barnes Rd. by airport,* ☎ *508/693–2540,* WEB *www.state.ma.us/dem/parks/corr.htm.* 🎟 *Free.* ☉ *Daily dawn–dusk.*

Dining and Lodging

$$$–$$$$ ✕🏠 **Lambert's Cove Country Inn.** A narrow road winds through pine woods and beside creeper-covered stone walls to this secluded inn surrounded by gardens and old stone walls. Rooms in the rambling 1790 farmhouse have light floral wallpapers and a sunny, country feel. Those in outbuildings have screened porches or decks. The soft candlelight and excellent contemporary cuisine make the restaurant ($$$–$$$$; reservations essential; BYOB) a destination for a special occasion. The fare is classic New England with an original spin. Especially good is the sautéed halibut with seedless grapes, wild mushrooms, shallots, lemon, and Vermouth. ✉ *Off Lambert's Cove Rd., West Tisbury (R.R. 1, Box 422, Vineyard Haven 02568),* ☎ *508/693–2298,* FAX *508/693–7890,* WEB *www.lambertscoveinn.com. 15 rooms. Restaurant, tennis court; no room phones, no room TVs, no smoking. AE, MC, V. BP.*

$ 🏠 **Martha's Vineyard International Hostel.** The only budget alternative in season, this hostel is one of the country's best. You'll catch up on local events from the bulletin board, and there is a large common kitchen. Doing morning chores is required in summer. ✉ *Edgartown–West Tisbury Rd. (Box 158, 02575),* ☎ *508/693–2665,* WEB *www.usahostels.org. 78 dorm-style beds. Volleyball, laundry facilities. MC, V. Closed early Nov.–Mar. 11* PM *curfew June–Aug.*

Nightlife and the Arts

WIMP (✉ Grange Hall, State Rd., ☎ 508/696–8475), the island's premier comedy improvisation troupe, performs Wednesday at 8 PM from mid-June to mid-October.

Outdoor Activities and Sports

Lambert's Cove Beach (✉ Lambert's Cove Rd.), on the Vineyard Sound, has fine sand and very clear water. In season the beach is restricted to residents and those staying in West Tisbury.Stop at the grammar school on Old County Road to reserve one of its hard-surface **tennis courts. Misty Meadows Horse Farm** (✉ Old County Rd., ☎ 508/693–1870) conducts trail rides.

Shopping

Granary Gallery (✉ Red Barn Emporium, Old County Rd., ☎ 508/693–0455 or 800/472–6279, WEB www.granarygallery.com) showcases sculptures, photography, and mostly representational paintings by island and international artists, including Margaret Bourke-White and Alfred Eisenstaedt.

Chilmark

㉒ *5½ mi southwest of West Tisbury*

Chilmark is a rural village whose ocean-view roads, rustic woodlands, and lack of crowds have drawn chic summer visitors and resulted in stratospheric real estate prices. Laced with rough roads and winding stone fences that once separated fields and pastures, Chilmark reminds people of what the Vineyard was like in an earlier time, before developers took over.

Dining and Lodging

$$–$$$$ ✕ **Feast of Chilmark.** Civilized and calming, the Feast is a welcome break from the Vineyard's busier joints. The seafood entrées, light appetizers, and fresh salads play up summer tastes and flavors, and the whole menu takes advantage of local produce. The works of renowned photographer Peter Simon (Carly's brother) hang on the walls. ⊠ *Beetlebung Corner,* ☎ *508/645–3553. AE, MC, V. BYOB. Closed Mon. and late Oct.–mid-May. No lunch.*

$$$$ ✕🏠 **Inn at Blueberry Hill.** Exclusive and secluded, this unique property comprising 56 acres of former farmland puts you in the heart of the rural Vineyard. The restaurant ($$$–$$$$; reservations essential) is relaxed and elegant, and the fresh, innovative, and health-conscious food is superb. Guest rooms are simply and sparsely decorated with Shaker-inspired island-made furniture. Some less-expensive rooms are on the small side; a number of rooms can be combined to create larger units. Though the restaurant serves only dinner, the cooks will prepare box lunches for guests. ⊠ *74 North Rd., 02535,* ☎ *508/645–3322 or 800/356–3322,* ℻ *508/645–3799,* 🌐 *www.blueberryinn.com. 25 rooms. Restaurant, tennis court, lap pool, gym, hot tub, massage, meeting room, airport shuttle; no kids under 12, no smoking. AE, MC, V. Closed Dec.–Apr. CP.*

Outdoor Activities and Sports

A dirt road leads off South Road to beautiful **Lucy Vincent Beach,** which in summer is open only to Chilmark residents and those staying in town.

Shopping

Apart from serving delicious handmade chocolates and sweets, **Chilmark Chocolates** (⊠ State Rd., ☎ 508/645–3013) provides employment opportunities for persons with disabilities.

Menemsha

★ ㉓ *1½ mi northwest of Chilmark.*

Unspoiled by the "progress" of the past few decades, the working port of Menemsha is a jumble of weathered fishing shacks, fishing and pleasure boats, drying nets, and lobster pots. Several scenes from the movie *Jaws* were filmed here. The village is a must-see for cyclists, who can stop for an ice cream cone or a cup of chowder.

Dining and Lodging

$$–$$$ ✕ **Homeport.** A classic seafood-in-the-rough experience since the ★   1930s, this breezy seasonal restaurant serves absolutely the freshest lobster around, plus steamers, scallops, and local fish. Sailors from all around southern New England savor the chance to pull into Menemsha for a meal at this stalwart, where commoners often rub shoulders with celebs. You can also get your meal to go and enjoy it on the lawn or by the dock overlooking the harbor. ⊠ *512 North Rd.,* ☎ *508/645–2679. No credit cards. BYOB. Closed mid-Oct.–mid-Apr. No lunch.*

$ ✕ **The Bite.** Fried everything—clams, fish-and-chips, you name it—is on the menu at this roadside shack, where two outdoor picnic tables are the only seating options. The Bite closes at 3 PM on weekdays and 7 PM on weekends. ⊠ *Basin Rd.,* ☎ *no phone. No credit cards. Closed Oct.–late Mar.*

$$$–$$$$
★
⊞ **Menemsha Inn and Cottages.** All with screened porches, fireplaces, and full kitchens, the cottages here are spaced on 10 acres; some have more privacy and better water views than others. The 1989 inn building and the pleasant three-bedroom Carriage House have plush blue or sea-green carpeting and Appalachian-pine reproduction furniture. All rooms have private decks, most with fine sunset views. The meal plan is for the inn and Carriage House only. ⊠ *North Rd. (Box 38, 02552),* ☎ *508/645–2521,* WEB *www.menemshainn.com. 15 rooms, 11 cottages, 1 carriage house. In-room data ports, in-room VCRs, some refrigerators, some kitchens, tennis court, gym. No credit cards. Closed Nov.–late-Apr. CP.*

Outdoor Activities and Sports

Menemsha Public Beach, adjacent to Dutcher's Dock, is a pebbly beach with gentle surf. The views to the west make it a great place to catch the sunset. There are rest rooms, food concessions, lifeguards, and parking spaces. **Menemsha Hills Reservation** (⊠ North Rd., just north of Menemsha) has 4 mi of some of the most challenging, breathtaking, and steep hiking trails on the island, including a stroll up to Martha's Vineyard's second-highest point and another ramble that descends down through the wind-swept valley to boulder-strewn Vineyard Sound Beach.

Shopping

Larsen's (⊠ Dutcher's Dock, ☎ 508/645–2680) is a retail fish store with reasonable prices and superb quality—they'll open oysters, stuff quahogs, and cook a lobster to order. The best deal is a dozen littlenecks or cherrystones for $7.50.

Aquinnah

❷❹ *6½ mi west of Menemsha, 10 mi southwest of West Tisbury, 17 mi southwest of Vineyard Haven.*

Aquinnah, called Gay Head until the town voted to change its name in 1997, is an official Native American township. The Wampanoag tribe is the guardian of the 420 acres that constitute the Aquinnah Native American Reservation. Aquinnah (pronounced a-*kwih*-nah), is Wampanoag for "land under the hill." The town is best known for the red-hued Aquinnah Cliffs.

Quitsa Pond Lookout (⊠ State Rd.) has a good view of the adjoining Menemsha and Nashaquitsa ponds, the woods, and the ocean beyond.

From a roadside iron pipe, **Aquinnah Spring** (⊠ State Rd.) gushes water cold enough to slake a cyclist's thirst on the hottest day. Feel free to fill a canteen. Locals come from all over the island to fill jugs. The spec-
★ tacular **Aquinnah Cliffs** (⊠ State Rd.), a National Historic Landmark, are part of the Wampanoag reservation land. These dramatically striated walls of red clay are the island's major attraction, as evidenced by the tour bus–filled parking lot. Native American crafts and food shops line the short approach to the overlook, from which you can see the Elizabeth Islands to the northeast across Vineyard Sound and Noman's Land Island—part wildlife preserve, part military bombing-practice site—3 mi off the Vineyard's southern coast. Adjacent to the cliffs overlook, the redbrick **Aquinnah Lighthouse** is stationed precariously atop the rapidly eroding cliffs. The lighthouse is open to the public on summer weekends at sunset, weather permitting; tours are by arrangement. ⊠ *Lighthouse Rd.,* ☎ *508/645–2211.* ☞ *$2.*

Dining and Lodging

$$$$ ✕⌖ **Outermost Inn.** Owned by Hugh (brother of singer James) and
★ Jeanne Taylor and standing alone on acres of moorland, the inn is
wrapped with windows revealing breathtaking views of sea and sky.
The restaurant ($$$$; reservations essential; BYOB) seats twice for dinner, at 6 and 8 PM four to six nights a week spring–fall. Dinners are
prix-fixe; try the crab cakes or baked stuffed seafood platter. The inn
is clean and contemporary with white walls, local art, and polished light-
wood floors. ⌧ *Lighthouse Rd. (R.R. 1, Box 171, 02535)*, ☏ *508/
645–3511*, 🄵🄰🅇 *508/645–3514*, 🅆🄴🄱 *www.outermostinn.com. 7 rooms.
Restaurant, some in-room hot tubs; no kids under 12, no smoking. AE,
D, MC, V. Closed mid-Oct.–May. BP.*

Martha's Vineyard A to Z

*To research prices, get advice from other travelers, and book travel ar-
rangements, visit www.fodors.com.*

AIR TRAVEL

Cape Air connects the Vineyard year-round with Boston (including an
hourly summer shuttle), Hyannis, Nantucket, Providence, and New Bedford. It offers joint fares and ticketing and baggage agreements with
several major carriers. Fares typically begin around $85 from Hyan-
nis to nearly $200 from Boston but vary depending on the time year.
Several charter airlines also serve the island—these come and go, so
it's best to check with the chamber of commerce. Martha's Vineyard
Airport is in West Tisbury, near the center of the island.
➤ CARRIER: **Cape Air** (☏ 800/352–0714, 🅆🄴🄱 www.flycapeair.com).
➤ AIRPORT INFORMATION: **Martha's Vineyard Airport** (⌧ Edgartown–
West Tisbury Rd., ☏ 508/693–7022).

BOAT AND FERRY TRAVEL

Car-and-passenger ferries travel to Vineyard Haven from Woods Hole
on Cape Cod year-round. In season, passenger ferries from Falmouth
and Hyannis on Cape Cod, and from New Bedford, serve Vineyard
Haven and Oak Bluffs. All provide overnight parking—fees are $6–
$12 nightly. Service below is often limited during the fall through
spring.

FROM FALMOUTH: The *Island Queen* makes the 35-minute trip to Oak
Bluffs from late May to early October. *Round-trip $10, bicycles $6.
One-way $6, bicycles $3.*

The **Falmouth–Edgartown Ferry** makes the one-hour trip to Edgartown
from late May to early October. *Round-trip $24, bicycles $6 additional.
One-way $13.50, bicycles $3 additional.*

FROM HYANNIS: Hy-Line makes the 1¾-hour run to Oak Bluffs between
May and October. Call to reserve a space in summer, because the parking lot often fills up. *One-way $13.50, bicycles $5 additional.*

FROM NANTUCKET: Hy-Line makes 2¼-hour runs to and from Oak Bluffs
from early June to mid-September—the only interisland passenger service. (To get a car from Nantucket to the Vineyard, you must return
to the mainland and drive from Hyannis to Woods Hole.) *One-way
$12, bicycles $5 additional.*

FROM NEW BEDFORD: The *Schamonchi* travels between Billy Woods
Wharf and Vineyard Haven from mid-May to mid-October. The 600-
passenger ferry makes the 1½-hour trip at least once a day, several times
in high season, allowing you to avoid Cape traffic. Note that round-
trip fares apply only for same-day travel; overnight stays require the

purchase of two one-way tickets. *Round-trip $18, bicycles $6 additional. One-way $10, bicycles $5 additional.*

FROM WOODS HOLE: The **Steamship Authority** runs the only car ferries, which make the 45-minute trip to Vineyard Haven year-round and to Oak Bluffs from late May through September. If you plan to take a car, you'll definitely need a reservation in summer or on weekends in the fall and spring (passenger reservations are not necessary). *Passengers one-way year-round $5.50, bicycles $3 additional. Car one-way mid-May–mid-Oct. $55; call for off-season rates.*

The three-car On Time ferry makes the five-minute run to Chappaquiddick Island. *Round-trip passenger $1.50, car $6, bicycle $4, moped $5.50, motorcycle $5. Memorial Day–mid-October, about every 5 mins, daily 7 AM–midnight, less frequently off-season.*

➤ BOAT AND FERRY INFORMATION: **Falmouth–Edgartown Ferry** (✉ Falmouth Marine, ☎ 508/548–9400, WEB www.falmouthferry.com). **Hy-Line** (✉ Ocean St. dock, ☎ 508/778–2600; 508/693–0112 in Oak Bluffs; WEB www.hy-linecruises.com). *Island Queen* (✉ Falmouth Harbor, ☎ 508/548–4800, WEB www.islandqueen.com). **On Time** (✉ Dock St., Edgartown, ☎ 508/627–9427). *Schamonchi* (☎ 508/997–1688 in New Bedford; Martha's Vineyard ticket office: ✉ Beach Rd., Vineyard Haven, ☎ 508/693–0125, WEB www.islandferry.com). **Steamship Authority** (☎ 508/477–8600 information and car reservations; 508/693–9130 on the Vineyard; WEB www.islandferry.com).

➤ TOWN HARBOR FACILITIES: **Edgartown** (☎ 508/627–4746). **Menemsha** (☎ 508/645–2846). **Oak Bluffs** (☎ 508/693–9644). **Vineyard Haven** (☎ 508/696–4249).

BIKE TRAVEL

Martha's Vineyard is superb terrain for biking—you can pick up a map that lists safety tips and shows the island's many dedicated bike paths from the chamber of commerce. Several shops throughout the island rent bicycles, many of them close to the ferry terminals. Martha's Vineyard Strictly Bikes rents bike racks for your car.

➤ BIKE RENTALS: **DeBettencourt's** (✉ Circuit Ave. Ext., Oak Bluffs, ☎ 508/693–0011). **Martha's Vineyard Strictly Bikes** (✉ 24 Union St., Vineyard Haven, ☎ 508/693–0782). **Wheel Happy** (✉ 8 S. Water St., Edgartown, ☎ 508/627–5928).

BUS TRAVEL

Bonanza Bus Lines travels to the Woods Hole ferry port on Cape Cod from Boston and other Northeast cities year-round. Martha's Vineyard Transit Authority (VTA) buses provide regular service to all six towns on the island, with frequent stops in peak season and quite limited service during the winter. The fare is 50¢ per town, with the exception of trips to South Beach, which are $1.50. The VTA also has three in-town minibus routes, two in Edgartown and one in Vineyard Haven. One-way fares are $1.50 or less; weekly, monthly, and seasonal passes are available.

➤ BUS LINES: **Bonanza Bus Lines** (☎ 888/751–8800, WEB www.bonanzabus.com). **Martha's Vineyard Transit Authority** (☎ 508/627–9663; 508/627–7448 for schedule; WEB www.vineyardtransit.com).

CAR RENTAL

You can book rentals through the Woods Hole ferry terminal free phone. The following agencies have rental desks at the airport; be aware, though, that cars rented from the airport incur a small surcharge. Rates start at about $50 daily in season.

➤ MAJOR AGENCIES: **All Island** (☎ 508/693–6868). **Budget** (☎ 508/693–1911). **Hertz** (☎ 508/693–2402). **Thrifty** (☎ 508/693–8143).

CAR TRAVEL

Traffic can be a challenge on the island, especially in season and in Vineyard Haven, Oak Bluffs, and Edgartown. If you really want to see the whole island, however, and to tour freely among the different towns, it's worth having a car here. Bringing one over on the ferry in summer, however, requires reservations far in advance, costs almost double what it does off-season, and necessitates standing in long lines—it's sometimes easier and more economical to rent a car once on the island, and then only for the days you plan on exploring. Where you stay and what you plan on seeing can greatly influence your transportation plans; as soon as you've booked a room, discuss the different options for getting around Martha's Vineyard with your innkeeper or hotel.

Note that permits, fees, and certain equipment is needed for driving on Katama Beach and Wasque Reservation. Contact the chamber of commerce or park rangers for details.

EMERGENCIES

Dial **911** for emergencies. Vineyard Medical Services provides walk-in care; call for days and hours. Leslie's Drug Store is open daily and has a pharmacist on 24-hour call for emergencies.

➤ HOSPITAL AND EMERGENCY SERVICE: **Martha's Vineyard Hospital** (⊠ Linton La., Oak Bluffs, ☎ 508/693–0410). **Vineyard Medical Services** (⊠ State Rd., Vineyard Haven, ☎ 508/693–6399).

➤ LATE-NIGHT PHARMACY: **Leslie's Drug Store** (⊠ 65 Main St., Vineyard Haven, ☎ 508/693–1010).

LODGING

BED-AND-BREAKFASTS

➤ RESERVATION SERVICES: **Martha's Vineyard and Nantucket Reservations** (☎ 508/693–7200, WEB www.mvreservations.com).

APARTMENT AND VILLA RENTALS

➤ RESERVATION SERVICES: **Martha's Vineyard Vacation Rentals** (☎ 800/556–4225, WEB www.mvvacationrentals.com). **Sandcastle Vacation Home Rentals** (☎ 508/627–5665, WEB www.sandcastlemv.com).

TAXIS

Muzik's Limousine Service provides limousine service on- and off-island.

➤ CONTACTS: **AdamCab** (☎ 800/281–4462, WEB www.adamcab.com). **All Island Taxi** (☎ 800/693–8294). **Martha's Vineyard Taxi** (☎ 877/454–5900). **Muzik's Limousine Service** (☎ 508/693–2212, WEB www.mvy.com/muzik).

TOURS

Martha's Vineyard Soaring conducts glider rides and instruction. See the island from the water on a charter through Edgartown Marine Harbor Tours. Martha's Vineyard Sightseeing gives narrated bus and trolley tours throughout the island, while Vineyard History Tours can take you for a colorful "ghost and scandal" walking excursion.

➤ TOUR-OPERATOR RECOMMENDATIONS: **Edgartown Marine Harbor Tours** (☎ 508/938–9282, WEB www.edgartownharbortours.com). **Martha's Vineyard Sightseeing** (☎ 888/546–6468, WEB www.mvtour.com). **Martha's Vineyard Soaring** (☎ 508/627–3833, WEB www.800soaring.com). **Vineyard History Tours** (☎ 508/627–8619).

VISITOR INFORMATION

Martha's Vineyard Chamber of Commerce is two blocks from the Vineyard Haven ferry. There are town information booths by the Vineyard

Haven Steamship terminal, on Circuit Avenue in Oak Bluffs, and on Church Street in Edgartown; these are generally open daily in season. ➤ TOURIST INFORMATION: **Martha's Vineyard Chamber of Commerce** (✉ Beach Rd. [Box 1698, Vineyard Haven 02568], ☎ 508/693–4486, WEB www.mvy.com).

NANTUCKET

Updated
by Sandy
MacDonald

At the height of its prosperity in the early 19th century, the little island of Nantucket was the foremost whaling port in the world. Its harbor bustled with whaling ships and merchant vessels; chandleries, cooperages, and other shops crowded the wharves. Burly ship hands loaded barrels of whale oil onto wagons, which they wheeled along cobblestone streets to refineries and candle factories. Sea breezes carried the smoke and smells of booming industry through town as its inhabitants eagerly took care of business. Shipowners and sea captains built elegant mansions, which today remain remarkably unchanged, thanks to a very strict building code initiated in the 1950s. The entire town of Nantucket is now an official National Historic District encompassing more than 800 pre-1850 structures within 1 square mi.

Day-trippers usually take in the architecture and historical sites, dine at one of the many delightful restaurants, and browse in the pricey boutiques, most of which stay open from mid-April through December. Signature items include Nantucket lightship baskets, originally crafted by sailors whiling away a long watch; artisans who continue the tradition now command prices of $700 and up, and the antiques are exponentially more expensive. Even if your time on-island is limited, try to get out of town as well, to explore the moors—swept with fresh salt breezes and scented with bayberry and wild roses—and the wide-open miles of white-sand beaches. If you do plan to linger, however, make reservations well in advance; for summer weekends, it wouldn't hurt to book a year ahead.

Nantucket Town

㉕ *30 mi southeast of Hyannis, 107 mi southeast of Boston.*

Nantucket Town has one of the country's finest historical districts, with beautiful 18th- and 19th-century architecture and a museum of whaling history. The **Nantucket Historical Association** (☎ 508/228–1894 NHA, WEB www.nha.org) maintains an assortment of venerable properties in town, including several museums. You can pay single admission at the Whaling Museum; to visit the others, you'll need to purchase an NHA Visitor Pass ($15), covering one visit to each the properties in the course of the season. Most NHA properties are open daily from Memorial Day to Columbus Day; hours vary from year to year, so call ahead.

The **Peter Foulger Museum** hosts engaging changing exhibits from the NHA's permanent collection, including portraits, historical documents, and furniture. ✉ *15 Broad St.,* ☎ *508/228–1655.* 🎫 *NHA pass.* ☉ *Memorial Day–mid-June and Columbus Day–Thanksgiving, weekends 11–3; mid-June–Labor Day, daily 10–5; Labor Day–Columbus Day, daily 11–3.*

★ An 1846 factory built for making spermaceti candles houses the excellent **Whaling Museum.** Exhibits include a fully rigged whaleboat, harpoons and other implements, portraits of sea captains, a large scrimshaw collection, and the skeleton of a 43-ft finback whale. Lectures on whaling history are given daily. ✉ *13 Broad St.,* ☎ *508/228–*

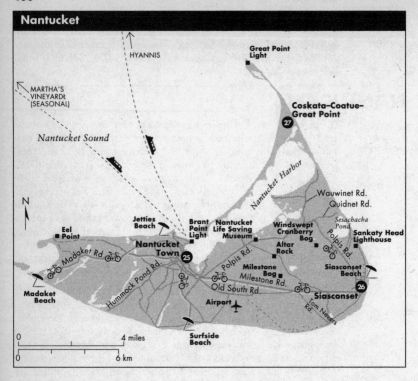

Nantucket

1894, 🌐 *www.nha.org.* ✉ *$8 or NHA pass.* ☉ *Jan.–Mar., Sat. 1–4; Apr. and Columbus Day–Nov., weekends 11–3; May (until Memorial Day), daily 11–3; Memorial Day–Columbus Day, daily 10–5.*

Built in 1818, the **Pacific National Bank,** at the corner of Main and Fair streets, is a monument to the Nantucket whaling ships it once financed.

At 93–97 Upper Main Street are the **"Three Bricks,"** identical redbrick Georgian mansions built between 1836 and 1838 by whaling merchant Joseph Starbuck for his three sons. A Starbuck daughter occupied one of the two white porticoed Greek Revival mansions across the street, built in 1845–46. The **Hadwen House** museum recaptures Nantucket's affluent whaling era. A guided tour points out the grand curving staircase, fine plasterwork, carved Italian marble fireplace mantels, and sterling silver doorknobs. ✉ *96 Main St.,* ☎ *508/228–1894,* 🌐 *www.nha.org.* ✉ *NHA pass.* ☉ *Apr.–Memorial Day, weekends 11–3; Memorial Day–Labor Day, daily 10–5; Labor Day–Columbus Day, daily 11–3.*

Several windmills sat on Nantucket hills in the 1700s, but only the **Old Mill,** a 1746 Dutch-style octagonal structure made of lumber salvaged from shipwrecks, remains. When the wind is strong enough, corn is ground into meal that is sold here. ✉ *50 Prospect St., at S. Mill St.,* ☎ *508/228–1894.* ✉ *NHA pass.* ☉ *Memorial Day–Columbus Day, daily 11–5.*

★ The tower of the **First Congregational Church** provides the best view of Nantucket—for those who climb the 92 steps. Rising 120 ft, the tower is capped by a weather vane depicting a whale catch. Peek in at the church's 1852 trompe l'oeil ceiling. ✉ *62 Centre St.,* ☎ *508/228–0950.* ✉ *Tour $2.50.* ☉ *Mid-June–mid-Oct., Mon.–Sat. 10–4; call for schedule of tower tours. Services Sun. at 8, 9, and 10:15 AM.*

The **Oldest House,** a 1686 saltbox also called the Jethro Coffin House, really is the oldest house on the island. The structure's most noteworthy element is the massive central brick chimney with a giant brick horseshoe adornment. Other highlights of the sparsely furnished interior are the enormous hearths and diamond-pane leaded-glass windows. Cutaway panels reveal 17th-century construction techniques. ⊠ *Sunset Hill Rd. (a 10- to 15-min walk up Centre St. and West Chester St. from Main St.),* ☎ *508/228–1894.* ⊠ *NHA pass.* ☉ *Memorial Day–Columbus Day, daily 10–5; call for off-season hrs.*

Twenty-six feet tall and gleaming white, **Brant Point Light** (⊠ end of Easton St., across a footbridge) juts into the mouth of Nantucket Harbor. The point was the site of the second-oldest lighthouse in the country (1746); the present, much-photographed light was built in 1902. The adjoining beach is a great place to watching the nautical traffic. Departing ferry goers, following tradition, often toss a penny from the boat to ensure their return to the island.

Dining and Lodging

$$$$ ✕ **American Seasons.** The culinary reference points that inform the menu
★ are geographic: owner Michael Getter has gathered specialties from the four corners of the continental United States. You can mix and match, with choices ranging from grilled Wyoming trout with a poblano–pinenut ensalada to oven-roasted catfish served atop grits in a pool of gumbo (name that provenance!). For all the fun involved, this festively accoutered cottage—the folk art is museum-grade—is also a strong contender in the romantic category. ⊠ *80 Centre St.,* ☎ *508/228–7111,* WEB *www.americanseasons.com. Reservations essential. AE, MC, V. Closed late Dec.–May. No lunch.*

$$$$ ✕ **Cap'n Tobey's.** At this rehabbed 1950s dive, silver paint has spruced up the once-scuffed captains' chairs, and a high-tech aqua laced with subtle halogen spotlights has brightened its smoky depths. Best of all, owners Kate and John O'Connor—who also own Atlantic Cafe—have a brilliant chef in Dante Benatti, who can dish out the requisite chowder but also come up with a knockout like the lobster "parfait": fresh chunks swirled amid tiny couscous with cucumber-papaya relish. Throw in free live jazz and you have one happening nightspot. ⊠ *Straight Wharf,* ☎ *508/228–0836. AE, D, DC, MC, V.*

$$$$ ✕ **Centre Street Bistro.** In summer you'll spot happy lunchers schmoozing on the stone patio in front of this onetime meetinghouse; in winter, the action reverts to the island's tiniest dining room (20 seats). It's one of the cutest, too, a skylit space decorated with bits of celestial découpage. Chef-owners Tim and Ruth Pitts put out an astounding three meals a day (cutting back slightly off-season), from the bounteous breakfasts to the often inventive dinners (the Vietnamese-style coconut chicken with red curry sauce is a perennial favorite). ⊠ *29 Centre St.,* ☎ *508/228–8470. No credit cards.*

$$$$ ✕ **Company of the Cauldron.** There's only one menu each night—luckily, just about anything coming out of this kitchen, beloved since the mid-'70s, is excellent. You might encounter fork-tender rack of lamb with blackberry merlot sauce, perhaps, or chocolate ganache cake with grilled fresh figs (upcoming menus are posted outside the door and on the Web site). The tiny dining room is a sconce-lit haven of handsome architectural salvage, with tables configured in clusters that tend to be more comradely than intimate. ⊠ *7 India St.,* ☎ *508/228–4016,* WEB *www.companyofthecauldron.com. Reservations essential. MC, V. No smoking. Closed mid-Dec.–Apr. No lunch.*

$$$$ ✕ **21 Federal.** The epitome of sophisticated dining, Nantucket-style
★ 21 Federal serves some of the island's best new American cuisine within a deceptively staid Greek Revival town house. The food has

enough spark to match the spirited clientele: a slow-roasted Portobello might turn up with Parmesan pudding; pan-crisped salmon, with curry aioli. For a foretaste, start with lunch on the cherry tree–shaded patio. ⊠ *21 Federal St.,* ☎ *508/228–2121,* WEB *www.21federal.net. AE, MC, V. Closed Jan.–Mar.*

$$$$ 🏠 **Beachside at Nantucket.** Only in Nantucket: an ultratasteful motel. Done up in cheerful florals and wicker, sitting between town and Jetties Beach (both are an easy 10-minute walk), this complex is popular with families—in part, no doubt, because of its heated outdoor pool, a relative rarity on-island. ⊠ *30 N. Beach St., 02554,* ☎ *508/228–2241 or 800/322–4433,* WEB *www.thebeachside.com. 90 rooms, 3 suites. Refrigerators, cable TV, pool, meeting rooms; no smoking. AE, D, DC, MC, V. Closed mid-Oct.–mid-Apr. CP.*

$$$$ 🏠 **Seven Sea Street Inn.** If this red-oak post-and-beam B&B looks awfully well preserved, that's because it was custom-built in 1987. Decked out in Early American style (fishnet-canopy beds, braided rugs), it provides the ambience of antiquity without the creaky drawbacks; instead, you can count on all the modern comforts and then some. ⊠ *7 Sea St., 02554,* ☎ *508/228–3577,* FAX *508/228–3578,* WEB *www. seeseastreetinn.com. 9 rooms. Refrigerators, cable TV, hot tub, steam room, library; no smoking. AE, D, MC, V. CP.*

$$$$ 🏠 **White Elephant.** A sister property to the Wauwinet since 1999, the White Elephant—a misnomered behemoth right on Nantucket Harbor—seems determined to keep raising the bar in terms of service and style. The complex, consisting of a main hotel plus several annexes, has a polished new American restaurant, Brant Point Grill, whose straightforward specialties include fire cone–roasted salmon (preparations on the open-air grill are quite dramatic). Rooms and common areas are elegantly appointed, in a fresh floral–white-wicker mode. ⊠ *Easton St. (Box 1139, 02554),* ☎ *508/228–2500; 800/475–2637 room reservations;* FAX *508/325–1195;* WEB *www.whiteelephanthotel.com. 24 rooms, 30 suites, 12 cottages. Room service, in-room data ports, refrigerators, cable TV, putting green, exercise equipment, dock, boccie, croquet, lounge, library, laundry service, concierge, business services, meeting rooms. AE, D, DC, MC, V. Closed late Oct.– mid-May. BP.*

$$$–$$$$ 🏠 **Centerboard Guest House.** Victoriana, surprisingly, is in short supply on Nantucket, but you'll find no dearth here. Stained-glass lamps and antique quilts adorn rooms ornate with original woodwork. Standouts include a first-floor suite with 11-ft ceilings and its own living room–library with parquet floors, fireplace, and bar; the green-marble bath boasts a whirlpool tub. ⊠ *8 Chester St. (Box 456, 02554),* ☎ *508/ 228–9696,* WEB *www.nantucket.net/lodging/centerboard. 6 rooms, 1 suite. Refrigerators, cable TV; no smoking. MC, V. CP.*

$$$–$$$$ 🏠 **Pineapple Inn.** Take a handsome 1835 Greek Revival captain's house, add gregarious owners with a restaurant background and impeccable taste, and you might approximate this ideal retreat. From the down quilts to the marble-finished baths, no expense was spared in retrofitting this unassuming house on a quiet street. Whaling captains used to display a pineapple on their stoops upon completion of a successful journey, to signal the neighbors and invite them to come celebrate. At the Pineapple Inn, that spirit prevails daily. ⊠ *10 Hussey St., 02554,* ☎ *508/228–9992,* WEB *www.pineappleinn.com. 12 rooms. In-room data ports, cable TV. AE, D, MC, V. CP.*

$$$–$$$$ 🏠 **Point Breeze Hotel.** A stone's throw from the snooty White Elephant, the Point Breeze is what you might call broken in, if not down; it debuted, after all, in 1892. Yet under the ministrations of creative local owners, it has lately recouped much of its former glory (in fact, it's a focal point for the glamorous Nantucket Film Festival). The in-house

restaurant, Chancellor's, is a boxy refectory the size of a basketball court; what it lacks in intimacy it makes up for in quality and affordability. ✉ *71 Easton St., 02554,* ☎ *508/228–0313 or 800/365–4371,* FAX *508/228–5763,* WEB *www.pointbreeze.com. 8 rooms, 14 suites, 7 cottages. Room service, in-room data ports, cable TV, airport shuttle. AE, MC, V. Closed mid-Oct.– late May. CP.*

Nightlife and the Arts

NIGHTLIFE

The **Brotherhood of Thieves** (✉ 23 Broad St., ☎ no phone), a faux-1840s whaling bar, presents folk musicians. The **Chicken Box** (a.k.a. the Box; ✉ 16 Dave St., off Lower Orange St., ☎ 508/228–9717) stages live music, from reggae to rock, six nights a week in season, weekends off-season. The **Muse** (✉ 44 Surfside Rd., ☎ 508/228–6873, WEB www.museack.com) attracts all ages with a variety of sounds from rock to reggae, both live and recorded. The **Rose & Crown** (✉ 23 S. Water St., ☎ 508/228–2595, WEB www.roseandcrown.com) is a friendly, noisy seasonal restaurant with a big bar, a small dance floor, live bands, DJs, and karaoke nights.

THE ARTS

Actors Theatre of Nantucket (✉ Methodist Church, 2 Centre St., at Main St., ☎ 508/228–6325, WEB www.nantuckettheatre.com) presents contemporary and classic plays between Memorial Day and Columbus Day, children's post-beach matinees in July and August, comedy nights, and other events. **Band concerts** (☎ 508/228–7213) are held at 6 PM Thursday and Sunday, July 4–Labor Day, at Children's Beach. The **Nantucket Musical Arts Society** (☎ 508/228–1287) presents Tuesday-evening concerts in July and August at the First Congregational Church (✉ 62 Centre St.). **Theatre Workshop of Nantucket** (✉ Bennett Hall, 62 Centre St., ☎ 508/228–4305, WEB www.theatreworkshop.com) stages plays, musicals, and readings.

Outdoor Activities and Sports

BEACHES

Children's Beach (✉ Harborview Way off S. Beach St.), a calm harbor beach suited to small children, is right in town. It has a park and playground, a lifeguard, food service, and rest rooms. Six miles west of town and accessible only by foot, **Eel Point** (✉ Eel Point Rd., off Cliff Rd. or Warren's Landing Rd. off Madaket Rd.) has clear, calm, shallow water. There are no services, just lots of birds, wild berries and bushes, and solitude.

Jetties Beach (✉ Hulbert Ave.), a short bike or shuttle ride from town, is the most popular beach for families because of its calm surf, lifeguards, bathhouse, snack bar, water-sports rentals, playground, and tennis. Known for great sunsets and lively surf, **Madaket Beach** is reached by shuttle bus or by the Madaket bike path (5½ mi) via Cliff Road. Lifeguards are on duty (the surf is sometimes too rough); there are no rest rooms. **Surfside** (✉ Surfside Rd.) is the premier bodysurfing beach, with lifeguards, rest rooms, a snack bar, and a wide strand of ivory sand. About 2 mi south of the center of town, the beach attracts young adults and families alike; it's also a great spot for kite flying and surf casting.

BOATING

Nantucket Community Sailing (✉ ☎ 508/228–5358, WEB www.nantucketsailing.com), a seasonal concession on Jetties Beach, has windsurfing, Sunfish and kayak rentals, plus optional instruction for all ages. If you'd rather leave the navigation to a pro, take a scenic harbor cruise aboard one of the beautiful sloops lined up along Straight

Wharf, such as the *Endeavor* (⊠ Slip 15, ☏ 508/228–5585, WEB www.endeavorsailing.com).

Cross Rip Outfitters (⊠ 24 Easy St., ☏ 508/228–4900, WEB www.crossrip.com) supplies and guides fly-fishers. An array of deep-sea fishing boats docked at Straight Wharf, including *Just Do It Too* (⊠ Slip 13, ☏ 508/228–7448, WEB www.justdoittoo.com), offer per-person rates as well as private charters.

Shopping

ANTIQUES

Lynda Willauer (⊠ 2 India St., ☏ 508/228–3631) has a stellar cache of furniture and fine collectibles. **Rafael Osona** (⊠ Box 2607, ☏ 508/228–3942, WEB www.nantucketonline.com/antiques/osona) holds Saturday auctions at the American Legion Hall from late May to early December: the stock is exquisite, the bidding heated. **Sylvia Antiques** (⊠ 6 Ray's Ct., ☏ 508/228–8760, WEB www.sylviaantiques.com) has the richest stash of island-related antiquities.

BOOKS

The stock at **Mitchell's Book Corner** (⊠ 54 Main St., ☏ 508/228–1080) has a special room dedicated to Nantucket and maritime titles.

CLOTHING

Murray's Toggery Shop (⊠ 62 Main St., ☏ 508/228–0437, WEB www.nantucketreds.com) stocks traditional footwear and clothing—including the famous Nantucket Reds (cotton clothing that fades to pink with washing)—for men, women, and children. Murray's outlet store (⊠ 7 New St., ☏ 508/228–3584) discounts merchandise up to 75%. **Vis-à-Vis Ltd.** (⊠ 34 Main St., ☏ 508/228–5527, WEB www.vis-a-vis-nantucket.com) captures the relaxed-luxe Nantucket look for women.

CRAFTS

Four Winds Craft Guild (⊠ 6 Ray's Ct., ☏ 508/228–9623, WEB www.sylviaantiques.com) sells antique and new scrimshaw and lightship baskets, as well as ship models, duck decoys, and a kit for making your own lightship basket. **Nantucket Looms** (⊠ 16 Main St., ☏ 508/228–5531) stocks luscious woven-on-the-premises textiles and chunky Susan Lister Locke jewelry, among other adornments for self and home.

GALLERIES AND GIFTS

The **Artists' Association of Nantucket** (⊠ 19 Washington St., ☏ 508/228–0772, WEB www.nantucketarts.org) is the best place to get an overview of the work being done on-island; many members have galleries of their own. **Leslie Linsley Nantucket** (⊠ 0 India St., ☏ 508/325–4900), the project of a widely published crafts aficionado, carries tasteful souvenirs and other decorative touches.

Siasconset

★ **26** *7 mi east of Nantucket Town.*

First a fishing outpost and then an artist's colony (Broadway actors favored it in the late 19th century), Siasconset—or 'Sconset, in the local vernacular—is a charming cluster of rose-covered cottages linked by driveways of crushed clamshells; at the edges of town, the former fishing shacks give way to magnificent sea-view mansions. The town per se consists of a market, post office, café, lunch room, and liquor store–cum–lending library.

★ The **Milestone Bog** (✉ off Milestone Rd., west of Siasconset) is a 200-acre cranberry bog surrounded by conservation land; always a beautiful sight to behold, it's especially colorful during the fall, when the berries turn red. At any time of year the open moor and bog land—technically called lowland heath and very rare in the United States—is worth exploring, via a disorienting maze of dirt roads and pathways.

Dining and Lodging

$$$$ ✕ **Chanticleer.** Since 1970, Brittany-born chef Jean-Charles Berruet has
★ been wowing the jet set with his superb French cuisine, served in a formal auberge-style setting. If you're seeking fanciful *nouvellerie,* forget it: this is classicism at its best—which may strike some modern palates as overly elaborate and heavy. Still, for many longtime fans, no Nantucket visit would be complete without getting dressed up and coming here. ✉ *9 New St.,* ☎ *508/257–6231,* WEB *www.thechanticleerinn. com. Jacket required. AE, MC, V. Closed Mon. and mid-Oct.–early May.*

$$$$ ✕ **'Sconset Café.** It may look like a modest lunchroom, but this tiny institution, treasured by summering locals since 1983, prepares wonderful breakfasts, great lunches, and outright astounding dinners. The nightly menus shift every two weeks to take advantage of seasonal bounty, with a focus on local seafood. If you can't get a table, order out and feast on the beach. ✉ *Post Office Sq.,* ☎ *508/257–4008. Reservations essential. No credit cards. BYOB. Closed Oct.–mid-May.*

$$$$ ✕🏠 **Summer House.** These rose-covered cottages encircling a flower-filled lawn perched above 'Sconset Beach pack surprising panache within: stripped-pine antiques, lavish linens, marble bathrooms with Jacuzzis. You can lunch at the pool house right on the beach and dine within the charming whitewashed restaurant ($$$$; reservations essential for dinner), as a pianist tinkles familiar tunes. The menu is robust new American, and romance rules the day—and night. ✉ *17 Ocean Ave. (Box 880, 02564),* ☎ *508/257–4577,* FAX *508/257–4590,* WEB *www.thesummerhouse.com. 8 cottages. Pool, some hot tubs, piano bar, concierge. AE, MC, V. Closed Nov.–late Apr. CP.*

$$–$$$$ 🏠 **Wade Cottages.** Managed by the same family since the 1920s, this complex of guest rooms, apartments, and cottages on a 'Sconset bluff feels just like home, especially if you're a beach lover. Furnishings are generally in somewhat worn beach style, with some antique pieces. Most of the rooms overlook the ocean. Typically, the quarters rent for a one-week minimum in high season, but you might find a shorter interval available; odds improve in the shoulder seasons. ✉ *Shell St. (Box 211, 02564),* ☎ *508/257–6308; 212/989–6423 off-season;* FAX *508/257–4602;* WEB *www.wadecottages.com. 8 rooms, 4 with bath; 6 apartments (1-wk minimum); 3 cottages (2-wk minimum). Badminton, Ping-Pong, beach, laundry facilities. AE, MC, V. Closed mid-Oct.–late May. CP.*

Outdoor Activities and Sports

BEACHES

Siasconset Beach (✉ end of Milestone Rd.) has a lifeguard (the surf runs moderate to heavy) but no facilities; restaurants are a short walk away.

BIKING

The 6½-mi **'Sconset Bike Path** starts at the rotary east of Nantucket Town and parallels Milestone Road, ending in 'Sconset. It is mostly level, with some gentle hills.

Wauwinet and Great Point

㉗ *13 mi northeast from Nantucket Town to Great Point, 11 mi north from Siasconset.*

Wauwinet Road leads to the gateway of **Great Point,** which harbors the **Coskata–Coatue Wildlife Refuge,** an all but deserted 1,117-acre tract spanning beaches, dunes, salt marshes, and oak and cedar stands. Entry on foot or bicycle is free; four-wheel-drive access is monitored by the nonprofit Trustees of the Reservations (☎ 508/228–2884, WEB www.thetrustees.org), who charge $85 per season for a beach permit ($75 for members). The three-hour, naturalist-led excursions conducted by the trustees from June to October are the most educational as well as eco-sensitive way to view the point, which provides a critical habitat for marsh hawks, oystercatchers, terns, gulls, and other birds, some of them endangered. With or without supervision (no lifeguards are on duty), swimming anywhere off the point is strongly discouraged, because of dangerous currents and riptides.

The **Nantucket Life Saving Museum,** en route to Great Point, is housed in a re-creation of an 1874 Life Saving Service station (a real one, now used as a youth hostel, survives on Surfside Beach). Exhibits include original rescue equipment and boats, artifacts recovered from the wreck *Andrea Doria,* and photos and accounts of daring rescues. ⊠ *158 Polpis Rd.,* ☎ *508/228–1885,* WEB *www.nantucket.net/museums/lifesaving.* ⌨ *$5.* ⊙ *Mid-June–mid-Oct., daily 9:30–4.*

★ At the end of Altar Rock Road off Polpis Road ½ mi past the Life Saving Museum, **Altar Rock,** Nantucket's second-highest spot, at a towering 108 ft, has spectacular views.

Dining and Lodging

$$$$ ✕🏨 **Wauwinet.** For those with deep enough pockets, this luxuriously
★ updated 19th-century hotel, mere steps from both bay and ocean beaches, is *the* place to stay. Living quarters, some with water views, are lavished with unfussy antiques. The restaurant, Toppers ($$$$; reservations essential), lays claim to being the best on-island, with such alluring dishes as sautéed lobster atop roe-pinkened fettuccine. If you're coming from town, you may use the complimentary jitney or arrive by launch from Straight Wharf. During the day, that same launch shuttles to an isolated stretch of beach on Coatue; the innkeeper runs a Land Rover tour of the Great Point preserve. ⊠ *120 Wauwinet Rd. (Box 2580, Nantucket 02584),* ☎ *508/228–0145 or 800/426–8718,* FAX *508/228–7135,* WEB *www.wauwinet.com. 25 rooms, 5 cottages. Restaurant, room service, 2 tennis courts, croquet, boating, mountain bikes, library, concierge, business services. AE, DC, MC, V. Closed Nov.– Apr. BP.*

Outdoor Activities and Sports

BIKING

The 8-mi **Polpis Bike Path** winds alongside slightly hilly Polpis Road and past Sesachacha Pond and Sankaty Light into Siasconset.

Nantucket A to Z

To research prices, get advice from other travelers, and book travel arrangements, visit www.fodors.com.

AIRPORTS

Nantucket Memorial Airport is about 3½ mi southeast of town via Old South Road; rental cars are available at the airport. American Eagle/American Airlines flies from Boston in season. Cape Air flies from Boston, Hyannis, New Bedford, and Providence year-round. US Airways Express has nonstops from New York (LaGuardia) year-round.
➤ AIRPORT INFORMATION: **Nantucket Memorial Airport** (☎ 508/325– 5300).

BIKE TRAVEL

Young's Bicycle Shop, open year-round, has been renting out bikes since 1931 and provides a free touring map. Daily rentals typically cost from $25 to $35 (inquire about family discounts); options include tandems and child trailers.

➤ BIKE RENTALS: **Young's Bicycle Shop** (✉ Steamboat Wharf, ☎ 508/228–1151, WEB www.youngsbicycleshop.com).

BOAT AND FERRY TRAVEL

The Steamship Authority runs car-and-passenger ferries to the island from Hyannis year-round (car ferry: one-way $13; bicycles $5; cars $165 May–Oct., $105 Nov.–Apr. High-speed: one-way $26; bicycles $5). The trip takes 2¼ hours. The passengers-only *Flying Cloud,* a high-speed catamaran, makes the crossing in an hour.

Regular Hy-Line ferries depart from Hyannis from early May to late October; the trip takes just under two hours. There is service from Oak Bluffs on Martha's Vineyard from early June to mid-September; that trip takes 2¼ hours and costs the same. Hy-Line's high-speed boat, *The Grey Lady* (regular ferry: one-way $13.50 or $22 for first class, not available interisland; bicycles $5. High-speed: one-way $33; bicycles $5), ferries passengers from Hyannis year-round; the trip takes just over an hour.

Reservations for the high-speed boats are available and strongly advised, especially in high season; you're required to arrive at least half an hour before departure. Also, all ferry schedules are subject to the weather, so always call ahead to confirm.

➤ BOAT AND FERRY INFORMATION: **Hy-Line** (☎ 508/778–2600 or 800/492–8082, WEB www.hy-linecruises.com). **Steamship Authority** (☎ 508/477–8600, WEB www.islandferry.com).

HARBOR FACILITIES

The Nantucket Boat Basin has marina services year-round, including fuel, electricity, cable TV and phone hookups, shower and laundry facilities, and a summer concierge.

➤ CONTACT: **Nantucket Boat Basin** (☎ 508/228–1333 or 800/626–2628, WEB www.nantucketboatbasin.com).

BUS TRAVEL

The Nantucket Regional Transit Authority runs shuttle buses around the island from late May through September 7 AM–11:30 PM; beach shuttles to Surfside and Jetties run mid-June through Labor Day 10 AM–6 PM. Fares are 50¢ in town and mid-island, $1 to 'Sconset, Surfside, or Madaket. Passes cost $10 for three days, $15 for seven, and $30 for one month; seasonal passes are also available.

➤ BUS INFORMATION: **Nantucket Regional Transit Authority** (✉ 22 Federal St., ☎ 508/228–7025, WEB www.nantucket.net/trans/nrta).

CAR RENTAL

➤ LOCAL AGENCIES: **Nantucket Windmill Auto Rental** (☎ 508/228–1227 or 888/228–1227, WEB www.nantucketautorental.com). **Young's** (☎ 508/228–1151, WEB www.youngsbicycleshop.com).

CHILDREN IN NANTUCKET

When the sun is out, children are in their natural element, with endless beaches and woods to explore. Rainy-day options include a movie matinee or story hour at the Nantucket Atheneum. For organized activities, the Murray Camp of Nantucket has a time-tested day camp, themed evenings, and adventure programs at Strong Wings, an ecologically oriented nonprofit organization. For supervised fun at home, the Nantucket Babysitters' Service provides a roster of well-trained sitters whose rates start at $20 per hour.

➤ INFORMATION: **Murray Camp of Nantucket** (☏ 508/325–4600). **Nantucket Babysitters' Service** (☏ 508/228–4970, WEB www. nantucketbabysitters.com). **Strong Wings** (☏ 508/228–1769, WEB www.strongwings.org).

EMERGENCIES

➤ HOSPITAL AND EMERGENCY SERVICES: **Police or fire** (☏ 911). **Nantucket Cottage Hospital** (✉ 57 Prospect St., ☏ 508/228–1200).
➤ LATE-NIGHT PHARMACY: **Nantucket Pharmacy** (✉ 45 Main St., ☏ 508/228–0180, WEB www.nantucketpharmacy.com).

LODGING

➤ RESERVATION AGENCIES: **Faraway Island Vacations** (✉ 30 Vestal St., Nantucket 02554, ☏ 508/228–3828, FAX 508/228–4162, WEB www. nantucket.net/lodging/faraway). **Nantucket Accommodations** (✉ 4 Dennis Dr. Nantucket 025454, ☏ 508/257–9559, WEB www. nantucketaccommodation.com).

MAIL AND SHIPPING

The main post office is in the center of town. Federal Express boxes are within the Steamship Wharf terminal and outside the FedEx office at the end of Old South Road near the airport. Packages can also be sent via Island Parcel Plus, a business center off Old South Road.

➤ MAIL AND SHIPPING INFORMATION: **Post Office** (✉ 5 Federal St., Nantucket 02554, ☏ 508/228–1067). **Federal Express** (☏ 800/328–5355, WEB www.fedex.com). **Island Parcel Plus** (✉ 2 Greglen Ave., Nantucket 02554, ☏ 508/257–2577).

MEDIA

A pair of widely distributed free papers, *Yesterday's Island* and the *Nantucket Map & Legend,* provide listings of local events and resources. For in-depth coverage, look to the weekly *Inquirer & Mirror,* published continuously since 1821.

TAXIS

➤ CONTACTS: **A-1 Taxi** (☏ 508/228–3330). **Aardvark Taxi** (☏ 508/228–2223). **Milestone Taxi** (☏ 508/228–5511).

TOURS

Sixth-generation Nantucketer Gail Johnson of Gail's Tours narrates a lively 1½-hour van tour of island highlights. The Rosewood Carriage Company conducts narrated carriage rides through Nantucket's historic district in season.

➤ TOUR-OPERATOR RECOMMENDATIONS: **Gail's Tours** (☏ 508/257–6557, WEB www.nantucket.net/tours/gails). **Rosewood Carriage Company** (☏ 508/228–9252).

VISITOR INFORMATION

The Nantucket Island Visitors Service and Information Bureau monitors room availability during the peak season and high-occupancy holidays. They can sometimes come up with last-minute bookings.

➤ TOURIST INFORMATION: **Nantucket Island Chamber of Commerce** (✉ 48 Main St., Nantucket 02554, ☏ 508/228–1700, WEB www. nantucketchamber.org). **Nantucket Visitor Services and Information Bureau** (✉ 25 Federal St., ☏ 508/228–0925, WEB www.nantucket.net/town/departments/visitor.html).

THE NORTH SHORE

Updated by
Carolyn Heller

The slice of Massachusetts's Atlantic Coast known as the North Shore extends past grimy docklands, through Boston's well-to-do northern suburbs, to the picturesque Cape Ann region, and beyond Cape Ann to Newburyport, just south of the New Hampshire border. In addition to miles of fine beaches, the North Shore encompasses Marblehead, a classic New England sea town; Salem, which thrives on a history of witches, millionaires, and the maritime trades; Gloucester, the oldest seaport in America; colorful Rockport, crammed with crafts shops and artists' studios; and Newburyport, with its redbrick center and rows of clapboard Federal-style mansions. Bright and bustling during the short summer season, the North Shore is calmer between November and June, with many restaurants, inns, and attractions operating during reduced hours or closing entirely. It's worth calling ahead off-season.

Marblehead

28 *17 mi north of Boston.*

Marblehead, with its narrow and winding streets, old clapboard houses, and sea captains' mansions, retains much of the character of the village founded in 1629 by fishermen from Cornwall and the Channel Islands. It's a sign of the times that today's fishing fleet is small compared to the armada of pleasure craft anchored in the harbor. This is one of New England's premier sailing capitals, and Race Week (usually the last week of July) attracts boats from all along the Eastern seaboard. Parking in town can be difficult; try the lot at the end of Front Street, the lot on State Street by the Landing restaurant, or the metered areas on the street.

Marblehead's 18th-century high society is exemplified in the **Jeremiah Lee Mansion,** now owned by the town's historical society. Colonel Lee was one of the wealthiest people in the colonies in 1768, and although few furnishings original to the house remain, the mahogany paneling, hand-painted wallpaper, and other appointments, as well as a fine collection of traditional North Shore furniture, provide clues into the life of an American gentleman. ⊠ *161 Washington St.,* ☎ *781/631–1069.* ⊠ *Guided tours $5.* ☉ *June–mid-Oct., Tues.–Sat. 10–4, Sun. 1–4.*

The town's Victorian-era municipal building, **Abbott Hall,** built in 1876, displays Archibald Willard's painting *The Spirit of '76,* one of the country's most beloved icons of patriotism. Many visitors, familiar since childhood with this image of the three Revolutionary veterans with fife, drum, and flag, are surprised to find the original in an otherwise unassuming town hall. Other artifacts on display include the original deed to Marblehead from the Native American Nanapashemets. ⊠ *188 Washington St.,* ☎ *781/631–0528.* ☉ *May–Oct., Mon.–Tues. and Thurs. 8–5, Wed. 7:30–7:30, Fri. 8–6, Sat. 9–6, Sun. 11–6; Nov.– Apr., Mon.–Tues. and Thurs. 8–5, Wed. 7:30–7:30, Fri. 8–1.*

Dining and Lodging

$$–$$$$ ✕ **The Landing.** Crisply outfitted in nautical blues and whites, this pleasant restaurant sits right on Marblehead harbor, with walls of windows on two sides and a deck that's nearly in the water. The menu mixes classic New England fare (clam chowder, lobster, broiled scrod) with more-contemporary dishes like salmon roasted on sherry-marinated plank and a roast pork tenderloin with a sage stuffing. Brunch is served on Sunday. There's also a pub with a lighter menu. ⊠ *81 Front St.,* ☎ *781/ 639–1266,* WEB *www.thelandingrestaurant.com. AE, D, DC, MC, V.*

The North Shore

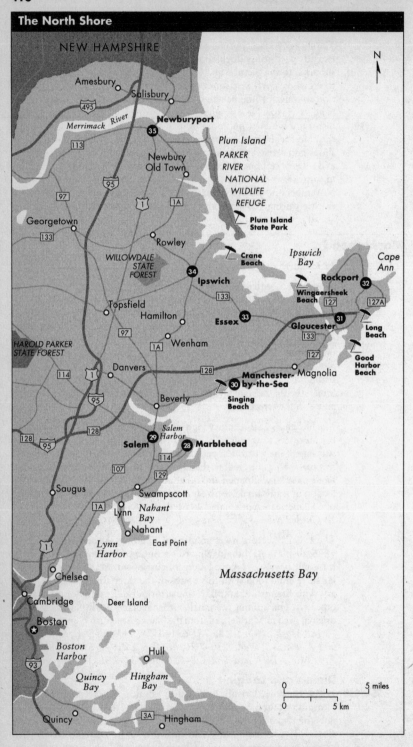

NEW HAMPSHIRE

N

Amesbury

Salisbury

495

Merrimack River

35 **Newburyport**

113

Newbury
Old Town

97

Plum Island

PARKER

RIVER

NATIONAL

WILDLIFE

REFUGE

Plum Island
State Park

Georgetown

133

Rowley

*WILLOWDALE
STATE
FOREST*

Crane
Beach

*Ipswich
Bay*

*Cape
Ann*

34 **Ipswich**

133

Rockport **32**

Wingaersheek
Beach

127

127A

Topsfield

Hamilton

97

Essex **33**

31

Gloucester **31**

Long
Beach

*HAROLD PARKER
STATE FOREST*

1A

Wenham

133

127

Good
Harbor
Beach

114

1

Danvers

128

**Manchester-
by-the-Sea** **30**

Magnolia

95

128

Beverly

Singing
Beach

128

95

*Salem
Harbor*

Salem **29**

28 **Marblehead**

107

114

129

Saugus

Swampscott

1A

Lynn

*Nahant
Bay*

Nahant

1

*Lynn
Harbor*

East Point

Massachusetts Bay

Chelsea

Cambridge

Deer Island

Boston

*Boston
Harbor*

Hull

93

*Quincy
Bay*

*Hingham
Bay*

0   5 miles

0   5 km

Quincy

3A

Hingham

\$\$–\$\$\$\$
★ 🏨 **Harbor Light Inn.** At this classic New England inn, there's a strong appeal to tradition in the stately antiques, four-poster and canopy beds, carved arched doorways, and wide-board floors. Most guest rooms have fireplaces, and several have whirlpool tubs or skylights. Afternoon tea (with fresh-baked cookies) and wine and cheese on winter Saturday nights help make a stay here special. ☒ *58 Washington St., 01945,* ☎ *781/631–2186,* FAX *781/631–2216,* WEB *www. harborlightinn.com. 21 rooms. Pool, meeting room. AE, MC, V. CP.*

\$\$–\$\$\$ 🏨 **Marblehead Inn.** The rambling mansard-roof mansion, built as a private home in 1872, sits on the main road between Salem and Marblehead. The two-room suites with Victorian-style furnishings have living rooms, bedrooms (some with four-poster beds that have a pineapple motif), and kitchenettes. Several have whirlpool tubs, and two have a private patio or terrace. ☒ *264 Pleasant St./Rte. 114, 01945,* ☎ *781/639–9999 or 800/399–5843,* FAX *781/639–9996,* WEB *www.marbleheadinn.com. 10 suites. Free parking; no smoking. AE, MC, V. CP.*

Outdoor Activities and Sports

BEACHES

Marblehead isn't known for sprawling beaches, but the ones it does have are well maintained and mostly used by "'headers" (natives of Marblehead) for family outings or quick ocean dips. **Deveraux Beach** (☒ Ocean Ave. before the causeway to Marblehead Neck), the most spacious, has some sandy and some pebbled areas, as well as a playground. Parking is \$5 for nonresidents.

BOATING

Marblehead is one of the North Shore's pleasure-sailing capitals, but the town has long waiting lists for mooring space. The **harbormaster** (☎ 781/631–2386) can inform you of nightly fees at public docks when space is available.

Salem

29 *16 mi northeast of Boston, 4 mi west of Marblehead.*

Salem unabashedly calls itself "Witch City." During the town's wildly popular October "Haunted Happenings," museums and businesses transform into haunted houses, graveyards, or dungeons as the town celebrates its spooky past. Witches astride broomsticks decorate the police cars; numerous witch-related attractions and shops, as well as resident witchcraft practitioners, recall the city's infamous connection with the witchcraft hysteria and trials of 1692. The incident began in January of that year, when several Salem-area girls fell ill and accused several townspeople of bewitching them. As the accusations continued and increased, more than 150 men and women were charged with practicing witchcraft, a crime punishable by death. After the resulting trials later that year, 19 innocent people were hanged

Witchcraft aside, Salem's charms include compelling museums, trendy waterfront stores and restaurants, and a wide common with a children's playground. Settled in 1626, the town has a rich maritime tradition; frigates out of Salem opened the Far East trade routes and generated the wealth that created America's first millionaires. Among its native sons are writer Nathaniel Hawthorne, navigator Nathaniel Bowditch, and architect Samuel McIntire.

A good place to start a Salem tour is the large **National Park Service Visitor Center,** which has many booklets and pamphlets, including a "Maritime Trail" and "Early Settlement Trail" for Essex County, and shows a free 27-minute film. ☒ *2 New Liberty St.,* ☎ *978/740–1650,* WEB *www.nps.gov/sama.* ☉ *Daily 9–5.*

One way to explore Salem is to follow the 1¾-mi **Heritage Trail** (painted in red on the sidewalk) around town. If you don't want to walk the Heritage Trail, the **Salem Trolley** leaves for a guided tour from near the National Park Visitor Center (call for exact schedule). You may get off and back on the trolley en route. In July and August, the trolleys continue to run in the early evening (from 5–8), although the narrated tours stop at 5. ⊠ *Trolley Depot, 191 Essex St.,* ☏ *978/744–5469 or 800/821–8179,* WEB *www.trolleydepot.com.* ⊡ *$10.* ☉ *Apr.–Oct., daily 10–5; Nov. and Mar., weekends 10–4.*

★ The **House of the Seven Gables,** immortalized in the classic novel by Nathaniel Hawthorne, should not be missed. Highlights of the house tour are the period furnishings, a secret staircase, and the garret containing an antique scale model of the house. The complex of 17th-century buildings includes the small house where Hawthorne was born in 1804; it was moved from its original location elsewhere in Salem. ⊠ *54 Turner St. (off Derby St.),* ☏ *978/744–0991,* WEB *www.7gables.org.* ⊡ *Guided tours $8.50; $14.50 combination ticket includes Salem 1630 Pioneer Village.* ☉ *Apr.–June and Nov.–Dec, daily 10–5; July–Oct., daily 10–7; mid-Jan.–Mar., Mon.–Sat. 10–5, Sun. noon–5.*

Near Derby Wharf is the 9¼-acre **Salem Maritime National Historic Site,** run by the National Park Service. The site focuses on Salem's heritage as a major seaport with a thriving overseas trade; it includes an orientation center with an 18-minute film; the 1762 home of Elias Derby, America's first millionaire; the 1819 Customs House, made famous in Nathaniel Hawthorne's *The Scarlet Letter*; and a replica of *The Friendship*, a 171-ft, three-masted 1797 merchant vessel. There's also an active lighthouse dating from 1871, as well as the nation's last surviving 18th-century wharves. ⊠ *174 Derby St.,* ☏ *978/740–1660,* WEB *www.nps.gov/sama.* ⊡ *Free; tours $5.* ☉ *Daily 9–5.*

Salem's vast maritime riches are celebrated at the **Peabody Essex Museum.** The galleries are filled with maritime art and history and spoils of the Asian export trade, ranging from 16th-century Chinese blue porcelain to an entire Japanese carrying litter to Indian Colonial silver. The museum is in the midst of a major renovation and expansion, designed by architect Moshe Safdie; at this writing the museum expected to close in the first half of 2003 and reopen mid-year. ⊠ *East India Sq.,* ☏ *978/745–9500 or 800/745–4054,* WEB *www.pem.org.* ⊡ *$10.* ☉ *Apr.–Oct., Mon.–Sat. 10–5, Sun. noon–5; Nov.–Mar., Tues.–Sat. 10–5, Sun. noon–5.*

For an informative, if somewhat hokey, introduction to the 1692 witchcraft hysteria, visit the **Salem Witch Museum.** A half-hour exhibit re-creates key scenes, using 13 sets, life-size models, and a taped narration. A 10-minute walk-through exhibit, "Witches' Evolving Perceptions," describes witch history and witch hunts through the years. The museum also sells an interesting pamphlet on the events that led to the witch trials. ⊠ *Washington Sq. N,* ☏ *978/744–1692,* WEB *www.salemwitchmuseum.com.* ⊡ *$6.50.* ☉ *Sept.–June, daily 10–5; July–Aug., daily 10–7.*

The **Salem Wax Museum of Witches and Seafarers** offers a multimedia presentation of sights and sounds culled from a century of Salem's tragedies and triumphs. At the **Salem Witch Village** across the street (and managed by the wax museum) you can learn about historic and modern witchcraft's spiritual and religious practices. ⊠ *282–288 Derby St.,* ☏ *978/740–2929,* WEB *www.salemwaxmuseum.com.* ⊡ *$5.50 each, $9.95 combination ticket.* ☉ *Nov.–Mar., Sun.–Fri. 11–4, Sat. 10–5; Apr.–June, daily 10–5; July–Sept., daily 10–7; Oct., daily 10–10.*

At the **Witch Dungeon Museum** you can get a guided tour of the dungeons where accused witches were kept. One trial is also reenacted, using the 1692 transcripts. ⊠ *16 Lynde St.,* ☎ *978/741–3570,* WEB *www.witchdungeon.com.* 🎫 *$6.* ☉ *Apr.–Nov., daily 10–5; evening hrs around Halloween.*

At the small **Salem 1630 Pioneer Village,** costumed interpreters re-create the Salem of the early 17th century, when it was a fishing village and the Commonwealth's first capital. Replicas of thatch-roof cottages, period gardens, and wigwams have been constructed at the site. ⊠ *Forest River Park, (follow Rte. 114 east, then turn left onto West Ave.),* ☎ *978/744–0991,* WEB *www.7gables.org/1630.html.* 🎫 *$7.50; $14.50 combination ticket includes House of the Seven Gables.* ☉ *Late Apr.– early Nov., Mon.–Sat. 10–5, Sun. noon–5.*

Dining and Lodging

$$–$$$ ✕ **Finz.** Walls of windows on three sides give this contemporary seafood restaurant on Pickering Wharf prime water views (there's a spacious deck, too). Fish-and-chips, seafood potpie, and San Diego–style fish tacos highlight the lunch menu, while in the evening, you might find Chilean sea bass with a lemon-thyme glaze, sesame-crusted tuna, or steamed lobster. There's live jazz occasionally; call for a schedule. ⊠ *76 Wharf St.,* ☎ *978/744–8485,* WEB *www.hipfinz.com. AE, D, DC, MC, V.*

$$–$$$ ✕ **The Grapevine.** Opposite Pickering Wharf, this inviting bistro serves contemporary northern Italian fare. The changing menu may include fish stew with Sardinian couscous, grilled lamb with black pepper vinaigrette, or capellini with arugula, garlic, and crab, as well as vegetarian selections. ⊠ *26 Congress St.,* ☎ *978/745–9335,* WEB *www.grapevinesalem.com. AE, D, MC, V. No lunch.*

$$$–$$$$ ✕🏨 **Hawthorne Hotel.** This imposing redbrick structure on the green is just a short walk from the commercial center, the waterfront, and other attractions. Guest rooms are appointed with reproduction 18th-century antiques, armchairs, and desks. The hotel's formal, chandelier-bedecked restaurant, Nathaniel's, is one of the more elegant eateries in Salem; the ambitious menu ($$–$$$$) may include lobster, pink peppercorn–crusted salmon, grilled sirloin, and wild mushroom ravioli. The bar has live entertainment on weekends. ⊠ *18 Washington Sq. W, 01970,* ☎ *978/744–4080 or 800/729–7829,* FAX *978/745–9842,* WEB *www.hawthornehotel.com. 83 rooms, 6 suites. Restaurant, gym, bar, lounge, meeting room. AE, D, DC, MC, V.*

$$–$$$$ 🏨 **Inn at Seven Winter Street.** Built in 1871, the inn has been restored to a Victorian-era appearance. The spacious rooms are well furnished, with heavy mahogany and walnut antiques. Some open to a deck, some have whirlpool tubs, some have marble fireplaces; the suites also have kitchenettes. Smoking isn't allowed. ⊠ *7 Winter St., 01970,* ☎ *978/745–9520 or 800/932–5547,* FAX *978/745–0523,* WEB *www.inn7winter.com. 8 rooms, 2 suites. Some kitchenettes, some in-room hot tubs, free parking. AE, MC, V. CP.*

$–$$$ 🏨 **Amelia Payson House.** Built in 1845, this Greek Revival house has been elegantly restored and converted into an airy bed-and-breakfast; it's near all the historic attractions. The pretty rooms are decorated with floral-print wallpaper, brass and canopy beds, nonworking marble fireplaces, and white wicker furnishings. The downstairs parlor has a grand piano. ⊠ *16 Winter St., 01970,* ☎ *978/744–8304,* WEB *www. ameliapaysonhouse.com. 4 rooms. Free parking; no smoking. AE, D, MC, V. Closed mid-Dec.–Mar. CP.*

Shopping

The best-known supernatural store is **Crow Haven Corner** (⊠ 125 Essex St., ☎ 978/745–8763), the former haunt of Laurie Cabot, once dubbed Salem's "official" witch. Her daughter Jody now presides over crystal balls, herbs, tarot decks, healing stones, and books about witchcraft. The **Pickering Wharf Antique Gallery** (☏ 978/741–3113) houses about 30 dealers.

Manchester-by-the-Sea

③⓪ *29 mi northeast of Boston; 13 mi northeast of Salem, via Beverly on Rte. 127.*

Manchester became a fashionable summer community for well-to-do urbanites in the mid-19th century. Today, the town is a small seaside commuter suburb built around a scenic harbor. Bostonians visit for its lovely, long **Singing Beach,** so called because of the whistling noise your feet make against the white sand. The beach has lifeguards, food stands, and rest rooms, but no parking; either take the commuter train from Boston or park in the private pay lot ($15 per day for nonresidents) by the railroad station. It's a ½-mi walk to the beach.

Gloucester

③① *37 mi northeast from Boston, 8 mi northeast from Manchester.*

On Gloucester's fine seaside promenade is a famous statue from 1923 of a man steering a ship's wheel, his eyes searching the horizon. The statue, which honors those "who go down to the sea in ships," was commissioned by the town citizens in celebration of Gloucester's 300th anniversary. The oldest seaport in the nation (and one with some of the North Shore's best beaches), this is still a major fishing port. One portrait of Gloucester's fishing community can be found in Sebastian Junger's best-selling 1997 book, *A Perfect Storm,* about the *Andrea Gail,* a Gloucester fishing boat caught in "the storm of the century" in October 1991; in 2000 the book was made into a movie, filmed on location in Gloucester.

The town's creative side thrives in the **Rocky Neck** neighborhood, the first-settled artists' colony in the United States. Its alumni include Winslow Homer, Maurice Prendergast, Jane Peter, and Cecilia Beaux. Today Rocky Neck is still a place that many artists call home; its galleries are usually open daily 10–10 during the busy summer months. From downtown, follow East Main Street.

Hammond Castle Museum is a stone "medieval" castle built in 1926 by the inventor John Hays Hammond Jr., who is credited with more than 500 patents. The museum contains medieval-style furnishings and paintings throughout, and the Great Hall houses an impressive, 8,200-pipe organ. Walk into the serene Patio Room, with its pool and garden, and you may feel as if you've entered a 15th-century village. From the castle you can see "Norman's Woe Rock," made famous by Longfellow in his poem "The Wreck of the Hesperus." In addition to being closed during the last two weeks of October, the museum often closes to host weddings or special events; call ahead. ⊠ *80 Hesperus Ave. (south side of Gloucester off Rte. 127),* ☏ *978/ 283–2080 or 978/283–7673,* WEB *www.hammondcastle.org.* ⊒ *$6.50.* ☉ *Memorial Day–Labor Day, daily 9–5; Labor Day–Memorial Day, weekends 10–3.*

Dining and Lodging

$$$ ✕ **Ristorante L'Amante.** A cozy bistro-style restaurant on the road to Rocky Neck, L'Amante offers regional Italian cuisine. Choices from the changing menu may include a caramelized onion and Gruyère tart, braised rabbit with polenta, or grilled sirloin with potato and celery-

root gratin. ⊠ *197 E. Main St.,* ☎ *978/282–4426. AE, DC, MC, V. Closed Mon.–Tues. and Jan. No lunch.*

$$ ✕ **Franklin Cape Ann.** Under the same ownership as the Franklin Café in Boston's South End, this funky nightspot brings hip comfort food to the North Shore. Think bistro-style chicken, roast cod, and upscale meat loaf, perfect for the late-night crowd (they're open until midnight). Tuesday evening generally brings live jazz. There's no sign, so look for the signature martini glass over the door. ⊠ *118 Main St.,* ☎ *978/283– 7888. AE, D, DC, MC, V. No lunch.*

$–$$$ ⊡ **Cape Ann Motor Inn.** On the sands of Long Beach, this three-story, shingled motel has guest rooms with balconies and ocean views. The Honeymoon Suite has a fireplace, a whirlpool bath, a king-size bed, and a private balcony. ⊠ *33 Rockport Rd., 01930,* ☎ *978/281–2900 or 800/464–8439,* FAX *978/281–1359,* WEB *www.capeannmotorinn.com. 30 rooms, 1 suite. Some kitchenettes, some in-room hot tubs, some pets allowed. AE, D, MC, V. CP.*

$$ ⊡ **Cape Ann's Marina Resort.** This year-round hostelry less than a mile from Gloucester really comes alive in summer, when a full-service restaurant (April–October), a whale-watching boat, and deep-sea fishing excursions operate on and from the premises. The rooms all have balconies and views of the water. ⊠ *75 Essex Ave., 01930,* ☎ *978/ 283–2116 or 800/626–7660 (outside Massachusetts only),* FAX *978/282– 4314,* WEB *www.capeannmarina.com. 53 rooms. Restaurant, pool. AE, D, DC, MC, V.*

Nightlife and the Arts

The **Gloucester Stage Company** (⊠ 267 E. Main St., ☎ 978/281–4099 or 978/281–4433) is a nonprofit professional group that stages new plays and revivals May–October. At the **Hammond Castle Museum** (⊠ 80 Hesperus Ave., ☎ 978/283–2080 or 978/283–7673) you can enjoy the summer chamber-music concert series. Concerts are held June–August; call for a schedule. The **Rhumb Line** (⊠ 40 Railroad Ave., ☎ 978/ 283–9732) has good food and live entertainment every night but Tuesday, with rock and roll on Friday and Saturday and acoustic music on Sunday.

Outdoor Activities and Sports

BEACHES

Gloucester has some of the best beaches on the North Shore. They generally have some facilities, such as bathrooms, changing rooms, showers, or concessions. From Memorial Day through mid-September, parking costs $15 on weekdays and $20 on weekends, when the lots often fill by 10 AM. **Good Harbor Beach** (⊠ signposted from Rte. 127A) is a huge, sandy, dune-backed beach with a rocky islet just offshore. For excellent sunbathing, visit **Long Beach** (⊠ off Rte. 127A on Gloucester–Rockport town line); parking here is only $5. **Wingaersheek Beach** (⊠ Exit 13 off Rte. 128) is a picture-perfect, well-protected cove of white sand and dunes, with the white Annisquam lighthouse in the bay.

BOATING

Consider a sail along the harbor and coast aboard the 65-ft schooner *Thomas E. Lannon,* crafted in Essex in 1996 and modeled after the great boats built a century before. From mid-May through October there are several two-hour sails, including sunset trips, lobster-bake sails, music cruises, and storytelling sails. The trips are on weekends only till mid-June and then daily after that. Advance reservations are strongly recommended. ⊠ *63 Rogers St., Seven Seas Wharf,* ☎ *978/281–6634,* WEB *www.schooner.org.*

FISHING

Captain Bill's Deep Sea Fishing/Whale Watch (✉ 30 Harbor Loop, ☎ 978/283–6995 or 800/339–4253, WEB www.cape-ann.com/captbill.html) offers half-day excursions July through Labor Day. **Coastal Fishing Charters** (✉ Rose's Wharf, 415 Main St., ☎ 978/283–5113 or 800/877–5110, WEB www.caww.com), under the same ownership as Cape Ann Whale Watch, operates day and evening fishing trips by private charter for up to six people. The **Yankee Fishing Fleet** (✉ 75 Essex Ave., ☎ 978/283–0313 or 800/942–5464, WEB www.yankee-fleet.com) conducts deep-sea fishing trips.

WHALE-WATCHING

The most popular special-interest tours on the North Shore are whale-sighting excursions. **Cape Ann Whale Watch** (✉ 415 Main St., ☎ 978/283–5110 or 800/877–5110, WEB www.caww.com) runs daily trips from mid-April to mid-October. **Captain Bill's Whale Watch** generally operates excursions between May and October. **Yankee Fishing Fleet** runs daily whale-watching trips from mid-June through September; call for spring and fall schedules.

Rockport

③② *41 mi northeast of Boston, 4 mi northeast of Gloucester on Rte. 127.*

Rockport, at the very tip of Cape Ann, derives its name from the local granite formations, and many Boston-area structures are made of stone cut from its long-gone quarries. Today, the town is a tourist center, with hilly rows of colorful clapboard houses, historic inns, and artists' studios. Rockport has refrained from going overboard with T-shirt emporia and other typical tourist-trap landmarks; shops sell good crafts, clothing, and cameras, and the restaurants serve quiche, seafood, or home-baked cookies rather than fast food.

Walk out to the end of Bearskin Neck for an impressive view of the Atlantic Ocean and the old, weather-beaten lobster shack known as "Motif No. 1" because of its popularity as a subject for amateur painters. The **Rockport Art Association Gallery** (✉ 12 Main St., ☎ 978/546–6604) displays the best work of local artists. It's open all year except January.

Dining and Lodging

$$–$$$ ✕ **Portside Chowder House.** One of the few restaurants in Rockport open year-round, this casual seafood spot has big picture windows overlooking the harbor. Upstairs, there's a deck with great harbor views, too. Chowder is the house specialty; it also serves lobster and crab plates, salads, burgers, and sandwiches. ✉ *Bearskin Neck*, ☎ 978/546–7045. *AE, D, MC, V. No dinner Mon.–Thurs. in winter.*

$–$$$ ✕ **Brackett's Oceanview Restaurant.** A big bay window in this quiet, homey restaurant gives an excellent view across Sandy Bay. The menu includes scallop casserole, fish cakes, and other seafood dishes. ✉ *25 Main St.,* ☎ 978/546–2797. *AE, D, DC, MC, V. Closed Nov.–Mar.*

$$$$ 🏨 **Yankee Clipper Inn.** This imposing Georgian mansion sits on a
★ rocky point jutting into the sea. Guest rooms vary somewhat in size, but most are spacious. Furnished with antiques, they have four-poster or canopy beds, some have balconies or sitting areas, and all but one have an ocean view. ✉ *127 Granite St., 01966,* ☎ 978/546–3407 or 800/545–3699, FAX 978/546–9730, WEB *www.yankeeclipperinn.com. 16 rooms. Pool, meeting room; no-smoking rooms. AE, D, DC, MC, V. Closed Dec.–Feb. BP.*

$$–$$$ 🏨 **Addison Choate Inn.** Just a minute's walk from the center of Rock-
★ port, this historic inn sits inconspicuously among private homes. The

sizable and beautifully decorated rooms have their share of antiques and local seascape paintings, as well as polished pine floors and large tile bathrooms; the navy-and-white captain's room contains a canopy bed, handmade quilts, and Oriental rugs. In the third-floor suite, huge windows look out over the rooftops to the sea. Two comfortably appointed duplex stable-house apartments have skylights, cathedral ceilings, and exposed wood beams. Rates include afternoon tea. ⊠ *49 Broadway, 01966,* ☎ *978/546–7543 or 800/245–7543,* FAX *978/546–7638,* WEB *www.addisonchoateinn.com. 5 rooms, 1 suite, 2 apartments. Dining room; no-smoking rooms. MC, V. CP.*

$$–$$$ 🏨 **Bearskin Neck Motor Lodge.** Almost at the end of Bearskin Neck, this small gray-shingle motel is convenient to the many gift shops and eateries. Rooms are comfortably but simply appointed with plain wood furnishings, but their real attraction is the view: all face the water. From the windows and private balconies all you see is the ocean, and at night you can hear it rolling in—or thundering—against the rocks below. You can sun or read on the motel's large deck. ⊠ *64 Bearskin Neck, 01966,* ☎ *978/546–6677 or 877/507–6272,* FAX *978/546–8591,* WEB *www.rockportusa.com/bearskin. 8 rooms. MC, V. Closed mid-Dec.–Mar. CP.*

$$–$$$ 🏨 **Seacrest Manor.** The distinctive 1911 clapboard mansion, surrounded by gardens, sits atop a hill overlooking the sea; the inn's motto is "Decidedly small, intentionally quiet." Two elegant sitting rooms are furnished with antiques and leather chairs; one has a huge looking glass salvaged from the old Philadelphia Opera House. The hall and staircase are hung with paintings—some depicting the inn—done by local artists. Guest rooms vary in size and character and combine simple traditional and antique furnishings; some have large, private decks. Rates include afternoon tea. ⊠ *99 Marmion Way, 01966,* ☎ *978/546–2211,* WEB *www.seacrestmanor.com. 8 rooms, 6 with bath. Dining room, 2 lounges; no-smoking rooms. No credit cards. Closed Dec.–Mar. BP.*

Essex

㉝ *30 mi northeast of Boston, 12 mi west of Rockport. Head west out of Cape Ann on Rte. 128, turning north on Rte. 133.*

The small, seafaring town of Essex, once an important shipbuilding center, is surrounded by salt marshes and is filled with antiques stores and seafood restaurants.

The **Essex Shipbuilding Museum,** which is still an active shipyard, has exhibits on 19th-century shipbuilding, including displays of period tools and ship models. One-hour tours are available, taking in the museum's several buildings and boats, including the *Evelina M. Goulart*—one of only seven remaining Essex-built schooners. ⊠ *66 Main St. (Rte. 133),* ☎ *978/768–7541,* WEB *www.essexshipbuildingmuseum.org.* 🎫 *$4.* ☉ *May–Columbus Day, Wed.–Sun. noon–4; call for winter hrs.*

To explore the area's salt marshes, rivers, and local wildlife, take a 1½-hour narrated cruise on the *Essex River Queen,* run by **Essex River Cruises.** ⊠ *Essex Marina, 35 Dodge St.,* ☎ *978/768–6981 or 800/748–3706,* WEB *www.essexcruises.com.* ☉ *Daily Apr.–Oct. Hrs vary; phone ahead.*

Dining

$$–$$$ ✕ **Jerry Pelonzi's Hearthside.** This 250-year-old converted farmhouse is the epitome of coziness; its small dining rooms have exposed beams and open fireplaces. Entrées include baked stuffed haddock, seafood

casserole, sirloin steak, lobster, and chicken. ⊠ *109 Eastern Ave./Rte.*
133, ☎ *978/768–6002. AE, MC, V. Closed Mon. in winter.*

$–$$$ ✕ **Woodman's of Essex.** Back in 1916, Lawrence "Chubby" Wood-
★ man dipped a shucked clam in batter and threw it into the french fryer
as a kind of joke, apparently creating the first fried clam in town. Today,
this large wooden shack with unpretentious booths is *the* place for
seafood in the rough. Besides fried clams, you can tuck into clam
chowder, lobster, or shellfish from the raw bar. ⊠ *121 Main St./Rte.*
133, ☎ *978/768–6451 or 800/649–1773,* WEB *www.woodmans.com.*
No credit cards.

Shopping

Essex is a popular antiquing destination. **Chebacco Antiques** (⊠ 38 Main
St., ☎ 978/768–7371) concentrates on American pine and country fur-
niture, as well as antique linens. **Howard's Flying Dragon Antiques** (⊠
136 Main St., ☎ 978/768–7282) is a general antiques shop that car-
ries statuary and glass.

Ipswich

③ *36 mi north of Boston, 6 mi northwest of Essex.*

Quiet little Ipswich, settled in 1633 and famous for its clams, is said
to have more 17th-century houses standing and occupied than any other
place in America; more than 40 were built before 1725. Information
and a booklet with a suggested walking tour are available at the **Vis-
itor Information Center** (⊠ 54 S. Main St., ☎ 978/356–2811)

The **Crane Estate,** a stretch of more than 2,000 acres along the Essex
and Ipswich rivers, encompasses Castle Hill, Crane Beach, and the Crane
Wildlife Refuge. Also on the estate is the Great House at Castle Hill,
a 59-room Stuart-style mansion built in 1927 for Richard Crane—of
the Crane plumbing company—and his family. Although the original
furnishings were sold at auction, the house has been elaborately re-
furnished in period style; photographs in most of the rooms show their
original appearance. One notable room is the library with ornate wood
carvings by 17th-century craftsman Grinling Gibbons. The Great
House is open for one-hour tours and also hosts concerts and other
special events. ⊠ *290 Argilla Rd.,* ☎ *978/356–4351,* WEB
www.thetrustees.org. 🎫 *House tours $7.* ☉ *Tours late May–early*
Sept., Wed.–Thurs. 10–4.

🐾 At **Russell Orchards,** a short drive from Crane Beach, you can pick what-
ever fruit is in season and buy apples and other produce, as well as
feed the friendly barnyard animals. The small winery here produces
hard cider and fruit wines. You can watch the regular cider being
made with wood presses in the back of the barn. ⊠ *123 Argilla Rd.,*
☎ *978/356–5366,* WEB *www.russellorchardsma.com.* ☉ *May–Nov.,*
daily 9–6.

Dining and Lodging

$–$$$ ✕ **Clam Box.** No visit to Ipswich is complete without a sampling of
the town's famous clams, and where better than at a restaurant shaped
like a box of fried clams? Since 1932, locals and tourists have come
to this casual spot for clams, fries, and onion rings. ⊠ *246 High*
St./Rte. 1A, ☎ *978/356–9707. Reservations not accepted. No credit*
cards. Closed Dec.–Feb.

$$$–$$$$ 🏨 **The Inn at Castle Hill.** Nothing but marsh, dunes, and ocean as far
as you can see—that's the view from the spectacular wraparound
porch at this secluded luxury retreat. On the grounds of the Crane Es-
tate and owned by the Trustees of Reservations, this former farmhouse
was built in the 1840s with Italianate flourishes. Furnishings range from

the traditional to the more contemporary and crisp, almost spare; the vistas from the top-floor rooms are especially dramatic. You can take your afternoon tea on the veranda or by the fire in the cozy sitting room. ⊠ *280 Argilla Rd., 01938,* ☎ *978/412–2555,* FAX *978/412–2556,* WEB *www.theinnatcastlehill.com. 9 rooms, 1 suite. No smoking. AE, MC, V. Closed Jan. CP.*

Nightlife and the Arts

The **Great House at Castle Hill** (⊠ 290 Argilla Rd., ☎ 978/356–4351) holds an annual picnic concert series of pop, folk, and classical music on Thursday evenings in July and August, plus a winter holiday-season concert and other special events.

Outdoor Activities and Sports

BEACHES

★ **Crane Beach,** one of the North Shore's most beautiful beaches, is a sandy, 4-mi-long stretch backed by dunes and a nature trail. There are lifeguards and changing rooms. Public parking is available. Sand Blast!, an annual sand-sculpture competition, is held here in late August. ⊠ *Argilla Rd.,* ☎ *978/356–4354,* WEB *www.thetrustees.org.* ⊠ *Mid-May–early Sept., parking $10 weekdays, $20 weekends; early Sept.–mid-May, parking $5.* ⊙ *Daily 8–sunset.*

Several small islands can be explored by taking a **Crane Island Tour** (☎ 978/356–4351) across the Castle Neck river. You can take a haywagon tour of Hog Island, view sets from the 1996 film *The Crucible* (filmed here and in nearby Essex), and admire the many birds and wildlife protected at this refuge. The tour lasts two hours; the 10-minute boat rides to the island leave at 10 and 2. Tours, which cost $12, run on selected Sundays in June, August, and September; call for the schedule. Advance reservations are recommended.

HIKING

The Massachusetts Audubon Society's **Ipswich River Wildlife Sanctuary** has trails through marshland hills, where there are remains of early Colonial settlements as well as abundant wildlife. Get a self-guiding trail map from the office. The Rockery Trail takes you to the perennial rock garden and the Japanese garden; the map details a further 10 mi of walking trails. You can also fish in the Parker and Ipswich rivers, both of which are stocked with trout each spring. ⊠ *87 Perkins Row, Topsfield (southwest of Ipswich, 1 mi off Rte. 97),* ☎ *978/887–9264,* WEB *www.massaudubon.org.* ⊠ *$4.* ⊙ *Office May–Oct., Tues.–Sun. and Mon. holidays 9–4; Nov.–Apr., Tues.–Sun. and Mon. holidays 10–4. Trails Tues.–Sun. and Mon. holidays, dawn–dusk.*

Newburyport

③⑤ *38 mi north of Boston, 12 mi north of Ipswich on Rte. 1A.*

Newburyport's High Street is lined with some of the finest examples of Federal-period (roughly, 1790–1810) mansions in New England. The city was once a leading port and shipbuilding center; the houses were built for prosperous sea captains. Although Newburyport's maritime significance ended with the decline of the clipper ships, the town's brick-front center is energetic once again. Inside the renovated buildings are restaurants, taverns, galleries, and shops that sell everything from nautical brasses to antique Oriental rugs. The civic improvements have been matched by private restorations of the town's housing stock, much of which dates from the 18th century, with a scattering of 17th-century homes in some neighborhoods.

Newburyport is a good walking city, and there's all-day free parking down by the water. A stroll through the **Waterfront Park and Promenade** gives a super view of the harbor and the fishing and pleasure boats that moor here. The **Custom House Maritime Museum,** built in 1835 in Classical Revival style, contains exhibits on maritime history, ship models, tools, and paintings, as well as a tidal tank housing lobsters, eels, and other marine life. ⊠ *25 Water St.,* ☎ *978/462–8681.* ⊠ *$5.* ☺ *Apr.–Dec., Mon.–Sat. 10–4, Sun. 1–4.*

A causeway leads from Newburyport to a narrow spit of land known as **Plum Island,** which harbors a summer colony (rapidly becoming year-round) at one end. The **Parker River National Wildlife Refuge** on Plum Island has 4,662 acres of salt marsh, freshwater marsh, beaches, and dunes; it's one of the few natural barrier beach–dune–salt marsh complexes left on the Northeast coast. Here you can bird-watch, fish, swim, and pick plums and cranberries. The refuge is such a popular place in summer, especially on weekends, that cars begin to line up at the gate before 7 AM. Only a limited number of cars are let in, although there's no restriction on the number of people using the beach. No pets are allowed in the refuge. ☎ *978/465–5753,* WEB *www.parkerriver.org.* ⊠ *Car $5, bicycle and walk-ins $2.* ☺ *Daily dawn–dusk. Beach sometimes closed during endangered species nesting season in spring and early summer.*

Dining and Lodging

$$–$$$ ★ ✕ **Scandia.** The Continental cuisine here is well known; house specialties include Caesar salad prepared table-side and a veal and lobster sauté. The Sunday brunch has hot entrées, cold salads, crepes, waffles, and omelets; at lunch, the menu offers upscale sandwiches, salads, and several seafood dishes. There are just 15 tables, so reservations are a good idea. ⊠ *25 State St.,* ☎ *978/462–6271. AE, D, MC, V.*

$$–$$$ ★ ▨ **Clark Currier Inn.** This 1803 Federal-style mansion with an elegant "good morning" staircase (so called because two small staircases join at the head of a large one, permitting people to greet one another on their way down to breakfast) has been restored with care, taste, and imagination. It's one of the best inns on the North Shore. Guest rooms are spacious and furnished with antiques, including one with a glorious, late-19th-century sleigh bed. Rates include afternoon tea. ⊠ *45 Green St., 01950,* ☎ *978/465–8363,* WEB *www.clarkcurrierinn.com. 8 rooms. Library; no smoking. AE, D, MC, V. CP.*

Nightlife and the Arts

The **Grog** (⊠ 13 Middle St., ☎ 978/465–8008, WEB www.thegrog.com) restaurant and bar hosts blues and rock bands several nights weekly.

Outdoor Activities and Sports

FISHING

Surf casting is popular—bluefish, pollack, and striped bass can be taken from the ocean shores of Plum Island; if you enter the refuge with fishing equipment in the daytime you can obtain a free permit to remain on the beach after dark. You don't need a permit to fish from the public beach at Plum Island; the best spot is around the mouth of the Merrimack River.

HIKING

Maudslay State Park (⊠ Curzon Mill Rd., I–95 to Rte. 113 east, then left on Noble St., ☎ 978/465–7223, WEB www.state.ma.us/dem/parks/maud.htm) has trails that wind through meadows, pine forests, and gardens. It's open daily 8 AM–sunset.

NORTH SHORE A TO Z

To research prices, get advice from other travelers, and book travel arrangements, visit www.fodors.com.

BUS TRAVEL

The Cape Ann Transportation Authority, or CATA, provides local bus service in the Gloucester, Rockport, and Essex region. The Coach Company bus line runs a commuter bus between Newburyport and Boston on weekdays. The ride takes 1–1¼ hours. MBTA buses leave daily from Boston's Haymarket Station for Marblehead and Salem. Travel time is about 1–1¼ hours.

➤ BUS INFORMATION: **Cape Ann Transportation Authority** (☎ 978/283–7916, WEB www.canntran.com). **Coach Company** bus line (☎ 800/874–3377, WEB www.coachco.com). **MBTA** (☎ 617/222–3200 schedules, WEB www.mbta.com).

CAR TRAVEL

The primary link between Boston and the North Shore is Route 128, which splits off from I–95 and follows the coast northeast to Gloucester. To pick up Route 128 from Boston, take I–93 north to I–95 north to Route 128. If you stay on I–95, you'll reach Newburyport. A less direct route is Route 1A, which leaves Boston via the Callahan Tunnel; once you're north of Lynn you'll pass through several pretty towns. Beyond Beverly, Route 1A travels inland toward Ipswich and Essex; at this point, Route 127 follows the coast to Gloucester and Rockport.

From Boston to Salem or Marblehead, follow Route 128 to Route 114 into Salem and on to Marblehead. A word of caution: this route is confusing and poorly marked, particularly returning to Route 128. An alternative route to Marblehead: follow Route 1A north, and then pick up Route 129 north along the shore through Swampscott and into Marblehead.

EMERGENCIES

➤ CONTACTS: **Police** (☎ 911). **Beverly Hospital** (⊠ 85 Herrick St., Beverly, ☎ 978/922–3000).

➤ LATE-NIGHT PHARMACIES: **CVS** (⊠ 53 Dodge St., Beverly, ☎ 978/927–3291, WEB www.cvs.com), open 24 hours. **Walgreens** (⊠ 201 Main St., Gloucester, ☎ 978/283–7361, WEB www.walgreens.com), open until 10 on weeknights, 6 on weekends.

TRAIN TRAVEL

MBTA trains travel from Boston's North Station to Salem (25–30 minutes), Manchester (40–50 minutes), Gloucester (55–60 minutes), Rockport (70 minutes), Ipswich (50–55 minutes), and Newburyport (60–65 minutes).

➤ TRAIN INFORMATION: **MBTA** (☎ 617/222–3200, WEB www.mbta.com). **Merrimack Valley Regional Transit Authority** (☎ 978/469–6878, WEB www.mvrta.com).

VISITOR INFORMATION

➤ TOURIST INFORMATION: **Cape Ann Chamber of Commerce** (⊠ 33 Commercial St., Gloucester 01930, ☎ 978/283–1601 or 800/321–0133, WEB www.capeannvacations.com). **Destination Salem** (⊠ 63 Wharf St., Salem 01970, ☎ 978/741–3252 or 877/725–3662, WEB www.salem.org). **Greater Newburyport Chamber of Commerce and Industry** (⊠ 29 State St., Newburyport 01950, ☎ 978/462–6680, WEB www.newburyportchamber.org). **Ipswich Visitor Information** (⊠ 20 S. Main St., Ipswich 01936, ☎ 978/356–8540, WEB www.ipswichma.com). **Marblehead Chamber of Commerce** (⊠ 62 Pleasant St. [Box 76, Marblehead 01945], ☎ 781/631–2868, WEB www. marbleheadchamber.org). **Rockport Chamber of Commerce** (⊠ 22 Broadway, Rockport 01966, ☎ 978/546–6575, WEB www. rockportusa.com).

THE PIONEER VALLEY

Updated by Andrew Collins

The Pioneer Valley, a string of historic settlements along the Connecticut River from Springfield in the south up to the Vermont border, formed the western frontier of New England from the early 1600s until the late 18th century. The river and its fertile banks first attracted farmers and traders, and the Connecticut later became a source of power and transport for the earliest industrial cities in America. The northern regions of the Pioneer Valley remain mostly rural and tranquil; farms and small towns reveal typically New England architecture. Farther south, the cities of Holyoke and Springfield are chiefly industrial but have come a long way toward reinventing themselves over the past decade. Educational pioneers came to this region as well—to form Mount Holyoke College, America's first college for women, and four other major colleges, as well as several well-known prep schools. Northampton and Amherst, the valley's two hubs of higher learning, have become increasingly desirable places to live, especially among empty nesters, recent college grads, artists, and telecommuters who relish in the ample natural scenery, sophisticated cultural venues, and lively dining and shopping.

Northfield

③⑥ *88 mi northwest of Boston; 50 mi north of Springfield; 20 mi south of Brattleboro, Vermont.*

Just south of the Vermont and New Hampshire borders, this country town is known mainly as a center for hikers, campers, and other lovers of the outdoors.

The **Northfield Mountain Recreation and Environmental Center** has 26 mi of hiking, horseback, and biking trails, and you can rent canoes, rowboats, and kayaks at the large campground at Barton Cove. From here you can paddle to the Munn's Ferry campground, accessible only by canoe. The center also runs 1½-hour riverboat tours of the Pioneer Valley, along a 12-mi stretch of the Connecticut River between Northfield and Gill, where you'll pass a nesting ground of bald eagles and pass through a dramatically narrow gorge. In winter, the center rents cross-country skis and snowshoes and offers lessons. ⊠ *99 Miller's Falls Rd.,* ☎ *413/863–9300 or 800/859–2960,* WEB *www.nu.com/northfield.* 🖼 *Free; riverboat tour $ 9.* ☉ *Riverboat tour mid-June–mid-Oct., Wed.– Sun. 11, 1:15 and 3. Reservations essential.*

Lodging

$$ 🖼 **Centennial House.** Once home to presidents of the town's Mount Hermon School, this 1811 Colonial bed-and-breakfast has three spacious, antiques-filled guest rooms (two of them can be booked with additional adjoining bedrooms) and a third-floor suite that sleeps four and has a kitchen. The inn's large, glassed-in sunroom (screened in summer) is a delightful place to curl up and read a book; the pine-paneled living room has a huge fireplace. You have 2½ acres of yard to play in or to just sit and watch the sun set. ⊠ *Main St., 01360,* ☎ *413/498–5921 or 877/ 977–5950,* FAX *413/498–2525,* WEB *www.thecentennialhouse.com. 3 rooms, 1 suite. Internet; no room phones, no TV in some rooms. AE, MC, V. BP.*

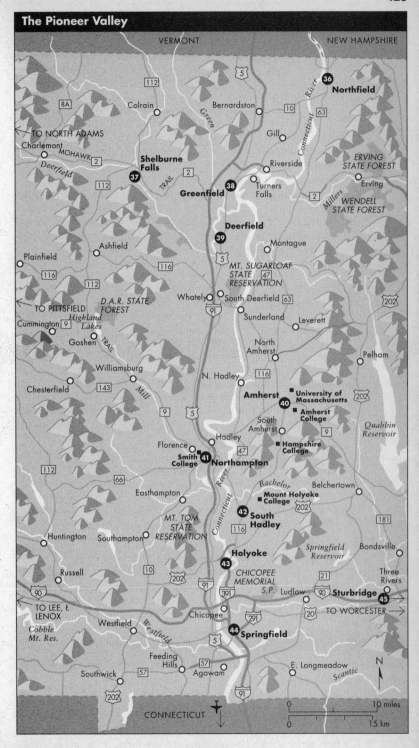

The Pioneer Valley

Shelburne Falls

③ *24 mi southwest of Northfield.*

The quintessence of small-town America, Shelburne Falls straddles the Deerfield River. A sprinkling of quality antiques shops and the Copper Angel Restaurant overlooking the river make the village a good place to spend a half day. From May to October an arched, 400-ft abandoned trolley bridge is transformed by Shelburne Falls' Women's Club into the **Bridge of Flowers** (⊠ at Water St., ☎ 413/625–2544), a gardened promenade bursting with colors. In the riverbed just downstream from the town are 50 immense **glacial potholes** ground out of granite during the last ice age.

Dining and Lodging

$$-$$$ ✕ **Copper Angel Restaurant.** This restaurant between the Deerfield River and State Street specializes in vegetarian cuisine but also serves poultry and fish. The organic produce–based menu includes lentil cutlets with vegetarian gravy, a tofu stir-fry with peanut sauce, stuffed chicken breast with garlic mashed potatoes, and orange-pepper shrimp. A deck overlooking the Bridge of Flowers is pleasant for summer dining. ⊠ *2 State St.,* ☎ *413/625–2727. Reservations not accepted. MC, V. Closed Tues.*

$ ⊡ **Penfrydd Farm.** In the middle of a 160-acre working farm, this serene B&B occupies a rejuvenated 1830s farmhouse and has exposed beams, wide floorboards, skylights, and a big hot tub. The ideal place to get away from it all, Penfrydd Farm has fabulous fall foliage and plenty of snow for snowshoeing and cross-country skiing in winter at nearby Cook State Forest. It's 8 mi north of Shelburne Falls. ⊠ *105 Hillman Rd. (R.R. 1, Box 100A, Colrain 01340),* ☎ *413/624–5516,* ⓌⒺⒷ *www.penfrydd.com. 4 rooms, 3 with shared bath. Some in-room hot tubs, hot tub; no kids under 10. AE, MC, V. CP weekends, BP weekdays.*

Outdoor Activities and Sports

You can raft along the Deerfield River at Charlemont, on the Mohawk Trail. From April to October **Zoar Outdoor** (☎ 800/532–7483, ⓌⒺⒷ www.zaroutdoor.com) operates one-day raft tours over 10 mi of Class II–III rapids daily as well as family float trips on the lower section of the Deerfield River. The outfit rents equipment and conducts canoe and kayak tours and rock climbs.

Shopping

The **Salmon Falls Artisans Showroom** (⊠ Ashfield St., ☎ 413/625–9833, ⓌⒺⒷ www.penguin-works.com/sfas) carries sculpture, pottery, glass (including handblown pieces by Josh Simpson), and furniture by more than 175 local artisans.

Greenfield

③ *13 mi south of Northfield, 14 mi east of Shelburne Falls.*

Once a prosperous trade and industrial center during much of its first 300 years, Greenfield declined during the latter half of the 20th century but has since become increasingly popular again for its bustling downtown and its wealthy residential neighborhoods dotted with immense Victorian mansions. It's a good base for exploring the northern half of the valley. Venture east into the highly walkable downtown, however, and you'll find independently owned shops, pubs, and eateries.

ⓒ Just west of downtown you can take a walk back in history at **Old Greenfield Village,** where stands a carefully documented replica of an 1895 New England town. Among the 15 buildings are a general store, a church, a schoolhouse, and a print shop. ⊠ *Rte. 2, Greenfield,* ☎ *413/774–7138,* WEB *users.crocker.com/greenfield/ogv.html.* ⊠ *$5.* ☉ *Mid-May–mid-Oct., Wed.–Mon. 10–4.*

Dining and Lodging

$$–$$$ ✕ **Blue Heron.** Set inside a red-clapboard 1830s mill on a rushing, ev-
★ ergreen-shrouded river southeast of Greenfield, this hard-to-find eatery is worth the adventure. The kitchen turns out contemporary southern European and North African–inspired fare, such as scallion potato pancakes with house-cured gravlax and Moroccan vegetable tagine with free-range chicken served over couscous with chermoula sauce. ⊠ *Greenfield Rd. (7 mi southeast of Greenfield),* ☎ *413/367–0200. MC, V. Closed Mon.–Tues. No lunch Wed.–Sat.*

$$–$$$ ☷ **Brandt House Country Inn.** The owner of this 16-room, turn-of-the-
★ 20th-century Colonial Revival mansion set on 3½ manicured acres is an interior decorator, and her touch is evident throughout. The sun-lit, spacious common rooms are filled with plants, plump easy chairs, and handsome contemporary furnishings; the elegantly appointed guest rooms have feather beds. The emphasis is on comfort and homi-ness. The stunning penthouse, with a full kitchen and sleeping loft, sleeps up to five. ⊠ *29 Highland Ave., Greenfield 01301,* ☎ *413/774–3329 or 800/235–3329,* FAX *413/772–2908,* WEB *www.brandt-house.com. 7 rooms, 6 with bath; 1 suite. Some in-room hot tubs, refrigerators, some in-room VCRs, tennis court, meeting room, some pets allowed. AE, D, MC, V. BP.*

Nightlife

A bohemian microbrewery in the center of town, **People's Pint** (⊠ 24 Federal St., ☎ 413/773–0333) books a wide range of folk and rock acts and serves healthful pub fare, fresh-baked breads, and robust handcrafted ales and porters.

Outdoor Activities and Sports

High on a ridge between downtown Greenfield and the Connecticut River, **Poet's Seat Tower** (⊠ Rocky Mountain, follow signs from Maple St.) makes for one of the valley's most rewarding short jaunts. It's a 1-mi hike from the parking area, and from the summit are inspiring 360-degree views of the countryside.

Shopping

Occupying a dramatic bank building in downtown Greenfield, **Pushkin Gallery** (⊠ 332 Main St., ☎ 413/774–2891 or 413/549–4564) carries the works of prominent Russian painters, both contemporary and vintage.

Deerfield

③⑨ *18 mi southeast of Shelburne Falls.*

In Deerfield, a horse pulling a carriage clip-clops past perfectly main-tained 18th-century homes, neighbors leave their doors unlocked and tip their hats to strangers, kids play ball in fields by the river, and the bell of the impossibly beautiful brick church peals from a white steeple. This is the perfect New England village, though not without a past dark-ened by tragedy. Settled by Native Americans more than 8,000 years ago, Deerfield was originally a Pocumtuck village—deserted after deadly epidemics and a war with the Mohawks that all but wiped out the tribe. English pioneers eagerly settled into this frontier outpost in the 1660s and 1670s, but two bloody massacres at the hands of the Native Americans and the French caused the village to be abandoned until 1707, when construction began on the buildings that remain today.

★ Although it has a turbulent past, **Historic Deerfield** now basks in a genteel aura. With 52 buildings on 93 acres, this village provides a vivid glimpse into 18th- and 19th-century America. The **Street**, a tree-lined avenue of 18th- and 19th-century houses, is protected and maintained as a museum site, with 14 of the preserved buildings open to the public year-round (in winter, homes are shown according to interest). Some homes contain antique furnishings and decorative arts; other buildings exhibit textiles, silver, pewter, or ceramics. The well-trained guides converse knowledgeably about the exhibits and Deerfield's history. Start your visit at the information center in Hall Tavern and don't miss the **Wells-Thorn House**, where rooms depict life as it changed from 1725 to 1850. Purchase of an all-house admission ticket includes access to the **Flynt Center of Early New England Life** (⊠ 37-D Old Main St.), which houses two exhibit galleries. One of the galleries holds 2,500 decorative objects from 1600 to the present. Quilts, Native American artifacts, furniture, and other objects are on display at **Memorial Hall Museum** (⊠ 8 Memorial St., ☎ 413/664–3768; ⬜ $6, or free with Historic Deerfield admission; ☉ May–Oct., daily 9:30–4:30), one of the oldest museums in the country. Plan to spend at least one full day at Historic Deerfield. ⊠ *The Street,* ☎ *413/774–5581,* WEB *www. historic-deerfield.org.* ⬜ *1-wk admission to all houses and museum $12, single-house admission $6.* ☉ *Daily 9:30–4:30.*

☾ Since it opened in fall 2001, **Magic Wings Butterfly Conservatory and Gardens** has rapidly developed into one of the region's favorite attractions. The facility comprises an indoor conservatory garden where you can stroll among thousands of fluttering butterflies, as well as an extensive three-season outdoor garden that's landscaped to attract local species. You can also observe the butterfly nursery, where throughout the day newborns first experience the joy of flight. An extensive garden shop sells statuary, tools, and butterfly-friendly plantings; there's also a snack bar and gift shop. ⊠ *281 Greenfield Rd. (U.S. 5/ Rte. 10), South Deerfield,* ☎ *413/665–2805,* WEB *www.magicwings.net.* ⬜ *$7.* ☉ *Daily 9–5 (until 6 in summer).*

☾ The flagship store of the national chain, **Yankee Candle Company** not only displays a full review of its product line—including scented candles in such outlandish aromas as cantaloupe, spiced pumpkin, and banana-nut bread—but an array of live exhibits. In a small candle-making museum off the main showroom, you can watch costumed docents practicing the art of candle-dipping, using historically accurate Colonial implements in a setting of antique furnishings. Highlights for younger kids include the Bavarian Christmas Village and Santa's Toy Factory, where electric trains chug by overhead and faux-snow falls lightly. You can have lunch at either the pleasant café or the full-service Chandler's American restaurant. The on-site car museum closed in 2001; plans are to add retail shops in the museum's former space. ⊠ *U.S. 5/Rte. 10, South Deerfield,* ☎ *413/665–2929,* WEB *www.yankeecandle.com.* ⬜ *Free.* ☉ *Daily 9:30–6.*

Dining and Lodging

$$–$$$ ✕ **Sienna.** The atmosphere here is soothing and the service well mannered, but the food is what really shines. Choices from the ever-changing menu might include a wild-mushroom crepe on a cantaloupe melon, with organic Roquefort cheese and scallion oil, followed by pan-seared sea basson Swiss chard, with fingerling potatoes, a sweet corn flan and white truffle oil. After an irresistible dessert such as a coconut panna cotta with persimmon compote, your evening ends with the personal touch of a handwritten check on stationery. ⊠ *6 Elm St., South Deerfield,* ☎ *413/665–0215. MC, V. Closed Mon.–Tues. No lunch.*

$$$$ ✕⊞ **Deerfield Inn.** Period wallpapers decorate the rooms in the main
★   inn, which was built in 1884; the rooms in an outbuilding have identical papers but are newer (1981) and closer to the parking lot. Rooms
are snug and handsomely appointed both with antiques and replicas;
some have four-poster or canopy beds. The restaurant ($$$–$$$$) show-
cases such creative American fare as pan-seared pheasant with crushed
peppercorns and wild mushrooms in a cognac cream sauce with a truf-
fle risotto cake. The tavern ($$–$$$) serves lighter fare. ⊠ *81 Old Main
St., 01342,* ☏ *413/774–5587 or 800/926–3865,* FAX *413/773–8712,* WEB
*www.deerfieldinn.com. 23 rooms. 2 restaurants, coffee shop, bar; no
smoking. AE, MC, V. BP.*

$$ ✕⊞ **Whately Inn.** Antiques and four-poster beds slope gently on old-
wood floors of the guest rooms at this informal Colonial inn. The din-
ing room ($$–$$$; no lunch) has a fireplace and exposed beams, tables
on a raised stage at one end, and some booths; it's dimly lighted, with
candles on the tables. Prime Angus steaks, baked lobster with shrimp
stuffing, rack of lamb, and other traditional entrées come with salad,
appetizer, dessert, and coffee. Sunday dinner begins at 1 PM. The full
menu is also served in the more casual lounge. ⊠ *Chestnut Plain Rd.,
Whately Center 01093,* ☏ *413/665–3044 or 800/942–8359,* WEB
www.whatelyinn.com 4 rooms. Restaurant. AE, D, MC, V.

$ ⊞ **Sunnyside Farm Bed and Breakfast.** Maple antiques and family heir-
looms decorate this circa-1800 Victorian farmhouse's country-style
rooms, all of which are hung with fine-art reproductions and have views
across the fields. A full country breakfast is served family-style in the
dining room. The 50-acre farm is about 8 mi south of Deerfield, convenient to cross-country skiing, mountain biking, and hiking. ⊠ *21
River Rd., Whately 01093,* ☏ *413/665–3113. 5 rooms without bath.
Pool. No credit cards. BP.*

Shopping

A short drive south of Historic Deerfield, **Richardson's Candy Kitchen**
(⊠ U.S. 5/Rte. 10, ☏ 413/772–0443) has been making and selling luscious chocolates and cream-filled truffles for more than a half century.

Amherst

④⓪   *10 mi southeast of Deerfield.*

Three of the Pioneer Valley's five major colleges—the University of
Massachusetts (UMass), Amherst College, and Hampshire College—
are in small but lively Amherst, which has a large village green. Bookstores, funky shops, bars, and cafés reflect the area's youthful orientation.

The poet Emily Dickinson (1830–86) was born and died in the **Emily
Dickinson Homestead.** The house contains some of the poet's belongings, but most of her manuscripts are elsewhere. Guided tours are the
only way to visit the house, and reservations are advisable. Next door,
you can also tour **The Evergreens** (⊠ 214 Main St., ☏ 413/253–5272),
an imposing Italianate Victorian mansion in which Emily's brother
Austin resided for more than 50 years. The house and grounds are currently undergoing a full restoration, during which guided tours are conducted May–September, Wednesday and Saturday 1–5. Admission is $5.
⊠ *280 Main St.,* ☏ *413/542–8161,* WEB *www.dickinsonhomestead.org.*
🖾 *$5.* ☉ *Mar.–mid-Dec., Wed.–Sun.; call for hrs.*

The **Amherst History Museum at the Strong House,** built in the mid-
1700s, displays an extensive collection of household tools, furniture,
china, and clothing that reflects changing styles of interior decoration.
Most items are Amherst originals, dating from the 18th to the mid-
20th century. ⊠ *67 Amity St.,* ☏ *413/256–0678,* WEB *www.*

amhersthistory.org. 🖼 *$4.* ⊙ *Feb.–Nov., Wed.–Sat. 12:30–3:30; call for Dec. hrs.*

NEED A
BREAK?
Newspapers and books are strewn about the tables at the **Black Sheep** (✉ 79 Main St., ☎ 413/253-3442), a funky downtown café specializing in flavored coffees, fancy desserts, and creative sandwiches that include the C'est la Brie (a baguette smothered with Brie, roasted peppers, spinach, and raspberry mustard) and the French Kiss (truffle pâté, Dijon mustard, and red onion on a baguette).

★ The effort to save Yiddish books and preserve Jewish culture has become a major movement, and the **National Yiddish Book Center** is its core. The center is housed in a thatched-roof building that resembles a cluster of structures typical of a shtetl, or traditional Eastern European Jewish village. Inside, a contemporary space contains more than 1.5 million books, a fireside reading area, a kosher dining area, and a visitor center with exhibits. The work here is performed out in the open: hundreds of books pour in daily, and workers come across everything from family keepsakes to rare manuscripts. ✉ *Harry and Jeanette Weinberg Bldg., Hampshire College, Rte. 116,* ☎ *413/256–4900,* 🕸 *www.yiddishbookcenter.org.* 🖼 *Free.* ⊙ *Sun.–Fri. 10–3:30.*

🐌 Scheduled at press time to open near the National Yiddish Book Center in November 2002, the **Eric Carle Museum of Picture Book Art** (✉ 125 W. Bay Rd., ☎ 413/586–8934, 🕸 www.picturebookart.org) will occupy a dramatic, contemporary space in an apple orchard beside the campus of Hampshire College. The museum's mission is to celebrate and preserve not only the works of renowned children's book author Eric Carle (who penned *The Very Hungry Caterpillar*) but also such luminaries as Maurice Sendak, Lucy Cousins, Petra Mathers, and Leo and Diane Dillon. The museum will also stage puppet shows, lectures, story-telling, dance, and music, and will contain an extensive children's-literature library.

Dining and Lodging

$–$$$ ✕ **Maplewood Farms Restaurant, Brewery, and Market.** What began as the area's first organic market has expanded over the years into a full microbrewery and restaurant, with a warm and rustic dining room. The menu specializes in creative, healthful American fare such as roasted butternut squash soup, grape salad with blue cheese and toasted walnuts, a barbecue pork tart with smoked bacon and cheddar, and horseradish-crusted salmon over fettuccine. The Fat Dog Stout is a favorite from the brewery. ✉ *138 Belchertown Rd./Rte. 9,* ☎ *413/256–3276. AE, D, MC, V. Closed Mon.*

$–$$ ✕ **Judie's.** Since 1977 students have crowded around small tables on the glassed-in porch, ordering chicken ravioli with walnuts, shrimp tempura, gumbo popovers, Gorgonzola-and-mushroom burgers—the list goes on and on. The atmosphere is hip and artsy; a painting on canvas covers each tabletop. ✉ *51 N. Pleasant St.,* ☎ *413/253-3491. Reservations not accepted. AE, D, MC, V. Closed Mon.*

$$–$$$ ✕🛏 **Lord Jeffery Inn.** This gabled brick inn sits regally over the town green. Many guest rooms have a light floral decor; others have stencils and pastel woodwork. In the formal dining room ($$–$$$$), with its dark paneling and prodigious fireplace, you might sample beef Wellington, Boston baked scrod, or grilled loin of venison. Burgers, salads, and the like are served at Boltwood's Tavern, which has a small bar and a wraparound porch. ✉ *30 Boltwood Ave., 01002,* ☎ *413/253–2576 or 800/742–0358,* 📠 *413/256–6152,* 🕸 *www.lordjefferyinn.com. 40 rooms, 8 suites. 2 restaurants, bar. AE, DC, MC, V.*

$$–$$$ ⊡ **Allen House Victorian and Amherst Inns.** A rare find, these late-19th-
★ century inns a block apart from each other have been gloriously restored with precision to the Aesthetic period of the Victorian era. Busy,
colorful wall coverings reach to the high ceilings. Antiques include a
burled-walnut headboard and dresser set, wicker "steamship" chairs,
screens, and carved golden-oak beds. Lace curtains and hand-stencil-
ing grace the rooms, which have supremely comfortable beds with goose-
down comforters. It's a short walk to downtown. Rooms in the Amherst
Inn tend to be larger and even more plush. Some rooms have nonworking
fireplaces. ⊠ *599 Main St., 01002,* ☎ *413/253–5000,* WEB *www.
allenhouse.com. 14 rooms. Massage, business services; no room TVs,
no kids under 10, no smoking. No credit cards. BP.*

$$ ⊡ **Campus Center Hotel.** Atop the UMass campus and convenient to
all of Amherst, this modern hotel has basic but pleasant motel-style
rooms with large windows that allow excellent views over campus and
countryside. You can use university exercise facilities—as well as the
pool and tennis courts—with prior reservation, and dine at several cam-
pus restaurants. Because the hotel is at a college, there's no hotel tax.
⊠ *University of Massachusetts, Murray D. Lincoln Tower, 01003,* ☎
413/549–6000, FAX *413/545–1210. 114 rooms, 2 suites. Business ser-
vices, meeting rooms. AE, D, DC, MC, V.*

Nightlife and the Arts

Major ballet and modern dance companies appear in season at the **UMass
Fine Arts Center** (⊠ Haigis Hall, ☎ 413/545–2511 or 800/999–8627).
The **William D. Mullins Memorial Center** (⊠ University Dr., University
of Massachusetts, ☎ 413/545–0505) hosts concerts, theatrical pro-
ductions, and other entertainment.

Outdoor Activities and Sports

BIKING

Valley Bicycles (⊠ 319 Main St., ☎ 413/256–0880) rents bikes and
dispenses cycling advice.

FISHING

The Connecticut River sustains shad, salmon, and several dozen other
fish species. From May to October, at **Waterfield Farms** (⊠ 500 Sun-
derland Rd./Rte. 116, Sunderland-Amherst border, ☎ 413/549–3558),
you pay $3 ($8 for a family of four) to drop your line, plus an amount
that varies depending on what fish you catch and the size. Poles can
be rented, and bait is sold.

Shopping

The **Leverett Crafts and Arts Center** (⊠ Montague Rd., Leverett, 5 mi
north of Amherst, ☎ 413/548–9070) houses 20 resident artists who
create jewelry, ceramics, glass, and textiles. An institution in the Pio-
neer Valley, **Atkins Farms Country Market** (⊠ Rte. 116, South Amherst,
☎ 413/253–9528 or 800/594–9537) is surrounded by apple orchards
and gorgeous views of the Holyoke Ridge. Hayrides are conducted in
the fall, and children's events are hosted year-round. The farm sells ap-
ples and has a bakery and deli.

Northampton

🕦 *8 mi southwest of Amherst.*

The small, bustling college town of Northampton, first settled in 1654,
is listed on the National Register of Historic Places. Tracy Kidder's 1999
nonfiction book *Home Town* describes how the community has suc-
cessfully absorbed an influx of new residents over the past few decades,
and author John Villani ranked Northampton No. 1 in his book *The
100 Best Small Art Towns in America*. Packed with ethnic restaurants,

live-music and dance clubs, and offbeat galleries and boutiques, the city attracts artsy types, academics, activists, lesbians and gays, and just about anyone else seeking the culture and sophistication of a big metropolis but the friendliness and easy pace of a small town.

The redbrick quadrangles of **Smith College,** the nation's largest liberal arts college for women, resemble the layouts of the women's colleges at Cambridge University, England, which were built around 1871, when this institution was founded. Worth visiting are the **Lyman Plant House** (☎ 413/585–2740; ⊙ daily 8:30–4) and the **botanic gardens,** which are undergoing an ambitious restoration.

Although it's closed for a massive renovation and expansion, the **Smith College Museum of Art** (☎ 413/585–2760) will reopen in spring 2003 (call ahead for hours) with a new floor of skylighted galleries, an expanded shop, an enclosed courtyard that will host occasional performances and receptions, and a high-tech art library. Highlights of the comprehensive permanent collection include European masterworks by Cézanne, Degas, Rodin, and Seurat; a vast survey of American painting; a fine representation of women's art that ranges from Mary Cassatt to Alice Neel; and significant African and Asian works.

Historic Northampton maintains three houses that are open for tours: Parsons House (1730), Shepherd House (1798), and Damon House (1813). Exhibits in the headquarters chronicle the history of Northampton with some 50,000 documents, photos, and collectibles. ⊠ *Headquarters, 46 Bridge St.,* ☎ *413/584–6011,* WEB *www.historic-northampton.org.* ⊠ *Headquarters exhibits by donation; houses $3. ⊙ Headquarters exhibits Tues.–Fri. 10–4; houses weekends noon–4.*

Northampton was the Massachusetts home of the 30th U.S. president, Calvin Coolidge. He practiced law here and served as mayor from 1910 to 1911. The **Coolidge Room,** which was renovated in 2001–2002, at the **Forbes Library** (⊠ 20 West St., ☎ 413/587–1011, WEB www.forbeslibrary.org/coolidge.html) contains a collection of his papers and memorabilia.

| NEED A BREAK? | One of the many student-filled hot spots in downtown Northampton, **Cha Cha Cha!** (⊠ 134 Main St., ☎ 413/586–7311) serves exceptionally tasty California-style burritos with Thai and Latin ingredients. On the lower level of Thorne's Marketplace, **Herrell's Ice Cream** (⊠ 8 Old South St., ☎ 413/586–9700) is famous for its chocolate-pudding, vanilla-malt, and cinnamon ice cream flavors, plus delicious homemade hot fudge sauce. |

☺ Within the 150-acre **Look Memorial Park** (⊠ 300 N. Main St./Rte. 9, Florence, ☎ 413/584–5457, WEB www.lookpark.org; ⊠ Apr.–Oct., $3 weekends, $2 weekdays; free Nov.–Mar.) are a small zoo, a wading pool, children's playgrounds, paddleboats, a train, and bumper boats. It's 5 mi west of Northampton.

At the wide place in the Connecticut River known as the Oxbow is the Massachusetts Audubon Society's 700-acre **Arcadia Nature Center and Wildlife Sanctuary,** where you can try the hiking and nature trails and scheduled canoe trips. ⊠ *127 Combs Rd., Easthampton (3 mi south of Northampton),* ☎ *413/584–3009.* ⊠ *$3. ⊙ Trails Tues.–Sun. 9–3.*

| OFF THE BEATEN PATH | **WILLIAM CULLEN BRYANT HOMESTEAD –** It's a scenic drive west on Route 9 to reach the country estate of poet and author William Cullen Bryant. In the scenic hills west of the Pioneer Valley, the wild 465-acre grounds over- |

look the Westfield River valley. Inside the Dutch Colonial 1783 mansion are furnishings and collectibles from Bryant's life, work, and travels. This is a great venue for bird-watching, cross-country skiing, snowshoeing, fishing, hiking, and picnics. ✉ *207 Bryant Rd., Cummington (20 mi northwest of Northampton),* ☎ *413/634–2244,* WEB *www.thetrustees.org.* ⛺ *House tour $5, grounds free, Rivulet Trail tour $4.* ☉ *House tours late June–early Sept., Fri.–Sun. 1–5; early Sept.–mid-Oct., weekends 1–5; grounds daily sunrise–sunset.*

Dining and Lodging

$$$–$$$$ ★ ✕ **Del Raye.** An upscale member of the esteemed Northampton dining empire that includes the more affordable but similarly outstanding Spoleto and Pizza Paradiso restaurants, this eatery is housed in a sexy, dimly lighted space with closely spaced tables and a swanky lounge. Among the world-beat creations are banana-encrusted sea scallops with dates, sweet tomatoes, and a cactus-fruit beurre rouge; and tangerine-glazed duck. ✉ *1 Bridge St.,* ☎ *413/586–2664. AE, MC, V. No lunch.*

$$ ★ ✕ **La Cazuela.** In a colorful painted-lady Victorian a block off Main Street, this spirited restaurant with both indoor and outdoor dining areas serves commendable and unusually—by New England standards—authentic southwestern and Mexican cooking. Ingredients are fresh and used to great effect: try the sweet-potato or smoky chicken–pasilla chile burros, or the fry bread stuffed with shredded beef. The list of kicky, never-frozen margaritas is extensive. ✉ *7 Old South St.,* ☎ *413/586–0400. AE, D, DC, MC, V.*

$$ ✕ **Mulino's** Cheerful, informal, yet romantic, this trattoria carefully prepares Sicilian-inspired home-style Italian food with authentic recipes and ingredients. You'll rarely taste a better carbonara sauce on this side of the Atlantic, and don't overlook the smoked salmon in a lemon-capershallot sauce tossed with fettuccine. Portions are huge, the wine list extensive. In the basement, the Bishop's Lounge has live jazz many evenings. ✉ *7 Old South St.,* ☎ *413/586–0400. AE, D, DC, MC, V. No lunch.*

$–$$ ✕ **Northampton Brewery.** In a rambling building behind the Thorne's Marketplace, this often-packed pub and microbrewery has extensive outdoor seating on an airy deck and serves tasty comfort-cooking. Good bets include chicken-and-shrimp jambalaya, the blackened blue burger (with blue cheese and caramelized onions), and homemade black-bean dip. ✉ *11 Brewster St.,* ☎ *413/584–9903. AE, D, DC, MC, V.*

$$$–$$$$ 🏨 **Hotel Northampton.** Room furnishings at this 1927 downtown hotel include Colonial reproductions and heavy curtains. Some rooms have four-poster beds, balconies overlooking a busy street or the parking lot, whirlpool tubs, and heated towel racks. Wiggins Tavern (no lunch) serves standard American fare and an elaborate Sunday brunch; the café serves lighter fare. ✉ *36 King St., 01060,* ☎ *413/584–3100 or 800/547–3529,* FAX *413/584–9455,* WEB *www.hotelnorthampton.com. 99 rooms, 6 suites, 2 efficiency units. 2 restaurants, gym, bar, meeting rooms. AE, D, DC, MC, V. CP.*

$$–$$$ ★ 🏨 **Clark Tavern Inn.** Early customers at this 1742 inn included minutemen on their way to fight in Concord and Lexington. Two centuries later, when the planned route for I–91 ran right through the property, two dedicated preservationists saved the house by moving it. Braided rugs, canopy beds, and stencils create a Colonial atmosphere. Fires warm two large but cozy common rooms; in summer, you can nap in the garden hammock or take a dip in the pool. Breakfast can be served fireside, on the screened-in porch, or in your room. ✉ *98 Bay Rd., Hadley 01035,* ☎ *413/586–1900,* WEB *www.clarktaverninn.com. 3 rooms. Inroom VCRs, pool. AE, D, DC, MC, V. BP.*

$ ⚅ **Twin Maples Bed and Breakfast.** Nearly 30 acres of fields and woods surround this 200-year-old farmhouse, which is 7 mi northwest of Northampton near the hilltop village of Williamsburg. Colonial and country antiques and reproductions furnish the small but enchanting rooms, which have restored brass beds. In winter you can watch maple-sugaring and attend a pancake breakfast. ⊠ *106 South St., Williamsburg 01096,* ☎ *413/268–7925,* FAX *413/268–7243,* WEB *www.hamphillsbandb.com/ twinmaples. 3 rooms without bath. No room phones, no room TVs. AE, MC, V. BP.*

Nightlife and the Arts

The convivial tavern **Fitzwilly's** (⊠ 23 Main St., ☎ 413/584–8666) draws a friendly and varied mix of locals and tourists for drinks and tasty pub fare. The **Iron Horse** (⊠ 20 Center St., ☎ 413/586–8686 or 800/ 843–8425) books some of the top folk and pop artists in the country, from Suzanne Vega to Patty Larkin. Spacious **Diva's** (⊠ 492 Pleasant St., ☎ 413/586–8161) serves the region's sizable lesbian and gay community with a cavernous dance floor and great music. **Pearl Street Nightclub** (⊠ 10 Pearl St., ☎ 413/584–0610) presents a varied slate of theme nights, from 18-and-over and live rock to dancing and top club DJs.

The **Center for the Arts in Northampton** (⊠ 17 New South St., ☎ 413/ 584–7327, WEB www.nohoarts.org) hosts more than 250 gallery exhibitions and theater, dance, and musical events each year, as well as First Night festivities New Year's Eve.

Outdoor Activities and Sports

The **Norwottuck Rail Trail,** part of the Connecticut River Greenway State Park (☎ 413/586–8706, WEB www.hadleyonline.com/railtrail), is a paved 10-mi path that links Northampton with Belchertown by way of Amherst. Great for cycling, rollerblading, jogging, and cross-country skiing, it runs along the old Boston & Maine Railroad Bed. **Sportsman's Marina Boat Rental Company** (⊠ Rte. 9, Hadley, ☎ 413/586– 2426) rents canoes and kayaks from summer through early fall.

Shopping

The 8,000-square-ft **Antique Center of Northampton** (⊠ 9½ Market St., ☎ 413/584–3600) houses 60 dealers. **P!nch** (☎ 413/586–4509 or 800/732–7091) sells contemporary ceramics, jewelry, and glass. **Thorne's Marketplace** (⊠ 150 Main St., ☎ 413/584–5582) is a funky four-floor indoor mall in a former department store. Among the 35 shops and eateries you'll find are **Dynamite Records** (☎ 413/584–1580); **Glimpse of Tibet** (☎ 413/586–1568), which sells authentic Tibetan crafts; and **Different Drummer's Kitchen** (☎ 413/586–7978), a well-stocked culinary shop. **Williamsburg General Store** (⊠ Village Center, Rte. 9, Williamstown, ☎ 413/268–3036), a Pioneer Valley landmark for more than a century, sells breads, specialty foods, penny candy, ice cream, and lots of gift items.

South Hadley

④ *10 mi southeast of Northampton.*

Although it remained a farming community well into the 20th century, South Hadley has long been known primarily as a college town. **Mount Holyoke College,** founded in 1837, was the first women's college in the United States. Among the college's alumnae are Emily Dickinson and playwright Wendy Wasserstein. The handsome wooded campus, encompassing two lakes and lovely walking or riding trails, was landscaped by Frederick Law Olmsted. ⊠ *Rte. 116,* ☎ *413/538–2000.*

Mount Holyoke's **College Art Museum,** scheduled at press time to re-open in late fall 2002 after an extensive renovation and expansion that will greatly increase the exhibit space, has more than 13,000 works of art spanning the globe and the ages. ⊠ *Lower Lake Rd.,* ☎ *413/538–2245,* WEB *www.mtholyoke.edu/offices/artmuseum.* ☜ *Free.* ☉ *Tues.–Fri. 11–5, weekends 1–5.*

Dining

$–$$ ✕ **Fedora's Tavern.** A favorite place with college students, moviego-ers, and shoppers wandering through the engaging shops at the Vil-lage Commons, this dark and cozy English pub serves up a nice range of pub foods. Try the Maine crab cakes, Portobello pasta, burgers, or a cup of what may be the best chili in the valley. ⊠ *25 College St.,* ☎ *413/534–8222. AE, D, MC, V.*

Outdoor Activities and Sports

Pinetum Farm Llamas (⊠ 7 Harris St., Granby, ☎ 413/467–7146), 6 mi east of South Hadley, customizes llama treks according to your abil-ity and interests.

Shopping

The **Hadley Antique Center** (⊠ 227 Russell St./Rte. 9, ☎ 413/586–4093) contains more than 70 different booths. The **Village Commons** (⊠ Col-lege St.), across from Mount Holyoke College, is an outdoor mall with a movie theater, several restaurants, and shops with everything from handmade picture frames to lingerie. Favorites include the **Odyssey Book-store** (☎ 413/534–7307), which stocks gifts, cards, and more than 50,000 new and used titles; and **Tailgate Picnic** (☎ 413/532–7597), a purveyor of bagels, sandwiches, cold pastas, wine, and crackers.

Holyoke

④ *5 mi south of South Hadley.*

Working hard to overcome its days as a textile-factory town, Holyoke has an imaginatively restored industrial city center with one of the most extensive and impressive collections of 19th-century commercial ar-chitecture in the country. Heritage Park sits in the middle of downtown and adjoins two museums. A walk along the streets near the park re-veals some wonderfully innovative adaptations of vintage mill and fac-tory buildings into office, condos, and retail space.

Ⓒ The **Heritage State Park** tells the story of this papermaking commu-nity, the nation's first planned industrial city. You can ride a vintage merry-go-round and admire its 48 hand-carved, hand-painted antique wooden horses. ⊠ *221 Appleton St.,* ☎ *413/534–1723.* ☜ *Free; merry-go-round $1 per ride.* ☉ *Tues.–Sun. 10:30–4:30.*

Ⓒ The **Children's Museum,** beside Heritage State Park in a converted mill by a canal, is packed with hands-on games and educational toys. Within the museum are a state-of-the-art TV station, a multitiered in-teractive exhibit on the body, a giant bubble maker, and a sand pen-dulum. ⊠ *444 Dwight St.,* ☎ *413/536–5437.* ☜ *$4.* ☉ *Tues.–Sat. 9:30–4:30, Sun. noon–5.*

Volleyball was invented at the Holyoke YMCA in 1895, and the **Vol-leyball Hall of Fame** pays homage to the sport with interactive videos and displays of memorabilia, and a Hitmaster and Jumpmaster to test your skills. ⊠ *444 Dwight St.,* ☎ *413/536–0926,* WEB *www.volleyhall.org.* ☜ *$3.50.* ☉ *Weekends noon–4:30.*

Wistariahurst Museum, the former home of silk magnate William Skin-ner, peers into the Pioneer Valley's prosperous industrial age. This

1874 Second Empire mansion with a sweeping Beaux Arts staircase and elaborately landscaped grounds overflows with antiques, paintings, and textiles. The house's leather wall coverings and meticulous woodwork remain perfectly intact. ✉ *238 Cabot St.,* ☎ *413/534–2216.* 🎫 *Donation suggested.* ⊘ *Apr.–Oct., Wed. and weekends 1–5; Nov.– Mar., Wed. and weekends noon–4.*

Dining and Lodging

$$$ ✕ **Delaney House.** Eating at this popular eatery 5 mi north of downtown always feels like an event, in part because of the elegantly set tables and tasteful Victorian decor. It's also because of the live music that flows out of the comfortable lounge. The biggest plus is the food, tasty and beautifully presented in ample portions. Most choices are standard American: prime rib, baked sea scallops, and rack of lamb. Among the more ambitious creations are the shellfish lasagna and the veal sautéed with lobster, artichokes, mushrooms, and couscous. ✉ *U.S. 5 at Smith's Ferry,* ☎ *413/532–1800. AE, D, DC, MC, V. No lunch.*

$$ ✕🏨 **Yankee Pedlar Inn.** Antiques and four-poster or canopy beds furnish the charming rooms at this sprawling inn at a busy crossroads near I–91. The elaborate Victorian bridal suite is heavy on lace and curtains; the beamed carriage house has rustic appointments and simple canopy beds. Chicken potpie and hazelnut-crusted salmon with a raspberry vinaigrette are among the dishes served in the Grill Room ($–$$$), which is painted burgundy and accented with stained glass. The more casual Oyster Bar hosts live music many nights. ✉ *1866 Northampton St., 01040,* ☎ *413/532–9494,* 🖷 *413/536–8877,* 🌐 *www.yankeepedlar.com. 21 rooms, 7 suites. Restaurant, bar, nightclub, meeting room. AE, D, DC, MC, V. CP.*

$$ 🏨 **Carlson Inn & Suites.** Opened beside Delaney House restaurant in October 2001, this attractive chain hotel has large and immaculate rooms, many with fireplaces and room to sleep four to six guests. Free local calls and morning papers are among the amenities. The hotel is just across from the Connecticut River, near Mt. Tom Reservation and 5 mi from both downtown Holyoke and Northampton. ✉ *U.S. 5 at Smith's Ferry, 01040,* ☎ *413/533–2100 or 800/456–4000,* 🖷 *413/539– 9761,* 🌐 *www.countryinns.com. 36 rooms, 25 suites. Some kitchens, indoor pool, health club, hot tub, Internet. AE, D, DC, MC, V. CP.*

Outdoor Activities and Sports

A 3⅓-mi round-trip hike at the **Mt. Tom State Reservation** (✉ U.S. 5, 5 mi north of downtown Holyoke, ☎ 413/527–4805) leads to the summit, whose sheer basalt cliffs were formed by volcanic activity 200 million years ago. At the top are excellent views over the Pioneer Valley and the Berkshires.

Springfield

㊹ *7 mi south of Holyoke; 90 mi west of Boston; 30 mi north of Hartford, Connecticut.*

Springfield is the largest city in the Pioneer Valley, an industrial town where modern skyscrapers rise between grand historic buildings. The city has several rewarding museums and historic sites. The late children's book author Theodore Geisel, also known as Dr. Seuss, was born here.

You can glimpse Springfield's prosperous industrial past by exploring either of the city's most noted neighborhoods—the Maple Hill Historic District (begins on Maple St., ½ mi south of State St.), which preserves several lavish mansions from the 1840s through the 1920s, and the McKnight Historic District (begins 1 mi east of Main St. at Worthington and Bowdoin Sts.)—where you'll see a bounty of ornate Stick, Queen Anne, shingle, Tudor Revival, and Italianate Victorian houses. Self-guided tours of both neighborhoods are available at the Greater Springfield Convention and Visitors Bureau.

★ Dr. James Naismith invented basketball in Springfield in 1891. The **Naismith Memorial Basketball Hall of Fame** has received a massive expansion, which at this writing was slated for completion in late fall 2002. Dedicated to preserving and promoting all facets of the sport, the new 80,000-square-ft facility includes a soaring domed arena, dozens of high-tech interactive exhibits, and video footage and interviews with former players. The Honors Rings pay tribute to the hall's nearly 250 enshrinees. The expansion is the cornerstone of a complete redevelopment of Springfield's waterfront along the Connecticut River—other elements include new shops, restaurants, and a hotel. ⊠ *1150 W. Columbus Ave.,* ☎ *413/781–6500 or 877/446–6752,* WEB *www.hoophall.com.* 🎫 *$10.* ⊙ *Daily 9:30–5:30.*

★ One of the most ambitious cultural venues in New England, the **Springfield Museums at the Quadrangle** comprises four impressive and historic facilities, as well as the dramatic 1912 Renaissance Revival **Springfield Library.** The most modest of them, the **Connecticut Valley Historical Museum** contains mostly quirky, rotating exhibits such as a collection of toy soldiers or a room of rare locally made violins. A key draw here is the in-depth genealogical library, where folks from all over the world come to research their family histories. The mustsee **George Walter Vincent Smith Art Museum** houses a varied but fascinating private art collection, which includes 19th-century American paintings by Frederic Church and Albert Bierstadt, and a Japanese antiquities room filled with armor, textiles, carved jade, and porcelain and rock-crystal snuff bottles. The **Museum of Fine Arts** has paintings by Gauguin, Renoir, Degas, Winslow Homer, J. Alden Weir, and Monet, as well as 18th-century American paintings and contemporary works by O'Keeffe, Frank Stella, George Bellows, and several WPA artists. Rotating exhibits are staged throughout the year. The **Springfield Science Museum** has an "Exploration Center" of touchable displays, the oldest American-built planetarium, an extensive collection of stuffed and mounted animals, dinosaur exhibits, and the African Hall, through which you can take an interactive tour of that continent's flora and ⓒ fauna. The latest addition to the Quadrangle is the **Dr. Seuss National Memorial,** an installation of five bronze statues set around the grounds and depicting scenes from Theodore Geisel's famously whimsical children's books. Geisel was born in Springfield on 1904 and inspired by the animals at Forest Park Zoo, of which his father was the director. The statues include a 4-ft-tall Lorax, a life-size elephant, and a 10-ft Yertle the Turtle. ⊠ *220 State St., at Chestnut St.,* ☎ *413/263–6800,* WEB *www.quadrangle.org.* 🎫 *$6 pass valid for all museums.* ⊙ *Wed.– Fri. noon–5, weekends 11–4.*

ⓒ **Forest Park,** Springfield's leafy 735-acre retreat, is an ideal urban green space. There are hiking paths, paddleboats on Porter Lake, tennis courts, picnic groves, a kiddie train, and a wonderful pond filled with hungry ducks. The **Zoo in Forest Park,** one of the highlights for children, is home to nearly 200 domestic and exotic animals, including black bear, bobcats, lemurs, wallabies, emus, and owls. ⊠ *Sumner Ave. (Rte. 83),* ☎ *413/787–6461; 413/733–2251 zoo.* 🎫 *Park $4 out-of-state cars weekdays, $2 in-state cars weekdays; $5 out-of-state cars weekends; $3 in-state cars weekends; zoo $3.50.* ⊙ *Park daily. Zoo mid-Apr.– Labor Day, daily 10–5; Labor Day–mid-Nov., daily 10–4; mid-Nov.– mid-Apr., weekends 10–3.*

NEED A
BREAK?
Springfield's South End is the home of a lively Little Italy that supports some excellent restaurants, as well as **La Fiorentina Pastry Shop** (⊠ 883 Main St., ☏ 413/732–3151), which has been doling out heavenly pastries, butter cookies, gelato, wedding cakes, and coffees since the 1940s.

★ ☺ **Six Flags New England.** New England's largest theme park and water park contains more than 160 rides and shows, including Batman–The Dark Knight floorless roller coaster and Superman–Ride of Steel, the tallest and fastest steel coaster on the East Coast. ⊠ 1623 Main St./Rte. 159, south from Rte. 57 west of Springfield, Agawam, ☏ 877/474–9352, WEB www.sixflags.com. 🎟 $39.99 ($26.99 after 4 PM); parking $10. ◷ Late Apr.–late May and early Sept.–late Oct., Fri.–Sat. 10–10; late May–early Sept., daily 10–10.

Dining

$$–$$$ ✕ **School Street Bistro.** It's worth the trip 15 mi west out to Westfield to sample first-rate contemporary cooking at this stately downtown eatery housed in a vintage 19th-century factory building. Top picks include black Angus tenderloin with a mushroom-Gorgonzola demiglace and pepper-grilled salmon with a port wine reduction, jasmine rice, and wilted greens. Thin-crust pizzas, pastas, and excellent salads are also available. ⊠ 29 School St., ☏ 413/562–8700. AE, D, MC, V. No lunch weekends.

$$–$$$ ✕ **Student Prince and Fort Restaurant.** Named after a 1930s operetta, this downtown restaurant established in 1935 is known for its rendition of classic German food—bratwurst, schnitzel, and sauerbraten—steaks, smoked pork chops with apple sauce, and broiled shrimp with garlic butter. It also holds a collection of more than 2,000 beer steins. ⊠ 8 Fort St., ☏ 413/734–7475. D, DC, MC, V.

$–$$$ ✕ **Nadina's Cafe Lebanon.** This casual eatery just a short walk down the hill from the Quadrangle museums serves such authentic Lebanese dishes as lamb shank simmered in tomato sauce with onions, charbroiled swordfish kabobs, and falafel with tahini sesame sauce. There's live belly-dancing on some Saturday evenings. ⊠ 141 State St., ☏ 413/737–7373. AE, D, DC, MC, V. No lunch weekends.

$–$$ ✕ **Theodore's.** "Booze, blues, and barbecue" are the specialties of this popular downtown restaurant, which stays open until 2 AM Friday–Sunday. You can dine saloon style in booths near the bar or in a small adjacent dining room. The decor is yard-sale eclectic, with framed old-time advertisements lending a whimsical air. The kitchen turns out barbecue, burgers, and pub fare—nothing special, but the point is more to listen to live blues and drink up a storm. ⊠ 201 Worthington St., ☏ 413/736–6000. AE, MC, V. No lunch weekends.

$$$ ✕▥ **Springfield Marriott.** One of the few luxury business hotels in the Pioneer Valley, the Marriott makes a good base for leisure travelers, especially on weekends, when the rates drop precipitously. Contemporary furnishings adorn the rooms, some of which face out toward the Connecticut River. The hotel adjoins the Baystate West Mall, with 70 shops and eateries. The hotel restaurant, Currents ($$–$$$$), is far better than you might expect of a chain hotel. Dine on such creative contemporary dishes as Block Island swordfish with sweet potato fries, citrus pesto, and ginger, garlic, and lime marinade. ⊠ Boland and Columbus Sts., 01115, ☏ 413/781–7111 or 800/229–9290, FAX 413/731–8932, WEB www.marriott.com. 264 rooms. Restaurant, room service, indoor pool, health club, hot tub, sauna, 2 bars, business services, parking (fee). AE, D, DC, MC, V. CP.

Nightlife and the Arts

Worthington Street, the city's nightlife center, is lined with bars, clubs, and cafés. If you're in the mood for a pint of Guinness and some friendly banter, drop by **Tilly's Irish Pub** (⊠ 1390 Main St., ☎ 413/732–3613), a favorite place to shoot pool and listen to live music on weekends.

The city's professional, nonprofit theater, **CityStage** (⊠ 1 Columbus Center, ☎ 413/733–2500 tickets; 413/788–7033 box office) showcases musicals, dramas, and comedy. The **Springfield Symphony Orchestra** (☎ 413/733–2291) performs at Symphony Hall (⊠ 75 Market Pl.) year-round and mounts a summer program of concerts in the Springfield area.

Sturbridge

㊺ *34 mi east of Springfield, 60 mi southwest of Boston, 20 mi southwest of Worcester.*

★ Sturbridge is best known as the home of an outstanding open-air museum. **Old Sturbridge Village,** one of the country's finest period restorations and the star attraction of central Massachusetts, is just east of the Pioneer Valley. The village is a model of an early 1800s New England town, with more than 40 historic buildings (moved here from other towns) on a 200-acre site. Some of the village houses are furnished with canopy beds and elaborate decoration; in the simpler, single-story cottages, interpreters wearing period costumes demonstrate home-based crafts like spinning, weaving, shoe making, and cooking. Also here are several mills, including a saw mill. On the informative short boat ride along the Quinebaug River, you can learn about river life in 19th-century New England and catch a glimpse of ducks, geese, turtles, and other local wildlife. The village store contains an amazing variety of goods necessary for everyday life in the 19th century. ⊠ *1 Old Sturbridge Village Rd.,* ☎ *508/347–3362 or 800/733–1830,* WEB *www.osv.org.* ☞ *$20, valid for 2 consecutive days.* ☉ *Apr.–Oct., daily 9–5; call for off-season hrs.*

OFF THE
BEATEN PATH

WORCESTER ART MUSEUM – Worcester, New England's third-largest city, has never been a huge tourist draw, but a number of engaging museums and attractions make it a worthwhile stop. Foremost among them, this nearly century-old museum provides a comprehensive survey of art from around the world, with especially strong concentrations of Islamic, pre-Columbian, Chinese, and Korean works. Highlights in the European galleries include works by William Hogarth and Paul Gauguin. American highlights include paintings by Copley, Cole, and Edward Hicks and silver service by Paul Revere. ⊠ *55 Salisbury St., Worcester (20 mi northeast of Sturbridge),* ☎ *508/799–4406,* WEB *www.worcesterart.org.* ☞ *$8.* ☉ *Wed., Fri., and Sun. 11–5; Thurs. 11–8; Sat. 10–5.*

For additional information on Worcester, contact the **Central Massachusetts Tourist Council** (⊠ 306 Main St., Worcester, ☎ 508/755–7400, WEB www.worcester.org).

Dining and Lodging

$$–$$$$ ✕ **Salem Cross Inn.** On a verdant 600-acre estate, the Salem Cross occupies a Colonial building built by the grandson of Peregrine White, the first child born on the *Mayflower.* It's a fitting legacy for a restaurant that prides itself on re-creating the early American dining experience, both in terms of decor and menu. A favorite event is the occasional Drover's Roasts, when prime rib of beef is spiced and slow-roasted for hours in a fieldstone pit—a lavish and lengthy feast fol-

lows. Other times you'll find traditional American and Continental fare, such as broiled lamb chops and baked stuffed fillet of sole with lobster sauce. ⊠ *Rte. 9, West Brookfield (12 mi northwest of Sturbridge),* ☎ *508/867–8337. AE, D, MC, V. Closed Mon. No lunch Sat.*

$$–$$$ ✕ **Cedar Street Restaurant.** This eatery, housed in a modest but charm-★ ing Victorian house, sits just off Main Street. Inside, candlelit tables decked with fresh flowers fill the intimate dining room. The menu tends toward the simple but creative, with an emphasis on healthful cooking. Choices include handmade parsnip ravioli with walnut pesto as well as molasses-brined pork chop with a mango-rum glaze, fried plantains, and a ginger-coconut custard. ⊠ *12 Cedar St.,* ☎ *508/347–5800. AE, MC, V. Closed Sun. No lunch.*

$$–$$$ ✕ **Tavern at Old Sturbridge Village.** Opened in February 2002, this brand-new building opposite the visitor center at Old Sturbridge Village looks right out of the Federal era. Decor recalls a vintage taproom and parlor, with wide-plank floors, authentic period-style light fixtures, and re-created 19th-century cutlery. The menu, however, tends toward the nouvelle, with such entrées as roast duck with cranberry barley hash, baby beets, and an apple-brandy sauce. Fireplace-cooking demonstrations are hosted from time to time, as well as live entertainment. ⊠ *Old Sturbridge Village, 1 Old Sturbridge Village Rd.,* ☎ *508/347–0395. AE, D, MC, V.*

$$–$$$ ✕🖬 **Publick House Historic Inn Complex.** Each of the three inns and the ★ motel in this complex has its own character. The 17 rooms in the Publick House, which dates to 1771, are Colonial in design, with uneven wide-board floors; some have canopy beds. The neighboring Chamberlain House consists of larger suites, and the Country Motor Lodge has more modern rooms. The Crafts Inn, about a mile away, has a library, lounge, pool, and eight rooms with four-poster beds and painted wood paneling (Continental breakfast is included in the price here). The big, bustling Publick House restaurant ($$$–$$$$) is busy on weekends. The fare is traditional Yankee with an inventive spin—pecan-dusted scrod, pan-seared barbecued scallops with bok choy and blue cheese–shallot–mashed potatoes. Lighter fare is served in two taverns and a bake shop. ⊠ *Rte. 131, On-the-Common, 01566,* ☎ *508/347–3313 or 800/782–5425,* FAX *508/347–5073,* WEB *www.publickhouse.com. 116 rooms, 9 suites. 4 restaurants, tennis court, pool, shuffleboard, cross-country skiing, bar, playground, meeting rooms. AE, D, DC, MC, V.*

$$–$$$ 🖬 **Sturbridge Country Inn.** The atmosphere at this 1840s Greek Revival farmhouse on Sturbridge's busy Main Street is between that of an inn and a plush business hotel. Guest rooms—all with working gas fireplaces and whirlpool tubs—have reproduction antiques; the best is the top-floor suite. ⊠ *530 Main St. (Box 60, 01566),* ☎ *508/347–5503,* FAX *508/347–5319,* WEB *www.sturbridgecountryinn.com. 6 rooms, 3 suites. In-room hot tubs, hot tub, bar. AE, D, MC, V. CP.*

$$ 🖬 **Sturbridge Host.** This hotel across the street from Old Sturbridge Village on Cedar Lake has luxuriously appointed bedrooms with Colonial decor and reproduction furnishings. Some rooms have fireplaces, balconies, or patios. Dinner is served nightly in Portobella's Italian Restaurant; the Oxhead Tavern serves a lunch and dinner pub menu, which includes club sandwiches and burgers. ⊠ *U.S. 20, 01566,* ☎ *508/347–7393 or 800/582–3232,* FAX *508/347–3944,* WEB *www. sturbridgehosthotel.com. 181 rooms, 39 suites. 2 restaurants, miniature golf, pool, health club, sauna, boating, fishing, basketball, racquetball, bar, video game room, meeting room. AE, D, DC, MC, V.*

Shopping

The **Seraph** (⊠ 420 Main St., ☎ 508/347–2241) sells high-quality reproduction furniture, all created authentically with period materials and designs. You'll also find tin, pewter, hand-forged hardware, and blown-glass accessories crafted in the Early America traditions. **Wild Bird Crossing** (✉ 4 Cedar St., ☎ 508/347–2473) carries every imaginable accoutrement for bird-watching, including birdbaths, nests, binoculars, suet feeders, and books.

Just a few miles west in Brimfield, one of New England's premier antiques-shopping hubs, **J&J Productions Antique & Collectibles** (✉ Auction Acres, U.S. 20, Brimfield, ☎ 413/245–3436, WEB www.jandj-brimfield.com) presents one of the region's most popular outdoor antiques shows three times per year (mid-May, mid-July, Labor Day weekend). U.S. 20 is also lined year-round with antiques shops.

The Pioneer Valley A to Z

To research prices, get advice from other travelers, and book travel arrangements, visit www.fodors.com.

AIRPORTS

Bradley International Airport in Windsor Locks, Connecticut, is the most convenient airport for flying into the Pioneer Valley—it's 20 mi south Springfield. American, America West, Continental, Delta, Midwest Express, Northwest, Southwest, United, and US Airways serve Bradley.

➤ AIRPORT INFORMATION: **Bradley International Airport** (✉ Rte. 20 [take Exit 40 off I–91], ☎ 860/292–2000, WEB www.bradleyairport.com).

BUS TRAVEL

Peter Pan Bus Lines links most major Northeast cities with Springfield, Holyoke, South Hadley, Northampton, Amherst, Deerfield, Greenfield, and Sturbridge and provides transportation to Bradley and Logan airports. Pioneer Valley Transit Authority provides service in 24 communities throughout the Pioneer Valley, including a Downtown Trolley that loops through Springfield on two vintage streetcars on weekdays.
➤ BUS INFORMATION: **Peter Pan Bus Lines** (☎ 413/781–2900 or 800/237–8747, WEB www.peterpanbus.com). **Pioneer Valley Transit Authority** (☎ 413/781–7882, WEB www.pvta.com).

CAR TRAVEL

A car is your best way for exploring the region, as distances between attractions can be significant and public transportation impractical for most visitors. Interstate 91 runs north–south through the valley. Interstate 90 links Springfield to Boston. Route 2 connects Boston with Greenfield and, via U.S. 5, Deerfield.

EMERGENCIES

➤ HOSPITALS AND EMERGENCY SERVICES: **Baystate Medical Center** (✉ 759 Chestnut St., Springfield, ☎ 413/794–0000). **Cooley Dickenson Hospital** (✉ 30 Locust St., Northampton, ☎ 413/582–2000). **Holyoke Hospital** (✉ 575 Beech St., Holyoke, ☎ 413/534–2500).

LODGING

BED-AND-BREAKFASTS

Berkshire Folkstone Bed & Breakfast Homes is a reservation service with listings throughout central and western Massachusetts.
➤ RESERVATION SERVICES: **Berkshire Folkstone Bed & Breakfast Homes** (☎ 413/268–7244 or 800/762–2751, FAX 413/268–7243, WEB www.berkshirebnbhomes.com).

TRAIN TRAVEL

Amtrak serves Springfield from Boston and New York City.

➤ Train Information: **Amtrak** (☎ 800/872–7245, WEB www. amtrak.com).

VISITOR INFORMATION

The Greater Springfield Convention and Visitors Bureau serves the entire Pioneer Valley; it also operates the Riverfront Visitor Information Center, next to the Basketball Hall of Fame. Both the Northampton and Amherst chambers of commerce have useful visitor centers and Web sites. Additionally, the Franklin County Chamber of Commerce has more specific information on the northern end of the valley, as well as a visitor center at the Route 2 exit of I–91. The Sturbridge Area Tourist Association is your best resource for that area.

➤ Tourist Information: **Amherst Area Chamber of Commerce** (⊠ 409 Main St., 01002, ☎ 413/253–0700, WEB www.amherstchamber.com). **Franklin County Chamber of Commerce** (⊠ 395 Main St. [Box 898, Greenfield 01302], ☎ 413/773–5463, WEB www.franklincc.org). **Greater Northampton Chamber of Commerce** (⊠ 99 Pleasant St., Northampton 01060, ☎ 413/584–1900 or 800/238–6869, WEB www. northamptonuncommon.com). **Greater Springfield Convention and Visitors Bureau** (⊠ 1441 Main St., Springfield 01103, ☎ 413/787–1548 or 800/723–1548, WEB www.valleyvisitor.com). **Riverfront Visitor Information Center** (⊠ 1200 W. Columbus Ave., Springfield). **Sturbridge Area Tourist Association** (⊠ 380 Main St., Sturbridge 01566, ☎ 508/ 347–7594 or 800/628–8379, WEB www.sturbridge.org).

THE BERKSHIRES

Updated by
Andrew Collins

More than a century ago, wealthy families from New York, Philadelphia, and Boston built "summer cottages" in western Massachusetts' Berkshire Hills—great country estates that earned Berkshire County the nickname "inland Newport." Many of those grand houses have been razed, and still others are now occupied by schools or hotels. But the region's legacy as a desirable vacation getaway and cultural hub continues unabated.

Occupying the far western end of the state, the Berkshires lie about 2½-hours by car from Boston and New York City, yet the region lives up to the storybook image of rural New England with wooded hills, narrow winding roads, and compact historic villages. Many cultural events take place in summer, among them the renowned Tanglewood classical music festival in Lenox. The foliage blazes brilliantly in fall, skiing is popular in winter, and spring is the time for maple sugaring. The scenic Mohawk Trail runs east to west across the northern section of the Berkshires.

North Adams

46 *130 mi northwest of Boston; 73 mi northwest of Springfield; 20 mi south of Bennington, Vermont.*

Established as the military outpost Fort Massachusetts in the mid-18th century, North Adams started out as a part of East Hoosac, later Adams, before incorporating as its own city in the late 19th century. By then its economy had become dependent upon its textile industry. After North Adams became a strong producer of electrical and radio parts, its fortunes waned just as they did in most other industrial New England cities following World War II.

In the past few years, however, the city has staged an impressive comeback as a center of contemporary art. In addition to the famous Mass MoCA arts space, North Adams has a bounty of mills and factory buildings that have been converted to artists' studios and residences. Additionally, Western Gateway Heritage State Park commemorates the city's industrial legacy. Downtown still is in somewhat of a transition, but preservation efforts continue to spruce things up, and new shops and eateries seem to open every few months.

The only natural bridge in North America caused by water erosion is the marble arch at 49-acre **Natural Bridge State Park,** which was the site of a marble quarry from 1810 through the mid-20th century. The bridge crosses a narrow 500-ft chasm containing numerous faults and fractures. There are picnic sites and hiking trails here, and in winter the property is popular for cross-country skiing. ⊠ *Rte. 8,* ☎ *413/663–6312.* 🖼 *$2 per vehicle.* ☉ *Late May–mid-Oct., weekdays 8:30–4:30, weekends 10–6.*

★ Opened in 1999 to much fanfare, the **Massachusetts Museum of Contemporary Arts,** or Mass MoCA, is the nation's largest center for contemporary performing and visual arts. The vast, 13-acre 19th-century complex of 27 buildings once housed the now-defunct Sprague Electric Co. Six of the factory buildings have been transformed into more than 250,000 square ft of galleries, studios, performance venues, cafés, and shops. Its size enables the museum to display monumentally scaled works such as Robert Rauschenberg's ¼ *Mile or 2 Furlong Piece.* Exhibits and performances include everything from art exhibitions to dance and music concerts and film presentations. ⊠ *87 Marshall St.,* ☎ *413/664–4481,* WEB *www.massmoca.org.* 🖼 *$7.* ☉ *June–Oct., daily 10–6; Nov.–May, Wed.–Mon. 10–5.*

The historic Beaver Mill, which occupies 27 acres of woodland adjacent to Natural Bridge State Park, houses the **Contemporary Artists Center (CAC),** a 130,000-square-ft artists' residence and studio. In this light-filled atelier you can tour many art studios, admiring work in virtually every medium. The CAC also hosts workshops, houses a small café that also hosts exhibits, and shows works in several galleries. ⊠ *189 Beaver St., off Rte. 8 north of Rte. 2,* ☎ *413/663–9555,* WEB *www. thecac.org.* 🖼 *Free.* ☉ *Daily; studio, café, and gallery hrs vary according to event (call ahead).*

Western Gateway Heritage State Park occupies the old Boston and Maine freightyard; it includes shops, a pub-restaurant, and a visitor center with exhibits that trace the impact of rail travel and the completion of the Hoosac Tunnel on the region's industrialization during the 19th century. A 30-minute documentary film provides a look at the intense labor that went into the construction of the Hoosac Tunnel. ⊠ *115 State St./Rte. 8, Bldg. 4,* ☎ *413/663–6312,* WEB *www.state.ma.us/dem/parks/wghp.htm.* 🖼 *Free.* ☉ *Grounds daily, visitor center daily 10–5.*

Dining and Lodging

$$–$$$ ✕ **Gramercy Bistro.** Occupying the space of an old downtown diner, this casual, upbeat eatery opened in summer 2001 and has quickly developed a loyal following. The tavernesque space, with a wood-beam ceiling and walls lined with black-and-white photos of the town, serves eclectic grills, burgers, and salads, plus a memorable weekend brunch. ⊠ *24 Marshall St.,* ☎ *413/663–5300. AE, MC, V.*

$–$$ ✕ **Freightyard Restaurant and Pub.** In an atmospheric space at the Heritage State Park, this busy and festive eatery serves half-pound burgers, prime rib, fajitas, and other down-home favorites. Dinner is served 'til 11 nightly, and the bar keeps going long after that. ⊠ *Heritage State Park,* ☎ *413/663–6547. D, MC, V.*

$ ✕ **Miss Adams Diner.** This 1949 classic Worcester lunch-car diner right in the center of downtown Adams has changed little over the years. You'll still find the original marble counters, cozy booths, and home-style cooking: burgers cooked to order, eggs Benedict (breakfast is served all day), and locally made Squeeze sodas. This is a real slice of Americana. Also, don't forget to try one of the fresh-baked doughnuts, pies, or cakes. ⊠ *53 Park St., Adams,* ☎ *413/743–5300. MC, V.*

$$$–$$$$ 🏨 **Porches Inn.** Opened in July 2001, this complex of once-dilapidated ★ 1890s mill workers' houses, across from Mass MoCA, has emerged as one of New England's most delightful and quirky small hotels. The design strikes a perfect balance between high-tech and historic—rooms have a mix of retro '40s and '50s lamps and Arts and Crafts–style fur-nishings along with such contemporary touches as stunning bath-rooms with slate floors, marble accents, Jacuzzi tubs, and mirrors fashioned out of old window frames. Some two-room suites have loft sleeping areas reached by spiral staircases and two bathrooms. Suites have pull-out sofas and can sleep up to six. ⊠ *231 River St., 01247,* ☎ *413/664–0400,* WEB *www.porches.com. 40 rooms, 12 suites. Some in-room hot tubs, some kitchens, pool, hot tub, sauna, bar, business services, concierge, meeting room. AE, MC, V. CP.*

$$–$$$ 🏨 **Blackinton Manor B&B.** Dan and Betsy Epstein's meticulously re-★ stored 1849 Italianate mansion is furnished with antiques and filled with music. The Epsteins are both professional musicians, and they often host concerts and chamber music workshops. Several of the elegantly appointed guest rooms have pianos. The mansion, built by a textiles baron, is notable for its intricate wrought-iron balconies, floor-to-ceil-ing windows, a spacious bay window, and decorative corbels. A kosher kitchen is available for stays of one week or longer. ⊠ *1391 Massa-chusetts Ave., 01247,* ☎ *413/663–5795 or 800/795–8613,* WEB *www. blackinton-manor.com. 5 rooms. Some in-room hot tubs, pool; no kids under 7, no smoking. MC, V. BP.*

Shopping

Delftree Mushroom Farm (⊠ 234 Union St./Rte. 2, ☎ 413/664–4907 or 800/243–3742) raises Japanese shiitake mushrooms inside a 19th-century mill; you can visit and see how the mushrooms are grown and buy them, too. In Adams, interior designers and home decorators rave about the many great finds at **Interior Alternative** (⊠ 5 Hoosac St., Adams, ☎ 413/743–1986), which carries factory seconds and firsts of wallpaper, bedding, and pillows—Waverly-print fabrics are a specialty.

Outdoor Activities and Sports

Picnic tables at the **Mohawk Trail State Forest** (⊠ Rte. 2, Charlemont, ☎ 413/339–5504) are set up under large evergreen trees. A few well-maintained hiking trails of a mile or so lead to a scenic lookout. A camp-ing area and a few log cabins are available; rates are $12 for sites and $25 and up for cabins.

En Route Many people approach the Berkshires along Route 2 from Boston and the East Coast. The **Mohawk Trail,** a 63-mi stretch from Orange to Williamstown, follows the path blazed long ago by Native Americans that ran along the Deerfield River through the Connecticut River val-ley to the Berkshire Hills. It is lovely in fall. Just beyond the town of Charlemont stands *Hail to the Sunrise,* a 900-pound bronze statue of an Indian facing east, with arms uplifted, dedicated to the five Native American nations that lived along the Mohawk Trail. Some mostly tacky "Indian trading posts" on the highway carry out the Mohawk theme. Also along the road are antiques stores, flea markets, and places to pull off the road, picnic, and take photos.

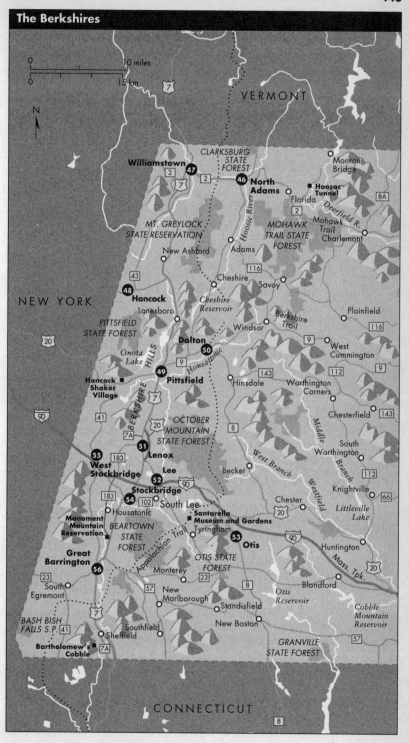

The Berkshires

0 —————— 10 miles
0 —————— 15 km

N

VERMONT

NEW YORK

CONNECTICUT

CLARKSBURG STATE FOREST

Williamstown 47

46 **North Adams**

Monroe Bridge

■ **Hoosac Tunnel**

Florida

Deerfield R.

Mohawk Trail *Charlemont*

8A

2

MT. GREYLOCK STATE RESERVATION

Hoosic River

New Ashford

Adams

MOHAWK TRAIL STATE FOREST

Cheshire

116

Savoy

Plainfield

116

48 **Hancock**

43

Cheshire Reservoir

Berkshire Trail

Lanesboro

PITTSFIELD STATE FOREST

20

Dalton 50

Windsor

9

West Cummington

9

Onota Lake

49

9

Housatonic

Pittsfield

143

Worthington Corners

112

9

Hinsdale

Hancock Shaker Village ■

Chesterfield

143

BERKSHIRE HILLS

7

90

41

OCTOBER MOUNTAIN STATE FOREST

20

8

South Worthington

112

7A

West Branch

Becket

Middle Branch

55 **West Stockbridge**

51 **Lenox**

183

Knightville

66

Lee

52

Westfield

Littleville Lake

54 **Stockbridge**

183

102

South Lee

90

Chester

20

Housatonic

■ **Santarella Museum and Gardens**

Tyringham

53 **Otis**

90

Huntington

20

Monument Mountain Reservation ■

BEARTOWN STATE FOREST

Appalachian Trail

OTIS STATE FOREST

Mass. Tpk.

Great Barrington

56

Monterey

23

8

Blandford

20

23

South Egremont

57

New Marlborough

Standisfield

Otis Reservoir

Cobble Mountain Reservoir

7

BASH BISH FALLS S.P.

41

Southfield

New Boston

57

Sheffield

Bartholomew's Cobble

7A

GRANVILLE STATE FOREST

Williamstown

47 *5 mi west of North Adams.*

When Colonel Ephraim Williams left money to found a free school in what was then known as West Hoosac, he stipulated that the name be changed to Williamstown. Williams College opened in 1793, and even today life in this placid town revolves around it, looking almost nothing like its gritty but colorful cousin to the east, North Adams. Graceful campus buildings like the Gothic cathedral, built in 1904, line wide Main Street. Down Spring Street, you'll find a handful of upscale shops and lively eateries. The collection and exhibits at the **Williams College Museum of Art** focus on American and 20th-century art. More than 11,000 works span a broad range of eras and cultures, but the emphasis is on modern and contemporary American works. ⊠ *Main St.,* ☎ *413/597–2429.* ⊡ *Free.* ⊘ *Tues.–Sat. 10–5, Sun. 1–5.*

★ The **Sterling and Francine Clark Art Institute** is one of the nation's notable small art museums. Its famous works include more than 30 paintings by Renoir (among them *Mademoiselle Fleury in Algerian Costume*), as well as canvases by Monet and Pissarro. *The Little Dancer,* an important sculpture by Degas, is another exceptional work. Other items include priceless English silver, European and American photography from the 1840s through the 1910s, and Flemish and Dutch masterworks from the 17th and 18th centuries. ⊠ *225 South St.,* ☎ *413/458–2303,* WEB *www.clarkart.edu.* ⊡ *July–Oct. $10; free rest of yr and Tues.* ⊘ *Sept.–June, Tues.–Sun. 10–5; July–Aug., daily 10–5.*

The **Chapin Library of Rare Books and Manuscripts** at Williams College contains original copies of the Four Founding Documents of the United States—the Declaration of Independence, the Articles of Confederation, the Constitution, and the Bill of Rights—and 50,000 books, 40,000 manuscripts, and illustrations dating from as far back as the 9th century. ⊠ *Stetson Hall, Main St.,* ☎ *413/597–2462,* WEB *www.williams.edu/resources/chapin.* ⊡ *Free.* ⊘ *Weekdays 10–noon and 1–5.*

Dining and Lodging

$$$ ✕ **Main Street Cafe.** Delicious northern Italian treats have earned this
★ dark and romantic restaurant rave reviews. A typical entrée is spinach-stuffed eggplant with fontina cheese. Continue on to pan-seared jumbo shrimp Toscana with prosciutto, sage, and fresh seasonal melon, or grilled filet mignon over spinach and roasted potatoes, with olive oil, fresh lemon juice, and cracked black pepper. You can always try the pizza of the day. ⊠ *16 Water St.,* ☎ *413/458–3210. AE, DC, MC, V. Closed Mon.*

$$–$$$ ✕ **101 North.** The restaurant's simple decor belies the ambitiousness of its menu. The menu changes frequently, featuring such dishes as osso buco, frogs' legs, a Japanese-inspired salmon cake appetizer, and an excellent apple strudel. The extensive wine list has been shrewdly selected, and a large fireplace adds coziness. A late-night menu is served in the bar and pool room. ⊠ *101 North St.,* ☎ *413/458–4000. AE, MC, V. Closed Mon. No lunch.*

$ ✕ **Arugula Cocina Latina.** This dapper storefront café with just a few
★ tables serves food until 8 but is mostly a lunch spot. With its contemporary art lining the walls and piped-in light Latin jazz, you'd expect to find this nifty hole-in-the-wall on a side street in Miami. Indeed, the Cuban sandwich is top-rate. You can also order empanadas, leafy green salads, chorizo sandwiches, rice-and-beans, and rich, hot white chocolate. ⊠ *25 Spring St.,* ☎ *413/458–2152. Closed Sun.*

$$$–$$$$ **✕▣ The Orchards Hotel.** Although it's right on Route 2 and sur-
★ rounded by parking lots, this thoroughly proper if rather stuffy hotel
compensates for these shortcomings with a beautiful central courtyard
with fruit trees and a pond stocked with koi. English antiques furnish
most of the spacious accommodations. The inner rooms, which have
one-way windows looking onto the courtyard, are best for summer stays.
The outer rooms have less-distinguished views, but their fireplaces add
appeal for winter visits. The restaurant ($$$–$$$$) serves such cre-
ative fare as sautéed scallops with a Russian banana–shiitake salad.
✉ *222 Adams Rd., 01267,* ☎ *413/458–9611 or 800/225–1517,* FAX
413/458–3273, WEB *www.orchardshotel.com. 49 rooms. Restaurant,
in-room data ports, some refrigerators, pool, gym, hot tub, sauna, bar,
meeting room. AE, DC, MC, V.*

$$$–$$$$ **▣ Field Farm Guest House.** Built in 1948, this house contains a fine
★ collection of art on loan from Williams College. It was donated as part
of a land trust by the former owners (art lovers who gave part of their
collection to Williams), and the 296-acre property is now run nonprofit
as a B&B. The large windows in the guest rooms have expansive views
of the grounds. Three rooms have private decks; two rooms have
working tiled fireplaces. You can prepare simple meals in the pantry.
The grounds, open to the public, include a pond, sculptures, a nature
center, and 4 mi of trails. ✉ *554 Sloan Rd., off Rte. 43, 01267,* ☎ FAX
413/458–3135, WEB *www.berkshireweb.com/trustees/field.html. 5
rooms. Tennis court, pool, fishing. D, MC, V. BP.*

$$–$$$ **▣ Berkshire Hills Motel.** All the rooms at this two-story brick-and-clap-
board motel about 3 mi south of Williamstown are furnished in Colonial
style. The lounge has a fireplace, and guests can use the barbecue on the
deck. Although the motel is close to the road, the spacious grounds in back
encompass a brook, woodlands, landscaped gardens, and an outdoor
heated pool. ✉ *1146 Cold Spring Rd./U.S. 7, 01267,* ☎ *413/458–3950
or 800/388–9677,* FAX *413/458–5878,* WEB *www.berkshirehillsmotel.com.
21 rooms. Pool, meeting room; no smoking. AE, D, MC, V. CP.*

$$ **▣ River Bend Farm.** One of the founders of Williamstown built this
Georgian Colonial farmhouse, now restored with complete authenticity.
The kitchen, through which guests enter, contains an open-range stove
and an oven hung with dried herbs. Some bedrooms have wide-plank
walls, curtains of unbleached muslin, and four-poster beds with canopies
or rope beds (yes, they really are comfortable). All rooms are sprinkled with antique pieces—chamber pots, washstands, wing chairs, and
spinning wheels. ✉ *643 Simonds Rd., 01267,* ☎ *413/458–3121. 4 rooms
without bath. No credit cards. Closed Nov.–Mar. CP.*

Nightlife and the Arts

Friday evening is folk music night; on Saturday jazz and blues are played
at the tavern in the **Williams Inn** (✉ On-the-Green, ☎ 413/458–9371).
The **Williamstown Theatre Festival** (✉ Williams College, Adams Memorial Theatre, ☎ 413/597–3400 tickets; 413/597–3399 information; WEB
www.wtfestival.org), which runs from June to August, presents well-
known theatrical works with famous performers on the Main Stage
and contemporary works on the Other Stage.

Shopping

Spring Street is downtown Williamstown's main drag, lined with upscale shops, cafés, and businesses. At **Library Antiques and More** (✉
70 Spring St., ☎ 413/458–3436), you'll find an array of prints, folk
art, jewelry, antiquarian books, and distinctive gifts. **Water Street
Books** (✉ 26 Water St., ☎ 413/458–8071) is a college bookstore with
local-history and general-interest titles. **Toonerville Trolley CDs &
Records** (✉ 131 Water St., ☎ 413/458–5229) carries hard-to-find
jazz, rock, and classical recordings.

Outdoor Activities and Sports

BIKING

The gently rolling Berkshire Hills are excellent cycling terrain. Mountain-bike trails can be found at the Mt. Greylock State Reservation. You can rent a bike from **Mountain Goat Bicycle Shop** (⊠ 130 Water St., ☎ 413/458–8445), which is about 7 mi northwest of Mt. Greylock.

GOLF

Waubeeka Golf Links (⊠ U.S. 7 and Rte. 43, ☎ 413/458–8355), an 18-hole, par-72 course, is open to the public and rents golf clubs. Greens fees are $30 weekdays and $35 weekends.

En Route   The centerpiece of the 10,327-acre **Mt. Greylock State Reservation** (⊠ Rockwell Rd., Lanesboro, ☎ 413/499–4262 or 413/499–4263, WEB www.state.ma.us/dem/parks/mgry.htm) is 3,491-ft-high Mt. Greylock, the highest point in Massachusetts. The reservation, south of Williamstown, has facilities for cycling, fishing, horseback riding, camping, and snowmobiling. Many treks—including a portion of the Appalachian Trail—start from the parking lot at the summit, an 8-mi drive from the base of the mountain. **Bascom Lodge** (☎ 413/743–1591 or 413/443–0011), also at the summit, provides overnight accommodations, snacks, and souvenirs from mid-May to mid-October. A visitor center at the base of the mountain is open daily, year-round. The Sperry Road turnoff leads to a camping-picnic area; there's a modest charge. In winter you can hike up to the summit from several points or visit by snowmobile. Summer access is from Lanesboro to the south, off Scott Road and U.S. 7; and from North Adams to the north, via Notch Road off Route 2.

Hancock

48   *15 mi south of Williamstown.*

Tiny, rural Hancock, the closest village to the Jiminy Peak ski resort, comes into its own during ski season. It's also a great base for outdoor enthusiasts year-round, with biking, hiking, and golf (in nearby Lanesboro) options during summer.

Lodging

$$$ 🏨 **Country Inn at Jiminy Peak.** Massive stone fireplaces in its lobby and lounge lend this hotel a ski-lodge atmosphere. The modern condo-style suites accommodate up to four people and have kitchenettes separated from the living area by a bar and high stools; the suites at the rear of the building overlook the slopes. Lodging-skiing packages are available. ⊠ *Corey Rd., 01237,* ☎ *413/738–5500 or 800/882–8859,* FAX *413/738–5513,* WEB *www.jiminypeak.com. 96 suites. 2 restaurants, kitchens, in-room VCRs, miniature golf, 5 tennis courts, pool, gym, 2 hot tubs, 2 saunas, fishing, hiking, cross-country skiing, downhill skiing, bar, video game room, meeting room. AE, D, DC, MC, V.*

$$ 🏨 **Hancock Inn.** This country Victorian inn, which dates from the late 1700s, provides cozy accommodations a mile from Jiminy Peak. Two small dining rooms have fireplaces, stained-glass windows, and candles on the tables—dinner is available only to guests and on weekends. ⊠ *Rte. 43, 01237,* ☎ *413/738–5873,* FAX *413/738–5719,* WEB *www. thehancockinn.com. 6 rooms. Restaurant. AE, D, MC, V. BP.*

Outdoor Activities and Sports

🐾   Established in the 1930s, the 600-acre **Ioka Valley Farm** (⊠ Rte. 43, ☎ 413/738–5915) is one of the best-known pick-your-own farms in the Berkshires. You can pick berries all summer, then apples and pumpkins in the fall. In winter you can cut your own Christmas tree. Other activities include hayrides, pedal tractors for kids, and a petting zoo with pigs, sheep, goats, and calves.

Ski Areas

BRODIE

The snow can be green, the beer is often green, and the decor is *always* green here. Yet it's more than the Irish ambience that attracts crowds for weekend and night skiing: the base lodge has a restaurant and bar with live entertainment, lodging (not fancy) is within walking distance of the lifts, and RV trailers are accommodated. Brodie and Jiminy Peak are under the same ownership, and a Value Card can be used at both areas. An express bus service shuttles from New York City on weekends. ✉ *U.S. 7, New Ashford 01237,* ☎ *413/443–4752; 413/443–4751 snow conditions.* WEB *www.skibrodie.com.*

Downhill. Almost all the 40 trails at Brodie are beginner and intermediate despite the black diamonds, which designate steeper (but not expert) runs; the vertical is 1,250 ft. Four double chairlifts and one surface lift serve the trails. Snowmaking covers 95% of the area's skiable terrain.

Tubing. The area's new tubing center is open Wednesday–Friday 4–10:30 and all day and night on weekends.

Child care. The nursery takes infants through age eight by the hour, half day, or full day. Afternoon, weekend, and holiday ski-instruction programs are available for children.

JIMINY PEAK

This area, three hours from New York City and Boston, has all the amenities of a major mountain resort. A high speed, six-passenger Berkshire Express chairlift whisks skiers ¾ mi to the summit (and the summit lodge) in just five minutes. Condominiums and an all-suites country inn are within walking distance of the ski lifts; more condominium complexes are nearby; and two restaurants and bars are at the slopes. Rentals are available on a nightly or weekly basis. ✉ *Corey Rd., 01237,* ☎ *413/738–5500; 888/454–6469 outside Massachusetts; 413/738–7325 snow conditions.* WEB *www.jiminypeak.com.*

Downhill. With a vertical of 1,150 ft, 40 trails, and nine lifts, Jiminy has near big-time status. It is mostly a cruising mountain—trails are groomed daily, and only on some are small moguls left to build up along the side of the slope. The steepest black-diamond runs are on the upper headwalls; longer, outer runs make for good intermediate terrain. There's skiing nightly in season, and snowmaking covers 93% of the skiable terrain.

Other activities. Jiminy has a snowboard park and an old-fashioned ice rink.

Child care. The nursery takes children from 6 months. Children ages 4–12 can take daily SKIwee lessons; those 6–15 can take a series of eight weekends of instruction with the same teacher. The kids' ski area has its own lift.

Summer activities. The resort has an alpine slide, a putting course, tennis courts, swimming facilities, and trout fishing. You can ride up the mountain on a high-speed chairlift.

Pittsfield

49 *21 mi south of Williamstown, 11 mi southeast of Hancock.*

A mere agricultural backwater at the time of the American Revolution, the seat of Berkshire county grew steadily throughout the 19th century into an industrial powerhouse of textile, paper, and electrical machinery manufacturing. As recently as the 1930s, the WPA guidebook on Massachusetts described Pittsfield as possessing a "prosperous, tranquil look of general comfort and cultivation which makes it one of the most attractive industrial cities in the state." Alas, the city's economy took a nosedive following World War II, and much of that apparent prosperity diminished.

Modern Pittsfield has brushed off some of its bruises and blemishes of the past several decades and reclaimed a number of intriguing industrial buildings. Still, this is a workaday city without the monied urbanity of Great Barrington or the quaint, rural demeanor of the comparatively small Colonial towns that surround it. Along North Street, several new shops and eateries have opened, perhaps signaling a return to downtown prosperity.

☺ Opened in 1903, the **Berkshire Museum** houses three floors of exhibits, which display a varied and sometimes curious collection of objects relating to history, the natural world, and art. A highlight of the latter is a collection of Hudson River School paintings, including works by Frederic Church and Albert Bierstadt. An aquarium contains 26 tanks of sea creatures, including a touch tank; a 10-ft-high, 26-ft-long "Wally" the Stegosaurus highlights the Dinosaurs and Paleontology gallery. At the Dino Dig, kids and adults can dig together for touchable replicas of dinosaur bones. An ancient civilization gallery displays Roman and Greek jewelry and an ancient Egyptian mummy. ⊠ *39 South St.,* ☎ *413/443–7171,* WEB *www.berkshiremuseum.org.* ⊠ *$8.* ☉ *Mon.–Sat. 10–5, Sun. noon–5.*

The **Herman Melville Memorial Room** at the Berkshire Athenaeum houses an extensive collection of books, letters, and memorabilia of the author of *Moby-Dick.* ⊠ *Berkshire Public Library, 1 Wendell Ave.,* ☎ *413/499–9486,* WEB *www.berkshire.net/pittsfieldlibrary.* ⊠ *Free.* ☉ *Call for hrs.*

Arrowhead, the gold-painted house Herman Melville purchased in 1850, is 4 mi south of downtown Pittsfield; the underwhelming tour includes the study in which *Moby-Dick* was written, which has stunning views out toward Mt. Greylock. ⊠ *780 Holmes Rd.,* ☎ *413/442–1793,* WEB *www.mobydick.org.* ⊠ *$5.* ☉ *Late May–Oct., daily 10–5, with guided tours on the hr; Nov.–late May, weekdays by appointment.*

★ **Hancock Shaker Village** was founded in the 1790s, the third Shaker community in America. At its peak in the 1840s, the village had almost 300 inhabitants, who made their living farming, selling seeds and herbs, making medicines, and producing crafts. The religious community officially closed in 1960, its 170-year life span a small miracle considering its population's vows of celibacy (they took in orphans to maintain their constituency). Many examples of Shaker ingenuity are visible at Hancock today: the **Round Stone Barn** and the **Laundry and Machine Shop** are two of the most interesting buildings. Also on-site are a farm, some period gardens, a museum shop with reproduction Shaker furniture, a picnic area, and a café. ⊠ *U.S. 20, 6 mi west of Pittsfield,* ☎ *413/443–0188 or 800/817–1137,* WEB *www.hancockshakervillage.org.* ⊠ *$15, $10 in winter.* ☉ *Late May–late Oct., daily 9:30–5 for self-guided tours; late Oct.–late May, daily 10–3 for guided tours.*

Dining and Lodging

$$–$$$ ✗ **Dakota.** Moose and elk heads watch over diners, and the motto is "Steak, seafood, and smiles" at this large and popular chain restaurant, decorated like a rustic hunting lodge. Meals cooked on the mesquite grill include steaks and salmon, shrimp, and trout; the 32-item salad bar has many organic foods. A hearty brunch buffet is served on Sunday. ⊠ *U.S. 7/20,* ☎ *413/499–7900. AE, D, DC, MC, V. No lunch Mon.–Sat.*

$$–$$$$ ⊞ **Crowne Plaza Pittsfield.** Two tiers of rooms surround the large, glass-dome swimming pool at this well-maintained 14-story downtown hotel. Most rooms have mountain views. ⊠ *Berkshire Common, 1 West St., 01201,* ☎ *413/499–2000 800/227–6963,* FAX *413/442–0449,* WEB *www.crowneplaza.com. 177 rooms, 2 suites. 2 restaurants, room service, in-room data ports, pool, gym, hot tub, sauna, bar, business services, meeting room, free parking. AE, D, DC, MC, V.*

Nightlife and the Arts

The **Albany Berkshire Ballet** (⊠ 51 North St., ☎ 413/445–5382) performs classical and contemporary works at several venues throughout the year; a highlight is *The Nutcracker* every December. On weekends in winter a DJ at the **Tamarack Lounge** (⊠ Dan Fox Dr., ☎ 413/442–2436), in the Bousquet ski area's base lodge, spins dance tunes.

Outdoor Activities and Sports

The **Housatonic River** flows south from Pittsfield between the Berkshire Hills and the Taconic Range toward Connecticut, where it eventually empties into Long Island Sound. You can rent canoes, rowboats, paddleboats, small motorboats, and even pontoon party boats from the **Onota Boat Livery** (⊠ 463 Pecks Rd., ☎ 413/442–1724), which also provides dock space on Onota Lake and sells fishing tackle and bait. **U-Drive Boat Rentals** (⊠ 1651 North St., ☎ 413/442–7020), on Pontoosuc Lake, rents boats.

Minor-league baseball's **Berkshire Black Bears** (⊠ Wahconah Park, Wahconah St., off North St., ☎ 413/448–2255), of the independent Northern League, plays late May–early September.

Ski Areas

BOUSQUET SKI AREA

Other areas have entered an era of glamour and high prices, but Bousquet remains an economical, no-nonsense place to ski. The inexpensive lift tickets are the same price every day, and there's night skiing except Sunday. You can go tubing for just $10 for the day when conditions allow. ⊠ *101 Dan Fox Dr., off U.S. 7, near Pittsfield Airport, 01201,* ☎ *413/442–8316; 413/442–2436 snow conditions;* WEB *www.bousquets.com.*

Downhill. Bousquet, with a 750-ft vertical drop, has 21 trails, but only if you count every change in steepness and every merging slope. Though this is a generous figure, you will find some good beginner and intermediate runs, with a few steeper pitches. There are three double chairlifts, two surface lifts, and a small snowboard park.

Child care. Bous-Care Nursery watches children age six months and up by the hour; reservations are suggested. Ski instruction classes are given twice daily on weekends and holidays for children ages five and up.

Summer and year-round activities. The facilities at the **Berkshire West Athletic Club** (⊠ Dan Fox Dr., ☎ 413/499–4600), across the street from Bousquet, include four handball courts, indoor and outdoor tennis courts, cardiovascular and weight machines, and indoor and outdoor pools.

Dalton

 8 mi northeast of Pittsfield.

The paper manufacturer Crane and Co., started by Zenas Crane in 1801, is the major employer in working-class Dalton. Exhibits at the **Crane Museum of Paper Making,** in the handsomely restored Old Stone Mill

(1844), trace the history of American papermaking from the 18th century to the present. A museum since 1930, the building sits on the banks of the Housatonic River. It's an impressive space with rough-hewn oak beams and Colonial-style chandeliers. ⊠ *E. Housatonic St., off Rte. 9,* ☎ *413/684–6481,* WEB *www.crane.com/about/crane-museum.* 🖼 *Free.* ☉ *June–mid-Oct., weekdays 2–5.*

Lodging

$$–$$$ 🏨 **Dalton House.** Cheerful guest rooms decorated in an eclectic mix of Shaker and period furnishings, folk art, plants, and collectibles are spread out in three interconnected buildings; the original structure was built in 1810 by a Hessian soldier. Common rooms include a living room with a stone fireplace and a sunny breakfast area. Two suites in the carriage house have sitting areas, exposed beams, and quilts. ⊠ *955 Main St., 01226,* ☎ *413/684–3854,* FAX *413/684–0203,* WEB *www.thedaltonhouse.com. 9 rooms, 2 suites. Pool; no smoking, no kids under 8. AE, MC, V. CP in winter, BP in summer.*

Outdoor Activities and Sports

Holiday Farm (⊠ Holiday Cottage Rd., ☎ 413/684–0444) has educational tours, hiking, maple-sugaring, stables, bike racing, and lots of barnyard animals to look at.

Lenox

🔟 *18 mi southwest of Dalton, 10 mi south of Pittsfield, 130 mi west of Boston.*

Long a bastion of privilege and immense wealth, Lenox is a small New England hamlet with a big reputation for even bigger mansions. Wealthy sorts from New York, Pennsylvania, and southern New England began building "summer cottages" here in the late 19th century. These lavish and majestic buildings often contained 20, 30, or even 40 rooms. Over the years some of the estates have burned, others have been razed, and still several more have been subdivided, but a decent number of them are now inns or B&Bs.

The famed Tanglewood music festival has been a fixture in Lenox for decades, and it's a part of the reason the town remains fiercely popular during the summer months. Booking a room here or in any of the nearby communities can set you back dearly when music or theatrical events are in town. Many of the town's most impressive homes are downtown; others you can only see by taking to the curving, tortuous back roads that traverse the region. In the center of the village, a few blocks of shabby-chic Colonial buildings contain shops and eateries.

★ **The Mount,** a mansion built in 1902 with myriad classical influences, was the former summer home of novelist Edith Wharton. The house and grounds were designed by Wharton, who is considered by many to have set the standard for 20th-century interior decoration. In designing the Mount, she followed the principles set forth in her book *The Decoration of Houses* (1897), creating a calm and well-ordered home. An extensive restoration of the property began in October 2001 and will be ongoing for some time. A "Women of Achievement" lecture series takes place here on Monday in July and August. ⊠ *2 Plunkett St.,* ☎ *413/637–1899 or 888/637–1902,* WEB *www.edithwharton.org.* 🖼 *$7.50.* ☉ *Late May–Oct., daily 9–5.*

Built in 1893, **Ventfort Hall,** was the summer "cottage" of Sarah Morgan, the sister of highfalutin financier J. P. Morgan. Inside is the **Museum of the Gilded Age,** which explores the role of Lenox and the Berkshires as the definitive mountain retreat during that fabled era. The building was in danger of being torn down when a group of preservationists formed to buy this 12-acre property in 1997. Since then a top restoration team has been hard at work repairing the elegant exterior brickwork and roofing, the ornate interior paneling and grand staircase, and the gabled carriage house. In summer 1998 Miramax films shot the orphanage scenes from *The Cider House Rules* movie here (other scenes were shot in Northampton). Although work continues on the building, tours are conducted. ⊠ *104 Walker St.,* ☎ *413/ 637–3206,* WEB *www.gildedage.org.* ▢ *$8.* ☉ *May–Oct., Mon.–Sat. tours on the hr 11:30–2:30; Nov.–Apr., Sat. tours at 10 and 11.*

The **Railway Museum,** in a restored 1903 railroad station in central Lenox, displays antique rail equipment, vintage exhibits, and a large working model railway. It's the starting point for the diesel-hauled **Berkshire Scenic Railway,** which travels for 15 minutes over a portion of the historic New Haven Railway's Housatonic Valley Line. ⊠ *Willow Creek Rd.,* ☎ *413/637–2210,* WEB *www.berkshireweb.com/culture/ railway.html.* ▢ *Rides $2.50, museum free.* ☉ *May–Oct., weekends 10–3:30.*

The sleek, modernist **Frelinghuysen Morris House & Studio** occupies a verdant 46-acre property and exhibits the works of American abstract artists Suzy Frelinghuysen and George L. K. Morris as well as those of contemporaries including Picasso, Braque, and Gris. For guided tours, reservations are requested 24 hours in advance. ⊠ *92 Hawthorne St.,* ☎ *413/ 637–0166,* WEB *www.frelinghuysen.org.* ▢ *$8.* ☉ *July–Aug., Thurs.– Sun. 10–4; Sept.–mid-Oct., Thurs.–Sat. 10–3; guided tours on the hr.*

Dining and Lodging

$$$–$$$$ ✕ **Bistro Zinc.** Crisp lemon-yellow walls, warm tile floors, and tall windows create a bright and inviting ambience at this stellar French bistro, which feels reminiscent of a country house in a Provence village. The kitchen turns out expertly prepared and refreshingly simple classics like steak frites, saddle of rabbit, and spinach lasagna. If you can overlook the occasionally self-important attitudes of the staff, Zinc is top-notch. ⊠ *56 Church St.,* ☎ *413/637–8800. MC, V. Closed Tues.*

$$$–$$$$ ✕ **Café Lucia.** *Bistecca alla fiorentina* (porterhouse steak grilled with olive oil, garlic, and rosemary) and ravioli *basilico e pomodoro* (homemade ravioli with fresh tomatoes, garlic, and basil) are among the dishes that change seasonally at this northern Italian restaurant. The sleek decor includes track lighting and photographs of the owners' Italian ancestors. Weekend reservations are essential up to a month ahead during Tanglewood. ⊠ *90 Church St.,* ☎ *413/637–2640. AE, DC, MC, V. Closed Mon. July–Oct. and Sun.–Mon. Nov.–June. No lunch.*

$$–$$$$ ✕ **Church Street Cafe.** A little more laid-back both in style and ambience than its nearby competitors, Church Street Cafe presents a no-less ambitious and intriguing menu of creative globally inspired dishes. From the punchy tortilla soup with avocado and smoked turkey to a memorable roasted Japanese sea bass with shrimp ravioli, dashi broth, and steamed spinach, it's hard to find a humdrum dish here. In warm weather, you can dine on a lovely tree-shaded outdoor deck. ⊠ *65 Church St.,* ☎ *413/637–2745. MC, V.*

$$–$$$ ✕ **Spigalina.** In an unprepossessing pale-green house in downtown
★ Lenox, Spigalina serves high-quality pan-Mediterranean fare in a quiet, diminutive dining room staffed by charming servers. The paella Valenciana—Spanish rice with slow-cooked chicken, seafood, peppers, chorizo, tomatoes, and cilantro—wins raves. Another standout is pan-seared New Zealand rack of lamb with a roasted-garlic risotto cake, Provençale ratatouille, and a kalamata-olive sauce. ⊠ *80 Main St.,* ☎ *413/637–4455. AE, D, MC, V. No lunch.*

\$\$–\$\$\$ ✕ **Trattoria Il Vesuvio.** *Proprietaria* Anna Arace, a native of Pompeii, is on hand nightly to assure that every dish meets her exacting standards. Among the house specialties are *arrosto di vitello,* roast breast of veal stuffed with sliced prosciutto and spinach, cooked in a brick oven and served with red wine sauce, and linguine with baby clams. Save room for Anna's homemade tiramisu. It's a short drive north of downtown, on the main road to Pittsfield. ⊠ *242 Pittsfield Rd.,* ☎ *413/637–4904. AE, D, MC, V. Closed Sun. Sept.–June. No lunch.*

\$\$\$\$ ✕🏨 **Blantyre.** Modeled after a castle in Scotland, this supremely elegant 1902 manor house sits amid nearly 100 acres of manicured lawns and woodlands. Lavishly decorated rooms in the main house have hand-carved four-poster beds, overstuffed chaise lounges, and Victorian bathrooms. The rooms in the carriage house are well appointed but can't compete with the formal grandeur of the main house. The restaurant (\$\$\$\$; reservations essential; jacket and tie) serves upscale country-house fare—no cream or heavy sauces, light on the butter. A typical entrée might be roasted Arctic char with fennel confit, crispy potatoes, mussels, crab, and saffron. After-dinner coffee and cognac are served in the music room, where a harpist plays. ⊠ *16 Blantyre Rd., off U.S. 20, 01240,* ☎ *413/637–3556,* ℻ *413/637–4282,* 🕸 *www. blantyre.com. 17 rooms, 5 suites, 1 cottage. Restaurant, 4 tennis courts, pool, some in-room hot tubs, hot tub, massage, sauna, croquet, hiking. AE, DC, MC, V. Closed early Nov.–early May. CP.*

\$\$\$\$ ✕🏨 **Wheatleigh Hotel.** Set amid 22 wooded acres, this mellow brick ★ estate based on a 16th-century Florentine palazzo has rooms with vaulted high ceilings, intricate plaster moldings, and an adroit and understated blend of sleek contemporary furnishings and neutral, earthy colors and tones. Smoke-glass fireplace screens, separate climate control for both the rooms and bathrooms, white-silk bedspreads, and limestone bathroom floors are among the swanky but low-key touches. The main restaurant (\$\$\$\$), a huge room with marble fireplaces and cut-glass chandeliers, serves such contemporary standouts as Texas antelope with a corn soufflé. The Library provides a more casual setting. ⊠ *Hawthorne Rd., 02140,* ☎ *413/637–0610,* ℻ *413/637–4507,* 🕸 *www.wheatleigh.com. 17 rooms, 2 suites. 2 restaurants, tennis court, pool, gym, bar, meeting room. AE, DC, MC, V.*

\$\$\$–\$\$\$\$ ✕🏨 **Gateways Inn.** The 1912 summer cottage of Harley Proctor (as ★ in Proctor and Gamble) has experienced some ups and downs during its tenure as a country inn. But under the skillful direction of innkeepers Fabrizio and Rosemary Chiariello, it looks better than ever. Rooms come in a variety of configurations and styles, most with working fireplaces, detailed moldings, and plush carpeting. In the restaurant (\$\$\$–\$\$\$\$; closed Mon.; no lunch weekdays) you might dine on sautéed medallions of venison or baked acorn squash with a wild rice–cranberry stuffing and roasted-chestnut ragout. The restaurant offers a light late-night menu during the Tanglewood season. The inn also makes sublimely delicious picnic lunches. You can sample dozens of rare grappas and single-malt whiskies in the bar. ⊠ *51 Walker St., 01240,* ☎ *413/637–2532,* ℻ *413/637–1432,* 🕸 *www.gatewaysinn.com. 11 rooms, 1 suite. Restaurant, in-room data ports, some in-room VCRs, bar, meeting room. AE, MC, V. BP.*

\$\$\$\$ 🏨 **Canyon Ranch.** This world-class spa resort provides a full slate of ★ vigorous activities and beauty and body treatments. Colonial-style rooms with floral bedspreads and light-wood furnishings are set inside a contemporary inn, while the ornate Bellefontaine Mansion houses the dining room, library, and activity areas. In the spa you can book everything from salt and seaweed treatments to deep-tissue massage. Rates are all-inclusive; there's a three-night minimum. Note that alcohol is not permitted in public areas or available anywhere for purchase. ⊠ *165 Kemble St., 01240,* ☎ *413/637–4100 or 800/742–9000,* FAX *413/637–0057,* WEB *www.canyonranch.com. 126 rooms. Dining room, tennis courts, 2 pools (1 indoor), aerobics, health club, hot tub, sauna, spa, bicycles, basketball, hiking, racquetball, squash, cross-country skiing; no kids under 14, no smoking. AE, D, MC, V. FAP.*

$$$$ ⊞ **Cranwell Resort, Spa, and Golf Club.** The best rooms in this 380-acre, five-building complex are in the century-old Tudor mansion; they're furnished with antiques and have marble bathrooms. Two smaller buildings have 20 rooms each, and there are several small cottages, each of which has a kitchen. Somewhat marring the property are an abundance of tightly spaced condos behind the hotel buildings. Most of the facilities are open to the public, as are the resort's restaurants, where you can dine formally or informally. There's also a full golf school. Opened in spring 2002, a 35,000-square-ft spa has a full complement of women's and men's treatments, plus several types of massage. ⊠ *55 Lee Rd., 02140,* ☎ *413/637–1364 or 800/272–6935,* FAX *413/637–4364,* WEB *www.cranwell.com. 107 rooms. 3 restaurants, 18-hole golf course, driving range, 4 tennis courts, pool, health club, spa, bicycles, hiking, cross-country skiing, concierge, meeting rooms. AE, D, DC, MC, V. CP.*

$$$–$$$$ ⊞ **Brook Farm Inn.** This 1870s Victorian and its gardens are tucked away in a beautiful wooded glen a short distance from Tanglewood. The innkeepers are music and literature aficionados and often have light opera, jazz, or Broadway tunes playing in the fireplace-lighted library, whose shelves contain copious volumes of verse. On Saturdays poetry is read at afternoon tea. Rooms have antiques, light-pastel color schemes, and in many cases four-poster beds. Even the smallest units, with their eaved ceilings and cozy configurations, are highly romantic. ⊠ *15 Hawthorne St., 01240,* ☎ *413/637–3013 or 800/285–7638,* WEB *www.brookfarm.com. 8 rooms, 1 suite. Pool, library; no room TVs, no kids under 15, no smoking. MC, V. BP.*

$$$–$$$$ ⊞ **Cliffwood Inn.** Six of the seven guest rooms in this 1889 Georgian Revival white-clapboard mansion have fireplaces, and four more fireplaces glow in the common areas, reflecting off the polished wooden floors. Many of the inn's ornate antiques come from Europe; most guest rooms have canopy beds. The patio and pool area are well designed; indoors there's a counter-current pool. ⊠ *25 Cliffwood St., 01240,* ☎ *413/637–3330 or 800/789–3331,* FAX *413/637–0221,* WEB *www.cliffwood.com. 6 rooms, 1 suite. Pool, some in-room hot tubs, some in-room VCRs, hot tub; no room phones, no TV in some rooms, no kids under 11, no smoking. No credit cards.*

$$$–$$$$ ⊞ **Garden Gables.** This 1780s summer cottage on 5 acres of wooded grounds has been an inn since 1947. The three common parlors have fireplaces, and one long, narrow room has a rare five-legged Steinway piano. Rooms come in various shapes, sizes, and colors and have American country-style antiques; some have brass beds, and others have pencil four-posters. Some rooms have sloping ceilings, fireplaces, whirlpool baths, or woodland views. Three have private decks. Breakfast is served buffet-style in the airy dining room. ⊠ *135 Main St. (Box 52, 01240),* ☎ *413/637–0193,* FAX *413/637–4554,* WEB *www.lenoxinn.com. 19 rooms. Some in-room hot tubs, pool; no TV in some rooms, no kids under 12, no smoking. AE, D, MC, V. BP.*

$$$–$$$$ ⊞ **Harrison House.** An inviting white Victorian house with a sweeping wraparound porch across from Lenox's White Church on the Hill, this upscale inn is particularly notable for its attractive, mature landscaping. Rooms are lavish with decadent furnishings—every unit has a working fireplace, and a few have four-poster or canopy beds. Plush duvets, ceiling fans, and Victorian-style wallpapers add to the sense of romance. It's a bit smaller and less busy than most of the inns in Lenox, and the hosts are friendly and enthusiastic. The inn is close enough to walk into town but set nicely on a hillside away from the tourist bustle. ✉ *174 Main St., 01240,* ☎ *413/637–1746,* WEB *www.harrison-house.com. 6 rooms. No phones in some rooms, no smoking. MC, V. BP.*

\$\$–\$\$\$\$
★
🏠 **Whistler's Inn.** The antiques decorating the parlor of this eccentric 1820s English Tudor mansion are ornate, with a touch of the exotic. The library, formal parlor, music room (with a Steinway grand piano and Louis XVI original furniture), and gracious dining room all impress. Designer drapes and bedspreads adorn the rooms, three of which have working fireplaces. The carriage house is only open May through October; one room in it has African decor, and another is done in southwestern style. The inn is nestled amid 7 acres of gardens and woods across from Kennedy Park. ✉ *5 Greenwood St., 01240,* ☎ *413/637–0975,* FAX *413/637–2190,* WEB *www.whistlersinnlenox.com. 14 rooms. Badminton, croquet, library. AE, D, MC, V. BP.*

\$–\$\$\$
★
🏠 **Yankee Inn.** Custom-crafted Amish canopy beds, gas fireplaces, and high-end fabrics decorate the top rooms at this immaculately kept property, one of several modern hotels and motels along U.S. 7. The more economical units contain attractive, if nondescript, country-style furnishings and such useful amenities as coffeemakers and irons with ironing boards. The same owners run an appealing B&B in downtown Lee, the Chambéry Inn. ✉ *461 Pittsfield Rd. (U.S. 7/Rte. 20), 01240,* ☎ *413/499–3700 or 800/835–2364,* FAX *413/499–3634,* WEB *www.yankeeinn.com. 96 rooms. In-room data ports, indoor pool, gym, hot tub. AE, D, MC, V. CP.*

Nightlife and the Arts

The **Robbins-Zust Family Marionettes** (☎ 413/698–2591) have been pleasing audiences for decades. Performances are Tuesday, Thursday, and Saturday at 11 and 2 at the **Lenox House Shops** (✉ U.S. 7/20) the first two weeks of July and the first two weeks in August, and year-round throughout the Berkshires.

Shakespeare and Company (✉ 70 Kemble St., ☎ 413/637–1199; 413/637–3353 tickets) performs the works of Shakespeare and Edith Wharton from late May through October at the 466-seat Founders' Theatre and the 99-seat Spring Lawn Theatre. Also under way is the re-creation of the Rose Playhouse, the original of which has stood on the South Bank of the London's Thames River since 1587.

Tanglewood (✉ West St., off Rte. 183, ☎ 413/637–5165; 617/266–1492; 617/266–1200 tickets from Symphony Charge; WEB www.bso.org), the 200-acre summer home of the Boston Symphony Orchestra, attracts thousands every year to concerts by world-famous performers from mid-June to Labor Day. The 5,000-seat main shed hosts larger concerts; the Seiji Ozawa Hall (named for the former BSO conductor—James Levine took the helm in 2002) seats around 1,200 and is used for recitals, chamber music, and more intimate performances by summer program students and soloists. One of the most rewarding ways to experience Tanglewood is to purchase lawn tickets, arrive early with blankets or lawn chairs, and have a picnic.

Outdoor Activities and Sports

Undermountain Farm (✉ 400 Undermountain Rd., ☎ 413/637–3365) gives horseback-riding lessons and conducts guided trail rides year-round, weather permitting.

Shopping

One of the foremost crafts centers in New England, **Hoadley Gallery** (✉ 21 Church St., ☎ 413/637–2814) shows American arts and crafts with a strong focus on pottery, jewelry, and textiles. Shop at **La Vie En**

Rose (⌂ 67 Church St., ☎ 413/637–3662) for [...] antiques, porcelain vases, and antique jewelry. [...] Church St., ☎ 413/637–1589) produces high-qual[...] and also sells estate and antique pieces. **Stone's Throw A[...]** Church St., ☎ 413/637–2733) carries fine 19th- and early [...] tury antiques, from gilt mirrors to delicate inkwells. The **Ute [...] Gallery** (⌂ 69 Church St., ☎ 413/637–3566) sells folk and con[...] porary art.

Evviva! (⌂ 22 Walker St., ☎ 413/637–9875) shows the top shoes, dresses, and accessories of several leading women's fashion designers. **Meanwheels** (⌂ 57A Housatonic St., ☎ 413/637–0644) rents and sells bikes and equipment. **Michael Charles Cabinetmaker** (⌂ 53 Church St., ☎ 413/637–3483) is famous for handcrafted, heirloom-quality furniture, all of it custom-designed and custom-made in the finest traditions of New England furniture making. **Nejaime's Wine Cellars** (⌂ 60 Main St., Lenox, ☎ 413/637–2221; ⌂ 444 Pittsfield–Lenox Rd., Pittsfield, ☎ 413/448–2274) prepares excellent picnics-to-go and is also a top-flight wine-and-cheese store.

Lee

🔢 *5 mi south of Lenox.*

Of all the towns in the Berkshires, Lee feels the most like a hybrid between the industrial urban centers and the elegant country villages. The town's water power made it ideal for paper mills during the early 19th century, and still today Mead Specialty Paper has a hulking redbrick mill on the Housatonic River, in South Lee. Lee never became a major mill town, however, and the construction of the Massachusetts Turnpike right through the heart of town helped turn it into a retail and services hub for Berkshires vacationers. The bustling downtown contains a mix of touristy and workaday shops, and an outlet shopping center sits just off the Mass Pike highway exit.

Santarella Museum and Gardens, which resembles a dwelling from the fairy tales of the Brothers Grimm, was the home and last studio of Sir Henry Hudson Kitson (1863–1947), sculptor of *The Minuteman* in Lexington and other renowned works. Today the studio is open as a museum and gallery, and the 4 acres of grounds designed by the artist-naturalist are a sculpture park. ⌂ *75 Main Rd., Tyringham, 7 mi south of Lee,* ☎ *413/243–3260.* 🎫 *$4.* ☼ *Late May–Oct., daily 10–5.*

Dining and Lodging

$$ ✕ **Sweet Basil.** Steps from the Historic Merrell and Federal House inns, this charming, laid-back trattoria in South Lee serves traditional red-sauce Italian fare at reasonable prices, including pork saltimbocca, grilled salmon, chicken with pesto over linguine, and calamari marinara. It's one of the few good restaurants in these parts with a children's menu. ⌂ *1575 Pleasant St./Rte. 102, South Lee,* ☎ *413/243–1114. AE, DC, MC, V. No lunch.*

$$$–$$$$ 🏨 **Applegate Inn.** This 1920s Georgian Revival mansion sits at the end
★ of a regal circular drive, overlooking 6 acres of lush lawns and apple trees, and a golf course across the road. The inn has been exquisitely decorated: one room has a spacious steam shower and a fireplace, and another contains a French reproduction sleigh bed with a manteled fireplace and stunning views out over the glorious grounds. A carriage house contains two superplush suites with stereos and wet bars; Godiva chocolates and crystal decanters filled with brandy add a touch of class. About the only negative is the slight hum of the Massachusetts Turn-

ath. ⊠ 279 W. Park St., 01238, ☎ 413/243–4451, ...inn.com. 6 rooms, 2 suites. Some in-room data ...m hot tubs, some in-room VCRs, pool; no kids ...ing. MC, V. BP.

This grand pale yellow-and-cream Federal-era manor ...atop a birch-shaded hillside dotted with a few quaint ...acres of rolling meadows—you'd be hard-pressed to ...matic setting in the Berkshires. The nine guest rooms ...le furnishings—many have Oriental rugs, lace-canopy ..., and working fireplaces. An immense penthouse suite is a favorite for special occasions, and a separate, contemporary cottage has its own kitchen with a pitched cathedral ceiling and private deck. A gracious pool and lanai sit behind the house. ⊠ 85 Stockbridge Rd., 01238, ☎ 413/243–3298 or 800/664–0880, FAX 413/243–1360, WEB www.devonfield.com. 6 rooms, 3 suites, 1 cottage. Some in-room hot tubs, some in-room VCRs, tennis court, pool, bicycles, cross-country skiing; no TV in some rooms, no kids under 12. MC, V. BP.

$$$–$$$$ ☷ **Federal House.** This well-maintained 1824 house with soaring columns and a Greek Revival facade cuts a dashing figure along Route 102—the original owner ran the paper mill just down the road. In your antiques-filled room, you'll find a queen-size four-poster bed and in many cases a fireplace, original wide-pine floors, and plush down comforters. The house's airy porches are ideal for whiling away a warm afternoon. Breakfast specialties include Grand Marnier French toast and a mushroom-onion frittata with hardwood-smoked bacon. ⊠ 1560 Pleasant St./Rte. 102, South Lee 01260, ☎ 413/243–1824 or 800/243–1824, FAX 413/243–1828, WEB www.federalhouseinn.com. 8 rooms, 1 suite. No kids under 12, no smoking. AE, D, MC, V. BP.

$$$ ☷ **Historic Merrell Inn.** Built in the 1780s as a private residence (it was later a stagecoach stopover), this inn has some good-size rooms, several with working fireplaces. Meticulously maintained, the Merrell has an unfussy yet authentic style, with polished wide-board floors, painted walls, and wood antiques. The sitting room has an open fireplace and contains the only intact "bird cage" Colonial bar—a semicircular bar surrounded by wooden slats—in the country. Breakfast is cooked to order. ⊠ 1565 Pleasant St./Rte. 102, South Lee 01260, ☎ 413/243–1794 or 800/243–1794, FAX 413/243–2669, WEB www.merrell-inn.com. 9 rooms, 1 suite. MC, V. BP.

Shopping

Prime Outlets at Lee (⊠ U.S. 20, at I–90 Exit 2, ☎ 413/243–8186) contains 65 shops, among them Geoffrey Beene, Coach, J. Crew, and Anne Klein.

Otis

❺❸ 15 mi southeast of Lee.

A more rustic alternative to the polish of Stockbridge and Lenox, Otis, with a ski area and 20 lakes and ponds, supplies plenty of what made the Berkshires desirable in the first place—the great outdoors. The dining options here are slim; your best bet is to pack a picnic of goodies from a Lenox gourmet shop. Nearby Becket hosts the outstanding Jacob's Pillow Dance Festival in summer.

Dining

$–$$ ✕ **Dream Away Lodge.** When the Dream Away reopened in 1998, folk-music fans hailed the revival of the "middle of nowhere" roadhouse once run by the late "Mama" Maria Fresca, a spirited hostess who befriended many performers (scenes from Bob Dylan's road-show movie Renaldo and Clara were filmed here). Wednesday is music night, with acoustic folk, blues, and other traditional sounds. The bar menu dishes up burgers, pastas, and spicy fries; four-course prix-fixe meals other nights might include roast cilantro chicken or salmon fillet in puff pastry. ⊠ *County Rd., Becket,* ☎ *413/623–8725. No credit cards. Closed Mon.–Tues.*

Nightlife and the Arts

For nine weeks each summer, the tiny town of Becket, 8 mi north of Otis, comes to life and becomes a mecca of the dance world during **Jacob's Pillow Dance Festival** (⊠ 358 George Carter Rd., at U.S. 20, Becket, ☎ 413/637–1322; 413/243–0745 box office mid-May–Aug.; WEB www.jacobspillow.org), which showcases world-renowned performers of ballet, modern, and ethnic dance. Before the main events, showings of works-in-progress and even of some of the final productions are staged outdoors, often free of charge. You can picnic on the grounds or eat at the restaurant.

Outdoor Activities and Sports

Deer Run Maples (⊠ 135 Ed Jones Rd., ☎ 413/269–7588) is one of several sugarhouses where you can spend the morning tasting freshly tapped maple syrup that's been drizzled onto a dish of snow. Sugaring season varies with the weather; it can be anytime between late February and early April.

You can hike, bike, or cross-country ski at the 3,800-acre **Otis State Forest** (⊠ Rte. 23, ☎ 413/269–6002). The 8,000-acre **Tolland State Forest** (⊠ Rte. 8, ☎ 413/269–6002) allows swimming in the Otis Reservoir and camping.

Ski Areas

OTIS RIDGE

The least expensive ski area in New England, Otis Ridge has long been a haven for beginners and families, but experts will find slopes here, too. The remote location is quite stunning, the buildings historic. ⊠ *Rte. 23, 01253,* ☎ *413/269–4444,* WEB *www.otisridge.com*

Downhill. There are six trails serviced by a pair of lifts.

Child care. Otis Ridge is home to the oldest operating ski camp in the country, having taught boys and girls ages 8–15 for more than 50 years. The camp also has a snowboarding program.

CANTERBURY FARM

This spectacular, high-country property in Becket has 12 mi of groomed cross-country ski trails, plus lessons and equipment. You can ski across a nearby lake or take to some 2,000 acres of unmaintained trails that surround the farm. ⊠ *Fred Snow Rd., Becket, 01223,* ☎ *413/623–0100.*

Stockbridge

54 *20 mi northwest of Otis, 7 mi south of Lenox.*

Stockbridge, a major tourist destination, has the look of small-town New England down pat. Its artistic and literary inhabitants have included sculptor Daniel Chester French, writers Norman Mailer and Robert Sherwood, and, fittingly enough, that champion of small-town America, painter Norman Rockwell, who lived here from 1953 until his death in 1978. James Taylor sung about the town in his hit "Sweet Baby James," and as told in balladeer Arlo Guthrie's famous Thanksgiving anthem "Alice's Restaurant," he tossed a mountain of garbage out the back of his Volkswagen bus down a Stockbridge hillside.

Indeed, Stockbridge is the stuff of story and legend, and it remains ever the quintessence of small-town New England charm—untainted by industry or large-scale development. The best hotel in town, the Red Lion Inn, is the very address travelers have been checking into since the late 1800s. You'll find a handful of engaging shops and eateries on the blocks surrounding the inn. The rest of Stockbridge is best appreciated via a country drive or bike ride over its hilly, narrow lanes.

★ The **Norman Rockwell Museum** owns more than 570 of the artist's works, beginning with the first *Saturday Evening Post* cover from 1916. The museum also mounts exhibits by other artists. On the 36-acre grounds is Rockwell's studio, complete with his brushes. You can picnic here or stroll along the river walk. ⊠ *Rte. 183 (2 mi from Stockbridge),* ☎ *413/298–4100,* WEB *www.nrm.org.* ☞ *$10.* ☉ *May–Oct., daily 10–5; Nov.–Apr., weekdays 10–4, weekends 10–5.*

★ **Chesterwood** was for 33 years the summer home of the sculptor Daniel Chester French (1850–1931), who created *The Minuteman* in Concord and the Lincoln Memorial in Washington, D.C. Tours are given of the house, which is maintained in the style of the 1920s, and of the studio, where you can view the casts and models French used to create the Lincoln Memorial. The beautifully landscaped 122-acre grounds also make for an enchanting stroll. ⊠ *Williamsville Rd. off Rte. 183,* ☎ *413/298–3579,* WEB *www.chesterwood.net.* ☞ *Tour $8.50; grounds only, $6.50.* ☉ *May–Oct., daily 10–5; call for limited Nov. hrs.*

The 15-acre **Berkshire Botanical Gardens** contain greenhouses, ponds, nature trails, and perennial, rose, day lilies, and herb gardens of both exotic and native plantings—some 2,500 varieties in all. Picnicking is encouraged. ⊠ *Rtes. 102 and 183, 2 mi east of downtown,* ☎ *413/ 298–3926,* WEB *www.berkshirebotanical.org.* ☞ *$7.* ☉ *May–Oct., daily 10–5.*

★ **Naumkeag,** a Berkshire cottage once owned by Joseph Choate, an ambassador during the administration of U.S. president William McKinley and a successful New York lawyer, provides a glimpse into the gracious living of the "gilded era of the Berkshires. The 26-room gabled mansion, designed by Stanford White in 1886, sits atop Prospect Hill. It is decorated with many original furnishings and art that spans three centuries; the collection of Chinese export porcelain is also noteworthy. The meticulously kept 8 acres of formal gardens designed by Fletcher Steele are themselves worth a visit. ⊠ *South Prospect Hill,* ☎ *413/298–3239,* WEB *www.thetrustees.org.* ☞ *$9.* ☉ *Late May–mid-Oct., daily 10–5.*

Dining and Lodging

$$ ✕ **Once Upon a Table.** The atmosphere is casual yet vaguely romantic at this little restaurant in an alley off Stockbridge's main street. The Continental and new American cuisine includes seasonal dishes, with appetizers such as escargots, and entrées that include seared crab cakes with horseradish-cream as well as lobster ravioli. ⊠ *36 Main St.,* ☎ *413/298–3870. Reservations essential AE, MC, V. No dinner some nights; call for hrs.*

$$–$$$$ ✕🏠 **Red Lion Inn.** An inn since 1773, the Red Lion has hosted five presidents and many celebrities over the years. It consists of a large main building and seven annexes, each of which is different (one is a converted fire station). Many rooms are small, and the furnishings are a tad worn in places; accommodations in the annex houses tend to be more appealing. All the rooms are furnished with antiques and reproductions and hung with Rockwell prints; some have Oriental rugs. The main dining room ($$–$$$$) has a somewhat formal ambience and serves such creative American fare as baked bluefish with almond-

mustard crust and watercress-citrus salad. In the Lion's Den, you'll find heartier dishes, including venison stew and grilled sausage, as well as live music many evenings. ⊠ *30 Main St., 02162,* ☎ *413/298–5545 or 413/298–1690,* FAX *413/298–5130,* WEB *www.redlioninn.com. 84 rooms, 70 with bath; 26 suites. 3 restaurants, some in-room VCRs, some in-room hot tubs, pool, gym, massage, bar, meeting room. AE, D, DC, MC, V. CP.*

$$$–$$$$ 🏨 **Inn at Stockbridge.** Antiques and feather comforters are among the
★ accents in the rooms of this 1906 Georgian Revival inn run by the attentive Alice and Len Schiller. The two serve breakfast in their elegant dining room, and every evening they provide wine and cheese. Each of the junior suites in the adjacent "cottage" building has a decorative theme such as Kashmir, St. Andrews, and Provence; the junior suites in the new "carriage" building have Berkshire themes. The airy and posh rooms have CD players, iron and ironing boards, hair dryers, and in some cases gas fireplaces. ⊠ *U.S. 7 (Box 618, 02162),* ☎ *413/298–3337 or 888/466– 7865,* FAX *413/298–3406,* WEB *www.stockbridgeinn.com. 8 rooms, 8 suites. Some in-room VCRs, some in-room hot tubs, pool; no TV in some rooms, no smoking. AE, D, MC, V. BP.*

Nightlife and the Arts

The **Berkshire Theatre Festival** (⊠ Main St., ☎ 413/298–5536; 413/ 298–5576 box office) stages nightly performances during summer in Stockbridge. Plays written by local schoolchildren are performed occasionally during the summer.

Shopping

The dynamic **Holsten Galleries** (⊠ 3 Elm St., ☎ 413/298–3044) shows wares of top contemporary glass sculptors of the Northeast, including Dale Chihuly. **Origins Gallery** (⊠ 36 Main St., ☎ 413/298–0002) is filled with colorful carved animals, baskets, stone sculpture from Zimbabwe, and other works from Africa.

West Stockbridge

55 *5 mi northwest of Stockbridge, 6 mi west of Lenox.*

The Williams River winds through this pretty little town, whose streets are dotted with galleries, antiques and specialty shops, and restaurants.

At the **Berkshire Center for Contemporary Glass** you can watch glassblowers create magnificent pieces and, in summer, create your own paperweight. This handsome gallery displays and sells the works of some of the country's foremost artists working in this medium. ⊠ *6 Harris St.,* ☎ *413/232–4666,* WEB *www.berkshireweb.com/bcfcg.* 🎫 *Free.* ☉ *Daily 10–6.*

Dining

$$–$$$ ✕ **Truc Orient Express.** Happy Pancake, Shaking Beef, and Beef on Rice
★ Noodles are just a few of the well-prepared Vietnamese specialties at this restaurant just across from the Berkshire Center for Contemporary Glass. Plenty of wood, windows, and artwork create a lovely setting. Portions tend to be on the small side but are beautifully presented. ⊠ *3 Harris St.,* ☎ *413/232–4204. AE, D, MC, V. No lunch.*

Shopping

Sawyer Antiques (⊠ Depot St., ☎ 413/232–7062) sells Early American furniture and accessories in a spare clapboard structure that was a Shaker mill.

Great Barrington

56 *11 mi south of West Stockbridge; 13 mi north of Canaan, Connecticut.*

The largest town in the southern Berkshires was the first place to free slaves under due process of law and was also the birthplace of W. E. B. Du Bois, the civil rights leader, author, and educator. The many ex–New Yorkers who live in Great Barrington expect great food and service, and the restaurants here deliver complex, toothsome fare. The town is also a favorite of antiques hunters, as are the nearby villages of South Egremont and Sheffield.

Bartholomew's Cobble, south of Great Barrington, is a natural rock garden beside the Housatonic River (the Native American name means "river beyond the mountains"). The 277-acre site is filled with trees, ferns, wildflowers, and 5 mi of hiking trails. The visitor center has a museum. ⊠ *Weatogue Rd./Rte. 7A,* ☎ *413/229–8600.* ⊡ *$4.* ☉ *Daily dawn–dusk.*

Dining and Lodging

$$–$$$$ ✕ **Pearl's.** Opened in 2001 by the same owners as Lenox's trendy Bistro Zinc, Pearl's adds a dash of big-city atmosphere to the Berkshires with its pressed-tin ceilings, tall booths, exposed brick walls, and well-coiffed crowd. The menu updates the old bigger-is-better steak-house tradition by serving thick and tender chops, prime rib, wild game, raw oysters, and fresh lobsters with innovative ingredients. Call ahead for a table on weekends, or simply hobnob and sip well-chosen wines and creative drinks at the elegant bar. ⊠ *47 Railroad St.,* ☎ *413/528–7767. AE, MC, V. No lunch.*

$$–$$$$ ✕ **Shiro.** Sushi and other Japanese fare have become increasingly com-
★ monplace in Great Barrington in recent years, helping solidify the town's reputation as the Berkshires' most sophisticated restaurant town. Shiro is a warmly lighted, art-filled space that serves superb sushi but also such delicious hot entrées as lightly battered and fried wasabi shrimp over wilted spinach, and tempura tuna and crab in seaweed roll served with a spicy aioli and caviar. A full range of sakes is available. ⊠ *105 Stockbridge Rd.,* ☎ *413/528–1898. AE, D, MC, V.*

$$–$$$ ✕ **Helsinki Tea Company.** The emphasis is on Finnish, Russian, and Jewish cuisines, prepared with lots of spices and served in big portions, at this restaurant, which suggests a lost world of Old European elegance. A hodgepodge of colorful cushions, fringed draperies, and objets d'art creates the feeling of an intimate café. It doesn't get much cozier than sitting by a roaring fire, tucking into an order of Midnight Train to Moscow (chicken-apple bratwurst, hot cabbage slaw, and potato latkes), and then lingering over one of the numerous tea choices (or something stronger—the restaurant has a full liquor license) and live music at the attached Club Helsinki. Sunday brunch is a popular affair. ⊠ *284 Main St.,* ☎ *413/528–3394. MC, V.*

$$–$$$ ✕ **Old Mill.** This rambling restaurant fashioned out of 1797 gristmill and blacksmith's shop has wide-plank floors and large windows overlooking the river below. With such a charmed setting, the kitchen could get away with serving old-hat American standbys, but the food here is at least as appealing as the space in which it is served. The menu lists a mix of regional New England and southern dishes, including a succulent oven-roasted poussin with garlic. A lighter menu is served in the cozy bar. ⊠ *Rte. 23, South Egremont,* ☎ *413/528–1421. AE, DC, MC, V. Closed Mon. No lunch.*

$$–$$$ ✕ **Verdura.** With all the fancy culinary hot spots that have opened in
★ Great Barrington in the past few years, this restaurant stands out as much as anything for its understatedly classy decor, youthful and friendly staff, and superbly executed Tuscan cooking. In a handsome

storefront space with sponge-dappled ocher and pale green walls, you can try saffron-lobster risotto with mascarpone or wood-grilled prosciutto-wrapped brook trout with lentils, roasted fennel, and sage-brown butter. The wild-mushroom pizza with leeks, chèvre, and white-truffle oil is another favorite. ⊠ *44 Railroad St.,* ☎ *413/528–8969. AE, MC, V.*

$ ✕ **Baba Louie's.** This intimate and always-crowded pizza spot with a rustic ambience serves delicious thin-crust pies with a riot of exotic ingredients. The pomodoro bianco comes topped with roasted Portobellos, roasted garlic, tomatoes, and chèvre; and the Isabella is covered with roasted sweet potatoes, roasted parsnips, caramelized onions, shaved fennel, and balsamic vinegar. Also try the tasty panini sandwiches, bruschetta, or Gorgonzola-pear salad. ⊠ *286 Main St.,* ☎ *413/528–8100. D, MC, V.*

$$$–$$$$ ✕🖭 **The Old Inn on the Green and Gedney Farm.** Five distinctive lodg-
★ ings make up this property in tranquil and historic New Marlborough. The 1760 Old Inn has five authentically restored, antiques-filled guest rooms. The ultradeluxe Thayer House includes five elegantly appointed rooms and a courtyard terrace with a pool. Just up the road is Gedney Farm, with two turn-of-the-20th-century, Normandy-style barns with 16 rooms and suites—all with queen beds and many with fireplaces. Other properties include the mid-19th-century Gedney Manor House with 12 guest rooms and the four-bedroom Colonial Hannah Stebbins House on the Green. The restaurant ($$$–$$$$) in the Old Inn is lit entirely by candlelight and has fireplaces in each dining room. It's worth the trip here to sample such splendid regional American creations as pan-seared yellowtail, snapper, garlic polenta, chorizo, and tomato-fennel ragout. ⊠ *Rte. 57, New Marlborough 01230,* ☎ *413/ 229–3131 or 800/286–3139,* 🅵🅰🆇 *413/229–8236,* 🆆🅴🅱 *www.oldinn.com. 37 rooms, 5 suites. Restaurant, some in-room hot tubs, pool, meeting rooms. AE, MC, V. CP.*

$$–$$$$ ✕🖭 **Egremont Inn.** The public rooms in this 1780 inn are enormous, and each has a fireplace. Bedrooms are on the small side but have four-poster beds (some have claw-foot baths) and, like the rest of the inn, unpretentious furnishings. Windows sweep around two sides of the stylish restaurant ($$$–$$$$; reservations essential on weekends in season), where flames flicker in a huge fireplace. The menu changes frequently but might include pan-seared Chilean sea bass with shiitakes and leeks or filet mignon with mashed potato and a caramelized-onion sauce. There's live jazz twice weekly. ⊠ *10 Old Sheffield Rd., South Egremont 01258,* ☎ *413/528–2111 or 800/859–1780,* 🅵🅰🆇 *413/528–3284,* 🆆🅴🅱 *www.egremontinn.com. 19 rooms, 1 suite. Restaurant, tennis court, pool, bar, meeting rooms; no room phones, no smoking. AE, D, MC, V. CP, MAP.*

$$$–$$$$ 🖭 **Weathervane Inn.** Originally a farmhouse, built in 1785, this inn with an 1835 Greek Revival addition on 10 landscaped acres has period-appointed guest rooms and comfortable sitting rooms. Home-baked cookies and cakes are served at afternoon tea, and the owners will prepare gourmet boxed picnic dinners and formal dinners for groups. Golf courses and tennis courts are nearby. ⊠ *Rte. 23 (Box 388, South Egremont 01258),* ☎ *413/528–9580 or 800/528–9580,* 🅵🅰🆇 *413/528–1713,* 🆆🅴🅱 *www.weathervaneinn.com. 10 rooms. Pool, bar, meeting rooms; no smoking. AE, MC, V. BP.*

$$–$$$ 🖭 **Race Brook Lodge.** This brook-side compound of haylofts, ice houses, and hoop sheds proudly promotes itself as a "chintz-free" lodging alternative. Indeed, the lodge and its several outbuildings have cozy and rustic rooms with plush touches and inviting designs including hand-hewn beams, wide-plank floors, country quilts, eclectic art, pitched ceilings, skylights, and hand-stenciling. Several of the

buildings contain just three or four guest rooms and kitchens, making
them ideal for families or friends traveling together. ✉ *864 S. Under-
mountain Rd./Rte. 41 01257,* ☎ *413/229–2916 or 888/725–6343,* FAX
413/229–6629, WEB *www.rblodge.com. 30 rooms, 28 with bath; 2
suites. Dining room, some kitchens, some room phones, Internet,
meeting room; no-smoking rooms. MC, V. BP.*

Nightlife and the Arts

Club Helsinki (✉ 284 Main St., ☎ 413/528–3394) draws some of the
region's top jazz, blues, soul, and folk acts in the region; it's open mike
on Sunday. Jazz musicians perform at the **Egremont Inn** (☞ Dining and
Lodging) on Friday and Saturday. In fall 2000, the **Berkshire Opera
Company** (✉ 14 Castle St., ☎ 413/644–9000; 413/644–9988 box office) purchased the 700-seat Mahaiwe Theatre in downtown Great Barrington; it now presents critically acclaimed operatic performances
throughout the summer in this beautifully restored 1905 venue.

Outdoor Activities and Sports

North of Great Barrington is the large and untamed **Beartown State
Forest,** which has miles of hiking trails and a small campground where
the fee for a site is $4 a night (first come, first served). ✉ *69 Blue Hill
Rd., Monterey,* ☎ *413/528–0904.*

Three miles north of Great Barrington, you can leave your car in a parking lot beside U.S. 7 and climb Squaw Peak in **Monument Mountain
Reservation** (☎ 413/298–3239). The 2½-mi circular hike (a trail map
is displayed in the parking lot) takes you up 900 ft, past glistening white
quartzite cliffs from which Native Americans are said to have leapt to
their deaths to placate the gods. The view of the surrounding mountains from the peak is superb.

GOLF

Great Barrington's **Egremont Country Club** (✉ Rte. 23, ☎ 413/528–
4222) ranks among the most challenging and scenic courses in western Massachusetts. It has a driving range and two tennis courts; greens
fees are $36 on weekends, $22 on weekdays.

Shopping

The Great Barrington area, including the small towns of Sheffield and
South Egremont, has the greatest concentration of antiques stores in
the Berkshires. Some shops are open sporadically, and many are closed
on Tuesday. For a list of storekeepers, send a self-addressed, stamped
envelope to the **Berkshire County Antiques Dealers Association** (✉ Box
95, Sheffield 01257, ☎ 413/229–3070).

The 200-plus dealers at **Coffman's Country Antiques Markets** (✉
Jenifer House Commons, U.S. 7, ☎ 413/528–9282) fill two buildings
with primitive to formal antiques. The **Splendid Peasant** (✉ Rte. 23
and Sheffield Rd., South Egremont, ☎ 413/528–5199) houses an extensive collection of museum-quality 18th- and 19th-century American folk art, including weather vanes, trade signs, and paintings.

Bradford Auction Galleries (✉ U.S. 7, Sheffield, ☎ 413/229–6667) holds
monthly auctions of furniture, paintings and prints, china, glass, silver, and Oriental rugs. A tag sale of household items occurs daily. Some
of the pottery on display at **Great Barrington Pottery** (✉ Rte. 41,
Housatonic, ☎ 413/274–6259) is crafted on-site. There are also gallery-
style showrooms, European and Japanese gardens, and a tearoom
where a full tea ceremony is performed Wednesday at noon in July and
August.

Foodies flock to **Guido's Quality Fruit & Produce** (✉ 760 S. Main St.,
Great Barrington, ☎ 413/528–9255; ✉ 1020 South St., Pittsfield, ☎

413/442–9912) for fine prepared foods, cheeses, fish, fruits and vegetables, and fresh-cut flowers. **Kenver Ltd.** (⊠ 39 Main St., South Egremont, ☎ 800/342–7547) carries elegant sports- and outdoors-wear, plus snowshoes, skis, skates, and other top-of-the-line equipment.

Ski Areas

CATAMOUNT SKI AREA

With a 1,000-ft vertical drop and 100% snowmaking capacity, this scenic slope on the New York state border is ideal for family skiing, with its slow and even grades. Nevertheless, the most varied terrain in the Berkshires is here, meaning that skiers of all abilities and tastes can find something to keep them happy. ⊠ *Rte. 23, South Egremont, 01258,* ☎ *413/528–1262; 800/342–1840 snow conditions;* WEB *www. catamountski.com.*

Downhill. There are 28 trails, served by seven lifts, plus a snowboard area called Megaplex Terrain Park, which is separated from the downhill area and has its own lift and a 400-ft halfpipe. A 2002 addition is the Sidewinder, an intermediate cruising trail, more than 1 mi from top to bottom. There's also lighted nighttime boarding and skiing.

Child care. Skiing and snowboarding programs are held for kids 4–12 and 7–12, respectively; a playroom caters to children ages 2–6.

SKI BUTTERNUT

This friendly resort has good base facilities, pleasant skiing, 100% snowmaking capabilities, and the longest quad lift in the Berkshires. Two top-to-bottom terrain parks are for snowboarders. Ski and snowboard lessons are available. Kids six and under ski free midweek on nonholidays if accompanied by a paying adult. ⊠ *Rte. 23, 01230,* ☎ *413/528–2000 ext. 112; 413/528–4433 ski school; 800/438–7669 snow conditions;* WEB *www.skibutternut.com.*

Downhill. Only a steep chute or two interrupt the mellow terrain on 22 trails, most of them intermediate. Eight lifts keep skier traffic spread out.

Cross-country. Butternut Basin has 8 km (6 mi) of groomed cross-country trails.

Child care. The nursery takes children ages 6 months–6 years. The ski school has programs for children ages 4–12.

The Berkshires A to Z

To research prices, get advice from other travelers, and book travel arrangements, visit www.fodors.com.

BIKE TRAVEL

The Ashuwillticook (pronounced *Ash*-oo-will-ti-cook) Rail Trail runs from the Pittsfield-Cheshire town line north up through Adams. Part of the trail is paved. It traces the old rail line and passes through rugged woodland and Cheshire Lake. This is also a great venue for strolling, jogging, in-line skating, and cross-country skiing. The Berkshire Visitors Bureau (☞ Visitor Information) distributes a free Berkshire Bike Touring Route, which is a series of relatively short excursions along area roads.

BUS TRAVEL

Bonanza Bus Lines connects Sheffield, Great Barrington, Stockbridge, Lenox, Lee, Pittsfield, Brodie Mountain, and Williamstown with Albany, New York City, and Providence. Peter Pan Bus Lines serves Lee, Lenox, and Pittsfield from Boston, Hartford, and Albany. Berkshire

Regional Transit Authority provides transportation throughout the Berkshires.

➤ Bus Information: **Berkshire Regional Transit Authority** (☎ 800/292–2782). **Bonanza Bus Lines** (☎ 800/556–3815, WEB www.bonanzabus.com). **Peter Pan Bus Lines** (☎ 413/781–2900 or 800/237–8747, WEB www.peterpanbus.com).

CAR TRAVEL

The Massachusetts Turnpike (I–90) connects Boston with Lee and Stockbridge and continues into New York, where it becomes the New York State Thruway. To reach the Berkshires from New York City take either I–87 or the Taconic State Parkway. The main north–south road within the Berkshires is U.S. 7. Route 2 runs from the northern Berkshires to Greenfield at the head of the Pioneer Valley and continues across Massachusetts into Boston. The scenic section of Route 2 known as the Mohawk Trail runs from Williamstown to Orange.

EMERGENCIES

➤ Hospitals: **Berkshire Medical Center** (✉ 725 North St., Pittsfield, ☎ 413/447–2000). **Fairview Hospital** (✉ 29 Lewis Ave., Great Barrington, ☎ 413/528–8600). **North Adams Regional Hospital** (✉ 71 Hospital Ave., North Adams, ☎ 413/663–3701).

LODGING
BED-AND-BREAKFASTS

Berkshire Folkstone Bed & Breakfast Homes is a reservation service with listings throughout central and western Massachusetts.

➤ Reservation Services: **Berkshire Folkstone Bed & Breakfast Homes** (☎ 413/268–7244 or 800/762–2751, FAX 413/268–7243, WEB www.berkshirebnbhomes.com).

MEDIA
NEWSPAPERS AND MAGAZINES

The daily *Berkshire Eagle* covers the area's arts festivals; from June to Columbus Day the *Eagle* publishes *Berkshires Week,* the summer bible for events information. The *Williamstown Advocate* prints general arts listings. The Thursday edition of the *Boston Globe* publishes news of major concerts.

OUTDOOR ACTIVITIES AND SPORTS
CANOEING

Pleasant canoe trips in the Berkshires include Lenox–Dalton (19 mi), Lenox–Stockbridge (12 mi), Stockbridge–Great Barrington (13 mi), and, for experts, Great Barrington–Falls Village (25 mi).

HIKING

Berkshire Region Headquarters of the state's Department of Environmental Management Division of Forests and Parks has information about trails and hiking in state parks. New England Hiking Holidays of North Conway, New Hampshire, organizes guided hiking vacations through the Berkshires, with overnight stays at country inns. Hikes cover from 5 to 9 mi per day.

➤ Contacts: **Division of Forests and Parks–Berkshire Region Headquarters** (✉ 740 South St., Pittsfield, ☎ 413/442–8928). **New England Hiking Holidays** (☎ 603/356–9696 or 800/869–0949, WEB www.nehikingholidays.com).

TAXIS

Abbott's Limousine and Livery Service, Inc. provides transportation to and from airports throughout the region, including New York, Boston, and Hartford. It requires 24-hr notice.

➤ CONTACT: **Abbott's Limousine and Livery Service, Inc.** (☎ 413/243–1645).

TRAIN TRAVEL

Amtrak runs the *Lake Shore Limited,* which stops at Pittsfield once daily in each direction on its route between Boston and Chicago.

➤ TRAIN INFORMATION: **Amtrak** (☎ 800/872–7245, WEB www.amtrak.com).

VISITOR INFORMATION

➤ TOURIST INFORMATION: **Berkshire Visitors Bureau** (✉ Berkshire Common, adjacent to Crowne Plaza, Pittsfield 01201, ☎ 413/443–9186 or 800/237–5747, WEB www.berkshires.org). **Mohawk Trail Association** (✉ Box 1044, North Adams 01247, ☎ 413/743–8127, WEB www.mohawktrail.com). **Northern Berkshires Chamber of Commerce** (✉ 57 Main St., North Adams, ☎ 413/663–3735, WEB www.nberkshirechamber.com).

MASSACHUSETTS A TO Z

To research prices, get advice from other travelers, and book travel arrangements, visit www.fodors.com.

AIRPORTS

Boston's Logan International Airport has scheduled flights by most major domestic and foreign carriers. Bradley International Airport in Windsor Locks, Connecticut, 18 mi south of Springfield on I–91, has scheduled flights by major U.S. airlines.

➤ AIRPORT INFORMATION: **Bradley International Airport,** (☎ 860/292–2000, WEB www.bradleyairport.com).**Logan International** (✉ I–93 N, Exit 24, ☎ 617/561–1800; 800/235–6426 24-hr information about parking and the ground transportation options).

BIKE TRAVEL

The Massachusetts Bicycle Coalition, an advocacy group that works to improve conditions for area cyclists, has information on organized rides and sells good bike maps of Boston and the state.

➤ CONTACT: The **Massachusetts Bicycle Coalition** (MassBike; ✉ 44 Bromfield St., Boston 02178, ☎ 617/542–2453, WEB www.massbike.org).

BUS TRAVEL

Bonanza Bus Lines serves Boston, as far as Woods Hole on Cape Cod, and the eastern part of the state from Providence, with connecting service to New York. Greyhound buses connect Boston with all major cities in North America. Peter Pan Bus Lines connects Boston with cities elsewhere in Massachusetts and in Connecticut, New Hampshire, and New York. Plymouth & Brockton buses link Boston with the South Shore and Cape Cod.

➤ BUS INFORMATION: **Bonanza Bus Lines** (☎ 800/556–3815, WEB www.bonanzabus.com). **Greyhound** (☎ 800/231–2222, WEB www.greyhound.com). **Peter Pan Bus Lines** (☎ 413/781–2900 or 800/237–8747, WEB www.peterpanbus.com). **Plymouth & Brockton Street Railway** (☎ 508/746–0378, WEB www.p-b.com).

CAR TRAVEL

Boston is the traffic hub of New England, with interstate highways approaching it from every direction. New England's chief coastal highway, I–95, skirts Boston; I–90 leads west through upstate New York. I–91 brings visitors to the Pioneer Valley in western Massachusetts from

Vermont and Canada to the north and Connecticut and New York to the south.

EMERGENCIES
➤ EMERGENCY SERVICES: **Ambulance, fire, police** (☎ 911).

LODGING
CAMPING

A list of private campgrounds throughout Massachusetts can be obtained free from the Massachusetts Office of Travel and Tourism (☞ Visitor Information). Berkshire Visitors Bureau has a room-booking service, but there's a $10 fee for using it. High season is generally from June through October.

➤ CONTACT: **Berkshire Visitors Bureau** (✉ Berkshire Common, adjacent to Crowne Plaza, Pittsfield 01201, ☎ 413/443–9186 or 800/237–5747, WEB www.berkshires.org).

OUTDOOR ACTIVITIES AND SPORTS
FISHING

For information about fishing and licenses, call the Massachusetts Division of Fisheries and Wildlife.

➤ CONTACT: **Massachusetts Division of Fisheries and Wildlife** (☎ 617/727–3151).

TRAIN TRAVEL
The Northeast Corridor service of Amtrak links Boston with the principal cities between it and Washington, D.C. High-speed Acela service is available between the two cities. The *Lake Shore Limited,* which stops at Springfield and the Berkshires, carries passengers from Chicago to Boston.

➤ TRAIN INFORMATION: **Amtrak** (☎ 800/872–7245, WEB www.amtrak.com).

VISITOR INFORMATION
➤ TOURIST INFORMATION: **Massachusetts Office of Travel and Tourism** (✉ 10 Park Plaza, Suite 4510, Boston 02116, ☎ 617/973–8500; 800/447–6277 brochures; WEB www.massvacation.com).

6 RHODE ISLAND

Though it's just 37 mi wide and 48 mi long, Rhode Island changes from pristine coastline to wooded hills to bustling city in the space of an hour's drive. From Newport, a city of gilded-age mansions and Colonial homes, it's a short, 25-mi trip to the Ocean State's capital, Providence; 20 mi farther north is the Blackstone Valley, birthplace of the American Industrial Revolution. Easily accessible and remarkably well preserved history, an abundance of natural beauty, and a lively culture of arts make Rhode Island an appealing New England destination.

Updated by
Paula M.
Bodah

WITH PROPER PLANNING, a traveler in Rhode Island can pick apples in the morning in the Blackstone Valley, tour a historic house in Providence by noon, spend the afternoon shopping for antiques in South County, and end the day with a sunset sail in Newport. Besides possessing such recreational opportunities, the smallest state in the nation—just 1,500 square mi (500 of that being water)—is packed with American history: the state holds 20% of the country's National Historic Landmarks and has more restored Colonial and Victorian buildings than anywhere else in the United States.

In May 1776, before the Declaration of Independence was issued, Rhode Island and Providence Plantations—the state's official name—passed an act removing the king's name from all state documents. This action was typical of the independent-thinking colony. A steadfast insistence upon separation of church and state made Rhode Island attractive to Baptists, Jews, and Quakers, who in the 17th and 18th centuries fled puritanical Massachusetts for Newport and Providence. The first public school was established in forward-thinking Newport in 1664. (Rhode Island continues to be a force in education, with 70,000 students at 10 colleges and universities.) In the 19th century the state flourished, as its entrepreneurial leaders constructed some of the nation's earliest cotton mills, textile mills, and foundries for jewelry. Industry attracted workers from French Canada, Italy, Ireland, England, and Eastern Europe, descendants of whom have retained much of their heritage in numerous ethnic enclaves all across the state.

The qualities that define Rhode Island's unique personality—its small size and diversity from community to community—also contribute to some less-attractive elements: crowded state highways, especially around Providence, and sprawling commercial development that has gone almost unchecked for the past two decades. But as tourism has grown into the state's biggest moneymaker, a more thoughtful approach to development seems to be the norm. Neighborhoods, remote villages, and even rough-hewn cities like Pawtucket and Woonsocket are now constructing bike paths, historic walkways, and visitor centers. Leading the way is the capital city of Providence, where leaders are aggressively reshaping the city.

Rhode Island's 39 towns and cities—none more than 50 mi apart—all hold architectural gems and historic sights. You can tour a gilded-age mansion in Newport and, an hour later, be inside the 1786 John Brown House in Providence, once considered the finest home in North America. Natural attractions such as Narragansett Bay—the second-largest bay on the East Coast and a mecca for world-class sailors—and the barrier beaches of South County round out Rhode Island's list of attractions; inspired culinary artistry and fine accommodations complement the mix. With so much to see in such a compact space, it's easy to explore the Rhode Island that fits your interests.

Pleasures and Pastimes

Beaches

Rhode Island has 400 mi of shoreline with more than 100 salt- and fresh-water beaches. Almost all the ocean beaches around the resort communities of Narragansett, Watch Hill, Newport, and Block Island are open to the public. Deep sands blanket most Rhode Island beaches, and their waters are clear and clean—in some places, the water takes on the turquoise color of the Caribbean Sea. Newport's harbor glim-

Rhode Island

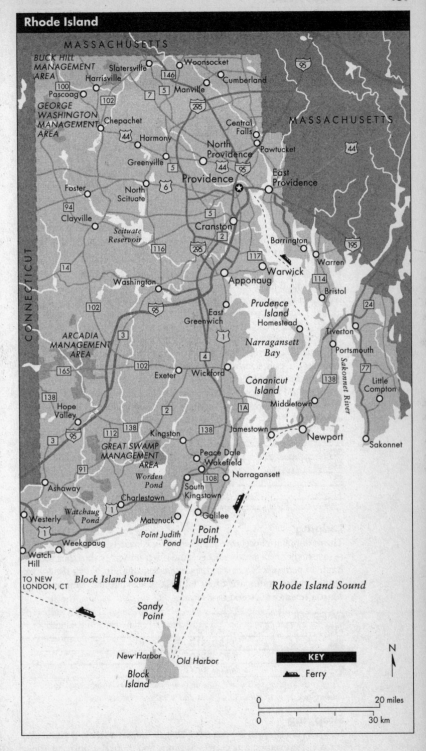

MASSACHUSETTS

BUCK HILL
MANAGEMENT
AREA

Slatersville
Woonsocket
Harrisville
Cumberland
100 Pascoag
102
GEORGE
WASHINGTON
MANAGEMENT
AREA
Chepachet
146
7
5 Manville
295
Central
Falls

MASSACHUSETTS

44 Harmony
44
North
Providence
Pawtucket
Greenville
5
44
95
Providence
East
Providence
Foster
North
Scituate
6
94
Clayville
5
Cranston
Scituate
Reservoir
2
295
Barrington
195
116
117
14
Warwick
Warren
Washington
Apponaug
114
95
Bristol
102
East
Greenwich
Prudence
Island
Homestead
24
ARCADIA
MANAGEMENT
AREA
3
1
Narragansett
Bay
Tiverton
Portsmouth
77
165
102
Exeter
Wickford
4
Conanicut
Island
138
Little
Compton
138
2
1A
Middletown
Hope
Valley
1A
95
112
138
Kingston
138
Jamestown
Newport
3
91
Peace Dale
Wakefield
108
Narragansett
Sakonnet
Ashaway
Worden
Pond
South
Kingstown
Charlestown
Galilee
Westerly
1
Watchaug
Pond
Matunuck
Point Judith
Pond
Point
Judith
1
Weekapaug
Watch
Hill
TO NEW
LONDON, CT

Block Island Sound

Rhode Island Sound

Sandy
Point

New Harbor   Old Harbor

Block
Island

KEY

Ferry

N

0   20 miles
0   30 km

mers from the beach at Fort Adams State Park; nearby Middletown has a long beach adjacent to a wildlife refuge; and Jamestown's Mackerel Cove Beach is sheltered from heavy surf, making it a good choice for families. With naturally occurring white sands and a rock reef to the north that's ideal for snorkeling, Mansion Beach on Block Island is one of the most splendid coastal stretches in New England.

Boating

It should come as no surprise that a place nicknamed the Ocean State would attract boaters. Colonial Newport prospered from shipbuilding and trading, and even today boating is the city's second-largest industry after tourism. Point Judith Pond, close to deep Atlantic waters, harbors New England's second-largest commercial fishing fleet (behind New Bedford, Massachusetts) and nearly four dozen sportfishing charter boats. Block Island's Great Salt Pond is New England's busiest summertime harbor, hosting more than 1,700 boats on weekends. At the head of Narragansett Bay, Waterplace—Providence's riverfront park—is a destination for small boats, canoes, and kayaks. Many tidal rivers and salt ponds in South County are ideal for kayaking and canoeing.

Dining

Rhode Island has been winning national accolades for its restaurants, which serve cuisine from every part of the world. You can still find regional fare such as johnnycakes, a corn cake–like affair cooked on a griddle, and the native clam, the quahog (pronounced "ko-hog"), which is served stuffed, fried, and in chowder. "Shore dinners" consist of clam chowder, steamed soft-shell clams, clam cakes, sausage, corn-on-the-cob, lobster, watermelon, and Indian pudding (a steamed pudding made with cornmeal and molasses). The Federal Hill neighborhood in Providence holds superlative Italian restaurants, and several dozen other restaurants in the city rival many of Boston's finest eateries.

CATEGORY	COST*
$$$$	over $25
$$$	$17–$25
$$	$9–$16
$	under $9

per person, for a main-course dinner

Lodging

The major chain hotels are represented in Rhode Island, but the state's many smaller bed-and-breakfasts and other inns provide a more down-home experience. Rates are very much seasonal; in Newport, for example, winter rates are often half those of summer. Many inns in coastal towns are closed in winter.

CATEGORY	COST*
$$$$	over $180
$$$	$130–$180
$$	$80–$130
$	under $80

All prices are for a standard double room during peak season and not including tax or gratuities. Some inns add a 15% service charge.

Shopping

Newport is a shopper's—but not a bargain hunter's—city. You can find antiques, souvenirs, fine crafts, clothing, and marine supplies in abundance. Antiques are a specialty of South County; more than 30 stores are within an hour's drive of each other. Villages such as Wickford and Watch Hill have unique shops in postcard waterside settings. An upscale shopping mall in downtown Providence has 150 stores and several movie theaters, and the city's ethnic communities sell specialties such as Italian groceries and Hmong (Laotian) clothing. Providence's student population supports secondhand boutiques and funky shops on Wickenden and Thayer streets. The Blackstone Valley contains myriad outlet stores; unlike suburban "factory outlets," these places, often modestly decorated, have great deals and are usually a short walk from the factory floor.

Exploring Rhode Island

The Blackstone Valley region and the capital city of Providence compose the northern portion of Rhode Island. South County to the west and Newport County to the east make up the southern portion of the state. The museums and country roads of the Blackstone Valley make it a good family destination; Providence has history, intellectual and cultural vitality, and great food. Both southerly regions have beaches, boating, and historical sights, with Newport being more historically significant, more upscale, and more crowded.

Numbers in the text and in the margin correspond to numbers on the maps: Central Providence, The Blackstone Valley, South County and Newport County, Block Island, Downtown Newport, and Greater Newport.

Great Itineraries

By car it's less than an hour from any one place in Rhode Island to another. Though the distances are short, the state is densely populated, and getting around its cities and towns can be confusing; it's best to map out your route in advance. In five days, you can visit all four regions of the state, as well as Block Island. On a shorter visit of several days, you can still take in two regions, such as Providence and Newport. Most of the sights in Providence can be seen in one day. The Blackstone Valley will also occupy one day, but during fall foliage season, you will want to spend more time here. Newport has many facets and will require two busy days. South County, with its superb beaches, is generally a relaxing two-day destination.

In Rhode Island, however, just one day can be an unforgettable adventure. A day-long drive from Watch Hill to Newport can include a beach hike at Napatree Point or go-cart rides in Misquamicut, a fishing trip out of Galilee, a tour of a Newport mansion, and dinner at an exquisite French restaurant.

IF YOU HAVE 3 DAYS

Spend a day and a half in the historic waterfront city of ▣ **Newport** ㊴–㊻, and then make the 40-minute drive north to ▣ **Providence** ①–⑯. Though this city's attractions are less packaged than Newport's, they include sophisticated restaurants, historic districts, two large city parks, and an outdoor skating rink.

IF YOU HAVE 5 DAYS

Spend your first three days in ▣ **Newport** ㊴–㊻ and ▣ **Providence** ①–⑯; then take two days to explore South County. With pristine beaches and no shortage of restaurants and inns, South County encourages a take-it-as-it-comes attitude that's just right for summer and fall touring. Shop and soak up the turn-of-the-20th-century elegance of ▣ **Watch Hill** ㉒, and then spend a day on the beach in **Charlestown** ㉔ or **South Kingstown** ㉕ (try **Misquamicut** ㉓ if you prefer beaches with a carnival atmosphere). ▣ **Narragansett** ㉖, which has great beaches and numerous B&Bs, is one option for a second South County night. A day trip to **Block Island** ㉘–㊲ allows enough time to see some of its treasures, but it's easy to linger longer.

When to Tour Rhode Island

The best time to visit Rhode Island is between May and October. Newport hosts several high-profile music festivals in summer; Providence is at its prettiest; and Block Island and the beach towns of South County are in full swing (though not nearly as crowded as Newport). Because of the light traffic and the often gorgeous weather, October is a great time to come to Rhode Island. The colorful fall foliage of the Blackstone Valley is as bright and varied as any in New England.

PROVIDENCE

Once regarded, even by its own residents, as an awkward stepchild of greater Boston (50 mi to the north), Providence has undergone an almost two-decades-long renovation. A once gritty wasteland that emptied out at the end of the workday has metamorphosed into a clean, modern city that entices people to enjoy it in the evenings or make a special trip on the weekend.

The focal point of this new Providence is Waterplace Park, a series of footbridges, walkways, and green spaces that run along both sides of the Providence River, which flows through the heart of downtown. Within walking distance of the park, a convention center and hotel, an outdoor ice rink that's larger than New York's Rockefeller Center rink, and Providence Place, a glittering, upscale shopping center, are additional jewels in the city's crown.

The second half of the 20th century was rough on Providence. The decline of its two main industries, textiles and jewelry, precipitated a population exodus in the 1940s and '50s. In the '60s and '70s, the state's major naval installations were phased out, and the 1990s began with a statewide banking crisis. But the bad news has ended, and New England's third-largest city (with a population of 200,000, behind Boston and Worcester) is starting the 21st century as a renaissance city. In the past decade, rivers have been rerouted and railroad tracks have been put underground. Dilapidated neighborhoods are being rejuvenated and luxury apartments and artists' lofts are sprouting up downtown. Many travelers now prefer the expanding T. F. Green State Airport to Boston's Logan International Airport.

Providence's renaissance isn't all looks. Besides the glitzy new apartment buildings, the shopping center, and hotels and parks, the city has cultivated a more worldly, sophisticated spirit. As a result, it has, in recent years, hosted the NCAA hockey finals, the annual meeting of the International Association of Culinary Professionals, and the National Governors Conference. The city also forged an annual cultural exchange program with Florence, Italy, that brings Italian artwork and artisans to Providence. Time spent courting Hollywood deal makers has resulted in a string of movies being filmed in the city, including *There's Something About Mary* and *Outside Providence,* as well as the popular NBC show *Providence*. With more restaurants per capita than any other major city in America, Providence—home to the Johnson and Wales University Culinary Institute—legitimately lays claim to being one of the nation's best places to get a bite to eat.

Roger Williams founded Providence in October 1635 as a refuge for freethinkers and religious dissenters escaping the dictates of the Puritans of Massachusetts Bay Colony. The city still embraces independent thinking in business, the arts, and academia. Brown University, the Rhode Island School of Design (RISD), and Trinity Square Repertory Company are major forces in New England's intellectual and cultural life. Playing to that strength, Providence is striving to have its once-abandoned downtown (now called Downcity, to erase the connotations of the old downtown) populated by artists and art studios. A state referendum has exempted such artists from income taxes. Such statewide support is not surprising, because improvements here are typically a boon to the rest of the state.

The narrow Providence River cuts through the city north to south. West of the river lies the compact business district. An Italian neighborhood, Federal Hill, pushes west from here along Atwells Ave. To the north you'll see the white-marble capitol. South Main and Benefit streets run parallel to the river, on the East Side. College Hill constitutes the western half of the East Side. At the top of College Hill, the area's primary thoroughfare, Thayer Street, runs north to south. Don't confuse East Providence, a city unto itself, with Providence's East Side.

A Good Walk and Tour

Begin at the **Rhode Island State House** ①, where the south portico looks down over the city of Providence and the farthest reach of Narragansett Bay. After touring the capitol, proceed to Smith Street, at the north end of the State House grounds. Follow the road east to **Roger Williams National Memorial** ②. **Benefit Street** ③ is one block east (up the hill). Walk south on this historic street to the **Museum of Art, Rhode Island School of Design** ④ and the **Providence Athenaeum** ⑤, with its changing exhibits from the library's collections.

Head east (away from the Providence River) on College Street and north (to the left) on Prospect Street to visit the **John Hay Library** ⑥ and its specialized collections. The handsome **Brown University** ⑦ campus is across the street. Walk east on Waterman Street; you can enter the grounds at Brown Street. After you've toured the campus, exit from the gate at George Street (to the south) and turn right, which will take you back to Benefit Street. Walk south for one block, where you'll see the Romanesque **First Unitarian Church of Providence** ⑧. The magnificent **John Brown House** ⑨ is two blocks south of here. From the Brown house, walk one block downhill on Power Street and turn right on South Main Street. Proceed north until you reach the **Market House** ⑩, a remnant of the Colonial economy, and, one block farther north, the Georgian **First Baptist Church in America** ⑪. Turn left at Steeple Street (also called Thomas Street), and you will shortly reach **Waterplace Park and Riverwalk** ⑫, centerpiece of the city's revitalization.

The Italian neighborhood of **Federal Hill** ⑬ and the fun shops of **Wickenden Street** ⑭ are best visited via car or taxi. The stately **Governor Henry Lippit House Museum** ⑮ and the **Museum of Rhode Island History at Aldrich House** ⑯ are four blocks apart in the eastern end of Providence; you'll need a car or taxi to visit them.

TIMING

The timing of the walk from the State House to Waterplace Park will vary greatly depending on how much time you spend at each sight. If you stop for a half hour at most sights and an hour at the RISD Museum of Art, the tour will take about six hours. To see the rest of the sights, add in several hours.

Sights to See

❸ **Benefit Street.** The centerpiece of any visit to Providence is the "mile of History," where a cobblestone sidewalk passes a row of early 18th- and 19th-century candy-color houses crammed shoulder-to-shoulder on a steep hill overlooking downtown. Romantic Benefit Street, with one of the nation's highest concentrations of historic architecture, is a

Central Providence

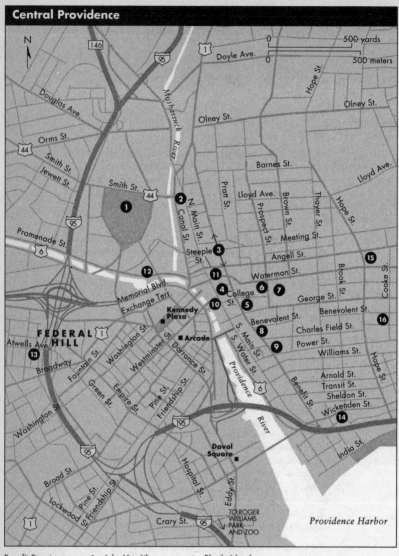

reminder of the wealth brought to Colonial Rhode Island through the triangular trade of slaves, rum, and molasses. The **Providence Preservation Society** (✉ 21 Meeting St., at Benefit St., East Side, ☎ 401/831–7440) distributes maps and pamphlets with self-guided tours.

❼ Brown University. The nation's seventh-oldest college, founded in 1764, is an Ivy League institution with more than 40 academic departments, including a school of medicine. Gothic and Beaux Arts structures dominate the campus, which has been designated a National Historic Landmark. University tours leave weekdays at 10, 11, 1, 3, and 4 from the admissions office, in the Corliss-Brackett House. The university is on College Hill, a neighborhood with handsome 18th- and 19th-century architecture well worth a stroll. Thayer Street is the campus's principal commercial thoroughfare. ✉ *Corliss-Brackett House, 45 Prospect St., East Side,* ☎ *401/863–2378; 401/863–2703 tour information.*

⓭ Federal Hill. You're as likely to hear Italian as English in this neighborhood, which is vital to Providence's culture and sense of self. The stripe down Atwells Avenue is repainted each year in red, white, and green, and a huge *pigna* (pinecone), an Italian symbol of abundance and quality, hangs on an arch soaring over the street. Hardware shops sell boccie sets and grocers sell pastas and Italian pastries. The neighborhood truly shines at the Columbus Weekend Festival (held on the Sunday of that weekend), with music, food stands, and parades.

⓫ First Baptist Church in America. This historic house of worship was built in 1775 for a congregation established in 1638 by Rhode Island founder Roger Williams and his fellow Puritan dissenters. The church, one of the finest examples of Georgian architecture in the United States, has a carved wood interior, a Waterford crystal chandelier, and graceful but austere Ionic columns. ✉ *75 N. Main St., East Side,* ☎ *401/751–2266.* 🎟 *Free; donations accepted.* ☉ *Weekdays 9–noon and 1–3; call ahead on Sat. Guided tours Memorial Day–Columbus Day, self-guided tours Columbus Day–Memorial Day. Sept.–June, Sun. service at 11, guided tour at 12:15; July–Aug., Sun. service at 10, guided tour at 11:15.*

❽ First Unitarian Church of Providence. This Romanesque house of worship made of Rhode Island granite was built in 1816. Its steeple houses a 2,500-pound bell, the largest ever cast in Paul Revere's foundry. ✉ *1 Benevolent St., at Benefit St., East Side,* ☎ *401/421–7970.* 🎟 *Free.* ☉ *Guided tours by appointment; Sun. service at 9:30 and 11.*

⓯ Governor Henry Lippit House Museum. The two-term Rhode Island governor made his fortune selling textiles to both armies during the Civil War, and he spared no expense in building his home, an immaculate Renaissance Revival mansion, in 1863. The floor of the billiard room is made with nine types of inlaid wood; the ceilings are intricately hand-painted (some look convincingly like tiger maple), and the neoclassical chandeliers are cast in bronze. The home was fitted with central heating and electricity, quite an extravagance at the time. ✉ *199 Hope St., East Side,* ☎ *401/453–0688.* 🎟 *$5.* ☉ *Daily. Tours by appointment only.*

★ ❾ John Brown House. John Quincy Adams called it "the most magnificent and elegant private mansion that I have ever seen on this continent." George Washington and other notables also visited the house. Designed by Joseph Brown for his brother in 1786, the three-story Georgian mansion has elaborate woodwork and is filled with decorative art, furniture, silver, and items from the China trade, which is how John Brown made his fortune. In addition to opening trade with China, Brown is famous for his role in the burning of the British customs ship *Gaspee*.

He was also a slave trader: his abolitionist brother, Moses, brought charges against him for illegally engaging in the buying and selling of human lives. John Brown donated the land for what became Brown University. Across the street and open Friday 1–4 is Nightingale House, built by Brown's chief rival in the China trade. ⊠ *52 Power St., East Side,* ☎ *401/331–8575,* WEB *www.rihs.org.* ⌑ *$6.* ☉ *Mar.–Dec., Tues.–Sat. 10–4:30, Sun. noon–4:30; Jan.–Feb., Mon.–Thurs. by appointment, Fri.–Sat. 10–5, Sun. noon–4.*

❻ John Hay Library. Built in 1910 and named for Abraham Lincoln's secretary, "The Hay" houses 11,000 items related to the 16th president. The noncirculating research library, part of **Brown University,** also stores American drama and poetry collections, 500,000 pieces of American sheet music, the Webster Knight Stamp Collection, the letters of horror and science-fiction writer H. P. Lovecraft, military prints, and a world-class collection of toy soldiers. ⊠ *20 Prospect St., East Side,* ☎ *401/863–2146.* ⌑ *Free.* ☉ *Weekdays 9–5.*

❿ Market House. Designed by Joseph Brown and now owned by the Rhode Island School of Design, this brick structure was central to Colonial Providence's trading economy. Tea was burned here in March 1775, and the upper floors were used as barracks for French soldiers during the Revolutionary War. From 1832 to 1878, Market House served as the seat of city government. A plaque shows the height reached by floodwaters during the Great Hurricane of 1938. The building is not open to the public. ⊠ *Market Sq. at S. Main St., Downtown.*

★ ❹ Museum of Art, Rhode Island School of Design. This small college museum is amazingly comprehensive. Many exhibitions, which change annually, are of textiles, a long-standing Rhode Island industry. The museum's permanent holdings include the Abby Aldrich Rockefeller collection of Japanese prints, Paul Revere silver, 18th-century porcelain, and French Impressionist paintings. Popular with children are the 10-ft statue of Buddha and the Egyptian mummy from the Ptolemaic period (circa 300 BC). Admission includes the adjoining **Pendleton House,** a replica of an early 19th-century Providence house. ⊠ *224 Benefit St., East Side,* ☎ *401/454–6500,* WEB *www.risd.edu.* ⌑ *$5.* ☉ *Tues.–Sun. 10–5.*

⑯ Museum of Rhode Island History at Aldrich House. The Federal-style Aldrich House, built in 1822, was given to the Rhode Island Historical Society in 1974 by the heirs of New York financier Winthrop W. Aldrich. The first comprehensive museum about Rhode Island history, it presents rotating exhibits. ⊠ *110 Benevolent St., East Side,* ☎ *401/331–8575,* WEB *www.rihs.org.* ⌑ *$2.* ☉ *Tues.–Fri. 9–5, Sun. 1–4; until 9 PM 3rd Thurs. of month.*

★ ❺ Providence Athenaeum. Established in 1753 and housed in a granite 1838 Greek Revival structure, this is among the oldest lending libraries in the world. The Athenaeum was the center of the intellectual life of old Providence. Here Edgar Allan Poe, visiting Providence to lecture at Brown, met and courted Sarah Helen Whitman, who was said to be the inspiration for his poem "Annabel Lee." The library holds Rhode Island art and artifacts, an original set of *Birds of America* prints by John J. Audubon, and one of the world's best collections of travel literature. Changing exhibits showcase parts of the collection. ⊠ *251 Benefit St., East Side,* ☎ *401/421–6970,* WEB *www.providenceathenaeum.org.* ⌑ *Free.* ☉ *June–Labor Day, Mon.–Thurs. 10–8, Fri. 10–5; Labor Day–May, Mon.–Thurs. 10–8, Fri.–Sat. 10–5, Sun. 1–5.*

❶ Rhode Island State House. Capitols are often planned to inspire awe (or at least respect), and this one, designed by the noted firm of McKim,

Mead & White and erected in 1900, achieves that effect. It has the first unsupported marble dome in the United States (and the fourth largest in the world), which was modeled on St. Peter's Basilica in Rome. The gilded statue *Independent Man* tops the ornate white Georgia marble exterior. Engraved on the south portico is a passage from the Royal Charter of 1663: "To hold forth a lively experiment that a most flourishing civil state may stand and best be maintained with full liberty in religious concernments." In the state room you'll see a full-length portrait of George Washington by Rhode Islander Gilbert Stuart, the same artist who created the likeness on the $1 bill. You'll also see the original parchment charter granted by King Charles to the colony of Rhode Island in 1663 and military accoutrements of Nathaniel Greene, Washington's second-in-command during the Revolutionary War. Booklets are available for self-guided tours, and a gift shop is on the basement level. ⊠ *82 Smith St., Downtown,* ☎ *401/222–2357.* ⊘ *Weekdays 8:30–4:30; guided tours by appointment.*

❷ **Roger Williams National Memorial.** Roger Williams contributed so significantly to the development of the concepts that underpin the Declaration of Independence and the Constitution that the National Park Service dedicated a 4½-acre park to his memory. Displays provide a quick glimpse into the life and times of Rhode Island's founder, who wrote the first-ever book on the languages of the native people of North America. ⊠ *282 N. Main St., Downtown,* ☎ *401/521–7266.* ⊠ *Free.* ⊘ *Daily 9–4:30.*

OFF THE
BEATEN PATH
ROGER WILLIAMS PARK AND ZOO – This beautiful 430-acre Victorian park is immensely popular. You can picnic, feed the ducks in the lakes, ride a pony, or rent a paddleboat or miniature speedboat. At Carousel Village, kids can ride the vintage carousel or a miniature train. The Museum of Natural History and the Cormack Planetarium are also here; the Tennis Center has Rhode Island's only public clay courts. More than 900 animals of 156 different species live at the zoo. Among the attractions are the Tropical Rain Forest Pavilion, the African Plains and Australasia exhibits, and an open-air aviary. To get here from downtown, take I–95 south to U.S. 1 south (Elmwood Avenue); the park entrance will be the first left turn. ⊠ *Elmwood Ave., South Providence,* ☎ *401/785–3510 zoo; 401/785–9457 museum.* ⊠ *$6.* ⊘ *Zoo daily 9–5 (until 4 in winter), museum daily 10–5.*

⑫ **Waterplace Park and Riverwalk.** Romantic Venetian-style footbridges, cobblestone walkways, and an amphitheater encircling a tidal pond set the tone at this 4-acre tract, which has won national and international design awards. The Riverwalk passes the junction of three rivers—the Woonasquatucket, Providence, and Moshassuck—a nexus of the shipping trade during the city's early years. It's the site of the popular Waterfire, a multimedia installation featuring music and nearly 100 burning braziers that rise from the water and are tended from boats; the dusk-to-midnight Waterfire attract 500,000 visitors annually and are held several times each year. The amphitheater hosts free concerts and plays. Ask about upcoming events at the visitor information center, in the clock tower. ⊠ *Boat House Clock Tower, 2 American Express Way, Downtown,* ☎ *401/751–1177.* ⊘ *Daily 10–4.*

⑭ **Wickenden Street.** The main artery in the Fox Point district, a working-class Portuguese neighborhood that is undergoing gentrification, Wickenden Street is chockablock with antiques stores, galleries, and trendy cafés. Professors, artists, and students are among the newer residents here. Many of the houses along Wickenden, Transit, Gano, and nearby streets are still painted the pastel colors of Portuguese homes.

Dining

American/Casual

$$–$$$ ✕ **Union Station Brewery.** The historic brick building that houses this brewpub was once the freight house for the Providence Train Station. You can wash down a tasty chipotle-glazed pork quesadilla, an old-fashioned chicken potpie, or ale-batter fish-and-chips with a pint of Providence cream ale or one of several other fine beers brewed here. ⌧ *36 Exchange Terr., Downtown,* ☎ *401/274–2739,* WEB *www. johnharvards.com. AE, D, DC, MC, V.*

Contemporary

$$–$$$$ ✕ **The Gatehouse.** A redbrick cottage houses this much-praised restaurant, where its dining room overlooks the serene Seekonk River. Soft candlelight and polished dark-wood furnishings make it feel elegant and romantic. Original works by the best area artists add to a sense of sophistication. Chef Mark Garofalo's menu stretches across the globe, from Asian-duck spring rolls to New Orleans–style barbecue shrimp to blackened yellowfin tuna to a simple American meat loaf. ⌧ *4 Richmond Sq., East Side,* ☎ *401/521–9229,* WEB *www.gatehouserestaurant.com. Reservations essential. AE, DC, MC, V. No lunch.*

$$$ ✕ **Neath's.** The large, open dining room of this converted warehouse is one reason why Neath's is a place to be seen. Views of the Providence River are nice, too, but it's the food that has made this the trendiest restaurant in town. Seafood with Asian accents is the primary focus, such as crisp Cambodian spring rolls with bean sprouts and grilled shrimp, and roasted sea bass with Chinese black bean marinade and jasmine rice. Don't pass up the chocolate-stuffed fried wontons for dessert. ⌧ *262 S. Water St., Downtown,* ☎ *401/751–3700,* WEB *www. neaths.com. AE, MC, V. Closed Mon. No lunch.*

$$–$$$ ✕ **Rue de l'Espoir.** At this homey, longtime Providence favorite, dishes are designed to be fun. A few of the many eclectic choices include a lobster Madeira crepe, Szechuan duck quesadillas, and Caribbean-spiced grilled pork porterhouse chops. Wide-plank pine floors, an ornate tin ceiling, and wooden booths set the mood in the dining room. The spacious barroom, where many locals prefer to dine, has a mural in bright pastels and a fine selection of jazz CDs. Breakfast is served on weekdays, brunch on weekends. ⌧ *99 Hope St., East Side,* ☎ *401/ 751–8890. AE, D, DC, MC, V. Closed Mon.*

French

$$$–$$$$ ✕ **Pot au Feu.** As night falls, business-driven downtown Providence
★   clears out, and this bastion of French country cuisine lights up. For more than a quarter century the chefs here have worked to perfect the basics, such as pâté du foie gras, beef bourguignonne, and potatoes au gratin. Such classically rendered dishes—and a distinctive list of French wines—have inspired a devoted corps of regulars. The dining experience is more casual at the downstairs Bistro than at the upstairs Salon. ⌧ *44 Custom House St., Downtown,* ☎ *401/273–8953. AE, DC, MC, V. Salon closed Sun.–Mon.*

Indian

$–$$ ✕ **India.** Mango chicken curry and swordfish kabobs are two of the entrées at this downtown restaurant filled with Oriental rugs, colorful paintings, and plants. India is known for its freshly made breads, including *paratha,* wheat bread cooked on a grill and stuffed with various fillings. ⌧ *123 Dorrance St., Downtown,* ☎ *401/278–2000. AE, MC, V.*

Italian

$$$ ✕ **Al Forno.** Rhode Island School of Design graduates George Germon
★   and Johanne Killeen's restaurant cemented the city's reputation as a

culinary center in New England. Try a wood-grilled pizza as an appetizer, followed by roasted clams and spicy sausage in a tomato broth, or charcoal-seared tournedos of beef with mashed potatoes (called "dirty steak" by regulars) and onion rings. Your dessert could be crepes with apricot puree or a fresh cranberry tart. Meals are served both upstairs, in the rustic dining room, and downstairs, in a room with white marble flooring. ⊠ *577 S. Main St., Fox Point,* ☏ *401/273–9760. Reservations not accepted. AE, DC, MC, V. Closed Sun.–Mon. No lunch.*

$$$ ✗ **L'Epicureo.** One of Providence's most refined restaurants was founded as half of a Federal Hill butcher shop called Joe's Quality. Joe's daughter Rozann and son-in-law Tom Buckner transformed the former market into an Italian bistro that has won high marks for its wood-grilled steaks, veal chops, and such pasta dishes as fettuccine tossed with arugula, garlic, and lemon. ⊠ *238 Atwells Ave., Federal Hill,* ☏ *401/454–8430. AE, D, DC, MC, V. Closed Sun.–Mon. No lunch.*

$$ ✗ **Angelo's Civita Farnese.** In the heart of Little Italy, lively (even boisterous) Angelo's is a family-run place with old-world charm. Locals come here for its good-size portions of fresh, simply prepared pasta. ⊠ *141 Atwells Ave., Federal Hill,* ☏ *401/621–8171. Reservations not accepted. No credit cards.*

Japanese

$–$$ ✗ **Tokyo Restaurant.** New carpeting and a fresh coat of paint may be in order at Tokyo, but the Japanese cuisine served here is the best in the state. Choose traditional or American seating—or take a stool at the sushi bar, where local fish such as tuna, mackerel, and eel are prepared alongside red snapper and fish from points beyond. The designer rolls include beef, squid, duck, and seaweed. Bring your own wine or beer. ⊠ *123 Wickenden St., Fox Point,* ☏ *401/331–5330. AE, D, MC, V.*

Seafood

$$$ ✗ **Providence Oyster Bar.** In a neighborhood long known as the place for Italian food, this seafood restaurant is a refreshing alternative. In a dining room handsomely turned out with polished wood floors, brick walls, and a tin ceiling, the raw bar serves more than a dozen varieties of fresh oysters from all over the country, including several from New England waters. For entrées, try plantain-encrusted swordfish in a creole sauce or salmon au poivre in a brandy cream sauce. ⊠ *283 Atwells Ave., Federal Hill,* ☏ *401/272–8866. AE, DC, MC, V. No lunch weekends.*

Steak

$$$ ✗ **Capital Grille.** Dry-aged beef is the star, but lobster and fish also highlight the menu at this cavernous steak house. The mashed potatoes, cottage fries, and Caesar salads are served in portions that will sate even the heartiest appetite. Leather, brass, mahogany, oil portraits, a mounted wooden canoe, and Bloomberg News ticking away in the barroom lend this establishment the feel of an opulent men's club. ⊠ *1 Cookson Pl., Downtown,* ☏ *401/521–5600,* 🕸 *www.thecapitalgrille.com. AE, D, DC, MC, V. No lunch weekends.*

Lodging

$$–$$$$ ▦ **Courtyard by Marriott Providence.** The newest of Providence's hotels is housed in a seven-story redbrick building, carefully designed to match the other buildings in its historic Union Station Plaza location. Nearly all of the oversizerooms in tones of green with mauve accents have views of either the Statehouse, Waterplace Park or the Financial District. The hotel is just steps away from the Providence Place mall. ⊠ *32 Exchange Terr., Downtown, 02903,* ☏ *401/272–1191 or 800/*

321–2211, FAX 401/272–1416, WEB *www.marriott.com. 210 rooms, 6 suites. Restaurant, indoor pool, gym, hot tub, Internet, meeting rooms. AE, D, DC, MC, V.*

$$–$$$$ 🏨 **Providence Marriott.** This chain hotel near the capitol lacks the old-fashioned grandeur of the Providence Biltmore, but it has all the modern conveniences. Tones of mauve and green grace the good-size rooms. The Bluefin Grille restaurant specializes in local seafood prepared with a French flair. ⊠ *Charles and Orms Sts. near Exit 23 off I–95, Downtown, 02904, ☎ 401/272–2400 or 800/937–7768, FAX 401/273–2686, WEB www.marriott.com. 351 rooms, 6 suites. Restaurant, 2 pools (1 indoor), health club, sauna, meeting rooms. AE, D, DC, MC, V.*

$$$ 🏨 **Providence Biltmore.** The Biltmore, completed in 1922, has a sleek Art Deco exterior, an external glass elevator with delightful views of Providence, a grand ballroom, and an Italian restaurant that rivals the best in the city. The personal attentiveness of its staff, with its European-style concierge system, the downtown location, and modern amenities make this hotel one of the city's best. ⊠ *Kennedy Plaza, Dorrance and Washington Sts., Downtown, 02903, ☎ 401/421–0700 or 800/294–7709, FAX 401/455–3040, WEB www.providencebiltmore.com. 84 rooms, 157 suites. Restaurant, café, health club, meeting room. AE, D, DC, MC, V.*

$$$ 🏨 **Westin Providence.** The multiturreted 25-story Westin towers over
★ Providence's compact downtown, connected by skywalks to the city's gleaming convention center and the Providence Place mall. Its rooms have reproduction period furniture, and half have king-size beds; many have views of the city. The redbrick hotel's Agora restaurant has a superb wine cellar. ⊠ *1 W. Exchange St., Downtown, 02903, ☎ 401/598–8000 or 800/937–8461, FAX 401/598–8200, WEB www.westin.com. 364 rooms, 22 suites. 2 restaurants, pool, health club, hot tub, 2 bars, meeting room. AE, D, DC, MC, V.*

$$–$$$ 🏨 **Old Court Bed & Breakfast.** This three-story Italianate inn on historic Benefit Street was built in 1863 as a rectory. Antique furniture, richly colored wallpaper, and memorabilia throughout the house reflect the best of 19th-century style. The comfortable, spacious rooms have high ceilings and chandeliers; most have nonworking marble fireplaces, and some have views of the statehouse and downtown. ⊠ *144 Benefit St., East Side, 02903, ☎ 401/751–2002, FAX 401/272–4830, WEB www.oldcourt.com. 10 rooms, 1 suite. AE, D, MC, V. BP.*

$$ 🏨 **State House Inn.** The beautifully restored rooms of this inviting, classy
★ inn near the statehouse are furnished with Shaker- or Colonial-style pieces, and a few have working fireplaces. Some rooms in the 1880s Colonial Revival home are on the small side. The neighborhood isn't great for a late-night stroll, but convenient parking is available. ⊠ *43 Jewett St., Downtown, 02903, ☎ 401/351–6111, FAX 401/351–4261, WEB www.providence-inn.com. 10 rooms. No smoking. AE, D, MC, V. BP.*

$–$$ 🏨 **C. C. Ledbetter's.** Innkeeper C. C. Ledbetter's mansard-roof 1770 home has a vibrant, welcoming interior and a great location on College Hill, the city's historic East Side. Lively art, photographs, quilts, and a shrewd blend of contemporary furnishings and antiques fill the place. The rooms at this B&B across from the John Brown House are reasonably priced, making it a favorite of the parents of Brown University students. ⊠ *326 Benefit St., East Side, 02903, ☎ FAX 401/351–4699. 5 rooms, 2 with bath. D, MC, V. CP.*

Nightlife and the Arts

For events listings, consult the daily *Providence Journal* and the weekly *Providence Phoenix* (free in restaurants and bookstores). Brown University and the Rhode Island School of Design often present free lectures and performances.

Nightlife

BARS

The sub-street-level **Custom House Tavern** (✉ 36 Weybosset St., Downtown, ☎ 401/751–3630) is a convivial gathering place, with a wooden bar stretching along most of one side of the narrow room. Fashionable with professionals, **Hot Club** (✉ 575 S. Water St., Fox Point, ☎ 401/861–9007) is where the waterside scenes in the movie *There's Something About Mary* were shot. **Oliver's** (✉ 83 Benevolent St., East Side, ☎ 401/272–8795), a popular hangout for Brown students that serves good pub food, has three pool tables. **Snookers** (✉ 145 Clifford St., Jewelry District, ☎ 401/351–7665) is a stylish billiard hall in the Jewelry District. Through a double doorway at the rear of the billiard room is a '50s-style lounge where food is served.

MUSIC CLUBS

AS220 (✉ 111 Empire St., Downtown, ☎ 401/831–9327) is a gallery and performance space; the musical styles run the gamut from techno-pop, hip-hop, and jazz to folk music. Talent shows and comedy nights are also scheduled. The **Call** (✉ 15 Elbow St., Jewelry District, ☎ 401/751–2255), a large blues bar, hosts such top local groups as Roomful of Blues. In the same building and under the same management as the Call is the **Century Lounge,** which hosts progressive bands. Proclaiming itself "Rhode Island's number one reason to party," the **Complex** (✉ 180 Pine St., Jewelry District, ☎ 401/751–4263) houses four different clubs, the most popular being for swing dancers. **Gerardo's Alternative Dance Club** (✉ 1 Franklin Sq., Downtown, ☎ 401/274–5560) is a popular gay and lesbian disco. The **Living Room** (✉ 23 Rathbone St., Downtown, ☎ 401/521–5200) presents live entertainment nightly, often by prominent local blues musicians. **Lupo's Heartbreak Hotel** (✉ 239 Westminster St., Downtown, ☎ 401/272–5876), a roadhouse-style nightclub, books mainly national jazz and blues acts, with a smattering of both contemporary and classic rock.

The Arts

FILM

The **Cable Car Cinema** (✉ 204 S. Main St., Downtown, ☎ 401/272–3970) is on the musty side, but the theater showcases a fine slate of alternative and foreign flicks. You sit on couches rather than seats, and street performers entertain prior to most shows. An espresso café substitutes for the traditional soda-and-popcorn concession. The **Providence Place** mall (✉ 1 Providence Pl., Downtown, ☎ 401/270–1000), near the Westin, has an IMAX theater and a multiscreen cinema.

GALLERY TOUR

The **ArTrolley** runs free tours of 20 galleries and museums on the third Thursday of every month. (✉ One Citizens Plaza, Downtown, ☎ 401/751–2628 schedule and list of galleries).

MUSIC

Rock bands and country acts occasionally perform at the 14,500-seat **Providence Civic Center** (✉ 1 LaSalle Sq., Downtown, ☎ 401/331–6700). The **Providence Performing Arts Center** (✉ 220 Weybosset St., Downtown, ☎ 401/421–2787), a 3,200-seat theater and concert hall that opened in 1928, hosts touring Broadway shows, concerts, and other large-scale happenings. Its lavish interior contains painted frescoes, Art Deco chandeliers, bronze moldings, and marble floors. The **Rhode Island Philharmonic** (☎ 401/831–3123) presents 18 concerts at Veterans Memorial Auditorium between October and May. **Veterans**

Memorial Auditorium (⊠ 69 Brownell St., Downtown, ☎ 401/222–3150) hosts concerts, plays, children's theater, and ballet.

THEATER

Brown University (⊠ Leeds Theatre, 77 Waterman St., East Side, ☎ 401/863–2838) mounts productions of contemporary, sometimes avant-garde, works as well as classics. **Sandra Feinstein-Gamm Theatre** (⊠ 31 Elbow St., Jewelry District, ☎ 401/831–2919), an ambitious offshoot of Trinity Square Repertory, presents innovative versions of classic and contemporary plays in a tiny, 75-seat space. **Trinity Square Repertory Company** (⊠ 201 Washington St., Downtown, ☎ 401/351–4242), one of New England's best theater companies, presents plays in the renovated Majestic movie house. The varied season generally includes classics, foreign plays, new works by groundbreaking young playwrights, and an annual version of *A Christmas Carol*.

Outdoor Activities and Sports

Basketball

The **Providence College Friars** play Big East basketball at the Providence Civic Center (⊠ 1 LaSalle Sq., Downtown, ☎ 401/331–6700 events information; 401/331–2211 tickets).

Biking

The best biking in the Providence area is along the 14½-mi **East Bay Bicycle Path,** which hugs the Narragansett Bay shore from India Point Park through four towns before it ends in Independence Park in Bristol. **Esta's Too** (⊠ 257 Thayer St., East Side, ☎ 401/831–2651), which rents bicycles, is near the East Bay Bicycle Path.

Boating

Prime boating areas include the Providence River, the Seekonk River, and Narragansett Bay. The **Narragansett Boat Club** (⊠ River Rd., East Side, ☎ 401/272–1838) has information about local boating.

Football

The **Brown Bears** (☎ 401/863–2773) of Brown University play at Brown Stadium (⊠ Elmgrove and Sessions Sts., East Side).

Golf

The 18-hole, par-72 **Triggs Memorial Golf Course** (⊠ 1533 Chalkstone Ave., North Providence, ☎ 401/521–8460) has lengthy fairways. The greens fee ranges from $25 to $30; an optional cart costs $24.

Hockey

The **Brown Bears** (☎ 401/863–2773) play high-energy hockey at Meehan Auditorium (⊠ 235 Hope St., East Side). The **Providence Bruins** (☎ 401/331–6700), a farm team of the Boston Bruins, play at the Providence Civic Center (⊠ 1 LaSalle Sq., Downtown).

Ice-skating

The popular **Fleet Skating Center** (⊠ Kennedy Plaza, Downtown, ☎ 401/331–5544), an outdoor ice rink, is open October–April, daily 10–8. Skates are available for rent.

Jogging

Three-mile-long **Blackstone Boulevard** draws joggers with its wide, level, and tree-lined trail.

Shopping

Antiques

Wickenden Street contains many antiques stores and several art galleries. **CAV** (⊠ 14 Imperial Pl., Jewelry District, ☎ 401/751–9164) is a large restaurant, bar, and coffeehouse (with music Friday and Saturday nights) in a revamped factory space. It sells fine rugs, tapestries, prints, portraits, and antiques. **Tilden-Thurber** (⊠ 292 Westminster St., Downtown, ☏ 401/272–3200) carries high-end Colonial- and Victorian-era furniture, antiques, and estate jewelry.

Art Galleries

The **Alaimo Gallery** (⊠ 301 Wickenden St., Fox Point, ☏ 401/421–5360) specializes in hand-colored engravings, magazine and playbill covers, political cartoons, antique prints and posters, and box labels. **JRS Fine Art** (⊠ 218 Wickenden St., Fox Point, ☏ 401/331–4380) sells works by national, regional, and Rhode Island artists. The **Peaceable Kingdom** (⊠ 116 Ives St., East Side, ☏ 401/351–3472) stocks folk art, including Native American crafts, Haitian paintings, Oriental rugs, kilims, and Hmong story cloths (from Laos).

Food

Constantino's Venda Ravioli (⊠ 265 Atwells Ave., Federal Hill, ☏ 401/421–9105) sells imported and homemade Italian foods. **Roma Gourmet Foods** (⊠ 310 Atwells Ave., Federal Hill, ☏ 401/331–8620) sells homemade pasta, bread, pizza, pastries, and meats and cheeses. **Tony's Colonial** (⊠ 311 Atwells Ave., Federal Hill, ☏ 401/621–8675), a superb Italian grocery and deli, stocks freshly prepared foods.

Malls

America's first shopping mall is the **Arcade** (⊠ 65 Weybosset St., Downtown, ☏ 401/598–1199), built in 1828. A National Historic Landmark, this graceful Greek Revival building has three tiers of shops and restaurants. Expect the unusual at **Copacetic Rudely Elegant Jewelry** (⊠ The Arcade, 65 Weybosset St., Downtown, ☏ 401/273–0470), which sells the work of more than 130 diverse artists. The **Game Keeper** (⊠ The Arcade, 65 Weybosset St., Downtown, ☏ 401/351–0362) sells board games, puzzles, and gadgets. Downtown's upscale **Providence Place** (⊠ 1 Providence Pl., at Francis and Hayes Sts., Downtown, ☏ 401/270–1000), with 150 shops, is anchored by Filene's, Lord & Taylor, and Nordstrom.

Maps

The **Map Center** (⊠ 671 N. Main St., East Side, ☏ 401/421–2184) carries maps of all types and nautical charts.

Providence A to Z

To research prices, get advice from other travelers, and book travel arrangements, visit www.fodors.com.

BUS TRAVEL TO AND FROM PROVIDENCE
Rhode Island Public Transit Authority buses run around town and to T. F. Green State Airport; the main terminal is in Kennedy Plaza. The fares range from $1 to $3.

➤ Bus Information: **Rhode Island Public Transit Authority** (RIPTA; ☏ 401/781–9400; 800/244–0444 in Rhode Island). Kennedy Plaza (⊠ Washington and Dorrance Sts., Downtown).

CAR TRAVEL
Overnight parking is not allowed on Providence streets, and during the day it can be difficult to find curbside parking, especially downtown and on Federal and College hills. The Westin Providence downtown has a large parking garage; parking is also available at the Providence Place Mall. To get from T. F. Green Airport to downtown Providence, take I–95 north to Exit 22.

EMERGENCIES

➤ Hospital: **Rhode Island Hospital** (⊠ 593 Eddy St., South Providence, ☎ 401/444–4000).

➤ 24-Hour Pharmacy: **Brooks Pharmacy** (⊠ 1200 N. Main St., ☎ 401/272–3048).

TAXIS

Fares are $2 at the flag drop, then $2 per mile. The ride from the airport to downtown takes about 15 minutes and costs about $22.

➤ Taxi Companies: **Airport Taxi** (☎ 401/737–2868). **Checker Cab** (☎ 401/273–2222). **Economy Cab** (☎ 401/944–6700). **Yellow Cab** (☎ 401/941–1122).

TOURS

Providence Preservation Society publishes a walking-tour guidebook ($2.50) to historic Benefit Street and leads house tours on the second weekend in June.

➤ Contact: **Providence Preservation Society** (⊠ 21 Meeting St., East Side, ☎ 401/831–7440, WEB www.providencepreservation.org).

VISITOR INFORMATION

➤ Tourist Information: **Greater Providence Convention and Visitors Bureau** (⊠ 1 W. Exchange St., Downtown, 02903, ☎ 401/274–1636, WEB www.providencecvb.com).

THE BLACKSTONE VALLEY

New England today calls up images of rural charm, but 200 years ago the region was being transformed by industry into the young nation's manufacturing powerhouse. Much of that industry is gone now, but its heritage remains to be explored. The 45-mi-long Blackstone River, a federally designated American Heritage River, runs from Worcester, Massachusetts, to Pawtucket, Rhode Island, where its power was first harnessed in 1790, setting off America's Industrial Revolution. Along the river and its tributaries are many old mill villages and towns separated by woods and farmland. Pawtucket and Woonsocket grew into large cities in the 1800s when a system of canals, and later railroads, became distribution channels for local industry, which attracted a steady flow of French, Irish, and Eastern European immigrants.

This area in the northern portion of the state is named for William Blackstone, who in 1628 became the first European to settle in Boston. In 1635, having grown weary of the ways of the Puritan settlers who had become his neighbors, this Anglican clergyman built a new home in what was wilderness and is now called Rhode Island. His cabin and his writings were destroyed in 1675, during the yearlong King Philip's War, a devastating conflict between European settlers and Native Americans.

In 1986 the National Park Service designated the Blackstone Valley a National Heritage Corridor. A planned bike path, to be completed in 2005, will run from Worcester to the Narragansett Bay, and the Museum of Work and Culture in Woonsocket relates the region's history through multimedia exhibits. The valley is gradually emerging as a destination for people interested in antiques, architecture, country drives, and fall foliage, as well as history. The visitor center in Pawtucket is a great place to begin a tour of the region.

Pawtucket

⑰ *5 mi north of Providence.*

In Algonquian, "petuket" (similar to standard Rhode Island pronunciation of the city's name, accent on the second syllable) means "water falls." A small village was established at the falls in 1670 by Joseph Jenks Jr., who considered the area a prime spot for an iron forge. When Samuel Slater arrived 120 years later, he was delighted to find a corps of skilled mechanics ready to assist him in his dream of organizing America's first factory system. Many older buildings were torn down as part of urban renewal projects in the 1970s, but significant portions of the city's history have been preserved and are worth a visit.

The **Blackstone Valley Visitor Center,** across the street from Slater Mill, has information kiosks, maps, and hospitable tourism consultants. A large screening room shows documentaries on the region. ⊠ *175 Main St.,* ☎ *401/724–2200 or 800/454–2882,* WEB *www.tourblackstone.com.* ☞ *Free.* ⊙ *Daily 9–5.*

In 1793, Samuel Slater and two Providence merchants built the first factory in America to produce cotton yarn from water-powered machines. The yellow clapboard **Slater Mill Historic Site** houses classrooms, a theater, and machinery illustrating the conversion of raw cotton to finished cloth. A 16,000-pound waterwheel powers an operational 19th-century machine shop; the shop and the adjacent 1758 Sylvanus Brown House are open to the public. ⊠ *67 Roosevelt Ave.,* ☎ *401/725–8638,* WEB *www.slatermill.org.* ☞ *$6.50.* ⊙ *June–Nov., Mon.–Sat. 10–5, Sun. 1–5; Mar.–May, weekends 1–5; Dec.–Feb., weekends, 1 PM tour only. Guided tours daily; call for times.*

Slater Memorial Park stretches along Ten Mile River. Within this stately grounds are picnic tables, tennis courts, playgrounds, a river walk, and two historic sites. Eight generations of Daggetts lived in the **Daggett House,** Pawtucket's oldest home, which was built in 1685. Among the 17th-century antiques on display are bedspreads owned by Samuel Slater. The **Loof Carousel,** built by Charles I. D. Loof, has 42 horses, three dogs, and a lion, camel, and giraffe that are the earliest examples of the Danish immigrant's work. ⊠ *Newport Ave./Rte. 1A,* ☎ *401/728–0500 park information.* ☞ *Park and carousel free, Daggett House $2.* ⊙ *Park daily dawn–dusk. Daggett House June–Sept., weekends 2–5. Carousel July–Labor Day, daily 10–5; late Apr.–June and Labor Day–Columbus Day, weekends 10–5.*

Dining

$–$$ ✕ **Modern Diner.** This 1941 Sterling Streamline eatery—a classic from the heyday of the stainless-steel diner—was the first diner to be listed on the National Register of Historic Places. The Modern serves standard diner fare and some specialty items, including lobster Benedict and French toast with custard sauce and berries. ⊠ *364 East Ave.,* ☎ *401/726–8390. No credit cards. No dinner.*

Outdoor Activities and Sports

The **Pawtucket Red Sox,** the Triple-A farm team of baseball's Boston Red Sox, play at McCoy Stadium (⊠ 1 Columbus Ave., ☎ 401/724–7300).

Woonsocket

⑱ *10 mi north of Pawtucket, 15 mi north of Providence.*

Rhode Island's sixth-largest city (population 40,000) was settled in the late 17th century, inhabited by a sawmill and Quaker farmers for its

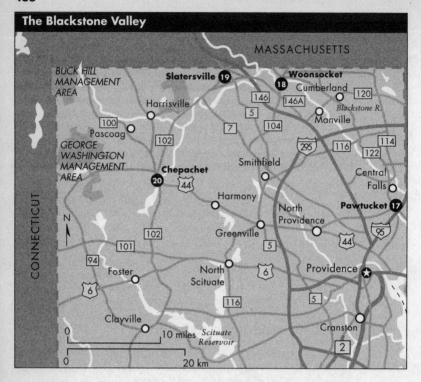

MASSACHUSETTS

BUCK HILL
MANAGEMENT
AREA

Slatersville **19**

Woonsocket **18**
Cumberland

Harrisville

146

146A

Blackstone R.

120

100

5

Manville

Pascoag

GEORGE
WASHINGTON
MANAGEMENT
AREA

102

7

104

295

116

114

122

Chepachet **20**
44

Smithfield

Central
Falls

CONNECTICUT

Harmony

North
Providence

Pawtucket **17**

N

102

Greenville

5

44

95

101

94

6

Foster

North
Scituate

6

Providence

116

5

Clayville

Scituate
Reservoir

Cranston

0   10 miles

2

0   20 km

first 100 years. A steep hill on the northern end of the city looks down
on the Blackstone River, which makes a dozen turns in its 5-mi course
through Woonsocket. The river's flow spawned textile mills that made
Woonsocket a thriving community in the 19th and early 20th centuries;
today a museum is dedicated to this industrial heritage. Manufacturing plants remain the city's leading employers.

Multimedia and more traditional exhibits at the **Museum of Work and
Culture** examine the lives of American factory workers and owners during the Industrial Revolution. The genesis of the textile workers' union
is described, as are the events that led to the National Textile Strike of
1934. A model of the triple-decker (a three-family tenement building)
demonstrates the practicality behind what was once the region's pre-
eminent style of home. Youngsters may be interested in presentations
about child labor. ⊠ *42 S. Main St.,* ☎ *401/769–9675.* ⌨ *$5.* ☉ *Week-
days 9:30–4, Sat. 10–5, Sun. 1–5.*

Dining and Lodging

$–$$ ✕ **Ye Olde English Fish & Chips.** Fresh fried fish and potatoes have been
served at this statewide institution for generations. Inside is unassuming—wood paneling and booths—so it must be the inexpensive and
consistently excellent food, served in red plastic baskets, that has kept
folks returning to this joint since 1922. ⊠ *Market Sq. at S. Main St.,*
☎ *401/762–3637. No credit cards. Closed Sun.–Mon.*

$–$$ 🏠 **Pillsbury House.** Stately Prospect Street stretches along the crest of
the ridge north of the Blackstone River; its mansions, like the mansard-
roof Pillsbury House, were built by mill owners in the late 1800s. The
common room has a baby grand piano, a parquet floor, and a fireplace with a maple hearth. The two guest rooms on the second floor
are furnished in Victorian style, with antiques, plants, high beds, and
fringed lamp shades; the third-floor suite favors a more rustic-coun-

try aesthetic. ⊠ *341 Prospect St., 02895,* ☎ *800/205–4112,* ☎ FAX *401/766–7983,* WEB *www.pillsburyhouse.com. 2 rooms, 1 suite. AE, D, DC, MC, V. BP.*

Nightlife and the Arts

The impressive entertainment lineup at **Chan's Fine Oriental Dining** (⊠ 267 Main St., ☎ 401/765–1900) includes blues, jazz, and folk performers. Reservations are essential; ticket prices range from $10 to $24.

Shopping

Storefront renovations have made for much better shopping along Main Street. **Main Street Antiques** (⊠ 32 Main St., ☎ 401/762–0805) is a good place to browse.

Slatersville

⑲ *3 mi west of Woonsocket.*

Samuel Slater's brother, John, purchased a small sawmill and blacksmith shop along the Branch River and turned the area (now part of the town of North Smithfield) into America's first company town, Slatersville, beginning in 1807. With their factory well removed from population centers, Slater and his partners built homes, a town green, a Congregational church, and a general store for their workers. The village, west of the junction of Routes 102 and 146, has been well preserved, and though it doesn't have many amenities for visitors, it is a fine place for an afternoon stroll.

Dining

$ ✕ **Wright's Farm Restaurant.** Chicken served family-style—all-you-can-eat bread, salad, roast chicken, pasta, and potatoes—a northern Rhode Island tradition, was born of a Woonsocket social club's need to feed many people efficiently. More than a dozen restaurants in the Blackstone Valley serve this food combo; Wright's Farm, the largest, dishes up 300 tons of chicken each year. ⊠ *84 Inman Rd., Burrillville, 2 mi west of Slatersville off Rte. 102,* ☎ *401/769–2856. No credit cards. Closed Mon.–Tues. No lunch.*

Chepachet

⑳ *12 mi south of Slatersville, 20 mi northwest of Providence.*

Antiques shops and other businesses line Main Street in the village of Chepachet, at the intersection of Routes 44 and 102 in the township of Glocester. The setting feels so much out of a storybook—it resembles a 19th-century stagecoach stop, with rustic wooden buildings along a tree-lined main street—you might find it jolting to see paved roads and automobiles upon exiting its many emporiums. **Snowhurst Farm** (⊠ 421 Chopmist Hill Rd., ☎ 401/568–8900) grows 16 varieties of apples that you pick yourself for 55¢ per pound, from late August until about Columbus Day. This working farm has cattle, horses, and sheep. From Chepachet, drive 2 mi south on U.S. 44 to Route 102; the farm is 2 mi south of the intersection.

Dining

$$ ✕ **Stagecoach Tavern.** Formerly a stagecoach stop between Providence and Hartford, this establishment serves hearty meat dishes and pastas at reasonable prices. Locals hang out at the casual bar. ⊠ *1157 Main St.,* ☎ *401/568–2275. AE, D, MC, V.*

Shopping

Established in 1809, **Brown & Hopkins Country Store** (⊠ 79 Main St., ☎ 401/568–4830) has been in operation longer than any other country store in America. Crafts, penny candy, a deli, antiques, and a pot-bellied stove await you.

Harold's (✉ 1191 Main St., ☎ 401/568–6030) specializes in antique lamps. The **Lion and the Swan** (✉ 1187 Main St., ☎ 401/568–1800) carries antique dark-wood furniture and dolls. **Old Chepachet Village** (✉ 11 Money Hill Rd., ☎ 401/568–3511) houses 30 crafts and antiques stores in a 10,000-square-ft building.

OFF THE BEATEN PATH	**BUCK HILL MANAGEMENT AREA** – Tucked away in the remote northwest corner of the state, 7 mi northwest of Chepachet, this area supports waterfowl, songbirds, deer, pheasant, owls, foxes, and wild turkeys. Hiking trails traverse the preserve and cross into Connecticut and Massachusetts. ✉ *Buck Hill Rd. off Rte. 100 (Wallum Lake Rd.)*, ☎ *401/222–2632.* ☒ *Free.* ☉ *Daily, from ½ hr before sunrise to ½ hr after sunset.*

Blackstone Valley A to Z

To research prices, get advice from other travelers, and book travel arrangements, visit www.fodors.com.

BUS TRAVEL
Rhode Island Public Transit Authority buses travel from Providence's Kennedy Plaza to towns in the Blackstone Valley.
➤ BUS INFORMATION: **Rhode Island Public Transit Authority** (RIPTA; ☎ 401/781–9400; 800/244–0444 in Rhode Island).

CAR TRAVEL
Pawtucket is north of Providence on I–95. To reach Woonsocket, take Route 146 northwest from Providence and head north at Route 99; from Woonsocket, take Route 146A west to Route 102 to get to Slatersville. Chepachet is southwest of Slatersville on Route 102 and west of Providence on U.S. 44.

The easiest way to explore the Blackstone Valley is by car, though a good map is needed because few signs exist. *Street Atlas Rhode Island* is available at most gas stations.

EMERGENCIES
➤ HOSPITAL: **Landmark Medical Center** (✉ 115 Cass Ave., Woonsocket, ☎ 401/769–4100).

TOURS
Blackstone Valley Explorer is a 49-passenger, canopied riverboat conducting various tours of the Blackstone River. Tours are given from April to October and depart from a number of landings along the river.
➤ CONTACT: *Blackstone Valley Explorer* (✉ 171 Main St., Pawtucket, ☎ 800/619–2628).

VISITOR INFORMATION
The Blackstone Valley Tourism Council operates the Blackstone Valley Visitor Center, a good starting point for northern Rhode Island. A complete list of factory stores is also available.
➤ TOURIST INFORMATION: **Blackstone Valley Tourism Council** (✉ 171 Main St., Pawtucket 02860, ☎ 401/724–2200 or 800/454–2882, WEB www.tourblackstone.com). **Northern Rhode Island Chamber of Commerce** (✉ 6 Blackstone Valley Pl., Suite 105, Lincoln 02865, ☎ 401/334–1000, WEB www.nrichamber.com).

SOUTH COUNTY

When the principal interstate traffic shifted from U.S. 1 to I–95 in the 1960s, coastal Rhode Island—known within the state as South County—was given a reprieve from the inevitabilities of development. In the past three decades, strong local zoning laws have been instituted and a park system established. In some communities, land trusts were set up to buy open space with monies generated from land-transaction fees. Always a summertime destination, South County is now growing into a region of year-round residents. The southern coast is, indeed, the fastest-growing region in the state, but the changes are being well managed by the respective communities, and the area's appeal as a summer playground has not diminished.

Westerly

㉑ *50 mi southwest of Providence, 100 mi southwest of Boston, 140 mi northeast of New York City.*

The city of Westerly is a busy little railroad town that grew up in the late 19th century around a major station on what is now the New York–Boston Amtrak corridor. The 30-square-mi community of 15 villages has since sprawled out along U.S. 1. Victorian and Greek Revival mansions line many streets off the town center, which borders Connecticut and the Pawcatuck River. During the Industrial Revolution and into the 1950s, Westerly was distinguished for its flawless red granite, from which monuments throughout the country were made.

Watch Hill and Misquamicut are summer communities recognized without mention of the city to which they belong, Westerly. Casinos in Uncasville and Ledyard, Connecticut (less than an hour away), are slowly changing Westerly's economic climate. Many residents work in the Mohegan Sun and Foxwoods casinos, and Westerly's B&Bs are becoming popular alternatives to casino hotels.

Wilcox Park (✉ 71½ High St., ☎ 401/596–8590), designed in 1898 by Warren Manning, an associate of Frederick Law Olmsted and Calvert Vaux, is an 18-acre park in the heart of town with a garden designed so that people with visual and other impairments can identify—by taste, touch, and smell—such plants as chives and thyme.

Dining and Lodging

$$$$ ✕⊞ **Weekapaug Inn.** Weekapaug is a picturesque coastal village 6 mi
★ southeast of Westerly center and 3 mi from Misquamicut Beach. This inn, with a peaked roof and huge wraparound porch, sits on a peninsula surrounded on three sides by salty Quonochontaug Pond. The rooms are cheerful, and most are big and bright, with wide windows and impressive views. The standards at the restaurant ($$$–$$$$), which has a full-time baker, are high: each daily menu emphasizes seafood and lists four to six entrées. You can choose to include breakfast and dinner in the price. ✉ *25 Spring Ave., Weekapaug 02891,* ☎ *401/322–0301,* FAX *401/322–1016. 55 rooms. Restaurant. No credit cards. Closed Oct.–May.*

$$–$$$ ✕⊞ **Shelter Harbor Inn.** This inn, about 6 mi east of downtown in a quiet, rural setting not far from the beach, started out as a summer musicians' colony. The rooms are furnished with a combination of Victorian antiques and reproduction pieces; bedspreads and curtains are in muted floral patterns. Many of the rooms have fireplaces and decks. The frequently changing menu at the excellent restaurant ($$–$$$) might include smoked scallops and capellini or pecan-crusted duck breast. Breakfast is good every day, but Sunday brunch is legendary. ✉ *10 Wag-*

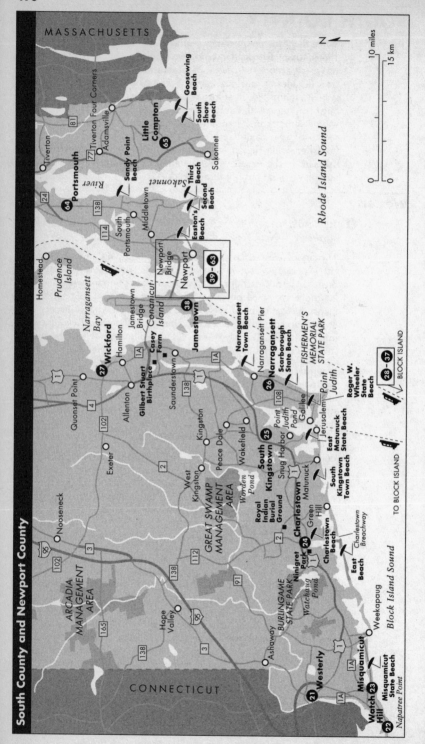

South County and Newport County

ner Rd., off U.S. 1, 02891, ☎ 401/322–8883 or 800/468–8883, FAX 401/322–7907. 23 rooms. Restaurant, hot tub, croquet, paddle tennis. AE, D, DC, MC, V. BP.

$$ 🖭 **Grandview Bed and Breakfast.** Relaxed and affordable, this B&B on a rise above Route 1A has comfortable, if nondescript, rooms (the front ones have ocean views). The common room has a TV with VCR. Breakfast is served on the porch year-round. ✉ 212 Shore Rd., Dunn's Corners (between Misquamicut and Weekapaug), 02891, ☎ 401/596–6384 or 800/447–6384, FAX 401/596–6384, WEB www.grandviewbandb.com. 9 rooms, 5 with bath. AE, MC, V. CP.

Watch Hill

★ ㉒ 5 mi south of downtown Westerly.

Watch Hill, a Victorian-era resort village, contains almost 2 mi of beautiful beaches. Many of its well-kept summerhouses are owned by wealthy families who have passed ownership down through generations. Sailing and socializing are the top activities for Watch Hill residents. This is a good place to tour the attractive streets, shop, and hit the beaches. Long before the first Europeans showed up, southern Rhode Island was inhabited by the Narragansetts, a powerful Native American tribe. The Niantics, ruled by Chief Ninigret in the 1630s, were one branch of the tribe. A statue of Ninigret stands watch over Bay Street, which is also a good place to shop for jewelry, summer clothing, and antiques.

☙ **Flying Horse Carousel,** at the beach end of Bay Street, is the oldest merry-go-round in America. It was built by the Charles W. F. Dare Co. of New York in about 1867. The horses, suspended from above, swing out when in motion. Each is hand-carved from a single piece of wood. Adults are not permitted to ride the carousel. ✉ Bay St. 🎟 50¢. ☉ Mid-June–Labor Day, weekdays 1–9, weekends 11–9.

The **Watch Hill Lighthouse,** an active U.S. Coast Guard station, has great views of the ocean and of Fishers Island, New York. A tiny museum contains exhibits about the lighthouse. Parking is for the elderly only; everyone else must walk from lots at the beach. The grounds here are worth a stroll, whether the museum is open or not. ✉ Lighthouse Rd., ☎ no phone. 🎟 Free. ☉ May–Sept., Tues. and Thurs. 1–3.

Dining and Lodging

$$–$$$ ✕ **Olympia Tea Room.** A step back in time, this small restaurant, which
★ opened in 1916, has varnished wood booths and a soda fountain behind a long marble counter. It also has a great reputation. The menu items are all memorable—some being Rhode Island classics (stuffed quahogs) and others the chef's own creations (duck egg rolls wrapped in phyllo dough). The "world-famous Avondale swan" dessert is a fantasy of ice cream, whipped cream, chocolate sauce, and puff pastry. ✉ 30 Bay St., ☎ 401/348–8211. Reservations not accepted. AE, MC, V. Closed Nov.–Mar.

$$$–$$$$ 🖭 **Ocean House.** The immensity of this yellow-clapboard Victorian hotel will just about take your breath away. Built by George Nash in 1868, the Ocean House helped earn Watch Hill its fame as a 19th-century resort. Though the place is a bit down at the heels these days, it has a private beach and one of the best seaside porches in New England. Casual, relaxing, and quiet, the inn has a reassuring, if faded, elegance. The furniture can best be described as maple eclectic. Ask for a room with an ocean view. ✉ 2 Bluff Ave., 02891, ☎ 401/348–8161. 59 rooms. Restaurant, beach, lounge. MC, V. Closed Sept.–June. BP, MAP.

Shopping

The **Book and Tackle Shop** (⊠ 7 Bay St., ☎ 401/596–1770) buys, sells, and appraises old and rare books, prints, autographs, and photographs. **Puffins of Watch Hill** (⊠ 60 Bay St., ☎ 401/596–1140) carries fine American crafts, collectibles, pottery, jewelry, and gifts. **Sun-Up Gallery** (⊠ 95 Watch Hill Rd., ☎ 401/596–0800) has an extensive selection of unique clothing as well as fine crafts, jewelry, and gifts.

Misquamicut

㉓ *2 mi northeast of Watch Hill.*

Strip motels jostle for attention in Misquamicut, where a giant water slide, a carousel, miniature golf, a game arcade, children's rides, batting cages, and fast-food stands attract visitors by the thousands. The mile-long beach is accessible year-round, but the amusements are open only between Memorial Day and Labor Day.

Atlantic Beach Park (⊠ 337 Atlantic Ave., ☎ 401/322–9298) has more games and rides for kids than any other Misquamicut facility.

Dining and Lodging

$$–$$$ ✕ **Maria's Seaside Cafe.** Although casual as a clam shack, this breezy and upbeat eatery serves such elegant dishes as fresh grilled salmon with lemon-thyme risotto, and sea scallops with Italian couscous. If you've got room, don't miss the grilled raspberry French toast for dessert. ⊠ *132 Atlantic Ave., ☎ 401/596–6886. AE, MC, V. No lunch; no dinner Mon.–Wed. Labor Day–Memorial Day.*

$–$$ ✕ **Paddy's Seafood Restaurant.** The food is good and the portions are generous at this no-frills, family-style beachside restaurant. Lobster, scrod, stuffed shrimp, grilled tuna, and other seafood plates rule the menu, but you can also order pastas and salads. ⊠ *159 Atlantic Ave., ☎ 401/596–2610. AE, D, MC, V. Closed Oct.–Apr.*

$$–$$$ ▣ **Breezeway Motel.** The Bellone family takes great pride in its accommodations: villas with fireplaces and hot tubs, suites, efficiencies, and airy and summery rooms with light wood furnishings. The grounds hold a swing set, shuffleboard, and floodlighted fountains. ⊠ *70 Winnapaug Rd. (Box 1368, 02891), ☎ 401/348–8953 or 800/462–8872, FAX 401/596–3207. 52 rooms, 14 suites, 2 villas. Refrigerators, pool, recreation room. AE, D, DC, MC, V. Closed Nov.–May. CP.*

Nightlife and the Arts

The **Windjammer** (⊠ 337 Atlantic Ave., ☎ 401/322–9298), open Memorial Day to Labor Day, hosts dancing to rock bands in a room that holds 1,500.

Outdoor Activities and Sports

Two-mile-long **Misquamicut State Beach** (⊠ Atlantic Ave., ☎ 401/596–9097) has parking, shower facilities, and a snack bar at the state-run beach pavilion.

Charlestown

㉔ *10 mi northeast of Misquamicut.*

Charlestown stretches along the Old Post Road (Route 1A). The 37-square-mi town has parks, the largest saltwater marsh in the state, 4 mi of pristine beaches, and many oceanfront motels, summer chalets, and cabins.

Ninigret Park (⊠ Park La. off Rte. 1A, ☎ 401/364–1222) is a 172-acre park with picnic grounds, ball fields, a bike path, tennis courts, nature trails, and a spring-fed pond. Also here is the **Frosty Drew Ob-**

servatory and Nature Center (☎ 401/364–9508), which presents nature and astronomy programs on Friday evenings.

Ninigret National Wildlife Refuge consists of two stretches of beach lands and marshes, plus the abandoned naval air station on Ninigret Pond. Nine miles of trails cross 400 acres of diverse upland and wetland habitats—including grasslands, shrub lands, wooded swamps, and freshwater ponds. ✉ *Rte. 1A,* ☎ *401/364–9124.* 🎫 *Free.* ☉ *Daily dawn–dusk.*

Many Narragansetts still live in the Charlestown area, but their historic sites are unmarked and easy to miss. The **Royal Indian Burial Ground,** on the left side of Narrow Lane north of U.S. 1, is the resting place of *sachems* (chiefs). You'll recognize it by the tall fences, but there's no sign. It's not open for visits except during the annual Narragansett meeting, usually the second Sunday in August, when tribal members from around the nation convene for costumed dancing and rituals.

Dining and Lodging

$$ ✕▥ **General Stanton Inn.** For helping pay the ransom of a native princess in 1655, the Narragansetts rewarded Thomas Stanton with the land where this inn stands. Since the 18th century, it has provided dining and lodging in a Colonial setting. The rooms have low ceilings, uneven floorboards, small windows, and period antiques and wallpapers. The dining rooms in the restaurant ($$–$$$; closed Nov.–Apr.) have brick fireplaces, beams, and wooden floors. Traditional New England fare—steaks, lobster, scrod, rack of lamb—is prepared. ✉ *4115-A Old Post Rd./Rte. 1A, 02813,* ☎ *401/364–8888,* ℻ *401/364–3333. 16 rooms. Restaurant, bar. AE, MC, V. BP.*

Outdoor Activities and Sports

The 2,100-acre **Burlingame State Park** (✉ 75 Burlingame Park Rd., ☎ 401/322–7337 or 401/322–7994) has nature trails, picnic and swimming areas, and campgrounds, as well as boating and fishing on Watchaug Pond.

BEACHES

The ½-mi **Charlestown Town Beach** (✉ Charlestown Beach Rd.) ends at a breachway that is part of Ninigret National Wildlife Refuge. Parking is at the end of East Beach Rd. Glorious **East Beach** (✉ East Beach Rd.), composed of 3½ mi of dunes backed by the crystal-clear waters of Ninigret Pond, is a 2-mi hike from the breachway at Charlestown Town Beach. You'll find a snack bar and rest rooms; parking is at the end of East Beach Road.

BOATING

Ocean House Marina (✉ 60 Town Dock Rd., ☎ 401/364–6040), at the Cross Mills exit off U.S. 1, is a full-service marina with boat rentals and fishing supplies.

Shopping

Artists Guild and Gallery (✉ 5429 Post Rd., off U.S. 1, ☎ 401/322–0506) exhibits 19th- and 20th-century art. **Fox Run Country Antiques** (✉ junction of U.S. 1 and Rte. 2, Crossland Park complex, ☎ 401/364–3160; 401/377–2581 appointments), open May–October, sells jewelry, lighting devices, Orientalia, antiques, china, and glassware.

The **Fantastic Umbrella Factory** (✉ 4920 Old Post Rd., off U.S. 1, ☎ 401/364–6616) comprises four rustic shops and a barn built around a wild garden. For sale are hardy perennials and unusual daylilies, greeting cards, kites, crafts, tapestries, and incense. There is also an art gallery, a greenhouse, and a café that serves organic foods.

South Kingstown

㉕ *4 mi northeast of Charlestown.*

In summer months, the 55-square-mi town of South Kingstown—encompassing Wakefield, Snug Harbor, Matunuck, Green Hill, Kingston, and 10 other villages—unfolds a wealth of history, outdoor recreation and beaches, and entertainment.

At the old **Washington County Jail,** built in 1792 in Wakefield, the largest South Kingstown village, you can view jail cells, rooms from the Colonial period, a Colonial garden, and exhibits about South County life. ⊠ *1348 Kingstown Rd.,* ☎ *401/783–1328.* ⊡ *Free.* ☉ *May–Oct., Tues., Thurs., and Sat. 1–4.*

Dining and Lodging

$$ ✕ **Mews Tavern.** The food at this cheery tavern is consistently excellent. Rhode Islanders consider it the best place in the state to get a hamburger (buy one, get one free on Thursday night), but you can also order seafood. Beer is also popular here; 69 varieties are on draft. ⊠ *465 Main St.,* ☎ *401/783–9370. Reservations not accepted. AE, D, MC, V.*

$$–$$$ ✕🏨 **Larchwood Inn.** This 1831 country inn with a Scottish flavor is set in a grove of larch trees. The dining room ($–$$) is open for three meals daily; the halibut stuffed with scallops is delicious. Ask for a table near the fireplace in winter or a patio spot under the trees in summer. Rooms range from suites with grand views to smaller, back-of-the-house affairs. ⊠ *521 Main St., Wakefield 02879,* ☎ *401/783–5454,* ℻ *401/783–1800,* WEB *www.xpos.com/larchwoodinn.html. 18 rooms. Restaurant. AE, D, DC, MC, V.*

$$ 🏨 **Admiral Dewey Inn.** Victorian antiques furnish the rooms of this inn, which was built in 1898 as a seaside hotel—it's across the road from Matunuck Beach—and is now on the National Register of Historic Places. Some rooms have views of the ocean; others are tucked cozily under the eaves. Smoking is permitted only on the wraparound veranda, which is filled with old-fashioned rocking chairs. ⊠ *668 Matunuck Beach Rd., 02881,* ☎ *401/783–2090,* WEB *www.admiraldewey.com. 10 rooms, 8 with bath. MC, V. CP.*

Nightlife and the Arts

Ocean Mist (⊠ 145 Matunuck Beach Rd., ☎ 401/782–3740) is a distinctive beachfront barroom with music nightly in summer and on weekends off-season. The hard-drinking crowd at this hangout of South County's younger generation can be as rough-hewn as the building. The barn-style **Theatre-by-the-Sea** (⊠ Cards Pond Rd., off U.S. 1, ☎ 401/782–8587), built in 1933 and listed on the National Register of Historic Places, presents musicals and plays in summer.

Outdoor Activities and Sports

BEACHES

East Matunuck State Beach (⊠ Succotash Rd.) is popular with the college crowd for its white sand and picnic areas. Crabs, mussels, and starfish populate the rock reef that extends to the right of **Matunuck Beach** (⊠ Succotash Rd.). Southward, the reef gives way to a sandy bottom. When the ocean is calm, you can walk on the reef and explore its tidal pools. **Roy Carpenter's Beach** (⊠ Matunuck Beach Rd.) is part of a cottage-colony of seasonal renters but is open to the public for a fee. **South Kingstown Town Beach** (⊠ Matunuck Beach Rd.), with a playground, picnic tables, grills, and showers draws many families.

FISHING

Gil's Custom Tackle (⊠ 101 Main St., Wakefield, ☎ 401/783–1370) sells recreational fishing gear. **Snug Harbor Marina** (⊠ 410 Gooseberry

Rd., Wakefield, ☎ 401/783–7766) sells bait, rents kayaks, and arranges fishing charters. At Snug Harbor it is not uncommon to see on the docks giant tuna and sharks weighing more than 300 pounds.

WATER SPORTS

The **Watershed** (⊠ 396 Main St., Wakefield, ☎ 401/789–3399) rents surfboards, Windsurfers, body boards, and wet suits. Owner Peter Pan gives lessons at nearby Narragansett Town Beach.

Shopping

Dove and Distaff Antiques (⊠ 365 Main St., Wakefield, ☎ 401/783–5714) is a good spot for Early American furniture. **Hera Gallery** (⊠ 327 Main St., Wakefield, ☎ 401/789–1488), a women's art cooperative, exhibits the work of emerging local artists. It's open Wednesday–Friday 1–5, Saturday 10–4.

Narragansett

❷❻ *2 mi east of South Kingstown.*

The popular beach town of Narragansett draws people for a scenic drive along the ocean (Route 1A) or for a stroll along its beach or its sea-wall. Set on the peninsula east of Point Judith Pond and the Pettaquamscutt River, the town has many grand old shingle houses that overlook the ocean and a handful of restaurants and shops directly across the street from the beach.

Narragansett Pier, the beach community often called simply the Pier, was named for an amusement wharf that no longer exists. The Pier—now populated by summertime "cottagers," college students, and commuting professionals—was a posh resort in the late 1800s linked by rail to New York and Boston. Many summer visitors headed for the Narragansett Pier Casino, which had a bowling alley, billiard tables, tennis courts, a rifle gallery, a theater, and a ballroom. The grand edifice burned to the ground in 1900. Only the **Towers** (⊠ Rte. 1A, ☎ 401/783–7121), the grand stone entrance to the former casino, remains. Most of the mansions built during Narragansett's golden age are along Ocean Road, from Point Judith to Narragansett Pier.

The village of **Galilee** is a busy, workaday fishing port from which whale-watching excursions, fishing trips, and the **Block Island Ferry** (⊠ Galilee State Pier, ☎ 401/783–4613) depart. The occasionally pungent smell of seafood and bait will lead you to the area's fine restaurants and markets. From the port of Galilee it's a short drive to the **Point Judith Lighthouse** (⊠ 1460 Ocean Rd., ☎ 401/789–0444) and a beautiful ocean view. The lighthouse is open from dawn to dusk.

☾ **Adventureland in Narragansett** has bumper boats, miniature golf, batting cages, and a go-cart track. ⊠ *Rte. 108,* ☎ *401/789–0030.* ⊡ *Combination tickets $1.50–$9.50.* ☉ *Mid-June–Labor Day, daily 10–10; Labor Day–Oct. and mid-Apr.–mid-June, weekends 10–10.*

☾ The seven buildings of the **South County Museum** house 20,000 artifacts dating from 1800 to 1933. Exhibits include a country kitchen, a carpentry shop, a cobbler's shop, a tack shop, a working print shop, and an antique carriage collection. ⊠ *Canonchet Farm, Anne Hoxie La., off Rte. 1A,* ☎ *401/783–5400.* ⊡ *$3.50.* ☉ *May–June and Sept.–Oct., Wed.–Sun. 11–4; July–Aug., Wed.–Mon. 10–4.*

Dining and Lodging

$$$ ✕ **Basil's.** French and Continental cuisine are served in intimate surroundings within walking distance of Narragansett Town Beach. Dark floral wallpaper and fresh flowers enrich the small dining room. The

specialty is veal topped with a light cream-and-mushroom sauce; among the other dishes are fish and duck à l'orange. ⊠ *22 Kingstown Rd.,* ☎ *401/789–3743. AE, DC, MC, V. Closed Oct.–June, Mon. and Tues. No lunch.*

$$–$$$ ✕ **Spain Restaurant.** South County's only Spanish restaurant is known
★ for its generous portions and fine service by well-trained professionals. Worthy appetizers include shrimp in garlic sauce, stuffed mushrooms, and Spanish sausages; lobster, steak, and paella are some of the main courses. Even basic dishes, such as chicken with rice, are unforgettable. Arched entryways and tall plants help create Mediterranean mood. ⊠ *1144 Ocean Rd.,* ☎ *401/783–9770. AE, D, DC, MC, V.*

$$ ✕ **Aunt Carrie's.** This popular family-owned restaurant has been serving up Rhode Island shore dinners, clam cakes and chowder, and fried seafood for nearly 80 years. At the height of the season the lines can be long; one alternative is to order from the take-out window and picnic on the grounds of the nearby lighthouse. ⊠ *Rte. 108 and Ocean Rd., Point Judith,* ☎ *401/783–7930. Reservations not accepted. MC, V. Closed Oct.–Mar. and Mon.–Thurs. Apr.–May and Sept.*

$$ ✕ **Coast Guard House.** This restaurant, housed in an 1888 building that served as a lifesaving station for 50 years, displays interesting photos of Narragansett Pier and the casino. Candles light the tables, and picture windows on three sides allow views of the ocean. The fare is American—seafood, pasta, veal, steak, and lamb. The upstairs lounge hosts entertainers and has a DJ on Friday and Saturday night. ⊠ *40 Ocean Rd.,* ☎ *401/789–0700. AE, D, DC, MC, V.*

$$ ✕ **George's of Galilee.** This restaurant at the mouth of the Point Judith harbor has been a must for tourists since 1948. The "stuffies" (baked stuffed quahogs) are some of the best in the state. The menu lists fried and broiled seafood, chicken, steak, and pasta, all at reasonable prices. Its proximity to the beach and its large outside bar on the second floor make George's a busy place all summer. ⊠ *Sand Hill Cove Rd., Port of Galilee,* ☎ *401/783–2306. Reservations not accepted. AE, D, MC, V. Closed Dec. and weekdays Nov. and Jan.*

$$ ✕ **Turtle Soup.** Be prepared to wait for a table at this lively spot, with its sweeping views of the ocean. The dining room oozes simplicity and comfort, with its gleaming wood paneling and wood floors; a sitting room provides a fireplace and overstuffed chairs. Although the menu focuses on American dishes such as steamed lobster and pecan-encrusted catfish, a smattering of Asian influences show up, such as the pot-sticker appetizer with a fiery Thai dipping sauce. ⊠ *113 Ocean Rd.,* ☎ *401/ 782–8683. Reservations not accepted. AE, MC, V. Closed Mon. No lunch Tues.–Fri.*

$–$$ 🏠 **The Richards.** Imposing and magnificent, this mansion has a broodingly Gothic mystique that is quite different from the spirit of the typical summerhouse. French windows in the wood-paneled common rooms downstairs open up to views of a lush landscape, and a grand swamp oak is the centerpiece of the garden. A fire crackles in the library fireplace on chilly afternoons. Some rooms have 19th-century English antiques, floral-upholstered furniture, and fireplaces. ⊠ *144 Gibson Ave., 02882,* ☎ *401/789–7746. 4 rooms, 1 suite. No credit cards. BP.*

Outdoor Activities and Sports

BEACHES

Popular **Narragansett Town Beach** (⊠ Rte. 1A) is within walking distance of many hotels and guest houses. Its pavilion has changing rooms, showers, and concessions. **Roger W. Wheeler State Beach** (⊠ Sand Hill Cove Rd., Galilee) has a pavilion; the beach, sheltered from ocean swells, also has picnic areas and a playground. **Scarborough State**

Beach (✉ Ocean Rd.), considered by many the jewel of the Ocean State's beaches, has a pavilion with showers and concessions. On weekends, teenagers and college students blanket the sands.

FISHING

The **Lady Frances** (✉ Frances Fleet, 2 State St., Point Judith, ☎ 401/ 783–4988 or 800/662–2824) operates day and overnight fishing trips. **Persuader** (☎ 401/783–5644) leads myriad sportfishing charters. Excursions on the **Prowler** (☎ 401/783–8487) include a variety of sportfishing. The **Seven B's V** (☎ 401/789–9250) runs sportfishing charters for all types of anglers. **Maridee Canvas–Bait & Tackle** (✉ 120 Knowlesway Ext., ☎ 401/789–5190) stocks supplies and provides helpful advice.

WHALE-WATCHING

Whale-watching excursions aboard the **Lady Frances** depart at 1 PM and return at 6 PM. The fare is $30. The trips operate Monday through Saturday from July to Labor Day.

Wickford

★ ➋ *10 mi north of Narragansett Pier, 15 mi south of Providence.*

The Colonial village of Wickford has a little harbor, dozens of 18th- and 19th-century homes, several antiques shops, and boutiques selling locally made jewelry and crafts, home accents and gifts, and clothing. This bay-side spot is the kind of almost-too-perfect salty New England period piece that is usually conjured up only in books and movies. In fact, Wickford was John Updike's model for the New England of his novel *The Witches of Eastwick.*

Old Narragansett Church, now called St. Paul's, was built in 1707. It's one of the oldest Episcopal churches in America. ✉ *55 Main St.,* ☎ *401/294–4357.* ☉ *July–Labor Day, Fri.–Sat. 11–4; Sun. services at 8 and 9:30.*

Smith's Castle, built in 1678 by Richard Smith Jr., is a beautifully preserved saltbox plantation house on the quiet shore of an arm of Narragansett Bay. It was the site of many orations by Roger Williams, from whom Smith bought the surrounding property. The grounds have one of the first military burial grounds (open during daylight hours) in the country: interred in a marked mass grave are 40 colonists killed in the Great Swamp battle of 1675. The Narragansetts were nearly annihilated, ending King Philip's War in Rhode Island. ✉ *55 Richard Smith Dr., 1 mi north of Wickford,* ☎ *401/294–3521.* ✍ *$3.* ☉ *May and Sept., Fri.–Sun. noon–4; June–Aug., Thurs.–Mon. noon–4. Castle tours by appointment Oct.–Apr.*

Historic **Silas Casey Farm,** off Route 1A south of Wickford, still functions much as it has since the 18th century. The farmhouse contains original furniture, prints, paintings, and 300 years of political and military documents. Nearly 30 mi of stone walls surround the 360-acre farmstead. ✉ *2325 Boston Neck Rd., Saunderstown,* ☎ *401/295–1030.* ✍ *$3.* ☉ *June–mid-Oct., Tues., Thurs., and Sat. 1–5.*

En Route Built in 1751, the **Gilbert Stuart Birthplace** was the home of America's foremost portraitist of George Washington. It lies on a pretty country road along little Mattatuxet River. The adjacent 18th-century snuff mill was the first in America. You can hike the trail along the river. ✉ *815 Gilbert Stuart Rd., Saunderstown,* ☎ *401/294–3001.* ✍ *$3.* ☉ *Apr.– Oct., Thurs.–Mon. 11–4:30.*

Shopping

ANTIQUES

The **Hour Glass** (⊠ 15 W. Main St., ☎ 401/295–8724) carries antique barometers, clocks, tide clocks, thermometers, and the like. **Mentor Antiques** (⊠ 7512 Post Rd., ☎ 401/294–9412) receives monthly shipments of antique English mahogany, pine, and oak furniture. **Wickford Antiques Centre** (⊠ 16 Main St., ☎ 401/295–2966) sells wooden kitchen utensils, country furniture, china, glass, linens, and jewelry.

CRAFTS

Needlepoint pillows, Florentine leather books, lamps, and woven throws are a few of the gifts and home furnishings at **Askham & Telham Inc.** (⊠ 12 Main St., ☎ 401/295–0891).

Outdoor Activities and Sports

BOATING

The **Kayak Centre** (⊠ 9 Phillip St., ☎ 401/295–4400), in bustling Wickford Harbor, rents kayaks and provides lessons.

South County A to Z

To research prices, get advice from other travelers, and book travel arrangements, visit www.fodors.com.

AIRPORTS

The closest major airport is T. F. Green State Airport (☞ Rhode Island A to Z) in Warwick, south of Providence. Westerly Airport is served by New England Airlines, which flies from Westerly to Block Island and operates charter flights.

➤ AIRPORT INFORMATION: **Westerly Airport** (⊠ Airport Rd., 2 mi south of Westerly off U.S. 1, ☎ 401/596–2460). **New England Airlines** (☎ 401/596–2460 or 800/243–2460).

BUS TRAVEL

Rhode Island Public Transit Authority provides service from Providence and Warwick to Kingston, Wakefield, and Narragansett.

➤ BUS INFORMATION: **Rhode Island Public Transit Authority** (RIPTA; ☎ 401/781–9400; 800/244–0444 in RI).

CAR TRAVEL

Interstate 95 passes 10 mi north of Westerly before heading inland toward Providence. U.S. 1 and Route 1A follow the coastline along Narragansett Bay and are the primary routes through the South County resort towns.

EMERGENCIES

➤ HOSPITALS: **South County Hospital** (⊠ 100 Kenyon Ave., Wakefield, ☎ 401/782–8000). **Westerly Hospital** (⊠ 25 Wells St., Westerly, ☎ 401/596–6000).

➤ 24-HOUR PHARMACY: **CVS Pharmacy** (⊠ Granite Shopping Center, 114 Granite St., Westerly, ☎ 401/596–0306).

TRAIN TRAVEL

Amtrak trains running between Washington and Boston stop in Westerly and Kingston.

➤ TRAIN INFORMATION: **Amtrak** (☎ 800/872–7245, WEB www.amtrak.com).

VISITOR INFORMATION

The state operates a visitor information center off I–95 at the Connecticut border.

➤ TOURIST INFORMATION: **Charlestown Chamber of Commerce** (⊠ 4945 Old Post Rd., Charlestown 02813, ☎ 401/364–3878). **Greater West-**

erly Chamber of Commerce (⌧ 74 Post Rd., Westerly 02891, ☎ 401/
596–7761 or 800/732–7636). **Narragansett Chamber of Commerce** (⌧
The Towers, Rte. 1A, Narragansett 02882, ☎ 401/783–7121). **South
County Tourism Council** (⌧ 4808 Tower Hill Rd., Wakefield 02879,
☎ 401/789–4422 or 800/548–4662).

BLOCK ISLAND

Block Island, 12 mi off Rhode Island's southern coast, has been a popular travel destination since the 19th century. Despite the many people who come here each summer, and thanks to the efforts of local conservationists, the island's beauty has been preserved; its 365 freshwater ponds support more than 150 species of migrating birds.

The original inhabitants of the island were Native Americans who called it Manisses, or "isle of the little god." Following a visit in 1614 by the Dutch explorer Adrian Block, the island was given the name Adrian's Eyelant, and later Block Island. In 1661 the island was settled by farmers and fishermen from Massachusetts Bay Colony. They gave Block Island what remains its second official name, the Town of New Shoreham, when it became part of Rhode Island in 1672.

Block Island is a laid-back community. Phone numbers are exchanged by the last four digits (466 is the prefix), and you can dine at any of the island's establishments in shorts and a T-shirt. Between May and Columbus Day is the island's busiest season—at other times, most restaurants, inns, stores, and visitor services close down. If you plan to stay overnight in summer, make reservations well in advance; for weekends in July and August, March is not too early.

Block Island has two harbors, Old Harbor and New Harbor. Approaching Block Island by sea from New London (Connecticut), Newport, or Point Judith, you'll see Old Harbor and its group of Victorian hotels. The Old Harbor area is the island's only village. Most of the inns, shops, and restaurants are here, and it's a short walk from the ferry landing to any hotel and to most of the interesting sights.

With the exception of a short strip called Moped Alley (actually Weldon's Way), where you can test-drive mopeds, you won't find a bad walk on all of Block Island. The West Side loop (West Side Road to Cooneymus Road) is gorgeous.

㉘ Three docks, two hotels, and four restaurants huddled in the southeast corner of the Great Salt Pond make up the **New Harbor** commercial area. The harbor itself—also called Great Salt Pond—shelters as many as 1,700 boats on busy weekends, hosts sail races and fishing tournaments, and is the landing point for two ferries that run from Montauk on Long Island (New York) to Block Island.

㉙ The **Island Cemetery**, ½ mi west on West Side Road from New Harbor, has held the remains of island residents since the 1700s. At this well-maintained graveyard you can spot the names of long-standing Block Island families (Ball, Rose, Champlin) and take in fine views of the Great Salt Pond, the North Light, and the Rhode Island coast; on a clear day, the Jamestown–Newport Bridge will be visible to the northeast.

To explore the island's lovely **west side,** head west from New Harbor on West Side Road; after the Island Cemetery, you will pass a horse farm and some small ponds. You get to the beach by turning right on Dories Cove Road or Cooneymus Beach Road; both dirt roads dead-end at the island's tranquil west shore. One mile past Dories Cove Road,

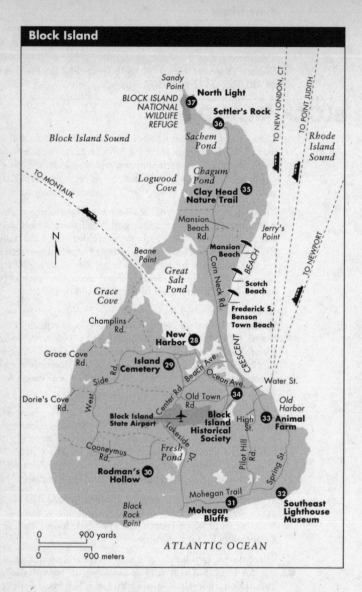

Block Island

Sandy Point

North Light 37

BLOCK ISLAND NATIONAL WILDLIFE REFUGE

Settler's Rock 36

Block Island Sound

Sachem Pond

TO NEW LONDON, CT

TO POINT JUDITH

Rhode Island Sound

Chagum Pond

Logwood Cove

Clay Head Nature Trail 35

Mansion Beach Rd.

Jerry's Point

Beane Point

Mansion Beach

Great Salt Pond

Corn Neck Rd.

Scotch Beach

Grace Cove

BEACH

Champlins Rd.

Frederick S. Benson Town Beach

TO NEWPORT

TO MONTAUK

N

New Harbor 28

Grace Cove Rd.

Island Cemetery 29

Beach Ave.

Ocean Ave.

CRESCENT

Water St.

Dorie's Cove Rd.

Side Rd.

West Rd.

Center Rd.

Old Town Rd.

Block Island Historical Society

Old Harbor

Animal Farm 33

34

High St.

Block Island State Airport

Lakeside Dr.

Pilot Hill Rd.

Spring St.

Cooneymus Rd.

Fresh Pond

Rodman's Hollow 30

Mohegan Bluffs 31

Mohegan Trail

Southeast Lighthouse Museum 32

Black Rock Point

0	900 yards
0	900 meters

ATLANTIC OCEAN

peaceful West Side Road jogs left and turns into Cooneymus Road. On your right ½ mi farther is a deep ravine.

★ 30 **Rodman's Hollow** (✉ off Cooneymus Rd.) is a fine example of a glacial outwash basin. This was the first piece of property purchased in the island's quarter-century-long tradition of land conservation, an effort that has succeeded in saving 25% of the island from development. At Rodman's you can descend along winding paths to the ocean, where you can hike the coastline, lie on beaches at the foot of sand and clay cliffs, or swim if the waters are calm.

31 The 200-ft cliffs along Mohegan Trail, the island's southernmost road, are called **Mohegan Bluffs**—so named for an Indian battle in which the local Manisses pinned down an attacking band of Mohegans at the base of the cliffs. From Payne Overlook, west of the Southeast Lighthouse Museum, you can see to Montauk Point, New York, and beyond. An intimidating set of stairs leads down to the beach.

③② The small **Southeast Lighthouse Museum** occupies a "rescued" 1873 red-brick beacon with gingerbread detail that was moved back from eroded cliffs. The lighthouse is a National Historic Landmark. ⊠ *Mohegan Trail,* ☎ *401/466–5009.* ⊠ *$5.* ☉ *Memorial Day–Labor Day, daily 10–4.*

③③ The owners of the 1661 Inn and Hotel Manisses run a small **Animal Farm** with a collection of llamas, emus, sheep, goats, and ducks. The animals happily coexist in a meadow next to the hotel. ⊠ *Off Spring or High St.,* ☎ *401/466–2063.* ⊠ *Free.* ☉ *Daily dawn–dusk.*

③④ Exhibits at the **Block Island Historical Society** describe the island's farming and maritime pasts. Many original pieces furnish the society's headquarters, an 1850 mansard-roof home that's well worth a visit. ⊠ *Old Town Rd.,* ☎ *401/466–2481 or 401/466–5009.* ⊠ *$2.* ☉ *July–Aug., daily 10–4; June and Sept., weekends 10–4.*

★ ③⑤ The outstanding **Clay Head Nature Trail** meanders past Clay Head Swamp and along 150-ft-high ocean-side cliffs. Songbirds chirp and flowers bloom along the paths that lead into the interior—an area called the Maze. The trailhead, recognizable by a simple white-post marker, is at the end of a dirt road that begins at Corn Neck Road, just past Mansion Beach Road. It's about a mile, but other trails lead off of it. Trail maps are available at the **Nature Conservancy** (⊠ *Ocean Ave.,* ☎ *401/466–2129*).

③⑥ **Settler's Rock,** on the spit of land between Sachem Pond and Cow Beach, is a monument that lists the names of the original settlers and marks the spot where they landed in 1661. Hiking 1 mi over sandy terrain will get you to the somber North Light.

★ ③⑦ **North Light,** an 1867 granite lighthouse on the northernmost tip of the Block Island National Wildlife Refuge, serves as a maritime museum. The protected area nearby is a temporary home to American oyster-catchers, piping plovers, and other rare migrating birds. From a parking lot at the end of Corn Neck Road, it's a mile-long hike over sand to the lighthouse. ⊠ *Corn Neck Rd.,* ☎ *401/466–3200.* ⊠ *$2.* ☉ *Mid-June–Labor Day, daily 10–4 (weather permitting).*

Dining and Lodging

$$–$$$ ✕ **Eli's.** Though the noise level is high and the napkins are paper, the
★ food keeps people coming back to Block Island's preferred restaurant. Pastas are the menu's mainstays, but the kitchen makes extensive excursions into local seafood, Asian dishes, and steaks like the Carpetbagger, a 12-ounce filet mignon filled with lobster, mozzarella, and sun-dried tomatoes, topped with a béarnaise sauce. ⊠ *Chapel St.,* ☎ *401/466–5230. Reservations not accepted. MC, V. Closed Jan.–Feb. and Mon.–Wed. Mar.–May.*

$$–$$$ ✕ **Finn's.** A Block Island institution, Finn's serves reliable fried and broiled seafood and prepares a wonderful smoked bluefish pâté. For lunch try the Workman's Special platter—a burger, coleslaw, and french fries. You can eat inside or out on the deck, or get food to go. Finn's raw bar is on an upstairs deck that overlooks Old Harbor. ⊠ *Ferry Landing,* ☎ *401/466–2473. Reservations not accepted. AE, MC, V. Closed mid-Oct.–May.*

$ ✕ **The BeacHead.** The food—especially the Rhode Island clam chowder—is very good, the price is right, and you won't feel like a tourist at this locals' hangout. Play pool, catch up on town gossip, or sit at the bar and stare out at the sea. The menu and service are unpretentious; burgers are served on paper plates with potato chips and pickles. ⊠ *Corn Neck Rd.,* ☎ *401/466–2249. Reservations not accepted. No credit cards.*

$$-$$$$ ✕⌾ **Atlantic Inn.** This long, white, classic Victorian resort has big win-
★   dows, high ceilings, and a sweeping staircase. Most of the oak and maple
furnishings in the rooms are original to the building. And then there
are the views: isolated from the hubbub of the Old Harbor area, you
can perch on a hillside, look out over the harbor, and contemplate the
shape of the island. Each morning the inn's pastry chef prepares a buf-
fet breakfast with fresh-baked goods. The restaurant ($$$–$$$$; reser-
vations essential; closed Nov.–Apr.; no lunch) serves creative prix-fixe
meals that use local ingredients. ✉ *High St. (Box 1788, 02807),* ☎
401/466–5883 or 800/224–7422, ⃝ *401/466–5678. 20 rooms, 1
suite. Restaurant, 2 tennis courts, croquet, playground, meeting room.
D, MC, V. Closed Nov.–Easter. CP.*

$$-$$$$ ✕⌾ **Hotel Manisses.** The chef at the island's premier restaurant ($$–
$$$; closed Nov.–Apr.) for American cuisine uses herbs and vegetables
from the hotel's garden and locally caught seafood to prepare superb
dishes such as littleneck clams Dijonnaise. Period furnishings and
knickknacks fill the rooms in the 1872 mansion. The extras here include picnic baskets, an animal farm, island tours, afternoon wine and
hors d'oeuvres in the parlor, and many rooms with whirlpool baths.
✉ *1 Spring St., 02807,* ☎ *401/466–2421 or 800/626–4773,* ⃝ *401/
466–3162,* ⃝ *www.blockislandresorts.com. 17 rooms. Restaurant, fans;
no kids under 12. MC, V. BP.*

$$$-$$$$ ⌾ **Blue Dory Inn.** This Old Harbor district inn has been a guest house
★   since its construction in 1898. Thanks to Ann Loedy, the dynamic
owner-manager, its main building and three small shingle-and-clap-
board outbuildings run efficiently. Though not large, the rooms are
tastefully appointed with Victorian antiques, and each has either an
ocean or a harbor view. Couples looking for a romantic hideaway often
enjoy the Tea House, which has a porch overlooking Crescent Beach.
✉ *Dodge St. (Box 488, 02807),* ☎ *401/466–2254 or 800/992–7290,*
⃝ *www.thebluedoryinn.com. 12 rooms, 4 cottages, 3 suites. AE, D,
MC, V. BP.*

$$$-$$$$ ⌾ **1661 Inn and Guest House.** If your island vacation fantasy includes
★   lounging in bed while gazing at swans in the marshes that overlook
the blue Atlantic, consider staying here. Loll on the inn's expansive
deck or curl up in a chair on the lawn; from both spots you'll enjoy
the panorama of the water below. The rooms reflect remarkable at-
tention to detail: floral wallpaper in one room matches the colors of
the hand-painted tiles atop its antique bureau, and another room has
a collection of wooden model ships. The ample breakfast buffet might
consist of fresh bluefish, corned-beef hash, sausage, Belgian waffles,
scrambled eggs, and fresh muffins. ✉ *Spring St., 02807,* ☎ *401/466–
2421 or 800/626–4773,* ⃝ *401/466–2858,* ⃝ *www.blockisland.
com/biresorts. 21 rooms, 19 with bath. Playground. AE, MC, V.
Closed mid-Nov.–mid-Apr. BP.*

$$-$$$ ⌾ **Barrington Inn.** Owners Joan and Howard Ballard run a tidy, invit-
ing place and enjoy helping you plan your days; the breakfast table
is known as "command central." The inn, meticulously clean, precisely
arranged, and thoroughly soundproofed, has views of Trims Pond, Great
Salt Pond, and Crescent Beach. Three rooms have private decks;
there's also a large common deck. Two apartments (rented by the week
in season) in a separate building are good options for families. ✉ *Beach
Ave. (Box 397, 02807),* ☎ *401/466–5510,* ⃝ *401/466–5880,* ⃝ *www.
blockisland.com/barrington. 6 rooms, 2 apartments. D, MC, V. CP.*

$$-$$$ ⌾ **Surf Hotel.** A stone's throw from the ferry dock, in the heart of the
Old Harbor area and near Crescent Beach, the Surf seems to have
changed little over the years; in fact, it's not hard to imagine what the
hotel must have been like when it first opened in 1876. Dimly lighted
hallways take you to small rooms furnished with a jumble of antique

furniture and odds and ends. The rooms have sinks but share toilets and baths. ⊠ *Dodge St. (Box C, 02807),* ☎ *401/466–2241. 38 rooms, 3 with bath. MC, V. Closed mid-Oct.–Apr. CP.*

Nightlife and the Arts

Block Island's nightlife is one of the island's highlights, and you'll find a good number of places to get a drink. Check the *Block Island Times* for band listings. **Captain Nick's Rock and Roll Bar** (⊠ 34 Ocean Ave., ☎ 401/466–5670), a fortress of summertime debauchery, has four bars and two decks on two floors. In season, bands play nightly. A 360-degree mural that depicts Block Island in the 1940s covers the walls at atmospheric **Club Soda** (⊠ 35 Connecticut Ave., ☎ 401/466–5397). **McGovern's Yellow Kittens Tavern** (⊠ Corn Neck Rd., ☎ 401/466–5855) has bands on weekend nights in summer.

Outdoor Activities and Sports

Beaches

The east side of the island has a number of beaches. The 2½-mi **Crescent Beach** runs from Old Harbor to Jerry's Point. **Frederick J. Benson Town Beach,** a family beach less than 1 mi down Corn Neck Road from Old Harbor, has a beach pavilion, parking, showers, and lifeguards. **Mansion Beach,** off Mansion Beach Road south of Jerry's Point, has deep white sand and is easily one of New England's most beautiful beaches. In the morning, you may spot deer on the dunes. Young summer workers congregate ½ mi north of Town Beach at **Scotch Beach** to play volleyball, to surf, and to sun themselves.

Boating

Block Island Boat Basin (⊠ West Side Rd., New Harbor, ☎ 401/466–2631) is the island's best-stocked ship's store. **New Harbor Kayak** (⊠ Ocean Ave., New Harbor, ☎ 401/466–2890) rents kayaks. **Oceans & Ponds** (⊠ Ocean and Connecticut Aves., ☎ 401/466–5131) rents kayaks and books charter-boat trips.

Fishing

Most of Rhode Island's record fish have been caught on Block Island. From almost any beach, skilled anglers can land tautog and bass. Bonito and fluke are often hooked in the New Harbor channel. Shellfishing licenses may be obtained at the town hall, on Old Town Road. **Oceans & Ponds** sells tackle and fishing gear, operates charter trips, and provides guide services. **Twin Maples** (⊠ Beach Ave., ☎ 401/466–5547) is the island's only bait shop.

Hiking

The **Greenway,** a well-maintained trail system, meanders across the island, but some of the best hikes are along the beaches. You can hike around the entire island in about eight hours. Trail maps for the Greenway are available at the **Chamber of Commerce** (⊠ Water St., ☎ 401/466–2982) and the **Nature Conservancy** (⊠ Ocean Ave. near Payne's Dock, ☎ 401/466–2129). The Nature Conservancy conducts nature walks; call for times or check the *Block Island Times.*

Water Sports

Island Outfitters (⊠ Ocean Ave., ☎ 401/466–5502) rents wet suits, spearguns, and scuba gear. PADI-certification diving courses are available, and beach gear and bathing suits are for sale. **Parasailing on Block Island** (⊠ Old Harbor Basin, ☎ 401/466–2474) will take you parasailing and also rents jet boats.

Shopping

Scarlet Begonia (✉ Dodge St., ☎ 401/466–5024) carries jewelry and crafts, including place mats and handmade quilts. **Spring Street Gallery** (✉ Spring St., ☎ 401/466–5374) shows and sells paintings, photographs, stained glass, serigraphs, and other work by island artists and artisans. **Watercolors** (✉ Dodge St., ☎ 401/466–2538) showcases distinctive jewelry and clothing, much of it locally made.

Block Island A to Z

To research prices, get advice from other travelers, and book travel arrangements, visit www.fodors.com.

AIRPORTS

Block Island Airport is served by a few small airlines. Action Air flies in from Groton, Connecticut, between June and October. New England Airlines flies from Westerly to Block Island and operates charter flights.
➤ AIRPORT INFORMATION: **Action Air** (☎ 203/448–1646 or 800/243–8623). **Block Island Airport** (✉ Center Rd., ☎ 401/466–5511). **New England Airlines** (☎ 401/466–5881 or 800/243–2460).

BIKE AND MOPED TRAVEL

The best way to explore the island is by bicycle (about $15 a day to rent) or moped (about $40). Most rental places are open spring through fall and have child seats for bikes, and all rent bicycles in a variety of styles and sizes, including mountain bikes, hybrids, tandems, and children's bikes.
➤ BIKE RENTALS: **Island Bike & Moped** (✉ Weldon's Way, ☎ 401/466–2700). **Moped Man** (✉ Weldon's Way, ☎ 401/466–5011). **Old Harbor Bike Shop** (✉ south of the ferry dock, Old Harbor, ☎ 401/466–2029).

BOAT AND FERRY TRAVEL

Interstate Navigation Co. operates ferry service from Galilee, a one-hour trip, for $16.30 round-trip; it runs six or seven trips a day. Make auto reservations well ahead. Foot passengers cannot make reservations; you should arrive 45 minutes ahead in high season—the boats do fill up. Ferries run daily from Memorial Day to October from Providence's India Street Pier to Newport's Fort Adams State Park, and to Block Island, and then return along the same route in the afternoon. The company also has summer service from New London, Connecticut. A high-speed ferry makes six round-trips a day (May 15–October 14) from Galilee, $26.50 adults, $12 children.

Nelseco Navigation operates an auto ferry from New London, Connecticut, in summer. Reservations are advised for the two-hour trip. One-way fares from New London are $15 per adult and $28 per vehicle. Viking Ferry Lines operates passenger and bicycle service from Montauk, Long Island (New York), from mid-May to mid-October. The trip, which takes 1¾ hours, costs $16 each way, plus $3 per bicycle.
➤ BOAT AND FERRY INFORMATION: **Interstate Navigation Co.** (✉ Galilee State Pier, Narragansett, ☎ 401/783–4613, WEB www.blockislandferry.com). **Island High-Speed Ferry** (✉ No. 3 State Pier, Narragansett, ☎ 877/733–9425, WEB www.islandhighspeedferry.com). **Nelseco Navigation** (✉ 2 Ferry Rd., New London, CT, ☎ 860/442–7891). **Viking Ferry Lines** (☎ 516/668–5709).

CAR RENTAL

➤ LOCAL AGENCY: **Block Island Car Rental** (☎ 401/466–2297).

CAR TRAVEL

Corn Neck Road runs north to Settler's Rock from Old Harbor. West Side Road loops west from New Harbor; to return to the Old Harbor area, take Cooneymus Road east and Lakeside Drive, Center Road, and Ocean Avenue north.

LODGING

Inns and hotels on Block Island are booked well in advance for weekends in July and August. Many visitors rent homes for stays of a week or more. Many houses, however, are booked solid by April.

➤ LOCAL AGENTS: **Ballard Hall Real Estate** (✉ Ocean Ave., 02807, ☎ 401/466–8883). **Sullivan Real Estate** (✉ Water St., 02807, ☎ 401/466–5521).

TAXIS

Taxis are plentiful at the Old Harbor and New Harbor ferry landings.
➤ CONTACTS: **Kirb's Cab** (☎ 401/466–2928). **Ladybird Taxi** (☎ 401/466–3133). **O. J.'s Taxi** (☎ 401/741–0500).

VISITOR INFORMATION

➤ TOURIST INFORMATION: **Block Island Chamber of Commerce** (✉ Drawer D, Water St., 02807, ☎ 401/466–2982).

NEWPORT COUNTY

Perched gloriously on the southern tip of Aquidneck Island and bounded on three sides by water, Newport is one of the great sailing cities of the world and the host to world-class jazz, blues, folk, and classical music festivals. Colonial houses and gilded-age mansions grace the city. Newport County encompasses the three communities of Aquidneck Island—Newport, Middletown, and Portsmouth—plus Conanicut Island, also known as Jamestown, and Tiverton and Little Compton, which abut Massachusetts to Newport's east. Little Compton is a remote, idyllic town that presents a strong contrast to Newport's quick pace.

Jamestown

38 *25 mi south of Providence, 3 mi west of Newport.*

Summer residents have come to Jamestown since the 1880s, but never to the same extent as to Watch Hill, Narragansett, or Newport. The locals' "We're not a T-shirt town" attitude has resulted in a relatively low number of visitors, even in July and August, making this a peaceful alternative to the bustle of nearby Newport and South County.

The east and west passages of Narragansett Bay encompass the 9-mi-long, 1-mi-wide landmass that goes by the names Jamestown and Conanicut Island. Valuable as a military outpost in days gone by, the island was once considered an impediment to commercial cross-bay shipping. In 1940 the Jamestown Bridge linked the island to western Rhode Island, and in 1969 the Newport Bridge completed the cross-bay route, connecting Newport to the entire South County area.

The water conditions range from tranquil to harrowing at **Beavertail State Park,** which straddles the southern tip of Conanicut Island. The currents and surf here are famously deadly during rough seas and high winds; but on a clear, calm day, the park's craggy shoreline seems intended for sunning, hiking, and climbing. The **Beavertail Lighthouse Museum,** in what was the lighthouse keeper's quarters, has displays about Rhode Island's lighthouses. ✉ *Beavertail Rd.,* ☎ *401/423–3270.* ✑ *Free.* ☾ *Museum June–Labor Day, daily 10–4. Park daily.*

Thomas Carr Watson's family had worked the **Watson Farm** for 190 years before he bequeathed it to the Society for the Preservation of New England Antiquities when he died in 1979. The 285-acre spread, dedicated to educating the public about agrarian history, has 2 mi of trails along Jamestown's southwestern shore with amazing views of Narragansett Bay and North Kingstown. ⊠ *455 North Rd.,* ☎ *401/423–0005.* ⊡ *$3.* ☉ *June–mid-Oct., Tues., Thurs., and Sun. 1–5.*

The English-designed **Jamestown Windmill,** built in 1789, ground corn for nearly 100 years—and it still works. Mills like this one were once common in Rhode Island. ⊠ *North Rd., east of Watson Farm,* ☎ *401/423–1798.* ⊡ *Free.* ☉ *Mid-June–Sept., weekends 1–4.*

A working 1859 hand tub and a horse-drawn steam pump are among ⏣ the holdings of the **Jamestown Fire Department Memorial Museum,** an informal display of fire-fighting equipment in a garage that once housed the fire company. ⊠ *50 Narragansett Ave.,* ☎ *401/423–0062.* ⊡ *Free.* ☉ *Daily 7–3; inquire next door at fire department if door is locked.*

Fort Wetherill State Park, an outcropping of stone cliffs at the tip of the southeastern peninsula, has been a picnic destination since the 1800s. There's great swimming at the small cove here, and it's a favorite spot for local snorkelers and scuba divers. ⊠ *Ocean St.,* ☎ *401/423–1771.* ⊡ *Free.* ☉ *Daily dawn–dusk.*

The **Jamestown and Newport Ferry Co.** stops in Newport at Bowen's Landing and Long Wharf and will stop on request at Fort Adams or Goat Island. The 26-ft passenger ferry departs on its half-hour voyage from Ferry Wharf about every 1½ hours, from 8:15 AM to 10 PM (11:30 PM on weekends). The last run leaves from Newport at 10:30 PM (midnight on weekends). The ferry operates from Memorial Day to mid-October. ⊠ *Ferry Wharf,* ☎ *401/423–9900.* ⊡ *About $6.*

Dining and Lodging

$$$ ✗ **Trattoria Simpatico.** A jazz trio plays on sunny weekends at Jamestown's signature restaurant, while patrons dine alfresco under a 275-year-old copper beech tree. An herb garden, fieldstone walls, and white linen complete the picture. You can munch on splendid salads, taste pasta dishes cooked northern-Italian style, or try meats prepared with a Continental flair. One memorable appetizer is crispy-skin duck confit with deep-fried fettuccine, savoy cabbage, and onion marmalade. Reservations are essential on summer weekends. ⊠ *13 Narragansett Ave.,* ☎ *401/423–3731. AE, D, MC, V. No lunch weekdays Labor Day–Memorial Day, no lunch weekends Memorial Day–Labor Day.*

$$ ✗ **Jamestown Oyster Bar.** Whether you're ordering clam chowder
★ and a dollar draft or grilled swordfish and a martini, you'll feel right at home here. Oysters are kept on ice behind the bar, where tenders pour fine microbrews and wines. The burgers are locally renowned, but for something more delicate, try one of the seafood specials listed on the chalkboard. ⊠ *22 Narragansett Ave.,* ☎ *401/423–3380. Reservations not accepted. AE, MC, V. No lunch weekdays.*

$$$$ ⊡ **Bay Voyage.** In 1889 this Victorian inn was shipped to its current location from Newport and named in honor of its trip. The one-bedroom suites, furnished in floral prints and pastels, have been sold as time-shares, which makes availability tight in summer months. The facilities are plentiful, the view memorable. The restaurant is known for its Sunday brunch, but dinner, where you might find juniper-rubbed venison in an espresso demiglace, is first-rate, too. ⊠ *150 Conanicus Ave., 02835,* ☎ *401/423–2100,* FAX *401/423–3209,* WEB *www.easternresorts.com. 32 suites. Restaurant, kitchenettes, pool, gym, sauna, bar. AE, D, DC, MC, V.*

$ 🏠 **East Bay B&B.** If Karen Montoya's three rooms aren't booked, you can get a great deal at her humble B&B. The circa-1896 Victorian is peaceful day and night, even though it's only a block from Jamestown's two main streets and bustling wharf. The original trim and bull-nose molding are all in great shape, as is the formal living room, which has a fireplace and Oriental rugs. ✉ *14 Union St., 02835,* ☎ *401/423–2715. 3 rooms, 1 with bath. No credit cards. CP.*

Outdoor Activities and Sports

BEACHES

Sandy **Mackerel Cove Beach** (✉ Beavertail Rd.) is sheltered from the currents of Narragansett Bay, making it a great spot for families. Parking costs $10 for nonresidents.

DIVING AND KAYAKING

Ocean State Scuba (✉ 79 N. Main Rd., ☎ 401/423–1662 or 800/933–3483) rents kayaks and diving equipment.

GOLF

Jamestown Country Club (✉ 245 Conanicus Ave., ☎ 401/423–9930) has a crisp 9-hole course, where for $10 you can play all day.

Newport

30 mi south from Providence, 80 mi south from Boston.

The island city of Newport preserves Colonial industry and gilded-age splendor like no other place in the country. Settled in 1639 by a small band of religious dissenters from Massachusetts, Newport earned a reputation for tolerance, and its prime location at the mouth of Narragansett Bay ensured its success in the Colonial period. The golden age of Newport ran from roughly 1720 to the 1770s, when products such as cheese, candles, clocks, and furniture, as well as livestock and the slave trade, put the city on a par with Charleston, South Carolina; the two cities trailed only Boston as centers of New World maritime commerce. In the mid-1700s, Newport employed the best shipbuilders in North America. Their small, swift, and reliable slave ships were the stars of the triangle trade (rum to Africa for slaves; slaves to the West Indies for molasses; molasses and slaves back to America, where the molasses was made into rum). This unsavory scheme guaranteed investors a 20% return on their money and earned Newport the dubious distinction of being the largest slave-trading port in the North. In 1774, progressive Rhode Island became the first colony to outlaw trading in slaves.

In the 19th century, Newport became a summer playground for the wealthy, the titans of the gilded age who built the fabulous "cottages" overlooking the Atlantic. Newport's mansions served as proving grounds for the country's best young architects. Richard Upjohn, Richard Morris Hunt, and firms like McKim, Mead & White have left a legacy of remarkable homes, many now open to the public.

Recreational sailing, a huge industry in Newport today, convincingly melds the attributes of two eras: the conspicuous consumption of the late 19th century and the nautical expertise of the Colonial era. Tanned young sailors often fill Newport bars and restaurants, where they talk of wind, waves, and expensive yachts. For those not arriving by water, a sailboat tour of the harbor is a great way to get your feet wet.

Newport in summer can be exasperating, its streets jammed with visitors, the traffic slowed by sightseeing buses (3½ million people visit the city each year). Yet the quality of Newport's sights and its arts festivals persuade many people to brave the crowds. In fall and spring, you can explore the city without having to stand in long lines.

Downtown Newport

More than 200 pre-Revolutionary buildings (mostly private residences) remain in Newport, more than in any other city in the country. Most of these treasures are in the neighborhood known as the Point.

A GOOD WALK

The ideal first sight in a walking tour is the Colonial-era **Hunter House** ㊴. Walk north from Hunter House on Washington Street. At Van Zandt Avenue, turn right and proceed to the **Common Burial Ground** ㊵. Cross aptly named Farewell Street through the cemetery, and then head southeast. At the Marlborough Street intersection you'll pass the country's oldest bar and restaurant, the **White Horse Tavern** ㊶. Across Farewell Street stands **Friends Meeting House** ㊷. To the east, Marlborough intersects Spring Street and Broadway; ahead on your right you'll see the **Wanton-Lyman-Hazard House** ㊸, the oldest home in Newport. Follow Spring Street three short blocks south to Washington Street, which heads west into Washington Square. Over your left shoulder is the imposing **Colony House** ㊹, site of a number of historic events. At the bottom of Washington Square is the **Museum of Newport History at the Brick Market** ㊺.

Walk two blocks east on Touro Street (on the south side of the square); **Touro Synagogue** ㊻, the country's oldest Jewish house of worship, will be on your left. Next door is the **Newport Historical Society** ㊼. Cross the road and follow High Street one block; then turn right on Church Street to see the immaculate **Trinity Church** ㊽. Proceed east on Church Street. Across Bellevue Avenue are the four pillars of the **Redwood Library** ㊾. The **Newport Art Museum and Art Association** ㊿ is one block south.

Timing. This walk covers 2½ mi. If you spend time inside each building, it should take about 4½ hours to reach Bellevue Avenue. It's best to do this walk one day and the mansions of Bellevue Avenue another. If you have only one day, you will have to limit the number of sights you visit.

SIGHTS TO SEE

㊹ **Colony House.** This redbrick structure above downtown Washington Square was where, on May 4, 1776, Rhode Island and Providence Plantations signed an act that removed King George's name from all state documents. The same year, from the balcony of this building, the Declaration of Independence was read to Newporters. In 1781, George Washington met here with French commander Count Rochambeau to plan the Battle of Yorktown, which led to the end of the Revolutionary War. ⊠ *Washington Sq.,* ☎ *401/846–2980.* ☉ *Tours by appointment.*

㊵ **Common Burial Ground.** Farewell Street is lined with historic cemeteries; the many tombstones at this 17th-century graveyard are fine examples of Colonial stone carving, much of it the work of John Stevens.

㊷ **Friends Meeting House.** Built in 1699, this is the oldest Quaker meetinghouse in the country. With its wide-plank floors, simple benches, balcony, and beam ceiling (considered lofty by Colonial standards), the two-story shingle structure reflects the quiet reserve and steadfast faith of Colonial Quakers. ⊠ *29 Farewell St.,* ☎ *401/846–0813.* ⊠ *$5.* ☉ *Tours by appointment.*

★ ㊴ **Hunter House.** The French admiral Charles Louis d'Arsac de Ternay used this lovely 1748 home as his Revolutionary War headquarters. The carved pineapple over the doorway was a symbol of welcome throughout Colonial America; a fresh pineapple placed out front signaled an invitation to neighbors to visit a returned seaman or to look

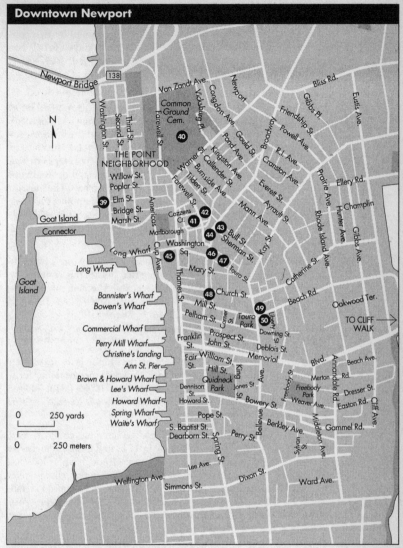

Downtown Newport

over a shop's new stock. The elliptical arch in the central hall is a typical Newport detail. Pieces made by Newport artisans Townsend and Goddard furnish much of the house, which also contains the first commissioned painting by a young Gilbert Stuart, best known for his portraits of George Washington. ⊠ *54 Washington St.,* ☎ *401/847–7516,* WEB *www.newportmansions.org.* ⌨ *$8.* ⊙ *May–Sept., daily 10–5; Oct., weekends 10–5.*

45 **Museum of Newport History at the Brick Market.** This restored building once used for slave trading houses a city museum with multimedia exhibits that explore Newport's social and economic influences. Antiques such as the printing press of James Franklin (Ben's brother) inspire the imagination. Built in 1760 and designed by Peter Harrison, who was also responsible for the Touro Synagogue and the Redwood Library, the building served as a theater and a town hall. The museum and the Gateway Information Center are departure points for walking tours of Newport; call for times. ⊠ *127 Thames St.,* ☎ *401/841–0813.* ⌨ *$5.* ⊙ *May–Nov., Mon. and Wed.–Sat. 10–5, Sun. 1–5; Dec.–Apr., Fri.–Sat. 10–4, Sun. 1–5.*

50 **Newport Art Museum and Art Association.** Richard Morris Hunt designed the Stick-style Victorian building that houses this community-supported center for the arts. The galleries exhibit contemporary works by New England artists. ⊠ *76 Bellevue Ave.,* ☎ *401/848–8200,* WEB *www.newportartmuseum.com.* ⌨ *$6.* ⊙ *Memorial Day–Labor Day, Mon.–Sat. 10–5, Sun. noon–5; Labor Day–Memorial Day, Fri.–Sat. 10–4, Sun. noon–4.*

47 **Newport Historical Society.** The headquarters of the historical society has a library and a small exhibit with Newport memorabilia, furniture, and maritime items. ⊠ *82 Touro St.,* ☎ *401/846–0813.* ⌨ *Free.* ⊙ *Mid-June–Aug., Tues.–Sat. 9:30–4:30; Sept.–mid-June, Tues.–Fri. 9:30–4:30, Sat. 9:30–noon.*

49 **Redwood Library.** This Roman templelike building, complete with Doric columns, was built as a library in 1747 and has been in use for that purpose ever since, a record in America. Although it may look like a Roman temple, it is actually made of wood; the exterior paint is mixed with sand to make it resemble cut stone. The library's paintings include works by Gilbert Stuart and Rembrandt Peale. ⊠ *50 Bellevue Ave.,* ☎ *401/847–0292,* WEB *www.redwood1747.org.* ⌨ *Free.* ⊙ *Mon.–Sat. 9:30–5:30.*

46 **Touro Synagogue.** Jews, like Quakers and Baptists, were attracted by Rhode Island's religious tolerance; they arrived from Amsterdam and Lisbon as early as 1658. The oldest surviving synagogue in the United States was dedicated in 1763. Although simple on the outside, the Georgian building, designed by Peter Harrison, has an elaborate interior. Its classical style influenced Thomas Jefferson in the building of Monticello and the University of Virginia. ⊠ *85 Touro St.,* ☎ *401/847–4794,* WEB *www.tourosynagogue.org.* ⌨ *Free.* ⊙ *July 4–Labor Day, Sun.–Fri. 10–5; Memorial Day–July 4 and Labor Day–Columbus Day, weekdays 1–3, Sun. 1–3; Columbus Day–Memorial Day, Sun. 1–3, weekdays for 2 PM tour only. Guided tours on the ½ hr. Services Fri. at 6 or 7 PM, Sat. at 8:45 AM; call to confirm.*

48 **Trinity Church.** This Colonial beauty was built in 1724 and modeled after London churches designed by Sir Christopher Wren. A special feature of the interior is the three-tier wineglass pulpit, the only one of its kind in America. The lighting, woodwork, and palpable feeling of history make attending Episcopal services here an unforgettable experience. ⊠ *Queen Anne Sq.,* ☎ *401/846–0660.* ⌨ *Free.* ⊙ *June–Sept.,* *daily 10–4; Oct.–May, daily 10–1. Sun services at 8 and 10, off-season (call for months) at 8 and 10:30.*

43 **Wanton-Lyman-Hazard House.** Newport's oldest residence dates from the mid-17th century and presents a window on the fascinating Colonial and Revolutionary history of Newport. The dark red building was site of the city's Stamp Act riot of 1765; after the British Parliament levied a tax on most printed material, the Sons of Liberty stormed the house, which was occupied by the English stamp master. ✉ *17 Broadway,* ☎ *401/846–0813.* *$4.* ⏲ *June–Aug., Thurs.–Sat. 11–3.*

41 **White Horse Tavern.** William Mayes, the father of a successful and notorious pirate, received a tavern license in 1687, which makes this building, built in 1673, the oldest tavern in America. Its gambrel roof, low dark-beam ceilings, cavernous fireplace, and uneven plank floors epitomize Newport's Colonial charm. ✉ *Marlborough and Farewell Sts.,* ☎ *401/849–3600,* WEB *www.whitehorsetavern.com.*

Greater Newport

The gilded-age mansions of Bellevue Avenue are what many people associate most with Newport. These late-19th-century homes are almost obscenely grand, laden with ornate rococo detail and designed with a determined one-upmanship. Also in this area are some museums.

The **Preservation Society of Newport County** (☎ 401/847–1000) maintains 12 mansions. Guided tours are given of each; you can purchase a combination ticket at any of the properties for a substantial discount. The hours and days the houses are open during the off-season are subject to change, so it's wise to call ahead. Chateau-sur-Mer, the Elms, and, in some years, the Marble House or the Breakers are decorated for Christmas and usually open for tours daily from Thanksgiving Day to Christmas Day.

A GOOD TOUR

At the corner of Memorial Boulevard and Bellevue Avenue is the **International Tennis Hall of Fame Museum at the Newport Casino** (51), birthplace of the U.S. Open. Before you visit the mansions (or stop by when you're done), you can walk south on Bellevue Avenue, make a right on Bowery Street, and turn left at Thames Street to visit the **International Yacht Restoration School** (52). Back on Bellevue Avenue, catercorner from Newport Casino is **Kingscote** (53), a Victorian "cottage." The neoclassical **Elms** (54) is two blocks south. Three blocks farther is the Gothic-style **Chateau-sur-Mer** (55), and **Rosecliff** (56), modeled after the Grand Trianon, is four more blocks in the same direction. **Astors' Beechwood** (57) and the **Marble House** (58), a Vanderbilt mansion, are on the same side of this lengthy block of palaces. Farther down, on the corner of Lakeview and Bellevue, is **Belcourt Castle** (59). Beyond this mansion, Bellevue Avenue turns 90 degrees west and dead-ends at what most consider the end of the Cliff Walk, a stunning promenade. From here you can take Cliff Walk down to **Rough Point** (60) to catch a backyard glimpse of the home of Doris Duke. Then you can stroll along the Rhode Island Sound to Newport's most renowned mansion, the **Breakers** (61), which can be reached from the Cliff Walk by heading west on Ruggles Avenue and north on Ochre Point Avenue.

You can walk the first part of this tour (although you may well prefer to save your energy for touring the houses), but you'll need a car to visit two sights. The **Museum of Yachting** (62) is at Fort Adams State Park. From downtown Newport, drive south on Thames Street to Wellington Avenue. Turn right and follow Wellington to the bend where Wellington becomes Halidon Avenue. Turn right on Harrison Avenue. One mile to the right is the entrance to the park; the museum is at the end of Fort Adams Road. To get back to town, follow Ocean Drive to Bellevue Avenue. To reach the **Naval War College Museum** ⑥, at the intersection with Memorial Boulevard, turn left; Memorial becomes America's Cup Avenue. At the cemetery, turn left on Farewell Street. Farewell runs into Bridge Access Road, where you will veer left to reach the Connell Highway traffic circle. Exit at the west end of the circle on Training Station Road. A small bridge will take you to Coasters Harbor Island. Park at the naval base entrance and walk two blocks along the same road to the museum, which is on a hill to your right.

Timing. If you have one day, it's best to tour two or three mansions and see the others only from the outside. To avoid long lines in summer, go early or choose the less-popular but still amazing mansions—the Elms, Kingscote, and Belcourt Castle. It's less than 2 mi from Kingscote to Belcourt—the first and last mansions on Bellevue Avenue. Plan on spending one hour at each mansion you visit. The full Cliff Walk is 3½ mi long. Seeing the Tennis Hall of Fame, three mansions, walking the length of Bellevue Avenue, and returning via the Cliff Walk takes five or six hours. The driving portion of the tour is about 11 mi long. You could easily spend an hour at each sight on the drive.

SIGHTS TO SEE

❺❼ **Astors' Beechwood.** The original mistress of this oceanfront mansion, Caroline Schermerhorn Astor, was the queen of American society in the late 19th century; her list of "The Four Hundred" was the first social register. Her husband, William Backhouse Astor, was a reserved businessman and a member of one of the wealthiest families in the nation (much of the Astors' fortune came from real estate, the China trade, and fur trading in North America). As you're guided through the 1857 mansion, actors in period costume play the family, their servants, and their household guests. ⊠ *580 Bellevue Ave.,* ☎ *401/846–3772,* WEB *www.astors-beechwood.com.* ⊑ *$9.* ☉ *Mid-May–Oct., daily 10–5; Nov.–Dec., daily 10–4; Feb.–mid-May, Fri.–Sun. 10–4; call about Christmas hrs and events.*

❺❾ **Belcourt Castle.** Richard Morris Hunt based this 1894 Gothic Revival mansion, built for banking heir Oliver H. P. Belmont, on Louis XIII's hunting lodge. The house is so filled with European and Asian treasures that locals have dubbed it the Metropolitan Museum of Newport. Sip tea and admire the stained glass and carved wood, and don't miss the Golden Coronation Coach. ⊠ *657 Bellevue Ave.,* ☎ *401/846–0669 or 401/849–1566.* ⊑ *$8.* ☉ *Apr.–Oct., daily 10–5; Nov.–Dec., daily 10–3; Feb.–Mar., daily 10–3.*

★ ❻❶ **The Breakers.** It's easy to understand why it took 2,500 workers in the early 1890s two years to build the most magnificent Newport palace, the 70-room home of railroad heir Cornelius Vanderbilt II. A few of the marvels within the four-story Italian Renaissance–style palace are a gold-ceiling music room, a blue marble fireplace, rose alabaster pillars in the dining room, and a porch with a mosaic ceiling that took Italian artisans six months, lying on their backs, to install. To build the Breakers today would cost $400 million. ⊠ *Ochre Point Ave.,* ☎ *401/847–6544,* WEB *www.newportmansions.org.* ⊑ *$12.* ☉ *Mar.–Oct., daily 10–5; Nov., weekends 10–4; open Dec. some years (call ahead).*

❺❺ **Chateau-sur-Mer.** Bellevue Avenue's first stone mansion was built in the Victorian Gothic style in 1852 for William S. Wetmore, a tycoon involved in the China trade, and enlarged in the 1870s by Richard Morris Hunt. The Gold Room by Leon Marcotte and the Renaissance Revival–style dining room and library by the Florentine sculptor Luigi

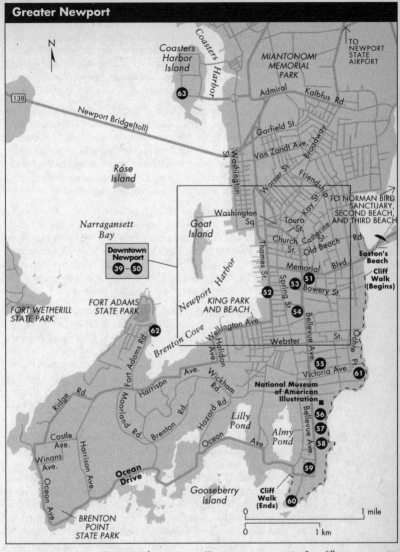

Greater Newport

N

TO NEWPORT STATE AIRPORT

Coasters Harbor Island

Coasters Harbor

MIANTONOMI MEMORIAL PARK

63

138

Newport Bridge(toll)

Admiral

Kalbfus Rd.

Garfield St.

Van Zandt Ave.

Broadway

Warner St.

Friendship

Rose Island

Washington St.

Washington Sq.

Key St.

TO NORMAN BIRD SANCTUARY, SECOND BEACH, AND THIRD BEACH

Narragansett Bay

Goat Island

Touro St.

Catherine St.

Church St.

Old Beach Rd.

Easton's Beach

Downtown Newport
39 – **50**

Thames St.

Memorial Blvd.

51

Cliff Walk (Begins)

Newport Harbor

52

Spring St.

53

Bowery St.

FORT WETHERILL STATE PARK

FORT ADAMS STATE PARK

KING PARK AND BEACH

54

Brenton Cove

Wellington Ave.

Webster St.

Ochre Pt.

Fort Adams Rd.

62

Holiday Ave.

Ridge Rd.

Harrison Ave.

Moorland Rd.

Wickham Rd.

55

Victoria Ave.

61

National Museum of American Illustration

Brenton Rd.

Hazard Rd.

Lilly Pond

Bellevue Ave.

56

57

Castle Ave.

Ocean Ave.

Almy Pond

58

Winans Ave.

Harrison Ave.

Ocean Drive

59

Ocean Ave.

Gooseberry Island

Cliff Walk (Ends)

60

BRENTON POINT STATE PARK

0   1 mile

0   1 km

Frullini are sterling examples of the work of leading 19th-century designers. Upstairs, the bedrooms are decorated in the English Aesthetic style with wallpaper by Arts and Crafts designers William Morris and William Burges. ⊠ *Bellevue Ave. at Shepard Ave.,* ☎ *401/847–1000,* WEB *www.newportmansions.org.* ⌧ *$9.* ☉ *May–Sept., daily 10–5; Oct.–Thanksgiving and Jan.–Mar., weekends 10–4; Thanksgiving– Dec. 23, daily 10–4; Apr., weekends 10–5.*

Chepstow. This Italianate villa with a mansard roof is not as grand as other Newport mansions, but it houses a remarkable collection of art and furniture gathered by the Morris family of New York City. Built in 1861, the home was designed by Newport architect George Champlin Mason and is the latest addition to the list of homes owned by the Preservation Society of Newport County. ⊠ *120 Narragansett Ave.,* ☎ *401/ 847–1000 ext. 165.* ⌧ *$10.* ☉ *May–Oct., Fri.–Sat. 10–5.*

★ **Cliff Walk.** Easton's Beach (also called First Beach) is the beginning of this spectacular 3½-mi path, which runs south along Newport's cliffs to Bailey's Beach. The promenade has views of sumptuous mansions on one side and the rocky coastline on the other; walking any section of it is worth the effort. The Cliff Walk can be accessed from any road running east off Bellevue Avenue. The unpaved sections can be difficult for small children or people with mobility problems.

⑤④ **The Elms.** In designing this graceful 48-room French neoclassical mansion, architect Horace Trumbauer paid homage to the style, fountains, broad lawn, and formal gardens of the Château d'Asnières near Paris. The Elms was built for Edward Julius Berwind, a bituminous-coal baron, in 1899. The energy magnate's home was one of the first in the nation to have central heat and to be piped for hot water. The trees throughout the 12-acre backyard are labeled, providing an exemplary botany lesson. ⊠ *Bellevue Ave.,* ☎ *401/842– 0546,* WEB *www.newportmansions.org.* ⌧ *$9.* ☉ *Daily 10–5.*

⑤① **International Tennis Hall of Fame Museum at the Newport Casino.** The photographs, memorabilia, and multimedia exhibits at the Hall of Fame provide a definitive chronicle of the game's greatest moments and characters. The magnificent, shingle-style Newport Casino, a social club, was designed by Stanford White and built in 1880 for publisher James Gordon Bennett Jr., who quit the nearby club, the Newport Reading Room, after a polo player—at Bennett's behest—rode a horse into the building and was subsequently banned. Bennett further retaliated by commissioning the Casino, which has 13 grass courts and one court-tennis facility (court tennis is the precursor to modern tennis). The Casino quickly became the social and recreational hot spot of the gilded age. ⊠ *194 Bellevue Ave.,* ☎ *401/849–3990,* WEB *www.tennisfame.com.* ⌧ *$8; tennis courts $35 per person per hr.* ☉ *Daily 9:30–5.*

⑤② **International Yacht Restoration School.** This school, off Thames Street in a former power plant, lets you watch shipwrights and students as they overhaul historically significant sailboats and powerboats. Placards recount each boat's past. The 1885 racing schooner *Coronet* and the original "cigarette boat" are two standouts. ⊠ *449 Thames St.,* ☎ *401/848–5777,* WEB *www.iyrs.org.* ⌧ *Free.* ☉ *Apr.–Nov., daily 9– 5; Dec.–Mar., Mon.–Sat. 10–5.*

Isaac Bell House. Considered one of the finest examples of American shingle-style architecture, this Bellevue Avenue home, currently being restored, is open to the public as a work in progress. The exterior has been completed; inside, a short film documents the effort to revitalize the McKim, Mead & White design, and you are given a tour of various rooms. Bell, who built the home in 1883, was a wealthy cotton broker. ✉ *Bellevue Ave. at Perry St.,* ☎ *401/847–1000,* WEB *www.newportmansions.org.* 🎫 *$9.* ⏲ *May–Oct., Fri.–Sat. 10–5.*

(53) **Kingscote.** This Victorian mansion, completed in 1841, was designed by Richard Upjohn for George Noble Jones, a plantation owner from Savannah, Georgia. (Newport was popular with Southerners before the Civil War.) Decorated with antique furniture, glass, and Asian art, it contains a number of Tiffany windows. ✉ *Bowery St., off Bellevue Ave.,* ☎ *401/847–1000,* WEB *www.newportmansions.org.* 🎫 *$9.* ⏲ *May–Sept., daily 10–5; Apr. and Oct., weekends 10–4.*

★ (58) **Marble House.** Perhaps the most opulent Newport mansion, the Marble House is known for its extravagant gold ballroom. The house was the gift of William Vanderbilt to his wife, Alva, in 1892. Alva divorced William in 1895 and married Oliver Perry Belmont, becoming the lady of Belcourt Castle. When Oliver died in 1908, she returned to Marble House. Mrs. Belmont was involved with the suffragist movement and spent much of her time campaigning for women's rights. The Chinese teahouse behind the estate was built in 1913. ✉ *Bellevue Ave., near Ruggles St.,* ☎ *401/847–1000,* WEB *www.newportmansions.org.* 🎫 *$9.* ⏲ *Apr.–Oct., daily 10–5; Jan.–Mar., weekends 10–4; open Dec. some years (call ahead).*

(62) **Museum of Yachting.** The museum has four galleries: Mansions and Yachts, Small Craft, America's Cup, and the Hall of Fame for Single-handed Sailors. Displays include an exhibit about the history of the Vanderbilts (of the Breakers and Marble House fame) and their yachts, many of which were America's Cup contenders and/or winners; the rescue boat used by Ida Lewis, keeper of the Limerock Light from 1860 to 1922, who rescued dozens of men over the years; and a scale model of *Courageous,* an America's Cup contender and the state yacht of RI. In summer, eight wooden yachts constitute a floating exhibition. ✉ *Ft. Adams State Park, Ocean Dr.,* ☎ *401/847–1018.* 🎫 *$3.* ⏲ *Mid-May–Oct., daily 10–5; Nov.–mid-May, by appointment.*

National Museum of American Illustration. In the renovated Vernon Court, an 1898 gilded-age mansion, the museum showcases original drawings and paintings created for books, advertisements, art prints, and periodicals, including works by Maxfield Parrish, Norman Rockwell, and N. C. Wyeth. ✉ *492 Bellevue Ave.,* ☎ *401/851–8949,* WEB *www.americanillustration.org.* 🎫 *$25.* ⏲ *By appointment.*

(63) **Naval War College Museum.** The Naval War College, the oldest school of its kind in the world, represents the pinnacle of education in the U.S. Navy. The museum's exhibits analyze the history of naval warfare and tactics and trace the history of the navy in Narragansett Bay. ✉ *Founders Hall, Gate 1, Naval Education and Training Center, Cushing Rd.,* ☎ *401/841–4052,* WEB *www.nwc.navy.mil/museum.* 🎫 *Free.* ⏲ *Oct.–May, weekdays 10–4; June–Sept., weekdays 10–4, weekends noon–4.*

Norman Bird Sanctuary. Eight miles of trails, from ¼-mi to 1⁷⁄₁₀-mi long, loop through the 450-acre sanctuary, which in summer provides refuge indeed from wharf-side Newport's hustle and bustle. Pheasants, rabbits, and numerous bird species live in the fields and woodlands; from the higher elevations you can see the ocean, some ponds, and the marshy lowlands. Exhibits at the visitor center explain the sanctuary's history and animal and plant life. ✉ *583 Third Beach Rd., Middletown,* ☎ *401/846–2577.* 🎫 *$4.* ⏲ *Thurs.–Tues. 9–5, Wed. until dark.*

(56) **Rosecliff.** Newport's most romantic mansion was built for Mrs. Hermann Oelrichs in 1902; her father had amassed a fortune from Nevada

silver mines. Stanford White modeled the palace after the Grand Trianon at Versailles. Rosecliff has a heart-shape staircase, and its 40 rooms include the Court of Love and a grand ballroom. ⊠ *Bellevue Ave. at Marine Ave.,* ☎ *401/847–5793,* WEB *www.newportmansions.org.* ⊠ *$9.* ⊘ *Apr.–Oct., daily 10–5.*

⑥⓪ **Rough Point.** The late tobacco heiress and preservationist Doris Duke hosted such celebs as Elizabeth Taylor at her Newport mansion, which is open for small tours that leave from the Newport Gateway visitor center. (And only from the center: you can't drive or walk here and be admitted.) The 105-room home was built in the English-manor style for an heir to the Vanderbilt railroad fortune. The furnishings range from the grand to the peculiar (count the mother-of-pearl bedroom suite among the latter), but Duke's taste in art, especially English portraiture, was pretty sharp: of all the Newport mansions, Duke's has the best art collection. ⊠ *Bellevue Ave. at Ocean Dr.,* ☎ *401/849–7300.* ⊠ *$25 (first-come, first-served basis).* ⊘ *Tours leave from the Newport Gateway visitor center (23 America's Cup Ave.) daily at 10, 12:30, and 3.*

Dining and Lodging

$$$–$$$$ ✕ **Asterix & Obelix.** Danish chef John Bach-Sorensen makes fine din-
★ ing as fun and colorful as the madcap French cartoon strip after which this eatery was named. An auto repair garage before Sorensen took it over, the restaurant has a concrete floor painted to look like it's been covered with expensive tiling. Asian twists enliven the French-influenced Mediterranean fare, accompanied by a carefully selected menu of wines, brandies, and aperitifs. Sunday brunch is served year-round. ⊠ *599 Thames St.,* ☎ *401/841–8833. AE, D, DC, MC, V. No lunch.*

$$$–$$$$ ✕ **The Black Pearl.** At this dignified, converted dock shanty, popular with yachters, clam chowder is sold by the quart. Dining is in the casual tavern or the formal Commodore's Room (reservations essential). The latter serves an appetizer of black-and-blue tuna with red-pepper sauce. The French and American entrées include duck breast with green peppercorn sauce and swordfish with Dutch pepper butter. ⊠ *Bannister's Wharf,* ☎ *401/846–5264. Jacket required. AE, MC, V.*

$$$–$$$$ ✕ **Clarke Cooke House.** Waiters in tuxedos and the richly patterned cushions on wood chairs and booths underscore this restaurant's luxurious Colonial setting. Formal dining is on the upper level, in a room with a timber-beam ceiling, green latticework, and water views; there's open-air dining in warm weather. The refined, pricey Mediterranean menu incorporates local seafood; game dishes often appear as specials. ⊠ *Bannister's Wharf,* ☎ *401/849–2900. Reservations essential. Jacket required. AE, D, DC, MC, V.*

$$$–$$$$ ✕ **Scales & Shells.** Busy, sometime noisy, but always excellent, this restaurant serves as many as 15 types of superbly fresh wood-grilled fish, including grilled lobster. The cooks occasionally send your server to the table with your future dinner so you'll know exactly how fresh the fish is. Similar dishes are available in the more formal dining room upstairs at Upscales. Reservations are not accepted downstairs. ⊠ *527 Thames St.,* ☎ *401/848–9378. No credit cards.*

$$$ ✕ **La Petite Auberge.** The colorful owner-chef, who once worked for General Charles de Gaulle, prepares such traditional delicacies as trout with almonds, duck flambé with orange sauce, and medallions of beef with goose-liver pâté. His exquisite cooking is served in a series of intimate rooms inside a Colonial house. In summer, dinner is served in the courtyard. ⊠ *19 Charles St.,* ☎ *401/849–6669. AE, MC, V.*

$$$ ✕ **White Horse Tavern.** The nation's oldest operating tavern, once a meetinghouse for Colonial Rhode Island's General Assembly, has intimate dining with black-tie service, a top-notch wine cellar, and con-

sistently excellent food. The tavern serves suave American cuisine, including local seafood and beef Wellington, along with more exotic entrées such as cashew-encrusted venison tenderloin topped with an apple-cider demiglace. ⊠ *Marlborough and Farewell Sts.,* ☎ *401/849–3600,* WEB *www.whitehorsetavern.com. Reservations essential. Jacket required. AE, D, DC, MC, V. No lunch Mon.–Wed.*

$$–$$$ ✕ **The Mooring.** The seafood chowder at this family-oriented restau-
★ rant won the local cook-off so many times that it was removed from further competition. Slowly braised beef short loin and any fish special are good choices. In fine weather you can dine on the enclosed patio overlooking the harbor; on chilly winter evenings, take advantage of the open fire in the sunken interior room. ⊠ *Sayer's Wharf,* ☎ *401/846–2260. AE, D, DC, MC, V.*

$$–$$$ ✕ **Restaurant Bouchard.** Regional takes on French cuisine fill the menu at this upscale yet homey restaurant. Sautéed local cod, for example, is topped with fresh Maine crab and asparagus, then finished with a light beurre blanc. ⊠ *505 Thames St.,* ☎ *401/846–0123. AE, D, MC, V.*

$$ ✕ **Flo's Clam Shack.** Fried seafood, steamed clams, cold beer, and the best raw bar in town keep the lines long here in summer. The rest of the year, Flo's, established in 1936, is a favorite with locals. An upstairs bar serves baked, chilled lobster, and outside seating is available. This place is across the street from First Beach. ⊠ *4 Wave Ave.,* ☎ *401/847–8141. Reservations not accepted. MC, V. Closed Jan.*

$$ ✕ **Puerini's.** The aroma of garlic and basil greets you as soon as you enter this laid-back neighborhood Italian restaurant. Lace curtains hang in the windows, and black-and-white photographs of Italy cover the soft-pink walls. The long and intriguing menu includes green noodles with chicken in marsala sauce, tortellini with seafood, and cavatelli with four cheeses. ⊠ *24 Memorial Blvd.,* ☎ *401/847–5506. Reservations not accepted. MC, V.*

$ ✕ **Ocean Coffee Roasters.** Known to locals as Wave Café, this nonchalant diner draws fans aplenty for fresh-roasted coffee and fresh-baked muffins as well as bagels, salads, and homemade Italian soups. Breakfast is served until 2 PM; lines can be long in summer. ⊠ *22 Washington Sq.,* ☎ *401/846–6060. Reservations not accepted. MC, V.*

$$$$ ✕🖼 **Vanderbilt Hall.** This former YMCA has been converted into the
★ city's most sophisticated inn and restaurant. A butler greets you on arrival, a musician solos nightly at the grand piano in the center of the home, and a classy billiard room beckons. Room 35 has a king-size bed and three windows with views of Newport Harbor and Trinity Church; suites have office space and sitting rooms. All the rooms are decorated with antiques. The butler serves canapés and cocktails in the common room while patrons peruse the options for dinner: Continental cuisine ($$$–$$$$), including beef Wellington, served on Wedgwood china at tables set with silver. ⊠ *41 Mary St., 02840,* ☎ *401/846–6200,* FAX *401/846–0701,* WEB *www.vanderbilthall.com. 40 rooms, 10 suites. Restaurant, in-room data ports, indoor pool, sauna, billiards. AE, D, DC, MC, V.*

$$$$ 🖼 **Cliffside Inn.** Grandeur and comfort come in equal supply at this
★ swank Victorian home on a tree-lined street near the Cliff Walk. The rooms are furnished with Victorian antiques, and more than 100 paintings by artist Beatrice Turner, who lived in the house for many years and painted hundreds of self portraits, are a signature touch. The Governor's Suite (named for Governor Thomas Swann, of Maryland, who built the home in 1880) has a two-sided fireplace, a whirlpool bath, a four-poster king-size bed, and a brass birdcage shower. Seven other rooms also have whirlpool baths; 10 have working fireplaces. ⊠ *2 Seaview Ave., 02840,* ☎ *401/847–1811 or 800/845–1811,* FAX *401/848–5850,* WEB *www.cliffsideinn.com. 16 rooms. AE, D, DC, MC, V. BP.*

$$$$ 🏠 **Elm Tree Cottage.** William Ralph Emerson, Ralph Waldo's cousin, designed the Elm Tree, a shingle-style house. This 1882 architectural treasure has massive guest rooms (most with fireplaces) furnished with English antiques and decorated by owner Priscilla Malone, an interior designer; her creative breakfasts are served on linen-bedecked tables. There's a two-night minimum weekends, three on holiday weekends. ⊠ *336 Gibbs Ave., 02840,* ☎ *401/849–1610 or 800/882–3356,* FAX *401/849–2084,* WEB *www.elm-tree.com. 5 rooms, 1 suite. Lounge; no smoking. AE, MC, V. BP.*

$$$$ 🏠 **Francis Malbone House.** The design of this stately painted-brick house
  ★   is attributed to Peter Harrison, the architect responsible for the Touro Synagogue and the Redwood Library. A lavish inn with period reproduction furnishings, the 1760 structure was tastefully doubled in size in the mid-1990s. The rooms in the main house are all in corners (with two windows) and look out over the courtyard, which has a fountain, or across the street to the harbor. Fifteen rooms have working fireplaces. ⊠ *392 Thames St., 02840,* ☎ *401/846–0392 or 800/846–0392,* FAX *401/848–5956,* WEB *www.malbone.com. 16 rooms, 2 suites. Some in-room hot tubs; no air-conditioning in some rooms. AE, MC, V. BP.*

$$$–$$$$ 🏠 **Castle Hill Inn and Resort.** Much of the furniture at this inn is orig-
  ★   inal to the structure, a summer home built in 1874 on a cliff at the mouth of the Narragansett Bay. Views over the bay are enthralling, and the public areas have tremendous charm. Castle Hill also has luxurious rooms in the more modern Beach Houses and Harbor Houses. The inn, 3 mi from the center of Newport, is famous for its Sunday brunches. On Sunday afternoons, the lawn is crowded with people enjoying cocktails. ⊠ *590 Ocean Dr., 02840,* ☎ *401/849–3800 or 888/466–1355,* FAX *401/849–3838,* WEB *www.castlehillinn.com. 35 rooms. Restaurant, 3 beaches. AE, D, MC, V. BP.*

$$$–$$$$ 🏠 **Hotel Viking.** An inn expressly built in 1926 for the guests of mansion owners, the redbrick Viking is elegantly situated at the north end of Bellevue Avenue. The wood paneling and original chandeliers evoke the hotel's sophisticated history. The stately rooms, adorned with reproduction Colonial furniture and appointments (draperies and spreads), resemble the grand homes of Colonial merchant seamen. ⊠ *1 Bellevue Ave., 02840,* ☎ *401/847–3300 or 800/556–7126,* FAX *401/848–4864,* WEB *www.hotelviking.com. 218 rooms, 9 suites. Restaurant, bar, refrigerators, in-room VCRs, indoor pool, hot tub, sauna, meeting room. AE, D, DC, MC, V.*

$$$–$$$$ 🏠 **Hyatt Regency Newport.** On Goat Island across from the Colonial Point District, the Hyatt has great views of the harbor and the Newport Bridge. Most rooms have water views. Although the hotel is a 15-minute walk to Newport's center, bike and moped rentals are nearby. All rooms have oak furnishings and multicolor jewel-tone fabrics. ⊠ *1 Goat Island, 02840,* ☎ *401/851–1234,* FAX *401/846–7210,* WEB *www.hyatt.com. 264 rooms. Restaurant, tennis court, indoor pool, saltwater pool, hair salon, health club, sauna, spa, boating, racquetball, meeting room, free parking. AE, D, DC, MC, V.*

$$$–$$$$ 🏠 **Inntowne.** This small town-house hotel is in the center of Newport, 1½ blocks from the harbor. The neatly appointed rooms are decorated in a floral motif. Light sleepers may prefer rooms on the upper floors, which let in less traffic noise. The staff members are on hand throughout the day to give sightseeing advice. ⊠ *6 Mary St., 02840,* ☎ *401/846–9200 or 800/457–7803,* FAX *401/846–1534,* WEB *www.inntowneinn.com. 26 rooms. AE, MC, V. CP.*

$$–$$$$ 🏠 **Admiral Fitzroy Inn.** This tidy 1854 Victorian Quiet provides restful retreat in the heart of Newport's bustling waterfront district. Period antiques decorate the rooms, each of which has either an antique brass or hand-carved wood bed. Two rooms have fireplaces, and one has a private deck with a harbor view. Kitchen facilities are available. Its namesake, Admiral Fitzroy, commanded the *Beagle,* who's most famous passenger was Charles Darwin. ⊠ *398 Thames St., 02840,* ☎ *866/848–8780 or 401/848–8006,* FAX *401/848–8006,* WEB *www.admiralfitzroy.com. 17 rooms. Cable TV. AE, D, MC, V. CP.*

$$–$$$$ 🖭 **Newport Marriott.** An atrium lobby with marble floors and a nautical theme unfold as you enter this luxury hotel on the harbor at Long Wharf. Rooms that don't border the atrium overlook the city or the waterfront. Fifth-floor rooms facing the harbor have sliding French windows that open onto large decks. Rates vary greatly according to season and location; harbor-view rooms cost more. ⊠ *25 America's Cup Ave., 02840,* ☎ *401/849–1000 or 800/228–9290,* FAX *401/849–3422,* WEB *www.courtyard.com. 317 rooms, 7 suites. Restaurant, indoor pool, health club, hot tub, sauna, racquetball, bar, meeting room. AE, D, DC, MC, V.*

$$$ 🖭 **Ivy Lodge.** The only B&B in the mansion district, this grand (though
★ small by Newport's standards) Victorian has gables and a Gothic turret. Designed by Stanford White, the home has 11 fireplaces, large and lovely rooms, a spacious dining room, window seats, and two common rooms. The defining feature is a Gothic-style oak entryway with a three-story turned-baluster staircase and a dangling wrought-iron chandelier. In summer, you can relax in wicker chairs on the wraparound porch. ⊠ *12 Clay St., 02840,* ☎ *401/849–6865,* FAX *401/849–2919,* WEB *www.ivylodge.com. 7 rooms, 1 suite. AE, MC, V. BP.*

$–$$ 🖭 **Harbor Base Pineapple Inn.** This basic, clean motel is the least expensive lodging in Newport. All rooms contain two double beds; some also have kitchenettes. Close to the naval base and jai alai, it's a five-minute drive from downtown. ⊠ *372 Coddington Hwy., 02840,* ☎ *401/847–2600,* WEB *www.newportrhodeisland.com/users/pineapple. 48 rooms. AE, D, DC, MC, V.*

Nightlife and the Arts

Detailed events calendars can be found in *Newport This Week* and the *Newport Daily News.*

NIGHTLIFE

For a sampling of Newport's lively nightlife, you need only stroll down **Thames Street** after dark. The **Candy Store** (⊠ Bannister's Wharf, ☎ 401/849–2900) in the Clarke Cooke House restaurant is a snazzy place for a drink. A DJ spins dance music in the summer at the **Cheeky Monkey** (⊠ 14 Perry Mill Wharf, ☎ 401/845–9494); the mood at the bar is lighthearted and casual year-round. **Newport Blues Café** (⊠ 286 Thames St., ☎ 401/841–5510) hosts great blues performers. **One Pelham East** (⊠ 270 Thames St., ☎ 401/847–9460) draws a young crowd for progressive rock, reggae, and R&B.

The **JVC Newport Jazz Festival** (☎ 401/847–3700) takes place in mid-August. Performers have included Ray Charles, Dave Brubeck, Cassandra Wilson, Natalie Cole, and Stefan Harris.

THE ARTS

Murder-mystery plays are performed on Thursday evening from June to October at 8 PM at the **Astors' Beechwood** (⊠ 580 Bellevue Ave., ☎ 401/846–3772). **Newport Children's Theatre** (⊠ Box 144, ☎ 401/848–0266) mounts several productions each year. The **Newport International Film Festival** (☎ 401/848–9443, WEB www.newportfilmfestival.com), a small but impressive five-day festival, takes place in June. **Newport Playhouse & Cabaret** (⊠ 102 Connell Hwy., ☎ 401/848–7529) stages comedies and musicals; dinner packages are available.

Outdoor Activities and Sports

BASEBALL

Sunset League Baseball (✉ America's Cup Ave. and Marlborough St., ☎ 401/847–5609), an amateur league, has played at Cardines Field since 1908. The ticket price is $1, and the talent level is impressive.

BEACHES

Easton's Beach (✉ Memorial Blvd.), also known as First Beach, is popular for its carousel. **Fort Adams State Park** (✉ Ocean Dr.), a small beach with a picnic area and lifeguards in summer, has views of Newport Harbor and is fully sheltered from ocean swells. **Sachuest Beach,** or Second Beach, east of First Beach in the Sachuest Point area of Middletown, is a beautiful sandy area adjacent to the Norman Bird Sanctuary and Sachuest Wildlife Reserve. Dunes and a campground make it popular with young travelers and families. **Third Beach,** in the Sachuest Point area of Middletown, is on the Sakonnet River. It has a boat ramp and is a favorite of windsurfers.

BIKING

The 12-mi swing down Bellevue Avenue, along Ocean Drive and back, is a great route to ride your wheels. **Ten Speed Spokes** (✉ 18 Elm St., ☎ 401/847–5609, WEB www.tenspeedspokes.com) rents bikes for $25 per day, performance mountain bikes for $45 per day.

BOATING

Adventure Sports (✉ The Inn at Long Wharf, America's Cup Ave., ☎ 401/849–4820) rents sailboats, kayaks, and canoes. **Newport Yacht Services** (✉ 580 Thames St., ☎ 401/846–7720) runs excursions from a day trip in Newport harbor to a seven-day trip to the Virgin Islands. **Oldport Marine Services** (✉ Sayer's Wharf, ☎ 401/847–9109) operates harbor tours and daily and weekly crewed yacht charters, rents moorings, and provides launch services. **Sail Newport** (✉ Ft. Adams State Park, ☎ 401/846–1983) rents sailboats by the hour.

DIVING

Newport Diving Center (✉ 550 Thames St., ☎ 401/847–9293) operates charter dive trips, refills Nitrox, conducts PADI training and certification, and has rentals, sales, and service.

FISHING

Fishin' Off (✉ American Shipyard, Goat Island Causeway, ☎ 401/849–9642) runs charter-fishing trips on a 36-ft Trojan. The **Saltwater Edge** (✉ 561 Thames St., ☎ 401/842–0062, WEB www.saltwateredge.com) sells fly-fishing tackle, gives lessons, and conducts guided trips. **Sam's Bait & Tackle** (✉ 36 Aquidneck Ave., ☎ 401/849–5909) stocks gear and live bait.

JAI ALAI

Newport Jai Alai (✉ 150 Admiral Kalbfus Rd., ☎ 401/849–5000, WEB www.newportgrand.com) hosts live jai alai from March to mid-September. Simulcast racing and video slot machines are available year-round.

Shopping

Many of Newport's art and crafts galleries and antiques shops are on Thames Street; others are on Spring Street, Franklin Street, and at Bowen's and Bannister's wharves. The Brick Market area—between Thames Street and America's Cup Avenue—has more than 40 shops. Bellevue Avenue just south of Memorial Boulevard (near the International Tennis Hall of Fame) contains a strip of pricey shops with high-quality merchandise.

ANTIQUES

Aardvark Antiques (⊠ 475 Thames St., ☎ 401/849–7233) carries architectural pieces such as mantels, doors, and stained glass; the nearby yard sells unique fountains and garden statuary. The 125 dealers at the **Armory** (⊠ 365 Thames St., ☎ 401/848–2398), a vast 19th-century structure, carry antiques, china, and estate jewelry. **Harbor Antiques** (⊠ 134 Spring St., ☎ 401/848–9711) stocks unusual furniture, prints, and glassware.

ART AND CRAFTS GALLERIES

Arnold Art Store and Gallery (⊠ 210 Thames St., ☎ 401/847–2273, WEB www.arnoldart.com) collects marine-inspired paintings and prints. **DeBlois Gallery** (⊠ 138 Bellevue Ave., ☎ 401/847–9977) exhibits the works of Newport's emerging artists. **MacDowell Pottery** (⊠ 140 Spring St., ☎ 401/846–6313) showcases the wares of New England potters. **Spring Bull Gallery** (⊠ 55 Bellevue Ave., ☎ 401/849–9166) displays exciting and diverse local art in Newport. The delicate, dramatic blown-glass gifts at **Thames Glass** (⊠ 688 Thames St., ☎ 401/846–0576) are designed by Matthew Buechner and created in the adjacent studio. **William Vareika Fine Arts** (⊠ 212 Bellevue Ave., ☎ 401/849–6149, WEB www.vareikafinearts.com) exhibits and sells American paintings and prints from the 18th to the 20th century.

BEACH GEAR

Water Brothers (⊠ 39 Memorial Blvd., ☎ 401/849–4990) is the place to go for surf supplies, including bathing suits, wet suits, sunscreen, sunglasses, and surfboards.

BOOKS

The **Armchair Sailor** (⊠ 543 Thames St., ☎ 401/847–4252) stocks marine and travel books, charts, and maps.

CLOTHING

JT's Ship Chandlery (⊠ 364 Thames St., ☎ 401/846–7256) stocks clothing, marine hardware, and equipment. **Michael Hayes** (⊠ 204 Bellevue Ave., ☎ 401/846–3090) sells upscale clothing for men, women, and children. **Tropical Gangsters** (⊠ 375 Thames St., ☎ 401/847–9113) stocks hip clothes for men and women.

JEWELRY

Angela Moore (⊠ 119 Bellevue Ave., ☎ 401/849–1900 or 800/927–5470) designs jewelry and other accessories that have been featured in *Vogue, InStyle,* and other publications.

Portsmouth

64 *8 mi north of Newport.*

Portsmouth is now mainly a bedroom community for professionals who work in other parts of Rhode Island and Massachusetts, but it also has a topiary garden and a beach. Its most significant resident was its founder, Anne Hutchinson. A religious dissident and one of the country's first feminists, she led a group of settlers to the area in 1638 after being banished from the Massachusetts Bay Colony.

Half the fun of a trip to Portsmouth is a ride on the **Old Colony & Newport Railway,** which follows an 8-mi route along Narragansett Bay. The vintage diesel train and coaches make three-hour round-trips. ⊠ *19 America's Cup Ave., Newport,* ☎ *401/624–6951,* WEB *www.ocnrr.com.* ☞ *$6.* ⊙ *May–mid-Nov.*

Green Animals, a large topiary garden on a Victorian estate, contains sculpted shrubs, flower gardens, winding pathways, and a variety of trees. Most notable are the animal-shape plants: an elephant, a camel, a giraffe, and even a teddy bear. Also on the grounds are a remarkable Victorian toy collection and a plant shop. ⊠ *Cory La. off Rte. 114,* ☎ *401/847–1000,* WEB *www.newportmansions.org.* ⌧ *$9.* ☉ *May–Oct., daily 10–5.*

Outdoor Activities and Sports

Sandy Point Beach (⊠ Sandy Point Ave.) is a choice spot for families and beginning windsurfers because of the calm surf along the Sakonnet River.

En Route   Route 77, the main thoroughfare to Little Compton, passes through **Tiverton Four Corners,** a great place to stretch your legs and catch your first breath of East Bay air. **Provender** (⊠ 3883 Main Rd., ☎ 401/624–8096), in a former general store and post office, is a gourmet food store, coffee shop, and bakery. It's also within walking distance of a half dozen galleries and gift shops. The delicious **Gray's Ice Cream** (⊠ junction of Rtes. 77 and 179, ☎ 401/624–4500) is produced and sold in this stout building.

Little Compton

⑥⑤   *19 mi southeast of Portsmouth.*

The rolling estates, lovely homes, farmlands, woods, and gentle western shoreline make Little Compton one of the Ocean State's prettiest areas. Little Compton and Tiverton were part of Massachusetts until 1747—to this day, residents here often have more roots in Massachusetts than in Rhode Island. "Keep Little Compton little" is a popular sentiment, but considering the town's remoteness and its steep land prices, there may not be all that much to worry about.

Little Compton Commons (⊠ Meetinghouse La.) is the epitome of a New England town square. As white as the clouds above, the spire of the Georgian-style United Congregational Church rises over the tops of adjacent oak trees. Within the triangular lawn is a cemetery with Colonial headstones, among them that of Elizabeth Padobie, said to be the first white girl born in New England. Surrounding the green is a rock wall and all the elements of a small community: town hall, a community center, the police station, and the school. You will find town squares only in a few northern Rhode Island towns, ones that were once a part of the Massachusetts Bay Colony. Rhode Islanders, adamant about separating church and state, did not favor this layout.

A neatly kept relic of Rhode Island living, the 1680 **Wilbor House** was occupied by eight generations of Wilburs—the first of which included 11 children born between 1690 and 1712. Curiously, later generations used a half dozen variations on the spelling of the same last name. The Common Room is 17th century; the living room 18th; the bedrooms 18th and 19th; and the kitchen 19th. The barn museum holds a one-horse shay, an oxcart, and a buggy and coach. ⊠ *548 W. Main Rd.,* ☎ *401/635–4035.* ⌧ *$4.* ☉ *Mid-June–mid-Sept., Thurs.–Sun. 2–5; mid-Sept.–early Oct., weekends 2–5.*

Sakonnet Point, a surreal spit of land, reaches out toward three tiny islands. The point begins where Route 77 ends. The ½-mi hike to the tip of Sakonnet Point passes tide pools, a beach composed of tiny stone, and outcroppings that recall the surface of the moon. Parking is sometimes available in the lot adjacent to Sakonnet Harbor.

Tours and tastings are free at **Sakonnet Vineyard,** New England's largest winery. A few of its brands are well known, including Eye of the Storm, which was born of compromise: a power outage caused by a hurricane forced the wine makers to blend finished wine with what was in the vats. ✉ *162 W. Main Rd.,* ☎ *401/635–8486,* WEB *www.sakonnetwines.com.* ⌑ *Free.* ⊙ *Oct.–May, daily 11–5, tours on the hr noon–4; June–Sept., daily 10–6, tours on the hr 11–5.*

Dining and Lodging

$$ ✕ **Abraham Manchester's.** Little Compton's former general store houses a restaurant with a menu of chicken, steak, seafood, and pasta. Antiques adorn the walls of the bar and the dimly lit, dark-paneled dining room, enhancing the feel of history. Take time to cross the street and look for the Rhode Island Red Monument (actually a plaque in the ground)—this community developed the famous Rhode Island Red breed of chicken. ✉ *Main Rd.,* ☎ *401/635–2700. MC, V.*

$–$$ ✕ **Commons Lunch.** This unpretentious old-Yankee restaurant, across from the church on the town square, opens daily at 5 AM. The food may not be spectacular, but it's reliable and priced to move. The menu is greasy-spoon standard, with Rhode Island favorites such as cabinets (milk shakes). ✉ *South of Commons Rd.,* ☎ *401/635–4388. No credit cards. No dinner.*

$$ ▦ **The Roost.** A former farmhouse amid the fields of Sakonnet Vineyards is an intimate B&B that's remote yet accessible to rural pleasures such as hiking, biking, and main-street shopping. Rooms are smartly furnished. Call well ahead for stays on summer weekends. ✉ *170 W. Main Rd., 02837,* ☎ *401/635–8486,* FAX *401/635–2101,* WEB *www.sakonnetwines.com. 3 rooms. AE, MC, V. CP.*

Outdoor Activities and Sports

FISHING

The 38-ft boat *Oceaneer* (✉ Sakonnet Point Marina, ☎ 401/635–4292) can accommodate up to six people on chartered fishing trips.

HIKING

Wilbur Woods (✉ Swamp Rd.), a 30-acre hollow with picnic tables and a waterfall, is a good place for a casual hike. A trail winds along and over Dundery Brook.

Newport County A to Z

To research prices, get advice from other travelers, and book travel arrangements, visit www.fodors.com.

AIRPORTS AND TRANSFERS

Newport State Airport is 3 mi northeast of Newport. Charters fly from here to T. F. Green State Airport in Warwick, south of Providence.
➤ AIRPORT INFORMATION: **Newport State Airport** (☎ 401/846–2200).

AIRPORT TRANSFERS

Cozy Cab runs a shuttle service ($15) between the airport and Newport's visitors bureau.
➤ TAXI: **Cozy Cab** (☎ 401/846–2500).

BOAT AND FERRY TRAVEL

The Jamestown and Newport Ferry Co. runs a passenger ferry about every 1½ hours from Newport's Bowen's Landing and Long Wharf (and, on request, Fort Adams and Goat Island) to Jamestown's Ferry Wharf. The ferry operates from Memorial Day to mid-October. Old Port Marine Company operates a water-taxi service for boaters in Newport Harbor.
➤ BOAT AND FERRY INFORMATION: **Jamestown and Newport Ferry Co.** (☎ 401/423–9900). **Old Port Marine Company** (☎ 401/847–9109).

BUS TRAVEL

Rhode Island Public Transit Authority buses leave from Providence for Newport and also serve the city from other Rhode Island destinations. ➤ BUS INFORMATION: **Rhode Island Public Transit Authority** (RIPTA; ☎ 401/847–0209; 800/244–0444 in Rhode Island).

CAR TRAVEL

From Providence take I–95 east into Massachusetts and head south on Route 24. From South County, take U.S. 1 north to Route 138 east. From Boston take I–93 south to Route 24 south. With the exception of Ocean Drive, Newport is a walker's city. In summer, traffic thickens, and the narrow one-way streets can constitute an unbearable maze. It's worth parking in a pay lot and leaving your car behind while you visit in-town sights; one lot is at the Gateway Information Center.

EMERGENCIES

➤ HOSPITAL: **Newport Hospital** (⊠ Friendship St., ☎ 401/846–6400). ➤ 24-HOUR PHARMACY: **Brooks Pharmacy** (⊠ 268 Bellevue Ave., ☎ 401/849–4600).

LODGING

➤ LOCAL AGENT: **Newport Reservations** (☎ 800/842–0102).

TOURS

More than a dozen yacht companies operate tours of Narragansett Bay and Newport Harbor. Outings usually last just two hours and cost about $25 per person. *Flyer Sailing,* a 57-ft catamaran, departs from Long Wharf. *Madeline,* a 72-ft schooner, departs from Bannister's Wharf. *RumRunner II,* a vintage 1929 motor yacht, once carried "hooch"; it leaves from Bannister's Wharf. *The Spirit of Newport,* a 200-passenger multideck ship, departs for tours of Narragansett Bay and Newport Harbor from the Newport Harbor Hotel, on America's Cup Avenue, from May to mid-October.

Viking Bus and Boat Tours of Newport conducts Newport tours in buses from April to October. One-hour boat tours of Narragansett Bay operate from mid-May to Columbus Day weekend. The Newport Historical Society sponsors walking tours on Saturday from May to November.

➤ TOUR OPERATORS: *Flyer Sailing* (☎ 401/848–2100). *Madeleine* (☎ 401/847–0298). **Newport Historical Society** (⊠ 82 Touro St., ☎ 401/846–0813). *RumRunner II* (☎ 401/847–0299). *The Spirit of Newport* (☎ 401/849–3575). **Viking Bus and Boat Tours of Newport** (⊠ Gateway Information Center, 23 America's Cup Ave., ☎ 401/847–6921).

VISITOR INFORMATION

Newport County Convention and Visitors Bureau shows an orientation film and provides maps and advice. ➤ TOURIST INFORMATION: **Newport County Convention and Visitors Bureau** (⊠ Gateway Information Center, 23 America's Cup Ave., ☎ 401/849–8048 or 800/326–6030, WEB www.gonewport.com).

RHODE ISLAND A TO Z

To research prices, get advice from other travelers, and book travel arrangements, visit www.fodors.com.

AIRPORTS

T. F. Green State Airport, 10 mi south of Providence, has scheduled daily flights by several major airlines, including American, Continental/Northwest, Southwest, United, and US Airways, with additional service by regional carriers. The main regional airports in Rhode Island are in Westerly, Newport State, and Block Island.

➤ AIRPORT INFORMATION: **T. F. Green State Airport** (✉ U.S. 1, Warwick, ☎ 401/737–4000).

BUS TRAVEL

Bonanza Bus Lines, Greyhound, and Peter Pan Bus Lines serve the Providence Bus Terminal. A shuttle service connects the Providence Bus Terminal with Kennedy Plaza in downtown Providence, where you can board the local public transit buses. Rhode Island Public Transit Authority buses crisscross the state.

➤ BUS INFORMATION: **Bonanza Bus Lines** (☎ 800/556–3815). **Greyhound** (☎ 800/231–2222). **Peter Pan Bus Lines** (☎ 800/237–8747). **Providence Bus Terminal** (✉ Bonanza Way, off Exit 25 from I–95, ☎ 401/751–8800; ✉ Kennedy Plaza, Washington and Dorrance Sts.). **Rhode Island Public Transit Authority** (RIPTA; ☎ 401/781–9400; 800/244–0444 in Rhode Island).

CAR TRAVEL

Interstate 95, which cuts diagonally across the state, is the fastest route to Providence from Boston, coastal Connecticut, and New York City. Interstate 195 links Providence with New Bedford and Cape Cod. Route 146 connects Providence to Worcester and I–90, passing through the northeastern portion of the Blackstone Valley. U.S. 1 follows much of the Rhode Island coast east from Connecticut before turning north to Providence. Route 138 heads east from Route 1 to Jamestown, Newport, and Tiverton in easternmost Rhode Island.

The speed limit on interstate highways varies from 55 mph to 65 mph; state routes vary, with 55 mph the top speed. Right turns are permitted on red lights after stopping, except in downtown Providence. Free state maps are available at all chambers of commerce and at visitor information centers in Providence and Newport and at T. F. Green State Airport. The detailed *Street Atlas Rhode Island,* published by Arrow Map, Inc., is available at many bookstores and gas stations.

EMERGENCIES

➤ CONTACTS: **Ambulance, fire, police** (☎ 911).

LODGING

BED-AND-BREAKFASTS

Bed and Breakfast of Rhode Island, Inc. represents about 100 B&Bs.
➤ RESERVATION SERVICE: **Bed and Breakfast of Rhode Island, Inc.** (✉ Box 3291, Newport 02840, ☎ 401/849–1298 or 800/828–0000, WEB www.visitnewport.com/bedandbreakfast).

OUTDOOR ACTIVITIES AND SPORTS

For information on pricing and where to buy licenses for freshwater fishing, contact the Department of Environmental Management's Division of Licensing. No license is needed for saltwater fishing.

One of the best trail guides for the region is the *AMC Massachusetts and Rhode Island Trail Guide,* available at local outdoors shops or from the Appalachian Mountain Club. The Rhode Island Audubon Society leads interesting hikes and field expeditions around the state.
➤ CONTACTS: **Appalachian Mountain Club** (AMC; ✉ 5 Joy St., Boston, MA 02114, ☎ 617/523–0636). **Division of Licensing** (☎ 401/222–3576). **Rhode Island Audubon Society** (✉ 12 Sanderson Rd., Smithfield 02917, ☎ 401/949–5454).

TRAIN TRAVEL

Amtrak service between New York City and Boston makes stops at Westerly, Kingston, and Providence. Providence Station is the city's main station. The MBTA commuter rail service connects Boston and Providence during weekday morning and evening rush hours for about half the cost of an Amtrak ride.

➤ TRAIN INFORMATION: **Amtrak** (☎ 800/872–7245, WEB www. amtrak.com). **MBTA** (☎ 617/722–3200). **Providence Station** (✉ 100 Gaspee St., ☎ 401/727–7379).

VISITOR INFORMATION

➤ TOURIST INFORMATION: **Rhode Island Department of Economic Development, Tourism Division** (✉ 1 W. Exchange St., Providence 02903, ☎ 401/222–2601 [ask to be transferred to Tourism Division] or 800/ 556–2484).

7 CONNECTICUT

The southern gateway to New England
is a small state with plenty of variety. In
southwestern Connecticut, commuters,
celebrities, and others enjoy its sophisticated
atmosphere and convenience to New York
City. The Connecticut River valley has a stretch
of river villages punctuated by a few small
cities and Hartford. The northwest's Litchfield
Hills have grand inns and rolling farmlands.
Along the southeastern coast are New Haven,
home to Yale and some fine museums,
and quiet shoreline villages. The sparsely
populated towns in the northeast's Quiet
Corner are known for their antiquing potential.

· Updated
by Michelle
Bodak Acri

C ONNECTICUT MAY BE the third-smallest state in the nation, but it is among the hardest to define. Indeed, you can travel from any point in the Nutmeg State, as it is known, to any other in less than two hours, yet the land you travel—fewer than 60 mi top to bottom and 100 mi across—is as varied as a drive across the country. Connecticut's 253 mi of shoreline blows salty sea air over such beach communities as Old Lyme and Stonington. The state's patchwork hills and peaked mountains fill the northwestern corner, and the once-upon-a-time mill towns line its rivers such as the Housatonic. Finally, Connecticut has seemingly endless farmland in the northeast, where cows just might outnumber people (and definitely outnumber the traffic lights), as well as chic bedroom communities of New York City such as Greenwich and New Canaan, where boutique shopping bags seem to be the dominant species. Each section of the state is unique; each defines Connecticut.

Just as diverse as the landscape are the state's residents, who numbered close to 3½ million at last count. There really is no such thing as the definitive Connecticut Yankee, however. Yes, families can trace their roots back to the 1600s, when Connecticut was founded as one of the 13 original colonies, but the state motto is also "He who transplanted still sustains." And so the face of the Nutmegger is that of the family from Naples who tend the pizza ovens in New Haven and the farmer in Norfolk whose land dates back five generations, the grandmother from New Britain who makes the state's best pierogi and the ladies who lunch from Westport, not to mention the celebrity nestled in the Litchfield Hills and the Bridgeport entrepreneur working to close the gap between Connecticut's struggling cities and its affluent suburbs.

A unifying characteristic of the Connecticut Yankee, however, is his or her propensity for inventiveness. You might say that Nutmeggers have been setting trends for centuries. They are historically known for both their intellectual abilities and their desire to have a little fun. As evidence of the former, consider that the nation's first public library was opened in New Haven in 1656 and its first statehouse built in Hartford in 1776; Tapping Reeve opened the first law school in Litchfield in 1784; and West Hartford's Noah Webster published the first dictionary in 1806. As proof of the latter, note that Lake Compounce in Bristol was the country's first amusement park, Bethel's P. T. Barnum staged the first three-ring circus, and the hamburger, the lollipop, the Frisbee, and the Erector set were all invented within the state's 5,009 square mi.

Not surprisingly, Nutmeggers have a healthy respect for their history. For decades, the Mystic Seaport museum, which traces the state's rich maritime past through living history exhibits, has been the premier tourist attraction. Today, however, slot machines in casinos in the southeastern woods of Connecticut are giving the sailing ships a run for their money. Foxwoods Casino near Ledyard, run by the Mashantucket Pequots, is the world's largest casino—it draws more than 40,000 visitors per day—and the Mohegan Sun Casino in nearby Uncasville, which completed an expansion in April 2002, is working hard to catch up. Thanks in large part to the lure of these casinos, not to mention the state's rich cultural attractions, cutting-edge restaurants, shopping outlets, first-rate lodgings, and abundance of natural beauty (including 92 state parks and 30 state forests), tourism is now the second leading industry in the state. Anyone who has explored even part of Connecticut will discover that a small state can have big diversity—and appeal.

Pleasures and Pastimes

Antiquing

Although you'll find everything from chic boutiques to vast outlet malls in Connecticut, the state is an antiquer's paradise. The Litchfield Hills region, in the state's northwest corner, is the heart of antiques country. The Quiet Corner, east of the Connecticut River, runs a close second, with several hundred dealers and complexes. Mystic, Old Saybrook, Essex, and other towns along the coast are filled with markets, galleries, and shops, many specializing in antique prints, maps, books, and collectibles.

Dining

Call it the fennel factor or the arugula influx: southern New England has witnessed a gastronomic revolution. Preparation and ingredients reflect the culinary trends of nearby Manhattan and Boston; indeed, the quality and diversity of Connecticut restaurants now rival those of such sophisticated metropolitan areas. Although traditional favorites remain—such as New England clam chowder, buttery lobster rolls, Yankee pot roast, and grilled haddock—Grand Marnier is now favored on ice cream over hot fudge sauce, sliced duck is wrapped in phyllo and served with a ginger-plum sauce (the orange glaze decidedly absent), and everything from lavender to fresh figs is used to season and complement dishes. Dining in the cities and suburbs is increasingly international: you'll find Indian, Vietnamese, Thai, Malaysian, South American, and Japanese restaurants, even Spanish tapas bars. The locals are also going a tad decadent; designer martinis are quite the rage, brewpubs have popped up all around the state—even caviar is making a comeback. The one drawback of this turn toward sophistication is that finding an under-$10 dinner entrée is difficult.

CATEGORY	COST*
$$$$	over $25
$$$	$17–$25
$$	$9–$16
$	under $9

*per person, for a main-course dinner

Fishing

Connecticut teems with possibilities for anglers, from deep-sea fishing in coastal waters to fly-fishing in the state's many streams. Try the Litchfield Hills region for freshwater fish: if you're just a beginner, don't fret—you'll be catching trout or bass in the Housatonic River in no time. Southeastern Connecticut is the charter- and party-boat capital of the state. Charter-fishing boats take passengers out on Long Island Sound for half-day, full-day, and overnight trips.

Lodging

Connecticut has plenty of business-oriented chain hotels and low-budget motels, but the state's unusual inns, resorts, bed-and-breakfasts, and country hotels are far more atmospheric and typical of New England. You'll pay dearly for rooms in summer on the coast and in autumn in the hills, where thousands peek at the changing foliage. Rates are lowest in winter, but so are the temperatures, making spring the best time for bargain seekers to visit.

CATEGORY	COST*
$$$$	over $180
$$$	$130–$180
$$	$80–$130
$	under $80

*All prices are for a standard double room during peak season and not including tax or gratuities. Some inns add a 15% service charge.

State Parks

Sixty percent of Connecticut is forest land, some of it under the jurisdiction of the state parks division, which also manages several beaches on the southern shoreline. Many parks have campgrounds. Trails meander through most of the parks—the hiking is especially spectacular around the cool, clear water at Lake Waramaug State Park and the 200-ft-high waterfall at Kent Falls State Park. Popular Gillette Castle State Park in East Haddam has several trails, some on former railroad beds. Some state parks have no entrance fees year-round. At others the fee varies ($5–$12), depending on the time of year, day of the week, and whether or not your car bears a Connecticut license plate.

Exploring Connecticut

Southwestern Connecticut contains the wealthy coastal communities. Moving east along the coast (in most states you usually travel north or south along the coast, but in Connecticut you actually travel east or west), you'll come to New Haven and the southeastern coast, which is broken by many small bays and inlets. The Quiet Corner in the northeast, bordered by Rhode Island to the east and Massachusetts to the north, provides a tranquil countryside with rolling hills. To the west are the fertile farmlands of the Connecticut River valley and the state's capital, Hartford. In the northwestern part of the state is the Litchfield Hills area, covered with miles of forests, lakes, and rivers.

Numbers in the text and in the margin correspond to numbers on the maps: Southwestern Connecticut, Connecticut River Valley, Downtown Hartford, Litchfield Hills, Southeastern Connecticut, Downtown New Haven, and The Quiet Corner.

Great Itineraries

The Nutmeg State is a confluence of different worlds, where farm country meets country homes, and fans of the New York Yankees meet Down-Easter Yankees. To get the best sense of this variety, especially if you have only a few days, start in the scenic Litchfield Hills, where you can see historic town greens and trendy cafés juxtaposed in a way that's uniquely Connecticut. If you have a bit more time, head south to the wealthy southwestern corner of the state and then over to New Haven, with its cultural pleasures. If you have five days or a week (the minimum time needed to truly sample the state's myriad flavors), take in the capital city of Hartford and the surrounding towns of the Connecticut River valley and head down to the southeastern shoreline. If you have kids or an interest in the sea, Mystic alone could occupy a few days.

IF YOU HAVE 1 DAY

Begin a day in the Litchfield Hills in **New Preston** ㉝ and then head for Lake Waramaug. In West Cornwall, near **Cornwall** ㉟, have a look at the state's largest covered bridge. Working your way north, stop in **Lakeville** ㊱ and **Salisbury** ㊲ (a good place to stop for lunch). Turning south, spend a couple of hours in **Litchfield** ㊸, where you can tour historic houses before continuing south via **Bethlehem** ㊺ to **Woodbury** ㊼ to visit the town's churches and antiques shops.

IF YOU HAVE 2 DAYS

Old Saybrook (61), once a lively shipbuilding and fishing town, is a picture-perfect example of the Connecticut shoreline. Start your day here with some shopping on Main Street or a stroll along the coastline. Next, head across the Connecticut River to **Old Lyme** (62), home to the Florence Griswold Museum, where members of the Old Lyme Impressionist Art Colony once lived and painted *en plein air.* Continue up the coast, stopping if you like in **Waterford** (63), to take in the

Connecticut

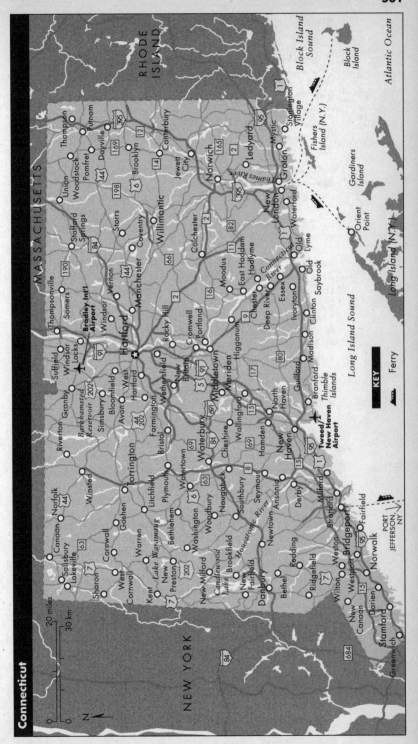

glorious water views at Harkness Memorial State Park, or in **Groton** ⑥⑦ to see the world's first nuclear-powered submarine and the Submarine Force Museum. On your way to **Mystic** ⑥⑧, stop in Noank for a late lunch or early dinner of lobster-in-the-rough seated at a picnic table at the edge of Noank Harbor. End your day in Mystic, where you'll find a wide assortment of hotels, inns, and restaurants to chose from. You won't have far to travel on day two: in Mystic, a visit to the highly esteemed Mystic Seaport Museum and Mystic Aquarium can easily fill your day. Afterward, if you have the stamina, head inland to **Ledyard** ⑥⑥ and try your luck at Foxwoods Resort Casino's 5,500-plus slot machines—it's open 24 hours.

IF YOU HAVE 3 DAYS

Greenwich ①, a wealthy community with grand homes and great restaurants, is a good starting point for a several-day tour that begins near New York. From here head to **Stamford** ②, where you can visit the Whitney Museum of American Art at Champion or hit the mall across the street. East along the coast is **Norwalk** ③, whose SoNo commercial district and Maritime Aquarium are popular attractions. Have dinner in **Westport** ⑨, and end your first day in 🖪 **Ridgefield** ⑥. After touring Ridgefield the next morning, head for the Litchfield Hills, driving north via **Cornwall** ㉟ to **Norfolk** ㊳. Then it's south to **Litchfield** ㊸ and 🖪 **New Preston** ㉝, where you may want to conclude your day. If not, travel a little farther south to charming 🖪 **Washington** ㊻. Begin day three in **Woodbury** ㊼ and then head to **New Haven** ㊿–㊐. Near the Yale University campus are many great museums, shops, and restaurants.

IF YOU HAVE 5 DAYS

With five days you can explore some of the state's cities as well as its historic interior towns and coastal villages. Spend the morning of your first day in **Hartford** ⑳–㉗ and the early part of the afternoon in **West Hartford** ㉘ before heading to 🖪 **Farmington** ㉙, which has two excellent house museums, and 🖪 **Simsbury** ㉚, where you can visit the Phelps Homestead. Spend the night in either town. On your second day, head west to **Woodbury** ㊼, stopping in **Litchfield** ㊸ and **Kent** ㉞. Stay the night in 🖪 **Washington** ㊻ or 🖪 **Ridgefield** ⑥. Begin your third day in southwestern Connecticut in **Greenwich** ①, followed by stops in **Stamford** ②, **Westport** ⑨, and **Bridgeport** ⑪. Spend the remainder of your day in 🖪 **New Haven** ㊿–㊐. Start your fourth day in **Essex** ⑬ and visit the Connecticut River Museum. At Gillette Castle State Park in **East Haddam** ⑯ you can tour the hilltop estate built by the actor William Gillette. From here, backtrack to the coastal town of **Old Saybrook** ㊱ and then cross the river to 🖪 **Old Lyme** ㊲, a former art colony. On the fifth day, continue touring the coast, starting in either **New London** ㊽ or **Groton** ⑥⑦, and head east toward **Mystic** ⑥⑧. Take time to visit Mystic Seaport before heading to the little village of **Stonington** ⑥⑨.

When to Tour Connecticut

Connecticut is lovely year-round, but fall and spring are particularly appealing times to visit. A drive in fall through the hills of the state's back roads or the Merritt Parkway (a National Scenic Byway) is a memorable experience. Leaves of yellow, orange, and red color the fall landscape, but the state blooms in springtime, too—town greens are painted with daffodils and tulips, and blooming trees punctuate the rich green countryside. Many attractions that close in winter reopen in April or May. Summer, of course, is prime time for most attractions; travelers have the most options then but also plenty of company, especially along the shore.

SOUTHWESTERN CONNECTICUT

Southwestern Connecticut is a rich swirl of old New England and new New York. This region consistently reports the highest cost of living and most expensive homes of any area in the country. Its bedroom towns are home primarily to white-collar executives; some still make the hour-plus dash to and from New York, but most enjoy a more civilized morning drive to Stamford, which is reputed to have more corporate headquarters per square mile than any other U.S. city. Strict zoning has preserved a certain privacy and rusticity uncommon in other such densely populated areas, and numerous celebrities—Paul Newman, David Letterman, Vince McMahon, and Mel Gibson, among them—live in Fairfield County.

Venture away from the wealthy communities, and you'll discover cities struggling in different stages of urban renewal: Stamford, Norwalk, Bridgeport, and Danbury. These four have some of the region's best cultural and shopping opportunities, but the economic disparity between Connecticut's troubled cities and its upscale towns is perhaps nowhere more visible than in Fairfield County.

Greenwich

① *28 mi northeast of New York City, 64 mi southwest of Hartford.*

You'll have no trouble believing that Greenwich is one of the wealthiest towns in the United States when you drive along U.S. 1 (called Route 1 by the locals, and which goes by the names West Putnam Avenue, East Putnam Avenue, and the Post Road, among others), where the streets are lined with ritzy car dealers, posh boutiques, and chic restaurants. The median price of a house sold in Greenwich is $550,000; the average is close to $1 million. In other words, bring your charge cards.

A section of the **Bruce Museum** devoted to environmental history has a wigwam, a spectacular mineral collection, a marine touch tank, and a 16th-century woodland diorama. Other permanent exhibits include a small but worthwhile collection of American Impressionist paintings. ⊠ *1 Museum Dr. (I–95, Exit 3),* ☎ *203/869–0376,* WEB *www.brucemuseum.com.* ☜ *$4, free Tues.* ☉ *Tues.–Sat. 10–5, Sun. 1–5.*

The small, barn-red **Putnam Cottage,** built in 1690 and operated as Knapp's Tavern during the Revolutionary War, was a frequent meeting place of Revolutionary War hero General Israel Putnam. You can meander through an herb garden and examine the cottage's Colonial furnishings and fieldstone fireplaces. ⊠ *243 E. Putnam Ave./U.S. 1,* ☎ *203/869-9697.* ☜ *$4.* ☉ *Apr.–Dec., Wed., Fri., and Sun. 1–4.*

The circa-1732 **Bush-Holley Historic Site,** a handsome central-chimney saltbox, contains a wonderful collection of 19th- and 20th-century artworks by sculptor John Rogers, potter Leon Volkmar, and painters Childe Hassam, Elmer Livingstone MacRae, and John Twachtman. The visitor center, set in the historic site's circa-1805 storehouse, holds exhibition galleries and a gift shop. ⊠ *39 Strickland Rd.,* ☎ *203/869-6899.* ☜ *$6.* ☉ *Jan.–Feb., weekends noon–4; Mar.–Dec., Tues.–Sun. noon–4*

More than 1,000 species of flora and fauna have been recorded at the 522-acre **Audubon Center** in northern Greenwich, where exhibits survey the local environment. Fifteen miles of trails traverse woods and fields. ⊠ *613 Riversville Rd.,* ☎ *203/869–5272,* WEB *www.greenwich.center.audubon.org.* ☜ *$3.* ☉ *Daily 9–5.*

Southwestern Connecticut

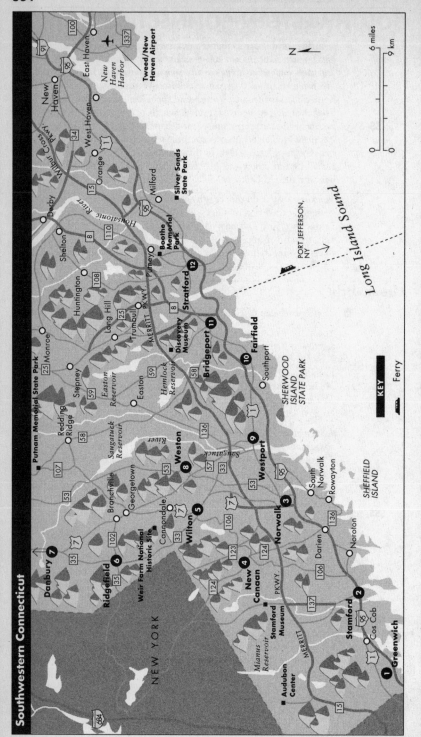

Dining and Lodging

$$$$ ✕ **Restaurant Jean-Louis.** Roses, Limoges china, and white tablecloths
★ with lace underskirts complement this restaurant's world-class cuisine.
On any given night, the five-course prix-fixe Celebration Menu might
include diced vegetables cooked in saffron bouillon with mussels and
scallops, served with a parsley coulis, or roast breast of duck on a bed
of wilted spinach. ✉ *61 Lewis St., 06830,* ☎ *203/622–8450. Jacket
required. AE, D, DC, MC, V. Closed Sun. No lunch Sat.*

$$–$$$$ ✕ **Dome.** Eclectic contemporary fare with shock appeal is served in a
sophisticated, arty space with colorful murals, faux leopard carpeting,
and bright blue banquettes. Standouts have included sesame-peanut
glass noodles and poppy and sesame-seed crusted tuna with jasmine
rice and baby bok choy. ✉ *253 Greenwich Ave., 06830,* ☎ *203/661–
3443. AE, DC, MC, V.*

$$$$ ✕🖫 **Homestead Inn.** A belvedere, ornate bracketed eaves, and an en-
★ closed wraparound Victorian porch grace this enormous Italianate
wood-frame house not far from the water. Rooms are decorated with
antiques, original artwork, and period reproductions, the beds layered
with luxe Frette linens. For all its architectural appeal, though, the
Homestead is becoming better known for the up-to-the-minute fine French
cuisine prepared by master chef–owner Thomas Henkelmann. The sea-
sonal menu ($$$$) might list Dover sole fillets poached and filled with
salmon mousse. Reservations are essential for dinner, for which a jacket
is required. ✉ *420 Field Point Rd., 06830* ☎ *203/869–7500,* FAX *203/
869–7502,* WEB *www.homesteadinn.com. 19 rooms, 7 suites. Restaurant,
in-room data ports, business services, meeting room. AE, DC, MC, V.*

$$$$ 🖫 **Delamar Greenwich Harbor.** This three-story luxury hotel with yel-
low stucco exterior and terra-cotta tile roof resembles a private villa
on the Italian Riviera. Handcrafted furnishings from all over the world
enrich all rooms; many have wrought-iron balconies overlooking
Greenwich Harbor and working fireplaces. Bathrooms have coral mar-
ble vanities, hand-painted framed mirrors, and deep cast-iron tubs. The
hotel has its own 600-ft private dock on the harbor for boat owners
to tie up; it's just a few blocks from downtown Greenwich and one
block from the train station. ✉ *500 Steamboat Rd., 06830,* ☎ *203/
661–9800,* FAX *203/661–2513,* WEB *www.thedelamar.com. 74 rooms, 9
suites. Restaurant, in-room data ports, gym. AE, D, DC, MC, V.*

$$$–$$$$ 🖫 **Hyatt Regency Greenwich.** The Hyatt's vast but comfortable atrium
contains a flourishing lawn and abundant flora. The rooms are spa-
cious, with modern furnishings and many amenities. The pleasant
Winfield's restaurant serves innovative renditions of classic dishes. ✉
1800 E. Putnam Ave., 06870, ☎ *203/637–1234,* FAX *203/629–9839,*
WEB *www.hyatt.com. 373 rooms, 14 suites. Restaurant, bar, in-room
data ports, indoor pool, hair salon, health club, sauna, shop, business
services, meeting room. AE, D, DC, MC, V.*

$$$–$$$$ 🖫 **Stanton House Inn.** The original structure of this Federal-style man-
sion, within walking distance of downtown, was built in 1840. In 1899,
under architect Stanford White's supervision, the house was enlarged.
The interior has been carefully decorated with a mixture of antiques
and reproductions; two rooms have fireplaces. ✉ *76 Maple Ave.,
06830,* ☎ *203/869–2110,* FAX *203/629–2116. 24 rooms, 2 suites. Pool;
no smoking. AE, D, DC, MC, V. CP.*

Stamford

➋ *6 mi northeast of Greenwich, 38 mi southwest of New Haven, 33 mi
northeast of New York City.*

Glitzy office buildings, chain hotels, and major department stores are
among the landmarks in Stamford, the most dynamic city on the south-

western shore. Restaurants, nightclubs, and shops line Atlantic and lower Summer streets, poised to harness the region's affluence and satisfy the desire of suburbanites to spend an exciting night on the town without having to travel to New York City.

Oxen, sheep, pigs, and other animals roam the **Stamford Museum and Nature Center,** a 118-acre New England–style farmstead with many nature trails to explore. Exhibits survey natural history, art, and Americana. Two enjoyable times to visit are spring harvest and maple-sugaring season—call for exact dates. ⊠ *39 Scofieldtown Rd./Rte. 137,* ☎ *203/322–1646,* WEB *www.stamfordmuseum.org.* ☞ *Grounds $6, planetarium an additional $2, observatory $3.* ☉ *Grounds Mon.–Sat. 9–5, Sun. 1–5; farm daily 9–5; planetarium shows Sun. 3 PM; observatory Fri. 8–10 PM.*

The 64-acre **Bartlett Arboretum,** owned by the University of Connecticut, holds natural woodlands, cultivated gardens, marked ecology trails, a swamp walk, and a pond. The wildflower garden is stunning in the spring. ⊠ *151 Brookdale Rd., off High Ridge Rd. (Merritt Pkwy., Exit 35),* ☎ *203/322–6971,* WEB *www.ucc.uconn.edu/~wwwbarad.* ☞ *Free.* ☉ *Grounds daily 8:30–dusk, visitor center weekdays 8:30–4:30.*

Dining and Lodging

$$–$$$ ✕ **Beacon.** Wraparound harbor views and a brick exterior highlight
★   this stylish waterfront restaurant. Its open kitchen prepares shared platters—try the one with lamb, chicken, and crisp braised pork shank— and stand-out entrées such as grass-fed rib-eye steak and herb-roasted salmon. If you want to linger before or after dinner, head to the bar upstairs for some lively chatter. ⊠ *183 Harbor Dr., 06902,* ☎ *203/327–4600. AE, DC, MC, V.*

$$–$$$ ✕ **Druid Restaurant.** Upscale contemporary Continental fare is the focus at this eatery on bustling Bedford Street. The Tudor-style dining room has elaborate woodwork, antiques, white linens, and gleaming oak floors reminiscent of an Irish manor house. Menu favorites include dishes such as pan-roasted pheasant and lamb carpaccio. ⊠ *120 Bedford St., 06901,* ☎ *203/316–8588. AE, DC, MC, V.*

$$ ✕ **Macarena.** The virgin of Macarena was the patron saint of bullfighting. This restaurant, which has infused a touch of Spain into downtown, has a colorful mural of a Spanish matador as the focus of its dining room. The cuisine ranges from such tasty tapas as tortilla española and roasted peppers stuffed with shrimp and saffron-flavored rice to hearty portions of paella. ⊠ *78 W. Park Pl., 06901,* ☎ *203/323–7421. AE, DC, MC, V. No lunch.*

$$$–$$$$ ☷ **Stamford Marriott Hotel.** The Marriott stands out for its up-to-date facilities and convenience to trains and airport buses. Furnishings are modern and comfortable. ⊠ *2 Stamford Forum, 06901,* ☎ *203/357–9555,* FAX *203/324–6897,* WEB *www.marriott.com. 500 rooms, 6 suites. 2 restaurants, bar, in-room data ports, indoor-outdoor pool, hair salon, health club, racquetball, meeting rooms. AE, D, DC, MC, V.*

$$$–$$$$ ☷ **Westin Stamford.** The ultramodern entrance of this downtown luxury hotel should prepare you for the dramatic atrium lobby, which has a brass-and-glass-enclosed gazebo. The attractive rooms are understated and elegant, with subdued colors and comfortable wing chairs; bathrooms are spacious. ⊠ *1 First Stamford Pl., 06901,* ☎ *203/967–2222,* FAX *203/967–3475,* WEB *www.starwood.com. 418 rooms, 28 suites. In-room data ports, restaurant, indoor pool, 2 tennis courts, health club, meeting rooms. AE, D, DC, MC, V. CP.*

Nightlife and the Arts

NIGHTLIFE

For alternative dance music try the **Art Bar** (⊠ 84 W. Park Pl., ☎ 203/973–0300), which draws a collegiate crowd. At the **Terrace Club** (⊠

1938 W. Main St., ☎ 203/961–9770) you can dance to everything from ballroom and country western to Top 40 and Latin. **Tigín Pub** (✉ 175 Bedford St., ☎ 203/353–8444) hosts live music Sunday nights.

THE ARTS

The **Connecticut Grand Opera and Orchestra** (☎ 203/327–2867) perform at the Palace Theatre. Opera season runs from October to May. The **Stamford Center for the Arts** (☎ 203/325–4466) presents everything from one-act plays and comedy shows to musicals and film festivals. Performances are held at the Rich Forum (✉ 307 Atlantic St.) and the Palace Theatre (✉ 61 Atlantic St.). The **Stamford Symphony Orchestra** (☎ 203/325–1407) stages performances from October to April, including a family concert series.

Outdoor Activities and Sports

The greens fee at the 18-hole, par-72 **Sterling Farms Golf Course** (✉ 1349 Newfield Ave., ☎ 203/461–9090) is $45; an optional cart costs $24.

Shopping

The **Stamford Town Center** (✉ 100 Greyrock Pl., ☎ 203/356–9700) houses 130 chiefly upscale shops, including Saks Fifth Avenue, Talbots, a Pottery Barn Studio Store, and Williams-Sonoma. Northern Stamford's **United House Wrecking** (✉ 535 Hope St., ☎ 203/348–5371) sells acres of architectural artifacts, decorative accessories, antiques, nautical items, and lawn and garden furnishings.

Norwalk

❸ *14 mi northeast of Stamford, 47 mi northeast of New York City.*

In the 19th century, Norwalk became a major New England port and also manufactured pottery, clocks, watches, shingle nails, and paper. It later fell into a state of neglect, in which it remained for much of the 20th century. During the past decade, however, Norwalk's coastal business district has been the focus of a major redevelopment project. Art galleries, restaurants, bars, and trendy boutiques have blossomed on and around Washington Street; the stretch is now known as the SoNo (short for South Norwalk) commercial district.

Norwalk is the home of Yankee Doodle Dandies: in 1756, Colonel Thomas Fitch threw together a motley crew of Norwalk soldiers and led them off to fight at Fort Crailo, near Albany, New York. Supposedly, Norwalk's women gathered feathers for the men to wear as plumes in their caps in an effort to give them some appearance of military decorum. Upon the arrival of these foppish warriors, one of the British officers sarcastically dubbed them "macaronis"—slang for dandies. The saying caught on, and so did the song.

★ ℭ The cornerstone of the SoNo district is the **Maritime Aquarium at Norwalk,** a 5-acre waterfront center that explores the ecology and history of Long Island Sound. The more than 20 habitats include the vast Open Ocean Tank; otter, seal, and sea turtle areas; and an Environmental Education Center. Besides the huge aquarium, the center also operates marine-mammal cruises aboard the *Oceanic* and an IMAX theater. Although not as popular as Mystic Seaport, the aquarium is one of the state's most worthwhile attractions—especially for families. ✉ *10 N. Water St.,* ☎ *203/852–0700,* WEB *www.maritimeaquarium.org.* ✆ *Aquarium $8.75, IMAX theater $6.75, combined $13.25.* ☉ *Labor Day–June, daily 10–5; July–Labor Day, daily 10–6.*

Restoration continues at the **Lockwood-Mathews Mansion Museum,** an ornate tribute to Victorian decorating that was the summer home of LeGrand Lockwood in the late 19th century. It's hard not to be impressed by the octagonal rotunda and 50 rooms of gilt, frescoes, marble, woodwork, and etched glass. ⊠ *295 West Ave.,* ☎ *203/838–9799,* WEB *www.lockwoodmathews.org.* ☑ *$8.* ☉ *Mid-Mar.–Jan. 1, Wed.–Sun. noon–5, or by appointment.*

The 3-acre park at the **Sheffield Island Lighthouse** is a prime spot for a picnic. The 1868 lighthouse has four levels and 10 rooms to explore. ⊠ *Ferry service from Hope Dock (corner of Washington and North Water Sts.),* ☎ *203/838–9444 ferry and lighthouse,* WEB *www.seaport.org.* ☑ *Round-trip ferry service and lighthouse tour $15.* ☉ *Ferry early May–mid-June and mid-Sept.–mid-Oct., weekends at 11 and 2; mid-June–Labor Day, weekdays at 11 and 2, weekends at 10, 1, and 4. Lighthouse open when ferry is docked.*

The colorful exhibits at the **Stepping Stones Museum for Children** encourage hands-on exploration for kids under 10 and incorporate the themes of science and technology, arts and culture, and heritage. An "I Spy Connecticut" exhibit, where kids can climb aboard a train, fly a helicopter, or submerge themselves in a research submarine, combines educational role playing with an introduction to the state's landmarks, landscapes, and history. ⊠ *Mathews Park, 303 West Ave.,* ☎ *203/899–0606,* WEB *www.steppingstonesmuseum.org.* ☑ *$6.* ☉ *Labor Day–Memorial Day, Tues.–Sat. 10–5, Sun. noon–5; Memorial Day–Labor Day, Mon.–Sat. 10–5, Sun. noon–5.*

Dining and Lodging

$$$–$$$$ ✕ **Match.** This chic South Norwalk hot spot is renowned for its imaginative designer pizza: potato (with roasted fingerling potatoes, caramelized onions, garlic, and mozzarella) and wild mushroom (with black truffles, mozzarella, goat cheese, and truffle oil) are two popular varieties. A centerpiece wood-burning stove also turns out entrées such as steak au poivre and pan-roasted salmon. ⊠ *98 Washington St., 06854,* ☎ *203/852–1088. AE, DC, MC, V. No lunch.*

$$ ✕ **Habana.** Ceiling fans, banana trees, and a high energy level characterize Habana, which serves contemporary Cuban cuisine with some Argentinian, Peruvian, Mexican, Puerto Rican, and Brazilian dishes thrown in for spice. Some favorites are roasted sea bass with a crispy plantain crust, empanadas stuffed with minced duck or chorizo, ceviche, and baby back ribs with guava sauce. ⊠ *70 N. Main St., 06854,* ☎ *203/852–9790. AE, D, MC, V. No lunch.*

$$–$$$ ✕▦ **Silvermine Tavern.** The simple rooms at this inn are furnished with hooked rugs and antiques along with some modern touches. The large, low-ceiling dining rooms ($$$–$$$$; closed Tues.) are romantic, with eclectic Colonial appointments; many tables overlook a millpond. Traditional New England favorites receive modern accents—roast breast of duck with mapled cranberries over risotto, for example. Sunday brunch is a local tradition. ⊠ *194 Perry Ave., 06850,* ☎ *203/847–4558,* FAX *203/847–9171,* WEB *www.silverminetavern.com. 10 rooms, 1 suite. Restaurant, shop. AE, DC, MC, V. CP.*

Nightlife and the Arts

Barcelona (⊠ 63 N. Main St., ☎ 203/899–0088), a wine bar, is a hot spot for Spanish tapas. Brewing memorabilia adorns the **Brewhouse** (⊠ 13 Marshall St., ☎ 203/853–9110), where you can choose from 15 draught and 15 bottled beers

Shopping

Along Washington Street in the South Norwalk (SoNo) area are some excellent art galleries and crafts dealers. **Stew Leonard's** (⊠ 100 Westport Ave., ☎ 203/847–7213), the self-proclaimed "Disneyland of Supermarkets," has a petting zoo and animated characters lining the aisles.

New Canaan

④ *5 mi northwest of Norwalk, 33 mi southwest of New Haven.*

So rich and elegant is the landscape in New Canaan that you may want to pick up a local street map and spend the afternoon driving around the estate-studded countryside, which includes everything from a Frank Lloyd Wright home and Philip Johnson's Glass House to imposing Georgians and clapboard farmhouses. Or you might prefer lingering on Main Street, which is loaded with upscale shops.

The **New Canaan Nature Center** comprises more than 40 acres of woods and habitats. You can try the hands-on natural science exhibits at the Discovery Center in the main building or walk along the many nature trails. Demonstrations take place in fall at the cider house and in spring at the maple sugar shed (reservations essential). ✉ *144 Oenoke Ridge,* ☎ *203/966–9577,* WEB *www.newcanaannature.org.* ✆ *Donation suggested for museum.* ☉ *Grounds daily dawn–dusk, museum Mon.–Sat. 9–4.*

Lodging

$$–$$$ 🏠 **Maples Inn.** This yellow clapboard structure a short drive from downtown has 13 gables, most of which are veiled by a canopy of maples. Bedrooms are furnished with antiques and queen-size canopy beds. Mahogany chests, gilt frames, and brass lamps gleam from energetic polishing. The Mural Room, whose walls are painted with images of New Canaan in each of the four seasons, is ideal for breakfast. ✉ *179 Oenoke Ridge, 06840,* ☎ *203/966–2927,* FAX *203/966–5003,* WEB *www.maplesinnct.com. 12 rooms. Cable TV; no smoking. AE, MC, V. CP.*

Wilton

⑤ *6 mi northeast of New Canaan, 27 mi southwest of New Haven.*

Quiet and unassuming, this lovely, tree-shaded town with graceful turn-of-the-20th-century houses is one of Fairfield County's many bedroom communities.

★ **Weir Farm National Historic Site** is dedicated to the legacy of painter J. Alden Weir (1852–1919), one of the earliest American Impressionists. Tours of Weir's studio and sculptor Mahonri Young's studio are given, and you can take a self-guided walk past Weir's painting sites. The property's 60 wooded acres include hiking paths, picnic areas, and a restored rose and perennial garden. ✉ *735 Nod Hill Rd.,* ☎ *203/834–1896,* WEB *www.nps.gov/wefa.* ✆ *Free.* ☉ *Grounds daily dawn–dusk, visitor center Wed.–Sun. 8:30–5.*

The forest and wetlands of 146-acre **Woodcock Nature Center** (✉ 56 Deer Run Rd., ☎ 203/762–7280, WEB www.wcol.net/woodcock) are the site of botany walks, birding and geology lectures, and hikes.

Shopping

Antiques sheds and boutiques can be found along and off U.S. 7. **Cannondale Village** (✉ off U.S. 7, ☎ 203/762–2233), a pre–Civil War farm village, overflows with antiques and arts-and-crafts vendors.

Ridgefield

⑥ *8 mi north of Wilton, 43 mi west of New Haven.*

In Ridgefield, you'll find a rustic Connecticut atmosphere within an hour of Manhattan. The town center, which you approach from Wilton on Route 33, is a largely residential sweep of lawns and majestic homes.

The **Aldrich Museum of Contemporary Art** presents changing exhibitions of cutting-edge work rivaling that of any small collection in New York and has an outstanding 2-acre sculpture garden. ⊠ *258 Main St.,* ☎ *203/438–4519,* WEB *www.aldrichart.org.* ⊡ *$5, free Tues.* ☉ *Tues.–Sun. noon–5.*

A British cannonball is lodged in a corner of the **Keeler Tavern Museum,** a historic inn and the former home of the noted architect Cass Gilbert (1859–1934). Furniture and Revolutionary War memorabilia fill the museum, where guides dressed in Colonial costumes conduct tours. The sunken garden is lovely in the spring. ⊠ *132 Main St.,* ☎ *203/438–5485,* WEB *www.keelertavernmuseum.org.* ⊡ *$4.* ☉ *Feb.–Dec., Wed. and weekends 1–4.*

Dining and Lodging

$$$–$$$$ ✕⊡ **The Elms Inn.** The best rooms here are in the frame house built by a Colonial cabinetmaker in 1760; antiques and reproductions furnish all the rooms. Chef Brendan Walsh presents fine new American cuisine in the restaurant ($$$–$$$$)—pan-roasted Maryland crab cakes with three-pepper relish, maple-thyme grilled loin of venison, and the like. ⊠ *500 Main St., 06877,* ☎ FAX *203/438–2541,* WEB *www.theelmsinn.com.* *23 rooms. Restaurant, pub. AE, DC, MC, V. CP.*

$$–$$$$ ✕⊡ **Stonehenge Inn & Restaurant.** The manicured lawns and bright white-clapboard buildings of Stonehenge are visible just off U.S. 7. Its tasteful rooms are a mix of Waverly and Schumacher fabrics; the gem of a restaurant ($$) is run by Bruno Crosnier. The ever-changing menu may include medallions of venison with dauphine potatoes (fried croquettes) laced with garlic and sweet green peppercorns or simple and elegant Dover sole. ⊠ *Stonehenge Rd. off U.S. 7, 06877,* ☎ *203/438–6511,* FAX *203/438–2478. 12 rooms, 4 suites. Restaurant. AE, D, MC, V. CP.*

Shopping

The **Hay Day Market** (⊠ 21 Governor St., ☎ 203/431–4400) stocks hard-to-find fresh produce, jams, cheeses, sauces, baked goods, flowers, and much more. Other locations are in Greenwich (☎ 203/637–7600) and Westport (☎ 203/254–5200).

Danbury

❼ *9 mi north of Ridgefield, 20 mi northwest of Bridgeport.*

A middle-class slice of suburbia, Danbury was the hat capital of America for nearly 200 years—until the mid-1950s. Rumors persist that the term "mad as a hatter" originated here. Hat makers suffered widely from the injurious effects of mercury poisoning, a fact that is said to explain the resultant "madness" of veteran hatters.

The **Military Museum of Southern New England** exhibits an impressive collection of U.S. and Allied forces memorabilia from World War II, plus 19 tanks dating from that war to the present. A computer program allows access to the names on the Vietnam Veterans Memorial in Washington. ⊠ *125 Park Ave.,* ☎ *203/790–9277,* WEB *www.usmilitarymuseum.org.* ⊡ *$4.* ☉ *Apr.–Nov., Tues.–Sat. 10–5, Sun. noon–5; Dec.–Mar., Fri.–Sat. 10–5, Sun. noon–5.*

☾ A station built in 1903 for the New Haven Railroad houses the **Danbury Railway Museum.** In the train yard are 20 or so examples of freight and passenger railroad stock, including a restored 1944 caboose, a 1948 Alco locomotive, and an operating locomotive turntable. Museum exhibits include vintage American Flyer model trains. ⊠ *120 White St.,* ☎ *203/778–8337,* WEB *www.danbury.org/drm.* ⊡ *$3.* ☉

Jan.–Mar., Wed.–Sat. 10–4, Sun. noon–4; Apr.–Dec., Tues.–Sat. 10–5, Sun. noon–5.

Dining

$$$$ ✕ **Ondine.** Drifts of flowers, soft lighting, handwritten menus, and waiters in white jackets make every meal feel like a celebration. The five-course prix-fixe traditional French menu, updated once a week, might list medallions of venison with a hunter's sauce made of dried cherries or fresh salmon with a crushed peppercorn crust served with red wine–butter sauce. Grand Marnier soufflé is the signature dessert. ⊠ *69 Pembroke Rd./Rte. 37, 06810,* ☎ *203/746–4900. AE, D, DC, MC, V. Closed Mon. No lunch Tues.–Sat.*

Outdoor Activities and Sports

The 18-hole, par-72 **Richter Park Golf Course** (⊠ 100 Aunt Hack Rd., ☎ 203/792–2550) is a superb, challenging public course. The greens fee is $48; an optional cart costs $24.

Shopping

The **Danbury Fair Mall** (⊠ I–84, Exit 3, ☎ 203/743–3247) has more than 200 shops as well as a huge working carousel in the food court. **Stew Leonard's** (⊠ 99 Federal Rd., ☎ 203/790–8030), with a petting zoo and animated characters in the aisles, is an experience as much as a supermarket.

Weston

8 *15 mi southeast of Danbury, 36 mi southwest of New Haven.*

Heavily wooded Weston is Fairfield County's version of a peaceful—and posh—New England town.

The 1,746 acres of woodlands, wetlands, and rock ledges at the **Nature Conservancy's Devil's Den Preserve** (⊠ 33 Pent Rd., ☎ 203/226–4991) include 20 mi of hiking trails. Trail maps are available in the parking-lot registration area, and guided walks take place year-round. There are no rest rooms, and pets and bikes are not allowed.

OFF THE
BEATEN PATH

PUTNAM MEMORIAL STATE PARK – In the winter of 1778–79, three brigades of Continental Army soldiers under the command of General Israel Putnam made their winter encampment at this site, known as Connecticut's Valley Forge. Superb for hiking, picnicking, and cross-country skiing, the park has a small history museum. ⊠ *Rtes. 58 and 107, West Redding (10 mi north of Weston),* ☎ *203/938–2285.* ⊡ *Donation suggested.* ☉ *Grounds daily 8 AM–dusk; museum May–Oct., weekends 10–5.*

Dining

$$–$$$$ ✕ **Cobb's Mill Inn.** Ducks and swans frolic in the waterfall outside this former mill and inn, now a charming restaurant. Start with either the crab cakes or escargots. The Continental menu is heavy on red meat dishes, but lighter fare might include grilled swordfish and roasted Chilean sea bass with a shiitake glaze. Sunday brunch is a favorite. ⊠ *12 Old Mill Rd., off Rte. 57,* ☎ *203/227–7221. AE, D, DC, MC, V. No lunch.*

Westport

9 *7 mi south of Weston, 47 mi northeast of New York City.*

Westport, an artists' community since the turn of the 20th century, continues to attract creative types. Despite commuters and corporations, the town remains more artsy and cultured than its neighbors: if the rest of Fairfield County is stylistically five years behind Manhattan, Westport lags by just five months. Paul Newman and Joanne Woodward have their main residence here.

Summer visitors to Westport congregate at **Sherwood Island State Park,** which has a 1½-mi sweep of sandy beach, two water's-edge picnic groves, sports fields, interpretive programs, and several food concessions (open seasonally). ⊠ *I–95, Exit 18,* ☎ *203/226–6983.* ⊠ *$5–$12.* ⊙ *Daily 8 AM–dusk.*

Dining and Lodging

$$–$$$$ ✕ **Tavern on Main.** This intimate restaurant takes the tavern concept
★   to a new level—fresh flowers and soft music included. In winter the glow of fireplaces reaches every table, and in summer a terrace with an awning beckons. The sophisticated comfort food includes starters such as wild mushroom ravioli and a roasted walnut and endive salad. Among the notable entrées are potato-wrapped sea bass with cabernet sauce and certified Black Angus steak with caramelized shallots. ⊠ *146 Main St., 06880,* ☎ *203/221–7222. AE, DC, MC, V.*

$$$ ✕ **Da Pietro's.** This romantic storefront café serves a savory mix of Italian and French specialties. Roasted monkfish with curry-coconut sauce, lasagna filled with snails and spinach, and sautéed veal tenderloins are possible choices. ⊠ *36 Riverside Ave., 06880,* ☎ *203/454–1213. AE, DC, MC, V. Closed Sun. No lunch.*

$$$$ ✕▦ **Inn at National Hall.** Each whimsically exotic room at this tower-
★   ing Italianate redbrick inn is a study in innovative restoration, wall-stenciling, and decorative painting—including magnificent trompe l'oeil designs. The furniture collection is exceptional. Some rooms and suites have sleeping lofts and 18-ft windows overlooking the Saugatuck River. At Miramar restaurant ($$–$$$$; no dinner Mon.; reservations essential on weekends), Todd English, a Boston superstar, turns out such dishes as grilled sirloin over Tuscan bruschetta and butternut squash tortellini with brown butter and sage. ⊠ *2 Post Rd. W, 06880,* ☎ *203/221–1351 or 800/628–4255,* ℻ *203/221–0276,* ⓌⒺⒷ *www.innatnationalhall.com. 8 rooms, 7 suites. Restaurant, refrigerators, in-room VCRs, meeting room. AE, D, DC, MC, V. CP.*

$$$ ✕▦ **Westport Inn.** Bedrooms in this upscale motor lodge have attractive contemporary furniture. Rooms surrounding the large indoor pool are set back nicely and are slightly larger than the rest. The on-site restaurant, Gennaro's of Westport ($$–$$$), serves updated Italian classics such as Black Angus filet mignon with cognac, Gorgonzola cheese, Portobello mushrooms, and fresh-picked lobster meat. ⊠ *1595 Post Rd. E,* ☎ *203/259–5236; 800/446–8997; 203/259–3456 restaurant;* ℻ *203/254–8439;* ⓌⒺⒷ *www.westportinn.com. 116 rooms, 2 suites. Restaurant, in-room data ports, indoor pool, health club, sauna, bar. AE, D, DC, MC, V.*

Nightlife and the Arts

The **Levitt Pavilion for the Performing Arts** (⊠ Jesup Rd., ☎ 203/221–4422) sponsors an excellent series of mostly free summer concerts that range from jazz to classical, folk rock to blues. The venerable **Westport Country Playhouse** (⊠ 25 Powers Ct., ☎ 203/227–4177) presents six productions each summer in a converted barn.

Shopping

J. Crew, Ann Taylor, Coach, Laura Ashley, Pottery Barn, and other fashionable shops have made Main Street in Westport the outdoor equivalent of upscale malls such as Stamford Town Center.

Fairfield

🔟 *9 mi east of Westport, 33 mi south of Waterbury.*

Fairfield, founded in 1639, was one of the first settlements along the old Post Road (Route 1). Although it was primarily an agricultural community in its early days, Fairfield turned its attention to the shipping industry in order to recover after it was burned to the ground by the British in 1779. Thousands of dogwood trees populate the Greenfield Hill section of town, which hosts the popular Dogwood Festival each May. Southport has grand estates and panoramic views of the Long Island Sound, while downtown Fairfield is just the place to browse through a bookstore and lick an ice cream cone.

The **Connecticut Audubon Center at Fairfield** (✉ 2325 Burr St., ☎ 203/259–6305, WEB www.ctaudubon.org/centers/fairfield) maintains a 160-acre wildlife sanctuary that includes 6 mi of rugged hiking trails and special walks for people with visual impairments and mobility problems.

The **Connecticut Audubon Birdcraft Museum** (✉ 314 Unquowa Rd., ☎ 203/259–0416, WEB www.ctaudubon.org/centers/birdcraft/birdcrafts.htm), operated by the Connecticut Audubon Society, has children's activities, 6 acres with trails, a pond that attracts waterfowl during their spring and fall migrations, and a nature center with natural history exhibits, a reference library, and a gift shop.

Dining

$$–$$$ ✕ **Voilà.** A stone fireplace and lace curtains add cozy warmth to this intimate French bistro. On any given day the menu may include escargots au Roquefort, pâté du chef, or veal chasseur. Save room for dessert: the tart Tatin is said to be a work of art. ✉ *70 Reef Rd., 06430,* ☎ *203/254–2070. AE, MC, V. No lunch Sun.*

$ ✕ **Rawley's Hot Dogs.** The legendary franks at this drive-in are deep-fried in vegetable oil, then grilled for a few seconds—a recipe the stand has been following since it opened in 1946. The cheesedog with the works is a favorite. ✉ *1886 Post Rd., 06430,* ☎ *203/259–9023. No credit cards. Closed Sun.*

Nightlife and the Arts

The **Quick Center for the Arts** (✉ Fairfield University, N. Benson Rd., ☎ 203/254–4010) hosts musical and theatrical performances, children's shows, and a lecture series with international speakers.

Bridgeport

⑪ *5 mi northeast of Fairfield, 63 mi west of New London.*

Bridgeport, a city that has endured some economic hard times, is working hard to overcome its negative image. Recent improvements by civic leaders, among them a new ballpark and sports and entertainment arena, as well as a number of unique attractions, make it a worthwhile stop.

Exhibits at the **Barnum Museum,** associated with past resident and former mayor P. T. Barnum, depict the life and times of the great showman, who presented performers such as General Tom Thumb and Jenny Lind, the Swedish Nightingale. You can tour a scaled-down model of Barnum's legendary five-ring circus. ✉ *820 Main St.,* ☎ *203/331–1104,* WEB *www.barnum-museum.org.* ☜ *$5.* ◷ *Tues.–Sat. 10–4:30, Sun. noon–4:30.*

The indoor walk-through South American rain forest at the **Beardsley Park and Zoological Gardens** alone justifies a visit. Also in the park, which has 36 acres of exhibits north of downtown Bridgeport, are a working carousel and museum and a New England farmyard. ✉ *1875 Noble Ave.*, ☎ *203/394–6565,* WEB *www.beardsleyzoo.org.* 🎫 *$6.* ☉ *Park daily 9–4, rain forest daily 10:30–3:30.*

Captain's Cove on historic Black Rock Harbor is the home port of the Lightship No. 112 *Nantucket.* Band concerts take place on Sunday afternoon in summer. The boardwalk, a popular warm-weather hangout, holds a small assortment of shops and a casual seafood restaurant. ✉ *1 Bostwick Ave. (I–95, Exit 26),* ☎ *203/335–1433,* WEB *www.captainscoveseaport.com.* 🎫 *Cove free, lightship tour $2.* ☉ *Call for tour info.*

🧒 The draws at the **Discovery Museum and Wonder Workshop** include a planetarium, several hands-on science exhibits, a computer-art exhibit, Hoop Smarts (a virtual basketball game), the *Challenger* learning center (which has a simulated space flight), and a children's museum. The Wonder Workshop schedules storytelling and arts-and-crafts, science, and other programs. ✉ *4450 Park Ave.,* ☎ *203/372–3521,* WEB *www.discoverymuseum.org.* 🎫 *$7.* ☉ *Sept.–June, Tues.–Sat. 10–5, Sun. noon–5; July–Aug., Mon.–Sat. 10–5, Sun. noon–5.*

Outdoor Activities and Sports
The **Bridgeport Bluefish** (✉ Harbor Yard, 500 Main St., off I–95, ☎ 203/345–4800) play in the Atlantic League of Professional Baseball Clubs. The **Bridgeport Sound Tigers** (✉ Arena at Harbor Yard, I–95, Exit 27, off I–95, ☎ 203/345–4800) play in the American Hockey League.

Stratford

⑫ *3 mi northeast of Bridgeport, 15 mi southwest of New Haven.*

Stratford, named after the English town Stratford-upon-Avon, has more than 150 historic homes, many of which are on Long Island Sound. The Academy Hill neighborhood, near the intersection of Main (Route 113) and Academy Hill streets, is a good area to stroll.

Boothe Memorial Park & Museum, a 32-acre complex with several unusual buildings, includes a blacksmith shop, carriage and tool barns, and a museum that traces the history of the trolley. Also on the grounds are beautiful rose gardens and a children's playground. ✉ *Main St.,* ☎ *203/381–2046.* 🎫 *Free.* ☉ *Park daily dawn–dusk; museum June–Oct., Tues.–Fri. 11–1, weekends 1–4.*

Southwestern Connecticut A to Z

To research prices, get advice from other travelers, and book travel arrangements, visit www.fodors.com.

BUS TRAVEL
Bonanza Bus Lines provides service to Danbury from Hartford, New York, and Providence. Peter Pan Bus Lines stops in Bridgeport en route from Hartford, Boston, and New York.

Connecticut Transit buses stop in Greenwich, Stamford, and Norwalk. The Greater Bridgeport Transit District's People Movers provide bus transportation in Norwalk, Bridgeport, Stratford, and Fairfield. Norwalk Transit provides bus service in Norwalk and Westport.
➤ Bus Information: **Bonanza Bus Lines** (☎ 888/751–8800, WEB www.bonanzabus.com). **Connecticut Transit** (☎ 203/327–7433, WEB www.cttransit.com). **Norwalk Transit** (☎ 203/852–0000 in Norwalk; ☎ 203/852–0000 in Westport; WEB www.norwalktransit.com). **People Movers** (☎ 203/333–3031, WEB www.gbtabus.com). **Peter Pan Bus Lines** (☎ 800/237–8747, WEB www.peterpanbus.com).

CAR TRAVEL

The main routes into southwestern Connecticut are Route 15 (called the Merritt Parkway in this area) and I–95 (also known as the Connecticut Turnpike). The Merritt Parkway and I–95 are the main arteries; both can have harrowing rush-hour snarls. Greenwich, Stamford, Norwalk, Westport, Fairfield, Bridgeport, and Stratford are on or just off I–95. From I–95 or the Merritt Parkway take Route 124 north to New Canaan; U.S. 7 north to Wilton or Danbury; U.S. 7 and Route 33 north to Ridgefield; and Route 53 north to Weston.

EMERGENCIES

➤ HOSPITALS: **Norwalk Hospital** (✉ 34 Maple St., Norwalk, ☎ 203/852–2000, WEB www.norwalkhosp.org). **St. Vincent's Medical Center** (✉ 2800 Main St., Bridgeport, ☎ 203/576–6000, WEB www.stvincents.org). ➤ 24-HOUR PHARMACY: **CVS** (✉ 235 Main St., Norwalk, ☎ 203/847–6057, WEB www.cvs.com).

TRAIN TRAVEL

Amtrak stops in Stamford and Bridgeport. Metro-North Railroad trains stop in Greenwich, Stamford, Norwalk, New Canaan, Wilton, Danbury, Redding, Westport, Fairfield, Bridgeport, and Stratford. ➤ TRAIN INFORMATION: **Amtrak** (☎ 800/872–7245, WEB www.amtrak.com). **Metro-North Railroad** (☎ 800/638–7646; 212/532–4900 in New York City; WEB www.mta.info).

VISITOR INFORMATION

➤ TOURIST INFORMATION: **Coastal Fairfield County Convention and Visitor Bureau** (✉ The Gate Lodge–Mathews Park, 297 West Ave., Norwalk 06850, ☎ 203/899–2799 or 800/866–7925, WEB www.coastalct.com). **Housatonic Valley Tourism District** (✉ 30 Main St., Danbury 06810, ☎ 203/743–0546 or 800/841–4488, WEB www.housatonic.org).

HARTFORD AND THE CONNECTICUT RIVER VALLEY

Westward expansion in the New World began along the meandering Connecticut River. Dutch explorer Adrian Block first explored the area in 1614, and in 1633 a trading post was set up in what is now Hartford. Within five years, throngs of restive Massachusetts Bay colonists had settled in this fertile valley. What followed was more than three centuries of shipbuilding, shad hauling, and river trading with ports as far away as the West Indies and the Mediterranean.

Less touristy than the coast and northwest hills, the Connecticut River valley is a swath of small villages and uncrowded state parks punctuated by a few small cities and a large one: the capital city of Hartford. To the south of Hartford, with the exception of industrial Middletown, genuinely quaint hamlets vie for a share of Connecticut's tourist crop with antiques shops, scenic drives, and trendy restaurants.

Essex

⓭ *29 mi east of New Haven.*

Essex, consistently named one of the best small towns in America, looks much as it did in the mid-19th century, at the height of its shipbuilding prosperity. So important to a young America was Essex's boat manufacturing that the British burned more than 40 ships here during the War of 1812. Gone are the days of steady trade with the West Indies, when the aroma of imported rum, molasses, and spices hung in the air. Whitewashed houses—many the former roosts of sea captains—line Main Street, which has shops that sell clothing, antiques, paintings and prints, and sweets.

In addition to pre-Colonial artifacts and displays, the **Connecticut River Museum** has a full-size reproduction of the world's first submarine, the *American Turtle*; the original was built by David Bushnell in 1775. Views of the river from the museum are spectacular. ⊠ *Steamboat Dock, 67 Main St.,* ☎ *860/767–8269,* WEB *www.ctrivermuseum.org.* 🖾 *$4.* ☾ *Tues.–Sun. 10–5.*

The **Essex Steam Train and Riverboat** travels alongside the Connecticut River and through the lower valley; if you wish to continue, you can take a riverboat up the river. The train trip lasts an hour; the riverboat ride, 90 minutes. Special trains, including a dinner train and a wine train, as well as a Santa Special and visits by Thomas the Tank Engine occur periodically throughout the year. ⊠ *Valley Railroad, 1 Railroad Ave./Rte. 9, Exit 3,* ☎ *860/767–0103,* WEB *www.essexsteamtrain.com.* 🖾 *Train fare $10.50, train-boat fare $18.50.* ☾ *May–Dec.; call for schedule.*

Dining and Lodging

$$$ ✕ **Steve's Centerbrook Café.** Latticework and gingerbread trim are among the architectural accents of the Victorian house that holds this bright café. The culinary accents lean toward the ornate as well, especially in the few classic French dishes. Although the menu changes regularly, you can usually find rack of lamb or grilled salmon. Save room for the *marjolaine,* a hazelnut torte covered with chocolate. ⊠ *78 Main St., Centerbrook 06409,* ☎ *860/767–1277. AE, MC, V. Closed Mon. No lunch.*

$$–$$$ ✕🏠 **Griswold Inn.** Two-plus centuries of catering to changing tastes at what's billed as America's oldest continuously operating inn has resulted in a kaleidoscope of decor—some Colonial, a touch of Federal, a little Victorian, and just as many modern touches as are necessary to meet present-day expectations. The chefs at the restaurant ($$$–$$$$) prepare country-style and more-sophisticated dishes—try the famous 1776 sausages, which come with sauerkraut and German potato salad. The Tap Room, built in 1738 as a schoolhouse, is ideal for after-dinner drinks. The "English Hunt Breakfast" is a Sunday event. ⊠ *36 Main St., 06426,* ☎ *860/767–1776,* FAX *860/767–0481,* WEB *www.griswoldinn.com. 17 rooms, 13 suites. Restaurant, bar; no-smoking rooms. AE, MC, V. CP.*

$$–$$$ 🏠 **Riverwind.** Antique furnishings, collectibles, and touches of stenciling enrich all the guest rooms at this whimsical inn. One room has a country-pine bed and a painted headboard; another holds a carved oak bed; a third contains an 18th-century bird's-eye-maple four-poster with a canopy. Co-owner Barbara Barlow serves a hearty country breakfast of Smithfield ham, her own baked goods, and several casseroles. Freshly brewed tea and coffee and home-baked cookies are always on hand, and you can relax in multiple common rooms. ⊠ *209 Main St., Deep River 06417,* ☎ *860/526–2014,* FAX *860/526–0875,* WEB *www.riverwindinn.com. 7 rooms, 1 suite. No kids under 12, no-smoking. AE, MC, V. BP.*

Ivoryton

⓮ *4 mi west of Essex.*

Ivoryton was named for its steady import of elephant tusks from Kenya and Zanzibar during the 19th century—piano keys were Ivoryton's leading export during this time. At one time, the Comstock-Cheney piano manufacturers processed so much ivory that Japan regularly purchased Ivoryton's surplus, using the scraps to make souvenirs. The

Connecticut River Valley

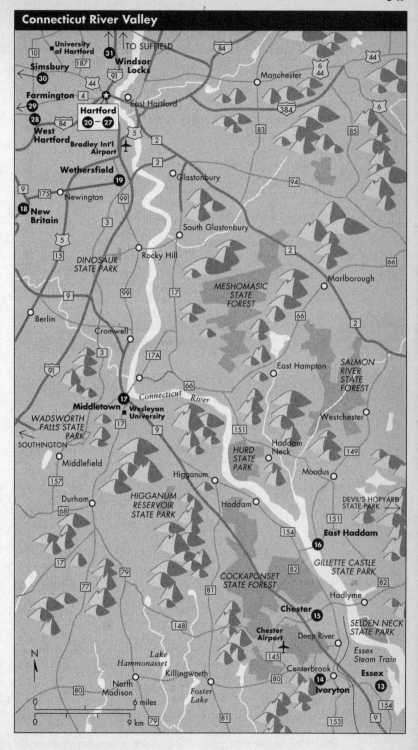

Depression closed the lid on Ivoryton's pianos, and what remains is a sleepy, shady hamlet.

The **Museum of Fife and Drum,** said to be the only one of its kind in the world, contains martial sheet music, instruments, and uniforms chronicling America's history of parades, from the Revolutionary War to the present. ⊠ 62 N. Main St., ☎ 860/767–2237 or 860/399–6519, WEB www.fifedrum.com/thecompany. ☜ $3. ⊙ June 30–Sept. 30, weekends 1–5 or by appointment. Free concerts on select Tues. at 7:30 July –Aug.

Dining and Lodging

$$–$$$$ ✕🏠 **Copper Beech Inn.** A magnificent copper beech tree shades the imposing main building of this Victorian inn, set on 7 wooded acres. The four rooms in the main house have an old-fashioned feel, right down to the claw-foot tubs; the nine rooms in the Carriage House are more modern and have decks. The distinctive country-French menu in the romantic dining room ($$$–$$$$; reservations essential; jacket and tie required; no lunch) changes seasonally. Specials might include the inn's renowned bouillabaisse or roasted boneless saddle of lamb with rosemary-scented tomato-and-lamb glaze. Dinner starts at 1 PM on Sunday. ⊠ 46 Main St., 06442, ☎ 860/767–0330 or 888/809–2056, WEB www.copperbeechinn.com. 13 rooms. Restaurant, in-room data ports; no-smoking rooms. AE, DC, MC, V. CP.

Chester

⑮ *5 mi north of Ivoryton, 24 mi northwest of New London.*

Upscale boutiques and artisans' studios fill chiefly 19th-century buildings along Chester's quaint and well-preserved Main Street. Chester sits on a portion of the Connecticut River that has been named "one of the last great places on earth" by the Nature Conservancy and is the starting point of the Chester-Hadlyme Ferry, which crosses the river in a grand total of five minutes.

Chester Airport arranges fantastic open-cockpit biplane rides over the lower Connecticut River valley. Bring your own bomber jacket and you're set. ⊠ Off Rte. 9, ☎ 860/526–4321 or 800/752–6371. ☜ ½ hr $85, 1 hr $160. ⊙ By appointment.

Sometimes the simple pleasures mean the most. The **Selden III** is the second-oldest continually operating ferry in the country. Although its trip across the Connecticut River to Hadlyme is swift, you'll still catch nice views of the valley and Gillette Castle. ⊠ 148 Ferry Rd., ☎ 860/ 526–2743. ☜ Vehicle and driver $2.25, each additional person 75¢. ⊙ Apr.–Nov., daily upon demand.

Dining

$$$$ ✕ **Restaurant du Village.** A black wrought-iron gate beckons you away from the antiques stores of Chester's Main Street, and an off-white awning draws you through the door of this classic little Colonial storefront, painted in historic Newport blue and adorned with flower boxes. Here you can sample exquisite classic French cuisine—escargots in puff pastry and filet mignon—while recapping the day's shopping coups. ⊠ 59 Main St., 06412, ☎ 860/526–5301. AE, MC, V. Closed Mon.–Tues. No lunch.

$$–$$$ ✕ **Fiddler's Seafood Restaurant.** The specialties at this fine fish house are the rich bouillabaisse and the lobster with a sauce of peaches, peach brandy, shallots, mushrooms, and cream. Blond-bentwood chairs, lacy stenciling on the walls, prints of famous schooners, and the amber glow of oil lamps lend the place a gentrified air. ⊠ 4 Water St., 06412, ☎ 860/526–3210. DC, MC, V. Closed Mon. No lunch Sun.

Shopping

Ceramica (✉ 36 Main St., ☎ 800/782–1238) carries hand-painted Italian tableware and decorative accessories. **Souleiado** (✉ 14 Main St., ☎ 860/526–1480) showcases a colorful collection of imported French percales, upholstery fabrics, table linens, furnishings, and decorative accessories for the home.

East Haddam

⑯ *7 mi north of Chester, 28 mi southeast of Hartford.*

Fishing, shipping, and musket-making were the chief enterprises at East Haddam, the only town in the state that occupies both banks of the Connecticut River. This lovely town retains much of its old-fashioned charm.

★ ☾ At **Allegra Farm and the Horsedrawn Carriage and Sleigh Museum of New England,** John and Kate Allegra not only run sleigh, hay, and carriage rides using authentic vehicles right out of a Currier & Ives scene, but they also have a post-and-beam barn museum that houses more than 30 restored antique carriages and sleighs. Children love the pony rides and the opportunity to visit the livery stable and its tenants—a donkey, llama, sheep, and 30 horses. ✉ *Junction of Rte. 82 and Petticoat La.,* ☎ *860/873–9658,* ⃢ *www.allegrafarm.com.* ☾ *Call for hrs and prices.*

★ **Gillette Castle State Park** holds the outrageous 24-room oak-and-field-stone hilltop castle built by the eccentric actor and dramatist William Gillette between 1914 and 1919; he modeled it after the medieval castles of the Rhineland. You can tour the castle and hike on trails near the remains of the 3-mi private railroad that chugged about the property until the owner's death in 1937. Gillette, who was born in Hartford, wrote two famous Civil War plays and was beloved for his play *Sherlock Holmes* (he performed the title role). In his will, Gillette demanded that the castle not fall into the hands of "some blithering saphead who has no conception of where he is or with what surrounded." To that end, the castle and 184-acre grounds were designated a state park that's an excellent spot for hiking and picnicking. ✉ *67 River Rd., off Rte. 82,* ☎ *860/526–2336.* ▣ *Castle $5, grounds free.* ☾ *Grounds daily 8–sunset. Castle Memorial Day–Columbus Day, daily 10–5 (last tour at 4:15); mid-Oct.–Thanksgiving, weekends 10–5 (last tour at 4:15).*

★ The upper floors of the 1876 Victorian gingerbread **Goodspeed Opera House** have served as a venue for theatrical performances for more than 100 years. In the 1960s the Goodspeed underwent a restoration that included the stage area, the Victorian bar, the sitting room, and the drinking parlor. More than 14 Goodspeed productions have gone on to Broadway, including *Annie.* The performance season runs from April to December. ✉ *Rte. 82,* ☎ *860/873–8668,* ⃢ *www.goodspeed.org.* ▣ *Tour $2.* ☾ *Tours Memorial Day–Columbus Day; call for times.*

St. Stephen's Church is listed in the *Guinness Book of Records* as having the oldest bell in the United States. Crafted in Spain in the year 815, the bell is believed to have been taken from a monastery by Napoléon and used for ballast in a ship. A Captain Andrews from East Haddam discovered it in Florida and brought it back to his hometown, where it now sits in the belfry of St. Stephen's, a small stone Episcopal church with cedar shingles. The church was built in 1794 and was moved to its present site in 1890. ✉ *Main St./Rte. 149,* ☎ *860/873–9547.* ☾ *Call for hrs and service times.*

The three formal herb gardens at the **Sundial Herb Garden**—a Persian-style knot garden of interlocking hedges, a typical 18th-century geometric garden with central sundial, and a topiary garden—surround an 18th-century farmhouse. An 18th-century barn serves as a formal tearoom and a shop with herbs, books, antiques, and rare and fine teas. Sunday afternoon teas and special programs take place throughout the year. ⊠ *59 Hidden Lake Rd., Higganum (6 mi from Higganum Center; head south on Rte. 81, turn right on Brault Hill Rd., and right again when road ends),* ☎ *860/345–4290,* WEB *www.sundialgardens.com.* ⊡ *$2.* ☉ *Jan.–mid-Oct., weekends 10–5; call for Christmas shop hrs Nov.–Dec.*

Sixty-foot cascades flow down Chapman Falls at the 860-acre **Devil's Hopyard State Park,** an idyllic spot for picnicking, fishing, camping, and hiking. ⊠ *366 Hopyard Rd., 3 mi north of junction of Rtes. 82 and 156,* ☎ *860/873–8566.* ⊡ *Free.* ☉ *Park daily 8 AM–dusk.*

Lodging

$$–$$$ 🛏 **Bishopsgate Inn.** An 1818 Federal-style inn near the landmark Good-speed Opera House, the Bishopsgate contains cozy and inviting rooms furnished with period reproductions, a smattering of antiques, and fluffy feather beds. Four rooms have fireplaces, and one has a sauna. You can order elaborate candlelight dinners served in your room. ⊠ *7 Norwich Rd./Rte. 82 (Box 290, 06423),* ☎ *860/873–1677,* FAX *860/873–3898,* WEB *www.bishopsgate.com. 6 rooms. No smoking. D, MC, V. BP.*

Middletown

🔟 *15 mi northwest of East Haddam, 24 mi northeast of New Haven.*

Middletown, once a bustling river city, was named for its location halfway between Hartford and Long Island Sound (it's also halfway between New York City and Boston). It is home to Wesleyan University. The wealthiest town in the state from about 1750 to 1800, Middletown had been in decline for more than a century before being chosen to take part in the National Trust for Historic Preservation's "Main Street Program." The town is currently undergoing a multiyear rehabilitation project to revitalize the downtown area.

The imposing campus of **Wesleyan University,** founded here in 1831, is traversed by High Street, which Charles Dickens once called "the loveliest Main Street in America"—even though Middletown's actual Main Street runs parallel to it a few blocks east. High Street is an architecturally eclectic thoroughfare. Note the massive, fluted Corinthian columns of the Greek Revival Russell House (circa 1828) at the corner of Washington Street, across from the pink Mediterranean-style Davison Arts Center, built just 15 years later; farther on are gingerbreads, towering brownstones, Tudors, and Queen Annes. A few hundred yards up on Church Street, which intersects High Street, is the Olin Library. The 1928 structure, Wesleyan University's library, was designed by Henry Bacon, the architect of the Lincoln Memorial.

The Federal **General Mansfield House** has 18th- and 19th-century decorative arts, Civil War memorabilia and firearms, and local artifacts. ⊠ *151 Main St.,* ☎ *860/346–0746.* ⊡ *$2.* ☉ *Sun. 2–4:30, Mon. 1–4, and by appointment.*

☾ Dinosaurs once roamed the area around **Dinosaur State Park,** north of Middletown. Tracks dating from the Jurassic period, 200 million years ago, are preserved here under a giant geodesic dome. From May to October you can make plaster casts of tracks on a special area of the property; call ahead to learn what materials you need to bring. An exhibit center with interactive displays interprets the dinosaurs, geology, and paleontology of the Connecticut River valley region. A pleasant place for easy hiking, the park has nature trails that run through woods, along a ridge, and through swamps on a boardwalk. ⊠ *400 West St., east of I–91, Exit 23, Rocky Hill,* ☎ *860/529–8423,* WEB *www.dinosaurstatepark.org.* ⌑ *$2.* ⊙ *Exhibits Tues.–Sun. 9–4:30, trails daily 9–4:30.*

You can pick your own fruits and vegetables—berries, peaches, pears, apples, and even pumpkins—at **Lyman Orchards** (⊠ Rtes. 147 and 157, Middlefield, ☎ 860/349–3673, WEB www.lymanorchards.com), just south of Middletown, from June to October. There's also a duck pond, picnic tables, and seasonal petting zoo.

Dining

$ ✕ **O'Rourke's Diner.** For a university town, Middletown has surprisingly few eateries. At this steel, glass, and brick diner, you'll find the expected diner fare, along with a tasty Irish stew, corned-beef hash, and regional delicacies such as steamed cheeseburgers (not served on weekends); it's all unusually good. The weekend breakfast menu is extensive. ⊠ *728 Main St.,* ☎ *860/346–6101. No credit cards. No dinner.*

Nightlife and the Arts

Wesleyan University's **Center for the Arts** (⊠ between Washington Terr. and Wyllys Ave., ☎ 860/685–3355) frequently hosts concerts, theater, films, and art exhibits. At last count, **Eli Cannon's** (⊠ 695 Main St., ☎ 860/347–3547) had 28 beers on tap and more than 100 bottled selections.

Outdoor Activities and Sports

Called by some "a public course with a private feel," the **Lyman Orchards Golf Club** (⊠ Rte. 157, Middlefield, ☎ 860/349–8055) has two 18-hole championship courses. The greens fee at both the par-72 course, designed by Robert Trent Jones, and par-71 course, designed by Gary Player, runs between $35 and $47. Carts ($11) are mandatory.

Shopping

Tours of the **Wesleyan Potters** (⊠ 350 S. Main St., ☎ 860/347–5925) pottery and weaving studios can be arranged in advance. Jewelry, clothing, baskets, pottery, weavings, and more are for sale.

Ski Areas

POWDER RIDGE

The trails here drop straight down from the 500-ft-high ridge for which this ski area is named. Half the 15 trails are designed for intermediate skiers, with the others split between beginner trails and expert black diamonds; all the trails are lighted for night skiing. One quad lift, two doubles, and a handle tow cover the mountain. Amenities include a snowtubing area, a snowboard park, an alpine park, a full-service restaurant, and ski instruction for children ages 4 and up. ⊠ *99 Powder Hill Rd., Middlefield 06455,* ☎ *877/754–74343.*

New Britain

18 *13 mi northwest of Middletown, 10 mi southwest of Hartford.*

New Britain got its start as a manufacturing center producing sleigh bells. From these modest beginnings, it soon became known as "Hardware City," distributing builders' tools, ball bearings, locks, and other such items. No longer a factory town, New Britain is home to the Central Connecticut State College University and a first-rate museum of American art.

The **New Britain Museum of American Art,** in a turn-of-the-20th-century house, holds 19 galleries and more than 5,000 works of art that survey the history of American art from 1740 to the present. Though the collection includes luminaries such as Thomas Cole, Georgia O'-Keeffe, and Thomas Hart Benton, the selection of Impressionist artists deserves special note—Mary Cassatt, William Merritt Chase, Childe Hassam, and John Henry Twachtman, among others. ✉ *56 Lexington St.,* ☎ *860/229–0257,* WEB *www.nbmaa.org.* ✇ *$5.* ⊘ *Tues., Thurs.–Fri., and Sun. noon–5; Wed. noon–7; Sat. 10–5.*

♻ The **Copernican Observatory & Planetarium,** on the campus of Central Connecticut State University, has one of the largest public telescopes in the nation and schedules programs geared to both children and adults. ✉ *1615 Stanley St.,* ☎ *860/832–3399.* ✇ *$3.50.* ⊘ *Shows Fri.–Sat.; call for times.*

Outdoor Activities and Sports

The **New Britain Rock Cats,** the Double-A affiliate of baseball's Minnesota Twins, play at New Britain Stadium (✉ Willow Brook Park, S. Main St., ☎ 860/224–8383) from April to September.

Wethersfield

⓳ *7 mi northeast of New Britain, 32 mi northeast of New Haven.*

Wethersfield, a vast Hartford suburb, dates from 1634 and has the state's largest—and, some say, most picturesque—historic district, with more than 100 buildings from before 1840. As was the case throughout early Connecticut, the Native Americans indigenous to these lands fought the arriving English with a vengeance; here their struggles culminated in the 1637 Wethersfield Massacre, when Pequot Indians killed nine settlers. Three years later, the citizens held a public election, America's first defiance of British rule, for which they were fined five British pounds.

The Joseph Webb House, Silas Deane House, and Isaac Stevens House, all built in the mid- to late 1700s, form one of the state's best historic-house museums, the **Webb-Deane-Stevens Museum.** The structures, well-preserved examples of Georgian architecture, reflect their owners' lifestyles as, respectively, a merchant, a diplomat, and a tradesman. The Webb House, a registered National Historic Landmark, was the site of the strategy conference between George Washington and the French general Jean-Baptiste Rochambeau that led to the British defeat at Yorktown. ✉ *211 Main St. (I–91, Exit 26),* ☎ *860/529–0612,* WEB *www.webb-deane-stevens.org.* ✇ *$8.* ⊘ *May–Oct., Wed.–Mon. 10–4; Nov.–Apr., weekends 10–4 (last tour at 3).*

Comstock Ferre & Co. (✉ 263 Main St., ☎ 860/571–6590, WEB www.comstockferre.com), founded in 1820, is the country's oldest continuously operating seed company. It sells more than 800 varieties of seeds and 3,000 varieties of perennials in an inviting chestnut post-and-beam building that dates from the late 1700s.

Hartford

4 mi north of Wethersfield, 45 mi northwest of New London, 81 mi northeast of Stamford.

Formerly one of the nation's most powerful cities, Connecticut's capital seems past its prime. Although the decline of the insurance and defense industries in the past two decades has left the once-lovely city in some disrepair, it still has many notable sights for travelers. Some ambitious long-term programs for downtown renewal are in the works, however, including riverfront beautification. America's insurance industry was born here in the early 19th century—largely in an effort to protect the Connecticut River valley's tremendously important shipping interests. Throughout the 19th century, insurance companies expanded their coverage to include fires, accidents, life, and (in 1898) automobiles. Through the years, Hartford industries have included the inspection and packing of tobacco (once a prominent industry in the northern river valley) and the manufacture of everything from bedsprings to artificial limbs, pool tables, and coffins. Hartford's distinctive office towers make what is actually an ever-expanding suburban development seem more urban.

㉒ The Federal **Old State House,** a building with an elaborate cupola and roof balustrade, was designed in the early 1700s by Charles Bulfinch, architect of the U.S. Capitol. The Great Senate Room, where everyone from Abraham Lincoln to George Bush has spoken, contains a Gilbert Stuart portrait of George Washington that remains in its commissioned location. For a chance to see a two-headed calf, drop by the small but distinctive museum of oddities upstairs. And at 12:15 every Tuesday, the trial of the Africans who mutinied on the *Amistad* in 1839 is reenacted in the very courtroom where it was first held. ⊠ *800 Main St.,* ☎ *860/522–6766.* ☜ *Free.* ☉ *Weekdays 10–4, Sat. 11–4. Closed last 2 wks in Aug.*

★ **㉑** With more than 50,000 artworks and artifacts spanning 5,000 years, the **Wadsworth Atheneum Museum of Art** is the second-largest public art museum in New England and the oldest in the nation, predating the Metropolitan Museum of Art in New York by 35 years. Among notable items to look for are five wall drawings by Connecticut's own Sol LeWitt, the well-known conceptual artist, as well as the first American acquisitions of works by Salvador Dalí and the Italian artist Caravaggio. Particularly impressive are the museum's collections of Baroque, Impressionist, and Hudson River School artists—including pieces by Frederic Church and Thomas Cole—as well as what some consider the world's finest collection of Pilgrim-era furnishings. The Museum Café is a lovely spot for lunch. ⊠ *600 Main St.,* ☎ *860/278–2670,* WEB *www.wadsworthatheneum.org.* ☜ *$7, free Sat. 11–noon and Thurs.* ☉ *Tues.–Sun. 11–5 (1st Thurs. of most months until 8).*

㉒ The **Center Church,** built in 1807, is a classic temple-with-spire design with a soaring, barrel-vaulted ceiling. The parish itself dates from 1632 and was started by Puritan clergyman Thomas Hooker (1586–1647), one of the chief founders of Hartford. Five of the stained-glass windows were created by Louis Tiffany. The Ancient Burying Ground, in the churchyard, is filled with granite and brownstone headstones, some dating from the 1600s. ⊠ *675 Main St.,* ☎ *860/249–5631.* ☜ *Free.* ☉ *By appointment.*

㉓ The **Butler-McCook Homestead,** built in 1782 and continuously occupied by the same family until 1971, has furnishings that show the evolution of American taste over time. An extensive collection of Japanese armor and Asian bronzes, a history center with interactive exhibits, Victorian-era toys, and a restored Victorian garden, originally designed by Jacob Weidenmann in 1865, enrich the experience. ⊠ *396 Main St.,* ☎ *860/522–1806 or 860/247–8996,* WEB *www.hartnet.org/als.* ☜ *$5.* ☉ *Wed.–Sun. noon–5 and by appointment.*

Bushnell Park, which fans out from the State Capitol building, was the first public space (1850) in the country with natural landscaping instead of a traditional village-green configuration. The park was created by the firm of Frederick Law Olmsted, the Hartford-born landscape architect who, with Calvert Vaux, designed New York City's Central

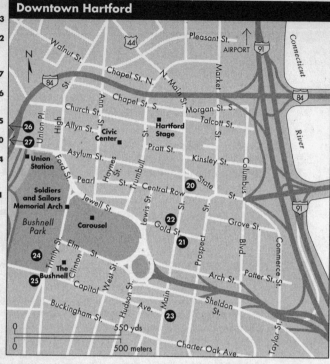

Downtown Hartford

Park. Amid Bushnell's 40 acres are 150 varieties of trees and such land-marks as a 1914 Stein & Goldstein carousel (open May–October) and the 100-ft-tall, 30-ft-wide medieval-style Soldiers and Sailors Memorial Arch, dedicated to Civil War soldiers.

24 Rising above Bushnell Park and visible citywide is the grandiose **State Capitol,** a colossal edifice composed of wholly disparate architectural elements. Built in 1879 of marble and granite, this gilt-dome wonder is replete with crockets, finials, and pointed arches. It houses the governor's office and legislative chambers and displays historic statuary, flags, and furnishings. ⊠ *210 Capitol Ave.,* ☎ *860/240–0222.* ☜ *Free.* ⊙ *Weekdays 9–3; tours on the hr Apr.–Oct., Mon.–Sat. 10:15–2:15, Nov.–Mar., weekdays 9:15–1:15*

25 The **Museum of Connecticut History** exhibits artifacts of Connecticut military, industrial, and political history, including the state's Colonial charter. It holds a vast assemblage of Samuel Colt firearms; the so-called Arm of Law and Order was manufactured in Hartford. ⊠ *231 Capitol Ave.,* ☎ *860/757–6535,* WEB *www.cslib.org/museum.htm.* ☜ *Free.* ⊙ *Weekdays 9–4, Sat. 10–4, Sun. noon–4.*

Nook Farm, a late-19th-century neighborhood, was home to several prominent families. Samuel Langhorne Clemens, better known as Mark Twain, built his Stick-style Victorian mansion here in 1874.

★ **26** During his residency at the 19-room **Mark Twain House,** he published seven major novels, including *Tom Sawyer, Huckleberry Finn,* and *The Prince and the Pauper.* Personal memorabilia and original furnishings are on display, and one-hour guided tours of the house discuss its spectacular Victorian interior and Twain's family life. Also on tour are the rooms of the family butler, George Griffin, a prominent member of Hartford's African-American community. A new Education and Visitors Center is scheduled to open in 2003. ⊠ *351 Farmington Ave., at Woodland*

St., ☎ *860/247–0998 ext. 26,* WEB *www.marktwainhouse.org.* 🖃 *$9.* ☉ *May–Oct. and Dec., Mon.–Sat. 9:30–4, Sun. noon–4; Jan.–Apr. and Nov., Mon. and Wed.–Sat. 9:30–4, Sun. noon–4.*

㉗ The **Harriet Beecher Stowe House,** a Victorian Gothic cottage erected in 1871, stands as a tribute to the author of one of 19th-century America's most popular and influential works of literature, the antislavery novel *Uncle Tom's Cabin.* Stowe (1811–96) spent her final years here. Inside are her personal writing table and effects, several of her paintings, a period pinewood kitchen, and a terrarium of native ferns, mosses, and wildflowers. ⊠ *77 Forest St.,* ☎ *860/522–9258,* WEB *www. harrietbeecherstowecenter.org.* 🖃 *$6.50.* ☉ *Memorial Day–Columbus Day and Dec., Mon.–Sat. 9:30–4:30, Sun. noon–4:30; mid-Oct.–Nov. and Jan.–Memorial Day, Tues.–Sat. 9:30–4:30, Sun. noon–4:30.*

Dining and Lodging

$$$–$$$$ ★ ✕ **Max Downtown.** One of restaurateur Richard Rosenthal's culinary creations, upscale Max Downtown serves cuisine from around the world—everything from smoked Chilean sea bass to porcini mushroom ravioli to fire-roasted pork tenderloin. A separate cigar bar serves classic port and single-malt liquor. ⊠ *CityPlace, 185 Asylum St., 06103,* ☎ *860/522–2530. Reservations essential. AE, DC, MC, V. No lunch weekends.*

$$$ ✕ **Hotep's.** This exotic restaurant—named for Imhotep, an Egyptian sage who lived in 2680 BC and was later deified—entices diners with international cuisine spiced with everything from Caribbean to Italian influences. You can muse at the decorative hieroglyphics and busts of Ramses and Nefertiti while sampling such starters as dahl soup and scallop ceviche. Favored entrées include jerk-roasted chicken and fresh grouper crusted with yucca. ⊠ *283–291 Asylum St.,* ☎ *860/548– 1675. AE, MC, V. Closed Sun.–Mon. No lunch Sat.*

$$–$$$ ✕ **Pastis.** Homey French cuisine such as steak frites, coq au vin, and beef bourguignonne highlights this Parisian-style brasserie. Tile floors, lace curtains, and French prints set the mood. ⊠ *201 Ann St., 06103,* ☎ *860/278–8852. AE, DC, MC, V. Closed Sun.*

$$–$$$ ✕ **Peppercorn's Grill.** This mainstay of Hartford's restaurant scene presents contemporary Italian cuisine in both a lively (colorful murals adorn the walls) and a formal (tables are topped with white linen) setting. Some of the specials might be smoked Sicilian swordfish carpaccio, grilled and roasted veal with a truffle and porcini glaze, or Tuscan seafood stew. ⊠ *357 Main St., 06016,* ☎ *860/547–1714. AE, DC, MC, V. Closed Sun.*

$$–$$$ ✕ **Trumbull Kitchen.** Mix and match is the way to go at this high-energy restaurant. Menu items are divided into categories including dim sum, tapas, and noshes; soups, noodles, and bowls; and fondues, stone pies, and sandwiches. Expect to find everything from cutting edge to home-style favorites, from nori rolls and Stilton cheese fritters with cranberry-orange chutney to pork-and-chive pot stickers and orange-glazed yellowfin tuna. You decide in what order you'd like them served. ⊠ *150 Trumbull St.,* ☎ *860/493–7412. AE, D, DC, MC, V. No lunch weekends.*

$–$$ ✕ **First and Last Tavern.** What looks to be a simple neighborhood joint south of downtown is actually one of the state's most hallowed pizza parlors. The long, old-fashioned wooden bar in one room is jammed most evenings with suburbia-bound daily-grinders shaking off their suits. The main dining room, which is just as noisy, has a brick outer wall covered with celebrity photos. ⊠ *939 Maple Ave., 06114,* ☎ *860/956– 6000. Reservations not accepted. AE, D, DC, MC, V.*

$$$–$$$$ 🏨 **Hilton Hartford Hotel.** At 15 stories, this is the city's largest hotel. It's not sumptuous, but touches of elegance such as the street-level lobby

abloom with fresh flowers abound. The Hilton connects to the Civic Center by an enclosed bridge and is within walking distance of the downtown area. ✉ *315 Trumbull St. (at the Civic Center Plaza), 06103,* ☎ *860/728–5151,* FAX *860/240–7246,* WEB *www.hilton.com. 390 rooms, 6 suites. Restaurant, in-room data ports, indoor pool, health club, hot tub, sauna, bar. AE, D, DC, MC, V.*

$$–$$$$ ★ 🏨 **Goodwin Hotel.** Connecticut's only truly grand city hotel looks a little odd in the downtown business district—the Civic Center dwarfs the ornate dark red structure, a registered historic landmark built in 1881. Its rooms are large and tastefully done in Colonial style and have Italian marble baths. The clubby, mahogany-panel Pierpont's Restaurant serves popular new American fare. ✉ *1 Haynes St., 06103,* ☎ *860/246–7500 or 800/922–5006,* FAX *860/247–4576,* WEB *www.goodwinhotel.com. 111 rooms, 13 suites. Restaurant, in-room data ports, gym, bar, meeting room. AE, D, DC, MC, V.*

$$ 🏨 **Parkside Hotel.** Adjacent to Bushnell Park, this hotel has an unobstructed view of the state capitol. Ask for a room in front—the ones facing the rear overlook the train station around the corner, a parking lot, and a busy highway. The restaurant serves steaks, hamburgers, and other traditional American fare. ✉ *440 Asylum St., 06103,* ☎ *860/ 246–6591,* FAX *860/728–1382. 96 rooms. Restaurant, in-room data ports. AE, D, DC, MC, V. CP.*

Nightlife and the Arts

NIGHTLIFE

The **Arch Street Tavern** (✉ 85 Arch St., ☎ 860/246–7610) hosts local rock bands. For barbecue and blues head to **Black-Eyed Sally's** (✉ 350 Asylum St., ☎ 860/278–7427). **Coach's Sports Bar** (✉ 187 Allyn St., ☎ 860/522–6224) is always a happening spot to watch the game. **Mozzicato–De Pasquale's Bakery, Pastry Shop & Caffe** (✉ 329 Franklin Ave., ☎ 860/296–0426) serves up late-night Italian pastries in the bakery and espresso, cappuccino, and gelato in the café, which has a full bar.

THE ARTS

The **Bushnell** (✉ 166 Capitol Ave., ☎ 860/246–6807) hosts the Hartford Symphony (☎ 860/244–2999) and tours of major musicals. The **Hartford Conservatory** (✉ 834 Asylum Ave., ☎ 860/246–2588) presents musical performances, with an emphasis on traditional works. The Tony Award–winning **Hartford Stage Company** (✉ 50 Church St., ☎ 860/527–5151) stages future Broadway hits, innovative productions of the classics, and new plays. The mammoth **Meadows Music Center** (✉ 61 Savitt Way, ☎ 860/548–7370) hosts nationally known popular music acts. The ensemble from the **National Theatre of the Deaf** (✉ 55 Van Dyke Ave., ☎ 860/724–5179) performs in sign and spoken language at various locations. **Real Art Ways** (✉ 56 Arbor St., ☎ 860/232–1006) presents modern and experimental musical compositions in addition to avant-garde and foreign films. **Theatreworks** (✉ 233 Pearl St., ☎ 860/527–7838), the Hartford equivalent of Off-Broadway, presents experimental new dramas.

Outdoor Activities and Sports

The **Hartford Wolf Pack** (☎ 860/246–7825) of the American Hockey League play at the 16,500-seat Civic Center (✉ 1 Civic Center Plaza).

Ski Areas

MT. SOUTHINGTON

This mountain, a 20-minute drive southwest of Hartford, has 14 trails off the 425 ft of vertical range, split equally among basic beginner, intermediate, and advanced. All trails are lighted for night skiing and are serviced by one triple chairlift, one double, two T-bars, one J-bar, and a handle tow. Snowboarders will find a halfpipe and terrain park. The ski school (with 150 instructors) includes a popular SKIwee program for kids ages 4–12. The Mountain Room provides respite for skiers and snowboarders alike. ⊠ *396 Mount Vernon Rd., Southington 06489,* ☎ *860/628–0954; 860/628–7669 snow conditions.*

West Hartford

28 *5 mi west of Hartford.*

More metropolitan than many of its suburban neighbors, West Hartford is alive with a sense of community. Gourmet-food and ethnic grocery stores abound, as do unusual boutiques and shops. A stroll around West Hartford Center (I–84, Exit 42) reveals well-groomed streets busy with pedestrians and lined with coffee shops.

★ ☺ A life-size walk-through replica of a 60-ft sperm whale greets patrons of the **Science Center of Connecticut,** whose attractions include a wildlife sanctuary and planetarium. The Kids Factory teaches about magnetics, motion, optics, sound, and light through colorful hands-on exhibits. Some "Mathmagical" toys in the lower exhibit hall are a giant bubble maker, a hands-on weather station, and "Kaleidovision"—a 30-ft by 9-ft walk-in kaleidoscope. ⊠ *950 Trout Brook Dr.,* ☎ *860/231–2824,* WEB *www.sciencecenterct.org.* ⊡ *Science Center $6, laser and planetarium shows an additional $3.* ☉ *Sept.–June, Tues.–Wed. and Fri.–Sat. 10–5, Thurs. 10–8, Sun. noon–5; July–Aug., Mon.–Wed. and Fri.–Sat. 10–5, Thurs. 10–8, Sun. noon–5.*

The **Noah Webster House/Museum of West Hartford History** is the birthplace of the famed author (1758–1843) of the *American Dictionary.* The 18th-century farmhouse contains Webster memorabilia and period furnishings. ⊠ *227 S. Main St.,* ☎ *860/521–5362,* WEB *www.ctstateu.edu/noahweb.* ⊡ *$5.* ☉ *Sept.–June, Mon. and Thurs.–Sun. 1–4; July–Aug., Mon. and Thurs.–Fri. 11–4, weekends 1–4.*

The **Museum of American Political Life** houses a staggering collection of rare political materials and memorabilia—buttons, posters, bumper stickers, and pamphlets—from the campaigns of U.S. presidents from George Washington to the present. A small section is devoted to memorabilia from the women's rights and temperance movements. ⊠ *University of Hartford, 200 Bloomfield Ave.,* ☎ *860/768–4090,* WEB *www.hartford.edu/polmus.* ⊡ *Donation suggested.* ☉ *Sept.–May, Tues.–Fri. 11–4, weekends noon–4; call for summer hrs.*

Dining

$$ ✕ **Butterfly Chinese Restaurant.** The piano entertainment suggests this is not your ordinary order-by-number Chinese restaurant; indeed, the food is authentic, the staff outgoing. Among the 140 mostly Cantonese (some Szechuan) entrées are Peking duck and sesame chicken. ⊠ *831 Farmington Ave., 06119,* ☎ *860/236–2816. AE, D, DC, MC, V.*

Farmington

29 *5 mi southwest of West Hartford*

Busy Farmington, incorporated in 1645, is a classic river town with lovely estates, a perfectly preserved main street, and the prestigious **Miss Porter's School** (⊠ *60 Main St.*), the late Jacqueline Kennedy Onassis's alma mater. Antiques shops can be found near the intersection of Routes 4 and 10, along with some excellent house-museums.

★ The **Hill-Stead Museum** was converted from a private home into a museum by its talented owner, Theodate Pope, a turn-of-the-20th-century

architect. The elaborate sunken garden stages poetry readings by nationally known writers every other week in summer. The Colonial Revival farmhouse contains a superb collection of French Impressionist
art displayed in situ. Paintings of haystacks by Monet hang at each end
of the drawing room, and Manet's *The Guitar Player* hangs in the middle. ⊠ *35 Mountain Rd.,* ☎ *860/677–4787,* WEB *www.hillstead.org.* 🈂
$9. ⊙ *May–Oct., Tues.–Sun. 10–5 (last tour at 4); Nov.–Apr., Tues.–*
Sun. 11–4 (last tour at 3).

A museum since the 1930s, the **Stanley-Whitman House** was built in
1720 and has a massive central chimney, an overhanging second story,
and superlative 18th-century furnishings. ⊠ *37 High St.,* ☎ *860/677–*
9222, WEB *www.stanleywhitman.org.* 🈂 *$5.* ⊙ *Nov.–Apr., Sun. noon–*
4 and by appointment; May–Oct., Wed.–Sun. noon–4.

Dining and Lodging

$$$ ✕ **Ann Howard's Apricots.** A white Colonial with dozens of windows
looking out over gardens and the Farmington River holds the area's
best eatery. Fine new American cuisine—such as the grilled filet mignon
with crispy fried Bermuda onions and a shiitake demiglace or the duck
with cashew wild rice—is presented in the quiet, cozy formal dining
room; less expensive fare is available in the convivial pub. ⊠ *1593 Farm-*
ington Ave., 06032, ☎ *860/673–5903. AE, DC, MC, V.*

$$ 🏨 **Farmington Inn.** Large guest rooms, tastefully appointed with antiques and reproductions, highlight this stately inn. Fresh flowers and
paintings by local artists add homey touches. Much nicer than a chain
hotel, the inn is very close to Miss Porter's and area museums. ⊠ *827*
Farmington Ave., 06032, ☎ *860/677–2821 or 800/648–9804,* FAX *860/*
677–8332, WEB *www.farmingtoninn.com. 59 rooms, 13 suites. Busi-*
ness services, meeting room. AE, D, DC, MC, V. CP.

Shopping

The upscale 160-shop **Westfarms Mall** (⊠ New Britain Ave., or I–84,
Exit 40, ☎ 860/561–3024) includes Nordstrom, April Cornell, Williams-
Sonoma, and Restoration Hardware.

Simsbury

③⓪   *12 mi north of Farmington via Rte. 10.*

Colonial-style shopping centers, a smattering of antiques shops, and
a proliferation of insurance-industry executives define this chic bedroom community near Hartford.

The highlight of the Simsbury Historical Society's **Phelps Tavern Mu-**
seum & Homestead is the period-furnished 1771 Colonial home of
Elijah Phelps and his family. A permanent exhibit highlights the use
of the home as a tavern from 1786 to 1849, when it was a stop on
the Farmington Canal. You'll also learn about the 300-year, largely
agrarian history of Simsbury, which was settled around 1640 and incorporated in 1670. Other buildings on the property include a Victorian carriage house (circa 1880), a 1795 cottage and herb garden,
a 1740 schoolhouse, and a replica of the town's original meetinghouse,
which can be seen on special tours. You can view the houses only on
a tour, but the highly strollable grounds are also accessible. ⊠ *800*
Hopmeadow St., ☎ *860/658–2500,* WEB *www.simsburyhistory.org.* 🈂
$6. ⊙ *Tues.–Sat. 10–4.*

The **Old New-Gate Prison and Copper Mine,** 7 mi north of Simsbury,
was the country's first chartered copper mine (in 1707) and, later (in
1773), Connecticut's first Colonial prison. Tours of the underground
mine (where temperatures rarely top 55°F) are a great way to chill out

in summer. There are hiking trails and a picnic area. ⊠ *Newgate Rd., East Granby,* ☎ *860/653–3563 or 860/566–3005.* 🎫 *$4.* ☉ *Mid-May–Oct., Wed.–Sun. 10–4:30.*

Lodging

$$$–$$$$ 🏨 **Avon Old Farms Hotel.** This 20-acre compound of redbrick Colonial-style buildings is set into the Avon countryside at the foot of Talcott Mountain, about midway between Farmington and Simsbury. An immense place that caters largely to business travelers, it has quietly elegant rooms. ⊠ *279 Avon Mountain Rd., Avon 06001,* ☎ *860/677–1651,* 🗺 *860/677–0364,* 🌐 *www.avonoldfarmshotel.com. 160 rooms. Restaurant, pool, gym, sauna, pub, business services, meeting room. AE, D, DC, MC, V. CP.*

$$$–$$$$ 🏨 **Simsbury 1820 House.** The rooms at this inn perched on a hillside contain a judicious mix of antiques and modern furnishings. The main house was built in 1820 and has an 1890 addition on its west side; each room and suite here has a special feature—a decorative fireplace or balcony, a patio, a wet bar, a dormer with a cozy window seat. Across the parking lot is a former carriage house with 10 rooms; the split-level Executive Suite has a private patio, entrance, and hot tub. ⊠ *731 Hopmeadow St., 06070,* ☎ *860/658–7658 or 800/879–1820,* 🗺 *860/651–0724,* 🌐 *www.simsbury1820house.com. 34 rooms, 3 suites. Restaurant, in-room data ports, meeting rooms. AE, D, DC, MC, V. CP.*

Outdoor Activities and Sports

ICE-SKATING

The **International Skating Center of Connecticut** is a world-class twin-rink facility used for practice by skating luminaries such as Viktor Petrenko, Ekaterina Gordeeva, and Scott Davis. Lessons and public skating sessions are offered, and ice shows are held periodically throughout the year. ⊠ *1375 Hopmeadow St.,* ☎ *860/651–5400.* 🎫 *Call for public hrs and rates.*

STATE PARK

A 1½-mi climb from the parking lot at the southern section of **Talcott Mountain State Park** and up the 165-ft Heublein Tower, a former private home, rewards you with spectacular views of the Farmington Valley and, some say, four states. ⊠ *Rte. 185,* ☎ *860/242–1158.* 🎫 *Free.* ☉ *Park daily 8 AM–sunset. Tower late Apr.–Labor Day, Thurs.–Sun. 10–5; Labor Day–late Oct., daily 10–5.*

Shopping

Arts Exclusive Gallery (⊠ 690 Hopmeadow St., ☎ 860/651–5824) represents more than 30 contemporary artists. The **Farmington Valley Arts Center** (⊠ 25 Arts Center La., Avon, ☎ 860/678–1867) displays the work of more than 20 artists in historic brownstone buildings and shows the works of nationally known artists in its gallery.

Windsor Locks

③① *13 mi northeast of Simsbury, 94 mi northeast of Greenwich, 48 mi northeast of New Haven, 56 mi northwest of New London.*

Windsor Locks was named for the locks of a canal built to bypass falls in the Connecticut River in 1833; in 1844 the canal closed to make way for a railroad line. You'll see long, low tobacco barns in the area. Bradley International Airport, the state's central transportation hub, resides here.

★ The more than 70 aircraft at the **New England Air Museum** include flying machines that date from 1870, among them gliders and helicopters.

A World War II–era P-47 Thunderbolt and B-29 Superfortress are on display, along with other vintage fighters and bombers. There's even a jet fighter simulator. ⊠ *Next to Bradley International Airport, off Rte. 75,* ☎ *860/623–3305,* WEB *www.neam.org.* ⊡ *$7.25.* ☉ *Daily 10–5.*

The **Phelps-Hatheway House,** 7 mi north of Windsor Locks, is one of the finest architectural specimens in New England. The walls of its neo-classical north wing (1794) still wear their original 18th-century French hand-blocked wallpaper. The double front doors and gambrel roof of the main house (1761) were typical accoutrements of Connecticut River valley homes. An ornate picket fence fronts the property. ⊠ *55 S. Main St. (take Rte. 75 north from Windsor Locks), Suffield,* ☎ *860/ 668–0055 or 860/247–8996.* ⊡ *$4.* ☉ *Mid-May–June and Sept.–mid-Oct., Wed. and weekends 1–4; July–Aug., Wed.–Sun. 1–4.*

Hartford and the Connecticut River Valley A to Z

To research prices, get advice from other travelers, and book travel arrangements, visit www.fodors.com.

AIRPORTS
Bradley International Airport, 12 mi north of Hartford, is served by American, Continental, Delta, Midwest Express, Northwest, Southwest, United, and US Airways.
➤ AIRPORT INFORMATION: **Bradley International Airport** (⊠ Rte. 20, Windsor Locks; take I–91, Exit 40, ☎ 860/627–3000, WEB www. bradleyairport.com).

BUS TRAVEL
Hartford's renovated Union Station is the main terminus for Greyhound and Peter Pan Bus Lines. Bus service is available to most major northeastern cities. Connecticut Transit provides bus service throughout the greater Hartford area. The fare varies according to destination.
➤ BUS INFORMATION: **Connecticut Transit** (☎ 860/525–9181, WEB www. cttransit.com). **Greyhound** (☎ 800/231–2222, WEB www.greyhound.com). **Peter Pan Bus Lines** (☎ 800/237–8747, WEB www.peterpanbus.com). **Union Station** (⊠ 1 Union Pl.).

CAR TRAVEL
Interstates 84 and 91, Route 2, and U.S. 44 intersect in Hartford. The junction of I–84 and I–91 in downtown Hartford is notorious for near-gridlock conditions during rush hour.

The major road through the valley is Route 9, which extends from south of Hartford at I–91 to I–95. Old Saybrook, Essex, Ivoryton, Chester, Middletown, and New Britain are all on or near Route 9; Wethersfield is east of Route 9. From just below Deep River to just above Higganum, Route 154 loops east of Route 9; head east from Route 154 on Route 151 to reach East Haddam. Farmington is west of Hartford on Route 4. To reach Simsbury head west from Hartford on U.S. 202/44 and north on U.S. 202. To reach Windsor Locks, take I–91 north from Hartford and head north on Route 159.

EMERGENCIES
➤ HOSPITALS: **Hartford Hospital** (⊠ 80 Seymour St., ☎ 860/545–5000, WEB www.hartfordhosp.org). **Middlesex Hospital** (⊠ 28 Crescent St., Middletown, ☎ 860/344–6000, WEB www.midhosp.org).
➤ LATE-NIGHT PHARMACIES: **CVS** (⊠ 1099 New Britain Ave., West Hartford, ☎ 860/236–6181; ⊠ 154 Main St., Old Saybrook, ☎ 860/388–1045; WEB www.cvs.com).

TRAIN TRAVEL

Hartford's renovated Union Station is the main terminus for Amtrak trains. Train service is available to most major northeastern cities. The fare varies according to destination.

➤ TRAIN INFORMATION: **Amtrak** (☎ 800/872–7245, WEB www. amtrak.com). **Union Station** (✉ 1 Union Pl. ☎ 860/247–5329).

VISITOR INFORMATION

➤ TOURIST INFORMATION: **Central Connecticut Tourism District** (✉ 1 Grove St., Suite 310, New Britain 06053, ☎ 860/225–3901, WEB www. centralct.org). **Connecticut's North Central Tourism Bureau** (✉ 111 Hazard Ave., Enfield 06082, ☎ 860/763–2578 or 800/248–8283, WEB www.cnctb.org). **Connecticut River Valley and Shoreline Visitors Council** (✉ 393 Main St., Middletown 06457, ☎ 860/347–0028 or 800/486–3346, WEB www.cttourism.org). **Greater Hartford Tourism District** (✉ 234 Murphy Rd., Hartford 06114, ☎ 860/244–8181 or 800/793–4480, WEB www.enjoyhartford.com).

THE LITCHFIELD HILLS

Here in the foothills of the Berkshires is some of the most spectacular and unspoiled scenery in Connecticut. Two scenic highways, I–84 and Route 8, form the southern and eastern boundaries of the region. New York, to the west, and Massachusetts, to the north, complete the rectangle. Grand old inns are plentiful, as are sophisticated eateries. Rolling farmlands abut thick forests, and trails—including a section of the Appalachian Trail—traverse the state parks and forests. Two rivers, the Housatonic and the Farmington, attract anglers and canoeing enthusiasts, and the state's three largest natural lakes, Waramaug, Bantam, and Twin, are here. Sweeping town greens and stately homes anchor Litchfield and New Milford. Kent, New Preston, and Woodbury draw avid antiquers, and Washington, Salisbury, and Norfolk provide a glimpse into New England village life as it might have existed two centuries ago.

Favorite roads for admiring fall foliage are U.S. 7, from New Milford through Kent and West Cornwall to Canaan; Route 41 to Route 4 from Salisbury through Lakeville, Sharon, Cornwall Bridge, and Goshen to Torrington; and Route 47 to U.S. 202 to Route 341 from Woodbury through Washington, New Preston, and Warren to Kent.

New Milford

32 *28 mi west of Waterbury, 46 mi northeast of Greenwich.*

If you're approaching the Litchfield Hills from the south, New Milford is a practical starting point to begin a visit. It was also a starting point for a young cobbler named Roger Sherman, who, in 1743, opened his shop where Main and Church streets meet. A Declaration of Independence signatory, Sherman also helped draft the Articles of Confederation and the Constitution. You'll find old shops, galleries, and eateries all within a short stroll of New Milford green—one of the longest in New England.

OFF THE BEATEN PATH

THE SILO – New Yorkers who miss Zabar's and Balducci's feel right at home in this silo and barn packed with *objets de cookery*, crafts, and assorted goodies and sauces. The founder and music director of the New York Pops, Skitch Henderson, and his wife, Ruth, own and operate this bazaar, where culinary superstars teach cooking classes between March and December. ✉ *44 Upland Rd., 4 mi north of the New Milford town green on U.S. 202,* ☎ *860/355–0300,* WEB *www. thesilo.com.* ⊘ *Daily 10–5.*

Dining and Lodging

$$–$$$ ✕ **Adrienne.** Set in an 18th-century farmhouse with terraced gardens, Adrienne serves American cuisine from a seasonal menu. You may be lucky enough to encounter seared scallops, garlic, rosemary, and spinach in a roasted tomato cream sauce over pasta or an Indonesian stew of chicken and potatoes with curry, coconut milk, and steamed broccoli. ⊠ *218 Kent Rd., 06776,* ☎ *860/354–6001. AE, D, DC, MC, V. Closed Mon.*

$–$$ ✕ **Bistro Café.** Copper pots and vintage black-and-white photos adorn the walls of this café in a redbrick corner building. The well-crafted regional American dishes change weekly—tender grilled swordfish with whipped potatoes, veggies, and a chive aioli one week, oven-roasted duck with pecans and cranberry coulis the next. You can sample buffalo, moose, antelope, kangaroo, alligator, or northern black bear—they're all farm-raised and low in cholesterol. Upstairs is a taproom where you can relax with a bottle of wine or feast from the same menu as downstairs. ⊠ *31 Bank St., 06776,* ☎ *860/355–3266. AE, MC, V.*

$$ 🏠 **Homestead Inn.** The Homestead, high on a hill overlooking New Milford's town green, was built in 1853 and opened as an inn in 1928. Life is casual here, and the owners, Rolf and Peggy Hammer, are always game for a leisurely chat. Breakfast is served in a cheery living room, where you can sit by the fire. The eight rooms in the main house have more personality than those in the motel-style structure next door. ⊠ *5 Elm St., 06776,* ☎ *860/354–4080,* FAX *860/354–7046,* WEB *www.homesteadct.com. 14 rooms. AE, D, DC, MC, V. CP.*

New Preston

㉝ *4 mi north of New Milford.*

The crossroads village of New Preston, perched above a 40-ft waterfall on the Aspetuck River, has a little town center that's packed with antiques shops specializing in everything from 18th-century furnishings to out-of-print books.

Lake Waramaug, north of New Preston on Route 45, is an area that reminds many of Austria and Switzerland. The lake is named for Chief Waramaug, one of the most revered figures in Connecticut's Native American history. A drive around the 8-mi perimeter of the lake takes you past beautiful inns—many of which serve delicious food—and homes. **Lake Waramaug State Park** (⊠ 30 Lake Waramaug Rd., ☎ 860/868–0220 or 860/868–2592), at the northwest tip of the lake, is an idyllic 75-acre spread, great for picnicking and lakeside camping.

The popular **Hopkins Vineyard,** overlooking Lake Waramaug, produces more than 13 varieties of wine, from sparkling to dessert. A weathered red barn houses a gift shop and a tasting room, and there's a picnic area. The wine bar serves a fine cheese-and-pâté board. ⊠ 25 Hopkins Rd., ☎ 860/868–7954, WEB www.hopkinsvineyard.com. 🆓 Free. ⊙ Jan.–Feb., Fri.–Sat. 10–5, Sun. 11–5; Mar.–Apr., Wed.–Sat. 10–5, Sun. 11–5; May–Dec., Mon.–Sat. 10–5, Sun. 11–5.

Dining and Lodging

$$$$ ✕🏠 **Boulders Inn.** The most idyllic and prestigious of the inns along
★ Lake Waramaug opened in 1940 but still looks like the private home it was a century ago. Apart from the main house, a carriage house and several guest houses command panoramic views of the countryside and the lake. The rooms, four with double whirlpool baths, contain Victorian antiques and wood-burning fireplaces. The exquisite menu at the window-lined, stone-wall dining room ($$$–$$$$) changes seasonally but might include chicken breast stuffed with goat cheese, leeks, and

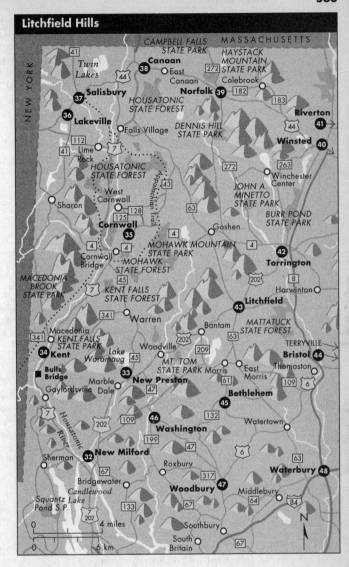

Litchfield Hills

arugula or red-wine braised lamb shank. ⊠ *E. Shore Rd./Rte. 45, 06777,* ☎ *860/868–0541 or 800/552–6853,* F̲A̲X̲ *860/868–1925,* W̲E̲B̲ *www.bouldersinn.com. 17 rooms. Restaurant, lake, beach, boating; no smoking. AE, MC, V. MAP.*

$$$–$$$$ ✕🏠 **Birches Inn.** One of the area's poshest inns, the Birches is some-
★ thing of a Lake Waramaug institution. Antiques and reproductions en-
rich the rooms; three on the waterfront have private decks. Executive
chef Frederic Faveau presides over the lake-view dining room ($$$; closed
Tues.–Wed.; no lunch). Among his signature dishes are grilled mari-
nated leg of lamb with herb risotto cake, sautéed mustard greens, and
a roasted garlic sauce. ⊠ *233 W. Shore Rd., 06777,* ☎ *860/868–
1735,* F̲A̲X̲ *860/868–1815,* W̲E̲B̲ *www.thebirchesinn.com. 8 rooms. Restaurant, beach; no kids under 10, no smoking. AE, MC, V. CP.*

$–$$ ✕🏠 **Hopkins Inn.** A grand 1847 Victorian atop a hill overlooking Lake
★ Waramaug, the Hopkins is one of the best bargains in the Hills.
Most rooms have plain white bedspreads, simple antiques, and pas-

tel floral wallpaper. In winter, the inn smells of burning firewood; year-round, it is redolent with the aromas from the rambling dining rooms ($$$; closed Jan.–late Mar.), which serve outstanding Swiss and Austrian dishes—sweetbreads Viennese are a favorite. When the weather is kind, you can dine on the terrace and view the lake. ⊠ *22 Hopkins Rd. (1 mi off Rte. 45), 06777,* ☎ *860/868–7295,* FAX *860/ 868–7464,* WEB *www.thehopkinsinn.com. 11 rooms. Restaurant, beach. AE, D, MC, V.*

Shopping

Ray Boas, Bookseller (⊠ 6 Church St., ☎ 860/868–9596) stocks thousands of antiquarian and out-of-print books. **J. Seitz & Co.** (⊠ Main St./Rte. 45, ☎ 860/868–0119) fills 5,000 square ft with stylish home furnishings, fashions, and gifts.

Kent

③④ *12 mi northwest of New Preston.*

Kent has the area's greatest concentration of art galleries, some nationally renowned. Home to a prep school of the same name, Kent once held many ironworks. The Schaghticoke Indian Reservation is also here. During the Revolutionary War, one hundred Schaghticokes helped defend the Colonies by transmitting messages of army intelligence from the Litchfield Hills to Long Island Sound, along the hilltops, by way of shouts and drum beats. **Bulls Bridge** (⊠ U.S. 7, south of Kent), one of three covered bridges in Connecticut, is open to cars.

Hardware-store buffs and vintage-tool aficionados will feel at home at the **Sloane-Stanley Museum.** Artist and author Eric Sloane (1905– 85) was fascinated by Early American woodworking tools, and his collection (on display) ranges from the 17th to the 19th century. The museum, a re-creation of Sloane's last studio, also encompasses the ruins of a 19th-century iron furnace. Sloane's books and prints, which celebrate vanishing aspects of American heritage such as barns and covered bridges, are on sale here. ⊠ *U.S. 7,* ☎ *860/927–3849 or 860/566– 3005.* ☜ *$3.50.* ☉ *Mid-May–Oct., Wed.–Sun. 10–4.*

Dining and Lodging

$$ ✕☰ **Fife 'n Drum.** If you like to shop, eat, and have a cozy place to rest your head, you can do all three at this family-owned inn, restaurant, and gift shop. The shop sells everything from cards and candles to jewelry and accessories. The eight inn rooms (most above the shop) are decorated with a pleasing assortment of antiques, reproductions, and flowery decorative accessories. The restaurant serves a mix of Continental and American choices such as six-cheese ravioli and shrimp-and-scallop brochette. ⊠ *53 N. Main St., 06757,* ☎ *860/927–3509,* FAX *860/927–4595,* WEB *www.fifendrum.com. 8 rooms. Restaurant, shop. AE, MC, V. Closed Tues.*

Outdoor Activities and Sports

The **Appalachian Trail**'s longest river walk, off Route 341, is the almost 8-mi hike from Kent to Cornwall Bridge along the Housatonic River. The early-season trout fishing is superb at 2,300-acre **Macedonia Brook State Park** (⊠ Macedonia Brook Rd. off Rte. 341, ☎ 860/ 927–3238), where you can also hike and cross-country ski.

Shopping

The **Bachelier-Cardonsky Gallery** (⊠ 10 Main St., ☎ 860/927–3129), one of the foremost galleries in the Northeast, exhibits works by local artists and contemporary masters such as Alexander Calder, Carol Anthony, and Jackson Pollock. The **Paris–New York–Kent Gallery** (⊠ Kent

Station, off U.S. 7, ☎ 860/927–4152) shows museum-quality contemporary works by local and world-famous artists. **Pauline's Place** (⊠ 79 N. Main St., ☎ 860/927–4475) specializes in Victorian, Georgian, Art Deco, Edwardian, and contemporary jewelry.

En Route   Heading north from Kent toward Cornwall, you'll pass the entrance to 295-acre **Kent Falls State Park** (⊠ U.S. 7, ☎ 860/927–3238), where you can hike a short way to one of the most impressive waterfalls in the state and picnic in the green meadows at the base of the falls.

Cornwall

③⑤   *12 mi northeast of Kent.*

Connecticut's Cornwalls can get confusing. (Try saying *that* five times fast.) There's Cornwall, Cornwall Bridge, West Cornwall, Cornwall Hollow, East Cornwall, and North Cornwall. What this quiet corner of the Litchfield Hills is known for is its fantastic vistas of woods and mountains and its covered bridge, which spans the Housatonic and is easily one of the most photographed spots in the state.

A romantic reminder of the past, the wooden, barn-red, one-lane, covered **Cornwall Bridge** is not in the town of the same name but several miles up U.S. 7 on Route 128 in West Cornwall. The bridge was built in 1841 and incorporates strut techniques that were copied by bridge builders around the country.

With many trails and nature walks, the **Sharon Audubon Center,** a 890-acre bird sanctuary, is one of the best places to hike in Connecticut. On-site are an exhibit center, a gift shop, and a picnic area. ⊠ *325 Cornwall Bridge Rd., Sharon,* ☎ *860/364–0520,* WEB *www.audubon.org/local/sanctuary/sharon.* ⊡ *$3.* ⊙ *Mon.–Sat. 9–5, Sun. 1–5; trails daily dawn–dusk.*

Dining and Lodging

$$$–$$$$ ✕☲ **The Cornwall Inn.** This 19th-century inn on scenic Route 7 combines country charm with contemporary elegance; eight rooms in the adjacent "lodge" are slightly more rustic in tone. The restaurant ($$–$$$$) serves a seasonally changing French menu with American accents. Entrées might include steak au poivre with cracked peppercorns and cognac sauce or fresh seafood entrées. ⊠ *270 Kent Rd./Rte. 7, 06754,* ☎ *860/672–6884 or 800/786–6884,* FAX *866/672–0352,* WEB *www.cornwallinn.com. 14 rooms. Restaurant, in-room data ports, pool, bar; no-smoking rooms. AE, D, MC, V. CP.*

Outdoor Activities and Sports

CANOEING AND KAYAKING

Clarke Outdoors (⊠ U.S. 7, West Cornwall, ☎ 860/672–6365) rents canoes and kayaks and operates 10-mi trips from Falls Village to Housatonic Meadows State Park from April to October.

FISHING

Housatonic Anglers (⊠ U.S. 7, West Cornwall, ☎ 860/672–4457), which operates half- and full-day tours, provides fly-fishing instruction for trout and bass on the Housatonic and its tributaries. **Housatonic River Outfitters** (⊠ Rte. 128, West Cornwall, ☎ 860/672–1010) operates a full-service fly shop, conducting guided trips of the region as well as classes in fly-fishing, fly-tying, and casting; it also stocks a good selection of vintage and antique gear.

STATE PARKS

Housatonic Meadows State Park (⊠ U.S. 7, Cornwall Bridge, ☎ 860/672–6772 or 860/927–3238) is marked by its tall pine trees near the

Housatonic River. Fly-fishers consider this 2-mi stretch of the river among the best places in New England to test their skills against trout and bass. The riverside campsites are excellent. **Mohawk Mountain State Park** (⊠ 1 mi south of Cornwall off Rte. 4, ☎ 860/927–3238) is a great spot for a picnic. The view at the top of 1,683-ft Mohawk Mountain is breathtaking, especially during fall foliage season; the hike up is 2½ mi.

Shopping

Cornwall Bridge Pottery Store (⊠ Rte. 128, West Cornwall, ☎ 860/672–6545) sells its own pottery and some glass by Simon Pearce. **Ian Ingersoll Cabinetmakers** (⊠ 1 Main St., by the Cornwall Bridge, West Cornwall, ☎ 860/672–6334) stocks Shaker-style furniture.

Ski Areas

MOHAWK MOUNTAIN

Mohawk's 23 trails, ranging down 650 vertical ft, include plenty of intermediate terrain, with a few trails for beginners and a few steeper sections toward the top of the mountain. A small section is devoted to snowboarders. Trails are serviced by one triple lift and four doubles; 14 are lit for night skiing. The base lodge has munchies and a retail shop, and the Pine Lodge, halfway up the slope, has an outdoor patio. Mohawk's SKIwee program is for kids ages 5–12. There are facilities for ice-skating. ⊠ 46 Great Hollow Rd., off Rte. 4, 06753, ☎ 860/672–6100.

Lakeville

 12 mi northwest of Cornwall.

You can usually spot an original Colonial home in handsome Lakeville by looking for the grapevine design cut into the frieze above the front door. It's the trademark of the builder of the town's first homes. Take a peak at the lake of Lakeville, **Lake Wononscopomuc,** as you drive along U.S. 44 or Route 41. A closer look is unlikely, however, as most of shoreline lies on private property.

The holdings of the **Holley-Williams House Museum,** which chronicles 18th- and 19th-century life, include a 1768 ironmaster's home with an 1808 Classical Revival wing filled with family furnishings, Colonial portraits, and a Holley Manufacturing Co. pocketknife exhibit. A popular hands-on exhibit, "From Corsets to Freedom," set in the 1870s, demonstrates the debate between women's rights versus "women's sphere" in the home. Tours are conducted. Admission also includes the on-site **Salisbury Cannon Museum,** which surveys the contributions of area residents and the local iron industry to the American Revolution. ⊠ 15 Millerton Rd., ☎ 860/435–2878. ☜ $3. ۞ Call for hrs.

Nightlife and the Arts

From mid-June to mid-September, **Music Mountain** (⊠ Falls Village, ☎ 860/824–7126) presents chamber music concerts on Sunday afternoon and some Saturday evenings and jazz concerts on Saturday nights.

Outdoor Activities and Sports

Auto racing at renowned **Lime Rock Park** (⊠ Rte. 112, ☎ 860/435–5000 or 800/722–3577) takes place on occasional Saturdays and holiday Mondays from late April to mid-October; amphitheater-style lawn seating allows for great views all around. **Rustling Wind Stables** (⊠ 160 Mountain Rd., Falls Village, ☎ 860/824–7634) gives riding lessons and operates pony rides for the kids by appointment.

Salisbury

 6 mi north of Lakeville.

Were it not for the obsolescence of its ironworks, Salisbury might today be the largest city in Connecticut. Instead, it settles for having both the state's highest mountain, Bear Mountain (2,355 ft), and its highest point, the shoulder of Mt. Frissel (2,380 ft)—whose peak is in Massachusetts. There's a spot on Mt. Frissel where, if the urge strikes you (as it does many), you can stretch your limbs across the Connecticut, Massachusetts, and New York borders.

Iron was discovered here in 1732, and for the next century, the slopes of Salisbury's Mt. Riga produced the finest iron in America. Swiss and Russian immigrants, and later Hessian deserters from the British army, worked the great furnaces. The spread of rail transport opened up better sources of ore, the region's lumber supply was depleted, and the introduction of the Bessemer process of steel manufacturing—partially invented by Salisbury native Alexander Holley—reduced the demand for iron products. Most signs of cinder heaps and slag dumps are long gone, replaced by grand summer homes and gardens.

Harney & Sons Fine Teas supplies its high-quality Darjeeling, Earl Grey, Keemun, and other blends to some of the world's best hotels and restaurants. The tasting room has samples of some of the 100 varieties, and a gift shop where you can buy them. If you call ahead you might even be able to schedule a tour, led by founder John Harney himself, of the factory, where the tea is blended and packaged. ⊠ *11 Brook St.,* ☎ *860/435–5050,* WEB *www.harney.com.* ⊠ *Free.* ☉ *Mon.–Sat. 10–5, Sun. 11–4.*

Dining and Lodging

$$$$ ✕☐ **Under Mountain Inn.** The nearest neighbors of this white-clapboard farmhouse are the horses grazing in the field across the road. Antiques, knickknacks, and objets d'art fill every space; chess and checkers are set up by the fireplace. The hospitality has a pronounced British flavor (there's a British video lounge and the Pub—a replica of an English taproom); dinner, too, recalls Britain with dishes such as hearty steak-and-kidney pie. You can work off some of those calories with a hike on the nearby Appalachian Trail. ⊠ *482 Under Mountain Rd./Rte. 41, 06068,* ☎ *860/435–0242,* FAX *860/435–2379. 7 rooms. Restaurant, hiking, pub, meeting rooms; no smoking. MC, V. MAP.*

Shopping

The **Salisbury Antiques Center** (⊠ 46 Library St., off U.S. 44, ☎ 860/435–0424) carries a varied selection of high-end American and English pieces. The **Village Store** (⊠ 19 Main St./U.S. 44, ☎ 860/435–9459) stocks quality sportswear, hiking boots, and maps, as well as bicycles, cross-country skis, and snowshoes for sale or rent.

Canaan

38 *10 mi northeast of Salisbury, 84 mi northeast of Stamford, 42 mi northwest of Hartford.*

Canaan is one of the more developed towns in the Litchfield region. It was the site of some important late-18th-century industry, including a gun-barrel factory and a paper mill, and was also the home of Captain Gershom Hewitt, who is credited with securing the plans of Fort Ticonderoga for Ethan Allen.

Dining

$$$ ✕ **Cannery Café.** The eggshell-color walls of this storefront American bistro are painted with a pattern of gleaming gold stars; elegant brass fixtures reflect the muted lighting. All is crisp and clean, the service chatty but refined. Pistachio-crusted salmon and grilled lamb are popular menu items. Sunday brunch is a favorite with locals. ⊠ *85 Main St./U.S. 44), 06018,* ☎ *860/824–7333. AE, MC, V. No lunch.*

$ ✕ **Collin's Diner.** There's no denying that this 1942 O'Mahony diner,
★ inspired by the jazzy railroad dining cars of the '20s and '30s, is a classic beauty. Locals count on Collin's for classic diner fare, but the specials are the biggest draw—on Friday usually baked stuffed shrimp is served, on Saturday its a meaty 2-inch cut of prime rib. The diner closes at 3 PM (at 1 PM on Wednesday); call for extended summer hours. ⊠ *U.S. 44, 06018,* ☎ *860/824–7040. No credit cards. No dinner.*

Shopping

The **Connecticut Woodcarvers Gallery** (⊠ U.S. 44, East Canaan, ☎ 860/824–0883) sells the work of wood-carver Joseph Cieslowski, whose unique relief carvings embellish clocks, mirrors, and decorative panels.

Norfolk

㊳ *7 mi southeast of Canaan, 59 mi north of New Haven.*

Norfolk, thanks to its severe climate and terrain, is one of the best-preserved villages in the Northeast. Notable industrialists have been summering here for two centuries, and many enormous homesteads still exist. The striking town green is at the junction of Route 272 and U.S. 44. At its southern corner is a fountain (designed by Augustus Saint-Gaudens and executed by Stanford White), a memorial to Joseph Battell, who turned Norfolk into a major trading center.

Dr. Frederick Shepard Dennis lavishly entertained guests, among them President Howard Taft and several Connecticut governors, in the stone pavilion at the summit of what is now **Dennis Hill State Park.** From its 1,627-ft height, you can see Haystack Mountain, New Hampshire, and, on a clear day, New Haven harbor, all the way across the state. Picnic on the park's 240-acre grounds or hike one of its many trails. ⊠ *Rte. 272,* ☎ *860/482–1817.* ☑ *Free.* ☉ *Daily 8 AM–dusk.*

Dining and Lodging

$$–$$$ ✕ **The Pub.** Bottles of trendy beers line the shelves of this down-to-earth
★ restaurant on the ground floor of a redbrick Victorian near the town green. Burgers and other pub fare are on the menu alongside strip steak and lamb burgers. This place is a real melting pot. ⊠ *U.S. 44, 06058,* ☎ *860/542–5716. AE, MC, V. Closed Mon.*

$$–$$$$ ☵ **Manor House.** Among this 1898 Bavarian Tudor's remarkable
★ appointments are its bibelots, mirrors, carpets, antique beds, and prints—not to mention the 20 stained-glass windows designed by Louis Comfort Tiffany. The vast Spofford Room has windows on three sides, a king-size canopy bed with a cheery fireplace opposite, and a balcony. The Morgan Room has the most remarkable feature—a private wood-panel elevator (added in 1939). It also has a private deck. ⊠ *69 Maple Ave. (Box 447, 06058),* ☎ FAX *860/542–5690,* WEB *www.manorhouse-norfolk.com. 8 rooms. Meeting room. AE, MC, V. BP.*

Nightlife and the Arts

The **Norfolk Chamber Music Festival** (☎ 860/542–3000), at the Music Shed on the Ellen Battell Stoeckel Estate at the northwest corner of the Norfolk green, presents world-renowned artists and ensembles on Friday and Saturday summer evenings. Students from the

Yale School of Music perform on Thursday evening and Saturday morning. Early arrivals can stroll or picnic on the 70-acre grounds or visit the art gallery. The newly renovated **Greenwoods Theatre at Norfolk** (⊠ U.S. 44, ☎ 860/542–0026) has its own professional resident company that performs June–September; a vintage film series runs the rest of the year.

Outdoor Activities and Sports

One of the most spectacular views in the state can be seen from **Haystack Mountain State Park** (⊠ Rte. 272, ☎ 860/482–1817), via its challenging trail to the top or a road halfway up. **Loon Meadow Farm** (⊠ 41 Loon Meadow Dr., ☎ 860/542–6085) runs horse-drawn carriage, hay, and sleigh rides.

Shopping

Norfolk Artisans Guild (⊠ 24 Greenwoods Rd. E, ☎ 860/542–5487) carries works by more than 60 local artisans—from hand-painted pillows to handcrafted baskets.

Winsted

40 *9 mi southeast of Norfolk, 28 mi north of Waterbury, 25 mi northwest of Hartford.*

With its rows of old homes and businesses seemingly untouched since the 1940s, Winsted still looks a bit like the set of a Frank Capra movie. Though it's far less fashionable than nearby Norfolk, the town, which was devastated by a major flood in 1955, is still worth a brief stop. You can drive around the hills and alongside the reservoirs.

Nightlife and the Arts

The **Gilson Café and Cinema** (⊠ 354 Main St., ☎ 860/379–6069), a refurbished Art Deco movie house, serves food and drinks unobtrusively during movies, every evening except Monday. You must be 21 or older for shows on the weekend.

Outdoor Activities and Sports

Main Stream Canoe and Kayaks (⊠ U.S. 44, New Hartford, ☎ 860/693–6791) rents and sells canoes and kayaks, conducts day trips on the Farmington River, and offers lessons. Moonlight trips take place on summer evenings. **North American Canoe Tours** (⊠ Satan's Kingdom State Recreation Area, U.S. 44, New Hartford, ☎ 860/739–0791) rents tubes and flotation devices for exhilarating self-guided tours along the Farmington River. The company is open for business on weekends from Memorial Day to June and daily from June to Labor Day.

Ski Area

SKI SUNDOWN

This area has the state's most challenging trails plus some neat touches—a sundeck on the top of the mountain and a Senior Spree social club for skiers 55 and older—as well as excellent facilities and equipment. The vertical drop is 625 ft. Of the 14 trails, 8 are for beginners, 3 for intermediates, and 3 for advanced skiers. All are lighted at night and serviced by three triple chairs and one double. Ski lessons are available for ages 4 and up. ⊠ *126 Ratlum Rd., New Hartford 06057, ☎ 860/379–7669 snow conditions.*

Riverton

41 *6 mi north of Winsted.*

Almost every New Englander has sat in a Hitchcock chair. Riverton, formerly Hitchcockville, is where Lambert Hitchcock built the first one, in 1826. The Farmington and Still rivers meet in this tiny hamlet. It's in one of the more unspoiled regions in the Hills, great for hiking and driving.

The **Hitchcock Museum,** showcasing beautiful examples of 18th- and 19th-century furniture, is in the gray granite Union Church. The nearby Hitchcock Factory Store, which sells first-quality merchandise at outlet prices and also has a seconds department, is open year-round and arranges tours. ⊠ *Rte. 20,* ☎ *860/379–4826.* ☞ *Free.* ☉ *By appointment only.*

Dining and Lodging

$$–$$$$ ✕🏠 **Old Riverton Inn.** This historic inn, built in 1796 and overlooking the west branch of the Farmington River and the Hitchcock Chair Factory, is a peaceful weekend retreat. Rooms are small—except for the fireplace suite—and the decorating, which includes Hitchcock furnishings, is for the most part ordinary, but the inn always delivers warm hospitality. The inviting dining room serves traditional New England fare ($$); the stuffed pork chops are local favorites. ⊠ *Rte. 20, 06065,* ☎ *860/379–8678 or 800/378–1796,* ℻ *860/379–1006. 11 rooms, 1 suite. Restaurant, bar. AE, D, DC, MC, V. BP.*

Outdoor Activities and Sports

American Legion and People's State Forests (⊠ off Rte. 181, ☎ 860/379–2469) border the west bank and the east bank, respectively, of the West Branch of the Farmington River—a designated National Wild and Scenic River. You can picnic beneath 200-year-old pines along the riverbank, and the hiking, fishing, tubing, and canoeing are superb.

Torrington

④ *14 mi southwest of Riverton.*

This old industrial town has a few hidden charms for those willing to overlook its rougher sections. Torrington's pines were for years used for shipbuilding, and its factories produced brass kettles, needles, pins, and bicycle spokes. Torrington was the birthplace of abolitionist John Brown and also of Gail Borden, who developed the first successful method for the production of evaporated milk.

The **Hotchkiss-Fyler House,** a 16-room century-old Queen Anne structure with a slate and brick exterior, is one of the better house museums in Connecticut. The design high points include hand-stenciled walls and intricate mahogany woodwork and ornamental plaster. European porcelains, American and British glass, and paintings by Winfield S. Clime are on display. If you plan to arrive around noon on a weekday, call ahead; the house sometimes closes briefly at lunchtime. ⊠ *192 Main St.,* ☎ *860/482–8260.* ☞ *$2.* ☉ *Tours Apr.–Oct. and last 2 wks in Dec., Tues.–Fri. 10–4, weekends noon–4.*

Nightlife and the Arts

The **Warner Theatre** (⊠ 68 Main St., ☎ 860/489–7180), an Art Deco former movie palace, presents live Broadway musicals, ballet, and concerts by touring pop, classical, and country musicians.

Outdoor Activities and Sports

The lures at 436-acre **Burr Pond State Park** (⊠ Rte. 8, ☎ 860/482–1817) are a crystal-clear pond, hiking paths, and wheelchair-accessible picnic grounds.

Litchfield

43 *5 mi southwest of Torrington, 48 mi north of Bridgeport, 34 mi west of Hartford.*

Everything in Litchfield, the wealthiest and most noteworthy town in the Litchfield Hills, seems to exist on a larger scale than in neighboring burgs, especially the impressive Litchfield Green and the white Colonial and Greek Revival homes that line the broad elm-shaded streets. Harriet Beecher Stowe, author of *Uncle Tom's Cabin,* and her brother, abolitionist preacher Henry Ward Beecher, were born and raised in Litchfield, and many famous Americans earned their law degrees at the Litchfield Law School. Today lovely but exceptionally expensive boutiques and hot-spot restaurants line the downtown, attracting celebrities and the town's monied citizens.

In 1773, Judge Tapping Reeve enrolled his first student, Aaron Burr, in what was to become the first law school in the country. (Before Judge Reeve, students studied the law as apprentices, not in formal classes.)

★ The **Tapping Reeve House and Law School** is dedicated to Reeve's remarkable achievement and to the notable students who passed through its halls: Oliver Wolcott Jr., John C. Calhoun, Horace Mann, three U.S. Supreme Court justices, and 15 governors, not to mention senators, congressmen, and ambassadors. This museum is one of the state's most worthy attractions, with interactive multimedia exhibits, an excellent introductory film, and beautifully restored facilities. ⊠ *82 South St.,* ☎ *860/567–4501,* WEB *www.litchfieldhistoricalsociety.org.* ⊡ *$5 (includes Litchfield History Museum).* ☉ *Mid-Apr.–late Nov., Tues.–Sat. 11–5, Sun. 1–5.*

The well-organized galleries at the **Litchfield History Museum** display decorative arts, paintings, and antique furnishings. The extensive reference library has information about the town's historic buildings, including the Sheldon Tavern (where George Washington slept on several occasions) and the Litchfield Female Academy, where in the late 1700s Sarah Pierce taught girls not just sewing and deportment but also mathematics and history. ⊠ *7 South St., at Rtes. 63 and 118,* ☎ *860/ 567–4501,* WEB *www.litchfieldhistoricalsociety.org.* ⊡ *$5 (includes Tapping Reeve House and Law School).* ☉ *Mid-Apr.–late Nov., Tues.– Sat. 11–5, Sun. 1–5.*

A stroll through the landscaped grounds of **White Flower Farm** is nearly always a pleasure, and gardeners will find many ideas here. The farm is the home base of a mail-order operation that sells perennials and bulbs to gardeners throughout the United States. ⊠ *Rte. 63 (3 mi south of Litchfield),* ☎ *860/567–8789,* WEB *www.whiteflowerfarm.com.* ⊡ *Free.* ☉ *Oct.–Mar., daily 10–5; Apr.–Sept., daily 9–6.*

Haight Vineyard and Winery flourishes despite the area's severe climate. You can stop in for vineyard walks, winery tours, and tastings. ⊠ *29 Chestnut Hill Rd./Rte. 118 (1 mi east of Litchfield),* ☎ *860/567– 4045,* WEB *www.ctwine.com/haight.html.* ⊡ *Free.* ☉ *Mon.–Sat. 10:30– 5, Sun. noon–5.*

The 4,000-acre **White Memorial Foundation and Conservation Center Museum,** Connecticut's largest nature center and wildlife sanctuary, contains fishing areas, bird-watching platforms, two self-guided nature trails, several boardwalks, and 35 mi of hiking, cross-country skiing, and horseback-riding trails. The main conservation center houses natural-history exhibits and a gift shop. ⊠ *U.S. 202 (2 mi west of village green),* ☎ *860/567–0857,* WEB *www.whitememorialcc.org.* ⊡ *Grounds free,* *conservation center $4.* ⊙ *Grounds daily; conservation center Mon.–Sat. 9–5, Sun. noon–4.*

The chief attractions at **Topsmead State Forest** are a Tudor-style cottage built by architect Henry Dana Jr. and a 40-acre wildflower preserve. The forest holds picnic grounds, hiking trails, and cross-country ski areas. ⊠ *Buell Rd. off E. Litchfield Rd.,* ☎ 860/567–5694. ⌷ *Free.* ⊙ *Forest daily 8 AM–dusk; house tours June–Oct., 2nd and 4th weekends of month.*

Dining and Lodging

$$$–$$$$ ✕ **West Street Grill.** This sophisticated dining room on the town green
★ is *the* place to see and be seen, both for patrons and for the state's up-and-coming chefs, many of whom have gotten their start here. Imaginative grilled fish, steak, poultry, and lamb dishes are served with fresh vegetables and pasta or risotto. The ice cream and sorbets, made by the restaurant, are worth every calorie. ⊠ *43 West St., 06759,* ☎ *860/567–3885. AE, MC, V.*

$–$$ ✕ **Village Restaurant.** The folks who run this storefront eatery in a redbrick town house serve food as tasty as any in town—inexpensive pub grub in one room, updated New England cuisine in the other. Whether you order burgers or homemade ravioli, you'll get plenty to eat. ⊠ *25 West St., 06759,* ☎ *860/567–8307. AE, MC, V.*

$$ ⊡ **The Litchfield Inn.** This reproduction Colonial-style inn lies little more than a mile west of the center of Litchfield. Period accents adorn its modern rooms, including themed "designer" rooms such as an "Irish" room (which has a four-poster bed draped in green floral chintz) and a "Western" room (which employs a rustic picket fence as a headboard). ⊠ *Rte. 202, 06759,* ☎ *860/567–4503 or 800/499–3444,* ᖴᴀX *860/567–5358,* ᴡᴇʙ *www.litchfieldinnct.com. 32 rooms. Restaurant, in-room data ports, bar. AE, MC, V. CP.*

Outdoor Activities and Sports

Lee's Riding Stables (⊠ 57 E. Litchfield Rd., ☎ 860/567–0785) conducts trail and pony rides. At **Mt. Tom State Park** (⊠ U.S. 202, ☎ 860/567–8870), you can boat, hike, swim, and fish in summer. The view from atop the mountain is outstanding.

Shopping

Black Swan Antiques (⊠ 17 Litchfield Commons/U.S. 202, ☎ 860/567–4429) carries 17th- and 19th-century English and Continental furniture and accessories. **Carretta Glass Studio** (⊠ 513 Maple St., ☎ 860/567–4851), open by appointment, makes and sells remarkable glass sculptures and works. The **P. S. Gallery** (⊠ 41 West St., ☎ 860/567–1059) showcases paintings, prints, and sculptures by area artists. **Susan Wakeen Dolls** (⊠ 425 Bantam Rd., ☎ 860/567–0007) creates stunning limited-edition and play dolls.

Bristol

④④ *17 mi southeast of Litchfield.*

There were some 275 clock makers in and around Bristol during the late 1800s—it is said that by the end of the 19th century just about every household in America told time to a Connecticut clock. Eli Terry (for whom nearby Terryville is named) first mass-produced clocks in the mid-19th century. Seth Thomas (for whom nearby Thomaston is named) learned under Terry and carried on the tradition.

★ ℭ **Lake Compounce,** which opened in 1846, is the oldest amusement park in the country. The rides and attractions at the 325-acre facility include an antique carousel, a classic wooden roller coaster, and a white-water raft ride. The park also has picnic areas, a beach, and a water playground with slides, spray fountains, and a wave pool. The Sky Coaster and Zoomerang are hair-raising rides. ⊠ *Rte. 229 N, I–84, Exit 31,* ☎ *860/583–3631,* ⩓ *www.lakecompounce.com.* ⛢ *$28.95.* ☉ *Memorial Day–late Sept.; call for hrs.*

★ The **Carousel Museum of New England** displays carousel art, much of it full-size pieces, in the Coney Island, Country Fair, and Philadelphia styles. Miniature carousels are also on display, and volunteers occasionally demonstrate the craft at the antique carving shop. ⊠ *95 Riverside Ave.,* ☎ *860/585–5411,* ⩓ *www.thecarouselmuseum.com.* ⛢ *$4.* ☉ *Apr.–Nov., Mon.–Sat. 10–5, Sun. noon–5; Dec.–Mar., Thurs.–Sat. 10–5, Sun. noon–5.*

You can set your watch by the **American Clock & Watch Museum**— one of the few in the country devoted entirely to clocks and watches. More than 3,000 timepieces are on display in an 1801 house. ⊠ *100 Maple St.,* ☎ *860/583–6070,* ⩓ *www.clockmuseum.org.* ⛢ *$5.* ☉ *Apr.–Nov., daily 10–5 or by appointment.*

Lodging

$$–$$$ 🏨 **Chimney Crest Manor.** All the rooms in this impressive circa-1930 Tudor mansion have spectacular views of the Farmington Valley. The 40-ft-long Garden Suite, in what was the mansion's ballroom, has gleaming hardwood floors, a fireplace, a queen-size canopy bed, its own kitchen, and tile walls with a dazzling sunflower motif. Breakfast, which might include yogurt pancakes, is served on fine china in the formal dining room or, more casually, on the grand fieldstone patio. Among the handsome public spaces are a sunroom and salon. ⊠ *5 Founders Dr., 06010,* ☎ *860/582–4219,* ⩓⩓ *860/584–5903. 5 rooms, 1 suite. Library; no smoking. AE, MC, V. BP.*

Bethlehem

④⑤ *16 mi west of Bristol.*

Come Christmas, Bethlehem is the most popular town in Connecticut. Cynics say that towns such as Canaan, Goshen, and Bethlehem were named primarily with the hope of attracting prospective residents and not truly out of religious deference. In any case, the local post office has its hands full postmarking the 220,000 pieces of holiday greetings mailed from Bethlehem every December.

The **Bethlehem Christmas Town Festival** (☎ 203/266–5557), which takes place in early December, draws quite a crowd. Year-round, the **Christmas Shop** (⊠ 18 East St., ☎ 203/266–7048) showcases the trimmings and trappings that help set the holiday mood.

The Benedictine nuns at the **Abbey of Regina Laudis,** who were made famous by their best-selling CD *Women in Chant,* make and sell fine handicrafts, honey, cheese, herbs, beauty products, and more. An 18th-century Neapolitan crèche with 80 hand-painted Baroque porcelain figures is on view from Easter to December. ⊠ *Flanders Rd.,* ☎ *203/266–7637,* ⩓ *www.abbeyofreginalaudis.com.* ☉ *Mon.–Tues. and Thurs.–Sun. 10–noon and 1:30–4.*

Washington

④⑥ *11 mi west of Bethlehem.*

The beautiful buildings of the Gunnery prep school mingle with stately Colonials and churches in Washington, one of the best-preserved Colonial towns in Connecticut. The Mayflower Inn, south of the Gunnery on Route 47, attracts an exclusive clientele. Washington, which was settled in 1734, became in 1779 the first town in the United States to be named for the first president.

Dining and Lodging

$$$$ ✕🏨 **Mayflower Inn.** Though the most-expensive suites at this inn cost
★   an unbelievable $1,300 a night, the Mayflower is always booked months in advance—and with good reason. Running streams, rambling stone walls, and rare specimen trees fill the inn's 28 manicured acres. Fine antiques, 18th- and 19th-century art, and four-poster canopy beds define each of the rooms. The colossal baths have mahogany wainscoting, marble, and handsome Belgian tapestries on the floors. At the posh restaurant ($$$–$$$$), the contemporary menu may list entrées such as potato-crusted Atlantic salmon or Asian barbecue pork chops. ✉ *118 Woodbury Rd. (Rte. 47), 06793,* ☎ *860/868–9466,* 𝔽𝔸𝕏 *860/ 868–1497,* 𝕎𝔼𝔹 *www.mayflowerinn.com. 17 rooms, 8 suites. Restaurant, in-room data ports, pool, tennis court, health club, spa, bar, meeting room. AE, MC, V.*

En Route   The **Institute for American Indian Studies,** between Roxbury and Washington, is a small but excellent and thoughtfully arranged collection of exhibits and displays that details the history of Northeastern Woodland Native Americans. Highlights include a replicated longhouse and nature trails. The institute is at the end of a forested residential road (just follow the signs from Route 199). ✉ *Curtis Rd. off Rte. 199,* ☎ *860/868–0518,* 𝕎𝔼𝔹 *www.instituteforaistudies.org.* 🎟 *$4.* ☉ *Jan.– Mar., Wed.–Sat. 10–5, Sun. noon–5; Apr.–Dec., Mon.–Sat. 10–5, Sun. noon–5.*

Woodbury

㊼   *10 mi southeast of Washington.*

There may very well be more antiques shops in the quickly growing town of Woodbury than in all the towns in the rest of the Litchfield Hills combined. Five magnificent churches and the Greek Revival King Solomon's Temple, formerly a Masonic lodge, line U.S. 6; they represent some of the finest-preserved examples of Colonial religious architecture in New England.

The **Glebe House** is the large gambrel-roof Colonial in which Dr. Samuel Seabury was elected America's first Episcopal bishop, in 1783. It holds an excellent collection of antiques. Renowned British horticulturist Gertrude Jekyll designed the historic garden. ✉ *Hollow Rd.,* ☎ *203/263–2855.* 🎟 *$5.* ☉ *Apr.–May and Sept.–Oct., Wed.–Sun. 1– 4; June–Aug. Wed.–Fri. and Sun. 1–4, Sat. 10–4; Nov., weekends 1– 4; Dec.–Mar. by appointment.*

Dining and Lodging

$$–$$$$ ✕ **Good News Café.** Carole Peck is a well-known name in these parts,
★   and her decision to open a restaurant in Woodbury was met with cheers. The emphasis is on healthful, innovative fare: braised veal shanks on pearl couscous with fiddlehead ferns and roasted tomatoes, wok-seared shrimp with new potatoes, grilled green beans, and a garlic aioli are good choices. You can drop by for cappuccino and munchies in a separate room decorated with fascinating vintage radios. ✉ *694 Main St. S, 06798,* ☎ *203/266–4663. AE, MC, V. Closed Tues.*

$$–$$$ 🏨 **The Heritage.** This sprawling resort has a modern Colonial look and extensive facilities. Guest rooms have dark traditional furniture and modern amenities; some have river or golf-course views. Drop by Schadrack's pub for light fare or a drink after a day on the greens. ✉ *522 Heritage Rd., Southbury 06488,* ☎ *203/264–8200 or 800/932–*

3466, FAX 203/264–5035, WEB www.d
suites. Restaurant, in-room data
courts, pool, health club, spa, r

$–$$ 🏨 **Curtis House.** Connecticut'
bury's antiques row, may also
$70. The inn has seen dozens of a
years, but the floorboards still creak
in some rooms look to be from the Ed S
downstairs, where the restaurant serves fill
potato genre. ⊠ 506 Main St. S/Rte. 6, 06798,
www.thecurtishouse.com. 18 rooms, 12 with ba
MC, V.

Shopping
Country Loft Antiques (⊠ 557 Main St. S, ☎ 203/266–45
18th- and 19th-century French antiques. **David Dunton** (⊠ Rte.
off Rte. 47, ☎ 203/263–5355) is a respected dealer of formal Ame
can Federal-style furniture. **Mill House Antiques** (⊠ 1068 Main St. N,
☎ 203/263–3446) carries formal and country English and French furniture and has the state's largest collection of Welsh dressers. The
Woodbury Pewterers (⊠ 860 Main St. S, ☎ 203/263–2668) factory
store has discounts on fine reproductions of Early American tankards,
Revere bowls, candlesticks, and more.

Outdoor Activities and Sports
G. E. M. Morgans (⊠ 75 N. Poverty Rd., Southbury, ☎ 203/264–
6196) conducts hay and carriage rides using registered Morgan horses.

Ski Areas
WOODBURY SKI AREA
This small, laid-back ski area with a 300-ft vertical drop has 18 downhill trails of varying difficulty that are serviced by a double chairlift,
three rope tows, a handle tow, and a T-bar. About half of the 15 km
(9 mi) of cross-country trails are groomed, and 2 km (1 mi) are lighted
and covered by snowmaking when necessary. There's a snowboard and
alpine park, a skateboard and in-line skating park, and a special area
for sledding and tubing serviced by two lifts and three tows. Snow-
biking and snowshoeing are other options. Ski parties are held on Friday and Saturday nights in the base lodge; lessons are given for adults
and for children ages 2 and up. ⊠ Rte. 47, 06798, ☎ 203/263–2203.

Waterbury

48 15 mi east of Woodbury, 28 mi southwest of Hartford, 28 mi north
of Bridgeport.

Waterbury, in the Naugatuck River valley, was once known as Brass
City for its role as the country's top producer of brass products in the
19th and early 20th centuries. Evidence of the prosperity of the city's
brass barons can still be seen in the hillside district northwest of downtown, where grand old Queen Anne, Greek and Georgian Revival, and
English Tudor homes remain, a few of which have been turned into
bed-and-breakfasts. Today Waterbury and its shops and restaurants
serves as the urban center for people in the nearby Litchfield Hills. The
dramatic 240-ft **Clock Tower** (⊠ 389 Meadow St.) in the historic
downtown was modeled after the city-hall tower in Siena, Italy.

Pick up a brochure at the **Waterbury Region Convention and
Visitors Bureau** (⊠ 21 Church St., ☎ 203/597–9527, WEB www.
waterburyregion.org) and follow its fascinating self-guided walking
tour of the downtown area.

he **Mattatuck Museum** has a fine collection of 19th- and 20th-cen-
ury Connecticut art and memorabilia documenting the state's industrial history, as well as a charming museum café. ⊠ *144 W. Main St.,*
☎ *203/753–0381,* WEB *www.mattatuckmuseum.org.* ⌦ *$4.* ☉ *Sept.–
June, Tues.–Sat. 10–5, Sun. noon–5; July–Aug., Tues.–Sat. 10–5.*

The **Timexpo Museum** curiously combines the history of Timex and
its predecessors with archaeological exhibits tracing the travels of Norwegian explorer Thor Heyerdahl. Additional components include a time-
piece collection, interactive exhibits, and crafts activities. A museum
store sells Timex watches, clocks, and related merchandise. ⊠ *175 Union
St., Brass Mill Commons,* ☎ *203/755–8463 or 800/225–7742,* WEB
www.timexpo.com. ⌦ *$6.* ☉ *Tues.–Sat. 10–5, Sun. noon–5.*

Dining and Lodging

$$$–$$$$ ✕ **Carmen Anthony Steak House.** A worthy re-creation of the steak
★ houses of old, Carmen Anthony has rich wood paneling, handsome
oil paintings on the walls, and white linen on the tables. You can order
Delmonico, filet mignon, porterhouse, and other steaks; the popular
"Italian" steaks are served on a bed of rotini pasta. ⊠ *496 Chase Ave.,
06704,* ☎ *203/757–3040. AE, D, DC, MC, V. No lunch weekends.*

$$–$$$$ ✕ **Diorio Restaurant and Bar.** The dining room at Diorio, a Waterbury
★ tradition for more than a half century, retains its original mahogany
bankers' booth, marble brass bar, high tin ceilings, exposed brick, and
white-tile floors. The dishes here are expertly prepared, from the juicy
shrimp scampi to the dozens of pasta, chicken, veal, steak, and seafood
plates. ⊠ *231 Bank St.,* ☎ *203/754–5111. AE, D, DC, MC, V. Closed
Sun. No lunch Sat.*

$$$ ⌂ **House on the Hill.** Owner-innkeeper Marianne Vandenburgh's fan-
ciful B&B is surrounded by lush gardens in a historic hillside neigh-
borhood. The three-story 1888 Victorian, former home of a brass
baron, has a glorious exterior color scheme of teal, sage green, red,
and ivory. The rich original woodwork and details remain, and guest
rooms are furnished in a welcoming blend of antiques and nostalgia.
⊠ *92 Woodlawn Terr., 06710,* ☎ *203/757–9901. 5 suites. Library. AE,
D, DC, MC, V. Closed mid-Dec.–mid-Jan. BP.*

Nightlife and the Arts

Seven Angels Theatre (⊠ Hamilton Park Pavilion, Plank Rd., ☎ 203/
757–4676) presents first-rate plays, musicals, children's theater, cabaret
concerts, and youth programs.

Shopping

Howland-Hughes (⊠ 120 Bank St., ☎ 203/753–4121) is stocked en-
tirely with items made in Connecticut, from Wiffle balls to Pez can-
dies, fine pottery to glassware.

Litchfield Hills A to Z

*To research prices, get advice from other travelers, and book travel ar-
rangements, visit www.fodors.com.*

AIR TRAVEL TO AND FROM LITCHFIELD HILLS
The airport nearest to the Litchfield Hills region is Hartford's Bradley
International Airport.

BUS TRAVEL
Bonanza Bus Lines operates daily buses between New York City's
Port Authority terminal and Southbury, in the southern part of the re-
gion. There is no local bus service in the Litchfield Hills.
➤ BUS INFORMATION: **Bonanza Bus Lines** (☎ 800/556–3815, WEB www.
bonanzabus.com).

CAR TRAVEL

U.S. 44 west and U.S. 6 south are the most direct routes from Hartford to the Litchfield Hills. To get here from New York, take I–684 to I–84, from which the roads off Exit 7 to Exit 18 head north into the hills.

U.S. 7 winds from New Milford through Kent, Cornwall Bridge, Cornwall, and West Cornwall to Canaan. Sharon is west of U.S. 7 on Route 4; continue north from Sharon on Route 41 to get to Lakeville and Salisbury. U.S. 44 heading east from Salisbury passes through Canaan, Norfolk, and Winsted. Route 63 travels southeast from South Canaan through Litchfield to Waterbury; at Watertown head west from Route 63 on U.S. 6 and north on Route 61 to get to Bethlehem. Southbury is at the junction of U.S. 6 and I–84. Route 8, the main north–south road through the eastern part of the Litchfield Hills, passes through Winsted, Torrington, and Waterbury; Bristol is east of Route 8 off U.S. 6, and Riverton is east of Route 8 on Route 20.

EMERGENCIES

➤ HOSPITALS: **New Milford Hospital** (✉ 21 Elm St., ☎ 860/355–2611, WEB www.newmilfordhospital.org). **Sharon Hospital** (✉ 50 Hospital Hill Rd., ☎ 860/364–4141, WEB www.sharonhospital.org).
➤ 24-HOUR PHARMACY: **CVS** (✉ 839 Farmington Ave., Bristol, ☎ 860/582–8167).

VISITOR INFORMATION

➤ TOURIST INFORMATION: **Litchfield Hills Visitors Council** (✉ Box 968, Litchfield 06759, ☎ 860/567–4506, WEB www.litchfieldhills.com).

NEW HAVEN AND THE SOUTHEASTERN COAST

As you drive northeast along I–95, culturally rich New Haven is the final urban obstacle between southwestern Connecticut's overdeveloped coast and southeastern Connecticut's quieter shoreline villages. The remainder of the jagged coast, which stretches all the way to the Rhode Island border, consists of small coastal villages, quiet hamlets, and undisturbed beaches. The only interruptions along this mostly undeveloped seashore are the industry and piers of New London and Groton. Mystic, Stonington, Old Saybrook, Clinton, and Guilford are havens for fans of antiques and boutiques. North of Groton, near the town of Ledyard, the Mashantucket Pequot Reservation owns and operates Foxwoods Casino and the Mashantucket Pequot Museum & Research Center. The Mohegan Indians run the Mohegan Sun casino in Uncasville.

Milford

49 *6 mi northeast of Stratford.*

Milford, established in 1639, is Connecticut's sixth-oldest municipality, and it retains the feel of a small-town coastal community despite its more than 48,000 residents and the commercial stretch of the Boston Post Road that runs through its center. The large town green is at the heart of this community, and it sparkles in winter with thousands of tiny white lights strung in its trees. The duck pond and waterfall behind city hall is a pleasant place to while away a spring afternoon, and Milford's many beaches, open to the public for the price of parking, are inviting in summer.

The **Connecticut Audubon Coastal Center,** an 840-acre reserve, where the Housatonic River meets the Long Island Sound, has an observa-

Southeastern Connecticut

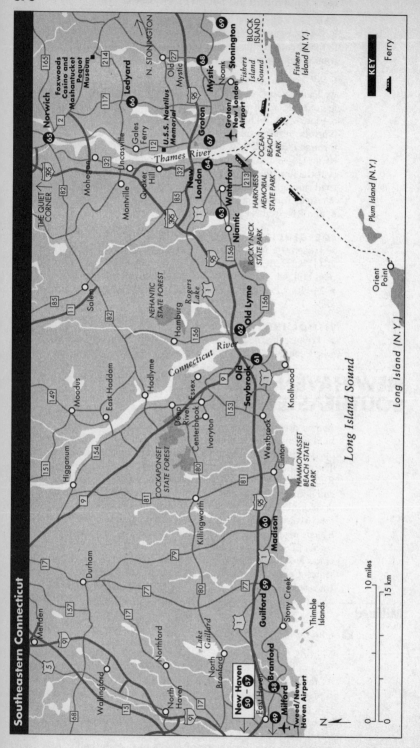

tion tower with a view of all the reserve has to offer: a boardwalk to a sandy beach for exploring (swimming is not allowed), observation platforms at the water's edge, a nature center, and an amazing assortment of birds year-round. Popular guided canoe trips through the salt marsh are scheduled from May to December. ⊠ *1 Milford Point Rd.,* ☎ *203/878–7440,* WEB *www.ctaudubon.org/centers/coastal.htm.* ☒ *Center $2, grounds free.* ☉ *Center Tues.–Sat. 10–4, Sun. noon–4; grounds daily dawn–dusk.*

Dining

\$\$ ✕ **Jeffrey's.** This popular restaurant serves up-to-the-minute new American cuisine in a refined yet welcoming setting that includes an antique Dutch armoire and a grand piano. Some of the changing specials have been wasabi-encrusted ahi tuna over basmati rice and pan-seared filet mignon with a horseradish potato tart. ⊠ *501 New Haven Ave., 06460,* ☎ *203/878–1910. AE, D, DC, MC, V. No lunch weekends.*

\$ ✕ **Paul's Famous Hamburgers.** "Not serving numbers, but generations" is the motto of this drive-in established in 1946. It's the place to go for extraordinarily friendly service and juicy burgers, hot dogs on toasted buns, fries, Reubens, and milk shakes thick enough to stand a spoon in. ⊠ *829 Boston Post Rd.,* ☎ *203/874–7586. No credit cards. Closed Sun.*

Outdoor Activities and Sports

BEACHES

Silver Sands State Park, with its signature beach and old-fashioned wooden boardwalk, is an inviting spot to while away an afternoon—whatever the season. You can walk out to Charles Island (where Captain Kidd is rumored to have buried his treasure) at low tide. ⊠ *600 E. Broadway,* ☎ *203/783–3280.* ☒ *Free.* ☉ *Daily 8 AM–dusk.*

BOATING

Milford Landing (⊠ 37 Helwig St., ☎ 203/874–1610), open April–November, is an attractive complex for temporary docking at the head of Milford Harbor. The 50 slips are for vessels up to 50 ft. Overnight slips are available; there are rest rooms, showers, a coin laundry, and tennis and basketball courts. Several restaurants are within walking distance.

New Haven

9 mi east of Milford, 46 mi northeast of Greenwich.

New Haven's history goes back to the 17th century, when its squares, including a lovely central green for the public, were laid out. The city, a cultural center, is home to Yale University. The historic district surrounding Yale and the shops, museums, theaters, and restaurants on nearby Chapel Street are handsome and prosperous. Be careful, however, about exploring areas away from the campus and city common at night.

50 Bordered on one side by the Yale campus, the **New Haven Green** (⊠ between Church and College Sts.) is a fine example of early urban planning. As early as 1638, village elders set aside the 16-acre plot as a town common. Three early 19th-century churches—the Gothic-style **Trinity Episcopal Church,** the Georgian-style **Center Congregational Church,** and the predominantly Federal-style **United Church**—contribute to its present appeal. Sculptor Ed Hamilton's three-sided, 14-ft-high *Amistad* memorial in front of City Hall (⊠ 165 Church St.) shows key incidents in the life of Joseph Cinque, one of the Africans kidnaped from Sierra Leone in 1839. Part of the Africans' battle for freedom took place in New Haven.

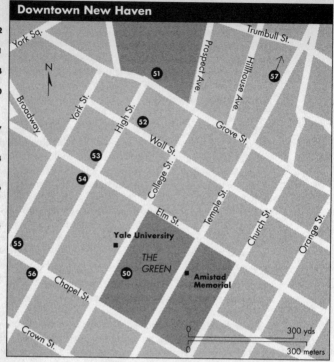

Downtown New Haven

🟡 A historic example of New Haven's innovation is the **Grove Street Cemetery** (⊠ 227 Grove St., ☎ 203/787–1443), the first planned public cemetery (1797) in the nation. Walk under the imposing Egyptian Revival arch, circa 1845, and you can see the final resting place of such Connecticut greats as Noah Webster, Eli Whitney, and Charles Goodyear.

New Haven is a manufacturing center dating from the 19th century, but the city owes its fame to merchant Elihu Yale. In 1718, Yale's contributions enabled the Collegiate School, founded in 1701, to settle in

★ New Haven, where it changed its name to **Yale University**, for which honor he never donated another dime to the school. This is one of the nation's great universities, and its campus holds some handsome neo-Gothic buildings and a number of noteworthy museums. The university's knowledgeable guides conduct one-hour walking tours that include Connecticut Hall in the Old Campus, which counts Nathan Hale, William Howard Taft, and Noah Webster among its past residents. ⊠ *Yale Visitors Center, 149 Elm St.,* ☎ *203/432–2300,* 🌐 *www.yale.edu.* ☉ *Tours weekdays at 10:30 and 2, weekends at 1:30. Tours start from 149 Elm St. on north side of New Haven Green.*

🟡 The collections at Yale's **Beinecke Rare Book and Manuscript Library** (⊠ 121 Wall St., ☎ 203/432–2977, 🌐 www.library.yale.edu/beinecke) include a Gutenberg Bible, illuminated manuscripts, and original Audubon bird prints, but the building is almost as much of an attraction—the walls are made of marble cut so thinly that the light shines through, making the interior a breathtaking sight on sunny days.

🟡 James Gamble Rogers, an American architect, created many buildings for Yale, his alma mater, including the **Sterling Memorial Library** (⊠ 120 High St., ☎ 203/432–2798, 🌐 www.library.yale.edu), which he designed in 1930 to be "a cathedral of knowledge and a temple of learning." This is evident in the major interior area, which resembles a Gothic cathedral.

54 The most notable example of the Yale campus's neo-Gothic architecture is the **Harkness Tower** (⊠ High St.), built between 1917 and 1921, which was modeled on St. Botolph's Tower in Boston, England. The university's famous motto, inscribed on Memorial Gate near the tower, is sometimes described as the world's greatest anticlimax: "For God, for country, and for Yale."

55 Since its founding in 1832, the **Yale University Art Gallery** has amassed more than 85,000 objects from around the world, dating from ancient Egypt to the present day. Highlights include works by van Gogh, Manet, Monet, Picasso, Winslow Homer, and Thomas Eakins, as well as Etruscan and Greek vases, Chinese ceramics and bronzes, and early Italian paintings. The gallery's collection of American decorative arts is considered one of the finest in the world. Be certain not to miss the re-creation of a Mithraic shrine downstairs. ⊠ *1111 Chapel St.,* ☎ *203/ 432–0600,* WEB *www.yale.edu/artgallery.* ⊠ *Free.* ☉ *Tues.–Sat. 10–5, Sun. 1–6.*

★ **56** The **Yale Center for British Art** has the most comprehensive collection of British art outside Britain and surveys the development of English art, life, and thought from the Elizabethan period to the present. The center's skylighted galleries, designed by Louis I. Kahn, contain works by Constable, Hogarth, Gainsborough, Reynolds, and Turner, to name but a few. You'll also find rare books and paintings documenting English history. ⊠ *1080 Chapel St.,* ☎ *203/432–2800,* WEB *www. yale.edu/ycba.* ⊠ *Free.* ☉ *Tues.–Sat. 10–5, Sun. noon–5.*

57 Yale's **Peabody Museum of Natural History** opened in 1876; with more than 9 million specimens, it's one of the largest natural history museums in the nation. In addition to exhibits on Andean, Mesoamerican, and Pacific cultures, the venerable museum has an excellent collection of birds, including a stuffed dodo and passenger pigeon. But the main attractions for children and amateur paleontologists alike are some of the world's earliest reconstructions of dinosaur skeletons. ⊠ *170 Whitney Ave.,* ☎ *203/432–5050,* WEB *www.peabody.yale.edu.* ⊠ *$5.* ☉ *Mon.–Sat. 10–5, Sun. noon–5.*

Dining and Lodging

$$–$$$$ ✕ **Hot Tomato's.** This café in the former 1912 Taft Hotel has a stately old-world elegance—cathedral-like windows, walls embellished with classic motifs in bas-relief, and a sweeping staircase that leads to a balcony dining room. Its contemporary menu includes everything from pork-and-vegetable wontons to fettuccine with lobster, mushrooms, and asparagus in a cream sauce. ⊠ *261 College St., 06510,* ☎ *203/624– 6331. AE, MC, V. No lunch weekends.*

$$–$$$ ✕ **Pika Tapas Café.** Chic and colorful, this cosmopolitan café serves delicate Spanish hors d'oeuvres meant for sharing; each region in Spain is well represented on the menu. *Gambas al ajillo* (shrimp sautéed in a pungent, good-to-the-last-drop garlic sauce) and baked goat cheese on parsley toast are among the popular tapas. A few salads and entrées— the roasted duck breast with avocado is a standout—are also prepared. ⊠ *39 High St., 06510,* ☎ *203/865–1933. AE, DC, MC, V. Closed Mon. No lunch Sun., Tues.*

$$ ✕ **Frank Pepe's.** Does this place serve the best pizza in the world, as some reviewers claim? If it doesn't, it comes close. Pizza is the only thing prepared here—try the famous white-clam pie. Expect to wait an hour or more for a table—or, on weekend evenings, come after 10. The **Spot** (☎ *203/865–7602*), right behind the restaurant, is owned by

Pepe's and is usually open when Pepe's is not. ⊠ *157 Wooster St., 06510,* ☎ *203/865–5762. Reservations not accepted. No credit cards. Closed Tues. No lunch Mon. or Wed.–Thurs.*

$ ✕ **Louis' Lunch.** This all-American luncheonette on the National Register of Historic Places claims to be the birthplace of the hamburger in America. The first-rate burgers are cooked in an old-fashioned, upright broiler and served with either a slice of tomato or cheese on two slices of toast. ⊠ *263 Crown St., 06510,* ☎ *203/562–5507. No credit cards. Closed Sun.–Mon. No dinner Tues.–Wed.*

$$$$ 🏨 **Omni New Haven Hotel at Yale.** This 19-floor Omni is the only large hotel in the city. With modern amenities and a view of the green, it's comfortable and convenient to the heart of New Haven. Galileo's, the rooftop restaurant is named for its lofty height, though the menu is somewhat more down to earth, with traditional hotel fare such as salmon and filet mignon at reasonable prices. ⊠ *155 Temple St., 06511,* ☎ *203/772–6664,* FAX *203/974–6777,* WEB *www.omnihotels.com. 306 rooms. Restaurant, in-room data ports, health club, lounge, business services, meeting room. AE, D, MC, V.*

$$$$ 🏨 **Three Chimneys Inn.** This 1870 Victorian mansion is one of the ★ classiest small inns in the state. Rooms have posh Georgian furnishings: mahogany four-poster beds, oversize armoires, Chippendale desks, and Oriental rugs. The sitting room and library have working fireplaces. ⊠ *1201 Chapel St., 06511,* ☎ *203/789–1201,* FAX *203/776–7363,* WEB *www.threechimneysinn.com. 11 rooms. In-room data ports, exercise equipment, library, business services, meeting room. AE, D, MC, V. BP.*

$$ 🏨 **New Haven Hotel.** A quiet spot in the heart of the city, the New Haven has the feel of a small, exclusive hotel, but the amenities are those of a large facility. The Queen Anne–style rooms are comfortable and modern, and the restaurant, Templeton's, serves innovative American cuisine. ⊠ *229 George St., 06510,* ☎ *203/498–3100,* FAX *203/498–0911,* WEB *www.newhavenhotel.com. 92 rooms. Restaurant, bar, in-room data ports, indoor lap pool, health club, hot tub, business services, meeting room. AE, D, DC, MC, V.*

Nightlife and the Arts

NIGHTLIFE

Anna Liffey's (⊠ 17 Whitney Ave., ☎ 203/773–1776) is one of the city's liveliest Irish pubs. **BAR** (⊠ Crown St. at College St., ☎ 203/495–1111) is a cross between a nightclub, a brick-oven pizzeria, and a brewpub. **Richter's** (⊠ 990 Chapel St., ☎ 203/777–0400) is famous for its half-yard glasses of beer. Alternative and traditional rock bands play at **Toad's Place** (⊠ 300 York St., ☎ 203/624–8623).

THE ARTS

The century-old **New Haven Symphony Orchestra** (☎ 203/865–0831) plays at Yale University's Woolsey Hall (⊠ College and Grove Sts.). The **SNET Oakdale Theatre** (⊠ 95 S. Turnpike Rd., ☎ 203/265–1501) in Wallingford, 18 mi north of New Haven, presents nationally known theatrical and musical performances. **Yale School of Music** (☎ 203/432–4157) presents an impressive roster of performers, from classical to jazz; most events take place in the Morse Recital Hall in Sprague Memorial Hall (⊠ College and Wall Sts.).

The well-regarded **Long Wharf Theatre** (⊠ 222 Sargent Dr., ☎ 203/787–4282) presents works by contemporary writers and imaginative revivals of neglected classics. The **Shubert Performing Arts Center** (⊠ 247 College St., ☎ 203/562–5666 or 800/228–6622) hosts Broadway musicals and dramas, usually following their run in the Big Apple, plus dance, classical music, and cabaret acts. The highly professional **Yale Repertory Theatre** (⊠ Chapel and York Sts., ☎ 203/432–1234) premieres new plays and mounts fresh interpretations of the classics. The **Yale Summer Cabaret** (⊠ 217 Park St., ☎ 203/432–1566) stages unusual plays during June, July, and August.

Outdoor Activities and Sports

A public beach, nature trails, excellent birding, and a stunning antique carousel in a century-old beach pavilion are attractions of the 88-acre **Lighthouse Point Park** (⊠ Lighthouse Rd. off Rte. 337, ☎ 203/946–8005), in southeastern New Haven.

The **New Haven Knights** (☎ 203/498–7825), members of the United Hockey League, play home games at Veterans Memorial Coliseum (⊠ George St.) from October to March.

The **New Haven Ravens** (☎ 800/728–3671), the Class AA affiliate of baseball's St. Louis Cardinals, play home games at Yale Field (⊠ 252 Derby Ave., West Haven) from April to September.

Shopping

Chapel Street, near the town green, has a pleasing assortment of shops and eateries. **Arethusa Book Shop** (⊠ 87 Audubon St., ☎ 203/624–1848) carries a huge selection of out-of-print and used books, including first editions. **Atticus Bookstore & Café** (⊠ 1082 Chapel St., ☎ 203/776–4040), in the heart of Yale University, was one of the first stores to combine books and food; it's been a favorite among museum groupies and theatergoers for years.

En Route   The oldest rapid-transit car and the world's first electric freight locomotive are among classic trolleys on display at the **Shoreline Trolley Museum.** Admission includes a 3-mi round-trip ride aboard a vintage trolley. ⊠ *17 River St., East Haven (midway between New Haven and Branford),* ☎ 203/467–6927, WEB *www.bera.org.* ⊠ *$6.* ☉ *Memorial Day–Labor Day, daily 10:30–4:30; May 1–Memorial Day, Labor Day–Oct., and Dec., weekends 10:30–4:30; Apr. and Nov., Sun. 10:30–4:30.*

Branford

58   *8 mi east of New Haven.*

Founded in 1644, Branford was a prosperous port and the site of a saltworks that during the Revolutionary War provided salt to preserve food for the Continental Army. Today it is a charming seaside town with a close-knit community of artists and craftspeople. The summer cottages are shoulder to shoulder, with tiny, well-kept yards and colorful gardens.

The small Branford village of Stony Creek, with a few tackle shops, antiques shops, a general store, and a marina, is the departure point for cruises around the **Thimble Islands.** This group of more than 90 tiny islands was named for its abundance of thimbleberries, which are similar to gooseberries. Legend has it that Captain Kidd buried pirate gold on one island. Two sightseeing vessels vie for your patronage, the *Volsunga IV* (☎ 203/488–9978, WEB www.thimbleislands.com) and the *Sea Mist II* (☎ 203/488–8905). Both depart from Stony Creek Dock, at the end of Thimble Island Road, from May to Columbus Day.

Dining

$$–$$$$ ✕ **USS Chowder Pot III.** There's no doubt about the specialty of the
★   house here: seafood with a capital "S"—clams, scallops, lobster, sole, and more. The casual, nautical surrounding (fish nets hang from every available surface) sets the mood for digging into the heaping fried seafood platters. One word of caution: the lines are often out the door. It's worth the wait, but try to arrive early or plan on drinks in the extensive bar-

lounge while you wait. ✉ *560 E. Main St., 06443,* ☎ *203/481–2356. Reservations not accepted. AE, DC, MC, V.*

$$–$$$ ✕ **Pesce.** White tablecloths, white china, and pale blue-and-white walls set the scene for a mix of seafood and Italian specialties at this restaurant. Old favorites like osso buco are on the menu alongside such trendier choices as big-eye tuna seared rare with porcini dust. Other entrées might include lobster bisque with cognac or Maine lobster and crabmeat cakes. ✉ *2 E. Main St.,* ☎ *203/483–5488. AE, D, DC, MC, V. Closed Mon. No lunch.*

Guilford

59   *5 mi northeast of Branford, 37 mi west of New London.*

The Guilford town green, crisscrossed by pathways, dotted with benches, and lined with historic homes and specialty shops, is considered by many to be the prettiest green in the state and is actually the third largest in the Northeast. The group of English settlers who founded Guilford in 1639 was led by the Reverend Henry Whitfield.

The **Henry Whitfield State Museum,** built by the Reverend Whitfield in 1639, is the oldest house in the state and the oldest stone house in New England. The furnishings in the medieval-style building were made between the 17th and 19th centuries. The visitor center has two exhibition galleries and a gift shop. ✉ *248 Old Whitfield St.,* ☎ *203/ 453–2457,* WEB *www.hbgraphics.com/whitfieldmuseum.* ⊡ *$3.50.* ☺ *Feb.–mid-Dec., Wed.–Sun. 10–4:30; mid-Dec.–Jan. by appointment.*

Dining

$$$ ✕ **Esteva.** A wall of windows overlooking stately Guilford Green and a colorful mural and open kitchen create a comfortable yet lively atmosphere perfect for enjoying the eclectic cuisine served here. You might find rack of lamb with a pomegranate and molasses glaze, monkfish and mahogany clams with green olives and prosciutto, or duck breast glazed with ponzu coloring your plate. ✉ *25 Whitfield St., 06437,* ☎ *203/458–1300. AE, MC, V. No lunch Mon.*

$–$$$ ✕ **Quattro's.** The two owner-chefs here are Ecuadoran but are trained
★ in the Italian style of cooking. Although their menu includes traditional pasta dishes, these pros really cut loose with the daily specials. Look for delicacies such as the smoky bacon-wrapped scallops served over a bed of lobster sauce and the filet mignon topped with fresh spinach, sautéed shrimp, and cognac sauce. ✉ *1300 Boston Post Rd., 06437,* ☎ *203/453–6575. Reservations essential. AE, DC, MC, V.*

Shopping

The **Guilford Handcrafts Center** (✉ 411 Church St., ☎ 203/453–5947) sponsors seven crafts exhibitions a year and has an excellent shop that represents more than 300 artists.

Madison

60   *5 mi east of Guilford, 62 mi northeast of Greenwich.*

Coastal Madison has an understated charm. Ice cream parlors, antiques stores, and quirky gift boutiques prosper along U.S. 1, the town's main street. Stately Colonial homes line the town green, site of many a summer antiques fair and arts and crafts festival. The Madison shoreline, particularly the white stretch of sand known as Hammonasset Beach and its parallel boardwalk, draws visitors year-round.

Hammonasset Beach State Park, the largest of the state's shoreline sanctuaries, has 2 mi of white-sand beaches, a nature center, excellent birding, and a hugely popular 541-site campground. ✉ *I–95, Exit 62,* ☎

203/245–2785 park; 203/245–1817 campground. ⬚ *Park $5–$12 Apr.–Sept., free Oct.–Mar.* ☉ *Park daily 8 AM–dusk.*

Dining and Lodging

$$$ ✕⬚ **Inn at Lafayette.** Skylights, painted murals, and handcrafted woodwork are among the design accents at this airy hostelry in a converted 1830s church. The rooms may be small, but they are decorated with beautiful fabrics and reproduction 17th- and 18th-century antique furniture. The modern marble baths come equipped with telephones. Fresh food and flawless service are highlights at Café Allegre ($$–$$$; closed Mon.), the inn's popular restaurant. The menu is largely southern Italian, with French accents. ✉ *725 Boston Post Rd., 06443,* ☎ *203/245–7773 or 866/623–7498,* FAX *203/245–6256,* WEB *www.allegrecafe.com. 5 rooms. Restaurant, bar, business services. AE, DC, MC, V. CP.*

En Route   Among the 70 upscale discount stores at **Clinton Crossing Premium Outlets** (✉ 20 Killingworth Turnpike, I–95, Exit 63, Clinton, ☎ 860/664–0700), you can find Off 5th–Saks Fifth Avenue, Donna Karan, Coach, Tommy Hilfiger, Barneys New York, and Lenox. Represented at **Westbrook Factory Stores** (✉ I–95, Exit 65, Westbrook, ☎ 860/399–8656) are Carter's, Springmaid/Wamsutta, Oneida, J. Crew, and Timberland, among more than 60 others.

Old Saybrook

61 *9 mi east of Madison, 29 mi east of New Haven.*

Old Saybrook, once a lively shipbuilding and fishing town, bustles with summer vacationers and antiques shoppers. In July and August a trolley run by the chamber of commerce shows you the sights, from restaurants to shops to the old-fashioned soda fountain where you can share a sundae with your sweetie.

Dining and Lodging

$$–$$$ ✕ **Aleia's.** This restaurant is as light, bright, and bountiful as the Italian countryside. Raffia, silk flowers, and hand-painted plates from Capri decorate the walls, and trompe l'oeil fruits, vegetables, and herbs adorn the tabletops. Chef-owner Kimberly Snow adds nouvelle touches to her mother's tried-and-true recipes, such as the grilled lamb steak with red bliss potatoes, Feta cheese, and sautéed spinach, and the seafood risotto with clams, shrimp, scallops, and chorizo. ✉ *1687 Boston Post Rd., 06475,* ☎ *860/399–5050. AE, MC, V. Closed Sun.–Mon. No lunch.*

$$–$$$ ✕ **Café Routier.** Duck-leg ragout in a rich red-wine sauce, fried oysters with a chipotle rémoulade, and steak au poivre with potatoes Dauphinois are among the entrées at this classy café. White tablecloths and candlelight complement the snappy French and American cuisine. Some of France's finest vintages are served from the copper wine bar. ✉ *1080 Boston Post Rd., 06475,* ☎ *860/388–6270. AE, D, DC, MC, V. Closed Mon. No lunch.*

$–$$ ✕ **Pat's Kountry Kitchen.** Upbeat service and traditional New England fare have made this home-style restaurant a local institution and a family favorite. Best-sellers are the fresh clam hash, pork chops, and apple-cranberry-raisin pie. ✉ *70 Mill Rock Rd. E, 06475,* ☎ *860/388–4784. AE, MC, V. Closed Wed.*

$$$–$$$$ ✕⬚ **Saybrook Point Inn & Spa.** Rooms at the Saybrook are furnished mainly in 18th-century style, with reproductions of British furniture and Impressionist art. The health club and pools overlook the inn's marina and the Connecticut River. The Terra Mar Grille ($$$–$$$$), which sits on the river, serves stylish Continental cuisine such as braised monkfish with celery root puree. ✉ *2 Bridge St., 06475,* ☎ *860/395–*

2000 or 800/243–0212, FAX *860/388–1504,* WEB *www.saybrook.com. 50 rooms, 12 suites. Restaurant, in-room data ports, 2 pools (1 indoor), spa, health club, marina, meeting room. AE, D, DC, MC, V.*

$$$$ 🏨 **Water's Edge Inn & Resort.** With its spectacular setting on Long Is-
★ land Sound, this traditional weathered gray-shingle compound in Westbrook is one of the Connecticut shore's premier resorts. The main
building has warm, bright public rooms furnished with antiques and
reproductions, and its upstairs bedrooms, with wall-to-wall carpeting
and clean, modern bathrooms, afford priceless views of the sound. ✉
1525 Boston Post Rd., Westbrook 06498, ☎ *860/399–5901 or 800/
222–5901,* FAX *860/399–6172,* WEB *www.watersedge-resort.com. 99
rooms, 67 suites. Restaurant, in-room data ports, 2 tennis courts, 2
pools (1 indoor), health club, spa, volleyball, beach, bar, business services, meeting room. AE, D, DC, MC, V.*

$$–$$$$ 🏨 **Deacon Timothy Pratt Bed & Breakfast.** Small but inviting, this
B&B is in the heart of the shopping and historic districts and within
a mile of a train station and beaches. Each room in the 1746 center-
chimney Colonial reflects the owner's attention to detail, respect for
history, and eye for romance. Three rooms have working fireplaces and
three have whirlpool baths. ✉ *325 Main St., 06475,* ☎ *860/395–1229,*
FAX *860/395–4748,* WEB *www.connecticut-bed-and-breakfast.com. 6
rooms. In-room data ports. AE, MC, V. BP.*

Outdoor Activities and Sports
Deep River Navigation Company (✉ Saybrook Point, ☎ 860/526–4954)
runs narrated cruises up the Connecticut River, along the shoreline, or
out into Long Island Sound.

Shopping
More than 120 dealers operate out of the **Essex-Saybrook Antiques
Village** (✉ 345 Middlesex Turnpike, ☎ 860/388–0689). **James Gallery
and Soda Fountain** (✉ 2 Pennywise La., ☎ 860/395–1229) sells both
watercolors and ice cream sodas in a historic former general store–phar-
macy. **North Cove Outfitters** (✉ 75 Main St., ☎ 860/388–6585) is Con-
necticut's version of L. L. Bean. **Saybrook Country Barn** (✉ 2 Main
St., ☎ 860/388–0891) has everything country, from tiger-maple din-
ing-room tables to hand-painted pottery.

Old Lyme

⓺ *4 mi east of Old Saybrook, 40 mi south of Hartford.*

Old Lyme, on the other side of the Connecticut River from Old Say-
brook, is renowned among art lovers for its history as America's fore-
most Impressionist-art colony. Artists continue to be attracted to the
area for its lovely countryside and shoreline. The town also has hand-
some old houses, many built for sea captains.

★ Central to Old Lyme's artistic reputation is the **Florence Griswold Mu-
seum,** a columned, Georgian-style former boardinghouse that hosted
members of the Old Lyme art colony, including Willard Metcalf, Clark
Voorhees, Childe Hassam, and Henry Ward Ranger, in the early 20th
century. Griswold, the descendant of a well-known family, offered
artistic encouragement as well as housing. The artists painted for their
hostess the double row of panels in the dining room that now serve as
the museum's centerpiece. Many of their other works are on display
in revolving exhibits, along with 19th-century furnishings and deco-
rative items. The landscaped 11-acre estate elegantly complements the
1817 late-Georgian mansion. The museum is part of the Connecticut
Impressionist Art Trail, a self-guided tour of nine sites. A new gallery
opened in July 2002 showcases a celebrated collection of more than

190 works donated to the museum by the Hartford Steam Boiler Inspection and Insurance Co., a former stop on the art trail. ☒ *96 Lyme St.,* ☎ *860/434–5542,* WEB *www.flogris.org.* 🎫 *$5.* ☼ *Jan.–Apr., Wed.–Sun. 1–5; May–Dec., Tues.–Sat. 10–5, Sun. 1–5.*

The **Lyme Academy of Fine Arts,** in a Federal-style home built in 1817, exhibits works by contemporary artists, including the academy's students and faculty. ☒ *84 Lyme St.,* ☎ *860/434–5232,* WEB *www.lymeacademy.edu.* 🎫 *$2 donation suggested.* ☼ *Tues.–Sat. 10–4, Sun. 1–4.*

Dining and Lodging

$$$–$$$$ ✕🏨 **Old Lyme Inn.** A white clapboard 1850s farmhouse with blue shutters is the centerpiece of this dining and lodging establishment in the heart of Old Lyme's historic district. Behind the ornate iron fence, tree-shaded lawn, and banister front porch are spacious guest rooms impeccably decorated with antiques and contemporary furnishings. The inn's elegant dining rooms ($$$–$$$$) serve creative American dishes such as honey-glazed lamb shoulder with shallot mashed potatoes and butternut squash ravioli. ☒ *85 Lyme St., 06371 (just north of I–95),* ☎ *860/434–2600 or 800/434–5352,* FAX *860/434–5352,* WEB *www.oldlymeinn.com. 13 rooms. Restaurant. AE, D, DC, MC, V. CP.*

$$–$$$$ ✕🏨 **Bee & Thistle Inn.** Behind a weathered stone wall in the Old Lyme
★ historic district is a three-story 1756 Colonial house with 5½ acres of broad lawns, formal gardens, and herbaceous borders. The scale of rooms throughout is small and inviting, with fireplaces in the parlors and dining rooms and light and airy curtains in the multipaned guest-room windows. Most rooms have canopy or four-poster beds; breakfast (not included in the price) can be brought to your room. Fireplaces and candlelight exude romance in the restaurant ($$$–$$$$; closed Tues. and 1st 3 wks in Jan.), where American cuisine—with entrées such as goat cheese ravioli and roasted rack of lamb—is served with style. ☒ *100 Lyme St., 06371,* ☎ *860/434–1667 or 800/622–4946,* FAX *860/434–3402,* WEB *www.beeandthistleinn.com. 11 rooms, 1 cottage. Restaurant; no smoking. AE, DC, MC, V.*

Waterford and Niantic

63 *13 mi east of Old Lyme (Waterford).*

Less cutesy than Mystic and less military than Groton, Waterford and Niantic are working shoreline towns, but not without their down-to-earth charms. In summer, crowds from all over flock to Niantic (actually a village of the town of East Lyme) to take in the salt-air pleasures of the crescent-shape beach at Rocky Neck State Park.

Harkness Memorial State Park, the former summer estate of Edward Stephen Harkness, a silent partner in Standard Oil, encompasses formal gardens, picnic areas, a beach for strolling and fishing (but not swimming), and the 42-room Italian villa–style mansion, Eolia. Classical, pop, and jazz talents perform at the **Summer Music at Harkness** (☎ 860/442–9199) festival in July and August. ☒ *275 Great Neck Rd./Rte. 213, Waterford,* ☎ *860/443–5725.* 🎫 *Memorial Day–Labor Day $4–$8, free Labor Day–Memorial Day.* ☼ *Daily 8 AM–dusk. House tours Memorial Day–Labor Day; call for hrs.*

☾ The **Children's Museum of Southeastern Connecticut,** about a mile from Waterford, uses a hands-on approach to engage kids in the fields of science, math, and current events. ☒ *409 Main St., Niantic,* ☎ *860/691–1255,* WEB *www.childmuseumsect.conncollege.edu.* 🎫 *$4.* ☼ *Labor Day–Memorial Day, Tues.–Thurs. and Sat. 9:30–4:30, Fri. 9:30–8, Sun. noon–5; Memorial Day–Labor Day, Mon.–Thurs. and Sat. 9:30–4:30, Fri. 9:30–8, Sun. noon–5.*

Outdoor Activities and Sports

In Waterford **Captain John's Dock** (☎ 860/443–7259) operates lighthouse cruises, as well as sightseeing tours in search of seals, bald eagles, or lighthouses aboard the 100-ft-long *Sunbeam Express*. Naturalists from Mystic Aquarium accompany the boat.

Among the attributes of **Rocky Neck State Park** are its picnic facilities, saltwater fishing, and historic stone-and-wood pavilion, which was built in the 1930s. The park's mile-long crescent-shape strand is one of the finest beaches on Long Island Sound. ✉ *Rte. 156 (off I–95, Exit 72), Niantic,* ☎ *860/739–5471.* ✉ *Apr.–Sept. $5–$12, free Oct.–Mar.* ☼ *Daily 8 AM–dusk.*

New London

64   *3 mi northeast of Waterford, 46 mi east of New Haven.*

New London, on the banks of the Thames River, has long had ties to the sea. In the mid-1800s it was the second-largest whaling port in the world. Today the U.S. Coast Guard Academy uses its campus on the Thames to educate and train its cadets. Ocean Beach Park, an old-fashioned beach resort with a wooden boardwalk, provides an up-close-and-personal view of New London's connection to the deep blue sea.

The 100-acre cluster of redbrick buildings at the **U.S. Coast Guard Academy** includes a museum and visitor's pavilion with a gift shop. The three-mast training bark, the USCGC *Eagle,* may be boarded on weekends when in port. ✉ *15 Mohegan Ave.,* ☎ *860/444–8270,* ⓦⒺⒷ *www.cga.edu.* ✉ *Free.* ☼ *Academy Nov.–Apr., daily 9–5; May–Oct., daily 10–5.*

The **Lyman Allyn Museum of Art,** at the southern end of the Connecticut College campus, was named by founder Harriet U. Allyn after her father, a whaling merchant. Housed in a neoclassical building designed by Charles Platt are collections of American fine arts from the country's earliest years through today. The galleries of Connecticut's decorative arts and American Impressionist paintings are noteworthy. ✉ *625 Williams St.,* ☎ *860/443–2545,* ⓦⒺⒷ *lymanallyn.conncoll.edu.* ✉ *$4.* ☼ *Tues.–Sat. 10–5, Sun. 1–5.*

The **Monte Cristo Cottage,** the boyhood home of Pulitzer and Nobel prizewinning playwright Eugene O'Neill, was named for the literary count, his actor-father's greatest role. The setting figures in two of O'Neill's landmark plays, *Ah, Wilderness!* and *Long Day's Journey into Night.* ✉ *325 Pequot Ave.,* ☎ *860/443–0051.* ✉ *$5.* ☼ *Memorial Day–Labor Day, Tues.–Sat. 10–5, Sun. 1–5.*

Dining and Lodging

$$ ✕ **Recovery Room.** It's a favorite game of Connecticut pizza parlors to declare "We're as good as Pepe's"—a reference to the famed New Haven eatery. But this white Colonial storefront eatery, presided over by the friendly Cash family, lives up to its claim. Plenty of "boutique" toppings are available, but don't ruin a great pizza with too many flavors. Perfection is realized by the three-cheese pizza with grated Parmesan, Romano, and Gorgonzola. ✉ *445 Ocean Ave., 06320,* ☎ *860/443–2619. MC, V. No lunch weekends.*

$$$$ ▥ **Lighthouse Inn Resort and Conference Center.** This Mediterranean-style mansion turned inn was built in 1902 as the summer home of a steel magnate. When it opened as an inn in 1927 it was a retreat for film stars such as Bette Davis and Joan Crawford. A spring 2002 restoration has returned the hotel to its original grandeur, including the grounds designed by renowned landscape architect Frederick Law Olmsted, designer of New York's Central Park. Rooms in the semi-circular mansion, which are appointed with a mix of antiques and period pieces, face either these gardens or the Long Island Sound. ⊠ 6 *Guthrie Pl., 06320,* ☎ *860/443–8411 or 888/443–8411,* FAX *860/437–7027,* WEB *www.lighthouseinn-ct.com. 52 rooms. Restaurant, beach, lounge, meeting rooms. AE, MC, V. CP.*

$$ 🏨 **Radisson Hotel.** The rooms are quiet and spacious at this downtown property convenient to State Street, I–95, and the Amtrak station. ⊠ *35 Gov. Winthrop Blvd., 06320,* ☎ *860/443–7000,* FAX *860/443–1239,* WEB *www.radisson.com. 116 rooms, 4 suites. Restaurant, bar, indoor pool, health club. AE, D, DC, MC, V.*

Nightlife and the Arts

The **El 'n' Gee Club** (⊠ 86 Golden St., ☎ 860/437–3800) presents heavy metal, reggae, and local and national bands. The **Garde Arts Center** (⊠ 325 State St., ☎ 860/444–7373) hosts national and international Broadway, music, dance, and theater touring companies. Connecticut College's **Palmer Auditorium** (⊠ Mohegan Ave., ☎ 860/439–2787) plans a full schedule of dance and theater programs.

Outdoor Activities and Sports

At **Fort Trumbull State Park,** (⊠ 90 Walbach St., ☎ 860/444–7591), a 19th-century fort on the Thames River and former location of the Naval Undersea Warfare Center, you'll find a visitors center, fishing pier, and picnic area. Along with its ½-mi-long beach, **Ocean Beach Park** (⊠ 1225 Ocean Ave., ☎ 860/447–3031) has an Olympic-size outdoor pool (with a triple water slide), a miniature golf course, a video arcade, a boardwalk, and a picnic area.

Norwich

⑥⑤ *15 mi north of New London, 37 mi southeast of Hartford.*

Outstanding Georgian and Victorian structures surround the triangular town green in Norwich, and more can be found downtown by the Thames River. The former mill town is hard at work at restoration and rehabilitation efforts. So eye-catching are these brightly colored structures that the town has been designated one of the "Prettiest Painted Places in New England" by the Paint Quality Institute.

The **Slater Memorial Museum & Converse Art Gallery,** on the grounds of the Norwich Free Academy, has the largest plaster-cast collection of classical statues in the country, including *Winged Victory, Venus de Milo,* and Michelangelo's *Pietà.* ⊠ *108 Crescent St.,* ☎ *860/887–2505 or 860/887–2506.* 🎫 *$3.* ◷ *Sept.–June, Tues.–Fri. 9–4, weekends 1–4; July–Aug., Tues.–Sun. 1–4.*

Lodging

$$$$ 🏨 **The Spa at Norwich Inn.** This posh Georgian-style inn is on 42 rolling acres right by the Thames River. The spa provides an entire spectrum of fitness classes, massages, and beauty treatments. You'll find four-poster beds, wood-burning fireplaces, and a complete galley kitchen in the posh villas as well as comfy country decor in the guest rooms. The inn's elegant restaurant serves both luxe Continental fare and lighter spa favorites. ⊠ *607 W. Thames St./Rte. 32, 06360,* ☎ *860/886–2401 or 800/275–4772,* FAX *860/886–4492,* WEB *www.thespaatnorwichinn.com. 49 rooms, 54 villas. Restaurant, in-room data ports, 18-hole golf course, 2 tennis courts, indoor pool, hair salon, spa. AE, DC, MC, V.*

Outdoor Activities and Sports

The **Norwich Navigators** (☎ 800/644–2867), the Class AA affiliate of baseball's New York Yankees, play at Senator Thomas J. Dodd Stadium (✉ 14 Stott Rd.).

Ledyard

66   *10 mi south of Norwich, 37 mi southeast of Hartford.*

There's no doubt that Ledyard, in the woods of southeastern Connecticut between Norwich and the coastline, is known first and foremost for the vast Mashantucket Pequot Tribal Nation's Foxwoods Resort Casino. With the opening of the excellent Mashantucket Pequot Museum & Research Center, however, the tribe has moved beyond gaming to educating the public about its history, as well as that of other Northeast Woodland tribes.

Foxwoods Resort Casino, on the Mashantucket Pequot Indian Reservation near Ledyard, is the world's largest gambling operation and a major draw. The skylighted compound draws more than 40,000 visitors daily to its more than 5,800 slot machines, 3,200-seat high-stakes bingo parlor, poker rooms, keno station, gaming area, theater, and Race Book room. This massive complex includes the Grand Pequot Tower, the Great Cedar Hotel, and Two Trees Inn, which have more than 1,400 rooms combined, as well as a full-service day spa, retail concourse, food court, and 24 restaurants. ✉ *Rte. 2, Mashantucket,* ☎ *860/312–3000 or 800/752–9244,* WEB *www.foxwoods.com.* ☉ *Daily.*

★ The **Mashantucket Pequot Museum & Research Center,** a large complex 1 mi from the Foxwoods Resort Casino, explores the history and culture of Northeastern Woodland tribes in general and the Pequots in particular with exquisitely researched detail. Some highlights include re-creations of a glacial crevasse, a caribou hunt from 11,000 years ago, and a 17th-century fort. Perhaps most remarkable is a sprawling "immersion environment"—a 16th-century village with life-size figures and real smells and sounds—in which you use audio devices to obtain detailed information about the sights. The research center, open to scholars and schoolchildren free of charge, holds thousands of books and artifacts. ✉ *110 Pequot Trail, Mashantucket,* ☎ *800/411–9671,* WEB *www.mashantucket.com.* 🎫 *$12.* ☉ *Memorial Day–Labor Day, daily 10–7; Labor Day–Memorial Day, Wed.–Mon. 10–6.*

The Mohegan Indians, known as the Wolf People, operate the **Mohegan Sun,** which currently has more than 300,000 square ft of gaming space, including 6,000 slot machines, more than 200 gaming tables, bingo, a theater, "Kids Quest" family entertainment complex, and, more than 40 food-and-beverage suppliers. For betting on the ponies or even on greyhounds, you'll find Race Book, a Simulcast theater with New York Racing Association broadcasts. Free entertainment, including nationally known acts, is presented nightly in the Wolf Den. An expansion completed in April 2002 includes a 1,200-room luxury hotel, 20 restaurants, a day spa, a 10,000-seat arena, 130,000-square-ft shopping mall, a cabaret, and an additional 115,000 square ft of gaming space. Uncasville is west of Ledyard, across the Thames River. For all the grandeur of this expansion, Mohegan Sun remains easier to navigate than Foxwoods Resort Casino and retains a more intimate, less intimidating feel. ✉ *Mohegan Sun Blvd. off I–395, Uncasville,* ☎ *888/226–7711,* WEB *www.mohegansun.com.*

Dining and Lodging

$$$$ ✕ **Paragon.** It's hard not to feel on top of the world at Paragon—it's on top of the tallest building at the largest casino in the world. It's no surprise, then, that the cuisine at this special-occasion restaurant is spectacular (though it should be mentioned you will pay dearly for it). Top choices include Cantonese-style steak dipped in tapioca flour and seared in a wok as well as seared lamb loin served with chorizo, grilled radicchio, and potato galette. ⊠ *Foxwoods Resort Casino, Rte. 2,* ☎ *860/312–3000. AE, D, DC, MC, V. Closed Mon.–Tues. No lunch.*

$$$–$$$$ ✕⊞ **Stonecroft.** A sunny 1807 Georgian Colonial on 6½ acres of green
★ meadows, woodlands, and rambling stone walls is the center of Stonecroft. Although individually thematic, the rooms here and in the historic barn are united in their refined but welcoming country atmosphere. At the restaurant ($$$–$$$$), try the pan-roasted filet mignon served with garlic mashed potatoes. ⊠ *515 Pumpkin Hill Rd., 06339,* ☎ *860/572–0771,* 🅵🅰🆇 *860/572–9161,* 🆆🅴🅱 *www.stonecroft.com. 10 rooms. Restaurant, croquet, horseshoes; no smoking. AE, D, MC, V. BP.*

$$$$ ⊞ **Mohegan Sun Hotel.** The emphasis of this 34-story hotel is on luxury. As you enter, towering impressionist red cedar trees form a canopy above you, gleaming glass and birch-lined walls surround you, and a stream and pool of water lead to the impressive Taughannick Falls across the lobby in the connecting Shops at Mohegan Sun. Guest rooms are large—a minimum of 450 square ft—and all have king or queen beds and marble baths. ⊠ *1 Mohegan Sun Blvd., Uncasville 06382,* ☎ *888/ 777–7922,* 🅵🅰🆇 *860/862–8328,* 🆆🅴🅱 *www.mohegansun.com. 1,020 rooms, 180 suites. Some kitchenettes, in-room data ports, pool, health club, spa, business services, meeting rooms. AE, MC, V.*

$$$–$$$$ ⊞ **Grand Pequot Tower.** Foxwoods' showcase hotel is an imposing 17 stories. Mere steps from the gaming floors, the expansive showpiece contains deluxe rooms and suites in pleasantly neutral tones. ⊠ *Rte. 2 (Box 3777, Mashantucket 06339),* ☎ *800/369–9663,* 🅵🅰🆇 *860/312– 5044,* 🆆🅴🅱 *www.foxwoods.com. 824 rooms. 4 restaurants, 2 18-hole golf courses, indoor pool, hair salon, health club, spa, 2 bars, meeting room. AE, D, DC, MC, V.*

Groton

⑥⑦ *10 mi south of Ledyard.*

Home to the United States naval submarine base and the Electric Boat Division of General Dynamics, designer and manufacturer of nuclear submarines, Groton is often referred to as the "submarine capital of the world." The submarine *Nautilus,* a National Historic Landmark, is a major draw, as is the Submarine Force Museum.

The world's first nuclear-powered submarine, the *Historic Ship Nautilus,* launched from Groton in 1954, is permanently berthed at the **Submarine Force Museum.** You're welcome to climb aboard and imagine yourself as a crew member during the boat's trip under the North Pole more than 40 years ago. The adjacent museum, outside the entrance to the submarine base, charts submarine history with memorabilia, artifacts, and displays, including working periscopes and controls. ⊠ *Crystal Lake Rd.,* ☎ *860/694–3174 or 800/343–0079,* 🆆🅴🅱 *www. ussnautilus.org.* 🎟 *Free.* ☉ *Mid-May–Oct., Wed.–Mon. 9–5, Tues. 1–5; Nov.–mid-May, Wed.–Mon. 9–4.*

Fort Griswold Battlefield State Park contains the remnants of a Revolutionary War fort. Historic displays at the museum mark the site of the massacre of American defenders by Benedict Arnold's British troops in 1781. Climb to the top of the Groton monument for a sweeping view of the shoreline. ⊠ *Monument St. and Park Ave.,* ☎ *860/445–1729,* 🆆🅴🅱 *www.revwar.com/ftgriswold.* 🎟 *Free.* ☉ *Park daily 8 AM–dusk. Museum and monument Memorial Day–Labor Day, daily 10–5.*

Lodging

$$$$ 🏨 **Mystic Marriott Hotel and Spa.** This six-story hotel, within Mystic Executive Park, has Georgian-style architecture. The old-world touches accent the modern rooms with rich fabrics, gleaming wood furnishings and elegant detailing. An Elizabeth Arden Red Door Spa is attached. ⊠ *625 North Rd./Rte. 117, 06340,* ☎ *860/446–2600 or 800/228–9290,* FAX *860/446–2696,* WEB *www.marriotthotels.com. 285 rooms, 6 suites. Restaurant, coffee shop, in-room data ports, some in-room hot tubs, pool, health club, sauna, spa, lounge, gift shop, business services, meeting rooms. AE, D, DC, MC, V.*

Outdoor Activities and Sports

Striped bass and blues are the catch of the day on **Hel-Cat II,** a 144-ft party fishing boat, from June to October. Cod, pollock, mackerel, blackfish, and sea bass are the goals in winter and spring. ⊠ *181 Thames St.,* ☎ *860/535–2066 or 860/445–5991.* 🎫 *$30–$48.* ☉ *Jan.–May, weekends; June–Oct., daily; call for hrs.*

Mystic

68 *8 mi east of Groton.*

Mystic has tried with dedication (if also with excessive commercialism) to recapture the seafaring spirit of the 18th and 19th centuries. This is where some of the nation's fastest clipper ships were built in the mid-19th century; today's Mystic Seaport is the state's most popular museum. Downtown Mystic has an interesting collection of boutiques and galleries.

★ ℭ **Mystic Seaport,** the world's largest marine museum, encompasses 17 acres of indoor and outdoor exhibits that provide a fascinating look at the area's rich maritime heritage. In the narrow streets and historic homes and buildings (some moved here from other sites), craftspeople give demonstrations of open-hearth cooking, weaving, and other skills of yesteryear. The museum's more than 480 vessels include the *Charles W. Morgan,* the last remaining wooden whaling ship afloat, and the 1882 training ship *Joseph Conrad.* You can climb aboard for a look or for sail-setting demonstrations and reenactments of whale hunts. Among the other attractions here are dozens of spectacular ship's figureheads, the world's largest collection of maritime art, cruises on 19th-century vessels, thousands of manuscripts and maps, and a period tavern. The museum can be very crowded in summer and early fall; if possible, plan to visit between October and May. In December, tours by lantern light are led by a costumed interpreter doing his 19th-century Christmas errands; reservations are essential. ⊠ *75 Greenmanville Ave.,* ☎ *860/572–0711,* WEB *www.mysticseaport.org.* 🎫 *$17.* ☉ *May–Oct., daily 9–5; Nov.–Apr., daily 10–4.*

★ ℭ Sea lions and penguins and whales—oh, my! The **Mystic Aquarium and Institute for Exploration,** with more than 3,500 specimens and 34 exhibits of sea life, includes Seal Island, a 2½-acre outdoor exhibit that shows off seals and sea lions from around the world; the Marine Theater, where California sea lions perform; and the beloved Penguin Pavilion. You'll also find exhibits such as a re-creation of the Alaska coastline, with the world's largest (750,000-gallon) outdoor beluga whale habitat. World-renowned ocean explorer Dr. Robert Ballard uses high-tech exhibits to take a simulated dive 3,000 ft below the ocean's surface. ⊠ *55 Coogan Blvd.,* ☎ *860/572–5955,* WEB *www.mysticaquarium.org.* 🎫 *$16.* ☉ *Labor Day–June, daily 9–5; July–Labor Day, daily 9–6.*

Dining and Lodging

$$–$$$ ✕ **Go Fish.** In this town by the sea, it's only right to dine on seafood,
★ and this sophisticated restaurant captures all the tastes—and colors—
of the ocean. The black granite sushi bar, with its myriad tiny, briny
morsels, is worth the trip in itself. The glossy blue tables in the two
large dining rooms perfectly complement the signature bouillabaisse
with aioli, fennel toast, and saffron-scented broth. The menu lists options for vegetarians and carnivores as well, but the lobster ravioli in
a light cream sauce is a must-try. ⊠ *Olde Mistick Village, Coogan Blvd.
(I–95, Exit 90), 06355,* ☎ *860/536–2662. AE, MC, V.*

$–$$$ ✕ **Abbott's Lobster in the Rough.** If you want some of the state's best
★ lobsters, mussels, crabs, or clams on the half shell, grab a bottle of wine
and slip down to this unassuming seaside lobster shack in sleepy
Noank, a few miles southwest of Mystic. Most seating is outdoors or
on the dock, where the views are magnificent. ⊠ *117 Pearl St., Noank
06340,* ☎ *860/536–7719. AE, MC, V. BYOB. Closed Columbus Day–
1st Fri. in May and weekdays Labor Day–Columbus Day.*

$–$$ ✕ **Mystic Pizza.** It's hard to say who benefited more from the success
of the 1988 sleeper film *Mystic Pizza:* then-budding actress Julia
Roberts or the pizza parlor on which the film is based (though no scenes
were filmed here). This joint, which is often teeming with customers
in summer, serves other dishes but is best known for its pizza, garlic
bread, and grinders. ⊠ *56 W. Main St., 06355,* ☎ *860/536–3700 or
860/536–3737. D, MC, V.*

$$$$ ✕⌂ **Inn at Mystic.** The highlight of this inn, which sprawls over 15
★ hilltop acres and overlooks picturesque Pequotsepos Cove, is the five-
bedroom Georgian Colonial mansion. Almost as impressive are the rambling four-bedroom gatehouse (where Lauren Bacall and Humphrey
Bogart honeymooned) and the unusually attractive motor lodge. The
convivial, sun-filled Flood Tide restaurant ($$$–$$$$) specializes in
contemporary Continental fare and New England classics such as
grilled veal medallions and jumbo sea scallops. Brunch fans flock here
on Sunday. ⊠ *U.S. 1 and Rte. 27, 06355,* ☎ *860/536–9604 or 800/
237–2415,* ⓕ *860/572–1635,* ⓦ *www.innatmystic.com. 67 rooms.
Restaurant, tennis court, pool, dock, boating. AE, D, DC, MC, V.*

$$–$$$ ✕⌂ **Whaler's Inn and Motor Court.** A perfect compromise between a
chain motel and a country inn, this complex with public rooms that con-
tain lovely antiques is one block from the Mystic River and downtown.
The motel-style guest rooms exude a Victorian ambience, with quilts
and reproduction four-poster beds. The restaurant, Bravo Bravo ($$–
$$$), serves nouvelle Italian food: the fettuccine might come with grilled
scallops, roasted apples, sun-dried tomatoes, and a Gorgonzola cream
sauce. ⊠ *20 E. Main St., 06355,* ☎ *860/536–1506 or 800/243–2588,*
ⓕ *860/572–1250,* ⓦ *www.whalersinnmystic.com. 41 rooms. Restau-
rant, outdoor café, in-room data ports, meeting room. AE, MC, V.*

$$$–$$$$ ⌂ **Steamboat Inn.** The rooms at this inn are named after famous Mys-
tic schooners, but it's hardly a creaky old establishment—many of the
rooms look as though they've been arranged for the cover shot of *House
Beautiful.* Six have wood-burning fireplaces, all have whirlpool baths,
and most have dramatic river views. Despite the inn's busy downtown
location (within earshot of the eerie hoot of the Bascule Drawbridge
and the chatter of tourists), the rooms are the most luxurious and ro-
mantic in town. Staterooms in the inn's classic yacht, moored along-
side the inn on the Mystic River, are also available for overnight rental.
⊠ *73 Steamboat Wharf, off W. Main St., 06355,* ☎ *860/536–8300,*
ⓕ *860/536–9528,* ⓦ *www.visitmystic.com/steamboat. 10 rooms.
AE, D, MC, V. CP.*

$$$ 🛏 **The Old Mystic Inn.** This cozy inn, built in 1784, when Mystic was noted for whaling, fishing, and shipbuilding, was once a bookshop specializing in antique books and maps. Today, all its rooms, some with working fireplaces and whirlpools, are named after authors. Each is a welcoming and comfortable mix of antiques and owner-innkeeper Michael Cardillo's personal touches. You can enjoy a game of checkers by the oversize Colonial hearth in the keeping room; a full country breakfast is served by the fire in the dining room. ⊠ *52 Main St., 06372,* ☎ *860/572–9422,* FAX *860/572–9954,* WEB *www.oldmysticinn.com. 8 rooms. No room phones, no room TVs. AE, MC, V. BP.*

Outdoor Activities and Sports

Private charter boats depart from **Noank Village Boatyard** (⊠ 38 Bayside Ave., Noank, ☎ 860/536–1770).

Shopping

Finer Line Gallery (⊠ 48 W. Main St., ☎ 860/536–8339) exhibits nautical and other prints. At the **Mystic Factory Outlets** (⊠ Coogan Blvd.), nearly two dozen stores discount famous-name clothing and other merchandise. **Olde Mistick Village** (⊠ Coogan Blvd. (off I–95, Exit 90), ☎ 860/536–1641), a re-creation of what an American village might have looked like in the early 1700s, is hokey yet picturesque. The stores here sell crafts, clothing, souvenirs, and food. **Tradewinds Gallery** (⊠ 42 W. Main St., ☎ 860/536–0119) represents some New England artists but specializes in antique maps and prints and marine art.

Stonington

69 *7 mi southeast of Mystic, 57 mi east of New Haven.*

The pretty village of Stonington pokes into Fishers Island Sound. Today a quiet fishing community clustered around white-spired churches, Stonington is far less commercial than Mystic. In the 19th century, though, this was a bustling whaling, sealing, and transportation center. Historic buildings line the town green and border both sides of Water Street up to the imposing Old Lighthouse Museum.

The **Captain Nathaniel B. Palmer House** is the Victorian home of the man who discovered Antarctica in 1820. Exhibits focus on both his career and family life. ⊠ *40 Palmer St.,* ☎ *860/535–8445,* WEB *www. stoningtonhistory.org/palmer.htm.* 🎟 *$4.* ☉ *May–Nov., Tues.–Sun. 10–4 (last tour at 3), or by appointment.*

The **Old Lighthouse Museum** has six rooms of exhibits depicting life in a coastal town circa 1649. It occupies a lighthouse built in 1823, which was moved to higher ground 17 years later. Climb to the top of the tower for a spectacular view of Long Island Sound and three states. ⊠ *7 Water St.,* ☎ *860/535–1440,* WEB *www.stoningtonhistory.org/light.htm.* 🎟 *$4.* ☉ *July–Aug., daily 10–5; May–June and Sept.–Oct., Tues.–Sun. 10–5; or by appointment.*

The **Stonington Vineyards,** a small coastal winery, grows premium vinifera, including chardonnay and French hybrid grape varieties. You can browse through the works of local artists in the small gallery or take a picnic lunch on the grounds. ⊠ *523 Taugwonk Rd.,* ☎ *860/ 535–1222,* WEB *www.stoningtonvineyards.com.* 🎟 *Free.* ☉ *Daily 11–5; tours at 2.*

Dining and Lodging

$$$$ ✕🛏 **Randall's Ordinary.** The waiters dress in Colonial garb at this inn known for its open-hearth cooking. The prix-fixe menu ($$$$; reservations essential for dinner) changes daily; choices might include tasty Nantucket scallops or roast rib eye of beef. The 17th-century John Ran-

dall House provides very simple accommodations, but all rooms have modern baths with whirlpool tubs and showers. The barn houses irregular-shape guest rooms, all with authentic early Colonial appointments. ⊠ *Rte. 2, 7 mi north of Stonington (Box 243, North Stonington 06359),* ☎ *860/599–4540,* ᴬˣ *860/599–3308,* ᴡᴱᴮ *www.randallsordinary.com. 14 rooms, 1 suite. Restaurant, meeting room. AE, MC, V.*

$$$$
★ 🍴 **Antiques & Accommodations.** The British influence is evident in the Georgian formality of this Victorian country home, built about 1861. Exquisite furniture and accessories decorate the rooms. An 1820 house has similarly furnished suites. Aromatic candles and fresh flowers create an inviting atmosphere. Some rooms have fireplaces. Breakfast is a grand four-course affair served by candlelight on fine china, sterling silver, and crystal. ⊠ *32 Main St., North Stonington, 7 mi north of Stonington, 06359,* ☎ *860/535–1736 or 800/554–7829,* ᴡᴱᴮ *www.visitmystic. com/antiques. 7 rooms, 1 suites. Some in-room hot tubs. MC, V. BP.*

$$$$
🍴 **The Inn at Stonington.** The views of Stonington Harbor and Fishers Island Sound are spectacular from this waterfront inn in the heart of Stonington Village. Each room is individually decorated; all have fireplaces, and most have whirlpool baths. Kayaks and bicycles are available for use. The inn also has a 400-ft deepwater pier if you are coming by boat. ⊠ *60 Water St., 06378,* ☎ *860/535–2000,* ᴬˣ *860/535–8193,* ᴡᴱᴮ *www.innatstonington.com. 12 rooms. Some in-room hot tubs, health club, bicycles; no kids under 16, no smoking. AE, MC, V. CP.*

New Haven and the Southeastern Coast A to Z

To research prices, get advice from other travelers, and book travel arrangements, visit www.fodors.com.

AIR TRAVEL TO AND FROM NEW HAVEN AND THE SOUTHEASTERN COAST

Tweed/New Haven Airport, 5 mi southeast of New Haven, is served by US Airways Express.

➤ AIRPORT INFORMATION: **Tweed/New Haven Airport** (⊠ 155 Burr St., off I–95, ☎ 203/466–8833 or 800/428–4322, ᴡᴱᴮ www. tweednewhavenairport.com). **US Airways Express** (☎ 203/466–8833 or 800/428–4322).

BOAT AND FERRY TRAVEL

From New London, Cross Sound Ferry operates year-round passenger and car service to and from Orient Point, Long Island, New York. Its high-speed ferry can make the trip in 40 minutes. Fishers Island Ferry has passenger and car service to and from Fishers Island, New York, from New London. Interstate Navigation Co. operates passenger and car service from New London to and from Block Island, Rhode Island, from June to early September.

➤ BOAT AND FERRY INFORMATION: **Cross Sound Ferry** (☎ 860/443–5281, ᴡᴱᴮ www.longislandferry.com). **Fishers Island Ferry** (☎ 860/443–6851). **Interstate Navigation Co.** (☎ 860/442–9553, ᴡᴱᴮ www.blockislandferry.com).

BUS TRAVEL

Peter Pan Bus Lines services New Haven from Boston, Hartford, and New York. Prime Time Shuttle provides shuttle service between New Haven and LaGuardia and John F. Kennedy airports in New York City. Connecticut Transit's local bus service connects New Haven and the surrounding towns, including service to and from Tweed/New Haven Airport.

➤ BUS INFORMATION: **Connecticut Transit** (☎ 203/624–0151, ᴡᴱᴮ www.cttransit.com). **Peter Pan Bus Lines** (☎ 800/237–8747, ᴡᴱᴮ www.

peterpanbus.com). **Prime Time Shuttle** (☎ 800/733–8267, WEB www.primetimeshuttle.com).

CAR TRAVEL

Interstate 95 and U.S. 1, which run mostly parallel but sometimes intertwine, are the main routes to and through southeastern Connecticut; the two roads intersect with I–91 (coming south from Hartford) in New Haven. Most of the southeastern Connecticut towns in New Haven and the southeastern coast are on or just off I–95 and U.S. 1, and a car is the easiest way to explore much of the area. Interstate 395 branches north from I–95 to Norwich.

EMERGENCIES

➤ HOSPITALS: **Lawrence & Memorial Hospital** (⊠ 365 Montauk Ave., New London, ☎ 860/442–0711, WEB www.lmhospital.org). **Yale–New Haven Hospital** (⊠ 20 York St., New Haven, ☎ 203/688–4242, WEB www.ynhh.org).

➤ LATE-NIGHT PHARMACY: **CVS** (⊠ 215 Whalley Ave., New Haven, ☎ 203/401–4661, WEB www.cvs.com).

TAXIS

Metro Taxi serves New Haven and environs.
➤ CONTACT: **Metro Taxi** (☎ 203/777–7777).

TRAIN TRAVEL

Amtrak trains make stops in New Haven, New London, and Mystic. Metro-North Railroad trains from New York stop in New Haven. The Connecticut Department of Transportation's Shore Line East operates commuter rail service (weekdays, westbound in the morning, eastbound in the evening) connecting New Haven, Branford, Guilford, Madison, Clinton, Westbrook, Old Saybrook, and New London.

FARES AND SCHEDULES
➤ TRAIN INFORMATION: **Amtrak** (☎ 800/872–7245, WEB www.amtrak.com). **Metro-North Railroad** (☎ 800/638–7646; 212/532–4900 in New York City; WEB www.mta.info). **Shore Line East** (☎ 800/255–7433 in Connecticut, WEB www.rideworks.com/sle).

VISITOR INFORMATION

➤ TOURIST INFORMATION: **Connecticut's Mystic and More** (⊠ 470 Bank St. [Box 89, New London 06320], ☎ 860/444–2206 or 800/863–6569, WEB www.mysticmore.com). **Connecticut River Valley and Shoreline Visitors Council** (⊠ 393 Main St., Middletown 06457, ☎ 860/347–0028 or 800/486–3346, WEB www.cttourism.org). **Greater New Haven Convention and Visitors Bureau** (⊠ 59 Elm St., Suite 100, New Haven 06510, ☎ 203/777–8550 or 800/332–7829, WEB www.newhavencvb.org). **Mystic Coast & Country Travel & Leisure Council** (☎ 800/692–6278, WEB www.mycoast.com).

THE QUIET CORNER

Few visitors to Connecticut experience the old-fashioned ways of the state's "Quiet Corner," a vast patch of sparsely populated towns that seem a world away from the rest of the state. The Quiet Corner has a reclusive allure: people used to leave New York City for the Litchfield Hills; now many are leaving for northeastern Connecticut, where the stretch of Route 169 from Brooklyn past Woodstock has been named a National Scenic Byway.

The cultural capital of the Quiet Corner is Putnam, a small mill city on the Quinebaug River whose formerly industrial town center has been

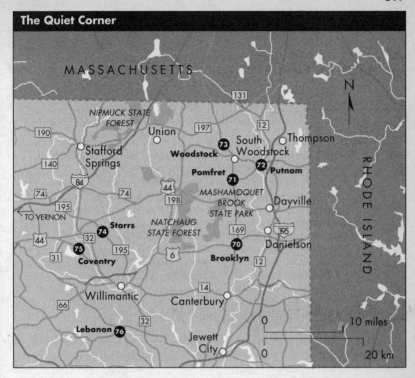

transformed into a year-round antiques mart. Smaller jewels in and around the Putnam area are Brooklyn, Pomfret, and Woodstock—three towns where authentic Colonial homesteads still seem to outnumber the contemporary, charmless clones that are springing up all too rapidly across the state.

Brooklyn

70 *45 mi east of Hartford.*

The village of Brooklyn bears no resemblance to the more famous borough of New York City that carries the same name. White picket fences and beautifully restored Colonial homes are the norm here.

The **New England Center for Contemporary Art,** housed in a four-story pre-Revolutionary barn, hosts changing exhibitions of 20th-century art and has a gift shop. ⊠ *Rte. 169,* ☎ *860/774–8899.* ✆ *Free.* ☺ *Apr.– Nov., Wed.–Sun. 1–5.*

Ever think that a Connecticut dairy farm is the home where buffalo roam? At **Creamery Brook Bison** they do. This working farm, with a herd of more than 70, leads wagon rides to the fields where the herd grazes and has a store with various buffalo-theme items such as T-shirts, stuffed animals, figurines, and even frozen buffalo meat. ⊠ *19 Purvis Rd.,* ☎ *860/779–0837,* WEB *www.creamerybrookbison.com.* ✆ *Wagon tours, $6.* ☺ *Weekdays 2–6, Sat. 9–2; wagon rides July–Sept., Sat. at 1:30.*

Logee's Greenhouses, a family business founded in 1892, has eight greenhouses overflowing with more than 1,500 varieties of indoor plants. Begonias—more than 400 varieties—are a specialty. ⊠ *141 North St., Danielson,* ☎ *860/774–8038,* WEB *www.logees.com.* ✆ *Free.* ☺ *Mon.– Sat. 9–5, Sun. 11–5.*

The **Prudence Crandall House** opened in 1833 as a boarding school and was the first of its kind to admit "girls of color." The 1805 home has a grand Palladian window in front and changing exhibits that deal with black, women's, and local history, period furnishings, a research library and a gift shop. Prudence Crandall, who lived here from 1831 to 1834, is Connecticut's state heroine. ⊠ *Rtes. 14 and 169, Canterbury 06331,* ☎ *860/546–9916 or 860/566–3005.* ⊠ *$2.50.* ☉ *Feb.–mid-Dec., Wed.–Sun. 10–4:30.*

Dining

$$$$ ✕ **Golden Lamb Buttery.** Connecticut's most unusual and magical dining experience has achieved almost legendary status. Eating here is far
★   more than a chance to enjoy good Continental food: it's a social and gastronomical event. There is one seating each for lunch and dinner in this converted barn. Owners Bob and Virginia "Jimmie" Booth have a vintage Jaguar roadster and a hay wagon that you can ride before dinner (a musician accompanies you). Choose from one of three daily soups and four entrées, which might include medallions of lamb or panfried beef tenderloin. ⊠ *499 Bush Hill Rd., off Rte. 169,* ☎ *860/774–4423. Reservations essential. No credit cards. Closed Jan.–early Apr. and Sun.–Mon. No dinner Tues.–Thurs.*

Pomfret

71 *6 mi north of Brooklyn.*

Pomfret, one of the grandest towns in the region, was once known as the inland Newport because it attracted the wealthy, who summered here in large "cottages." Today it is a quiet stopping-off point along Route 169, designated one of the 10 most scenic byways in the country. Some of Connecticut's loveliest views are seen from the hilltop campus of the Pomfret School.

Sharpe Hill Vineyard is centered on an 18th-century-style barn in the hills of Pomfret. Tours and tastings are given, and you can nibble on smoked salmon and fruit and cheese in the European-style wine garden or the Fireside Tavern, which also serves dinner on periodic Friday evenings. ⊠ *108 Wade Rd.,* ☎ *860/974–3549,* WEB *www.sharpehill.com.* ⊠ *Free.* ☉ *Fri.–Sun. 11–5.*

The **Connecticut Audubon Center at Pomfret** is adjacent to the Connecticut Audubon Bafflin Sanctuary's 700 acres of rolling meadows, grassland habitats, forests, and streams. The nature center conducts environmental education programs for all ages, seasonal lectures and workshops, and changing natural history exhibits. Miles of self-guided trails provide excellent birding; the center also leads day and evening hikes. ⊠ *189 Pomfret St./Rte.169,* ☎ *860/928–4948,* WEB *www.ctaudubon.org/centers/pomfret/pomfret.htm.* ⊠ *Free.* ☉ *Daily dawn–dusk.*

Dining

$$–$$$$ ✕ **The Harvest.** This romantic country restaurant is alive with fresh flowers, glimmering candles, antiques, and touches of chintz. It serves seafood, vegetable, and pasta dishes. Its large assortment of "prime entrées" includes steaks, fillets, and chops with your choice of such accompaniments as shiitake mushrooms with wasabi béarnaise sauce or roasted garlic and tomatoes. ⊠ *37 Putnam Rd., 06258,* ☎ *860/928–0008. AE, MC, V. No lunch weekends.*

$–$$ ✕ **Vanilla Bean Café.** A perfect stop for lunch, this tan Colonial-style barn serves salads and hearty sandwiches in an informal dining room. Dinner entrées such as smoked mozzarella and basil ravioli and roast pork with winter vegetables are served until 8. From May to October, you can dine on fare from the outside grill on the patio until 9; the indoor grill is fired up for burgers year-round. The cheesecake gets rave reviews. Breakfast is available on weekends. ✉ *450 Deerfield Rd. (off U.S. 44, Rte. 97, and Rte. 169), 06258,* ☎ *860/928–1562. No credit cards. No dinner Mon.–Tues.*

Outdoor Activities and Sports

Mashamoquet Brook State Park was formed by combining Mashamoquet Brook, Wolf Den, and Saptree Run into an 860-acre park with an attractive trail system. The park also has swimming, fishing, and camping facilities. ✉ *U.S. 44,* ☎ *860/928–6121.* *Memorial Day–Labor Day $5–$8; Labor Day–Memorial Day free.* ⏲ *Daily 8 AM–dusk.*

Shopping

Majilly (✉ 56 Babbitt Hill Rd., ☎ 860/974–3714), an upscale line of hand-painted ceramic pottery crafted in Italy, is based in a 150-year-old barn. Open Tuesday through Saturday, the outlet sells still-gorgeous seconds at 50%–70% off the retail prices. **Martha's Herbary** (✉ 589 Pomfret St., ☎ 860/928–0009), in a 1780 home, is an herb-theme gift shop and garden. Classes in the demonstration kitchen cover everything from cooking with herbs to making herbal facial masks.

Putnam

72 *5 mi northeast of Pomfret.*

Ambitious antiques dealers have reinvented Putnam, a mill town 30 mi west of Providence, Rhode Island, that became neglected after the Depression. Putnam's downtown, with more than 400 antiques dealers, is the heart of the Quiet Corner's antiques trade. The first weekend in November is usually Antiquing Weekend, when nearly two dozen area shops offer discounts and give workshops.

Dining and Lodging

$$–$$$ ✕ **The Vine.** This stylish trattoria-bistro is *the* place to go for a break from antiquing. Don't miss the eggplant rollatini (thinly sliced eggplant rolled with ricotta, mozzarella, Parmesan, and sun-dried tomatoes with a marinara sauce), a starter. You can follow with the house special: Pasta D'Vine (sautéed chicken breast with artichoke hearts, tomatoes, black olives, mushrooms, and homemade angel-hair pasta). ✉ *85 Main St., 06260,* ☎ *860/928–1660. Reservations essential. AE, MC, V. Closed Mon.*

$ **King's Inn.** Less than 2 mi from downtown Putnam, the King's Inn is a good base for antiquers. Half the rooms, which are decorated with cream-color walls or print wallpaper and straightforward wood furnishings, overlook a pond. ✉ *5 Heritage Rd., 06260,* ☎ *860/928–7961 or 800/541–7304,* FAX *860/963–2463,* WEB *www.kingsinnputnam.com. 40 rooms, 1 suite. Restaurant, pool, bar, meeting rooms. AE, D, DC, MC, V. CP.*

Nightlife and the Arts

The **Theatre of Northeastern Connecticut at the Bradley Playhouse** (✉ 30 Front St., ☎ 860/928–7887) produces some eight shows a year in a turn-of-the-20th-century vaudeville theater. Dinner-theater packages with area restaurants are available.

Shopping

The four-level **Antiques Marketplace** (✉ 109 Main St., ☎ 860/928–0442) houses the wares of nearly 300 dealers, from fine furniture to tchotchkes and collectibles. **Arts & Framing** (✉ 88 Main St., ☎ 860/963–0105) sells antique art and also provides art restoration and framing services. **Brighton Antiques** (✉ 91 Main St., ☎ 860/928–1419) carries furniture and accessories from the 18th through 20th century. The

30,000-square-ft **Great Atlantic Co.** (✉ 83 Main St., ☎ 860/928–1905) stocks everything from chandeliers and architectural elements to dining-room sets and antique books.

Woodstock

73 *5 mi northwest of Putnam.*

The landscape of this enchanting town is splendid in every season—the rolling hills seem to stretch for miles. Scenic roads take you past antiques shops, a country inn in the grand tradition, orchards, grassy fields and grazing livestock, and the fairgrounds of one of the state's oldest—and most popular—agricultural fairs held each Labor Day weekend.

Roseland Cottage, probably the region's most notable historic dwelling, is a pink board-and-batten Gothic Revival house built in 1846 by New York publisher and merchant Henry Bowen. The pride of its grounds is an 1850s boxwood parterre garden that four presidents—Ulysses S. Grant, Rutherford B. Hayes, Benjamin Harrison, and William McKinley—have visited. ✉ *556 Rte. 169,* ☎ *860/928–4074,* WEB *www.spnea.org/visit/homes/bowen.htm.* ✑ *$4.* ◷ *June–mid-Oct., Wed.–Sun. 11–5. Tours on the hr (last tour at 4.)*

Dining and Lodging

$$–$$$ ✕▥ **Inn at Woodstock Hill.** This inn on a hill overlooking the countryside has sumptuous rooms with antiques, four-poster beds, fireplaces, pitched ceilings, and timber beams. The chintz-and-prints restaurant ($$–$$$; reservations essential) next door serves excellent Continental and American variations on seafood, veal, beef, pork, and chicken dishes. ✉ *94 Plaine Hill Rd., South Woodstock 06267,* ☎ *860/928–0528,* FAX *860/928–3236,* WEB *www.woodstockhill.com. 19 rooms, 3 suites. Restaurant, in-room data ports, meeting room. D, MC, V. CP.*

Shopping

Chocolate Saltbox Stenciler (✉ 1250 Rte. 171, ☎ 860/974–1437), with a library of more than 10,000 stencil designs, sells hand-stenciled table linens, clothing, and accessories. The **Christmas Barn** (✉ 835 Rte. 169, ☎ 860/928–7652) has 12 rooms of country and Christmas goods. **Scranton's Shops** (✉ 300 Rte. 169, ☎ 860/928–3738) sells antiques and the wares of 90 local artisans. **Whispering Hill Farm** (✉ Rte. 169, ☎ 860/928–0162) sells supplies for rug hooking and braiding, quilting, and needlework mixed with an assortment of antiques.

Storrs

74 *25 mi southwest of Woodstock.*

The majority hillside and farmland of Storrs is occupied by the 4,400 acres and some 12,000 students of the main campus of the University of Connecticut (UConn). Many cultural programs, sporting events, and other happenings take place here. University Parking Services and the Student Union supply campus maps.

Hand puppets, rod puppets, body puppets, shadow puppets, marionettes—the **Ballard Institute and Museum of Puppetry** has more than 2,000 puppets in its extraordinary collection. Half were created by Frank Ballard, a master of puppetry who established the country's first complete undergraduate and graduate degree program in puppetry at UConn more than three decades ago. Exhibits change seasonally. If you're lucky you might even catch Oscar the Grouch from *Sesame Street* on display. ✉ *Univ. of Connecticut Depot Campus, 6 Bourn Place, U-212,* ☎ *860/486–4605.* ✑ *$2.* ◷ *Late Apr.–early Nov., Fri.–Sun. noon–5.*

The permanent collection of the **William Benton Museum of Art** includes European and American paintings, drawings, prints, and sculptures from the 16th century to the present. ⊠ *Univ. of Connecticut, 245 Glenbrook Rd.,* ☎ *860/486–4520,* WEB *www.benton.uconn.edu.* ✆ *Free.* ☉ *Tues.–Fri. 10–4:30, weekends 1–4:30. Closed between exhibitions.*

Talk about diversity—the **University of Connecticut Greenhouses** are internationally acclaimed for their more than 3,000 different kinds of plants, from 900 varieties of exotic orchids to banana plants and a redwood tree. Organized tours are given weekends by advance appointment. ⊠ *Univ. of Connecticut, 75 N. Eagleville Rd.,* ☎ *860/486–4052.* ✆ *Free.* ☉ *Weekdays 8–4.*

From mollusks and fossils to sharks and wigwams, the natural and cultural history of Connecticut is the focus of the **Connecticut State Museum of Natural History.** More than 200 events and programs are held each year, including workshops, lectures, nature hikes and field trips. The museum also houses the Office of State Archaeology, with more than 600,000 artifacts. ⊠ *Univ. of Connecticut, 2019 Hillside Rd.,* ☎ *860/486–4460,* WEB *www.mnh.uconn.edu.* ✆ *Free.* ☉ *Weekdays 10–4 and some weekends.*

Lodging

$$–$$$ 🏨 **Nathan Hale Inn and Conference Center.** Opened in October 2001, this five-floor inn and conference center on the University of Connecticut campus is the long-awaited answer to a serious lack of lodging in the area. The contemporary, spartan rooms are comfortable with a lot of mahogany appointments. ⊠ *855 Bolton Rd., 06268,* ☎ *860/427–7888,* FAX *860/427–7850,* WEB *www.nathanhaleinn.com. 100 rooms. Restaurant, in-room data ports, some microwaves, some refrigerators, pool, health club, hot tub, lounge, business services, meeting rooms. AE, D, DC, MC, V.*

Nightlife and the Arts

The **Jorgenson Auditorium** (⊠ Univ. of Connecticut, 2132 Hillside Rd., ☎ 860/486–4226) presents music, dance, and theater programs. Downstairs in the Jorgenson Auditorium in the Harriet S. Jorgensen Theatre (a.k.a. "Baby" Jorgensen), the **Connecticut Repertory Theatre** (☎ 860/486–3969) produces musicals, Shakespeare, and modern dramas. **Mansfield Drive-In** (⊠ Rtes. 31 and 32, Mansfield, ☎ 860/423–4441), with three big screens, is one of the state's few remaining drive-in theaters.

Shopping

The **Mansfield Marketplace** (⊠ Mansfield Drive-In, Rtes. 31 and 32, Mansfield, ☎ 860/456–2578), with between 150 and 200 vendors selling everything from T-shirts to toys and jewelry, unfolds on Sunday from March through December.

Coventry

⑦⑤ *5 mi southwest of Storrs.*

Historians will recognize Coventry as the birthplace of the Revolutionary War hero Captain Nathan Hale, who was hanged as a spy by the British in 1776. It was Hale who spoke the immortal last words, "I only regret that I have but one life to lose for my country." Gardeners and herbalists, on the other hand, regard Coventry first and foremost as the home of Caprilands Herb Farm, which the late Adelma Grenier Simmons built into a center of worldwide renown.

The **Nathan Hale Homestead** was rebuilt by Deacon Richard Hale, Nathan's father, in 1776. Ten Hale children, six of whom served in the Revolutionary War, were raised here. Family artifacts are on exhibit in the completely furnished house. The grounds include a corncrib and an 18th-century barn. ⊠ 2299 *South St.*, ☏ *860/742–6917.* ⊡ *$4.* ☺ *Mid-May–mid-Oct., Wed.–Sun. 1–4.*

Coventry's **Caprilands Herb Farm** (⊠ 534 Silver St., ☏ 860/742–7244, WEB www.caprilands.com) has more than 30 gardens with more than 300 varieties of herbs, which are for sale. A noon luncheon-lecture program is hosted on Saturday from May through December, and tea is held on Sunday (phone for reservations for both).

Lebanon

76   *20 mi southeast of Coventry.*

Lebanon is a quiet town known for its expansive town green—it stretches 1 mi head to toe—and the Trumbulls: Revolutionary resident Jonathan Trumbull was royal governor of the colony of Connecticut. He was the only Colonial governor to side with the Continentals and provided highly valuable food supplies to the starving soldiers during the winter of 1780. President George Washington is said to have written in his diary, "No other man than Trumbull would have procured them and no other state could have furnished them." The Governor's son, artist John Trumbull, created the Washington's rendition of the U.S. $1 bill.

Governor Jonathan Trumbull House, the circa-1735 home of the only Connecticut governor (1769–84) to turn against the Crown and support the Colonies' War for Independence, is furnished in period decor. Also on the property is the Wadsworth Stable where George Washington's *horse* slept! ⊠ *West Town St.*, ☏ *860/642–7558.* ⊡ *$2.* ☺ *Mid-May–mid-Oct., Tues.–Sat. 1–5.*

The **Lebanon Historical Society Museum & Visitor Center** includes permanent and changing exhibits on local history and a historical and genealogical research center. You can also pick up information on other historic sites around Lebanon Green, including the Revolutionary War Office where men such as Washington, Lafayette, John Adams, and Benjamin Franklin met to strategize. ⊠ *865 Trumbull Hwy.*, ☏ *860/642–6579,* WEB *www.lebanonct.org.* ⊡ *$3.* ☺ *Wed. 9–1, Sat. 1–5, and by appointment.*

The Quiet Corner A to Z

To research prices, get advice from other travelers, and book travel arrangements, visit www.fodors.com.

CAR TRAVEL

You'll need a car to reach and explore the Quiet Corner. Many Nutmeggers live their entire lives without even noticing I–395, let alone driving on it, but this is the main highway connecting Worcester, Massachusetts, with New London—and it passes right through the Quiet Corner. From Hartford take I–84 east to U.S. 44 east, and from Providence, Rhode Island, take either U.S. 44 or 6 west. The main towns in the Quiet Corner are on or near historic Route 169.

EMERGENCIES

➤ HOSPITALS: **Rockville General Hospital** (⊠ 31 Union St., Vernon, ☏ 860/872–5100, WEB www.echn.org/rgh.htm). **Windham Community Memorial Hospital** (⊠ 112 Mansfield Ave., Willimantic, ☏ 860/456–9116, WEB www.windhamhospital.org).
➤ PHARMACY: **CVS** (⊠ Mansfield Shopping Plaza, Storrs, ☏ 860/487–0223, WEB www.cvs.com).

VISITOR INFORMATION
➤ TOURIST INFORMATION: **Northeast Connecticut Visitors District** (✉ 13 Canterbury Rd., Suite 3 [Box 145, Brooklyn 06234], ☎ 860/779–6383 or 888/628–1228, WEB www.ctquietcorner.org).

CONNECTICUT A TO Z

To research prices, get advice from other travelers, and book travel arrangements, visit www.fodors.com.

AIRPORTS

Many people visiting Connecticut fly into New York City's John F. Kennedy International Airport or LaGuardia Airport, both of which are served by many major carriers. Another option is Bradley International Airport, north of Hartford.

➤ AIRPORT INFORMATION: **Bradley International Airport,** (☎ 860/292–2000, WEB www.bradleyairport.com). **John F. Kennedy International Airport** (☎ 718/244–4444, WEB www.panynj.gov/aviation/jfkframe.htm). **LaGuardia Airport** (☎ 718/533–3400, WEB www.panynj.gov/aviation/jgaframe/htm).

AIRPORT TRANSFERS

The Airport Connection has scheduled service from Bradley to Hartford's Union Station, as well as door-to-door service. Connecticut Limo operates bus and van service between Connecticut and the New York airports and to and from Bradley International Airport. Prime Time Shuttle serves New Haven and Fairfield counties with service to and from both New York airports.

➤ TAXIS AND SHUTTLES: **Airport Connection** (☎ 860/529–7865). **Connecticut Limo** (☎ 800/472–5466, WEB www.ctlimo.com). **Prime Time Shuttle** (☎ 800/733–8267, WEB www.primetimeshuttle.com).

BUS TRAVEL

Bonanza Bus Lines connects Hartford, Farmington, Southbury, Waterbury, Manchester, and Danbury with Boston and New York. Greyhound links Connecticut with most major cities in the United States. Peter Pan Bus Lines serves the eastern seaboard, including many New England cities.

➤ BUS INFORMATION: **Bonanza Bus Lines** (☎ 800/556–3815, WEB www.bonanzabus.com). **Greyhound** (☎ 800/231–2222, WEB www.greyhound.com). **Peter Pan Bus Lines** (☎ 800/237–8747, WEB www.peterpanbus.com).

CAR TRAVEL

From New York City head north on I–95, which hugs the Connecticut shoreline into Rhode Island or, to reach the Litchfield Hills and Hartford, head north on I–684, then east on I–84. From Springfield, Massachusetts, go south on I–91, which bisects I–84 in Hartford and I–95 in New Haven. From Boston take I–95 south through Providence or take the Massachusetts Turnpike west to I–84. Interstate 395 runs north–south from southeastern Connecticut to Massachusetts.

The interstates are the quickest routes between many points in Connecticut, but they are busy and ugly. The speed limits on Connecticut's interstates change, sometimes going from 65 mph to 45 mph and back quite quickly through the cities. Be certain to check for posted speed limits. Right turns on red are legal unless posted otherwise.

If time allows, skip the interstates in favor of the historic Merritt Parkway (Route 15), which winds between Greenwich and Middletown; U.S. 7 and Route 8, extending between I–95 and the Litchfield Hills;

Route 9, which heads south from Hartford through the Connecticut River valley to Old Saybrook; and scenic Route 169, which meanders through the Quiet Corner. Maps are available free from the Connecticut Office of Tourism (☞ Visitor Information).

EMERGENCIES
➤ CONTACT: **Ambulance, fire, police** (☎ 911).

LODGING
BED-AND-BREAKFASTS
RESERVATION SERVICES: **B&B, Ltd.** (☎ 203/469–3260). **Covered Bridge B&B Reservation Service** (☎ 860/542–5944). **Nutmeg B&B Agency** (☎ 860/236–6698, WEB www.bnb-link.com).

OUTDOOR ACTIVITIES AND SPORTS
For information about fishing licenses and regulations and a copy of the annual angler's guide to state lakes and ponds and the fish that inhabit them, call the Fisheries Division of the Department of Environmental Protection.
➤ CONTACT: **Fisheries Division of the Department of Environmental Protection** (☎ 860/424–3474).

TOURS
The Connecticut Freedom Trail has 40 historic sights associated with the state's African-American heritage. The Connecticut Impressionist Art Trail is a self-guided tour of nine museums important to the 19th-century American Impressionist movement. Write to the below address for a map. The Connecticut Wine Trail travels between 11 member vineyards.
➤ CONTACTS: **Connecticut Freedom Trail** (✉ Connecticut Historical Commission, 59 S. Prospect St., Hartford 06106, ☎ 860/566–3005, WEB www.ctfreedomtrail.com). **Connecticut Impressionist Art Trail** (✉ Box 793, Old Lyme 06371, WEB www.ctwine.com). **Connecticut Wine Trail** (✉ 131 Tower Rd., Brookfield 06804, ☎ 203/775–1616, WEB www.arttrail.org).

TRAIN TRAVEL
Amtrak runs from New York to Boston, stopping in Stamford, Bridgeport, and New Haven before heading either north to Hartford or east to Mystic. Metro-North Railroad trains from New York stop locally between Greenwich and New Haven, and a few trains head inland to New Canaan, Danbury, and Waterbury.
➤ TRAIN INFORMATION: **Amtrak** (☎ 800/872–7245, WEB www.amtrak.com). **Metro-North Railroad** (☎ 800/638–7646; 212/532–4900 in New York City; WEB www.mta.nyc.ny.us).

VISITOR INFORMATION
State welcome centers, in Darien and Westbrook on I–95 northbound, North Stonington on I–95 southbound, Danbury on I–84 eastbound, and Willington on I–84 westbound, have visitor information.
➤ TOURIST INFORMATION: **Antiquarian and Landmarks Society** (✉ 66 Forest St., Hartford 06105, ☎ 860/247–8996, WEB www.hartnet.org/als). **Connecticut Campground Owners Association** (✉ 14 Rumford St., West Hartford 06107, ☎ 860/521–4704, WEB www.campconn.org). **Connecticut Office of Tourism** (✉ 505 Hudson St., Hartford 06106, ☎ 800/282–6863 brochures, WEB www.ctbound.org). **Connecticut State Golf Association** (✉ 35 Cold Spring Rd., Suite 212, Rocky Hill 06067, ☎ 860/257–4171, WEB www.csgalinks.org). **State Parks Division Bureau of Parks and Forests** (✉ 79 Elm St., Hartford 06106, ☎ 860/424–3200).

INDEX

Fodor's Key to the Guides

America's guidebook leader publishes guides for every kind of traveler. Check out our many series and find your perfect match.

Fodor's Gold Guides
America's favorite travel-guide series offers the most detailed insider reviews of hotels, restaurants, and attractions in all price ranges, plus great background information, smart tips, and useful maps.

Fodor's Road Guide USA
Big guides for a big country—the most comprehensive guides to America's roads, packed with places to stay, eat, and play across the U.S.A. Just right for road warriors, family vacationers, and cross-country trekkers.

COMPASS AMERICAN GUIDES
Stunning guides from top local writers and photographers, with gorgeous photos, literary excerpts, and colorful anecdotes. A must-have for culture mavens, history buffs, and new residents.

Fodor's CITYPACKS
Concise city coverage with a foldout map. The right choice for urban travelers who want everything under one cover.

Fodor's EXPLORING GUIDES
Hundreds of color photos bring your destination to life. Lively stories lend insight into the culture, history, and people.

Fodor's POCKET GUIDES
For travelers who need only the essentials. The best of Fodor's in pocket-size packages for just $9.95.

Fodor's To Go
Credit-card–size, magnetized color microguides that fit in the palm of your hand—perfect for "stealth" travelers or as gifts.

Fodor's FLASHMAPS
Every resident's map guide. 60 easy-to-follow maps of public transit, parks, museums, zip codes, and more.

Fodor's CITYGUIDES
Sourcebooks for living in the city: Thousands of in-the-know listings for restaurants, shops, sports, nightlife, and other city resources.

Fodor's AROUND THE CITY WITH KIDS
68 great ideas for family days, recommended by resident parents. Perfect for exploring in your own backyard or on the road.

Fodor's ESCAPES
Fill your trip with once-in-a-lifetime experiences, from ballooning in Chianti to overnighting in the Moroccan desert. These full-color dream books point the way.

Fodor's FYI
Get tips from the pros on planning the perfect trip. Learn how to pack, fly hassle-free, plan a honeymoon or cruise, stay healthy on the road, and travel with your baby.

Fodor's Languages for Travelers
Practice the local language before hitting the road. Available in phrase books, cassette sets, and CD sets.

Karen Brown's Guides
Engaging guides to the most charming inns and B&Bs in the U.S.A. and Europe, with easy-to-follow inn-to-inn itineraries.

Baedeker's Guides
Comprehensive guides, trusted since 1829, packed with A–Z reviews and star ratings.

At bookstores everywhere.   www.fodors.com/books